k_{Nom}	Nominal risk-free rate of interest
k_p	Cost of preferred stock
k_{RF}	Rate of return on a risk-free security
k_s	(1) Cost of retained earnings
	(2) Required return on a stock
M	Maturity value of a bond
M/B	Market to book ratio
MCC	Marginal cost of capital
n	(1) Life of a project
	(2) Number of shares outstanding
NPV	Net present value
NWC	Net working capital
P	(1) Price of a share of stock; P_0 = price of the stock today
	(2) Sales price per unit of product sold
P/E	Price/earnings ratio
PMT	Periodic level payment or annuity
PV	Present value
PVA_n	Present value of an annuity
PVIF	Present value interest factor for a lump sum
PVIFA	Present value interest factor for an annuity
Q	Quantity produced or sold
r	(1) Rate of return
	(2) Correlation coefficient
ROA	Return on assets
ROE	Return on equity
RP	Risk premium
S	(1) Total market value of a firm's stock
	(2) Sales
SML	Security market line
Σ	Summation sign (capital sigma)
σ	Standard deviation (lower case sigma)
σ^2	Variance
t	Time period
T	Marginal income tax rate
TIE	Times-interest-earned ratio
V	(1) Variable cost per unit
	(2) Market value of a firm
VC	Total variable costs
YTM	Yield to maturity

Fundamentals of
Financial Management

Fifth Edition

Fundamentals of Financial Management

Fifth Edition

Eugene F. Brigham
University of Florida

The Dryden Press

Chicago   New York   San Francisco   Philadelphia   Montreal   Toronto   London   Sydney   Tokyo

Acquisitions Editor: Ann Heath
Developmental Editor: Judy Sarwark
Project Editor: Cate Rzasa
Design Director: Alan Wendt
Production Manager: Barb Bahnsen
Director of Editing, Design, and Production: Jane Perkins

Text and Cover Designer: C. J. Petlick, Hunter Graphics
Copy Editor: Judith Lary
Compositor: The Clarinda Company
Text Type: 10/12 ITC Garamond Light

Library of Congress Cataloging-In Publication Data

Brigham, Eugene F., 1930–
  Fundamentals of financial management/Eugene F. Brigham.
    p.   cm.
  Includes bibliographical references and index.
  ISBN 0-03-025482-5
  1. Corporations—Finance.   I. Title.
  HG4026.B6693   1989
  658.1'5—dc 19   88-25631

Printed in the United States of America
901-039-987654321

Address orders:
The Dryden Press
Orlando, FL 32887

Address editorial correspondence:
The Dryden Press
908 N. Elm Street
Hinsdale, IL 60521

The Dryden Press
Holt, Rinehart and Winston
Saunders College Publishing

The Dryden Press Series in Finance

Preface

Fundamentals of Financial Management is intended for use in the introductory finance course. It begins, in Part I, with a discussion of such basic concepts as security markets, interest rates, taxes, risk analysis, time value of money, and valuation models. In subsequent parts, we go on to explain how financial managers can help maximize the value of a firm by making better decisions in such areas as capital budgeting, working capital management, and choice of capital structure. This organization has three important advantages:

1. Explaining early in the book how financial markets operate, and how security prices are determined within these markets, helps students see how financial management can affect the value of the firm. Also, early coverage of risk analysis, time value, and valuation models permits us to use and reinforce these key concepts throughout the remainder of the book.

2. Structuring the book around markets and valuation concepts enhances continuity—students can better see how the various topics relate to one another.

3. Most students—even those who do not plan to major in finance—are generally interested in stock and bond valuation, rates of return, and the like. Since people's ability to learn a subject is a function of their interest and motivation, and since *Fundamentals* begins by showing the relationship between security markets, security values, and financial management, this organization is good from a pedagogic standpoint.

CHANGES IN THE FIFTH EDITION

The theory and practice of finance are dynamic, and as new developments occur, they should be incorporated into a textbook such as this one. Also, we and a team of reviewers are constantly on the lookout for ways to improve the book in terms of clarity and understanding. As a result, we have made several important changes in this edition, including the following:

1. All sections were updated to reflect the latest tax laws, interest rates, and other financial developments.

2. At the suggestion of reviewers, the section on capital budgeting was expanded from two to three chapters. This expansion allowed us to cover such topics as inflation effects, replacement chains, and equivalent annual annuities. However, we structured the book in modular form so that some topics (and even chapters) can be omitted by instructors who prefer not to cover them in the introductory course.

3. The expanded coverage of capital budgeting also allowed us to devote an entire chapter (Chapter 10) to cash flow estimation. Indeed, we were able to expand the discussion and simplify the analysis by use of an income statement/cash flow statement approach that is much clearer than the formulas used in the fourth edition.

4. Risk analysis was moved from Chapter 6 to Chapter 4, so that it follows immediately the chapter on interest rates and capital markets and precedes the chapter on valuation models. This arrangement provides for a smoother, more logical transition from the discussion of interest rates and risk premiums to risk-adjusted rates of return, then on to time value of money and valuation models.

5. A new section on business ethics was added to Chapter 1, and special attention was given to pointing out ethical issues throughout the remainder of the book.

6. The statement of changes in financial position was replaced with a statement of cash flows to reflect the recent change in financial accounting standards.

7. The discussion of zero coupon bonds was completely rewritten to reflect the current tax treatment of these bonds.

8. A discussion on putable bonds has been added to Chapter 13, Long-Term Debt, and the coverage of bond indentures has been updated to include material on the impact of LBO strategies on the bond rating of firms such as RJR Nabisco.

9. International finance is no longer covered as a separate chapter. Important topics are now covered in a special international section at the end of selected chapters.

10. Numbered equations are now set in blue type. Highlighting the most important equations serves as an effective study and review tool for students.

11. We also added to the end-of-chapter problems for each chapter an integrative problem that covers in a comprehensive manner all the major concepts discussed in the chapter. These problems can be used as the basis for lectures, or they can be used by students as comprehensive study problems. To facilitate their use as lecture problems, we wrote the *Instructor's Manual* solutions in a lecture note format, and we developed a set of transparency masters that can be used to make transparencies for overhead projectors. Furthermore, since students often get left behind when instructors use overheads, we developed a new ancillary,

Blueprints: A Problem Notebook. Designed as a note-taking or study tool, *Blueprints* comes with each new copy of the book and corresponds to the integrative problems in the text. Each integrative problem is restated in *Blueprints,* space is provided for taking notes, and graph set-ups and other features designed to help students take clear notes or think through the problems are provided. Using *Blueprints* as a guide, students will be able to take good notes and still have time to follow the lecture.

12. The number of end-of-chapter problems was increased, and the range of difficulty was expanded. Also, a separate section, entitled Computer-Related Problems, was added to most chapters, and a diskette that contains *Lotus 1-2-3* models for these problems is available to instructors from The Dryden Press. The computerized problems are designed to show students the power of computers in financial analysis; however, no knowledge of computers or programming is needed to use them.

13. The old chapter summaries were replaced by new sections entitled Summary and Key Concepts, in which we summarize key concepts covered in each chapter in bulleted lists. The new format makes it easier for students to review the concepts than did the narrative format used previously.

ANCILLARY MATERIALS

Blueprints: A Problem Notebook. This supplement is supplied free of charge with each new textbook. It contains a statement of the integrative problems developed for each chapter, space for taking notes or for solving the problem and discussing the concepts involved, and graph set-ups to facilitate working the problems.

A number of other items are included in the *Fundamentals* package and are available free of charge to adopting instructors.

1. **Instructor's Manual.** A comprehensive manual is available to instructors who adopt the book. The manual contains answers to all text questions and problems, a detailed set of lecture notes (including suggestions for use of the acetate transparencies described in the next section), detailed solutions to integrative lecture problems with transparency masters to illustrate them, sample exams, and suggested course outlines.

2. **Transparencies.** A comprehensive set of acetate transparencies (six to eight per chapter), including 40 color acetates, is available to instructors who adopt the text. Also, an extensive set of transparency masters (six to eight per chapter) was developed for use with the integrative lecture problems.

3. **Test Bank.** A revised and enlarged test bank with more than 1,000 class-tested questions and problems, in objective format, is available both in

book form and on IBM computer diskettes (5¼″ and 3½″). The new questions are more challenging than those in many test banks, and they are well suited for exams. Also, the topics covered, the degree of difficulty, and the correct answer are provided in the margin for each question.

4. **Supplemental Problems.** A set of additional problems, organized according to topic and level of difficulty, is also available to instructors.

5. **Problem Diskette.** A diskette (5¼″ and 3½″) containing *Lotus 1-2-3* models for the computer-related end-of-chapter problems is also available. To obtain the diskette, complete the insert card found at the front of the *Instructor's Manual.*

A number of additional items are available for purchase by students:

1. **Study Guide.** This supplement outlines the key sections of each chapter, provides students with self-test questions, and provides a set of problems and solutions similar to those in the text and in the *Test Bank.*

2. **Casebook.** The tax update edition of *Cases in Managerial Finance,* sixth edition (Dryden Press, 1987), by Roy L. Crum and Eugene F. Brigham, is well suited for use with this text. The cases provide real-world applications of the methodologies and concepts developed in the text.

3. **Readings Book.** A readings book, *Issues in Managerial Finance,* third edition (Dryden Press, 1987), edited by Ramon E. Johnson, provides an excellent mix of theoretical and practical articles which can be used to supplement the text.

4. **Finance with Lotus 1-2-3: Text, Cases, and Models.** This text by Eugene F. Brigham, Dana A. Aberwald, and Susan E. Ball (Dryden Press, 1988), enables students to learn, on their own, how to use *Lotus 1-2-3* and explains how many commonly encountered problems in financial management can be analyzed with electronic spreadsheets.

5. **PROFIT +.** This software supplement by James Pettijohn of Southwest Missouri State University contains 18 user-friendly programs that include the time value of money, forecasting, and capital budgeting. The program includes a user's manual, and it is available for the IBM PC.

ACKNOWLEDGMENTS

This book reflects the efforts of a great many people over a number of years. First, I would like to thank the following, whose reviews and comments on prior editions and companion books have contributed to this edition: Mike Adler, Ed Altman, Bruce Anderson, Ron Anderson, Bob Angell, Vince Apilado, Bob Aubey, Gil Babcock, Peter Bacon, Kent Baker, Tom Bankston, Les Barenbaum, Charles Barngrover, Bill Beedles, Moshe Ben Horim, Bill Beranek, Tom

Berry, Bill Bertin, Roger Bey, John Bildersee, Russ Boisjoly, Keith Boles, Geof Booth, Kenneth Boudreaux, Oswald Bowlin, Don Boyd, Pat Boyer, Joe Brandt, Elizabeth Brannigan, Greg Brauer, Mary Broske, Dave Brown, Kate Brown, Bill Brueggeman, Kirt Butler, Bill Campsey, Bob Carleson, Severin Carlson, David Cary, Steve Celec, Don Chance, Antony Chang, Susan Chaplinsky, Jay Choi, S. K. Choudhury, Lal Chugh, Maclyn Clouse, Margaret Considine, Phil Cooley, Joe Copeland, David Cordell, John Cotner, David Crary, Roy Crum, Brent Dalrymple, Bill Damon, Joel Dauten, Steve Dawson, Sankar De, Miles Delano, Fred Dellva, Bernard Dill, Greg Dimkoff, Les Dlabay, Mark Dorfman, Gene Drzycimski, Dean Dudley, David Durst, Ed Dyl, Dick Edelman, Charles Edwards, John Ellis, Dave Ewert, John Ezzell, Michael Ferri, Jim Filkins, John Finnerty, Susan Fischer, Steve Flint, Russ Fogler, Dan French, Michael Garlington, Jim Garvin, Adam Gehr, Jim Gentry, Philip Glasgo, Rudyard Goode, Walt Goulet, Bernie Grablowsky, Ed Grossnickle, John Groth, Alan Grunewald, Manak Gupta, Sam Hadaway, Don Hakala, Gerald Hamsmith, William Hardin, John Harris, Paul Hastings, Bob Haugen, Steve Hawke, Del Hawley, Robert Hehre, George Hettenhouse, Haws Heymann, Kendall Hill, Roger Hill, Tom Hindelang, Ralph Hocking, Ronald Hoffmeister, Jim Horrigan, John Houston, John Howe, Keith Howe, Steve Isberg, Jim Jackson, Kose John, Craig Johnson, Keith Johnson, Ramon Johnson, Ray Jones, Manuel Jose, Gus Kalogeras, Mike Keenan, Bill Kennedy, Joe Kiernan, Rick Kish, Don Knight, Dorothy Koehl, Jaroslaw Komarynsky, Duncan Kretovich, Harold Krogh, Charles Kronke, Joan Lamm, P. Lange, Howard Lanser, Martin Laurence, Ed Lawrence, Wayne Lee, Jim LePage, John Lewis, Chuck Linke, Bill Lloyd, Susan Long, Jim Longstreet, Judy Maese, Bob Magee, Ileen Malitz, Phil Malone, Terry Maness, Chris Manning, Terry Martell, D. J. Masson, John Mathys, John McAlhany, Andy McCollough, Bill McDaniel, Jamshid Mehran, Larry Merville, Rick Meyer, Jim Millar, Ed Miller, John Mitchell, Carol Moerdyk, Bob Moore, Barry Morris, Gene Morris, Fred Morrissey, Chris Muscarella, David Nachman, Tim Nantell, Don Nast, Bill Nelson, Bob Nelson, Bob Niendorf, Tom O'Brien, Dennis O'Connor, John O'Donnell, Jim Olsen, Robert Olsen, Jim Pappas, Stephen Parrish, Glenn Petry, Jim Pettijohn, Rich Pettit, Dick Pettway, Hugo Phillips, John Pinkerton, Gerald Pogue, R. Potter, Franklin Potts, R. Powell, Chris Prestopino, Jerry Prock, Howard Puckett, Herbert Quigley, George Racette, Bob Radcliffe, Bill Rentz, Ken Riener, Charles Rini, John Ritchie, Pietra Rivoli, Antonio Rodriguez, E. N. Roussakis, Dexter Rowell, Jim Sachlis, Abdul Sadik, Thomas Scampini, Kevin Scanlon, Mary Jane Scheuer, Carl Schweser, John Settle, Alan Severn, Sol Shalit, Frederic Shipley, Ron Shrieves, Neil Sicherman, J. B. Silvers, Clay Singleton, Joe Sinkey, Stacy Sirmans, Jaye Smith, Steve Smith, Don Sorenson, David Speairs, Ken Stanly, Ed Stendardi, Alan Stephens, Don Stevens, Jerry Stevens, Glen Strasburg, Philip Swensen, Ernie Swift, Paul Swink, Gary Tallman, Dennis Tanner, Russ Taussig, Ted Teweles, Andrew Thompson, George Trivoli, George Tsetsekos, Mel Tysseland, David Upton, Howard Van Auken, Pretorious Van den Dool, Pieter Vanderburg, Paul Vanderheiden, Jim Verbrugge, Patrick Vincent, Steve Vinson, Susan Visscher, John Wachowicz, Mike Walker, Sam Weaver, Kuo Chiang Wei, Bill

Welch, Fred Weston, Norm Williams, Tony Wingler, Ed Wolfe, Don Woods, Michael Yonan, Dennis Zocco, and Kent Zumwalt.

In addition, the following professors reviewed the manuscript and provided detailed comments and suggestions for improving the fifth edition:

Robert Balik	Carol Kiefer	Patricia Smith
Scott Besley	Larry Lang	Dulal Talukdar
James Desreumaux	Thomas McCue	William Tozer
Robert Hollinger	S. K. Mansinghka	

Dana Aberwald and Susan Ball worked closely with me at every stage of the revision; their assistance was absolutely invaluable. Also, Chris Barry, Texas Christian University, wrote many of the small business sections; Dilip Shome, Virginia Polytechnic Institute, helped greatly with the capital structure chapter; Art Herrmann, University of Hartford, coauthored the bankruptcy appendix; and William Tozer, Washington State University, reviewed the manuscript and also worked through the end-of-chapter problems, including the computer problems, to help ensure that they are as clear, accurate, and relevant as possible. Louis Gapenski worked closely with me on the integrative problems and the *Blueprints,* and offered advice on many other parts of the book. In addition, several students and colleagues at the University of Florida worked through and/or discussed with me all or major parts of the book and ancillaries to help eliminate errors and confusing sections: Brian Butler, Kimberly McCollough, and Craig Tapley. Carol Stanton and Bob Karp typed and helped proof the various manuscripts. Finally, The Dryden Press staff, especially Barb Bahnsen, Ann Heath, Judy Lary, Jane Perkins, Cate Rzasa, Judy Sarwark, Bill Schoof, Alan Wendt, and Betsy Webster, helped greatly with all phases of the revision.

ERRORS IN THE TEXT

At this point, most authors make a statement like this: "I appreciate all the help I received from the people listed above, but any remaining errors are, of course, my own responsibility." And generally there are more than enough remaining errors. As a part of my quest for clarity, I resolved to avoid this problem in *Fundamentals,* and as a result of the error detection procedures we used, I am convinced that it is virtually free of mistakes.

Some of my colleagues suggested that if I am so confident about the book's accuracy, I should offer a reward to people who find errors. With this in mind, but primarily because I want to detect any remaining errors and correct them in subsequent printings, I hereby offer a reward of $7.50 per error (misspelled word, arithmetic mistake, and the like) to the first person who reports it to me. (Any error that has follow-through effects is counted as two errors only.) Two accounting students have set up a foolproof audit system to make sure I pay—accounting students tend to be skeptics! Please report any errors to me at the address below.

CONCLUSION

Finance is, in a real sense, the cornerstone of the enterprise system—good financial management is vitally important to the economic health of business firms, and, hence, to the nation and the world. Because of its importance, finance should be widely and thoroughly understood, but this is easier said than done. The field is relatively complex, and it is undergoing constant change in response to shifts in economic conditions. All of this makes finance stimulating and exciting, but also challenging and sometimes perplexing. I sincerely hope that *Fundamentals* will meet its own challenge by contributing to a better understanding of our financial system.

Eugene F. Brigham
College of Business
University of Florida
Gainesville, Florida 32611

December 1988

Contents in Brief

Contents

I Fundamental Concepts in Financial Management

1

An Overview of Financial Management

DIFFERENCES IN FINANCIAL POLICY: DELTA VS. EASTERN

In 1964 Eastern Airlines' stock sold for more than $60 per share, whereas Delta's sold for $10. By 1988, Delta had become one of the strongest airlines, and its stock sold for $60, a gain of 500 percent. Eastern, on the other hand, no longer exists as an independent company — it was acquired recently in a "shotgun merger" at less than $10 per share by Texas Air, the company that owns Continental Airlines and New York Air. Delta's earnings, dividends, and stock price all soared during the 1970s and 1980s. Eastern, on the other hand, paid its last dividend in 1969, and it suffered losses totaling over $1 billion between 1969 and its acquisition. Further, Delta's employees have reasonably secure, well-paid positions, while Eastern has been laying off people and slashing the salaries of those who remain. Even Eastern's chairman, ex-astronaut Frank Borman, lost his job.

Although many factors combined to produce these divergent results, financial decisions exerted a major influence. Eastern had traditionally used a great deal of debt, while Delta had a policy of financing mostly with common equity. For example, in 1988 Delta had about 44 percent debt versus Eastern's debt ratio of over 90 percent. The dramatic increase in interest rates (the prime business loan rate rose from 6 percent in the 1960s to 21 percent in the early 1980s) greatly increased Eastern's costs and lowered its profits, but it had only a minor effect on Delta. Further, when fuel price increases of over 1,000 percent made it imperative for the airlines to buy new, fuel-efficient planes, Delta was able to do so but Eastern was not. Finally, when the airlines were deregulated in the late 1970s, Delta was strong enough to expand into developing markets and to cut prices as necessary to attract business, but Eastern was not.

Similar stories could be told about hundreds of companies in scores of industries — autos, computers, insurance, banking, or you name it. One company does well while another goes bankrupt — and a major reason for the divergent results is a difference in some basic financial policy. In this chapter we outline the major types of financial decisions that must be made. Then, in the remainder of the book, we discuss how these decisions should be made.

WHAT role does "finance" play within the firm? What specific tasks are assigned to the financial staff, and what tools and techniques are available to it for improving the firm's performance? On a broader scale, what is the role of finance in the U.S. economy, and how can financial management be used to further our national goals? As we shall see, proper financial management will help any business provide better products to its customers at lower prices, pay higher wages and salaries to its workers and managers, and still provide greater returns to the investors who put up the capital needed to form and then operate the company. Since the economy — both national and worldwide — consists of customers, employees, and investors, sound financial management contributes both to individual well-being and to the well-being of the general population.

THE FINANCIAL MANAGER'S RESPONSIBILITIES

The financial manager's primary task is to plan for the acquisition and use of funds so as to maximize the value of the firm. Put another way, he or she makes decisions about alternative sources and uses of funds. Here are some specific activities which are involved:

1. *Forecasting and planning.* The financial manager must interact with other executives as they jointly look ahead and lay the plans which will shape the firm's future position.

2. *Major investment and financing decisions.* On the basis of long-run plans, the financial manager must raise the capital needed to support growth. A successful firm usually achieves a high rate of growth in sales, which requires increased investments in the plant, equipment, and current assets necessary to produce goods and services. The financial manager must help determine the optimal rate of sales growth, and he or she must help decide on the specific investments to be made as well as on the types of funds to be used to finance these investments. Decisions

must be made about the use of internal versus external funds, the use of debt versus equity, and the use of long-term versus short-term debt.

3. *Coordination and control.* The financial manager must interact with executives in other parts of the business if the firm is to operate as efficiently as possible. All business decisions have financial implications, and all managers — financial and otherwise — need to take this into account. For example, marketing decisions affect sales growth, which in turn changes investment requirements. Thus, marketing decision makers must take account of how their actions affect (and are affected by) such factors as the availability of funds, inventory policies, and plant capacity utilization.

4. *Interaction with capital markets.* The financial manager must deal with the money and capital markets. As we shall see in the next chapter, each firm affects and is affected by the general financial markets, where funds are raised, where the firm's securities are traded, and where its investors are either rewarded or penalized.

In sum, the central responsibilities of financial managers involve decisions such as which investments their firms should make, how these projects should be financed, and how the firm can most effectively manage its existing resources. If these responsibilities are performed optimally, financial managers will help to maximize the values of their firms, and this will also maximize the long-run welfare of those who buy from or work for the firm.

THE CHANGING ROLE OF FINANCIAL MANAGEMENT

Finance consists of three interrelated areas: (1) *money and capital markets,* or macro finance, which deals with many of the topics covered in macroeconomics; (2) *investments,* which focuses on the decisions of individuals and financial institutions as they choose securities for their investment portfolios; and (3) *financial management,* or "business finance," which involves the management of the firm. Each of these areas interacts with the others, so a corporate financial manager must have a good knowledge of both capital market operations and the way investors appraise securities.

Financial management has undergone significant changes over the years. When it first emerged as a separate field of study in the early 1900s, the emphasis was on the legal aspects of such matters as mergers, consolidations, the formation of new firms, and the various types of securities issued by corporations. Industrialization was sweeping the country, and the critical problem firms such as U.S. Steel and Reynolds Tobacco faced was obtaining capital for expansion. The capital markets were relatively primitive, which made transfers of funds from individual savers to businesses difficult. The earnings and asset values reported in accounting statements were unreliable, and stock trading by insiders and manipulators caused prices to fluctuate wildly. Consequently, investors were reluctant to purchase stocks and bonds. As a result of these environmental conditions, finance in the early 1900s focused on legal issues relating to the issuance of securities.

The emphasis remained on securities through the 1920s. However, radical changes occurred during the depression of the 1930s, when an unprecedented number of business failures shifted the focus to bankruptcy and reorganization, to corporate liquidity, and to governmental regulation of securities markets. Finance was still a descriptive, legalistic subject, but the emphasis changed from expansion to survival.

During the 1940s and early 1950s, finance continued to be taught as a descriptive, institutional subject, viewed from the standpoint of an outsider rather than from that of management. However, financial management techniques designed to help firms maximize their profits and stock prices were beginning to receive attention.

A movement toward rigorous analysis developed during the late 1950s. Also, the major emphasis began to shift from the right-hand side of the balance sheet (liabilities and equity) to asset analysis. Computers were beginning to be used, and models were being developed to help manage inventories, cash, accounts receivable, and fixed assets. Increasingly, the focus of finance shifted from the outsider's to the insider's point of view, and financial decisions within the firm came to be recognized as the critical issue in corporate finance. Descriptive, institutional materials on capital markets and financing instruments were still studied, but these topics were considered in terms of their effects on corporate financial decisions.

The 1960s and 1970s witnessed a renewed interest in the liabilities and equity side of the balance sheet, with a focus on (1) the optimal mix of securities and (2) the way in which individual investors make investment decisions, or *portfolio theory*, and the implications of both topics for corporate finance. Corporate financial management was redesigned to help general management take actions that would maximize the value of the firm and the wealth of its stockholders, giving recognition to the fact that the results of corporate financial decisions depend upon how investors react to them. This recognition produced a blending of investment theory into corporate finance.

In the 1980s, four issues have received emphasis: (1) inflation and its effects on interest rates, (2) deregulation of financial institutions and the accompanying trend away from specialized institutions toward broadly diversified financial service corporations, (3) a dramatic increase in the use of telecommunications for transmitting information and computers for analyzing financial decisions, and (4) new and innovative methods for financing long-term investments. Inflation, including ways to combat it and to deal with it when it heats up, is being worked into the fabric of both financial theories and financial decision processes. New financial institutions and products have been created; for example, money market funds and interest rate futures. Also, older institutions have made major structural changes; so much so that today it is hard to tell a bank from a savings and loan association, or an insurance company from a brokerage firm. For example, Prudential Insurance owns a stock brokerage firm; Merrill Lynch offers checking account services; and Sears, Roebuck is one of the largest U.S. financial institutions, owning such firms as Allstate Insurance, the Dean Witter brokerage house, and Coldwell Banker, the largest U.S. real estate brokerage company. Technological developments in the computer hardware and telecommunications areas, and the availability of software packages that make otherwise very difficult numerical analyses relatively easy, are bringing about fundamental changes in the way managers manage. Data storage, transmittal, and retrieval techniques are reducing the "judgmental" aspects of management, as financial managers can now obtain relatively precise estimates of the effects of alternative courses of action.

Several innovative financing techniques have emerged in the 1980s in response to changing economic conditions. For example, a market for high-risk, high-yield bonds known as *junk bonds* was developed to finance mergers and management buyouts of their own firms. *Floating rate debt,* in which the interest rate is changed periodically to reflect current market conditions, was introduced in the early 1980s to protect investors from the adverse effects of high inflation and fluctuating interest rates. These and other long-term financing techniques will be discussed in detail in Chapter 13.

INCREASING IMPORTANCE OF
FINANCIAL MANAGEMENT

The events discussed above have greatly increased the importance of financial management. In earlier times the marketing manager would project sales, the engineering and production staffs would determine the assets necessary to meet those demands, and the financial manager's job was simply to raise the money needed to purchase the required plant, equipment, and inventories. This mode of operation is no longer prevalent; decisions are now made in a much more coordinated manner, and the financial manager generally has direct responsibility for the control process.

Public Service of Indiana (PSI) can be used to illustrate this change. A few years ago, PSI's economic forecasters would project power demand on the basis of historical trends and give those forecasts to the engineers, who would then proceed to build the new plants necessary to meet the forecasted demand. The finance department simply had the task of raising the capital the engineers told them was needed. However, inflation, environmental regulations, and other factors combined to double or even triple plant construction costs, and this caused a corresponding increase in the need for new capital. At the same time, rising fuel costs led to dramatic increases in electricity prices, which lowered the quantity of electricity demanded and made some of the new construction unnecessary. Thus, PSI found itself building a nuclear power plant that it did not really need, and, as the true situation became clear to investors, they refused to provide PSI with the capital needed to complete the plant. Eventually, a $2.5 billion investment had to be written off, and the price of the company's stock declined from about $35 in the late 1970s to a 1985 low of $6.88. (As this was being written early in 1988, PSI's stock price had risen to $13.50, but that was still far below its high of $35.) As a result of this experience, PSI (and most other companies) now places far more emphasis on the planning and control process, and this has greatly increased the importance of its finance staff.

The direction in which business is moving, as well as the increasing importance of finance, was described in a *Fortune* article several years ago. After pointing out that well over half of the then current top executives had majored in business administration versus about 25 percent a few years earlier, the *Fortune* article continued:

> Career patterns have followed the educational trends. Like scientific and technical schooling, nuts-and-bolts business experience seems to have become less important. The proportion of executives with their primary experience in production, operations, engineering, design, and research and development has fallen from a third of the total to just over a quarter. And the number of top officers with legal and financial backgrounds has increased more than enough to make up the difference. Lawyers and financial people now head two out of five corporations.
>
> It is fair to assume that the changes in training, and in the paths that led these people to the top, reflect the shifting priorities and needs of their corporations. In fact, the expanding size and complexity of corporate organizations, coupled with their continued expansion overseas, have greatly increased the importance of financial planning and controls. And the growth of government regulation and of obligations companies face under the law has heightened the need for legal advice. The engineer and the production expert have become, in consequence, less important in management than the financial executive and the lawyer.
>
> Today's chief executive officers have obviously perceived the shift in emphasis, and many of them wish they had personally been better prepared for it. Interestingly enough, a majority of them say they would have benefited from additional formal training, mainly in business administration, accounting, finance, and law.[1]

Recent surveys indicate that these trends are continuing, and they are also evident at lower levels within firms of all sizes, as well as in nonprofit and governmental organizations. Thus, it is becoming increasingly important for people in marketing, accounting, production, personnel, and other areas to understand finance in order to do a good job in their own fields. Marketing people, for instance, must understand how marketing decisions affect and are affected by funds availability, by inventory levels, by excess plant capacity, and so on. Similarly, accountants must understand how accounting data are used

---

[1]Charles G. Burck, "A Group Profile of the Fortune 500 Chief Executive," *Fortune*, May 1976, 173.

in corporate planning and are viewed by investors. The function of accounting is to provide quantitative financial information for use in making economic decisions, whereas the main functions of financial management are to plan for, acquire, and utilize funds in order to maximize the efficiency and value of the enterprise.[2]

Thus, there are financial implications in virtually all business decisions, and nonfinancial executives simply must know enough finance to work these implications into their own specialized analyses.[3] This point should make every student of business, regardless of major, concerned with finance.

ALTERNATIVE FORMS OF BUSINESS ORGANIZATION

There are three main forms of business organization: the sole proprietorship, the partnership, and the corporation. In terms of numbers, about 80 percent of business firms are operated as sole proprietorships, while the remainder are divided equally between partnerships and corporations. By dollar value of sales, however, about 80 percent of business is conducted by corporations, about 13 percent by sole proprietorships, and about 7 percent by partnerships. Because most business is conducted by corporations, we will concentrate on them in this book. However, it is important to understand the differences among the three forms, as well as their advantages and disadvantages.

Proprietorship

proprietorship
A business owned by one individual.

A **proprietorship** is a business owned by one individual. Going into business as a single proprietor is easy — one merely begins business operations. However, most cities require even the smallest establishments to be licensed, and occasionally state licenses are required as well.

The proprietorship has two important advantages for small operations: (1) It is easily and inexpensively formed, and it is subject to few government regulations. (2) The business pays no corporate income taxes; as we shall see, however, this is not always a net advantage, as all earnings of the firm, whether they are reinvested in the business or withdrawn, are subject to personal income taxes at the owner's tax rate.

The proprietorship also has three important limitations: (1) it is difficult for a proprietorship to obtain large sums of capital; (2) the proprietor has unlimited personal liability for business debts, which can result in losses greater than the money invested in the company; and (3) the life of a business

---

[2]American Institute of Certified Public Accountants, *AICPA Professional Standards,* Section 100, (New York, November 1987.)

[3]It is an interesting fact that the course "Financial Management for Nonfinancial Executives" has the highest enrollment in most executive development programs.

organized as a proprietorship is limited to the life of the individual who created it. For these three reasons, the individual proprietorship is restricted primarily to small business operations. However, businesses are frequently started as proprietorships and then converted to corporations if and when their growth causes the disadvantages of being a proprietorship to outweigh its advantages.

Partnership

partnership
An unincorporated business owned by two or more persons.

A **partnership** exists whenever two or more persons associate to conduct a business. Partnerships may operate under different degrees of formality, ranging from informal, oral understandings to formal agreements filed with the secretary of the state in which the partnership does business. The major advantage of a partnership is its low cost and ease of formation. The disadvantages are similar to those associated with proprietorships: (1) unlimited liability, (2) limited life of the organization, (3) difficulty of transferring ownership, and (4) difficulty of raising large amounts of capital. The tax treatment of a partnership is similar to that for proprietorships, and when compared to that of a corporation, this can be either an advantage or a disadvantage, depending on the situation; this point is illustrated in Chapter 2, where we discuss the federal tax system.

Regarding liability, the partners must risk all of their personal assets, even those assets not invested in the business, for under partnership law each partner is liable for the business's debts. This means that if any partner is unable to meet his or her pro rata claim in the event the partnership goes bankrupt, the remaining partners must take over the unsatisfied claims, drawing on their personal assets if necessary.[4]

The first three disadvantages — unlimited liability, impermanence of the organization, and difficulty of transferring ownership — cause the fourth, the difficulty partnerships have in attracting substantial amounts of capital. This is no particular problem for a slow-growing business, but if a business's products really catch on, and if it needs to raise large amounts of capital to expand and thus capitalize on its opportunities, the difficulty in attracting capital becomes a real drawback. Thus, growth companies such as Hewlett-Packard and Apple Computer generally begin life as proprietorships or partnerships, but at some point they find it necessary to convert into corporations.

Corporation

corporation
A legal entity created by a state, separate and distinct from its owners and managers, having unlimited life, easy transferability of ownership, and limited liability.

A **corporation** is a legal entity, or "person," created by a state. It is separate and distinct from its owners and managers. This separateness gives the corpo-

---

[4]However, it is possible to limit the liabilities of some of the partners by establishing a *limited partnership,* wherein certain partners are designated *general partners* and others *limited partners.* Limited partnerships are quite common in the area of real estate investment, but they do not work well with most types of businesses because one partner is rarely willing to assume all the business's risk.

ration three major advantages: (1) it has an *unlimited life* — it can continue after its original owners and managers are deceased; (2) it permits *easy transferability of ownership interest,* because ownership interests can be divided into shares of stock, which in turn can be transferred far more easily than can partnership interests; and (3) it permits *limited liability.* To illustrate the concept of limited liability, suppose you invested $10,000 in a partnership which then went bankrupt owing $1 million. Because the owners are liable for the debts of a partnership, you could be assessed for a share of the company's debt, and you could be held liable for the entire $1 million if your partners could not pay their shares. Thus, an investor in a partnership is exposed to unlimited liability. On the other hand, if you invested $10,000 in the stock of a corporation which then went bankrupt, your potential loss on the investment would be limited to your $10,000 investment.[5] These three factors — unlimited life, easy transferability of ownership interest, and limited liability — make it much easier for corporations than proprietorships or partnerships to raise money in the general capital markets.

The corporate form offers significant advantages over proprietorships and partnerships, but it does have two primary disadvantages: (1) Corporate earnings are subject to double taxation — the earnings of the corporation are taxed, and then any earnings paid out as dividends are taxed again as income to the stockholders. (2) Setting up a corporation is more complex and time-consuming than setting up a proprietorship or a partnership. Although a proprietorship or a partnership can commence operations without much paperwork, setting up a corporation requires that the incorporators prepare a charter and a set of bylaws, or hire a lawyer to do it for them. The *charter* includes the following information: (1) name of the proposed corporation, (2) types of activities it will pursue, (3) amount of capital stock, (4) number of directors, and (5) names and addresses of directors. The charter is filed with the secretary of the state in which the firm will be headquartered, and, when it is approved, the corporation is officially in existence.

The *bylaws* are a set of rules drawn up by the founders of the corporation to aid in governing the internal management of the company. Included are such points as (1) how directors are to be elected (all elected each year or, say, one-third each year for three-year terms); (2) whether the existing stockholders will have the first right to buy any new shares the firm issues; (3) what provisions there are for management committees, such as an executive committee or a finance committee, and the duties of such committees; and (4) what procedures there are for changing the bylaws themselves, should conditions require it. Attorneys have standard forms for charters and bylaws in their word processors, and they can set up a corporation with very little effort. A business can be incorporated for about $500.

---

[5]In the case of small corporations, the limited liability feature is often a fiction, since bankers and credit managers frequently require personal guarantees from the stockholders of small, weak businesses.

The value of any business other than a very small one will probably be maximized if it is organized as a corporation. The reasons are as follows:

1. Limited liability reduces the risks borne by investors, and, other things held constant, *the lower the firm's risk, the higher its value.*

2. A firm's value is dependent on its *growth opportunities,* which in turn are dependent on the firm's ability to attract capital. Since corporations can attract capital more easily than can unincorporated businesses, they have superior growth opportunities.

3. The value of an asset also depends on its *liquidity,* which means the ease of selling the asset and converting it to cash. Since an investment in the stock of a corporation is much more liquid than a similar investment in a proprietorship or partnership, this too means that the corporate form of organization can enhance the value of a business.

4. Corporations are taxed differently than proprietorships and partnerships, and *under certain conditions the tax laws favor corporations.* This point is discussed in detail in Chapter 2.

As we will see later in the chapter, most firms are managed with value maximization in mind, and this, in turn, has caused most large businesses to be organized as corporations.

FINANCE IN THE ORGANIZATIONAL STRUCTURE OF THE FIRM

Organization structures vary from firm to firm, but Figure 1-1 presents a fairly typical picture of the role of finance within a corporation. The chief financial officer — who has the title of vice-president: finance — reports to the president. The financial vice-president's key subordinates are the treasurer and the controller. The treasurer has direct responsibility for managing the firm's cash and marketable securities, for planning its financial structure, for selling stocks and bonds to raise capital, and for overseeing the corporate pension fund. Also under the treasurer (but in some firms under the controller) are the credit manager, the inventory manager, and the director of capital budgeting (who analyzes decisions related to investments in fixed assets). The controller is responsible for the activities of the accounting and tax departments.

stockholder wealth maximization
The appropriate goal for management decisions; considers the risk and timing associated with expected earnings per share in order to maximize the price of the firm's common stock.

THE GOALS OF THE CORPORATION

Decisions are not made in a vacuum but, rather, with some objective in mind. *Throughout this book we operate on the assumption that management's primary goal is* **stockholder wealth maximization.** As we shall see, this translates

Figure 1-1   Place of Finance in a Typical Business Organization

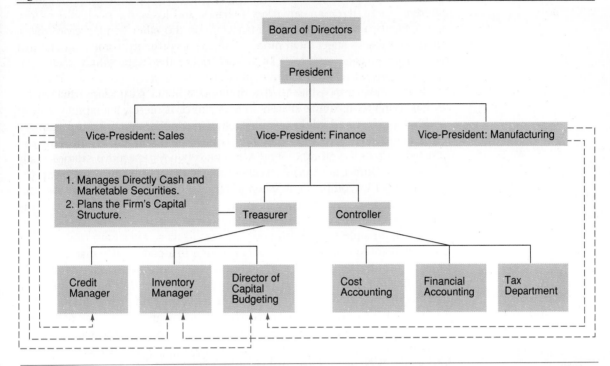

into *maximizing the price of the common stock.* Firms do, of course, have other objectives; managers, who make the actual decisions, are interested in their own personal satisfaction, in employees' welfare, and in the good of the community and society at large. Still, for the reasons set forth in the sections that follow, *stock price maximization is the most important goal of most corporations,* and it is a reasonable operating objective on which to build decision rules in a book such as this one.

Managerial Incentives to Maximize Shareholder Wealth

Stockholders own the firm and elect the management team. Management, in turn, is supposed to operate in the best interests of the stockholders. We know, however, that because the stock of most large firms is widely held, the managers of such firms have a great deal of autonomy. This being the case, might not managers pursue goals other than stock price maximization? For example, some have argued that the managers of a large, well-entrenched corporation could work to keep stockholder returns at a "fair" or "reasonable" level and then devote part of their efforts and resources to public service activities, to employee benefits, to higher executive salaries, or to golf.

Similarly, a firmly entrenched management might avoid risky ventures, even when the possible gains to stockholders were high enough to warrant taking the gamble. The theory behind this argument is that since stockholders are generally well diversified in the sense that they hold portfolios of many different stocks, if a company takes a chance and loses, the stockholders lose only a small part of their wealth. Managers, on the other hand, are not diversified, so setbacks affect them more seriously. Accordingly, some maintain that corporate managers tend to "play it safe" rather than aggressively seeking to maximize the prices of their firms' stocks.

It is almost impossible to determine whether a particular management team is trying to maximize shareholder wealth or is merely attempting to keep stockholders satisfied while pursuing other goals. For example, how can we tell whether employee or community benefit programs are in the long-run best interests of the stockholders? Are relatively high executive salaries really necessary to attract and retain excellent managers, who in turn will keep the firm ahead of its competition? When a risky venture is turned down, does this reflect management conservatism, or is it a correct judgment regarding the risks of the venture versus its potential rewards?

It is impossible to give definitive answers to these questions. However, we do know that the managers of a firm operating in a competitive market will be forced to undertake actions that are reasonably consistent with shareholder wealth maximization. If they depart from this goal, they run the risk of being removed from their jobs through a **hostile takeover** or a **proxy fight**.

A hostile takeover is the purchase by one company of the stock of another over the opposition of its management, whereas a proxy fight involves an attempt to gain control by getting stockholders to vote a new management group into office. Both actions are facilitated by low stock prices, so for the sake of self-preservation management will try to keep its stock value as high as possible. The dominant view is that takeovers rarely present a serious threat to a well-entrenched management team if that team has succeeded in maximizing the firm's value, for people attempt to take over undervalued, bargain companies, not fully valued ones. So, while it may be true that some managers are more interested in their own personal positions than in maximizing shareholder wealth per se, the threat of losing their jobs still motivates them to try to maximize stock prices.

Social Responsibility

hostile takeover
The purchase by one company of the stock of another over the opposition of its management.

proxy fight
An attempt to gain control of a firm by soliciting stockholders to vote for a new management team.

social responsibility
The concept that businesses should be actively concerned with the welfare of society at large.

Another issue that deserves consideration is **social responsibility**: Should businesses operate strictly in their stockholders' best interests, or are firms also partly responsible for the welfare of their employees, customers, and the communities in which they operate? Certainly firms have an ethical responsibility to provide a safe working environment for their employees, to ensure that their production processes are not endangering the environment, to engage in fair hiring practices, and to produce products that are safe for consumers. However, socially responsible actions such as these have costs to businesses, and it is questionable whether businesses would incur these costs voluntarily. It is clear, however, that if some firms act in a socially responsible manner while other firms do not, then the socially responsible firms will be at a dis-

normal profits/rates of return
Those profits and rates of return that are close to the average for all firms.

advantage in attracting investors. To see why this is so, consider first those firms whose **profits** and **rates of return on investment** are close to **normal,** that is, close to the average for all firms. If one company attempts to exercise social responsibility, its costs and product prices will have to increase to cover the costs of these actions. If the other businesses in the industry do not follow suit, their costs and prices will remain constant. The socially responsible firm will not be able to compete, and it thus will be forced to abandon its efforts. Thus, any voluntary socially responsible acts that raise costs will be difficult, if not impossible, in industries that are subject to keen competition.

What about oligopolistic firms with profits above normal levels — cannot such firms devote resources to social projects? Undoubtedly they can, and many large, successful firms do engage in community projects, employee benefit programs, and the like to a greater degree than would appear to be called for by pure profit or wealth maximization goals.[6] Still, publicly owned firms are constrained in such actions by capital market factors. To illustrate, suppose a saver who has funds to invest is considering two alternative firms. One firm devotes a substantial part of its resources to social actions, while the other concentrates on profits and stock prices. Most investors are likely to shun the socially oriented firm, thus putting it at a disadvantage in the capital market. After all, why should the stockholders of one corporation subsidize society to a greater extent than those of other businesses? For this reason, even highly profitable firms (unless they are closely held rather than publicly owned) are generally constrained against taking unilateral cost-increasing social actions.

Does all this mean that firms should not exercise social responsibility? Not at all, but it does mean that most significant cost-increasing actions will have to be put on a *mandatory* rather than a voluntary basis, at least initially, to insure that their burdens fall uniformly across all businesses. Thus, such social benefit programs as fair hiring practices, minority training, product safety, pollution abatement, and antitrust actions are most likely to be effective if realistic rules are established initially and then enforced by government agencies. Of course, it is critical that industry and government cooperate in establishing the rules of corporate behavior, that the costs as well as the benefits of such actions be accurately estimated and taken into account, and that firms follow the spirit as well as the letter of the law in their actions. In such a setting, the rules of the game become constraints. Throughout this book, we shall assume that managers are stock price maximizers who operate subject to a set of socially imposed constraints.

Business Ethics

Related to the issue of social responsibility is the question of business ethics. Ethics is defined in Webster's dictionary as "standards of conduct or moral behavior." Business ethics can be thought of as a company's attitude and conduct toward its employees, customers, community, and stockholders. High

---

[6]Even firms like these often find it necessary to justify such projects at stockholder meetings by stating that these programs will contribute to long-run profit maximization.

standards of ethical behavior demand that a firm treat each of these constituents in a fair and honest manner. A firm's commitment to business ethics can be measured by the tendency of the firm and its employees to adhere to laws and regulations relating to product safety and quality, fair employment practices, fair marketing and selling practices, the use of confidential information for personal gain, community involvement, bribery, and illegal payments to foreign governments to obtain business.

There are many instances of firms engaging in unethical behavior. For example, in 1988 employees of several prominent Wall Street investment banking houses were sentenced to prison terms for illegally using insider information on proposed mergers for their own personal gain, and E. F. Hutton, the stock brokerage firm, lost its independence through a forced merger after it was convicted of cheating its banks out of millions of dollars in a check kiting scheme. However, the results of a recent Business Roundtable study indicate that the executives of most major firms in the United States believe that their firms should, and do, try to maintain high ethical standards in all of their business dealings.[7] In fact, most executives believe that there is a positive correlation between ethics and long-run profitability. For example, Chemical Bank suggested that ethical behavior has increased its profitability by allowing the firm (1) to avoid fines and legal expenses, (2) to build public trust, (3) to gain business from customers who appreciate and support its policies, (4) to attract and keep employees of the highest caliber, and (5) to support the economic viability of the community in which it operates.

Most firms today have in place strong codes of ethical behavior, and they put on training programs designed to ensure that all employees understand the correct behavior in different business situations. However, it is imperative that top management — the chairman, president, and vice-presidents — be openly committed to ethical behavior, and that they communicate this commitment through their own personal actions as well as through company policies, directives, and punishment/reward systems.

Stock Price Maximization and Social Welfare

If firms attempt to maximize stock prices, is this good or bad for society? In general, it is good. Aside from such illegal actions as attempting to form monopolies, violating safety codes, and failing to meet pollution control requirements — all of which are constrained by the government — *the same actions that maximize stock prices also benefit society.* First, stock price maximization requires efficient, low-cost operations that produce the desired quality and quantity of output at the lowest possible cost. Second, stock price maximization requires the development of products that consumers want and need, so the profit motive leads to new technology, to new products, and to new jobs. Finally, stock price maximization necessitates efficient and courteous

---

[7]The Business Roundtable, *Corporate Ethics: A Prime Business Asset* (New York, February 1988).

service, adequate stocks of merchandise, and well-located business establishments — these factors are all necessary to make sales, and sales are necessary for profits. Therefore, the types of actions that help a firm increase the price of its stock are also directly beneficial to society at large. This is why profit-motivated, free-enterprise economies have been so much more successful than socialistic and other types of economic systems. Since financial management plays a crucial role in the operation of successful firms, and since successful firms are absolutely necessary for a healthy, productive economy, it is easy to see why finance is important from a social standpoint.[8]

THE AGENCY PROBLEM

In a very important article, Michael Jensen and William Meckling defined an *agency relationship* as a contract under which one or more people (the principals) hire another person (the agent) to perform some service on their behalf and delegate some decision-making authority to that agent.[9] Within the financial management framework, agency relationships exist (1) between stockholders and managers and (2) between debtholders and stockholders. These relationships are discussed in the following sections.

Stockholders versus Managers

agency problem
A potential conflict of interest between (1) the principals (outside shareholders) and the agent (manager) or (2) stockholders and debtholders.

Jensen and Meckling demonstrated that a potential **agency problem** arises whenever the manager of a firm owns less than 100 percent of the firm's common stock. If a firm is a proprietorship managed by the owner, we can assume that the owner-manager will take every possible action to improve his or her own welfare, with welfare measured primarily in the form of increased personal wealth but also in more leisure or perquisites.[10] However, if the owner-manager relinquishes a portion of his or her ownership by incorporating and selling some of the firm's stock to outsiders, a potential conflict of

---

[8]People sometimes argue that firms, in their efforts to raise profits and stock prices, increase product prices and gouge the public. In a reasonably competitive economy, which we have, prices are constrained by competition and consumer resistance. If a firm raises its prices beyond reasonable levels, it will simply lose its market share. Even giant firms like General Motors lose business to the Japanese and Germans, as well as to Ford and Chrysler, if they set prices over what will cover production costs plus a "normal" profit. Of course, firms *want* to earn more, and they constantly try to cut costs, to develop new products, and so on, and thereby to earn above-normal profits. Note, though, that if they are indeed successful and do earn above-normal profits, those very profits will attract competition and eventually drive prices down, so again the main long-term beneficiary is the consumer.

[9]See Michael C. Jensen and William H. Meckling, "Theory of the Firm: Managerial Behavior, Agency Costs, and Ownership Structure," *Journal of Financial Economics,* October 1976, 305–360. The discussion of agency theory which follows draws heavily from their work.

[10]*Perquisites* are executive fringe benefits such as luxurious offices, use of corporate planes and yachts, personal assistants, and so on.

interests immediately arises. For example, the owner-manager may now decide either to lead a more relaxed life and not work as strenuously to maximize shareholder wealth, because less of this wealth will go to him or her, or to take a higher salary or consume more perquisites, because part of these costs will now fall on the outside stockholders. This potential conflict between two parties, the principals (outside shareholders) and the agent (manager), is one type of agency problem.

leveraged buyout
A situation in which a group, often the firm's management, uses credit to purchase the outstanding shares of the company's stock.

tender offer
An offer to buy the stock of a firm directly from its shareholders.

Another potential conflict between management and stockholders arises in a **leveraged buyout**, a term used to describe the situation in which management itself (1) arranges a line of credit, (2) makes an offer, called a **tender offer**, to the stockholders to buy the stock not already owned by the management group, and (3) "takes the company private" after it has bought the outstanding shares. Dozens of such buyouts of New York Stock Exchange listed companies have occurred recently, and a potential conflict clearly exists whenever one is contemplated. For example, the management of Cone Mills, the largest U.S. producer of denim, recently decided to make a leveraged buyout offer to the outside stockholders. It was in management's best interests to have the stock price minimized, not maximized, prior to the offer. Aware of this, Cone's management, like most who contemplate leveraged buyouts, obtained an outside opinion about the value of the stock so as to head off lawsuits. Also, Cone's management's offer, like most, was contested by competing offers from other parties. In spite of competing offers, Cone Mills' managers were able to purchase the stock of the company at a price which they regarded as less than its true value. Thus, leveraged buyouts constitute a type of agency problem arising between the stockholders and the managers of a firm.

agency costs
The costs associated with monitoring management's actions to insure that those actions are consistent with contractual agreements between managers, stockholders, and debtholders.

To insure that its managers act in the best interests of the outside shareholders, the firm must incur **agency costs**, which may take several forms: (1) expenditures to monitor managerial actions, (2) expenditures to structure the organization so that the possibility of undesirable managerial behavior will be limited, and (3) opportunity costs associated with lost profit opportunities resulting from an organizational structure which does not permit managers to take actions on as timely a basis as would be possible if the managers were also the owners.

There are two extreme positions regarding how to deal with the agency problem. At one extreme, if a firm's managers were compensated only with shares of the firm's stock, agency costs would be low because the managers would have less incentive to take excessive leisure, salary, or perquisites. However, it would be difficult to hire managers under these terms. At the opposite extreme, owners could closely monitor every managerial activity, but this solution would be extremely costly and inefficient. The optimal solution lies somewhere between the extremes, where executive compensation is tied to performance, but some monitoring is also done. Several mechanisms which tend to force managers to act in the shareholders' best interests are discussed next. These include (1) the threat of firing, (2) the threat of takeover, and (3) the proper structuring of managerial incentives.

The Threat of Firing. Until recently, the probability of a large firm's management being ousted by its stockholders was so remote that it posed little threat. This situation existed because ownership of most firms was so widely distributed, and management's control over the proxy mechanism was so strong, that it was almost impossible for dissident stockholders to gain enough votes to overthrow the managers. However, stock ownership is being increasingly concentrated in the hands of large institutions rather than individuals, and the institutional money managers have the clout, if they choose to use it, to exercise considerable influence over a firm's operations.

To illustrate, consider the case of GAF Corporation, a leading producer of building materials and industrial chemicals with 1987 sales of about $750 million. GAF's stock price was as high as $41 in 1965, after which it began a long slide; by the 1980s it was selling below $8. At that point, institutions began to buy heavily, and their ownership increased from 15 to 40 percent. Many bought shares with the expectation that GAF's chairman, Jesse Werner, would retire soon and that the company would be broken up or acquired by another firm. This expectation was fueled by the fact that Mr. Werner, who had been chairman since 1964, announced that GAF would sell eight marginally profitable businesses representing about half of its sales. Analysts figured that this would make the company cash-rich and a likely takeover candidate, and thus that the price of its stock would rise. Indeed, the stock price more than doubled in one year, from $7.75 to $16.375.

But Mr. Werner decided to keep his job. He obtained a new five-year contract and announced that the firm would reinvest internally most of the $212 million it had received from the sale of the eight divisions. These actions caused GAF's stock price to drop back below $9. This prompted Samuel Heyman, a Connecticut shopping center owner who held 4.2 percent of GAF's stock, to wage a proxy fight. Mr. Heyman obtained proxies representing about 60 percent of the shares, so he was able to oust Mr. Werner.

The victory for the dissidents was made possible because of support from large institutional holders. "We've got to outperform the market," explained one money manager. "Our clients have many money managers, and if we're performing poorly, the meter starts running, and pretty soon we'll be cut from the list." Another money manager said, "We simply can't afford to have much patience with poor management." So, whereas individual investors may be uninformed, lazy, or simply willing to "vote with their feet" by selling shares in companies whose performance is sub-par, institutional investors are more likely to work actively to oust an inefficient management. Recognizing this fact, people like Mr. Heyman are now more likely to "run against" a firmly entrenched management than would have been true some years ago.

The Threat of Takeover. Hostile takeovers (where management does not want the firm to be taken over) are most likely to occur when a firm's stock is undervalued relative to its potential because of poor managerial decisions. In a hostile takeover, the managers of the acquired firm are generally fired, and any who are able to stay on lose the autonomy they had prior to the acquisition. Thus, managers have a strong incentive to take actions which maximize share price. In the words of one company president, "If you want to keep control, don't let your company's stock sell at a bargain price."

Actions to increase the firm's stock price and to keep it from being a bargain are obviously good from the standpoint of the stockholders, but other tactics that managers can take to ward off a hostile takeover may not be. Two examples of questionable tactics are poison pills and greenmail. A **poison pill** is an action that a firm can take which practically kills it and thus makes it unattractive to potential suitors. Examples include Walt Disney's plan to sell large blocks of its stock at low prices to "friendly" parties, Scott Industries' decision to make all of its debt immediately payable if its management changed, and Carleton Corporation's decision to give huge retirement bonuses, which represented a large part of the company's wealth, to its managers if the firm was taken over (such payments are called *golden parachutes*). **Greenmail**, which is like blackmail, occurs when this sequence of events takes place: (1) A potential acquirer (firm or individual) buys a block of stock in a company, (2) the target company's management becomes frightened that the acquirer will make a tender offer and gain control of the company, and (3) to head off a possible takeover, management offers to pay greenmail, buying the stock of the potential raider at a price above the existing market price without offering the same deal to other stockholders. A good example of greenmail was Texaco's recent buy-back of 13 million shares of its stock from the Bass Brothers' organization at a price of $50 a share at a time when the stock sold in the market at less than $40. As this book goes to press, the SEC and Congress are considering legislation to protect stockholders from poison pills, greenmail, and the like.

Structuring Managerial Incentives. More and more, firms are tying managers' compensation to the company's performance, and research suggests that this motivates managers to operate in a manner consistent with stock price maximization.[11]

Performance-based incentive plans have become an accepted management tool. In the 1950s and 1960s, most of these plans involved **executive stock options**, which allowed managers to purchase stock at some time in the future at a given price; the options would be valuable if the market price of the stock rose above the option purchase price. The firms which used these plans believed that allowing managers to purchase stock at a fixed price would provide an incentive for them to take actions which would maximize the stock's price. This type of managerial incentive lost favor in the 1970s, however, because the

poison pill
An action taken by a firm to make it unattractive to potential buyers in an attempt to avoid a hostile takeover.

greenmail
A situation in which a firm, in trying to avoid a takeover, offers to buy back stock from a raider at a price above the existing market price.

executive stock option
A type of incentive plan that allows managers to purchase stock at some time in the future at a given price.

---

[11]See Wilbur G. Lewellen, "Management and Ownership in the Large Firm," *Journal of Finance,* May 1969, 299–322. Lewellen concluded that managers seem to make decisions that are largely oriented toward stock price maximization. Economic events since his study was published suggest that the incentives for stock price maximization are even stronger today than they were during the period his data covered.

options generally did not pay off. The general stock market declined, and stock prices did not necessarily reflect companies' earnings growth. Incentive plans ought to be based on those factors over which managers have control, and since they cannot control the general stock market, stock option plans have proved to be weak incentive devices. Therefore, whereas 61 of the 100 largest U.S. firms used stock options as their sole incentive compensation in 1970, not even one of the largest 100 companies relied exclusively on such plans in 1987.

performance shares
A type of incentive plan in which managers are awarded shares of stock on the basis of their performance over given intervals with respect to earnings per share or other measures.

One important incentive plan now is **performance shares**, which are shares of stock given to executives on the basis of performance as measured by earnings per share, return on assets, return on equity, and so on. For example, Honeywell uses growth in earnings per share as its primary performance measure. The firm has two overlapping four-year performance periods, beginning two years apart. At the start of each period, the participating executives are allocated a certain number of performance shares, say, 10,000 shares for the president down to 1,000 shares for a lower-ranking manager. If the company achieves, say, a targeted 13 percent annual average growth in earnings per share, the managers will earn 100 percent of their shares. If the corporate performance is above the target, Honeywell's managers can earn even more shares, up to a maximum of 130 percent, which requires a 16 percent growth rate. However, if growth is below 13 percent, they get less than 100 percent of the shares, and below a 9 percent growth rate, they get zero. Executives must remain with Honeywell through the performance period (four years) in order to receive the bonus shares.

Performance shares have a value even if the company's stock price remains constant because of a poor general stock market, whereas, under similar conditions, stock options might have no value even though managers had been successful in boosting earnings. Of course, the *value* of the shares received is dependent on market price performance, because 1,000 shares of Honeywell stock are a lot more valuable if the stock sells for $200 than if it sells for only $100.

All incentive compensation plans — executive stock options, performance shares, profit-based bonuses, and so forth — are supposed to accomplish two things. First, they offer executives incentives to act on those factors under their control in a manner that will contribute to stock price maximization. Second, the existence of such performance plans helps companies attract and retain top-level executives. Well-designed plans can accomplish both goals.[12]

---

[12]One interesting aspect of incentive plans which involve stock rather than cash is their effects on reported corporate profits. To illustrate, suppose a company has operating income of $10 million before executive compensation. If it paid its executives $1 million in salary and cash bonuses, then it would report operating income of $9 million. However, if it gave them stock options worth $1 million, this would have no effect on reported profits, even though there is truly a cost to the company, because it will later have to sell shares at a bargain price, which will reduce earnings available to the other stockholders. The Financial Accounting Standards Board is currently exploring ways to deal with this problem and thus to make reported profits more realistic and consistent across companies.

Stockholders versus Creditors

The second agency problem arises because of potential conflicts between stockholders and creditors. Creditors lend funds to the firm at rates that are based on (1) the riskiness of the firm's existing assets, (2) expectations concerning the riskiness of future asset additions, (3) the firm's existing capital structure (that is, the amount of debt financing it uses), and (4) expectations concerning future capital structure changes. These are the factors that determine the riskiness of the firm's cash flows and hence the safety of its debt issues, so creditors set their required rates of return, and hence the cost of debt to the firm, on expectations regarding these factors.

Now suppose the stockholders, acting through management, cause the firm to take on new projects that have greater risks than were anticipated by the creditors. This increased risk will cause the required rate of return on the firm's debt to increase, which in turn will cause the value of the outstanding debt to fall.[13] If the riskier capital investments turn out to be successful, all of the benefits will go to the stockholders, because the creditors get only a fixed return, but if things go sour, the bondholders will have to share the losses. What we would have, from the stockholders' point of view, is a game of "heads I win, tails you lose," which is obviously not a good game from the creditors' standpoint. Similarly, if the firm increases its level of debt in an effort to boost profits, the value of the old debt will decrease, because the old debt's bankruptcy protection will be lessened by the issuance of the new debt. In both of these situations, stockholders would be gaining at the expense of the firm's creditors.

Can and should stockholders, through their managers/agents, try to expropriate wealth from the firm's creditors? In general, the answer is no. First, because such attempts have been made in the past, creditors today protect themselves reasonably well against such stockholder actions through restrictions in credit agreements. Second, if creditors perceive that the firm is trying to take advantage of them in unethical ways, they will either refuse to deal further with the firm or else will require a much higher than normal rate of interest to compensate for the risks of such possible exploitation. Thus, firms which try to deal unfairly with creditors either lose access to the debt markets or are saddled with higher interest rates, which can lead to a decrease in the long-run value of the stock.

In view of these constraints, it follows that the goal of maximizing shareholder wealth requires fair play with creditors: Stockholder wealth depends on continued access to capital markets, and access depends on fair play and abiding with both the letter and the spirit of credit agreements. Therefore, the managers, as agents of both the creditors and the shareholders, must act in a manner which is fairly balanced between the interests of these two classes of security holders. Similarly, because of other constraints and sanctions, manage-

---

[13]In general, the higher the required rate of return on an existing debt issue, the lower its value. In Chapter 6 we will present some models which illustrate this point.

ment actions which would expropriate wealth from the firm's employees, customers, suppliers, or community will ultimately be to the detriment of shareholders. We conclude that in our society the goal of shareholder wealth maximization requires the fair treatment of other groups.

MANAGERIAL ACTIONS TO MAXIMIZE SHAREHOLDER WEALTH

profit maximization
The maximization of the firm's net income.

earnings per share (EPS)
The net income of the firm divided by the number of shares of common stock outstanding.

To maximize the long-run value of a firm's stock, what types of actions should its management take? First, consider the question of stock prices versus profits: Will **profit maximization** also result in stock price maximization? In answering this question, we must analyze the matter of total corporate profits versus **earnings per share (EPS)**.

For example, suppose Xerox had 100 million shares outstanding and earned $400 million, or $4 per share, and you owned 100 shares of the stock, so your share of the total profits would be $400. Now suppose Xerox sold another 100 million shares and invested the funds received in assets which produced $100 million of income. Total income would rise to $500 million, but earnings per share would decline from $4 to $500/200 = $2.50. Now your share of the firm's earnings would be only $250, down from $400. You (and other current stockholders) would have suffered an earnings dilution, even though total corporate profits had risen. Therefore, other things held constant, *if management is interested in the well-being of its current stockholders, it should concentrate on earnings per share rather than on total corporate profits.*

Will maximization of expected earnings per share always maximize stockholder welfare, or should other factors be considered? Think about the *timing of the earnings.* Suppose Xerox had one project that would cause earnings per share to rise by $0.20 per year for 5 years, or $1 in total, while another project would have no effect on earnings for 4 years but would increase earnings by $1.25 in the fifth year. Which project is better — in other words, is $0.20 per year for 5 years better or worse than $1.25 in Year 5? The answer depends on which project adds the most to the value of the stock, which in turn depends on the time value of money to investors. Thus, timing is an important reason to concentrate on wealth as measured by the price of the stock rather than on earnings alone.

Still another issue relates to *risk.* Suppose one project is expected to increase earnings per share by $1, while another is expected to raise earnings by $1.20 per share. The first project is not very risky; if it is undertaken, earnings will almost certainly rise by about $1 per share. However, the other project is quite risky, so although our best guess is that earnings will rise by $1.20 per share, we must recognize the possibility that there may be no increase whatsoever, or even a loss. Depending on how averse stockholders are to risk, the first project may be preferable to the second.

The riskiness inherent in projected earnings per share (EPS) also depends on *how the firm is financed.* As we shall see, many firms go bankrupt every year, and the greater the use of debt, the greater the threat of bankruptcy. *Consequently, while the use of debt financing may increase projected EPS, debt also increases the riskiness of projected future earnings.*

Still another issue is the matter of paying dividends to stockholders versus retaining earnings and reinvesting them in the firm, thereby causing the earnings stream to grow over time. Stockholders like cash dividends, but they also like the growth in EPS that results from plowing earnings back into the business. The financial manager must decide exactly how much of the current earnings to pay out as dividends rather than to retain and to reinvest — this is called the **dividend policy decision**. The optimal dividend policy is the one that maximizes the firm's stock price.

We see, then, that the firm's stock price is dependent on the following factors:

dividend policy decision
The decision as to how much of current earnings to pay out as dividends rather than to retain and to reinvest in the firm.

1. Projected earnings per share
2. Timing of the earnings stream
3. Riskiness of these projected earnings
4. The firm's use of debt
5. Dividend policy

Every significant corporate decision should be analyzed in terms of its effect on these factors and hence on the price of the firm's stock. For example, suppose Exxon's coal division is considering opening a new mine. If this is done, can it be expected to increase EPS? Is there a chance that costs will exceed estimates, that prices and output will fall below projections, and that EPS will be reduced because the new mine was opened? How long will it take for the new mine to start showing a profit? How should the capital required to open the mine be raised? If debt is used, how much will this increase Exxon's riskiness? Should Exxon reduce its current dividends and use the cash thus saved to finance the project, or should it maintain its dividends and finance the mine with external capital? Financial management is designed to help answer questions like these, plus many more.

THE ECONOMIC ENVIRONMENT

Although managers can take actions which affect the values of their firms' stocks, there are additional factors which influence stock prices. Included among them are external constraints, the general level of economic activity, taxes, and conditions in the stock market. Figure 1-2 diagrams these general relationships. Working within the set of external constraints shown in the box at the extreme left, management makes a set of long-run strategic policy decisions which chart a future course for the firm. These policy decisions, along

Figure 1-2   Summary of Major Factors Affecting Stock Prices

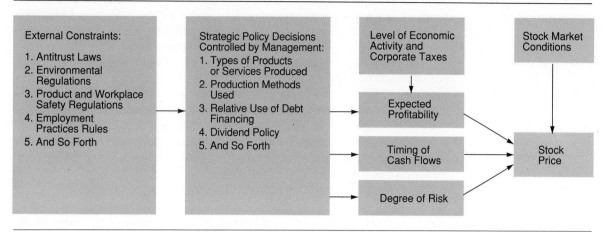

with the general level of economic activity and the level of corporate income taxes, influence the firm's expected profitability, the timing of its earnings, the eventual transfer of earnings to stockholders in the form of dividends, and the degree of uncertainty (or risk) inherent in projected earnings and dividends. Profitability, timing, and risk all affect the price of the firm's stock, but so does another factor, the state of the stock market as a whole, because all stock prices tend to move up and down together to some extent.

ORGANIZATION OF THE BOOK

Part I contains fundamental background materials upon which the book builds. Finance cannot be studied in a vacuum — financial decisions are profoundly influenced by the economic and social environment in which they are made. An introduction to the economic side of this environment is presented in Chapters 2 and 3. Then, in Chapters 4, 5, and 6, we go on to develop some financial models which can be used to help evaluate financial decisions. The specific tasks of financial managers include (1) coordinating the planning process, (2) administering the control process, (3) handling specialized finance functions such as raising capital, and (4) analyzing strategic long-term investment decisions. To perform these tasks properly, it is necessary to estimate stockholders' reactions to alternative actions or events. Accordingly, a major task in Part I is to develop a set of *valuation models,* which can be used to gain insights into how different actions are likely to affect the price of the firm's stock. The concepts and models developed in Part I are used extensively throughout the remainder of the book.

Part II, which includes Chapters 7 and 8, examines financial statements and financial forecasting. Because both long- and short-run plans are analyzed in terms of future financial statements, it is important to understand how these statements are developed and used by both managers and investors. We concentrate first on analyzing reports of past operations, then on projecting financial statements into the future under different strategic plans and operating conditions.

Beginning with Part III, in Chapters 9, 10, and 11, we move into the execution phase of the long-range strategic planning process, considering the vital subject of long-term investment decisions, or *capital budgeting*. Since major capital expenditures take years to plan and execute, and since decisions in this area are generally not reversible and hence affect operations for many years, their effect on the value of the firm is obvious.

Parts IV and V focus on long-term financial decisions: What are the principal sources and forms of long-term capital, how much does each type cost, and how does the method of financing affect the value of the firm? These sections use most of the valuation concepts developed earlier in the book to analyze such key issues as the optimal debt/equity mix and dividend policy. These sections also serve to integrate the long-term, strategic aspects of the book and to show how the parts fit together.

Finally, in Part VI we examine the management of current assets and current liabilities. From accounting we know that assets which are expected to be converted to cash within a year, such as inventories and accounts receivable, are called *current assets,* and that liabilities which must be paid off within a year are called *current liabilities.* The management of current assets and current liabilities is known as *working capital management,* and Part VI addresses that topic.

International

THE INTERNATIONAL ENVIRONMENT

In theory, the concepts and procedures discussed in various parts of the text are valid for both domestic and multinational operations. However, several problems uniquely associated with the international environment increase the complexity of the manager's task in a multinational corporation and often force us to alter the way alternative courses of action are evaluated and compared. Five major factors complicate the situation and thus distinguish financial management as practiced by firms operating entirely in a single country versus those that operate in several different countries:

1. Cash flows in various parts of a multinational corporate system are denominated in different currencies. Hence, an analysis of exchange rates, and the effects of changing currency values, must be included in all types of financial analyses.

2. Each country in which the firm operates will have its own unique political and economic institutions. Institutional differences among countries can cause significant problems when the corporation tries to coordinate and control the worldwide operations of its subsidiaries. For example, differences in tax laws among countries can cause a given economic transaction to have

strikingly dissimilar after-tax consequences, depending on where it occurred. Similarly, differences in the legal systems of host nations, such as the Common Law of Great Britain versus the French Civil Law, complicate many matters, from the simple recording of a business transaction to the role played by the judiciary in resolving conflicts. Such differences can restrict the flexibility of multinational corporations to deploy resources as they wish and can even make illegal procedures in one part of the company that are required in another part. These differences also make it difficult for executives trained in one country to operate effectively in another.

3. Even within geographic regions that have long been considered relatively homogeneous, different countries have unique cultural heritages which shape values and influence the role of business in the society. Multinational corporations find that such matters as defining the appropriate goals of the firm, attitudes toward risk-taking, dealings with employees, the ability to curtail unprofitable operations, and so on, can vary dramatically from one country to the next.

4. Most traditional models in finance assume the existence of a competitive marketplace, in which the terms of competition are determined by the participants. The government, through its power to establish basic ground rules, is involved in this process, but its participation is minimal. Thus, the market provides both the primary barometer of success and an indicator of the actions that must be taken to remain competitive. This view

of the process is reasonably correct for the United States and a few other major Western industrialized nations, but it does not accurately describe the situation in the majority of countries. Frequently, the terms under which companies compete, actions that must be taken or avoided, and the terms of trade on various transactions are determined not in the marketplace but by direct negotiation between the host government and the multinational corporation. This is essentially a political process, and it must be treated as such. Thus, our traditional financial models have to be recast to include political and other noneconomic facets of the decision.

5. The distinguishing characteristic of a nation state that differentiates it from a multinational corporation is that the nation state exercises sovereignty over the people and property in its territory. Hence, a nation state is free to place constraints on the transfer of corporate resources and even to expropriate without compensation the assets of the firm. This is a political risk, and it tends to be largely a given rather than a variable which can be changed by negotiation. Political risk varies from country to country, and it must be addressed explicitly in any financial analysis.

These five factors complicate financial management within the multinational firm, and they increase the risk faced by the firms involved. However, higher prospects for profit often make it well worthwhile for firms to accept these risks, and to learn how to minimize or at least live with them.

**Small
Business**

GOALS AND RESOURCES IN THE SMALL FIRM

Small businesses are critically important in the U.S. economy. The Small Business Administration (SBA) reports more than 98 percent of all businesses are considered small by SBA standards. Further, these small businesses provide approximately 60 percent of U.S. business employment, plus almost 100 percent of *new* jobs in American industry. Also, the SBA reports that more than half of all product and service innovations developed in the United States

since World War II have been developed by independent small business entrepreneurs.[14]

Although small business is a vital contributor to the financial health of our economy, the businesses

---

[14]Small Business Administration, *Facts about Small Business and the U.S. Small Business Administration* (Washington, D.C.: U.S. Government Printing Office, 1981).

themselves are often fragile and susceptible to failure because of their poor management, particularly their financial management.

Significant differences exist between small and big businesses: the way they are owned, the way they are managed, and the financial and managerial resources they have at their disposal. These differences affect the financial management function in small firms, and they make it necessary to modify the standard financial management principles for application in the small business area. Two especially important differences are resource shortages and goal conflicts.

Resource Shortages

John Thompson owns 75 percent of the stock in Circuit Products Corporation, a small but growing manufacturer of semiconductor components. The remainder of the stock is owned by his friends and relatives. The company began operation with about $250,000 in cash, and it has developed a promising line of products. However, the firm has used up nearly all of its original capital.

In addition to Thompson, the company has 12 employees; 10 are engineers or technicians involved in the development and testing of new products, and the other two are clerical/secretarial personnel. Thompson uses the services of an outside accounting firm to process the company's monthly statements, which typically are completed approximately six weeks after the end of the month.

Thompson has full responsibility for the management of Circuit Products except for product development, which is run by Vice-President Roland Smith. Smith is a technical whiz with no interest or background in business management, but he does have an impressive list of technical credentials. He recently left a senior engineering position at a large electronics company to join Thompson's company.

Thompson's responsibilities include making contacts with potential customers, handling all personnel decisions, giving final approval to all proposed new products presented by the technical staff, overseeing investor relations, handling legal issues both in the patent area and in the issuance of the firm's stock, managing the firm's relations with the bank, and managing the firm's finances. He has not taken a day off in six months, and he does not expect to do so for several more months.

Thompson is not unusual. Management in small firms is often spread very thin, with one or two key individuals taking on far more responsibility than they can handle properly. Thompson, for example, believes that other priorities in the business are too important to let him spend time putting together a budget or checking regularly to see how well the company is doing against such a budget. He argues, "I have a pretty good feel for how we're doing cash-wise, and I really don't have the time to go into any more detail. Making budgets doesn't make money."

Given a request by the technical staff for some new and expensive testing equipment for development purposes, Thompson would make the decision to buy or not to buy the equipment with little or no formal analysis, proceeding on the basis of his "gut feelings." He sees the analysis as being too time-consuming in view of the fact that he must this week put together a presentation for a potential customer and talk with a venture capital firm about providing Circuit Products with capital to get its products into new markets.

Not only is management often spread thin in small firms, but smaller firms have great difficulty acquiring the new funds needed for business expansion. Until Circuit Products achieves a fairly substantial size, say $15 million or so in sales, the company cannot sell stock or bonds to the general public. Further, if the company does have a public stock offering at the first opportunity, its costs will be quite high in comparison to larger firms' costs of issuing stock. Thus, Circuit Products has very limited access to public capital markets. Access to nonpublic markets is also limited. For example, its banks are reluctant to lend Circuit Products substantial amounts of money because of the firm's lack of financial history.

Small firms thus have constraints both on their managerial talent and on their ability to obtain adequate financial resources. It is no wonder small firms often fail, given their poor (or overworked) management and lack of capital.

Goal Setting

Small businesses also differ from large firms with regard to corporate goals. Earlier in the chapter we pointed out that share price maximization is taken to be the goal of all firms. Thompson, however, is a good example of an owner whose life is tied up in his company. He depends on the firm for his liveli-hood, and he has bet his future on the success of the company. His personal wealth portfolio is not at all diversified: he has put everything he owns into the company. Given his level of commitment to the company and his lack of a fallback position, Thomp-son takes a very different posture toward risk-taking by his firm than would a typical investor in a public company. Most public investors hold a number of other investments, and thus a well-diversified port-folio of holdings, and investors' employment in-comes generally come from jobs in altogether separate industries. On the other hand, both Thompson's salary and investment income are de-pendent on the success of one company, Circuit Products. This makes his risk exposure quite high.

The owner-managers of small firms are very much interested in the value of their firms, even if this value cannot be observed in the market. Thompson and others in similar positions generally have in mind "taking the firm public" or having it acquired by a larger firm at some future date — at the highest possible price. But the motives of small business owners are complex, and some owners may be motivated primarily by such considerations as the desire to be their "own boss," even if this means not letting the firm grow at the fastest rate possible or be as profitable as it could be. In other words, there is value to being in control, and that value is not easily measurable. As a result, we often observe small businesses taking actions, such as re-fusing to bring in new stockholders even when they badly need new capital, that do not make sense when judged on the basis of value maximization but that do make sense when seen in the light of the personal objectives of the owners.

To the extent that the goals of the small firm differ from value maximization, some of the pre-scriptions in this text may not be entirely applica-ble. However, most of the tools we develop will be useful for small businesses, even though the tools may have to be modified somewhat. In any event, brief "Small Business" sections in various chapters will serve as a vehicle for discussing issues of spe-cial importance to small firms.

SUMMARY AND KEY CONCEPTS

This chapter has provided an overview of financial management. The key con-cepts covered are listed below.

- **Financial managers** are responsible for obtaining and using funds in a way that will maximize the value of the firm.

- The three main forms of business organization are the **sole proprietorship**, the **partnership**, and the **corporation**.

- Although each form of organization offers some advantages and disadvantages, **most business is conducted by corporations because this organizational form maximizes their values.**

- The primary goal of management should be to **maximize stockholders' wealth,** and this means **maximizing the price of the firm's stock.**

- An **agency problem** is a potential conflict of interest that can arise between (1) the owners of the firm and its management or (2) the stockholders and the debtholders.

- There are a number of ways to **motivate managers to act in the best interests of stockholders,** including (1) the threat of firing, (2) the threat of takeovers, and (3) properly structured managerial compensation packages.

- The **price of the firm's stock** depends on the firm's projected earnings per share, the timing of earnings, the riskiness of projected earnings, the firm's use of debt, and the firm's dividend policy.

- **International operations** are becoming increasingly important to individual firms and to the national economy. We shall discuss international operations throughout the text.

- **Small businesses** are quite important in the aggregate. Again, we discuss small businesses issues throughout the text.

The book's organization reflects the stock price maximization goal. First, we discuss the economic and social environment, after which we develop valuation models that can be used to show how corporate actions will affect stock prices. Then, in the remainder of the book, we examine specific actions that management can take to achieve stock price maximization.

For the most part, we address issues faced by and techniques used by medium and large companies operating in the domestic economy. However, we do, in various sections throughout the book, point out aspects of both multinational financial management and financial management within small firms.

Questions

1-1 What are the three principal forms of business organization? What are the advantages and disadvantages of each?

1-2 Would the "normal" rate of return on investment be the same in all industries? Would "normal" rates of return change over time? Explain.

1-3 Would the role of the financial manager be likely to increase or decrease in importance relative to other executives if the rate of inflation increased? Explain.

1-4 Should stockholder wealth maximization be thought of as a long-run or a short-run goal — for example, if one action would probably increase the firm's stock price from a current level of $20 to $25 in 6 months and then to $30 in 5 years, but another action would probably keep the stock at $20 for several years but then increase it to $40 in 5 years, which action would be better? Can you think of some corporate actions which might have these general tendencies?

1-5 Drawing on your background in accounting, can you think of any accounting procedure differences that might make it difficult to compare the relative performance of different firms?

1-6 Would the management of a firm in an oligopolistic or in a competitive industry be more likely to engage in what might be called "socially conscious" practices? Explain your reasoning.

1-7 What is the difference between stock price maximization and profit maximization? Under what conditions might profit maximization not lead to stock price maximization?

1-8   If you were the president of a large, publicly owned corporation, would you make decisions to maximize stockholders' welfare or your own personal interests? What are some actions stockholders could take to insure that management's interests and those of stockholders coincided? What are some other factors that might influence management's actions?

1-9   The president of Union Semiconductor Corporation made this statement in the Company's annual report: "Union's primary goal is to increase the value of the common stockholders' equity over time." Later on in the report, the following announcements were made:

a. The Company contributed $1 million to the symphony orchestra in its home office city.

b. The Company is spending $300 million to open a new plant in South America. No revenues will be produced by the plant for 3 years, so earnings will be depressed during this period versus what they would have been had the decision been made not to open the new plant.

c. The Company is increasing its relative use of debt. Whereas assets were formerly financed with 40 percent debt and 60 percent equity, henceforth the financing mix will be 50-50.

d. The Company uses a great deal of electricity in its manufacturing operations, and it generates most of this power itself. Plans are to utilize nuclear fuel rather than coal to produce electricity in the future.

e. The Company has been paying out half of its earnings as dividends and retaining the other half. Henceforth, it will pay out only 20 percent as dividends.

Discuss how each of these factors might affect Union's stock price.

Self-Test Problem

Key terms

ST-1   Define each of the following terms:

a. Proprietorship; partnership; corporation
b. Stockholder wealth maximization
c. Hostile takeover; proxy fight; tender offer
d. Social responsibility
e. Normal profits; normal rate of return
f. Agency problem; agency costs
g. Leveraged buyout
h. Poison pill; greenmail
i. Performance shares; executive stock option
j. Profit maximization
k. Earnings per share
l. Dividend policy decision
m. Multinational corporation; multinational financial management
n. Small business versus large business

Solution to Self-Test Problem

ST-1   Refer to the marginal glossary definitions or relevant chapter sections to check your responses.

2 Financial Statements, Taxes, and Cash Flows

WHAT CORPORATE REPORT CARDS MEASURE: APPLE COMPUTER'S SUCCESS

What do Apple Computer, Hewlett-Packard, and Safeway Stores all have in common? They, and most other big businesses, all started out as proprietorships, later became partnerships, and eventually converted to corporations. Why does this pattern emerge? The answer is that organizational form affects risk, returns, and growth opportunities — and hence the market value — of a business. This chapter will give you some insights into why Apple Computer is a corporation rather than a partnership or proprietorship, and also some ideas about the form of organization you should choose if you decide to go into business for yourself.

Apple's stock value is based on its current and projected earnings, which in turn depend on the company's assets and liabilities. Income, assets, and liabilities are all reported in Apple's financial statements. Consequently, the information given in these statements is important to anyone thinking of investing in Apple's stock. The firm's balance sheets and income statements show where it has been, where it is now, and where it seems to be headed in the future. In a sense, Apple's financial statements are like its report card; analysts can examine the statements and determine whether the company should receive an A, B, C, D, or F. The central task of Apple's management is to take actions now, in the current year, that will lead to good "report cards" in future years.

> Also, you should recognize that Apple and other companies have a major "silent partner" who takes a large (but somewhat controllable) share of the profits, and that this same silent partner takes a further share of all the interest and dividends Apple pays to its investors. This silent partner is, of course, the Internal Revenue Service, which takes its share of the pie as taxes. The Tax Code is quite complicated, and, depending on how a firm is structured and the types of actions it takes, the firm can pay rates as high as 39 percent or as low as zero. Studying the tax issues discussed in this chapter will not assure anyone of achieving Apple's success, but it will give you a good idea of how the U.S. tax system operates and of how to live with the system.

FINANCIAL management cannot be studied in a vacuum; if the value of a firm is to be maximized, the financial manager must understand the legal environment in which financial decisions are made. This requires a consideration of the types of financial statements firms must provide to investors and the types of securities they may issue. Further, the value of any asset — be it a *financial asset* such as a stock or a bond, or a real (physical) asset such as land, buildings, equipment, or inventories — depends on the usable, or *after-tax,* cash flows the asset produces. Accordingly, this chapter presents some background information on financial statements, on the major types of securities used by businesses, and on the federal income tax system.[1]

FINANCIAL STATEMENTS AND SECURITIES

Any business must have *assets* if it is to operate, and in order to acquire assets, the firm must raise *capital.* Capital comes in two basic forms, *debt* and *equity.* There are many different types of debt — long-term and short-term, interest-bearing and non-interest-bearing, secured and unsecured, and so on. Similarly, there are different types of equity. For example, the equity of a proprietorship is called *proprietor's interest* or *proprietor's net worth,* whereas for a partnership, the word *partner* is inserted in lieu of *proprietor.* For a corporation, equity is represented by *preferred stock* and *common stockholders' equity.* Common equity, in turn, includes both *paid-in capital* and *retained earnings.*

Table 2-1 shows a simplified balance sheet for Teletron Electronics Company, a large electronics components manufacturer, as of December 31, 1988. Teletron began life in 1957 as a proprietorship, then became a partnership, and finally converted to a corporation in 1965. Its 1988 sales were $401 mil-

---

[1]This chapter contains essential information, but many business students will have been exposed to some or all of it in economics or accounting courses. Even if they have not, the material is both straightforward and descriptive. Therefore, some instructors may prefer to have students cover Chapter 2 on their own rather than cover it in class.

Table 2-1   Teletron Electronics Company:
Balance Sheet as of December 31, 1988
(Millions of Dollars)

Assets		Liabilities and Equity	
Cash and marketable securities	$ 12.0	Accounts payable	$ 23.8
Accounts receivable	50.3	Notes payable to banks	30.0
Inventories	91.6	Accrued wages and taxes	2.6
Prepaid expenses and other current		Other current liabilities	5.0
assets	1.6	Total current liabilities	$ 61.4
Total current assets	$155.5	Long-term bonds	107.0
		Preferred stock (112,000 shares)	11.2
Gross fixed assets	149.7	Common stockholders' equity:	
Less depreciation	25.0	Common stock	
Net fixed assets	$124.7	(1,706,351 shares)	10.4
		Retained earnings	90.2
		Total common equity	$100.6
Total assets	$280.2	Total liabilities and equity	$280.2

lion, and the $280 million of assets shown in Table 2-1 were necessary to support these sales. Teletron and other companies obtain the bulk of the funds used to buy assets (1) by buying on credit from their suppliers (accounts payable); (2) by borrowing from banks, insurance companies, pension funds, and other institutions (notes payable and long-term bonds); (3) by selling preferred and common stock to investors; and (4) by "saving money" (retained earnings) as reflected in the retained earnings account. (Recall from your accounting courses that a corporation saves whenever the company pays dividends which are less than its net income, and the savings that have accumulated since the company began are reported as retained earnings on its balance sheet.) Also, because wages and taxes are not paid on a daily basis, Teletron obtains some "credit" from its labor force and from the government in the form of accrued wages and taxes.

The first claim against Teletron's income and assets is by its creditors — all those claims items listed on the right-hand side of the balance sheet above preferred stock. However, the creditors' claims are limited to fixed amounts. For example, most of the long-term debt bears interest at a rate of 9 percent per year, so the bondholders in total get interest of about $0.09 \times \$107$ million = $9.6 million per year. If Teletron did extremely well and had profits of, say, $80 million, the bondholders would still get only $9.6 million. However, if Teletron lost money, the bondholders would nevertheless get their $9.6 million; assets would be sold, the cash raised would be used to pay the bond interest, and the value of the common equity would decline. Further, if the company's situation were so bad that it simply could not generate the cash needed to make the required payments to the bondholders and other creditors (if this occurs, the firm is said to have *defaulted* on its debt), (1) the company would be forced into bankruptcy, (2) the assets would be sold off (generally at less than the values stated on the balance sheet), (3) the creditors would receive the proceeds from the bankruptcy liquidation, and (4) the claims of the common stockholders would probably be wiped out.[2]

The preferred stockholders stand next in line, after the creditors, for the firm's income and assets. Teletron has 112,000 shares of preferred stock, each with a par value of $100. This preferred pays a dividend of $8.125 per year, or 8.125 percent on its $100 par value. The preferred dividends must be paid before any dividends can be paid on the common, and, in the event of bankruptcy, the preferred must be paid off in full before anything goes to the common stockholders.

After everyone else has been paid, the remaining income, often called *residual income,* belongs to the common stockholders. This income may be retained for reinvestment in the firm, or it may be paid out as dividends to the common stockholders. Firms like Teletron typically retain some earnings to support growth and then pay the rest out as dividends. Teletron has 1,706,351 shares of common stock outstanding. Investors actually paid the company about $6.09 on the average for these shares ($10,400,000/1,706,351 = $6.09), but the company has saved through retention of earnings $90,200,000/1,706,351 = $52.86 per share since it was incorporated in 1965.[3] Therefore, stockholders on the average have a total investment of $6.09 + $52.86 = $58.95 per share in the company; this is the stock's *book value.*

Teletron's debt and preferred stock are held primarily by its suppliers, by five banks, and by some institutions, such as life insurance companies and pension funds. The debt is rarely if ever traded, because this particular set of investors tends to hold debt until it matures. Teletron's common stock, on the other hand, is actively traded. Individuals own about 65 percent of the stock, whereas institutions own the remaining 35 percent; these are typical percentages. In the fall of 1988, the stock traded in the general range of $60 to $70 per share, and it has ranged from a high of $75 to a low of $10 during the past 12 years. The price rises and falls depending (1) on how the company is doing at a given point in time, (2) on what is happening to other stock prices, and (3) most important, on how investors expect the company to do in the future. The *market value* (or price) does not depend directly on, and is usually dif-

---

[2]If anything were left from the proceeds of the asset sale after creditors had been paid off, this residual would go to the stockholders. The status of the different types of investors, and bankruptcy proceedings in general, are discussed in more detail in Appendix 13A. As a general rule, the order of priority of different claimants in the event of bankruptcy is: (1) secured creditors' claims from the proceeds from the sale of the specific assets securing their loans, such as a building which secures a mortgage; (2) employees for accrued wages; (3) federal and state governments for accrued taxes; (4) unfunded pension plan benefits; (5) unsecured creditors; (6) preferred stockholders; and (7), last in line, common stockholders. This priority system has a major effect on the riskiness and consequently on the rates of return on different classes of securities.

[3]The $10.4 million shown in the common stock account indicates the actual dollars the company received for the 1,706,351 shares it has issued. As we discuss in Chapter 12, the common stock account is sometimes split into two accounts, one of which is called "par value" and the other called "paid-in capital," or the amount received in excess of par.

Table 2-2   Teletron Electronics Company: Income Statement for Year Ended December 31, 1988 (Millions of Dollars Except per Share Data)

Sales	$401.0
Cost of goods sold (excluding depreciation)	280.7
Other operating expenses	79.6
Depreciation	4.9
Total operating costs	$365.2
Earnings before interest and taxes	$ 35.8
Interest expense	12.6
Earnings before taxes	$ 23.2
Taxes (34%)	7.9
Net income	$ 15.3
Preferred dividends	0.9
Income available to common stockholders	$ 14.4
Common dividends	6.0
Additions to retained earnings	$ 8.4
Net cash flow (Net income + depreciation)	$ 19.3
Earnings per share (EPS)	$ 8.44
Dividends per share (DPS)	$ 3.52

ferent from, the book value. Book value, or the firm's common equity per share, is determined by accountants as the sum of assets valued at their original costs minus accumulated depreciation, minus all borrowed capital, minus preferred stockholders' claims, all divided by common shares outstanding. Market value, on the other hand, is a function of the cash expected to flow to stockholders in the future. It is easy to imagine a situation in which assets that were purchased years ago are worth far more today, and hence it is easy to see why market values can be above (or below) book values.

Teletron's income statement for 1988 is shown in Table 2-2. We can see that Teletron had earnings available to common stockholders of $14.4 million, so the company earned $8.44 per share of stock outstanding. Of this amount, Teletron paid out $6 million, or $3.52 per share, in dividends, and it retained $8.4 million. When you studied income statements in accounting, the emphasis was probably on determining the net income of the firm. In finance, however, we focus on *cash flows*. The value of an asset (or a whole firm) is determined by the cash flows it generates. The firm's net income is important, but cash flows are even more important, because dividends must be paid in cash, and cash is also necessary to purchase the assets required to continue operations.

As we discussed in Chapter 1, the goal of the firm should be to maximize the price of its stock. Since the value of any asset, including a share of stock, depends on the cash flows produced by the asset, managers should strive to maximize cash flows available to investors over the long run. A business's cash flows are generally equal to cash from sales, minus cash operating costs, minus interest charges, and minus taxes. Depreciation is an operating cost, so the greater the firm's depreciation charge, the lower its profits. However, depreciation is not a cash expenditure. Firms do not write checks to pay for depreciation, as they do for labor, materials, and taxes. Hence, a firm's cash flow in any year can be found by adding to its net income its depreciation expense. The greater the level of depreciation, other things held constant, the larger the firm's cash flows, because depreciation reduces taxable income and, hence, taxes.

To see more clearly how depreciation affects cash flows, consider the following simplified income statement (Column 1) and cash flow statement (Column 2). Here we assume that all sales revenues are received in cash during the year and that all costs except depreciation are paid in cash during the year. Cash flows are seen to equal net income plus depreciation:

	Income Statement (1)	Cash Flows (2)	
Sales revenue	$1,000	$1,000	
Costs except depreciation	700	700	
Depreciation	100	—	
Total costs	$ 800	$ 700	(Cash costs)
Taxable income	$ 200	$ 300	(Pretax cash flow)
Taxes (40%)	80	80	(From Column 1)
Net income	$ 120	$ 220	(Net cash flow)
Add back depreciation	100		
Net cash flow	$ 220		

Now suppose Congress changes the tax laws and permits the company to depreciate its assets faster, which causes depreciation to rise from $100 to $200. Sales revenues and other costs remain unchanged. What effect will the change in depreciation have on net income and cash flows? The answer is worked out below:

	Income Statement (1)	Cash Flows (2)	
Sales revenue	$1,000	$1,000	
Costs except depreciation	700	700	
Depreciation	200	—	
Total costs	$ 900	$ 700	(Cash costs)
Taxable income	$ 100	$ 300	(Pretax cash flow)
Taxes (40%)	40	40	(From Column 1)
Net income	$ 60	$ 260	(Net cash flow)
Add back depreciation	200		
Net cash flow	$ 260		

Thus, we see that the increase in depreciation caused the firm's net cash flows to increase from $220 to $260, or by $40.

You might at this point notice that the increase in depreciation caused a decline in net income (from $120 to $60) and wonder if that is not bad. In other words, is the increase in depreciation good because it increases net cash flows or bad because it reduces net income? In this case, the assets are not wearing out any faster — all that has happened is that Congress has allowed the company to deduct larger depreciation charges before calculating its tax bill. The firm can, if it chooses, tell its accountants to calculate income for tax purposes as shown above but to use a *different* (lower) amount of depreciation when they calculate the income they report to stockholders. Thus, because the increase in depreciation increases cash flows yet need not adversely affect net income as calculated by the accountants, the change in depreciation is unambiguously good. We will discuss this point in more detail later in the chapter, and also in Appendix 2A.

THE FEDERAL INCOME TAX SYSTEM

The value of any financial asset, such as a share of stock, a bond, or a mortgage, as well as the values of most real assets, such as plants or even entire firms, depends on the stream of cash flows produced by the asset. Cash flows from an asset consist of *usable* income plus depreciation. Usable income means income *after taxes.* Proprietorship and partnership income must be reported by the owners, and it is taxed as their personal income. Most corporations, however, must first pay taxes on the corporation's own income, and then stockholders must pay additional taxes on all corporate after-tax income distributed as dividends. Therefore, both *personal* and *corporate* income taxes are important in the determination of the cash flows produced by financial assets.

Our tax laws can be changed by Congress, and in recent years changes have occurred almost every year. Indeed, a nontrivial change has occurred, on average, every 1½ years since 1913, when our federal income tax system began. Further, certain parts of our tax system are tied to the rate of inflation, so changes automatically occur each year, depending on the rate of inflation during the previous year. Therefore, although this chapter will give you a good background on the basic nature of our tax system, you should consult current rate schedules and other data published by the Internal Revenue Service (and available in U.S. post offices) before you file your personal or business tax return!

Currently (1988), federal income tax rates for individuals go up to 33 percent, and when state and city income taxes are included, the marginal tax rate on an individual's income can exceed 40 percent. Business income is also taxed heavily. The income from partnerships and proprietorships is reported by the individual owners as personal income and, consequently, is taxed at rates going up to 40 percent or more. Corporate profits are subject to federal income tax rates of up to 39 percent, in addition to state income taxes. Because of the magnitude of the tax bite, taxes play an important role in many financial decisions.

Because the U.S. government is running a large fiscal deficit, most experts predict that tax rates will be raised in the not-too-distant future. Thus, by the time you read this chapter, rates may well be higher. Still, if you understand the chapter, you will be able to apply the new tax rates.

Taxes are so complicated that university law schools offer master's degrees in taxation to practicing lawyers, many of whom also have CPA certification. In a field complicated enough to warrant such detailed study, we can cover only the highlights. This is really enough, though, because business managers and investors should and do rely on tax specialists rather than trust their own limited knowledge. Still, it is important to know the basic elements of the tax system as a starting point for discussions with tax experts.

Individual Income Taxes

progressive tax
A tax that requires a higher percentage payment on higher incomes. The personal income tax in the United States, which goes from a rate of 0 percent on the lowest increments of income to 33 percent and then back to 28 percent on the highest increments, is progressive.

taxable income
Gross income minus exemptions and allowable deductions as set forth in the Tax Code.

marginal tax rate
The tax applicable to the last unit of income.

average tax rate
Taxes paid divided by taxable income.

Individuals pay taxes on wages and salaries, on investment income (dividends, interest, and profits from the sale of securities), and on the profits of proprietorships and partnerships. Our tax rates are **progressive** — that is, the higher one's income, the larger the percentage paid in taxes.[4] Table 2-3 gives the tax rates for single individuals and married couples filing joint returns under the rate schedules in effect in 1988. Here are the highlights of the table:

1. **Taxable income** is defined as gross income less a set of exemptions and deductions which are spelled out in the instructions to the tax forms individuals must file. In 1988, each taxpayer received an exemption of $1,950 for each dependent, including the taxpayer, which reduces taxable income. This exemption will rise to $2,000 in 1989, and thereafter it will be indexed to rise with inflation. However, high-income taxpayers must pay a surtax, which takes away the value of personal exemptions. Also, certain expenses, such as mortgage interest paid, state and local income taxes paid, and charitable contributions, can be deducted and thus be used to reduce taxable income.

2. The **marginal tax rate** is defined as the tax on the last unit of income. Marginal rates begin at 15 percent, rise to 28 and then to 33 percent, and finally fall back to 28 percent. The average tax rate on all taxable income rises from zero to approximately 28 percent.

3. One can calculate **average tax rates** from the data in Table 2-3. For example, if Carol Stanton, a single individual, had taxable income of $30,000, her tax bill would be $2,678 + ($30,000 − $17,850)(0.28) = $2,678 + $3,402 = $6,080. Her *average tax rate* would be $6,080/$30,000 = 20.3% versus a *marginal rate* of 28 percent. If Carol received a raise of $1,000, bringing her income to $31,000, she would have to pay $280 of it as taxes, so her after-tax raise would be $720.

---

[4]Prior to the 1986 Tax Code revisions, individual rates were more steeply progressive, going from 11 percent to 50 percent, but higher-income taxpayers were able to use a variety of tax shelters that lowered effective tax rates substantially. Indeed, many people had cash income in the millions of dollars yet were able to completely avoid taxes. The 1986 changes eliminated most tax shelters. Also, the revisions increased dramatically the tax rate on capital gains, most of which are earned by wealthy individuals. Therefore, in reality, the new law did not lower the progressivity of our tax system.

Table 2-3   Individual Tax Rates for 1988

Single Individuals

If Your Taxable Income Is	You Pay This Amount on the Base of the Bracket	Plus This Percentage on the Excess over the Base	Average Tax Rate at Top of Bracket
Up to $17,850	$ 0	15%	15.0%
$17,850–$43,150	2,678	28	22.6
$43,150–$100,480	9,762	33	28.0
Over $100,480	28,680	28	28.0

Married Couples Filing Joint Returns

If Your Taxable Income Is	You Pay This Amount on the Base of the Bracket	Plus This Percentage on the Excess over the Base	Average Tax Rate at Top of Bracket
Up to $29,750	$ 0	15%	15.0%
$29,750–$71,900	4,462	28	22.6
$71,900–$171,090	16,264	33	28.0
Over $171,090	48,997	28	28.0

Notes:

a. The tax rates are for 1988 and beyond. However, the income ranges at which the 28 percent rate takes effect, as well as the ranges for the surtax discussed below, are scheduled to be indexed with inflation beyond 1988, so they will change from those shown in the table.

b. Technically, a surtax of 5 percent is imposed on income in the range $43,150 to $100,480 for single individuals and in the range $71,900 to $171,090 for married couples. This surtax is designed to eliminate the effects of the 15 percent rate on the first increments of income and to eliminate the benefits of the personal exemption. The surtax ceases when the personal exemption has been fully offset, and hence the dollar amount at which the marginal rate drops back to 28 percent depends on the number of exemptions claimed. The amounts shown in this table assume one exemption for a single individual and two exemptions for a married couple. Different tables, similar to the one we present but with different numbers of exemptions, are available from the Internal Revenue Service.

bracket creep
A situation that occurs when progressive tax rates combine with inflation to cause a greater portion of each taxpayer's real income to be paid as taxes.

4.   As indicated in the notes to the table, current legislation provides for tax brackets to be indexed to inflation to avoid the **bracket creep** that occurred during the 1970s and that de facto raised tax rates substantially.[5]

Taxes on Dividend and Interest Income. Dividend and interest income received by individuals from corporate securities is added to other income and thus is taxed at rates going up to 33 percent. Since corporations pay dividends out of earnings that have already been taxed, there is *double taxation* of corporate income.

---

[5]For example, if you were single and had a taxable income of $17,850, your tax bill would be $2,678. Now suppose inflation caused prices to double and your income, being tied to a cost of living index, rose to $35,700. Because our tax rates are progressive, if tax brackets were not indexed, your taxes would jump to $7,676. Your after-tax income would thus increase from $15,172 to $28,024, but, because prices have doubled, your real income would *decline* from $15,172 to $14,012 (calculated as one-half of $28,024). You would be in a higher tax bracket, so you would be paying a higher percentage of your real income in taxes. If this happened to everyone, and if Congress failed to change tax rates sufficiently, real disposable incomes would decline because the federal government would be taking a larger share of the national product. This is called the federal government's "inflation dividend." However, since tax brackets are indexed, if your income doubled due to inflation, your tax bill would double, but your after-tax real income would remain constant at $15,172. Bracket creep was a real problem during the 1970s and early 1980s, but indexing — if it stays in the law — will put an end to it.

It should be noted that under U.S. tax laws, interest on most state and local government bonds, called *municipals* or *"munis,"* is not subject to federal income taxes. Thus, investors get to keep all of the interest received from most municipal bonds but only a fraction of the interest received from bonds issued by corporations or by the U.S. government. This means that a lower-yielding muni can provide the same after-tax return as a higher-yielding corporate bond. For example, a taxpayer in the 33 percent marginal tax bracket who could buy a muni that yielded 9 percent would have to receive a before-tax yield of 13.43 percent on a corporate or U.S. Treasury bond to have the same after-tax income:

$$\frac{\text{Equivalent pretax yield}}{\text{on taxable bond}} = \frac{\text{Yield on muni}}{1 - \text{Marginal tax rate}} = \frac{9\%}{1 - 0.33} = 13.43\%.$$

$$\frac{\text{Yield on}}{\text{muni}} = \frac{\text{Pretax yield}}{\text{on taxable}} - \left(\frac{\text{Pretax yield}}{\text{on taxable}}\right)\left(\frac{\text{Tax}}{\text{rate}}\right) = 13.43\% - (13.43\%)(0.33) = 9.0\%.$$

This exemption from federal taxes stems from the separation of federal and state powers, and its primary effect is to help state and local governments borrow at lower rates than would otherwise be available to them.

Capital Gains versus Ordinary Income. Assets such as stocks, bonds, and real estate are defined as *capital assets*. If you buy a capital asset and later sell it for more than your purchase price, the profit is called a **capital gain**; if you suffer a loss, it is called a **capital loss**. An asset sold within 6 months of the time it was purchased produces a *short-term gain or loss,* whereas one held for more than 6 months produces a *long-term gain or loss.* Thus, if you buy 100 shares of GE stock for $70 per share and sell it for $80 per share, you make a capital gain of 100 × $10, or $1,000. However, if you sell the stock for $60 per share, you will have a $1,000 capital loss. If you hold the stock for more than 6 months, the gain or loss is long-term; otherwise, it is short-term. If you sell the stock for exactly $70 per share, you make neither a gain nor a loss; you simply get your $7,000 back, and no tax is due.

From 1921 through 1986, long-term capital gains were taxed at substantially lower rates than ordinary income. For example, in 1986 long-term capital gains were taxed at only 40 percent of the tax rate on ordinary income. However, the tax law changes which took effect in 1987 eliminated this differential, and all capital gains income (both long-term and short-term) is now taxed as if it were ordinary income.

There was a great deal of controversy over the elimination of the preferential rate for capital gains. It was argued that lower tax rates on capital gains (1) stimulated the flow of venture capital to new, start-up businesses (which generally provide capital gains as opposed to dividend income) and (2) caused companies to retain and reinvest a high percentage of their earnings in order to provide their stockholders with capital gains as opposed to highly taxed dividend income. Thus, it was argued that elimination of the favorable rates on capital gains would retard investment and economic growth. The proponents of preferential capital gains tax rates lost the argument in 1986, but they

capital gain or loss
The profit (loss) from the sale of a capital asset for more (less) than its purchase price.

Table 2-4   Corporate Tax Rates

If a Corporation's Taxable Income Is	It Pays This Amount on the Base of the Bracket	Plus This Percentage on the Excess over the Base	Average Tax Rate at Top of Bracket
Up to $50,000	$ 0	15%	15.0%
$50,000 to $75,000	7,500	25	18.3
$75,000 to $100,000	13,750	34	22.3
$100,000 to $335,000	22,250	39	34.0
Over $335,000	113,900	34	34.0

Notes:

a. The rates shown here are for 1988 and beyond.

b. For income in the range of $100,000 to $335,000, a surtax of 5% is added to the base rate of 34%. This surtax, which eliminates the effects of the lower rates on income below $75,000, results in a marginal tax rate of 39% for income in the $100,000 to $335,000 range.

did succeed in keeping in the law all the language dealing with capital gains, which will make it easy to reinstate the differential if economic conditions suggest that it is indeed needed to encourage growth. Therefore, you should not be surprised if the capital gains differential is reinstated in the future.

When capital gains were taxed at favorable rates, this had implications for dividend policy (it favored lower payouts and hence higher earnings retention). It also favored stock investments over bond investments, because part of the income from stock normally comes from capital gains. Thus, one can anticipate changes in corporate dividend and capital structure policy as a result of the elimination of the differential.

Corporate Income Taxes

The corporate tax structure, shown in Table 2-4, is relatively simple. To illustrate, if a firm had $100,000 of taxable income, its tax bill would be:

$$\text{Taxes} = \$13,750 + 0.34(\$25,000)$$

$$= \$13,750 + \$8,500$$

$$= \$22,250,$$

and its average tax rate would be $22,250/$100,000 = 22.25\%$. Note that for all income over $335,000, one can disregard the surtax and simply calculate the corporate tax as 34 percent of all taxable income. Thus, the corporate tax is progressive up to $335,000 of income, but it is constant thereafter.[6]

[6] Prior to 1987, many large, profitable corporations such as General Electric and Boeing paid zero income taxes. The reasons why this happened were as follows: (1) expenses, especially depreciation, were defined differently for calculating taxable income than for reporting earnings to stockholders, so some companies reported positive profits to stockholders but losses — hence no taxes — to the Internal Revenue Service; and (2) some companies which did have tax liabilities used various tax credits, including the investment tax credit (discussed later in the chapter) to offset taxes that would otherwise have been payable. This situation was drastically curtailed in 1987.

Interest and Dividend Income Received by a Corporation. Interest income received by a corporation is taxed as ordinary income at regular corporate tax rates. However, 70 percent of the dividends received by one corporation from another is excluded from taxable income, while the remaining 30 percent is taxed at the ordinary tax rate. Thus, a corporation earning over $335,000 and paying a 34 percent marginal tax rate would pay only $(0.30)(0.34) = 0.102 = 10.2\%$ of its dividend income as taxes, so its effective tax rate on intercorporate dividends would be 10.2 percent. If this firm had $10,000 in pretax dividend income, its after-tax dividend income would be $8,980:

$$\begin{aligned} \frac{\text{After-tax}}{\text{income}} &= \text{Before-tax income} - \text{Taxes} \\[6pt] &= \text{Before-tax income} - (\text{Before-tax income})(\text{Effective tax rate}) \\[6pt] &= \text{Before-tax income}(1 - \text{Effective tax rate}) \\[6pt] &= \$10,000\,[1 - (0.30)(0.34)] \\[6pt] &= \$10,000(1 - 0.102) \\[6pt] &= \$10,000(0.898) = \$8,980. \end{aligned}$$

If the corporation passes its own after-tax income on to its stockholders as dividends, the income is ultimately subjected to *triple taxation:* (1) The original corporation is first taxed, (2) the second corporation is then taxed on the dividends it received, and (3) the individuals who receive the final dividends are taxed again. This is the reason for the 70 percent exclusion on intercorporate dividends.

If a corporation has surplus funds that can be invested in marketable securities, the tax factor favors investment in stocks, which pay dividends, rather than in bonds, which pay interest. For example, suppose IBM had $100,000 to invest, and it could buy bonds that paid interest of $7,000 per year or preferred stock that paid dividends of $6,600. IBM is in the 34 percent tax bracket; therefore, its tax on the interest, if it bought bonds, would be $0.34(\$7,000) = \$2,380$ and its after-tax income would be $4,620. If it bought preferred stock, its tax would be $0.34[(0.3)(\$6,600)] = \$673$ and its after-tax income would be $5,927. Other factors might lead IBM to invest in bonds, but the tax factor certainly favors stock investments when the investor is a corporation.[7]

---

[7]This illustration demonstrates why corporations favor investing in lower-yielding preferred stocks to higher-yielding bonds. When tax consequences are considered, the yield on the preferred stock, $[1 - 0.34(0.30)](6.6\%) = 5.927\%$, is higher than the yield on the bond, $(1 - 0.34)(7.0\%) = 4.620\%$. Also note that corporations are restricted in their use of borrowed funds to purchase other firms' preferred or common stocks. Without such restrictions, firms could engage in *tax arbitrage,* whereby the interest on borrowed funds reduces taxable income on a dollar-for-dollar basis but taxable income is increased by only $0.30 per dollar of dividend income. Thus, current tax laws reduce the 70 percent dividend exclusion in proportion to the amount of borrowed funds used to purchase the stock.

Table 2-5 Cash Flows to Investors under Bond and Stock Financing

	Use Bonds	Use Stock
Income before interest and taxes	$2,000,000	$2,000,000
Interest	2,000,000	0
Taxable income	$ 0	$2,000,000
Federal plus state taxes (40%)	0	800,000
After-tax income	$ 0	$1,200,000
Income to investors	$2,000,000	$1,200,000
Advantage to bonds	$ 800,000	

Interest and Dividends Paid by a Corporation. A firm's operations can be financed either with debt or equity capital. If it uses debt, it must pay interest on this debt, whereas if it uses equity, it will pay dividends to the equity investors (stockholders). The interest paid by a corporation is deducted from its operating income to obtain its taxable income, but dividends paid are not deductible. Therefore, a firm needs $1 of pretax income to pay $1 of interest, but if it is in the 40 percent federal-plus-state tax bracket, it needs

$$\frac{\$1}{1 - \text{Tax rate}} = \frac{\$1}{0.60} = \$1.6667$$

of pretax income to pay $1 of dividends.

To illustrate, Table 2-5 shows the situation for a firm whose assets produced $2 million of income before interest and taxes. If the firm were financed entirely by bonds, and if it made interest payments of $2 million, its taxable income would be zero, taxes would be zero, and its investors would receive the entire $2 million. (The term *investors* includes both stockholders and bondholders.) If the firm had no debt and was therefore financed only by stock, all of the $2 million of operating income would be taxable income to the corporation, the tax would be $2,000,000(0.40) = $800,000, and investors would receive only $1.2 million versus $2 million under debt financing.

Of course, it is generally not possible to finance exclusively with debt capital, and the risk of doing so would offset the benefits of the higher expected income. *Still, the fact that interest is a deductible expense has a profound effect on the way businesses are financed — our tax system favors debt financing over equity financing.* This point is discussed in more detail in Chapters 16 and 17.

Corporate Capital Gains. Before 1987, corporate long-term capital gains were taxed at rates lower than ordinary income, just as with individuals. Under current law, however, corporations' capital gains are taxed at the same rates as their operating income.

Corporate Loss Carry-Back and Carry-Forward. Ordinary corporate operating losses can be carried back (**carry-back**) to each of the preceding 3 years and

tax loss carry-back and carry-forward
Losses that can be carried backward or forward in time to offset taxable income in a given year.

forward (**carry-forward**) for the following 15 years to offset taxable income in those years. For example, an operating loss in 1989 could be carried back and used to reduce taxable income in 1986, 1987, and 1988, and forward, if necessary, and used in 1990, 1991, and so on, to the year 2004. The loss must be applied first to the earliest year, then to the next earliest year, and so on, until losses have been used up or the 15-year carry-forward limit has been reached.

To illustrate, suppose Manhattan Manufacturing, Inc., had a $1 million *pretax* profit (taxable income) in 1986, 1987, and 1988, and then, in 1989, Manhattan lost $6 million. The company would use the carry-back feature to recompute its taxes for 1986, using $1 million of the 1989 operating losses to reduce the 1986 pretax profit to zero. This would permit it to recover the amount of taxes paid in 1986. Therefore, in 1990 Manhattan would receive a refund of its 1986 taxes because of the loss experienced in 1989. Because $5 million of the unrecovered losses would still be available, Manhattan would repeat this procedure for 1987 and 1988. Thus, in 1990 the company would pay zero taxes for 1989 and also would receive a refund for taxes paid from 1986 through 1988. Manhattan would still have $3 million of unrecovered losses to carry forward, subject to the 15-year limit, until the entire $6 million loss had been used to offset taxable income. The purpose of permitting this loss treatment is, of course, to avoid penalizing corporations whose incomes fluctuate substantially from year to year.

Improper Accumulation to Avoid Payment of Dividends. Corporations could refrain from paying dividends to permit their stockholders to avoid personal income taxes on dividends. To prevent this, the Tax Code contains an **improper accumulation** provision which states that earnings accumulated by a corporation are subject to penalty rates *if the purpose of the accumulation is to enable stockholders to avoid the personal income tax.* A cumulative total of $250,000 (the balance sheet item "retained earnings") is by law exempted from the improper accumulation tax. This is a benefit primarily to small corporations.

The improper accumulation penalty applies only if the retained earnings in excess of $250,000 are *shown to be unnecessary to meet the reasonable needs of the business.* A great many companies do indeed have legitimate reasons for retaining more than $250,000 of earnings. For example, earnings may be retained and used to pay off debt, to finance growth, or to provide the corporation with a cushion against possible cash drains caused by losses. How much a firm should properly accumulate for uncertain contingencies is a matter of judgment. We shall consider this matter again in Chapter 18, which deals with corporate dividend policy.

Consolidated Corporate Tax Returns. If a corporation owns 80 percent or more of another corporation's stock, it can aggregate income and file one consolidated tax return; thus, the losses of one company can be used to offset the profits of another. (Similarly, one division's losses can be used to offset another division's profits.) No business ever wants to incur losses (you can go

improper accumulation Retention of earnings by a business for the purpose of enabling stockholders to avoid personal income taxes.

broke losing $1 to save 34¢ in taxes), but tax offsets do make it more feasible for large, multidivisional corporations to undertake risky new ventures or ventures that will suffer losses during a developmental period.

Taxation of Small Businesses: S Corporations

The Internal Revenue Code provides that small businesses which meet certain restrictions as spelled out in the code may be set up as corporations and thus receive the benefits of the corporate form of organization — especially limited liability — yet still be taxed as proprietorships or partnerships rather than as corporations. These corporations are called **S corporations**. See the small business section at the end of this chapter for more information on S corporations.

S corporation
A small corporation which under Subchapter S of the Internal Revenue Code elects to be taxed as a proprietorship or a partnership yet retains limited liability and other benefits of the corporate form of organization.

DEPRECIATION

Suppose a firm buys a milling machine for $100,000 and uses it for 5 years, after which it is scrapped. The cost of the goods produced by the machine must include a charge for the machine, and this charge is called *depreciation*. Because depreciation reduces profits as calculated by the accountants, the higher a firm's depreciation charges, the lower its reported net income. However, depreciation is not a cash charge, so higher depreciation levels do not reduce cash flows. Indeed, higher depreciation levels *increase* cash flows, because the greater a firm's depreciation, the lower its tax bill.

Companies generally calculate depreciation one way when figuring taxes and another way when reporting income to investors: most use the *straight line* method for stockholder reporting (or "book" purposes), but they use the fastest rate permitted by law (Congress) for tax purposes. Under the straight line method, one normally takes the cost of the asset, subtracts its estimated salvage value, and divides the net amount by the asset's economic life. For an asset with a 5-year life, which costs $100,000 and has $15,000 salvage value, the annual straight line depreciation charge is ($100,000 − $15,000)/5 = $17,000.

For tax purposes, Congress changes the permissible tax depreciation methods from time to time. Prior to 1954, the straight line method was required for tax purposes, but in 1954 *accelerated* methods (double declining balance and sum-of-years'-digits) were permitted. Then, in 1981, the old accelerated methods were replaced by a simpler procedure known as the **Accelerated Cost Recovery System (ACRS)**. The ACRS system was changed again in 1986 as a part of the Tax Reform Act.

Accelerated Cost Recovery System (ACRS)
A depreciation system that allows businesses to write off the cost of an asset over a period much shorter than its operating life.

Tax Depreciation Calculations

For tax purposes, the cost of an asset is expensed over its depreciable life. Historically, an asset's depreciable life was determined by its estimated useful economic life; it was intended that an asset would be fully depreciated at ap-

Table 2-6	Major Classes and Asset Lives for ACRS Under the Tax Reform Act of 1986

Class	Type of Property
3-year	Computers and equipment used in research.
5-year	Automobiles, tractor units, light-duty trucks, computers, and certain special manufacturing tools.
7-year	Most industrial equipment, office furniture, and fixtures.
10-year	Certain longer-lived types of equipment.
27.5-year	Residential rental real property such as apartment buildings.
31.5-year	All nonresidential real property, including commercial and industrial buildings.

proximately the same time that it reached the end of its useful economic life. However, ACRS totally abandoned that practice and set simple guidelines which created several classes of assets, each with a more-or-less arbitrarily prescribed life called a *recovery period* or *class life*. The ACRS class life bears only a rough relationship to the expected economic life.

A major effect of the ACRS system has been to shorten the depreciable lives of assets, thus giving businesses larger tax deductions and thereby increasing their cash flows available for reinvestment. Table 2-6 describes the types of property that fit into the different class life groups, and Table 2-7 sets forth the ACRS recovery allowances (depreciation rates) for the various classes of investment property.

Consider Table 2-6 first. The first column gives the ACRS class life, while the second column describes the types of assets which fall into each category. Property in the 27.5- and 31.5-year categories (real estate) must be depreciated by the straight line method, but 3-, 5-, 7-, and 10-year property can be depreciated either by the straight line or by an accelerated method which uses the rates shown in Table 2-7.[8]

As we saw earlier in the chapter, higher depreciation expenses result in lower taxes and hence higher cash flows. Therefore, when a firm has the option of using straight line or the ACRS rates shown in Table 2-7, it should elect to use the ACRS rates. The yearly recovery allowance, or depreciation expense, is determined by multiplying each asset's *depreciable basis* by the applicable recovery percentage, as shown in Table 2-7. Calculations are discussed in the following sections.

half-year convention
A feature of ACRS in which assets are assumed to be put into service at mid-year and thus are allowed a half-year's depreciation regardless of when they actually go into service.

Half-Year Convention. Under the 1986 Act, the assumption is generally made that property is placed in service in the middle of the first year. Thus, for 3-year class life property, the recovery period begins in the middle of the year the asset is placed in service and ends three years later. The effect of the **half-**

---

[8]As a benefit to very small companies, the Tax Code also permits companies to *expense*, which is equivalent to depreciating over one year, up to $10,000 of equipment. Thus, if a small company bought one asset worth up to $10,000, it could write the asset off in the year it was acquired. This is called "Section 179 expensing." We shall disregard this provision throughout the book.

Table 2-7   Recovery Allowance Percentages for
Personal Property (not Real Estate)

Ownership Year	Class of Investment			
	3-Year	5-Year	7-Year	10-Year
1	33%	20%	14%	10%
2	45	32	25	18
3	15	19	17	14
4	7	12	13	12
5		11	9	9
6		6	9	7
7			9	7
8			4	7
9				7
10				6
11				3
	100%	100%	100%	100%

Notes:

a. We developed these recovery allowance percentages based on the 200 percent declining balance method prescribed in the 1986 Tax Act with a switch to straight line depreciation at some point in the asset's life. For example, consider the 5-year recovery allowance percentages. The straight line percentage would be 20 percent per year, so the 200 percent declining balance multiplier is $2.0(20\%) = 40\% = 0.4$. However, because the half-year convention applies, the ACRS percentage for Year 1 is 20 percent. For Year 2, there is 80 percent of the depreciable basis remaining to be depreciated, so the recovery allowance percentage is $0.40(80\%) = 32\%$. In Year 3, $20\% + 32\% = 52\%$ of the depreciation has been taken, leaving 48%, so the percentage is $0.4(48\%) \approx 19\%$. In Year 4, the percentage is $0.4(29\%) \approx 12\%$. After 4 years, straight line depreciation exceeds the declining balance depreciation, so a switch is made to straight line (this is permitted under the law). However, the half-year convention must also be applied at the end of the class life, and hence the remaining 17 percent of depreciation must be taken (amortized) over 1.5 years. Thus, the percentage in Year 5 is $17\%/1.5 \approx 11\%$, and in Year 6, $17\% - 11\% = 6\%$. We rounded to the nearest whole number.

b. Residential rental property (apartments) is depreciated over a 27.5-year life, whereas commercial and industrial structures are depreciated over 31.5 years. In both cases, straight line depreciation must be used. The depreciation allowance for the first year is based, pro rata, on the month the asset was placed in service, with the remainder of the first year's depreciation being taken in the 28th or 32nd year.

year convention is to extend the recovery period out one more year, so 3-year class life property is depreciated over 4 calendar years, 5-year property is depreciated over 6 calendar years, and so on. This convention is incorporated into Table 2-7's recovery allowance percentages.[9]

depreciable basis
The portion of an asset's value which can be depreciated for tax purposes. The depreciable basis under ACRS is equal to the cost of the asset, including shipping and installation charges.

Depreciable Basis. The depreciable basis is a critical element of ACRS, because each year's allowance (depreciation expense) depends jointly on the asset's depreciable basis and its ACRS class life. The depreciable basis under ACRS is equal to the purchase price of the asset plus any shipping and installation costs. The basis is not adjusted for salvage value (which is the estimated

[9]The half-year convention also applies if the straight line option is used, with half of one year's depreciation taken in the first year, a full year's depreciation taken in each of the remaining years of the asset's class life, and the remaining half-year's depreciation taken in the year following the end of the class life. You should recognize that virtually all companies have computerized depreciation systems. Each asset's depreciation pattern is programmed into the system at the time of its acquisition, and the computer aggregates the depreciation allowances for all assets when the accountants close the books and prepare the financial statements and tax returns.

market value of the asset at the end of its useful life) regardless of whether ACRS or the straight line method is used.

investment tax credit (ITC)
A specified percentage of the cost of new assets that businesses are sometimes allowed by law to deduct as a credit against their income taxes.

Investment Tax Credit. An **investment tax credit (ITC)** provides for a direct reduction of taxes, and its purpose is to stimulate business investment. ITCs were first introduced during the Kennedy administration in 1961, and they have subsequently been put in and taken out of the tax system, depending on how Congress feels about the need to stimulate business investment versus the need for federal revenues. Immediately prior to the 1986 Tax Reform Act, ITCs applied to depreciable personal property with a life of 3 or more years, and the credit amounted to 6 percent for short-lived assets and 10 percent for longer-lived assets. The credit was determined by multiplying the cost of the asset by the applicable percentage. However, ITCs were eliminated by the 1986 tax revision. Nevertheless, you should be aware of what ITCs are, because there is a good chance that they will be reinstated at some future date if Congress deems that they are needed to stimulate investment.

Sale of a Depreciable Asset. If a depreciable asset is sold, the sale price (actual salvage value) minus the then-existing undepreciated book value is added to operating income and taxed at the firm's marginal tax rate. For example, suppose a firm buys a 5-year class life asset for $100,000 and sells it at the end of the fourth year for $32,000. The asset's book value is equal to $100,000(0.11 + 0.06) = $100,000(0.17) = $17,000. Therefore, $32,000 − $17,000 = $15,000 is added to the firm's operating income and is taxed.

ACRS Illustration. Assume that Manhattan Manufacturing buys a $100,000 computer, which falls into the ACRS 5-year class life, and places it into service on March 15, 1989. Manhattan must pay an additional $20,000 for delivery and installation. Salvage value is not considered, so the computer's depreciable basis is $120,000. (Delivery and installation charges are included in the depreciable basis rather than expensed in the year incurred.) Each year's recovery allowance (tax depreciation expense) is determined by multiplying the depreciable basis by the applicable recovery allowance percentage. Thus, the depreciation expense for 1989 is 0.20($120,000) = $24,000, and for 1990 it is 0.32($120,000) = $38,400. Similarly, the depreciation expense is $22,800 for 1991, $14,400 for 1992, $13,200 for 1993, and $7,200 for 1994. The total depreciation expense over the 6-year recovery period is $120,000, which is equal to the depreciable basis of the machine.

CASH FLOW ANALYSIS

As noted earlier, management's primary goal is stock price maximization. As we shall see in Chapters 5 and 6, a stock's value is based on the *present value of the cash flows* which investors expect it to provide in the future. Although

cash flow
The actual net cash, as opposed to accounting net income, that flows into (or out of) a firm during some specified period.

accounting profit
A firm's net income as reported on its income statement.

any individual investor could sell the stock and receive cash for it, the **cash flow** provided by the stock itself is the expected future dividend stream, and that expected dividend stream provides the fundamental basis for the stock's value.

Because dividends are paid in cash, a company's ability to pay dividends depends on its cash flows. Cash flows are generally correlated with **accounting profit,** which is simply net income as reported on the income statement. Companies with relatively high accounting profits generally have relatively high cash flows, but the relationship is not precise. Therefore, investors are concerned about cash flow projections as well as profit projections.

Firms can be thought of as having two separate but related bases of value: *existing assets,* which provide profits and cash flows, and *growth opportunities,* which represent opportunities to make new investments that will increase future profits and cash flows. The ability to take advantage of growth opportunities often depends on the availability of the cash needed to buy new assets, and the cash flow from existing assets is often the primary source for the funds needed for profitable new investments. This is another reason for both investors and managers to be concerned with cash flows as well as profits.

For our purposes, it is useful to divide cash flows into two classes: (1) *operating cash flows* and (2) *other cash flows.* **Operating cash flows** are those that arise from normal operations, and they are, in essence, the difference between sales revenues and cash expenses, including taxes paid. Other cash flows arise from the issuance of stock, from borrowing, or from the sale of fixed assets, as illustrated by CBS's recent sale of Dryden Press (the company that published this book) and its other textbook operations to Harcourt Brace Jovanovich for $550 million. Our focus here is on operating cash flows.

operating cash flows
Those cash flows that arise from normal operations; the difference between sales revenues and cash expenses.

Operating cash flows can differ from accounting profit (or net income) for two primary reasons:

1. All the taxes reported on the income statement may not have to be paid during the current year, or, under certain circumstances, the actual cash payments for taxes may exceed the tax figure deducted from sales to calculate net income. The reasons for these tax cash flow differentials are discussed in detail in accounting courses, but we summarize them in Appendix 2A to this chapter.

2. Sales may be on credit, hence not represent cash, and some of the expenses (or costs) deducted from sales to determine profits may not be cash costs. Most important, depreciation is not a cash cost.

Thus, operating cash flows could be larger or smaller than accounting profits during any given year. The effects of the major noncash expense, depreciation, were discussed earlier in this chapter, and we consider the cash flow implications of credit sales in a later chapter.

TAXES AND THE SMALL FIRM

Small firms face inherent disadvantages in the competition for funds. For this reason, our tax laws contain some special provisions designed to encourage the flow of equity capital to them. These are not tax loopholes; rather, they are measures purposefully designed to aid small business. This section considers two provisions that help small businesses grow: S corporation tax status and Section 1244 stock. These provisions, along with lower tax rates on corporate income below $75,000, provide significant benefits to smaller companies.

S Corporation Tax Status

Subchapter S of the Internal Revenue Code allows small businesses, known as *S corporations,* to enjoy the limited-liability benefits of the corporate form of organization yet obtain the benefits of being taxed as a partnership. To qualify for S corporation status, a corporation must meet the legal definition of a small business, must be a domestic corporation, must be owned by no more than 35 individuals, and must make a proper S corporation election.[10]

Owners of S corporations are taxed as if they were partners in a partnership. This tax treatment is especially beneficial in the early stages of a firm's development, when it is both making heavy investments in fixed assets and incurring start-up costs, which lead to operating losses. If such firms were not corporations, the businesses' losses would be used to offset the owners' other income. *S corporation status allows the corporation to pass on those benefits as if the firm were a partnership, with the shareholders receiving the benefits on a pro rata basis in accordance with their fractional ownership of the firm's equity.*

If the firm is profitable during a year in which S corporation status is elected, the earnings are added to the individual owners' ordinary incomes. Likewise, if an S corporation has an unprofitable year, the losses reduce the owners' ordinary incomes. This feature of Subchapter S tax treatment can be either an advantage or a disadvantage. If the corporation has income in excess of $75,000, Subchapter S (1) allows the firm's income to be taxed at the maximum personal rate of 33 percent versus a corporate rate of 39 (or 34) percent, and it also (2) allows the firm to avoid double taxation when earnings are paid out as dividends. On the other hand, if the owners wish to retain all earnings in the firm to finance continued growth, and if income is less than $75,000, S corporation status may be a disadvantage. On balance, though, the new tax law has led most qualifying corporations to file for S corporation status.

Many factors other than taxes bear on the question of whether or not a firm should be organized as a corporation. However, the provision for S corporation status makes it possible for most small businesses to enjoy the benefits of a corporation, yet avoid double taxation problems.

Section 1244 Stock

Small businesses also enjoy benefits with regard to capital gains and losses. Long-term capital gains are taxed at a maximum tax rate of 33 percent under current law, but the Tax Code permits only $3,000 of net capital losses to be used to offset ordinary income per year. Thus, if you invested $10,000 in a stock and the company went bankrupt, you could normally deduct a maximum of $3,000 in any one year. However, Section 1244 of the Code contains a provision that gives favored tax treatment to capital losses incurred on the stocks of small businesses: Up to $50,000 annually, rather than the normal $3,000, can be deducted if the stock is that of a small business as defined in Section 1244 of the Tax Code. For an individual in a high tax bracket, this feature greatly reduces the downside risk of investment. For example, if an investor in the 33 percent tax bracket has made a $50,000 investment in Sec-

---

[10]The full set of conditions that must be met to qualify for S corporation status is spelled out in the Tax Code. Because these provisions are subject to change by Congress, it is important to consult the current version of the Tax Code.

tion 1244 stock that becomes worthless, the investor in effect gets back $16,500 in the form of reduced taxes. This treatment provides a significant enhancement to the value of an investment in a small, high-risk firm, and hence it encourages investment in small businesses.

Because Section 1244 stock is designed to help small firms compete for investment capital, it is restricted to small firms, defined as those with less than $1,000,000 in invested capital. Furthermore, it applies only to the original holders of the stock, and then only to individuals or partnerships — corporations and trusts cannot obtain Section 1244 benefits.[11]

---

[11]An interesting presentation of the advantages of Section 1244 stock and the conditions for qualifying for Section 1244 treatment is given in Dick Levin, *Buy Low, Sell High, Collect Early, and Pay Late* (Englewood Cliffs, N.J.: Prentice-Hall, 1983), Chapter 4.

SUMMARY AND KEY CONCEPTS

This chapter presented some background information on financial statements, business securities, income taxes, and cash flows. The key concepts covered are listed below.

- Firms need capital to acquire assets, and they raise this capital by issuing **debt** and **equity** securities.

- **Debtholders,** or **creditors,** have first claim to the firm's earnings and assets, whereas the **common equity holders** (the firm's owners) have claims against all earnings and assets remaining after everyone else has been paid. Stockholders' rewards can be high, but they can also be low.

- The value of any asset depends on the stream of **after-tax cash flows** it produces. Tax rates and other aspects of our tax system are changed by Congress every year or so.

- Fixed assets are **depreciated** over time to reflect the decline in value of the assets. **Depreciation** is a tax-deductible, but noncash, expense for the firm. The higher the firm's depreciation, the lower its taxes and the higher its cash flows, other things held constant.

- Current tax laws require fixed assets to be depreciated using the **Accelerated Cost Recovery System (ACRS).** Tax depreciation rules have a major impact on the profitability of capital investments.

- **Operating cash flows** differ from reported **accounting income.** Investors should be more interested in a firm's projected cash flows than reported earnings, because it is cash, not paper profits, that is paid out as dividends and plowed back into the business to produce growth.

Questions

2-1 Suppose you owned 100 shares of General Motors stock, and the company earned $6 per share during the last reporting period. Suppose further that GM could either pay all its earnings out as dividends (in which case you would receive $600) or retain the earnings in the business, buy more assets, and cause the price of the stock to go up by $6 per share (in which case the value of your stock would rise by $600).

a. How would the tax laws influence what you, as a typical stockholder, would want the company to do?

b. Would your choice be influenced by how much other income you had? Why might the desires of a 45-year-old physician differ with respect to corporate dividend policy from those of a pension fund manager or a retiree living on a small income?

c. How might the corporation's decision about dividend policy influence the price of its stock?

2-2   What does *double taxation of corporate income* mean?

2-3   If you were starting a business, what tax considerations might cause you to prefer to set it up as a proprietorship or a partnership rather than as a corporation?

2-4   Explain how the federal income tax structure affects the choice of financing (use of debt versus equity) of U.S. business firms.

2-5   How can the federal government influence the level of business by adjusting the ITC?

2-6   For someone planning to start a new business, is the average or the marginal tax rate more relevant?

Self-Test Problems   *(Solutions Appear on Page 60)*

Key terms

ST-1   Define each of the following terms:
a. Progressive tax
b. Taxable income
c. Marginal and average tax rates
d. Bracket creep
e. Capital gain or loss
f. Tax loss carry-back and carry-forward
g. Improper accumulation
h. ACRS depreciation; half-year convention; depreciable basis
i. Investment tax credit (ITC)
j. Cash flow; operating cash flow; accounting profit

Effect of form of organization on taxes

ST-2   Craig Vermeil is planning to start a new business, CV Enterprises, and he must decide whether to incorporate or to do business as a sole proprietorship. Under either form, Vermeil will initially own 100 percent of the firm, and tax considerations are important to him. He plans to finance the firm's expected growth by drawing a salary just sufficient for his family living expenses, which he estimates will be about $30,000, and by retaining all other income in the business. Assume that as a married man with one child, Vermeil has income tax exemptions of 3 × $2,000 = $6,000, and he estimates that his itemized deductions will be $5,800. He expects CV Enterprises to grow and to earn income of $50,000 in 1990, $80,000 in 1991, and $100,000 in 1992. Which form of business organization will allow Vermeil to pay the lowest taxes (and retain the most income) during the period 1990 to 1992?

Problems

(Note: by the time this book is published, Congress may have changed tax rates and other provisions. Work all problems on the assumption that the information in the chapter is still current.)

Corporate tax liability

2-1   The Kendrick Aluminum Company has 1989 income of $350,000 from operations after all operating costs but before (1) interest charges of $40,000, (2) dividends paid of $30,000, and (3) income taxes. What is Kendrick's income tax liability and after-tax income?

Corporate tax liability; taxation of interest and dividends

2-2   The Pennington Corporation had $600,000 of taxable income from operations in 1989.
  a. What is the company's federal income tax bill for the year?
  b. Assume the firm receives an additional $50,000 of interest income from some bonds it owns. What is the tax on this interest income?
  c. Now assume that the firm does not receive the interest income but does receive an additional $50,000 as dividends on some stock it owns. What is the tax on this dividend income?

Loss carry-back, carry-forward

2-3   The Maguire Company has made $200,000 before taxes in each of the last 15 years, and it expects to make $200,000 a year before taxes in the future. However, last year (1988) Maguire incurred a loss of $1,200,000. Maguire claimed a tax credit at the time it filed its 1988 income tax returns and received a check from the U.S. Treasury. Show how it calculated this credit, and then indicate Maguire's expected tax liability for each of the next 5 years. To ease the calculations, assume a 30 percent tax rate on *all* income.

Loss carry-back, carry-forward

2-4   The projected taxable income of the Lancing Corporation, formed in 1989, is indicated in the following table. (Losses are shown in parentheses.) What is the projected corporate tax liability for each year? Use tax rates as shown in the text.

Year	Taxable Income
1989	($80,000)
1990	60,000
1991	50,000
1992	70,000
1993	(120,000)

Income and cash flow analysis

2-5   The Ressard Corporation expects to have sales of $10 million in 1989. Costs other than depreciation are expected to be 70 percent of sales, and depreciation is expected to amount to $1 million. All sales revenues will be collected in cash, and costs other than depreciation must be paid for during the year. Ressard's federal-plus-state tax rate is 40 percent.
  a. Set up an income and a cash flow statement (in two columns of one statement). What is Ressard's expected cash flow from operations?
  b. Suppose that Congress changed the tax laws so that Ressard's depreciation expenses doubled. No changes in operations occurred. What would happen to reported profits and to cash flows?
  c. Now suppose that Congress, instead of doubling Ressard's depreciation, reduced it by 50 percent. How would profits and cash flows be affected?

d. If this were your company, would you prefer Congress to cause your depreciation expense to be doubled or halved? Why?

e. In the situation in which depreciation doubled, would this possibly have an adverse effect on the company's stock price and on its ability to borrow money? What could the firm's accountants do to alleviate any possible problems? (Hint: See Appendix 2A.)

Effect of form of organization on taxes   **2-6**   Robert Gould has operated his small repair shop as a sole proprietorship for several years, but projected changes in his business's income have led him to consider incorporating.

Gould is married and has two children. His family's only income, an annual salary of $40,000, is from operating the business. (The business actually earns more than $40,000, but Gould reinvests the additional earnings in the business.) His itemized income tax deductions are $6,100, and with four exemptions he has total exemptions of 4 × $2,000 = $8,000. Thus, his taxable income, given a salary of $40,000, would be $40,000 − $6,100 − $8,000 = $25,900. (We assume that the personal exemption will remain constant at $2,000 through 1991 for the base-case problem.) Of course, his actual taxable income, if he does not incorporate, would be higher by the amount of reinvested income. Gould estimates that his business earnings before salary and taxes for the period 1989 to 1991 will be as follows:

Year	Earnings before Salary and Taxes
1989	$50,000
1990	70,000
1991	90,000

a. What would be the tax advantage to incorporation? (Hint: 1989 tax as a corporation = $5,385 and 1989 tax as a proprietorship = $6,184.)

b. Should Gould incorporate his business? Discuss.

(Note: Answer Parts c, d, and e of this problem in words only. Problem C2-1 deals with quantifying these answers.)

c. In Part a, we assumed that the personal deduction would remain constant. Beginning in 1990, however, the personal deduction is scheduled to increase with the rate of inflation. Assume that Gould believes inflation will be 5 percent in 1990 and 1991 and, therefore, that the personal deduction will increase to $2,100 in 1990 and to $2,205 in 1991. Assume further that Gould intends to raise the salary he pays himself to keep up with inflation. Thus, his salary will rise to $42,000 in 1990 and to $44,100 in 1991. Without doing any calculations, discuss the effect of these changes on Gould's tax liability if he incorporates and if he does not incorporate.

d. Suppose Gould decides to pay out (1) 50 percent or (2) 100 percent of the after-salary corporate income in each year as dividends. Would such dividend policy changes affect Gould's decision about whether or not to incorporate? Assume the facts as stated in Part c. Answer in words only.

e. Suppose business improves, and actual earnings before salary and taxes in each year are twice the original estimate. However, Gould will continue to receive the salary specified in Part c and to reinvest additional earnings in the business. (No dividends will be paid.) What would be the effect of this increase in business income on Gould's tax liability?

Personal taxes   **2-7**   Jill Triffs has the following situation for the year 1989: salary of $50,000; dividend income of $10,000; interest on IBM bonds of $5,000; interest on state of Florida municipal bonds of $8,000; proceeds of $12,500 from the sale of 100 shares of IBM stock purchased in 1981 at a cost of $6,000; and proceeds of $12,500 from the sale of 100 shares of IBM stock purchased in October 1989 at a cost of $12,000. Triffs gets one exemption ($2,000), and she has itemized deductions of $4,000; these amounts will be deducted from her gross income to determine her taxable income.

    a. What is Triffs' tax liability for 1989? Assume she is single.

    b. What are her marginal and average tax rates?

    c. If she had $100,000 to invest and was offered a choice of either Florida bonds with a yield of 9 percent or more IBM bonds with a yield of 11 percent, which should she choose, and why?

    d. At what marginal tax rate would Triffs be indifferent to the choice between the Florida and the IBM bonds?

Depreciation   **2-8**   The Ewald Printing Company purchased a new printing press in 1989 at a cost of $240,000. Ewald also paid $65,000 to have the press delivered and installed. The press has an estimated useful life of 12 years, but it will be depreciated using ACRS over its 7-year class life.

    a. What is the depreciable basis of the printing press?

    b. What will be the depreciation allowance in each year on the 7-year class life printing press?

Depreciation   **2-9**   The Apex Corporation is commencing operations on January 1, 1989. Here are some data on the company: Sales revenues for 1989 are projected at $1,000,000; labor and materials costs are projected at $700,000; on January 1, the company purchased $100,000 of equipment, which had a 5-year ACRS class life; Apex received $10,000 of dividends on some stock the company owned and $10,000 of interest on some bonds it owned; also on January 1, the company issued $500,000 of long-term bonds, which carried an interest rate of 12 percent. Apex will pay its shareholders a dividend of $40,000 during 1989.

    a. What is the depreciation expense in each year on the 5-year class life equipment? (Hint: Depreciation for Year 1 is $20,000.)

    b. What is Apex's 1989 tax liability?

    c. Suppose Apex had forecasted higher costs and lower revenues for the first few years of its operations. Thus, when you developed the income statement, you found a loss and hence no taxes. Would this mean the company would lose the tax benefits of the loss? How would you recommend that it handle the situation? Assume for purposes of this question that losses were projected for 5 years, and after this start-up period, substantial profits were projected.

Depreciation and cash flows   **2-10**   Electronics Systems Incorporated (ESI) will commence operations on January 1, 1989. It expects to have sales of $200,000 in 1989, $250,000 in 1990, and $350,000 in 1991. It also forecasts that operating expenses will total 60 percent of sales in each year over this period and that it will have interest expenses of $10,000 in 1989, $12,500 in 1990, and $17,500 in 1991. ESI will make an investment of $100,000 on January 1, 1989, in fixed assets. The assets will be depreciated over their 3-year class life using ACRS.

a. What is the depreciation expense in each year on the 3-year class life equipment?

b. What is ESI's tax liability in each year?

c. What is ESI's cash flow in each year?

Cash flow analysis
(*Integrative*)

2-11   After graduating with a degree in landscape architecture and spending several years with a large landscaping company, Gary Powell has decided to go into business for himself. Initially, he will be the only employee of Powell's Garden Service, and he plans to pay himself a salary of $25,000 per year. He must purchase $10,000 of equipment to get started, and although the equipment should last at least 7 years, assume that it will be depreciated over a 3-year ACRS class life. Powell estimates that his first year revenues will be $40,000 and that his customer base, and hence his revenues, will grow by 10 percent a year thereafter. Powell also estimates that his operating expenses (for fertilizer, gasoline, oil, parts, and so forth) will equal 20 percent of annual revenues. If his business grows as expected, he will hire additional employees after three years.

Powell believes that for liability reasons the business should be incorporated after three years, when he brings in additional employees, but he is not certain about whether he should incorporate it now. Consequently, he hired Michelle DelaTorre, a consultant, to develop his projected income statements and to advise him on the form of organization that will minimize his taxes and maximize his cash flows over the first three years of operation. Powell is single, so his personal exemption is $2,000. In addition, he estimates that his itemized deductions will be $4,500 during each of the three years. Since this is Powell's first experience running his own business, he has asked DelaTorre to help him understand the reasons behind her recommendations. Consequently, she has developed the following list of questions which, when answered, will give Powell the information he needs to make his decision.

a. What is depreciation? How is depreciation calculated? Why must depreciation be included in the income statement? What effect does depreciation have on the firm's cash flows?

b. Calculate the depreciation expense over the life of his equipment. Will this expense be the same or different under a proprietorship versus a corporation?

c. If he incorporates, what will the corporation's tax bill, after-tax income, and cash flows be for each of the first three years? Assume that the company's only income is from garden maintenance services, and that its only expenses are Powell's salary, the company's operating expenses, and depreciation.

d. Assume that Powell incorporates and pays himself a salary of $25,000 per year, that this is his only income, and that the personal exemption is $2,000 in each year. Also, assume that Powell can take deductions of $4,500 per year. Under these assumptions, what will his personal taxes be in each of the three years?

e. What would Powell's total corporate and personal taxes be if he incorporates?

f. Now assume that Powell does not incorporate, and he operates the business as a sole proprietorship. What will his tax bill be in each of the three years?

g. Strictly on the basis of minimizing taxes during Years 1 to 3, should Powell incorporate?

h. Now suppose Powell estimates that his business will require inventories equal to 10 percent and cash equal to 5 percent of sales revenues for the coming year, and that accounts receivable will be equal to 10 percent of the past year's sales. Powell will supply $10,000, which is all of his savings, and he will borrow any additional funds needed from his bank. If in any year he has any excess cash, he will invest it in short-term Treasury bills. On the basis of these assumptions, develop approximate balance sheets for the business just before it commences operations and at the end of each of the first three years. Assume that all expenses are paid in cash and that Powell has elected to incorporate. Ignore interest.

i. If he wanted to, could Powell organize his business as a corporation and still be taxed as if it were a proprietorship? Could he do the reverse? Under what conditions would it be desirable to elect one of these options?

j. Suppose Powell's business had an additional $20,000 of expenses in Year 2. What would this do to his taxes and his after-tax income in each of the three years (1) if he incorporates and (2) if he operates as a proprietorship?

k. What does the term "progressive tax system" mean? Does such a system exist in the United States? Do the data in this problem illustrate such a system?

l. How would dividend income be treated by Powell as an individual? By the corporation? What about interest income?

m. Suppose Powell decided to incorporate, and the company was quite successful. Retained earnings in the amount of $500,000 were built up, and these funds were simply held as cash in the bank. How could Powell get the $500,000 for his personal use, and what would be the tax consequences of this action?

Computer-Related Problem

Effect of form of organization on taxes

C2-1   Do this problem only if your instructor has supplied you with the computer problem diskette. The problem requires a rework of Problem 2-6, using the data provided in Parts c, d, and e.

a. Rework Part c of Problem 2-6, using the file C2 on the computer problem diskette. Check your verbal answer given in Problem 2-6c against your numerical answer obtained here.

b. Rework Part d of Problem 2-6, using the file C2 on the computer problem diskette. Check your verbal answer given for Problem 2-6d.

c. Rework Part e of Problem 2-6, using the file C2 on the computer problem diskette. Check your verbal answer given for Problem 2-6e.

Solutions to Self-Test Problems

ST-1   Use the marginal glossary definitions to check your responses.

ST-2

	1990	1991	1992
Vermeil's Taxes as a Corporation			
Income before salary & taxes	$50,000	$80,000	$100,000
Less salary	(30,000)	(30,000)	(30,000)
Taxable income, corporate	$20,000	$50,000	$ 70,000
Total corporate tax	3,000[a]	7,500	12,500
Salary	$30,000	$30,000	$ 30,000
Less exemptions and deductions	(11,800)	(11,800)	(11,800)
Taxable personal income	$18,200	$18,200	$ 18,200
Total personal tax	2,730[b]	2,730	2,730
Combined corporate and personal tax:	$ 5,730	$10,230	$ 15,230
Vermeil's Taxes as a Proprietorship			
Total income	$50,000	$80,000	$100,000
Less exemptions and deductions	11,800	11,800	11,800
Taxable personal income	$38,200	$68,200	$ 88,200
Tax liability of proprietorship	$ 6,828[c]	$15,228	$ 21,643
Advantage to being a corporation:	$ 1,098	$ 4,998	$ 6,413

[a]Corporate tax in 1990 = (0.15)($20,000) = $3,000.

[b]Personal tax (if Vermeil incorporates) in 1990 = (0.15)($18,200) = $2,730.

[c]Proprietorship tax in 1990 = $4,462 + (0.28)($38,200 − $29,750)
$$= \$4,462 + \$2,366$$
$$= \$6,828.$$

The corporate form of organization allows Vermeil to pay the lowest taxes in each year; therefore, on the basis of taxes over the 3-year period, Vermeil should incorporate his business. However, note that to get money out of the corporation so he can spend it, Vermeil will have to have the corporation pay dividends, which will be taxed to Vermeil, and thus he will, sometime in the future, have to pay additional taxes.

2A   Effects of Depreciation Methods on Taxes, Net Income, and Cash Flows

Managers and financial analysts are concerned primarily with the stream of cash flows firms generate from operations. As we saw in Chapter 2, net income and cash flows are rarely, if ever, the same. We also saw that a firm's cash flows are approximately equal to its net income plus depreciation. However, we noted that taxes paid can differ from reported taxes, and this too can affect cash flows. We explore all this in this appendix, and in the process we show how a firm's choice of depreciation accounting affects both its cash flows and its accounting profits.

Depreciation for Tax Purposes versus Reporting Purposes

All firms are required to use either the Accelerated Cost Recovery System (ACRS) method or the straight line method when depreciating their assets for tax purposes. Most firms use the most rapid method, ACRS. The reason is that since depreciation is a tax-deductible expense, larger depreciation write-offs decrease current tax liabilities, and it is better to pay taxes later rather than sooner because the firm has the use of the money in the meantime. However, larger depreciation expenses also reduce firms' reported net income.

Generally accepted accounting principles, which specify the accounting methods a firm may use to determine its income as reported to its stockholders, state that a firm should depreciate its assets for reporting purposes using the method which most accurately reflects the decline in the value of the assets over time. For most firms, this method is straight line depreciation. A few firms use ACRS for both tax and reporting purposes, but it is far more common for firms to use ACRS for calculating taxes and straight line for reporting income to investors.

Effects on Taxes and Net Income. Table 2A-1 shows pretax income, taxes, and net income for a firm which has sales of $100 million a year, costs equal to 50 percent of sales, and a single asset which cost $100 million. This asset has a 10-year economic life, and it will have zero salvage value at the end of the 10 years. Section 1 of the table shows the calculation of actual taxes owed using the ACRS method; Section II shows the calculation of taxes and net income for reporting purposes using the straight line method; and Section III shows the income statements the company would report to investors if it used ACRS depreciation for both tax and reporting purposes.[1]

In Year 1, the firm reports to the Internal Revenue Service $20 million in depreciation and $30 million of taxable income, and it pays $10.2 million in taxes. If it uses ACRS for stockholder reporting, as shown in Section III, it reports net income of $19.8 million. However, if it uses straight line depreciation for stockholder reporting, as shown in Section II, it reports $10 million in depreciation, $10.2 + $3.4 = $13.6 million in taxes, and net income of $26.40 million, even though the actual tax bill is only $10.2 million. The difference of $13.6 − $10.2 = $3.4 million in reported versus paid taxes is shown on the income statement as *deferred taxes* — that is, the firm has been able to defer paying these taxes until a later date by using an accelerated depreciation method for calculating taxable income.

Notice in Section III that net income using ACRS depreciation fluctuates for several years, then is stable at a level above net income as reported to stockholders.

---

[1]We do not show it, but if the straight line method had been used for both stockholder reporting and tax purposes, pretax income would have been $40 million each year (disregarding the half-year convention). Therefore, taxes would have been 0.34 × $40 = $13.6 million each year, or 10 × $13.6 = $136 million in total. This is exactly the same total as when ACRS is used for tax purposes, but the timing of the tax payments is quite different.

Table 2A-1   Effects of Depreciation on Taxes and Profits

1. The firm has a single asset which cost $100 million, has a 10-year economic life, and has a zero salvage value. Revenues are $100 million per year over the 10 years, and costs other than depreciation are $50 million per year. The firm's tax rate is 34 percent, and it has 10 million shares of stock outstanding.
2. Straight line depreciation charges are $100,000,000/10 = $10,000,000 per year. The asset has a 5-year tax life, so it can, under ACRS, be depreciated at the following rates (millions of dollars):

Year	ACRS Rate	Depreciation
1	0.20	$ 20.00
2	0.32	32.00
3	0.19	19.00
4	0.12	12.00
5	0.11	11.00
6	0.06	6.00
		$100.00

3. In the following table we show (1) how the tax liability is calculated and (2) how income is reported to investors (millions of dollars):

I. Tax Calculations

	Year						
	1	2	3	4	5	6	7 . . . 10[a]
Sales	$100.00	$100.00	$100.00	$100.00	$100.00	$100.00	$100.00
Costs	50.00	50.00	50.00	50.00	50.00	50.00	50.00
Depreciation (D)	20.00	32.00	19.00	12.00	11.00	6.00	0.00
Pretax income	$ 30.00	$ 18.00	$ 31.00	$ 38.00	$ 39.00	$ 44.00	$ 50.00
Taxes payable at 34% (T)	10.20	6.12	10.54	12.92	13.26	14.96	17.00

II. Income Statements Reported to Stockholders: Straight Line Depreciation with Deferred Taxes

	Year						
	1	2	3	4	5	6	7 . . . 10[a]
Sales	$100.00	$100.00	$100.00	$100.00	$100.00	$100.00	$100.00
Costs	50.00	50.00	50.00	50.00	50.00	50.00	50.00
Depreciation (D)	10.00	10.00	10.00	10.00	10.00	10.00	10.00
Pretax income	$ 40.00	$ 40.00	$ 40.00	$ 40.00	$ 40.00	$ 40.00	$ 40.00
Taxes paid, 34% (T) (from Section I)	10.20	6.12	10.54	12.92	13.26	14.96	17.00
Deferred taxes (DT)[b]	3.40	7.48	3.06	0.68	0.34	(1.36)	(3.40)
Net income after all taxes (NI)	$ 26.40	$ 26.40	$ 26.40	$ 26.40	$ 26.40	$ 26.40	$ 26.40
Earnings per share	$ 2.64	$ 2.64	$ 2.64	$ 2.64	$ 2.64	$ 2.64	$ 2.64

III. Income Statements Reported to Stockholders: ACRS Depreciation

	Year						
	1	2	3	4	5	6	7 . . . 10[a]
Sales	$100.00	$100.00	$100.00	$100.00	$100.00	$100.00	$100.00
Costs	50.00	50.00	50.00	50.00	50.00	50.00	50.00
Depreciation (D)	20.00	32.00	19.00	12.00	11.00	6.00	0.00
Pretax income	$ 30.00	$ 18.00	$ 31.00	$ 38.00	$ 39.00	$ 44.00	$ 50.00
Taxes payable at 34% (T)	10.20	6.12	10.54	12.92	13.26	14.96	17.00
Net income after taxes (NI)	$ 19.80	$ 11.88	$ 20.46	$ 25.08	$ 25.74	$ 29.04	$ 33.00
Earnings per share	$ 1.98	$ 1.19	$ 2.05	$ 2.51	$ 2.57	$ 2.90	$ 3.30

[a]The income statements do not change for Years 7 through 10.

[b]DT = (Pretax income)(Tax rate) − Taxes paid from Part I = $40(0.34) − $10.2 = $3.4 in Year 1.

Table 2A-2   Effects of Depreciation on Cash Flows

I. ACRS Depreciation Used for Stockholder Reporting

	Year						
	1	2	3	4	5	6	7 . . . 10[a]
Net income after taxes	$19.80	$11.88	$20.46	$25.08	$25.74	$29.04	$33.00
Depreciation	20.00	32.00	19.00	12.00	11.00	6.00	0
Deferred taxes	0	0	0	0	0	0	0
Cash flows[b]	$39.80	$43.88	$39.46	$37.08	$36.74	$35.04	$33.00

II. Straight Line Depreciation Used for Stockholder Reporting

	Year						
	1	2	3	4	5	6	7 . . . 10[a]
Net income after taxes	$26.40	$26.40	$26.40	$26.40	$26.40	$26.40	$26.40
Depreciation	10.00	10.00	10.00	10.00	10.00	10.00	10.00
Deferred taxes	3.40	7.48	3.06	0.68	0.34	(1.36)	(3.40)
Cash flows[b]	$39.80	$43.88	$39.46	$37.08	$36.74	$35.04	$33.00

[a]Cash flows do not change in Years 7 through 10.

[b]Cash flows = Net income + Depreciation + Deferred taxes.

Income reported to stockholders using straight line depreciation is stable during the entire period. For this reason, firms that use deferred tax accounting are said to be using a "normalization" procedure, where "normalize" means "stabilize." To the extent that investors (1) give weight to reported accounting profits and (2) prefer stable or growing earnings to fluctuating earnings, there is an advantage to using straight line depreciation for reporting purposes.

If the firm had Year 1 costs of $80 million, its taxable income, hence taxes paid, would be zero, yet if it used deferred taxes, it would report a profit to stockholders. General Electric, Boeing, and a number of other successful companies have in recent years been in such a situation; they did not actually pay any federal income taxes, yet they reported high profits. This situation helped create a political climate that led to much higher corporate taxes in 1987 and thereafter. An alternative minimum tax has also been imposed on corporations. The alternative minimum tax is too complicated to cover in this text, but it insures that any company that reports profits to stockholders will pay at least some tax.

Effects on Cash Flows. The cash flows which accrue to the firm are calculated in Table 2A-2. Notice that cash flows, which are equal to net income plus depreciation plus deferred taxes, are the same regardless of the depreciation method used for reporting purposes. This result always occurs. Thus, we can see that the depreciation method has no effect on the cash flows which accrue to a firm from its assets — provided that the firm uses ACRS for tax purposes. The important point is that both depreciation and deferred taxes must be added to net income to calculate cash flows.

Effects on the Balance Sheet. The cumulative deferred taxes for each year are reported on the balance sheet under the account "Deferred taxes." Deferred taxes are regarded as a liability — in effect, a loan from the federal government. Our hypothetical company in Table 2A-1, Part II, would show deferred taxes on its end-of-Year 1 balance sheet of $3.40 million. The amount shown at the end of Year 2 would be $3.40 + $7.48 = $10.88 million, and the account would peak at $14.96 million at the end of Year 5. Then, in Year 6, the account would be reduced by $1.36 million, and in Years 7 through 10, the account would be reduced by $3.40 million per year. Finally, the account would show a zero balance at the end of Year 10.

3

Financial Markets, Institutions, and Interest Rates

KNOWING WHEN TO BORROW: CATERPILLAR AND FINANCIAL CORPORATION OF AMERICA

"Money Men Are Minding the Store: The Financial Brains Have Taken Charge in Retailing." This caption appeared in a recent issue of *The New York Times*. The article went on to explain how financial executives were taking over the top spots of major U.S. retailing chains from marketing executives. The primary reason behind this shift of power is that finance people best understand the markets wherein companies raise capital for expansion and where stock prices, which firms seek to maximize, are established.

Another article, this one in *Business Week*, illustrates the impact that financial timing can have. Caterpillar Company executives delayed a $300 million bond issue on the grounds that the 10.5 percent interest rate the company would have had to pay was too high. Subsequently, interest rates rose sharply rather than falling as the Caterpillar executives had expected, and a year later, with rates at 15 percent, the company's cash needs forced management to go ahead with the issue — at an additional cost of $13.5 million per year.

Caterpillar was a victim of bad luck (or bad forecasting), but rising interest rates have been far more painful to many other companies. For example,

65

Financial Corporation of America, one of the largest financial institutions in the United States, borrowed money on a short-term basis and then loaned it out on a long-term, fixed rate basis. This was profitable as long as short-term rates were lower than long-term rates, but when short rates rose above long rates, Financial Corp found itself with an asset portfolio that was yielding about 11 percent and liabilities which had an average cost of about 14 percent. The Federal Deposit Insurance Corporation had to pump billions of dollars into FCA, and it was acquired by Robert Bass, the Texas billionaire, in 1988. Many of Financial Corp's managers have already been demoted or fired, and more will surely follow.

To some extent the problems of Caterpillar, Financial Corp, and the thousands of other companies that have been hurt by high interest rates were the result of bad luck; it is hard to predict interest rates. However, some of these problems might have been avoided had these firms' financial managers had a better understanding of financial markets and institutions, and of the way interest rates are established in these markets. These topics are discussed in this chapter.

A knowledge of the environment in which financial managers operate is critical to an understanding of financial management. In this chapter we examine the markets where capital is raised, securities are traded, and stock prices are established, as well as the institutions through which such transactions are conducted. In the process, we shall see how money costs are determined, and we shall explore the principal factors that determine the level of interest rates in the economy.

THE FINANCIAL MARKETS

Business firms, as well as individuals and government units, often need to raise capital. For example, suppose Pacific Gas & Electric Company (PG&E) forecasts an increase in the demand for electricity in Northern California, and the company decides to build a new power plant. Because PG&E almost certainly will not have the $2 billion or so necessary to pay for the plant, the company will have to raise this capital in the market. Or suppose Mr. Jones, the proprietor of a Dallas hardware store, decides to expand into appliances. Where will he get the money to buy the initial inventory of TV sets, washers, and freezers? Similarly, if the Smith family wants to buy a home that costs $100,000, but they have only $20,000 in savings, how can they raise the additional $80,000? If the City of Sacramento wants to borrow $20 million to finance a new sewer plant, or if the federal government needs $150 billion or so to cover its projected 1989 deficit, they too need sources for raising this capital.

On the other hand, some individuals and firms have incomes which are greater than their current expenditures, so they have funds available to invest. For example, Edgar Rice has an income of $36,000, but his expenses are only $30,000. In 1988, Ford Motor Company had accumulated over $9 billion of excess cash, which it could make available for investment.

People and organizations wanting to borrow money are brought together with those having surplus funds in the *financial markets*. Note that "markets" is plural — there are a great many different financial markets, each one consisting of many institutions, in a developed economy such as ours. Each market deals with a somewhat different type of instrument in terms of the instrument's maturity and the assets backing it. Also, different markets serve different sets of customers, or operate in different parts of the country. Here are some of the major types of markets:

1. *Physical asset markets* and *financial asset markets* must be distinguished. *Physical asset markets* (also called "tangible" or "real" asset markets) are those for such products as wheat, autos, real estate, computers, and machinery. *Financial markets* deal with stocks, bonds, notes, mortgages, and other *claims on real assets.*

2. *Spot markets* and *futures markets* are terms that refer to whether the assets are being bought or sold for "on the spot" delivery (literally, within a few days) or for delivery at some future date, such as six months or a year in the future. The futures markets (which could include the *options markets*) are growing in importance, but we shall not discuss them until much later in the text.

money markets
The financial markets in which funds are borrowed or loaned for short periods (less than one year).

3. **Money markets** are the markets for debt securities with maturities of less than one year. The New York money market is the world's largest, and it is dominated by the major U.S. banks, although branches of foreign banks are also active there. London, Tokyo, and Paris are other major money market centers.

capital markets
The financial markets for stocks and for long-term debt (one year or longer).

4. **Capital markets** are the markets for long-term debt and corporate stocks. The New York Stock Exchange, which handles the stocks of the largest U.S. corporations, is a prime example of a capital market.

5. *Mortgage markets* deal with loans on residential, commercial, and industrial real estate, and on farmland.

6. *Consumer credit markets* involve loans on autos and appliances, as well as loans for education, vacations, and so on.

7. *World, national, regional,* and *local markets* also exist. Thus, depending on an organization's size and scope of operations, it may be able to borrow all around the world, or it may be confined to a strictly local, even neighborhood, market.

primary markets
Markets in which corporations raise capital by issuing new securities.

8. **Primary markets** are the markets in which corporations raise new capital, and in which newly issued securities are involved. If IBM were to sell a new issue of common stock to raise capital, this would be a primary

market transaction. The corporation selling the stock receives the proceeds from the sale in a primary market transaction.

secondary markets
Markets in which securities and other financial assets are traded among investors after they have been issued by corporations.

9. **Secondary markets** are markets in which existing, outstanding securities are traded among investors. Thus, if John Mitchell decided to buy 1,000 shares of IBM stock, the purchase would (except for a new issue) occur in the secondary market. The New York Stock Exchange is a secondary market, since it deals in outstanding as opposed to newly issued stocks and bonds. Secondary markets also exist for mortgages, various other types of loans, and other financial assets. The corporation whose securities are being traded is not involved in a secondary market transaction and, thus, does not receive any funds from such a sale.

Other classifications could be made, but this breakdown is sufficient to show that there are many types of financial markets.

A healthy economy is dependent on efficient transfers of funds from people who are net savers to firms and individuals who need capital — that is, the economy depends on *efficient financial markets*. Without efficient transfers, the economy simply could not function: Pacific Gas & Electric could not raise capital, so San Francisco's citizens would have no electricity; the Smith family would not have adequate housing; Edgar Rice would have no place to invest his savings; and so on. Obviously, the level of employment and productivity, and hence our standard of living, would be much lower, so it is absolutely essential that our financial markets function efficiently — not only quickly, but also at a low cost.[1]

FINANCIAL INSTITUTIONS

Transfers of capital between savers and those who need capital take place in the three different ways diagrammed in Figure 3-1:

1. *Direct transfers* of money and securities, as shown in the top section, occur when a business sells its stocks or bonds directly to savers, without going through any type of intermediary. Dollars flow from savers to the business, which then gives securities to the savers.

2. As shown in the middle section, transfers may also go through an *investment banking house* such as Merrill Lynch, which serves as a middleman and facilitates the issuance of securities. The company sells its stocks or bonds to the investment bank, which in turn sells them to ultimate savers. The businesses' securities and the savers' money merely

---

[1] When organizations like the United Nations design plans to aid developing nations, just as much attention must be paid to the establishment of cost-efficient financial markets as to electrical power, transportation, communications, and other infrastructure systems. Economic efficiency is simply impossible without a good system for allocating capital within the economy.

Figure 3-1   Diagram of the Capital Formation Process

1. Direct Transfers

2. Indirect Transfers through Investment Bankers

3. Indirect Transfers through a Financial Intermediary

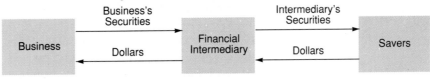

"pass through" the investment banking house. However, the investment bank does buy the securities, and it is taking a chance — it may not be able to resell them to savers for as much or more than it paid, but the company is sure of getting the funds it needs. Because the corporation receives money from the sale, this is a primary market transaction.

3. Transfers can also be made through a *financial intermediary* such as a bank or mutual fund, which obtains funds from savers and then issues its own securities in exchange. For example, a saver might give dollars to a bank, receiving from it a certificate of deposit, and then the bank might lend the money to a small business in the form of a mortgage loan. Thus, intermediaries literally create new forms of capital — in this case, certificates of deposit, which are more liquid than mortgages and hence are better securities for most savers to hold — and this increases general market efficiency.

For simplicity, we assumed that the entity which needs capital is a business, and specifically a corporation, although it is easy to visualize the demander of capital as a potential home purchaser, a government unit, and so on.

Direct transfers of funds from savers to businesses are possible and do occur on occasion, but it is generally more efficient for a business to obtain the services of an **investment banking house**. Merrill Lynch, Salomon Brothers, and Dean Witter are examples of financial service corporations which offer investment banking services. Such organizations (1) help corporations design

investment banking house
A financial institution that underwrites and distributes new investment securities and helps businesses obtain financing.

securities with the features that will be most attractive to investors, (2) buy these securities from the corporation, and (3) then resell them to savers. Although the securities are sold twice, this process is really one primary market transaction, with the investment banker acting as a middleman in the process of transferring capital from savers to businesses.

financial intermediaries
Specialized financial firms that facilitate the transfer of funds from savers to demanders of capital.

As noted previously, the **financial intermediaries** shown in the third section of Figure 3-1 do more than simply transfer money and securities between firms and savers — they literally create new financial products. Since the intermediaries are generally large, they gain economies of scale in analyzing the creditworthiness of potential borrowers, in processing and collecting loans, and in pooling risks and thus helping individual savers diversify, which means "not putting all their financial eggs in one basket." Further, a system of specialized intermediaries can enable savings to do more than just draw interest. For example, people can put money into banks and get both interest income and a convenient way of making payments (checking), put money into life insurance companies and get both interest income and protection for their beneficiaries, and so on.

In the United States and other developed nations, a large set of specialized, highly efficient financial intermediaries has evolved. The situation is changing rapidly, however, and different types of institutions are performing services that were formerly reserved for others, causing institutional distinctions to become blurred. Still, there is a degree of institutional identity, and here are the major classes of intermediaries:

1. *Commercial banks,* which are the traditional "department stores" of finance, serve a wide variety of savers and those with needs for funds. Historically, the commercial banks were the major institutions for handling checking accounts and through which the Federal Reserve System expanded or contracted the money supply. Today, however, some of the other institutions also provide checking services and significantly influence the effective money supply. Conversely, commercial banks now provide an ever widening range of services, including stock brokerage services and insurance.

    Note that commercial banks are quite different from "investment banks." Commercial banks lend money, whereas investment bankers help companies raise capital from other parties. Prior to 1933, commercial banks offered investment banking services, but the Glass–Steagall Act, which was passed in that year, prohibited commercial banks from engaging in investment banking. Thus, the Morgan Bank was broken up into two separate organizations, one of which is now the Morgan Guaranty Trust Company, while the other is Morgan Stanley, a major investment banking house.

2. *Savings and loan associations (S&Ls),* which have traditionally served individual savers and residential and commercial mortgage borrowers, take the funds of many small savers and then lend this money to home buyers and other types of borrowers. Because the savers are provided a

degree of liquidity that would be absent if they bought the mortgages or other securities directly, perhaps the most significant economic function of the S&Ls is to "create liquidity" which would otherwise be lacking. Also, the S&Ls have more expertise in analyzing credit, setting up loans, and making collections than individual savers could possibly have, so they reduce the cost and increase the availability of real estate loans. Finally, the S&Ls hold large, diversified portfolios of loans and other assets and thus spread risks in a manner that would be impossible if small savers were making mortgage loans directly. Because of these factors, savers benefit by being able to invest their savings in more liquid, better managed, and less risky accounts, whereas borrowers benefit by being able to obtain more capital, and at lower costs, than would otherwise be possible.

3. *Mutual savings banks,* which are similar to S&Ls, operate primarily in the northeastern states, accept savings primarily from individuals, and lend mainly on a long-term basis to home buyers and consumers.

4. *Credit unions* are cooperative associations whose members have a common bond, such as being employees of the same firm. Members' savings are loaned only to other members, generally for auto purchases, home improvements, and the like. Credit unions often are the cheapest source of funds available to the individual borrower.

5. *Pension funds* are retirement plans funded by corporations or government agencies for their workers and administered primarily by the trust departments of commercial banks or by life insurance companies. Pension funds invest in bonds, stocks, mortgages, and real estate.

6. *Life insurance companies* take savings in the form of annual premiums, then invest these funds in stocks, bonds, real estate, and mortgages, and finally make payments to the beneficiaries of the insured parties. In recent years life insurance companies have also offered a variety of tax-deferred savings plans designed to provide benefits to the participants when they retire.

mutual fund
A corporation that invests the pooled funds of many savers, thus obtaining economies of scale in investing and reducing risk by diversification.

7. **Mutual funds** are corporations which accept dollars from savers and then use these dollars to buy stocks, long-term bonds, or short-term debt instruments issued by businesses or government units. These organizations pool funds and thus reduce risks by diversification. They also gain economies of scale, which lowers the costs of analyzing securities, managing portfolios, and buying and selling securities. Different funds are designed to meet the objectives of different types of savers. Hence, there are bond funds for those who desire safety, stock funds for savers who are willing to accept significant risks in the hope of higher returns, and still other funds that are used as interest-bearing checking accounts (the **money market funds**). There are literally hundreds of different mutual funds with dozens of different goals and purposes.

money market fund
A mutual fund that invests in short-term, low-risk securities and allows investors to write checks against their accounts.

Financial institutions have historically been heavily regulated, with the primary purpose of this regulation being to insure the safety of the institutions and thus to protect depositors. However, these regulations — which have taken the form of prohibitions on nationwide branch banking, restrictions on the types of assets the institutions can buy, ceilings on the interest rates they can pay, and limitations on the types of services they can provide — have tended to impede the free flow of capital from surplus to deficit areas and thus have hurt the efficiency of our capital markets. Recognizing this fact, Congress has authorized some major changes, and more will be forthcoming.

financial service corporation
A firm which offers a wide range of financial services, including investment banking, brokerage operations, insurance, and commercial banking.

The end result of the ongoing regulatory changes is a blurring of the distinctions between the different types of institutions. Indeed, the trend in the United States today is toward huge **financial service corporations**, which own banks, S&Ls, investment banking houses, insurance companies, pension plan operations, and mutual funds, and which have branches across the country and even around the world. Sears, Roebuck is, interestingly, one of the largest financial service corporations. It owns Allstate Insurance, Dean Witter (a leading brokerage and investment banking firm), Coldwell Banker (the largest real estate brokerage firm), a huge credit card business, and a host of other related businesses. Other financial service corporations, most of which started in one area and have now diversified to cover the full financial spectrum, include Transamerica, Merrill Lynch, American Express, Citicorp, and Prudential.

THE STOCK MARKET

As noted earlier, secondary markets are those in which outstanding, previously issued securities are traded. By far the most active secondary market, and the most important one to financial managers, is the *stock market*. It is here that the prices of firms' stocks are established. Since the primary goal of financial management is to maximize the firm's stock price, a knowledge of the market in which this price is established is essential for anyone involved in managing a business.

organized security exchanges
Formal organizations having tangible physical locations that conduct auction markets in designated ("listed") securities. The two major U.S. stock exchanges are the New York Stock Exchange (NYSE) and the American Stock Exchange (AMEX).

The Stock Exchanges

There are two basic types of stock markets — the *organized exchanges,* which include the New York Stock Exchange (NYSE), the American Stock Exchange (AMEX), and several regional exchanges, and the less formal *over-the-counter markets.* Since the organized exchanges have actual physical market locations and are easier to describe and understand, we shall consider them first.

The **organized security exchanges** are tangible physical entities. Each of the larger ones occupies its own building, has specifically designated members, and has an elected governing body — its board of governors. Members are said to have "seats" on the exchange, although everybody stands up. These seats, which are bought and sold, give the holder the right to trade on the exchange. In 1979 seats on the NYSE sold for as little as $40,000, but in May 1987, they hit an all-time high price of $1.1 million.

Most of the larger investment banking houses operate *brokerage departments,* which own seats on the exchanges and designate one or more of their officers as members. The exchanges are open on all normal working days, with the members meeting in a large room equipped with telephones and other electronic equipment that enable each member to communicate with his or her firm's offices throughout the country.

Like other markets, security exchanges facilitate communication between buyers and sellers. For example, Merrill Lynch (the largest brokerage firm) might receive an order in its Atlanta office from a customer who wants to buy 100 shares of General Motors stock. Simultaneously, Dean Witter's Denver office might receive an order from a customer wishing to sell 100 shares of GM. Each broker communicates by wire with the firm's representative on the NYSE. Other brokers throughout the country are also communicating with their own exchange members. The exchange members with *sell orders* offer the shares for sale, and they are bid for by the members with *buy orders.* Thus, the exchanges operate as *auction markets.*[2]

The Over-the-Counter Market

over-the-counter market A large collection of brokers and dealers, connected electronically by telephones and computers, that provides for trading in unlisted securities.

In contrast to the organized security exchanges, the **over-the-counter market** is a nebulous, intangible organization. An explanation of the term "over-the-counter" will help clarify exactly what this market is. The exchanges operate as auction markets; buy and sell orders come in more or less simultaneously, and exchange members match these orders. If a stock is traded less frequently,

---

[2]The NYSE is actually a modified auction market, wherein people (through their brokers) bid for stocks. Originally — a hundred or so years ago — brokers would literally shout, "I have 100 shares of Union Pacific for sale; how much am I offered?" and then sell to the highest bidder. If a broker had a buy order, he or she would shout, "I want to buy 100 shares of Union Pacific; who'll sell at the best price?" The same general situation still exists, although the exchanges now have members known as *specialists* who facilitate the trading process by keeping an inventory of shares of the stocks in which they specialize. If a buy order comes in at a time when no sell order arrives, the specialist will sell off some inventory. Similarly, if a sell order comes in, the specialist will buy and add to inventory. The specialist sets a *bid price* (the price the specialist will pay for the stock) and an *asked price* (the price at which shares will be sold out of inventory). The bid and asked prices are set at levels designed to keep the inventory in balance. If many buy orders start coming in because of favorable developments, or sell orders come in because of unfavorable events, the specialist will raise or lower prices to keep supply and demand in balance. Bid prices are somewhat lower than asked prices, with the difference, or *spread,* representing the specialist's profit margin.

Special facilities are available to help institutional investors such as mutual funds or pension funds sell large blocks of stock without depressing their prices. In essence, brokerage houses which cater to institutional clients will purchase blocks (defined as 10,000 or more shares) and then resell the stock to other institutions or individuals. Also, when a firm has a major announcement which is likely to cause its stock price to change sharply, it will ask the exchanges to halt trading in its stock until the announcement has been made and digested by investors. Thus, when Texaco announced that it planned to acquire Getty Oil, trading was halted for one day in both Texaco and Getty stocks.

perhaps because it is the stock of a new or a small firm, few buy and sell orders come in, and matching them within a reasonable length of time would be difficult. To avoid this problem, some brokerage firms maintain an inventory of such stocks; they buy when individual investors want to sell and sell when investors want to buy. At one time the inventory of securities was kept in a safe, and the stocks, when bought and sold, were literally passed over the counter.

Today, the over-the-counter markets are defined as all facilities that provide for any security transactions not conducted on the organized exchanges. These facilities consist of (1) the relatively few *dealers* who hold inventories of over-the-counter securities and who are said to "make a market" in these securities, (2) the thousands of brokers who act as *agents* in bringing these dealers together with investors, and (3) the computers, terminals, and electronic networks that provide for communications between dealers and brokers. The dealers who make a market in a particular stock continuously post a price at which they are willing to buy the stock (the *bid price*) and a price at which they will sell shares (the *asked price*). These prices, which are adjusted as supply and demand conditions change, can be read off computer screens all across the country. The spread between bid and asked prices represents the dealer's markup, or profit.

Brokers and dealers who make up the over-the-counter market are members of a self-regulating body known as the *National Association of Security Dealers (NASD)*, which licenses brokers and oversees trading practices. The computerized trading network used by NASD is known as the NASD Automated Quotation System (NASDAQ), and *The Wall Street Journal* and other newspapers contain information on NASDAQ transactions.

In terms of numbers of issues, the majority of stocks are traded over-the-counter. However, because the stocks of larger companies are listed on the exchanges, about two-thirds of the dollar volume of stock trading takes place on the exchanges.

Some Trends in Security Trading Procedures

From the NYSE's inception in the 1800s until the 1970s, the vast majority of all stock trading occurred on the Exchange and was conducted by member firms. The NYSE established a set of minimum brokerage commission rates, and no member firm could charge a commission lower than the set rate. This was a monopoly, pure and simple. However, on May 1, 1975, the Securities and Exchange Commission (SEC), with strong prodding from the Antitrust Division of the Justice Department, forced the NYSE to abandon its fixed commissions. Commission rates declined dramatically, falling in some cases as much as 90 percent from former levels. These changes were a boon to the investing public, but not to the brokerage industry. A number of "full service" brokerage houses went bankrupt, and others were forced to merge with stronger firms. Many Wall Street experts predict that once the dust settles, the number of brokerage houses will have declined from literally thousands in the 1960s to a much smaller number of large, strong, nationwide companies, all of which are units of diversified financial service corporations. Deregulation has spawned a number of small "discount brokers," some of which are affiliated with commercial banks or savings and loans; several of these will be among the survivors.[3]

THE COST OF MONEY

Capital in a free economy is allocated through the price system. *The interest rate is the price paid to borrow capital, whereas in the case of equity capital, investors' returns come in the form of dividends and capital gains.* The factors which affect the supply of and the demand for investment capital, and hence the cost of money, are discussed in this section.

production opportunities
The returns available within an economy from investment in productive (cash-generating) assets.

time preferences for consumption
The preferences of consumers for current consumption as opposed to saving for future consumption.

The two most fundamental factors affecting the cost of money are (1) **production opportunities** and (2) **time preferences for consumption**. To see how these factors operate, visualize an isolated island community where the people live on fish. They have a stock of fishing gear which permits them to survive reasonably well, but they would like to have more fish. Now suppose Mr. Crusoe had a bright idea for a new type of fishnet that would enable him to double his daily catch. However, it would take him a year to perfect his design, to build his net, and to learn how to use it efficiently, and Mr. Crusoe would probably starve before he could put his new net into operation. Therefore, he might suggest to Ms. Robinson, Mr. Friday, and several others that if they would give him one fish each day for a year, he would return two fish a day during all of the next year. If someone accepted the offer, then the fish which Ms. Robinson or one of the others gave to Mr. Crusoe would constitute *savings;* these savings would be *invested* in the fishnet; and the extra fish the net produced would constitute a *return on the investment.*

Obviously, the more productive Mr. Crusoe thought the new fishnet would be, the higher his expected return on the investment would be and the more he could offer to pay Ms. Robinson, Mr. Friday, or other potential investors for their savings. In this example we assume that Mr. Crusoe thought he would be able to pay, and thus he offered, a 100 percent rate of return — he offered to give back two fish for every one he received. He might have tried to attract savings for less; for example, he might have decided to offer only 1.5 fish next year for every one he received this year, which would represent a 50 percent rate of return to Ms. Robinson or the other potential savers.

How attractive Mr. Crusoe's offer would appear to potential savers would depend in large part on their *time preferences for consumption.* For example,

---

[3]Full service brokers give investors information on different stocks and make recommendations as to which stocks to buy. Discount brokers do not give advice—they merely execute orders. Some brokerage houses (institutional houses) cater primarily to institutional investors such as pension funds and insurance companies, while others cater to individual investors and are called retail houses. Large firms such as Merrill Lynch generally have both retail and institutional brokers.

Ms. Robinson might be thinking of retirement, and she might be willing to trade fish today for fish in the future on a one-for-one basis. On the other hand, Mr. Friday might have a wife and several young children and need his current fish, so he might be unwilling to "lend" a fish today for anything less than three fish next year. Mr. Friday would be said to have a high time preference for consumption and Ms. Robinson a low time preference. Note also that if the entire population were living right at the subsistence level, time preferences for current consumption would necessarily be high, aggregate savings would be low, interest rates would be high, and capital formation would be difficult.

In a more complex society there are many businesses like Mr. Crusoe's, many goods other than fish, and many savers like Ms. Robinson and Mr. Friday. Further, people use money as a medium of exchange rather than barter with fish. *Still, the interest rate paid to savers depends in a basic way on (1) the rate of return producers expect to earn on invested capital and (2) consumers'/savers' time preferences for current versus future consumption.* Producers' expected returns on their business investments set an upper limit on how much they can pay for savings, while consumers' time preferences for consumption establish how much consumption they are willing to defer and hence how much they will save at different levels of interest offered by producers.[4]

INTEREST RATE LEVELS

Capital is allocated among firms by interest rates: Firms with the most profitable investment opportunities are willing and able to pay the most for capital, so they tend to attract it away from inefficient firms or from those whose products are not in demand. Of course, our economy is not completely free in the sense of being influenced only by market forces. Thus, the federal government has agencies which help individuals or groups, as stipulated by Congress, to obtain credit on favorable terms. Among those eligible for this kind of assistance are small businesses, certain minorities, and firms willing to build plants in areas with high unemployment. Still, most capital in the U.S. economy is allocated through the price system.

Figure 3-2 shows how supply and demand interact to determine interest rates in two capital markets. Markets A and B represent two of the many capital markets in existence. The going interest rate, k, is 10 percent for the low-risk securities in Market A. Borrowers whose credit is strong enough to qualify for this market can obtain funds at a cost of 10 percent, and investors who want to put their money to work at low risk can obtain a 10 percent return. Riskier

---

[4]The term "producers" is really too narrow. A better word might be "borrowers," which would include corporations, home purchasers, people borrowing to go to college, or even people borrowing to buy autos or to pay for vacations. Also, the wealth of a society influences its people's ability to save and hence their time preferences for current versus future consumption.

Figure 3-2   Interest Rates as a Function of Supply and Demand for Funds

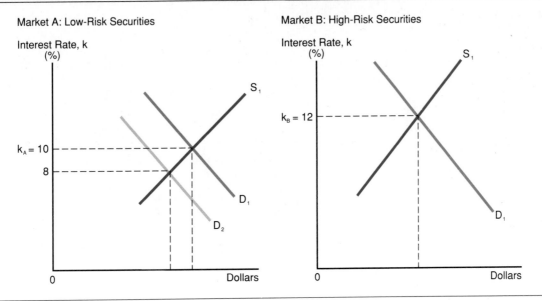

Market A: Low-Risk Securities

Market B: High-Risk Securities

borrowers must obtain higher-cost funds in Market B. Investors who are more willing to take risks invest in Market B with the expectation of receiving a 12 percent return but also with the realization that they might receive much less.

If the demand for funds in a market declines, as it typically does during a business recession, the demand curves will shift to the left, as shown in Curve D_2 in Market A. The market-clearing, or equilibrium, interest rate in this example declines to 8 percent. Similarly, you should be able to visualize what would happen if the Federal Reserve tightened credit: The supply curve, S_1, would shift to the left, and this would raise interest rates and lower the current level of borrowing in the economy.

Capital markets are interdependent. For example, if Markets A and B were in equilibrium before the demand shift to D_2 in Market A, then investors were willing to accept the higher risk in Market B in exchange for a *risk premium* of 12% − 10% = 2%. After the shift to D_2, the risk premium would initially increase to 12% − 8% = 4%. In all likelihood, this much larger premium would induce some of the lenders in Market A to shift to Market B; this, in turn, would cause the supply curve in Market A to shift to the left (or up) and that in Market B to shift to the right. This transfer of capital between markets would raise the interest rate in Market A and lower it in Market B, thus bringing the risk premium back closer to the original level, 2 percent.

There are many capital markets in the United States. U.S. firms also invest and raise capital throughout the world, and foreigners both borrow and lend capital in the United States. There are markets in the United States for home

Figure 3-3   Long- and Short-Term Interest Rates, 1953–1988

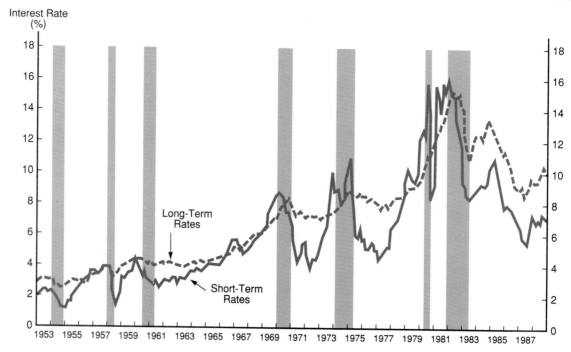

Notes:

a. The shaded areas designate business recessions.

b. Short-term rates are measured by four- to six-month loans to very large, strong corporations and long-term rates by AAA corporate bonds.

Source: *Federal Reserve Bulletin.*

loans; farm loans; business loans; federal, state, and local government loans; and consumer loans. Within each category, there are regional markets as well as different types of submarkets. For example, in real estate there are separate markets for first and second mortgages, and for loans on owner-occupied homes, apartments, office buildings, shopping centers, vacant land, and so on. Within the business sector, there are dozens of types of debt and also several sharply differentiated markets for common stocks.

There is a price for each type of capital, and these prices change over time as shifts occur in supply and demand conditions. Figure 3-3 shows how long- and short-term interest rates to business borrowers have varied since the 1950s. Notice that short-term interest rates are especially prone to rise during booms and then fall during recessions. (The shaded areas of the chart indicate recessions.) When the economy is expanding, firms need capital, and this demand for capital pushes rates up. Also, inflationary pressures are strongest during business booms, so at such times the Federal Reserve tends to tighten the money supply, which also exerts an upward pressure on rates. Conditions are reversed during recessions — slack business reduces the demand for

Figure 3-4 Relationship between Annual Inflation Rates and Long-Term Interest Rates, 1953–1988

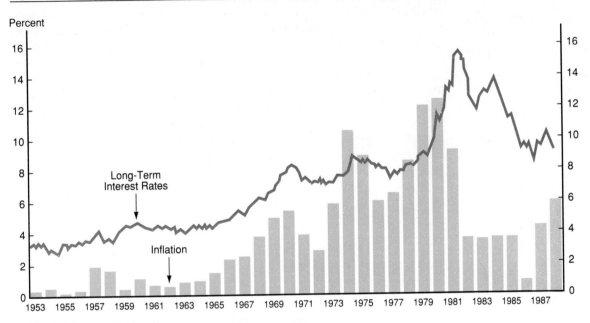

Notes:
a. Interest rates are those on AAA long-term corporate bonds.
b. Inflation is measured as the annual rate of change in the Consumer Price Index (CPI).

Source: *Federal Reserve Bulletin.*

credit, the Fed increases the money supply, and the result is a drop in interest rates. In addition, inflationary pressures are normally weakest during recessions, and this too helps keep interest rates down.

These tendencies do not hold exactly — the period after 1984 is a case in point. The price of oil decreased dramatically in 1985 and 1986, reducing inflationary pressures on other prices and easing fears of serious long-term inflation. Earlier, these fears had pushed interest rates to record levels. The economy from 1984 to 1987 was fairly strong, but the declining fears about inflation more than offset the normal tendency of interest rates to rise during good economic times, and the net result was lower interest rates.[5]

The relationship between inflation and long-term interest rates is highlighted in Figure 3-4, which plots rates of inflation along with long-term interest rates. Prior to 1965, when the average rate of inflation was about 1.0 percent, interest rates on AAA-rated bonds generally ranged from 4 to 5 percent.

---

[5]Short-term rates are responsive to current economic conditions, whereas long-term rates primarily reflect long-run expectations for inflation. As a result, short-term rates are sometimes above and sometimes below long-term rates. The relationship between long-term and short-term rates is called the *term structure of interest rates.* This topic is discussed later in the chapter.

As the war in Vietnam accelerated in the mid-1960s, the rate of inflation increased, and interest rates began to rise. The rate of inflation dropped after 1970, and so did long-term interest rates. However, the 1973 Arab oil embargo was followed by a quadrupling of oil prices in 1974, which caused a spurt in the price level, which in turn drove interest rates to new record highs in 1974 and 1975. Inflationary pressures eased in late 1975 and 1976 but then rose again after 1976. In 1980, inflation rates hit the highest level on record, and fears of continued double-digit inflation pushed interest rates up to historic highs. From 1981 through 1986, the inflation rate dropped steadily, and in 1986 inflation was only 1.1 percent, the lowest level in 25 years. Early in the period, investors' fears of a renewal of double-digit inflation kept long-term interest rates at relatively high levels, but as confidence built that inflation was under control, interest rates declined. Currently (1988), inflation is up to about 6 percent, and interest rates have moved up accordingly.

THE DETERMINANTS OF MARKET INTEREST RATES

In general, the nominal (or stated) interest rate on a debt security, k, is composed of a pure rate of interest, k^*, plus several premiums that reflect inflation, the riskiness of the security, and the security's marketability (or liquidity). This relationship can be expressed as follows:

$$\text{Market rate} = k = k^* + IP + DRP + LP + MRP, \tag{3-1}$$

which can also be expressed as

$$k = k_{RF} + DRP + LP + MRP. \tag{3-2}$$

Here

k = the nominal, or stated, rate of interest on a given security.[6] There are many different securities, hence many different stated interest rates.

k^* = the real risk-free rate of interest; k^* is pronounced "k-star," and it is the rate that would exist on a riskless security if zero inflation were expected.

k_{RF} = the nominal risk-free rate of interest. This is the stated interest rate on a security such as a U.S. Treasury bill which is free of default risk. k_{RF} does include a premium for expected inflation, so $k_{RF} = k^* + IP$.

---

[6]The term *nominal* as it is used here means the *stated* rate as opposed to the *real* rate, which is adjusted for inflation. If you bought a 10-year Treasury bond in March 1988, the stated, or nominal, rate would be about 8 percent, but if inflation averages 5 percent over the next 10 years, the real rate would be about $8\% - 5\% = 3\%$. In Chapter 5 we will use the term nominal in yet another way: to distinguish between stated rates and effective annual rates when compounding occurs more frequently than once a year.

IP = inflation premium. IP is equal to the average expected inflation rate over the life of the security.

DRP = default risk premium. This premium reflects the possibility that the issuer will not pay interest or principal on a security at the stated time and in the stated amount.

LP = liquidity premium. This is a premium charged by lenders to reflect the fact that some securities cannot be converted to cash on short notice at a "reasonable" price.

MRP = maturity risk premium. As we explain later, longer-term bonds are exposed to more risk of price declines, and this premium is charged by lenders to reflect this risk.

We discuss the components whose sum makes up the stated, or nominal, rate in the following sections.

The Real Risk-Free Rate of Interest, k*

real risk-free rate of interest, k*
The rate of interest that would exist on default-free U.S. Treasury securities if no inflation were expected.

The **real risk-free rate of interest, k***, is defined as the interest rate that would exist on a riskless security if no inflation were expected, and it may be thought of as the rate of interest that would exist on short-term U.S. Treasury securities in an inflation-free world. The real risk-free rate is not static — it changes over time depending on economic conditions, especially (1) the rate of return corporations and other borrowers can expect to earn on productive assets and (2) people's time preferences for current versus future consumption. Borrowers' expected returns on real asset investments set an upper limit on how much they can afford to pay for borrowed funds, whereas savers' time preferences for consumption establish how much consumption they are willing to defer and hence the amount of funds they will lend at different levels of interest. It is difficult to measure k* precisely, but most experts think that in the United States it has fluctuated in the range of 1 to 4 percent in recent years.

The Nominal "Risk-Free" Rate of Interest, k_{RF}

nominal risk-free rate, k_{RF}
The rate of interest on a security that is free of all risk; k_{RF} is proxied by the T-bill rate or the T-bond rate. k_{RF} includes an inflation premium.

The **nominal risk-free rate, k_{RF}**, is the real risk-free rate plus a premium for expected inflation: $k_{RF} = k^* + IP$. To be strictly correct, the risk-free rate should mean the interest rate on a totally risk-free security — one that has no risk of default, no maturity risk, no liquidity risk, and no risk of loss if inflation increases. There is no such security, and hence there is no observable truly risk-free rate. However, there is one security that is free of most risks, a U.S. Treasury bill (T-bill), which is short-term debt issued by the U.S. government. Treasury bonds (T-bonds), which are longer-term government securities, are free of default and liquidity risks, but T-bonds are exposed to some risk due to changes in the general level of interest rates.

If the term "risk-free rate" is used without either the modifier "real" or the modifier "nominal," people generally mean the nominal rate, and we will follow that convention in this book. Therefore, when we use the term risk-free rate, k_{RF}, we mean the nominal risk-free rate, which includes an inflation premium equal to the average expected inflation rate over the life of the security. In general, we use the T-bill rate to approximate the short-term risk-free rate, and the T-bond rate to approximate the long-term risk-free rate. So, whenever you see the term "risk-free rate," assume that we are referring either to the U.S. T-bill rate or the T-bond rate.

Inflation Premium (IP)

Inflation has a major impact on interest rates because it erodes the purchasing power of the dollar and lowers the real rate of return on investments. To illustrate, suppose you save $1,000 and invest it in a Treasury bond that matures in 1 year and pays 5 percent interest. At the end of the year you will receive $1,050 — your original $1,000 plus $50 of interest. Now suppose the rate of inflation during the year is 10 percent, and it affects all items equally. If beer had cost $1 per bottle at the beginning of the year, it would cost $1.10 at the end. Therefore, your $1,000 would have bought $1,000/$1 = 1,000 bottles at the beginning of the year but only $1,050/$1.10 = 955 bottles at the end. Thus, in *real terms,* you would be worse off — you would receive $50 of interest, but it would not be sufficient to offset inflation. You would thus be better off buying 1,000 bottles of beer (or some other storable asset such as land, timber, apartment buildings, wheat, or gold) than buying bonds.

inflation premium (IP)
A premium for anticipated or expected inflation that investors add to the real risk-free rate of return.

Investors are well aware of all this, so when they lend money, they add an **inflation premium (IP)** equal to the expected inflation rate over the life of the security to the rate they would have been willing to accept in the absence of inflation. As discussed previously, for a short-term, default-free U.S. Treasury bill, the actual interest rate charged, $k_{T\text{-bill}}$, would be the real risk-free rate, k^*, plus the inflation premium (IP):

$$k_{T\text{-bill}} = k_{RF} = k^* + IP.$$

Therefore, if the real risk-free rate of interest were $k^* = 3\%$, and if inflation were expected to be 4 percent (and hence IP = 4%) during the next year, then the rate of interest on 1-year T-bills would be 7 percent. In March of 1988, the expected 1-year inflation rate was about 5 percent, and the yield on 1-year T-bills was about 6.5 percent. This implies that the real risk-free rate at that time was about 1.5 percent. The real risk-free rate is not observable, but on the basis of observed yields on Treasury securities and reported expected inflation rates, we know that the real risk-free rate varies over time and that it is generally in the range of 1 to 4 percentage points.

It is important to note that the rate of inflation built into interest rates is the *rate of inflation expected in the future,* not the rate experienced in the past. Thus, the latest reported figures might show an annual inflation rate of 3 percent, but that is for a past period. If people on the average expect a 6 percent inflation rate in the future, then 6 percent would be built into the current rate of interest. Note also that the inflation rate reflected in the interest rate on any security is the *average rate of inflation expected over the security's life*. Thus, the inflation rate built into a 1-year bond is the expected inflation rate for the next year, but the inflation rate built into a 30-year bond is the average rate of inflation expected over the next 30 years.[7]

Expectations for future inflation are closely related to, although not perfectly correlated with, rates experienced in the recent past. Therefore, if the inflation rate reported for last month increased, people would tend to raise their expectations for future inflation, and this change in expectations would cause an increase in interest rates.

Default Risk Premium (DRP)

The risk that a borrower will *default* on a loan, which means that the borrower does not pay the interest or pay off the principal, also affects the market interest rate on a security: the greater the default risk, the higher the interest rate lenders charge. Treasury securities have no default risk, and hence they carry the lowest interest rates on taxable securities in the United States. For corporate bonds, the higher the bond's rating, the lower its default risk, and, consequently, the lower its interest rate.[8] Here are some representative interest rates on long-term bonds during February of 1988:

U.S. Treasury	8.4%
AAA	9.1
AA	9.4
A	9.8

default risk premium (DRP)
The difference between the interest rate on a U.S. Treasury bond and a corporate bond of equal maturity and marketability.

The difference between the interest rate on a T-bond and that on a corporate bond with similar maturity, liquidity, and other features is the **default risk premium (DRP)**. Therefore, if the bonds listed previously were otherwise similar, the default risk premium would be DRP = 9.1% − 8.4% = 0.7 percentage points for AAA corporate bonds, 1.0 percentage points for AA, and 1.4 percentage points for A corporate bonds. Default risk premiums vary somewhat over time, but the February 1988 figures are representative of levels in recent years.

---

[7]To be theoretically precise, we should use a *geometric average*. Also, since millions of investors are active in the market, it is impossible to determine exactly the consensus expected inflation rate. Survey data are available, however, which give us a reasonably good idea of what investors expect over the next few years. For example, in 1980 the University of Michigan's Survey Research Center reported that people expected inflation during the next year to be 11.9 percent and that the average rate of inflation expected over the next 5 to 10 years was 10.5 percent. Those expectations led to record high interest rates. However, the economy cooled in 1981 and 1982, and, as Figure 3-4 showed, actual inflation dropped sharply after 1980. This led to gradual reductions in the *expected future* inflation rate. In 1988, as we write this, the expected future inflation rate is about 5 percent. As inflationary expectations dropped, so did the market rate of interest.

[8]Bond ratings, and bonds' riskiness in general, will be discussed in Chapter 13. For now, merely note that bonds rated AAA are judged to have less default risk than bonds rated AA, AA bonds are less risky than A bonds, and so on.

Liquidity Premium (LP)

liquid asset
An asset that can be readily converted to spendable cash.

A highly **liquid asset** is one that can be sold at a predictable price and thus be converted to a well-specified amount of spendable cash on short notice. Active markets, which provide liquidity, exist for government bonds and for the stocks and bonds of the larger corporations. Also, claims on certain financial intermediaries such as bank time deposits are highly liquid because banks will redeem them for cash. Real estate, as well as securities issued by small companies that are not known by many investors, are *illiquid* — they can be sold to raise cash, but not quickly and not at a predictable price. If a security is *not* liquid, investors will add a **liquidity premium (LP)** when they establish the market interest rate on the security. It is very difficult to measure liquidity premiums with precision, but a differential of at least two and probably four or five percentage points is thought to exist between the least liquid and the most liquid financial assets of similar default risk and maturity.

liquidity premium (LP)
A premium added to the equilibrium interest rate on a security that cannot be converted to cash on short notice.

Maturity Risk Premium (MRP)

U.S. Treasury securities are free of default risk in the sense that one can be virtually certain that the federal government will pay interest on its bonds and also pay them off when they mature. Therefore, the default risk premium on Treasury securities is essentially zero. Further, active markets exist for Treasury securities, so their liquidity premiums are also close to zero. Thus, as a first approximation, the rate of interest on a Treasury bond should be the risk-free rate, k_{RF}, which is equal to the real rate, k^*, plus an inflation premium, IP. However, an adjustment is needed for long-term Treasury bonds. The prices of long-term bonds decline sharply whenever interest rates rise, and since interest rates can and do occasionally rise, all long-term bonds, even Treasury bonds, have an element of risk called **interest rate risk**. As a general rule, the bonds of any organization, from the U.S. government to Eastern Airlines, have more interest rate risk the longer the maturity of the bond.[9] Therefore, a **maturity risk premium (MRP)**, which is higher the longer the years to maturity, must be included in the required interest rate.

interest rate risk
The risk of capital losses to which investors are exposed because of changing interest rates.

maturity risk premium (MRP)
A premium which reflects interest rate risk.

The effect of maturity risk premiums is to raise interest rates on long-term bonds relative to those on short-term bonds. This premium, like the others, is extremely difficult to measure, but (1) it seems to vary over time, rising when interest rates are more volatile and uncertain and falling when they are more stable, and (2) in recent years, the maturity risk premium on 30-year T-bonds appears to have generally been in the range of one or two percentage points.[10]

---

[9]For example, if you bought a 30-year Treasury bond for $1,000 in 1972, when the long-term interest rate was 7 percent, and held it until 1981, when long-term T-bond rates were about 14.5 percent, the value of your bond would have declined to about $513. That would represent a loss of almost half your money, and it demonstrates that long-term bonds, even U.S. Treasury bonds, are not riskless. However, had you invested in short-term bills in 1972 and subsequently reinvested your principal each time the bills matured, you still would have had $1,000. This point will be discussed in detail in Chapter 6.

[10]The MRP has averaged 1.7 percentage points over the last 61 years. See *Stocks, Bonds, Bills, and Inflation: 1988 Yearbook* (Chicago: Ibbotson Associates, 1988).

reinvestment rate risk
Risk that a decline in interest rates will lead to lower income when bonds mature and funds are reinvested.

We should mention that although long-term bonds are heavily exposed to interest rate risk, short-term bonds are heavily exposed to **reinvestment rate risk**. When short-term bonds mature and the funds are reinvested, or "rolled over," a decline in interest rates would result in reinvestment at a lower rate and hence a decline in interest income. To illustrate, suppose you had $100,000 invested in 1-year T-bonds, and you lived on the income. In 1981, short-term rates were about 15 percent, so your income would have been about $15,000. However, your income would have declined to about $9,000 by 1983, and to just over $6,000 by 1988. Had you invested your money in long-term bonds, your income (but not the value of the principal) would have been stable.[11] Thus, although the principal is preserved, the interest income provided by short-term bonds varies from year to year, depending on reinvestment rates.

THE TERM STRUCTURE OF INTEREST RATES

A study of Figure 3-3 reveals that at certain times, such as 1988, short-term interest rates are lower than long-term rates, whereas at other times, such as 1980 and 1981, short-term rates are higher than long-term rates. The relationship between long- and short-term rates, which is known as the **term structure of interest rates**, is important to corporate treasurers, who must decide whether to borrow by issuing long- or short-term debt. The term structure of interest rates is also important to investors, who must decide whether to buy long- or short-term bonds. Thus, it is important to understand (1) how long- and short-term rates are related to each other and (2) what causes shifts in their relative positions.

term structure of interest rates
The relationship between yields and maturities of securities.

To begin, we can look up in a source such as *The Wall Street Journal* or the *Federal Reserve Bulletin* the interest rates on bonds of various maturities at a given point in time. For example, the tabular section of Figure 3-5 presents interest rates for Treasury issues of different maturities on two dates. The set of data for a given date, when plotted on a graph such as that in the Figure 3-5 graph, is called the **yield curve** for that date. The yield curve changes both in position and in slope over time. In March of 1980, all rates were relatively high, and short-term rates were higher than long-term rates, so the yield curve on that date was *downward sloping*. However, in July of 1987, all rates had fallen, and short-term rates were lower than long-term rates, so the yield curve at that time was *upward sloping*. Had we drawn the yield curve during January

yield curve
A graph showing the relationship between yields and maturities of securities.

---

[11]Long-term bonds also have some reinvestment rate risk. To actually earn the stated rate on a long-term bond, the interest payments must be reinvested at the stated rate. However, if interest rates fall, the interest payments would be reinvested at a lower rate, and hence the realized return would be less than the stated rate. Note, though, that the premium added for reinvestment rate risk is lower on a long-term bond than on a short-term bond because only the interest payments (rather than interest plus principal) on the long-term bond are exposed to reinvestment rate risk. Only zero coupon bonds, discussed in Chapter 13, are free of reinvestment rate risk.

Figure 3-5   U.S. Treasury Bond Interest Rates on Different Dates

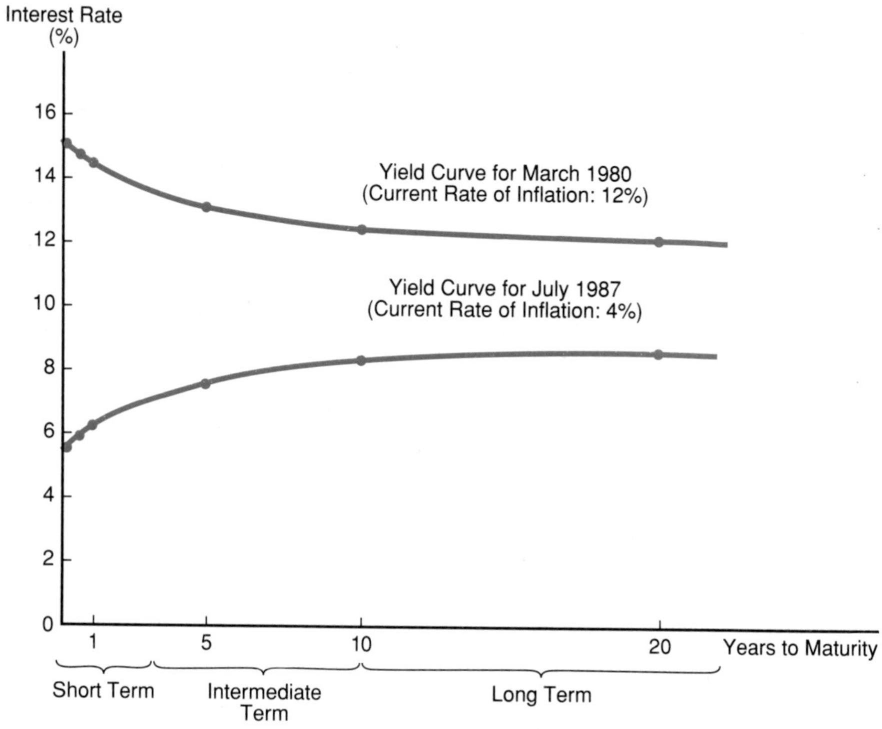

Interest Rate
(%)

Term to Maturity	Interest Rate	
	March 1980	July 1987
6 months	15.0%	5.9%
1 year	14.0	6.2
5 years	13.5	8.0
10 years	12.8	8.4
20 years	12.5	8.5

---

of 1982, it would have been essentially horizontal, for long-term and short-term bonds on that date had about the same rate of interest. (See Figure 3-3.)

Figure 3-5 shows yield curves for U.S. Treasury securities, but we could have constructed them for corporate bonds; for example, we could have developed yield curves for IBM, General Motors, Eastern Airlines, or any other company that borrows money over a range of maturities. Had we constructed such curves and plotted them on Figure 3-5, the corporate yield curves would have been above those for Treasury securities on the same date because the corporate yields would include default risk premiums, but they would have had the same general shape as the Treasury curves. Also, the riskier the corporation, the higher its yield curve; thus, Eastern, which was on the verge of bankruptcy, would have had a yield curve substantially higher than that of IBM, which is an extremely strong company.

Historically, in most years long-term rates are above short-term rates, so usually the yield curve is upward sloping. For this reason, people often call an upward-sloping yield curve a **"normal" yield curve** and a yield curve which slopes downward an **inverted,** or **"abnormal," yield curve.** Thus, in Figure 3-5 the yield curve for March 1980 was inverted, but the one for July 1987 was normal. We explain in the next section why an upward slope is the normal situation, but briefly, the reason is that short-term securities are less risky than longer-term securities, and hence short-term rates are normally lower than long-term rates.

Term Structure Theories

Several theories have been used to explain the shape of the yield curve. The three major ones are (1) the *market segmentation theory,* (2) the *liquidity preference theory,* and (3) the *expectations theory.*

Market Segmentation Theory. Briefly, the **market segmentation theory** states that each lender and each borrower has a preferred maturity. For example, a person borrowing to buy a long-term asset like a house, or an electric utility company borrowing to build a power plant, would want a long-term loan. However, a retailer borrowing in September to build its inventory for Christmas would prefer a short-term loan. Similar differences exist among savers, and a person saving up to take a vacation next summer would want to lend in the short-term market, but someone saving for retirement 20 years hence would probably buy long-term securities.

The thrust of the market segmentation theory is that the slope of the yield curve depends on supply/demand conditions in the long-term and short-term markets. Thus, according to this theory, the yield curve could at any given time be either upward sloping or downward sloping. An upward-sloping yield curve would occur when there was a large supply of funds relative to demand in the short-term market but a relative shortage of funds in the long-term market. Similarly, a downward-sloping curve would indicate relatively strong demand in the short-term market compared to that in the long-term market.

Liquidity Preference Theory. The **liquidity preference theory** states that long-term bonds normally yield more than short-term bonds for two reasons: (1) Investors generally prefer to hold short-term securities, because such securities are more liquid in the sense that they can be converted to cash with little danger of loss of principal. Investors will, therefore, accept lower yields on short-term securities. (2) At the same time, borrowers react in exactly the opposite way — borrowers generally prefer long-term debt, because short-term debt exposes them to the risk of having to repay the debt under adverse conditions. Accordingly, borrowers are willing to pay a higher rate, other things held constant, for long-term funds than for short-term funds. Taken together,

"normal" yield curve
An upward-sloping yield curve.

inverted ("abnormal") yield curve
A downward-sloping yield curve.

market segmentation theory
The theory that each borrower and lender has a preferred maturity and that the slope of the yield curve depends on the supply of and demand for funds in the long-term market relative to the short-term market.

liquidity preference theory
The theory that lenders prefer to make short-term loans rather than long-term loans; hence, they will lend short-term funds at lower rates than long-term funds.

these two sets of preferences — and hence the liquidity preference theory — imply that under normal conditions, the maturity risk premium (MRP) is positive and increases with maturity, and, hence, that the yield curve should be upward sloping.

expectations theory
The theory that the shape of the yield curve depends on investors' expectations about future inflation rates.

Expectations Theory. The **expectations theory** states that the yield curve depends on expectations about future inflation rates. Specifically, k_t, the nominal interest rate on a U.S. Treasury bond that matures in t years, is found as follows:

$$k_t = k^* + IP_t.$$

Here k^* is the real, default-free interest rate, IP_t is an inflation premium which is equal to the average expected rate of inflation over the t years before the bond matures, and the maturity risk premium (MRP) is assumed to be zero.

To illustrate, suppose that in late December of 1988 the real default-free rate of interest was $k^* = 3\%$ and expected inflation rates for the next 3 years were as follows:[12]

	Expected Annual (1-Year) Inflation Rate	Expected Average Inflation Rate from 1988 to Indicated Year
1989	4%	4%/1 = 4.0%
1990	6%	(4% + 6%)/2 = 5.0%
1991	8%	(4% + 6% + 8%)/3 = 6.0%

Given these expectations, the following pattern of interest rates should exist:

	Real Default-free Rate (k^*)		Inflation Premium, Which is Equal to the Average Expected Inflation Rate (IP_t)		Treasury Bond Rate for Each Maturity $(k_{T\text{-bond}})$
1-year bond	3%	+	4.0%	=	7.0%
2-year bond	3%	+	5.0%	=	8.0%
3-year bond	3%	+	6.0%	=	9.0%

Had the pattern of expected inflation rates been reversed, with inflation expected to fall from 8 percent to 6 percent and then to 4 percent, the following situation would have existed:

	Real Default-free Rate		Average Expected Inflation Rate		Treasury Bond Rate for Each Maturity
1-year bond	3%	+	8.0%	=	11.0%
2-year bond	3%	+	7.0%	=	10.0%
3-year bond	3%	+	6.0%	=	9.0%

---

[12]Technically, we should be using geometric averages rather than arithmetic averages, but the differences are not material in this example. For a discussion of this point, see Robert C. Radcliffe, *Investment: Concepts, Analysis, and Strategy,* 2nd ed. (Glenview, Ill.: Scott, Foresman, 1987), Chapter 6.

Figure 3-6   Hypothetical Example of the Term Structure of Interest Rates

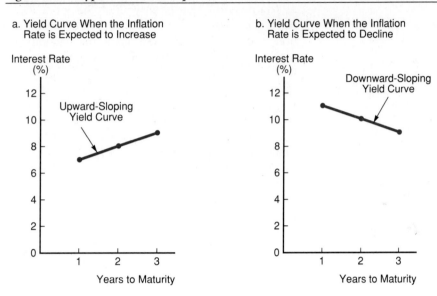

a. Yield Curve When the Inflation
   Rate is Expected to Increase

b. Yield Curve When the Inflation
   Rate is Expected to Decline

These hypothetical data are plotted in Figure 3-6. According to the expectations theory, whenever the annual rate of inflation is expected to decline, the yield curve must be downward sloping, whereas it must be upward sloping if inflation is expected to increase.

Various tests of the theories have been conducted, and these tests indicate that all three theories have some validity. Thus, the shape of the yield curve at any given time is affected (1) by supply-demand conditions in long- and short-term markets, (2) by liquidity preferences, and (3) by expectations about future inflation. One factor may dominate at one time, another at another time, but all three affect the structure of interest rates.

OTHER FACTORS THAT INFLUENCE INTEREST RATE LEVELS

In addition to inflationary expectations, liquidity preferences, and normal supply-demand fluctuations, other factors also influence the general level of interest rates and the shape of the yield curve. The four most important ones are (1) Federal Reserve policy, (2) the level of the federal budget deficit, (3) the foreign trade balance, and (4) the level of business activity.

Federal Reserve Policy

As you probably learned in your studies of economics, (1) the money supply has a major effect on both the level of economic activity and the rate of inflation, and (2) in the United States the Federal Reserve System controls the money supply. If the Fed wants to stimulate the economy, it increases growth in the money supply. The initial effect of such an action is to cause interest rates to decline, but the action may also lead to an increase in the expected rate of inflation, which in turn could push interest rates up. The reverse holds if the Fed tightens the money supply.

To illustrate, in 1981 inflation was quite high, so the Fed tightened up the money supply. The Fed deals primarily in the short-term end of the market, so this tightening had the direct effect of pushing short-term interest rates up sharply. At the same time, the very fact that the Fed was taking strong action to reduce inflation led to a decline in expectations for long-run inflation, which led to a drop in long-term bond yields. Short-term rates decreased shortly thereafter.

During periods when the Fed is actively intervening in the markets, the yield curve will be distorted. Short-term rates will be temporarily "too high" if the Fed is tightening credit and "too low" if it is easing credit. Long-term rates are not affected as much by Fed intervention, except to the extent that such intervention affects expectations for long-term inflation.

Federal Deficits

If the federal government spends more than it takes in from tax revenues, it runs a deficit, and that deficit must be covered either by borrowing or by printing money. If the government borrows, this added demand for funds pushes up interest rates. If it prints money, this increases expectations for future inflation, which also drives up interest rates. Thus, the larger the federal deficit, other things held constant, the higher the level of interest rates. Whether long- or short-term rates are more affected depends on how the deficit is financed, so we cannot state, in general, how deficits will affect the slope of the yield curve.

Foreign Trade Balance

Businesses and individuals in the United States buy from and sell to people and firms in other countries. If we buy more than we sell (that is, import more than we export), we are said to run a *foreign trade deficit*. When trade deficits occur, they must by financed, with the main source of financing being debt. In other words, if we import $200 billion of goods but export only $100 billion, we run a trade deficit of $100 billion. We must borrow the $100 billion.[13]

---

[13]The deficit could also be financed by selling assets, including gold, corporate stocks, entire companies, and real estate. The U.S. has financed its massive trade deficits by all of these means in recent years, but the primary method has been by borrowing.

Therefore, the larger our trade deficit, the more we must borrow, and as we increase our borrowing, this drives up interest rates. Also, foreigners are willing to hold U.S. debt if and only if the interest rate on this debt is competitive with interest rates in other countries. Therefore, if the Federal Reserve attempts to lower interest rates in the United States, causing our rates to fall below rates abroad, then foreigners will sell U.S. bonds, those sales will depress bond prices, and the result will be higher U.S. rates.

The United States has been running annual trade deficits since the mid-1970s, and the cumulative result of these deficits is that the United States is by far the largest debtor nation of all time. As a result, interest rates are very much influenced by the annual trade deficit situation (larger trade deficits lead to higher U.S. interest rates), and also by interest rate trends in other countries around the world (higher rates abroad lead to higher U.S. rates). Because of all this, U.S. corporate treasurers must keep up with developments in the world economy.

Business Activity

Figure 3-3, presented earlier, can be examined to see how business conditions influence interest rates. Here are the key points revealed by the graph:

1. Because inflation has generally been increasing since 1953, the general tendency has been toward higher interest rates.

2. Until 1966, short-term rates were almost always below long-term rates. Thus, in those years the yield curve was almost always "normal" in the sense that it was upward sloping.

3. The shaded areas in the graph represent recessions, during which the demand for money falls and, at the same time, the Federal Reserve tends to increase the money supply in an effort to stimulate the economy. As a result, there is a tendency for interest rates to decline during recessions.

4. During recessions, short-term rates experience sharper declines than long-term rates. This occurs because (1) the Fed operates mainly in the short-term sector and hence its intervention has a major effect here, and (2) long-term rates reflect the average expected inflation rate over the next 20 to 30 years, and this expectation generally does not change much, even when the current rate of inflation is low because of a recession.

INTEREST RATE LEVELS AND STOCK PRICES

Interest rates have two effects on corporate profits: (1) Because interest is a cost, the higher the rate of interest, the lower a firm's profits, other things held constant; and (2) interest rates affect the level of economic activity, and, hence, corporate profits. Interest rates obviously affect stock prices because of their effects on profits, but, perhaps even more important, they have an effect due to competition in the marketplace between stocks and bonds. If interest rates rise sharply, investors can get higher returns in the bond market, which induces them to sell stocks and to transfer funds from the stock market to the bond market. Such transfers in response to rising interest rates obviously depress stock prices. Of course, the reverse occurs if interest rates decline. Indeed, the bull market of 1985–1987, when the Dow Jones Industrial Index rose from 1100 to over 2700, was caused almost entirely by the sharp drop in long-term interest rates.

The experience of Commonwealth Edison, the electric utility serving the Chicago area, can be used to illustrate the effects of interest rates on stock prices. In 1984 Commonwealth's stock sold for $21 per share, and since the company paid a $3 dividend, the dividend yield was $3/$21 = 14.3%. Commonwealth's bonds at the time also yielded about 14.3 percent. Thus, if someone had $100,000 and invested it in either the stock or the bonds, his or her annual income would have been about $14,300. (The investor might also have expected the stock price to grow over time, providing some capital gains, but that point is not relevant for the example.)

By 1988, all interest rates were much lower, and Commonwealth's bonds were yielding only 10.5 percent. If the stock still yielded 14.3 percent, investors could switch $100,000 out of the bonds and into the stock and, in the process, increase their annual income from $10,500 to $14,300. Many people did exactly that — as interest rates dropped, orders poured in for the stock, and its price was bid up. In July 1988, Commonwealth's stock sold for $28, up 33 percent over the 1984 level, and the dividend yield (10.7%) was very close to the bond yield (10.5%).

INTEREST RATES AND BUSINESS DECISIONS

The yield curve for July 1987, shown earlier in Figure 3-5, indicates how much the U.S. government had to pay in 1987 to borrow money for 1 year, 5 years, 10 years, and so on. A business borrower would have had to pay somewhat more, but assume for the moment that we are back in 1987 and that the yield curve for that year also applies to your company. Now suppose your company has decided (1) to build a new plant with a 20-year life which will cost $1 million and (2) to raise the $1 million by selling an issue of debt (or borrowing) rather than by selling stock. If you borrowed in 1987 on a short-term basis — say, for one year — your interest cost for that year would be only 6.2 percent, or $62,000, whereas if you used long-term (20-year) financing, your cost would be 8.5 percent, or $85,000. Therefore, at first glance it would seem that you should use short-term debt.

However, this could prove to be a horrible mistake. If you use short-term debt, you will have to renew your loan every year, and the rate charged on each new loan will reflect the then-current short-term rate. Interest rates could return to their March 1980 levels, so by 1990 you could be paying 14 percent, or $140,000, per year. These high interest payments would cut into and perhaps eliminate your profits. Your reduced profitability could easily increase your firm's risk to the point where its bond rating would be lowered, causing lenders to increase the risk premium built into the interest rate they charge, which in turn would force you to pay even higher rates. These very high interest rates would further reduce your profitability, worrying lenders even more, and making them reluctant to renew your loan. If your lenders refused to renew the loan and demanded payment, as they have every right to do, you might have trouble raising the cash. If you had to make price cuts to convert physical assets to cash, you might incur heavy operating losses, or even bankruptcy.

On the other hand, if you used long-term financing in 1987, your interest costs would remain constant at $85,000 per year, so an increase in interest rates in the economy would not hurt you. You might even be able to buy up some of your bankrupt competitors at bargain prices — bankruptcies increase dramatically when interest rates rise, primarily because many firms do use short-term debt.

Does all this suggest that firms should always avoid short-term debt? Not necessarily. If inflation remains low in the next few years, so will interest rates. If you had borrowed on a long-term basis for 8.5 percent in July 1987, your company would be at a major disadvantage if its debt were locked in at 8.5 percent while its competitors (who used short-term debt in 1987 and thus rode interest rates down in subsequent years) had a borrowing cost of only 6 or 7 percent. On the other hand, large federal deficits might drive inflation and interest rates up to new record levels. In that case, you would wish you had borrowed on a long-term basis in 1987.

Financing decisions would be easy if we could develop accurate forecasts of future interest rates. Unfortunately, predicting future interest rates with consistent accuracy is somewhere between difficult and impossible — people who make a living by selling interest rate forecasts say it is difficult, but many others say it is impossible.

Even if it is difficult to predict future interest rate *levels,* it is easy to predict that interest rates will *fluctuate* — they always have, and they always will. This being the case, sound financial policy calls for using a mix of long- and short-term debt, as well as equity, in such a manner that the firm can survive in most interest rate environments. Further, the optimal financial policy depends in an important way on the nature of the firm's assets — the easier it is to sell off assets and thus to pay off debts, the more feasible it is to use large amounts of short-term debt. This makes it more feasible to finance current assets than fixed assets with short-term debt. We will return to this issue later in the book, when we discuss working capital management.

International

EUROCURRENCY MARKET

Investors buy securities sold by the U.S. government and U.S. corporations, but they also invest internationally by purchasing stocks, bonds, and various money market instruments issued by governments of foreign countries and corporations headquartered in Europe, the Far East, and elsewhere. Investments in the foreign capital markets may be made in the Eurocurrency market or the international bond markets. The Eurocurrency market is essentially a short-term money market — most deposits and loans are for less than one year. However, because corporations and governments also need long-term debt capital, international bond markets also have been developed. We focus on the Eurocurrency market here, and we discuss the international bond markets in Chapter 13.

A *Eurodollar* is a U.S. dollar deposited in a bank outside the United States. (Although they are called Eurodollars because they originated in Europe, Eurodollars may be deposited in any part of the world.) The bank in which the deposit is made may be a host country institution, such as Barclay's Bank in London, the foreign branch of a U.S. bank, such as Citibank's Paris branch, or even a foreign branch of a third-country bank, such as Barclay's Munich branch. Most Eurodollar deposits are for $500,000 or more, and they have maturities ranging from overnight to 5 years.

The major difference between regular U.S. time deposits and Eurodollar deposits is their geographic locations. The deposits do not involve different currencies — in both cases, dollars are on deposit. However, Eurodollars are outside the direct control of the U.S. monetary authorities; therefore, U.S. banking regulations, such as fractional reserves, interest rate ceilings, and FDIC insurance premiums, do not apply. The absence of these costs means that the interest rate paid on Eurodollar deposits tends to be higher than domestic U.S. rates on equivalent instruments.

Interest rates on Eurodollar deposits (and loans) are tied to a standard rate known by the acronym *LIBOR*, which stands for *London Inter-Bank Offer Rate*. LIBOR is the rate of interest offered by the largest London banks on deposits of other large banks of the highest credit standing. In July 1988, LIBOR rates were approximately six-tenths of a percentage point above domestic U.S. bank rates on time deposits of the same maturity — 7.9 percent for 3-month CDs versus 8.5 percent for LIBOR CDs.

Although the dollar is the leading international currency, German marks, Swiss francs, Japanese yen, and other currencies are also deposited outside their home countries; these *Eurocurrencies* are handled in exactly the same way as Eurodollars.

SUMMARY AND KEY CONCEPTS

In this chapter we discussed the nature of financial markets, the types of institutions that operate in these markets, how interest rates are determined, and some of the ways in which interest rates affect business decisions. The key concepts covered are listed below.

- There are many different types of **financial markets**. Each market serves a different set of customers or deals with a different type of security.

- Transfers of capital between borrowers and savers take place (1) by **direct transfers** of money and securities, (2) by transfers through an **investment banking house** which acts as a middleman, and (3) by transfers through **financial intermediaries**, which create new securities.

- The **stock market** is an especially important market for financial managers because it is where stock prices (which are used to "grade" managers' performances) are established.

- There are two basic types of stock markets — the **organized exchanges** and the **over-the-counter markets**.

- Capital is allocated through the price system — a price is charged to "rent" money. Lenders charge **interest** on funds they lend, while equity investors receive dividends and capital gains in return for letting the firm use their money.

- Two fundamental factors affect the cost of money: (1) **production opportunities** and (2) **time preferences for consumption**.

- The **risk-free rate of interest** (k_{RF}) is defined as the real risk-free rate (k^*) plus an inflation premium (IP): $k_{RF} = k^* + IP$.

- The **nominal interest rate** on a debt security, **k**, is composed of the real risk-free rate, k^*, plus premiums that reflect inflation (IP), default risk (DRP), liquidity (LP), and maturity risk (MRP): $k = k^* + IP + DRP + LP + MRP$.

- If the **real risk-free rate of interest and the various premiums were constant over time**, interest rates in the economy would be **stable**. However, the **premiums** — especially the premium for expected inflation — **do change over time, causing market interest rates to change**. Also, Federal Reserve intervention to increase or decrease the money supply, as well as international currency flows, lead to fluctuations in interest rates.

- The relationship between the yields on securities and the securities' maturities is known as the **term structure of interest rates**, and the **yield curve** graphs this relationship.

- The yield curve is normally **upward sloping** — this is called a **normal yield curve** — but the curve can slope downward if the demand for short-term funds is relatively strong, or if the rate of inflation is expected to decline.

- **Interest rate levels have a profound effect on stock prices.** Higher interest rates (1) depress the economy, (2) increase interest expenses, and (3) produce more competition from the bond market. Each of these factors tends to depress stock prices.

- **Eurodollars** are U.S. dollars deposited in banks outside the United States. Interest rates on Eurodollars are tied to **LIBOR**, the London Inter-Bank Offer Rate.

Interest rate levels have a significant influence on corporate financial policy. Because interest rate levels are difficult if not impossible to predict, sound financial policy calls for using a mix of short- and long-term debt, and also for positioning the firm to survive in any future interest rate environment.

Questions

3-1   What are financial intermediaries, and what economic functions do they perform?

3-2   Suppose interest rates on residential mortgages of equal risk were 9 percent in California and 11 percent in New York. Could this differential persist? What forces might tend to equalize rates? Would differentials in borrowing costs for businesses of equal risk located in California and New York be more or less likely than those on residential mortgages? Would differentials in the cost of money for New York and California firms be more likely to exist if the firms being compared were very large or if they were very small? What are the implications of all this for the pressure now being put on Congress to permit banks to engage in nationwide branching?

3-3   What would happen to the standard of living in the United States if people lost faith in the safety of our financial institutions?

3-4   How does a cost-efficient capital market help reduce the prices of goods and services?

3-5   Which fluctuate more, long-term or short-term interest rates? Why?

3-6   Suppose you believe that the economy is just entering a recession. Your firm must raise capital immediately, and debt will be used. Should you borrow on a long-term or a short-term basis?

3-7   Suppose the population of Area Y is relatively young whereas that of Area O is relatively old, but everything else about the two areas is equal.
a. Would interest rates likely be the same or different in the two areas? Explain.
b. Would a trend toward nationwide branching by banks and S&Ls, and the development of diversified nationwide financial corporations, affect your answer to Part a?

3-8   Suppose a new type of computer-controlled industrial robot were developed which was quite expensive but which would, in time, triple the productivity of the labor force. What effect would this have on interest rates?

3-9   Suppose a new and much more liberal Congress and administration were elected, and their first order of business was to take away the independence of the Federal Reserve System and to force the Fed to expand greatly the money supply. What effect would this have
a. On the level and slope of the yield curve immediately after the announcement?
b. On the level and slope of the yield curve that would probably exist two or three years in the future?

3-10   It is a fact that the federal government (1) encouraged the development of the S&L industry; (2) virtually forced the industry to make long-term, fixed interest rate mortgages; and (3) also forced the S&Ls to obtain most of their capital as deposits that were withdrawable on demand.
a. Would S&Ls be better off in a world with a "normal" or an inverted yield curve?

     b. If federal actions like deficit spending and expansion of the money supply produced a sharp increase in inflation, why might a federal bailout of the S&L industry be necessary?

3-11   Suppose interest rates on Treasury bonds rose from 10 to 15 percent. Other things held constant, what do you think would happen to the price of an average company's common stock?

Self-Test Problems   *(Solutions Appear on Page 100)*

Key terms

ST-1   Define each of the following terms:
    a. Money market; capital market
    b. Primary market; secondary market
    c. Investment banker; financial service corporation
    d. Financial intermediary
    e. Mutual fund; money market fund
    f. Organized security exchanges; over-the-counter market
    g. Production opportunities; time preferences for consumption
    h. Real risk-free rate of interest, k^*
    i. Nominal risk-free rate of interest, k_{RF}
    j. Inflation premium (IP)
    k. Default risk premium (DRP)
    l. Liquid asset; liquidity premium (LP)
    m. Interest rate risk; maturity risk premium (MRP)
    n. Reinvestment rate risk
    o. Term structure of interest rates; yield curve
    p. "Normal" yield curve
    q. Eurodollars

Inflation and interest rates

ST-2   Assume that it is now January 1, 1989. The rate of inflation is expected to average 5 percent throughout 1989. However, increased government deficits and renewed vigor in the economy are then expected to push inflation rates higher. Investors expect the inflation rate to be 6 percent in 1990, 7 percent in 1991, and 8 percent in 1992. The real risk-free rate, k^*, is currently 3 percent. Assume that no maturity risk premiums are required on bonds with 5 years or less to maturity. The current interest rate on 5-year T-bonds is 10 percent. Disregard maturity premiums.
    a. What is the average expected inflation rate over the period 1989–1992?
    b. What should be the prevailing interest rate on 4-year T-bonds?
    c. What is the implied expected inflation rate in 1993, or Year 5, given that bonds which mature in that year yield 10 percent?

Problems

Yield curves

3-1   Suppose you and most other investors expect the rate of inflation to be 8 percent next year, to fall to 6 percent during the following year, and then to run at a rate of 4 percent thereafter. Assume that the real risk-free rate, k^*, is 2 percent and that maturity risk premiums on Treasury securities rise from zero on very short-term bonds (those that mature in a few days) by 0.2 percentage points for each year to maturity, up to a limit of 1.0 percentage points on 5-year or longer T-bonds.

a. Calculate the interest rate on 1-, 2-, 3-, 4-, 5-, 10-, and 20-year Treasury securities, and plot the yield curve.

b. Now suppose IBM, an AAA-rated company, has bonds with the same maturities as the Treasury bonds. As an approximation, plot an IBM yield curve on the same graph with the Treasury bond yield curve. (Hint: Think about the default risk premium on IBM's long-term versus its short-term bonds.)

c. Now plot the approximate yield curve of Eastern Airlines, which has serious financial problems.

Yield curves   **3-2**   The following yields on U.S. Treasury securities were taken from *The Wall Street Journal* of November 13, 1987:

Term	Rate
6 months	6.5%
1 year	7.1
2 years	7.7
3 years	8.0
4 years	8.2
5 years	8.3
10 years	8.8
20 years	9.2
30 years	8.9

Plot a yield curve based on these data. (Note: If you looked up the data in the *Journal,* you would find that some of the bonds — for example, the 3 percent issue which matures in February 1995 — show very low yields. These are "flower bonds," which are generally owned by older people and are associated with funerals, because they can be turned in and used at par value to pay estate taxes. Thus, flower bonds always sell at close to par and have a yield which is close to the coupon yield, irrespective of the "going rate of interest." Also, because the yields quoted in the *Journal* are not for the same point in time for all bonds, random variations will appear. An interest rate series that is purged of flower bonds and random variations, and hence provides a better picture of the true yield curve, is known as the "constant maturity series" and can be obtained from the *Federal Reserve Bulletin.*)

Expected rate of interest   **3-3**   Suppose the annual yield on a 2-year Treasury bond is 10.5 percent, while that on a 1-year bond is 9 percent.

a. Using the expectations theory, forecast the interest rate on a 1-year bond during the second year. (Hint: Under the expectations theory, the yield on a 2-year bond is equal to the average yield on 1-year bonds in Years 1 and 2, and the maturity risk premium is zero.)

b. What is the expected inflation rate in Years 1 and 2, assuming $k^* = 3\%$?

Expected interest rates   **3-4**   Assume that the real risk-free rate is 3 percent and that the maturity risk premium is zero. If the nominal rate of interest on 1-year bonds is 11 percent and that on comparable-risk 2-year bonds is 13 percent, what inflation rate is expected during Year 2? What is the 1-year interest rate that is expected for Year 2? Comment on why the average interest rate during the 2-year period differs from the 1-year interest rate expected for Year 2.

Inflation and
interest rates

3-5   In late 1980 the U.S. Commerce Department released new figures which showed that inflation was running at an annual rate of close to 15 percent. However, many investors expected that the new Reagan administration would be more effective in controlling inflation than the Carter administration had been. At the time the prime rate of interest was 21 percent, a record high. However, many observers believed that the extremely high interest rates and generally tight credit, which resulted from the Federal Reserve System's attempts to curb the inflation rate, would shortly bring about a recession, which in turn would lead to a decline in the inflation rate as well as in the rate of interest. Assume that at the beginning of 1981 the expected rate of inflation for 1981 was 12 percent; for 1982, 10 percent; for 1983, 8 percent; and for 1984 and thereafter, 6 percent.

a. What was the average expected inflation rate over the 5-year period 1981–1985? (Use the arithmetic average.)

b. What average *nominal* interest rate would, over the 5-year period, produce a 2 percent real rate of return?

c. Assuming a real risk-free rate of 2 percent and a maturity risk premium which starts at 0.1 percent and increases by 0.1 percent each year, estimate the interest rate in January 1981 on bonds that mature in 1, 2, 5, 10, and 20 years, and draw a yield curve based on these data.

d. Describe the general economic conditions that could be expected to produce an upward-sloping yield curve.

e. If the consensus view of investors in early 1981 had been that the expected rate of inflation for every future year was 10 percent (that is, $I_t = I_{t+1} = 10\%$ for $t = 1$ to ∞), what do you think the yield curve would have looked like? Consider all the factors that are likely to affect the curve. Does your answer here make you question the yield curve you drew in Part c?

Financial markets
and institutions
(*Integrative*)

3-6   Christopher Sarwark recently graduated with a degree in finance and just reported to work as an investment advisor at the firm of Martin and Shore, Inc. Sarwark's first assignment is to explain the nature of the U.S. financial markets and institutions to Manuel Perez, a professional baseball player who has just come to the United States from Chile. Perez is a highly rated pitcher who expects to invest substantial amounts of money through Martin and Shore. He is also very bright, and, therefore, he would like to understand in general terms what will happen to his money. Sarwark has developed the following questions, which he will ask and answer to explain the U.S. financial system to Perez.

a. What is a financial market? How are financial markets differentiated from markets for physical assets?

b. Differentiate between money markets and capital markets.

c. Differentiate between a primary market and a secondary market. If Apple Computer decided to issue additional common stock, and Perez purchased 100 shares of this stock from Merrill Lynch, the underwriter, would this transaction be a primary market transaction or a secondary market transaction? Would it make a difference if Perez purchased previously outstanding Apple stock?

d. Describe the three primary ways in which capital is transferred between savers and borrowers.

e. Securities can be traded on organized exchanges or in the over-the-counter market. Define each of these markets, and describe how stocks are traded in each of them.

f. What do we call the price that a borrower must pay for debt capital? What is the price of equity capital? What are the two most fundamental factors that affect the cost of money, or the general level of interest rates, in the economy?

g. What is the real risk-free rate of interest (k^*)? The nominal risk-free rate (k_{RF})? How are these two rates measured?

h. Define the terms (a) inflation premium, IP, (b) default risk premium, DRP, (c) liquidity premium, LP, and (d) maturity risk premium, MRP. Which of these premiums is included when determining the interest rate on (1) short-term U.S. Treasury securities, (2) long-term U.S. Treasury securities, (3) short-term corporate securities, and (4) long-term corporate securities? Explain how the premiums would vary over time and among the different securities listed above.

i. What is the term structure of interest rates? What is a yield curve? At any given time, how would the yield curve facing a given company such as IBM or Colt Industries (whose bonds are classified as "junk bonds") compare with the yield curve for U.S. Treasury securities?

j. Several theories have been advanced to explain the shape of the yield curve. The three major ones are (1) the *market segmentation theory*, (2) the *liquidity preference theory*, and (3) the *expectations theory*. Briefly describe each of these theories. Which one do economists regard as being "true"?

k. Suppose most investors expect the rate of inflation to be 5 percent next year, 6 percent the following year, 7 percent the third year, and 8 percent thereafter. The real risk-free rate is 3 percent, and the maturity premium is zero for bonds that mature in 1 year or less, 0.1 percent for 2-year bonds, and it increases by 0.1 percent per year thereafter for 20 years, after which it is stable. What is the interest rate on 1-year, 5-year, and 20-year Treasury bonds? Draw a yield curve with these data. Is your yield curve consistent with the three structure theories?

Solutions to Self-Test Problems

ST-1   Refer to the marginal glossary definitions or relevant chapter sections to check your responses.

ST-2   a. Average = (5% + 6% + 7% + 8%)/4 = 26%/4 = 6.50%.
   b. $k_{T\text{-bond}}$ = k* + IP = 0.03 + 0.0650 = 0.0950 = 9.50%.
   c. If the 5-year T-bond rate is 10 percent, the inflation rate is expected
      to average approximately 10% − 3% = 7% during the next 5 years.
      Thus, the implied Year 5 inflation rate is 9.0 percent:

$$7\% = (5\% + 6\% + 7\% + 8\% + I_5)/5$$

$$35\% = 26\% + I_5$$

$$I_5 = 9\%.$$

4 Risk and Rates of Return

WHY RISK VARIES: HOMESTAKE VERSUS DU PONT OR GE

Common sense tells us that required rates of return on investments increase as the investments increase in risk. However, it does not tell us how to measure risk, and, indeed, the proper measurement of risk is rather subtle. To illustrate, consider these two examples:

1. Homestake Mining Company is a leading U.S. gold producer. Gold prices are volatile, and since Homestake's profits vary with the price of gold, its earnings also fluctuate widely from year to year. Moreover, it is one of the few New York Stock Exchange companies whose profits have declined so badly in recent years that it was forced to cut its dividend. All this suggests that Homestake is relatively risky, and hence that the required rate of return on its stock, k_s, should be higher than those of most other NYSE companies. However, Homestake's k_s in 1988, and all other years, was quite low in relation to those of most other companies. This indicates that investors regard Homestake as being a low-risk company in spite of its uncertain profits and its unstable dividend stream.

2. Such large, strong, well-diversified companies as Du Pont and General Electric (GE) have more predictable earnings and dividends than does Homestake or most of the other 1,600 or so smaller NYSE firms. This suggests that Du Pont, GE, and other giant companies should have much less risk, and, consequently, a much lower required rate of return,

than the smaller companies. However, this is not the case: a careful analysis indicates that Du Pont, GE, and other giant firms are not perceived to be much less risky than Homestake and other smaller, more volatile companies.

The reason for these somewhat counterintuitive facts has to do with diversification and its effects on risk. It so happens that Homestake's stock price rises with inflationary expectations, whereas other stocks tend to decline as inflation heats up. Therefore, holding Homestake in a portfolio of "normal" stocks tends to stabilize returns on the entire portfolio. In the case of Du Pont and GE, it turns out that investors, by forming portfolios of the stocks of smaller companies, can and do diversify away much of the risk that would otherwise be inherent in such firms.

IN this chapter we take an in-depth look at how investment risk should be measured, as well as at how both risk and inflation affect rates of return. Recall that in Chapter 3, when we examined the determinants of interest rates, we defined the real risk-free rate, k*, to be the rate of interest on a risk-free security in the absence of inflation. The actual interest rate on a particular debt security was shown to be equal to the real risk-free rate plus several premiums which reflect both inflation and the riskiness of the security in question. In this chapter we define more precisely the term *risk* as it relates to securities, we examine procedures managers use for measuring risk, and we discuss the relationship between risk and return. Then, in Chapters 5 and 6, we extend these relationships to show how security prices are determined in the financial markets. Financial managers should understand these concepts and use them as they plan the actions which will shape their firms' futures.

We will demonstrate in this chapter that each investment — stock, bond, or physical asset — has two different types of risk: (1) *diversifiable risk* and (2) *nondiversifiable risk*. The sum of these two components is the investment's *total risk*. Diversifiable risk is not important to rational, informed investors, because they will eliminate its effects by diversifying it away. The really meaningful risk is nondiversifiable risk — this risk is bad in the sense that it cannot be eliminated, and if you invest in anything other than riskless assets such as short-term Treasury Bills, you will be exposed to it. In the balance of the chapter we will explain these risk concepts and will give you an understanding of how risk enters into the financial decision process.

DEFINING AND MEASURING RISK

risk
The chance that some unfavorable event will occur.

Risk is defined in *Webster's* as "a hazard; a peril; exposure to loss or injury." Thus, risk refers to the chance that some unfavorable event will occur. If you engage in skydiving, you are taking a chance with your life — skydiving is risky.

If you bet on the horses, you are risking your money. If you invest in speculative stocks (or, really, *any* stock), you are taking a risk in the hope of making an appreciable return.

To illustrate the riskiness of financial assets, suppose an investor buys $100,000 of short-term government bonds with an expected return of 10 percent. In this case, the rate of return on the investment, 10 percent, can be estimated quite precisely, and the investment is defined as being risk-free. However, if the $100,000 were invested in the stock of a company just being organized to prospect for oil in the mid-Atlantic, then the investment's return could not be estimated precisely. One might analyze the situation and conclude that the *expected* rate of return, in a statistical sense, is 20 percent, but the investor should also recognize that the *actual* rate of return could range from, say, +1,000 percent to −100 percent. Because there is a significant danger of actually earning a return considerably less than the expected return, the stock would be described as being relatively risky.

Investment risk, then, is related to the probability of earning a return less than the expected return — the greater the chance of low or negative returns, the riskier the investment. However, we can define risk more precisely, and it is useful to do so.

Probability Distributions

An event's *probability* is defined as the chance that the event will occur. For example, a weather forecaster might state, "There is a 40 percent chance of rain today and a 60 percent chance that it will not rain." If all possible events, or outcomes, are listed, and if a probability is assigned to each event, the listing is called a **probability distribution**. For our weather forecast, we could set up the following probability distribution:

probability distribution
A listing of all possible outcomes, or events, with a probability (chance of occurrence) assigned to each outcome.

Outcome (1)	Probability (2)	
Rain	0.4 =	40%
No rain	0.6 =	60
	1.0 =	100%

The possible outcomes are listed in Column 1, while the probabilities of these outcomes, expressed both as decimals and as percentages, are given in Column 2. Notice that the probabilities must sum to 1.0, or 100 percent.

Probabilities can also be assigned to the possible outcomes (or returns) from an investment. If you buy a bond, you expect to receive interest on the bond, and those interest payments provide you with a rate of return on your investment. The possible outcomes from this investment are (1) that the issuer will make the interest payments or (2) that the issuer will fail to make the interest payments. The higher the probability of failure to make the interest payments, the riskier the bonds, and the higher your required rate of return on the bond. If instead of buying a bond you invest in a stock, you will again do so to earn a return on your money. In the case of a stock, the return will come from dividends plus capital gains. Again, the riskier the stock — which means the higher the probability (1) that the firm will fail to pay expected dividends or (2) that the stock price will not increase as much as you expected — the higher the expected return must be to induce you to invest in it.

With this in mind, consider the possible rates of return (dividend yield plus capital gain or loss) that you might earn next year on a $10,000 investment in the stock of either Kelly Products, Inc., or U.S. Water Company. Kelly manufactures and distributes computer terminals and equipment for the rapidly growing data transmission industry. Because its sales are cyclical, its profits rise and fall with the business cycle. Further, its market is extremely competitive, and some new company could develop better products which could literally bankrupt Kelly. U.S. Water, on the other hand, supplies an essential service, and because it has city franchises which protect it from competition, its sales and profits are relatively stable and predictable.

The rate-of-return probability distributions for the two companies are shown in Table 4-1. Here we see that there is a 30 percent chance of a boom, in which case both companies will have high earnings, pay high dividends, and enjoy capital gains; there is a 40 percent probability of a normal economy and moderate returns; and there is a 30 percent probability of a recession, which will mean low earnings and dividends as well as capital losses. Notice, however, that Kelly Products' rate of return could vary far more widely than that of U.S. Water. There is a fairly high probability that the value of the Kelly stock will drop substantially, resulting in a loss of 70 percent, while there is no chance of a loss for U.S. Water.[1]

EXPECTED RATE OF RETURN

expected rate of
return, $\hat{k}$
The rate of return
expected to be realized
from an investment; the
mean value of the
probability distribution
of possible results.

If we multiply each possible outcome by its probability of occurrence and then sum these products, as in Table 4-2, we have a *weighted average* of outcomes. The weights are the probabilities, and the weighted average is the **expected rate of return, $\hat{k}$,** called "k-hat."[2] The expected rates of return for both Kelly Products and U.S. Water are shown in Table 4-2 to be 15 percent. This type of table is known as a *payoff matrix*.

---

[1] It is, of course, completely unrealistic to think that any stock has no chance of a loss. Only in hypothetical examples could this occur. To illustrate, the price of IBM's stock dropped from $135 on October 18 to $103 on October 19, 1987, a decline of 23 percent in one day, as the Dow Jones Industrial average plummeted 22.6 percent. All investors were reminded that any stock is exposed to some risk of loss, and those investors who bought IBM, or almost any stock, on October 18 learned this lesson the hard way.

[2] In this section we discuss only returns on stocks; thus, the subscript s is unnecessary, and we use the term $\hat{k}$ rather than $\hat{k}_s$. In Chapter 6, we will use k_d to signify the return on a debt instrument and k_s to signify the return on a stock.

Table 4-1   Probability Distributions for Kelly Products and U.S. Water

State of the Economy	Probability of This State Occurring	Rate of Return on Stock if This State Occurs	
		Kelly Products	U.S. Water
Boom	0.3	100%	20%
Normal	0.4	15	15
Recession	0.3	−70	10
	1.0		

Table 4-2   Calculation of Expected Rate of Return: Payoff Matrix

State of the Economy (1)	Probability of This State Occurring (2)	Kelly Products		U.S. Water	
		Rate of Return if This State Occurs (3)	Product: (2) × (3) = (4)	Rate of Return if This State Occurs (5)	Product: (2) × (5) = (6)
Boom	0.3	100%	30%	20%	6%
Normal	0.4	15	6	15	6
Recession	0.3	−70	−21	10	3
	1.0		$\hat{k} = $ 15%		$\hat{k} = $ 15%

The expected rate of return calculation can also be expressed as an equation which does the same thing as the payoff matrix table:[3]

$$\text{Expected rate of return} = \hat{k} = P_1k_1 + P_2k_2 + \cdots + P_nk_n$$

$$= \sum_{i=1}^{n} P_ik_i. \qquad (4\text{-}1)$$

Here k_i is the ith possible outcome, P_i is the probability of the ith outcome, and n is the number of possible outcomes. Thus, $\hat{k}$ is a weighted average of the possible outcomes (the k_i values), with each outcome's weight being equal to its probability of occurrence. Using the data for Kelly Products, we obtain its expected rate of return as follows:

$$\hat{k} = P_1(k_1) + P_2(k_2) + P_3(k_3)$$

$$= 0.3(100\%) + 0.4(15\%) + 0.3(-70\%)$$

$$= 15\%.$$

---

[3]The second form of the equation is simply a shorthand expression in which sigma (Σ) signifies "sum up," or add the values of n factors. If i = 1, then $P_ik_i = P_1k_1$; if i = 2, then $P_ik_i = P_2k_2$; and so on until i = n, the last possible outcome. The symbol $\sum_{i=1}^{n}$ simply says, "Go through the following process: First, let i = 1 and find the first product; then let i = 2 and find the second product; then continue until each individual product up to i = n has been found, and then add these individual products to find the expected rate of return."

Figure 4-1   Probability Distributions of Kelly Products' and U.S. Water's Rates of Return

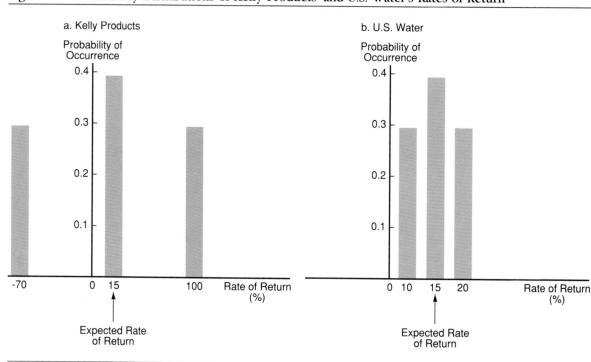

U.S. Water's expected rate of return is also 15 percent:

$$\hat{k} = 0.3(20\%) + 0.4(15\%) + 0.3(10\%)$$

$$= 15\%.$$

We can graph the rates of return to obtain a picture of the variability of possible outcomes; this is shown in the bar charts in Figure 4-1. The height of each bar signifies the probability that a given outcome will occur. The range of probable returns for Kelly Products is from +100 to −70 percent, with an expected return of 15 percent. The expected return for U.S. Water is also 15 percent, but its range is much narrower.

Continuous Probability Distributions

Thus far, we have assumed that only three states of the economy can exist: recession, normal, and boom. Actually, of course, the state of the economy could range from a deep depression to a fantastic boom, and there are an unlimited number of possibilities in between. Suppose we had the time and patience to assign a probability to each possible state of the economy (with the sum of the probabilities still equaling 1.0), and to assign a rate of return

**Figure 4-2   Continuous Probability Distributions of Kelly Products'
and U.S. Water's Rates of Return**

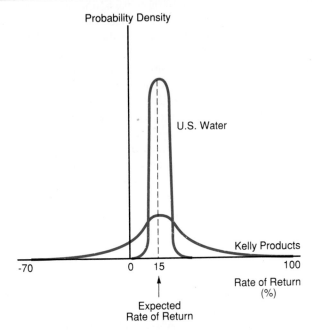

Note: The assumptions regarding the probabilities of various outcomes have been changed from those in Figure 4-1. There the probability of obtaining exactly 15 percent was 40 percent; here it is *much smaller,* because there are many possible outcomes instead of just three. With continuous distributions, it is more appropriate to ask what the probability is of obtaining at least some specified rate of return than to ask what the probability is of obtaining exactly that rate. This topic is covered in detail in statistics courses.

to each stock for each state of the economy. We would have a table similar to Table 4-2, except that it would have many more entries in each column. This table could be used to calculate expected rates of return as shown previously, and the probabilities and outcomes could be approximated by continuous curves such as those presented in Figure 4-2. Here we have changed the assumptions so that there is essentially a zero probability that Kelly Products' return will be less than −70 percent or more than 100 percent, or that U.S. Water's return will be less than 10 percent or more than 20 percent, but virtually any return within these limits is possible.

The tighter, or more peaked, the probability distribution, the more likely it is that the actual outcome will be close to the expected value, and, consequently, the less likely it is that the actual return will end up far below the expected return. Thus, the tighter the probability distribution, the lower the risk assigned to a stock. Since U.S. Water has a relatively tight probability distribution, its *actual return* is likely to be closer to its 15 percent *expected return* than is that of Kelly Products.

Measuring Risk: The Standard Deviation

Risk is a difficult concept to grasp, and a great deal of controversy has surrounded attempts to define and measure it. However, a common definition, and one that is satisfactory for many purposes, is stated in terms of probability distributions such as those presented in Figure 4-2: *The tighter the probability distribution of expected future returns, the smaller the risk of a given investment.* According to this definition, U.S. Water is less risky than Kelly Products, because the chance that the actual return will end up far below the expected return is smaller for U.S. Water than for Kelly Products.

standard deviation, σ
A statistical measurement of the variability of a set of observations.

To be most useful, any measure of risk should have a definite value — we need a measure of the tightness of the probability distribution. One such measure is the **standard deviation**, the symbol for which is σ, pronounced "sigma." The smaller the standard deviation, the tighter the probability distribution, and, accordingly, the lower the riskiness of the stock.[4] To calculate the standard deviation, we proceed as shown in Table 4-3, taking the following steps:

1. We calculate the expected rate of return:

$$\text{Expected rate of return} = \hat{k} = \sum_{i=1}^{n} P_i k_i.$$

For Kelly, we previously found $\hat{k} = 15\%$.

2. In Column 1 of Table 4-3, we subtract the expected rate of return ($\hat{k}$) from each possible outcome (k_i) to obtain a set of deviations about $\hat{k}$:

$$\text{Deviation}_i = k_i - \hat{k}.$$

3. In Columns 2 and 3 of the table, we square each deviation, then multiply the result by the probability of occurrence for its related outcome, and sum these products to obtain the **variance** of the probability distribution:

variance, σ²
The square of the standard deviation.

$$\text{Variance} = \sigma^2 = \sum_{i=1}^{n} (k_i - \hat{k})^2 P_i. \tag{4-2}$$

4. Finally, we take the square root of the variance to obtain the standard deviation:

$$\text{Standard deviation} = \sigma = \sqrt{\sum_{i=1}^{n} (k_i - \hat{k})^2 P_i}. \tag{4-3}$$

Thus, the standard deviation is a probability-weighted average deviation from the expected value; it gives you an idea of how far above or below the expected value the actual value is likely to be. Kelly's standard deviation is seen

---

[4]Since we defined risk in terms of the chances of returns being less than expected, it would seem logical to measure risk in terms of the probability of returns below the expected return rather than by the entire distribution. Measures of below-expected returns, which are known as *semivariance measures,* have been developed, but they are difficult to analyze. Additionally, if the distribution is reasonably symmetric, which is often the case for security returns, the standard deviation is as good a risk measure as the semivariance.

Table 4-3   Calculating Kelly Products' Standard Deviation

$k_i - \hat{k}$ (1)		$(k_i - \hat{k})^2$ (2)	$(k_i - \hat{k})^2 P_i$ (3)
100 − 15 =	85	7,225	(7,225)(0.3) = 2,167.5
15 − 15 =	0	0	(0)(0.4) = 0.0
−70 − 15 =	−85	7,225	(7,225)(0.3) = 2,167.5
			Variance = σ^2 = 4,335.0

$$\text{Standard deviation} = \sigma = \sqrt{\sigma^2} = \sqrt{4,335} = 65.84\%.$$

in Table 4-3 to be $\sigma = 65.84\%$. Using these same procedures, we find U.S. Water's standard deviation to be 3.87 percent. Since Kelly's standard deviation is larger, it is the riskier stock, according to this measure of risk.

If a probability distribution is normal, the *actual* return will be within ±1 standard deviation of the *expected* return 68.26 percent of the time. Figure 4-3 illustrates this point, and it also shows the situation for ±2σ and ±3σ. For

Figure 4-3   Probability Ranges for a Normal Distribution

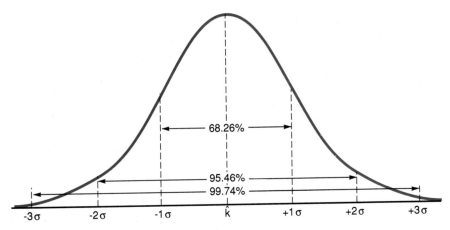

Notes:
a. The area under the normal curve equals 1.0, or 100 percent. *Thus, the areas under any pair of normal curves drawn on the same scale, whether they are peaked or flat, must be equal.*
b. Half of the area under a normal curve is to the left of the mean, indicating that there is a 50 percent probability that the actual outcome will be less than the mean, and half is to the right of $\hat{k}$, indicating a 50 percent probability that it will be greater than the mean.
c. Of the area under the curve, 68.26 percent is within ± 1σ of the mean, indicating that the probability is 68.26 percent that the actual outcome will be within the range $\hat{k} - 1\sigma$ to $\hat{k} + 1\sigma$.
d. Procedures exist for finding the probability of other ranges. These procedures are covered in statistics courses.
e. For a normal distribution, the larger the value of σ, the greater the probability that the actual outcome will vary widely from, and hence perhaps be far below, the expected, or most likely, outcome. *Since the probability of having the actual result turn out to be far below the expected result is one definition of risk, and since σ measures this probability, we can use σ as a measure of risk.* This definition may not be a good one, however, if we are dealing with an asset held in a diversified portfolio. This point is covered later in the chapter.

Kelly Products, $\hat{k} = 15\%$ and $\sigma = 65.84\%$, whereas $\hat{k} = 15\%$ and $\sigma = 3.87\%$ for U.S. Water. Thus, there is a 68.26 percent probability that the actual return for Kelly Products will be in the range of 15 ± 65.84 percent, or from -50.84 to 80.84 percent. For U.S. Water, the 68.26 percent range is 15 ± 3.87 percent, or from 11.13 to 18.87 percent. With such a small σ, there is only a small probability that U.S. Water's return will be significantly less than expected, so the stock is not very risky. For the average firm listed on the New York Stock Exchange, σ has been close to 30 percent in recent years.[5]

coefficient of variation
Standardized measure of the risk per unit of return; calculated as the standard deviation divided by the expected return.

Another useful measure of risk is the **coefficient of variation**, which is the standard deviation divided by the expected return. The coefficient of variation (CV) shows the risk per unit of return, and it provides a more meaningful basis for comparison when the expected returns on two alternatives are not the same. Since U.S. Water and Kelly Products have the same expected return, the coefficient of variation is not particularly useful in this case. The firm with the larger standard deviation, Kelly, must have the larger coefficient of variation when the means are equal. In fact, the coefficient of variation for Kelly is $65.84/15 = 4.39$, and that for U.S. Water is $3.87/15 = 0.26$. Thus, Kelly is almost 17 times more risky than U.S. Water on the basis of this criterion.

For a case where the coefficient of variation is especially useful, consider two projects, X and Y, which have different expected rates of return and differ-

---

[5]In the example we described the procedure for finding the mean and standard deviation when the data are in the form of a known probability distribution. If only sample returns data over some past period are available, the standard deviation of returns can be estimated using this formula:

$$\text{Estimated } \sigma = S = \sqrt{\frac{\sum_{t=1}^{n} (\bar{k}_t - \bar{k}_{Avg})^2}{n - 1}}. \tag{4-3a}$$

Here $\bar{k}_t$ ("k bar t") denotes the past realized rate of return in Period t, and $\bar{k}_{Avg}$ is the average annual return earned during the last n years. Here is an example:

Year	$\bar{k}_t$
1986	15%
1987	-5
1988	20

$$\bar{k}_{Avg} = \frac{(15 - 5 + 20)}{3} = 10.0\%.$$

$$\text{Estimated } \sigma \text{ (or S)} = \sqrt{\frac{(15 - 10)^2 + (-5 - 10)^2 + (20 - 10)^2}{3 - 1}}$$

$$= \sqrt{\frac{350}{2}} = 13.2\%.$$

Often the historical σ is used as an estimate of the future σ. Much less often, and generally incorrectly, $\bar{k}_{Avg}$ for some past period is used as an estimate of $\hat{k}$, the expected future return. Because past variability is likely to be repeated, σ may be a good estimate of future risk, but it is much less reasonable to expect that the past *level* of return (which could have been as high as $+100\%$ or as low as -50%) is the best expectation of what investors think will happen in the future.

ent standard deviations. Project X has a 30 percent expected rate of return and a 10 percent standard deviation, while Project Y has an expected return of 10 percent and a standard deviation of 5 percent. Is Project X riskier, since it has the larger standard deviation? If we calculate the coefficients of variation for these two projects, we find that Project X has a coefficient of variation of 10/30 = 0.33, and Project Y has a coefficient of variation of 5/10 = 0.50. Thus, we see that Project Y actually has more risk per unit of return than Project X, in spite of the fact that X's standard deviation is larger. Therefore, by the coefficient of variation measure, Project Y is riskier. Where such differences occur, the coefficient of variation is generally the better risk measure.

Risk Aversion and Required Returns

Suppose you had worked hard and saved $1 million, which you now plan to invest. You can buy a 10 percent U.S. Treasury note, and at the end of 1 year you will have a sure $1.1 million, which is your original investment plus $100,000 in interest. Alternatively, you can buy stock in R&D Enterprises. If R&D's research programs are successful, your stock will increase in value to $2.2 million; however, if the research is a failure, the value of your stock will go to zero, and you will be penniless. You regard R&D's chances of success or failure as being 50-50, so the expected value of the stock investment is 0.5($0) + 0.5($2,200,000) = $1,100,000. Subtracting the $1 million cost of the stock leaves an expected profit of $100,000, or an expected (but risky) 10 percent rate of return:

$$\frac{\text{Expected rate}}{\text{of return}} = \frac{\text{Expected ending value} - \text{Cost}}{\text{Cost}}$$

$$= \frac{\$1,100,000 - \$1,000,000}{\$1,000,000}$$

$$= \frac{\$100,000}{\$1,000,000} = 10\%.$$

Thus, you have a choice between a sure $100,000 profit (representing a 10 percent rate of return) on the Treasury note or a risky expected $100,000 profit (also representing a 10 percent expected rate of return) on the R&D Enterprises stock. Which one would you choose? *If you choose the less risky investment, you are risk averse. Most investors are indeed risk averse, and certainly the average investor is risk averse, at least with regard to his or her "serious money." Because this is a well-documented fact, we shall assume* **risk aversion** *throughout the remainder of the book.*

risk aversion
A dislike for risk. Risk-averse investors have higher required rates of return for higher-risk securities.

What are the implications of risk aversion for security prices and rates of return? The answer is that, other things held constant, the higher a security's risk, the lower its price, and the higher its required return. To see how this works, we can analyze the situation with U.S. Water and Kelly Products stocks. Suppose that each stock sold for $100 per share and that each had an expected rate of return of 15 percent. Investors are averse to risk, so there would be a general preference for U.S. Water. People with money to invest would bid for U.S. Water rather than Kelly stock, and Kelly's stockholders would start selling their stock and using the money to buy U.S. Water stock. The buying pressure would tend to drive up the price of U.S. Water stock, and the selling pressure would simultaneously cause Kelly's price to decline.

These price changes, in turn, would cause changes in the expected rates of return on the two securities. Suppose, for example, that the price of U.S. Water stock was bid up from $100 to $150, whereas the price of Kelly's stock declined from $100 to $75. This would cause U.S. Water's expected return to fall to 10 percent, while Kelly's expected return would rise to 20 percent. The difference in returns, 20% − 10% = 10%, is a **risk premium, RP**, which represents the compensation investors require for assuming the additional risk of Kelly stock.

risk premium, RP
The difference between the expected rate of return on a given risky asset and that on a less risky asset.

This example demonstrates a very important principle: *In a market dominated by risk-averse investors, riskier securities will have higher expected returns, as estimated by the average investor, than will less risky securities, for if this situation does not hold, actions will occur in the market to force it to occur.* We will consider the question of how much higher the returns on risky securities must be later in the chapter, after we see how diversification affects the way risk should be measured. Then, in Chapter 6, we will see how risk-adjusted rates of return affect the price investors are willing to pay for a security.

PORTFOLIO RISK AND THE CAPITAL ASSET PRICING MODEL

In the preceding section we considered the riskiness of a stock held in isolation. Now we analyze the riskiness of stocks held in portfolios.[6] As we shall see, a stock held as part of a portfolio is less risky than the same stock held in isolation. This fact has been incorporated into a generalized framework for analyzing the relationship between risk and rates of return; this framework is called the **Capital Asset Pricing Model**, or **CAPM**. The CAPM framework is an extremely important analytical tool in both financial management and investment analysis. In the following sections we discuss the elements of the CAPM.[7]

Capital Asset Pricing Model (CAPM)
A model based on the proposition that any stock's required rate of return is equal to the risk-free rate of return plus its risk premium, where risk reflects diversification.

[6]A *portfolio* is a collection of investment securities. If you owned some General Motors stock, some Exxon stock, and some IBM stock, you would be holding a three-stock portfolio. For reasons set forth in this section, the majority of all stocks are held as parts of portfolios.

[7]The CAPM is a relatively complex subject, and we present only the basic conclusions in this text. For a more detailed discussion, see any standard investments textbook.

Portfolio Risk and Return

Most financial assets are not held in isolation; rather, they are held as parts of portfolios. Banks, pension funds, insurance companies, mutual funds, and other financial institutions are required by law to hold diversified portfolios. Even individual investors — at least those whose security holdings constitute a significant part of their total wealth — generally hold stock portfolios, not the stock of only one firm. This being the case, from an investor's standpoint the fact that a particular stock goes up or down is not very important; *what is important is the return on his or her portfolio, and the portfolio's risk. Logically, then, the risk and return of an individual security should be analyzed in terms of how that security affects the risk and return of the portfolio in which it is held.* The CAPM analysis requires us to determine how the security affects the riskiness of the portfolio, and it then provides an equation for calculating the required return of the stock, given its risk.

expected return on a portfolio, $\hat{k}_p$
The weighted average expected return on the stocks held in the portfolio.

Portfolio Returns. The **expected return on a portfolio, $\hat{k}_p$,** is simply the weighted average expected return of the individual stocks in the portfolio, with the weights being the fraction of the total portfolio invested in each stock:

$$\hat{k}_p = w_1\hat{k}_1 + w_2\hat{k}_2 + \ldots + w_n\hat{k}_n$$

$$= \sum_{i=1}^{n} w_i\hat{k}_i. \tag{4-4}$$

Here the $\hat{k}_i$'s are the expected returns on the individual stocks, and the w_i's are the weights. There are n stocks in the portfolio. Note (1) that w_i is the proportion of the portfolio's dollar value invested in Stock i (that is, the value of the investment in Stock i divided by the total value of the portfolio), and (2) that the w_i's must sum to 1.0.

In March 1988, a security analyst estimated that the following returns could be attached to four leading computer software companies:

	Expected Return, $\hat{k}$
Lotus Development	14%
Microsoft	13%
Cullinet	20%
Computer Sciences	18%

If we formed a $100,000 portfolio, investing $25,000 in each stock, the expected portfolio return would be 16.25%:

$$\hat{k}_p = w_1\hat{k}_1 + w_2\hat{k}_2 + w_3\hat{k}_3 + w_4\hat{k}_4$$

$$= 0.25(14\%) + 0.25(13\%) + 0.25(20\%) + 0.25(18\%)$$

$$= 16.25\%.$$

Of course, after the fact and a year later, the actual *realized* rates of return on the individual stocks — the $\bar{k}_i$ values — will almost certainly be different from their expected values, so $\bar{k}_p$ will be somewhat different from $\hat{k}_p = 16.25\%$. For example, Lotus stock might double in price and provide a return of $+100\%$, whereas Cullinet stock might have a terrible year, fall sharply, and have a return of -75%. Note, though, that those two events would be somewhat offsetting, so the portfolio's return might still be close to its expected return, even though the individual stocks' returns were far from their expected returns.

Portfolio Risk. As we just saw, the expected return on a portfolio is simply a weighted average of the expected returns on the individual stocks in the portfolio. However, unlike returns, the riskiness of a portfolio, σ_p, is generally *not* a weighted average of the standard deviations of the individual securities in the portfolio; the portfolio's risk will be *smaller* than the weighted average of the stocks' σs. In fact, it may even be theoretically possible to combine two stocks which are individually quite risky as measured by their standard deviations and to form a portfolio which is completely riskless, with $\sigma_p = 0$.

To illustrate, consider the situation in Figure 4-4. The bottom section gives data on rates of return both for Stocks W and M individually, and for a portfolio invested 50 percent in each stock. The three top graphs show plots of the data in a time series format, and the lower graphs show the probability distributions of returns, assuming that the future is expected to be like the past. The two stocks would be quite risky if they were held in isolation, but when they are combined to form Portfolio WM, they are not risky at all. (Note: These stocks are called W and M because their returns graphs in Figure 4-4 resemble a W and an M.)

The reason Stocks W and M can be combined to form a riskless portfolio is that their returns move countercyclically to each other—when W's returns fall, those of M rise, and vice versa. The tendency of two variables to move together is called *correlation*, and the **correlation coefficient, r,** measures this tendency.[8] In statistical terms, we say that the returns on Stocks W and M are *perfectly negatively correlated*, with $r = -1.0$.

correlation coefficient, r
A measure of the degree of relationship between two variables.

The opposite of perfect negative correlation, with $r = -1.0$, is *perfect positive correlation*, with $r = +1.0$. Returns on two perfectly positively correlated stocks would move up and down together, and a portfolio consisting of two such stocks would be just as risky as the individual stocks. This point is illustrated in Figure 4-5, where we see that the portfolio's standard deviation is equal to that of the individual stocks. Thus, diversification does nothing to reduce risk if the portfolio consists of perfectly positively correlated stocks.

Figures 4-4 and 4-5 demonstrate that when stocks are perfectly negatively correlated ($r = -1.0$), all risk can be diversified away, but when stocks are perfectly positively correlated ($r = +1.0$), diversification does no good whatsoever. In reality, most stocks are positively correlated, but not perfectly so.

---

[8]The *correlation coefficient, r,* can range from $+1.0$, denoting that the two variables move up and down in perfect synchronization, to -1.0, denoting that the variables always move in exactly opposite directions. A correlation coefficient of zero suggests that the two variables are not related to each other—that is, changes in one variable are *independent* of changes in the other.

Figure 4-4   **Rate of Return Distributions for Two Perfectly Negatively Correlated Stocks (r = −1.0) and Portfolio WM**

a. Rate of Return

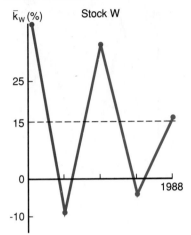

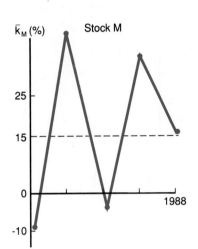

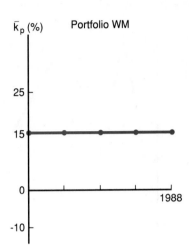

b. Probability Distribution of Returns

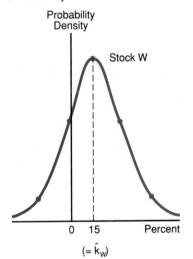

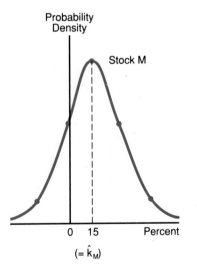

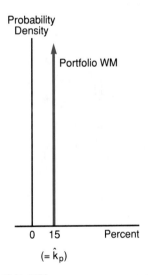

Year	Stock W ($\bar{k}_W$)	Stock M ($\bar{k}_M$)	Portfolio WM ($\bar{k}_p$)
1984	40%	−10%	15%
1985	−10	40	15
1986	35	−5	15
1987	−5	35	15
1988	15	15	15
Average return	15%	15%	15%
Standard deviation	22.6%	22.6%	0.0%

**Figure 4-5   Rate of Return Distributions for Two Perfectly Positively
Correlated Stocks (r = +1.0) and Portfolio MM′**

a. Rate of Return

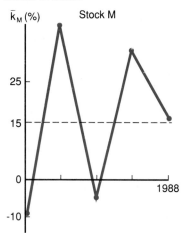
Stock M

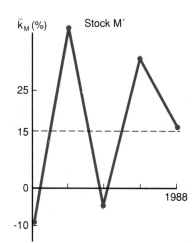
Stock M′

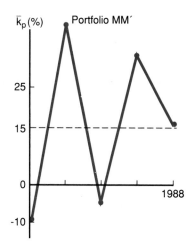
Portfolio MM′

b. Probability Distribution of Returns

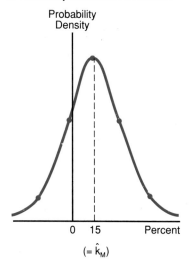

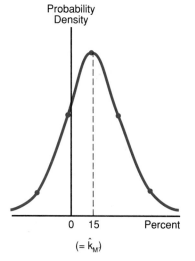

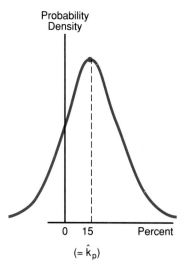

Year	Stock M $(\bar{k}_M)$	Stock M′ $(\bar{k}_{M'})$	Portfolio MM′ $(\bar{k}_p)$
1984	−10%	−10%	−10%
1985	40	40	40
1986	− 5	− 5	− 5
1987	35	35	35
1988	15	15	15
Average return	15%	15%	15%
Standard deviation	22.6%	22.6%	22.6%

On average, the correlation coefficient for the returns on two randomly selected stocks would be about +0.6, and for most pairs of stocks, r would lie
in the range of +0.5 to +0.7. *Under such conditions, combining stocks into
portfolios reduces risk but does not eliminate it completely.* Figure 4-6 illustrates this point with two stocks whose correlation coefficient is r = +0.65.
The portfolio's average return is 15.0 percent, which is exactly the same as the
average return for each of the two stocks, but its standard deviation is 20.6
percent, which is less than the standard deviation of either stock. Thus, the
portfolio's risk is *not* an average of the risks of its individual stocks — diversification has reduced, but not eliminated, risk.

From these two-stock portfolio examples, we have seen that in one extreme case (r = −1.0), risk can be completely eliminated, while in the other
extreme case (r = +1.0), diversification does no good whatever. In between
these extremes, combining two stocks into a portfolio reduces, but does not
eliminate, the riskiness inherent in the individual stocks.

What would happen if we included more than two stocks in the portfolio?
*As a rule, the riskiness of a portfolio will be reduced as the number of stocks
in the portfolio increases.* If we added enough partially correlated stocks, could
we completely eliminate risk? In general, the answer is no, but the extent to
which adding stocks to a portfolio reduces its risk depends on the *degree of
correlation* among the stocks: The smaller the correlation coefficient, the
lower the remaining risk in a large portfolio. If we could find a set of stocks
whose correlation coefficients were zero or negative, all risk could be eliminated. *In the typical case, where the correlations among the individual stocks
are positive but less than +1.0, some, but not all, risk can be eliminated.*

To test your understanding, would you expect to find higher correlations
between the returns on two companies in the same or in different industries?
For example, would the correlation of returns on Ford's and General Motors's
stocks be higher, or would the correlation coefficient be higher between either Ford or GM and IBM, and how would those correlations affect the risk of
portfolios containing them?

Answer: Ford's and GM's returns have a correlation coefficient of about 0.9
with one another, but only about 0.6 with those of IBM.

Implications: A two-stock portfolio consisting of Ford and GM would be
riskier than a two-stock portfolio consisting of Ford or GM, plus IBM. Thus, to
minimize risk, portfolios should be diversified across industries.

Company-Specific Risk versus Market Risk. As noted earlier, it is very difficult,
if not impossible, to find stocks whose expected returns are not positively
correlated — most stocks tend to do well when the national economy is strong
and badly when it is weak.[9] Thus, even very large portfolios end up with a
substantial amount of risk, but not as much risk as if all the money were invested in only one stock.

---

[9]It is not too hard to find a few stocks that happened to rise because of a particular set of
circumstances in the past while most other stocks were declining; it is much harder to find
stocks that could logically be *expected* to go up in the future when other stocks are falling.

Figure 4-6   Rate of Return Distributions for Two Partially Correlated
Stocks (r = +0.65) and Portfolio WY

a. Rate of Return

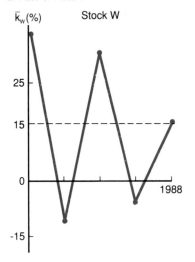

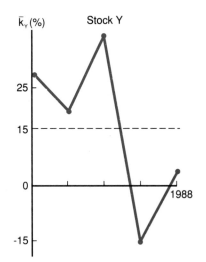

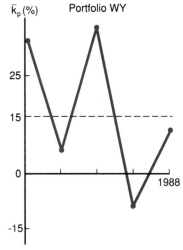

b. Probability Distribution of Returns

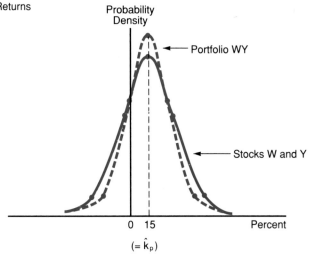

Year	Stock W (k_W)	Stock Y (k_Y)	Portfolio WY (k_p)
1984	40%	28%	34%
1985	− 10	20	5
1986	35	41	38
1987	− 5	− 17	− 11
1988	15	3	9
Average return	15%	15%	15%
Standard deviation	22.6%	22.6%	20.6%

Figure 4-7   Effects of Portfolio Size on Portfolio Risk for Average Stocks

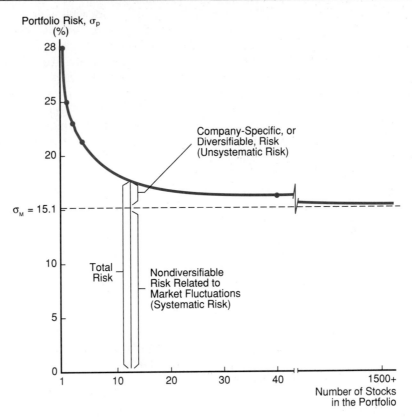

To see more precisely how portfolio size affects portfolio risk, consider Figure 4-7, which shows how portfolio risk is affected by forming larger and larger portfolios of randomly selected NYSE stocks. Standard deviations are plotted for an average one-stock portfolio, a two-stock portfolio, and so on, up to a portfolio consisting of all 1,500-plus common stocks that were listed on the NYSE at the time the data were graphed. The graph illustrates that, in general, the riskiness of a portfolio consisting of average NYSE stocks tends to decline and to asymptotically approach a limit as the size of the portfolio increases. According to data accumulated in recent years, σ_1, the standard deviation of a one-stock portfolio (or an average stock), is approximately 28 percent. A portfolio consisting of all stocks, which is called the *market portfolio,* would have a standard deviation of about 15.1 percent. The market portfolio's standard deviation is given the symbol σ_M, so $\sigma_M = 15.1\%$.

Thus, almost half of the riskiness inherent in an average individual stock can be eliminated if the stock is held in a reasonably well-diversified portfolio, one containing about 40 stocks. Some risk always remains, however, so it is virtually impossible to diversify away the effects of broad stock market movements that affect almost all stocks.

That part of the risk of a stock which can be eliminated is called *diversifiable,* or *company-specific,* or *unsystematic, risk;* that part which cannot be eliminated is called *nondiversifiable,* or *market,* or *systematic, risk.* The name is not especially important, but the fact that a large part of the riskiness of any individual stock can be eliminated is vitally important.

company-specific risk
That part of a security's risk associated with random events; can be eliminated by proper diversification.

Company-specific risk is caused by such things as lawsuits, strikes, successful and unsuccessful marketing programs, the winning and losing of major contracts, and other events that are unique to a particular firm. Since these events are essentially random, their effects on a portfolio can be eliminated by diversification — bad events in one firm will be offset by good events in another. **Market risk,** on the other hand, stems from factors which systematically affect all firms, such as war, inflation, recessions, and high interest rates. Since all stocks will tend to be negatively affected by these factors, systematic risk cannot be eliminated by diversification.

market risk
That part of a security's risk that cannot be eliminated by diversification.

We know that investors demand a premium for bearing risk; that is, the higher the riskiness of a security, the higher the expected return required to induce investors to buy (or to hold) it. However, if investors are primarily concerned with *portfolio risk* rather than the risk of the individual securities in the portfolio, how should the riskiness of an individual stock be measured? The answer, as provided by the Capital Asset Pricing Model (CAPM), is this: *The relevant riskiness of an individual stock is its contribution to the riskiness of a well-diversified portfolio.* In other words, the riskiness of Lotus Development's stock to a doctor who has a portfolio of 40 stocks, or to a trust officer managing a 150-stock portfolio, is the contribution that the Lotus stock makes to the portfolio's riskiness. The stock might be quite risky if held by itself, but if most of its risk can be eliminated by diversification, then its **relevant risk,** which is its *contribution to the portfolio's risk,* may be small.

relevant risk
The risk of a security that cannot be diversified away, or market risk. This reflects a security's contribution to the risk of a portfolio.

A simple example will help make this point clear. Suppose you can flip a coin once; if a head comes up, you win $10,000, but if it comes up tails, you lose $8,000. This is a good bet — the expected return is 0.5($10,000) + 0.5(−$8,000) = $1,000. However, it is a highly risky proposition, because you have a 50 percent chance of losing $8,000. Thus, you might well refuse to make the bet. Alternatively, suppose you were offered the chance to flip a coin 100 times, and you would win $100 for each head but lose $80 for each tail. It is possible that you would flip all heads and win $10,000, and it is also possible that you would flip all tails and lose $8,000, but the chances are very high that you would actually flip about 50 heads and about 50 tails, winning a net $1,000. Although each individual flip is a risky bet, collectively you have a low-risk proposition, because you have diversified away most of the risk. This is the idea behind holding portfolios of stocks rather than just one stock, except that with stocks all of the risk cannot be eliminated by diversification — those risks related to broad, systematic changes in the stock market will remain.

Are all stocks equally risky in the sense that adding them to a well-diversified portfolio would have the same effect on the portfolio's riskiness? The answer is no. Different stocks will affect the portfolio differently, so different securities have different degrees of relevant risk. How can the relevant risk of an individual stock be measured? As we have seen, all risk except that related to broad market movements can, and presumably will, be diversified away. After all, why accept risk that can easily be eliminated? *The risk that remains after diversifying is market risk, or risk that is inherent in the market, and it can be measured by the degree to which a given stock tends to move up and down with the market.* In the next section, we develop a measure of a stock's market risk, and then, in a later section, we introduce an equation for determining the required rate of return on a stock, given its market risk.

The Concept of Beta

beta coefficient, b
A measure of the extent
to which the returns on
a given stock move with
the stock market.

The tendency of a stock to move with the market is reflected in its **beta coefficient, b**, which is a measure of the stock's volatility relative to that of an average stock. Beta is a key element of the CAPM.

An *average-risk stock* is defined as one that tends to move up and down in step with the general market as measured by some index, such as the Dow Jones Industrials, the S&P 500, or the New York Stock Exchange Index. Such a stock will, by definition, have a beta, b, of 1.0, which indicates that, in general, if the market moves up by 10 percent, the stock will also move up by 10 percent, while if the market falls by 10 percent, the stock will likewise fall by 10 percent. A portfolio of such b = 1.0 stocks will move up and down with the broad market averages, and it will be just as risky as the averages. If b = 0.5, the stock is only half as volatile as the market — it will rise and fall only half as much — and a portfolio of such stocks will be half as risky as a portfolio of b = 1.0 stocks. On the other hand, if b = 2.0, the stock is twice as volatile as an average stock, so a portfolio of such stocks will be twice as risky as an average portfolio.

Figure 4-8 shows betas in a graphic sense. The data below the graph assume that in 1986 the "market," defined as a portfolio consisting of all stocks, had a total return (dividend yield plus capital gains yield) of 10 percent, and Stocks H, A, and L (for High, Average, and Low risk) also had returns of 10 percent. In 1987 the market went up sharply, and the return on the market portfolio was $\bar{k}_M = 20\%$. Returns on the three stocks also went up: H soared to 30 percent; A went up to 20 percent, the same as the market; and L only went up to 15 percent. Now suppose that the market dropped in 1988, and the market return was $\bar{k}_M = -10\%$. The three stocks' returns also fell, H plunging to −30 percent, A falling to −10 percent, and L going down only to $\bar{k}_L = 0\%$. Thus, the three stocks all moved in the same direction as the market, but H, the high-beta stock, was by far the most volatile; A was just as volatile as the market; and L was less volatile.

Betas can be calculated by plotting lines like those in Figure 4-8. The slopes of the lines show how each stock moves in response to a movement in the general market — *indeed, the slope coefficient of such "regression lines" is defined as the beta coefficient.* (Procedures for actually calculating betas are

Figure 4-8   Beta Graph

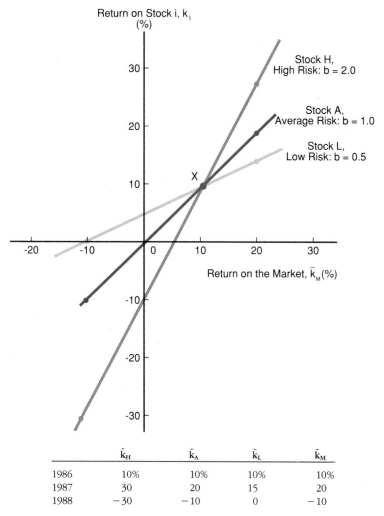

	$\bar{k}_H$	$\bar{k}_A$	$\bar{k}_L$	$\bar{k}_M$
1986	10%	10%	10%	10%
1987	30	20	15	20
1988	−30	−10	0	−10

Note: These three stocks plot exactly on their regression lines. This indicates that they are exposed only to market risk. Mutual funds which concentrate on stocks with a specific degree of market risk would have patterns similar to those shown in the graph.

described in Appendix 4A.) Betas for literally thousands of companies are cal-culated and published by Merrill Lynch, Value Line, and numerous other or-ganizations. The beta coefficients of some well-known companies are shown in Table 4-4. Most stocks have betas in the range of 0.50 to 1.50, and the average for all stocks is 1.0 by definition.[10]

---

[10]The betas we have been discussing are called *historic,* or *ex post,* betas because they are based strictly on historic, or past, data. Another type of beta, the *fundamental beta,* which is based partly on past actions and partly on expected future conditions not yet reflected in historic data, is also used.

Table 4-4   Illustrative List of Beta Coefficients

Stock	Beta
Georgia-Pacific	1.45
Apple Computer	1.40
General Electric	1.10
General Motors	1.05
IBM	1.00
Johnson & Johnson	1.00
Anheuser Busch	0.95
Procter & Gamble	0.90
Pacific Gas & Electric	0.85
Gerber Products	0.85
Boston Edison	0.70
Energen Corp.[a]	0.50

Source: *Value Line,* October 30, 1987.

[a]Energen is a gas distribution company. It has a monopoly in much of Alabama, and its rates are adjusted every 3 months so as to keep its return on equity within the range of 13.75 to 14.25 percent.

If a higher-beta-than-average stock (one whose beta is greater than 1.0) is added to an average-beta (b = 1.0) portfolio, then the beta, and consequently the riskiness, of the portfolio will increase. Conversely, if a lower-beta-than-average stock (one whose beta is less than 1.0) is added to an average-risk portfolio, the portfolio's beta and risk will decline. *Thus, since a stock's beta measures its contribution to the riskiness of a portfolio, beta is a theoretically correct measure of the stock's riskiness.*

The preceeding analysis of risk in a portfolio setting is called the Capital Asset Pricing Model, and we can summarize our discussion to this point as follows:

1. A stock's risk consists of two components, market risk and company-specific risk.

2. Company-specific risk can be eliminated by diversification, and most investors do indeed diversify, either directly or by purchasing shares in a mutual fund. We are left, then, with market risk, which is caused by general movements in the stock market and which reflects the fact that all stocks are systematically affected by certain overall economic events like war, recessions, and inflation. Market risk is the only relevant risk to a rational, diversified investor, because he or she should have already eliminated company-specific risk.

3. Investors must be compensated for bearing risk — the greater the riskiness of a stock, the higher its required return. However, compensation is required only for risk which cannot be eliminated by diversification. If risk premiums existed for diversifiable risk, well-diversified investors would start buying these securities and bidding up their prices, and their final (equilibrium) expected returns would reflect only nondiversifiable market risk.

If this point is not clear, an example may help clarify it. Suppose half of Stock A's risk is market risk (it occurs because Stock A moves up and down with the market, and the market can go down). The other half of A's risk is diversifiable. You hold only Stock A, and hence you are exposed to all of its risk. To compensate you for bearing so much risk, you want a risk premium of 8 percent over the T-bond rate, which is 10 percent. Thus, your required return is $k_A = 10\% + 8\% = 18\%$. But suppose other investors, including your professor, are well diversified; if they hold Stock A, they will eliminate its diversifiable risk and thus be exposed to only half as much risk as you. Therefore, their risk premium will be only half as large as yours, and their required rate of return will be $k_A = 10\% + 4\% = 14\%$.

If the stock were yielding more than 14 percent in the market, others, including your professor, would buy it. If it were yielding more than 18 percent, you would be willing to buy it, but well-diversified investors would bid its price up and its yield down, and keep you from getting it. In the end, you would have to accept a 14 percent return or else keep your money in the bank. Thus, risk premiums in the market reflect only market risk.

4.   The market risk of a stock is measured by its beta coefficient, which is an index of the stock's relative volatility. Some benchmark betas follow:

   $b = 0.5$: Stock is only half as volatile, or risky, as the average stock.

   $b = 1.0$: Stock is of average risk.

   $b = 2.0$: Stock is twice as risky as the average stock.

5.   *Since a stock's beta coefficient determines how it affects the riskiness of a diversified portfolio, beta is the most relevant measure of a stock's risk.*

Portfolio Beta Coefficients

A portfolio consisting of low-beta securities will itself have a low beta, because the beta of any set of securities is a weighted average of the individual securities' betas:

$$b_p = \sum_{i=1}^{n} w_i b_i. \tag{4-5}$$

Here b_p is the beta of the portfolio, which reflects how volatile the portfolio is in relation to the market; w_i is the fraction of the portfolio invested in the ith stock; and b_i is the beta coefficient of the ith stock. For example, if an investor holds a $100,000 portfolio consisting of $10,000 invested in each of 10 stocks, and each of the stocks has a beta of 0.8, then the portfolio's beta will be $b_p = 0.8$. Thus, the portfolio will be less risky than the market: it should experience relatively narrow price swings and have relatively small rate-of-return fluctuations.

Now suppose one of the existing stocks is sold and replaced by a stock with $b_i = 2.0$. This action will increase the riskiness of the portfolio from $b_{p1} = 0.8$ to $b_{p2} = 0.92$:

$$b_{p2} = \sum_{i=1}^{n} w_i b_i = 0.9(0.8) + 0.1(2.0)$$

$$= 0.92.$$

Had a stock with $b_i = 0.2$ been added, the portfolio beta would have declined from 0.8 to 0.74. Adding a low-beta stock, therefore, would reduce the riskiness of the portfolio.

THE RELATIONSHIP BETWEEN RISK AND RATES OF RETURN

In the preceding section we saw that under the CAPM theory, beta is the appropriate measure of a stock's relevant risk. Now we must specify the relationship between risk and return: For a given level of beta, what rate of return will investors require on a stock in order to compensate them for assuming the risk? To begin, let us define the following terms:

$\hat{k}_i$ = expected rate of return on the ith stock.

k_i = required rate of return on the ith stock. Note that if $\hat{k}_i$ is less than k_i, you would not purchase this stock, or you would sell it if you owned it. If $\hat{k}_i$ were greater than k_i, you would want to buy the stock, and you would be indifferent if $\hat{k}_i = k_i$.

k_{RF} = risk-free rate of return, in this context generally measured by the return on long-term U.S. Treasury bonds.

b_i = beta coefficient of the ith stock. The beta of an average stock is $b_A = 1.0$.

k_M = required rate of return on a portfolio consisting of all stocks, which is the market portfolio. k_M is also the required rate of return on an average ($b_A = 1.0$) stock.

$RP_M = (k_M - k_{RF})$ = market risk premium. This is the additional return over the risk-free rate required to compensate an average investor for assuming an average amount of risk. Average risk means $b_A = 1.0$.

$RP_i = (k_M - k_{RF})b_i$ = risk premium on the ith stock. The stock's risk premium is less than, equal to, or greater than the premium on an average stock, depending on whether its beta is less than, equal to, or greater than 1.0. If $b_i = b_A = 1.0$, then $RP_i = RP_M$.

market risk premium, RP_M
The additional return over the risk-free rate needed to compensate investors for assuming an average amount of risk.

The **market risk premium, RP_M,** depends on the degree of aversion that investors in the aggregate have to risk.[11] Let us assume that at the current time, Treasury bonds yield k_{RF} = 8% and an average share of stock has a required return of k_M = 12%. Therefore, the market risk premium is 4 percent:

$$RP_M = k_M - k_{RF} = 12\% - 8\% = 4\%.$$

It follows that if one stock were twice as risky as another, its risk premium would be twice as high, and, conversely, if its risk were only half as much, its risk premium would be half as large. Further, we can measure a stock's relative riskiness by its beta coefficient. Therefore, if we know the market risk premium, RP_M, and the stock's risk as measured by its beta coefficient, b_i, we can find its risk premium as the product $(RP_M)b_i$. For example, if b_i = 0.5 and RP_M = 4%, then RP_i is 2 percent:

$$\text{Risk premium for Stock i} = RP_i = (RP_M)b_i \qquad (4\text{-}6)$$

$$= (4\%)(0.5)$$

$$= 2.0\%.$$

To summarize, given estimates of k_{RF}, k_M, and b_i, we can find the required rate of return on Stock i:

$$k_i = k_{RF} + (k_M - k_{RF})b_i \qquad (4\text{-}7)$$

$$= k_{RF} + (RP_M)b_i$$

$$= 8\% + (12\% - 8\%)(0.5)$$

$$= 8\% + 4\%(0.5)$$

$$= 10\%.$$

If some other stock, j, were riskier than Stock i and had b_j = 2.0, then its required rate of return would be 16 percent:

$$k_j = 8\% + (4\%)2.0 = 16\%.$$

An average stock, with b = 1.0, would have a required return of 12 percent, the same as the market return:

$$k_A = 8\% + (4\%)1.0 = 12\% = k_M.$$

---

[11]This concept, as well as other aspects of CAPM, is discussed in more detail in Chapter 2 of Brigham and Gapenski, *Intermediate Financial Management*. It should be noted that the risk premium of an average stock, $k_M - k_{RF}$, cannot be measured with great precision because it is impossible to obtain precise values for k_M. However, empirical studies suggest that where long-term U.S. Treasury bonds are used to measure k_{RF} and where k_M is the expected return on the S&P 400 Industrial Stocks, the market risk premium varies somewhat from year to year, and it has generally ranged from 4 to 8 percent during the last 20 years.

Chapter 2 of *Intermediate Financial Management* also discusses the assumptions embodied in the CAPM framework. Some of the assumptions of the CAPM theory are unrealistic, and, because of this, the theory does not hold exactly.

Figure 4-9   The Security Market Line (SML)

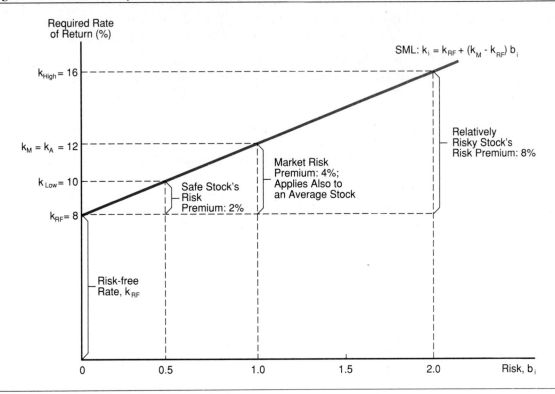

Equation 4-7 is called the **Security Market Line (SML)** equation, and it is often expressed in graph form, as in Figure 4-9, which shows the SML when $k_{RF} = 8\%$ and $k_M = 12\%$. Note the following points:

1. Required rates of return are shown on the vertical axis, while risk as measured by beta is shown on the horizontal axis. This graph is quite different from the one shown in Figure 4-8, where the returns on individual stocks were plotted on the vertical axis and returns on the market index were shown on the horizontal axis. The slopes of the three lines in Figure 4-8 represent the three stocks' betas, and these three betas are then plotted as points on the horizontal axis in Figure 4-9.

2. Riskless securities have $b_i = 0$; therefore, k_{RF} appears as the vertical axis intercept in Figure 4-9.

3. The slope of the SML reflects the degree of risk aversion in the economy; the greater the average investor's aversion to risk, (1) the steeper the slope of the line, (2) the greater the risk premium for any stock, and (3)

the higher the required rate of return on stocks.[12] These points are discussed further in a later section.

4. The values we worked out for stocks with $b_i = 0.5$, $b_i = 1.0$, and $b_i = 2.0$ agree with the values shown on the graph for k_{Low}, k_A, and k_{High}.

Both the Security Market Line and a company's position on it change over time due to changes in interest rates, investors' risk aversion, and individual companies' betas. Such changes are discussed in the following sections.

The Impact of Inflation

As we learned in Chapter 3, interest amounts to "rent" on borrowed money, or the price of money; thus, k_{RF} is the price of money to a riskless borrower. We also learned that the risk-free rate as measured by the rate on U.S. Treasury securities is called the *nominal rate,* and it consists of two elements: (1) a *real inflation-free rate of return, k*,* and (2) an *inflation premium, IP,* equal to the anticipated rate of inflation.[13] Thus, $k_{RF} = k^* + IP$. The real rate on long-term Treasury bonds has historically ranged from 2 to 4 percent, with a mean of about 3 percent. Therefore, if no inflation were expected, long-term Treasury bonds would tend to yield about 3 percent. However, as the expected rate of inflation increases, a premium must be added to the real rate of return to compensate investors for the loss of purchasing power that results from inflation. Therefore, the 8 percent k_{RF} shown in Figure 4-9 might be thought of as consisting of a 3 percent real rate of return plus a 5 percent inflation premium: $k_{RF} = k^* + IP = 3\% + 5\% = 8\%$.

If the expected rate of inflation rose to 7 percent, this would cause k_{RF} to rise to 10 percent. Such a change is shown in Figure 4-10. Notice that under the CAPM, the increase in k_{RF} also causes an *equal* increase in the rate of return on all risky assets, because the inflation premium is built into the required rate of return of both riskless and risky assets.[14] For example, the rate of return on an average stock, k_M, increases from 12 to 14 percent. Other risky securities' returns also rise by two percentage points.

---

[12]Students sometimes confuse beta with the slope of the SML. This is a mistake. The slope of any line is equal to the "rise" divided by the "run," or $(Y_1 - Y_0)/(X_1 - X_0)$. Consider Figure 4-9. If we let $Y = k$ and $X = $ beta, and we go from the origin to $b = 1.0$, we see that the slope is $(k_M - k_{RF})/(beta_M - beta_{RF}) = (12 - 8)/(1 - 0) = 4$. Thus, the slope of the SML is equal to $(k_M - k_{RF})$, the market risk premium. In Figure 4-9, $k_i = 8\% + 4b_i$, so a unitary increase in beta (for example, from 1.0 to 2.0) would produce a 4 percentage point increase in k_i.

[13]Long-term Treasury bonds also contain a maturity risk premium, MRP. Here we include the MRP in k^* to simplify the discussion.

[14]Recall that the inflation premium for any asset is equal to the average expected rate of inflation over the life of the asset. Thus, in this analysis we must assume either that all securities plotted on the SML graph have the same life or else that the expected rate of future inflation is constant.

It should also be noted that k_{RF} in a CAPM analysis can be proxied by either a long-term rate (the T-bond rate) or a short-term rate (the T-bill rate). Traditionally, the T-bill rate was used, but in recent years there has been a movement toward use of the T-bond rate because there is a closer relationship between T-bond yields and stocks than between T-bill yields and stocks. See Ibbotson and Sinquefield, *Stocks, Bonds, Bills, and Inflation; 1988 Yearbook* (Chicago: Ibbotson & Associates, 1988), for a discussion.

Figure 4-10   Shift in the SML Caused by an Increase in Inflation

---

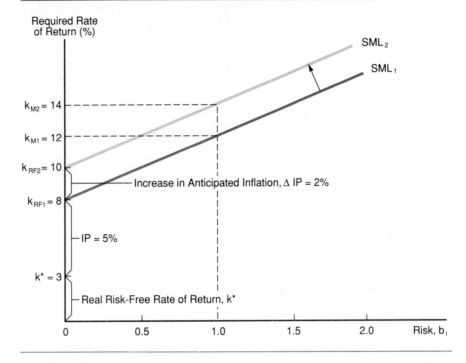

Changes in Risk Aversion

The slope of the Security Market Line also reflects the extent to which investors are averse to risk — the steeper the slope of the line, the greater the average investor's risk aversion. If investors were indifferent to risk and if k_{RF} were 8 percent, then risky assets would also sell to provide an expected return of 8 percent: With no risk aversion, there would be no risk premium, so the SML would be horizontal. As risk aversion increases, so does the risk premium and, thus, the slope of the SML.

Figure 4-11 illustrates an increase in risk aversion. The market risk premium rises from 4 to 6 percent, and k_M rises from 12 to 14 percent. The returns on other risky assets also rise, with the effect of this shift in risk aversion being more pronounced on riskier securities. For example, the required return on a stock with $b_i = 0.5$ increases by only one percentage point, from 10 to 11 percent, whereas that on a stock with $b_i = 1.5$ increases by three percentage points, from 14 to 17 percent.

Changes in a Stock's Beta Coefficient

As we shall see later in the book, a firm can affect its market, or beta, risk through changes in the composition of its assets as well as through its use of debt financing. A company's beta can also change as a result of external factors,

Figure 4-11   Shift in the SML Caused by Increased Risk Aversion

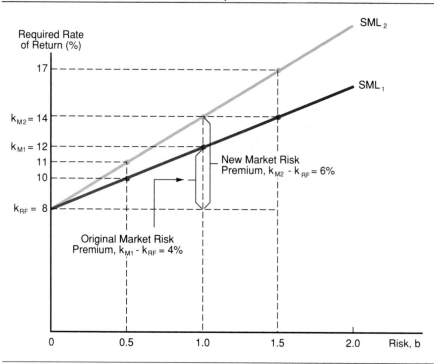

such as increased competition in its industry, the expiration of basic patents, and the like. When such changes occur, the required rate of return also changes, and, as we shall see in Chapter 6, this will affect the price of the firm's stock. For example, consider Teletron Electronics Corporation, with a beta equal to 1.0. Now suppose some action occurred that caused Teletron Electronics' beta to increase from 1.0 to 1.5. If the conditions depicted in Figure 4-9 held, Teletron's required rate of return would increase from

$$k_1 = k_{RF} + (k_M - k_{RF})b_i$$

$$= 8\% + (12\% - 8\%)1.0$$

$$= 12\%$$

to

$$k_2 = 8\% + (12\% - 8\%)1.5$$

$$= 14\%.$$

Any change which affects the required rate of return on a security, such as a change in its beta coefficient or in expected inflation, will have an impact on the price of the security. We will look at the relationship between a security's rate of return and its stock price in Chapter 6.

PHYSICAL ASSETS VERSUS SECURITIES

In a book on the financial management of business firms, why do we spend so much time on the riskiness of security investments? Why not begin by looking at the riskiness of such business assets as plant and equipment? *The reason is that, for a management whose goal is stock price maximization, the overriding consideration is the riskiness of the firm's stock, and the relevant risk of any physical asset must be measured in terms of its effect on the stock's risk.* For example, suppose Goodyear Tire Company is considering a major investment in a new product, recapped tires. Sales of recaps and hence earnings on the new operation are highly uncertain, so it would appear that the new venture is quite risky. However, suppose that returns on the recap business are negatively correlated with Goodyear's regular operations; when times are good and people have plenty of money, they buy new tires, but when times are bad, they tend to buy more recaps. Therefore, returns would be high on regular operations and low on the recap division during good times, but the opposite situation would occur during recessions. The result might be a pattern like that shown in Figure 4-4 earlier in the chapter for Stocks W and M. Thus, what appears to be a risky investment when viewed on a stand-alone basis might not be very risky when viewed within the context of the company as a whole.

This analysis can be extended to the corporation's owners, the stockholders. Because the stock of Goodyear and other companies is owned by stockholders, the real issue each time a company makes a major asset investment is this: How does this investment affect the risk of our stockholders? Again, the stand-alone risk of an individual project may look quite high, but viewed in the context of a project's effect on stockholders' risk, it may not be very large. We will address this subject again in Chapter 11.

A WORD OF CAUTION

A word of caution about betas and the Capital Asset Pricing Model is in order. Although these concepts are logical, the entire theory is based on *ex ante,* or expected, conditions, yet we have available only *ex post,* or past, data. Thus, the betas we calculate show how volatile a stock has been in the *past,* but conditions may change, and its *future volatility,* which is the item of real concern to investors, might be quite different from its past volatility. Although the CAPM represents a significant step forward in security pricing theory, it does have some potentially serious deficiencies when applied in practice, so estimates of k_i found through use of the SML may be subject to considerable error.

International

THE RISK OF FOREIGN INVESTMENT

Thus far in Chapter 4 we have implicitly focused on the risk and return of *domestic investments.* Although the same concepts are involved when we move to the international scene, some important differences must also be observed. For example, someone who invests on a world-wide basis must be concerned with (1) sovereign risk and (2) exchange rate risk. *Sovereign risk* is the risk that the sovereign country in which the real assets backing an investment are located will take some action, such as nationalization without adequate compensation, that will decrease the value of the investment. Enron Corporation, a multibillion dollar U.S.-based energy company, experienced exactly this situation when Peru nationalized an Enron subsidiary in 1985, resulting in a sharp drop in Enron's stock price. Sovereign risk is diversifiable, but it is something that concerns both international investors and multinational corporations.

The second type of international risk, *exchange rate risk,* stems from the fact that different countries use different currencies, and the values of those currencies change over time. To illustrate, in 1985, the exchange rate between yen and dollars was 251:1, meaning that one dollar could buy 251 yen. In 1988, the exchange rate had dropped to 135:1. This change, which is called a *decline in the value of the dollar* because a dollar would now buy fewer yen, had a major effect on both U.S. and Japanese firms and investors. First, suppose a U.S. investor bought 100 shares of Toyota stock at a price of 1,000 yen per share, or 100,000 in total. That investment would have a dollar cost of 100,000/251 = $398.41. If the yen price of Toyota's stock had remained constant at 1,000, the decline in the value of the dollar would have caused the dollar value of the stock to rise from $398.41 to 100,000/135 = $740.74, an 86 percent increase. Since the dollar also fell against most other major currencies, this same experience was repeated in other international capital markets, and, as a result, those U.S. investors who included foreign stocks in their portfolios did well from 1985 to 1988. Of course, foreign stocks will drop if the dollar rises in the future.

One might think that because of the additional risks of international operations, U.S. firms that do business abroad would be viewed as being riskier than firms operating solely in the U.S. If this were true, international firms would have higher betas, hence higher required rates of return, than purely domestic firms. However, a recent study of 84 multinational firms and 52 purely domestic firms showed that the betas of multinational firms are both lower and more stable than those of domestic firms.[15]

The results of this study indicate that international diversification reduces the degree of systematic (market) risk for the firm. Systematic risk depends in large part on the economy of the country in which the firm operates. A multinational firm operates in many countries, and the economies of these countries are not perfectly correlated with each other, or with the firm's home country's economy. Hence, the effects of a poor economy in one country may be offset by strong economies in its other operating areas. As a result, a multinational firm is exposed to less systematic risk than a purely domestic firm. According to the CAPM, only systematic risk need be compensated with higher expected rates of return. Since firms operating in international markets appear to have less systematic risk than domestic firms, international firms should have lower betas, lower required rates of return, and lower costs of capital than otherwise comparable domestic firms.

---

[15]Ali M. Fatemi, "Shareholder Benefits from Corporate International Diversification," *Journal of Finance,* December 1984, 1325–1344.

SUMMARY AND KEY CONCEPTS

The primary goals of this chapter were (1) to show how risk is measured in financial analysis and (2) to explain how risk affects rates of return. The key concepts covered are listed below.

- **Risk** can be defined as the chance that some unfavorable event will occur.
- Most rational investors hold **portfolios of stocks** and are more concerned with the risks of their portfolios than with the risks of individual securities.
- The **expected return** on an investment is the mean value of the probability distribution of its possible returns.
- The **higher the probability** that the actual return will be far below the expected return, the **greater the risk** associated with owning an asset.
- The average investor is **risk averse** and must be compensated for holding risky securities; therefore, riskier securities must have higher expected returns than less risky securities.
- A stock's risk consists of **company-specific risk**, which can be eliminated by **diversification**, plus **market risk**, which cannot be eliminated by diversification.
- The **relevant risk** of an individual security is its contribution to the riskiness of a well-diversified **portfolio**, which in turn is the security's **market risk**. Since market risk cannot be eliminated by diversification, investors must be compensated for it.
- A stock's **beta coefficient, b,** is a measure of the stock's market risk, or the extent to which its returns move with the stock market.
- A **high-beta stock** is more volatile than an average stock, while a **low-beta stock** is less volatile than average. An **average stock** has $b = 1.0$ by definition.
- The **beta of a portfolio** is a **weighted average** of the betas of the individual securities in the portfolio.
- The **Security Market Line (SML)** shows the relationship between securities' risks and rates of return. The return required for any security i is equal to the risk-free rate plus the market risk premium times the security's beta: $k_i = k_{RF} + (k_M - k_{RF})b_i$.
- The equation shown above is sometimes referred to as the **Capital Asset Pricing Model (CAPM) Equation.**
- Even though expected rates of return on stocks are generally equal to their required returns, a number of things can happen to cause required rates of return to change: **the risk-free rate can change** because of changes in anticipated inflation; **a stock's beta can change**; or **investors' aversion to risk can change.**

- Foreign investments are similar to domestic investments, but sovereign risk and exchange rate risk must be considered. **Sovereign risk** is the risk that the foreign government will take some action which will decrease the value of the investment, while **exchange rate risk** is the risk of losses due to fluctuations in the value of the dollar relative to the values of foreign currencies.

In the next two chapters, we will see how a security's rate of return affects the value investors place on the asset. Then, in the remainder of the book, we will examine the ways in which a firm's management can influence a stock's riskiness and hence its price.

Questions

4-1   The probability distribution of a less risky expected return is more peaked than that of a riskier return. What shape would the probability distribution have for (a) completely certain returns and (b) completely uncertain returns?

4-2   Security A has an expected return of 6 percent, a standard deviation of expected returns of 30 percent, a correlation coefficient with the market of −0.25, and a beta coefficient of −0.5. Security B has an expected return of 11 percent, a standard deviation of returns of 10 percent, a correlation with the market of 0.75, and a beta coefficient of 1.0. Which security is more risky? Why?

4-3   Suppose you owned a portfolio consisting of $500,000 worth of long-term U.S. government bonds.
a. Would your portfolio be riskless?
b. Now suppose you hold a portfolio consisting of $500,000 worth of 30-day Treasury bills. Every 30 days your bills mature and you reinvest the principal ($500,000) in a new batch of bills. Assume that you live on the investment income from your portfolio and that you want to maintain a constant standard of living. Is your portfolio truly riskless?
c. You should have concluded that both long-term and short-term portfolios of government securities have some element of risk. Can you think of any asset that would be completely riskless?

4-4   A life insurance policy is a financial asset. The premiums paid represent the investment's cost.
a. How would you calculate the expected return on a life insurance policy?
b. Suppose the owner of the life insurance policy has no other financial assets — the person's only other asset is "human capital," or lifetime earnings capacity. What is the correlation coefficient between returns on the insurance policy and returns on the policyholder's human capital?
c. Life insurance companies have to pay administrative costs and sales representatives' commissions; hence, the expected rate of return on insurance premiums is generally low or even negative. Use the portfolio concept to explain why people buy life insurance in spite of negative expected returns.

4-5   If investors' aversion to risk increased, would the risk premium on a high-beta stock increase more or less than that on a low-beta stock? Explain.

Self-Test Problems   *(Solutions Appear on Page 142)*

Key terms

ST-1   Define the following terms, using graphs or equations to illustrate your answers wherever feasible:
a. Risk; probability distribution
b. Expected rate of return, $\hat{k}$
c. Standard deviation, σ; variance, σ^2; coefficient of variation
d. Risk aversion
e. Risk premium for Stock i, RP_i; market risk premium, RP_M
f. Capital Asset Pricing Model (CAPM)
g. Expected return on a portfolio, $\hat{k}_p$
h. Correlation coefficient, r
i. Market risk; company-specific risk; relevant risk
j. Beta coefficient, b; average stock's beta, b_A
k. Security Market Line (SML); SML equation
l. Slope of SML as a measure of risk aversion
m. Sovereign risk; exchange rate risk

Realized rates of return   **ST-2**   Stocks A and B have the following historical returns:

Year	Stock A's Returns, k_A	Stock B's Returns, k_B
1984	−12.24%	− 5.00%
1985	23.67	19.55
1986	35.45	44.09
1987	5.82	1.20
1988	28.30	21.16

a. Calculate the average rate of return for each stock during the period 1984 through 1988. Assume that someone held a portfolio consisting of 50 percent of Stock A and 50 percent of Stock B. What would have been the realized rate of return on the portfolio in each year from 1984 through 1988? What would have been the average return on the portfolio during this period?
b. Now calculate the standard deviation of returns for each stock and for the portfolio.
c. On the basis of the extent to which the portfolio has a lower risk than the stocks held individually, would you guess that the correlation coefficient between returns on the two stocks is closer to 0.9 or to −0.9?
d. If you added more stocks at random to the portfolio, what is the most accurate statement of what would happen to σ_p?
1. σ_p would remain constant.
2. σ_p would decline to somewhere in the vicinity of 15 percent.
3. σ_p would decline to zero if enough stocks were included.

Problems

Expected returns

4-1   Stocks A and B have the following probability distributions of expected future returns:

Probability	A	B
0.1	−25%	−40%
0.2	5	0
0.4	15	16
0.2	30	40
0.1	45	66

a. Calculate the expected rate of return, $\hat{k}$, for Stock B. ($\hat{k}_A = 15\%$.)
b. Calculate the standard deviation of expected returns for Stock A. (That for Stock B is 27.0 percent.) Now calculate the coefficient of variation for Stock B. Is it possible that most investors might regard Stock B as being *less* risky than Stock A? Explain.

Required rate of return

4-2   Suppose $k_{RF} = 10\%$, $k_M = 13\%$, and $b_C = 1.4$.
a. What is k_C, the required rate of return on Stock C?
b. Now suppose k_{RF} (1) increases to 11 percent or (2) decreases to 9 percent. The slope of the SML remains constant. How would this affect k_M and k_C?
c. Now assume k_{RF} remains at 10 percent but k_M (1) increases to 15 percent or (2) falls to 12 percent. The slope of the SML does not remain constant. How would these changes affect k_C?

Expected returns

4-3   Suppose you were offered (1) $1 million or (2) a gamble in which you would get $2 million if a head were flipped but zero if a tail came up.
a. What is the expected value of the gamble?
b. Would you take the sure $1 million or the gamble?
c. If you choose the sure $1 million, are you a risk averter or a risk seeker?
d. Suppose you actually take the sure $1 million. You can invest it in either a U.S. Treasury bond that will return $1,075,000 at the end of a year or a common stock that has a 50-50 chance of being either worthless or worth $2,300,000 at the end of the year.
   1. What is the expected dollar profit on the stock investment? (The expected profit on the T-bond investment is $75,000.)
   2. What is the expected rate of return on the stock investment? (The expected rate of return on the T-bond investment is 7.5 percent.)
   3. Would you invest in the bond or the stock?
   4. Exactly how large would the expected profit (or the expected rate of return) have to be on the stock investment to make *you* invest in the stock, given the 7.5 percent return on the bond?
   5. How might your decision be affected if, rather than buying one stock for $1 million, you could construct a portfolio consisting of 100 stocks with $10,000 invested in each? Each of these stocks has the same return characteristics as the one stock — that is, a 50-50 chance of being worth either zero or $23,000 at year-end. Would the correlation between returns on these stocks matter?

Security Market Line   **4-4**   The Mitchell Investment Fund has total capital of $400 million invested in five stocks:

Stock	Investment	Stock's Beta Coefficient
A	$120 million	0.5
B	100 million	2.0
C	60 million	4.0
D	80 million	1.0
E	40 million	3.0

The beta coefficient for a fund like Mitchell Investment can be found as a weighted average of the fund's investments. The current risk-free rate is 7 percent, whereas market returns have the following estimated probability distribution for the next period:

Probability	Market Return
0.1	8%
0.2	10
0.4	12
0.2	14
0.1	16

a. What is the estimated equation for the Security Market Line (SML)? (Hint: Determine the expected market return.)
b. Compute the fund's required rate of return for the next period.
c. Suppose John Mitchell, the president, receives a proposal for a new stock. The investment needed to take a position in the stock is $50 million; it will have an expected return of 16 percent; and its estimated beta coefficient is 2.5. Should the new stock be purchased? At what expected rate of return should Mitchell be indifferent to purchasing the stock?

Realized rates of return   **4-5**   Stocks A and B have the following historical returns:

Year	Stock A's Returns, k_A	Stock B's Returns, k_B
1984	− 20.00%	− 11.04%
1985	20.00	19.44
1986	33.17	43.61
1987	− 1.98	− 6.26
1988	25.80	11.24

a. Calculate the average rate of return for each stock during the period 1984 through 1988.
b. Assume that someone held a portfolio consisting of 50 percent of Stock A and 50 percent of Stock B. What would have been the realized rate of return on the portfolio in each year from 1984 through 1988? What would have been the average return on the portfolio during this period?
c. Calculate the standard deviation of returns for each stock and for the portfolio.
d. Calculate the coefficient of variation for each stock and for the portfolio.

e. If you are a risk-averse investor, would you prefer to hold Stock A, Stock B, or the portfolio? Why?

Risk and return
(Integrative)

4-6   Jan Berger, who recently graduated with a major in finance, has landed a job in the trust department of a large regional bank. Her first assignment is to invest $100,000 from an estate for which the bank is trustee. Because the estate is expected to be distributed to heirs in about one year, Berger has been instructed to plan for a one-year holding period. Further, her boss has restricted her to the following investment alternatives:

State of the Economy	Probability	T-Bills	Estimated Rate of Return High Tech	Goldmines	U.S. Rubber	Market Portfolio
Recession	0.1	8.0%	− 22.0%	28.0%	10.0%	− 13.0%
Below average	0.2	8.0	− 2.0	14.7	− 10.0	1.0
Average	0.4	8.0	20.0	0.0	7.0	15.0
Above average	0.2	8.0	35.0	− 10.0	45.0	29.0
Boom	0.1	8.0	50.0	− 20.0	30.0	43.0
	1.0					

The bank's economic and forecasting staff developed probability estimates for the state of the economy, and the trust department has a sophisticated computer program which estimated the rate of return on each alternative under each state of the economy. High Tech, Inc., is an electronics firm; Goldmines Corporation owns gold mines in the United States and Canada; and U.S. Rubber manufactures tires and various other rubber and plastics products. The bank also maintains an "index fund" which owns a market-weighted fraction of all publicly traded stocks, and Berger can invest in that fund and thus obtain average stock market results. Place yourself in Berger's position, and answer the following questions:

a. Why is the T-bill return independent of the state of the economy? Do T-bills promise a completely risk-free return? Why do High Tech's returns move with the economy whereas Goldmines' are estimated to move counter to the economy?

b. Calculate the expected rate of return on each alternative. Based solely on expected returns, which alternative should Berger choose?

c. Berger recognizes that basing a decision solely on expected returns is only appropriate for risk-neutral individuals. Since the beneficiaries of Berger's trust, like virtually everyone, are risk-averse, the riskiness of each alternative is an important aspect of the decision. One possible measure of risk is the standard deviation of returns. Calculate this value for each alternative. What type of risk is measured by the standard deviation?

d. Berger just remembered that the coefficient of variation (CV) is generally regarded as being a better measure of total risk than the standard deviation when the alternatives being considered have widely differing expected returns. Calculate the CVs for the different securities. Does the CV produce the same risk rankings as the standard deviation?

e. Berger wondered what would happen if she created a two-stock portfolio by investing $50,000 in High Tech and $50,000 in Goldmines. What is the expected return and the standard deviation for this portfolio? How does the riskiness of the portfolio compare to the riskiness of the individual stocks?

f. The expected rates of return and the beta coefficients of the alternatives as supplied by the bank's computer program are as follows:

Security	Return ($\hat{k}$)	Risk (Beta)
High Tech	17.4%	1.29
Market	15.0	1.00
U.S. Rubber	13.8	0.68
T-bills	8.0	0.00
Goldmines	1.7	−0.86

What is a beta coefficient, and how is it used in risk analysis? Do the expected returns appear to be related to each alternative's market risk? Is it possible to choose among the alternatives on the basis of the information developed thus far?

g. Construct a Security Market Line (SML) and use it to calculate the required rate of return on each alternative. How do the expected rates of return compare with the required rates of return? Does the fact that Goldmines has a negative required rate of return make any sense? What is the market risk and the required return of a 50-50 portfolio of High Tech and Goldmines? Of High Tech and U.S. Rubber?

h. Suppose investors raised their inflation expectations by 3 percentage points over current estimates as reflected in the 8 percent T-bill rate. What effect would this have on the SML and on the returns of high- and low-risk securities? Suppose instead that investors' risk aversion increased enough to cause the market risk premium to increase by 3 percentage points. What effect would this have on the SML and on returns of high- and low-risk securities?

Computer-Related Problem

(Work the problem in this section only if you are using the computer problem diskette.)

Realized rates of return   **C4-1**   Using the computerized model for Problem C4-1 in the file C4, rework Problem 4-5, assuming that a third stock, Stock C, is available for inclusion in the portfolio. Stock C has the following historical returns:

Year	Stock C's Returns, k_C
1984	37.19%
1985	−13.31
1986	7.75
1987	30.50
1988	−5.13

a. Calculate (or read from the computer screen) the average return, standard deviation, and coefficient of variation for Stock C.

b. Assume that the portfolio now consists of 33.33 percent of Stock A, 33.33 percent of Stock B, and 33.33 percent of Stock C. How does this affect the portfolio return, standard deviation, and coefficient of variation versus when 50 percent was invested in A and in B?

c. Make some other changes in the portfolio, making sure that the percentages sum to 100 percent. For example, enter 25 percent for Stock A, 25 percent for Stock B, and 50 percent for Stock C. (Note that the program will not allow you to enter a zero for the percentage in Stock C.) Notice that k_p remains constant and that σ_p changes. Why do these results occur?

d. In Problem 4-5, the standard deviation of the portfolio decreased only slightly because Stocks A and B were highly positively correlated with one another. In this problem, the addition of Stock C causes the standard deviation of the portfolio to decline dramatically, even though $\sigma_C = \sigma_A = \sigma_B$. What does this indicate about the correlation between Stock C and Stocks A and B?

e. Would you prefer to hold the portfolio described in Problem 4-5 consisting only of Stocks A and B or a portfolio that also included Stock C? If others react similarly, how might this affect the stocks' prices and rates of return?

Solutions to Self-Test Problems

ST-1   Refer to the marginal glossary definitions and appropriate sections of the text to check your responses.

ST-2   a. The average rate of return for each stock is calculated by simply averaging the returns over the five-year period. The average return for each stock is 16.20 percent, calculated for Stock A as follows:

$$k_{Avg} = (-12.24\% + 23.67\% + 35.45\% + 5.82\% + 28.30\%)/5$$

$$= 16.20\%.$$

The realized rate of return on a portfolio made up of Stock A and Stock B would be calculated by finding the average return in each year as $k_A(\%$ of Stock A$) + k_B(\%$ of Stock B$)$ and then averaging these yearly returns.

Year	Portfolio AB's Return, k_{AB}
1984	− 8.62%
1985	21.61
1986	39.77
1987	3.51
1988	24.73
	k_{Avg} = 16.20%

b. The standard deviation of returns is estimated, using Equation 4-3a, as follows (see Footnote 5):

$$\text{Estimated } \sigma = S = \sqrt{\frac{\sum_{t=1}^{n}(\bar{k}_t - \bar{k}_{Avg})^2}{n - 1}}. \qquad (4\text{-}3a)$$

For Stock A, the estimated σ is 19.3 percent:

$$\sigma_A = \sqrt{\frac{(-12.24 - 16.2)^2 + (23.67 - 16.2)^2 + \ldots + (28.30 - 16.2)^2}{5 - 1}}$$

$$= \sqrt{\frac{1,489.35}{4}} = 19.3\%.$$

The standard deviation of returns for Stock B and for the portfolio are similarly determined, and they are as follows:

	Stock A	Stock B	Portfolio AB
Standard deviation	19.3	19.3	18.9

c. Since the risk reduction from diversification is small (σ_{AB} falls only from 19.3 to 18.9 percent), the most likely value of the correlation coefficient is 0.9. If the correlation coefficient were -0.9, the risk reduction would be much larger. In fact, the correlation coefficient between Stocks A and B is 0.93.

d. If more randomly selected stocks were added to the portfolio, σ_p would decline to somewhere in the vicinity of 15 percent; see Figure 4-7. σ_p would remain constant only if the correlation coefficient were $+1.0$, which is most unlikely. σ_p would decline to zero only if the correlation coefficient, r, were equal to zero and a large number of stocks were added to the portfolio, or if the proper proportions were held in a two-stock portfolio with $r = -1.0$.

4A   Calculating Beta Coefficients

The CAPM is an *ex ante* model, which means that all of the variables represent before-the-fact, *expected* values. In particular, the beta coefficient used in the SML equation should reflect the expected volatility of a given stock's return versus the return on the market during some *future* period. However, people generally calculate betas using data from some *past* period and then assume that the stocks' relative volatility will be the same in the future as it was in the past.

Figure 4A-1   Calculating Beta Coefficients

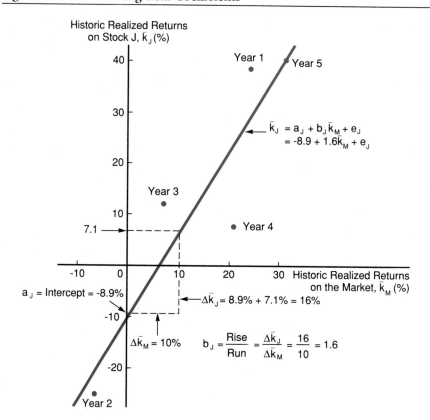

Year	Stock J($\bar{k}_J$)	Market ($\bar{k}_M$)
1	38.6%	23.8%
2	−24.7	−7.2
3	12.3	6.6
4	8.2	20.5
5	40.1	30.6
Average $\bar{k}$	14.9%	14.9%
$\sigma_{\bar{k}}$	26.5%	15.1%

To illustrate how betas are calculated, consider Figure 4A-1. The data at the bottom of the figure show the historical realized returns for Stock J and for the market over the last five years. The data points have been plotted on the scatter diagram, and a regression line has been drawn. If all the data points had fallen on a straight line, as they did in Figure 4-8 in Chapter 4, it would be easy to draw an accurate line. If they do not, as in Figure 4A-1, then you must fit the line either "by eye" as an approximation or by statistical procedures.

Recall what the term *regression line,* or *regression equation,* means: The equation $Y = a + bX + e$ is the standard form of a simple linear regression. It states that the dependent variable, Y, is equal to a constant, a, plus b times X, where b is the slope coefficient (or parameter) and X is the independent variable, plus an error term, e. Thus, the rate of return on the stock during a given time period (Y) depends on what happens to the general stock market, which is measured by $X = \bar{k}_M$.

Once the line has been drawn on graph paper, we can estimate its intercept and slope, the a and b values in $Y = a + bX$. The intercept, a, is simply the point where the line cuts the vertical axis. The slope coefficient, b, can be estimated by the "rise over run" method. This involves calculating the amount by which $\bar{k}_J$ increases for a given increase in $\bar{k}_M$. For example, we observe in Figure 4A-1 that $\bar{k}_J$ increases from -8.9 to $+7.1$ percent (the rise) when $\bar{k}_M$ increases from 0 to 10.0 percent (the run). Thus b, the beta coefficient, can be measured as follows:

$$b = \text{Beta} = \frac{\text{Rise}}{\text{Run}} = \frac{\Delta Y}{\Delta X} = \frac{7.1 - (-8.9)}{10.0 - 0.0} = \frac{16.0}{10.0} = 1.6.$$

Note that rise over run is a ratio, and it would be the same if measured using any two arbitrarily selected points on the line.

The regression line equation enables us to predict a rate of return for Stock J, given a value of $\bar{k}_M$. For example, if $\bar{k}_M = 15\%$, we would predict $\bar{k}_J = -8.9\% + 1.6(15\%) = 15.1\%$. However, the actual return would probably differ from the predicted return. This deviation is the error term, e_J, for the year, and it varies randomly from year to year depending on company-specific factors.

In actual practice, monthly rather than annual returns are generally used for $\bar{k}_J$ and $\bar{k}_M$, and five years of data are employed; thus, there would be $5 \times 12 = 60$ dots on the scatter diagram. Also, in practice one would use the *least squares method* for finding the regression coefficients a and b; this procedure minimizes the squared values of the error terms. It is discussed in statistics courses.

The least squares value of beta can be obtained quite easily with a computer or even with a calculator that has statistical functions. The procedures that follow explain how to find the values of beta and the slope using either a Texas Instruments, a Hewlett-Packard, or a Sharp financial calculator.

Texas Instruments BA, BA-II, or MBA Calculator

1. Press **2nd** **Mode** until "STAT" shows in the display.

2. Enter the first X value ($\bar{k}_M = 23.8$ in our example), press **x≶y**, and then enter the first Y value ($\bar{k}_J = 38.6$) and press **Σ+**.

3. Repeat Step 2 until all values have been entered.

4. Press **2nd** **b/a** to find the value of Y at $X = 0$, which is the value of the Y intercept (a), -8.9219, and then press **x≶y** to display the value of the slope (beta), 1.6031.

5. You could also press **2nd** **Corr** to obtain the correlation coefficient, r, which is 0.9134.

Putting it all together, you should have this regression line:

$$\bar{k}_J = -8.92 + 1.60\bar{k}_M.$$

$$r = 0.9134.$$

Hewlett-Packard 12C[1]

1. Press $\boxed{f}$ $\boxed{CLx}$ to clear your memory registers.
2. Enter the first Y value ($\bar{k}_J = 38.6$ in our example), press $\boxed{ENTER}$, and then enter the first X value ($\bar{k}_M = 23.8$) and press $\boxed{\Sigma+}$.
3. Repeat Step 2 until all values have been entered.
4. Press $\boxed{0}$ $\boxed{g}$ $\boxed{\hat{y},r}$ to find the value of Y at X = 0, which is the value of the Y intercept (a), -8.9219.
5. Press $\boxed{STO}$ $\boxed{0}$ to store the value of the Y intercept for use in calculating the slope (beta).
6. Press $\boxed{0}$ $\boxed{g}$ $\boxed{\hat{x},r}$ to find the value of X at Y = 0, which is the value of the X intercept, 5.5655.
7. Press $\boxed{RCL}$ $\boxed{0}$ $\boxed{CHS}$ $\boxed{x \leqslant y}$ $\boxed{\div}$ to calculate and display the value of the slope (beta), 1.6031.
8. You can also press $\boxed{0}$ $\boxed{g}$ $\boxed{\hat{y},r}$ $\boxed{x \leqslant y}$ to obtain the correlation coefficient, r, which is 0.9134 in this case.
    Putting it all together, you should have this regression line:

$$\bar{k}_J = -8.92 + 1.60\bar{k}_M.$$

$$r = 0.9134.$$

Sharp EL-733

1. Press $\boxed{2nd\ F}$ $\boxed{Mode}$ until "STAT" shows in the lower right corner of the display.
2. Press $\boxed{2nd\ F}$ $\boxed{CA}$ to clear all memory registers.
3. Enter the first X value ($k_M = 23.8$ in our example), press $\boxed{(x,y)}$, and then enter the first Y value ($k_J = 38.6$) and press $\boxed{DATA}$.
4. Repeat Step 3 until all values have been entered.
5. Press $\boxed{2nd\ F}$ $\boxed{a}$ to find the value of Y at X = 0, which is the value of the Y intercept (a), -8.9219, and then press $\boxed{2nd\ F}$ $\boxed{b}$ to display the value of the slope (beta), 1.6031.
6. You can also press $\boxed{2nd\ F}$ $\boxed{r}$ to obtain the correlation coefficient, r, which is 0.9134.

---

[1]The new Hewlett-Packard calculator, the 17B, is even easier to use. If you have one, see Chapter 9 of the *Owner's Manual*.

Putting it all together, you should have this regression line:

$$\bar{k}_j = -8.92 + 1.60\bar{k}_M.$$

$$r = 0.9134.$$

Problems

Beta coefficients and rates of return

4A-1   You are given the following set of data:

	Historic Rates of Return ($\bar{k}$)	
Year	Stock Y($\bar{k}_Y$)	NYSE ($\bar{k}_M$)
1	3.0%	4.0%
2	18.2	14.3
3	9.1	19.0
4	− 6.0	− 14.7
5	− 15.3	− 26.5
6	33.1	37.2
7	6.1	23.8
8	3.2	− 7.2
9	14.8	6.6
10	24.1	20.5
11	18.0	30.6
Mean	9.8%	9.8%
$\sigma_{\bar{k}}$	13.8	19.6

a. Construct a scatter diagram graph (*on graph paper*) showing the relationship between returns on Stock Y and the market as in Figure 4A-1; then draw a freehand approximation of the regression line. What is the approximate value of the beta coefficient? (If you have a calculator with statistical functions, use it to calculate beta.)

b. Give a verbal interpretation of what the regression line and the beta coefficient show about Stock Y's volatility and relative riskiness as compared with other stocks.

c. Suppose the scatter of points had been more spread out but the regression line was exactly where your present graph shows it. How would this affect (1) the firm's risk if the stock were held in a one-asset portfolio and (2) the actual risk premium on the stock if the CAPM held exactly? How would the degree of scatter (or the correlation coefficient) affect your confidence that the calculated beta will hold true in the years ahead?

d. Suppose the regression line had been downward sloping and the beta coefficient had been negative. What would this imply about (1) Stock Y's relative riskiness and (2) its probable risk premium?

e. Construct an illustrative probability distribution graph of returns (see Figure 4-6) on portfolios consisting of (1) only Stock Y, (2) 1 percent each of 100 stocks with beta coefficients similar to that of Stock Y, and (3) all stocks (that is, the distribution of returns on the market). Use as the expected rate of return the arithmetic mean as given previously for both Stock Y and the market, and assume that the distributions are normal. Are the expected returns "reasonable" — that is, is it reasonable that $\hat{k}_Y = \hat{k}_M = 9.8\%$?

f. Now suppose that in the next year, Year 12, the market return was 27 percent but Firm Y increased its use of debt, which raised its perceived risk to investors. Do you think that the return on Stock Y in Year 12 could be approximated by this historical characteristic line?

$$\hat{k}_Y = 3.8\% + 0.62(\hat{k}_M) = 3.8\% + 0.62(27\%) = 20.5\%.$$

g. Now suppose $\hat{k}_Y$ in Year 12, after the debt ratio was increased, had actually been 0 percent. What would the new beta be, based on the most recent 11 years of data (that is, Years 2 through 12)? Does this beta seem reasonable — that is, is the change in beta consistent with the other facts given in the problem?

Security Market Line   **4A-2**   You are given the following historical data on market returns, $\bar{k}_M$, and the returns on Stocks A and B, $\bar{k}_A$ and $\bar{k}_B$:

Year	$\bar{k}_M$	$\bar{k}_A$	$\bar{k}_B$
1	37.2%	37.2%	26.1%
2	23.8	23.8	19.4
3	− 7.2	− 7.2	3.9
4	6.6	6.6	10.8
5	20.5	20.5	17.7
6	30.6	30.6	22.8

k_{RF}, the risk-free rate, is 10 percent. Your probability distribution for k_M for next year is as follows:

Probability	k_M
0.1	− 15%
0.2	0
0.4	15
0.2	30
0.1	45

a. Determine graphically the beta coefficients for Stocks A and B.
b. Graph the Security Market Line and give its equation.
c. Calculate the required rates of return on Stocks A and B.
d. Suppose a new stock, C, with $\hat{k}_C = 16$ percent and $b_C = 2.0$ becomes available. Is this stock in equilibrium; that is, does the required rate of return on Stock C equal its expected return? Explain. If the stock is not in equilibrium, explain how equilibrium will be restored.

5

Time Value of Money

HOW THE VALUE OF MONEY CHANGES
OVER TIME, *or* WHAT BANK OF
AMERICA BONDS, YOUR COLLEGE
EDUCATION, AND A GM ELECTRIC
CAR HAVE IN COMMON

The managers of IBM's pension plan were recently offered the opportunity to buy some Bank of America bonds which cost $590 per bond, pay *zero* interest during their lifetime, but then will pay $1,000 when they mature 5 years later. At the same time, IBM's fund managers were offered "regular" Bank of America bonds which cost $830, pay interest of $87.50 per year, and then will return $1,000 when they mature in 13 years. Which is the better buy, the zero interest bonds or the "regular" bonds?

A father, concerned about the rapidly rising cost of a college education, is planning a savings program to put his daughter through college. She is now 13 years old, plans to enroll in the university in 5 years, and should take 4 years to complete her education. Currently, the cost per year (for everything—food, clothing, tuition, books, transportation, and so forth) is $8,000, but a 6 percent inflation rate in these costs is forecasted. The daughter recently received $5,000 from her grandfather's estate; this money is invested in a bank account which pays 9 percent interest, compounded annually. How much will the father have to deposit each year from now to the time his daughter starts college in order to put her through school?

Suppose that in January 1989 General Motors' engineers informed top management that they had just made a breakthrough which would permit them to produce an electric car capable of operating at an energy cost of

149

about 3 cents per mile versus an energy cost of about 5 cents for a comparable gasoline-powered car. If GM produces the electric car, it should be able to regain the market share previously lost to the Japanese. However, the investment required to complete development of the new batteries, to design the new car, and to tool up for production would amount to $6 billion per year for 5 years, starting immediately. Cash flows from the $30 billion investment should amount to $4 billion per year for 15 years, starting 5 years from now, or $60 billion in total. Assuming these costs and cash flow estimates are correct (and they are obviously subject to more forecasting errors than if GM simply bought $30 billion of Treasury bonds), should management give the go-ahead for full-scale electric car production? These are the types of questions this chapter is designed to help you answer.

IN Chapter 1 we saw that the primary goal of the financial manager is to maximize the value of a firm's stock. We also saw that stock values depend in part on the timing of the cash flows investors expect to receive from an investment—a dollar expected soon is worth more than a dollar expected in the distant future. Therefore, it is essential that financial managers have a clear understanding of discounted cash flow analysis and its impact on the value of the firm. These concepts are extended and made more precise in this chapter, where we show how the timing of cash flows affects asset values and rates of return.

The principles of discounted cash flow analysis as developed here also have many other applications, ranging from setting up schedules for paying off loans to making decisions about whether to acquire new equipment. *In fact, of all the techniques used in finance, none is more important than the concept of the time value of money, or discounted cash flow (DCF) analysis.* Since this concept is used throughout the remainder of the book, it is vital that you understand the material in this chapter thoroughly before going on to other topics.[1]

---

[1]This chapter, and indeed the entire book, is written on the assumption that some students may not have financial calculators. The cost of these calculators is falling rapidly, however, so many students will have them. As a result, procedures for obtaining financial calculator solutions are set forth in each of the major sections, along with procedures for obtaining solutions by using regular calculators or tables. It is highly desirable for each student to obtain a financial calculator and to learn how to use it, for calculators — and not clumsy, rounded, and incomplete tables — are used exclusively in well-run, efficient businesses.

Even though financial calculators are efficient, they do pose a danger: People sometimes learn how to use them in a "cookbook" fashion without understanding the logical processes that underlie the calculations, and then, when confronted with a new type of problem, they cannot figure out how to set it up. Therefore, you are urged not only to get a good calculator and to learn how to use it but also to work through the illustrative problems "the long way" to insure that you understand the concepts involved.

FUTURE VALUE

compounding
The arithmetic process of determining the final value of a payment or series of payments when compound interest is applied.

A dollar in hand today is worth more than a dollar to be received next year because, if you had it now, you could invest it, earn interest, and end up next year with more than one dollar. The process of finding future values is called **compounding**. To illustrate compounding, let us suppose you had $100 which you deposited in a bank savings account that paid 5 percent interest compounded annually. How much would you have at the end of 1 year? Let us define terms as follows:

PV = $100 = present value of your account, or the beginning amount.

k = 5% = interest rate the bank pays you per year. Expressed as a decimal, k = 0.05. On financial calculators, the term i is frequently used rather than k.

I = dollars of interest you earn during the year = k(PV).

FV_n = future value, or ending amount, of your account at the end of n years. Whereas PV is the value now, at the *present* time, FV_n is the value n years into the *future,* after compound interest has been earned. Note also that FV_0 is the future value *zero* years into the future, which is the *present,* so FV_0 = PV.

n = number of years or, more generally, periods, involved in the transaction.

In our example, n = 1, so FV_n = FV_1, is calculated as follows:

$$FV_1 = PV + I$$

$$= PV + PV(k)$$

$$= PV(1 + k). \tag{5-1}$$

future value, FV
The amount to which a payment or series of payments will grow over a given future time period when compounded at a given interest rate.

In words, the **future value, FV**, at the end of 1 period is the present value times 1 plus the interest rate.

We can now use Equation 5-1 to find how much your $100 will be worth at the end of 1 year at a 5 percent interest rate:

$$FV_1 = \$100(1 + 0.05) = \$100(1.05) = \$105.$$

Your account will earn $5 of interest (I = $5), so you will have $105 at the end of the year.

Now suppose you leave your funds on deposit for 5 years; how much will you have at the end of the fifth year? The answer is $127.63; this value is worked out in Table 5-1. Notice the following points: (1) You start with $100, earn $5 of interest during the first year, and end the year with $105 in your account. (2) You start the second year with $105, earn $5.25 on this now larger account, and end the second year with $110.25. Your second-year earnings, $5.25, were higher because you earned interest on the first year's interest. (3) This process continues, and because in each year the beginning balance is

Table 5-1   Compound Interest Calculations

Year	Amount at Beginning of Year, PV	×	(1 + k)	=	Amount at End of Year, FV_n	Interest Earned, PV(k)
1	$100.00		1.05		$105.00	$ 5.00
2	105.00		1.05		110.25	5.25
3	110.25		1.05		115.76	5.51
4	115.76		1.05		121.55	5.79
5	121.55		1.05		127.63	6.08
						$27.63

higher, your interest income increases. (4) The total interest earned, $27.63, is reflected in the ending balance, $127.63.

Notice that the Table 5-1 value for FV_2, the value of the account at the end of Year 2, is equal to

$$FV_2 = FV_1(1 + k)$$
$$= PV(1 + k)(1 + k)$$
$$= PV(1 + k)^2$$
$$= \$100(1.05)^2$$
$$= \$110.25.$$

Continuing, we see that FV_3, the balance after Year 3, is

$$FV_3 = FV_2(1 + k)$$
$$= PV(1 + k)^3$$
$$= \$100(1.05)^3$$
$$= \$115.76.$$

In general, FV_n, the future value at the end of n years, is found as follows:

$$FV_n = PV(1 + k)^n. \tag{5-2}$$

Applying Equation 5-2 to our 5-year, 5 percent case, we obtain

$$FV_5 = \$100(1.05)^5$$
$$= \$100(1.2763) \quad \text{ANNUAL}$$
$$= \$127.63,$$

which is the same as the value worked out in Table 5-1.

We can solve future value problems in three ways:

1. **Use a regular calculator.** One can simply use a regular calculator, either by multiplying (1 + k) by itself n − 1 times or by using the exponential function to raise (1 + k) to the *n*th power. In our example, you would

Table 5-2   Future Value of $1 at the End of n Periods:

$$FVIF_{k,n} = (1 + k)^n$$

Period (n)	1%	2%	3%	4%	5%	6%	7%	8%	9%	10%
1	1.0100	1.0200	1.0300	1.0400	1.0500	1.0600	1.0700	1.0800	1.0900	1.1000
2	1.0201	1.0404	1.0609	1.0816	1.1025	1.1236	1.1449	1.1664	1.1881	1.2100
3	1.0303	1.0612	1.0927	1.1249	1.1576	1.1910	1.2250	1.2597	1.2950	1.3310
4	1.0406	1.0824	1.1255	1.1699	1.2155	1.2625	1.3108	1.3605	1.4116	1.4641
5	1.0510	1.1041	1.1593	1.2167	1.2763	1.3382	1.4026	1.4693	1.5386	1.6105
6	1.0615	1.1262	1.1941	1.2653	1.3401	1.4185	1.5007	1.5869	1.6771	1.7716
7	1.0721	1.1487	1.2299	1.3159	1.4071	1.5036	1.6058	1.7138	1.8280	1.9487
8	1.0829	1.1717	1.2668	1.3686	1.4775	1.5938	1.7182	1.8509	1.9926	2.1436
9	1.0937	1.1951	1.3048	1.4233	1.5513	1.6895	1.8385	1.9990	2.1719	2.3579
10	1.1046	1.2190	1.3439	1.4802	1.6289	1.7908	1.9672	2.1589	2.3674	2.5937

enter $1 + k = 1.05$ and multiply it by itself four times, or else enter 1.05, enter 5, and then press the y^x (or exponential) function key. In either case, you would get the factor $(1.05)^5 = 1.2763$, which you would then multiply by $100 to get the final answer, $127.63.

future value interest factor for k,n, ($FVIF_{k,n}$) The future value of $1 left in an account for n periods paying k percent per period, which is equal to $(1 + k)^n$.

2. **Use compound interest tables.** The term **future value interest factor for k,n ($FVIF_{k,n}$)** is defined as being equal to $(1 + k)^n$, and tables have been constructed for values of $(1 + k)^n$ for a wide range of k and n values. Table 5-2 is illustrative, and a more complete table, with more years and more interest rates, is given in Table A-3 in Appendix A at the end of the book.[2]

Equation 5-2 can be written as $FV_n = PV(FVIF_{k,n})$. It is necessary only to go to an appropriate interest table (5-2 or A-3) to find the proper interest factor. For example, the correct interest factor for our 5-year, 5 percent illustration can be found in Table 5-2. We look down the period column to 5 and then across this row to the 5 percent column to find the interest factor, 1.2763. Then, using this interest factor, we find the value of $100 after 5 years to be $FV_5 = PV(FVIF_{5\%, 5\ years}) = \$100(1.2763) = \$127.63$, which is identical to the value obtained by the long method in Table 5-1.

3. **Use a financial calculator.** Financial calculators have been programmed to solve most future value problems. In effect, the calculators first generate the $FVIF_{k,n}$ factors for a specified pair of k and n values, and then multiply the computed factor by the PV to produce the FV. In our illustrative problem, you simply enter PV = $100, k = i = 5%, and

---

[2]Notice that we have used the word *period* rather than *year* in Table 5-2. As we shall see later in the chapter, compounding can occur over periods of time other than one year. Thus, although interest is often compounded on an annual basis, it can be compounded quarterly, semiannually, monthly, or over any other period.

Figure 5-1   Relationship between Future Value Interest Factors, Interest Rates, and Time

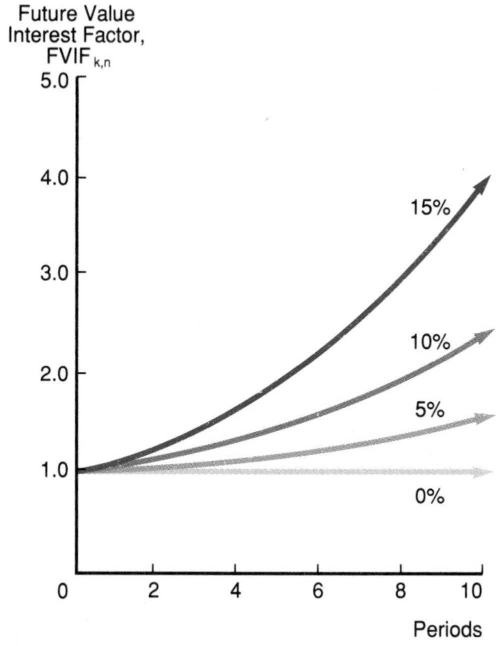

n = 5, then press the FV key, and the answer, $127.63 rounded to two decimal places, will appear. (The FV will appear with a minus sign on some calculators. The logic behind the negative output is that you put in the initial amount (the PV) and take out the ending amount (the FV), so one is an inflow and the other is an outflow, and the negative sign reminds you of that. At this point, though, you can ignore the minus sign.)

The most efficient way to solve most problems is to use a financial calculator. Therefore, you should get one and learn how to use it. However, you ought to understand how the tables are developed and used, and you should also understand the logic and the math that underlie all types of financial analysis. Otherwise, you simply will not understand stock and bond valuation, lease analysis, capital budgeting, and other critically important topics.

Graphic View of the Compounding Process: Growth

Figure 5-1 shows how $1 (or any other sum) grows over time at various rates of interest. The 5 and 10 percent curves are based on the values given in Table 5-2. The higher the rate of interest, the faster the rate of growth. The interest rate is, in fact, a growth rate. If a sum is deposited and earns 5 percent, then the funds on deposit grow at the rate of 5 percent per period. Note that these formulas can be applied to anything that is growing — sales, population, earnings per share, or what have you. If you ever need to figure the growth rate of anything, the formulas in this chapter can be used.

PRESENT VALUE

Suppose you are offered the alternative of receiving either $127.63 at the end of 5 years or X dollars today. There is no question that the $127.63 will be paid in full (perhaps the payer is the U.S. government). Having no current need for the money, you would deposit the X dollars in a bank account that pays 5 percent interest. (Five percent is defined to be your *opportunity cost,* or the rate of interest you could earn on alternative investments of equal risk.) What value of X would make you indifferent in your choice between X dollars today and the promise of $127.63 five years hence?

From Table 5-1 we saw that the initial amount of $100 growing at 5 percent a year will be worth $127.63 at the end of 5 years. Thus, you should be indifferent to the choice between $100 today and $127.63 at the end of 5 years. The $100 is defined as the **present value**, or **PV**, of $127.63 due in 5 years when the opportunity cost rate is 5 percent. Therefore, if X is anything less than $100, you should prefer the promise of $127.63 in 5 years to X dollars today; if X were greater than $100, you should prefer X.

In general, the present value of a sum due n years in the future is the amount which, if it were on hand today, would grow to equal the future sum. Since $100 would grow to $127.63 in 5 years at a 5 percent interest rate, $100 is the present value of $127.63 due 5 years in the future when the appropriate interest rate is 5 percent.

Finding present values — or **discounting**, as it is commonly called — is simply the reverse of compounding, and Equation 5-2 can be transformed into a present value formula:

$$FV_n = PV(1 + k)^n, \qquad (5\text{-}2)$$

which, when solved for PV, gives

$$PV = \frac{FV_n}{(1 + k)^n} = FV_n(1 + k)^{-n} = FV_n\left(\frac{1}{1 + k}\right)^n. \qquad (5\text{-}3)$$

Tables have been constructed for the term in parentheses for various values of k and n; Table 5-3 is an example. (For a more complete table, see Table A-1 in Appendix A at the end of the book.) For our illustrative case, look down the 5 percent column in Table 5-3 to the fifth row. The figure shown there, 0.7835, is the **present value interest factor** ($PVIF_{k,n}$) used to determine the present value of $127.63 payable in 5 years, discounted at 5 percent:

present value, PV
The value today of a future payment or series of payments discounted at the appropriate discount rate.

discounting
The process of finding the present value of a payment or a series of future cash flows; the reverse of compounding.

present value interest factor ($PVIF_{k,n}$)
The present value of $1 due n periods in the future discounted at k percent per period.

Table 5-3   Present Value of $1 Due at the End of n Periods:

$$PVIF_{k,n} = \frac{1}{(1 + k)^n} = \left(\frac{1}{1 + k}\right)^n$$

Period (n)	1%	2%	3%	4%	5%	6%	7%	8%	9%	10%
1	.9901	.9804	.9709	.9615	.9524	.9434	.9346	.9259	.9174	.9091
2	.9803	.9612	.9426	.9246	.9070	.8900	.8734	.8573	.8417	.8264
3	.9706	.9423	.9151	.8890	.8638	.8396	.8163	.7938	.7722	.7513
4	.9610	.9238	.8885	.8548	.8227	.7921	.7629	.7350	.7084	.6830
5	.9515	.9057	.8626	.8219	.7835	.7473	.7130	.6806	.6499	.6209
6	.9420	.8880	.8375	.7903	.7462	.7050	.6663	.6302	.5963	.5645
7	.9327	.8706	.8131	.7599	.7107	.6651	.6227	.5835	.5470	.5132
8	.9235	.8535	.7894	.7307	.6768	.6274	.5820	.5403	.5019	.4665
9	.9143	.8368	.7664	.7026	.6446	.5919	.5439	.5002	.4604	.4241
10	.9053	.8203	.7441	.6756	.6139	.5584	.5083	.4632	.4224	.3855

$$PV = FV_5(PVIF_{5\%, 5\ years})$$

$$= \$127.63(0.7835)$$

$$= \$100.$$

Again, you could use a regular calculator to find the PVIF and a financial calculator to find the PV of $100. With a financial calculator, just enter n = 5, k = i = 5, and FV = 127.63, and then press the PV button to find PV = $100. (On some calculators, the PV will be given as −$100. Also, on some calculators you may need to press the Compute key before pressing the PV button.)

Graphic View of the Discounting Process

Figure 5-2 shows how interest factors for discounting decrease as the discounting period increases. The curves in the figure, which were plotted with data taken from Table 5-3, show that the present value of a sum to be received at some future date decreases as the payment date is extended further into the future, and the rate of decrease is steeper as the interest (or discount) rate increases. If relatively high discount rates apply, funds due in the future are worth very little today, and even at relatively low discount rates, the present values of funds due in the distant future are quite small. For example, $1 due in 10 years is worth about 61 cents today if the discount rate is 5 percent, but it is worth only 25 cents at a 15 percent discount rate. Similarly, $1 due in 5 years at 10 percent is worth 62 cents today, but at the same discount rate $1 due in 10 years is worth only 39 cents today. At a 15 percent discount rate, $1 due in 50 years is worth only $0.0009, or 9/10,000 of $1, today.

Figure 5-2   Relationship between Present Value Interest Factors, Interest Rates, and Time

---

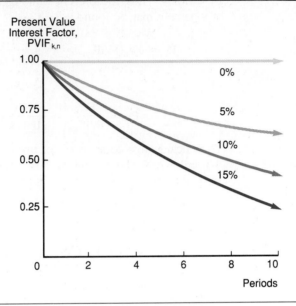

FUTURE VALUE VERSUS PRESENT VALUE

Equation 5-2, the basic equation for compounding, was developed from the logical sequence set forth in Table 5-1; the equation merely presents in mathematical form the steps outlined in the table. The present value interest factor ($PVIF_{k,n}$) in Equation 5-3, the basic equation for discounting or finding present values, was found as the *reciprocal* of the future value interest factor ($FVIF_{k,n}$) for the same k,n combination:

$$PVIF_{k,n} = \frac{1}{FVIF_{k,n}}.$$

Therefore, since the *future value* interest factor for 5 percent over 5 years is seen in Table 5-2 to be 1.2763, the *present value* interest factor for 5 percent over 5 years must be the reciprocal of 1.2763:

$$PVIF_{5\%,5\ years} = \frac{1}{1.2763} = 0.7835.$$

The $PVIF_{k,n}$ found in this manner does, of course, correspond with that shown in Table 5-3.

The reciprocal nature of the relationship between present values and future values permits us to find present values in two ways—by multiplying or by dividing. Thus, the present value of $1,000 due in 5 years and discounted at 5 percent may be found as

$$PV = FV_n(PVIF_{k,n}) = FV_5\left(\frac{1}{1 + k}\right)^5 = \$1,000(0.7835) = \$783.50,$$

or as

$$PV = \frac{FV_n}{FVIF_{k,n}} = \frac{FV_5}{(1 + k)^5} = \frac{\$1,000}{1.2763} = \$783.50.$$

To conclude this comparison of present and future values, compare Figures 5-1 and 5-2. Notice that the vertical intercept is at 1.0 in each case, but future value interest factors rise whereas present value interest factors decline.[3]

FUTURE VALUE OF AN ANNUITY

annuity
A series of payments of an equal amount for a specified number of periods.

An **annuity** *is defined as a series of payments of an equal, or constant, amount of money at fixed intervals for a specified number of periods.* Payments are given the symbol PMT, and if they occur at the end of each period, as they typically do, then we have an *ordinary annuity,* sometimes called a *deferred annuity.* If payments are made at the beginning of each period, then we have an *annuity due.* Since ordinary annuities are far more common in finance, when the word *annuity* is used in this book you may assume that payments are received at the end of each period unless otherwise indicated.

Ordinary Annuities

ordinary (deferred) annuity
An annuity whose payments occur at the end of each period.

A promise to pay $1,000 a year for 3 years is a 3-year annuity, and if each payment is made at the end of the year, it is an **ordinary (deferred) annuity.** If you were to receive such an annuity and then deposited each annual payment in a savings account that paid 4 percent interest, how much would you have at the end of 3 years? The answer is shown graphically as a *time line* in Figure 5-3. The first payment is made at the end of Year 1, the second at the end of Year 2, and the third at the end of Year 3. Thus, the first payment is compounded over a 2-year period; the second payment is compounded for 1 year; and the last payment is not compounded at all. When the future values of each of the payments are summed, their total is the future value of the annuity. In the example, this total is $3,121.60.

---

[3]Notice that Figure 5-2 is not a mirror image of Figure 5-1. The curves in Figure 5-1 approach ∞ as n increases; in Figure 5-2 the curves approach zero, not $-\infty$.

Figure 5-3   Time Line for an Ordinary Annuity:
Future Value with k = 4%

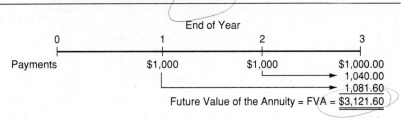

Future Value of the Annuity = FVA = $3,121.60

FVA$_n$
The future value of an annuity over n periods.

FVIFA$_{k,n}$
The future value interest factor for an annuity of n periodic payments compounded at k percent.

Expressed algebraically, with **FVA$_n$**, the sum of an annuity, defined as the future value of the annuity over n periods, PMT as the periodic payment, and **FVIFA$_{k,n}$** as the future value interest factor for the annuity, the formula is

$$FVA_n = PMT(1 + k)^{n-1} + PMT(1 + k)^{n-2} +$$
$$\ldots + PMT(1 + k)^1 + PMT(1 + k)^0$$

$$= PMT[(1 + k)^{n-1} + (1 + k)^{n-2} +$$
$$\ldots + (1 + k)^1 + (1 + k)^0]$$

$$= PMT \sum_{t=1}^{n} (1 + k)^{n-t}$$

$$= PMT(FVIFA_{k,n}) = \text{future value of an annuity.} \qquad (5\text{-}4)$$

The expression in parentheses, FVIFA$_{k,n}$, has been calculated for various combinations of k and n. An illustrative set of these annuity interest factors is given in Table 5-4.[4] (A more complete set of annuity future value factors is given in Table A-4 of Appendix A.) To find the answer to the 3-year, $1,000 annuity problem, simply refer to Table 5-4, look down the 4 percent column to the row of the third period, and multiply the factor 3.1216 by $1,000. The answer is the same as the one derived by the long method illustrated in Figure 5-3:

$$FVA_n = PMT(FVIFA_{k,n})$$

$$FVA_3 = \$1,000(FVIFA_{4\%, 3 \text{ years}})$$

$$= \$1,000(3.1216) = \$3,121.60.$$

You could find FVA$_n$ directly with a financial calculator. Just enter n = 3, k = i = 4, and PMT = 1,000, and then press the FV button to get the answer, FVA$_3$ = $3,121.60 (on some calculators, − $3,121.60). The calculator first cal-

---

[4]The equation given at the top of Table 5-4 recognizes that an FVIFA factor is the sum of a geometric progression. It is easy to use the equation to develop annuity factors; this is especially useful if you need the FVIFA for some interest rate not given in the tables — for example, 6.5 percent. The equation is also useful for finding factors for fractional periods — for example, 2.5 years — but one needs a calculator with an exponential function for this.

Table 5-4   Future Value of an Annuity of $1 per Period for n Periods:

$$FVIFA_{k,n} = \sum_{t=1}^{n}(1 + k)^{n-t} = \frac{(1 + k)^n - 1}{k}$$

Number of Periods (n)	1%	2%	3%	4%	5%	6%	7%	8%	9%	10%
1	1.0000	1.0000	1.0000	1.0000	1.0000	1.0000	1.0000	1.0000	1.0000	1.0000
2	2.0100	2.0200	2.0300	2.0400	2.0500	2.0600	2.0700	2.0800	2.0900	2.1000
3	3.0301	3.0604	3.0909	3.1216	3.1525	3.1836	3.2149	3.2464	3.2781	3.3100
4	4.0604	4.1216	4.1836	4.2465	4.3101	4.3746	4.4399	4.5061	4.5731	4.6410
5	5.1010	5.2040	5.3091	5.4163	5.5256	5.6371	5.7507	5.8666	5.9847	6.1051
6	6.1520	6.3081	6.4684	6.6330	6.8019	6.9753	7.1533	7.3359	7.5233	7.7156
7	7.2135	7.4343	7.6625	7.8983	8.1420	8.3938	8.6540	8.9228	9.2004	9.4872
8	8.2857	8.5830	8.8923	9.2141	9.5491	9.8975	10.2598	10.6366	11.0285	11.4359
9	9.3685	9.7546	10.1591	10.5828	11.0266	11.4913	11.9780	12.4876	13.0210	13.5795
10	10.4622	10.9497	11.4639	12.0061	12.5779	13.1808	13.8164	14.4866	15.1929	15.9374

culates FVIFA and then multiplies it by PMT = $1,000. Financial calculators also handle fractional years and fractional interest rates with no trouble.

For all positive interest rates, the $FVIFA_{k,n}$ for the sum of an annuity is always equal to or greater than the number of periods the annuity runs. Note also that the entry for each period n in Table 5-4 is equal to 1.0 plus the sum of the entries in Table 5-2 up to and including Period n − 1; for example, the entry for Period 3 under the 4 percent column in Table 5-4 is equal to 1.000 + 1.0400 + 1.0816 = 3.1216.

Annuity Due

annuity due
An anniuty whose payments occur at the beginning of each period.

Had the three $1,000 payments in the previous example each been made at the beginning of each year, the annuity would have been an **annuity due**. In terms of Figure 5-3, each payment would have been shifted to the left, so there would have been a $1,000 under Period 0 and a zero under Period 3; thus, each payment would be compounded for one extra year.

We can modify Equation 5-4 to handle annuities due as follows:

$$FVA_n(\text{Annuity due}) = PMT(FVIFA_{k,n})(1 + k). \tag{5-4a}$$

Each payment is compounded for one extra year, and multiplying the term $PMT(FVIFA_{k,n})$ by $(1 + k)$ takes care of this extra compounding. Applying Equation 5-4a to the previous example, we obtain

$$FVA_n(\text{Annuity due}) = \$1,000(3.1216)(1.04) = \$3,246.46$$

versus $3,121.60 for the ordinary annuity. Since its payments come in faster, the annuity due is more valuable.

Annuity due problems can also be solved with financial calculators, most of which have a switch or key marked "Due" or "Beginning" that permits you to convert from ordinary annuities to annuities due. Be careful, though. People sometimes change the setting to work an annuity due problem, then forget to switch the calculator back and consequently get wrong answers to subsequent ordinary annuity problems.

PRESENT VALUE OF AN ANNUITY

Suppose you were offered the following alternatives: (1) a 3-year annuity with payments of $1,000 at the end of each year or (2) a lump sum payment today. You have no need for the money during the next 3 years, so if you accept the annuity, you would simply deposit the payments in a savings account that pays 4 percent interest. Similarly, the lump sum payment would be deposited in an account paying 4 percent, compounded annually. How large must the lump sum payment be to make it equivalent to the annuity?

The time line shown in Figure 5-4 will help explain the problem. The present value of the first payment is $PMT[1/(1 + k)]$, the PV of the second is $PMT[1/(1 + k)]^2$, and so on. Defining **PVA$_n$** as the present value of an annuity of n periods, and **PVIFA$_{k,n}$** as the present value interest factor for the annuity, we may write the following equation in its several equivalent forms:

PVA$_n$
The present value of an annuity of n periods.

PVIFA$_{k,n}$
The present value interest factor for an annuity of n periodic payments discounted at k percent.

$$PVA_n = PMT\left(\frac{1}{1 + k}\right)^1 + PMT\left(\frac{1}{1 + k}\right)^2 + \ldots + PMT\left(\frac{1}{1 + k}\right)^n$$

$$= PMT\left[\frac{1}{(1 + k)^1} + \frac{1}{(1 + k)^2} + \ldots + \frac{1}{(1 + k)^n}\right]$$

$$= PMT \sum_{t=1}^{n}\left(\frac{1}{1 + k}\right)^t$$

$$= PMT(PVIFA_{k,n}). \tag{5-5}$$

Again, tables have been worked out for PVIFA$_{k,n}$. Table 5-5 is illustrative, and a more complete listing is found in Table A-2 in Appendix A. From Table 5-5, the PVIFA$_{k,n}$ for a 3-year, 4 percent annuity is found to be 2.7751. Multiplying this factor by the $1,000 annual payment gives $2,775.10, the present value of the annuity:

$$PVA_n = PMT(PVIFA_{k,n})$$

$$PVA_3 = \$1,000(PVIFA_{4\%,3 \text{ years}})$$

$$= \$1,000(2.7751) = \$2,775.10.$$

This value is identical to the long-method answer shown in Figure 5-4.

**Figure 5-4   Time Line for an Ordinary Annuity:
Present Value with k = 4%**

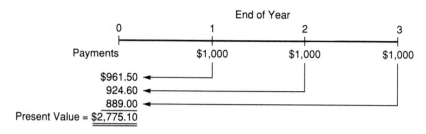

Note: $961.50 compounded for one year at 4 percent equals $1,000, $924.60 compounded for two years equals $1,000, and $889.00 compounded for three years equals $1,000.

Again, this problem can be solved directly with a financial calculator. Just enter n = 3, k = i = 4, and PMT = 1,000, and then press the PV button to find PVA_n = $2,775.09. The penny difference results from rounding.

Notice that the entry for each value of n in Table 5-5 is equal to the sum of the entries in Table 5-3 up to and including Period n. For example, the PVIFA for 4 percent, 3 periods, as shown in Table 5-5, could have been calculated by summing values from Table 5-3:

$$0.9615 + 0.9246 + 0.8890 = 2.7751.$$

Table 5-5   Present Value of an Annuity of $1 per Period for n Periods:

$$PVIFA_{k,n} = \sum_{t=1}^{n} \frac{1}{(1 + k)^t} = \frac{1 - \dfrac{1}{(1 + k)^n}}{k} = \frac{1}{k} - \frac{1}{k(1 + k)^n}$$

Number of Periods (n)	1%	2%	3%	4%	5%	6%	7%	8%	9%	10%
1	0.9901	0.9804	0.9709	0.9615	0.9524	0.9434	0.9346	0.9259	0.9174	0.9091
2	1.9704	1.9416	1.9135	1.8861	1.8594	1.8334	1.8080	1.7833	1.7591	1.7355
3	2.9410	2.8839	2.8286	2.7751	2.7232	2.6730	2.6243	2.5771	2.5313	2.4869
4	3.9020	3.8077	3.7171	3.6299	3.5460	3.4651	3.3872	3.3121	3.2397	3.1699
5	4.8534	4.7135	4.5797	4.4518	4.3295	4.2124	4.1002	3.9927	3.8897	3.7908
6	5.7955	5.6014	5.4172	5.2421	5.0757	4.9173	4.7665	4.6229	4.4859	4.3553
7	6.7282	6.4720	6.2303	6.0021	5.7864	5.5824	5.3893	5.2064	5.0330	4.8684
8	7.6517	7.3255	7.0197	6.7327	6.4632	6.2098	5.9713	5.7466	5.5348	5.3349
9	8.5660	8.1622	7.7861	7.4353	7.1078	6.8017	6.5152	6.2469	5.9952	5.7590
10	9.4713	8.9826	8.5302	8.1109	7.7217	7.3601	7.0236	6.7101	6.4177	6.1446

For all positive interest rates, $PVIFA_{k,n}$ for the *present value* of an annuity is always less than the number of periods the annuity runs, whereas $FVIFA_{k,n}$ for the *future value* of an annuity is equal to or greater than the number of periods.

Present Value of an Annuity Due

Had the payments in the preceding example occurred at the beginning of each year, the annuity would have been an *annuity due*. In terms of Figure 5-4, each payment would have been shifted to the left, so $1,000 would have appeared under Period 0 and a zero would have appeared under Period 3. Each payment occurs one period earlier, so it has a higher PV. To account for these shifts, we multiply Equation 5-5 by $(1 + k)$ to find the present value of an annuity due:

$$PVA_n(\text{Annuity due}) = PMT(PVIFA_{k,n})(1 + k). \qquad (5\text{-}5a)$$

Our illustrative 4 percent, 3-year annuity, with payments made at the beginning of each year, thus has a present value of $2,886.10 versus a value of $2,775.10 on an ordinary annuity basis:

$$PVA_3 = \$1,000(2.7751)(1.04)$$

$$= \$2,775.10(1.04)$$

$$= \$2,886.10.$$

Since each payment comes earlier, an annuity due is worth more than an ordinary annuity.

PERPETUITIES

Most annuities call for payments to be made over some definite period of time — for example, $1,000 per year for 3 years. However, some annuities go on indefinitely; here the payments constitute an *infinite series,* and the series is defined as a **perpetuity**. The present value of a perpetuity is found by applying Equation 5-6:[5]

perpetuity
A stream of equal payments expected to continue forever.

$$PV(\text{perpetuity}) = \frac{\text{Payment}}{\text{Interest rate}} = \frac{PMT}{k}. \qquad (5\text{-}6)$$

Perpetuities can be illustrated by some British securities issued after the Napoleonic Wars. In 1815, the British government sold a huge bond issue and used the proceeds to pay off many smaller issues that had been floated in prior

[5]The derivation of Equation 5-6 is given in Appendix 3A of Eugene F. Brigham and Louis C. Gapenski, *Intermediate Financial Management,* 2nd ed. (Hinsdale, Ill: Dryden Press, 1987).

consol
A perpetual bond issued by the British government to consolidate past debts; in general, any perpetual bond.

years to pay for the wars. Since the purpose of the new bonds was to consolidate past debts, the bonds were called **consols**. Suppose each consol promised to pay $90 interest per year in perpetuity. (Actually, interest was stated in pounds.) What would each bond be worth if the going rate of interest, or the discount rate, were 8 percent? The answer is $1,125:

$$\text{Value} = \$90/0.08 = \$1,125 \text{ if k is } 8\%.$$

Suppose interest rates rose to 12 percent; what would that do to the consol's value? The answer changes to $750:

$$\text{Value} = \$90/0.12 = \$750 \text{ if k is } 12\%.$$

If k fell to 4 percent, the consol's value would rise to $2,250.

We see, then, that the value of a perpetuity changes dramatically when interest rates change. Perpetuities are discussed further in Chapter 6, where procedures for finding the values of various types of securities (stocks and bonds) are analyzed.

PRESENT VALUE OF AN UNEVEN SERIES OF PAYMENTS

The definition of an annuity includes the words *constant amount* — in other words, annuities involve situations in which cash flows are *identical* in every period. Although many financial decisions do involve constant cash flows, some important decisions are concerned with *uneven* flows of cash; for example, common stocks are typically expected to pay an increasing series of dividends over time, and capital budgeting projects do not normally provide constant cash flows. Consequently, it is necessary to expand our analysis to deal with **uneven payment streams**.

uneven payment stream
A series of payments in which the amount varies from one period to the next.

The PV of an uneven stream of future income is found as the sum of the PVs of the individual components of the stream. For example, suppose we are trying to find the PV of the stream of payments shown in Figure 5-5, discounted at 6 percent. As shown in the lower part of the figure, we multiply each payment by the appropriate $\text{PVIF}_{k,n}$ (taken from Appendix A, Table A-1) and then sum these products to obtain the PV of the stream, $1,413.24. The graph gives a pictorial view of the cash flow stream.[6]

The PV of the payments shown in Figure 5-5 for Years 2 through 5 can

---

[6]This general equation may be used to find the PV of an uneven series of payments:

$$PV = \sum_{t=1}^{n} PMT_t \left(\frac{1}{1+k}\right)^t = \sum_{t=1}^{n} PMT_t(PVIF_{k,t}),$$

where PMT_t is the payment in any Year t.

Figure 5-5   Time Line for an Uneven Cash Flow Stream: Present Value with k = 6%

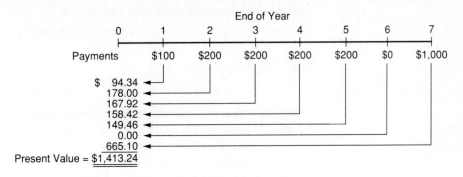

Present Value = $1,413.24

Year	Payment	×	PVIF$_{6\%,n}$	= PV of Individual Payments
1	$ 100		0.9434	$ 94.34
2	200		0.8900	178.00
3	200		0.8396	167.92
4	200		0.7921	158.42
5	200		0.7473	149.46
6	0		0.7050	0
7	1,000		0.6651	665.10
			PV = Sum =	$1,413.24

also be found by using the annuity equation. This alternative solution process involves the following steps:

Step 1. Find the PV of $100 due in Year 1:

$$\$100(0.9434) = \$94.34.$$

Step 2. Recognize that a $200 annuity will be received during Years 2 through 5. Thus, we could determine the value of a 5-year annuity, subtract from it the value of a 1-year annuity, and have remaining the value of a 4-year annuity whose first payment is due in 2 years. This result is achieved by subtracting the PVIFA for a 1-year, 6 percent annuity from that for a 5-year annuity and then multiplying the difference by $200:

$$PV \text{ of the annuity} = \$200(PVIFA_{6\%,5 \text{ years}}) - \$200(PVIFA_{6\%,1 \text{ year}})$$
$$= \$200(PVIFA_{6\%,5 \text{ years}} - PVIFA_{6\%,1 \text{ year}})$$
$$= \$200(4.2124 - 0.9434)$$
$$= \$200(3.2690) = \$653.80.$$

Thus, the present value of the annuity component of the uneven stream is $653.80.[7]

Step 3. Find the PV of the $1,000 due in Year 7:

$$\$1,000(0.6651) = \$665.10.$$

Step 4. Sum the components:

$$(\$94.34 + \$653.80 + \$665.10) = \$1,413.24.$$

Either the Figure 5-5 method or the method utilizing the annuity formula can be used to solve problems of this type. However, the alternative annuity solution is much easier if the annuity component runs for many years. For example, the alternative solution would be clearly superior for finding the PV of a stream consisting of $100 in Year 1, $200 in Years 2 through 29, and $1,000 in Year 30.

The present value of a stream of future cash flows can always be found by summing the present values of each individual cash flow. However, cash flow regularities within the stream may allow the use of shortcuts, such as finding the present value of several cash flows that compose an annuity. Also, in some instances we may want to find the value of a stream of payments at some point other than the present (Year 0). In this situation, we proceed as before but compound and discount to some other point in time, say Year 2 rather than Year 0.

Problems involving unequal cash flows can be solved quite easily with most financial calculators. Most of these calculators permit you to input the separate cash flows plus the interest rate; then, when you press the PV (or NPV) button, you obtain the solution. This feature is not found on all financial calculators, but it is found on the better ones. Some of the newer financial calculators even allow you to specify annuities within the cash flow stream. For example, you could specify 1 payment of $100, 4 payments of $200, 1 payment of $0, and 1 payment of $1,000, along with an interest rate of 6 percent, to find the present value of the cash flow stream given in Figure 5-5.

The future value of a series of uneven payments, often called the *terminal value*, is found by compounding each payment and then summing the individual future values:

$$\text{Terminal value} = TV_n = FV_n = \sum_{t=1}^{n} PMT_t(1 + k)^{n-t}.$$

We are generally more interested in the present value of a stream of payments from an asset than in the future (or terminal) value, because the PV is the

---

[7]An alternative method for finding the present value of the annuity component of the cash flow stream would be (1) to find the value of the annuity at the end of Year 1 = $200(PVIFA_{6\%,4 \text{ years}})$ = $200(3.4651) = 693.02 and (2) to discount this lump sum value back one year to the present, $693.02(PVIF_{6\%,1 \text{ year}})$ = $693.02(0.9434) = $653.80.

value today and hence the market value of the asset. However, we will use the terminal value concept in Chapter 9, when we deal with capital budgeting.

DETERMINING INTEREST RATES

We can use the basic equations that were developed earlier in the chapter to determine the interest rates explicit in financial contracts.

Example 1. A bank offers to lend you $1,000 if you sign a note to pay $1,610.50 at the end of 5 years. What rate of interest would the bank be charging you?

1. Recognize that $1,000 is the PV of $1,610.50 due in 5 years:

$$PV = \$1,000 = \$1,610.50(PVIF_{k,5 \text{ years}}).$$

2. Solve for $PVIF_{k,5 \text{ years}}$:

$$PVIF_{k,5 \text{ years}} = \$1,000/\$1,610.50 = 0.6209.$$

3. Now turn to Table 5-3 (or Table A-1). Look across the row for Period 5 until you find the value 0.6209. It is in the 10 percent column, so you would be paying a 10 percent rate of interest if you were to take out the loan.

4. Financial calculators are especially useful for finding interest rates in problems like this. Enter $PV = 1,000$, $n = 5$, and $FV = 1,610.5$, and then press the $k = i$ button to obtain the interest rate. The calculator blinks a few times, and 10.00 percent appears. Your calculator may require that either the PV or FV be entered as a negative in recognition of the fact that the PV is an inflow and the FV is an outflow. If you get an error message, try entering $FV = -1,610.5$.

Example 2. A bank offers to lend you $25,000 to buy a home. You must sign a mortgage calling for payments of $2,545.16 at the end of each of the next 25 years. What interest rate is the bank offering you?

1. Recognize that $25,000 is the PV of a 25-year, $2,545.16 annuity:

$$PV = \$25,000 = \sum_{t=1}^{25} \$2,545.16 \frac{1}{(1 + k)^t}$$

$$\$25,000 = \$2,545.16(PVIFA_{k,25 \text{ years}}).$$

2. Solve for $PVIFA_{k,25 \text{ years}}$:

$$PVIFA_{k,25 \text{ years}} = \$25,000/\$2,545.16 = 9.8226.$$

3. Turn to Table A-2. Looking across the row for 25 periods, you will find 9.8226 under the column for 9 percent. Therefore, the rate of interest on this mortgage loan is 9 percent.

4. To solve this problem with a financial calculator, enter PV = 25,000, n = 25, and PMT = 2,545.16 (or − 2,545.16), and then press the k = i button to find the interest rate of 9 percent. Consider also the situation in which the mortgage calls for annual payments of $2,400. In that case, $PVIFA_{k,n}$ = $25,000/$2,400 = 10.4167. In Table A-2, this value lies between the $PVIFA_{k,n}$ for 8 and 9 percent, but it is closer to 8 percent. The approximate rate for the mortgage could be found by "linear interpolation," a topic discussed in algebra texts, but today we would use a financial calculator and find the interest rate simply by pressing the i button. The rate in this example is 8.2887 percent.

Although the tables can be used to find the interest rate implicit in single payments and annuities, it is more difficult to find the interest rate implicit in an uneven series of payments. One can use a trial-and-error procedure, a financial calculator with an IRR feature (IRRs are discussed in Chapter 9), or a graphic procedure (which is also discussed in Chapter 9). We will defer further discussion of this problem for now, but we will take it up later in our discussion of bond values and again in the capital budgeting chapters.

SEMIANNUAL AND OTHER COMPOUNDING PERIODS

In all of our examples thus far, we have assumed that returns are received once a year, or annually. Suppose, however, that you put your $1,000 into a bank account which pays 6 percent compounded *semiannually*. How much will you have at the end of 1 year, 2 years, or some other period? Semiannual compounding means that interest is paid each 6 months. The procedures for semiannual compounding are illustrated in Section 2 of Table 5-6, and they are compared with annual compounding as set forth in Section 1. For semiannual compounding, the annual interest rate is divided by 2, but twice as many compounding periods are used because interest is paid twice a year. Comparing the amount in the account at the end of each year, we see that the $1,000 grows faster under semiannual compounding, so a 6 percent semiannual rate is better than a 6 percent annual rate from a saver's standpoint. This result occurs because under semiannual compounding you earn *interest on interest* more frequently.

Throughout the economy, different compounding periods are used for different types of investments. For example, bank accounts generally pay interest monthly or daily; most bonds pay interest semiannually; stocks pay dividends quarterly; and many loans pay interest annually.[8] Thus, if we are to

---

[8]Many banks and savings and loans even pay interest compounded continuously. Continuous compounding and discounting are discussed in Appendix 5A.

compare securities with different compounding periods, we need to put them on a common basis. This means that we must distinguish between the *nominal, or stated, interest rate* and the *effective annual rate (EAR).*[9]

nominal (stated) interest rate
The contracted, or stated, interest rate.

effective annual rate
The annual rate of interest actually being earned as opposed to the stated rate.

The **nominal, or stated, interest rate** is the quoted rate; thus, in our example, the nominal rate is 6 percent. The nominal interest rate is often called the *annual percentage rate (APR)* when it is reported by banks and other lending institutions.[10] The **effective annual rate** is the rate that would have produced the final compound value, $1,060.90, under annual rather than semiannual compounding. In this case, the effective annual rate is 6.09 percent, found by solving for k in the following equation:

$$\$1,000(1 + k) = \$1,060.90$$

$$k = \frac{\$1,060.90}{\$1,000} - 1 = 0.0609 = 6.09\%.$$

Thus, if one bank offered 6 percent with semiannual compounding while another offered 6.09 percent with annual compounding, they would both be paying the same effective annual rate of interest. This point is demonstrated in Section 3 of Table 5-6.

In general, we can determine the effective annual rate, given the nominal rate, by solving Equation 5-7:

$$\text{Effective annual rate} = \left(1 + \frac{k_{Nom}}{m}\right)^m - 1.0. \qquad (5\text{-}7)$$

Here k_{Nom} is the nominal, or stated, interest rate, and m is the number of compounding periods per year. For example, to find the effective annual rate if the nominal rate is 6 percent and semiannual compounding is used, we make the following calculation:

$$\text{Effective annual rate} = \left(1 + \frac{0.06}{2}\right)^2 - 1.0$$

$$= (1.03)^2 - 1.0$$

$$= 1.0609 - 1.0$$

$$= 0.0609 = 6.09\%.$$

Semiannual compounding is handled easily with a financial calculator. Simply set i = 3, n = 2, and PV = 1,000, and then press the FV button to get the solution, FV = $1,060.90.

---

[9]The term *nominal* as it is used here has a different meaning than the way it is used in Chapter 3. There, nominal interest rates meant market rates as opposed to real (inflation-adjusted) rates. In this chapter, the term *nominal rate* means the stated rate as opposed to the effective annual rate, which gives consideration to compounding more frequently than once a year.

[10]The nominal interest rate, or the APR, is the rate reported by banks. Although this is a widespread practice, and it apparently meets the minimum requirements of the "truth in lending" laws, it is somewhat deceptive because the true effective interest rate, which ought to be reported to borrowers, exceeds the nominal rate except where annual compounding is used.

Table 5-6   Future Value Calculations: Semiannual versus Annual Compounding

---

1. Annual Compounding at a 6% Rate

Year	Beginning Amount, PV	×	(1 + k)	Ending Amount, FV_n
1	$1,000.00		(1.06)	$1,060.00
2	1,060.00		(1.06)	1,123.60
3	1,123.60		(1.06)	1,191.02

Total interest earned over 3 years at a 6%, annual compounding: $191.02

2. Semiannual Compounding at a 6% Nominal Rate

6-Month Period	Beginning Amount, PV	×	(1 + k/2)	Ending Amount, FV_n
1	$1,000.00		(1.03)	$1,030.00
2	1,030.00		(1.03)	1,060.90[a]
3	1,060.90		(1.03)	1,092.73
4	1,092.73		(1.03)	1,125.51[a]
5	1,125.51		(1.03)	1,159.27
6	1,159.27		(1.03)	1,194.05[a]

Total interest earned over 3 years at 6%, semiannual compounding: $194.05

[a]End of year

3. Annual Compounding at an Effective Annual Rate of 6.09%

Year	Beginning Amount, PV	×	(1 + k)	Ending Amount, FV_n
1	$1,000.00		(1.0609)	$1,060.90
2	1,060.90		(1.0609)	1,125.51
3	1,125.51		(1.0609)	1,194.05

Notes:

a. Sections 1 and 2 demonstrate that if a given interest rate (6%) is paid each 6 months (semiannually), more interest is earned over time than if the same interest rate is paid annually.

b. Section 3 demonstrates that there is some annual interest rate, called the *effective annual rate,* which is equivalent to the *stated* (or *nominal*) semiannual rate. For a 6% nominal rate paid semiannually, the effective annual rate is 6.09%, found as follows:

$$\text{Effective annual rate} = \left(1 + \frac{k_{Nom}}{m}\right)^m - 1.0 = \left(1 + \frac{0.06}{2}\right)^2 - 1.0 = 0.0609 = 6.09\%.$$

Here m = number of compounding periods per year.

The points made about semiannual compounding can be generalized as follows. When compounding periods are more frequent than once a year, we use a modified version of Equation 5-2 to find the future value of a lump sum:

$$\text{Annual compounding: } FV_n = PV(1 + k)^n. \tag{5-2}$$

$$\text{More frequent compounding: } FV_n = PV\left(1 + \frac{k_{Nom}}{m}\right)^{mn}. \tag{5-2a}$$

Here m is the number of times per year compounding occurs, and n is the number of years. For example, when banks compute daily interest, the value of m is set at 365 and Equation 5-2a is applied.[11]

To illustrate further the effects of compounding more frequently than annually, consider the interest rate charged on credit cards. In March 1988, most interest rates had declined sharply from earlier levels. For example, the yield on 30-year Treasury bonds was 8.5 percent, down from 14.2 percent in December 1985. However, credit card rates (the rate of interest charged to credit card users who do not pay within the no-interest period) were generally unchanged from earlier levels. Most states set maximum rates for credit card loans, and most banks charge the allowed limit, which ranges from 12 to 21 percent, but averages 19 percent.

Certain members of Congress raised this question: Why haven't credit card rates dropped along with other rates? Is there some conspiracy among bankers to keep these rates up, thus helping bank profits but exploiting those consumers who borrow on credit cards? As expected, the bankers replied that both administrative costs and bad debt losses are high on credit card loans, and that the rates charged are completely justified. The interesting thing to note for our purposes, though, is that the rate the banks are actually charging is higher than the rate they say they are charging. For example, if a bank charges 1½ percent per month, it will state that its annual percentage rate (APR) is 1½ × 12 = 18%. Actually, though, the true rate is the effective annual rate of 19.6%:

$$\text{Effective annual rate} = (1.015)^{12} - 1.0 = 0.196 = 19.6\%.$$

If the bank states that it charges 21 percent, the true rate is 23.1%. Whether or not those rates are really justified is a moot question, but it surely pays to pay credit card bills within the interest-free period!

The interest tables can often be used when compounding occurs more than once a year. Simply divide the nominal, or stated, interest rate by the number of times compounding occurs, and multiply the years by the number of compounding periods per year. For example, to find the amount to which $1,000 will grow after 5 years if semiannual compounding is applied to a stated 8 percent interest rate, divide 8 percent by 2 and multiply the 5 years by 2. Then look in Table A-3 under the 4 percent column and in the row for Period 10. You will find an interest factor of 1.4802. Multiplying this by the initial $1,000 gives a value of $1,480.20, the amount to which $1,000 will grow in 5 years at 8 percent, compounded semiannually. This compares with $1,469.30 for annual compounding.

It should be clear that the tables in this book are not complete enough to handle much variability of interest rates. For example, to handle 9 percent,

---

[11]To illustrate, the future value of $1 invested at 10 percent for 1 year under daily compounding is $1.1052:

$$FV_n = \$1\left(1 + \frac{0.10}{365}\right)^{365(1)} = \$1(1.105156) = \$1.1052.$$

compounded quarterly, we would need a table for 2¼ percent; 10 percent quarterly would require a table for 2½ percent; and so on. However, any compounding period can be handled easily with a financial calculator. Thus, to work our illustrative problem, simply enter $i = k_{Nom}/m = 4$, $n = m \times n = 10$, and then proceed as before.

Semiannual and other compounding periods can be used for discounting, single payments, and annuities. To illustrate semiannual discounting in finding the present value of an annuity, consider the case described in the section "Present Value of an Annuity": $1,000 a year for 3 years, discounted at 4 percent. With annual discounting, the interest factor is 2.7751 and the present value of the annuity is $2,775.10. For semiannual discounting, look under the 2 percent column and in the Period 6 row of Table 5-5 to find an interest factor of 5.6014. This is multiplied by half of $1,000, or the $500 received each six months, to get the present value of the annuity, $2,800.70. The payments come a little more rapidly — the first $500 is paid after only six months (similarly with other payments) — so the annuity is a little more valuable if payments are received semiannually rather than annually.

By letting m approach infinity, Equation 5-2a can be modified to the special case of **continuous compounding**. Continuous compounding is useful in theoretical finance, and it also has practical applications — for example, banks and savings associations sometimes pay interest on a continuous basis. Continuous compounding is discussed in Appendix 5A.

continuous compounding
A situation in which interest is added continuously rather than at discrete points in time.

AMORTIZED LOANS

One of the most important applications of compound interest involves loans that are to be paid off in installments over time. Included are automobile loans, home mortgage loans, and most business debt other than very short-term loans. If a loan is to be repaid in equal periodic amounts (monthly, quarterly, or annually), it is said to be an **amortized loan**.[12]

amortized loan
A loan that is repaid in equal payments over its life.

To illustrate, suppose a firm borrows $1,000 to be repaid in 3 equal payments at the end of each of the next 3 years. The lender is to receive 6 percent interest on the loan balance that is outstanding at the beginning of each period. The first task is to determine the amount the firm must repay each year, or the annual payment. To find this amount, recognize that the $1,000 represents the present value of an annuity of PMT dollars per year for 3 years, discounted at 6 percent:

$$\text{PV of annuity} = \frac{PMT}{(1 + k)^1} + \frac{PMT}{(1 + k)^2} + \frac{PMT}{(1 + k)^3}$$

---

[12]The word *amortized* comes from the Latin *mors,* meaning "death," so an amortized loan is one that is "killed off" over time.

Table 5-7   Loan Amortization Schedule

Year	Beginning Amount (1)	Payment (2)	Interest[a] (3)	Repayment of Principal[b] (4)	Remaining Balance (5)
1	$1,000.00	$ 374.11	$ 60.00	$ 314.11	$685.89
2	685.89	374.11	41.15	332.96	352.93
3	352.93	374.11	21.18	352.93	0.00
		$1,122.33	$122.33	$1,000.00	

[a]Interest is calculated by multiplying the loan balance at the beginning of the year by the interest rate. Therefore, interest in Year 1 is $1,000(0.06) = $60; in Year 2 it is $685.89(0.06) = $41.15; and in Year 3 it is $352.93(0.06) = $21.18.

[b]Repayment of principal is equal to the payment of $374.11 minus the interest charge for each year.

$$\$1,000 = \frac{PMT}{(1.06)} + \frac{PMT}{(1.06)^2} + \frac{PMT}{(1.06)^3}$$

$$= PMT\left[\frac{1}{1.06} + \frac{1}{(1.06)^2} + \frac{1}{(1.06)^3}\right]$$

$$= PMT(PVIFA_{6\%,3 \text{ years}}).$$

The PVIFA is found in Table 5-5 to be 2.6730, so

$$\$1,000 = PMT(2.6730).$$

Solving for PMT, we obtain

$$PMT = \$1,000/2.6730 = \$374.11.$$

If the firm pays the lender $374.11 at the end of each of the next 3 years, the percentage cost to the borrower, and the rate of return to the lender, will be 6 percent.

The payment can also be found using a financial calculator. Simply enter n = 3, i = 6, and PV = 1,000, and then press PMT. The solution, PMT = $374.11 (or −$374.11) will appear.

amortization schedule
A schedule showing precisely how a loan will be repaid. It gives the required payment on each specified date and a breakdown of the payment showing how much constitutes interest and how much constitutes repayment of principal.

Each payment consists partly of interest and partly of a repayment of principal. This breakdown is given in the **amortization schedule** shown in Table 5-7. The interest component is largest in the first year and declines as the outstanding balance of the loan goes down. For tax purposes, a business borrower reports as a deductible cost each year the interest payments in Column 3, while the lender reports these same amounts as taxable income.

SUMMARY AND KEY CONCEPTS

Financial decisions often involve situations in which someone pays money at one point in time and receives money at some later time. Dollars that are paid or received at two different points in time are different, and this difference is

Figure 5-6   Illustration for Chapter Summary (k = 4%)

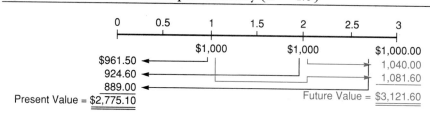

recognized and accounted for in *time value of money, or discounted cash flow (DCF), analysis*. We summarize the types of DCF analysis and the key concepts covered in this chapter below, using the data shown in Figure 5-6 to illustrate the various points. Refer to the figure constantly, and find in it an example of the point covered, as you go through this section.

- **Compounding** is the process of determining the **future value** (FV) of a payment or a series of payments. The compounded amount, or future value, is equal to the beginning amount plus the interest earned.

- Future value: $FV_n = PV(1 + k)^n = PV(FVIF_{k,n})$.
  (single payment)

  Example: $961.50 compounded for 1 year at 4%.

$$FV_1 = \$961.50(1.04)^1 = \$1,000.$$

- **Discounting** is the process of finding the **present value** (PV) of a future payment or a series of payments; discounting is the reverse of compounding.

- Present value: $PV = FV_n\left(\dfrac{1}{1 + k}\right)^n = FV_n(1 + k)^{-n}$
  (single payment)

$$= FV_n(PVIF_{k,n}).$$

  Example: $1,000 discounted back for 2 years at 4%.

$$PV = \$1,000\left(\frac{1}{1.04}\right)^2 = \$1,000(0.9246) = \$924.60.$$

- An **annuity** is defined as a series of equal, periodic payments (PMT) for a specified number of periods.

- Future value: $FVA_n = PMT(1 + k)^{n-1} + PMT(1 + k)^{n-2}$
  (annuity)

$$+ \ldots + PMT(1 + k)^{n-n}$$

$$= PMT \sum_{t=1}^{n} (1 + k)^{n-t}$$

$$= PMT\left[\frac{(1 + k)^n - 1}{k}\right]$$

$$= PMT(FVIFA_{k,n}).$$

Example: FVA of 3 payments of $1,000 when $k = 4\%$:

$$FVA_3 = 3.1216(\$1,000) = \$3,121.60.$$

- Present value:
  (annuity)

$$PVA_n = PMT\sum_{t=1}^{n}\left[\frac{1}{1 + k}\right]^t$$

$$= PMT\left[\frac{1 - \dfrac{1}{(1 + k)^n}}{k}\right]$$

$$= PMT(PVIFA_{k,n}).$$

Example: PVA of 3 payments of $1,000 when $k = 4\%$.

$$PVA = 2.7751(\$1,000) = \$2,775.10.$$

- An annuity that has payments occurring at the *end* of each period is called an **ordinary annuity**. The formulas above are for ordinary annuities.
- If each payment occurs at the beginning of the period rather than at the end, then we have an **annuity due**. In Figure 5-6, the payments would be shown at Years 0, 1, and 2 rather than at 1, 2, and 3. The PV of each payment would be larger, because each payment would be discounted back one year less, and hence the PV of the annuity would also be larger. Similarly, the FV of the annuity due would also be larger, because each payment would be compounded for an extra year. These formulas can be used to convert the PV and FV of an ordinary annuity to an annuity due:

  PVA(annuity due) = PVA of an ordinary annuity × (1 + k).

  FVA(annuity due) = FVA of an ordinary annuity × (1 + k).

- If the time line in Figure 5-6 were extended out forever, so that the $1,000 payments went on forever, we would have a **perpetuity** whose value could be found as follows:

$$\text{Value of perpetuity} = \frac{PMT}{k} = \frac{\$1,000}{0.04} = \$25,000.$$

- If the payments in Figure 5-6 were unequal, we could not use the annuity formulas. To find the PV or FV of the series, find the PV or FV of each individual payment and then sum them. However, if some of the payments constitute an annuity, then the annuity formula could be used to calculate the present value of that part of the payment stream.
- **Financial calculators** have built-in programs which perform all of the operations discussed in this chapter. It is very helpful to get such a

calculator and to learn how to use it. However, it is essential that you also understand the logical processes involved.

- If you know the payments and the PV (or FV) of a payment stream, you can **determine the interest rate**. For example, in the Figure 5-6 illustration, if you were given the information that a loan (or bond) called for 3 payments of $1,000 each, and that the loan (or bond) had a value today of PV = $2,775.10, then you could find the interest rate that caused the sum of the PVs of the payments to equal $2,775.10. Since we are dealing with an annuity, we could proceed as follows:
  a. Recognize that PVA = $2,775.10 = $1,000(PVIFA$_{k,3}$).
  b. Solve for PVIFA$_{k,3}$:

$$PVIFA_{k,3} = \$2,775.10/\$1,000 = 2.7751.$$

  c. Look up 2.7751 in Table A-2, on the third row. It is in the 4% column, so the interest rate must be 4 percent. If the factor did not appear in the table, this would indicate that the interest rate was not a whole number. In this case, you could not use this procedure to find the exact rate. In practice, though, this is not a problem, because people use financial calculators to find interest rates.

- Thus far in the summary we have assumed that payments are made, and interest is earned, at the end of each year, or annually. However, many contracts call for more frequent payments; for example, mortgage and auto loans call for monthly payments, and most bonds pay interest semiannually. Similarly, most banks compute interest daily. When compounding occurs more frequently than once a year, this fact must be recognized. We can use the Figure 5-6 example to illustrate the procedures. First, the following formula is used to find an **effective annual rate**:

$$\text{Effective annual rate} = \left(1 + \frac{k_{Nom}}{m}\right)^m - 1.0.$$

For semiannual compounding, the effective annual rate is 4.04%:

$$\left(1 + \frac{0.04}{2}\right)^2 - 1.0 = (1.02)^2 - 1.0 = 1.0404 - 1.0 = 0.0404 = 4.04\%.$$

This rate could then be used (with a calculator but not with the tables) to find the PV or FV of each payment, or of the annuity, in Figure 5-6.

If the $1,000 per year payments were actually payable as $500 each six months, you would simply redraw Figure 5-6 to show $500 each six months.

- An **amortized loan** is one that is paid off in equal payments over a specified period. An **amortization schedule** shows how much of each payment constitutes interest, how much is used to reduce the principal, and the remaining balance of the loan at each point in time.

The concepts covered in this chapter will be used throughout the remainder of the book. In Chapter 6 we apply present value concepts to the process of valuing stocks and bonds; there we will see that the market prices of securities are established by determining the present values of the cash flows they are expected to provide. In later chapters, the same basic concepts are applied to corporate decisions involving both expenditures on capital assets and the types of capital that should be used to pay for assets.

Questions

5-1   Is it true that for all positive interest rates the following conditions hold: $FVIF_{k,n} \geq 1.0$; $PVIF_{k,n} \leq 1.0$; $FVIFA_{k,n} \geq$ number of periods the annuity lasts; and $PVIFA_{k,n} \leq$ number of periods the annuity lasts?

5-2   An *annuity* is defined as a series of payments of a fixed amount for a specific number of periods. Thus, $100 a year for 10 years is an annuity, but $100 in Year 1, $200 in Year 2, and $400 in Years 3 through 10 does *not* constitute an annuity. However, the second series *contains* an annuity. Is this statement true or false?

5-3   If a firm's earnings per share grew from $1 to $2 over a 10-year period, the *total growth* would be 100 percent, but the *annual growth rate* would be *less than* 10 percent. Why is this so?

5-4   Would you rather have a savings account that pays 5 percent interest compounded semiannually or one that pays 5 percent interest compounded daily? Explain.

5-5   To find the present value of an uneven series of payments, you can use the $PVIF_{k,n}$ tables; the $PVIFA_{k,n}$ tables can never be of use, even if some of the payments constitute an annuity (for example, $100 each for Years 3, 4, 5, and 6), because the entire series is not an annuity. Is this statement true or false?

5-6   The present value of a perpetuity is equal to the payment on the annuity, PMT, divided by the interest rate, k: $PV = PMT/k$. What is the *sum,* or future value, of a perpetuity of PMT dollars per year? (Hint: The answer is infinity, but explain why.)

Self-Test Problems   *(Solutions Appear on Page 185)*

Key terms

ST-1   Define each of the following terms:
a. PV; k; I; FV_n; n; PVA_n; FVA_n
b. $FVIF_{k,n}$; $PVIF_{k,n}$; $FVIFA_{k,n}$; $PVIFA_{k,n}$
c. Opportunity cost
d. Annuity; lump sum payment; uneven payment stream
e. Ordinary (deferred) annuity; annuity due
f. Perpetuity; consol
g. Financial calculator versus regular calculator
h. Compounding; discounting
i. Annual, semiannual, quarterly, monthly, daily, and continuous compounding

j. Effective annual rate; nominal (stated) interest rate; APR
k. Amortization schedule; principal component versus interest component of a payment

Future value   **ST-2**   Assume that it is now January 1, 1989. On January 1, 1990, you will deposit $1,000 into a savings account paying an 8 percent interest rate.
   a. If the bank compounds interest annually, how much will you have in your account on January 1, 1993?
   b. What would your January 1, 1993, balance be if the bank used quarterly compounding rather than annual compounding?
   c. Suppose you deposited the $1,000 in 4 payments of $250 each on January 1 of 1990, 1991, 1992, and 1993. How much would you have in your account on January 1, 1993, based on 8 percent annual compounding?
   d. Suppose you deposited 4 equal payments in your account on January 1 of 1990, 1991, 1992, and 1993. Assuming an 8 percent interest rate, how large would each of your payments have to be for you to obtain the same ending balance you calculated in Part a?

Discounted cash flow analysis   **ST-3**   Assume that it is now January 1, 1989, and you will need $1,000 on January 1, 1993. Your bank compounds interest at an 8 percent rate annually.
   a. How much must you deposit on January 1, 1990, to have a balance of $1,000 on January 1, 1993?
   b. If you want to make equal payments on each January 1 from 1990 through 1993 to accumulate the $1,000, how large must each of the 4 payments be?
   c. If your father were to offer either to make the payments calculated in Part b ($221.92) or to give you a lump sum of $750 on January 1, 1990, which would you choose?
   d. If you have only $750 on January 1, 1990, what interest rate, compounded annually, would you have to earn to have the necessary $1,000 on January 1, 1993?
   e. Suppose you can deposit only $186.29 each January 1 from 1990 through 1993, but you still need $1,000 on January 1, 1993. What interest rate, with annual compounding, must you seek out to achieve your goal?
   f. To help you reach your $1,000 goal, your father offers to give you $400 on January 1, 1990. You will get a part-time job and make 6 additional payments of equal amounts each 6 months thereafter. If all of this money is deposited in a bank which pays 8 percent, compounded semiannually, how large must your payments be?
   g. What is the effective annual rate being paid by the bank in Part f?
   h. *Reinvestment rate risk* was defined in Chapter 3 as being the risk that maturing securities (and coupon payments on bonds) will have to be reinvested at a lower rate of interest than they were previously earning. Is there a reinvestment rate risk implied in the preceding analysis? If so, how might this risk be eliminated?

Effective annual rates   **ST-4**   Bank A pays 8 percent interest, compounded quarterly, on its money market account. The managers of Bank B want its money market account to equal Bank A's effective annual rate, but interest is to be compounded on a monthly basis. What nominal, or stated, rate must Bank B set?

Problems

Present and future values for different periods	**5-1** Find the following values *without using tables,* and then work the problems with tables to check your answers. If you have a financial calculator, use it to check your answers. Disregard rounding errors. a. An initial $300 compounded for 1 year at 8 percent. b. An initial $300 compounded for 2 years at 8 percent. c. The present value of $300 due in 1 year at a discount rate of 8 percent. d. The present value of $300 due in 2 years at a discount rate of 8 percent.
Present and future values for different interest rates	**5-2** Use the tables to find the following values. Check your work with a financial calculator if you have one. a. An initial $300 compounded for 10 years at 8 percent. b. An initial $300 compounded for 10 years at 16 percent. c. The present value of $300 due in 10 years at a 8 percent discount rate. d. The present value of $1,323.42 due in 10 years at a 16 percent discount rate and at an 8 percent rate. Give a verbal definition of the term *present value,* and illustrate it with data from this problem. As a part of your answer, explain why present values are dependent upon interest rates.
Time for a lump sum to double	**5-3** To the closest year, how long will it take $200 to double if it is deposited and earns the following rates? (Note: This problem cannot be solved with some financial calculators. For example, if you enter 200, − 400, and 7 in a HP-12C, and then press the n key, you will get 11 years for Part a. The correct answer is 10.2448, which rounds to 10, but the calculator rounds up. However, the HP-17B gives the correct answer. You should look up FVIF = 400/200 = 2 in the tables for Parts a, b, and c, but figure out Part d.) a. 7 percent. b. 9 percent. c. 12 percent. d. 100 percent.
Future value of an annuity	**5-4** Find the *future value* of the following annuities. The first payment in these annuities is made at the *end* of Year 1; that is, they are *ordinary annuities.* a. $200 per year for 10 years at 10 percent. b. $100 per year for 5 years at 5 percent. c. $200 per year for 5 years at 0 percent. d. Now rework Parts a, b, and c assuming that payments are made at the *beginning* of each year; that is, they are *annuities due.*
Present value of an annuity	**5-5** Find the *present value* of the following *ordinary annuities:* a. $200 per year for 10 years at 10 percent. b. $100 per year for 5 years at 5 percent. c. $200 per year for 5 years at 0 percent. d. Now rework Parts a, b, and c assuming that payments are made at the *beginning* of each year; that is, they are *annuities due.*
Uneven cash flow stream	**5-6** a. Find the present values of the following cash flow streams. The appropriate discount rate is 10 percent.

Year	Cash Stream A	Cash Stream B
1	$100	$300
2	400	400
3	400	400
4	400	400
5	300	100

b. What is the value of each cash flow stream at a 0 percent discount rate?

Uneven cash flow stream

5-7   Find the present value of the following cash flow stream, discounted at 5 percent: Year 1, $100; Year 2, $400; Years 3 through 20, $300.

Present value comparison

5-8   Which amount is worth more at 10 percent: $1,000 in hand today or $2,000 due after 8 years?

Growth rates

5-9   Snyder Corporation's 1988 sales were $10 million. Sales were $5 million 5 years earlier (in 1983).
a. To the nearest percentage point, at what rate have sales been growing?
b. Suppose someone calculated the sales growth for Snyder Corporation in Part a as follows: "Sales doubled in 5 years. This represents a growth of 100 percent in 5 years, so, dividing 100 percent by 5, we find the growth rate to be 20 percent per year." Explain what is wrong with this calculation.

Effective rate of interest

5-10   Find the interest rates, or rates of return, on each of the following:
a. You borrow $600 and promise to pay back $648 at the end of 1 year.
b. You lend $600 and receive a promise of $648 at the end of 1 year.
c. You borrow $60,000 and promise to pay back $129,534 at the end of 10 years.
d. You borrow $6,000 and promise to make payments of $1,664.45 per year for 5 years.

Expected rate of return

5-11   The Carver Company buys a machine for $30,000 and expects a return of $7,155.64 per year for the next 10 years. What is the expected rate of return on the machine?

Expected rate of return

5-12   Oregon-Pacific invests $2 million to clear a tract of land and to set out some young pine trees. The trees will mature in 10 years, at which time Oregon-Pacific plans to sell the forest at an expected price of $4 million. What is Oregon-Pacific's expected rate of return?

Effective rate of interest

5-13   Your broker offers to sell you a note for $14,500 that will pay $2,250 per year for 10 years. If you buy the note, what rate of interest (to the closest percent) will you be earning?

Effective rate of interest

5-14   A mortgage company offers to lend you $80,000; the loan calls for payments of $7,494.30 per year for 25 years. What interest rate is the mortgage company charging you?

Required lump sum payment

5-15   To complete your last year in business school and then go through law school, you will need $8,000 per year for 4 years, starting next year (that is, you will need to withdraw $8,000 one year from today). Your rich uncle offers to put you through school, and he will deposit in a bank time deposit paying 8 percent interest a sum of money that is sufficient to provide the four payments of $8,000 each. His deposit will be made today.

a. How large must the deposit be?

b. How much will be in the account immediately after you make the first withdrawal? After the last withdrawal?

Repaying a loan   **5-16**   While Carol Stanton was a student at the University of Florida, she borrowed $12,000 in student loans at an annual interest rate of 8 percent. If Carol repays $1,800 per year, how long, to the nearest year, will it take her to repay the loan?

Reaching a financial goal   **5-17**   If you deposit $1,500 per year in an account which pays 12 percent interest compounded annually, how long will it take you to accumulate a balance of $10,000? (Note that some calculators automatically round up to the nearest whole period. For example, if the solution to a problem is 3.2 periods, the answer will be displayed as 4 periods. These calculators show the correct number of payments — you cannot make 3.2 payments — but fail to indicate that the final payment would be smaller than the previous payments. You should be aware of that potential discrepancy when working this problem.)

Future value for various compounding periods   **5-18**   Find the amount to which $200 will grow under each of the following conditions:

a. 12 percent compounded annually for 5 years.

b. 12 percent compounded semiannually for 5 years.

c. 12 percent compounded quarterly for 5 years.

d. 12 percent compounded monthly for 1 year.

Present value for various compounding periods   **5-19**   Find the present value of $200 due in the future under each of the following conditions:

a. 12 percent nominal rate, semiannual compounding, discounted back 5 years.

b. 12 percent nominal rate, quarterly compounding, discounted back 5 years.

c. 12 percent nominal rate, monthly compounding, discounted back 1 year.

Future value of an annuity for various compounding periods   **5-20**   Find the future values of the following regular annuities:

a. FV of $200 each 6 months for 5 years at a nominal rate of 12 percent, compounded semiannually.

b. FV of $100 each 3 months for 5 years at a nominal rate of 12 percent, compounded quarterly.

c. The annuities described in Parts a and b have the same amount of money paid into them during the 5-year period and both earn interest at the same nominal rate, yet the annuity in Part b earns $50.80 more than the one in Part a over the 5 years. Why does this occur?

Effective versus nominal interest rates   **5-21**   The First City Bank pays 9 percent interest, compounded annually, on time deposits. The Second City Bank pays 8 percent interest, compounded quarterly.

a. In which bank would you prefer to deposit your money?

b. Could your choice of banks be influenced by the fact that you might want to withdraw your funds during the year as opposed to the end of the year? In answering this question, assume that funds must be left on deposit during the entire compounding period in order for you to receive any interest.

Present value of a perpetuity	**5-22**	What is the present value of a perpetuity of $100 per year if the appropriate discount rate is 5 percent? If interest rates in general were to double, and the appropriate discount rate rose to 10 percent, what would happen to the present value of the perpetuity?
Amortization schedule	**5-23**	a. Set up an amortization schedule for a $20,000 loan to be repaid in equal installments at the end of the next 3 years. The interest rate is 10 percent.
		b. How large must each annual payment be if the loan is for $40,000? Assume that the interest rate remains at 10 percent and that the loan is paid off over 3 years.
		c. How large must each payment be if the loan is for $40,000, the interest rate is 10 percent, and the loan is paid off in equal installments at the end of the next 6 years? This loan is for the same amount as the loan in Part b, but the payments are spread out over twice as many periods. Why are these payments not half as large as the payments on the loan in Part b?
Effective rates of return	**5-24**	IBM's pension fund managers recently had to choose between two investments. Their choices were (1) a bond which costs $590 today, pays nothing during its life, and then pays $1,000 after 5 years or (2) a bond which costs $830 today, pays $87.50 in interest at the end of each of the next 12 years, and pays $1,087.50 interest and principal at the end of Year 13.
		a. Which alternative would have provided the higher rate of return?
		b. Assume that the market interest rate dropped to 10 percent immediately after the bonds were purchased and that rates remained at that level for the next 13 years. If IBM holds the bonds until they mature, what annual rates of return would it realize on the two bond alternatives over the 13-year holding period?
Required annuity payments	**5-25**	A father is planning a savings program to put his daughter through college. His daughter is now 13 years old. She plans to enroll at the university in 5 years, and it should take her 4 years to complete her education. Currently, the cost per year (for everything — food, clothing, tuition, books, transportation, and so forth) is $10,000, but a 5 percent inflation rate in these costs is forecasted. The daughter recently received $5,000 from her grandfather's estate; this money, which is invested in a bank account paying 9 percent interest compounded annually, will be used to help meet the costs of the daughter's education. The rest of the costs will be met by money the father will deposit in the savings account. He will make equal deposits to the account in each year from now until his daughter starts college. These deposits will also earn 9 percent interest.
		a. What will be the present value of the cost of four years of education at the time the daughter becomes 18? (Hint: Calculate the future value of the cost in each year of her education and then discount these costs back to the year in which she turns 18.)
		b. What will be the value of the $5,000 which the daughter received from her grandfather's estate at the time she turns 18?
		c. If the father is planning to make the first of 6 deposits today, how large must each deposit be for him to be able to put his daughter through college?

d. How large would each payment need to be if the interest rate on both the money from the grandfather's estate and the annual deposit made by the father were 8 percent?

Present value of an annuity

5-26 Suppose that in January 1989 General Motors' engineers informed top management that they had just made a breakthrough which would permit them to produce an electric car capable of operating at an energy cost of about 3 cents per mile versus an energy cost of about 5 cents for a comparable gasoline-powered car. If GM produces the electric car, it should be able to regain the market share it previously lost to the Japanese. However, the investment required to complete development of the new batteries, to design the new car, and to tool up for production would amount to $6 billion per year for 5 years, starting immediately. Cash inflows from the $30 billion investment should amount to $4 billion per year for 15 years, or $60 billion total, starting 5 years from now. If the electric car project is not undertaken, GM will invest the $6 billion per year for 5 years in investments which earn 10 percent, compounded annually.

a. What is the present value of GM's costs to develop the electric car?
b. What is the present value of the cash flows GM will receive if it develops the electric car?
c. Based on these cost and cash inflow estimates, should GM's management give the go-ahead for full-scale electric car production?

Time value of money analysis
(*Integrative*)

5-27 Answer the following questions concerning time value of money analysis:
a. Why are discounted cash flow (time value of money) concepts so important in financial analysis? What is a time line? What is a lump sum cash flow? An annuity? An uneven cash flow stream?
b. 1. What is the future value of $100 after 3 years if it is invested in an account paying 10 percent annual interest?
   2. What is the present value of $100 to be received in 3 years if the appropriate interest rate is 10 percent?
c. What is the difference between an ordinary, or regular, annuity and an annuity due? What type of annuity is this? How would you change it to the other type of annuity?

d. What is the future value of a 3-year ordinary annuity of $100 if the appropriate interest rate is 10 percent? What is the present value of the annuity? What would the future and present values be if the annuity were an annuity due?
e. What is the present value of the following cash flow stream? The appropriate interest rate is 10 percent.

Year	CF
0	$ 0
1	100
2	300
3	300
4	(50)

f. What annual interest rate will cause $100 to grow to $125.97 in 3 years?

g. What is the result of compounding more often than annually? What is the difference between the stated, or nominal, rate and the effective annual rate? What is the effective annual rate for a nominal rate of 10 percent, compounded semiannually? Compounded quarterly? Compounded daily? What is the future value of $100 after 3 years under 10 percent semiannual compounding? Quarterly compounding?

h. What is the value at the end of Year 3 of the following cash flow stream if the interest rate is 10 percent, compounded semiannually? What is the PV of the same stream? Is the stream an annuity?

i. Construct an amortization schedule for a $1,000, 10 percent annual rate loan with 3 equal installments. What is the annual interest expense for the borrower, and the annual interest income for the lender?

Computer-Related Problems

(Work the problems in this section only if you are using the computer problem diskette.)

Amortization schedule   **C5-1**   Use the computerized model for Problem C5-1 in the file C5 to solve this problem.

a. Set up an amortization schedule for a $20,000 loan to be repaid in equal installments at the end of each of the next 20 years at an interest rate of 10 percent. What is the annual payment?

b. Set up an amortization schedule for a $40,000 loan to be repaid in 20 equal annual installments at an interest rate of 10 percent. What is the annual payment?

c. Set up an amortization schedule for a $40,000 loan to be repaid in 20 equal annual installments at an interest rate of 20 percent. What is the annual payment?

Required annuity payments   **C5-2**   Use the computerized model for Problem C5-2 in the file C5 to solve this problem.

a. Refer back to Problem 5-25. How large must each deposit be if the interest rate is expected to remain at 9 percent for 2 years and then to fall to 8 percent for the remainder of the time until the daughter graduates from college? (Assume that the interest rate on the grandfather's money will also decline because this money is in a savings account.)

b. Using the interest rate as given in Part a, how large would each payment need to be if inflation were expected to be 8 percent rather than 5 percent?

Present value of an annuity   **C5-3**   Use the computerized model for Problem C5-3 in the file C5 to solve this problem.

a. Refer to Problem 5-26. Suppose inflation is expected to average 5 percent per year during the 19-year forecast period. Therefore, all forecasted cash inflows and outflows will increase by 5 percent per year. On the basis of these revised cash flows, should GM produce the electric car?

b. In the original problem (Problem 5-26), the present value of the electric car project was negative, but it was positive in the scenario described in Part a. Why did inflation have so much greater an effect on the cash inflows than on the cash outflows?

c. At what forecastable rate of inflation would GM be indifferent to the electric car project? (Change the inflation rate by trial-and-error until the present value of the project is zero.)

Solutions to Self-Test Problems

ST-1 Refer to the marginal glossary definitions or appropriate sections of the chapter to check your responses.

ST-2 a.

1/1/89	1/1/90	1/1/91	1/1/92	1/1/93
$1,000				

$1,000 is being compounded for 3 years, so your balance on January 1, 1993, is $1,259.71:

$$FV = PV(1 + k)^n = \$1,000(1 + 0.08)^3 = \$1,259.71.$$

b. The effective annual rate for 8 percent, compounded quarterly, is

$$\begin{align*}
\text{Effective annual rate} &= \left(1 + \frac{0.08}{4}\right)^4 - 1.0 \\
&= (1.02)^4 - 1.0 = 0.0824 = 8.24\%.
\end{align*}$$

Therefore, FV = $1,000(1.0824)^3 = \$1,000(1.2681) = \$1,268.10$. Alternatively, use FVIF for 2%, $3 \times 4 = 12$ periods:

$$FV = \$1,000(FVIF_{2\%,12 \text{ periods}}) = \$1,000(1.2682) = \$1,268.20.$$

(Calculator solution = $1,268.24.)

Note that since the interest factors are carried to only four decimal places, rounding errors occur. Rounding errors also occur between calculator and tabular solutions.

c.

1/1/89	1/1/90	1/1/91	1/1/92	1/1/93
	$250	$250	$250	$250

As you work this problem, keep in mind that the tables assume that payments are made at the end of each period. Therefore, you may solve this problem by finding the future value of an annuity of $250 for 4 years at 8 percent:

$$PMT(FVIFA_{k,n}) = \$250(4.5061) = \$1,126.53.$$

d. FV = $1,259.71; k = 8\%; n = 4$.

$$PMT(FVIFA_{8\%,4 \text{ years}}) = FV$$

$$PMT(4.5061) = \$1,259.71$$

$$PMT = \$1,259.71/4.5061 = \$279.56.$$

Therefore, you would have to make 4 payments of $279.56 each to have a balance of $1,259.71 on January 1, 1993.

ST-3 a. Set up a time line like those in the preceding problem, and note that your deposit will grow for 3 years at 8 percent. The fact that it is now January 1, 1989, is irrelevant. The deposit on January 1, 1990, is the PV, and the $1,000 = FV. Here is the solution:

$$FV = \$1,000; n = 3; k = 8\%.$$

$$FV(PVIF_{8\%, 3 \text{ years}}) = PV$$

$$PV = \$1,000(0.7938) = \$793.80 = \text{Initial deposit to accumulate } \$1,000.$$

$$(\text{Calculator solution} = \$793.83.)$$

b. Here we are dealing with a 4-year annuity whose first payment occurs one year from today, on 1/1/90, and whose future value must equal $1,000. You should set up a time line to help visualize the situation. Here is the solution:

$$FV = \$1,000; n = 4; k = 8\%.$$

$$PMT(FVIFA_{8\%, 4 \text{ years}}) = FV$$

$$PMT = \frac{FV}{(FVIFA_{8\%, 4 \text{ years}})}$$

$$= \frac{\$1,000}{4.5061}$$

$$= \$221.92 = \text{Payment necessary to accumulate } \$1,000.$$

c. This problem can be approached in several ways. Perhaps the simplest is to ask this question: "If I received $750 on 1/1/90 and deposited it to earn 8 percent, would I have the required $1,000 on 1/1/93?" The answer is no:

$$\$750(1.08)(1.08)(1.08) = \$944.78.$$

This indicates that you should let your father make the payments rather than accept the lump sum of $750.

You could also compare the $750 with the PV of the payments:

$$PMT = \$221.92; k = 8\%; n = 4.$$

$$PMT(PVIFA_{8\%, 4 \text{ years}}) = PV$$

$$\$221.92(3.3121) = \$735.02 = \text{Present value of the required payments.}$$

This is less than the $750 lump sum offer, so your initial reaction might be to accept the lump sum of $750. However, this would be a mistake. As we saw before, if you were to deposit the $750 on January 1, 1990, at an 8 percent interest rate, to be withdrawn on January 1, 1993, interest would be compounded for only 3 years, from January 1, 1990, to December 31, 1992, and the future value would be only

$$PV(FVIF_{8\%,3 \text{ years}}) = \$750(1.2597) = \$944.78.$$

The problem is that when you found the $735.02 PV of the annuity, you were finding the value of the annuity *today*, on January 1, 1989. You were comparing $735.02 today with the lump sum of $750 one year from now. This is, of course, invalid. What you should have done was take the $735.02, recognize that this is the PV of an annuity as of January 1, 1989, multiply $735.02 by 1.08 to get $793.82, and compare $793.82 with the lump sum of $750. You would then take your father's offer to make the payments rather than take the lump sum on January 1, 1990.

d. $PV = \$750$; $FV = \$1,000$; $n = 3$; $k = ?$

$$PV(FVIF_{k,3 \text{ years}}) = FV$$

$$FVIF_{k,3 \text{ years}} = \frac{FV}{PV}$$

$$= \frac{\$1,000}{\$750} = 1.3333.$$

Use the Future Value of $1 table (Table A-3 at the end of the book) for 3 periods to find the interest rate corresponding to an FVIF of 1.3333. Look across the Period 3 row of the table until you come to 1.3333. The closest value is 1.3310, in the 10 percent column. Therefore, you would require an interest rate of approximately 10 percent to achieve your $1,000 goal. The exact rate required, found with a financial calculator, is 10.0642 percent.

e. $FV = \$1,000$; $PMT = \$186.29$; $n = 4$; $k = ?$

$$PMT(FVIFA_{k,4 \text{ years}}) = FV$$

$$\$186.29(FVIFA_{k,4 \text{ years}}) = \$1,000$$

$$FVIFA_{k,4 \text{ years}} = \frac{\$1,000}{\$186.29} = 5.3680.$$

Using Table A-4 at the end of the book, we find that 5.3680 corresponds to a 20 percent interest rate. You might be able to find a borrower willing to offer you a 20 percent interest rate, but there would be some risk involved — he or she might not actually pay you your $1,000!

(Calculator solution = 19.9997%.)

f.

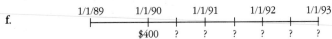

Find the future value of the original $400 deposit:

$$FV = PV(FVIF_{4\%,6}) = \$400(1.2653) = \$506.12.$$

This means that on January 1, 1993, you need an additional sum of $493.88:

$$\$1,000.00 - \$506.12 = \$493.88.$$

This will be accumulated by making 6 equal payments which earn 8 percent compounded semiannually, or 4 percent each 6 months:

$$FV = \$493.88; n = 6; k = 4\%.$$

$$PMT(FVIFA_{4\%,6}) = FV$$

$$PMT = \frac{FV}{(FVIFA_{4\%,6})}$$

$$= \frac{\$493.88}{6.6330} = \$74.46.$$

g.   Effective annual rate $= \left(1 + \frac{k_{Nom}}{m}\right)^m - 1.0$

$$= \left(1 + \frac{0.08}{2}\right)^2 - 1 = (1.04)^2 - 1$$

$$= 1.0816 - 1 = 0.0816 = 8.16\%.$$

h. There is a reinvestment rate risk here, because we assumed that funds will earn an 8 percent return in the bank. In fact, if interest rates in the economy fall, the bank will lower its deposit rate because it will be earning less when it lends out the funds you deposited with it. If you buy certificates of deposit (CDs) that mature on the date you need the money (1/1/93), you will avoid the reinvestment risk, but that will work only where you are making the deposit today. Other ways of reducing reinvestment rate risk will be discussed later in the text.

ST-4   Bank A's effective annual rate is 8.24 percent:

$$\text{Effective annual rate} = \left(1 + \frac{0.08}{4}\right)^4 - 1.0$$

$$= (1.02)^4 - 1 = 1.0824 - 1$$

$$= 0.0824 = 8.24\%.$$

Now Bank B must have the same effective annual rate:

$$\left(1 + \frac{k}{12}\right)^{12} - 1.0 = 0.0824$$

$$\left(1 + \frac{k}{12}\right)^{12} = 1.0824$$

$$1 + \frac{k}{12} = (1.0824)^{1/12}$$

$$1 + \frac{k}{12} = 1.00662$$

$$\frac{k}{12} = 0.00662$$

$$k = 0.07944 = 7.94\%.$$

5A

Continuous Compounding and Discounting

In Chapter 5, we implicitly assumed that growth occurs at discrete intervals — annually, semiannually, and so forth. For some purposes it is better to assume instantaneous, or *continuous,* growth. In this appendix, we discuss present value and future value relationships when the interest rate is compounded continuously.

Continuous Compounding

The relationship between discrete and continuous compounding is illustrated in Figure 5A-1. Panel a shows the annual compounding case, in which interest is added once a year; in Panel b compounding occurs twice a year; and in Panel c, interest is earned continuously. As the graphs show, the more frequent the compounding period, the larger the final compound amount, because interest is earned on interest more often.

In Chapter 5, Equation 5-2a was developed to allow for any number of compounding periods per year:

$$FV_n = PV\left(1 + \frac{k_{Nom}}{m}\right)^{mn}. \tag{5-2a}$$

Here k_{Nom} = the stated interest rate, m = the number of compounding periods per year, and n = the number of years. To illustrate, let PV = \$100, k = 10%, and n = 5. At various compounding periods per year, we obtain the following future values at the end of 5 years:

$$\text{Annual: } FV_5 = \$100\left(1 + \frac{0.10}{1}\right)^{1(5)} = \$100(1.10)^5 = \$161.05.$$

$$\text{Semiannual: } FV_5 = \$100\left(1 + \frac{0.10}{2}\right)^{2(5)} = \$100(1.05)^{10} = \$162.89.$$

$$\text{Monthly: } FV_5 = \$100\left(1 + \frac{0.10}{12}\right)^{12(5)} = \$100(1.0083)^{60} = \$164.53.$$

$$\text{Daily: } FV_5 = \$100\left(1 + \frac{0.10}{365}\right)^{365(5)} = \$164.86.$$

$$\text{Hourly: } FV_5 = \$100\left(1 + \frac{0.10}{8,760}\right)^{365(24)(5)} = \$164.88.$$

We could keep going, compounding every minute, every second, every 1/1,000th of a second, and so on. At the limit, we could compound every instant, or *continuously.* The equation for continuous compounding is

$$FV_n = PV(e^{kn}), \tag{5A-1}$$

Figure 5A-1   Annual, Semiannual, and Continuous Compounding: Future Value with k = 25%

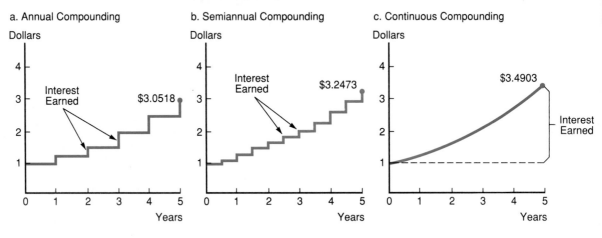

a. Annual Compounding

b. Semiannual Compounding

c. Continuous Compounding

---

where e is the value 2.7183 . . . .[1] If $100 is invested for 5 years at 10 percent compounded continuously, then FV_5 is computed as follows:

$$\text{Continuous: } FV_5 = \$100[e^{0.10(5)}] = \$100(2.7183 \ldots)^{0.5}$$

$$= \$164.872.$$

Continuous Discounting

Equation 5A-1 can be transformed into Equation 5A-2 and used to determine present values under continuous discounting:

$$PV = \frac{FV_n}{e^{kn}} = FV_n e^{-kn}. \tag{5A-2}$$

Thus, if $1,649 is due in 10 years, and if the appropriate *continuous* discount rate, k, is 5 percent, then the present value of this future payment is

$$PV = \$1,649\left[\frac{1}{(2.7183 \ldots)^{0.5}}\right] = \frac{\$1,649}{1.649} = \$1,000.$$

---

[1]Calculators with exponential functions can be used to evaluate Equation 5A-1.

6 Bond and Stock Valuation

PICKING WINNERS AND AVOIDING LOSERS IN THE BOND AND STOCK MARKETS

In February 1988, some bonds Alabama Power had issued several years earlier for $1,000 were selling for only $875, while some other Alabama Power bonds that had also been issued at $1,000 were selling for $1,060. In the same month, U.S. Treasury bonds originally sold to investors for $1,000 ranged in price from $785 to $1,480. Coleco had some $1,000 bonds that were selling for only $321, while Compaq Computer's bonds were selling well above par, at $1,250. Why had the holders of some of Alabama Power's bonds suffered large capital losses while others were making substantial gains? Why were the Compaq bonds selling so high, and the Coleco bonds so low? How could one invest in U.S. Treasury securities and lose money?

At the same time, some interesting things were happening in the stock market. The stock of CBS, the broadcasting company, was selling for $164 per share, down from its high of $226 a few months earlier. Still, CBS stockholders had not done badly. Just two years ago the stock had sold for $115, and in 1983 it could have been bought for as little as $62. Thus, although CBS's stock price had fallen dramatically just recently, the stock had still gained an average of more than 21 percent per year during the last five years. The stock market generally increased during this period, but not all stocks had done as well as CBS. For example, Apple Computer was selling for $41, down from its record high a few months earlier of $59 and up only $9 per share from its 1983 price. For the five years from 1983 until 1988, Apple's stock had gained an average of only 5 percent per year. Why was CBS stock worth $164 per share and Apple $41? More important, what actions can managers take to increase their firms' stock prices, and how can investors decide what a stock or bond is worth, and which securities are likely to rise in value rather than fall?

You will be able to answer some of these questions, and will gain insights into the others, after reading this chapter. Study hard, and perhaps you can pick the winners and avoid the losers.

IN Chapter 1 we noted that financial managers should work to maximize the value of their firms. Then, in Chapter 4, we saw how investors determine the rates of return they require on securities, and in Chapter 5 we examined time value of money, or discounted cash flow (DCF), analysis. These DCF concepts are used by managers and investors to establish the worth of any asset whose value is derived from future cash flows; such assets include real estate, factories, machinery, oil wells, coal mines, farmland, stocks, and bonds. In this chapter we use time value of money techniques to explain how financial managers and investors go about establishing the values of stocks and bonds. The material covered in the chapter is obviously important to investors and potential investors, and it is equally important to financial managers. *Indeed, since all important corporate decisions should be analyzed in terms of how they will affect the price of the firm's stock, it is essential that managers know how stock prices are determined.*

BOND VALUES

Corporations raise capital in two primary forms — debt and common equity. Our first task in this chapter is to examine the valuation process for bonds, the principal type of long-term debt.

bond
A long-term debt instrument.

A **bond** is a long-term promissory note issued by a business or governmental unit. For example, on January 2, 1989, the Teletron Electronics Company borrowed $50 million by selling 50,000 individual bonds for $1,000 each. Teletron received the $50 million and promised to pay the bondholders annual interest and to repay the $50 million on a specified date. The lenders were willing to give Teletron $50 million, so the value of the bond issue was $50 million. But how did the investors decide that the issue was worth $50 million? As a first step in explaining how the values of this and other bonds are determined, we need to define some terms:

par value
The nominal or face value of a stock or bond.

1. *Par value.* The **par value** is the stated face value of the bond; it is usually set at $1,000, although multiples of $1,000 (for example, $5,000) are used on occasion. The par value generally represents the amount of money the firm borrows and promises to repay at some future date.

maturity date
A specified date on which the par value of a bond must be repaid.

original maturity
The number of years to maturity at the time a bond is issued.

call provision
A provision in a bond contract that gives the issuer the right to redeem the bonds under specified terms prior to the stated maturity date.

coupon payment
Specified dollars of interest paid each period, generally each six months, on a bond.

coupon interest rate
The stated annual rate of interest on a bond.

2. *Maturity date.* Bonds generally have a specified **maturity date** on which the par value must be repaid. Teletron's bonds, which were issued on January 2, 1989, will mature on January 1, 2004; thus, they had a 15-year maturity at the time they were issued. Most bonds have **original maturities** (the maturity at the time the bond is issued) of from 10 to 40 years, but any maturity is legally permissible. Of course, the effective maturity of a bond declines each year after it has been issued. Thus, Teletron's bonds had a 15-year original maturity, but in 1990 they will have a 14-year maturity, and so on.

3. *Call provisions.* Some bonds have a provision whereby the issuer may pay them off prior to maturity. This feature is known as a **call provision**, and it is discussed in detail in Chapter 13. If a bond is callable, and if interest rates in the economy decline, then the company can sell a new issue of low-interest-rate bonds and use the proceeds to retire the old high-interest-rate issue, just as a homeowner can refinance a home mortgage.

4. *Coupon interest rate.* The bond requires the issuer to pay a specified number of dollars of interest each year (or, more typically, each six months). When this **coupon payment**, as it is called, is divided by the par value, the result is the **coupon interest rate**. For example, Teletron Electronics' bonds have a $1,000 par value, and they pay $150 in interest each year. The bond's coupon interest is $150, so its coupon interest rate is $150/$1,000 = 15 percent. The $150 is the yearly "rent" on the $1,000 loan. This payment, which is fixed at the time the bond is issued, remains in force, by contract, during the life of the bond. Incidentally, some time ago, most bonds literally had a number of small (½-by-2-inch) dated coupons attached to them, and on the interest payment date, the owner would clip off the coupon for that date and either cash it at his or her bank or mail it to the company's paying agent, who then mailed back a check for the interest. A 30-year, semiannual bond started with 60 coupons, whereas a 5-year annual payment bond would start with only 5 coupons. Today, however, most bonds are *registered* — no coupons are involved, and interest checks are mailed automatically to the registered owners of the bonds. Even so, we continue to use the terms *coupon* and *coupon interest rate,* even for registered bonds.

5. *New issues versus outstanding bonds.* As we shall see, a bond's market price is determined primarily by its coupon interest payments — the higher the coupon, other things held constant, the higher the market price of the bond. At the time a bond is issued, the coupon is generally set at a level that will force the market price of the bond to equal its par value. If a lower coupon were set, investors simply would not be willing to pay $1,000 for the bond, while if a higher coupon were set, investors would clamor for the bond and bid its price up over $1,000. Investment bankers can judge quite precisely the coupon rate that will cause a bond to sell at its $1,000 par value.

A bond that has just been issued is known as a *new issue. (The Wall Street Journal* classifies a bond as a new issue for about two weeks after it has first been issued.) Once the bond has been on the market for a while, it is classified as an *outstanding bond,* also called a *seasoned issue.* Newly issued bonds generally sell very close to par, but the prices of outstanding bonds vary widely from par. Coupon interest payments are constant, so when economic conditions change, a bond with a $150 coupon that sold at par when it was issued will sell for more or less than $1,000 thereafter.

The Basic Bond Valuation Model[1]

As we noted previously, bonds call for the payment of a specified amount of interest for a stated number of years, and for the repayment of the par value on the bond's maturity date. Thus, a bond represents an annuity plus a lump sum, and its value is found as the present value of this payment stream.

The following equation is used to find a bond's value:[2]

$$\text{Value} = V = \sum_{t=1}^{n} I\left(\frac{1}{1 + k_d}\right)^t + M\left(\frac{1}{1 + k_d}\right)^n$$

$$= I(\text{PVIFA}_{k_d,n}) + M(\text{PVIF}_{k_d,n}). \tag{6-1}$$

Here

I = dollars of interest paid each year = coupon interest rate × par value.
M = par value, or maturity value, which is typically $1,000.
k_d = appropriate rate of interest on the bond.[3]
n = number of years until the bond matures; n declines each year after the bond is issued, so a bond that had a maturity of 30 years when it was issued (original maturity = 30 years) becomes a 29-year bond a year later, then a 28-year bond, and so on.

We can use Equation 6-1 to find the value of Teletron's bonds when they were issued. Simply substitute $150 for I, $1,000 for M, and the values of PVIFA

---

[1]In finance the term *model* refers to an equation or set of equations designed to show how one or more variables affect some other variable. Thus, a bond valuation model shows the mathematical relationship between a bond's price and the set of variables that determine the price.

[2]Actually, since most bonds pay interest semiannually, not annually, it is necessary for us to modify our valuation equation slightly. The modification is discussed later in the chapter. Also, we should note that some bonds issued in recent years either pay no interest during their lives (zero coupon bonds) or else pay very low coupon rates. Such bonds are sold at a discount below par, and hence they are called *original issue discount bonds.* The "interest" earned on a zero coupon bond comes at the end, when the company pays off at par ($1,000) a bond which was purchased for, say, $321.97. The discount of $1,000 − $321.97 = $678.03 substitutes for interest. Original issue discount bonds are discussed at greater length in Chapter 13.

[3]The appropriate interest rate on debt securities was discussed in Chapter 3. The bond's riskiness and years to maturity, as well as supply and demand conditions in the capital markets, all have an influence.

Figure 6-1   Time Line for Teletron Electronics Bonds

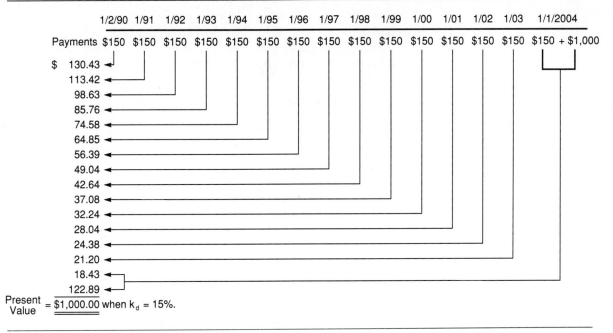

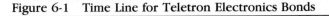

and PVIF at 15 percent, 15 periods, as found in Tables A-2 and A-1 at the end of the book:

$$V = \$150(5.8474) + \$1,000(0.1229)$$

$$= \$877.11 + \$122.90$$

$$= \$1,000.01 \approx \$1,000 \text{ when } k_d = 15\%.$$

Figure 6-1 shows the same result in a time line graph.

You can also find the value of these bonds with many financial calculators. Enter n = 15, PMT = 150, FV = 1,000, and k_d = i = 15, and then press the PV key. The answer, \$1,000 (or −\$1,000), will appear.

If k_d remained constant at 15 percent, what would the value of the bond be 1 year after it was issued? We can find this value using Equation 6-1, but now the term to maturity is only 14 years — that is, n = 14. We see that V remains at \$1,000:

$$V = \$150(5.7245) + \$1,000(0.1413)$$

$$= \$999.98 \approx \$1,000.$$

With a financial calculator, just replace n = 15 with n = 14, press the PV button, and you will get the same answer. The value of the bond will remain at $1,000 as long as the appropriate interest rate for it remains constant at 15 percent.[4]

Now suppose interest rates in the economy fell after the Teletron bonds were issued, and, as a result, k_d *decreased* from 15 to 10 percent. Both the coupon interest payments and the maturity value remain constant, but now 10 percent values for PVIF and PVIFA would have to be used in Equation 6-1. The value of the bond at the end of the first year would be $1,368.31:

$$V = \$150(\text{PVIFA}_{10\%,14 \text{ years}}) + \$1,000(\text{PVIF}_{10\%,14 \text{ years}})$$

$$= \$150(7.3667) + \$1,000(0.2633)$$

$$= \$1,105.01 + \$263.30$$

$$= \$1,368.31.$$

Thus, the bond would sell above, or at a *premium* over, its par value.

The arithmetic of the bond value increase should be clear, but what is the logic behind it? The fact that k_d has fallen to 10 percent means that if you had $1,000 to invest, you could buy new bonds like Teletron's (every day some 10 to 12 companies sell new bonds), except that they would pay $100 of interest each year rather than $150. Naturally, you would prefer $150 to $100, so you would be willing to pay more than $1,000 for Teletron bonds to obtain its higher coupons. All investors would recognize these facts, and, as a result, the Teletron bonds would be bid up in price to $1,368.31, at which point they would provide the same rate of return to a potential investor as the new bonds — 10 percent.

Assuming that interest rates remain constant at 10 percent for the next 14 years, what would happen to the value of a Teletron bond? It would fall gradually from $1,368.31 at present to $1,000 at maturity, when Teletron Electronics must redeem each bond for $1,000. This point can be illustrated by calculating the value of the bond 1 year later, when it has 13 years remaining to maturity:

$$V = \$150(\text{PVIFA}_{10\%,13 \text{ years}}) + \$1,000(\text{PVIF}_{10\%,13 \text{ years}})$$

$$= \$150(7.1034) + \$1,000(0.2897) = \$1,355.21.$$

Thus, the value of the bond will have fallen from $1,368.31 to $1,355.21, or by

---

[4]The bond prices quoted by brokers are calculated as described. However, if you bought a bond between interest payment dates, you would have to pay the basic price plus accrued interest. Thus, if you purchased a Teletron Electronics bond 6 months after it was issued, your broker would send you an invoice stating that you must pay $1,000 as the basic price of the bond plus $75 interest, representing one-half the annual interest of $150. The seller of the bond would receive $1,075. If you bought the bond the day before its interest payment date, you would pay $1,000 + (364/365)($150) = $1,149.59. Of course, you would receive an interest payment of $150 at the end of the next day. See Self-Test Problem 3 for a detailed discussion of bond quotations between interest payment dates.

Throughout the chapter we assume that the bond is being evaluated immediately after an interest payment date. The better financial calculators have a built-in calendar which permits the calculation of exact values between interest payment dates.

$13.10. If you were to calculate the value of the bond at other future dates, the price would continue to fall as the maturity date approached.

Notice that if you purchased the bond at a price of $1,368.31 and then sold it 1 year later with k_d still at 10 percent, you would have a capital loss of $13.10, or a total return of $150.00 − $13.10 = $136.90. Your percentage rate of return would consist of an *interest yield* (also called a *current yield*) plus a *capital gains yield,* calculated as follows:

$$\text{Interest, or current, yield} = \$150/\$1,368.31 = 0.1096 = 10.96\%$$
$$\text{Capital gains yield} = -\$13.10/\$1,368.31 = -0.0096 = -0.96\%$$
$$\text{Total rate of return, or yield} = \$136.90/\$1,368.31 = 0.1001 \approx \underline{10.00\%}$$

Had interest rates risen from 15 to 20 percent during the first year after issue rather than fallen, the value of Teletron bonds would have declined to $769.49:

$$V = \$150(\text{PVIFA}_{20\%,14 \text{ years}}) + \$1,000(\text{PVIF}_{20\%,14 \text{ years}})$$

$$= \$150(4.6106) + \$1,000(0.0779)$$

$$= \$691.59 + \$77.90$$

$$= \$769.49.$$

In this case, the bond would sell at a *discount* of $230.51 below its par value:

$$\text{Discount} = \text{Price} - \text{Par value} = \$769.49 - \$1,000.00$$
$$= -\$230.51.$$

The total expected future yield on the bond would again consist of a current yield and a capital gains yield, but now the capital gains yield would be *positive.* The total yield would be 20 percent.

The discount or premium on a bond may also be calculated as follows:

$$\frac{\text{Discount}}{\text{or premium}} = \left[\begin{array}{c}\text{Interest payment} \\ \text{on the old bond}\end{array} - \begin{array}{c}\text{Interest payment} \\ \text{on the new bond}\end{array}\right](\text{PVIFA}_{k_d,n}),$$

where n = years to maturity on the old bond and k_d = current rate of interest on a new bond. For example, if interest rates had risen to 20 percent 1 year after the Teletron bonds were issued, the discount on them would have been calculated as follows:

$$\text{Discount} = (\$150 - \$200)(4.6106) = -\$230.53.$$

(The minus sign indicates discount.) This value agrees, except for rounding, with the −$230.51 value calculated previously. From these calculations, we see that the discount is equal to the present value of the interest payment you sacrifice when you buy a low-coupon old bond rather than a high-coupon new bond. The longer the bond has left to maturity, the greater the sacrifice, and hence the greater the discount.

Figure 6-2 graphs the values of the bond over time, assuming that interest rates in the economy (1) remain constant at 15 percent, (2) fall to 10 percent

Figure 6-2   Time Path of the Value of a 15% Coupon, $1,000 Par Value Bond When Interest Rates are 10%, 15%, and 20%

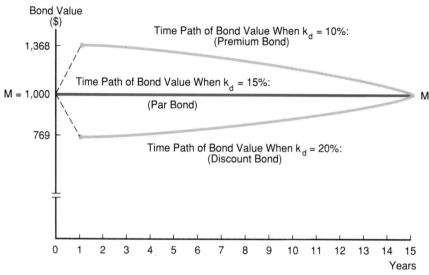

Note: The curves for 10% and 20% have a slight bow.

and then remain constant at that level, or (3) rise to 20 percent and remain constant at that level. Of course, if interest rates do *not* remain constant, then the price of the bond will fluctuate. However, regardless of what future interest rates do, the bond's price will approach $1,000 as it nears the maturity date (barring bankruptcy, in which case the bond's value might drop to zero).

Figure 6-2 illustrates the following key points:

1.   Whenever the going rate of interest, k_d, is equal to the coupon rate, a bond will sell at its par value. Normally, the coupon rate is set at the going interest rate when a bond is issued, so it sells at par initially.

2.   Interest rates change over time, but the coupon rate remains fixed after the bond has been issued. Whenever the going rate of interest is *greater than* the coupon rate, a bond will sell *below* its par value. Such a bond is called a **discount bond.**

3.   Whenever the going rate of interest is *less than* the coupon rate, a bond will sell *above* its par value. Such a bond is called a **premium bond.**

4.   Thus, an *increase* in interest rates will cause the price of an outstanding bond to *fall,* whereas a *decrease* in rates will cause it to *rise.*

5.   The market value of a bond will always approach its par value as its maturity date approaches, provided the firm does not go bankrupt.

These points are very important, for they show that bondholders may suffer capital losses or make capital gains, depending on whether interest rates rise or fall. And, as we saw in Chapter 3, interest rates do indeed change over time.

discount bond
A bond that sells below its par value; occurs when the coupon rate is lower than the going rate of interest.

premium bond
A bond that sells above its par value; occurs when the coupon rate is above the going rate of interest.

Finding the Interest Rate on a Bond: Yield to Maturity

yield to maturity (YTM)
The rate of return
earned on a bond if it is
held to maturity.

Suppose you were offered a 14-year, 15 percent coupon, $1,000 par value bond at a price of $1,368.31. What rate of interest would you earn on your investment if you bought the bond and held it to maturity? This rate is called the bond's **yield to maturity (YTM)**, and it is the interest rate discussed by bond traders when they talk about rates of return. To find the yield to maturity, you could solve Equation 6-1 for k_d:

$$V = \$1{,}368.31 = \frac{\$150}{(1 + k_d)^1} + \ldots + \frac{\$150}{(1 + k_d)^{14}} + \frac{\$1{,}000}{(1 + k_d)^{14}}$$

$$= \$150(\text{PVIFA}_{k_d,14}) + \$1{,}000(\text{PVIF}_{k_d,14}).$$

You can substitute values for PVIFA and PVIF until you find a pair that "works" and forces this equality:

$$\$1{,}368.31 = \$150(\text{PVIFA}_{k_d,14}) + \$1{,}000(\text{PVIF}_{k_d,14}).$$

What would be a good interest rate to use as a starting point? First, you know that because the bond is selling at a premium over its par value ($1,368.31 versus $1,000), the bond's yield to maturity must be *below* its 15 percent coupon rate. Therefore, you might try a rate of 12 percent. Substituting factors for 12 percent, you obtain

$$\$150(6.6282) + \$1{,}000(0.2046) = \$1{,}198.83 \neq \$1{,}368.31.$$

The calculated bond value, $1,198.83, is *below* the actual market price, so the YTM is *not* 12 percent. To raise the calculated value, you must *lower* the interest rate used in the process. Inserting interest factors for 10 percent, you obtain

$$V = \$150(7.3667) + \$1{,}000(0.2633)$$

$$= \$1{,}105.01 + \$263.30$$

$$= \$1{,}368.31.$$

This calculated value is equal to the market price of the bond; thus, 10 percent is the bond's yield to maturity: $k_d = \text{YTM} = 10.0\%$.[5]

---

[5]A few years ago, bond traders all had specialized tables called *bond tables* that gave yields on bonds of different maturities selling at different premiums and discounts. Because calculators are so much more efficient (and accurate), bond tables are rarely used any more.

R. J. Rodriquez recently developed a formula that can be used to find the *approximate* YTM on a bond:

$$\text{Approximate } k_d = \text{Approximate YTM} \approx \frac{I + (M - V)/n}{(M + 2V)/3}.$$

The numerator gives the average total return (coupon plus capital gain or loss) over the life of the bond, while the denominator is the average price of the bond. In our example, I = $150, M = $1,000, V = $1,368.31, and n = 14, so

$$\text{Approximate } k_d \approx \frac{\$150 + (\$1{,}000 - \$1{,}368.31)/14}{(\$1{,}000 + \$2{,}736.62)/3} = 0.0993 = 9.93\%.$$

The exact value is 10 percent, so Rodriquez's formula provides a close approximation.

As you might guess, by far the easiest way to find the bond's YTM is with a financial calculator. In this example, enter n = 14, PMT = 150, FV = 1,000, and PV = 1,368.31 (−1,368.31 on some calculators). Now press the i button. The calculator will blink for several seconds, and then the answer, 10 percent, will appear.[6]

The yield to maturity is identical to the total rate of return discussed in the preceding section. The YTM for a bond that sells at par consists entirely of an interest yield, but if the bond sells at a price other than par value, the YTM consists of the interest yield plus a positive or negative capital gains yield. Note also that a bond's yield to maturity changes whenever interest rates in the economy change, and this is almost daily. One who purchases a bond and holds it until it matures will receive the YTM that existed on the purchase date, but the bond's calculated YTM will change frequently between the purchase date and the maturity date.

Yield to Call

If you purchased a bond that was callable, and the company called it, you would not have the option of holding it until it matured, so the yield to maturity would not be applicable. For example, if Teletron Electronics' 15 percent coupon bonds were callable, and if interest rates fell from 15 percent to 10 percent, the company could call in the 15 percent bonds, replace them with 10 percent bonds, and save $150 − $100 = $50 interest per bond per year. This would be beneficial to the company, but not to its bondholders.

If current interest rates are well below an outstanding bond's coupon rate, then a callable bond is likely to be called, and investors should estimate the expected rate of return on the bond as the **yield to call (YTC)** rather than as the yield to maturity. To calculate the YTC, solve this equation for k_d:

yield to call (YTC)
The rate of return earned on a bond if it is called before its maturity date.

$$\text{Price of bond} = \sum_{t=1}^{N} \frac{I}{(1 + k_d)^t} + \frac{\text{Call price}}{(1 + k_d)^N}.$$

Here N is the number of years until the company can call the bond; call price is the price the company must pay in order to call the bond (it is often set equal to the par value plus one year's interest); and k_d is the YTC. In the balance of the chapter, we assume that bonds are not callable unless otherwise noted, but some of the end-of-chapter problems deal with yield to call.

Call provisions can have a profound effect on a bond's value. Consider the following example. In 1984, the Duval County (Florida) Housing Authority sold some 30-year zero coupon bonds (zeros) to yield 11.5 percent tax-exempt interest. The price of the bonds was $38.17 — an investor would pay $38.17, and 30 years later he or she would get back $1,000. The money the housing

---

[6]If you are using a Sharp calculator, make sure that it is *not* in BGN mode, and press the compute key before pressing the i button. With an HP 17B, go into the TVM menu, END Mode, enter the values, and press PV to get the answer.

authority received was made available to low-income home buyers; these home buyers were able to obtain mortgage money for 11.5 percent versus about 14.5 percent, which was the going mortgage loan rate at the time.

A provision in the bonds stated that if the Housing Authority received cash from home buyers who were paying off their loans, then that cash could be used to call and pay off the zeros, with the call price being set at $38.17(1.115)^n$, with n being the number of years since the bonds were issued. However, because the rate home buyers were paying in 1984 was so far below the going mortgage rate, few investors thought homeowners would want to pay off their mortgages, and hence the call provision in the zeros was ignored.

In 1986, interest rates dropped sharply, and the rate on tax-exempt bonds fell from 11.5 to 8 percent. The Duval zeros' price shot up from $38.17 to $89.55, at which point they yielded 9 percent:

$$\$89.55 = \frac{\$1,000}{(1 + k_d)^{28}},$$

which solves to $k_d = 9\%$. (On a financial calculator, enter n = 28, PV = 89.55 or −89.55, and FV = 1,000, and then press the k = i key to obtain the yield, $8.999 \approx 9$ percent.) The 9 percent tax-exempt interest looked high in comparison to the 8 percent return on new municipal bonds with the same degree of risk, so some University of Florida professors bought heavily. That turned out to be a big mistake. Because mortgage rates had dropped to 10 percent, homebuyers whose mortgages were at 11.5 percent started refunding (that is, paying off their old mortgages and replacing them with lower-interest ones). Duval County began receiving cash, so it started calling the bonds at a price of $38.17(1.115)^2 = \$47.45$. Thus, people who had bought the bonds for $89.55 a few months earlier ended up with $47.45 per bond. They learned an expensive lesson about the implications of call provisions!

Bond Values with Semiannual Compounding

Although some bonds pay interest annually, most actually pay interest semiannually. To evaluate semiannual payment bonds, we must modify the valuation model (Equation 6-1) as follows:

1. Divide the annual coupon interest payment by 2 to determine the amount of interest paid each 6 months.
2. Multiply the years to maturity, n, by 2 to determine the number of semiannual periods.
3. Divide the annual interest rate, k_d, by 2 to determine the semiannual interest rate.

By making these changes, we obtain the following equation for finding the value of a bond that pays interest semiannually:

$$V = \sum_{t=1}^{2n} \frac{I}{2}\left(\frac{1}{1 + k_d/2}\right)^t + M\left(\frac{1}{1 + k_d/2}\right)^{2n}$$

$$= \frac{I}{2}(PVIFA_{k_d/2,2n}) + M(PVIF_{k_d/2,2n}). \qquad (6\text{-}1a)$$

To illustrate, assume now that Teletron Electronics' bonds pay \$75 interest each 6 months rather than \$150 at the end of each year. Thus, each interest payment is only half as large, but there are twice as many of them. When the going rate of interest is 10 percent, the value of this 15-year bond is found as follows:[7]

$$V = \$75(PVIFA_{5\%,30\ periods}) + \$1,000(PVIF_{5\%,30\ periods})$$

$$= \$75(15.3725) + \$1,000(0.2314)$$

$$= \$1,152.94 + \$231.40$$

$$= \$1,384.34.$$

With a financial calculator, you would enter $n = 30$, $k = i = 5$, PMT = 75, FV = 1,000, and then press the PV key to obtain the bond's value, \$1,384.31. The value with semiannual interest payments is slightly larger than \$1,380.32, the value when interest is paid annually. This higher value occurs because interest payments are received somewhat faster under semiannual compounding.

Students sometimes want to discount the maturity value at 10 percent over 15 years rather than at 5 percent over 30 six-month periods. This is incorrect. Logically, all cash flows in a given contract must be discounted on the same basis, semiannually in this instance. For consistency, bond traders *must* apply semiannual compounding to the maturity value, and they do.

Interest Rate Risk on a Bond

As we saw in Chapter 3, interest rates go up and down over time, and as rates change, the values of outstanding bonds also fluctuate. Suppose you bought some 15 percent Teletron bonds at a price of \$1,000 and interest rates subsequently rose to 20 percent. As we saw before, the price of the bonds would fall to \$769.49, so you would have a loss of \$230.51 per bond.[8] Interest rates

---

[7]We are also assuming a change in the effective annual interest rate, from 10 percent to
$$(1.05)^2 - 1 = 1.1025 - 1.0 = 0.1025 = 10.25\%.$$
Most bonds pay interest semiannually, and the rates quoted, generally the YTM, are on a semiannual basis, so the effective annual rates are somewhat higher than the quoted rates.

[8]You would have an *accounting* (and tax) loss only if you sold the bond; if you held it to maturity, you would not have such a loss. However, even if you did not sell, you would still have suffered a *real economic loss in an opportunity cost sense,* because you would have lost the opportunity to invest at 20 percent and would be stuck with a 15 percent bond in a 20 percent market. Thus, in finance we regard "paper losses" as being just as bad as realized accounting losses.

can and do rise, and rising rates cause a loss of value for bondholders. Thus, people or firms who invest in bonds are exposed to risk from changing interest rates, or **interest rate risk.**

interest rate risk
The risk to which investors are exposed due to changing interest rates.

One's exposure to interest rate risk is higher on bonds with long maturities than on those maturing in the near future. This point can be demonstrated by showing how the value of a 1-year bond with a 15 percent coupon fluctuates with changes in k_d and then comparing these changes with those on a 14-year bond as calculated previously. The 1-year bond's values at different interest rates are shown here:

Value at $k_d = 10\%$:

$$\begin{aligned} V &= \$150(\text{PVIFA}_{10\%,1 \text{ year}}) + \$1,000(\text{PVIF}_{10\%,1 \text{ year}}) \\ &= \$150(0.9091) + \$1,000(0.9091) \\ &= \$136.37 + \$909.10 \\ &= \$1,045.47. \end{aligned}$$

Value at $k_d = 15\%$:

$$\begin{aligned} V &= \$150(0.8696) + \$1,000(0.8696) \\ &= \$130.44 + \$869.60 \\ &= \$1,000.04 \approx \$1,000. \end{aligned}$$

Value at $k_d = 20\%$:

$$\begin{aligned} V &= \$150(0.8333) + \$1,000(0.8333) \\ &= \$125.00 + \$833.30 \\ &= \$958.30. \end{aligned}$$

You could obtain the first value with a financial calculator by entering n = 1, PMT = 150, FV = 1,000, and i = 10, and then pressing PV to get \$1,045.45. With everything still in your calculator, enter i = 15 to override the old i = 10, and press PV to find the bond's value at k_d = i = 15; it is \$1,000. Then enter i = 20 and press the PV key to find the last bond value, \$958.33.

The values of the 1-year and 14-year bonds at several current market interest rates are summarized and plotted in Figure 6-3. Notice how much more sensitive the price of the long-term bond is to changes in interest rates. At a 15 percent interest rate, both the long- and the short-term bonds are valued at \$1,000. When rates rise to 20 percent, the long-term bond falls to \$769.47, but the short-term bond falls only to \$958.33. A similar situation occurs when rates fall below 15 percent.

For bonds with similar coupons, this differential sensitivity to changes in interest rates always holds true—the longer the maturity of the bond, the greater its price changes in response to a given change in interest rates. Thus, even if the risk of default on two bonds is exactly the same, the one with the longer maturity is typically exposed to more risk from a rise in interest rates.

The logical explanation for this difference in interest rate risk is simple. Suppose you bought a 14-year bond that yielded 15 percent, or \$150 a year. Now suppose interest rates on comparable-risk bonds rose to 20 percent. You

Figure 6-3   Value of Long- and Short-Term 15% Annual Coupon Rate Bonds at Different Market Interest Rates

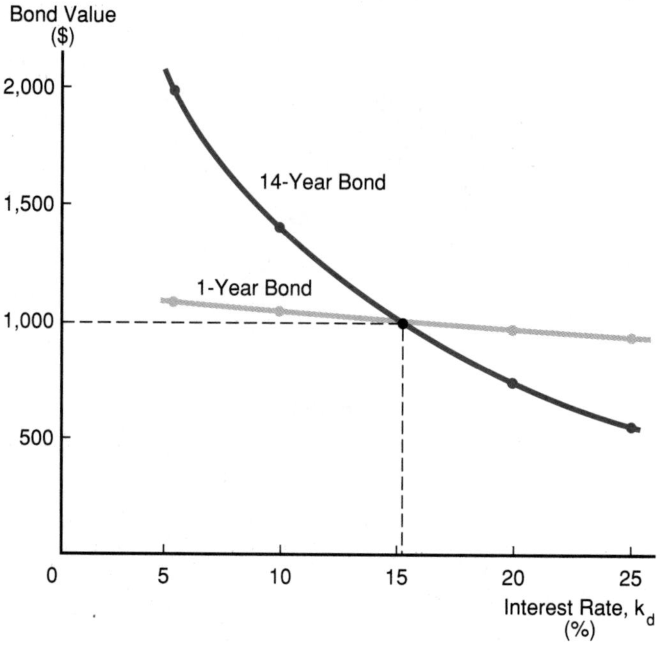

	Value of	
Current Market Interest Rate, k_d	1-Year Bond	14-Year Bond
5%	$1,095.24	$1,989.86
10	1,045.45	1,368.33
15	1,000.00	1,000.00
20	958.33	769.47
25	920.00	617.59

Note: Bond values were calculated using a financial calculator.

would be stuck with only $150 of interest for the next 14 years. On the other hand, had you bought a 1-year bond, you would have a low return for only 1 year. At the end of the year, you would get your $1,000 back, and you could then reinvest it and receive 20 percent, or $200 per year, for the next 13 years. Thus, interest rate risk reflects the length of time one is committed to a given investment.[9]

---

[9]If a 10-year bond were plotted in Figure 6-3, its curve would lie between those of the 14-year bond and the 1-year bond. The curve of a 1-month bond would be almost horizontal, indicating that its price would change very little in response to an interest rate change, but a perpetuity would have a very steep slope.

Although a 1-year bond has less interest rate risk than a 14-year bond, the 1-year bond exposes the buyer to more **reinvestment rate risk**. Suppose you bought a 1-year bond that yielded 15 percent, and then interest rates on comparable-risk bonds fell to 10 percent. After 1 year, when you got your $1,000 back, you would have to invest it at only 10 percent, so you would lose $150 − $100 = $50 in annual interest. Had you bought the 14-year bond, you would have continued to receive $150 in annual interest payments even if rates fell. Of course, if you intended to spend the $1,000 after 1 year, investing in a 1-year bond would guarantee (ignoring bankruptcy) that you would get your $1,000 back (plus interest) after 1 year. The 14-year bond investment, on the other hand, if sold after 1 year, would return less than $1,000 if interest rates had risen.[10]

Bond Prices in Recent Years

We know from Chapter 3 that interest rates fluctuate, and we have just seen that the prices of outstanding bonds rise and fall inversely with changes in interest rates. Figure 6-4 shows what has happened to the price of a typical bond, Alabama Power's 8½ percent, 30-year bond which matures in 2001. When this bond was issued in 1971 it was worth $1,000, but at the 1981 interest rate peak, it sold for only $530. However, the recent drop in interest rates caused the price of the bond to rise, and by 1988 it was back over par, selling at a premium. The graph also shows that if interest rates remain at the 1988 level, the price of the bond will gradually fall, and it will sell for $1,000 (plus accrued interest) just before it matures in 2001.

Bond Markets

Corporate bonds are traded primarily in the over-the-counter market. Most bonds are owned by and traded among the large financial institutions (for example, life insurance companies, mutual funds, and pension funds, all of which deal in very large blocks of securities), and it is relatively easy for the over-the-counter bond dealers to arrange the transfer of large blocks of bonds among the relatively few holders of the bonds. It would be much more difficult to conduct similar operations in the stock market among the literally millions of large and small stockholders, so most stock trades occur on the exchanges.

Information on bond trades in the over-the-counter market is not published, but a representative group of bonds is listed and traded on the bond division of the NYSE. Figure 6-5 gives a section of the bond market page of *The Wall Street Journal* on trading for December 11, 1987. A total of 728 issues were traded on that date, but we show only the bonds of Alabama Power. Note that Alabama Power had 10 different bonds traded on December 11; the com-

---

[10]A broader definition of reinvestment rate risk is "the risk that cash flows (interest plus principal) from a bond will have to be reinvested at a rate less than the YTM." This point is covered in detail in investments courses.

**Figure 6-4   Alabama Power 8½%, 30-Year Bond:
Market Value as Interest Rates Change**

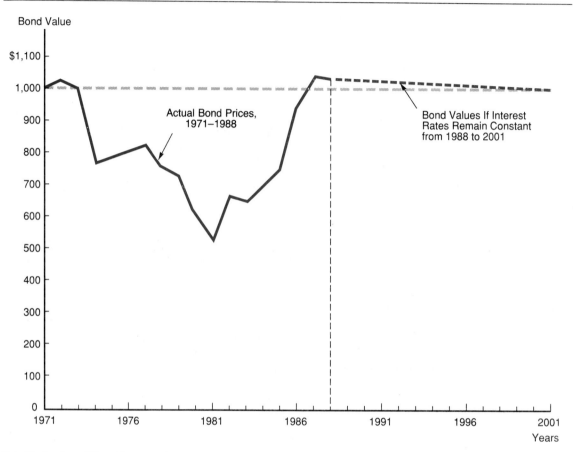

Note: The line from 1988 to 2001 appears linear, but it actually has a slight curve.

pany actually had more than 20 bond issues outstanding, but some of them did not trade on that date.

The Alabama Power and other bonds can have various denominations, but most have a par value of $1,000 — this is how much per bond the company borrowed and how much it must someday repay. However, since other denominations are possible, for trading and reporting purposes bonds are quoted as percentages of par. Looking at the first bond listed, which is the one we plotted in Figure 6-4, we see that there is an 8½ just after the company's name; this indicates that the bond is of the series which pays 8½ percent interest, or 0.0850($1,000) = $85.00 of interest per year. The 8½ percent is the bond's *coupon rate*. The 01 which comes next indicates that this bond

**Figure 6-5   NYSE Bond Market Transactions,
December 11, 1987**

Bonds	Cur Yld	Vol	High	Low	Close	Net Chg.
AlaP 8½s01	9.9	5	86¼	86¼	86¼	− 1¾
AlaP 7¾s02	9.7	10	80⅜	80¼	80¼	− 1¾
AlaP 8⅞s03	10.2	10	87½	87	87	− 2
AlaP 9¾s04	10.3	9	94⅝	94⅝	94⅝	+ ⅛
AlaP 10⅞s05	10.7	5	101⅞	101⅞	101⅞	− 1⅛
AlaP 8¾s07	10.3	7	85⅛	85⅛	85⅛	− 1⅞
AlaP 9¼s07	10.2	10	90¾	90¾	90¾	+ ¾
AlaP 9½s08	10.3	5	92½	92½	92½	− ½
AlaP 9⅝s08	10.3	25	93¾	93¾	93¾	− ¼
AlaP 12⅝s10	11.7	16	108	108	108	+ 2

Source: *The Wall Street Journal,* December 14, 1987.

current yield
The annual interest payment on a bond divided by its current market value.

matures and must be repaid in the year 2001; it is not shown in the table, but this bond was issued in 1971, so it had a 30-year original maturity. The 9.9 in the third column is the bond's **current yield**, which is defined as the annual interest payment divided by the closing price of the bond: Current yield = $85/$862.50 = 9.86%, rounded to 9.9 percent. The 5 in the fourth column indicates that 5 of these bonds were traded on December 11, 1987. Since the prices shown are expressed as a percentage of par, the high of 86¼ percent translates to $862.50; the low also was $862.50; and the bond closed at $862.50, down $17.50 from the previous day's close. (Question: Since in Figure 6-5 the bond is selling at 86¼, why is its current value as shown in Figure 6-4 above the $1,000 line? Answer: The graph was plotted earlier in 1987, and after it was constructed, interest rates rose and bond prices fell. As an exercise, update the graph to make it consistent with the data in Figure 6-5.)

Companies generally set their coupon rates at levels which reflect the "going rate of interest" on the day a bond is issued. If the rates were set lower, investors simply would not buy the bonds at the $1,000 par value, so the company would not borrow the money it needed. Thus, bonds generally sell at their par values when they are issued, but their prices fluctuate thereafter as interest rates change.

As you can see from Figure 6-5, Alabama Power's 8½ percent bonds maturing in 2001 were recently selling for $862, while its 12⅝ percent bonds maturing in 2010 were selling for $1,080. This difference reflects the fact that the going rate of interest in 1972, when the 8½s were sold, was lower than recent interest rates, so the bonds now sell at a discount. On the other hand, the 12⅝s were sold in 1980, when interest rates were higher than recent rates, so those bonds now sell at a premium.

All of the bonds traded on a given day are listed in the newspaper (and hence in Figure 6-5) in alphabetical order by company and in the order of the dates on which they were originally issued, beginning with the earliest bond issued. Thus, the coupon rates shown in Figure 6-5 are generally rising as we move down the list, reflecting the facts (1) that interest rates have generally risen in recent years and (2) that Alabama Power has not had to raise any new debt capital since interest rates declined.

PREFERRED STOCK VALUATION

Preferred stock is a *hybrid* — it is similar to bonds in some respects and to common stock in others. Preferred dividends are similar to interest payments on bonds in that they are fixed in amount and generally must be paid before common stock dividends can be paid. However, like common dividends, preferred dividends can be omitted without bankrupting the firm if earnings are low. In addition, some preferred stock is similar to common stock in that it has no maturity date and is not callable; hence, such issues are never retired.

Most preferred stocks entitle their owners to regular fixed dividend payments. If the payments last forever, the issue is a perpetuity whose value V_{ps}, is found as follows:

$$V_{ps} = \frac{D_{ps}}{k_{ps}}. \qquad (6\text{-}2)$$

V_{ps} is the value of the preferred stock, D_{ps} is the dividend, and k_{ps} is the required rate of return. (We discussed required rates of return in Chapter 4.) Teletron has preferred stock outstanding which pays a dividend of $8.125 per year. If the required rate of return on this preferred stock is 10 percent, its value is $81.25, found by solving Equation 6-2 as follows:

$$V_{ps} = \frac{\$8.125}{0.10} = \$81.25.$$

If we know the current price of a preferred stock and its dividend, we can solve for the current rate being earned, as

$$k_{ps} = \frac{D_{ps}}{V_{ps}}.$$

COMMON STOCK VALUATION

Common stock represents the ownership of a corporation, but to the typical investor, a share of common stock is simply a piece of paper distinguished by two features:

1. It entitles its owner to dividends, but only if the company has earnings out of which dividends can be paid and if management chooses to pay dividends rather than to retain all the earnings. Whereas a bond contains a *promise* to pay interest, common stock provides no such promise (in a legal sense) to pay dividends — if you own a stock you may *expect* a dividend, but your expectations may not in fact be met. To illustrate, Long Island Lighting Company (Lilco) had paid dividends on its common stock for more than 50 years, and people expected these dividends to

continue. However, when the company encountered severe problems a few years ago, it stopped paying dividends. Note, though, that Lilco continued to pay interest on its bonds; if it had not, then it would have been declared bankrupt, and the bondholders would have taken over the company.

2. Stock can be sold at some future date, hopefully at a price greater than the purchase price. If the stock is actually sold at a price above its purchase price, the investor will receive a *capital gain.* Generally, at the time people buy common stocks, they expect to receive capital gains; otherwise, they would not buy the stocks. However, after the fact one can end up with capital losses rather than capital gains. Lilco's stock price dropped from $17.50 in 1983 to $3.75 in 1984, so *expected* capital gains on that stock turned out to be *actual* capital losses.

Definitions of Terms Used in the Stock Valuation Models

Common stocks provide an expected future cash flow stream, and a stock's value is found in the same manner as the values of other financial assets — namely, as the present value of an expected future cash flow stream. The expected cash flows consist of two elements: (1) the dividends expected in each year and (2) the price investors expect to receive when they sell the stock. The expected final stock price includes the return of the original investment plus a capital gain.

We saw in Chapter 1 that managers seek to maximize the value of their firm's stocks. Through their actions, managers affect both the stream of income to investors and the riskiness of that stream. Managers need to know how alternative actions will affect stock prices. Therefore, at this point we develop some models to help show how the value of a share of stock is determined. We begin by defining the following terms:

D_t = dividend the stockholder *expects* to receive at the end of Year t. D_0 is the most recent dividend, which has already been paid; D_1 is the first dividend expected, and it will be paid at the end of this year; D_2 is the dividend expected at the end of 2 years; and so forth. D_1 represents the first cash flow a new purchaser of the stock will receive. Note that D_0, the dividend which has just been paid, is known with certainty. However, all future dividends are expected values, so the estimate of D_t may differ among investors.[11]

---

[11]Stocks generally pay dividends quarterly, so theoretically we should evaluate them on a quarterly basis. However, in stock valuation, most analysts work on an annual basis because the data generally are not precise enough to warrant the refinement of a quarterly model. For additional information on the quarterly model, see Charles M. Linke and J. Kenton Zumwalt, "Estimation Biases in Discounted Cash Flow Analysis of Equity Capital Cost in Rate Regulation," *Financial Management,* Autumn 1984, 15–21.

market price, P_0
The price at which a stock sells in the market

intrinsic value, $\hat{P}_0$
The value of an asset that in the mind of a particular investor is justified by the facts; may be different from the asset's current market price, its book value, or both.

growth rate, g
The expected rate of growth in dividends per share.

required rate of return, k_s
The minimum rate of return on a common stock that a stockholder considers acceptable.

expected rate of return, $\hat{k}_s$
The rate of return on a common stock that an individual stockholder expects to receive.

actual (realized) rate of return, $\bar{k}_s$
The rate of return on a common stock actually received by stockholders. $\bar{k}_s$ may be greater than or less than $\hat{k}_s$ and/or k_s.

dividend yield
The expected dividend divided by the current price of a share of stock.

capital gains yield
The capital gain during any one year divided by the beginning price.

P_0 = actual **market price** of the stock today.

$\hat{P}_t$ = expected price of the stock at the end of each Year t (pronounced "P hat t"). $\hat{P}_0$ is the **intrinsic,** or *theoretical,* **value** of the stock today as seen by the particular investor doing the analysis; $\hat{P}_1$ is the price expected at the end of 1 year; and so on. Note that $\hat{P}_0$ is the intrinsic value of the stock today based on a particular investor's estimate of the stock's expected dividend stream and riskiness. Hence, whereas P_0 is fixed and is identical for all investors, $\hat{P}_0$ could differ among investors depending on how optimistic they are regarding the company. The caret, or "hat," is used to indicate that $\hat{P}_t$ is an estimated value. $\hat{P}_0$, the investor's estimate of the intrinsic value today, could be above or below P_0, the current stock price, but an investor would buy the stock only if his or her estimate of $\hat{P}_0$ were equal to or greater than P_0.

Since there are many investors in the market, there can be many values for $\hat{P}_0$. However, we can think of an "average," or "marginal," investor whose actions actually determine the market price. For this marginal investor, P_0 must equal $\hat{P}_0$; otherwise, a disequilibrium would exist, and buying and selling in the market would change P_0 until $P_0 = \hat{P}_0$ for the marginal investor.

g = expected **growth rate** in dividends as predicted by the marginal investor. (If we assume that dividends are expected to grow at a constant rate, g is also equal to the expected rate of growth in the stock's price.) Different investors may use different g's to evaluate a firm's stock, but the market price, P_0, is set on the basis of the g estimated by marginal investors.

k_s = minimum acceptable, or **required, rate of return** on the stock, considering both its riskiness and the returns available on other investments. Again, this term generally relates to the marginal investor. The determinants of k_s were discussed in detail in Chapter 4.

$\hat{k}_s$ = **expected rate of return** which an investor who buys the stock actually expects to receive. $\hat{k}_s$ (pronounced "k hat s") could be above or below k_s, but one would buy the stock only if $\hat{k}_s$ were equal to or greater than k_s.

$\bar{k}_s$ = **actual,** or **realized,** *after the fact* **rate of return,** pronounced "k bar s." You may *expect* to obtain a return of $\hat{k}_s = 15$ percent if you buy Exxon stock today, but if the market goes down, you may end up next year with an actual realized return that is much lower, perhaps even negative.

D_1/P_0 = expected **dividend yield** on the stock during the coming year. If the stock is expected to pay a dividend of $1 during the next 12 months, and if its current price is $10, then the expected dividend yield is $1/$10 = 0.10 = 10%.

$\dfrac{\hat{P}_1 - P_0}{P_0}$ = expected **capital gains yield** on the stock during the coming year. If the stock sells for $10 today, and if it is expected to rise to

$10.50 at the end of 1 year, then the expected capital gain is $\hat{P}_1 - P_0 = \$10.50 - \$10.00 = \$0.50$, and the expected capital gains yield is $\$0.50/\$10 = 0.05 = 5\%$.

Expected total return. The sum of the expected dividend yield and the expected capital gains yield on a share of stock.

Expected total return = expected dividend yield (D_1/P_0) plus expected capital gains yield $[(\hat{P}_1 - P_0)/P_0] = \hat{k}_s$. In our example, the **expected total return** $= \hat{k}_s = 10\% + 5\% = 15\%$.

Expected Dividends as the Basis for Stock Values

In our discussion of bonds, we found the value of a bond as the present value of interest payments over the life of the bond plus the present value of the bond's maturity (or par) value:

$$V = \frac{I}{(1 + k_d)^1} + \frac{I}{(1 + k_d)^2} + \cdots + \frac{I}{(1 + k_d)^n} + \frac{M}{(1 + k_d)^n}.$$

Stock prices are likewise determined as the present value of a stream of cash flows, and the basic stock valuation equation is similar to the bond valuation equation. What are the cash flows that corporations provide to their stockholders? First, think of yourself as an investor who buys a stock with the intention of holding it (in your family) forever. In this case, all that you (and your heirs) will receive is a stream of dividends, and the value of the stock today is calculated as the present value of an infinite stream of dividends:

Value of stock $= \hat{P}_0 =$ PV of expected future dividends

$$= \frac{D_1}{(1 + k_s)^1} + \frac{D_2}{(1 + k_s)^2} + \cdots + \frac{D_\infty}{(1 + k_s)^\infty}$$

$$= \sum_{t=1}^{\infty} \frac{D_t}{(1 + k_s)^t}. \tag{6-3}$$

What about the more typical case, in which you expect to hold the stock for a finite period and then sell it — what will be the value of $\hat{P}_0$ in this case? *The value of the stock is again determined by Equation 6-3.* To see this, recognize that for any individual investor, expected cash flows consist of expected dividends plus the expected sale price of the stock. However, the sale price the current investor receives will depend on the dividends some future investor expects. Therefore, for all present and future investors in total, expected cash flows must be based on expected future dividends. To put it another way, unless a firm is liquidated or sold to another concern, the cash flows it provides to its stockholders consist only of a stream of dividends; therefore, the value of a share of its stock must be established as the present value of that expected dividend stream.

The general validity of Equation 6-3 can also be confirmed by asking the following question: Suppose I buy a stock and expect to hold it for 1 year. I will receive dividends during the year plus the value $\hat{P}_1$ when I sell out at the end of the year, but what will determine the value of $\hat{P}_1$? The answer is that it will be determined as the present value of the dividends during Year 2 plus the stock price at the end of that year, which in turn will be determined as the present stock value of another set of future dividends and an even more distant stock price. This process can be continued ad infinitum, and the ultimate result is Equation 6-3.[12]

Equation 6-3 is a generalized stock valuation model in the sense that the time pattern of D_t can be anything: D_t can be rising, falling, or constant, or it can even fluctuate randomly, and Equation 6-3 will still hold. Often, however, the projected stream of dividends follows a systematic pattern, in which case we can develop a simplified (that is, easier to evaluate) version of the stock valuation model expressed in Equation 6-3. In the following sections we consider the cases of zero growth, constant growth, and nonconstant growth.

Stock Values with Zero Growth

zero growth stock
A common stock whose future dividends are not expected to grow at all; that is, g = 0.

Suppose dividends are expected not to grow at all but to remain constant. Here we have a **zero growth stock,** for which the dividends expected in future years are equal to some constant amount — that is, $D_1 = D_2 = D_3$ and so on. Therefore, we can drop the subscripts on D and rewrite Equation 6-3 as follows:

$$\hat{P}_0 = \frac{D}{(1 + k_s)^1} + \frac{D}{(1 + k_s)^2} + \ldots + \frac{D}{(1 + k_s)^n} + \ldots + \frac{D}{(1 + k_s)^\infty}. \qquad (6\text{-}3a)$$

As we noted in Chapter 5 in connection with the British consol bond, and also in our discussion of preferred stocks, a security that is expected to pay a constant amount each year forever is called a perpetuity. Therefore, a zero growth stock may be thought of as a perpetuity. Although the stock is expected to provide a constant stream of dividends into the indefinite future, each dividend has a smaller present value than the preceding one, and as n gets very large, the present value of the individual future dividends approaches zero. To illustrate, suppose $D = \$1.82$ and $k_s = 16\% = 0.16$. We can rewrite Equation 6-3a as follows:

$$\hat{P}_0 = \frac{\$1.82}{(1.16)^1} + \frac{\$1.82}{(1.16)^2} + \frac{\$1.82}{(1.16)^3} + \ldots + \frac{\$1.82}{(1.16)^{50}} + \ldots + \frac{\$1.82}{(1.16)^{100}} + \ldots$$

$$= \$1.57 \;\; + \$1.35 \;\; + \$1.17 \;\; + \ldots + \$0.001 \;\; + \ldots + \$0.000001 + \ldots.$$

We can also show the perpetuity in graph form, as in Figure 6-6. The horizontal line shows the constant dividend stream, $D_t = \$1.82$. The descend-

---

[12]We should note that investors periodically lose sight of the long-run nature of stocks as investments and forget that in order to sell a stock at a profit, one must find a buyer who will pay the higher price. If you analyzed a stock's value in accordance with Equation 6-3, concluded that the stock's market price exceeded a reasonable value, and then bought the stock anyway, then you would be following the "bigger fool" theory of investment — you think that you may be a fool to buy the stock at its excessive price, but you also think that when you get ready to sell it, you can find someone who is an even bigger fool. The bigger fool theory was widely followed in the summer of 1987, just before the stock market lost over one-third of its value.

Figure 6-6   Present Values of Dividends of a Zero Growth Stock (Perpetuity)

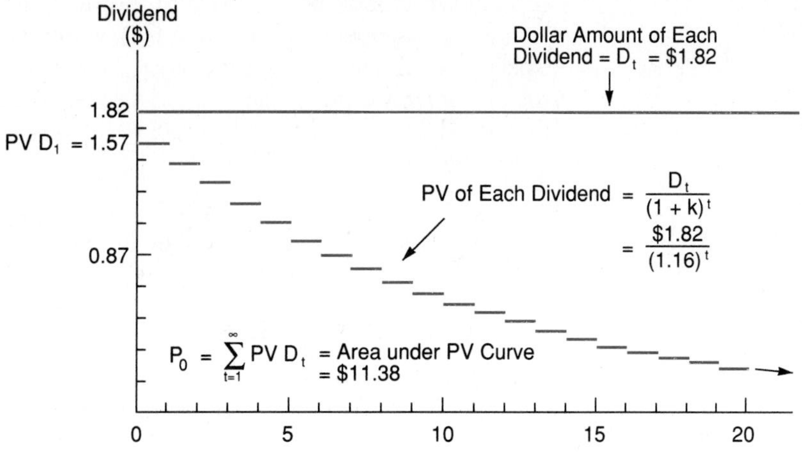

ing step function curve shows the present value of each future dividend. If we extended the analysis on out to infinity and then summed the present values of all the future dividends, the sum would be equal to the value of the stock.

As we saw in Chapter 5, the value of any perpetuity is simply the cash flow divided by the discount rate, so the value of a zero growth stock reduces to this formula:

$$\hat{P}_0 = \frac{D}{k_s}. \tag{6-4}$$

Therefore, in our example the value of the stock is $11.38:

$$\hat{P}_0 = \frac{\$1.82}{0.16} = \$11.38.$$

If you extended Figure 6-6 on out forever and then added up the present value of each individual dividend, you would end up with the intrinsic value of the stock, $11.38.[13] The actual market value of the stock, P_0, could be greater than, less than, or equal to $11.38, depending on other investors' perceptions of the dividend pattern and riskiness of the stock.

We could transpose the $\hat{P}_0$ and the k_s in Equation 6-4 and solve for k_s to produce Equation 6-5:

---

[13]If you think that having a stock pay dividends forever is unrealistic, then think of it as lasting only for 50 years. Here you would have an annuity of $1.82 per year for 50 years. The PV of a 50-year annuity would be $1.82(6.2463) = $11.37, which would differ by only a penny from that of the perpetuity. Thus, the dividends from Years 51 to infinity would not contribute much to the value of the stock.

$$\hat{k}_s = \frac{D}{P_0}. \qquad (6\text{-}5)$$

We could then look up the price of the stock and the latest dividend, P_0 and D, in the newspaper, and the value D/P_0 would be the rate of return we could expect to earn if we bought the stock. Since we are dealing with an *expected rate of return,* we put a "hat" on the k value. Thus, if we bought the stock at a price of $11.38 and expected to receive a constant dividend of $1.82, our expected rate of return would be

$$\hat{k}_s = \frac{\$1.82}{\$11.38} = 0.16 = 16\%.$$

Normal, or Constant, Growth

Although the zero growth model is applicable to some companies, the earnings and dividends of most companies are expected to increase each year. Expected growth rates vary from company to company, but dividend growth in general is expected to continue in the foreseeable future at about the same rate as that of the nominal gross national product (real GNP plus inflation). On this basis, it is expected that the dividend of an average, or "normal," company will grow at a rate of 6 to 8 percent a year. Thus, if a **normal, or constant, growth** company's last dividend, which has already been paid, was D_0, its dividend in any future Year t may be forecast as $D_t = D_0(1 + g)^t$, where g is the constant expected rate of growth. For example, if Teletron Electronics just paid a dividend of $1.82 (that is, $D_0 = \$1.82$) and if investors expect a 10 percent growth rate, the estimated dividend 1 year hence will be $D_1 = \$1.82(1.10) = \$2.00$; D_2 will be $2.20; and the estimated dividend 5 years hence will be

normal (constant) growth
Growth which is expected to continue into the foreseeable future at about the same rate as that of the economy as a whole; g = a constant.

$$D_t = D_0(1 + g)^t = \$1.82(1.10)^5 = \$2.93.$$

Using this method of estimating future dividends, we can determine the current value, $\hat{P}_0$, using Equation 6-3 as set forth above — in other words, we can find the expected future cash flow stream (the dividends), calculate the present value of each dividend payment, and then sum these present values to find the value of the stock. Thus, the intrinsic value of the stock is equal to the present value of its expected future dividends.

However, if g is constant, Equation 6-3 may be simplified as follows:[14]

$$\hat{P}_0 = \frac{D_0(1 + g)}{k_s - g} = \frac{D_1}{k_s - g}. \qquad (6\text{-}6)$$

Inserting values into Equation 6-6, we find the value of our illustrative stock to be $33.33:

---

[14]Equation 6-6 is derived in Appendix 3A of Eugene F. Brigham and Louis C. Gapenski, *Intermediate Financial Management,* 2nd ed. (Hinsdale, Ill.: Dryden Press, 1987).

Figure 6-7   **Present Values of Dividends of a Constant Growth Stock:**
$D_0 = \$1.82, g = 10\%, k_s = 16\%$

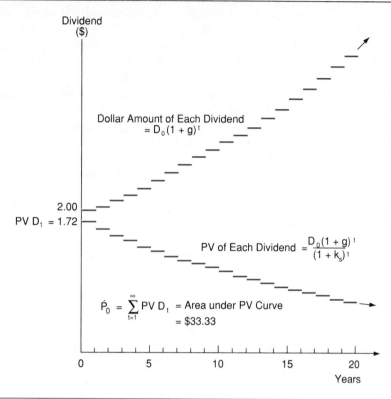

$$\hat{P}_0 = \frac{\$1.82(1.10)}{0.16 - 0.10} = \frac{\$2.00}{0.06} = \$33.33.$$

constant growth model
Also called the Gordon
Model, it is used to find
the value of a constant
growth stock.

The **constant growth model** expressed in Equation 6-6 is often called the Gordon Model, after Myron J. Gordon, who did much to develop and popularize it.

Note that Equation 6-6 is sufficiently general to encompass the zero growth case described above: If growth is zero, this is simply a special case of constant growth, and Equation 6-6 is equal to Equation 6-4. Note also that a necessary condition for the derivation of Equation 6-6 is that k_s is greater than g. If the equation is used where k_s is not greater than g, the results will be meaningless.

The concept underlying the valuation process for a constant growth stock is graphed in Figure 6-7. Dividends are growing at the rate g = 10%, but because $k_s > g$, the present value of each future dividend is declining. For example, the dividend in Year 1 is $D_1 = D_0(1 + g)^1 = \$1.82(1.10) = \$2.00$. However, the present value of this dividend, discounted at 16 percent, is

$PV(D_1) = \$2.00/(1.16)^1 = \$2.00/1.16 = \$1.72$. The dividend expected in Year 2 grows to $\$2.00(1.10) = \$2.20$, but the present value of this dividend falls to $\$1.64$. Continuing, $D_3 = \$2.42$ and $PV(D_3) = \$1.55$, and so on. Thus, the expected dividends are growing, but the present value of each successive dividend is declining.

If we summed the present values of each future dividend, this summation would be the value of the stock, $\hat{P}_0$. As we have seen, when g is a constant, this summation is equal to $D_1/(k_s - g)$, as shown in Equation 6-6. Therefore, if we extended the lower step function curve in Figure 6-7 on out to infinity and added up the present values of each future dividend, the summation would be identical to the value given by Equation 6-6, $\$33.33$.

Growth in dividends occurs primarily as a result of growth in *earnings per share (EPS)*. Earnings growth, in turn, results from a number of factors, including (1) inflation and (2) the amount of earnings the company reinvests. Regarding inflation, if output (in units) is stable, and if both sales prices and input costs rise at the inflation rate, then EPS also will grow at the inflation rate. EPS will also grow as a result of the reinvestment, or plowback, of earnings. If the firm's earnings are not all paid out as dividends (that is, if some fraction of earnings is retained), the dollars of investment behind each share will rise over time, which should lead to growth in earnings and dividends.

Expected Rate of Return on a Constant Growth Stock

We can solve Equation 6-6 for k_s, again using the hat to denote that we are dealing with an expected rate of return:[15]

$$\begin{matrix} \text{Expected rate} \\ \text{of return} \end{matrix} = \begin{matrix} \text{Expected} \\ \text{dividend} \\ \text{yield} \end{matrix} + \begin{matrix} \text{Expected growth} \\ \text{rate, or capital} \\ \text{gains yield} \end{matrix}$$

$$\hat{k}_s \quad = \quad \frac{D_1}{P_0} \quad + \quad g. \tag{6-7}$$

Thus, if you buy a stock for a price $P_0 = \$33.33$, and if you expect the stock to pay a dividend $D_1 = \$2.00$ one year from now and to grow at a constant rate $g = 10\%$ in the future, your expected rate of return is 16 percent:

$$\hat{k}_s = \frac{\$2.00}{\$33.33} + 10\% = 6\% + 10\% = 16\%.$$

In this form, we see that $\hat{k}_s$ is the *expected total return* and that it consists of an *expected dividend yield, $D_1/P_0 = 6\%$*, plus an *expected growth rate or capital gains yield, g = 10\%*.

---

[15]The k_s value of Equation 6-6 is a *required* rate of return, but when we transform to obtain Equation 6-7, we are finding an *expected* rate of return. Obviously, the transformation requires that $k_s = \hat{k}_s$. This equality holds if the stock market is in equilibrium, a condition that will be discussed later in the chapter.

Suppose this analysis had been conducted on January 1, 1989, so $P_0 = \$33.33$ is the January 1, 1989, stock price and $D_1 = \$2.00$ is the dividend expected at the end of 1989. What should the stock price be at the end of 1989 (or the beginning of 1990)? We would again apply Equation 6-6, but this time we would use the 1990 dividend, $D_2 = D_1(1 + g) = \$2.00(1.10) = \$2.20$:

$$\hat{P}_{1/1/1990} = \frac{D_{1990}}{k_s - g} = \frac{\$2.20}{0.16 - 0.10} = \$36.67.$$

Now notice that \$36.67 is 10 percent greater than P_0, the \$33.33 price on January 1, 1989:

$$\$33.33(1.10) \approx \$36.67.$$

Thus, we would expect to make a capital gain of $\$36.67 - \$33.33 = \$3.34$ during the year, and a capital gains yield of 10 percent:

$$\text{Capital gains yield} = \frac{\text{Capital gain}}{\text{Beginning price}} = \frac{\$3.34}{\$33.33} = 0.10 = 10\%.$$

We could extend the analysis on out, and in each future year the expected capital gains yield would always equal g, the expected dividend growth rate.

The dividend yield in 1990 could be estimated as follows:

$$\text{Dividend yield}_{1990} = \frac{D_{1990}}{\hat{P}_{1/1/90}} = \frac{\$2.20}{\$36.67} = 0.06 = 6\%.$$

The dividend yield for 1991 could also be calculated, and again it would be 6 percent. Thus, *for a constant growth stock,* the following conditions must hold:

1. The dividend is expected to grow forever at a constant rate, g.
2. The stock price is expected to grow at this same rate.
3. The expected dividend yield is a constant.
4. The expected capital gains yield is also a constant, and it is equal to g.
5. The expected total rate of return, $\hat{k}_s$, is equal to the expected dividend yield plus the expected growth rate: $\hat{k}_s = $ dividend yield $+ g$.

The term *expected* should be clarified — it means expected in a probabilistic sense, as the most likely outcome. Thus, if we say the growth rate is expected to remain constant at 10 percent, we mean that the most likely growth rate in any future year is 10 percent, not that we literally expect the growth rate to be exactly equal to 10 percent in each future year. In this sense, the constant growth assumption is a reasonable one for many large, mature companies.

Supernormal, or Nonconstant, Growth

Firms typically go through *life cycles.* During the early part of their lives, their growth is much faster than that of the economy as a whole; then they match the economy's growth; and finally their growth is slower than that of the econ-

Figure 6-8   Illustrative Dividend Growth Rates

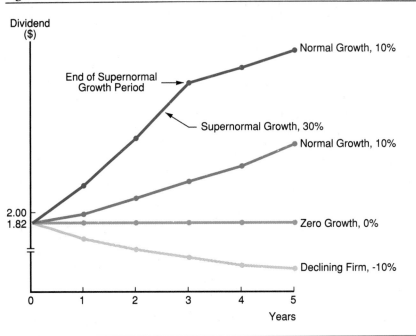

omy.[16] Automobile manufacturers in the 1920s and computer software firms such as Lotus in the 1980s are examples of firms in the early part of the cycle; these firms are called **supernormal**, or **nonconstant, growth** firms. Figure 6-8 illustrates such nonconstant growth and compares it with normal growth, zero growth, and negative growth.[17]

In the figure, the dividends of the supernormal growth firm are expected to grow at a 30 percent rate for 3 years, after which the growth rate is expected to fall to 10 percent, the assumed average for the economy. The value of this firm, like any other, is the present value of its expected future dividends as

supernormal (nonconstant) growth
The part of the life cycle of a firm in which its growth is much faster than that of the economy as a whole.

---

[16]The concept of life cycles could be broadened to *product cycle,* which would include both small, start-up companies and large companies like IBM, which periodically introduce new products that typically give sales and earnings a boost. We should also mention *business cycles,* which alternately depress and boost sales and profits. The growth rate just after a major new product has been introduced, or as a firm emerges from the depths of a recession, is likely to be much higher than the "long-run average growth rate," which is the proper number for a DCF analysis.

[17]A negative growth rate indicates a declining company. A mining company whose profits are falling because of a declining ore body is an example. Someone buying such a company would expect its earnings, and consequently its dividends and stock price, to decline each year, and this would lead to capital losses rather than capital gains. Obviously, a declining company's stock price will be low, and its dividend yield must be high enough to offset the expected capital loss and still produce a competitive total return. Students sometimes argue that they would not be willing to buy a stock whose price was expected to decline. However, if the annual dividends are large enough to *more than offset* the falling stock price, the stock still could provide a good return.

determined by Equation 6-3. In the case in which D_t is growing at a constant rate, we simplified Equation 6-3 to $\hat{P}_0 = D_1/(k_s - g)$. In the supernormal case, however, the expected growth rate is not a constant — it declines at the end of the period of supernormal growth. To find the value of such a stock, or any nonconstant growth stock when the growth rate will eventually stabilize, we proceed in three steps:

1.   Find the PV of the dividends during the period of nonconstant growth.

2.   Find the price of the stock at the end of the nonconstant growth period, at which point it has become a constant growth stock, and discount this price back to the present.

3.   Add these two components to find the intrinsic value of the stock, $\hat{P}_0$.

To illustrate the process for valuing nonconstant growth stocks, suppose the following facts exist:

k_s = stockholders' required rate of return = 16%.
N = years of supernormal growth = 3.
g_s = rate of growth in both earnings and dividends during the supernormal growth period = 30%. (Note: The growth rate during the supernormal growth period could vary from year to year.)
g_n = rate of constant growth after the supernormal period = 10%.
D_0 = last dividend the company paid = $1.82.

The valuation process is diagrammed in Figure 6-9, and it is explained in the steps set forth below the time line. The value of the stock is calculated to be $53.86.

Comparing Companies with Different Expected Growth Rates

It is useful to summarize our discussion of stock valuation models by comparing companies with the four growth situations that were graphed in Figure 6-8. There we have a zero growth company, one with a constant 10 percent expected growth rate, one whose earnings are expected to decline at the rate of 10 percent a year, and one whose growth rate is nonconstant.

We can use the valuation equations developed previously to determine the stock prices, dividend yields, capital gains yields, total expected returns, and price/earnings (P/E) ratios for the four companies; these are shown in Table 6-1.[18] We assume that each firm had earnings per share (EPS) of $3.41 during

---

[18]Price/earnings (P/E) ratios relate a stock's price to its earnings per share (EPS). The higher the P/E ratio, the more investors are willing to pay for a dollar of the firm's current earnings. Other things held constant, investors will pay more per dollar of current earnings for a rapidly growing firm than for a slow growth company; hence, rapid growth companies generally have high P/E ratios. These ratios are discussed in more detail in Chapter 7. The relationships among the P/E ratios, shown in the last column of Table 6-1, are similar to what one would intuitively expect — the higher the expected growth rate (all other things the same), the higher the P/E ratio.

Differences in P/E ratios among firms can also arise from differences in the required rates of return, k_s, which investors use in capitalizing the future dividend streams. If one company has a higher P/E ratio than another, this could be caused by a higher g, a lower k_s, or a combination of these two factors.

Figure 6-9   Process for Finding the Value of a
Supernormal Growth Stock

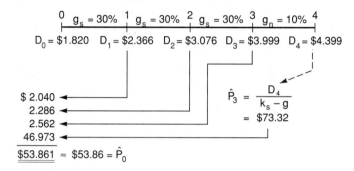

Step 1. Find the dividends paid (D_t) at the end of Years 1 to 3, and then the present values of these dividends (PV D_t), using the following procedure:

D_0	×	FVIF$_{30\%,t}$	=	D_t	×	PVIF$_{16\%,t}$	=	PV D_t
D_1: $1.82	×	1.3000	=	$2.366;	×	0.8621	=	$2.040
D_2: 1.82	×	1.6900	=	3.076;	×	0.7432	=	2.286
D_3: 1.82	×	2.1970	=	3.999;	×	0.6407	=	2.562
						Sum of PVs of supernormal period dividends	=	$6.888

Step 2. The stock price at the end of Year 3 is the PV of the dividends expected from Year 4 to infinity. To find this, we first (a) find the expected value of the stock at the end of Year 3 and then (b) find the present value of the Year 3 stock price:

a. $\hat{P}_3 = \dfrac{D_4}{k_s - g_n} = \dfrac{D_0(1 + g_s)^3(1 + g_n)}{k_s - g_n} = \dfrac{D_3(1 + g_n)}{0.16 - 0.10}$

$= \dfrac{\$3.999(1.10)}{0.06} = \dfrac{\$4.399}{0.06} = \$73.32.$

b. PV $\hat{P}_3 = \$73.32(\text{PVIF}_{16\%,3 \text{ years}}) = \$73.32(0.6407) = \$46.97.$

Step 3. Find $\hat{P}_0$, the value of the stock today:

$$\hat{P}_0 = \$6.89 + \$46.97 = \$53.86.$$

Note: You would normally calculate the stream of dividends and their present values with a financial calculator rather than with FVIF and PVIF factors, but the steps would be the same.

Table 6-1   Stock Prices, Dividend Yields, and Price/Earnings Ratios for 16 Percent Returns under Different Growth Assumptions

		Price	Current Dividend Yield (D_1/P_0)	Capital Gains Yield in Year 1 $[(\hat{P}_1 - P_0)/P_0]$	Total Expected Return	P/E Ratio[a]
Declining constant growth (-10%)	$\hat{P}_0 = \dfrac{D_1}{k_s - g} = \dfrac{\$1.64}{0.16 - (-0.10)} = \$ 6.31$		26%	-10.0%	16%	1.85
Zero growth (0%)	$\hat{P}_0 = \dfrac{D}{k_s} = \dfrac{\$1.82}{0.16} = 11.38$		16	0.0	16	3.34
Normal constant growth (10%)	$\hat{P}_0 = \dfrac{D_1}{k_s - g} = \dfrac{\$2.00}{0.16 - 0.10} = 33.33$		6	10.0	16	9.77
Supernormal growth	$\hat{P}_0 = $ (See Steps 1–3, Figure 6-9) $ = 53.86$		4.4	11.6^b	16	15.79

[a]It was assumed at the beginning of this example that each company is earning $3.41 initially. This $3.41, divided into the various prices, gives the indicated P/E ratios.

As the supernormal growth rate declines toward the normal rate (or as the time when this decline will occur becomes more imminent), the high P/E ratio must approach the normal P/E ratio — that is, the P/E of 15.79 will decline year by year and equal 9.77, that of the normal growth company, in the third year.

Note that D_1 differs for each firm. It is calculated as follows:

$$D_1 = EPS_0(1 + g)(\text{Fraction of earnings paid out}) = \$3.41(1 + g)(0.533).$$

For the declining firm, $D_1 = \$3.41(0.90)(0.533) = \$1.64.$

[b]With k = 16% and D_1/P_0 = 4.4%, the capital gains yield must be 16.0% − 4.4% = 11.6%. We could calculate the expected price of the stock at the end of the year, $\hat{P}_1$, using the supernormal growth procedures, to confirm that the capital gains yield in Year 1 is indeed 11.6 percent, but this is not necessary.

the preceding reporting period (that is, $EPS_0 = \$3.41$) and that each paid out 53.3 percent of its reported earnings as dividends. Therefore, dividends per share last year, D_0, were $1.82 for each company, but the values of D_1 differ among the firms.

The value of each stock equals its market price, and the expected and required return is 16 percent on each; thus, $\hat{k}_s = k_s = 16\%$. For the declining firm, this return consists of a high current dividend yield, 26 percent, combined with a capital loss amounting to 10 percent a year. For the zero growth firm there is neither a capital gain nor a capital loss expectation, so that 16 percent return has to be obtained entirely from the dividend yield. The normal growth firm provides a 6 percent current dividend yield plus a 10 percent capital gains expectation. Finally, the supernormal growth firm has a low current dividend yield but a high capital gains expectation.

What is expected to happen to the prices of the four illustrative firms' stocks over time? Three of the four cases are straightforward: The zero growth firm's price is expected to be constant; the declining firm is expected to have a falling stock price; and the constant growth firm's stock price is expected to grow at a constant rate, 10 percent. We do not prove it here, but we could show that the supernormal firm's stock price growth rate starts at 11.6 percent per year, but it declines to 10 percent as the supernormal growth period ends.

STOCK MARKET EQUILIBRIUM

Recall from Chapter 4 that the required return on Stock X, k_X, can be found using the Security Market Line (SML) equation as it was developed in our discussion of the Capital Asset Pricing Model (CAPM):

$$k_X = k_{RF} + (k_M - k_{RF})\, b_X.$$

If the risk-free rate of return is 8 percent, if the market risk premium is 4 percent, and if Stock X has a beta of 2, then the marginal investor will require a return of 16 percent on Stock X, calculated as follows:

$$k_X = 8\% + (12\% - 8\%)\, 2.0$$

$$= 16\%.$$

This 16 percent required return is shown as a point on the SML in Figure 6-10.

The marginal investor will want to buy Stock X if the expected rate of return is more than 16 percent, will want to sell it if the expected rate of return is less than 16 percent, and will be indifferent, hence hold but not buy or sell, if the expected rate of return is exactly 16 percent. Now suppose the investor's portfolio contains X, and he or she analyzes the stock's prospects and concludes that its earnings, dividends, and price can be expected to grow at a constant rate of 5 percent per year. The last dividend was $D_0 = \$2.8571$, so the next expected dividend is

$$D_1 = \$2.8571(1.05) = \$3.$$

Our marginal investor observes that the present price of the stock, P_0, is \$30. Should he or she purchase more of Stock X, sell the present holdings, or maintain the present position?

The investor can calculate Stock X's *expected rate of return* as follows:

$$\hat{k}_X = \frac{D_1}{P_0} + g = \frac{\$3}{\$30} + 5\% = 15\%.$$

This value is plotted on Figure 6-10 as Point X, which is below the SML. Because the expected rate of return is less than the required return, this marginal investor will want to sell the stock, as will other holders. However, few people will want to buy at the \$30 price, so present owners will be unable to find buyers unless they cut the price of the stock. Thus, the price will decline, and this decline will continue until the stock's price reaches \$27.27, at which point the market for this security will be in **equilibrium**, because the expected rate of return, 16 percent, will be equal to the required rate of return:

equilibrium
The condition under which the expected return on a security is just equal to its required return, $\hat{k} = k$, and the price is stable.

$$\hat{k}_X = \frac{\$3}{\$27.27} + 5\% = 16\% = k_X.$$

Had the stock initially sold for less than \$27.27, say at \$25, events would have been reversed. Investors would have wanted to buy the stock because its

---

Figure 6-10 Expected and Required Returns on Stock X

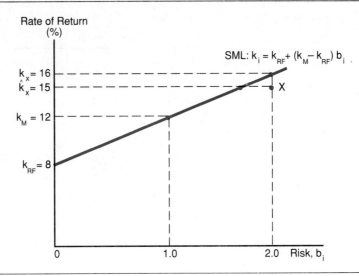

expected rate of return would have exceeded its required rate of return, and buy orders would have driven the stock's price up to $27.27.

To summarize, in equilibrium these two conditions must hold:

1. The expected rate of return as seen by the marginal investor must equal the required rate of return: $\hat{k}_i = k_i$.

2. The actual market price of the stock must equal its intrinsic (DCF) value as estimated by the marginal investor: $P_0 = \hat{P}_0$.

Of course, some individual investors will believe that $\hat{k}_i > k$ and $\hat{P}_0 > P_0$, and hence they will invest most of their funds in the stock, while other investors will have an opposite view and will sell all of their shares. However, it is the marginal investor who establishes the actual market price, and for this investor, $\hat{k}_i = k_i$ and $P_0 = \hat{P}_0$. If these conditions do not hold, trading will occur until they do hold.

Changes in Equilibrium Stock Prices

Stock market prices are not constant — they undergo violent changes at times. For example, on October 19, 1987, the Dow Jones average dropped 508 points, and the average stock lost about 23 percent of its value in just one day. Some stocks lost over half of their value that day. To see how such changes can occur, let us assume that Stock X is in equilibrium, selling at a price of $27.27 per share. If all expectations were exactly met, during the next year the price would gradually rise to $28.63, or by 5 percent. However, many different events could occur to cause a change in the equilibrium price of the stock. To illustrate, consider again the set of inputs used to develop Stock X's price of $27.27, along with a new set of assumed input variables:

	Variable Value	
	Original	New
Risk-free rate, k_{RF}	8%	7%
Market risk premium, $k_M - k_{RF}$	4%	3%
Stock X's beta coefficient, b_X	2.0	1.0
Stock X's expected growth rate, g_X	5%	6%
D_0	$2.8571	$2.8571
Price of Stock X	$27.27	?

The first three variables influence k_X, which declines from 16 to 10 percent as a result of the new set of variables:

$$\text{Original } k_X = 8\% + 4\%(2.0) = 16\%.$$

$$\text{New } k_X = 7\% + 3\%(1.0) = 10\%.$$

Using these values, together with the new g value, we find that $\hat{P}_0$, and consequently P_0, rises from $27.27 to $75.71.[19]

$$\text{Original } \hat{P}_0 = \frac{\$2.8571(1.05)}{0.16 - 0.05} = \frac{\$3}{0.11} = \$27.27.$$

$$\text{New } \hat{P}_0 = \frac{\$2.8571(1.06)}{0.10 - 0.06} = \frac{\$3.0285}{0.04} = \$75.71.$$

At the new price, the expected and required rates of return will be equal:[20]

$$\hat{k}_X = \frac{\$3.0285}{\$75.71} + 6\% = 10\% = k_X.$$

Evidence suggests that stocks, and especially those of large NYSE companies, adjust rapidly to disequilibrium situations. Consequently, equilibrium ordinarily exists for any given stock, and, in general, required and expected returns are equal. Stock prices certainly change, sometimes violently and rapidly, but this simply reflects changing conditions and expectations. There are, of course, times when a stock continues to react for several months to a favorable or unfavorable development, but this does not signify a long adjustment period; rather, it simply illustrates that as more new bits of information about the situation become available, the market adjusts to them. The ability of the market to adjust to new information is discussed in the next section.

---

[19]A price change of this magnitude is by no means rare. The prices of *many* stocks double or halve during a year. For example, during 1987 Franklin Computer increased in value by 588 percent; on the other hand, Todd Shipyards fell from 24½ to 1⅝, a 93 percent loss.

[20]It should be obvious by now that actual realized rates of return are not necessarily equal to expected and required returns. Thus, an investor might have *expected* to receive a return of 15 percent if he or she had bought Franklin Computer or Todd Shipyards stock in 1987, but after the fact, the realized return on Franklin was far above 15 percent, whereas that on Todd was far below.

The Efficient Markets Hypothesis

Efficient Markets Hypothesis (EMH)
The hypothesis that securities are typically in equilibrium — that they are fairly priced in the sense that the price reflects all publicly available information on each security.

A body of theory called the **Efficient Markets Hypothesis (EMH)** holds (1) that stocks are always in equilibrium and (2) that it is impossible for an investor to consistently "beat the market." Essentially, those who believe in the EMH note that there are some 100,000 or so full-time, highly trained, professional analysts and traders operating in the market, while there are fewer than 3,000 major stocks. Therefore, if each analyst followed 30 stocks (which is about right, as analysts tend to specialize in the stocks in a specific industry), there would be 1,000 analysts following each stock. Further, these analysts work for organizations such as Citibank, Merrill Lynch, Prudential Insurance, and the like, which have billions of dollars available with which to take advantage of bargains. As a result of SEC disclosure requirements and electronic information networks, as new information about a stock becomes available, these 1,000 analysts all receive and evaluate it at approximately the same time. Therefore, the price of the stock adjusts almost immediately to reflect any new developments.

Financial theorists generally define three forms, or levels, of market efficiency:

1. The *weak-form* of the EMH states that all information contained in past price movements is fully reflected in current market prices. Therefore, information about recent trends in a stock's price is of no use in selecting stock — the fact that a stock has risen for the past three days, for example, gives us no useful clues as to what it will do today or tomorrow. People who believe that weak-form efficiency exists also believe that "tape watchers" and "chartists" are wasting their time.[21]

2. The *semistrong-form* of the EMH states that current market prices reflect all *publicly available* information. If this is true, no abnormal returns can be gained by analyzing stocks.[22] Thus, if semistrong-form efficiency exists, it does no good to pore over annual reports or other published data, because market prices will have adjusted to any good or bad news contained in such reports as soon as they came out. However, insiders (say, the presidents of companies), even under semistrong-form efficiency, can still make abnormal returns on their own companies' stocks.

3. The *strong-form* of the EMH states that current market prices reflect all pertinent information, whether publicly available or privately held. If this form holds, even insiders would find it impossible to earn abnormal returns in the stock market.[23]

---

[21]Tape watchers are people who watch the NYSE tape, while chartists plot past patterns of stock price movements. Both are called "technicians," and both believe that they can see if something is happening to the stock that will cause its price to move up or down in the near future.

[22]An abnormal return is one that exceeds the return justified by the riskiness of the investment — that is, a return that plots above the SML in a graph like Figure 6-10.

[23]Several cases of illegal insider trading have made the news headlines recently. These cases involved employees of several major investment banking houses and even an employee of the SEC. In the most famous case, Ivan Boesky admitted to making $50 million by purchasing the stock of firms he knew were about to merge. He went to jail, and he had to pay a large fine, but he helped disprove the strong-form EMH.

Many empirical studies have been conducted to test for the three forms of market efficiency. Most of these studies suggest that the stock market is indeed highly efficient in the weak form and reasonably efficient in the semistrong form, at least for the larger and more widely followed stocks. However, the strong-form EMH does not hold, so abnormal profits can be made by those who possess insider information.

What bearing does the EMH have on financial decisions? Since stock prices do reflect public information, most stocks do seem to be fairly valued. This does not mean that new developments could not cause a stock's price to soar or to plummet, but it does mean that stocks, in general, are neither overvalued nor undervalued — they are fairly priced and in equilibrium. However, there are cases in which financial managers do have information not known to outsiders.

If the EMH is correct, it is a waste of time for most of us to analyze stocks by looking for those that are undervalued. If stock prices already reflect all available information and hence are fairly priced, one can "beat the market" only by luck, and it is difficult, if not impossible, for anyone to consistently outperform the market averages. Empirical tests have shown that the EMH is, in its weak and semi-strong forms, valid. However, people such as corporate officers who have insider information can do better than the averages, and individuals and organizations that are especially good at digging out information on small, new companies also seem to do consistently well. Also, some investors may be able to analyze and react more quickly than others to releases of new information, and these investors may have an advantage over others. However, the buy-sell actions of these investors quickly bring market prices into equilibrium. Therefore, it is generally safe to assume that $\hat{k} = k$, that $\hat{P}_0 = P_0$, and that stocks plot on the SML.[24]

Actual Stock Prices and Returns

Our discussion thus far has focused on *expected* stock prices and *expected* rates of return. Anyone who has ever invested in the stock market knows that there can be and generally there are large differences between *expected* and *realized* prices and returns.

We can use IBM's experience during the 1980s to illustrate this point. On January 1, 1981, IBM's stock price was $67.875 per share. Its 1980 dividend, D_0, had been $3.44, and the consensus view among security analysts was that IBM would experience a growth rate of about 11 percent in the future. Thus, an average investor who bought IBM at $67.875 would have expected to earn a return of about 16.6 percent:

---

[24]Market efficiency also has important implications for managerial decisions, especially those pertaining to common stock issues, stock repurchases, and tender offers. Stocks appear to be fairly valued, so decisions based on a stock's being undervalued or overvalued must be approached with caution. However, managers do have better information about their own companies than outsiders have, and this information can legally be used to the companies' (but not the managers' own) advantage.

$$\hat{k}_s = \frac{\text{Expected dividend}}{\text{yield}} + \frac{\text{Expected growth rate, or}}{\text{expected capital gains yield}}$$

$$= \frac{D_0(1 + g)}{P_0} + g$$

$$= \frac{\$3.82}{\$67.875} + 11\%$$

$$= 5.6\% + 11.0\% = 16.6\%.$$

IBM's bonds at the time had a yield of about 13 percent.

In fact, things did not work out as expected. The economy in 1981 was weaker than had been predicted, so IBM's earnings did not grow as fast as expected, and its dividend remained at $3.44. Further, interest rates soared during 1981, and capital was attracted out of the stock market and into the bond market to take advantage of the high interest rates. As a result of these two events, IBM stock's price declined, and it closed on December 31, 1981, at $56.875, down $11 for the year. Thus, on a beginning-of-the-year investment of $67.875, the actual return on IBM for 1981 was −11.1 percent:

$$\bar{k}_s = \text{Actual dividend yield} + \text{Actual capital gains yield}$$

$$= \frac{\$3.44}{\$67.875} + \frac{-\$11}{\$67.875}$$

$$= 5.1\% - 16.2\% = -11.1\%.$$

Most other stocks performed similarly to IBM's in 1981.

The economy improved after 1981, however, and IBM's dividend and stock price improved apace. The total realized return on IBM in 1982 increased dramatically to 77 percent; in 1983 it was a strong 30 percent; it was only 5 percent in 1984; it was back up to 30 percent in 1985; and in 1986 the total return was a negative 19 percent, even though the market as a whole was strong. IBM's total return was −1.0 percent in 1987, slightly below the market average. On average, the realized return on IBM stock during the 1980s has been about 17 percent, which is about equal to the rate of return investors expected. However, in every single year, the realized return differed significantly from the expected return.

Panel a of Figure 6-11 shows how the price of an average share of stock has varied in recent years, and Panel b shows how total realized returns have varied. The market has gone up in some years and down in others, and the stocks of individual companies have likewise gone up and down. We know from theory that expected returns as estimated by a marginal investor are always positive, but in some years, as Panel b shows, negative returns have been realized. Of course, even in bad years some individual companies do well, so the "name of the game" in security analysis is picking the winners. Financial managers attempt to take actions which will put their companies into the winners' column, but they do not always succeed. In subsequent chapters, we will

Figure 6-11 New York Stock Exchange Prices and Total Returns, 1953–1988

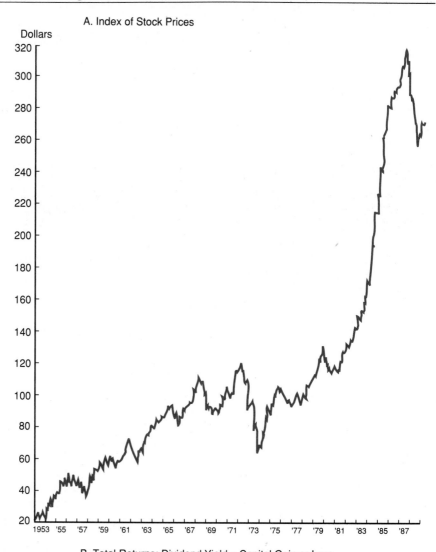

A. Index of Stock Prices

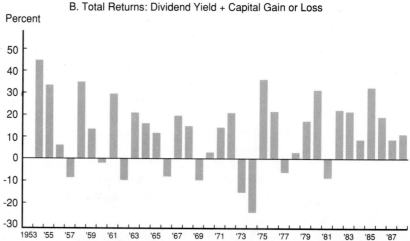

B. Total Returns: Dividend Yield + Capital Gain or Loss

Note: 1988 results are through July.

Figure 6-12 Stock Market Transactions, December 11, 1987

52 Weeks High	52 Weeks Low	Stock	Div.	Yld %	P-E Ratio	Sales 100s	High	Low	Close	Net Chg.
		– A–A–A –								
25⅝	14	AAR s	.36	2.3	14	110	15½	14¾	15½	+ ⅝
12	8¾	ACM G n	.21e	1.8	...	x302	11½	11¼	11½	– ⅛
32½	19	AFG s	.16	.7	8	126	23½	23⅛	23⅛	– ⅜
27	10½	AGS s		...	12	112	13⅜	13	13⅜	...
10½	6¼	AMCA		...	...	4	6½	6½	6½	– ⅛
9⅜	3¼	AM Intl		...	31	1292	4¾	4⅜	4⅜	– ¼
33¾	17	AM Int pf	2.00	10.1	...	7	20⅛	19¾	19¾	– ⅜
65½	26¾	AMR		...	8	3603	29⅝	28¾	29⅛	– ⅛
12¼	6⅜	ARX s		...	7	220	7	6⅞	7	...
73½	35⅛	ASA	2.00a	3.8	...	975	53	51⅞	53	+ ⅝
22⅜	9½	AVX		...	16	106	12¼	12⅛	12¼	...
67	40	AbtLab	1.00	2.2	17	3630	45½	44¾	44⅞	– ⅜
28	15⅜	Abitibi g		...	...	170	18¾	18½	18¾	+ ⅜
16¾	8½	AcmeC	.40	4.0	14	114	10⅛	10	10	...
10½	6⅛	AcmeE	.32b	4.6	24	10	7	7	7	...
20	14⅛	AdaEx	3.34e	22.3	...	59	15⅛	15	15	– ¼
19½	6⅞	AdmM s	.24	2.9	6	102	8½	8¼	8¼	...
35	16⅝	AdvSys		...	12	454	26½	26	26¼	...

Source: *The Wall Street Journal,* December 14, 1987.

examine the actions that managers can take to increase the odds of their firms doing relatively well in the marketplace.

Stock Market Reporting

Figure 6-12, taken from a daily newspaper, is a section of the stock market page on stocks listed on the NYSE. For each stock it provides specific data on the trading that took place on December 11, 1987, as well as other, more general, information. Similar information is available on stocks listed on the other exchanges, as well as on stocks traded over-the-counter.

Stocks are listed alphabetically, from AAR Industries to Zurn Industries; the data in Figure 6-12 were taken from the top of the listing. We will examine the data for Abbott Laboratories, AbtLab, shown about half the way down the page. The two columns on the left show the highest and lowest prices at which the stocks have sold during the past year; Abbott Labs has traded in the range from \$67 to \$40 during the preceding 52 weeks. The figure just to the right of the company's abbreviated name is the dividend; Abbott Labs had a current indicated annual dividend rate of \$1.00 per share and a dividend yield (which is the dividend divided by the closing stock price) of 2.2 percent. Next comes the ratio of the stock's price to its annual earnings (the P/E ratio), followed by the volume of trading for the day: 363,000 shares of Abbott Labs stock were traded on December 11, 1987. Following the volume come the high and low prices for the day, and then the closing price. On December 11, Abbott Labs traded as high as \$45½ and as low as \$44¾, while the last trade was at \$44⅞. The last column gives the change from the closing price on the previous day. Abbott Labs was down ⅜, or \$0.375, so the previous close must have been \$44.875 + \$0.375 = \$45.25.

There are three other points to note in Figure 6-12. First, the "pf" follow-ing the stock name of the second AM Int listing tells us that it is a preferred stock rather than a common stock. Second, a "u" preceding a stock's daily high indicates that the price is a new 52-week high, whereas a "d" preceding the daily low indicates a new 52-week low. None of the stocks shown in Figure 6-12 achieved new highs or lows on December 11. Third, an "x" preceding a stock's sales volume indicates that the stock went ex-dividend that day; this means that someone who buys the stock will not receive the next dividend. We discuss ex-dividend effects in detail in Chapter 18.

RECENT DEVELOPMENTS

We close this chapter by discussing some recent events in the bond and stock markets.

1. As this is being written (July 1988), the bond market is fairly strong — interest rates have dropped recently, and bond prices have risen. Fears of inflation are not strong, and the economy is sluggish, so there is not a great demand for money, which would put upward pressure on interest rates.

2. In the opening to this chapter, we stated that some Alabama Power bonds were selling for $875 while others were selling for $1,060, and that U.S. Treasury bonds which were originally sold to the public for $1,000 ranged in price from $785 to $1,480. As this indicates, there is a wide range of prices in the bond market. Alabama Power bonds, as well as U.S. Treasury bonds, sell at different prices because they were issued at different times under different interest rate environments, and thus they carry higher or lower coupon rates.

3. On October 19, 1987, the NYSE experienced the greatest one-day decline in its history. The Dow Jones Industrial Average fell by 508 points, from 2246 to 1738. During the months that followed, the Dow Jones average has fluctuated greatly, registering 7 of its 10 biggest one-day gains ever (all 10 of the biggest gains occurred during 1987 and 1988), but also registering many of its biggest declines. By July 1988, the Dow Jones average had climbed back over the 2000 mark.

4. During the October 1987 stock market crash, the prices of most stocks fell substantially. Although most stocks go up when the market does well and decline when the market is off, there is still a tendency for well-managed firms to "buck the tide" and to do better than average in both up and down markets. In the following chapters, we will explain how good financial management can help lead to good stock market performance.

Small
Business

VALUATION OF SMALL FIRMS

In this chapter we have presented several equations for valuing a firm's common stock. These equations had one common element: they all assumed that the firm is currently paying a dividend. However, many small firms, even highly profitable ones whose stock is traded in the market, have never paid a dividend. How does one value the stock of such firms? We will see in a moment that if a firm is expected to begin paying dividends in the future, we can modify the equations presented in the chapter and use them to determine the value of the stock.

A new business often expects to have very low sales during its first few years of operation as it develops and begins to market its product. Then, if the product really catches on, sales will grow quite rapidly for several years. For example, Compaq Computer Company had only three employees when it was incorporated in 1982. Its first year was devoted to product development, and 1982 sales were zero. In 1983, however, Compaq began marketing its personal computer, and its sales hit $111 million, a record first-year volume for any new firm. By 1986 Compaq was included in Fortune's 500 largest U.S. industrial firms. Obviously, Compaq has been more successful than most new businesses, but it is common for small firms to have growth rates of 100 percent, 500 percent, or even 1,000 percent during their first few years of operation, if their products are successful.

Sales growth brings with it the need for additional assets — Compaq could not have increased its sales as it did without also increasing its assets, and asset growth requires an increase in liability and/or equity accounts. Small firms generally can obtain some bank credit, but they must maintain a reasonable balance between debt and equity. Thus, additional bank borrowings require increases in equity. Getting the equity capital needed to support growth can be difficult for small firms. They have limited access to the capital markets, and, even when they can sell common stock, the owners of small firms are reluctant to do so for fear of losing voting control. Therefore, the best source of equity for most small businesses is retained earnings, and for this reason most small firms pay no dividends during their rapid growth years. Eventually, successful firms do pay dividends, and those dividends generally grow rapidly at first and then begin to grow at a constant rate once the firm reaches maturity.

If a small firm currently pays no dividend but is expected to pay dividends in the future, the value of its stock can be found as follows:

1. Estimate when dividends will be paid, the amount of the first dividend, the growth rate during the supernormal growth period, the length of the supernormal period, the long-run (constant) growth rate, and the rate of return required by investors.

2. Use the constant growth model to determine the price of the stock at the time the firm is expected to reach a stable growth situation.

3. Set out the cash flows (dividends during the supernormal growth period and the stock price once the constant growth state is reached), and then find the present value of these cash flows. That present value represents the value of the stock today.

To illustrate this process, consider the situation for WonderLure, Inc., a company that was set up in 1987 to produce and market a new high-tech fishing lure. WonderLure's sales are currently growing at a rate of 200 percent per year. The company expects to experience a high but declining rate of growth in sales and earnings during the next 10 years, after which analysts estimate that it will grow at a steady 10 percent per year. The firm's management has announced that it will pay no dividends for 5 years, but if earnings materialize as forecasted, it will pay a dividend of $0.20 per share at the end of Year 6, $0.30 in Year 7, $0.40 in Year 8, $0.45 in Year 9, and $0.50 in Year 10. After Year 10, current plans are to increase the dividend by 10 percent per year.

WonderLure's investment bankers estimate that investors require a 15 percent return on similar stocks. Therefore, we find the value of a share of WonderLure's stock as follows:

$$P_0 = \frac{\$0}{(1.15)^1} + \ldots + \frac{\$0}{(1.15)^5} + \frac{\$0.20}{(1.15)^6}$$

$$+ \frac{\$0.30}{(1.15)^7} + \frac{\$0.40}{(1.15)^8} + \frac{\$0.45}{(1.15)^9} + \frac{\$0.50}{(1.15)^{10}}$$

$$+ \left(\frac{\$0.50(1.10)}{0.15 - 0.10} \right) \left(\frac{1}{(1.15)^{10}} \right)$$

$$= \$3.30.$$

Thus, we see that the valuation concepts discussed in the chapter can be applied to small firms which currently pay no dividends, if an estimate of future dividends can be made.

SUMMARY AND KEY CONCEPTS

Corporate decisions should be analyzed in terms of how alternative courses of action are likely to affect the value of a firm. However, it is necessary to know how bond and stock prices are established before attempting to measure how a given decision will affect a specific firm's value. Accordingly, this chapter showed how bond and stock values are determined, as well as how investors go about estimating the rates of return they expect to earn. The key concepts covered in this chapter are summarized below.

- A **bond** is a long-term promissory note issued by a business or governmental unit. The firm receives the selling price of the bond in exchange for a promise to make interest payments and to repay the principal on a specified future date.

- The **value of a bond** is found as the present value of an **annuity** (the interest payments) plus the present value of a lump sum (the **principal**). The bond is evaluated at the appropriate periodic interest rate over the number of periods for which interest payments are made.

- The equation used to find the value of an annual coupon bond is:

$$V = \sum_{t=1}^{n} \frac{I}{(1 + k_d)^t} + \frac{M}{(1 + k_d)^n}$$

$$= I(PVIFA_{k_d,n}) + M(PVIF_{k_d,n}).$$

An **adjustment** to the formula must be made if the bond pays interest **semiannually**: divide I and k_d by 2, and multiply n by 2.

- The return earned on a bond held to maturity is defined as the bond's **yield to maturity (YTM)**. If the bond can be redeemed before maturity, the return investors will receive is defined as the bond's **yield to call (YTC)**. The YTC is found as the present value of the interest payments received while the bond is outstanding plus the present value of the call price (the par value plus a call premium).

- The longer the maturity of a bond, the greater its price will change in response to a given change in interest rates; this is called **interest rate**

risk. Bonds with short maturities, however, expose the investor to high **reinvestment rate risk,** or the risk that income will fall because funds received from maturing short-term investments will have to be reinvested at lower rates, thus lowering income.

- Since most preferred stocks are **perpetuities,** the value of a share of preferred stock is found as the dividend divided by the required rate of return:

$$V_{ps} = \frac{D_{ps}}{k_{ps}}.$$

- The **value of a share of stock** is calculated as the **present value of the stream of dividends** to be received in the future.

- The equation used to find the **value of a constant, or normal, growth stock** is: $\hat{P}_0 = D_1/(k_s - g)$.

- The **expected total rate of return** from a stock consists of an **expected dividend yield** and an **expected capital gains yield.** For a constant growth firm, both the expected dividend yield and the expected capital gains yield are constant.

  The equation for the **expected rate of return on a constant growth stock** can be expressed as: $k_s = D_1/P_0 + g$.

- A **zero growth stock** is one whose future dividends are not expected to grow at all, while a **supernormal growth stock** is one whose earnings and dividends are expected to grow much faster than the economy as a whole over some specified time period.

- To find the **present value of a supernormal growth stock,** (1) find the PV of the dividends during the supernormal growth period, (2) find the price of the stock at the end of the supernormal growth period, (3) discount this price back to the present, and (4) sum these two components.

- The **Efficient Markets Hypothesis (EMH)** holds (1) that stocks are always in equilibrium and (2) that it is impossible for an investor to consistently "beat the market." Therefore, stocks are always fairly valued ($\hat{P}_0 = P_0$), the required return on a stock is equal to its expected return, and stocks' expected returns plot on the SML.

- If a **small firm** does not pay dividends, the value of its stock can be determined by (1) estimating when dividends will be paid, the dividends which will be paid during the supernormal growth period, and the required rate of return, (2) using the constant growth model to determine the price at the end of the supernormal growth period, and (3) finding the present value of those cash flows.

Finally, in this chapter we saw that differences can and do exist between expected and actual returns in the stock and bond markets — only for short-term, risk-free assets are expected and actual (or realized) returns equal.

Questions

6-1   Two investors are evaluating AT&T's stock for possible purchase. They agree on the expected value of D_1 and also on the expected future dividend growth rate. Further, they agree on the riskiness of the stock. However, one investor normally holds stocks for 2 years, while the other normally holds stocks for 10 years. Based on the type of analysis done in this chapter, they should both be willing to pay the same price for AT&T's stock. True or false? Explain.

6-2   A bond that pays interest forever and has no maturity date is a perpetual bond. In what respect is a perpetual bond similar to a no-growth common stock and to a share of preferred stock?

6-3   Is it true that the following equation can be used to find the value of an n-year bond that pays interest once a year?

$$\text{Value} = \sum_{t=1}^{n} \frac{\text{Annual interest}}{(1 + k_d)^t} + \frac{\text{Par value}}{(1 + k_d)^n}.$$

6-4   "The values of outstanding bonds change whenever the going rate of interest changes. In general, short-term interest rates are more volatile than long-term interest rates. Therefore, short-term bond prices are more sensitive to interest rate changes than are long-term bond prices." Is this statement true or false? Explain.

6-5   The rate of return you would get if you bought a bond and held it to its maturity date is called the bond's yield to maturity. If interest rates in the economy rise after a bond has been issued, what will happen to the bond's price and to its YTM? Does the length of time to maturity affect the extent to which a given change in interest rates will affect the bond price?

6-6   If you buy a *callable* bond and interest rates decline, will the value of your bond rise by as much as it would have if the bond had not been callable?

6-7   If you bought a share of common stock, you would typically expect to receive dividends plus capital gains. Would you expect the distribution between dividend yield and capital gains to be influenced by the firm's decision to pay more dividends rather than to retain and reinvest more of its earnings?

6-8   The next expected dividend, D_1, divided by the current price of a share of stock, P_0, is called the stock's expected dividend yield. What is the relationship between the dividend yield, the total yield, and the remaining years of supernormal growth for a supernormal growth firm?

6-9   Is it true that the following expression can be used to find the value of a constant growth stock?

$$\hat{P}_0 = \frac{D_0}{k_s + g}.$$

Self-Test Problems *(Solutions Appear on Page 243)*

Key terms

ST-1 Define each of the following terms:
a. Bond
b. Par value; maturity date; call provision
c. Coupon payment; coupon interest rate
d. Premium bond; discount bond
e. Current yield (on a bond); yield to maturity (YTM); yield to call (YTC)
f. Interest rate risk; reinvestment rate risk
g. Intrinsic value ($\hat{P}_0$); market price (P_0)
h. Required rate of return, k_s; expected rate of return, $\hat{k}_s$; actual, or realized, rate of return, $\bar{k}_s$
i. Capital gains yield; dividend yield; expected total return
j. Zero growth stock
k. Normal, or constant, growth; supernormal, or nonconstant, growth
l. Equilibrium
m. Efficient Markets Hypothesis (EMH)

Stock growth rates and valuation

ST-2 You are considering buying the stocks of two companies that operate in the same industry and have very similar characteristics except for their dividend payout policies. Both companies are expected to earn $3 per share this year. However, Company D (for "dividend") is expected to pay out all of its earnings as dividends, while Company G (for "growth") is expected to pay out only one-third of its earnings, or $1 per share. D's stock price is $20. G and D are equally risky. Which of the following is most likely to be true?
a. Company G will have a faster growth rate than Company D. Therefore, G's stock price should be greater than $20.
b. Although G's growth rate should exceed D's, D's current dividend exceeds that of G, and this should cause D's price to exceed G's.
c. An investor in Stock D will get his or her money back faster because D pays out more of its earnings as dividends. Thus, in a sense, D is like a short-term bond, and G is like a long-term bond. Therefore, if economic shifts cause k_d and k_s to increase, and if the expected streams of dividends from D and G remain constant, Stocks D and G will both decline, but D's price should decline further.
d. D's expected and required rate of return is $\hat{k}_s = k_s = 15\%$. G's expected return will be higher because of its higher expected growth rate.
e. On the basis of the available information, the best estimate of G's growth rate is 10 percent.

Bond valuation

ST-3 The Franklin Corporation issued a new series of bonds on January 1, 1967. The bonds were sold at par ($1,000), have a 12 percent coupon, and mature in 30 years, on December 31, 1996. Coupon payments are made semiannually (on June 30 and December 31).
a. What was the YTM of Franklin's bonds on January 1, 1967?
b. What was the price of the bond on January 1, 1972, 5 years later, assuming that the level of interest rates had fallen to 10 percent?
c. Find the current yield and capital gains yield on the bond on January 1, 1972, given the price as determined in Part b.

d. On July 1, 1987, Franklin's bonds sold for $896.64. What was the YTM at that date?

e. What were the current yield and capital gains yield on July 1, 1987?

f. Now assume that you purchased an outstanding Franklin bond on March 1, 1987, when the going rate of interest was 15.5 percent. How large a check must you have written to complete the transaction? This is a hard question!

Constant growth stock valuation   **ST-4**   Ambrose Company's current stock price is $24, and its last dividend was $1.60. In view of Ambrose's strong financial position and its consequent low risk, its required rate of return is only 12 percent. If dividends are expected to grow at a constant rate, g, in the future, and if k_s is expected to remain at 12 percent, what is Ambrose's expected stock price 5 years from now?

Supernormal growth stock valuation   **ST-5**   Woerheide Computer Chips, Inc., is experiencing a period of rapid growth. Earnings and dividends are expected to grow at a rate of 18 percent during the next 2 years, at 15 percent in the third year, and at a constant rate of 6 percent thereafter. Woerheide's last dividend was $1.15, and the required rate of return on the stock is 12 percent.

a. Calculate the value of the stock today.

b. Calculate $\hat{P}_1$ and $\hat{P}_2$.

c. Calculate the dividend yield and capital gains yield for Years 1, 2, and 3.

Problems

Bond valuation   **6-1**   The Hayes Company has two bond issues outstanding. Both bonds pay $100 annual interest plus $1,000 at maturity. Bond L has a maturity of 15 years and Bond S a maturity of 1 year.

a. What will be the value of each of these bonds when the going rate of interest is (1) 6 percent, (2) 9 percent, and (3) 12 percent? Assume that there is only one more interest payment to be made on Bond S.

b. Why does the longer-term (15-year) bond fluctuate more when interest rates change than does the shorter-term bond (1-year)?

Yield to maturity   **6-2**   The Coronet Company's bonds have 4 years remaining to maturity. Interest is paid annually; the bonds have a $1,000 par value; and the coupon interest rate is 8 percent.

a. What is the yield to maturity at a current market price of (1) $825 or (2) $1,107?

b. Would you pay $825 for one of these bonds if you thought that the appropriate rate of interest was 10 percent — that is, if $k_d = 10\%$? Explain your answer.

Bond valuation   **6-3**   Suppose Exxon sold an issue of bonds with a 10-year maturity, a $1,000 par value, a 12 percent coupon rate, and semiannual interest payments.

a. Two years after the bonds were issued, the going rate of interest on bonds such as these fell to 8 percent. At what price would the bonds sell?

b. Suppose that 2 years after the initial offering, the going interest rate had risen to 14 percent. At what price would the bonds sell?

c. Suppose that the conditions in Part a existed — that is, interest rates fell to 8 percent 2 years after the issue date. Suppose further that the interest rate remained at 8 percent for the next 8 years. What would happen to the price of the Exxon bonds over time?

Perpetual bond valuation   **6-4**   The bonds of the Stanroy Corporation are perpetuities with a 12 percent coupon. Bonds of this type currently yield 10 percent, and their par value is $1,000.
a. What is the price of the Stanroy bonds?
b. Suppose interest rate levels rise to the point where such bonds now yield 15 percent. What would be the price of the Stanroy bonds?
c. At what price would the Stanroy bonds sell if the yield on these bonds were 12 percent?
d. How would your answers to Parts a, b, and c change if the bonds were not perpetuities but had a maturity of 20 years?

Perpetual bond yield to maturity   **6-5**   The yield to maturity (YTM) is the interest rate earned on a bond that is held to maturity. What will be the yield to maturity of a perpetual bond with a $1,000 par value, a 9 percent coupon rate, and a current market price of (a) $700, (b) $900, (c) $1,000, and (d) $1,300? Assume interest is paid annually.

Constant growth stock valuation   **6-6**   Your broker offers to sell you some shares of Jasper Carriage Company common stock that paid a dividend of $2 *last year*. You expect the dividend to grow at the rate of 5 percent per year for the next 3 years, and if you buy the stock you plan to hold it for 3 years and then sell it.
a. Find the expected dividend for each of the next 3 years; that is, calculate D_1, D_2, and D_3. Note that $D_0 = \$2$.
b. Given that the appropriate discount rate is 12 percent and that the first of these dividend payments will occur 1 year from now, find the present value of the dividend stream; that is, calculate the PV of D_1, D_2, and D_3, and then sum these PVs.
c. You expect the price of the stock 3 years from now to be $34.73; that is, you expect $\hat{P}_3$ to equal $34.73. Discounted at a 12 percent rate, what is the present value of this expected future stock price? In other words, calculate the PV of $34.73.
d. If you plan to buy the stock, hold it for 3 years, and then sell it for $34.73, what is the most you should pay for it?
e. Use Equation 6-6 to calculate the present value of this stock. Assume that $g = 5\%$, and it is constant.
f. Is the value of this stock dependent upon how long you plan to hold it? In other words, if your planned holding period were 2 years or 5 years rather than 3 years, would this affect the value of the stock today, $\hat{P}_0$?

Return on common stock   **6-7**   You buy a share of Ferri Corporation stock for $35.33. You expect it to pay dividends of $1.06, $1.1236, and $1.1910 in Years 1, 2, and 3, respectively, and you expect to sell it at a price of $42.08 at the end of 3 years.
a. Calculate the growth rate in dividends.
b. Calculate the expected dividend yield.
c. Assuming that the calculated growth rate is expected to continue, you can add the dividend yield to the expected growth rate to get the

expected total rate of return. What is this stock's expected total rate of return?

Constant growth stock valuation   **6-8**   Investors require a 20 percent rate of return on Delva Company's stock ($k_s = 20\%$).

a. What will be Delva's stock value if the previous dividend was $D_0 = \$2$ and if investors expect dividends to grow at a constant compound annual rate of (1) -5 percent, (2) 0 percent, (3) 5 percent, and (4) 15 percent?

b. Using data from Part a, what is the Gordon (constant growth) model value for Delva's stock if the required rate of return is 20 percent and the expected growth rate is (1) 20 percent or (2) 25 percent? Are these reasonable results? Explain.

c. Is it reasonable to expect that a constant growth stock would have $g > k_s$?

Stock price reporting   **6-9**   Look up the prices of IBM's stock and bonds in *The Wall Street Journal* (or some other newspaper which provides this information).

a. What was the stock's price range during the last year?

b. What is IBM's current dividend? What is its dividend yield?

c. What change occurred in IBM's stock price the day the newspaper was published?

d. If IBM were to sell a new issue of $1,000 par value long-term bonds, approximately what coupon interest rate would it have to set on the bonds if it wanted to bring them out at par?

e. If you had $10,000 and wanted to invest it in IBM, what return would you expect to get if you bought the bonds and what return if you bought IBM's stock? (Hint: Think about capital gains when you answer the latter part of this question.)

Discount bond valuation   **6-10**   In February 1956 the Los Angeles Airport authority issued a series of 3.4 percent, 30-year bonds. Interest rates rose substantially in the years following the issue, and as they did, the price of the bonds declined. In February 1969, 13 years later, the price of the bonds had dropped from $1,000 to $650. In answering the following questions, assume that the bond calls for annual interest payments.

a. Each bond originally sold at its $1,000 par value. What was the yield to maturity of these bonds at their time of issue?

b. Calculate the yield to maturity in February 1969.

c. Assume that interest rates stabilized at the 1969 level and stayed there for the remainder of the life of the bonds. What would have been the bonds' price in February 1981, when they had 5 years remaining to maturity?

d. What would the price of the bonds have been the day before they matured in 1986? (Disregard the last interest payment.)

e. In 1969 the Los Angeles Airport bonds were classified as "discount bonds." What happens to the price of a discount bond as it approaches maturity? Is there a "built-in capital gain" on such bonds?

f. The coupon interest payment divided by the market price of a bond is called the bond's *current yield.* Assuming the conditions in Part c, what would have been the current yield of a Los Angeles Airport bond (1) in February 1969 and (2) in February 1981? What would have been its capital gains yields and total yields (total yield equals yield to maturity) on those same two dates?

Declining growth stock valuation

6-11   Ellis Mining Company's ore reserves are being depleted, so its sales are falling. Also, its pit is getting deeper each year, so its costs are rising. As a result, the company's earnings and dividends are declining at the constant rate of 10 percent per year. If $D_0 = \$6$ and $k_s = 15\%$, what is the value of Ellis Mining's stock?

Supernormal growth stock valuation

6-12   It is now January 1, 1989. Severn Electric, Inc., has just developed a solar panel capable of generating 200 percent more electricity than any solar panel currently on the market. As a result, Severn is expected to experience a 20 percent annual growth rate for the next 5 years. By the end of 5 years, other firms will have developed comparable technology, and Severn's growth rate will slow to 6 percent per year indefinitely. Stockholders require a return of 10 percent on Severn's stock. The most recent annual dividend (D_0), which was paid yesterday, was $1.50 per share.

a. Calculate Severn's expected dividends for 1989, 1990, 1991, 1992, and 1993.

b. Calculate the value of the stock today, $\hat{P}_0$. Proceed by finding the present value of the dividends expected at the end of 1989, 1990, 1991, 1992, and 1993 plus the present value of the stock price which should exist at the end of 1993. The year-end 1993 stock price can be found by using the constant growth equation. Notice that to find the December 31, 1993, price, you use the dividend expected in 1994, which is 6 percent greater than the 1993 dividend.

c. Calculate the expected dividend yield, D_1/P_0, the capital gains yield expected in 1989, and the expected total return (dividend yield plus capital gains yield) for 1989. (Assume that $\hat{P}_0 = P_0$, and recognize that the capital gains yield is equal to the total return minus the dividend yield.) Also calculate these same three yields for 1993.

d. How might an investor's tax situation affect his or her decision to purchase stocks of companies in the early stages of their lives, when they are growing rapidly, versus stocks of older, more mature firms? When does Severn's stock become "mature" in this example?

e. Suppose your boss tells you that she believes that Severn's annual growth rate will be only 15 percent during the next 5 years and that the firm's normal growth rate is only 5 percent. Without doing any calculations, what effect would these growth-rate changes have on the price of Severn's stock?

f. Suppose your boss also tells you that she regards Severn as being quite risky and that she believes the required rate of return is 13 percent, not 10 percent. Again without doing any calculations, how would the higher required rate of return affect the price of the stock?

Supernormal growth stock valuation

6-13   Overseas Motor Corporation (OMC) has been growing at a rate of 25 percent per year in recent years. This same growth rate is expected to last for another 2 years.

a. If $D_0 = \$2$, $k = 14\%$, and $g_n = 6\%$, what is OMC's stock worth today? What are its expected dividend yield and capital gains yield?

b. Now assume that OMC's period of supernormal growth is to last another 5 years rather than 2 years. How does this affect its price, dividend yield, and capital gains yield? Answer in words only.

c. What will be OMC's dividend yield and capital gains yield the year after its period of supernormal growth ends? (Hint: These values will be the same regardless of whether you examine the case of 2 or 5 years of supernormal growth; the calculations are trivial.)

d. Of what interest to investors is the changing relationship between dividend yield and capital gains yield over time?

Yield to call   **6-14**   It is now January 1, 1989, and you are considering the purchase of an outstanding Teweles Corporation bond that was issued on January 1, 1987. The Teweles bond has a 10.5 percent annual coupon and a 30-year original maturity (it matures in 2017). There is a 5-year call protection (until December 31, 1991), after which time the bond can be called at 110 (that is, at 110 percent of par, or $1,100). Interest rates have declined since the bond was issued, and the bond is now selling at 115.174 percent of par, or $1,151.74. You want to determine both the yield to maturity and the yield to call for this bond. (Note: The yield to call considers the effect of a call provision on the bond's probable yield. In the calculation, we assume that the bond will be outstanding until the call date, at which time it will be called. Thus, the investor will have received interest payments for the call-protected period and then will receive the call price — in this case, $1,100 — on the call date.)

a. What is the yield to maturity in 1989 for the Teweles bond? What is its yield to call?

b. If you bought this bond, which return do you think you would actually earn? Explain your reasoning.

c. Suppose the bond had sold at a discount. Would the yield to maturity or the yield to call have been more relevant?

Equilibrium stock price   **6-15**   The risk-free rate of return, k_{RF}, is 10 percent; the required rate of return on the market, k_M, is 15 percent; and Mathys Company's stock has a beta coefficient of 1.6.

a. If the dividend expected during the coming year, D_1, is $2.50, and if g = a constant 5%, at what price should Mathys' stock sell?

b. Now suppose the Federal Reserve Board increases the money supply, causing the risk-free rate to drop to 9 percent and k_M to fall to 14 percent. What would this do to the price of the stock?

c. In addition to the change in Part b, suppose investors' risk aversion declines; this fact, combined with the decline in k_{RF}, causes k_M to fall to 13 percent. At what price would Mathys' stock sell?

d. Now suppose Mathys has a change in management. The new group institutes policies that increase the expected constant growth rate to 6 percent. Also, the new management stabilizes sales and profits and thus causes the beta coefficient to decline from 1.6 to 1.3. After all these changes, what is Mathys' new equilibrium price? (Note: D_1 goes to $2.52.)

Beta coefficients   **6-16**   Suppose Kriegal Chemical Company's management conducts a study and concludes that if Kriegal expanded its consumer products division (which is less risky than its primary business, industrial chemicals), the firm's beta would decline from 1.2 to 0.9. However, consumer products have a somewhat lower profit margin, and this would cause Kriegal's constant growth rate in earnings and dividends to fall from 7 to 5 percent.

a. Should management make the change? Assume the following: k_M = 12%; k_{RF} = 9%; D_0 = $2.

b. Assume all the facts as given above except the change in the beta coefficient. How low would the beta have to fall to cause the expansion to be a good one? (Hint: Set $\hat{P}_0$ under the new policy equal to $\hat{P}_0$ under the old one, and find the new beta that will produce this equality.)

Expected rate of return   **6-17**   The beta coefficient for Stock C is b_c = 0.4, whereas that for Stock D is b_D = −0.5. (Stock D's beta is negative, indicating that its rate of return rises whenever returns on most other stocks fall. There are very few negative beta stocks, although gold mining stocks are sometimes cited as an example.)

a. If the risk-free rate is 9 percent and the expected rate of return on an average stock is 13 percent, what are the required rates of return on Stocks C and D?

b. For Stock C, suppose the current price, P_0, is $25; the next expected dividend, D_1, is $1.50; and the stock's expected constant growth rate is 4 percent. Is the stock in equilibrium? Explain, and describe what will happen if the stock is not in equilibrium.

Bond/stock valuation   **6-18**   Robert Balik and Carol Kiefer are senior vice presidents of the Mutual of
(Integrative)   Chicago Insurance Company. They are co-directors of the company's pension fund management division, with Balik having responsibility for fixed income securities (primarily bonds), and Kiefer being responsible for equity investments. A major new client, the California League of Cities, has requested that Mutual of Chicago present an investment seminar to the mayors of the represented cities, and Balik and Kiefer, who will make the actual presentation, have asked you to help them by answering the following questions.

Part I: a. How is the value of any asset whose value is based on expected
Bond valuation   future cash flows determined? How is the discount rate determined?

b. How is the value of a bond determined? What is the value of a 1-year, $1,000 par value bond with a 10 percent annual coupon if its required rate of return is 10 percent? What is the value of a similar 10-year bond?

c. What would be the value of the bonds described in Part b if investors required a 13 percent return? A 7 percent return? What would happen to the value of the 10-year bond over time if the required rate of return remained at 13 percent? Remained at 7 percent?

d. What is the yield to maturity on a 10-year, 10 percent annual coupon, $1,000 par value bond that sells for $887.00? That sells for $1,134.20? What is the current yield and capital gains yield in each case?

e. What is interest rate risk? Which bond in Part b has more interest rate risk, the 1-year bond or the 10-year bond? What is reinvestment rate risk? Which bond in Part b has more reinvestment rate risk, assuming a 10-year investment horizon?

f. Redo Parts b and c, assuming that the bonds have semiannual coupons.

g. What is the value of a perpetual bond with an annual coupon of $100 if its required rate of return is 10 percent? 13 percent? 7 percent? Assess the following statement: "Because perpetual bonds match an infinite investment horizon, they have little interest rate risk."

h. Suppose a 10-year, 10 percent, semiannual coupon bond having a par value of $1,000 is currently selling for $1,135.90, producing a yield to maturity of 8.0 percent. However, the bond can be called after 5 years for a price of $1,050. What is the bond's yield to call? If you bought this bond, do you think you would earn the YTM or the YTC?

Part II:
Stock valuation

To illustrate the common stock valuation process, Balik and Kiefer have asked you to analyze the Bon Temps Company, an employment agency that supplies word processors and computer programmers to other businesses to help their permanent staffs meet temporary heavy workloads. You are to answer the following questions.

a. What formula can be used to value any stock, regardless of its dividend pattern? What is a constant growth stock? How are constant growth stocks valued? What happens if $g > k_s$? Will many stocks have $g > k_s$?

b. Assume that Bon Temps has a beta coefficient of 1.2. Further, assume that the risk-free rate (yield on T-bonds) is 10 percent and the required rate of return on the market is 15 percent. What is Bon Temps's required rate of return?

c. Assume that Bon Temps is a constant growth stock company whose last dividend (D_0, which was paid yesterday) was $2.00. The dividend is expected to grow at a 6 percent rate. What is Bon Temps's expected dividend stream over the next 3 years? What is Bon Temps's current value? What is the stock's expected value in one year? What is the expected dividend yield and capital gains yield for the first year? What is the expected total yield during the first year?

d. Now assume that Bon Temps's stock is currently selling at $21.20. What is the expected rate of return on the stock?

e. What would Bon Temps's stock be worth if its dividends were expected to have zero growth?

f. Now assume that Bon Temps will experience supernormal growth of 30 percent in the next 3 years and then return to its steady-state constant growth rate of 6 percent. What is its value under these conditions? What is its expected dividend yield and capital gains in Year 1? In Year 4?

g. Suppose Bon Temps is expected to experience no growth during the first 3 years and then to resume its steady-state growth of 6.0 percent. What is the stock's value now? What is its expected dividend yield and capital gains yield in Year 1? In Year 4?

h. Finally, assume that Bon Temps's dividends are expected to grow at a constant -6.0 percent rate; that is, the dividend is expected to decline by 6 percent each year. What would be Bon Temps stock's current value? What would be the dividend yield and capital gains yield in each year?

Computer-Related Problems

(Work the problems in this section only if you are using the computer problem diskette.)

Supernormal growth stock valuation

C6-1   Use the model on the computer problem diskette for Problem C6-1 in the file C6 to solve this problem.

    a. Refer back to Problem 6-12. Rework Part e, using the computerized model to determine what Severn's expected dividends and stock price would be under the conditions given.

    b. Suppose your boss tells you that she regards Severn as being quite risky and that she believes the required rate of return should be higher than the 10 percent originally specified. Rework the problem under the conditions given in Part e, except change the required rate of return to (1) 13 percent, (2) 15 percent, and (3) 20 percent to determine the effects of the higher required rates of return on Severn's stock price.

Supernormal growth stock valuation

C6-2   Use the model on the computer problem diskette for Problem C6-2 in the file C6 to solve this problem.

    a. Refer back to Problem 6-13. What will be OMC's stock price, dividend yield, and capital gains yield if the supernormal growth period is 5 years rather than 2 years? Assume that the supernormal growth rate will be 25 percent, $D_0 = \$2$, $k = 14\%$, and $g_n = 6\%$.

    b. What will be the price, dividend yield, and capital gains yield if the required rate of return is 16 percent rather than 14 percent and the supernormal growth period is 5 years?

Yield to call

C6-3   Use the model on the computer problem diskette for Problem C6-3 in the file C6 to solve this problem.

    a. Refer back to Problem 6-14. Suppose that on January 1, 1990, the Teweles bond is selling for $1,200. What does this indicate about the level of interest rates in 1990 as compared with interest rates a year earlier? What will be the yield to maturity and the yield to call on the Teweles bond on this date? Note that the bond now has 27 years remaining until maturity and 2 years until it can be called. Which rate should an investor expect to receive if he or she buys the bond on this date?

    b. Suppose that instead of increasing the price, the Teweles bond falls to $800 on January 1, 1990. What will be the yield to maturity and the yield to call on this date? Which rate should an investor expect to receive?

Solutions to Self-Test Problems

ST-1   Refer to the marginal glossary definitions or appropriate sections of the text to check your responses.

ST-2   a. This is not necessarily true. Because G plows back two-thirds of its earnings, its growth rate should exceed that of D, but D pays more dividends ($3 versus $1). We cannot say which stock should have the higher price.

b. Again, we just do not know which price would be higher.

c. This is false. The changes in k_d and k_s would have a greater effect on G — its price would decline more.

d. The total expected return for D is $\hat{k}_D = D_1/P_0 + g = 15\% + 0\% = 15\%$. The total expected return for G will have D_1/P_0 less than 15 percent and g greater than 0 percent, but $\hat{k}_G$ should be neither greater nor smaller than D's total expected return, 15 percent, because the two stocks are equally risky.

e. We have eliminated a, b, c, and d, so e should be correct. On the basis of the available information, D and G should sell at about the same price, $20; thus, $\hat{k}_s = 15\%$ for both D and G. G's current dividend yield is $1/$20 = 5\%. Therefore, g = 15\% − 5\% = 10\%.

ST-3   a. Franklin's bonds were sold at par; therefore, the original YTM equaled the coupon rate of 12%.

b.
$$V = \sum_{t=1}^{50} \frac{\$120/2}{\left(1 + \dfrac{0.10}{2}\right)^t} + \frac{\$1,000}{\left(1 + \dfrac{0.10}{2}\right)^{50}}$$

$$= \$60(\text{PVIFA}_{5\%,50}) + \$1,000(\text{PVIF}_{5\%,50})$$

$$= \$60(18.2559) + \$1,000(0.0872)$$

$$= \$1,095.35 + \$87.20 = \$1,182.55.$$

c.
$$\text{Current yield} = \text{Annual coupon payment/Price}$$

$$= \$120/\$1,182.55$$

$$= 0.1015 = 10.15\%.$$

$$\text{Capital gains yield} = \text{Total yield} - \text{Current yield}$$

$$= 10\% - 10.15\% = -0.15\%.$$

d.
$$\$896.64 = \sum_{t=1}^{19} \frac{\$60}{(1 + k_d/2)^t} + \frac{\$1,000}{(1 + k_d/2)^{19}}.$$

Use the approximate YTM formula to get a starting point:

$$\text{Approximate YTM} = \frac{I + (M - V)/n}{(M + 2V)/3}$$

$$= \frac{\$60 + (\$1,000 - \$896.64)/19}{(\$1,000 + \$1,793.28)/3}$$

$$= 7.03\%.$$

Therefore, $k_d \approx 7.03(2) = 14.06\%$.
Try $k_d = 14\%$:

$$V = I(\text{PVIFA}_{7\%,19}) + M(\text{PVIF}_{7\%,19})$$

$$\$896.64 = \$60(10.3356) + \$1,000(0.2765)$$

$$= \$620.14 + \$276.50 = \$896.64.$$

Therefore, the YTM on July 1, 1987, was 14 percent.

e. $$\text{Current yield} = \$120/\$896.64 = 13.38\%.$$

$$\text{Capital gains yield} = 14\% - 13.38\% = 0.62\%.$$

f. The following time line illustrates the years to maturity of the bond:

1/1/87   7/1/87   1/1/88   7/1/88   1/1/89   12/31/96

3/1/87

Thus, on March 1, 1987, there were 19⅔ periods left before the bond matures. Bond traders actually use the following procedure to determine the price of the bond:

1. Find the price of the bond on the next coupon date, July 1, 1987.

$$V_{7/1/87} = \$60(\text{PVIFA}_{7.75\%,19}) + \$1,000(\text{PVIF}_{7.75\%,19})$$

$$= \$60(9.7788) + \$1,000(0.2421)$$

$$= \$828.83.$$

Note that we could use a calculator to solve for $V_{7/1/87}$ or we could substitute $k = 7.75\%$ and $n = 19$ periods into the equations for PVIFA and PVIF:

$$\text{PVIFA} = \frac{1 - \dfrac{1}{(1 + k)^n}}{k} = \frac{1 - \dfrac{1}{(1 + 0.0775)^{19}}}{0.0775} = 9.7788.$$

$$\text{PVIF} = \frac{1}{(1 + k)^n} = \frac{1}{(1 + 0.0775)^{19}} = 0.2421.$$

2. Add the coupon, $60, to the bond price to get the total value, TV, of the bond on the next interest payment date: TV = $828.83 + $60.00 = $888.83.
3. Discount this total value back to the purchase date:

$$\text{Value at purchase date (March 1, 1987)} = \$888.83(\text{PVIF}_{7.75\%,4/6})$$

$$= \$888.83(0.9515)$$

$$= \$845.72.$$

Here

$$\text{PVIF}_{7.75\%,2/3} = \frac{1}{(1 + 0.0775)^{2/3}} = \frac{1}{1.0510} = 0.9515.$$

4. Therefore, you would have written a check for $845.72 to complete the transaction. Of this amount, $20 = (1/3)($60) would represent accrued interest and $825.72 would represent the bond's basic value. This breakdown would affect both your taxes and those of the seller.
5. This problem could be solved *very* easily using a financial calculator with a bond valuation function, such as the HP 12C or the HP 17B.

ST-4   The first step is to solve for g, the unknown variable, in the constant growth equation. Since D_1 is unknown but D_0 is known, substitute $D_0(1 + g)$ as follows:

$$\hat{P}_0 = P_0 = \frac{D_1}{k_s - g} = \frac{D_0(1 + g)}{k_s - g}$$

$$\$24 = \frac{\$1.60(1 + g)}{0.12 - g}.$$

Solving for g, we find the growth rate to be 5 percent:

$$\$2.88 - \$24g = \$1.60 + \$1.60g$$

$$\$25.60g = \$1.28$$

$$g = 0.05 = 5\%.$$

The next step is to use the growth rate to project the stock price 5 years hence:

$$\hat{P}_5 = \frac{D_0(1 + g)^6}{k_s - g}$$

$$= \frac{\$1.60(1.05)^6}{0.12 - 0.05}$$

$$= \$30.63.$$

(Alternatively, $\hat{P}_5 = \$24(1.05)^5 = \$30.63$.)

Therefore, Ambrose Company's expected stock price 5 years from now, $\hat{P}_5$, is $30.63.

ST-5   a. 1. Calculate the PV of the dividends paid during the supernormal growth period:

$$D_1 = \$1.1500(1.18) = \$1.3570.$$

$$D_2 = \$1.3570(1.18) = \$1.6013.$$

$$D_3 = \$1.6013(1.15) = \$1.8415.$$

$$\text{PV D} = \$1.3570(0.8929) + \$1.6013(0.7972) + \$1.8415(0.7118)$$

$$= \$1.2117 + \$1.2766 + \$1.3108$$

$$= \$3.7991 \approx \$3.80.$$

2. Find the PV of Woerheide's stock price at the end of Year 3:

$$\hat{P}_3 = \frac{D_4}{k_s - g} = \frac{D_3(1 + g)}{k_s - g}$$

$$= \frac{\$1.8415(1.06)}{0.12 - 0.06}$$

$$= \$32.53.$$

$$\text{PV } \hat{P}_3 = \$32.53(0.7118) = \$23.15.$$

3. Sum the two components to find the value of the stock today:

$$\hat{P}_0 = \$3.80 + \$23.15 = \$26.95.$$

b. $\hat{P}_1 = \$1.6013(0.8929) + \$1.8415(0.7972) + \$32.53(0.7972)$

$\quad = \$1.4298 + \$1.4680 + \$25.9329$

$\quad = \$28.8307 \approx \$28.83.$

$\hat{P}_2 = \$1.8415(0.8929) + \$32.53(0.8929)$

$\quad = \$1.6443 + \$29.0460$

$\quad = \$30.6903 \approx \$30.69.$

c.

Year	Dividend Yield	+	Capital Gains Yield	=	Total Return
1	$\dfrac{\$1.3570}{\$26.95} = 5.04\%$		$\dfrac{\$28.83 - \$26.95}{\$26.95} = 6.98\%$		$\approx 12\%$
2	$\dfrac{\$1.6013}{\$28.83} = 5.55\%$		$\dfrac{\$30.69 - \$28.83}{\$28.83} = 6.45\%$		$\approx 12\%$
3	$\dfrac{\$1.8415}{\$30.69} = 6.00\%$		$\dfrac{\$32.53 - \$30.69}{\$30.69} = 6.00\%$		$\approx 12\%$

II Financial Statements and Financial Forecasting

7 Analysis of Financial Statements

REAPING THE REWARDS OF PROPER FINANCIAL STATEMENT ANALYSIS

Ascher Edelman, a well-known Wall Street raider, taught a finance course at Columbia University in 1987. Many Wall Streeters teach courses in New York-area universities, but what made Edelman's course so unusual was that he offered his students a prize — he promised $100,000 to any student who, through financial analysis, could identify an undervalued firm which Edelman could take over. Presumably, the winning student would get an A in the course, along with the $100,000.

Needless to say, Edelman's course was oversubscribed. Perhaps less obviously, his offer led to a furor within the faculty. One faculty group thought Edelman's offer was fine; it would motivate students to learn, and it would give them a chance to see how a real pro did what they were in school learning to do. A larger faculty group, however, argued that Edelman's offer would corrupt the academic environment; if his offer were allowed to stand, other professors might begin using students to help with their consulting, and who could tell where all this would lead? Edelman was forced to withdraw his offer, much to the dismay of his students!

What was required of Edelman's students to earn either the $100,000 or the A? Essentially, they had to go through the type of analysis set forth in this chapter, studying the financial statements of various companies to identify firms whose managers were not using their financial resources as fully as possible. The students would then use computers to simulate what would happen to the firms' earnings and stock prices if different financial policies were followed.

There are, literally, platoons of finance graduates doing essentially the same thing all over the country, including loan officers for Citibank and Prudential Insurance, stock analysts for Merrill Lynch and Shearson Lehman Hutton, and credit analysts for Exxon and General Electric. Any time a large loan is made or a large block of stock is purchased, the type of analysis that Edelman's students were learning, and that we cover in this chapter, comes into play.

Financial managers are just as concerned with analyzing their firms' statements as are outsiders, for such analyses can point out weak spots that need improvement and identify strengths that can be used to the firm's advantage. Managers are learning that it is better to do these things themselves than to have raiders like Edelman's troops move in and do it for them!

In Part I we examined the time value of money concept, developed bond and stock valuation models, discussed the concept of risk, and saw how risk affects the value of financial assets. Up to this point, however, we have abstracted from the actual data used in financial analysis. In this chapter, we examine the basic financial data available to managers and investors, and then we look at some analytical techniques used by both investors and managers to appraise firms' relative riskiness, profit potential, and general performance.

If management is to maximize the value of the firm's stock price, it must take advantage of the firm's strengths and correct its weaknesses. Financial statement analysis involves a comparison of the firm's performance relative to that of other firms in the same industry. This helps management identify deficiencies and then take actions to improve the firm's performance. In this chapter, we discuss how financial managers (and investors) calculate and interpret financial ratios. Then, in the next chapter, we will see how managers forecast future financial statements and ratios, and then use these forecasts to determine the effect of specific decisions on the firm's future performance.

As you go through this chapter, it is important to remember that security values are based on *cash flows,* yet accounting statements concentrate primarily on *reported profits.* Recall from Chapter 2 that there can be major differences between profits as reported by accountants and actual cash flows. This makes it necessary to "look behind the accounting numbers," both when appraising the performance of management and when setting a value for the firm. For the most part, accounting numbers are valid — high accounting profits generally signify high cash flows and the ability to pay high dividends. However, there are enough exceptions to this rule to warrant a critical examination of all accounting data.

FINANCIAL STATEMENTS AND REPORTS

annual report
A report issued annually by a corporation to its stockholders that contains basic financial statements as well as management's opinion of the past year's operations and the firm's future prospects.

Of the various reports corporations issue to their stockholders, the **annual report** is by far the most important. Two types of information are given in this report. First, there is a verbal section, often presented as a letter from the president, which describes the firm's operating results during the past year and discusses new developments that will affect future operations. Second, the annual report presents four basic financial statements — the *income statement,* the *balance sheet,* the *statement of retained earnings,* and the *statement of cash flows.* Taken together, these statements give an accounting picture of the firm's operations and financial position. Detailed data are provided for the two most recent years, along with historical summaries of key operating statistics for the past five or ten years.[1]

The quantitative and verbal information are equally important. The financial statements report *what has actually happened* to earnings and dividends over the past few years, whereas the verbal statements attempt to explain why things turned out the way they did. For example, Salomon Inc.'s earnings dropped sharply from $516 million in 1986 to $130 million in 1987. Management reported that the drop resulted from losses associated with the stock market crash of 1987 and from increased costs due to excessive growth. However, it then went on to paint a more optimistic picture for the future, stating that the operations had been scaled back, that several less profitable businesses had been eliminated, and that 1988 profits were expected to rise sharply. Of course, an increase in profitability may not occur, and analysts should compare management's past statements with subsequent results. In any event, *the information contained in the annual report is used by investors to form expectations about future earnings and dividends, and about the riskiness of these expected values.* Therefore, the annual report is obviously of great interest to investors.

The Income Statement

income statement
A statement summarizing the firm's revenues and expenses during an accounting period.

Table 7-1 gives the 1987 and 1988 **income statements** for National Metals Company, a producer of fabricated aluminum products. Net sales are shown at the top of each statement, after which variable costs, including income taxes, are subtracted to obtain the net income available to common stockholders. A report on earnings and dividends per share is given at the bottom of the statement. In financial management, earnings per share (EPS) is called "the bottom line," denoting that of all the items on the income statement, EPS is the most

---

[1]Firms also provide quarterly reports, but these are much less comprehensive than the annual reports. In addition, larger firms file even more detailed statements, giving breakdowns for each major division or subsidiary, with the Securities and Exchange Commission (SEC). These reports, called *10-K reports,* are made available to stockholders upon request to a company's secretary. Finally, many larger firms also publish *statistical supplements,* which give financial statement data and key ratios going back ten years.

Table 7-1   National Metals Company:
Income Statements for Years Ending December 31
(Thousands of Dollars, Except for Per-Share Data)

	1988	1987
Net sales	$3,000	$2,850
Costs and expenses:		
Labor and materials	2,544	2,413
Depreciation	100	90
Selling expenses	22	20
General and administrative expenses	40	35
Lease payments on buildings	28	28
Total operating costs	$2,734	$2,586
Net operating income, or earnings before interest and taxes (EBIT)	$ 266	$ 264
Less interest expense:		
Interest on notes payable	$ 8	$ 2
Interest on first mortgage bonds	40	42
Interest on debentures	18	3
Total interest	$ 66	$ 47
Earnings before taxes	$ 200	$ 217
Federal and state taxes (at 40%)	80	87
Net income before preferred dividends	$ 120	$ 130
Dividends to preferred stockholders	8	8
Net income available to common stockholders	$ 112	$ 122
Disposition of net income:		
Dividends to common stockholders	$ 92	$ 82
Addition to retained earnings	$ 20	$ 40
Per share of common stock:		
Stock price (year-end)	$26.50	$27.00
Earnings per share (EPS)[a]	$ 2.24	$ 2.44
Dividends per share (DPS)[a]	$ 1.84	$ 1.64

[a]There are 50,000 shares outstanding; see Table 7-2. Note that EPS is based on earnings after preferred dividends — that is, on net income available to common stockholders. Calculations of EPS and DPS for 1988 are as follows:

$$\text{EPS} = \frac{\text{Net income after tax}}{\text{Shares outstanding}} = \frac{\$112,000}{50,000} = \$2.24.$$

$$\text{DPS} = \frac{\text{Dividends paid to common stockholders}}{\text{Shares outstanding}} = \frac{\$92,000}{50,000} = \$1.84.$$

important.[2] National Metals earned $2.24 per share in 1988, down from $2.44 in 1987, but it still increased the dividend from $1.64 to $1.84.

The Balance Sheet

balance sheet
A statement of the firm's financial position at a specific point in time.

The left-hand side of National Metals' year-end 1987 and 1988 **balance sheets**, which are given in Table 7-2, shows the firm's assets, while the right-hand side shows the liabilities and equity, or the claims against these assets. The assets

[2]Dividends are important too, but the firm's ability to pay dividends is dependent on its long-run cash flows, which in turn are dependent primarily on its earnings.

Table 7-2   National Metals Company:
December 31 Balance Sheets
(Thousands of Dollars)

Assets	1988	1987	Liabilities and Equity	1988	1987
Cash	$ 50	$ 55	Accounts payable	$ 60	$ 30
Marketable securities	0	25	Notes payable	100	60
Accounts receivable	350	315	Accrued wages	10	10
Inventories	300	215	Accrued taxes	130	120
Total current assets	$ 700	$ 610	Total current liabilities	$ 300	$ 220
Gross plant and equipment	$1,800	$1,470	First mortgage bonds	$ 500	$ 520
Less depreciation	500	400	Debentures	300	60
Net plant and equipment	$1,300	$1,070	Total long-term debt	$ 800	$ 580
			Stockholders' equity:		
			Preferred stock (20,000 shares, $1 par value)	$ 20	$ 20
			Common stock (50,000 shares, $1 par)	50	50
			Additional paid-in capital	80	80
			Retained earnings	750	730
			Total stockholders' equity	$ 900	$ 880
Total assets	$2,000	$1,680	Total liabilities and equity	$2,000	$1,680

Note: The first mortgage bonds have a sinking fund requirement of $20,000 a year. Sinking funds are discussed in Chapter 13, but in brief, a sinking fund simply involves the repayment of long-term debt. Thus, National Metals was required to pay off $20,000 of its mortgage bonds during 1988. The current portion of the long-term debt is included in notes payable here, although in a more detailed balance sheet, it would be shown as a separate item under current liabilities.

are listed in order of their "liquidity," or the length of time it typically takes to convert them to cash. The claims are listed in the order in which they must be paid: Accounts payable must generally be paid within 30 days, notes are payable within 90 days, and so on, down to the stockholders' equity accounts, which represent ownership and never need to be "paid off."

Some additional points about the balance sheet are worth noting:

1. **Cash versus other assets.** Although the assets are all stated in terms of dollars, only cash represents actual money. Receivables are bills others owe National Metals; inventories show the dollars the company has invested in raw materials, work-in-process, and finished goods available for sale; and fixed assets reflect the amount of money National Metals paid for its plant and equipment when it acquired those assets at some time in the past. National Metals can write checks at present for a total of $50,000 (versus current liabilities of $300,000 due within a year). The noncash assets should produce cash flows eventually, but they do not represent cash-in-hand, and the amount of cash they will eventually produce could be higher or lower than the values at which they are carried on the books.

2. **Liabilities versus stockholders' equity.** The claims against assets are of two types — liabilities (or money the company owes) and the

stockholders' equity (net worth)
The capital supplied by stockholders—capital stock, paid-in capital, retained earnings, and, occasionally, certain reserves. *Common equity* is total equity minus preferred stock.

stockholders' ownership position.[3] The **stockholders' equity**, or **net worth**, is a residual:

$$\text{Assets} \quad - \quad \text{Liabilities} \quad = \quad \text{Stockholders' equity.}$$
$$\$2,000,000 \ - \ \$1,100,000 \ = \qquad \$900,000.$$

Suppose assets decline in value — for example, suppose some of the accounts receivable are written off as bad debts. Liabilities remain constant, so the value of the stockholders' equity must decline. Therefore, the risk of asset value fluctuations is borne by the stockholders. Note, however, that if asset values rise (perhaps because of inflation), these benefits will accrue exclusively to the stockholders.

3. **Breakdown of the stockholders' common equity account.** A detailed discussion of the common equity accounts is given in Chapter 12, "Common Stock and the Investment Banking Process," but a brief preview of that discussion is useful here. First, note that the equity section is divided into four accounts — preferred stock, common stock, paid-in capital, and retained earnings — and that the last three, in total, equal common equity. The **retained earnings** account is built up over time by the firm "saving" a part of its earnings rather than paying all earnings out as dividends. The other two common equity accounts arise from the sale of stock by the firm to raise capital. Accountants generally assign a *par value* to common stock — National Metals' stock has a par value of $1 per share.[4] Now suppose National Metals were to sell 1,000 additional shares at a price of $30 per share. The company would raise $30,000, and the cash account would go up by this amount. Of the total, $1,000 would be added to common stock and $29,000 to **paid-in capital**. Thus, after the sale, common stock would show $50,000 + $1,000 = $51,000, paid-in capital would show $80,000 + $29,000 = $109,000, and there would be 51,000 shares outstanding.

retained earnings
That portion of the firm's earnings that is saved rather than paid out as dividends.

paid-in capital
Funds received in excess of par value when a firm sells stock.

The breakdown of the common equity accounts is important for some purposes but not for others. For example, a potential stockholder would want to know whether the company actually earned the funds reported in its equity accounts or whether funds came mainly from selling stock. A potential creditor, on the other hand, is more interested in the amount of money the owners put up than in the form in which the money was put up. In the remainder of this chapter, we generally

---

[3]One could divide liabilities into (1) debts owed to someone and (2) other items, such as deferred taxes, reserves, and so on. Because we do not make this distinction, the terms *debt* and *liabilities* are used synonymously. It should be noted that firms occasionally set up reserves for certain contingencies, such as the potential costs involved in a lawsuit currently in the courts. These reserves represent an accounting transfer from retained earnings to the reserve account. If the company wins the suit, retained earnings will be credited and the reserve will be eliminated. If it loses, cash will be reduced and the reserve will be eliminated.

[4]See Chapter 12 for a discussion of par value.

aggregate the three common equity accounts and call this sum *common equity* or *net worth.*

4. **Inventory accounting.** National Metals uses the FIFO (first-in, first-out) method to determine the inventory value shown on its balance sheet ($300,000). It could have used the LIFO (last-in, first-out) method. During a period of rising prices, FIFO shows a higher value for reported inventories than LIFO does. For example, if costs are rising at an annual rate of 10 percent, inventory items that were just acquired would cost 10 percent more than identical items that were acquired a year ago. Since National Metals uses FIFO, and since inflation has been occurring, (1) its costs are relatively low as compared to what they would have been under LIFO, (2) its reported profits are therefore relatively high, and (3) its balance sheet inventories are higher than they would have been had it used LIFO. In National Metals' case, had the company elected to use LIFO in 1988, EPS would have been lowered by 30 cents, to $1.94, and its balance sheet figure for inventories would have been $275,000 rather than $300,000. Thus, the inventory valuation method can have a significant effect on the financial statements.

5. **Depreciation methods.** Companies often use the ACRS method to calculate depreciation for tax purposes but use straight line based on a longer life for stockholder reporting. However, National Metals, IBM, and some other companies have elected to use rapid depreciation (ACRS) for both stockholder reporting and tax purposes. Had National Metals elected to use straight line instead of ACRS for stockholder reporting, its depreciation expense would have been almost $25,000 less, so net income would have been higher, as would its EPS. The $1,300,000 shown for "net plant" on its balance sheet, and hence its retained earnings, would also have been approximately $25,000 higher.

6. **The time dimension.** The balance sheet may be thought of as a snapshot of the firm's financial position *at a point in time* — for example, on December 31, 1988. Thus, on December 31, 1987, National Metals had $25,000 of marketable securities, but this account had been reduced to zero by the end of 1988. The income statement, on the other hand, reports on operations *over a period of time* — for example, during the calendar year 1988. National Metals had sales of $3,000,000, and its net income available to common stockholders was $112,000. The balance sheet changes every day as inventories are increased or decreased, as fixed assets are added or retired, as bank loans are increased or decreased, and so on. Companies whose businesses are seasonal have especially large changes in their balance sheets. For example, most retailers have large inventories just before Christmas but low inventories and high accounts receivable after Christmas. Therefore, their balance sheets will look materially different, depending on the date chosen to construct the statement.

The Cash Flow Cycle

As a company like National Metals goes about its business, it makes sales, which lead (1) to a reduction of inventories, (2) to an increase in cash, and, (3) if the sales price exceeds the cost of the item sold, to a profit. These transactions cause the balance sheet to change, and they also are reflected in the income statement. It is critically important for you to understand (1) that businesses deal with *physical* units like autos, computers, or aluminum, (2) that physical transactions are translated into dollar terms through the accounting system, and (3) that the purpose of financial analysis is to examine the accounting numbers to determine how efficient the firm is at making and selling physical goods and services.

Several factors make financial analysis difficult. One of them is variations in accounting methods among firms. As was discussed in the previous section, different methods of inventory valuation and depreciation can lead to differences in reported profits for otherwise identical firms, and a good financial analyst must be able to adjust for these differences if he or she is to make valid comparisons among companies. Another factor involves timing — an action is taken at one point in time, but its full effects cannot be accurately measured until some later period.

cash flow cycle
The way in which actual net cash, as opposed to accounting net income, flows into or out of the firm during some specified period.

To understand how timing influences the financial statement, one must understand the **cash flow cycle** within a firm, as set forth in Figure 7-1. Rectangles represent balance sheet accounts — assets and claims against assets — whereas circles represent actions taken by the firm. Each rectangle may be thought of as a reservoir, and the wavy lines designate the amount of the asset or liability in the reservoir (account) on a balance sheet date. Various transactions cause changes in the accounts, just as adding or subtracting oil changes the level in an oil reservoir.

The cash account is the focal point of the figure. Certain events, such as collecting accounts receivable or borrowing money from the bank, will cause the cash account to increase, while the payment of taxes, interest, dividends, and accounts payable will cause it to decline. Similar comments could be made about all the balance sheet accounts — their balances rise, fall, or remain constant depending on events that occur during the period under study, which for National Metals is January 1, 1988, through December 31, 1988.

Projected sales increases may require the firm to raise cash by borrowing from its bank or selling new stock. For example, if National Metals anticipates an increase in sales, (1) it will expend cash to buy or build fixed assets through the capital budgeting process; (2) it will step up purchases of raw materials, thereby increasing both raw materials inventories and accounts payable; (3) it will increase production, which will cause an increase in both accrued wages and work-in-process; and (4) it will eventually build up its finished goods inventory. Some cash will have been expended and hence removed from the cash account, and the firm will have obligated itself to expend still more cash within a few weeks to pay off its accounts payable and its accrued wages. These events will have occurred *before* any new cash has been generated from sales.

Figure 7-1   Cash and Materials Flows within the Firm

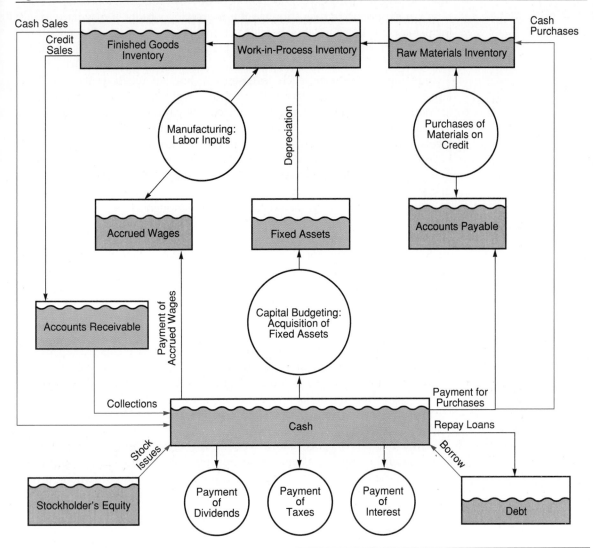

Even when the expected sales do occur, there will still be a lag in the generation of cash until receivables are collected — because National Metals grants
credit for 30 days, it will have to wait 30 days after a sale is made before cash
comes in. Depending on how much cash the firm had at the beginning of the
build-up, on the length of its production-sales-collection cycle, and on how
long it can delay payment of its own payables and accrued wages, the company
may have to obtain substantial amounts of additional cash by selling stock or
bonds, or by borrowing from the bank.

If the firm is profitable, its sales revenues will exceed its costs, and its cash inflows will eventually exceed its cash outlays. However, even a profitable business can experience a cash shortage if it is growing rapidly. It may have to pay for plant, materials, and labor before cash from the expanded sales starts flowing in. For this reason, rapidly growing firms generally require large bank loans, or capital from other sources.

An unprofitable firm, such as Eastern Airlines in recent years, will have larger cash outlays than inflows. This, in turn, will typically cause a slowdown in the payment of accrued wages and accounts payable, and it may also lead to heavy borrowings. Accordingly, liabilities generally build up to excessive levels in unprofitable firms. Similarly, an overly ambitious expansion plan will be reflected in an excessive buildup of inventories and fixed assets, while a poor credit/collection policy will result in bad debts and reduced profits that first show up as high accounts receivable.

If a firm runs out of cash and cannot obtain enough to meet its obligations, then it cannot operate, and it will have to declare bankruptcy. Therefore, a good cash flow forecast is a critical element in a good financial plan. Financial analysts are well aware of all this, and they use the analytical techniques discussed in the remainder of this chapter to help discover cash flow problems before they become too serious.

Statement of Retained Earnings

statement of retained earnings
A statement reporting how much of the firm's earnings were not paid out in dividends. The figure for retained earnings that appears here is the sum of the annual retained earnings for each year of the firm's history.

Changes in the common equity accounts between balance sheet dates are reported in the **statement of retained earnings**. National Metals' statement is shown in Table 7-3. The company earned $112,000 during 1988, paid out $92,000 in dividends, and plowed $20,000 back into the business. Thus, the balance sheet item "Retained earnings" increased from $730,000 at the end of 1987 to $750,000 at the end of 1988.

Note that the balance sheet account "Retained earnings" represents a *claim against assets,* not assets per se. Further, firms retain earnings primarily to expand the business — this means investing in plant and equipment, inventories, and so on, *not* in a bank account. *Thus, retained earnings as reported on the balance sheet do not represent cash, and they are not "available" for the payment of dividends or anything else.*[5]

---

[5]The amount recorded in the retained earnings account is *not* an indication of the amount of cash the firm has. That amount (as of the balance sheet date) is found in the cash account — an asset account. A positive number in the retained earnings account indicates only that in the past, according to generally accepted accounting principles, the firm has earned an income, but its dividends have been less than its reported income. Also, recall our earlier discussion of cash flow and the difference between accrual and cash accounting. Even though a company reports record earnings and shows an increase in the retained earnings account, it still may be short of cash.

The same situation holds for individuals. You might own a new BMW (with no loan), lots of clothes, and an expensive stereo set, and hence have a high net worth, but if you have only 23 cents in your pocket plus $5 in your checking account, you would still be short of cash.

Table 7-3   National Metals Company:
Statement of Retained Earnings for
Year Ending December 31, 1988
(Thousands of Dollars)

Balance of retained earnings, December 31, 1987	$730
Add: Net income, 1988	112
Less: Dividends to stockholders	(92)[a]
Balance of retained earnings, December 31, 1988	$750

[a]Here, and throughout the book, parentheses are used to denote negative numbers.

Statement of Cash Flows

statement of cash flows
A statement reporting
the impact of a firm's
operating, investing, and
financing activities on
cash flows over an
accounting period.

The graphic cash flow analysis set forth in Figure 7-1 is converted into numerical form and reported in annual reports as the **statement of cash flows**. This statement is designed (1) to show how the firm's operations have affected its liquidity, as measured by its cash flows, and (2) to show the relationships among cash flows from operating, investing, and financing activities. It helps answer questions such as: Is the firm generating the cash needed to purchase additional fixed assets for growth? Is growth so rapid that external financing is required both for maintaining operations and for investment in new fixed assets? Does the firm have excess cash flows that can be used to repay financing from earlier periods or to invest in new products? This information is useful both for investment analysis and for corporate planning, so the statement of cash flows is an important part of the annual report.

Before we discuss the cash flow statement in detail, we should reflect for a moment on one of its most important elements — depreciation. First, what is depreciation? Recall from Chapter 2 that depreciation is an annual charge against income based on the estimated dollar cost of the capital equipment used up in the production process. For example, suppose a machine with an ACRS class life of 5 years and a zero expected salvage value was purchased in 1987 for $100,000. This $100,000 cost is not expensed in the purchase year; rather, it is charged against production over the machine's 5-year depreciable life. If the depreciation expense were not taken, profits would be overstated, and taxes would be too high. The annual depreciation allowance is deducted from sales revenues, along with such other costs as labor and raw materials, to determine income. However, because funds were expended back in 1987, the depreciation charged against the income in 1988 through 1992 is not a cash outlay, as are labor or raw materials charges. *Depreciation is a noncash charge, so it must be added back to net income to obtain an estimate of the cash flow from operations.*

Preparing the Sources and Uses of Funds Statement. The first step in preparing a statement of cash flows is to identify which balance sheet items provided cash and which used cash during the year. This is done on a sources and uses of funds statement. The change in each balance sheet account is determined, and this change is recorded as either a source or a use of funds in accordance with the following rules:

Sources

1. Any increase in a liability or equity account. Borrowing from the bank is an example of a source of funds.

2. Any decrease in an asset account. Selling some fixed assets, or reducing inventories, are examples of sources of funds.

Uses

1. Any decrease in a liability or equity account. Paying off a loan is an example of a use of funds.

2. Any increase in an asset account. Buying fixed assets or building inventories are examples of uses of funds.

Thus, sources of funds include bank loans and retained earnings, as well as money generated by selling assets, by collecting receivables, and even by drawing down the cash account. Uses include acquiring fixed assets, building up receivables or inventories, and paying off debts.

Table 7-4 shows the changes that occurred in National Metals' balance sheet accounts during the calendar year 1988, with each change designated as a source or a use. Sources and uses each total $470,000.[6] Note that the table does not contain any summary accounts, such as total current assets or net plant and equipment. If we included summary accounts in Table 7-4 and then used these accounts to prepare the statement of cash flows, we would be "double counting."

The data in Table 7-4 are used next to prepare the formal statement of cash flows. The one in National Metals' annual report is shown in Table 7-5.[7] Each balance sheet item change from Table 7-4 is classified as resulting from (1) operations, (2) long-term investments, or (3) financing activities. Operating cash flows are those associated with the production and sale of goods and services. Net income is the primary operating cash flow, but changes in accounts payable, accounts receivable, inventories, and accruals are also operating cash flows. Investment cash flows arise from the purchase or sale of plant, property, and equipment. Financing cash inflows result from issuing debt or

---

[6]Adjustments would have to be made if fixed assets were sold during the year. National Metals had no sales of assets during 1988.

[7]There are two different formats for presenting the cash flow statement. The method we present here is called the *indirect method*. Cash flows from operations are calculated by starting with net income, adding back expenses not paid out of cash, and subtracting revenues not providing cash. Using the *direct method*, operating cash flows are found by summing all revenues providing cash and then subtracting all expenses using cash. Both produce the same result, and both formats are accepted by the Financial Accounting Statements Board.

Table 7-4 National Metals Company:
Sources and Uses of Funds during 1988
(Thousands of Dollars)

	12/31/88	12/31/87	Change Source	Change Use
Cash	$ 50	$ 55	$ 5	
Marketable securities	0	25	25	
Accounts receivable	350	315		$ 35
Inventories	300	215		85
Gross plant and equipment	1,800	1,470		330
Accumulated depreciation[a]	500	400	100	
Accounts payable	60	30	30	
Notes payable	100	60	40	
Accrued wages	10	10		
Accrued taxes	130	120	10	
Mortgage bonds	500	520		20
Debentures	300	60	240	
Preferred stock	20	20		
Common stock	50	50		
Paid-in capital	80	80		
Retained earnings	750	730	20	
Totals			$470	$470

[a]Depreciation is a *contra-asset*, not an asset; hence, an increase in depreciation is treated as a source of funds.

common stock, while financing outflows occur when the firm pays dividends or repays debt. The cash inflows and outflows from these three activities are summed to determine their impact on the firm's liquidity position, which is measured by the change in the cash and marketable securities accounts.

Note that every item in the "change" columns of Table 7-4 is carried over to Table 7-5 except retained earnings. Table 7-5 reports net income as a source and dividends paid as a use rather than netting these items out and simply reporting the increase in retained earnings. Also, note that cash and marketable securities are combined in Table 7-5. Like most companies, National Metals considers its marketable securities to be cash equivalents, so with regard to financial position, they are treated as cash.

Table 7-5 pinpoints the sources and uses of National Metals' net cash flow, where net cash flow is defined as the change in cash and marketable securities. The top part shows funds generated by and used in operations — for National Metals, operations provided net cash flows of $140,000. The major sources of operating cash flows were net income and depreciation, while the primary use was to increase inventories. The second section shows long-term investing activities. National Metals purchased fixed assets totaling $330,000; this was its only investment activity during 1988. National Metals' financing activities, shown in the lower section of Table 7-5, consisted of borrowing from banks

Table 7-5   National Metals Company
Statement of Cash Flows for 1988
(Thousands of Dollars)

Cash Flows from Operations:		
Net income	$120	
Additions (sources of cash):		
Depreciation[a]	100	
Increase in accounts payable	30	
Increase in accrued taxes	10	
Subtractions (uses of cash):		
Increase in accounts receivable	($ 35)[b]	
Increase in inventories	(85)	
Net cash flows from operations		$140
Cash Flows Associated with Long-Term Investments:		
Acquisition of fixed assets		($330)
Cash Flows Associated with Financing Activities:		
Increase in notes payable	$ 40	
Increase in debentures	240	
Repayment of mortgage bonds	(20)	
Common and preferred dividends paid	(100)	
Net cash flows from financing		$160
Net reduction in cash and marketable securities		($ 30)

[a]Depreciation is a noncash expense that was deducted when calculating net income. It must be added back to show the correct cash flow from operations. You might look back at Chapter 2 for a further discussion of why depreciation is regarded as a source of funds.

[b]Recall that parentheses denote negative numbers here and throughout the book.

(notes payable), selling debentures, paying off part of its mortgage bonds, and paying dividends on its common and preferred stock. National Metals raised $280,000 from the capital markets but repaid $20,000 on its mortgage loan, and paid $100,000 in dividends, so its net inflow of funds from financing activities during 1988 was $160,000.

When all of these sources and uses of cash are totaled, we see that National Metals had a $30,000 cash shortfall during 1988. It met that shortfall by selling off marketable securities ($25,000) and by reducing its cash balance ($5,000), as can be seen from Table 7-4.

National Metals is a strong, well-managed company, and its statement of cash flows shows nothing unusual or alarming. It does show a cash drain which resulted primarily from the purchase of fixed assets, but it also shows positive cash flows from operations. If the company chooses to cut back on its fixed asset expansion, it will generate positive cash flows. Thus, the cash outflow does not appear likely to continue, and to bleed the company to death.

Earnings and Dividends

In addition to the four statements previously described, most annual reports today also give a summary of earnings and dividends over the last few years. For National Metals, these data are analyzed in Figure 7-2. Earnings were variable, but there was a definite upward trend during the period. In 1988 a strike caused earnings to drop somewhat, but management expects the growth trend to resume in 1989.

Although dividends and dividend policy are discussed in detail in Chapter 18, we can make several comments about dividends at this point:

1. Dividends per share (DPS) represent the basic cash flows passed from the firm to its stockholders. As such, dividends are a key element in the stock valuation models developed in earlier chapters.

2. DPS in any given year can exceed EPS, but in the long run dividends are paid from earnings, so DPS normally is smaller than EPS. The percentage of earnings paid out in dividends, or the ratio of DPS to EPS, is called the *dividend payout ratio.* National Metals' payout ratio has varied from year to year, but it has averaged about 80 percent.

3. In a graph such as that in Figure 7-2, the DPS line is typically below the EPS line, but the two lines generally have about the same slope, indicating that EPS and DPS generally grow at about the same rate. As the data in Figure 7-2 indicate, National Metals' earnings and dividends have both been growing at an average rate of 5 percent per year. If the type of analysis undertaken in the next section suggests that this trend will continue, then 5 percent is the value of g that will be used in the discounted cash flow valuation model to calculate the company's stock price.

RATIO ANALYSIS

Financial statements report both on a firm's position at a point in time and on its operations over some past period. However, the real value of financial statements lies in the fact that they can be used to help predict the firm's future earnings and dividends. From an investor's standpoint, *predicting the future is what financial statement analysis is all about,* while from management's standpoint, *financial statement analysis is useful both as a way to anticipate future conditions and, more important, as a starting point for planning actions that will influence the future course of events.*

An analysis of the firm's ratios is generally the first step in a financial analysis. The ratios are designed to show relationships between financial statement accounts. For example, Firm A might have debt of $5,248,760 and interest charges of $419,900, while Firm B might have debt of $52,647,980 and interest charges of $3,948,600. The true burden of these debts, and the companies'

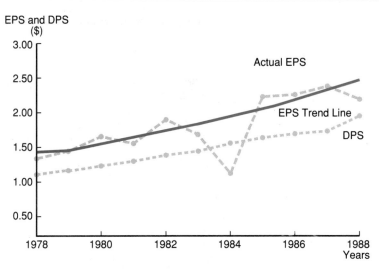

**Figure 7-2   National Metals Company:
Earnings and Dividends, 1978–1988**

Year	Earnings per Share	Dividends per Share
1978	$1.41	$1.10
1979	1.44	1.15
1980	1.67	1.20
1981	1.53	1.25
1982	1.88	1.35
1983	1.66	1.40
1984	1.10	1.50
1985	2.25	1.55
1986	2.27	1.60
1987	2.44	1.64
1988	2.24	1.84

10-year growth rate: EPS = 5%
DPS = 5%

Note: Growth rates were obtained by linear regression. The logs of EPS and DPS were regressed against years, and the slope coefficient represents the growth rate. The graph above plots EPS and DPS over time and gives a trend line for EPS fitted by least squares regression. (The DPS growth is so smooth that a trend line is unnecessary.) By dividing the trend line figure for EPS in 1988 ($2.24) into the trend line figure for 1978 ($1.41), we obtain a PVIF for 10 years (not 11 years; 11 years of data are needed to estimate 10 years of *growth*). We can look up PVIF = $1.41/$2.24 = 0.629464 in Table A-1 in Appendix A across the row for 10 periods. The calculated interest factor is closest to 0.6139, the factor for 5 percent; thus, the growth rate in EPS is approximately 5 percent.

Calculated growth rates can be highly sensitive to the beginning and ending points — for example, National Metals' growth rate in EPS was negative from 1978 to 1984 but positive from 1978 to 1988. A great deal of judgment, plus qualitative information about the company, is needed when interpreting past trends and forecasting future DPS growth rates. Indeed, the historic growth rate can almost never be used as more than a starting point for estimating the expected future growth rate. See Brigham and Gapenski, *Intermediate Financial Management,* 2nd ed., Chapter 4, for a further discussion of growth rates.

ability to repay them, can be ascertained (1) by comparing each firm's debt to its assets and (2) by comparing the interest it is charged to the income it has available for payment of interest. Such comparisons are made by *ratio analysis.*

In the paragraphs which follow, we will calculate the 1988 financial ratios for National Metals.[8] We will also evaluate those ratios in relation to the industry averages. Note that all dollar amounts in the ratio calculations are in thousands.

Liquidity Ratios

One of the first concerns of most financial analysts is liquidity: Will the firm be able to meet its maturing obligations? National Metals has debts totaling $300,000 that must be paid off within the coming year. Will it have trouble satisfying those obligations? A full liquidity analysis requires the use of cash budgets (described in Chapter 20), but by relating the amount of cash and other current assets to the current obligations, ratio analysis provides a quick, easy-to-use measure of liquidity. Two commonly used **liquidity ratios** are discussed in this section.

liquidity ratios
Ratios that show the relationship of a firm's cash and other current assets to its current obligations.

Current Ratio. The **current ratio** is computed by dividing current assets by current liabilities:

current ratio
The ratio computed by dividing current assets by current liabilities; indicates the extent to which the claims of short-term creditors are covered by assets expected to be converted to cash in the near future.

$$\text{Current ratio} = \frac{\text{Current assets}}{\text{Current liabilities}} = \frac{\$700}{\$300} = 2.3 \text{ times.}$$

$$\text{Industry average} = 2.5 \text{ times.}$$

Current assets normally include cash, marketable securities, accounts receivable, and inventories. Current liabilities consist of accounts payable, short-term notes payable, current maturities of long-term debt, accrued income taxes, and other accrued expenses (principally wages).

If a company is getting into financial difficulty, it begins paying its bills (accounts payable) more slowly, building up bank loans, and so on. If these current liabilities are rising faster than current assets, the current ratio will fall, and this could spell trouble. Because the current ratio provides the best single indicator of the extent to which the claims of short-term creditors are covered by assets that are expected to be converted to cash in a period roughly corresponding to the maturity of the claims, it is the most commonly used measure of short-term solvency.

National Metals' current ratio is slightly below the average for its industry, 2.5, but it is not low enough to cause concern. It appears that National Metals

---

[8]In addition to the ratios discussed in this section, financial analysts also employ a tool known as *common size* balance sheets and income statements. To form a common size balance sheet, one simply divides each asset and liability item by total assets and then expresses the result as a percentage. The resultant percentage statement can be compared with statements of larger or smaller firms, or those of the same firm over time. To form a common size income statement, one simply divides each item by sales.

is about in line with most other aluminum manufacturers. Since current assets are scheduled to be converted to cash in the near future, it is highly probable that they could be liquidated at close to their stated value. With a current ratio of 2.3, National Metals could liquidate current assets at only 43 percent of book value and still pay off current creditors in full.[9]

Although industry average figures are discussed later in some detail, it should be stated at this point that an industry average is not a magic number that all firms should strive to maintain — in fact, some very well-managed firms will be above the average while other good firms will be below it. However, if a firm's ratios are far removed from the average for its industry, the analyst must be concerned about why this variance occurs. Thus, a deviation from the industry average should signal the analyst (or management) to check further.

quick (acid test) ratio
This ratio is computed by deducting inventories from current assets and dividing the remainder by current liabilities.

Quick, or Acid Test, Ratio. The **quick**, or **acid test**, **ratio** is calculated by deducting inventories from current assets and dividing the remainder by current liabilities:

$$\text{Quick, or acid test, ratio} = \frac{\text{Current assets} - \text{Inventories}}{\text{Current liabilities}} = \frac{\$400}{\$300} = 1.3 \text{ times.}$$

$$\text{Industry average} = 1.0 \text{ times.}$$

Inventories are typically the least liquid of a firm's current assets, and hence they are the assets on which losses are most likely to occur in the event of liquidation. Therefore, a measure of the firm's ability to pay off short-term obligations without relying on the sale of inventories is important.

The industry average quick ratio is 1.0, so National Metals' 1.3 ratio compares favorably with the ratios of other firms in the industry. If the accounts receivable can be collected, the company can pay off its current liabilities even without selling any inventory.

Asset Management Ratios

asset management ratios
A set of ratios which measures how effectively a firm is managing its assets.

The second group of ratios, the **asset management ratios**, measures how effectively the firm is managing its assets. These ratios are designed to answer this question: Does the total amount of each type of asset as reported on the balance sheet seem reasonable, too high, or too low in view of current and projected operating levels? National Metals and other companies must borrow or obtain capital from other sources to acquire assets. If they have too many assets, their interest expenses will be too high and hence their profits will be depressed. On the other hand, if assets are too low, profitable sales may be lost.

---

[9]$1/2.3 = 0.43$, or 43 percent. Note that $0.43(\$700) = \$300$, the amount of current liabilities.

inventory turnover ratio
The ratio computed by dividing sales by inventories; also called the *inventory utilization ratio*.

Inventory Turnover. The **inventory turnover ratio**, also called the *inventory utilization ratio*, is defined as sales divided by inventories:

$$\text{Inventory turnover, or utilization, ratio} = \frac{\text{Sales}}{\text{Inventory}} = \frac{\$3,000}{\$300} = 10 \text{ times.}$$

$$\text{Industry average} = 9 \text{ times.}$$

As a rough approximation, each item of National Metals' inventory is sold out and restocked, or "turned over," 10 times per year.[10]

National Metals' turnover of 10 times compares favorably with the industry average of 9 times. This suggests that the company does not hold excessive stocks of inventory; excess stocks are, of course, unproductive and represent an investment with a low or zero rate of return. National Metals' high inventory turnover ratio also reinforces our faith in the current ratio. If the turnover were low — say, 3 or 4 times — we might wonder whether the firm was holding damaged or obsolete goods not actually worth their stated value.

Two problems arise in calculating and analyzing the inventory turnover ratio. First, sales are stated at market prices, so if inventories are carried at cost, as they generally are, the calculated turnover overstates the true turnover ratio. Therefore, it would be more appropriate to use cost of goods sold in place of sales in the numerator of the formula. However, established compilers of financial ratio statistics, such as Dun & Bradstreet, use the ratio of sales to inventories carried at cost. To develop a figure that can be compared with those published by Dun & Bradstreet and similar organizations, it is necessary to measure inventory turnover with sales in the numerator, as we do here.

The second problem lies in the fact that sales occur over the entire year, whereas the inventory figure is for one point in time. This makes it better to use an average inventory measure.[11] If the firm's business is highly seasonal, or if there has been a strong upward or downward sales trend during the year, it is essential to make some such adjustment. To maintain comparability with industry averages, however, we did not use the average inventory figure.

average collection period (ACP)
The ratio computed by dividing average sales per day into accounts receivable; indicates the average length of time the firm must wait after making a sale before receiving payment.

Average Collection Period. The **average collection period (ACP)** is used to appraise accounts receivable, and it is computed by dividing average daily sales into accounts receivable to find the number of days' sales tied up in receiv-

---

[10]"Turnover" is a term that originated many years ago with the old Yankee peddler, who would load up his wagon with goods, then go off on his route to peddle his wares. The merchandise was his "working capital," because it was what he actually sold, or "turned over," to produce his profits, whereas his "turnover" was the number of trips he took each year. Annual sales divided by inventory equaled turnover, or trips per year. If he made 10 trips per year, stocked 100 pans, and made a gross profit of $5 per pan, his annual gross profit would be $(100)(\$5)(10) = \$5,000$. If he speeded up and made 20 trips per year, his gross profit would double, other things held constant.

[11]Preferably, the average inventory value should be calculated by summing the monthly figures during the year and dividing by 12. If monthly data are not available, one can add the beginning and ending figures and divide by 2; this will adjust for growth but not for seasonal effects.

ables. Thus, the ACP represents the average length of time that the firm must wait after making a sale before receiving cash. The calculations for National Metals show an average collection period of 42 days, slightly above the 36-day industry average.[12]

$$ACP = \begin{array}{c} \text{Average} \\ \text{collection} \\ \text{period} \end{array} = \frac{\text{Receivables}}{\text{Average sales per day}} = \frac{\text{Receivables}}{\text{Annual sales/360}}$$

$$= \frac{\$350}{\$3,000/360} = \frac{\$350}{\$8.333} = 42 \text{ days}.$$

Industry average = 36 days.

The ACP can also be evaluated by comparison with the terms on which the firm sells its goods. For example, National Metals' sales terms call for payment within 30 days, so the 42-day collection period indicates that customers, on the average, are not paying their bills on time. If the trend in the collection period over the past few years has been rising, but the credit policy had not changed, this would be even stronger evidence that steps should be taken to expedite the collection of accounts receivable.

fixed assets turnover ratio
The ratio of sales to net fixed assets; also called the *fixed assets utilization ratio.*

Fixed Assets Turnover. The **fixed assets turnover ratio**, also called the *fixed assets utilization ratio,* measures how effectively the firm uses its plant and equipment, and it is the ratio of sales to net fixed assets:

$$\begin{array}{c} \text{Fixed assets turnover,} \\ \text{or utilization, ratio} \end{array} = \frac{\text{Sales}}{\text{Net fixed assets}} = \frac{\$3,000}{\$1,300} = 2.3 \text{ times}.$$

Industry average = 3.0 times.

National Metals' ratio of 2.3 times compares poorly with the industry average of 3 times, indicating that the firm is not using its fixed assets to as high a percentage of capacity as are the other firms in the industry. The financial manager should bear this in mind when production people request funds for new capital investments.

A major potential problem exists with the use of the fixed assets turnover ratio for comparative purposes. Recall that all assets except cash and accounts receivable reflect the historic cost of the assets. Inflation has caused the value

---

[12]Because information on credit sales is generally unavailable, total sales must be used. Since all firms do not have the same percentage of credit sales, there is a chance that the average collection period will be somewhat in error. Also, note that by convention the financial community generally uses 360 rather than 365 as the number of days in the year for purposes such as this. Finally, it would be better to use *average* receivables, either an average of the monthly figures or (beginning + ending)/2 = ($315 + $350)/2 = $332.5 in the formula. Had the annual average been used, National Metals' ACP would have been $332.5/$8.333 = 40 days. The 40-day figure is the more accurate one, but because the industry average was based on year-end receivables, we used 42 days for our comparison. The ACP is discussed further in Chapter 21. Finally, note that the ACP is sometimes called Days' Sales Outstanding (DSO); ACP and DSO mean the same thing.

of many assets that were purchased in the past to be seriously understated. Therefore, if we were comparing an old firm which had acquired many of its fixed assets years ago at low prices with a new company which had acquired its fixed assets only recently, we probably would find that the old firm reported a higher turnover. However, this would be more reflective of the inability of accountants to deal with inflation than of any inefficiency on the part of the new firm. The accounting profession is trying to devise ways of making financial statements more reflective of current than of historic values. If balance sheets were stated on a current value basis, this would eliminate the problem of comparisons, but at the moment the problem still exists. Since financial analysts typically do not have the data necessary to make adjustments, they simply recognize that a problem exists and deal with it judgmentally. In National Metals' case, the issue is not a serious one because all firms in the industry have been expanding at about the same rate; thus, the balance sheets of the comparison firms are indeed comparable.[13]

total assets turnover ratio
The ratio computed by dividing sales by total assets; also called the *total assets utilization ratio.*

Total Assets Turnover. The final asset management ratio, the **total assets turnover ratio**, measures the turnover, or utilization, of all of the firm's assets; it is calculated by dividing sales by total assets:

$$\text{Total assets turnover,} \atop \text{or utilization, ratio} = \frac{\text{Sales}}{\text{Total assets}} = \frac{\$3,000}{\$2,000} = 1.5 \text{ times.}$$

$$\text{Industry average} = 1.8 \text{ times.}$$

National Metals' ratio is somewhat below the industry average, indicating that the company is not generating a sufficient volume of business for the size of its total asset investment. Sales should be increased, some assets should be disposed of, or a combination of these steps should be taken.

Debt Management Ratios

financial leverage
The extent to which a firm uses debt financing.

The extent to which a firm uses debt financing, or **financial leverage**, has three important implications. (1) By raising funds through debt, the owners can maintain control of the firm with a limited investment. (2) Creditors look to the equity, or owner-supplied funds, to provide a margin of safety; if the owners have provided only a small proportion of total financing, the risks of the enterprise are borne mainly by its creditors. (3) If the firm earns more on investments financed with borrowed funds than it pays in interest, the return on the owners' capital is magnified, or "leveraged."

The first point is obvious, but to understand better how the use of debt, or financial leverage, affects risk and return, consider Table 7-6. Here we are analyzing two companies that are identical except for the way they are fi-

---

[13]See FASB #33, *Financial Reporting and Changing Prices* (September 1979), for a discussion of the effects of inflation on financial statements and what the accounting profession is trying to do to provide better and more useful balance sheets and income statements.

Table 7-6   Effect of Financial Leverage on Stockholders' Returns

Firm U (Unleveraged)

Current assets	$ 50	Debt	$ 0
Fixed assets	50	Common equity	100
Total assets	$100	Total liabilities and equity	$100

	Expected Conditions (1)	Bad Conditions (2)
Sales	$100.00	$82.50
Operating costs	70.00	80.00
Operating income (EBIT)	$ 30.00	$ 2.50
Interest	0.00	0.00
Taxable income	$ 30.00	$ 2.50
Taxes (40%)	12.00	1.00
Net income (NI)	$ 18.00	$ 1.50
ROE_U = NI/Common equity = NI/$100 =	18.00%	1.50%

Firm L (Leveraged)

Current assets	$ 50	Debt (k_d = 15%)	$ 50
Fixed assets	50	Common equity	50
Total assets	$100	Total liabilities and equity	$100

	Expected Conditions (1)	Bad Conditions (2)
Sales	$100.00	$82.50
Operating costs	70.00	80.00
Operating income (EBIT)	$ 30.00	$ 2.50
Interest	7.50	7.50
Taxable income	$ 22.50	($ 5.00)
Taxes (40%)	9.00	(2.00)
Net income (NI)	$ 13.50	($ 3.00)
ROE_L = NI/Common equity = NI/$50 =	27.00%	− 6.00%

nanced. Firm U (for "unleveraged") has no debts, whereas Firm L (for "leveraged") is financed half with equity and half with debt that has an interest rate of 15 percent. Both companies have $100 of assets and $100 of sales. Their expected ratio of operating income (also called earnings before interest and taxes, or EBIT) to assets, or the *basic earning power ratio,* is EBIT/Total assets = $30/$100 = 0.30 = 30%. Of course, things could turn out badly, in which case the basic earnings power ratio would be lower. Even though both companies' assets have the same expected earning power, Firm L provides its stockholders with an expected return on equity of 27 percent versus only 18 percent for Firm U. This difference is caused by Firm L's use of debt.

Financial leverage raises the expected rate of return to stockholders for two reasons: (1) Since interest is deductible, the use of debt financing lowers the tax bill and leaves more of the firm's operating income available to its investors; and (2) if the rate of return on assets (EBIT/Total assets) exceeds the interest rate on debt, as it generally does, then a company can use debt to finance assets, pay the interest on the debt, and have something left over as a "bonus" for its stockholders. For our hypothetical firms, these two effects have combined to push Firm L's expected rate of return on equity up to 1.5 times that of Firm U, a gain of 50 percent. Thus, debt can be used to "leverage up" the expected rate of return on equity.

However, financial leverage can cut both ways; as we show in Column 2 of the income statements, if sales are lower and costs are higher than were expected, the return on assets will be lower than was expected. Consequently, the leveraged firm's return on equity will fall sharply, and losses can occur. For example, under the "bad conditions" in Table 7-6, the unleveraged firm still shows a profit, but the firm which uses debt shows a loss and a negative return on equity. Firm U, because of its strong balance sheet, could ride out the recession and be ready for the next boom. Firm L, on the other hand, would be under great pressure. Because of its losses, its cash would be depleted, requiring it to raise funds. However, because it would be running a loss, Firm L would have a hard time selling stock to raise capital, and the losses would cause lenders to raise the interest rate, increasing L's problems still further. As a final result, Firm L just might not be around to enjoy the next boom.

We see, then, that firms with relatively high debt ratios are exposed to more risk of loss when the economy is in a recession, but they also have higher expected returns when the economy booms. Conversely, firms with low debt ratios are less risky, but they also forgo the opportunity to leverage up their return on equity. The prospects of high returns are desirable, but investors are averse to risk. Therefore, decisions about the use of debt require firms to balance higher expected returns against increased risk. Determining the optimal amount of debt for a given firm is a complicated process, and we defer a discussion of this topic until Chapter 17, when we will be better prepared to deal with it. For now we will simply look at the two ways analysts examine the firm's use of debt in a financial statement analysis: (1) They check balance sheet ratios to determine the extent to which borrowed funds have been used to finance assets, and (2) they review income statement ratios to determine the number of times fixed charges are covered by operating profits. These two sets of ratios are complementary, and most analysts use both types.

Total Debt to Total Assets. The ratio of total debt to total assets, generally called the **debt ratio**, measures the percentage of the total funds that was provided by creditors:

debt ratio
The ratio of total debt to total assets.

$$\text{Debt ratio} = \frac{\text{Total debt}}{\text{Total assets}} = \frac{\$1,100}{\$2,000} = 55\%.$$

$$\text{Industry average} = 40\%.$$

Debt is defined to include both current liabilities and long-term debt. Creditors prefer low debt ratios, since the lower the ratio, the greater the cushion against creditors' losses in the event of liquidation. The owners, on the other hand, may seek high leverage either to magnify earnings or because selling new stock would mean giving up some degree of control.

National Metals' debt ratio is 55 percent; this means that its creditors have supplied more than half the firm's total financing. Since the average debt ratio for this industry — and for manufacturing generally — is about 40 percent, National Metals would find it difficult to borrow additional funds without first raising more equity capital. Creditors would be reluctant to lend the firm more money, and management would probably be subjecting the firm to the risk of bankruptcy if it sought to increase the debt ratio any further by borrowing additional funds.[14]

times-interest-earned (TIE) ratio
The ratio of earnings before interest and taxes (EBIT) to interest charges; measures the ability of the firm to meet its annual interest payments.

Times Interest Earned. The **times-interest-earned (TIE) ratio** is determined by dividing earnings before interest and taxes (EBIT in Table 7-1) by the interest charges:

$$\text{Times-interest-earned (TIE) ratio} = \frac{\text{EBIT}}{\text{Interest charged}} = \frac{\$266}{\$66} = 4 \text{ times.}$$

$$\text{Industry average} = 6 \text{ times.}$$

The TIE ratio measures the extent to which operating income can decline before the firm is unable to meet its annual interest costs. Failure to meet this obligation can bring legal action by the firm's creditors, possibly resulting in bankruptcy. Note that earnings before interest and taxes is used in the numerator. Because interest is a deductible cost, the ability to pay current interest is not affected by taxes.

National Metals' interest is covered 4 times. Since the industry average is 6 times, the company is covering its interest charges by a relatively low margin of safety. Thus, the TIE ratio reinforces our conclusion based on the debt ratio that the company would face some difficulties if it attempted to borrow additional funds.

fixed charge coverage ratio
This ratio expands upon the TIE ratio to include the firm's annual long-term lease obligations.

Fixed Charge Coverage. The **fixed charge coverage ratio** is similar to the times-interest-earned ratio, but it is more inclusive in that it recognizes that many firms lease assets and incur long-term obligations under lease contracts.[15]

---

[14]The ratio of debt to equity is also used in financial analysis. The debt to assets (D/A) and debt to equity (D/E) ratios are simply transformations of each other:

$$D/E = \frac{D/A}{1 - D/A}, \text{ and } D/A = \frac{D/E}{1 + D/E}.$$

Both ratios increase as a firm of a given size (total assets) uses a greater proportion of debt, but D/A rises linearly and approaches a limit of 100 percent, whereas D/E rises exponentially and approaches infinity.

[15]Generally, a long-term lease is defined as one that extends for more than 1 year. Thus, rent incurred under a 6-month lease would not be included in the fixed charge coverage ratio, but rental payments under a 1-year or longer lease would be defined as fixed charges and would be included.

Leasing has become widespread in certain industries in recent years, making this ratio preferable to the times-interest-earned ratio for many purposes. Fixed charges are defined as interest plus annual long-term lease obligations, and the fixed charge coverage ratio is defined as follows:

$$\text{Fixed charge coverage ratio} = \frac{\text{EBIT} + \text{Lease payments}}{\text{Interest charges} + \text{Lease payments}}$$

$$= \frac{\$266 + \$28}{\$66 + \$28} = \frac{\$294}{\$94} = 3.1 \text{ times.}$$

$$\text{Industry average} = 5.5 \text{ times.}$$

National Metals' fixed charges are covered only 3.1 times, as opposed to an industry average of 5.5 times. Again, this indicates that the firm is somewhat weaker than creditors would prefer it to be, and it points up the difficulties National Metals would probably encounter if it attempted to increase its debt.

Cash Flow Coverage. National Metals has preferred stock outstanding which requires the payment of $8,000 in dividends per year. It also must make annual repayments of principal (sinking fund payments) of $20,000 per year on its debt obligations. To the numerator of the fixed charge coverage ratio we add depreciation, which is a noncash charge, and to the denominator we add the preferred dividends and principal repayments, both put on a before-tax basis by dividing each by $(1 - T)$ to reflect the fact that neither is a tax-deductible expense.[16] These adjustments produce the **cash flow coverage ratio**, which shows the margin by which operating cash flows cover financial requirements:

cash flow coverage ratio
This ratio shows the margin by which the firm's operating cash flows cover its financial requirements.

$$\text{Cash flow coverage ratio} = \frac{\text{EBIT} + \text{Lease payments} + \text{Depreciation}}{\text{Interest plus lease payments} + \frac{\text{Dividends on preferred stock}}{1 - T} + \frac{\text{Debt repayment}}{1 - T}}$$

$$= \frac{\$266 + \$28 + \$100}{\$94 + \$8/0.6 + \$20/0.6} = \frac{\$394}{\$141} = 2.8 \text{ times.}$$

$$\text{Industry average} = 3.2 \text{ times.}$$

Again, National Metals does not come up to industry standards.

Profitability Ratios

Profitability is the net result of a large number of policies and decisions. The ratios examined thus far provide some information about the way the firm is

---

[16]Dividing an after-tax number by $(1-T)$ is often called "grossing up" the net after-tax number. Because preferred dividends and sinking fund payments must be made from income remaining after payment of income taxes, dividing by $(1 - T)$ "grosses up" the payments and shows the before-tax amounts necessary to produce a given after-tax amount. For example, to pay $8,000 of preferred dividends, National Metals needs $8,000/(1 - T) = $8,000/0.6 = $13,333.33 of pre-tax income. Proof: $13,333.33 - 0.4($13,333.33) = $13,333.33 - $5,333.33 = $8,000.

profitability ratios
A group of ratios which show the combined effects of liquidity, asset management, and debt management on operating results.

operating, but the **profitability ratios** show the combined effects of liquidity, asset management, and debt management on operating results.

Profit Margin on Sales. The **profit margin on sales**, computed by dividing net income after taxes by sales, gives the profit per dollar of sales:

profit margin on sales
This ratio measures income per dollar of sales; computed by dividing net profit after taxes by sales.

$$\text{Profit margin on sales} = \frac{\text{Net income available to common stockholders}}{\text{Sales}} = \frac{\$112}{\$3,000} = 3.7\%.$$

$$\text{Industry average} = 5\%.$$

National Metals' profit margin is somewhat below the industry average of 5 percent, indicating that its sales prices are relatively low, that its costs are relatively high, or both.

basic earning power ratio
This ratio indicates the power of the firm's assets to generate operating income; computed by dividing EBIT by total assets.

Basic Earning Power. The **basic earning power ratio** is calculated by dividing earnings before interest and taxes (EBIT) by total assets:

$$\text{Basic earning power ratio} = \frac{\text{EBIT}}{\text{Total assets}} = \frac{\$266}{\$2,000} = 13.3\%.$$

$$\text{Industry average} = 17.2\%.$$

This ratio shows the raw earning power of the firm's assets, before the influence of taxes and leverage, and it is useful for comparing firms in different tax situations and with different degrees of financial leverage. Because of its low turnover ratio and low profit margin on sales, National Metals is not getting as much return on its assets as is the average aluminum products company.[17]

Return on Total Assets. The ratio of net income to total assets measures the **return on total assets (ROA)** after interest and taxes:

return on total assets (ROA)
The ratio of net income after taxes to total assets.

$$\text{Return on total assets (ROA)} = \frac{\text{Net income available to common stockholders}}{\text{Total assets}} = \frac{\$112}{\$2,000} = 5.6\%.$$

$$\text{Industry average} = 9\%.$$

National Metals' 5.6 percent return is well below the 9 percent average for the industry. This low rate results from the company's low basic earning power plus its above-average use of debt, both of which cause its net income to be relatively low.

---

[17]Notice that EBIT is earned throughout the year, whereas the total assets figure is as of the end of the year. Therefore, it would be conceptually better to calculate this ratio as EBIT/Average assets = EBIT/[(Beginning assets + Ending assets)/2]. We have not made this adjustment because the published ratios used for comparative purposes do not include it, but when we construct our own comparative ratios, we do make the adjustment. Incidentally, the same adjustment would also be appropriate for the next two ratios, ROA and ROE.

Return on Common Equity. The ratio of net income after taxes to common equity measures the **return on common equity (ROE)**, or the rate of return on the stockholders' investment:

return on common equity (ROE)
The ratio of net income after taxes to common equity; measures the rate of return on common stockholders' investment.

$$\text{Return on common equity (ROE)} = \frac{\text{Net income available to common stockholders}}{\text{Common equity}} = \frac{\$112}{\$880} = 12.7\%.$$

Industry average = 15.0%.

National Metals' 12.7 percent return is below the 15.0 percent industry average, but it is not as far below as the return on total assets. This results from the firm's greater use of debt, a point that is analyzed in detail later in the chapter.

Market Value Ratios

market value ratios
A set of ratios that relate the firm's stock price to its earnings and book value per share.

A final group of ratios, **market value ratios**, relates the firm's stock price to its earnings and book value per share. These ratios give management an indication of what investors think of the company's past performance and future prospects. If the firm's liquidity, asset management, debt management, and profitability ratios are all good, then its market value ratios will be high, and its stock price will probably be as high as can be expected.

price/earnings (P/E) ratio
The ratio of the price per share to earnings per share; shows the dollar amount investors will pay for $1 of current earnings.

Price/Earnings Ratio. The **price/earnings (P/E) ratio**, which was discussed in Chapter 6, shows how much investors are willing to pay per dollar of reported profits. National Metals' stock sells for $26.50, so with an EPS of $2.24 its P/E ratio is 11.8:

$$\text{Price/earnings (P/E) ratio} = \frac{\text{Price per share}}{\text{Earnings per share}} = \frac{\$26.50}{\$2.24} = 11.8 \text{ times.}$$

Industry average = 12.5 times.

As we saw in Chapter 6, P/E ratios are higher for firms with high growth prospects, other things held constant, but they are lower for riskier firms. National Metals' P/E ratio is slightly below those of other aluminum producers, which suggests that the company is regarded as being somewhat riskier than most, as having poorer growth prospects, or both.

Market/Book Ratio. The ratio of a stock's market price to its book value gives another indication of how investors regard the company. Companies with relatively high rates of return on equity generally sell at higher multiples of book value than those with low returns. National Metals' book value per share is $17.60:

$$\text{Book value per share} = \frac{\text{Common equity}}{\text{Shares outstanding}} = \frac{\$880}{50} = \$17.60.$$

market/book ratio
The ratio of a stock's market price to its book value.

Dividing the price per share by the book value gives a **market/book ratio** of 1.5 times:

$$\text{Market/book ratio} = \frac{\text{Market price per share}}{\text{Book value per share}} = \frac{\$26.50}{\$17.60} = 1.5 \text{ times.}$$

$$\text{Industry average} = 1.8 \text{ times.}$$

Investors are willing to pay slightly less for National Metals' book value than for that of an average aluminum products company.

The typical railroad, which has a very low rate of return on assets, has a market/book value ratio of less than 0.5. On the other hand, very successful firms like IBM achieve high rates of return on their assets, and they have market values well in excess of their book values. In May 1988, IBM's book value per share was $60 and it was selling for $108, so its market/book ratio was $108/$60 = 1.8.

Trend Analysis

trend analysis
An analysis of a firm's financial ratios over time; used to determine the improvement or deterioration of its financial situation.

It is important to analyze trends in ratios as well as their absolute levels, for trends give clues about whether the financial situation is improving or deteriorating. To do a **trend analysis**, one simply graphs a ratio against years, as shown in Figure 7-3. This graph shows that National Metals' rate of return on common equity has been declining since 1985, even though the industry average has been relatively stable. Other ratios could be analyzed similarly.

Summary of Ratio Analysis: The Du Pont System

Du Pont chart
A chart designed to show the relationships between return on investment, asset turnover, and the profit margin.

Table 7-7 summarizes National Metals' ratios, whereas Figure 7-4, which is called a modified **Du Pont chart** because that company's managers developed the general approach, shows the relationships between return on investment, asset turnover, and the profit margin. The left-hand side of the chart develops the *profit margin on sales.* The various expense items are listed and then summed to obtain National Metals' total costs. Subtracting costs from sales yields the company's net income. When we divide net income by sales, we find that 3.7 percent of each sales dollar is left over for stockholders. If the profit margin is low or trending down, one can examine the individual expense items to identify and then correct the problem.

The right-hand side of Figure 7-4 lists the various categories of assets, totals them, and then divides sales by total assets to find the number of times National Metals "turns its assets over" each year. The company's total assets turnover ratio is 1.5 times.

Du Pont equation
A formula that gives the rate of return on assets by multiplying the profit margin by the total assets turnover.

The profit margin times the total assets turnover is called the **Du Pont equation**, and it gives the rate of return on assets (ROA):

$$\text{ROA} = \text{Profit margin} \times \text{Total assets turnover}$$

$$= \frac{\text{Net income}}{\text{Sales}} \times \frac{\text{Sales}}{\text{Total assets}} \qquad (7\text{-}1)$$

$$= 3.7\% \times 1.5 = 5.6\%.$$

Figure 7-3   National Metals Company:
Rate of Return on Common Equity, 1984–1988

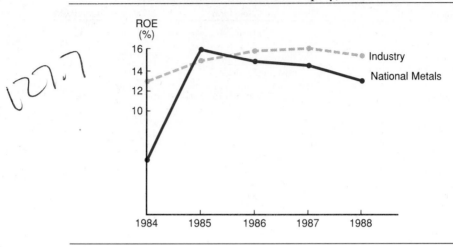

National Metals made 3.7 percent, or 3.7 cents, on each dollar of sales, and assets were "turned over" 1.5 times during the year, so the company earned a return of 5.6 percent on its assets.

If the company had used only equity, the rate of return on assets would have equaled the rate of return on equity. However, in the actual case, 55 percent of the firm's capital was supplied by creditors, and since the 5.6 percent return on total assets all goes to stockholders, who put up only 45 percent of the capital, the return on equity is higher than 5.6 percent. Specifically, the rate of return on assets (ROA) must be multiplied by the *equity multiplier,* which is the ratio of assets to common equity, to obtain the rate of return on equity (ROE):

$$\text{ROE} = \text{ROA} \times \text{Equity multiplier}$$

$$= \frac{\text{Net income}}{\text{Total assets}} \times \frac{\text{Total assets}}{\text{Common equity}} \tag{7-2}$$

$$= \quad 5.6\% \quad \times \quad \$2{,}000/\$880$$

$$= \quad 5.6\% \quad \times \quad 2.27$$

$$= \quad 12.7\%.$$

We can combine Equations 7-1 and 7-2 to form the extended Du Pont equation:

Table 7-7 National Metals Company: Summary of Financial Ratios (Thousands of Dollars)

Ratio	Formula for Calculation	Calculation	Ratio	Industry Average	Comment
Liquidity					
Current	$\dfrac{\text{Current assets}}{\text{Current liabilities}}$	$\dfrac{\$700}{\$300}$	$= 2.3\times$	$2.5\times$	Slightly low
Quick, or acid test	$\dfrac{\text{Current assets} - \text{Inventories}}{\text{Current liabilities}}$	$\dfrac{\$400}{\$300}$	$= 1.3\times$	$1\times$	Good
Asset Management					
Inventory turnover	$\dfrac{\text{Sales}}{\text{Inventory}}$	$\dfrac{\$3,000}{\$300}$	$= 10\times$	$9\times$	OK
Average collection period (ACP)	$\dfrac{\text{Receivables}}{\text{Sales}/360}$	$\dfrac{\$350}{\$8.333}$	$= 42$ days	36 days	High
Fixed assets turnover	$\dfrac{\text{Sales}}{\text{Net fixed assets}}$	$\dfrac{\$3,000}{\$1,300}$	$= 2.3\times$	$3\times$	Low
Total assets turnover	$\dfrac{\text{Sales}}{\text{Total assets}}$	$\dfrac{\$3,000}{\$2,000}$	$= 1.5\times$	$1.8\times$	Low
Debt Management					
Debt to total assets	$\dfrac{\text{Total debt}}{\text{Total assets}}$	$\dfrac{\$1,100}{\$2,000}$	$= 55\%$	40%	High
Times-interest-earned (TIE)	$\dfrac{\text{Earnings before interest and taxes}}{\text{Interest charges}}$	$\dfrac{\$266}{\$66}$	$= 4\times$	$6\times$	Low
Fixed charge coverage	$\dfrac{\text{Earnings before interest and taxes} + \text{Lease obligations}}{\text{Interest charges} + \text{Lease obligations}}$	$\dfrac{\$294}{\$94}$	$= 3.1\times$	$5.5\times$	Low
Cash flow coverage	$\dfrac{\text{Cash inflows}}{\text{Interest plus lease payments} + \dfrac{\text{Preferred stock dividends}}{1 - T} + \dfrac{\text{Debt repayment}}{1 - T}}$	$\dfrac{\$394}{\$141}$	$= 2.8\times$	$3.2\times$	Low
Profitability					
Profit margin on sales	$\dfrac{\text{Net income available to common stockholders}}{\text{Sales}}$	$\dfrac{\$112}{\$3,000}$	$= 3.7\%$	5%	Low
Basic earning power	$\dfrac{\text{Earnings before interest and taxes}}{\text{Total assets}}$	$\dfrac{\$266}{\$2,000}$	$= 13.3\%$	17.2%	Low
Return on total assets (ROA)	$\dfrac{\text{Net income available to common stockholders}}{\text{Total assets}}$	$\dfrac{\$112}{\$2,000}$	$= 5.6\%$	9%	Very low
Return on common equity (ROE)	$\dfrac{\text{Net income available to common stockholders}}{\text{Common equity}}$	$\dfrac{\$112}{\$880}$	$= 12.7\%$	15%	Low
Market Value					
Price/earnings (P/E)	$\dfrac{\text{Price per share}}{\text{Earnings per share}}$	$\dfrac{\$26.50}{\$2.24}$	$= 11.8\times$	$12.5\times$	Slightly low
Market/book	$\dfrac{\text{Market price per share}}{\text{Book value per share}}$	$\dfrac{\$26.50}{\$17.60}$	$= 1.5\times$	$1.8\times$	Slightly low

Figure 7-4 Modified Du Pont Chart Applied to
National Metals Company
(Thousands of Dollars)

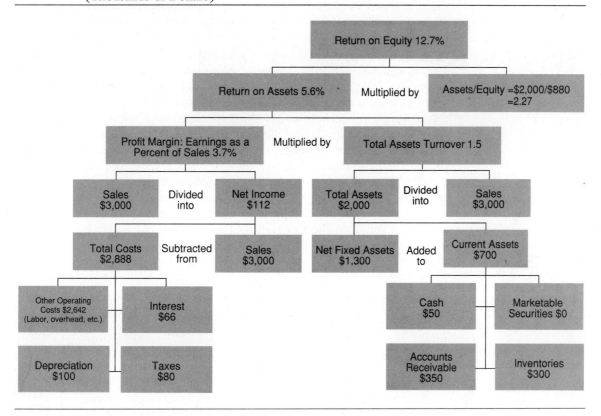

$$ROE = (\text{Profit margin})(\text{Total assets turnover})(\text{Equity multiplier})$$

$$= \left(\frac{\text{Net income}}{\text{Sales}}\right)\left(\frac{\text{Sales}}{\text{Total assets}}\right)\left(\frac{\text{Total assets}}{\text{Common equity}}\right) \qquad (7\text{-}3)$$

$$= \frac{\text{Net income}}{\text{Common equity}}.$$

Thus, for National Metals, we have

$$ROE = (3.73\%)(1.5)(2.27)$$

$$= 12.7\%.$$

The 12.7 percent rate of return could, of course, be calculated directly: Net income after taxes/Common equity = $112/$880 = 12.7%. However, the Du

Pont equation shows how the profit margin, the total asset turnover ratio, and the use of debt interact to determine the return on equity.[18]

National Metals can use the Du Pont system to analyze ways of improving the firm's performance. On the left, or "profit margin," side of its Du Pont chart, National's marketing people study the effects of raising sales prices (or lowering them to increase volume), of moving into new products or markets with higher margins, and so on. The company's cost accountants can study various expense items and, working with engineers, purchasing agents, and other operating personnel, can seek ways of holding down costs. On the "turn-over" side, National's financial analysts, working with both production and marketing people, can investigate ways of minimizing investments in various types of assets. At the same time, the treasury staff can analyze the effects of alternative financing strategies, seeking to hold down interest expenses and the risks of debt while still using debt to increase the rate of return on equity.

As a result of such an analysis, John Mitchell, National's president, recently announced a series of moves designed to cut operating costs by more than 20 percent per year. Mitchell also announced that National intended to concentrate its capital in markets where profit margins are reasonably high, and that if competition increased in certain of its product markets (such as the low-price end of the aluminum siding market), National would withdraw from those markets. National is seeking a high return on equity, and Mitchell recognizes that if competition drives profit margins too low in a particular market, it then becomes impossible to earn high returns on the capital invested to serve that market. Therefore, if it is to achieve a high ROE, National may have to develop new products and shift capital into new areas. National's future depends on this type of analysis, and if it succeeds in the future, the Du Pont system will have helped it achieve that success.

COMPARATIVE RATIOS

comparative ratio analysis
An analysis based on a comparison of a firm's ratios with those of other firms in the same industry.

The preceding analysis of National Metals Company pointed out the usefulness of a **comparative ratio analysis**. Comparative ratios are available from a number of sources. One useful set of comparative data is compiled by Dun & Bradstreet, Inc., (D&B), which provides 14 ratios calculated for a large number of industries; nine of these ratios are shown for a small sample of firms in Table 7-8. Useful ratios can also be found in the *Annual Statement Studies*

[18]Another ratio that is frequently used is the following:

$$\text{Rate of return on investors' capital} = \frac{\text{Net income after taxes} + \text{Interest}}{\text{Debt} + \text{Equity}}.$$

The numerator shows the dollar returns to investors, the denominator shows the total amount of money investors have put up, and the ratio itself shows the rate of return on all investors' capital. This ratio is especially important in the public utility industries, where regulators are concerned about the companies' using their monopoly positions to earn excessive returns on investors' capital. In fact, regulators try to set utility prices (service rates) at levels that will force the return on investors' capital to equal a company's cost of capital as defined in Chapter 16.

Table 7-8 Dun & Bradstreet Ratios for Selected Industries: Upper Quartile, Median, and Lower Quartile[a]

SIC Codes, Line of Business, and Number of Concerns Reporting	Quick Ratio	Current Ratio	Total Liabilities to Net Worth	Average Collection Period	Net Sales to Inventory	Total Assets to Net Sales	Return on Net Sales	Return on Total Assets	Return on Net Worth
	×	×	%	Days	×	%	%	%	%
2879 Agricultural chemicals (61)	1.4	2.7	41.5	21.2	11.5	33.6	5.3	15.2	23.7
	1.0	2.0	86.0	38.7	7.6	42.7	4.2	9.6	17.3
	0.6	1.4	171.5	64.1	5.3	64.4	0.7	3.9	6.4
3724 Aircraft parts, including engines (86)	2.4	4.1	28.7	32.8	11.3	44.7	13.0	12.7	16.7
	1.3	2.5	66.3	47.3	5.5	64.7	9.0	8.4	14.2
	0.7	1.7	162.9	67.7	3.7	88.6	3.9	3.8	7.9
2051 Bakery products (170)	2.0	2.9	33.4	16.8	62.8	23.5	5.4	11.9	28.3
	1.1	1.9	84.8	24.5	40.9	31.4	2.5	5.9	15.2
	0.6	1.1	187.9	33.9	21.5	44.8	1.2	2.0	4.3
2086 Beverages (168)	2.2	4.2	21.2	18.9	26.9	26.9	6.5	13.0	21.8
	1.2	2.3	52.9	24.8	18.8	39.7	3.6	8.3	13.4
	0.8	1.6	114.2	32.4	13.3	59.4	1.4	3.0	5.8
3312 Blast furnaces and steel mills (118)	1.5	2.6	57.6	34.0	13.3	39.4	5.2	7.9	20.5
	0.9	1.9	153.4	43.8	8.2	57.6	2.4	3.7	7.8
	0.7	1.3	316.8	57.1	5.5	78.2	(0.1)	(3.0)	(9.2)
2731 Book publishing (393)	2.2	4.9	24.8	27.7	11.7	41.9	10.4	13.4	25.7
	1.1	2.3	77.9	53.6	5.2	62.8	5.2	6.1	13.2
	0.7	1.4	183.5	85.1	3.0	107.0	1.4	2.1	4.2

Source: Industry Norms and Key Business Ratios, 1987 Edition, Dun & Bradstreet Credit Services.

[a]The median and quartile ratios can be illustrated by an example. The median quick ratio for agricultural chemical manufacturers, as shown in Table 7-8, is 1.0. To obtain this figure, the ratios of current assets to current debt for each of the 61 concerns were arranged in a graduated series, with the largest ratio at the top and the smallest at the bottom. The median ratio of 1.0 is the ratio halfway between the top and the bottom. The ratio of 1.4, representing the upper quartile, is one-quarter of the way down from the top (or halfway between the top and the median). The ratio 0.6, representing the lower quartile, is one-quarter of the way up from the bottom (or halfway between the median and the bottom.) SIC codes are "Standard Industrial Classification" codes used by the U.S. government to classify companies.

published by Robert Morris Associates, which is the national association of bank loan officers. The U.S. Commerce Department's *Quarterly Financial Report,* which is found in most libraries, gives a set of ratios for manufacturing firms by industry group and size of firm. Trade associations and individual firms' credit departments also compile industry average financial ratios. Finally, financial statement data for thousands of publicly owned corporations are available on magnetic tapes and diskettes, and since brokerage houses, banks, and other financial institutions have access to these data, security analysts can and do generate comparative ratios tailored to their specific needs.

Each of the data-supplying organizations uses a somewhat different set of ratios designed for its own purposes. For example, D&B deals mainly with small firms, many of which are proprietorships, and it sells its services primarily to banks and other lenders. Therefore, it is concerned largely with the creditor's viewpoint, and its ratios emphasize current assets and liabilities, not market value ratios. Therefore, when you select your comparative data source, you should be sure that your emphasis is similar to that of the agency whose ratios you use. Additionally, there are often definitional differences in the ratios presented by different sources, so before using a source, be sure to verify the exact definitions of the ratios to insure consistency.

USES AND LIMITATIONS OF RATIO ANALYSIS

As noted earlier, ratio analysis is used by three main groups: (1) *managers,* who employ ratios to help analyze, control, and thus improve the firm's operations; (2) *credit analysts,* such as bank loan officers or credit managers for industrial companies, who analyze ratios to help ascertain a company's ability to pay its debts; and (3) *security analysts,* including both stock analysts, who are interested in a company's efficiency and growth prospects, and bond analysts, who are concerned with a company's ability to pay interest on its bonds as well as with the liquidating value of the assets that would be available to bondholders in the event the company went bankrupt. In later chapters we will look more closely at the basic factors which underlie each ratio; this will give you a better idea about how to interpret and use ratios.

We should also note that although ratio analysis can provide useful information concerning a company's operations and financial condition, it does have some inherent problems and limitations that necessitate care and judgment. Potential problems are listed below:

1. Many large firms operate a number of different divisions in quite different industries, and in such cases it is difficult to develop a meaningful set of industry averages for comparative purposes. This tends to make ratio analysis more useful for small, narrowly-focused firms than for large, multidivisional ones.

2. Most firms want to be better than average (although half will be above and half below the median), so merely attaining average performance is not necessarily good. As a target for high-level performance, it is preferable to look at the industry leaders' ratios.

3. Inflation has badly distorted firms' balance sheets — recorded values are often substantially different from "true" values. Further, since this affects both depreciation charges and inventory costs, profits are also affected. Thus, a ratio analysis for one firm over time, or a comparative analysis of firms of different ages, must be interpreted with care and judgment.

4. Seasonal factors can also distort ratio analysis. For example, the inventory turnover ratio for a food processor will be radically different if the balance sheet figure used for inventory is the one just before versus the one just after the close of the canning season. This problem can be minimized by using monthly averages for inventory when calculating ratios such as turnover.

"window dressing" techniques
Techniques employed by a firm to make its financial statements look better to credit analysts.

5. Firms can employ **"window dressing" techniques** to make their financial statements look better to credit analysts. To illustrate, a Chicago builder borrowed on a two-year basis on December 29, 1988, held the proceeds of the loan as cash for a few days, and then paid off the loan ahead of time on January 5, 1989. This improved his current and quick ratios, and made his year-end 1988 balance sheet look good. However, the improvement was strictly temporary; a week later the balance sheet was back at the old level.

6. Different operating and accounting practices can distort comparisons. As noted earlier, inventory valuation and depreciation methods can affect the financial statements and thus distort comparisons among firms that use different accounting procedures. Also, if one firm leases a substantial amount of its productive equipment, then its assets may be low relative to sales because leased assets often do not appear on the balance sheet. At the same time, the lease liability may not be shown as a debt, so leasing can artificially improve both the debt and turnover ratios. The accounting profession has recently taken steps to reduce this problem, as we discuss in Chapter 14.

7. It is difficult to generalize about whether a particular ratio is "good" or "bad." For example, a high current ratio may indicate a strong liquidity position, which is good, or excessive cash, which is bad because excess cash in the bank is a nonearning asset. Similarly, a high fixed assets turnover ratio may denote either a firm that uses assets efficiently or one that is undercapitalized and simply cannot afford to buy enough assets.

8. A firm may have some ratios which look "good" and others which look "bad," making it difficult to tell whether the company is, on balance, in a strong or weak position. However, statistical procedures can be used to analyze the *net effects* of a set of ratios. Many banks and other lending organizations use statistical procedures to analyze firms' financial ratios,

and, on the basis of their analyses, classify companies according to their probability of getting into financial distress.[19]

Ratio analysis is useful, but analysts should be aware of these problems and make adjustments as necessary. Ratio analysis conducted in a mechanical, unthinking manner is dangerous; however, used intelligently and with good judgment, it can provide useful insights into a firm's operations. Your judgment in interpreting a set of ratios is necessarily weak at this point, but it will improve as you go through the remainder of the book.

---

[19]The technique used is discriminant analysis. For a discussion, see Edward I. Altman, "Financial Ratios, Discriminant Analysis, and the Prediction of Corporate Bankruptcy," *Journal of Finance,* September 1968, 589–609, or Eugene F. Brigham and Louis C. Gapenski, *Intermediate Financial Management,* 2nd ed., Chapter 20.

Small Business

FINANCIAL ANALYSIS IN THE SMALL FIRM

Financial ratio analysis is especially useful for small businesses. Readily available sources of key financial ratios provide comparative data by size, with the class size varying down to some very small firms. For example, Robert Morris Associates provides comparative ratios for a number of small-firm classes, including the size range of zero to $250,000 in annual sales. Nevertheless, the financial analysis of small firms presents some unique problems that are related to risks and to depth and quality of management. We examine here some of those problems from the standpoint of a bank loan officer, one of the most frequent users of ratio analysis.

When examining a small-business credit prospect, a banker is essentially making a prediction about the ability of the company to repay its debt if the bank extends credit. In making this prediction, the banker will be especially concerned about indicators of liquidity and about continuing prospects for profitability. The banker will elect to do business with a new customer if it appears that loans will be paid off on a timely basis and that the company will remain in business and therefore be a customer of the bank for years to come. Thus, both short-run and long-run viability are of interest to the banker. On the other hand, the banker's percep-

tions about the business are important to the owner-manager, because the bank may become a vital source of funds as the firm's needs increase in the future.

The first problem the banker is likely to encounter is that, unlike the bank's bigger customers, the small firm may not have audited financial statements. Furthermore, the statements that are available may have been produced on an irregular basis (for example, in some months or quarters but not in others). If the firm is young, it may have historical financial statements for only one year, or perhaps it has none at all. Also, the banker will probably require that periodic financial statements be produced by a reputable accounting firm, not by the owner's brother-in-law.

The quality of its financial data may therefore be a problem for a small business that is attempting to establish a banking relationship. This may keep the firm from getting credit even though it is really on solid financial ground. Therefore, it is in the owner's interest to make sure that the firm's financial data are credible, even if it is more expensive to do so. Furthermore, if the banker is uncomfortable with the data, the firm's management should also be uncomfortable: Because many managerial decisions depend on the numbers in the firm's accounting statements, those numbers should be as accurate as possible.

For a given set of financial ratios, a small firm may be riskier than a larger one. Often small firms produce a single product or else rely heavily on a single customer, or both. For example, several years ago a company called Yard Man, Inc., manufactured and sold lawn equipment. Most of Yard Man's sales were to Sears, so most of Yard Man's revenues and profits were due to the Sears account. When Sears decided to drop Yard Man as a supplier, the company was left without its most important customer. Yard Man is no longer in business. Because large firms typically have a broad customer base, they are not as susceptible to a loss of such a large portion of their business.

A similar danger applies to a single-product company. Just as the loss of a key customer can be disastrous for a small business, so can a shift in the tides of consumer interest in a particular fad. For example, Coleco manufactured and sold the extremely popular Cabbage Patch dolls. The phenomenal popularity of the dolls was a great boom for Coleco, but the public is fickle. One can never predict when such a fad will die out, leaving the company with a great deal of capacity to make a product that no one will buy and with a large amount of overvalued inventory. Exactly this situation hit Coleco, and it was forced into bankruptcy in 1988.

The extension of credit to a small company, and especially a small owner-managed company, often involves yet another risk that is less of a problem for larger firms — namely, dependence on the leadership of a single key individual whose unexpected death could cause the company to fail. Similarly, if the company is family owned and managed, there is typically one key decision maker, although perhaps several other family members are involved in helping to manage the company. In the case of the family business, the loss of the top person may not wipe out the company, but it may create the equally serious problem of who will assume the leadership role. The loss of a key family member is often a highly emotional event, and it is not at all unusual for it to be followed by an ugly and prolonged struggle for control of the business. It is in the family's interest, and certainly in the creditors' interests, to see that a plan of management succession is clearly specified before trouble arises. If no good plan can be worked out, perhaps the firm should be forced to carry "key person insurance," payable to the bank and used to retire the loan in the event of the key person's death.

In summary, to determine the creditworthiness of a small firm, the financial analyst must look beyond the basic financial ratios and analyze the viability of the firm's products, customers, management, and market. It is not an easy task, but it must be done. Ratio analysis is only the starting point.

SUMMARY AND KEY CONCEPTS

The primary purposes of this chapter were (1) to describe the basic financial statements and (2) to discuss techniques used by investors and managers to analyze them. The key concepts covered are listed below.

- The four basic statements contained in the annual report are the **balance sheet**, the **income statement**, the **statement of retained earnings**, and the **statement of cash flows**. Investors use the information contained in these statements to form expectations about the future levels of earnings and dividends, and about the riskiness of these expected values.

- **Financial statement analysis** generally begins with the calculation of a set of **financial ratios** designed to reveal the relative strengths and weaknesses of a company as compared to other companies in the same industry, and to show whether the firm's position has been improving or deteriorating over time.

- **Liquidity ratios** show the relationship of a firm's current assets to its current obligations.
- **Asset management ratios** measure how effectively a firm is managing its assets.
- **Debt management ratios** reveal (1) the extent to which the firm is financed with debt and (2) the firm's ability to meet its debt obligations. ·
- **Profitability ratios** show the combined effects of liquidity, asset management, and debt management on operating results.
- **Market value ratios** relate the firm's stock price to its earnings and book value per share.
- **Trend analysis** is important because it reveals whether the firm's ratios have improved or deteriorated over time.
- The **Du Pont system** is designed to show how the profit margin on sales, the asset turnover ratio, and the use of debt interact to determine the rate of return on equity.
- In analyzing a small firm's financial position, **ratio analysis** is only the starting point. The analyst must also (1) examine the quality of the financial data, (2) insure that the firm is sufficiently diversified to withstand shifts in customers' buying habits, and (3) insure that the firm has a plan for the succession of its management.

Ratio analysis has limitations, but used with care and judgment, it can be most helpful.

Questions

7-1   What four statements are contained in most annual reports?

7-2   Is it true that if a "typical" firm reports $20 million of retained earnings on its balance sheet, its directors could declare a $20 million cash dividend without any qualms whatsoever?

7-3   Financial ratio analysis is conducted by four groups of analysts: managers, equity investors, long-term creditors, and short-term creditors. What is the primary emphasis of each of these groups in evaluating ratios?

7-4   Why would the inventory turnover ratio be more important to a grocery store than to a shoe repair store?

7-5   Profit margins and turnover ratios vary from one industry to another. What are some industry characteristics that help explain these variations?

7-6   How does inflation distort ratio analysis comparisons both for one company over time (trend analysis) and when different companies are compared? Are only balance sheet items or both balance sheet and income statement items affected?

7-7   If a firm's ROE is low and management wants to improve it, explain how using more debt might help.

7-8   Suppose a firm used debt to leverage up its ROE, and in the process its EPS was also boosted. Would this necessarily lead to an increase in the price of the firm's stock? Assume the payout ratio remains constant.

7-9   How might (a) seasonal factors and (b) different growth rates distort a comparative ratio analysis? Give some examples. How might these problems be alleviated?

7-10   Indicate the effects of the transactions listed in the following table on total current assets, current ratio, and net profit. Use (+) to indicate an increase, (−) to indicate a decrease, and (0) to indicate either no effect or an indeterminate effect. Be prepared to state any necessary assumptions, and assume an initial current ratio of more than 1.0. (Note: A good accounting background is necessary to answer some of these questions; if yours is not strong, just answer the questions you can handle.)

	Total Current Assets	Current Ratio	Effect on Net Income
a. Cash is acquired through issuance of additional common stock.	____	____	____
b. Merchandise is sold for cash.	____	____	____
c. Federal income tax due for the previous year is paid.	____	____	____
d. A fixed asset is sold for less than book value.	____	____	____
e. A fixed asset is sold for more than book value.	____	____	____
f. Merchandise is sold on credit.	____	____	____
g. Payment is made to trade creditors for previous purchases.	____	____	____
h. A cash dividend is declared and paid.	____	____	____
i. Cash is obtained through short-term bank loans.	____	____	____
j. Short-term notes receivable are sold at a discount.	____	____	____
k. Marketable securities are sold below cost.	____	____	____
l. Advances are made to employees.	____	____	____
m. Current operating expenses are paid.	____	____	____
n. Short-term promissory notes are issued to trade creditors for past due accounts receivable.	____	____	____
o. Ten-year notes are issued to pay off accounts payable.	____	____	____
p. A fully depreciated asset is retired.	____	____	____
q. Accounts receivable are collected.	____	____	____
r. Equipment is purchased with short-term notes.	____	____	____
s. Merchandise is purchased on credit.	____	____	____
t. The estimated taxes payable are increased.	____	____	____

Self-Test Problems   (Solutions Appear on Page 299)

Key terms

ST-1   Define each of the following terms:
a. Annual report; income statement; balance sheet
b. Equity, or net worth; paid-in capital; retained earnings

c. Cash flow cycle

d. Statement of retained earnings; statement of cash flows; sources and uses of funds statement

e. Depreciation; inventory valuation methods

f. Liquidity ratios; current ratio; quick, or acid test, ratio

g. Asset management ratios; inventory turnover ratio; average collection period (ACP); fixed assets turnover ratio; total assets turnover ratio

h. Debt management ratios; debt ratio; times-interest-earned (TIE) ratio; fixed charge coverage ratio; cash flow coverage ratio

i. Profitability ratios; profit margin on sales; basic earning power ratio; return on total assets (ROA); return on common equity (ROE)

j. Market value ratios; price/earnings (P/E) ratio; market/book (M/B) ratio; dividend payout ratio; book value per share

k. Trend analysis; comparative analysis

l. Du Pont chart; Du Pont equation

m. "Window dressing"; seasonal effects on ratios

Debt ratio   **ST-2**   A. L. Kaiser & Co. had earnings per share of $4 last year, and it paid a $2 dividend. Book value per share at year-end was $40, and total retained earnings increased by $12 million during the year. Kaiser has no preferred stock, and no new common stock was issued during the year. If Kaiser's year-end debt (which equals its total liabilities) was $120 million, what was the company's year-end debt/assets ratio?

Ratio analysis   **ST-3**   The following data apply to Cadwalader & Company (millions of dollars):

Cash and marketable securities	$100.00
Fixed assets	$283.50
Sales	$1,000.00
Net income	$50.00
Quick ratio	2.0×
Current ratio	3.0×
ACP	40 days
ROE	12%

Cadwalader has no preferred stock — only common equity, current liabilities, and long-term debt.

a. Find Cadwalader's (1) accounts receivable (A/R), (2) current liabilities, (3) current assets, (4) total assets, (5) ROA, (6) common equity, and (7) long-term debt.

b. In Part a, you should have found Cadwalader's accounts receivable (A/R) = $111.1 million. If Cadwalader could reduce its ACP from 40 days to 30 days while holding other things constant, how much cash would it generate? If this cash were used to buy back common stock (at book value) and thus reduced the amount of common equity, how would this affect (1) the ROE, (2) the ROA, and (3) the total debt/total assets ratio?

Problems

Ratio analysis   **7-1**   Data for the Mainframe Computer Company and its industry averages follow.

a. Calculate the indicated ratios for Mainframe.

b. Construct the extended Du Pont equation for both Mainframe and the industry.

c. Outline Mainframe's strengths and weaknesses as revealed by your analysis.

d. Suppose Mainframe had doubled its sales as well as its inventories, accounts receivable, and common equity during 1988. How would that information affect the validity of your ratio analysis? (Hint: Think about averages and the effects of rapid growth on ratios if averages are not used. No calculations are needed.)

Mainframe Computer Company: Balance Sheet as of December 31, 1988

Cash	$ 155,000	Accounts payable	$ 258,000
Receivables	672,000	Notes payable	168,000
Inventory	483,000	Other current liabilities	234,000
Total current assets	$1,310,000	Total current liabilities	$ 660,000
Net fixed assets	585,000	Long-term debt	513,000
		Common equity	722,000
Total assets	$1,895,000	Total liabilities and equity	$1,895,000

Mainframe Computer Company: Income Statement for Year Ended December 31, 1988

Sales		$3,215,000
Cost of goods sold:		
Materials	$1,434,000	
Labor	906,000	
Heat, light, and power	136,000	
Indirect labor	226,000	
Depreciation	83,000	2,785,000
Gross profit		$ 430,000
Selling expenses		230,000
General and administrative expenses		60,000
Earnings before interest and taxes		$ 140,000
Interest expense		49,000
Net income before taxes		$ 91,000
Federal and state income taxes (40%)		36,400
Net income		$ 54,600

Ratio	Mainframe	Industry Average
Current assets/current liabilities	_____	2.0×
Average collection period	_____	35 days
Sales/inventories	_____	6.7×
Sales/total assets	_____	2.9×
Net income/sales	_____	1.2%
Net income/total assets	_____	3.4%
Net income/equity	_____	8.5%
Total debt/total assets	_____	60.0%

Liquidity ratios   **7-2**   The Speairs Company has $1,750,000 in current assets and $700,000 in current liabilities. Its initial inventory level is $500,000, and it will raise funds as additional notes payable and use them to increase inventory. How much can Speairs's short-term debt (notes payable) increase without violating a current ratio of 2 to 1? What will be the firm's quick ratio after Speairs has raised the maximum amount of short-term funds?

Ratio calculations   **7-3**   The Dlabay Company had a quick ratio of 1.4, a current ratio of 3.0, an inventory turnover of 6 times, total current assets of $675,000, and cash and marketable securities of $100,000 in 1988. What were Dlabay's annual sales and its ACP for that year?

Balance sheet analysis   **7-4**   Complete the balance sheet and sales information in the table that follows for Hastings Software Company, using the following financial data:

Debt ratio: 50%
Quick ratio: 0.80×
Total assets turnover: 1.5×
Average collection period: 36 days
Gross profit margin: 25%
Inventory turnover ratio: 5×

Balance Sheet			
Cash	_____	Accounts payable	_____
Accounts receivable	_____	Long-term debt	40,000
Inventories	_____	Common stock	_____
Fixed assets	_____	Retained earnings	65,000
Total assets	200,000	Total liabilities and equity	_____
Sales	_____	Cost of goods sold	_____

Du Pont analysis   **7-5**   The Blacksburg Furniture Company, a manufacturer and wholesaler of high-quality home furnishings, has been experiencing low profitability in recent years. As a result, the board of directors has replaced the president of the firm with a new president, Jerry Stevens, who has asked you to make an analysis of the firm's financial position using the Du Pont system. The most recent industry average ratios and Blacksburg's financial statements are as follows:

Industry Average Ratios			
Current ratio	2×	Sales/fixed assets	6×
Debt/total assets	30%	Sales/total assets	3×
Times-interest-earned	7×	Net profit on sales	3%
Sales/inventory	10×	Return on total assets	9%
Average collection period	24 days	Return on common equity	12.8%

Blacksburg Furniture Company:
Balance Sheet as of
December 31, 1988
(Millions of Dollars)

Cash	$ 30	Accounts payable	$ 30
Marketable securities	22	Notes payable	30
Net receivables	44	Other current liabilities	14
Inventories	106	Total current liabilities	$ 74
Total current assets	$202	Long-term debt	16
Gross fixed assets	150	Total liabilities	$ 90
Less depreciation	52	Common stock	76
Net fixed assets	$ 98	Retained earnings	134
		Total stockholders' equity	$210
Total assets	$300	Total liabilities and equity	$300

Blacksburg Furniture Company:
Income Statement for Year Ended
December 31, 1988
(Millions of Dollars)

Net sales	$530
Cost of goods sold	440
Gross profit	$ 90
Selling expenses	49
Depreciation expense	8
Interest expense	3
Total expenses	$ 60
Net income before tax	30
Taxes (40%)	12
Net income	$ 18

a. Calculate those ratios that you think would be useful in this analysis.
b. Construct an extended Du Pont equation for Blacksburg, and compare the company's ratios to the composite ratios for the industry as a whole.
c. Do the balance sheet accounts or the income statement figures seem to be primarily responsible for the low profits?
d. Which specific accounts seem to be most out of line in relation to other firms in the industry?
e. If Blacksburg had a pronounced seasonal sales pattern, or if it grew rapidly during the year, how might that affect the validity of your ratio analysis? How might you correct for such potential problems?

Statement of cash flows   **7-6**   The consolidated balance sheets for the Vanderheiden Lumber Company at the beginning and end of 1988 follow. The company bought $150 million worth of fixed assets. The charge for depreciation in 1988 was $30 million. Earnings after taxes were $76 million, and the company paid out $20 million in dividends.
a. Fill in the amount of each source or use in the appropriate column.

Vanderheiden Lumber Company:
Balance Sheets at
Beginning and End of 1988
(Millions of Dollars)

			Change	
	Jan. 1	Dec. 31	Source	Use
Cash	$ 30	$ 14	_____	_____
Marketable securities	22	0	_____	_____
Net receivables	44	60	_____	_____
Inventories	106	150	_____	_____
Total current assets	$202	$224	_____	_____
Gross fixed assets	150	300	_____	_____
Less depreciation	(52)	(82)	_____	_____
Net fixed assets	$ 98	$218	_____	_____
Total assets	$300	$442	_____	_____
Accounts payable	$ 30	$ 36	_____	_____
Notes payable	30	6	_____	_____
Other current liabilities	14	30	_____	_____
Long-term debt	16	52	_____	_____
Common stock	76	128	_____	_____
Retained earnings	134	190	_____	_____
Total liabilities and equity	$300	$442	_____	_____

Note: Total sources must equal total uses.

b. Prepare a statement of cash flows.
c. Briefly summarize your findings.

Du Pont analysis   **7-7**   The Hardin Electronic Corporation's (HEC) balance sheets for 1988 and 1987 are as follows (millions of dollars):

	1988	1987
Cash	$ 21	$ 45
Marketable securities	0	33
Receivables	90	66
Inventories	225	159
Total current assets	$336	$303
Gross fixed assets	450	225
Less accumulated depreciation	(123)	(78)
Net fixed assets	$327	$147
Total assets	$663	$450
Accounts payable	$ 54	$ 45
Notes payable	9	45
Accruals	45	21
Total current liabilities	$108	$111
Long-term debt	78	24
Common stock	192	114
Retained earnings	285	201
Total long-term capital	$555	$339
Total liabilities and equity	$663	$450

Additionally, Hardin's 1988 income statement is as follows (millions of dollars):

Sales	$1,365
Cost of goods sold	888
General expenses	300
EBIT	$ 177
Interest	10
EBT	$ 167
Taxes (40%)	67
Net income	$ 100

a. What was Hardin's dividend payout ratio in 1988?
b. The following extended Du Pont equation is the industry average for 1988:

Profit margin × Asset turnover × Equity multiplier = ROE

$$6.52\% \quad \times \quad 1.82 \quad \times \quad 1.77\cdot \quad = 21.00\%.$$

Construct Hardin's 1988 extended Du Pont equation. What does the Du Pont analysis indicate about HEC's expense control, asset utilization, and debt utilization? What is the industry's debt to assets ratio?
c. Construct Hardin's 1988 statement of cash flows. What does it suggest about the company's operations?

Ratio analysis **7-8** The Bangor Corporation's forecasted 1989 financial statements follow, along with some industry average ratios.
a. Calculate Bangor's forecasted ratios, compare them with the industry average data, and comment briefly on Bangor's strengths and weaknesses.
b. What do you think would happen to Bangor's ratios if the company initiated cost cutting measures that allowed it to hold lower levels of inventory and substantially decreased the cost of goods sold? Answer in words only. Think about which ratios would be affected by changes in these two accounts.

Bangor Corporation:
Pro Forma Balance Sheet as of December 31, 1989

Cash	$ 72,000
Accounts receivable	439,000
Inventory	894,000
Total current assets	$1,405,000
Land and building	238,000
Machinery	132,000
Other fixed assets	61,000
Total assets	$1,836,000
Accounts and notes payable	$ 432,000
Accruals	170,000
Total current liabilities	$ 602,000
Long-term debt	404,290
Common stock	575,000
Retained earnings	254,710
Total liabilities and equity	$1,836,000

Bangor Corporation:
Pro Forma Income Statement for 1989

Sales	$4,290,000
Cost of goods sold	3,580,000
Gross operating profit	$ 710,000
General administrative and selling expenses	236,320
Depreciation	159,000
Miscellaneous	134,000
Taxable income	$ 180,680
Taxes (40%)	72,272
Net income	$ 108,408
Number of shares outstanding	23,000

Per-Share Data:

EPS	$4.71
Cash dividends	$0.95
P/E ratio	5×
Market price (average)	$23.57

Industry Financial Ratios (1989)[a]	
Quick ratio	1.0×
Current ratio	2.7×
Inventory turnover[b]	7×
Average collection period	32 days
Fixed assets turnover[b]	13.0×
Total assets turnover[b]	2.6×
Return on total assets	9.1%
Return on equity	18.2%
Debt ratio	50%
Profit margin on sales	3.5%
P/E ratio	6×

[a]Industry average ratios have been constant for the past four years.
[b]Based on year-end balance sheet figures.

Financial statement analysis (Integrative)

7-9   Donna Jamison was recently hired as a financial analyst by Computron Industries, a manufacturer of electronic components. Her first task was to conduct a financial statement analysis of the firm covering the last two years. To begin the analysis, she gathered the following financial data:

	1987	1988
Balance Sheets		
Cash	$ 57,600	$ 52,000
Accounts receivable	351,200	402,000
Inventory	715,200	836,000
Total current assets	$1,124,000	$1,290,000
Gross fixed assets	491,000	527,000
Less accumulated depreciation	146,200	166,200
Net fixed assets	344,800	360,800
Total assets	$1,468,800	$1,650,800

	1987	1988
Balance Sheets		
Accounts payable	$ 145,600	$ 175,200
Notes payable	200,000	225,000
Accruals	136,000	140,000
Total current liabilities	$ 481,600	$ 540,200
Long-term debt	323,432	424,612
Common stock	460,000	460,000
Retained earnings	203,768	225,988
Total equity	$ 663,768	$ 685,988
Total liabilities and equity	$1,468,800	$1,650,800
Income Statements		
Sales	$3,432,000	$3,850,000
Cost of goods sold	2,864,000	3,250,000
Other expenses	340,000	430,300
Depreciation	18,900	20,000
EBIT	$ 209,100	$ 149,700
Interest expense	62,500	76,000
EBT	$ 146,600	$ 73,700
Taxes (40%)	58,640	29,480
Net income	$ 87,960	$ 44,220
Other Data		
December 31 stock price	$ 8.50	$ 6.00
Number of shares	100,000	100,000
Dividend per share	$ 0.22	$ 0.22
Lease payments	$ 40,000	$ 40,000

Jamison also developed the following industry average data for 1988:

Ratio	Industry Average
Current	2.7×
Quick	1.0×
Inventory turnover	7.0×
Average collection period (ACP)	32.0 days
Fixed assets turnover	10.7×
Total assets turnover	2.6×
Debt	50.0%
TIE	2.5×
Fixed charge coverage	2.1×
Profit margin	3.5%
Basic earning power	19.1%
ROA	9.1%
ROE	18.2%
Price/earnings	14.2×
Market/book	1.4×

Jamison plans to structure her analysis around a series of questions. Give her a hand by performing the following tasks and answering the following questions:

a. Convert Computron's 1988 income statement to a statement of cash flows. (If done properly, the bottom line — net cash flow — should equal − $5,600, the change in the cash account from 1987 to 1988.) Explain the cash flow statement.

b. Define liquidity within a financial statement analysis context. What are Computron's current and quick ratios? Assess Computron's liquidity position.

c. What are Computron's inventory turnover, average collection period, fixed assets turnover, and total assets turnover ratios? How does the firm's asset utilization stack up against that of the industry?

d. What are the firm's debt, times-interest-earned, and fixed charge coverage ratios? How does Computron compare with the industry with respect to financial leverage?

e. Calculate and interpret the firm's profitability ratios — that is, profit margin, basic earning power, return on assets (ROA), and return on equity (ROE).

f. Analyze Computron's market value ratios — that is, its price/earnings ratio and market/book ratio.

g. Use the extended Du Pont equation (ROE = Profit margin × Total assets turnover × Equity multiplier) to obtain an overview of Computron's financial condition.

h. Although financial statement analysis can provide useful information about a company's operations and financial condition, it does have some inherent problems and limitations that necessitate care and judgment. Discuss these problems and limitations.

Computer-Related Problem

(Work the problem in this section only if you are using the computer problem diskette.)

Ratio analysis   **C7-1**   Use the computerized model for Problem C7-1 in the file C7 to solve this problem.

a. Refer back to Problem 7-8. Suppose that Bangor Corporation is considering installing a new computer system which would provide tighter control of inventory, accounts receivables, and accounts payable. If the new system is installed, the following data are projected (rather than the data given in Problem 7-8) for the indicated balance sheet and income statement accounts:

Accounts receivable	$400,000
Inventory	$771,000
Other fixed assets	$91,000
Accounts payable	$300,000
Accruals	$133,000
Cost of goods sold	$3,510,000
Administrative and selling expense	$228,320
P/E	6×

How do these changes affect the projected ratios and the comparison with the industry averages? (Note that any changes to the income statement will change the amount of retained earnings; therefore, the model is set up to calculate 1989 retained earnings as 1988 retained earnings plus net income minus dividends paid. The model also adjusts the cash balance so that the balance sheet balances.)

b. If the new computer were even more efficient than Bangor's management had estimated and thus caused the cost of goods sold to decrease by $100,000 from the projections in Part a, what effect would that have on the company's financial position?

c. If the new computer were less efficient than Bangor's management had estimated and caused the cost of goods sold to increase by $100,000 from the projections in Part a, what effect would that have on the company's financial position?

d. Change, one by one, the other items in Part a. Then think about, and write a paragraph describing, how computer models like this one can be used to help make better decisions about the purchase of such things as a new computer system.

Solutions to Self-Test Problems

ST-1   Refer to the marginal glossary definitions and appropriate sections of the text to check your responses.

ST-2   Kaiser paid $2 in dividends and retained $2 per share. Since total retained earnings rose by $12 million, there must be 6 million shares outstanding. With a book value of $40 per share, total common equity must be $40(6 million) = $240 million. Since Kaiser has $120 million of debt, its debt ratio must be 33.3 percent:

$$\frac{\text{Debt}}{\text{Assets}} = \frac{\text{Debt}}{\text{Debt} + \text{Equity}} = \frac{\$120 \text{ million}}{\$120 \text{ million} + \$240 \text{ million}}$$

$$= 0.333 = 33.3\%.$$

ST-3   a. In answering questions like this, always begin by writing down the relevant definitional equations, then start filling in numbers.

$$(1) \qquad \text{ACP} = \frac{\text{Accounts receivable}}{\text{Sales}/360}$$

$$40 = \frac{\text{A/R}}{\$1,000/360}$$

$$\text{A/R} = 40(\$2.778) = \$111.1 \text{ million.}$$

$$(2) \quad \text{Quick ratio} = \frac{\text{Current assets} - \text{Inventories}}{\text{Current liabilities}} = 2.0$$

$$= \frac{\text{Cash and marketable securities} + \text{A/R}}{\text{Current liabilities}} = 2.0$$

$$2.0 = \frac{\$100 + \$111.1}{\text{Current liabilities}}$$

$$\text{Current liabilities} = (\$100 + \$111.1)/2 = \$105.5 \text{ million.}$$

(3)

$$\text{Current ratio} = \frac{\text{Current assets}}{\text{Current liabilities}} = 3.0$$

$$= \frac{\text{Current assets}}{\$105.5} = 3.0.$$

$$\text{Current assets} = 3.0(\$105.5) = \$316.50 \text{ million.}$$

(4)

$$\text{Total assets} = \text{Current assets} + \text{Fixed assets}$$

$$= \$316.5 + \$283.5 = \$600 \text{ million.}$$

(5)

$$\text{ROA} = \text{Profit margin} \times \text{Total assets utilization}$$

$$= \frac{\text{Net income}}{\text{Sales}} \times \frac{\text{Sales}}{\text{Total assets}}$$

$$= \frac{\$50}{\$1,000} \times \frac{\$1,000}{\$600}$$

$$= 0.05 \times 1.667 = 0.833 = 8.33\%.$$

(6)

$$\text{ROE} = \text{ROA} \times \frac{\text{Assets}}{\text{Equity}}$$

$$12.0\% = 8.33\% \times \frac{\$600}{\text{Equity}}$$

$$\text{Equity} = \frac{(8.33\%)(\$600)}{12.0\%}$$

$$= \$416.50 \text{ million.}$$

(7)

$$\text{Total assets} = \text{Total claims} = \$600$$

$$\text{Current liabilities} + \text{Long-term debt} + \text{Equity} = \$600$$

$$\$105.5 + \text{Long-term debt} + \$416.5 = \$600$$

$$\text{Long-term debt} = \$600 - \$105.5 - \$416.5 = \$78 \text{ million.}$$

Note: We could have found equity as follows:

$$\text{ROE} = \frac{\text{Net income}}{\text{Equity}}$$

$$12.0\% = \frac{\$50}{\text{Equity}}$$

$$\text{Equity} = \$50/0.12$$

$$= \$416.67 \text{ million (rounding error difference).}$$

Then we could have gone on to find current liabilities and long-term debt.

b. Cadwalader's average sales per day were $1,000/360 = $2.777777 million. Its ACP was 40, so A/R = 40($2,777,777) = $111,111,080. Its new ACP of 30 would cause A/R = 30($2,777,777) = $83,333,310. The reduction in receivables would be $111,111,080 − $83,333,310 = $27,777,770, which would equal the amount of cash generated.

(1)

$$\text{New equity} = \text{Old equity} - \text{Stock bought back}$$

$$= \$416,500,000 - \$27,777,770$$

$$= \$388,722,230.$$

Thus,

$$\text{New ROE} = \frac{\text{Net income}}{\text{New equity}}$$

$$= \frac{\$50,000,000}{\$388,722,230}$$

$$= 12.86\% \text{ (versus old ROE of 12.0\%).}$$

(2)

$$\text{New ROA} = \frac{\text{Net income}}{\text{Total assets} - \text{Reduction in A/R}}$$

$$= \frac{\$50,000,000}{\$600,000,000 - \$27,777,770}$$

$$= 8.74\% \text{ (versus old ROA of 8.33\%).}$$

(3) The old debt is the same as the new debt:

$$\text{Debt} = \text{Total claims} - \text{Equity}$$

$$= \$600 - \$416.5 = \$183.5 \text{ million.}$$

$$\text{Old total assets} = \$600 \text{ million.}$$

$$\text{New total assets} = \text{Old total assets} - \text{Reduction in A/R}$$

$$= \$600 - \$27.78$$

$$= \$572.22 \text{ million.}$$

Therefore,

$$\frac{\text{Debt}}{\text{Old total assets}} = \frac{\$183.5}{\$600} = 30.6\%,$$

whereas

$$\frac{\text{New debt}}{\text{New total assets}} = \frac{\$183.5}{\$572.22} = 32.1\%.$$

8 Financial Forecasting

DETAILS MAGAZINE: LACK OF FINANCIAL FORECASTING LEADS TO LOSS OF CONTROL

In 1982 Annie Flanders, a former model, department store buyer, fashion columnist, security analyst, and Ethiopian leather factory manager, founded a magazine called *Details. Details* broke even on its very first issue, and it grew quickly from then on. The faster it grew, however, the worse its cash position became; as it grew, its costs for labor, materials, and so forth increased *ahead of sales,* but cash flows came in *after* sales.

In early 1984 Flanders was desperate for cash. Then Gary Bogard, former owner of the *London Tatler,* offered her $300,000 for controlling interest in *Details,* and Flanders accepted. With the new money, *Details* took off. Although Flanders lost financial control, Bogard let her retain editorial control of "her baby." In 1987, however, Bogard sold his controlling interest to Alan Patricof, a New York venture capitalist, and Patricof almost immediately sold out to Advanced Publications, a huge media chain, for $2 million. Thus, Flanders sold stock for $300,000 that 3 years later fetched $2 million, and she lost control of her creation in the process. Flanders reportedly does not mind working for a chain rather than being her own boss, but she must have some regrets about having to sell out just before *Details* reached the take-off stage.

The story of how Annie Flanders lost *Details* is, unfortunately, typical. Someone has a good idea, executes it well, and obtains good results. However, growth requires cash, and if a venture starts off undercapitalized, cash shortfalls soon become critical. If Flanders had read Chapter 8, perhaps she could have been better able to anticipate events, and perhaps she would still have control of *Details*.

FIRMS need assets to make sales, and if sales are to grow, assets must also increase. Further, a sales expansion requires a prior investment in new current assets, and if the firm is operating at full capacity, fixed assets must also be added. Capital will be needed to finance these new assets, and while some of the required capital can be obtained by retaining earnings, if the growth rate is high, even a highly profitable firm will need external capital. Since it takes time to raise capital, it is important for firms to have reasonably accurate estimates of their forecasted capital requirements so that plans may be made to obtain funds well in advance of the need.

This planning process is an integral part of the financial manager's job. As we will see in subsequent chapters, long-term debt and equity funds are raised infrequently and in large amounts, primarily because of the fixed cost involved in selling securities. Thus, it is necessary for the firm to estimate its needs for funds for the next few years if it is to properly time its long-term security offerings. Also, because both managers and investors are vitally concerned with *future* cash flows, financial managers should consider how alternative growth and financing actions will affect the firm's cash flows. To project cash flows, one needs projected financial statements. Therefore, in this chapter we discuss briefly how projected financial statements are constructed, after which we show how they are used to help estimate the need for different types of capital.

SALES FORECASTS

sales forecast
A forecast of a firm's unit and dollar sales for some future period; generally based on recent sales trends plus forecasts of the economic prospects for the nation, region, industry, and so forth.

The **sales forecast** generally starts with a review of sales during the past five to ten years, expressed in a graph such as that in Figure 8-1. The first part of the graph shows actual sales for Telecomp Corporation, a manufacturer of computer and telecommunications equipment, from 1978 through 1988. During this 10-year period, sales grew from $175 million to $500 million, or at a compound growth rate of 11.1 percent. However, the growth rate has accelerated sharply in recent years, primarily as a result of the breakup of AT&T and the separation of its manufacturing and telephone operations, which permitted companies like Telecomp to compete for sales to telephone operating companies. Also, Telecomp's research and development program has been especially successful, so when the telecommunications market broke open, Telecomp was ready.

On the basis of the recent trend in sales, on new product introductions, and on Telecomp's economics staff's forecast that the national economy will

---

Figure 8-1 Telecomp Corporation: 1989 Sales Projection

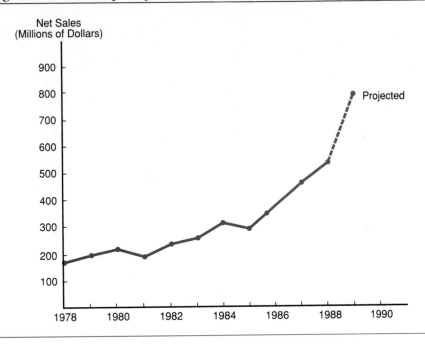

be quite strong during the coming year, Telecomp's planning group projects a 50 percent growth rate during 1989, to a sales level of $750 million. That forecast was developed as follows:

1. To begin, Telecomp's sales are divided into three major product groups: (1) sales to telephone companies of equipment used in telephone networks; (2) sales of equipment such as PBXs used by hotels, motels, and businesses to route calls among rooms; and (3) sales of electronic components to computer manufacturers. Sales in each of these areas during the past 10 years are plotted, the trend is observed, and a "first approximation forecast," assuming a continuation of past trends, is made.

2. Next, the level of business activity for each of the company's market areas is forecast — for example, what will be the level of hotel, motel, and office building construction in 1989? These forecasts are used as a basis for modifying the demand forecasts in each of Telecomp's business areas.

3. Telecomp's planning group next looks at the firm's probable shares of each major market. Consideration is given to such factors as the company's capacity, its competitors' capacity, and new products or product improvements that either Telecomp or its competitors may plan. Pricing strategies are also considered — for example, does the company have plans to raise prices to boost profit margins, or to lower prices to

gain market share and thus cut production costs as a result of gaining economies of scale? Such actions could greatly affect sales forecasts. In addition, since Telecomp has some export sales and also faces competition from Japanese and European firms in its U.S. markets, changes in exchange rates and the value of the dollar can have an important influence on its market share.

4. Advertising campaigns, promotional discounts, credit terms, and the like also affect sales, so probable developments in these areas are also factored in.

5. Order backlogs and recent trends in new orders (or cancellations) are taken into account.

6. Forecasts are made for each product group both in the aggregate (for example, sales to telephone companies) and on an individual product basis. The individual product sales forecasts are summed and then compared with the aggregate product group forecasts. Differences are reconciled, and the end product is a sales forecast for the company as a whole but with breakdowns by major divisions and for individual products.

If the sales forecast is off, the consequences can be serious. First, if the market expands *more* than Telecomp has expected and geared up for, the company will not be able to meet its customers' needs. Orders will back up, delivery times will lengthen, repairs and installations will be harder to schedule, and customer dissatisfaction will increase. Customers will end up going elsewhere, and Telecomp will lose market share and will have missed a major opportunity. On the other hand, if its projections are overly optimistic, Telecomp could end up with too much plant, equipment, and inventory. This would mean low turnover ratios, high costs for depreciation and storage, and, possibly, write-offs of obsolete inventory and equipment. All of this would result in a low rate of return on equity, which in turn would depress the company's stock price. If Telecomp had financed the expansion with debt, its problems would, of course, be compounded. Thus, an accurate sales forecast is critical to the well-being of the firm.[1]

FORECASTING FINANCIAL REQUIREMENTS: THE PERCENTAGE OF SALES METHOD

pro forma financial statement
A projected financial statement that shows how an actual statement will look if certain specified assumptions are realized.

Several methods are used to develop **pro forma**, or forecasted, **financial statements**. In this chapter we focus on the percentage of sales method. We also explain when this method can and cannot be used, and we discuss the growing use of computerized models for forecasting financial statements.

---

[1] A sales forecast is actually the *expected value of a probability distribution* of possible levels of sales. Because any sales forecast is subject to a greater or lesser degree of uncertainty, for financial planning we are often just as interested in the degree of uncertainty inherent in the sales forecast (σ sales) as we are in the expected value of sales.

Table 8-1   Telecomp Corporation:
1988 Financial Statements
(Millions of Dollars)

Balance Sheet, December 31

Cash	$ 10	Accounts payable	$ 40
Receivables	85	Notes payable	10
Inventories	100	Accrued wages and taxes	25
Total current assets	$195	Total current liabilities	$ 75
Net fixed assets	150	Mortgage bonds	72
		Common stock	150
		Retained earnings	48
Total assets	$345	Total liabilities and equity	$345

Summary Income Statement

Sales	$500 million
Net income	20 million
Dividends paid	8 million

**percentage of
sales method**
A method of forecasting
financial requirements
by expressing various
balance sheet items as a
percentage of sales and
then multiplying these
percentages by expected
future sales to construct
pro forma balance
sheets.

The **percentage of sales method** is a simple but often practical method of forecasting financial statement variables. The procedure is based on two assumptions: (1) that most balance sheet accounts are tied directly to sales, and (2) that the current levels of all assets are optimal for the current sales level. We illustrate the process with Telecomp Corporation, whose December 31, 1988, balance sheet and summary income statement are given in Table 8-1. Telecomp operated its fixed assets at full capacity in 1988 to support its $500 million of sales, and it had no unnecessary current assets. Its profit margin on sales was 4 percent, and it paid out 40 percent of its net income to stockholders as dividends. If Telecomp's sales increase to $750 million in 1989, what will be its pro forma December 31, 1989, balance sheet, and how much additional financing will the company require during 1989?

The first step in the percentage of sales forecast is to identify those balance sheet items that vary directly with sales. Since Telecomp has been operating at full capacity, each asset item must increase if the higher level of sales is to be attained. More cash will be needed for transactions; receivables will be higher; additional inventory must be stocked; and new plant must be added.[2]

If Telecomp's assets are to increase, its liabilities and equity must likewise rise — the balance sheet must balance. Therefore, any increase in assets must be financed in some manner. **Spontaneously generated funds** will come from such sources as accounts payable and accruals, which rise spontaneously with sales: As sales increase, so will Telecomp's own purchases, and larger purchases will automatically result in higher levels of accounts payable. Thus, if sales double, accounts payable will also double. Similarly, a higher level of

**spontaneously
generated funds**
Funds that are obtained
automatically from
routine business
transactions.

---

[2]Some assets, such as marketable securities, are not tied directly to operations and hence do not vary directly with sales. Also, as we shall see later in the chapter, if some assets are not being fully utilized, sales can increase without increasing those assets.

operations will require more labor, so accrued wages will increase, and, assuming profit margins are maintained, an increase in profits will pull up accrued taxes. Retained earnings will also increase, but not in direct proportion to the increase in sales. Neither notes payable, mortgage bonds, nor common stock will rise spontaneously with sales — higher sales do not *automatically* trigger increases in these items.

We can construct a pro forma balance sheet for December 31, 1989, proceeding as outlined in the following paragraphs.

Step 1. In Table 8-2, Column 1, we express those balance sheet items that vary directly with sales as a percentage of 1988 sales. An item such as notes payable that does not automatically vary with sales is designated "not applicable."

Step 2. We multiply these percentages (their fractions, really) by the $750 million projected 1989 sales to obtain the projected amounts as of December 31, 1989. These are shown in Column 2 of the table.

Step 3. We simply insert figures for notes payable, mortgage bonds, and common stock from the December 31, 1988, balance sheet. At least one of these accounts will have to be changed later in the analysis.

Step 4. We add the estimated addition to retained earnings for 1989 to the December 31, 1988, balance sheet figure for retained earnings to obtain the December 31, 1989, projected retained earnings. Recall that Telecomp expects to earn 4 percent on 1989 sales of $750 million, or $30 million, and expects to pay 40 percent of this out in dividends to stockholders; thus the **dividend payout ratio** is 40 percent, and dividends paid will be 0.4($30 million) = $12 million. Therefore, retained earnings for the year are projected to be $30 million − $12 million = $18 million. Adding this $18 million to the $48 million beginning retained earnings gives the $66 million projected retained earnings shown in Column 2.

dividend payout ratio
The percentage of earnings paid out in dividends.

Step 5. We sum the asset accounts, obtaining a total projected assets figure of $518 million for 1989, and we also sum the projected liabilities and net worth items to obtain $396 million, the estimate of available funds. Since liabilities and equity must total $518 million, but only $396 million is projected, we have a shortfall of $122 million which we designate **additional funds needed**, or **AFN**; it will presumably be raised by bank borrowing, by issuing securities, or both. For simplicity, we disregard depreciation by assuming that cash flows generated by depreciation will be used to replace worn-out fixed assets.

additional funds needed (AFN)
Funds that a firm must acquire through borrowing or by selling new common or preferred stock.

Step 6. Telecomp could use short-term bank loans (notes payable), mortgage bonds, common stock, or a combination of these securities to make up the shortfall. Ordinarily, it would make this choice on the basis of the relative costs of these different types of securities, subject to certain constraints. For example, in Telecomp's case, the company has a contractual agreement with its

Table 8-2   Telecomp Corporation:
December 31, 1988, Balance Sheet
Expressed as a Percentage of Sales and
December 31, 1989, Pro Forma Balance Sheet
(Millions of Dollars)

	Balance Sheet Items on 12/31/88 (as a % of the $500 1988 Sales) (1)	Pro Forma Balance Sheet on 12/31/89 (= Projected Sales of $750 Times Column 1) (2)
Cash	2.0%	$ 15
Receivables	17.0	128
Inventories	20.0	150
Total current assets	39.0%	$293
Net fixed assets	30.0	225
Total assets	69.0%	$518
Accounts payable	8.0%	$ 60
Notes payable	n.a.[a]	10[b]
Accrued wages and taxes	5.0	38
Total current liabilities	n.a.	$108
Mortgage bonds	n.a.	72[b]
Common stock	n.a.	150[b]
Retained earnings	n.a.	66[c]
Funds available		$396
Additional funds needed (AFN)		122[d]
Total liabilities and equity		$518

[a]n.a. = not applicable. (Item does not vary spontaneously and directly with sales.)

[b]Initially projected to remain constant at the 1988 level. Later financing decisions might change this level.

[c]Balance in the retained earnings account at December 31, 1988, plus the 1989 projected addition to retained earnings as explained in Step 4 in the text.

[d]"Additional funds needed" is a balancing figure: $518 projected assets − $396 projected funds available = $122 additional funds needed.

bondholders to keep total debt at or below 50 percent of total assets and also to keep the current ratio at a level of 2.5 or greater. These provisions restrict the financing choices as follows:[3]

1. *Restriction on additional debt:*
   Maximum debt permitted = (0.5)(Total assets)
   $$= (0.5)(\$518 \text{ million}) = \$259 \text{ million}$$
   Less debt already projected for December 31, 1989:

Current liabilities	$108 million	
Mortgage bonds	72 million =	180 million
Maximum additional debt		= $ 79 million

---

[3]As we shall see in Chapter 13, restrictions like these are contained in virtually all long-term debt agreements. They are designed to protect bondholders against managerial decisions that would increase the risk the bondholders face.

2. *Restriction on additional current liabilities:*

Maximum current liabilities = Projected current assets/2.5	
= \$293 million/2.5 = \$117 million	
Less current liabilities already projected	108 million
Maximum additional current liabilities	\$ 9 million

3. *Common equity requirements:*

Total additional funds needed (from Table 8-2)	\$122 million
Maximum additional debt permitted	79 million
Common equity funds required	\$ 43 million

We see, then, that Telecomp needs a total of \$122 million from external sources. Its existing debt contract limits new debt to \$79 million, and only \$9 million of that amount can be short-term debt. Thus, since Telecomp wants to make maximum use of debt financing, it must plan to sell additional common stock in the amount of \$43 million to cover its financial requirements. Here is a summary of its projected nonspontaneous external financings:

Short-term debt (notes payable)	\$ 9 million
Long-term debt	70 million
New common stock	43 million
Total	\$122 million

Projected Financial Statements and Ratios

Telecomp's financial staff can now construct a set of projected, or pro forma, financial statements and then analyze the ratios that are implied therein. Parts I and II of Table 8-3 give abbreviated versions of the final projected balance sheet and income statement; Part III gives the statement of cash flows; and Part IV gives a few key ratios. These statements can be used by the financial manager to show the other executives the implications of the planned sales increase. For example, the projected rate of return on equity is 11.6 percent. Is this a reasonable target, or can it be improved? The preliminary forecast also calls for the sale of \$43 million of common stock — but does top management really want to sell any new stock? Suppose just over 50 percent of Telecomp's stock is owned by Robert Balik, and he does not want the company to sell any stock and thereby cause him to lose his majority control. How then could the needed funds be raised, or what adjustments could be made? In the remainder of the chapter, we look at approaches to answering questions like these.

Relationship between Sales and Capital Requirements

Although the forecast of capital requirements can be made by constructing pro forma balance sheets as described previously, under certain conditions it is easier to use a simple forecasting formula. The formula can also be used to highlight the relationship between sales growth and financial requirements:

Table 8-3   Telecomp Corporation:
Projected Financial Statements for 1989
(Millions of Dollars)

I. Projected Balance Sheet, December 31, 1989

Cash	$ 15	Accounts payable	$ 60
Accounts receivable	128	Notes payable	19
Inventories	150	Accruals	38
Total current assets	$293	Total current liabilities	$117
Net fixed assets	225	Long-term debt	142
		Common stock	193
		Retained earnings	66
		Total equity	$259
Total assets	$518	Total liabilities and equity	$518

II. Projected Income Statement, 1989

Sales	$750
Total costs	700
Net income before taxes	$ 50
Taxes (40%)	20
Net income after taxes	$ 30
Dividends (40% of income)	12
Addition to retained earnings	$ 18

III. Projected Statement of Cash Flows, 1989

Cash Flows from Operations		
Net income	$30	
Additions (sources of cash):[a]		
Increase in accounts payable	20	
Increase in accruals	13	
Subtractions (uses of cash):		
Increase in accounts receivables	(43)	
Increase in inventories	(50)	
Total cash flows from operations		($ 30)
Cash Flows Associated with Long-Term Investments		
Increase in fixed assets		(75)
Cash Flows from Financing Activities		
Increase in notes payable	$ 9	
Proceeds from sale of bonds	70	
Proceeds from sale of common stock	43	
Dividends paid	(12)	
Net cash flows from financing activities		110
Net increase in cash		$ 5

IV. Key Ratios Projected for December 31, 1989[b]

1. Current ratio	2.5 times
2. Quick ratio	1.2 times
3. Total debt/total assets	50%
4. Rate of return on ending equity	11.6%

[a] The figure for cash flows from operations normally includes depreciation. Here we have assumed that depreciation is reinvested in fixed assets; that is, we netted it out against fixed asset additions.

[b] Other ratios could be calculated and analyzed by the Du Pont system.

$$
\begin{array}{ccccc}
\text{Additional} & & \text{Required} & \text{Spontaneous} & \text{Increase in} \\
\text{funds} & = & \text{increase} & - \quad \text{increase in} & - \quad \text{retained} \\
\text{needed} & & \text{in assets} & \text{liabilities} & \text{earnings}
\end{array}
$$

$$
\text{AFN} \quad = \quad (A/S)\Delta S \quad - \quad (L/S)\Delta S \quad - MS_1(1 - d). \qquad (8\text{-}1)
$$

Here

AFN = additional funds needed.

A/S = assets that must increase if sales are to increase as a percentage of sales, or required dollar increase in assets per \$1 increase in sales. A/S = 69%, or 0.69, for Telecomp from Column 1 of Table 8-2. Thus, for every \$1 increase in sales, assets must increase by \$0.69.

L/S = liabilities that increase spontaneously with sales as a percentage of sales, or spontaneously generated financing per \$1 increase in sales. L/S = 13.0%, or 0.13, for Telecomp. Thus, every \$1 increase in sales generates \$0.13% of spontaneous financing.

S_1 = total sales projected for next year. Note that S_0 designates last year's sales. S_1 = \$750 million for Telecomp.

ΔS = change in sales = $S_1 - S_0$ = \$750 million − . \$500 million = \$250 million for Telecomp.

M = profit margin, or rate of profit per \$1 of sales. M = 4%, or 0.04, for Telecomp.

d = percentage of earnings paid out in dividends, or the dividend payout ratio; d = 40%, or 0.40, for Telecomp. Notice that 1 − d = 1.0 − 0.4 = 0.6, or 60 percent, is the percentage of earnings that Telecomp retains. The term (1 − d) is called the **retention rate**, or *retention ratio*.

retention rate
The percentage of its earnings retained by the firm, which is equal to 1 minus the dividend payout ratio.

Inserting values for Telecomp into Equation 8-1, we find the additional funds needed to be \$122 million:

$$
\text{AFN} = 0.69(\Delta S) - 0.13(\Delta S) - 0.04(S_1)(1 - 0.4)
$$

$$
= 0.69(\$250 \text{ million}) - 0.13(\$250 \text{ million}) - 0.04(\$750 \text{ million})(0.6)
$$

$$
= \$172.5 \text{ million} - \$32.5 \text{ million} - \$18 \text{ million}
$$

$$
= \$122 \text{ million}.
$$

To increase sales by \$250 million, Telecomp must increase assets by \$172.5 million. The \$172.5 million of new assets must be financed in some manner. Of the total, \$32.5 million will come from a spontaneous increase in liabilities, while another \$18 million will be obtained from retained earnings. The remaining \$122 million must be raised from external sources. This value agrees with the figure developed earlier in Table 8-2.

Relationship between Growth and Financial Requirements

The faster Telecomp's growth rate in sales, the greater its need for external financing; we can use Equation 8-1, which is plotted in Figure 8-2, to quantify this relationship. The lower section shows Telecomp's external financial re-

Figure 8-2   Relationship between Growth in Sales and Financial Requirements, Assuming S_0 = $500 Million (Millions of Dollars)

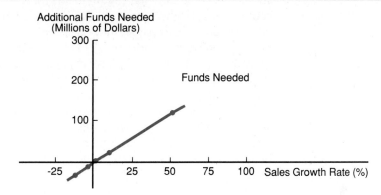

Growth Rate in Sales (1)	Increase (Decrease) in Sales, ΔS (2)	Forecasted Sales, S_1 (3)	Additional Funds Needed (4)
50%	$250	$750	$122.0
10	50	550	14.8
4.478	22.39	522.39	0.0
0	0	500	(12.0)
−10	(50)	450	(38.8)

Explanation of Columns:

Column 1: Growth rate in sales, g.

Column 2: Increase (decrease) in sales, $\Delta S = g(S_0) = g(\$500)$.

Column 3: Forecasted sales, $S_1 = S_0 + g(S_0) = S_0(1 + g) = \$500(1 + g)$.

Column 4: Additional funds needed $= 0.69(\Delta S) - 0.13(\Delta S) - 0.024(S_1)$.

quirements at various growth rates, and these data are plotted in the graph. The figure illustrates the following important points:

Financial Planning. At low growth rates, Telecomp needs no external financing and even generates surplus cash. However, if the company grows faster than 4.478 percent, it must raise capital from outside sources.[4] Further, the faster the growth rate, the greater the capital requirements. If management foresees difficulties in raising the required capital, perhaps because Telecomp's current stockholders do not want to sell additional stock, then management should reconsider the feasibility of the expansion plans.

---

[4]We found the 4.478 percent growth rate by setting AFN equal to zero, substituting gS_0 for ΔS and $S_0 + g(S_0)$ for S_1 in the AFN equation, and then solving the equation $0 = 0.69(g)(S_0) - 0.13(g)(S_0) - 0.04(S_0 + gS_0)(1 - 0.4)$ for g. The g that solved this equation was 0.04478, or 4.478 percent.

Effect of Dividend Policy on Financing Needs. Dividend policy as reflected in the payout ratio (d in Equation 8-1) also affects external capital requirements — the higher the payout ratio, the smaller the addition to retained earnings, and hence the greater the requirements for external capital. Therefore, if Telecomp foresees difficulties in raising capital, it might want to consider a reduction in the dividend payout ratio. This would lower (or shift to the right) the line in Figure 8-2, indicating smaller external capital requirements at all growth rates. However, before changing its dividend policy, management should consider the effects of such a decision on stock prices. These effects are discussed in Chapter 18.

Notice that the line in Figure 8-2 does *not* pass through the origin; thus, at low growth rates (below 4.478 percent), surplus funds will be produced, because new retained earnings plus spontaneous funds will exceed the required asset increases. Only if the dividend payout ratio were 100 percent, meaning that the firm did not retain any of its earnings, would the "funds needed" line pass through the origin.

Capital Intensity. The amount of assets required per dollar of sales, A/S in Equation 8-1, is often called the **capital intensity ratio**. This factor has a major effect on capital requirements per unit of sales growth. If the capital intensity ratio is low, sales can grow rapidly without much outside capital. However, if the firm is capital intensive, even a small growth in output will require a great deal of new outside capital.

> **capital intensity ratio**
> The amount of assets required per dollar of sales (A/S).

Profit Margin. The profit margin, M, is also an important determinant of the funds-required equation — the higher the margin, the lower the funds requirements, other things held constant. Telecomp's profit margin is 4 percent. Now suppose M increased to 6 percent. This new value could be inserted into the funds-needed formula, and the effect would be to reduce the additional funds needed at all positive growth rates. In terms of the graph, an increase in the profit margin would cause the line to shift down, and its slope would also become less steep. Because of the relationship between profit margins and external capital requirements, some very rapidly growing firms do not need much external capital. For example, for many years Xerox grew at a rapid rate with very little borrowing or stock sales. However, as the company lost patent protection and as competition intensified in the copier industry, Xerox's profit margin declined, its needs for external capital rose, and it began to borrow from banks and other sources. IBM has had a similar experience.

FORECASTING FINANCIAL REQUIREMENTS WHEN THE BALANCE SHEET RATIOS ARE SUBJECT TO CHANGE

To this point we have been assuming that the balance sheet ratios of assets and liabilities to sales (A/S and L/S) remain constant over time, which in turn requires the assumption that each "spontaneous" asset and liability item in-

**Figure 8-3   Three Possible Ratio Relationships
(Millions of Dollars)**

a. Constant Ratios

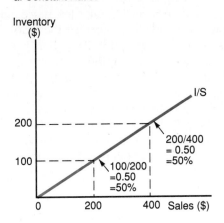

b. Economies of Scale; Declining Ratios

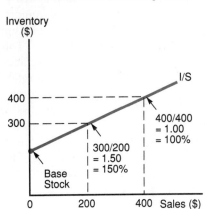

c. Lumpy Assets

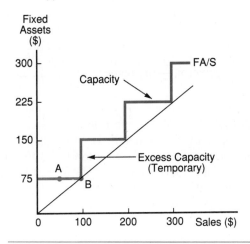

creases at the same rate as sales. In graph form, this implies the type of relationship shown in Panel a of Figure 8-3, a relationship that is linear and passes through the origin. Under those conditions, if the company's sales increase from $200 million to $400 million, inventory will increase proportionately, from $100 million to $200 million.

The assumption of constant ratios is appropriate at times, but there are times when it is incorrect. Three such conditions are described in the following sections.

Economies of Scale

There are economies of scale in the use of many kinds of assets, and when economies occur, the ratios are likely to change over time as the size of the firm increases. For example, firms often need to maintain base stocks of different inventory items, even if current sales levels are quite low. As sales expand, inventories grow less rapidly than sales, so the ratio of inventory to sales (I/S) declines. This situation is depicted in Panel b of Figure 8-3. Here we see that the inventory/sales ratio is 1.5, or 150 percent, when sales are $200 million, but the ratio declines to 1.0 when sales climb to $400 million.

The relationship used to illustrate economies of scale is linear, but this is not necessarily the case. Indeed, as we shall see in Chapters 20 and 21, if the firm uses the most popular model for establishing inventory levels, the EOQ model, inventories will rise with the square root of sales. In this case, the graph in Figure 8-3b will be a curved line whose slope decreases at higher sales levels.

"Lumpy" Assets

"lumpy" assets
Assets that cannot be acquired in small increments but must be obtained in large, discrete amounts.

In many industries, technological considerations dictate that if a firm is to be competitive it must add fixed assets in large, discrete units; such assets are often referred to as **"lumpy" assets**. In the paper industry, for example, there are strong economies of scale in basic paper mill equipment, so when a paper company expands capacity, it must do so in large, or lumpy, increments. This type of situation is depicted in Panel c of Figure 8-3. Here we assume that the minimum economically efficient plant has a cost of $75 million and that such a plant can produce enough output to attain a sales level of $100 million. If the firm is to be competitive, it simply must have at least $75 million of fixed assets.

This situation has a major effect on fixed assets/sales (FA/S) ratios at different sales levels and, consequently, on financial requirements. At Point A in Figure 8-3c, which represents a sales level of $50 million, the fixed assets are $75 million, so the ratio FA/S = $75/$50 = 1.5. Sales can expand by $50 million, out to $100 million, with no additions to fixed assets. At that point, represented by Point B, the ratio FA/S = $75/$100 = 0.75. However, if the firm is operating at capacity (sales of $100 million), even a small increase in sales would require a doubling of plant capacity, so a small projected sales increase would bring with it a very large financial requirement.[5]

---

[5]Several other points should be noted about Panel c of Figure 8-3. First, if the firm is operating at a sales level of $100 million or less, any expansion that calls for a sales increase above $100 million will require a *doubling* of the firm's fixed assets. A much smaller percentage increase would be involved if the firm were large enough to be operating a number of plants. Second, firms generally go to multiple shifts and take other actions to minimize the need for new fixed asset capacity as they approach Point B. However, these efforts can go only so far, and eventually a fixed asset expansion will be required. Third, firms often make arrangements to share excess capacity with other firms in their industry. For example, consider the situation in the electric utility industry, which is very much like that depicted in Panel c. Electric companies often build jointly owned plants, or else they "take turns" building plants and then buy power from or sell power to other utilities to avoid building new plants that may be underutilized.

Cyclical Changes

Panels a, b, and c of Figure 8-3 all focus on target, or projected, relationships between sales and assets. Actual sales, however, are often different from projected sales, and the actual asset/sales ratio for a given period may thus be quite different from the planned ratio. To illustrate, the firm depicted in Panel b of Figure 8-3 might, when its sales are $200 million and its inventories $300 million, project a sales expansion to $400 million and then increase its inventories to $400 million in anticipation of the sales expansion. Yet suppose an unforeseen economic downturn holds sales to only $300 million. In this case, actual inventories would be $400 million, but inventories of only $350 million would be needed to support actual sales of $300 million. From this situation, if the firm were making its forecast for the following year, it would have to recognize that sales could expand by $100 million with no increase whatever in inventories, but that any sales expansion beyond $100 million would require additional financing to build inventories.

MODIFYING THE FORECAST OF
ADDITIONAL FUNDS NEEDED

If any of the conditions noted previously apply (economies of scale exist, excess capacity exists, or asset additions are lumpy), the A/S ratio will not be a constant, and the simple percentage of sales forecasting method should not be used. Rather, other techniques must be used to forecast asset levels and the resulting external financing requirements. Two of these methods — linear regression and specific item forecasting — are discussed in the following sections.

Simple Linear Regression

If we assume that the relationship between a certain type of asset and sales is linear, then we can use simple linear regression techniques to estimate the requirements for that type of asset for any given sales increase. For example, Telecomp's levels of sales, receivables, inventories, and net fixed assets over the last 11 years are shown in the lower section of Figure 8-4, and each current asset item is plotted in the upper section as a scatter diagram versus sales. Estimated regression equations as found with a hand calculator are also shown with each graph. For example, the estimated relationship between inventories and sales (in millions of dollars) is

$$\text{Inventories} = \$20 + 0.16(\text{Sales}).$$

The plotted points are quite close to the regression line, which indicates a

Figure 8-4   Telecomp Corporation: Linear Regression Models
(Millions of Dollars)

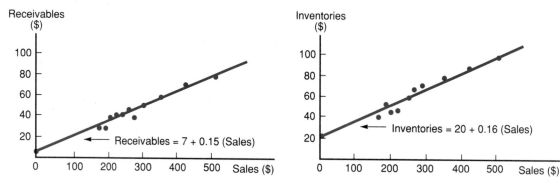

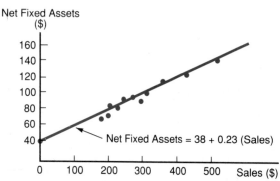

Year	Sales	Accounts Receivable	Inventories	Net Fixed Assets
1978	$175	$33	$ 44	$ 78
1979	200	38	48	83
1980	215	44	53	86
1981	185	35	57	79
1982	235	43	60	91
1983	265	45	66	98
1984	300	52	73	106
1985	280	47	70	101
1986	350	61	78	118
1987	420	71	90	135
1988	500	85	100	150

high degree of correlation. In fact, the correlation coefficient between inventories and sales is 0.98, indicating that there is a very strong linear relationship between these two variables.

We can use the estimated relationship between inventories and sales to forecast 1989 inventory levels. Since 1989 sales are projected at $750 million, 1989 inventories should be $140 million:

$$\text{Inventories} = \$20 + 0.16(\$750) = \$140 \text{ million.}$$

This is $10 million less than our earlier forecast based on the percentage of sales method. The difference occurs because the percentage of sales method assumed that the ratio of inventories to sales would remain constant, while in fact it will probably decline, because the regression line in Figure 8-4 does not pass through the origin. Note also that although our graphs show linear relationships, we could have easily used a non-linear regression model had such a relationship been indicated.

Specific Item Forecasting

Consider again the Telecomp example set forth in Tables 8-1 and 8-2. Now suppose a ratio analysis along the lines described in Chapter 7 suggests that the ratios of cash, receivables, and inventories to sales as indicated in Table 8-2 are appropriate, as are the liability ratios and the retained earnings calculations, but that excess capacity exists in fixed assets. Specifically, fixed assets in 1988 were being utilized to only 80 percent of capacity. If fixed assets had been used at full capacity, 1988 sales could have been as high as $625 million:

$$\begin{array}{l}\text{Full} \\ \text{capacity} \\ \text{sales}\end{array} = \frac{\text{Current sales}}{\begin{array}{c}\text{Percentage of capacity} \\ \text{at which fixed assets} \\ \text{were operated}\end{array}} = \frac{\$500 \text{ million}}{0.80} = \begin{array}{l}\$625 \text{ million sales} \\ \text{at full capacity.}\end{array}$$

This suggests that Telecomp's target for the fixed assets (FA) to sales ratio should be

$$\begin{array}{l}\text{Target} \\ \text{FA/Sales} \\ \text{ratio}\end{array} = \frac{\text{Fixed assets}}{\text{Full capacity sales}} = \frac{\$150 \text{ million}}{\$625 \text{ million}} = 0.24,$$

not the 0.30 that actually existed. Therefore, at the projected sales level of $750 million, Telecomp would require fixed assets of only 0.24($750 million) = $180 million, up only $30 million from the $150 million currently on hand, rather than up $75 million.[6]

We estimated earlier that Telecomp would need an additional $122 million of capital. However, those estimates were based on the assumption that $75 million of additional fixed assets would be required. If Telecomp could attain a sales level of $750 million with an addition of only $30 million of fixed assets, then the external funds needed would decline by $75 − $30 = $45 million, to a total of $122 − $45 = $77 million.

---

[6]This $30 million of required new fixed assets could also be determined by noting (1) that sales could grow from $500 million to $625 million without any increase in fixed assets but (2) that the sales increase from $625 million to $750 million would require new fixed assets of (FA/S)(ΔS) = 0.24($125 million) = $30 million.

COMPUTERIZED FINANCIAL PLANNING MODELS

Although the type of financial forecasting described in this chapter can be done with a hand calculator, most well-managed firms with sales greater than a few million dollars use some type of computerized financial planning model. Such models can be programmed to show the effects of different sales levels, different ratios of sales to operating assets, and different assumptions about sales prices and input costs. Plans are then made regarding how financial requirements are to be met — by borrowing from banks, thus increasing short-term notes payable; by selling long-term bonds; or by selling new common stock. Pro forma balance sheets and income statements are generated under the different financing plans, and earnings per share are projected, along with such risk measures as the current ratio, the debt/assets ratio, and the times-interest-earned ratio.

Depending on how these projections look, management may modify its initial plans. For example, the firm may conclude that its sales forecast must be cut because the requirements for external capital exceed the firm's ability to raise money. Alternatively, management may decide to reduce dividends and thus generate more funds internally. The company also may decide to investigate production processes that require fewer fixed assets, or it may consider the possibility of buying rather than manufacturing certain components, thus eliminating raw materials and work-in-process inventories as well as certain manufacturing facilities.

In subsequent chapters we will look in detail at ways to analyze policy changes such as those mentioned above. In all such considerations, the basic issue is the effect that a specific action will have on future earnings and cash flows, on the firm's risk, and hence on the price of its stock. Since computerized planning models help management assess these effects, they are playing an increasingly important role in corporate management. An illustrative *Lotus 1-2-3* forecasting model is described in Appendix 8A, and others are used to solve the computer-related problems for this chapter.[7]

---

[7]It is becoming increasingly easy for companies to develop planning models as a result of the dramatic improvements that have been made in computer hardware and software in recent years. *Lotus 1-2-3* is the most widely used system, although many companies also employ more complex and elaborate modeling systems. Increasingly, a knowledge of *1-2-3* or some similar planning system is becoming a requirement for getting even an entry-level job in many corporations. Indeed, surveys indicate that the probability of a business student getting an attractive job offer increases dramatically if he or she has a working knowledge of *1-2-3*. In addition, starting salaries are materially higher for those students who have such a knowledge.

Note also that we have concentrated on long-run, or strategic, financial planning. Within the framework of the long-run strategic plan, firms also develop short-run financial plans. For example, in Table 8-2 we saw that Telecomp Corporation expects to need $122 million by the end of 1989, and that it plans to raise this capital by using short-term debt, long-term debt, and common stock. However, we do not know when during the year the need for funds will occur, or when Telecomp will obtain each of its different types of capital. To address these issues, the firm must develop a short-run financial plan, the centerpiece of which is the *cash budget,* which is a projection of cash inflows and outflows on a daily, weekly, or monthly basis during the coming year (or other budget period). We will discuss cash budgeting in Chapter 20.

International

CURRENCY EXCHANGE RATES

Financial forecasting is more difficult for a multinational corporation than for a purely domestic one because the results for overseas operations must be "translated" from foreign currencies into U.S. dollars. For example, IBM might have correctly forecasted its Japanese subsidiary's results in terms of yen, but then missed the consolidated corporate forecast badly because of an unanticipated change in the rate at which yen can be exchanged into dollars. If the number of dollars a yen would buy rose, IBM's Japanese subsidiary's contribution to consolidated profits would exceed the forecasted level, and vice versa if the value of the yen fell.

Exchange rates also affect unit sales, sales prices, and costs — and thus financial forecasts — in yet another way. To illustrate, suppose Blount-Raulerson Honda, the Gainesville Honda dealer, planned to import 600 autos at an average cost of 1,600,000 yen each. In the winter of 1988, when these plans were being made, one dollar could be exchanged for 125 yen, so the cost per car was 1,600,000/125 = $12,800. Assume further that the dealer would incur $1,000 of transportation costs, and that it planned to mark up the cars by another $1,000 and sell them for $14,800 each. Thus, Blount-Raulerson expected a gross profit of 600 × $1,000 = $600,000.

Suppose, however, that the yen/dollar exchange rate changed from ¥125:$1 to ¥100:$1. That exchange rate change would mean that Blount-Raulerson would have to pay 1,600,000/100 = $16,000 per car, so with the same transportation cost and profit per car, the retail sales price would have to be $18,000. Now something would have to change. If customers were willing to buy 600 cars at a price of $14,800, they would certainly buy fewer cars if prices were raised by 22 percent, to $18,000. Thus, Blount-Raulerson would have to either negotiate a lower price from Honda, cut its profit margin drastically, or sell fewer cars. In fact, Honda dealers all across the United States took all three of these actions in 1987, when a similar increase in the value of the yen occurred. Honda Motors had to lay off workers in Japan, and its profits fell. Toyota, Sony, and other Japanese manufacturers were also hurt by the rise in the value of the yen, but Ford, GM, and other U.S. companies were helped — their sales and profits rose, and they hired new workers to help meet demand.

From the end of World War II to 1971, exchange rates were *fixed* by agreement among the central bankers of the major trading nations. However, since 1971 rates have *floated,* moving up or down depending on supply and demand forces. Here are the exchange rates between dollars and some selected currencies in several recent years.[8]

| | Units of Foreign Currency Required to Buy One U.S. Dollar | | | |
	May 1988	July 1986	April 1985	April 1984
British pound	0.54	0.66	0.81	0.71
Canadian dollar	1.24	1.36	1.37	1.28
Japanese yen	124.52	159.98	250.25	225.65
French franc	5.75	6.97	9.41	8.25
West German mark	1.70	2.17	3.10	2.68

From 1984 to 1985, the dollar *strengthened,* or *appreciated,* against other currencies — it took more of those currencies to buy a dollar in 1985 than it had in 1984. However, from 1985 to 1986, the dollar *weakened,* or *depreciated* — it took fewer yen, francs, and so forth to buy a dollar. The dollar weakened further from 1986 to 1988.

We have already seen the implications of changing exchange rates; the weaker dollar in 1988 vis-à-vis 1986 hurt Japanese (and other) manufacturers because it raised the price of Japanese goods in the United States. Conversely, U.S. firms were helped, because U.S. goods became more competitive in world markets. As a corollary, employment rose in the United States, but it fell in Japan and other countries whose currency values rose. Note, though, that the situation from 1984 to 1985 was just the reverse — exchange rate changes hurt U.S. industry and helped foreign firms.

---

[8]Typically, the British pound and Canadian dollar are quoted as U.S. dollars required to buy one unit of the foreign currency. Thus, in May 1988 the pound quote would have been 1/0.54 = 1.85 and the Canadian dollar quote would have been 1/1.24 = 0.81. We do not know why this convention exists, but it does.

The preceding discussion focused on the effects of exchange rates on exports and imports between countries, and hence on economic conditions within countries. Exchange rate fluctuations also make financial forecasting and planning difficult. Therefore, many people would like to see the world return to a fixed exchange rate system. However, that probably cannot be done. To understand why, recognize first that exchange rates are simply prices — the price of $1 to a Japanese importer is 125 yen, whereas to a Canadian merchant the price of a U.S. dollar is $1.24 Canadian. Like other prices, exchange rates move up and down in response to changes in supply and demand. Suppose, for illustrative purposes, that the United States traded only with Japan. U.S. importers would order Japanese goods, and they would have to make payment for these goods in yen. Thus, U.S. importers would receive Japanese goods, sell them and receive dollars, and then take those dollars and buy yen in the foreign exchange market to pay the Japanese exporters. If the Japanese were simultaneously buying U.S. goods, Japanese merchants would need U.S. dollars, so they would be buying dollars with yen.

Now suppose U.S. importers want to buy $20 billion of Japanese goods, but Japanese importers want to buy only $10 billion of U.S. goods. There will be a demand for $20 billion of yen but a supply of only $10 billion of yen. The supply of dollars in the foreign exchange market will exceed the demand for dollars, whereas the reverse will be true for the yen. Therefore, the price of the dollar will fall, and the price of the yen will rise. If the initial exchange rate was 125 yen per $1, the dollar might depreciate to a rate of 100 yen per dollar. This change would make U.S. goods less expensive in Japan and Japanese goods more expensive in the United States, and that, in turn, would alter the balance of trade from the $20 billion imports versus $10 billion exports level. Eventually, an equilibrium would be established, with imports equalling exports, but only a freely working floating exchange rate system can bring about an equilibrium.

This discussion has only touched the surface of exchange rates. They are also affected by relative inflation rates in different countries, by capital movements among nations (that is, by net borrowing by the citizens of one nation from those of another), by central bank intervention, and so on. Given the importance of exchange rates — indeed, of international operations generally — business students would be well advised to learn more about international financial systems.

SUMMARY AND KEY CONCEPTS

This chapter described in broad outline how firms project their financial statements and determine their capital requirements. The key concepts covered are listed below.

- Management establishes a **target balance sheet** on the basis of ratio analysis.

- **Financial forecasting** generally begins with a forecast of the firm's sales, in terms of both units and dollars, for some future time period.

- **Pro forma**, or **projected**, **financial statements** are developed to determine the firm's financial requirements.

- The **percentage of sales method** of forecasting financial statements is based on the assumptions (1) that most balance sheet accounts vary directly with sales and (2) that the firm's existing level of assets is optimum for its sales volume.

- A firm can determine the amount of **additional funds needed (AFN)** by estimating the amount of new assets necessary to support the forecasted level of sales and then subtracting from that amount the spontaneous funds that will be generated from operations. The firm can then plan to raise the AFN through bank borrowing, by issuing securities, or both.

- The **higher a firm's sales growth rate**, the **greater** will be its need for external financing. Similarly, the **larger a firm's dividend payout ratio**, the **greater** its need for external funds.

- The percentage of sales method cannot be used if **economies of scale** exist in the use of assets, if **excess capacity** exists, or if some assets must be added in "**lumpy**" **increments**.

- **Linear regression** and **specific item forecasting techniques** can be used to forecast asset requirements in situations in which the percentage of sales method is not appropriate.

- Financial forecasting is especially difficult for multinational firms, because **exchange rate fluctuations** make it difficult to estimate the dollars that overseas operations will produce.

The type of forecasting described in this chapter is important for several reasons. First, if the projected operating results are unsatisfactory, management can "go back to the drawing board," reformulate its plans, and develop more reasonable targets for the coming year. Second, it is possible that the funds required to meet the sales forecast simply cannot be obtained; if so, it is obviously better to know this in advance and to scale back the projected level of operations than to suddenly run out of cash and have operations grind to a halt. Third, even if the required funds can be raised, it is desirable to plan for their acquisition well in advance. As we shall see in later chapters, raising capital takes time, and both time and money can be saved by careful forward planning.

Questions

8-1   Certain liability and net worth items generally increase spontaneously with increases in sales. Put a check ($\checkmark$) by those items that typically increase spontaneously:

Accounts payable   _____
Notes payable to banks   _____
Accrued wages   _____
Accrued taxes   _____
Mortgage bonds   _____
Common stock   _____
Retained earnings   _____
Marketable securities   _____

8-2   The following equation can, under certain assumptions, be used to forecast financial requirements:

$$\text{AFN} = (A/S)(\Delta S) - (L/S)(\Delta S) - MS_1(1 - d).$$

Under what conditions does the equation give satisfactory predictions, and when should it not be used?

8-3   Assume that an average firm in the office supply business has a 6 percent after-tax profit margin, a 40 percent debt/assets ratio, a total assets turnover of 2 times, and a dividend payout ratio of 40 percent. Is it true that if such a firm is to have *any* sales growth (g > 0), it will be forced to borrow or to sell common stock (that is, it will need some nonspontaneous, external capital even if g is very small)?

8-4   Is it true that computerized corporate planning models were a fad during the 1970s but, because of a need for flexibility in corporate planning, they have been dropped by most firms?

8-5   Suppose a firm makes the following policy changes. If the change means that external, nonspontaneous financial requirements for any rate of sales growth will increase, indicate this by a (+); indicate a decrease by a (−); and indicate indeterminate or no effect by a (0). Think in terms of the immediate, short-run effect on funds requirements.
   a. The dividend payout ratio is increased.   _____
   b. The firm contracts to buy rather than make certain
       components used in its products.   _____
   c. The firm decides to pay all suppliers on delivery, rather
       than after a 30-day delay, to take advantage of discounts
       for rapid payment.   _____
   d. The firm begins to sell on credit (previously all sales
       had been on a cash basis).   _____
   e. The firm's profit margin is eroded by increased
       competition; sales are steady.   _____
   f. Advertising expenditures are stepped up.   _____
   g. A decision is made to substitute long-term mortgage
       bonds for short-term bank loans.   _____
   h. The firm begins to pay employees on a weekly basis
       (previously it had paid at the end of each month).   _____

Self-Test Problems   *(Solutions Appear on Page 333)*

Key terms

ST-1   Define each of the following terms:
   a. Sales forecast
   b. Percentage of sales method
   c. Spontaneously generated funds
   d. Dividend payout ratio; retention rate
   e. Pro forma financial statement
   f. Additional funds needed (AFN)
   g. Capital intensity ratio
   h. "Lumpy" assets
   i. Exchange rates

Growth rate

ST-2   K. Billingsworth and Company has the following ratios: A/S = 1.6; L/S = 0.4; profit margin = 0.10; and dividend payout ratio = 0.45, or 45 percent. Sales last year were $100 million. Assuming that these ratios will remain constant and that all liabilities increase spontaneously with increases in sales, what is the maximum growth rate Billingsworth can achieve without having to employ nonspontaneous external funds?

External funds needed **ST-3** Suppose Billingsworth's financial consultants report (1) that the inventory turnover ratio is sales/inventory = 3 times, versus an industry average of 4 times, and (2) that Billingsworth could reduce inventories and thus raise its turnover to 4 without affecting sales, the profit margin, or the other asset turnover ratios. Under these conditions, what amount of external funds would Billingsworth require during each of the next 2 years if sales grew at a rate of 20 percent per year?

Problems

Pro forma balance sheet **8-1** A group of investors is planning to set up a new company, The Running Shoe, Ltd., to manufacture and distribute a novel type of running shoe. To help determine the new company's financial requirements, Barry Morris, the president, has asked you to construct a pro forma balance sheet for December 31, 1989, the end of the first year of operations, and to estimate Running Shoe's external financing requirements for 1989. Sales for 1989 are projected at $10 million, and the following are industry average ratios for athletic shoe companies:

Sales to common equity	5×
Current debt to equity	50%
Total debt to equity	80%
Current ratio	2.2×
Net sales to inventory	9×
Accounts receivable to sales	10%
Fixed assets to equity	70%
Profit margin	3%
Dividend payout ratio	30%

a. Complete the pro forma balance sheet that follows, assuming that 1989 sales are $10 million and that the firm maintains industry average ratios.

The Running Shoe, Ltd.:
Pro Forma Balance Sheet
December 31, 1989
(Millions of Dollars)

Cash	$	Current debt	$
Accounts receivable		Long-term debt	
Inventories	_____	Total debt	
Total current assets			
Fixed assets	_____	Equity	_____
Total assets	$_____	Total liabilities and equity	$_____

b. If the investor group supplies all the equity, how much capital (exclusive of retained earnings) will it be required to put up during 1989?

Long-term financing needed

8-2   At year-end 1988, total assets for Shipley, Inc., were $4.8 million. Sales, which in 1988 were $10 million, are expected to increase by 25 percent in 1989. The 1988 ratio of assets to sales will be maintained in 1989. Accounts payable were 15 percent of sales in 1988, and this ratio will be maintained in 1989. Common stock amounted to $1,700,000 in 1988, and retained earnings were $1,180,000. Shipley plans to sell new common stock in the amount of $300,000. Net income after taxes is expected to be 6 percent of sales; 50 percent of earnings will be paid out as dividends. If Shipley has no current liabilities other than accounts payable, (a) what was Shipley's total debt in 1988, and (b) how much new, long-term debt financing will be needed in 1989? (Hint: AFN − New stock = New long-term debt.)

Pro forma statements and ratios

8-3   Cordell Computers makes bulk purchases of small computers, stocks them in conveniently located warehouses, and ships them to its chain of retail stores. Cordell's balance sheet as of December 31, 1988, is shown here (millions of dollars):

Cash	$ 3.5	Accounts payable	$ 9.0
Receivables	26.0	Notes payable	17.5
Inventories	58.0	Accruals	9.0
Total current assets	$ 87.5	Total current liabilities	$ 35.5
Net fixed assets	35.0	Mortgage loan	6.0
		Common stock	15.0
		Retained earnings	66.0
Total assets	$122.5	Total liabilities and equity	$122.5

Sales for 1988 were $350 million, while net income after taxes for the year was $10.5 million. Cordell paid dividends of $4.2 million to common stockholders. The firm is operating at full capacity.

a. If sales are projected to increase by $70 million, or 20 percent, during 1989, what are Cordell's projected external capital requirements?

b. Construct Cordell's pro forma balance sheet for December 31, 1989. Assume that all external capital requirements are met by bank loans and are reflected in notes payable.

c. Now calculate the following ratios, based on your projected December 31, 1989, balance sheet. Cordell's 1988 ratios and industry average ratios are shown here for comparison:

	Cordell Computers		Industry Average
	12/31/89	12/31/88	12/31/88
Current ratio	————	2.5×	3×
Debt/total assets	————	33.3%	30%
Rate of return on equity	————	12.1%	12%

d. Now assume that Cordell grows by the same $70 million but that the growth is spread over 5 years — that is, that sales grow by $14 million each year.

1. Calculate total additional financial requirements over the 5-year period. (Hint: Use 1988 ratios, $\Delta S = 70$, but *total* sales for the 5-year period.)

2. Construct a pro forma balance sheet as of December 31, 1993, using notes payable as the balancing item.
3. Calculate the current ratio, debt/assets ratio, and rate of return on net worth as of December 31, 1993. [Hint: Be sure to use *total sales*, which amount to $1,960 million, to calculate retained earnings but use 1993 profits to calculate the rate of return on equity — that is, return on equity = (1993 profits)/(12/31/93 equity).]

e. Do the plans outlined in Parts c and d seem feasible to you? In other words, do you think Cordell could borrow the required capital, and would the company be raising the odds on its bankruptcy to an excessive level in the event of some temporary misfortune?

Additional funds needed   8-4   Houston Textile's 1988 sales were $48 million. The percentage of sales of each balance sheet item that varies directly with sales is as follows:

Cash	3%
Receivables	20
Inventories	25
Net fixed assets	40
Accounts payable	15
Accruals	10

The dividend payout ratio is 40 percent; the profit margin is 5 percent; the December 31, 1987, balance sheet account for retained earnings was $16.4 million; and both common stock and mortgage bonds are constant and equal to the amounts shown on the balance sheet that follows.

a. Complete the following balance sheet as of December 31, 1988:

Houston Textile:
Balance Sheet as of
December 31, 1988
(Thousands of Dollars)

Cash	$	Accounts payable	$
Receivables		Notes payable	4,400
Inventories	_____	Accruals	_____
Total current assets		Total current liabilities	
Net fixed assets		Mortgage bonds	4,000
		Common stock	4,000
		Retained earnings	_____
Total assets	$_____	Total liabilities and equity	$_____

b. Now suppose 1989 sales are projected to increase by 10 percent over 1988 sales. Determine the additional funds needed. Assume that the company was operating at full capacity in 1988, that it cannot sell off any of its fixed assets, and that any required financing will be borrowed as notes payable. Use Equation 8-1 to answer this question.
c. Develop a pro forma balance sheet for December 31, 1989. Assume that any required financing is borrowed as notes payable. Note that 12/31/88 retained earnings are $17,840,000.

Excess capacity   **8-5**   Weiss Lumber's 1988 sales were $72 million. The percentage of sales of each balance sheet item except notes payable, mortgage bonds, and common stock is given here:

Cash	4%
Receivables	25
Inventories	30
Net fixed assets	50
Accounts payable	15
Accruals	5
Profit margin (after taxes) on sales	5

The dividend payout ratio is 60 percent; the December 31, 1987, balance sheet account for retained earnings was $41.8 million; and both common stock and mortgage bonds are constant and equal to the amounts shown on the balance sheet that follows.

a. Complete the following balance sheet.

Weiss Lumber:
Balance Sheet as of
December 31, 1988
(Thousands of Dollars)

Cash	$	Accounts payable	$
Receivables		Notes payable	6,840
Inventories	———	Accruals	———
Total current assets		Total current liabilities	
Net fixed assets		Mortgage bonds	10,000
		Common stock	4,000
	———	Retained earnings	———
Total assets	$ ═══	Total liabilities and equity	$ ═══

b. Assume that the company was operating at full capacity in 1988 with regard to all items *except* fixed assets; had the fixed assets been used to full capacity, the fixed assets/sales ratio would have been 40 percent in 1988. By what percentage could 1989 sales increase over 1988 sales without the need for an increase in fixed assets?

c. Now suppose that 1989 sales increase by 20 percent over 1988 sales. How much additional external capital will be required? Assume that Weiss Lumber cannot sell any fixed assets. (Hint: Equation 8-1 can no longer be used. You must develop a pro forma balance sheet as in Table 8-2.) Assume that any required financing is borrowed as notes payable. (Another hint: Notes payable = $10,728.)

d. Suppose that industry averages for receivables and inventories are 20 percent and 25 percent, respectively, and that Weiss Lumber matches these figures in 1989 and then uses the funds released to reduce equity. (It could pay a special dividend out of retained earnings.) What would this do to the rate of return on year-end 1989 equity?

Additional funds needed   8-6   The 1988 sales of Koehlman Technologies, Inc., were $3 million. The dividend payout ratio is 50 percent. Retained earnings as shown on the December 31, 1987, balance sheet were $105,000. The percentage of sales in each balance sheet item that varies directly with sales is expected to be as follows:

Cash	4%
Receivables	10
Inventories	20
Net fixed assets	35
Accounts payable	12
Accruals	6
Profit margin (after taxes) on sales	3

a. Complete the balance sheet that follows, assuming that common stock and notes payable did not change during 1988.
b. Suppose that in 1989, sales will increase by 10 percent over 1988 sales. How much additional capital will be required? Assume the firm operated at full capacity in 1988.
c. Construct the year-end 1989 balance sheet. Assume 50 percent of the additional capital required will be financed by selling common stock and the remainder by borrowing as notes payable.
d. If the profit margin after taxes remains at 3 percent and the dividend payout rate remains at 50 percent, at what growth rate in sales will the additional financing requirements be exactly zero? (Hint: Set AFN equal to zero and solve for g.)

Koehlman Technologies, Inc.:
Balance Sheet as of December 31, 1988

Cash	$	Accounts payable	$
Receivables		Notes payable	130,000
Inventories	_____	Accruals	_____
Total current assets		Total current liabilities	
Fixed assets		Common stock	1,250,000
		Retained earnings	_____
Total assets	$_____	Total liabilities and equity	$_____

External financing   8-7   The 1988 balance sheet for the Sorrell Company follows. Sales in 1988
requirements   totaled $7 million. The ratio of net profits to sales was 3 percent, while the dividend payout ratio was 60 percent of net income.
a. The firm operated at full capacity in 1988. It expects sales to increase by 20 percent during 1989. Use the percentage of sales method to determine how much outside financing is required, then develop the firm's pro forma balance sheet using AFN as the balancing item.
b. If the firm must maintain a current ratio of 2.5 and a debt ratio of 40 percent, how much financing will be obtained using notes payable, long-term debt, and common stock?

Sorrell Company:
Balance Sheet as of
December 31, 1988
(Thousands of Dollars)

Assets		Liabilities	
Cash	$ 105	Accounts payable	$ 70
Accounts receivable	245	Accruals	35
Inventory	525	Notes payable	245
Total current assets	$ 875	Total current liabilities	$ 350
Fixed assets	2,625	Long-term debt	1,050
		Total debt	$1,400
		Common stock	1,225
		Retained earnings	875
Total assets	$3,500	Total liabilities and equity	$3,500

Financial forecasting
(Integrative)

8-8

Dan Edwards, financial manager of Watson Laboratories, is currently working on his firm's financial forecast for the coming year. Watson's balance sheet for last year is as follows (in thousands of dollars):

Cash	$ 450	Accounts payable	$ 300
Receivables	750	Accruals	150
Inventory	1,500	Notes payable	375
Current assets	$2,700	Current liabilities	$ 825
Net fixed assets	6,000	Long-term debt	3,600
		Total debt	$4,425
		Common stock	3,000
		Retained earnings	1,275
Total assets	$8,700	Total liabilities and equity	$8,700

Watson was operating at full capacity last year and had sales of $15 million. Watson's marketing department is forecasting a 20 percent sales increase for the coming year. Further, the firm has had a profit margin of 5 percent and a 60 percent payout ratio over the last several years, and these values are expected to continue in the near term. In preparing his forecast, Edwards proceeds by answering the following questions and completing the indicated tasks:

a. Use the percentage of sales method to prepare the coming year's pro forma balance sheet. What is the external funds requirement? What assumptions are necessary to use the percentage of sales approach?

b. For planning purposes, Edwards assumes that the additional funds needed will be raised as 10 percent short-term debt (notes payable), 40 percent long-term debt, and 50 percent common stock. What dollar amounts are needed to cover Watson's forecasted deficiency? Recast the pro forma balance sheet to reflect the additional financing.

c. A simple forecasting formula can be used to estimate additional funds needed (AFN) when the percentage of sales method is used. Use this formula to forecast Watson's funds requirements.

d. Use the forecasting formula to estimate Watson's additional funds needed at sales growth rates of 10 percent and 30 percent. Repeat the analysis assuming zero sales growth. What effect does sales growth have on funds requirements?

e. What is the maximum sales growth rate Watson can achieve without using outside financing? (Hint: Use the forecasting formula and set AFN = $0.)

f. What effects do a firm's dividend policy, profitability, and capital intensity have on its external financing requirements?

g. Now assume that Watson is operating at only 80 percent of capacity with regard to fixed assets. (1) What is the firm's additional financing requirement in this situation, assuming that sales are forecasted to increase to $18 million? (2) What would it be if Watson were operating at 90 percent of capacity?

Computer-Related Problems

(Work the problems in this section only if you are using the computer problem diskette.)

Forecasting

C8-1   Use the model for Problem C8-1 in the file C8 to solve this problem.

The 1988 sales of Pettijohn Industries, Inc., were $100 million. The percentage of sales of each balance sheet item except for long-term debt and common stock (which do not vary directly with sales) is as follows:

Cash	5%
Receivables	15
Inventories	25
Net fixed assets	50
Accounts payable	10

The dividend payout ratio is 40 percent, and the profit margin is 5 percent. Long-term debt at December 31, 1988, was $20 million; notes payable were $5 million; common stock was $25 million; and the balance sheet amount for retained earnings was $35 million. Projected annual sales growth for the next 5 years is 20 percent.

a. Pettijohn plans to finance its additional funds needed with 50 percent short-term debt and 50 percent long-term debt. Prepare the 1988 balance sheet, as well as pro forma balance sheets for 1989 through 1993, and then determine (1) additional funds needed, (2) the current ratio, (3) the debt ratio, and (4) the return on equity.

b. Sales growth could be 5 percentage points above or below the projected 20 percent. Determine the effect of such variances on AFN and the key ratios.

c. Perform an analysis to determine the sensitivity of AFN and the key ratios for 1993 to changes in the profit margin and the dividend payout ratio as specified below, assuming sales grow at a constant 20 percent:

1. Profit margin (a) rises from 5 to 6 percent or (b) falls from 5 to 4 percent.

2. With the profit margin at 5 percent, the dividend payout ratio (a) is raised from 40 to 70 percent or (b) is lowered from 40 to 20 percent.

External financing
requirements

C8-2   Use the model for Problem C8-2 in the file C8 to solve this problem.

a. Refer back to Problem 8-7. Suppose that the Sorrell Company expects sales to increase by 40 percent during 1989 and that its current ratio must be at least 2.5 but its debt ratio could be as high as 50 percent. Under this situation, how much external financing would the firm require and how would those funds be obtained?

b. What is the maximum rate of sales growth the firm could sustain without having to sell common stock, given the debt constraints in Part a?

Pro forma balance sheet   **C8-3**   Use the model for Problem C8-3 in the file C8 to solve this problem.

Erie Steel Company is a wholesale steel distributor which purchases steel in carload lots and sells to several thousand steel users. The nature of the steel business requires that the company maintain large inventories to take care of customer requirements in the event of mill strikes or other delays.

In examining records from 1982 to 1987, the company found consistent relationships among the following accounts as a percent of sales:

Current assets	60%
Net fixed assets	30
Accounts payable	5
Other current liabilities	5
Profit margin	3

The company's sales for 1988 were $15 million, and its balance sheet on December 31, 1988, follows. The company expects sales to grow by $2 million per year over the next 5 years. The company wants to project its financial requirements for each of the next 5 years, assuming that the projected sales levels are achieved. Assume further that the company pays out 40 percent of earnings as dividends.

a. Construct pro forma balance sheets for the end of each of the next 5 years, assuming that 25 percent of external financing requirements are met by increasing notes payable, 25 percent by issuing long-term debt, and 50 percent by selling new common stock.

b. What was the critical assumption you made in your projection?

Erie Steel Company:
Balance Sheet as of
December 31, 1988
(Thousands of Dollars)

Assets			Liabilities	
Current assets	$ 9,000		Accounts payable	$ 750
Fixed assets	4,500		Notes payable	2,000
			Other current liabilities	750
			Total current liabilities	$ 3,500
			Long-term debt	1,500
			Common stock	2,750
			Retained earnings	5,750
Total assets	$13,500		Total liabilities and equity	$13,500

Solutions to Self-Test Problems

ST-1   Refer to the marginal glossary definitions to check your responses.

ST-2   To solve this problem, we will define ΔS as the change in sales and g as the growth rate in sales. We then use the three following equations:

$$\Delta S = gS_0.$$

$$S_1 = S_0(1 + g).$$

$$AFN = (A/S)(\Delta S) - (L/S)(\Delta S) - MS_1(1 - d).$$

Set AFN = 0, substitute in known values for A/S, L/S, M, d, and S_0, and then solve for g:

$$0 = 1.6(\$100g) - 0.4(\$100g) - 0.10[\$100(1 + g)](0.55)$$

$$= \$160g - \$40g - 0.055(\$100 + \$100g)$$

$$= \$160g - \$40g - \$5.5 - \$5.5g$$

$$\$114.5g = \$5.5$$

$$g = \$5.5/\$114.5 = 0.048 = 4.8\%$$

$$= \text{Maximum growth rate without external financing.}$$

ST-3   Assets consist of cash, marketable securities, receivables, inventories, and fixed assets. Therefore, we can break the A/S ratio into its components — cash/sales, inventories/sales, and so forth. Then,

$$\frac{A}{S} = \frac{A - \text{Inventories}}{S} + \frac{\text{Inventories}}{S} = 1.6.$$

We know that the inventory turnover ratio is sales/inventories = 3 times, so inventories/sales = 1/3 = 0.3333. Further, if the inventory turnover ratio can be increased to 4 times, then the inventory/sales ratio will fall to 1/4 = 0.25, a difference of 0.3333 − 0.2500 = 0.0833. This, in turn, causes the A/S ratio to fall from A/S = 1.6 to A/S = 1.6 − 0.0833 = 1.5167.

This change has two effects: first, it changes the AFN equation, and second, it means that Billingsworth currently has excessive inventories. Because it is costly to hold excess inventories, Billingsworth will want to reduce its inventory holdings by not replacing inventories until the excess amounts have been used. We can account for this by setting up the revised AFN equation (using the new A/S ratio), estimating the funds that will be needed next year if no excess inventories are currently on hand, and then subtracting out the excess inventories which are currently on hand:

Present conditions:

$$\frac{\text{Sales}}{\text{Inventories}} = \frac{\$100}{\text{Inventories}} = 3,$$

so

$$\text{Inventories} = \$100/3 = \$33.3 \text{ million at present.}$$

New Conditions:

$$\frac{\text{Sales}}{\text{Inventories}} = \frac{\$100}{\text{Inventories}} = 4,$$

so

New level of inventories = $100/4 = $25 million.

Therefore,

Excess inventories = $33.3 − 25 = $8.3 million.

Forecast of Funds Needed, First Year:

ΔS in first year = 0.2($100 million) = $20 million.

$\text{AFN} = 1.5167(\$20) - 0.4(\$20) - 0.1(0.55)(\$120) - \$8.3$

$\qquad = \$30.3 - \$8 - \$6.6 - \$8.3$

$\qquad = \$7.4$ million.

Forecast of Funds Needed, Second Year:

ΔS in second year = gS_1 = 0.2($120 million) = $24 million.

$\text{AFN} = 1.5167(\$24) - 0.4(\$24) - 0.1(0.55)(\$144)$

$\qquad = \$36.4 - \$9.6 - \$7.9$

$\qquad = \$18.9$ million.

8A   Microcomputers and Financial Forecasting

In Chapter 8 we presented a method of forecasting financial requirements, the percentage of sales method, which required only paper, pencil, and a calculator. Although this simple procedure is helpful for understanding the basics of financial forecasting, pencil and paper computations are no longer used in the forecasting process by corporations — virtually all corporate forecasts are made with the aid of computerized forecasting models. Such models vary greatly in complexity, ranging from simple electronic spreadsheet models that can be run on personal computers to complex models that require mainframe computers. In this appendix, we discuss computerized forecasting models in general, and we illustrate the use of an electronic spreadsheet model which forecasts earnings and calculates key financial ratios for the Telecomp Corporation.

Computerized Forecasting Models

The simplest computerized financial models are based on electronic spreadsheets. The user inputs historical data and formulas, which the computer then processes to calculate key relationships between sales and both income statement and balance sheet items. Projected future sales levels or sales growth rates are also fed in, and the computer then performs essentially the same calculations as the forecaster would have done using a calculator.

Electronic spreadsheet models have two major advantages over pencil and paper calculations. First, it is much faster to construct a spreadsheet model than to make a "by hand" forecast if the forecast period extends beyond two or three years, and, second, the spreadsheet model instantaneously recomputes all forecasts if one of the input variables is changed, thus permitting the user to analyze the sensitivity of the model's output to input changes.

Electronic spreadsheets, which are run on personal computers, are simply computer programs which (1) set up an electronic matrix as a series of rows and columns (that is, like a sheet of accounting paper) and then (2) do arithmetic on the rows and columns automatically. For example, Column 1 can be set up as last year's balance sheet, and Columns 2, 3, and so forth can be used for the balance sheets for Years 1, 2, and so forth, with each account programmed to increase at a specified rate. A lower section of the spreadsheet can be designated as a corresponding series of projected income statements, and a still lower section can be used to calculate the projected ratios for each year. By far the most popular spreadsheet is *Lotus 1-2-3*.[1]

Even small firms, such as retail stores and auto repair shops, are finding that they simply cannot compete effectively if they do not use computers for planning and control purposes. Indeed, now that hardware and software costs have fallen so drastically, most businesses larger than shoeshine stands can use computers in a cost-effective way — and competing in business without a computer is almost like competing on a finance exam without a calculator. Thus, our advice is this: If you want to be a success (or even a non-failure) in the business world, learn something about computers!

---

[1]Various surveys indicate that *Lotus 1-2-3* has between 80 and 90 percent of the spreadsheet market. We have also found, in our consulting and other work with businesses, that we can *always* exchange data and models set up with *1-2-3*, and recruiters tell us that *1-2-3* is the spreadsheet that they would prefer students to know. Finally, *1-2-3* is, in a fundamental sense, the "grandfather" of spreadsheets, so if someone knows how to use it, he or she can learn to use others in short order should the occasion arise. For all these reasons, we decided to concentrate on *1-2-3* in this book and the ancillaries we developed for it.

Spreadsheet models can do many different types of things, such as (1) setting up schedules for paying off mortgages (amortization schedules), (2) figuring taxes, (3) managing security portfolios, (4) analyzing proposed capital budgeting projects, (5) analyzing bond refunding decisions, (6) analyzing lease proposals, (7) analyzing alternative capital structures for a firm, and an almost limitless list of other applications. Because of the power of these models and the ease with which one can learn to use them, most business schools now require students to learn how to use software packages rather than how to program in FORTRAN, BASIC, or other languages.

A Simplified Financial Forecasting Model

We can best demonstrate the usefulness of financial forecasting systems by discussing one such model. In Table 8A-1 we show a simplified electronic spreadsheet model, based on *Lotus 1-2-3*, which we used to make a six-year financial forecast for Telecomp Corporation. The model was constructed under the following assumptions: (1) sales and assets will grow at 20 percent a year; (2) the additional funds requirement will be met by using debt; (3) fixed costs will grow at 10 percent a year; (4) variable costs, including interest, will grow at 22 percent a year (variable costs will grow at a faster rate than sales because in this particular case the firm's debt level, hence interest, will increase at a faster rate than sales); (5) both the dividend payout ratio and the common stock account will remain constant. The model calculates net income, additions to retained earnings, and the forecasted level of assets, and it then solves for the level of debt needed to finance those assets. The model also computes the company's key financial ratios.

The *Lotus 1-2-3* spreadsheet designates columns as A, B, C, . . . and rows as 1, 2, 3, . . . , and each cell in the matrix has a designation, such as A1, A2, B1, B2, and so forth. Thus, in Table 8A-1, the years are in Row 1; sales are in Row 2; fixed costs are in Row 3; and so forth. Column A provides the row labels; Column B shows the formulas used in the model; and Columns C through H give data for the different years. Thus, Cell C3 gives the 1988 value for fixed costs (FC), Cell C4 gives the 1988 value for variable costs (VC), and so on. The 1989 value for sales is the 1988 value increased by 20 percent, and the electronic spreadsheet automatically computes this using the formula C2*1.2, repeated for 1989 through 1993. Similarly, fixed costs, variable costs, and assets are increased each year. The remainder of the income statement and balance sheet items are calculated, and the ratios are then developed.

We can see from Table 8A-1, Rows 15, 16, and 17, that as Telecomp's sales grow, its profit margin, ROE, and ROA also increase. This result occurs in part because a larger percentage of assets is being financed by debt than by equity. In fact, Row 18 shows that from 1988 until 1993, the firm's debt ratio is projected to increase from 43 percent of assets to 59 percent.

The model allows us to examine the trends in the firm's profitability and debt ratios; however, it does not show us what is happening to the firm's liquidity and activity ratios. It would be easy enough to provide more detail regarding projected income statement and balance sheet items, and this might show us that Telecomp's current ratio was weak, that the firm was holding excess stocks of inventory, or what have you. We could also build in constraints, such as requirements that the debt ratio not exceed 50 percent and that the current ratio be maintained at 2.0 times or higher.

It is extremely easy to change the assumptions built into computer models to see the results under alternative scenarios. For example, if we wanted to see what would happen if sales grew at a rate of 10 percent rather than 20 percent, we would simply move the cursor to Cell B2, delete the "2" and replace it with a "1" (leaving the cell +C2*1.1), and the computer would immediately and automatically recalculate everything and produce a new Table 8A-1. Similar changes could be made with the profit margin, the tax rate, and so on. This type of analysis is called "sensitivity" or "what if" analysis — "What if the sales growth rate drops 10 percent or the profit margin increases to 5 percent? How sensitive are the results to such a change?" Being able to answer this type of question is extremely useful in all forms of financial planning.

Table 8A-1   Simplified Forecasting Model for the Telecomp Corporation

(A)	(B)	(C)	(D)	(E)	(F)	(G)	(H)
1 Year		1988	1989	1990	1991	1992	1993
2 Sales	+C2*1.2	500	600	720	864	1037	1244
3 FC	+C3*1.1	175	193	212	233	256	282
4 VC	+C4*1.22	288	351	429	523	638	778
5 EBT	+C2−C3−C4	37	56	80	108	143	184
6 Tax (46%)	+C5*.46	17	26	37	50	66	85
7 Net income	+C5−C6	20	30	43	58	77	99
8 Dividend payout	+C8	.5	.5	.5	.5	.5	.5
9 Dividends	+C7*C8	10	15	21	29	38	50
10 Addition to RE	+C7−C9	10	15	21	29	38	50
11 Assets	+C11*1.2	345	414	497	596	715	858
12 Debt	+C11−C13−C14	147	201	262	332	413	506
13 Common stock	+C13	150	150	150	150	150	150
14 RE	+C14+D10	48	63	85	114	152	202
15 Profit margin	+C7/C2	0.04	0.05	0.06	0.07	0.07	0.08
16 ROE	+C7/(C13 + C14)	0.10	0.14	0.18	0.22	0.25	0.28
17 ROA	+C7/C11	0.06	0.07	0.09	0.10	0.11	0.12
18 D/A	+C12/C11	0.43	0.49	0.53	0.56	0.58	0.59

Note: The formulas in Column B would not normally appear on the printout of an actual *Lotus 1-2-3* model; they are presented here to show the relationships among items in the income statements and balance sheets from one year to the next year.

We have illustrated computer modeling with a simple financial forecast. It should be noted that computerized models are used to analyze many of the financial decisions covered in this book, including cash budgeting, capital budgeting, capital structure analysis, lease analysis, and bond refunding decisions.[2]

Finally, most chapters of this book have problems designated "computer-related problems." You can get a diskette from your instructor which contains *Lotus 1-2-3* models for each of these computer problems. You can work through them fairly rapidly and, in the process, gain a good understanding of just how useful computer models can be in dealing with many of the issues addressed in this book.

---

[2]Illustrations of such models are provided in Brigham, Aberwald, and Ball, *Finance with Lotus 1-2-3: Text, Cases, and Models* (Hinsdale, Ill.: Dryden, 1988).

III Strategic Long-Term Investment Decisions

9

The Basics of Capital Budgeting

LOCKHEED'S TRI-STAR PROJECT: FLAWED CAPITAL BUDGETING ANALYSIS LEADS TO FAILURE

Businesses invest hundreds of billions of dollars in fixed assets each year. By their very nature, such investments affect a firm's fortunes for many years. A good decision can boost earnings sharply and increase the price of a firm's stock. A bad decision can lead to bankruptcy.

A classic example of a bad capital budgeting decision which could easily have been avoided involved Lockheed's production of the L-1011 Tri-Star commercial aircraft. When Lockheed made the final decision to go forward with Tri-Star production, it estimated the breakeven volume at about 200 planes. The company had orders for about 180 planes, and it was sure of getting at least 20 more orders. Consequently, it decided to commit $1 billion and to commence production.

However, Lockheed's analysis was flawed; it failed to account for the cost of the capital tied up in the project. Had its analysts appraised the project correctly, they would have found that the breakeven point was far above 200 planes — so far above that the Tri-Star program was almost certainly doomed to fail. This mistake contributed to a decline in Lockheed's stock price from $73 per share to $3. Had Lockheed's managers read Chapter 9 and heeded its advice, at least some of that loss might have been avoided.

capital budgeting
The process of planning expenditures on assets whose returns are expected to extend beyond one year.

IN previous chapters we have seen how investors value corporate securities and how investors determine required rates of return. Now we turn to investment decisions involving fixed assets, called *capital budgeting*. The term *capital* refers to fixed assets used in production, whereas a *budget* is a plan which details projected inflows and outflows during some future period. Thus, the *capital budget* outlines the planned expenditures on fixed assets, and **capital budgeting** is the whole process of analyzing projects and deciding whether they should be included in the capital budget. This process is of fundamental importance to the success or failure of the firm, for its capital budgeting decisions, more than anything else, determine its future.

Our treatment of capital budgeting is divided into three parts. First, Chapter 9 gives an overview and explains the basic techniques used in capital budgeting analysis. Then, in Chapter 10, we go on to consider how cash flows are estimated. Finally, in Chapter 11, we discuss how risk is brought into the analysis.

IMPORTANCE OF CAPITAL BUDGETING

A number of factors combine to make capital budgeting decisions perhaps the most important ones financial managers must make. First and foremost, since the results of capital budgeting decisions continue over an extended period, the decision maker loses some of his or her flexibility. For example, the purchase of an asset with an economic life of ten years requires a long waiting period before the final results of the action can be known. Further, because asset expansion is fundamentally related to expected future sales, a decision to buy a fixed asset that is expected to last 10 years involves an implicit 10-year sales forecast.

An erroneous forecast of asset requirements can have serious consequences. If the firm has invested too much in assets, it will incur unnecessarily heavy expenses. On the other hand, if it has not spent enough on fixed assets, two problems may arise. First, the firm's equipment may not be sufficiently modern to enable it to produce competitively. Second, if it has inadequate capacity, it may lose a portion of its share of the market to rival firms, and regaining lost customers typically requires heavy selling expenses, price reductions, and product improvements, all of which are costly.

Another aspect of capital budgeting is timing — capital assets must be ready to come "on line" at the time they are needed. Edward Ford, executive vice president of Western Design, a decorative tile company, gave the author an illustration of the importance of capital budgeting. His firm tried to operate near capacity most of the time. During a four-year period, Western experienced intermittent spurts in the demand for its product, which forced it to turn away orders. After these sharp increases in demand, the firm would add capacity by renting an additional building, then purchasing and installing the appropriate equipment. It would take six to eight months to get the additional capacity ready, but frequently by that time Western found that there was no demand for its increased output — other firms had already expanded their operations and had taken an increased share of the market. If Western had properly forecasted demand and had planned its increase in capacity six months to a year in advance, it would have been able to maintain or perhaps even increase its share of the market.

Effective capital budgeting will improve both the timing of asset acquisitions and the quality of assets purchased. A firm which forecasts its needs for capital assets in advance will have the opportunity to purchase and install the assets before its sales are at capacity. In practice, though, most firms do not order capital goods until they approach full capacity. If sales increase because of an increase in general market demand, all firms in the industry will tend to order capital goods at about the same time. This often results in backlogs, long waiting times for machinery, a deterioration in the quality of the capital goods, and an increase in their prices. The firm which foresees its needs and purchases capital assets early can avoid these problems. Note, though, that if a firm forecasts an increase in demand and expands capacity to meet the anticipated demand, and if sales then do not expand, it will be saddled with excess capacity and abnormally high costs. This can lead to losses or even bankruptcy. Thus, the sales forecast is critical.

Finally, capital budgeting is also important because asset expansion typically involves substantial expenditures, and before a firm spends a large amount of money, it must make the proper plans — large amounts of funds are not available automatically. A firm contemplating a major capital expenditure program may need to arrange its financing several years in advance to be sure of having the funds required for the expansion.

OBTAINING IDEAS FOR CAPITAL PROJECTS

The same general concepts are involved in both capital budgeting and security analysis. However, whereas a set of stocks and bonds exists in the securities market, and investors select from this set, *capital budgeting projects are created by the firm*. For example, a sales representative may report that customers are asking for a particular product that the company does not now produce. The sales manager then discusses the idea with the marketing research group to determine the size of the market for the proposed product. If it appears likely that a significant market does exist, cost accountants and engineers will be asked to estimate production costs. If it appears that the product can be produced and sold to yield a sufficient profit, the project will be undertaken.

A firm's growth and development, even its ability to remain competitive and to survive, depend upon a constant flow of ideas for new products and for ways to make existing products better, or to produce them at a lower cost. Accordingly, a well-managed firm will go to great lengths to develop good capital budgeting proposals. For example, the executive vice-president of one very successful corporation indicated that his company takes the following steps to generate projects:

> Our R&D department is constantly searching for new products and also for ways to improve existing products. In addition, our executive committee, which consists of senior executives in marketing, production, and finance, identifies the products and markets in which our company will compete, and the committee sets long-run targets for each division. These targets, which are formulated in the corporation's **strategic business plan,** provide a general guide to the operating executives who must meet them. These executives then seek new products, set expansion plans for existing products, and look for ways to reduce production and distribution costs. Since bonuses and promotions are based in large part on each unit's ability to meet or exceed its targets, these economic incentives encourage our operating executives to seek out profitable investment opportunities.
>
> While our senior executives are judged and rewarded on the basis of how well their units perform, people further down the line are given bonuses for specific suggestions, including ideas that lead to profitable investments. Additionally, a percentage of our corporate profit is set aside for distribution to nonexecutive employees. Our objective is to encourage employees at all levels to keep on the lookout for good ideas, including those that lead to capital investments.

strategic business plan
A long-run plan which outlines in broad terms the firm's basic strategy for the next 5 to 10 years.

If a firm has capable and imaginative executives and employees, and if its incentive system is working properly, many ideas for capital investment will be advanced. Since some ideas will be good ones while others will not, procedures must be established for screening projects, as we discuss in the remainder of the chapter.

PROJECT CLASSIFICATIONS

Analyzing capital expenditure proposals is not a costless operation — benefits can be gained from a careful analysis, but such an investigation does have a cost. For certain types of projects, a relatively detailed analysis may be warranted; for others, cost/benefit studies suggest that simpler procedures should be used. Accordingly, firms generally classify projects into the following categories and analyze those in each category somewhat differently:

1. **Replacement: maintenance of business.** Category 1 consists of expenditures necessary to replace worn-out or damaged equipment used to produce profitable products. These projects are necessary if the firm is to continue in its current businesses. The only issues here are (1) should we continue to produce these products or services and (2) should we continue to use our existing plant and equipment? Usually, the answers are "yes," so maintenance decisions are normally made without going through an elaborate decision process.

2. **Replacement: cost reduction.** This group includes expenditures to replace serviceable but obsolete equipment. The purpose of these expenditures is to lower the costs of labor, materials, or other items such as electricity. These decisions are somewhat more discretionary, so a more detailed analysis is generally required to support the expenditure.

3. **Expansion of existing products or markets.** Expenditures to increase output of existing products, or to expand outlets or distribution facilities in markets now being served, are included here. These decisions are more complex, because they require an explicit consideration of future demand in the firm's product markets. Mistakes are more likely, so still more detailed analysis is required, and the final decision is made at a higher level within the firm.

4. **Expansion into new products or markets.** These are expenditures necessary to produce a new product or to expand into a geographic area not currently being served. These projects involve strategic decisions that could change the fundamental nature of the business, and they normally require the expenditure of large sums of money over long periods. Invariably, a very detailed analysis is required, and final decisions on new product or market decisions are generally made by the board of directors as a part of the strategic plan. Mergers and acquisitions often are analyzed as a part of the capital budgeting process, and they are used to implement the strategic plan.

5. **Safety and/or environmental projects.** Expenditures necessary to comply with government orders, labor agreements, or insurance policy terms fall into this category. These expenditures are often called *mandatory investments,* or *nonrevenue-producing projects.* How they are handled depends on their size, with small ones being treated much like the Category 1 projects described previously.

6. **Other.** This catch-all includes office buildings, parking lots, executive aircraft, and so on. How they are handled also depends on their size.

In general, relatively simple calculations and only a few supporting documents are required for replacement decisions, especially maintenance-type investments in profitable plants. More detailed analysis is required for cost reduction replacements, for expansion of existing product lines, and especially for investments in new products or areas. Also, within each category, projects are broken down by their dollar costs: The larger the required investment, the more detailed the analysis, and the higher the level of the officer who must authorize the expenditure. Thus, although a plant manager may be authorized to approve maintenance expenditures up to $10,000 on the basis of a relatively unsophisticated analysis, the full board of directors may have to approve decisions which involve either amounts over $1 million or expansions into new products or markets. Statistical data are generally lacking for new product decisions, so here judgments, as opposed to detailed cost data, are a key element in the decision process.

RELATIONSHIP BETWEEN CAPITAL BUDGETING AND SECURITY VALUATION

Conceptually, the capital budgeting process involves exactly the same six steps that are used in security analysis as described in Chapter 6:

1. First, the cost of the project must be determined. This is similar to finding the price that must be paid for a stock or bond.

2. Next, management estimates the expected cash flows from the project, including the value of the asset at a specified terminal date. This is similar to estimating the future dividend or interest payment stream on a stock or bond.

3. Third, the riskiness of the projected cash flows must be estimated. To do this, management needs information about the probability distributions of the cash flows.

4. Then, given the riskiness of the projected cash flows and the general level of money costs in the economy as reflected in the risk-free rate, k_{RF}, management determines the appropriate discount rate, or cost of capital, at which the project's cash flows are to be discounted. This is equivalent to finding the required rate of return on a stock, as we did in Chapter 4.

5. Next, the expected cash flows are put on a present value basis to obtain an estimate of the asset's value to the firm. This is equivalent to finding the present value of expected future dividends.

6. Finally, the present value of the expected cash inflows is compared with the required outlay, or cost, of the project; if the asset's present value exceeds its cost, the project should be accepted. Otherwise, the project should be rejected. (Alternatively, the expected rate of return on the project can be calculated, and if this rate of return exceeds the project's required rate of return, the project is accepted.)

If an individual investor identifies and invests in a stock or bond whose market price is less than its true value, the value of the investor's portfolio will increase. Similarly, if a firm identifies (or creates) an investment opportunity with a present value greater than its cost, the value of the firm will increase. Thus, there is a very direct link between capital budgeting and stock values: The more effective the firm's capital budgeting procedures, the higher its growth rate, and hence the higher the price of its stock.

CAPITAL BUDGETING RANKING CRITERIA

ranking methods
Methods used to evaluate capital expenditure proposals.

Four major methods are used to rank projects and to decide whether or not they should be accepted for inclusion in the capital budget. These **ranking methods** are: (1) payback, (2) net present value (NPV), (3) regular internal rate

Table 9-1   Cash Flows for Projects S and L

Year (t)	Expected After-Tax Net Cash Flow, CF$_t$	
	Project S	Project L
0	($1,000)[a]	($1,000)[a]
1	500	100
2	400	300
3	300	400
4	100	600

[a]Represents the net investment outlay, or initial cost. The parentheses indicate a negative number, or cash outflow.

of return (IRR), and (4) modified internal rate of return (IRR*). We first explain how each ranking criterion is calculated, and then we evaluate how well each performs in terms of identifying those projects which will maximize the firm's stock price.[1]

We use the cash flow data shown in Table 9-1 for Projects S and L to illustrate each method, and throughout this chapter we assume that the projects are equally risky. The cash flows, CF$_t$, are expected values, and they include depreciation, salvage values, and tax effects. Also, since many projects require an investment in both fixed assets and working capital, the investment outlays shown as CF$_0$ include any necessary changes in net working capital.[2] Finally, we assume that all cash flows occur at the end of the designated year. Incidentally, the S stands for *short* and the L for *long*: Project S is a short-term project in the sense that its cash inflows tend to come in sooner than L's.

Payback Period

The **payback period**, defined as the expected number of years required to recover the original investment, was the first formal method used to evaluate capital budgeting projects. The easiest way to calculate the payback period is to accumulate the project's net cash flows and see when they sum to zero. For

payback period The length of time required for the net revenues of an investment to return the cost of the investment.

[1]Various types of "accounting rates of return" are occasionally used in project evaluation, but all of these methods have serious flaws, and hence we omit them from this text. Another DCF method, the *profitability index*, or *benefit/cost ratio*, which is found by dividing the PV of the inflows by the PV of the costs, and which consequently shows the benefits per dollar of costs, is sometimes used in practice. This method is not as good as the NPV and IRR methods.

[2]The most difficult part of the capital budgeting process is the estimation of the relevant cash flows. For simplicity, the net cash flows are treated as a given in this chapter, which allows us to focus on our main idea of concern, the capital budgeting ranking criteria. However, in Chapter 10 we will discuss cash flow estimation in detail. Also, note that *working capital* is defined as the firm's current assets and that *net working capital* is current assets minus current liabilities.

example, the annual and cumulative net cash flows of Project S are shown in the following table:

cost of Capital $ 1,000 [handwritten annotation]

Year (t)	S's Net Cash Flows	
	Annual	Cumulative
0	($1,000)	($1,000)
1	500	(500)
2	400	(100)
3	300	200
4	100	300

[handwritten annotations: N=1 455; N=2 331; N=3 225; N=4 68; 900 bracketing 500 and 400; below table: 1,000 - 900 - (100) log + 2.3]

Thus, the investment is recovered by the end of Year 3. Assuming that cash flows occur evenly during the year, the recovery actually occurs one-third of the way into Year 3: $100 remains to be recovered at the end of Year 2, and since Year 3 produces $300 in net cash flow, the payback period for Project S is 2⅓ years.

Using the same procedure, we find the payback of Project L to be 3⅓ years. Thus,

$$\text{Payback}_S\text{: } 2\frac{1}{3} \text{ years.}$$

$$\text{Payback}_L\text{: } 3\frac{1}{3} \text{ years.}$$

The shorter the payback period, the better the project is judged to be. Thus, if the firm required a payback of three years or less, Project S would be accepted but Project L would be rejected. If the projects were **mutually exclusive**, S would be ranked over L because S has the shorter payback. *Mutually exclusive* means that if one project is taken on, the other must be rejected. For example, the installation of a conveyor-belt system in a warehouse and the purchase of a fleet of forklift trucks for the same warehouse would be mutually exclusive projects — accepting one implies rejection of the other. *Independent* projects are projects whose cash flows are independent of one another.

Some firms use a variant of the regular payback, the *discounted payback period,* which is similar to the regular payback period except that the expected cash flows are discounted by the project's cost of capital, or the required rate of return for the project.[3] Thus, the discounted payback period is defined as the number of years required to recover the investment from *discounted* cash flows. Table 9-2 contains the discounted net cash flows for Projects S and L, assuming a 10 percent cost of capital. To construct Table 9-2, each cash inflow in Table 9-1 is divided by $(1 + k)^t = (1.10)^t$, where t is the year in which the cash flow occurs and k is the project's cost of capital. After 3 years, Project S will have generated $1,011 in discounted cash inflows. Since the cost is $1,000,

mutually exclusive projects
A set of projects of which only one can be accepted.

[3]The project's cost of capital reflects the return required by the firm's investors, which in turn reflects the riskiness of the project being evaluated. Higher risk projects have higher required rates of return, just as higher risk stocks or bonds have higher required returns. All of this will be discussed in detail in Chapter 16.

Table 9-2   Discounted Cash Flows for Projects S and L

Year (t)	Project S Annual	Project S Cumulative	Project L Annual	Project L Cumulative
0	($1,000)	($1,000)	($1,000)	($1,000)
1	455	(545)	91	(909)
2	331	(214)	248	(661)
3	225	11	301	(360)
4	68	79	410	50

[handwritten annotations: "1,000 INVESTMENT", "786 - 1,000", "214", "225", "2.95 years"]

the discounted payback is just under 3 years, or, to be precise, 2 + ($214/ $225) = 2.95 years. Project L's discounted payback is 3.88 years. Thus,

$$\text{Discounted payback}_S: 2.0 + 214/225 = 2.95 \text{ years.}$$

$$\text{Discounted payback}_L: 3.0 + 360/410 = 3.88 \text{ years.}$$

For Projects S and L, the rankings are the same regardless of which payback method is used; that is, Project S is preferred to Project L, and Project S would still be selected if the firm were to require a payback of three years or less. However, it is possible for the regular and the discounted paybacks to produce conflicting rankings.

Note that the payback is a type of "breakeven" calculation in the sense that if cash flows come in at the expected rate until the payback year, the project will break even in an accounting sense. However, the regular payback does not take account of the cost of capital: The cost of the debt and equity used to undertake the project is not reflected in the cash flows or the calculation. The discounted payback does take account of capital costs — it shows the breakeven year after covering debt and equity costs. However, as we shall see, both payback methods have serious deficiencies. Therefore, other procedures lead to better project acceptance decisions.

It should be noted that the payback period does provide information about how long funds will be tied up in a project. Thus, the shorter the payback period, other things held constant, the greater the project's *liquidity*. Also, cash flows expected in the distant future are generally regarded as being riskier than near-term cash flows. *Therefore, the payback is often used as a measure of both the liquidity and the riskiness of a project.*

discounted cash flow (DCF) techniques
Methods of ranking investment proposals that employ time value of money concepts; two of these are the net present value and internal rate of return methods.

Net Present Value (NPV)

As flaws in the payback method were recognized, people began to search for methods to improve project evaluations. This led to the development of **discounted cash flow (DCF) techniques**, which take into account the time value

net present value (NPV) method
A method of ranking investment proposals using the NPV, which is equal to the present value of future cash flows, discounted at the marginal cost of capital.

of money. One DCF method is the **net present value (NPV) method.** To implement this approach, one proceeds as follows:

1. Find the present value of each cash flow, including both inflows and outflows, discounted at the project's cost of capital.

2. Sum these discounted cash flows; this sum is the project's NPV.

3. If the NPV is positive, the project should be accepted; if the NPV is negative, it should be rejected; and if two projects are mutually exclusive, the one with the higher positive NPV should be chosen.

The NPV can be expressed as follows:

$$NPV = \sum_{t=0}^{n} \frac{CF_t}{(1 + k)^t} = \sum_{t=0}^{n} CF_t(PVIF_{k,t}). \qquad (9\text{-}1)$$

Here CF_t is the expected net cash flow in Period t, and k is the project's cost of capital. Cash outflows (expenditures on the project, such as the cost of buying equipment or building factories) are treated as *negative* cash flows. In evaluating Projects S and L, only CF_0 is negative, but for many large projects, such as the Alaska Pipeline, an electric generating plant, or IBM's new series of mainframe computers, outflows occur for several years before operations begin and cash flows turn positive, and for these projects the first few values of CF_t are negative.

At a 10 percent cost of capital, the NPV of Project S is $78.82. The NPV can be found using a time line approach, as shown in Figure 9-1, or using Equation 9-1, as follows:

$$NPV_s = \frac{-\$1,000}{(1.10)^0} + \frac{\$500}{(1.10)^1} + \frac{\$400}{(1.10)^2} + \frac{\$300}{(1.10)^3} + \frac{\$100}{(1.10)^4}$$

$$= -\$1,000 + \$454.55 + \$330.58 + \$225.39 + \$68.30$$

$$= \$78.82.$$

By a similar process, we find $NPV_L = \$49.18$. On this basis, both projects should be accepted if they are independent, but S should be the one chosen if they are mutually exclusive. (Note: With many financial calculators, you can input the five cash flows, enter i = 10, and press the NPV key to find the net present value.)

Rationale for the NPV Method. The rationale for the NPV method is straightforward. The value of a firm is the sum of the values of its parts. If a firm takes on a project with a zero NPV, the wealth of its current stockholders is unchanged — the firm becomes larger by the amount of the investment, but the value of its stock remains constant. However, if the firm takes on a project with a positive NPV, the wealth of the current stockholders is increased. In our example, current stockholders' wealth would increase by $78.82 if the firm takes on Project S, but by only $49.18 if it takes on Project L. Thus, it is easy to

Figure 9-1   NPV of Project S at a 10% Cost of Capital

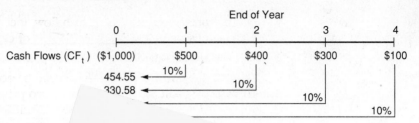

End of Year

	0	1	2	3	4
Cash Flows (CF_t)	($1,000)	$500	$400	$300	$100

454.55 ◄── 10%

330.58 ◄──── 10%

───── 10%

────── 10%

Net Present

see why S ... the logic of the
NPV appr

Intern

In Ch ... d to maturity (YTM),
or r ... d hold it to maturity,
you ... tly the same concepts
are ... rate of return (IRR)
m ... te which *forces the pres-*
e ... *the present value of the*

...osts.

internal rate of return (IRR) method
A method of ranking investment proposals using the rate of return on an asset investment, calculated by finding the discount rate that equates the present value of future cash inflows to the investment's cost.

...osts = 0

$$\frac{\bar{r}_t}{IRR)^t} = 0, \qquad (9\text{-}2)$$

IRR
The discount rate wh forces the PV of a project's inflows to equal the PV of its costs.

[a]This ... ified. Both analysts and investors anticipate that ... PV projects, and stock prices reflect these expectations. Thus, stoc ... its of new capital projects only to the extent that such projects were no ... in this sense, we may think of a firm's value as consisting of two parts: (1) the value of ... g assets and (2) the value of its "growth opportunities," or projects with positive NPVs. AT&T is a good example of this: the company has the world's largest long-distance network plus telephone manufacturing facilities, both of which provide earnings and cash flows, and it has Bell Labs, which has the *potential* for coming up with new products in the computer/telecommunication area that could be extremely profitable. Security analysts (and investors) thus analyze AT&T as a company with a set of cash-producing assets plus a set of growth opportunities that will materialize if and only if it can come up with positive NPV projects through its capital budgeting process.

Figure 9-2   IRR for Project S

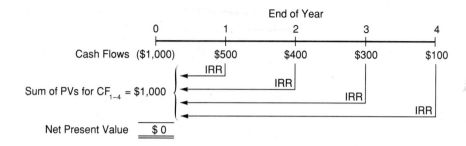

IRR$_s$ = 14.5% = discount rate which forces the sum of the PVs
of CF$_{1-4}$ to equal the project's cost, $1,000.

which can also be written as

$$\sum_{t=0}^{n} CF_t(PVIF_{IRR,t}) = 0. \tag{9-2a}$$

For our Project S, here is the set-up:

$$\frac{-\$1,000}{(1 + IRR)^0} + \frac{\$500}{(1 + IRR)^1} + \frac{\$400}{(1 + IRR)^2} + \frac{\$300}{(1 + IRR)^3} + \frac{\$100}{(1 + IRR)^4} = 0,$$

or

$$-\$1,000 + \$500(PVIF_{IRR,1}) + \$400(PVIF_{IRR,2}) + \$300(PVIF_{IRR,3}) + \$100(PVIF_{IRR,4}) = 0.$$

These cash flows can also be laid out on a time line, as shown in Figure 9-2. Here we know the value of each CF$_t$, but we do not know the value of IRR. Thus, we have an equation with one unknown, and we can solve for the value of IRR. *The solution value is the IRR.*

Notice that the internal rate of return formula, Equation 9-2, is simply the NPV formula, Equation 9-1, solved for the particular discount rate that forces the NPV to equal zero. Thus, the same basic equation is used for both methods, but in the NPV method the discount rate, k, is specified and the NPV is found, whereas in the IRR method the NPV is specified to equal zero and the value of IRR that forces this equality is determined.

Equation 9-2 (or 9-2a) can be solved to find the IRR in several ways:

1. **Trial and error.** Substitute in different values for IRR until you find the value that forces the NPV to equal zero. This is an extremely tedious and inefficient process.

2. **Mathematical procedures.** One can select values of IRR in a systematic manner so that the equation quickly converges on zero. Methods exist for solving polynomial equations, and they are discussed in math books

and used in calculators and computers to solve IRR problems quickly and efficiently.

3. **Financial calculators or computers.** Better financial calculators and computer spreadsheet packages such as *Lotus 1-2-3* have IRR functions which solve Equation 9-2 rapidly (very rapidly with a computer, and after several seconds with a calculator). Simply input the cash flows, and the computer or calculator finds the IRR.

Since internal rates of return can be calculated very easily with financial calculators or computers, most firms now have computerized their capital budgeting processes and automatically generate IRRs, NPVs, and paybacks for all projects. (See Problem 9-2 at the end of this chapter.) Thus, businesses have no difficulty whatever with the mechanical side of capital budgeting, and a serious business student should have a financial calculator capable of finding IRRs. All IRRs reported hereafter in this and the following chapters have been obtained by using a financial calculator (or a PC). By keying in the cash flows and then pressing the IRR button, we find that project S has $IRR_S = 14.5\%$, whereas $IRR_L = 11.8\%$. If both projects have a cost of capital of 10 percent, the internal rate of return rule indicates that if the projects are independent, both should be accepted — both of them are expected to earn more than the cost of the capital needed to finance them. If they are mutually exclusive, S ranks higher and should be accepted, whereas L should be rejected. If the cost of capital is more than 14.5 percent, both projects should be rejected.

Rationale and Use of the IRR Method. Why is the particular discount rate that equates a project's cost with the present value of its receipts (the IRR) so special? To answer this question, let us first assume that our illustrative firm obtains the $1,000 needed to take on Project S by borrowing from a bank at an interest rate of 14.5 percent. Since the internal rate of return was calculated to be 14.5 percent, the same as the cost of the bank loan, the firm can invest in the project, use the cash flows generated by the investment to pay off the principal and interest on the loan, and come out exactly even on the transaction. This point is demonstrated in Table 9-3, which shows that Project S provides cash flows that are just sufficient to pay 14.5 percent interest on the unpaid balance of the bank loan, retire the loan over the life of the project, and end up with a balance that differs from zero only by a rounding error of 32 cents.

Table 9-3   Analysis of Project S's IRR as a Loan Rate

Beginning Loan Balance (1)	Cash Flow (2)	Interest on the Loan at 14.5% $0.145 \times (1) = (3)$	Repayment of Principal $(2) - (3) = (4)$	Ending Loan Balance $(1) - (4) = (5)$
$1,000.00	$500	$145.00	$355.00	$645.00
645.00	400	93.53	306.47	338.53
338.53	300	49.09	250.91	87.62
87.62	100	12.70	87.30	0.32

If the internal rate of return exceeds the cost of the funds used to finance a project, a surplus remains after paying for the capital, and this surplus accrues to the firm's stockholders. Therefore, taking on a project whose IRR exceeds its cost of capital increases the value of the firm's stock. On the other hand, if the internal rate of return is less than the cost of capital, taking on the project imposes a cost on existing stockholders. It is this (breakeven) characteristic that makes the IRR useful in evaluating capital projects.[5]

EVALUATION OF THE DECISION RULES

We have presented three possible capital budgeting rules, all of which are used to a greater or lesser extent in practice, and we shall discuss a fourth method later in the chapter. However, because the methods can lead to different capital budgeting decisions, we need to answer this question: Which method is best, where "best" is defined as the method that selects from all available projects that particular set of projects which maximizes the firm's value and hence its shareholders' wealth? If more than one method does this, then the best method would be the one that is easiest to use in practice.

There are three properties which must be exhibited by a selection method if it is to lead to consistently correct capital budgeting decisions:

 NPV ≯ D Payback

1. The method must consider all cash flows throughout the entire life of a project.

2. The method must consider the time value of money; that is, it must reflect the fact that dollars which come in sooner are more valuable than dollars which are received in the distant future.

only NPV → 3. When the method is used to select from a set of mutually exclusive projects, it must choose that project which maximizes the firm's stock price.

How do the various methods stand in regard to the required properties? Both the regular and the discounted payback methods violate Property 1 — they do not consider all cash flows. Additionally, the undiscounted payback method also violates Property 2. The NPV and IRR methods satisfy Properties 1 and 2, and both lead to identical (and correct) accept/reject decisions for independent projects. However, only the NPV method satisfies Property 3 under all conditions, because there are certain conditions under which the IRR method fails to identify correctly that project, within a set of mutually exclusive projects, which maximizes the firm's stock price. This point is explored in depth in the following sections.

----

[5]This example illustrates the logic of the IRR method, but for technical correctness, the capital used to finance the project should be assumed to come from both debt and equity, not from debt alone.

COMPARISON OF THE NPV AND IRR METHODS

We have noted that the NPV method exhibits all the desired decision rule properties, and, for this reason, it is the best method for evaluating projects. Because the NPV method is better than the IRR, we were tempted to explain NPV only, to state that it should be used as the basis for capital budgeting decisions, and to go on to the next topic. However, the IRR method is familiar to many corporate executives, and it is widely entrenched in industry. Indeed, surveys continually show that business executives prefer the IRR method to the NPV approach, apparently because they are more used to thinking in terms of rates of return rather than dollars of NPV. Therefore, it is important to explain why, at times, a project with a lower IRR may be preferable to one with a higher IRR.

NPV Profiles

net present value profile
A curve showing the relationship between a project's NPV and the firm's cost of capital.

A graph which shows how a project's NPV is related to the firm's cost of capital is called the project's **net present value profile**; NPV profiles for Projects L and S are shown in Figure 9-3. To construct the profiles, we first note that at a zero cost of capital, the NPV is simply the sum of a project's undiscounted cash flows; thus, at a zero cost of capital, $NPV_S = \$300$ and $NPV_L = \$400$. These values are plotted as the vertical axis intercepts in Figure 9-3. Next, we calculate the projects' NPVs at three possible costs of capital, say 5, 10, and 15 percent, and plot these values. The four points plotted on our graphs are shown at the bottom of the figure.

Recall that the IRR is defined as the discount rate at which a project's NPV equals zero. Therefore, *the point at which a project's net present value profile crosses the horizontal axis indicates its internal rate of return.* Since we calculated IRR_S and IRR_L in an earlier section, we have two other points which we can use in plotting the projects' NPV profiles.

When we connect the plot points, we have the net present value profiles.[6] NPV profiles are useful in project analysis, and we will use them often in the remainder of the chapter.

NPV Rankings Depend on the Cost of Capital

We saw in Figure 9-3 that the NPV profiles of both Project L and Project S decline as the cost of capital increases. However, look again at the figure and notice that Project L has the higher NPV at a low cost of capital, but Project S has

---

[6]Notice that the NPV profiles are curved — they are *not* straight lines. Also, the NPVs approach the $t = 0$ cash flow (the cost of the project) as the cost of capital increases without limit. The reason is that, at an infinitely high cost of capital, the PV of the inflows would be zero, so NPV = CF_0, which in our example is − \$1,000. Under certain conditions the NPV profiles can cross the horizontal axis several times or never cross it. This point is discussed later in the chapter.

Figure 9-3   Net Present Value Profiles:
NPVs of Projects S and L at Different Costs of Capital

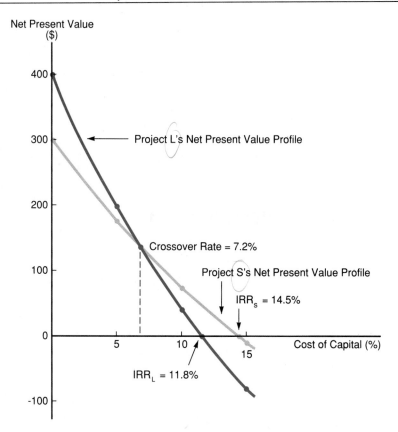

Cost of Capital	NPV$_S$	NPV$_L$
0%	$300.00	$400.00
5	180.42	206.50
10	78.82	49.18
15	(8.33)	(80.14)

crossover rate
The discount rate at which the NPV profiles of two projects cross and at which the projects' NPVs are equal.

the higher NPV if the cost of capital is above the 7.2 percent **crossover rate.** Notice also that Project L's NPV is "more sensitive" to changes in capital costs than is NPV$_S$; that is, Project L's net present value profile has the steeper slope, indicating that a given change in k has a larger effect on NPV$_L$ than on NPV$_S$.

To see why L has the greater sensitivity, recall first that the cash flows from S are received faster than those from L; in a payback sense, S is a short-term project, whereas L is a long-term project. Next, recall the equation for the NPV:

$$NPV = \frac{CF_0}{(1 + k)^0} + \frac{CF_1}{(1 + k)^1} + \frac{CF_2}{(1 + k)^2} + \frac{CF_3}{(1 + k)^3} + \cdots + \frac{CF_t}{(1 + k)^t}.$$

Now notice that the denominators of the terms in this equation increase as k and t increase, and because the increase is exponential, the effect of an increase in k is greater if t is larger. To understand this point more clearly, consider the following data:

PV of a $100 cash flow due in 1 year, discounted at 5%	$95.24
PV of a $100 cash flow due in 1 year, discounted at 10%	$90.91
Effect on PV of a doubling of k when t = 1	− $ 4.33, or −4.5%
PV of a $100 cash flow due in 10 years, discounted at 5%	$61.39
PV of a $100 cash flow due in 10 years, discounted at 10%	$38.55
Effect on PV of a doubling of k when t = 10	− $22.84, or −37.2%

A doubling of the discount rate causes only a 4.5 percent decline in the PV of a Year 1 cash flow, but the same increase in the discount rate causes the PV of a Year 10 cash flow to fall by 37 percent. Thus, if a project has most of its cash flows coming in the early years, its NPV will not be lowered very much by a capital cost increase, but a project whose cash flows come later will be severely penalized by such an increase. Accordingly, Project L, which has most of its cash flows in the later years, is hurt badly when the cost of capital is high, whereas Project S, which has relatively rapid cash flows, is less affected by rising capital costs. The slopes of the NPV profiles reflect this situation.

Independent Projects

independent project
A project whose cash flows are unaffected by the decision to accept or reject some other project.

If two projects are **independent**, the NPV and IRR criteria always lead to the same accept/reject decision: if NPV says accept, IRR also says accept. To see why this is so, look back at Figure 9-3 and focus on Project L. Notice (1) that the IRR criterion for acceptance is that the project's cost of capital is less than (or to the left of) the IRR and (2) that whenever the project's cost of capital is less than the IRR, its NPV is positive. Thus, for any cost of capital less than 11.8 percent, Project L is acceptable by both the NPV and the IRR criteria, whereas both methods reject the project if the cost of capital is greater than 11.8 percent. Project S, and all other independent projects under consideration, could be analyzed similarly, and it will always turn out that if a project's IRR is greater than k, its NPV is also greater than 0. Thus, if a project is acceptable by the IRR criterion, it must also be acceptable by the NPV criterion.

Mutually Exclusive Projects

Now assume that Projects S and L are *mutually exclusive* rather than independent. In other words, we can choose either Project S or Project L, or we can reject both, but we cannot accept both projects. Notice in Figure 9-3 that as long as the cost of capital is *greater than* the crossover rate of 7.2 percent, (1) NPV_S is greater than NPV_L and (2) IRR_S is also greater than IRR_L. Therefore, if k is greater than the crossover rate, the two methods must lead to the selection of the same project. However, if the cost of capital is *less than* the crossover rate, the NPV method ranks Project L higher, but the IRR method indicates that

Project S is better. Thus, a conflict exists: NPV says choose mutually exclusive Project L, whereas IRR says take S. Which answer is correct? Logic suggests that the NPV method is better, since it selects that project which adds the most to shareholder wealth.

There are two basic conditions which cause NPV profiles to cross and thus create potential conflicts between NPV and IRR: (1) *the projects differ in size (or scale),* meaning that the cost of one project is larger than that of the other, or (2) *they differ in the time patterns of cash flows,* meaning that the cash flows of one project come in relatively early as compared with the cash flows of the other project, as occurred with Projects L and S.[7]

When either size or timing differences occur, the firm will have different amounts of funds to invest in the various years, depending on which of the two mutually exclusive projects it chooses. For example, if one project costs more than the other, the firm will have additional funds to invest at t = 0 if it selects the smaller project. Similarly, for projects of equal size, the one with the larger early cash inflows provides more funds for reinvestment in the early years. Given this situation, the rate of return at which differential cash flows can be invested is quite important. In the next section, we prove that the NPV/IRR conflict is caused by the different **reinvestment rate assumptions** that are inherent in the two decision rules.

reinvestment rate assumption
The assumption that cash flows from a project can be reinvested (1) at the cost of capital, if using the NPV method, or (2) at the internal rate of return, if using the IRR method.

THE REINVESTMENT RATE (OPPORTUNITY COST) ASSUMPTION

Conflicts between mutually exclusive projects arise as a result of scale- or timing-induced cash flow differentials. Therefore, the critical issue in resolving conflicts between mutually exclusive projects is this: How beneficial is it to have cash flows earlier rather than later? The answer depends on what the firm can do with the additional funds, or the *opportunity cost rate* at which it can invest differential early years' cash flows. *The NPV method implicitly assumes that the cash flows generated by a project can be reinvested at the cost of capital, whereas the IRR method assumes that the firm has the opportunity to reinvest at the IRR.* These assumptions are inherent in the mathematics of the discounting processes for the two methods. Thus, the NPV method discounts cash flows at the cost of capital, whereas the IRR method discounts cash flows at the project's IRR. The cash flows may actually be withdrawn as dividends by the stockholders and spent on beer and pizza, but the assumption of reinvestment opportunity is still implicit in IRR and NPV calculations.

Which is the better assumption — that cash flows can be reinvested at the cost of capital or that they will be reinvested at the project's IRR? It can be demonstrated that the best assumption is that projects' cash flows are rein-

---

[7]Of course, it is possible for mutually exclusive projects to differ with respect to both scale and timing. Also, if mutually exclusive projects have different lives (as opposed to different cash flow patterns over a common life), this introduces further complications, and for meaningful comparisons, some mutually exclusive projects must be evaluated over a common life. This point is discussed in Chapter 10.

vested at the cost of capital.[8] Therefore, we conclude that *the best reinvestment rate assumption is the cost of capital, which is implicit in the NPV method.* This, in turn, leads us to prefer the NPV method, at least for firms willing and able to obtain capital at a cost reasonably close to their current cost of capital. In Chapter 11, when we discuss capital rationing, we will see that under certain conditions the NPV rule may be questionable, but for most firms at most times, NPV is conceptually better than IRR.

We should reiterate that when projects are independent, the NPV and IRR methods both lead to exactly the same accept/reject decision. However, *for evaluating mutually exclusive projects, the NPV method is better.* We should also note that there is one other situation in which the IRR approach may not be usable — this is when one is evaluating "nonnormal" projects. A *normal* capital project is one that has one or more cash outflows (costs) followed by a series of cash inflows. If, however, a project calls for a large cash outflow either sometime during or at the end of its life, it is considered to be a *nonnormal* project. Nonnormal projects can present unique difficulties when evaluated by the IRR method. The most common problem encountered when evaluating nonnormal projects is multiple IRRs, which we discuss later in the chapter.

MODIFIED INTERNAL RATE OF RETURN (IRR*)

In spite of a strong academic preference for the NPV, surveys indicate that business executives prefer the IRR over the NPV by a margin of 3 to 1. Apparently, managers find it intuitively more appealing to analyze investments in terms of percentage rates of return than dollars of NPV. Given this fact, can we devise a percentage evaluator that is better than the regular IRR? The answer is yes — we can modify the IRR to make it a better indicator of relative profitability and hence better for use in capital budgeting. The new measure is called the **modified IRR**, or **IRR***, and it is defined as follows:[9]

modified IRR (IRR*)
The discount rate at which the present value of a project's cost is equal to the present value of its terminal value, where the terminal value is found as the future value of the cash inflows, compounded at the firm's cost of capital.

$$PV\ costs = PV\ terminal\ value$$

$$\sum_{t=0}^{n} \frac{COF_t}{(1+k)^t} = \frac{\sum_{t=0}^{n} CIF_t(1+k)^{n-t}}{(1+IRR^*)^n}$$

$$PV\ costs = \frac{TV}{(1+IRR^*)^n} \qquad (9\text{-}2b)$$

---

[8]See Eugene F. Brigham and Louis C. Gapenski, *Intermediate Financial Management,* 2nd ed., Chapter 7, for a demonstration of this point.

[9]Although IRR* appears to be widely used by financial managers, the author has never seen a discussion of it in the academic literature. However, such a discussion was presented by Samuel Weaver, Director of Financial Analysis for Hershey Corporation, in October 1987 at the Financial Management Association Conference in Las Vegas. A year later, at the October 1988 FMA conference, all executives who spoke on capital budgeting indicated that they relied heavily upon IRR*. Also, note that IRR* can be computed on some of the better financial calculators. For the exact procedure, see the Hewlett-Packard 12-C or 17B owners' handbook.

Here COF refers to cash outflows, or the cost of the project, and CIF refers to cash inflows. The term on the left is simply the PV of the investment outlays when discounted at the cost of capital, and the numerator of the term on the right is the future value of the inflows, assuming that the cash inflows are reinvested at the cost of capital. The compounded sum in the numerator is also called the *terminal value,* or *TV.* The discount rate that forces the PV of the costs to equal the PV of the TV is defined as IRR*.

If the investment costs are all incurred at t = 0, and if the first operating inflow occurs at t = 1, as is true for our illustrative Projects S and L, the following equation may be used:

$$\text{Cost} = \frac{TV}{(1 + IRR^*)^n} = \frac{\sum_{t=1}^{n} CIF_t(1 + k)^{n-t}}{(1 + IRR^*)^n}. \tag{9-2c}$$

We can illustrate the calculation with Project S:

$$\$1{,}000 = \frac{\$500(1.10)^{4-1} + \$400(1.10)^{4-2} + \$300(1.10)^{4-3} + \$100(1.10)^{4-4}}{(1 + IRR^*)^4}$$

$$= \frac{\$665.50 + \$484.00 + \$330.00 + \$100.00}{(1 + IRR^*)^4} = \frac{\$1{,}579.50}{(1 + IRR^*)^4}.$$

Using a financial calculator, enter PV = 1,000, FV = 1,579.5 (or −1,579.5), and n = 4, and press the i button to find IRR^*_S = 12.1%. Similarly, we find IRR^*_L = 11.3%. We can also illustrate this process with a time line; this is shown for Project S in Figure 9-4.

The modified IRR has a significant advantage over the regular IRR. IRR* assumes that cash flows from all projects are reinvested at the cost of capital, whereas the regular IRR assumes that the cash flows from each project are reinvested at the project's own IRR. Since reinvestment at k is generally more correct, the modified IRR is a better indicator of a project's true profitability. Therefore, if managers want to choose from among alternative projects the one with the highest rate of return, IRR* gives a better picture of the "true" rate of return. This is why financial executives are adopting IRR*.

Is IRR* as good as NPV for selecting among competing (mutually exclusive) projects? If the two projects are of equal size, NPV and IRR* will always lead to the same project selection decision. Thus, for any two projects like our Projects S and L, if $NPV_S > NPV_L$, then $IRR^*_S > IRR^*_L$, and the kinds of conflict we encountered between NPV and the regular IRR will not occur. However, if the projects differ in size, conflicts can still occur. Thus, if we were comparing a large project with a smaller mutually exclusive one, we might find $NPV_L > NPV_S$, but $IRR^*_S > IRR^*_L$.

Our conclusion is that IRR* is superior to the regular IRR as an indicator of a project's "true" rate of return or "expected long-term rate of return," but the NPV method is still best, especially for choosing among competing projects that differ in size, because it provides a better indicator of how much each project will cause the value of the firm to increase.

Figure 9-4 IRR* for Project S at a 10% Cost of Capital

I. Find the terminal value (TV) of the cash
inflows at the 10 percent discount rate.

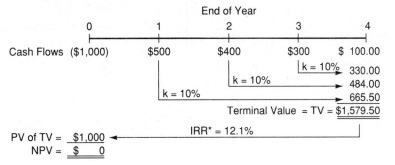

Notes:
a. Compound the cash inflows to the terminal year at the cost of capital, k. It is assumed that the cash inflows are reinvested at k.
b. Discount the TV at a rate which causes the PV of the TV to equal the cost of the project; this equalizing discount rate is called IRR*.

We can close this section by asking this question: "Which would most firms prefer, a 30 percent return on a $10,000,000 investment or a 100 percent return on a $1 investment?" Most would prefer the large project with the lower return. NPV would lead to that choice, but both IRR and IRR* would rank the smaller project higher.

MULTIPLE IRRs

A fairly common problem occurs when one uses the regular IRR method: If negative cash flows occur after a project has gone into operation, then when we solve Equation 9-2,

$$\sum_{t=0}^{n} \frac{CF_t}{(1 + IRR)^t} = 0, \qquad (9\text{-}2)$$

it is possible to obtain more than one positive value of IRR, which means that there are multiple IRRs.

To illustrate this problem, suppose a firm is considering an expenditure of $1.6 million at Year 0 to develop a strip mine (Project M). The mine will produce a cash flow of $10 million at the end of Year 1. Then, at the end of Year 2, $10 million must be expended to restore the land to its original condition. Therefore, the project's expected net cash flows are as follows (in millions of dollars):

	Expected Net Cash Flow	
Year 0	End of Year 1	End of Year 2
− $1.6	+ $10	− $10

Figure 9-5   NPV Profile for Project M

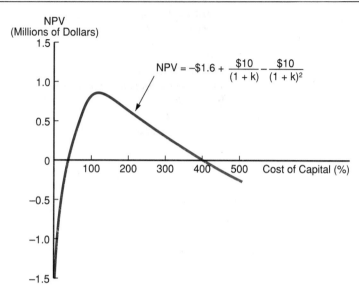

These values can be substituted into Equation 9-2:

$$\frac{-\$1.6 \text{ million}}{(1 + \text{IRR})^0} + \frac{\$10 \text{ million}}{(1 + \text{IRR})^1} + \frac{-\$10 \text{ million}}{(1 + \text{IRR})^2} = 0.$$

When solved, we find that NPV = 0 when IRR = 25% and also when IRR = 400%.[10] Therefore, the IRR of the investment is both 25 and 400 percent. This relationship is depicted graphically in Figure 9-5.[11] Note that no dilemma would arise if either the NPV method or the IRR* method were used; we would simply find NPV or IRR* and use it to evaluate the project. If Project M's cost of capital is 10 percent, its NPV is − $0.77 million, and the project should be rejected. Also, IRR* is − 20.9 percent, which is less than the cost of capital, so the IRR* method also indicates that the project should be rejected.

The author encountered a good example of problems caused by multiple internal rates of return when a major California bank *borrowed* funds from an

---

[10]If you attempted to find the IRR of this project with many financial calculators, you would get an error message; this message occurs if a project has more than one IRR. We actually found our project's IRRs by using *Lotus 1-2-3* to calculate NPVs at a number of different values for k and then plotting the NPV profile. The intersections with the X-axis gave a good idea of the IRR values. We then could use either trial and error or the *Lotus 1-2-3* IRR function to find the exact value of k which forces the equation to zero. The HP 17B calculator will also calculate IRRs.

[11]Does Figure 9-5 suggest that the firm should try to *raise* its cost of capital to about 100 percent in order to maximize the NPV of the project? Certainly not. Logically, the firm should seek to *minimize* its cost of capital; this will cause the price of its stock to be maximized. Actions taken to raise the cost of capital might make this particular project look good, but those actions would be terribly harmful to the firm's more numerous normal projects. Only if the firm's cost of capital is high, in spite of efforts to keep it down, will the illustrative project have a positive NPV.

insurance company and then used these funds (plus an initial investment of its own) to buy a number of jet engines, which it then leased to a major airline. The bank expected to receive positive net cash flows (lease payments plus tax savings minus interest on the insurance company loan) for a number of years, then have several large negative cash flows as it repaid the insurance company loan, and, finally, have a large inflow from the sale of the engines when the lease expired.[12]

The bank discovered two IRRs and wondered which was correct. It could not ignore the IRR and use the NPV method, since the lease was already on the books, and the bank's senior loan committee, as well as Federal Reserve bank examiners, wanted to know the return on the lease. The author recommended that the bank use IRR*, discounting its cash outflows back to the initial decision point at the bank's cost of funds, compounding its cash inflows forward to the end of the lease's life at that same rate, and then finding IRR* as the discount rate which equated the PV of the costs with the PV of the TV of the inflows. This procedure satisfied both the loan committee and the bank examiners.[13]

The examples just presented illustrate one problem — multiple IRRs — that can arise when the IRR criterion is used with a project that has nonnormal cash flows. Use of the IRR method on nonnormal cash flow projects could produce other problems, such as no IRR or an IRR which leads to an incorrect accept/reject decision. In all such cases, either the NPV or the IRR* criterion could easily be applied, and the NPV leads to conceptually correct capital budgeting decisions.

THE POST-AUDIT

post-audit
A comparison of the actual and expected results for a given capital project.

An important aspect of the capital budgeting process is the **post-audit**, which involves (1) comparing actual results with those predicted by the project's sponsors and (2) explaining why any differences occurred. For example, many firms require that the operating divisions send a monthly report for the first six months after a project goes into operation, and a quarterly report thereafter, until the project's results are up to expectations. From then on, reports on the project are handled like those of other operations.

The post-audit has several purposes, including the following:

1. **Improve forecasts.** When decision makers systematically compare their projections to actual outcomes, there is a tendency for estimates to improve. Conscious or unconscious biases are observed and eliminated; new forecasting methods are sought as the need for them becomes apparent; and people simply tend to do everything better, including forecasting, if they know that their actions are being monitored.

---

[12]The situation described here is a *leveraged lease*. Leasing is covered in Chapter 14.

[13]For additional insights into the multiple root problem, see William H. Jean, "On Multiple Rates of Return," *Journal of Finance,* March 1968, 187–192.

2.   **Improve operations**. Businesses are run by people, and people can perform at higher or lower levels of efficiency. When a divisional team has made a forecast about a new installation, its members are, in a sense, putting their reputations on the line. If costs are above predicted levels, sales below expectations, and so on, executives in production, sales, and other areas will strive to improve operations and to bring results into line with forecasts. In a discussion related to this point, an IBM executive made this statement: "You academicians worry only about making good decisions. In business, we also worry about making decisions good."

The post-audit is not a simple process. There are a number of factors that can cause complications. First, we must recognize that each element of the cash flow forecast is subject to uncertainty, so a percentage of all projects undertaken by any reasonably venturesome firm will necessarily go awry. This fact must be considered when appraising the performances of the operating executives who submit capital expenditure requests. Second, projects sometimes fail to meet expectations for reasons beyond the control of the operating executives and for reasons that no one could realistically be expected to anticipate. For example, the decline in oil prices in the mid-1980s adversely affected many energy-related projects, as well as real estate projects in Texas and other oil-producing areas. Third, it is often difficult to separate the operating results of one investment from those of a larger system. Although some projects stand alone and permit ready identification of costs and revenues, the actual cost savings that result from a new computer system, for example, may be very hard to measure. Fourth, it is often hard to assess blame or praise, because the executives who were actually responsible for a given decision may have moved on by the time the results of long-term investments are known.

Because of these difficulties, some firms tend to play down the importance of the post-audit. However, observations of both businesses and governmental units suggest that the best-run and most successful organizations are the ones that put the greatest stress on post-audits. Accordingly, we regard the post-audit as being one of the most important elements in a good capital budgeting system.

Small Business

CAPITAL BUDGETING IN THE SMALL FIRM

The allocation of capital in small firms is as important as it is in large ones. In fact, given their lack of access to the capital markets, it is often more important in the small firm, because the funds necessary to correct a mistake may not be available. Also, large firms with capital budgets of $100 million or more allocate capital to numerous projects, so a mistake on one project can be offset by successes with others.

In spite of the importance of capital expenditures to small business, studies of the way capital budgeting decisions are made generally suggest that many small firms use "back-of-the-envelope" analysis, or perhaps even no analysis at all. For example, in a study of small manufacturing firms in Iowa, Robert Soldofsky found that more than 50 percent of the companies relied exclusively on payback or some similar criterion, and over 40 percent used no formal analysis at all.[14] Similarly, L. R. Runyon studied 214 firms with net worths of from $500,000 to $1,000,000. He found that almost 70 percent relied upon either payback or some other incorrect criteria; only 14 percent used a discounted cash flow analysis; and about 9 percent indicated that they used no formal analysis at all.[15] Studies of larger firms, on the other hand, generally find that most support their capital budgeting decisions with discounted cash flow techniques.

We are left with a puzzle. Capital budgeting is clearly important to small firms, yet the firms neglect to use the tools that have been developed to improve these decisions. Why does this situation exist? One argument is that managers of small firms are simply not well trained; they are unsophisticated. This argument suggests that the managers would use the more sophisticated techniques if they understood them better.

Another argument relates to the fact that management talent is a scarce resource in small firms. That is, even if the managers were exceptionally sophisticated, perhaps the demands on their time are such that they simply cannot take the time to use elaborate techniques to analyze a proposed project. In other words, small business managers may be capable of doing careful discounted cash flow analysis, but it would be irrational for them to allocate the time required for such an analysis.

A third argument relates to the cost of analyzing capital projects. To some extent, these costs are fixed; the costs may be larger for bigger projects, but not by much. To the extent that the costs of analysis are indeed fixed, it may not be economical to incur these costs if the project itself is relatively small. This argument suggests that small firms with projects that are comparatively small may in some cases be making the sensible decision when they rely upon management's "gut feeling."

Note also that a major part of the capital budgeting process in large firms involves lower level analysts marshalling facts needed by higher level decision makers. This step is less necessary in the small firm. Thus, a cursory examination of a small firm's decision process might suggest that capital budgeting decisions are based on snap judgment, but if that judgment is exercised by someone with a total knowledge of the firm and its markets, it could represent a better decision than one based on an elaborate analysis by a lower-level analyst in a large firm.

Also, as Soldofsky reported in his study of manufacturing firms, small firms tend to be cash oriented. They are concerned with basic survival, so they tend to look at expenditures from the standpoint of their near-term effects on cash. This cash and survival orientation leads the firm to focus on a relatively short time horizon, and this, in turn, leads to an emphasis on the payback period. The limitations of payback are well known, but in spite of those limitations, the technique is popular in small business, as it gives the firm a feel for when the cash committed to an investment will be recovered and thus available for new opportunities. Small firms that are cash oriented and have limited managerial resources may find the payback method an appealing compromise between the need for extensive analysis on the one hand and the high costs of analysis on the other.

Small firms also face greater uncertainty in the cash flows they might generate beyond the immediate future. Large firms such as IBM and General Motors have "staying power" — they can make an investment and then ride out business downturns or situations of excess capacity in an industry. Such periods are called "shake-outs," and it is the smaller firms that generally get shaken out. Therefore, most small business managers are uncomfortable making forecasts beyond a few years. Since discounted cash flow techniques require explicit estimates of cash flows through the life of the project, small business managers may not take seriously an analysis that hinges on "guesstimate" numbers which, if wrong, could lead to bankruptcy.

The Value of the Firm and Capital Budgeting

The single most appealing argument for the use of net present value in capital expenditure decisions is

[14]Robert M. Soldofsky, "Capital Budgeting Practices in Small Manufacturing Companies," in *Studies in the Factor Markets for Small Business Firms,* ed. Dudley G. Luckett (Washington, DC: Small Business Administration, 1964).

[15]L. R. Runyon, "Capital Expenditure Decision Making in Small Firms," *Journal of Business Research,* September 1983, 389–397.

that NPV gives an explicit measure of the effect of the investment on the value of the firm: if NPV is positive, the investment will increase the value of the firm and make its owners wealthier. In small firms, however, it is often the case that the stock is not traded in public markets, so its value cannot be easily observed. Also, for reasons of control, many small business owners and managers may not want to broaden ownership by going public.

It is difficult to argue for value-based techniques when the value of the firm itself is unobservable. Furthermore, in a closely-held firm the objectives of the individual owner-manager may extend beyond the firm's monetary value. For example, the owner-manager often values the firm's reputation for quality and service and therefore may make an investment that would be rejected on purely economic grounds. In addition, the owner-manager may not hold a well-diversified investment portfolio but may instead have all of his or her eggs in this one basket. In that case, the manager would logically be sensitive to the total risk of the firm, not just to its systematic or undiversifiable component. Thus, one project might be viewed as desirable because of its contribution to risk reduction in the firm as a whole, whereas another project with a low beta but high unsystematic risk might be unacceptable, even though in a CAPM framework it would be judged acceptable.

Another problem faced by a firm that is not publicly traded is that its cost of equity capital is not easily determined — the P_0 term in the cost of equity equation $k = D_1/P_0 + g$ is not observable, nor is its beta. Since a cost of capital estimate is required to use either the NPV or IRR methods, a small firm in an industry of small firms may simply have no basis for estimating its cost of capital.

Conclusions

Small firms make less extensive use of DCF techniques than larger firms. This may be a rational decision resulting from a conscious or subconscious conclusion that the costs of sophisticated analyses outweigh their benefits; it may reflect nonmonetary goals of small businesses' owner-managers; or it may reflect difficulties in estimating the cost of capital, which is required for DCF analyses but not for payback. However, nonuse of DCF methods may also reflect a weakness in many small business organizations. We simply do not know. We do know that small businesses must do all they can to compete effectively with big business, and to the extent that a small business fails to use DCF methods because its manager is unsophisticated or uninformed, it may be putting itself at a serious competitive disadvantage.

SUMMARY AND KEY CONCEPTS

This chapter discussed the capital budgeting process, and the key concepts covered are listed below.

- **Capital budgeting** is the process of analyzing potential expenditures on fixed assets and deciding whether the firm should undertake those investments.

- The capital budgeting process requires the firm (1) to determine the **cost of the project**, (2) to estimate the **expected cash flows** from the project and the riskiness of those cash flows, (3) to determine the appropriate **cost of capital** at which to discount the cash flows, and (4) to determine the **present values** of the expected cash flows and of the project.

- The **payback period** is defined as the expected number of years required to recover the original investment. The payback method ignores cash flows beyond the payback period, and it does not consider the time value of money. The payback does, however, provide an indication of a project's risk and liquidity, because it shows how long the original capital will be "at risk."

- The **discounted payback method** is similar to the regular payback method except that it discounts cash flows at the project's cost of capital. Like the regular payback method, it ignores cash flows beyond the discounted payback period.

- The **net present value (NPV) method** discounts all cash flows at the project's cost of capital and then sums those cash flows. The project is accepted if this sum, called the NPV, is positive.

- The **internal rate of return (IRR)** is defined as the rate of return on an investment that forces the present value of the future cash inflows to equal the cost of the investment. The project is accepted if the IRR is greater than the project's cost of capital.

- The NPV and IRR methods make the same accept/reject decisions for **independent projects,** but if projects are **mutually exclusive,** then ranking conflicts can arise. If conflicts arise, the NPV method should be used. Both the NPV and IRR methods are superior to the payback, but NPV is better than IRR.

- The NPV method assumes that cash flows will be reinvested at the firm's cost of capital, while the IRR method assumes reinvestment at the project's IRR. It is because **reinvestment at the cost of capital is the better assumption** that the NPV is superior to the IRR.

- The **modified IRR (IRR*) method** corrects some of the problems with the regular IRR. IRR* involves finding the terminal value (TV) of the cash inflows at the firm's cost of capital and then determining the rate (IRR*) which forces the TV to equal the present value of the outflows.

- The **post-audit** is one of the most important aspects of capital budgeting. By comparing actual results with predicted results, and then determining why differences occurred, decision makers can improve both their operations and their forecasts of projects' outcomes.

- Small firms tend to use the payback method rather than the discounted cash flow method. This may be a rational decision if (1) the **cost** of the DCF analysis **outweighs the benefits** for the project being considered, (2) **the firm's cost of capital cannot be estimated accurately,** or (3) the small business owner is trying to accomplish **nonmonetary goals.**

Although this chapter has presented the basic elements of the capital budgeting process, there are many other aspects of this crucial topic. Some of the more important ones are discussed in the following two chapters.

Questions

9-1   How is a project classification scheme (for example, replacement, expansion into new markets, and so forth) used in the capital budgeting process?

9-2   Explain why the NPV of a relatively long-term project, defined as one for which a high percentage of its cash flows is expected in the distant future, is more sensitive to changes in the cost of capital than is the NPV of a short-term project.

9-3   Explain why, if two mutually exclusive projects are being compared, the short-term project might have the higher ranking under the NPV criterion if the cost of capital is high, but the long-term project might be deemed better if the cost of capital is low. Would changes in the cost of capital ever cause a change in the IRR ranking of two such projects?

9-4   In what sense is a reinvestment rate assumption embodied in the NPV, IRR, and IRR* methods? What is the implicitly assumed reinvestment rate of each method?

9-5   "If a firm has no mutually exclusive projects, only independent ones, and it also has a constant cost of capital, and normal projects in the sense that each project has one or more outflows followed by a stream of inflows, then the NPV and IRR methods will always lead to identical capital budgeting decisions." Discuss this statement. What does it imply about using the IRR method in lieu of the NPV method? If each of the assumptions made in the question were changed (one by one), how would these changes affect your answer?

9-6   Are there conditions under which a firm might be better off if it were to choose a machine with a rapid payback rather than one with a larger NPV?

9-7   A firm has $100 million available for capital expenditures. It is considering investing in one of two projects; each has a cost of $100 million. Project A has an IRR of 20 percent and an NPV of $9 million. It will be terminated at the end of one year at a profit of $20 million, resulting in an immediate increase in earnings per share (EPS). Project B, which cannot be postponed, has an IRR of 30 percent and an NPV of $50 million. However, the firm's short-run EPS will be reduced if it accepts Project B, because no revenues will be generated for several years.
    a. Should the short-run effects on EPS influence the choice between the two projects?
    b. How might situations like the one described here influence a firm's decision to use payback as a part of the capital budgeting process?

Self-Test Problems   *(Solutions Appear on Page 374)*

Key terms

ST-1   Define each of the following terms:
    a. The capital budget; capital budgeting
    b. Regular payback period; discounted payback period
    c. DCF techniques; net present value (NPV) method
    d. Internal rate of return (IRR) method
    e. Modified internal rate of return (IRR*) method
    f. NPV profile; crossover rate
    g. Independent projects; mutually exclusive projects
    h. Project cost of capital
    i. Reinvestment rate assumption
    j. Post-audit

Project analysis

ST-2   You are a financial analyst for Porter Electronics Company. The director of capital budgeting has asked you to analyze two proposed capital investments, Projects S and L. Each project has a cost of $10,000, and the cost of capital for each project is 12 percent. The projects' expected net cash flows are as follows:

| Year | Expected Net Cash Flow | |
	Project S	Project L
0	($10,000)	($10,000)
1	6,500	3,500
2	3,000	3,500
3	3,000	3,500
4	1,000	3,500

a. Calculate each project's payback period, net present value (NPV), internal rate of return (IRR), and modified internal rate of return (IRR*).
b. Which project or projects should be accepted if they are independent?
c. Which project should be accepted if they are mutually exclusive?
d. How might a change in the cost of capital produce a conflict between the NPV and IRR rankings of these two projects? Would this conflict exist if k were 5%? (Hint: Plot the NPV profiles.)
e. Why does the conflict exist?

Problems

Payback, NPV, and
IRR calculations

9-1   Project L has a cost of $65,000, and its expected net cash inflows are $15,000 per year for 8 years.
a. What is the project's payback period (to the closest year)?
b. The cost of capital is 14 percent. What is the project's NPV?
c. What is the project's IRR? (Hint: Recognize that the project is an annuity.)

NPVs and IRRs for
independent projects

9-2   Parrish Engineering is considering including two pieces of equipment, a truck and an overhead pulley system, in this year's capital budget. The projects are not mutually exclusive. The cash outlay for the truck is $17,350, and that for the pulley system is $24,225. The firm's cost of capital is 15 percent. After-tax cash flows, including depreciation, are as follows:

Year	Truck	Pulley
1	$5,300	$8,100
2	5,300	8,100
3	5,300	8,100
4	5,300	8,100
5	5,300	8,100

Calculate the IRR and NPV for each project, and indicate the correct accept/reject decision for each.

NPVs and IRRs for
mutually exclusive
projects

9-3   Besley Industries must choose between a gas-powered and an electric-powered forklift truck for moving materials in its factory. Since both forklifts perform the same function, the firm will choose only one. (They are mutually exclusive investments.) The electric-powered truck will cost more, but it will be less expensive to operate; it will cost $22,000, whereas the gas-powered truck will cost $17,600. The cost of capital that applies to both investments is 10 percent. The life for both types of truck is estimated to be 6 years, during which time the net cash flows for the electric-powered truck will be $6,600 per year and those for the gas-powered truck will be $5,300 per year. Annual net cash flows include depreciation expenses. Calculate the NPV and IRR for each type of truck, and decide which to recommend for purchase.

Capital budgeting methods   **9-4**   Project S costs $10,000 and is expected to produce benefits (cash flows) of $3,000 per year for five years. Project L costs $25,000 and is expected to produce cash flows of $7,400 per year for five years. Calculate the two projects' NPVs, IRRs, and IRR*s, assuming a cost of capital of 12 percent. Which project would be selected, assuming they are mutually exclusive, using each ranking method? Which should actually be selected?

NPV and IRR analysis   **9-5**   Rivoli Products Company is considering two mutually exclusive investments. The projects' expected net cash flows are as follows:

| Year | Expected Net Cash Flow | |
	Project A	Project B
0	($300)	($405)
1	(387)	134
2	(193)	134
3	(100)	134
4	600	134
5	600	134
6	850	134
7	(180)	0

a. Construct NPV profiles for Projects A and B.
b. What is each project's IRR?
c. If you were told that each project's cost of capital was 10 percent, which project should be selected? If the cost of capital was 17 percent, what would the proper choice be?
d. What is each project's IRR* at a cost of capital of 10 percent? At k = 17%?
e. What is the crossover rate, and what is its significance?

Timing differences   **9-6**   The Texas Oil Exploration Company is considering two mutually exclusive plans for extracting oil on property for which it has mineral rights. Both plans call for the expenditure of $10,000,000 to drill development wells. Under Plan A, all the oil will be extracted in one year, producing a cash flow at t = 1 of $12,000,000. Under Plan B, cash flows will be $1,750,000 per year for 20 years.

a. What are the annual incremental cash flows that will be available to Texas Oil Exploration if it undertakes Plan B rather than Plan A? (Hint: Subtract Plan A's flows from B's.)
b. If Texas Oil accepts Plan A, then invests the extra cash generated at the end of Year 1, what rate of return (reinvestment rate) would cause the cash flows from reinvestment to equal the cash flows from Plan B?

c. Suppose a company has a cost of capital of 10 percent. Is it logical to assume that it would take on all available independent projects (of average risk) with returns greater than 10 percent? Further, if all available projects with returns greater than 10 percent have been taken on, would this mean that cash flows from past investments would have an opportunity cost of only 10 percent, because all the firm could do with these cash flows would be to replace money that has a cost of 10 percent? Finally, does this imply that the cost of capital is the correct rate to assume for the reinvestment of a project's cash flows?

d. Construct NPV profiles for Plans A and B, identify each project's IRR, and indicate the crossover rate of return.

Scale differences   **9-7**   The McDaniel Publishing Company is considering two mutually exclusive expansion plans. Plan A calls for the expenditure of $50 million on a large-scale, integrated plant which will provide an expected cash flow stream of $8 million per year for 20 years. Plan B calls for the expenditure of $15 million to build a somewhat less efficient, more labor-intensive plant which has an expected cash flow stream of $3.4 million per year for 20 years. McDaniel's cost of capital is 10 percent.

a. Calculate each project's NPV and IRR.

b. Set up a Project Δ which has cash flows equal to the difference between the cash flows for Plan A and for Plan B. In other words, if McDaniel goes with the larger plant, Plan A, its investment will be $35 million larger than if it built the smaller plant and its annual cash flows will be $4.6 million larger. What are the NPV and the IRR for this Project Δ?

c. Graph the NPV profiles for Plan A, Plan B, and Project Δ.

d. Give a logical explanation, based on reinvestment rates and opportunity costs, as to why the NPV method is better than the IRR method when the firm's cost of capital is constant at some value, such as 10 percent.

Multiple rates of return   **9-8**   The Stenardi Uranium Company is deciding whether or not it should open a strip mine, the net cost of which is $4.4 million. Net cash inflows are expected to be $27.7 million, all coming at the end of Year 1. The land must be returned to its natural state at a cost of $25 million, payable at the end of Year 2.

a. Plot the project's NPV profile.

b. Should the project be accepted if k = 8%? If k = 14%? Explain your reasoning.

c. Can you think of some other capital budgeting situations in which negative cash flows during or at the other end of the project's life might lead to multiple IRRs?

Multiple rates of return   **9-9**   The Wei Development Company (WDC) has many excellent investment opportunities, but it has insufficient cash to undertake them all. WDC has been offered the chance to borrow $2 million from the Pacific City Retirement Fund at 10 percent, with the loan to be repaid at the end of one year. Also, a "consulting fee" of $700,000 will be paid to Pacific City's mayor at the end of one year for helping to arrange the credit. Of the $2 million received, $1 million will be used immediately to buy an old city-owned hotel and to convert it to a gambling casino. The other $1 million will be invested in other lucrative WDC projects that otherwise would have to be forgone because of a lack of capital. For two years, all cash generated by the casino will be plowed back into the casino project. At the end of two years, the casino sold for $2 million.

Assuming that (1) the deal has been worked out in the sunshine and is completely legal and (2) cash from the other WDC Company operations will be available to make the required payments at the end of Year 1, under what rate-of-return conditions should WDC accept the offer? Disregard taxes.

Present value of costs   **9-10**   The Scampini Coffee Company is evaluating the within-plant distribution system for its new roasting, grinding, and packing plant. The two alternatives are (1) a conveyor system with a high initial cost but low annual operating costs and (2) several forklift trucks, which cost less but have considerably higher operating costs. The decision to construct the plant has already been made, and the choice here will have no effect on the overall revenues of the project. The cost of capital for the plant is 8 percent, and the projects' expected net costs are listed in the table:

Year	Expected Net Cash	
	Conveyor	Forklift
0	($500,000)	($200,000)
1	(110,000)	(160,000)
2	(110,000)	(160,000)
3	(110,000)	(160,000)
4	(110,000)	(160,000)
5	(110,000)	(160,000)

a. What is the IRR of each alternative?
b. What is the present value of costs of each alternative? Which method should be chosen?

Basics of capital budgeting (Integrative)   **9-11**   George Bryant, director of capital budgeting for Bayside Marine, has just completed estimating the cash flows of two projects that the firm is considering. Project L is the code name for an upgraded Loran navigation receiver, and Project S is a sonar-based depth sounder. Both projects involve the production and sale of new models of marine electronics equipment, but they differ significantly in their production and sales schedules. L's cash flows will increase over time, while S's will decline. The projects both have 3-year lives, because Bayside is expecting to market a new generation of devices at that time. The following is Bryant's net cash flow estimates (in thousands of dollars):

Year	Expected Net Cash Flow	
	Project L	Project S
0	($100)	($100)
1	10	70
2	60	50
3	80	20

Depreciation, salvage values, net working capital requirements, and tax effects are included in these cash flows.

Also, Bryant made a subjective risk assessment of both projects, and he concluded that they both have risk characteristics similar to those of Bayside's other projects. The firm's overall cost of capital is 10 percent. Now Bryant must determine whether the projects should be accepted or rejected, and then make a presentation to the company's board of directors. Bryant plans to conduct his analysis and presentation by asking and then answering the following questions:

a. What is capital budgeting? Is there any similarity between firms' capital budgeting decisions and individuals' investment decisions?

b. What is the difference between independent and mutually exclusive projects? Between normal and nonnormal projects?

c. What is the payback period? Find the paybacks for Projects L and S. What is the rationale for using payback? According to the payback method, which project or projects would be accepted if Bayside's maximum acceptable payback were 2 years and the projects were independent? Mutually exclusive? What is the difference between payback and discounted payback? What is the main disadvantage of payback? Does the payback method provide any useful information when making a capital budgeting decision such as this one?

d. Define the term net present value (NPV). What is each project's NPV? What is the rationale behind NPV? According to NPV, which project or projects would be accepted if they were independent? Mutually exclusive? Would the NPV change if the cost of capital changed?

e. Define the term internal rate of return (IRR). What is each project's IRR? What is the logic behind IRR? According to IRR, which project or projects would be accepted if they were independent? Mutually exclusive? Would the projects' IRRs change if the cost of capital changed?

f. What is the underlying cause of ranking conflicts between NPV and IRR? Under what conditions can conflicts occur? Which method is better? Why?

g. What are the three properties that a capital budgeting evaluation method must exhibit if it is to lead to correct capital budgeting decisions? Which of the methods we discussed have these properties?

h. Draw the NPV profiles for Projects L and S. At what cost of capital do the profiles cross? What are the implications of the NPV profiles regarding the acceptability of Projects L and S using NPV and IRR, assuming that the projects are independent? Assuming that they are mutually exclusive? What condition could cause a ranking conflict?

i. Assume that Bayside Marine is considering sponsoring a pavilion at the upcoming World's Fair (Project F). The pavilion would cost $800,000, and it is expected to generate $5 million in cash flow during its year of operation. However, it would then take another year and $5 million to demolish the building and return the site to its original condition. Thus, Project F's expected net cash flows look like this (in millions of dollars):

Year	Cash Flow
0	($0.8)
1	5
2	(5)

The project is estimated to have average risk, and hence its cost of capital is 10 percent. What is Project F's NPV? What is its IRR? Draw Project F's NPV profile. Does Project F have normal or nonnormal cash flows? Should the project be accepted?

j. Define the modified IRR (IRR*). Find IRR* for Projects L, S, and F. Why is IRR* better than IRR? Is IRR* as good as NPV?

Computer-Related Problem

(Work the problem in this section only if you are using the computer problem diskette.)

NPV and IRR analysis

C9-1   Use the model for Problem C9-1 in the file C9 to solve this problem.
Northeast Chemical Company (NCC) is considering two mutually exclusive investments. The projects' expected net cash flows are as follows:

| | Expected Net Cash Flow | |
Year	Project A	Project B
0	($39,000)	($53,000)
1	(18,000)	17,000
2	36,000	17,000
3	36,000	17,000
4	36,000	17,000
5	(24,000)	17,000

a. Construct NPV profiles for Projects A and B.
b. Calculate each project's IRR and IRR*. Assume the cost of capital is 12 percent.
c. If the cost of capital for each project is 12 percent, which project should Northeast select? If the cost of capital were 8 percent, what would be the proper choice? If the cost of capital were 16 percent, what would be the proper choice?
d. At what rate do the NPV profiles of the two projects cross?
e. Project A has a large negative outflow in Year 5 associated with ending the project. NCC's management is confident of Project A's cash flows in Years 0 to 4 but is uncertain about what its Year 5 cash flow will be. (There is no uncertainty about Project B's cash flows.) Under a worst case scenario, Project A's Year 5 cash flow will be − $30,000, whereas under a best case scenario, the cash flow will be − $20,000. Redo Parts a, b, and d for each scenario, assuming a 12 percent cost of capital. Press the F10 function key (in the lower left corner of the keyboard) to see the new NPV profiles. If the cost of capital for each project is 12 percent, which project should be selected under each scenario?

Solutions to Self-Test Problems

ST-1   Refer to the marginal glossary definitions and appropriate sections of the text to check your responses.

ST-2   a. *Payback:*
To determine the payback, construct the cumulative cash flows for each project:

| | Cumulative Cash Flow | |
Year	Project S	Project L
0	($10,000)	($10,000)
1	(3,500)	(6,500)
2	(500)	(3,000)
3	2,500	500
4	3,500	4,000

$$\text{Payback}_S = 2 + \frac{\$500}{\$3,000} = 2.17 \text{ years.}$$

$$\text{Payback}_L = 2 + \frac{\$3,000}{\$3,500} = 2.86 \text{ years.}$$

Net Present Value (NPV):

$$\text{NPV}_S = -\$10,000 + \frac{\$6,500}{(1.12)^1} + \frac{\$3,000}{(1.12)^2} + \frac{\$3,000}{(1.12)^3} + \frac{\$1,000}{(1.12)^4}$$

$$= \$966.01$$

$$\text{NPV}_L = -\$10,000 + \frac{\$3,500}{(1.12)^1} + \frac{\$3,500}{(1.12)^2} + \frac{\$3,500}{(1.12)^3} + \frac{\$3,500}{(1.12)^4}$$

$$= \$630.72.$$

Internal Rate of Return (IRR):
To solve for each project's IRR, find the discount rates which equate each NPV to zero:

$$\text{IRR}_S = 18.0\%.$$

$$\text{IRR}_L = 15.0\%.$$

Modified Internal Rate of Return (IRR*):
To obtain each project's IRR*, begin by finding each project's terminal value (TV) of cash inflows:

$$\text{TV}_S = \$6,500(1.12)^3 + \$3,000(1.12)^2$$

$$+ \$3,000(1.12)^1 + \$1,000 = \$17,255.23.$$

$$\text{TV}_L = \$3,500(1.12)^3 + \$3,500(1.12)^2$$

$$+ \$3,500(1.12)^1 + \$3,500 = \$16,727.65.$$

Now, each project's IRR* is that discount rate which equates the PV of the TV to each project's cost, $10,000:

$$\text{IRR}^*_S = 14.61\%.$$

$$\text{IRR}^*_L = 13.73\%.$$

b. The following table summarizes the project rankings by each method:

	Project Which Ranks Higher
Payback	S
NPV	S
IRR	S
IRR*	S

Note that all methods rank Project S over Project L. In addition, both projects are acceptable under the NPV, IRR, and IRR* criteria. Thus, both projects should be accepted if they are independent.

c. In this case, we would choose the project with the higher NPV at k = 12%, or Project S.

d. To determine the effects of changing the cost of capital, plot the NPV profiles of each project. The crossover rate occurs at about 6 to 7 percent.

NPV Profiles for Projects S and L

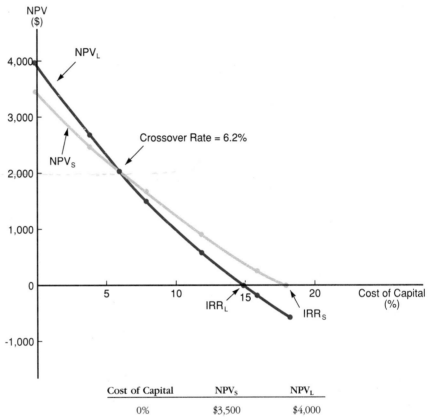

Cost of Capital	NPV$_S$	NPV$_L$
0%	$3,500	$4,000
4	2,546	2,705
8	1,707	1,592
12	966	630
16	307	(206)
18	5	(585)

If the firm's cost of capital is less than 6 percent, a conflict exists because NPV$_L$ > NPV$_S$, but IRR$_S$ > IRR$_L$. Therefore, if k were 5 percent, a conflict would exist. Note, however, that when k = 5.0%, IRR*$_S$ = 10.64% and IRR*$_L$ = 10.83%; hence the modified IRR ranks the projects correctly, even if k is to the left of the crossover point.

e. The basic cause of the conflict is differing reinvestment rate assumptions between NPV and IRR. NPV assumes that cash flows can be reinvested at the cost of capital, while IRR assumes reinvestment at the (generally) higher IRR. The high reinvestment rate assumption under IRR makes early cash flows especially valuable, and hence short-term projects look better under IRR.

10

Cash Flow Estimation, Replacement, and Other Topics in Capital Budgeting

FEDERAL EXPRESS LEARNS THE IMPORTANCE OF ACCURATE CASH FLOW ESTIMATION

Federal Express recently abandoned its ZapMail electronic delivery service. The system had worked like this: ZapMail customers would lease a state-of-the-art facsimile machine capable of transmitting documents via a special satellite communications network. Then, in just seconds, a customer in Atlanta, for example, could transmit a document to another customer, say in Boise. ZapMail was intended to replace overnight air delivery as the best way to ship important documents to far-flung locations.

Federal Express expected to spend about $200 million on ZapMail, and it expected to earn a high return on this investment. However, because potential customers resisted the cost of the service (initially $35, but eventually lowered to $25, for up to 10 pages) the system never generated the expected revenues. At the same time, software and hardware problems pushed the investment requirement to well over $300 million. As a result, ZapMail had operating losses of $132 million on revenues of only $33 million in its first year, so the project was terminated and the investment was written off as a loss.

Federal Express used the correct capital budgeting technique, NPV, yet the ZapMail project was still a failure. Revenues were projected too high and costs too low, so cash flows failed to meet the forecasted levels. This example demonstrates a basic truth — if cash flow estimates are not reasonably accurate, any analytical technique, no matter how sophisticated, can lead to poor decisions and hence to operating losses and lower stock prices.

THE basic principles of capital budgeting were covered in Chapter 9. Now we examine some additional issues, including (1) cash flow estimation, (2) replacement decisions, (3) mutually exclusive projects with unequal lives, and (4) the effects of inflation on capital budgeting analysis.

CASH FLOW ESTIMATION

*vs. investment outlays
cash inflows due
to implementation of
project*

cash flow
The actual net cash, as opposed to accounting net income, that flows into (or out of) a firm during some specified period.

*unit sales
unit Price
operating costs
capital outlays
(LAND)*

The most important, but also the most difficult, step in the analysis of a capital project is estimating its **cash flows** — the investment outlays and the annual net cash inflows after the project goes into operation. Many variables are involved in cash flow forecasting, and many individuals and departments participate in the process. For example, the forecasts of unit sales and sales prices are normally made by the marketing group, based on their knowledge of price elasticity, advertising effects, the state of the economy, competitors' reactions, and trends in consumers' tastes. Similarly, the capital outlays associated with a new product are generally obtained from the engineering and product development staffs, while operating costs are estimated by cost accountants, production experts, personnel specialists, purchasing agents, and so forth.

Because it is difficult to make accurate forecasts of the costs and revenues associated with a large, complex project, forecast errors can be quite large. For example, when several major oil companies decided to build the Alaska Pipeline, the original cost forecasts were in the neighborhood of $700 million, but the final cost was closer to $7 billion. Similar (or even worse) miscalculations are common in forecasts of product design costs, such as the costs to develop a new personal computer. Further, as difficult as plant and equipment costs are to estimate, sales revenues and operating costs over the life of the project are generally even more uncertain. For example, when Federal Express developed its ZapMail project, it envisaged large sales, yet it turned out that virtually no one was willing to pay the price required to cover the project's costs. Because of its financial strength, Federal Express was able to absorb losses on the project with no problem, but the ZapMail venture could have forced a weaker firm into bankruptcy.

The financial staff's role in the forecasting process includes (1) coordinating the efforts of the other departments, such as engineering and marketing, (2) ensuring that everyone involved with the forecast uses a consistent set of economic assumptions, and (3) making sure that no biases are inherent in the forecasts. This last point is extremely important, because division managers often become emotionally involved with pet projects or develop empire-building complexes, both of which tend to lead to cash flow forecasting biases

Table 10-1   Accounting Profit versus Net Cash Flow (Thousands of Dollars)

	Accounting Profits	Cash Flows
I. 1990 Situation		
Sales	$100,000	$100,000
Costs except depreciation	50,000	50,000
Depreciation	30,000	0
Operating income	$ 20,000	$ 50,000
Federal-plus-state taxes (40%)	8,000	8,000
Net income or net cash flow	$ 12,000	$ 42,000

Net cash flow = Net income plus depreciation = $12,000 + $30,000 = $42,000.

	Accounting Profits	Cash Flows
II. 1995 Situation		
Sales	$100,000	$100,000
Costs except depreciation	50,000	50,000
Depreciation	10,000	0
Operating income	$ 40,000	$ 50,000
Federal-plus-state taxes (40%)	16,000	16,000
Net income or net cash flow	$ 24,000	$ 34,000

Net cash flow = $24,000 + $10,000 = $34,000.

which make bad projects look good — on paper. The ZapMail project is an example of this problem.

It is almost impossible to overstate the difficulties one can encounter in cash flow forecasts. It is also difficult to overstate the importance of these forecasts. Still, observing the principles discussed in the next several sections will help to minimize forecast errors.

IDENTIFYING THE RELEVANT CASH FLOWS

One important element in cash flow estimation is the identification of *relevant cash flows,* which are defined as the specific set of cash flows that should be considered in the decision at hand. Errors are often made here, but there are two cardinal rules which can help financial analysts avoid mistakes: (1) Capital budgeting decisions must be based on *cash flows,* not accounting income, and (2) only *incremental cash flows* are relevant to the accept/reject decision. These two rules are discussed in detail in the following sections.

Cash Flow versus Accounting Income

In capital budgeting analysis, *annual cash flows, not accounting profits,* are used. Cash flows and accounting profits can be very different. To illustrate, consider Table 10-1, which shows how accounting profits and cash flows are related to each other. We assume that HBJ Publishing is planning to start a new

NI + Dep =
Net cash flows

available
for other
investments

division at the end of 1989; that sales and all costs except depreciation represent actual cash flows and are projected to be constant over time; and that the division will use accelerated depreciation, which, as we discussed in Chapter 2, will cause its reported depreciation charges to decline over time.

The top section of the table shows the situation in the first year of operations, 1990. Accounting profits are $12 million, but the division's net cash flow — money which is available to HBJ — is $42 million. The bottom part of the table shows the situation projected for 1995. Here reported profits have doubled (because of the decline in depreciation), but the net cash flow is down sharply. Accounting profits are important for some purposes, but for purposes of setting a value on a project using DCF techniques, cash flows are what is relevant. Therefore, in capital budgeting, we are interested in net cash flows, defined as

$$\text{Net cash flow} = \text{Net income after taxes} + \text{Depreciation},$$

not in accounting profits per se.[1]

Incremental Cash Flows *$ coming directly from project*

In evaluating a capital project, we are concerned only with those cash flows that result directly from the project. These cash flows, called **incremental cash flows**, represent the change in the firm's total cash flows that occurs as a direct result of accepting or rejecting the project. Four special problems in determining incremental cash flows are discussed next.

Sunk Costs. Sunk costs are not incremental costs, and they should not be included in the analysis.[2] A **sunk cost** is an outlay that has already been committed or that has already occurred and hence is not affected by the accept/reject decision under consideration. To illustrate, in 1989 Northeast BankCorp was considering the establishment of a branch office in a newly developed section of Boston. To help with its evaluation, Northeast had, back in 1988, hired a consulting firm to perform a site analysis at a cost of $100,000; this amount was expensed for tax purposes in 1988. Is this 1988 expenditure a relevant cost with respect to the 1989 capital budgeting decision? The answer is no —

incremental cash flow
The net cash flow attributable to an investment project.

sunk cost
A cash outlay that has already been incurred and which cannot be recovered regardless of whether the project is accepted or rejected.

---

[1] Actually, net cash flow should be adjusted to reflect all noncash charges, not just depreciation. However, for most firms, depreciation is by far the largest noncash charge. Also, notice that Table 10-1 ignores interest charges, which would be present if the firm used debt. Most firms do use debt and hence finance part of their investments in capital projects with debt. Therefore, the question has been raised as to whether or not interest charges should be reflected in capital budgeting cash flow analysis. The consensus is that interest charges should *not* be dealt with explicitly in capital budgeting — rather, the effects of debt financing are reflected in the cost of capital which is used to discount the cash flows. The cost of capital is discussed in Chapter 16.

[2] For a classic example of the improper treatment of sunk costs by a major corporation, see U. E. Reinhardt, "Break-Even Analysis for Lockheed's TriStar: An Application of Financial Theory," *Journal of Finance,* September 1973, 821–838.

the $100,000 is a sunk cost, and Northeast cannot recover it regardless of whether or not the new branch is built. It often turns out that a particular project has a negative NPV when all the associated costs, including sunk costs, are considered. However, on an incremental basis the project may be a good one, because the incremental cash flows are large enough to produce a positive NPV on the incremental investment.

opportunity cost
The return on the best *alternative* use of an asset; the highest return that will *not* be earned if funds are invested in a particular project.

Opportunity Costs. The second potential problem relates to **opportunity costs**, defined here as the cash flows that can be generated from assets the firm already owns if they are not used for the project in question. To illustrate, Northeast BankCorp already owns a piece of land that is suitable for the branch location. When evaluating the prospective branch, should the cost of the land be disregarded because no additional cash outlay would be required? The answer is no, because there is an opportunity cost inherent in the use of the property. In this case, the land could be sold to yield $150,000 after taxes. Use of the site for the branch would require forgoing this inflow, so the $150,000 must be charged as an opportunity cost against the project. Note that the proper land cost in this example is the $150,000 market-determined value, irrespective of whether Northeast originally paid $50,000 or $500,000 for the property. (What Northeast paid would, of course, have an effect on taxes and hence on the after-tax opportunity cost.)

externalities
Effects of a project on cash flows in other parts of the firm.

Effects on Other Parts of the Firm: Externalities. The third potential problem involves the effects of a project on other parts of the firm, which economists call **externalities**. For example, some of Northeast's customers who would use the new branch are already banking with Northeast's downtown office. The loans and deposits, and hence profits, generated by these customers would not be new to the bank; rather, they would represent a transfer from the main office to the branch. Thus, the net revenues produced by these customers should not be treated as incremental income in the capital budgeting decision. On the other hand, having a suburban branch would help the bank attract new business to its downtown office, because some potential customers could now make transactions both from home and from work. In this case, the additional revenues that would actually flow to the downtown office should be attributed to the branch. Although often difficult to quantify, externalities such as these must be considered.

Shipping and Installation Costs. When a firm acquires fixed assets, it often must incur substantial costs for shipping and installing the equipment. These charges are added to the invoice price of the equipment when the cost of the project is being determined. Also, the full cost of the equipment, including shipping and installation costs, is used as the depreciable basis when depreciation charges are being calculated. Thus, if Northeast BankCorp bought a computer with an invoice price of $100,000, and paid another $10,000 for shipping and installation, then the full cost of the computer, and its depreciable basis, would be $110,000.

CHANGES IN NET WORKING CAPITAL

change in net working capital
The increased current assets resulting from a new project minus the increased current liabilities.

Normally, additional inventories are required to support a new operation, and expanded sales also lead to additional accounts receivable. Both of these asset increases must be financed. However, accounts payable and accruals will increase spontaneously as a result of the expansion, and this will reduce the net cash needed to finance inventories and receivables. The difference between the increase in current assets and the spontaneous increase in current liabilities is the **change in net working capital**. If this change is positive, as it generally is for expansion projects, this indicates that additional financing, over and above the cost of the fixed assets, is needed to fund the increase in current assets.

As the project approaches termination, inventories are sold off and not replaced, and receivables also are converted to cash. As these changes occur, the firm receives an end-of-project cash flow that is equal to the net working capital requirement that occurred when the project was begun.

CAPITAL BUDGETING PROJECT EVALUATION

Up to this point, we have discussed several important aspects of cash flow analysis, but we have not seen how they affect the capital budgeting decision. In this section, we illustrate these effects by examining two types of capital budgeting decisions — new expansion project analysis and replacement project analysis.

Expansion Projects

expansion project
A project that is intended to increase sales.

New facility

An **expansion project** is defined as one that calls for the firm to invest in new facilities to increase sales. We will illustrate expansion project analysis by examining a project that is being considered by Brandt-Quigley Corporation (BQC), an Atlanta-based technology company. BQC's research and development department has been applying its expertise in microprocessor technology to develop a small computer specifically designed to control home appliances. Once programmed, the computer would automatically control the heating and air conditioning systems, security system, hot water heater, and even small appliances such as a coffee maker. By increasing a home's energy efficiency, the computer can save enough on costs to pay for itself within a few years. Developments have now reached the stage at which a decision must be made about whether or not to go forward with production.

BQC's marketing department plans to target sales of the appliance computer toward the owners of larger homes; the computer is cost effective only in homes with 2,000 or more square feet of heated/air-conditioned space. The marketing vice-president believes that annual sales would be 20,000 units if the units were priced at $2,000 each, so annual sales are estimated at $40 million. The engineering department has reported that the firm would need additional manufacturing capability, and BQC currently has an option to purchase an existing building at a cost of $12 million which would meet this need. The building would be bought and paid for in one year, on December 31, 1989, and for depreciation purposes would fall into the ACRS 31.5-year class.

The necessary equipment would be purchased and installed late in 1989, and it would also be paid for on December 31, 1989. The equipment would fall into the ACRS 5-year class, and it would cost $8 million, including transportation and installation.

The project also would require an initial investment of $6 million in net working capital. The initial working capital investment would also be made on December 31, 1989. The project's estimated economic life is 4 years. At the end of that time, the building is expected to have a market value of $7.5 million and a book value of $10.74 million, whereas the equipment would have a market value of $2 million and a book value of $1.36 million. The production department has estimated that variable manufacturing costs would total 60 percent of sales and that fixed overhead costs, excluding depreciation, would be $5 million a year. Depreciation expenses would vary from year to year in accordance with the ACRS rates (which were discussed in Chapter 2).

BQC's marginal federal-plus-state tax rate is 40 percent; its cost of capital is 12 percent; and for capital budgeting purposes, the company's policy is to assume that cash flows occur at the end of each year. Because the plant would begin operations on January 1, 1990, the first operating cash flows would occur on December 31, 1990.

As one of the company's financial analysts, you have been assigned the task of supervising the capital budgeting analysis. For now, you may assume that the project has the same amount of risk as the firm's average project, and you may use the corporate required rate of return, 12 percent, for this project. In Chapter 11, we will examine additional information about the riskiness of the project, but at this point assume that the project is of average risk.

Analysis of the Cash Flows. The first step in the analysis is to summarize the investment outlays required for the project; this is done in the first column of Table 10-2. For BQC's computer project, the cash outlays consist of the purchase price of the building, the price of the needed equipment, and the required investment in net working capital (NWC).

Having estimated the capital requirements, we must now estimate the cash flows that will occur once production begins; these are set forth in the remaining columns of Table 10-2. The operating cash flow estimates are based on information provided by BQC's various departments. The depreciation amounts were obtained by multiplying the depreciable basis by the ACRS recovery allowance rates set forth in Note b to Table 10-2.

The investment in net working capital will be recovered in 1993. Also, an estimate of the cash flows from the salvage values is required, and Table 10-3 summarizes this analysis. The building has an estimated salvage value which is

Table 10-2   BQC Expansion Project
Net Cash Flows, 1989–1993
(Thousands of Dollars)

	1989	1990	1991	1992	1993
Building	($12,000)				
Equipment	(8,000)				
Increase in NWC[a]	(6,000)				
Sales		$40,000	$40,000	$40,000	$40,000
Variable costs (60% of sales)		24,000	24,000	24,000	24,000
Fixed costs		5,000	5,000	5,000	5,000
Depreciation (building)[b]		180	360	360	360
Depreciation (equipment)[b]		1,600	2,560	1,520	960
Earnings before taxes		$ 9,220	$ 8,080	$ 9,120	$ 9,680
Taxes (40%)		3,688	3,232	3,648	3,872
Net income		$ 5,532	$ 4,848	$ 5,472	$ 5,808
Add back depreciation		1,780	2,920	1,880	1,320
Cash flow from operations		$ 7,312	$ 7,768	$ 7,352	$ 7,128
Return of NWC					6,000
Net salvage value (see Table 10-3)					10,540
Net cash flow	($26,000)	$ 7,312	$ 7,768	$ 7,352	$23,668
Net present value (12%)	$ 6,996				

[a]NWC = net working capital. These funds will be recovered at the end of the project's operating life, 1993, as inventories are sold off and not replaced and as receivables are collected.

[b]ACRS depreciation expenses were calculated using the following rates:

Year	1	2	3	4
Depreciation rates (building)	1.5%	3.0%	3.0%	3.0%
Depreciation rates (equipment)	20.0%	32.0%	19.0%	12.0%

These percentages were multiplied by the depreciable basis ($12,000,000 for the building and $8,000,000 for the equipment) to determine the depreciation expense for each year. The allowances have been rounded for ease of computation. See Chapter 2 for a review of ACRS.

less than its book value — it will be sold at a loss for tax purposes. This loss will reduce taxable income and thus will generate a tax savings. In effect, the company has been depreciating the building too slowly, and it will write off the loss against its ordinary income, saving taxes that it would otherwise have to pay. The equipment, on the other hand, will be sold for more than its book value, and the company will have to pay taxes on the $640,000 profit. In both cases, the book value is calculated as the initial cost minus the accumulated depreciation. The total cash flow from salvage is merely the sum of the net salvage values of the building and equipment components.

Making the Decision. To summarize the data and get them ready for evaluation, it is useful to combine all of the net cash flows on a time line like the one shown in Figure 10-1, using data taken from Table 10-2. Figure 10-1 also shows the payback period, IRR, IRR*, and NPV (at the 12 percent cost of capital). The project appears to be acceptable using the NPV, IRR, and IRR* meth-

Table 10-3   Net Salvage Values, 1993

	Building	Equipment
Initial cost	$12,000,000	$8,000,000
Salvage (market) value	7,500,000	2,000,000
Book value[a]	10,740,000	1,360,000
Gain (loss) on sale[b]	($ 3,240,000)	$ 640,000
Taxes (40%)	(1,296,000)	256,000
Net salvage value[c]	$ 8,796,000	$1,744,000

Total cash flow from salvage value = $8,796,000 + $1,744,000 = $10,540,000.

[a]The book values equal depreciable basis (initial cost in this case) minus accumulated ACRS depreciation. For the building, accumulated depreciation equals $1,260,000, so book value equals $12,000,000 − $1,260,000 = $10,740,000; for the equipment, accumulated depreciation equals $6,640,000, so book value equals $8,000,000 − $6,640,000 = $1,360,000.

[b]Building: $7,500,000 market value − $10,740,000 book value = − $3,240.000. This represents a shortfall in depreciation taken versus "true" depreciation, and it is treated as an operating expense for 1993.

Equipment: $2,000,000 market value − $1,360,000 book value = $640,000. Here the depreciation charge exceeds the "true" depreciation, and the difference is called "depreciation recapture." It is taxed as ordinary income in 1993.

[c]Net salvage value equals salvage (market) value minus taxes. For the building, the loss results in a tax credit.

ods, and it also would be acceptable if BQC required a payback period of four years or less. Note, however, that the analysis thus far has been based on the assumption that the project has the same degree of risk as the company's average project. If the project were judged to be riskier than an average project, it would be necessary to increase the cost of capital, which in turn might cause the NPV to become negative and IRR and IRR* to fall below k. In Chapter 11, we will extend the evaluation of this project to include a risk analysis.

Replacement Analysis

Brandt-Quigley's appliance control computer project was used to show how an expansion project is analyzed. All companies, including this one, also make replacement decisions, and the analysis relating to replacements is somewhat different from that for expansion because the cash flows from the old asset must be considered. **Replacement analysis** is illustrated with another BQC example, this time from the company's research and development (R&D) division.

replacement analysis
An analysis involving the decision of whether or not to replace an existing asset that is still productive with a new one.

A lathe for trimming molded plastics was purchased 10 years ago at a cost of $7,500. The machine had an expected life of 15 years at the time it was purchased, and management originally estimated, and still believes, that the salvage value will be zero at the end of the 15-year life. The machine is being depreciated on a straight line basis; therefore, its annual depreciation charge is $500, and its present book value is $2,500.[3]

---

[3]This machine was purchased prior to the Tax Act of 1981, so ACRS was not in place at the time. The company chose to depreciate the lathe on a straight line basis.

Figure 10-1   Time Line of Consolidated Net Cash Flows, 1989–1993

1989	1990	1991	1992	1993
($26,000,000)	$7,312,000	$7,768,000	$7,352,000	$23,668,000

Payback period: 3.15 years.
IRR: 21.9% versus a 12% cost of capital.
IRR*: 18.9% versus a 12% cost of capital.
NPV: $6,995,624.

The R&D manager reports that a new special-purpose machine can be purchased for $12,000 (including freight and installation), and, over its 5-year life, it will reduce labor and raw materials usage sufficiently to cut operating costs from $7,000 to $4,000. This reduction in costs will cause before-tax profits to rise by $7,000 − $4,000 = $3,000 per year.

It is estimated that the new machine can be sold for $2,000 at the end of 5 years; this is its estimated salvage value. The old machine's actual current market value is $1,000, which is below its $2,500 book value. If the new machine is acquired, the old lathe will be sold to another company rather than exchanged for the new machine. The company's marginal federal-plus-state tax rate is 40 percent, and the replacement project is of average risk. Net working capital requirements will also increase by $1,000 at the time of replacement. By an IRS ruling, the new machine falls into the 3-year ACRS class, and, since the cash flows are relatively certain, the project's cost of capital is only 11.5 percent. Should the replacement be made?

Table 10-4 shows the worksheet format the company uses to analyze replacement projects. Each line is numbered, and a line-by-line description of the table follows.

Line 1. The top section of the table, Lines 1 through 5, sets forth the cash flows which occur at (approximately) t = 0, the time the investment is made. Line 1 shows the purchase price of the new machine, including installation and freight charges. Since it is an outflow, it is negative.

Line 2. Here we show the price received from the sale of the old equipment.

Line 3. Since the old equipment would be sold at less than book value, the sale would create a loss which would reduce the firm's taxable income and hence its next quarterly income tax payment. The tax saving is equal to (Loss)(T) = ($1,500)(0.40) = $600, where T is the marginal corporate tax rate. The Tax Code defines this loss as an operating loss, because it reflects the fact that inadequate depreciation was taken on the old asset. If there had been a profit on the sale (that is, if the sales price had exceeded book value), Line 3 would have shown taxes *paid*, a cash outflow. In the actual case, the equipment

Table 10-4 Replacement Analysis Worksheet

I. Net Cash Flow at the Time the Investment Is Made (t = 0)

1. Cost of new equipment	($12,000)
2. Market value of old equipment	1,000
3. Tax savings on sale of old equipment	600
4. Increase in net working capital	(1,000)
5. Total net investment	($11,400)

(handwritten: 3,000, 3,000)

	Year:	0	1	2	3	4	5

II. Operating Inflows over the Project's Life

	0	1	2	3	4	5
6. After-tax decrease in costs		$1,800	$1,800	$1,800	$1,800	$1,800
7. Depreciation on new machine		$3,960	$5,400	$1,800	$ 840	$ 0
8. Depreciation on old machine		500	500	500	500	500
9. Change in depreciation (7 − 8)		$3,460	$4,900	$1,300	$ 340	($ 500)
10. Tax savings from depreciation (0.4 × 9)		1,384	1,960	520	136	(200)
11. Net operating cash flows (6 + 10)		$3,184	$3,760	$2,320	$1,936	$1,600

III. Terminal Year Cash Flows

	0	1	2	3	4	5
12. Estimated salvage value of new machine						$2,000
13. Tax on salvage value						(800)
14. Return of net working capital						1,000
15. Total termination cash flows						$2,200

IV. Net Cash Flows

	0	1	2	3	4	5
16. Total net cash flows	($11,400)	$3,184	$3,760	$2,320	$1,936	$3,800

(handwritten: NEW)

V. Results

Payback period: 4.1 years.
IRR: 10.1% versus an 11.5% cost of capital.
IRR*: 10.7% versus an 11.5% cost of capital.
NPV: − $388.77

would be sold at a loss, so no taxes would be paid, and the company would realize a tax savings of $600.[4]

Line 4. The investment in additional net working capital (new current asset requirements minus increases in accounts payable and accruals) is shown here. This investment will be recovered at the end of the project's life (see Line 14). No taxes are involved.

---

[4]If the old asset were being exchanged for the new asset, rather than being sold to a third party, the tax consequences would be different. In an exchange of similar assets, no gain or loss is recognized. If the market value of the old asset is greater than its book value, the depreciable basis of the new asset is decreased by the excess amount. Conversely, if the market value of the old asset is less than its book value, the depreciable basis is increased by the shortfall.

Line 5. Here we show the total net cash outflow at the time the replacement is made. The company writes a check for $12,000 to pay for the machine, and another $1,000 is invested in net working capital. However, these outlays are partially offset by proceeds from the sale of the old equipment and reduced taxes.

Line 6. Section II of the table shows the *incremental operating cash flows,* or benefits, that are expected if the replacement is made. The first of these benefits is the reduction in operating costs shown on Line 6. Cash flows increase because operating costs are reduced by $3,000, but reduced costs also mean higher taxable income and hence higher income taxes:

Reduction in costs = Δ cost =	$3,000
Associated increase in taxes = T(Δ cost) = 0.4($3,000) =	1,200
Increase in net after-tax cash flows due to cost reduction = Δ NCF =	$1,800
Note also that Δ NCF = (Δ cost)(1 − T) = ($3,000)(0.6) =	$1,800

Had the replacement resulted in an increase in sales in addition to the reduction in costs (that is, if the new machine had been both larger and more efficient), then this amount would also be reported on Line 6 (or a separate line could be added). Also, note that the $3,000 cost savings is constant over Years 1 through 5; had the annual savings been expected to change over time, this fact would have to have been built into the analysis.

Line 7. The depreciable basis of the new machine, $12,000, is multiplied by the appropriate ACRS recovery allowance for 3-year class property (see Page 49) to obtain the depreciation figures shown on Line 7. Note that if you summed across Line 7, the total would be $12,000, the depreciable basis.

Line 8. Line 8 shows the $500 straight line depreciation on the old machine.

Line 9. The depreciation expense on the old machine as shown on Line 8 can no longer be taken if the replacement is made, but the new machine's depreciation will be available. Therefore, the $500 depreciation on the old machine is subtracted from that on the new machine to show the net change in annual depreciation. The change is positive in Years 1 through 4 but negative in Year 5. The Year 5 negative net change in annual depreciation signifies that the purchase of the replacement machine results in a *decrease* in depreciation expense during that year.

Line 10. The net change in depreciation results in a tax reduction which is equal to the change in depreciation multiplied by the tax rate: Depreciation tax savings = T(Change in depreciation) = 0.40($3,460) = $1,384 for Year 1. Note that the relevant cash flow is the tax savings on the *net change* in depreciation, not just the depreciation on the new equipment. Capital budgeting decisions are based on *incremental* cash flows, and since BQC will lose $500 of depreciation if it replaces the old machine, that fact must be taken into account.

Line 11. Here we show the net operating cash flows over the project's 5-year life. These flows are found by adding the after-tax cost decrease to the depreciation tax savings, or Line 6 + Line 10.

Line 12. Part III shows the cash flows associated with the termination of the project. To begin, Line 12 shows the estimated salvage value of the new machine at the end of its 5-year life, $2,000.[5]

Line 13. Since the book value of the new machine at the end of Year 5 is zero, the company will have to pay taxes of $2,000(0.4) = $800.

Line 14. An investment of $1,000 in net working capital was shown as an outflow at t = 0. This investment, like the new machine's salvage value, will be recovered when the project is terminated at the end of Year 5. Accounts receivable will be collected, inventories will be drawn down and not replaced, and the result is an inflow of $1,000 at t = 5.

Line 15. Here we show the total cash flows resulting from terminating the project.

Line 16. Part IV shows, on Line 16, the total net cash flows in a form suitable for capital budgeting evaluation. In effect, Line 16 is a "time line."

Part V of the table, "Results," shows the replacement project's payback, IRR, IRR*, and NPV. Because of the nature of the project, it is less risky than the firm's average project, so a cost of capital of only 11.5 percent is appropriate. However, even at this cost of capital, the project is not acceptable, and hence the old lathe should not be replaced.

COMPARING PROJECTS WITH UNEQUAL LIVES[6]

A replacement decision involves two mutually exclusive projects: the retention of the old asset or the purchase of a new one. To simplify matters, in our replacement example we assumed that the new machine had a life equal to

---

[5]In this analysis, the salvage value of the old machine is zero. However, if the old machine was expected to have a positive salvage value at the end of 5 years, replacing the old machine now would eliminate this cash flow. Thus, the after-tax salvage value of the old machine would represent an opportunity cost to the firm, and it would be included as a Year 5 cash outflow in the terminal cash flow section of the worksheet.

[6]This section may be omitted without loss of continuity.

Table 10-5   Expected Net Cash Flows for Projects C and F

Year	Project C	Project F
0	($40,000)	($20,000)
1	8,000	7,000
2	14,000	13,000
3	13,000	12,000
4	12,000	—
5	11,000	—
6	10,000	—
NPV at 11.5%	$ 7,165	$ 5,391

the remaining life of the old machine. If, however, we were choosing between two mutually exclusive alternatives with substantially different lives, an adjustment would be necessary. We now discuss two procedures — the replacement chain method and the equivalent annual annuity method — both to illustrate the problem and to deal with it.

Suppose Brandt-Quigley is planning to modernize its production facilities, and as a part of the process, it is considering either a conveyor system (Project C) or a forklift truck (Project F) for moving materials from the parts department to the main assembly line. Table 10-5 shows both the expected net cash flows and the NPV for each of these mutually exclusive alternatives. We see that Project C, when discounted at an 11.5 percent cost of capital, has the higher NPV, and hence it appears to be the better project.

Replacement Chain (Common Life) Approach

Although the analysis in Table 10-5 suggests that Project C should be selected, this analysis is incomplete, and the decision to choose Project C is actually incorrect. If BQC chooses Project F, it will have the opportunity to make a similar investment after 3 years, and if cost and revenue conditions continue at the Table 10-5 levels, this second investment also will be profitable. However, if the company chooses Project C, it will not have this second investment opportunity. Therefore, to make a proper comparison of Projects C and F, we must find the NPV of Project F over a 6-year period and then compare this extended NPV with the NPV of Project C over the same 6 years. This method is called the **replacement chain approach**.

The NPV for Project C as calculated in Table 10-5 is already over a 6-year life. For Project F, however, we must take three additional steps: (1) determine the NPV of a second Project F three years hence, (2) discount this NPV back to the present, and (3) sum these two component NPVs:

1. If we assume (1) that Project F's cost and annual cash inflows will not change if the project is repeated in 3 years and (2) that BQC's cost of capital will remain at 11.5 percent, then Project F's second-stage NPV will

replacement chain approach
A method of comparing projects of unequal lives which assumes that each project can be replicated as many times as necessary to reach a common life span; the NPVs over this life span are then compared, and the project with the higher common life NPV is chosen.

[handwritten margin note: 2nd Investment Opportunity]

Figure 10-2   Time Line View of Replacement Chain Analysis

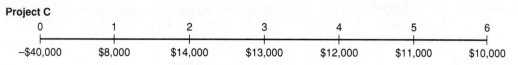

Project C

0	1	2	3	4	5	6
−$40,000	$8,000	$14,000	$13,000	$12,000	$11,000	$10,000

NPV_C at 11.5% = $7,165.

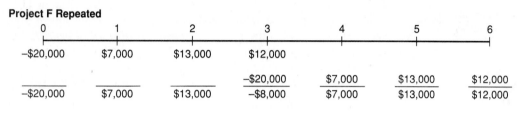

Project F Repeated

0	1	2	3	4	5	6
−$20,000	$7,000	$13,000	$12,000			
			−$20,000	$7,000	$13,000	$12,000
−$20,000	$7,000	$13,000	−$8,000	$7,000	$13,000	$12,000

NPV_F at 11.5% = $9,280.

remain the same as its first-stage NPV, $5,391. However, the second NPV would not accrue for 3 years, and hence we must discount it back 3 years.

2.   The present value (at t = 0) of the replicated Project F is determined by discounting the second NPV (at t = 3) back 3 years at 11.5 percent: $5,391/(1.115)^3 = $3,889.

3.   The "true" NPV of Project F is $5,391 + $3,889 = $9,280. This is the value which should be compared with the NPV of Project C, $7,165. Because the true NPV of Project F is greater than the NPV of Project C, Project F should be selected.

Figure 10-2 shows the analysis of Projects C and F in a time-line format. Note that NPV_F can be found either by evaluating the two separate 3-year projects' cash flow streams as described above or by evaluating the 6-year cash flow stream, which shows a net cash flow of − $8,000 in Year 3, as shown in Figure 10-2.

Equivalent Annual Annuity Approach[7]

Although the preceding example illustrates why an extended analysis is necessary if we are comparing mutually exclusive projects with different lives, the arithmetic is generally more complex in practice. For example, one project

---

[7]This section may be omitted without loss of continuity.

equivalent annual
annuity method (EAA)
A method which
calculates the annual
payments a project
would provide if it were
an annuity. When
comparing projects of
unequal lives, the one
with the higher
equivalent annual
annuity should be
chosen.

might have an 8-year life and the other an 11-year life. This would require an analysis over 88 years, the lowest common denominator of the two lives. In such a situation, it is often simpler to use a second procedure, the **equivalent annual annuity method (EAA)**, which involves three steps:

1. Find each project's NPV over its initial life. In the previous example, we found $NPV_C = \$7,165$ and $NPV_F = \$5,391$.

2. Find the annuity cash flow that has the same present value as each project's NPV. For example, for Project C, enter 7,165 as the PV, $k = i = 11.5$, and $n = 6$ in your calculator and solve for PMT. The answer is $\$1,718$. This cash flow stream, when discounted back 6 years at 11.5 percent, has a present value equal to Project C's original NPV, $\$7,165$. The value $\$1,718$ is called the project's *equivalent annual annuity (EAA)*. The EAA for Project F is found similarly to be $\$2,225$. Thus, Project C has an NPV which is equivalent to an annuity of $\$1,718$ per year for 6 years, whereas Project F's NPV is equivalent to an annuity of $\$2,225$ for 3 years.

3. Assuming that continuous replacements can and will be made each time the asset's life ends, these EAAs will continue on out to infinity; that is, they will constitute perpetuities. Recognizing that the value of a perpetuity is $V = $ Annual receipt/k, we can find the net present values of the infinite EAAs of Projects C and F as follows:

$$\text{Infinite horizon } NPV_C = \$1,718/0.115 = \$14,939.$$

$$\text{Infinite horizon } NPV_F = \$2,225/0.115 = \$19,348.$$

In effect, the EAA method assumes that each asset will, if taken on, be replaced each time it wears out, and that it will provide cash flows equivalent to the calculated annuity value. The PV of this infinite annuity is then the infinite horizon NPV for the project. Since the infinite horizon NPV of F exceeds that of C, Project F should be accepted. Therefore, the EAA method leads to the same decision as the simple replacement chain method — accept Project F.

The EAA method is generally easier to apply than the replacement chain method. However, the replacement chain method is often easier to explain to decision makers, and it does not require the assumption of an infinite time horizon. Still, the two methods always lead to the same decision if consistent assumptions are used. Note that Step 3 of the EAA method is not really necessary; we could have stopped after Step 2, because the project with the higher EAA will always have the higher NPV over any common life.

When should one worry about unequal life analysis? As a general rule, the unequal life issue does not arise for independent projects, but it can arise if mutually exclusive projects with substantially different lives are being evaluated. Even for mutually exclusive projects, however, it is not always appropriate to extend the analysis to a common life. This should only be done if there is a high probability that the projects will actually be replicated beyond their initial lives.

We should note several potentially serious weaknesses inherent in this type of unequal life analysis. First, if inflation is expected, replacement equipment will have a higher price, and both sales prices and operating costs will probably change; thus, the static conditions built into the analysis will be invalid. Second, replacements that occur down the road will probably employ new technology, which in turn might change the cash flows. This factor is not built into either replacement chain analysis or the EAA approach. Finally, because it is difficult enough to estimate the lives of most projects, estimating the lives of a series of projects is often just a speculation.

In view of these problems, no experienced financial analyst would be too concerned about comparing mutually exclusive projects with lives of, say, 8 years and 10 years. Given all the uncertainties in the estimation process, such projects could, for all practical purposes, be assumed to have the same life. Still, it is important for you to recognize that a problem could exist if mutually exclusive projects which are likely to be repeated do have substantially different lives. When we encounter such problems in practice, we build expected inflation or possible efficiency gains directly into the cash flow estimates and then use the replacement chain approach (but not the equivalent annual annuity method). The cash flow estimation is more complicated, but the concepts involved are exactly the same as in our example.

ADJUSTING FOR INFLATION[8]

Because inflation is a fact of life in the United States and most other nations, it must be considered in any sound capital budgeting analysis. Inflation raises costs and hence reduces the purchasing power of cash flows to be received in the future. As we discussed in Chapter 3, investors recognize this problem, so they incorporate expectations about inflation into their required rates of return. Suppose, for example, that investors require a *real rate of return, k_r,* of 8 percent on an investment with a given degree of risk. Suppose further that they anticipate the average annual rate of inflation, i, to be 6 percent. Then, to end up with an 8 percent real rate of return, the *nominal rate of return, k_n,* must be 14 percent, found as follows:

$$k_n = k_r + i$$

$$= 8\% + 6\% = 14\%.$$

Here the inflation rate, i, is equivalent to the inflation premium, IP, that we discussed in Chapter 3.

The "market" automatically adjusts required rates of return for inflation; that is, rates quoted in the market, or nominal rates, include a premium for expected inflation. Therefore, it is necessary in capital budgeting analysis to

---

[8]This section may be omitted without loss of continuity.

develop nominal cash flows that are also adjusted for inflation. Earlier, when we analyzed the Brandt-Quigley computer project, we assumed for simplicity that there would be no inflation. If we had assumed that inflation would occur, however, we would have identified those cash flow items likely to increase with inflation, and we would have adjusted them. For example, we might have assumed that sales prices and fixed overhead costs would increase at the forecasted rate of inflation, say 6 percent annually. Then we would have built into our model an increase of 6 percent per year for those two items. Note that variable costs would then also increase automatically with inflation, because they were defined to be a fixed percentage of dollar sales. Note too that we could have assumed different rates of inflation for sales prices and fixed overhead. For example, Brandt-Quigley might be using a building under a long-term lease which results in keeping a portion of its fixed expenses constant, and this might lower the average increase in fixed overhead from i = 6% to only 5 percent. In any event, inflation should be built into the capital budgeting analysis, with the specific adjustments reflecting as accurately as possible the most likely set of circumstances.

The present value of the cash flow in any year t is defined as follows:

$$PV\ CF_t = \frac{CF_t}{(1 + k)^{t'}}$$

In capital budgeting, the term k is a nominal, market cost rate, and, as we saw in Chapter 3, it includes a premium for expected inflation. Therefore, the higher the expected rate of inflation, the higher k will be. Normally, if inflation exists, a project's cash flows will also tend to rise over time; this will automatically happen if both costs and sales prices rise because of inflation and if prices exceed costs. In the PV equation, note that if k includes inflation, the denominator will be increased, and this will lower the PV of the cash flow in Year t. Thus, if inflation is included in k but not in CF_t, the PV of CF_t will be biased downward. *Because inflation is automatically reflected in k by the market, if the firm does not reflect inflation's effects in its forecasts of future cash flows, its calculated NPVs will be downward biased.*

An example will help clarify this point. Suppose you are considering buying an apartment building which costs $100,000 and which has an expected cash flow of $15,000 per year. Your cost of capital is 14 percent, the building is expected to last for 15 years, and the expected inflation rate is 5 percent. Should you buy the building? On the basis of a standard NPV analysis, you would find a NPV of − $7,867 and therefore would reject the purchase:

$$NPV = \sum_{t=1}^{15} \frac{\$15,000}{(1.14)^t} - \$100,000$$

$$= PVIFA_{14\%,15}(\$15,000) - \$100,000$$

$$= 6.1422(\$15,000) - \$100,000$$

$$= -\$7,867.$$

If you increased the cash flows to reflect the 5 percent expected inflation rate, however, you would find a NPV of $24,042:

$$NPV = \sum_{t=1}^{15} \frac{\$15,000(1.05)^t}{(1.14)^t} - \$100,000 = \$24,042.$$

More arithmetic is required to obtain the inflation-adjusted NPV, but this is a small price to pay for the improved accuracy of the analysis.

In summary, because inflation can have major effects on businesses, it is critically important, and it must be recognized and dealt with. The most effective way to deal with inflation is to build it into each cash flow element, using the best available information about how each element will be affected. Since one cannot estimate future inflation rates with precision, errors are bound to be made. Therefore, inflation adds to the uncertainty, or riskiness, of capital budgeting, as well as to its complexity. Fortunately, computers and spreadsheet models are available to help with inflation analysis; thus, in practice, the mechanics of inflation adjustments are not difficult.

CAPITAL RATIONING

Capital budgeting decisions are typically made as described in this and the preceding chapter — independent projects are accepted if their NPVs are positive, and choices among mutually exclusive projects are made by selecting the one with the highest NPV. In this analysis, it is assumed that if in a particular year the firm has an especially large number of good projects, management simply will go into the financial markets and raise whatever funds are required to finance all of the acceptable projects. However, some firms set limits on the amount of funds they are willing to raise, and, if this is done, the capital budget must also be limited. This situation is known as **capital rationing**.

capital rationing
A situation in which a constraint is placed on the total size of the firm's capital investment during a particular period.

Elaborate and mathematically sophisticated models have been developed to help firms maximize their values when they are subject to capital rationing. However, a firm which subjects itself to capital rationing is deliberately forgoing profitable projects, and hence it is not truly maximizing its value. This point is well known, so few sophisticated firms ration capital today. Therefore, we shall not discuss it further, but you should know what the term *capital rationing* means.[9]

---

[9]See Eugene F. Brigham and Louis C. Gapenski, *Intermediate Financial Management,* 2nd ed., Chapter 10, for a further discussion of capital rationing.

International

CASH FLOW ANALYSIS OF INTERNATIONAL INVESTMENTS

Cash flow analysis is much more complex when capital investments are being made in a foreign country. *The relevant cash flows from a foreign investment are the dollar cash flows that would be returned, or repatriated, to the parent company.* Since cash flows are earned in the currency of the foreign country, they must be converted to dollars, and thus they are subject to future exchange rate fluctuations.

International cash flow analysis can be illustrated by International Electronics Corporation's (IEC) analysis of a proposed plant in Venezuela to assemble television sets for sale in South America. If the plant is built, a new IEC subsidiary, wholly owned by the parent company, will be incorporated in Venezuela. IEC has reached an agreement with the Venezuelan government allowing all of the subsidiary's earnings to be repatriated to the parent company. The investment, to be made in January 1990, will cost 50 million Venezuelan bolivars. IEC has agreed to sell the subsidiary to Venezuelan investors at the end of five years at its expected book value of 25 million bolivars. Therefore, its investment time horizon extends only to 1994.

Table 10-6 summarizes the projected cash inflows from the investment. IEC will evaluate the investment at a required rate of return of 15 percent. The subsidiary will have to pay income taxes of 20 percent to the Venezuelan government. In addition, IEC will have to pay U.S. income taxes on the earnings of the subsidiary, but it will receive credit for the Venezuelan taxes paid by the subsidiary. IEC's marginal U.S. tax rate is 34 percent, and U.S. taxes are calculated as (Income before Venezuelan taxes)(U.S. tax rate − Venezuelan tax rate). Therefore, if the subsidiary has earnings of 20 million bolivars in 1990, it would pay Venezuelan taxes of 4 million bolivars, and then the parent company would pay (20 million bolivars)(0.34 − 0.20) = 2.8 million bolivars in U.S. taxes.

Table 10-7 converts the annual cash flows from bolivars to dollars and then calculates the present value of the dollar cash flows. Line 1 gives the annual cash flows in bolivars, while the estimated exchange rate, set equal to the current rate of 7.5 bolivars to the dollar, is shown on Line 2. Dividing the cash flows in bolivars by the exchange rate gives the expected cash flows in dollars as shown on Line 3. The present value of the expected dollar flows at a 15 percent required rate of return is $1.9 million, and the IRR of 24.2 percent exceeds the 15 percent required rate of return.

Since the investment's NPV is positive, it appears to be acceptable. Note, however, that the actual value of the investment to IEC will depend on the exchange rate that exists when the earnings are

---

Table 10-6   Projected Cash Inflows, 1990–1994 (Millions of Venezuelan Bolivars)

	1990	1991	1992	1993	1994
(1) Revenues	50.0	55.0	60.0	65.0	70.0
(2) Total costs (60%)	30.0	33.0	36.0	39.0	42.0
(3) Income before taxes	20.0	22.0	24.0	26.0	28.0
(4) Venezuelan tax (20%)	4.0	4.4	4.8	5.2	5.6
(5) Net income	16.0	17.6	19.2	20.8	22.4
(6) Earnings repatriated	16.0	17.6	19.2	20.8	22.4
(7) U.S. tax (34% − 20%)	2.8	3.1	3.4	3.6	3.9
(8) Proceeds from sale					25.0
(9) After-tax cash flows	13.2	14.5	15.8	17.2	43.5

Table 10-7   Cash Flows and NPV to Parent Company
(in millions)

	1990	1991	1992	1993	1994
(1) Cash flows (bolivars)	13.2	14.5	15.8	17.2	43.5
(2) Exchange rate (bolivars per dollar)	7.5	7.5	7.5	7.5	7.5
(3) Cash flows (dollars = bolivars/exchange rate)	$1.8	$1.9	$2.1	$2.3	$5.8
(4) Present value of cash flows at 15%					$8.6
(5) Less initial investment of 50 million bolivars at 7.5 bolivars per dollar, or $6.7 million					6.7
(6) NPV of investment at 15%					$ 1.9
(7) IRR of investment					24.2%

repatriated. If U.S. exports increase relative to imports, then there will be an increase in the demand for dollars by foreigners to pay for the net U.S. exports. This would drive up the value of the dollar vis-à-vis currencies such as the bolivar. For example, the dollar might rise in value from 7.5 bolivars to $1 as shown on Line 2 to 10.0 bolivars to $1. That, in turn, would mean that the repatriated bolivars would purchase fewer dollars, so the dollar cash flows and hence the value of the investment would decline. For simplicity, we assumed in Table 10-7 that the exchange rate which existed when the project was undertaken would remain constant during the life of the investment. In reality, however, exchange rates change daily, and long-run trends associated with inflation and other fundamental factors occur, but not in a very predictable manner. Therefore, over a 5-year period, substantial changes could occur, but it is exceedingly difficult to predict what they will be. These exchange rate changes make international capital budgeting analysis quite complex, and they also increase the riskiness of foreign investments.[10]

___

[10]However, in a portfolio sense, foreign investments may be less risky than purely domestic investments, because the economies of different countries are not perfectly correlated, and, hence, international diversification can stabilize portfolio returns.

SUMMARY AND KEY CONCEPTS

This chapter discussed four issues in capital budgeting: cash flow estimation, replacement decisions, unequal life analyses, and inflation adjustments. The key concepts covered are listed below.

- The most important, but most difficult, step in analyzing a capital budgeting project is **estimating the incremental after-tax cash flows** the project will produce.

- **Net cash flows** consist of (1) sales revenues minus cash operating costs, reduced by taxes plus (2) a depreciation cash flow equal to the amount of depreciation taken during the period, multiplied by the tax rate.

- In determining incremental cash flows, **opportunity costs** (the return on the best alternative investment available) must be included, but **sunk costs** (cash outlays that have been made and that cannot be recouped) are not included. Any **externalities** (effects of a project on other parts of the firm) also should be included in the analysis.

- Capital projects often require additional investment in **net working capital (NWC)**. An increase in NWC must be included as an initial cash outlay in Year 0 and then shown as a cash inflow in the final year of the project.

- When choosing between **mutually exclusive projects** with different lives, it is necessary to adjust the NPVs using either the **replacement chain method** or the **equivalent annual annuity (EAA) method**. Both methods produce the same results.

- The **replacement chain (common life) method** assumes that both projects can be replicated as many times as is necessary to reach a common life. The NPVs are calculated for each replication, then they are discounted back to the present, and, finally, they are summed to find the total NPV of the project. The project which has the higher total NPV is chosen.

- The **equivalent annual annuity (EAA) method** finds each project's NPV over its initial life and then determines the annuity cash flow which would produce this NPV. The project with the higher EAA is chosen.

- Expected **inflation** should be accounted for in capital budgeting analysis. The most efficient way to deal with inflation is to build it into each cash flow element.

- **Capital rationing** occurs when management places a constraint on the size of the firm's capital investment during a particular period.

- **International capital budgeting** is more complex than domestic capital budgeting because cash flows must be translated from foreign currencies to U.S. dollars.

In Chapter 11, we will examine the effects of risk on capital budgeting analyses.

Questions

10-1   Cash flows rather than accounting profits are listed in Table 10-2. What is the basis for this emphasis on cash flows as opposed to net income?

10-2   Why is it true, in general, that a failure to adjust expected cash flows for expected inflation biases the calculated NPV downward?

10-3   Suppose a firm is considering two mutually exclusive projects. One has a life of 4 years and the other a life of 10 years. Would the failure to employ some type of replacement chain analysis bias an NPV analysis against one of the projects? Explain.

10-4   Look at Table 10-4 and answer these questions:
   a. Why is the salvage value shown on Line 12 reduced for taxes on Line 13?
   b. Why is depreciation on the old machine deducted on Line 8 to get Line 9?
   c. What would happen if the new machine permitted a *reduction* in net working capital?
   d. Why are the cost savings on Line 6 reduced by multiplying the before-tax figure by $(1 - T)$, whereas the change in depreciation figure on Line 9 is multiplied by T?

10-5   Explain why sunk costs should not be included in a capital budgeting analysis, but opportunity costs and externalities should be included.

10-6   Explain how net working capital is recovered at the end of a project's life, and why it is included in a capital budgeting analysis.

10-7   In general, is an explicit recognition of incremental cash flows more important in new project or replacement analysis? Why?

Self-Test Problems   *(Solutions Appear on Page 405)*

Key terms

ST-1   Define each of the following terms:
   a. Cash flow; accounting income
   b. Incremental cash flow; sunk cost; opportunity cost
   c. Change in net working capital
   d. Salvage value
   e. Replacement analysis
   f. Replacement chain approach
   g. Equivalent annual annuity method
   h. Capital rationing

New project analysis

ST-2   You have been asked by the president of Ellis Construction Company, headquartered in Toledo, to evaluate the proposed acquisition of a new earthmover. The mover's basic price is $50,000, and it will cost another $10,000 to modify it for special use by Ellis Construction. Assume that the mover falls into the ACRS 3-year class. It will be sold after 3 years for $20,000, and it will require an increase in net working capital (spare parts inventory) of $2,000. The earthmover purchase will have no effect on revenues, but it is expected to save Ellis $20,000 per year in before-tax operating costs, mainly labor. Ellis's marginal federal-plus-state tax rate is 40 percent.
   a. What is the company's net investment if it acquires the earthmover? (That is, what are the Year 0 cash flows?)
   b. What are the operating cash flows in Years 1, 2, and 3?
   c. What are the additional (nonoperating) cash flows in Year 3?
   d. If the project's cost of capital is 10 percent, should the earthmover be purchased?

Replacement project analysis

ST-3   The Dauten Toy Corporation currently uses an injection molding machine that was purchased 2 years ago. This machine is being depreciated on a straight line basis toward a $500 salvage value, and it has 6 years of remaining life. Its current book value is $2,600, and it can be sold for $3,000 at this time. Thus, the annual depreciation expense is ($2,600 − $500)/6 = $350 per year.

Dauten is offered a replacement machine which has a cost of $8,000, an estimated useful life of 6 years, and an estimated salvage value of $800. This machine falls into the ACRS 5-year class, and under current law it does not qualify for an investment tax credit. The replacement machine would permit an output expansion, so sales would rise by $1,000 per year; even so, the new machine's much greater efficiency would still cause operating expenses to decline by $1,500 per year. The new machine would require that inventories be increased by $2,000, but accounts payable would simultaneously increase by $500.

Dauten's marginal federal-plus-state tax rate is 40 percent, and its cost of capital is 15 percent. Should it replace the old machine?

Problems

Depreciation effects

10-1 Ronald Clay, great grandson of the founder of Clay Tile Products and current president of the company, believes in simple, conservative accounting. In keeping with his philosophy, he has decreed that the company shall use alternative straight line depreciation, based on the ACRS class lives, for all newly acquired assets. Your boss, the financial vice-president and the only non-family officer, has asked you to develop an exhibit which shows how much this policy costs the company in terms of market value. Mr. Clay is interested in increasing the value of the firm's stock because he fears a family stockholder revolt which might remove him from office. For your exhibit, assume that the company spends $50 million each year on new capital projects, that the projects have on average a 10-year class life, that the company has a 10 percent cost of debt, and that its tax rate is 34 percent. (Hint: Show how much the NPV of projects in an average year would increase if Clay used the standard ACRS recovery allowances.)

New project analysis

10-2 You have been asked by the president of your company to evaluate the proposed acquisition of a new spectrometer for the firm's R&D department. The equipment's basic price is $70,000, and it would cost another $15,000 to modify it for special use by your firm. The spectrometer, which falls into the ACRS 3-year class, would be sold after 3 years for $30,000. Use of the equipment would require an increase in net working capital (spare parts inventory) of $4,000. The spectrometer would have no effect on revenues, but it is expected to save the firm $25,000 per year in before-tax operating costs, mainly labor. The firm's marginal federal-plus-state tax rate is 40 percent.

a. What is the net cost of the spectrometer? (That is, what is the Year 0 net cash flow?)

b. What are the net operating cash flows in Years 1, 2, and 3?

c. What is the additional (nonoperating) cash flow in Year 3?

d. If the project's cost of capital is 10 percent, should the spectrometer be purchased?

New project analysis

10-3 The Clouse Company is evaluating the proposed acquisition of a new milling machine. The machine's base price is $180,000, and it would cost another $25,000 to modify it for special use by your firm. The machine falls into the ACRS 3-year class, and it would be sold after 3 years for $80,000. The machine would require an increase in net working capital (inventory) of $7,500. The milling machine would have no effect on revenues, but it is expected to save the firm $75,000 per year in before-tax operating costs, mainly labor. Clouse's marginal tax rate is 34 percent.

a. What is the net cost of the machine for capital budgeting purposes? (That is, what is the Year 0 net cash flow?)

b. What are the net operating cash flows in Years 1, 2, and 3?

c. What is the additional (nonoperating) cash flow in Year 3?

d. If the project's cost of capital is 10 percent, should the machine be purchased?

Replacement analysis   **10-4**   Niendorf Company is considering the purchase of a new machine tool to replace an obsolete one. The machine being used for the operation has both a tax book value and a market value of zero; it is in good working order, however, and will last physically for at least another 10 years. The proposed replacement machine will perform the operation so much more efficiently that Niendorf engineers estimate it will produce after-tax cash flows (labor savings and depreciation) of $6,000 per year. The new machine will cost $24,000 delivered and installed, and its economic life is estimated to be 10 years. It has zero salvage value. The firm's cost of capital is 12 percent, and its marginal tax rate is 40 percent. Should Niendorf buy the new machine?

Replacement analysis   **10-5**   Long Beach Shipyards is considering the replacement of an 8-year-old riveting machine with a new one that will increase earnings before depreciation from $25,000 to $50,000 per year. The new machine will cost $60,000, and it will have an estimated life of 8 years and no salvage value. The new machine will be depreciated over its 5-year ACRS recovery period. The applicable corporate tax rate is 40 percent, and the firm's cost of capital is 12 percent. The old machine has been fully depreciated and has no salvage value. Should the old riveting machine be replaced by the new one?

Replacement analysis   **10-6**   The Nelson Equipment Company purchased a machine 5 years ago at a cost of $100,000. The machine had an expected life of 10 years at the time of purchase and an expected salvage value of $10,000 at the end of the 10 years. It is being depreciated by the straight line method toward a salvage value of $10,000, or by $9,000 per year.

A new machine can be purchased for $150,000, including installation costs. During its 5-year life, it will reduce cash operating expenses by $50,000 per year. Sales are not expected to change. At the end of its useful life, the machine is estimated to be worthless. ACRS depreciation will be used, and the machine will be depreciated over its 3-year class life rather than its 5-year economic life.

The old machine can be sold today for $65,000. The firm's tax rate is 34 percent. The appropriate discount rate is 15 percent.

a. If the new machine is purchased, what is the amount of the initial cash flow at Year 0?

b. What incremental operating cash flows will occur at the end of Years 1 through 5 as a result of replacing the old machine?

c. What incremental nonoperating cash flow will occur at the end of Year 5 if the new machine is purchased?

d. What is the NPV of this project? Should Nelson replace the old machine?

Replacement analysis   **10-7**   The Tanner Bottling Company is contemplating the replacement of one of its bottling machines with a newer and more efficient one. The old machine has a book value of $500,000 and a remaining useful life of 5 years. The firm does not expect to realize any return from scrapping the old machine in 5 years, but it can sell it now to another firm in the industry for $200,000. The old machine is being depreciated toward a zero salvage value, or by $100,000 per year, using the straight line method.

The new machine has a purchase price of $1.2 million, an estimated useful life and ACRS class life of 5 years, and an estimated salvage value of $175,000. It is expected to economize on electric power usage, labor, and repair costs, as well as to reduce the number of defective bottles. In total, an annual savings of $275,000 will be realized if the new machine is installed. The company is in the 40 percent federal-plus-state tax bracket, and it has a 10 percent cost of capital.

a. What is the initial cash outlay required for the new machine?

b. Calculate the annual depreciation allowances for both machines, and compute the change in the annual depreciation expense if the replacement is made.

c. What are the operating cash flows in Years 1 through 5?

d. What is the cash flow from the salvage value in Year 5?

e. Should the firm purchase the new machine? Support your answer.

f. In general, how would each of the following factors affect the investment decision, and how should each be treated?

(1) The expected life of the existing machine decreases.

(2) The cost of capital is not constant but is increasing.

Unequal lives   **10-8**   Toddler Clothes, Inc., is considering the replacement of its old, fully depreciated knitting machine. Two new models are available: Machine 190-3, which has a cost of $190,000, a 3-year expected life, and after-tax cash flows (labor savings and depreciation) of $87,000 per year; and Machine 360-6, which has a cost of $360,000, a 6-year life, and after-tax cash flows of $98,300 per year. Knitting machine prices are not expected to rise, because inflation will be offset by cheaper components (microprocessors) used in the machines. Assume that Toddler's cost of capital is 14 percent.

a. Should the firm replace its old knitting machine, and, if so, which new machine should it buy?

b. Suppose the firm's basic patents will expire in 9 years, and the company expects to go out of business at that time. Assume further that the firm depreciates its assets using the straight line method, that its marginal federal-plus-state tax rate is 40 percent, and that the used machines can be sold at their book values. Under these circumstances, should the company replace the machine and, if so, which new model should the company purchase?

Inflation adjustments   **10-9**   The Rothfield Company is considering an average risk investment in a mineral water spring project that has a cost of $150,000. The project will produce 1,000 cases of mineral water per year indefinitely. The current sales price is $138 per case, and the current cost per case (all variable) is $105. Rothfield is taxed at a rate of 34 percent. Both prices and costs are expected to rise at a rate of 6 percent per year. Rothfield uses only equity, and it has a cost of capital of 15 percent. Assume that cash flows consist of only after-tax profits, since the spring has an indefinite life and will not be depreciated.

a. Should Rothfield accept the project? (Hint: The project is a perpetuity, so you must use the formula for a perpetuity to find the NPV. Determine the net after-tax cash flow and then the NPV of this cash flow at a real rate of 9 percent.)

b. If total costs consisted of a fixed cost of $10,000 per year and variable costs of $95 per unit, and if only the variable costs were expected to increase with inflation, would this make the project better or worse? Continue with the assumption that the sales price will rise with inflation. (Do not do any calculations.)

Cash flow estimation
(Integrative)

10-10 Citrus Grove Corporation, a leading producer of fresh, frozen, and made-from-concentrate citrus juice, is currently evaluating a new product, fresh lemon juice. The new product would cost more, but it is superior to the competing reconstituted lemon juices. Steve Johnson, a recent finance graduate, has been asked to analyze the project and to present his findings to the company's executive committee.

The production line would be set up in an unused section of Citrus Grove's main plant. The machinery is relatively inexpensive, costing an estimated $200,000, but shipping and installation would cost an additional $40,000. Further, Citrus Grove's inventories would have to be NWC increased by $25,000 to handle the new line, but accounts payable would rise by $5,000. The machinery falls into the ACRS 3-year class, is expected to be used for 4 years, and is expected to have a salvage value of $25,000 at the end of this time.

The new product is expected to generate incremental net revenues (before taxes and excluding depreciation) of $125,000 in each of the next 4 years. Citrus Grove's federal-plus-state tax rate is 40 percent, and its required rate of return is 10 percent.

Johnson plans to perform the following tasks and to answer the following questions in performing his analysis.

a. Define *incremental cash flow*. Construct the project's incremental cash flow statement for its first year of operation. Does this cash flow statement include any financial flows, such as interest expense? Why or why not?

b. Suppose the firm had spent $10,000 last year to rehabilitate the production line site in preparation for another project that had subsequently been abandoned. Should this cost be included in the analysis? Further, assume that the plant space could be leased out to another firm at $5,000 a year. Should this be included in the analysis? Finally, assume that the lemon juice product is expected to decrease sales of the firm's frozen lemonade by $20,000 per year. Should this be considered in the analysis? Be sure to explain your answers fully.

c. What is Citrus Grove's net investment outlay (t = 0 cost) on this project? What is the net cash flow at the end of the project's operating life?

d. Estimate the operating cash flows during Years 2, 3, and 4. What is the project's estimated net cash flow stream? What is its NPV? Should the project be undertaken?

e. Now assume that the project is a replacement project rather than a new, or expansion, project. Describe in words how the analysis would have to be changed to deal with a replacement project.

f. In an unrelated analysis, Johnson was asked to choose between the two following mutually exclusive projects:

	Expected Net Cash Flow	
Year	Project S	Project L
0	($100,000)	($100,000)
1	60,000	33,500
2	60,000	33,500
3	—	33,500
4	—	33,500

Both of these projects are in Citrus Grove's main line of business, orange juice, and whichever is chosen is expected to be replicated into the foreseeable future. Each project should be evaluated at the firm's 10 percent required rate of return. What is each project's NPV over its original life? Now apply the replacement chain approach to make a decision. Repeat the analysis using the equivalent annual annuity method. Which project, if either, should be chosen?

Computer-Related Problems

(Work the problems in this section only if you are using the computer problem diskette.)

Expansion project

C10-1   Use the computerized model for Problem C10-1 in the file C10 to work this problem.

Sunshine State Bakers, Inc. (SSB), has an opportunity to invest in a new dough machine. SSB needs more productive capacity, so the new machine will not replace an existing machine. The new machine costs $180,000 and will require modifications costing $20,000. It has an expected useful life of 10 years, will be depreciated using the ACRS method over its 5-year class life, and has an expected salvage value of $20,000 at the end of Year 10. The machine will require a $30,000 investment in net working capital. It is expected to generate additional sales revenues of $150,000 per year, but its use also will increase annual cash operating expenses by $80,000. SSB's cost of capital is 12 percent, and its marginal tax rate is 40 percent. The machine's book value at the end of Year 10 will be zero, so SSB will have to pay taxes on the $20,000 salvage value.

a. What is the NPV of this expansion project? Should SSB purchase the new machine?

b. Should SSB purchase the new machine if it is expected to be used for only 5 years and then sold for $50,000? (Note that the model is set up to handle a 5-year life; you need only enter the new life and salvage value.)

c. Would the machine be profitable if revenues increased by only $120,000 per year? Assume a 10-year project life and a salvage value of $20,000.

d. Suppose that revenues rose by $150,000 but that expenses rose by $95,000. Would the machine be acceptable under these conditions? Assume a 10-year project life and a salvage value of $20,000.

Replacement project

C10-2   Use the computerized model for Problem C10-2 in the file C10 to solve this problem.

Refer back to Problem 10-5. Now assume that the machine to be replaced is not fully depreciated but, rather, has a current book value of $20,000 and a remaining life of 8 years. The old machine was purchased in 1981, and it is being depreciated using the straight line method toward a zero salvage value, or by $2,500 per year. If replaced now, it can be sold for $12,000. The new machine being considered will have a salvage value of $8,000 at the end of Year 8. Under these conditions, should the replacement be made?

Replacement project

C10-3   Use the computerized model for Problem C10-3 in the file C10 to solve this problem.

a. Refer back to Problem 10-7. Suppose that Tanner Bottling Company can purchase an alternative new bottling machine from another supplier. This machine's purchase price would be $1,050,000, and its salvage value would be $165,000. Purchase of the alternative machine would result in lower annual operating savings of $225,000. Should Tanner purchase this machine?

b. If the annual savings on the new machine were $235,000 rather than $225,000, how would this affect the decision? At what amount of annual savings would Tanner be indifferent in its choice between the two new machines?

c. Suppose that the salvage value on the new machine were $190,000 rather than $165,000. How would this affect the decision? Assume annual savings of $225,000.

Solutions to Self-Test Problems

ST-1   Refer to the marginal glossary definitions and appropriate sections of the text to check your responses.

ST-2   a. *Estimated investment requirements:*

Price	($50,000)
Modification	(10,000)
Change in net working capital	(2,000)
Total investment	($62,000)

b. *Operating cash flows:*

	Year 1	Year 2	Year 3
1. After-tax cost savings[a]	$12,000	$12,000	$12,000
2. Depreciation[b]	19,800	27,000	9,000
3. Depreciation tax savings[c]	7,920	10,800	3,600
Net cash flow (1 + 3)	$19,920	$22,800	$15,600

[a]$20,000 (1 − T)
[b]Depreciable basis = $60,000; the ACRS percentage allowances are 0.33, 0.45, and 0.15 in Years 1, 2, and 3, respectively; hence, depreciation in Year 1 = 0.33($60,000) = $19,800, and so on. There will remain $4,200, or 7 percent, undepreciated after Year 3; it would normally be taken in Year 4.
[c]Depreciation tax savings = T(Depreciation) = 0.4($19,800) = $7,920 in Year 1, and so on.

c. *End-of-project cash flows:*

Salvage value	$20,000
Tax on salvage value[a]	(6,320)
Net working capital recovery	2,000
	$15,680

[a]Sale price	$20,000
Less book value	4,200
Taxable income	$15,800
Tax at 40%	$ 6,320

Book value = Depreciable basis − Accumulated depreciation

= $60,000 − $55,800 = $4,200.

d. *Project NPV:*

$$\text{NPV} = -\$62,000 + \frac{\$19,920}{(1.10)^1} + \frac{\$22,800}{(1.10)^2} + \frac{\$31,280}{(1.10)^3}$$

$$= -\$1,547.$$

Because the earthmover has a negative NPV, it should not be purchased.

ST-3 *First determine the net cash flow at t = 0:*

Purchase price	($8,000)
Sale of old machine	3,000
Tax on sale of old machine	(160)[a]
Change in net working capital	(1,500)[b]
Total investment	($6,660)

[a]The market value is $3,000 − $2,600 = $400 above the book value. Thus, there is a $400 recapture of depreciation, and Dauten would have to pay 0.40($400) = $160 in taxes.

[b]The change in net working capital is a $2,000 increase in current assets minus a $500 increase in current liabilities, which totals to $1,500.

Now, examine the operating cash inflows:

Sales increase	$1,000
Cost decrease	1,500
Increase in pretax operating revenues	$2,500

After-tax operating revenue increase:

$$\$2,500(1 - T) = \$2,500(0.60) = \underline{\underline{\$1,500.}}$$

Depreciation:

Year	1	2	3	4	5	6
New[a]	$1,600	$2,560	$1,520	$ 960	$ 880	$ 480
Old	350	350	350	350	350	350
Change	$1,250	$2,210	$1,170	$ 610	$ 530	$ 130
Depreciation Tax savings[b]	$ 500	$ 884	$ 468	$ 244	$ 212	$ 52

[a]Depreciable basis = $8,000. Depreciation expense in each year equals depreciable basis times the ACRS percentage allowances of 0.20, 0.32, 0.19, 0.12, 0.11, and 0.06 in Years 1–6, respectively.

[b]Depreciation tax savings = $T(\Delta$ Depreciation) = $0.4(\Delta$ Depreciation).

Now recognize that at the end of Year 6 Dauten would recover its net working capital investment of $1,500, and it would also receive $800 from the sale of the replacement machine. However, since the machine would be fully depreciated, the firm must pay 0.40($800) = $320 in taxes on the sale. Also, by undertaking the replacement now, the firm forgoes the right to sell the old machine for $500 in Year 6; thus, this $500 in Year 6 must be considered an opportunity cost in that year. No tax would be due, because the $500 salvage value would equal the old machine's Year 6 book value.

Finally, place all the cash flows on a time line:

	0	1	2	3	4	5	6
Net investment	($6,660)						
After-tax revenue increase		$1,500	$1,500	$1,500	$1,500	$1,500	$1,500
Depreciation tax savings		500	884	468	244	212	52
Working capital recovery							1,500
Salvage value on new machine							800
Tax on salvage value of new machine							(320)
Opportunity cost of old machine							(500)
Net cash flow	($6,660)	$2,000	$2,384	$1,968	$1,744	$1,712	$3,032

The net present value of this incremental cash flow stream, when discounted at 15 percent, is $1,335. Thus, the replacement should be made.

11 Risk Analysis in Capital Budgeting[1]

LILCO AND FPC: DIFFERENT APPROACHES TO RISK ANALYSIS LEAD TO VERY DIFFERENT OUTCOMES

Capital budgeting is, in theory, relatively straightforward and mechanical — we simply estimate the cost of a project and its expected future cash flows, find the PV of the cash flows, and, if this PV exceeds the project's cost, accept it. This is fine if we have an accurate estimate of the project's cost and its future cash flows. However, if the cost and cash flow estimates are wrong, what initially looked like a good project can turn out to be a disaster.

To illustrate, Long Island Lighting Company (LILCO) decided to build the Shoreham nuclear power plant in the 1970s. At the time, the demand for electricity was growing at a rate of 7 percent per year, so it looked as though LILCO would have to double its generating capacity every 10 years to meet the electrical needs of its area. Thus, LILCO began the construction of Shoreham at a forecasted cost of $500 million.

The project turned out to be a fiasco. First, growth in the demand for power began to fall shortly after Shoreham was started, but LILCO failed to make adequate adjustments to its demand forecast. Second, the cost of building the plant had been drastically underestimated — by 1987, construction

---

[1]This chapter is relatively technical, and it can be omitted in the first finance course without loss of continuity.

costs were estimated at about $6 billion versus the originally forecasted $0.5 billion, a 1,100 percent error!

With lower revenues and a higher initial cost, Shoreham's projected positive NPV turned out to be a huge negative one. As this book goes to press, the future of Shoreham is uncertain — the final cost of the plant is uncertain, as is demand for its output. Further, the state of New York is concerned about how population near the plant could be evacuated if an accident should occur, and, on the basis of this issue, the state has blocked the plant's startup. As a result of all this, LILCO is no longer able to pay dividends, and if the plant is abandoned and LILCO is forced to write it off, the company will be bankrupt. Its stockholders have already lost millions, as have its bondholders, and the company's top executives have lost their jobs. LILCO's customers have also suffered, as they must pay close to the highest electric rates in the nation, largely as a result of the Shoreham project.

About the same time LILCO decided to build Shoreham, Florida Power Corporation (FPC) was also studying the feasibility of a new nuclear plant. Several University of Florida finance professors met with the FPC planners and discussed with them the topics contained in this chapter as applied to their capital budgeting decision. FPC rejected nuclear energy and built a plant fueled by coal. Its stock price has increased 500 percent, and today's FPC's financial position is as good as LILCO's is bad. If you learn the lessons of this chapter, it may help you make good decisions like that of FPC and avoid LILCO-type disasters.

market, or beta, risk
That part of a project's risk that cannot be eliminated by diversification; it is measured by the project's beta coefficient.

within-firm total risk
Risk not considering the effects of diversification; it is measured by a project's effect on the firm's earnings variability.

stand-alone total risk
The risk an asset would have if it were a firm's only asset; it is measured by the variability of the asset's expected returns.

RISK analysis is important in all financial decisions, especially those relating to capital budgeting. As we saw in Chapter 4, the higher an investment's risk, the higher its required rate of return. This is equally true when the investor is a corporation and the investment is a capital project. In this chapter we discuss procedures (1) for measuring the riskiness of potential capital projects, (2) for incorporating this information into the capital budgeting decision, and (3) for determining a firm's optimal capital budget.

INTRODUCTION TO RISK ASSESSMENT

Three separate and distinct types of project risk can be identified: (1) **market, or beta, risk**, which assesses project risk from the standpoint of an investor who holds a highly diversified portfolio; (2) **within-firm total risk**, which looks at the effects a project has on the company's total risk, without considering the effects of the stockholders' own personal diversification; and (3) the project's own **stand-alone total risk**, or its risk disregarding the facts that it is but one asset within the firm's portfolio of assets and that the firm in question is but one stock in most investors' stock portfolios. As we shall see, a particular project may have high stand-alone risk, yet taking it on may not have much effect on either the firm's risk or that of its owners because of portfolio effects.

A project's stand-alone risk is measured by the variability of the project's expected returns; its within-firm risk is measured by its impact on the firm's earnings variability; and its market risk is measured by its effect on the firm's beta coefficient. Taking on a project with a high degree of either stand-alone or within-firm risk will not necessarily affect the firm's beta to any great extent. However, if the project has highly uncertain returns, and if those returns are highly correlated with those of the firm's other assets and most other assets in the economy, the project will have a high degree of all types of risk. For example, suppose General Motors decides to undertake a major expansion to build solar-powered autos. GM is not sure how its technology will work on a mass production basis, so there are great risks in the venture — its stand-alone risk is high. Management also estimates that the project will have a higher probability of success if the economy is strong, for then people will have money to spend on the new autos. This means that the project will tend to do well if GM's other divisions also do well and to do badly if other divisions do badly. In this case, the project will have high within-firm risk. Finally, since GM's prospects are highly correlated with those of most other firms, the project's beta coefficient will be high. Thus, it will be risky by all three measures.

Market risk is important because of its direct effect on a firm's stock price: Beta affects k, and k affects the stock price. Within-firm risk, often called *corporate risk,* is also important for three primary reasons:

1. Undiversified stockholders, including the owners of small businesses, are more concerned about corporate risk than about market risk.

2. Empirical studies of the determinants of required rates of return (k) generally find both market and corporate risk to be important. This suggests that investors, even those who are well diversified, consider factors other than market risk when they establish required returns.

3. The firm's stability is important to its managers, workers, customers, suppliers, and creditors, as well as to the community in which it operates. Firms that are in serious danger of bankruptcy, or even of suffering low profits and reduced output, have difficulty attracting and retaining good managers and workers. Also, both suppliers and customers are reluctant to depend on weak firms, and such firms have difficulty borrowing money except at high interest rates. These factors tend to reduce risky firms' profitability and hence the prices of their stocks, and, thus, they make corporate risk significant.

For these reasons, corporate risk is important even if a firm's stockholders are well diversified.

TECHNIQUES FOR MEASURING STAND-ALONE RISK

What about a project's stand-alone risk — is it of any importance to anyone? In theory, this type of risk should be of little or no concern. However, it is of great importance, for the following reasons:

1. It is much easier to estimate a project's stand-alone risk than its within-firm risk, and it is far easier to measure stand-alone risk than market risk.

2. In the vast majority of cases, all three types of risk are highly correlated — if the general economy does well, so will the firm, and if the firm does well, so will most of its projects. Thus, stand-alone risk is generally a good proxy for hard-to-measure market risk.

3. Because of Points 1 and 2, if management wants a reasonably accurate assessment of a project's riskiness, it ought to spend considerable effort on ascertaining the riskiness of the project's own cash flows — that is, its stand-alone risk.

The starting point for analyzing a project's stand-alone risk involves determining the uncertainty inherent in the project's cash flows. This analysis can be handled in a number of ways, ranging from informal judgments to complex economic and statistical analyses involving large-scale computer models. To illustrate what is involved, we shall refer to Brandt-Quigley Corporation's appliance control computer project that we discussed back in Chapter 10. Many of the individual cash flows that were shown back in Table 10-2 are subject to uncertainty. For example, sales for each year were projected at 20,000 units to be sold at a net price of $2,000 per unit, or $40 million in total. Actual unit sales would almost certainly be somewhat higher or lower than 20,000, however, and the sales price would probably turn out to be different from the projected $2,000 per unit. *In effect, the sales quantity and the sales price estimates are really expected values taken from probability distributions, as are many of the other values that were shown in Table 10-2.* The distributions could be relatively "tight," reflecting small standard deviations and low risk, or they could be "flat," denoting a great deal of uncertainty about the final value of the variable in question and hence a high degree of stand-alone risk.

The nature of the individual cash flow distributions, and their correlations with one another, determine the nature of the NPV distribution and, thus, the project's stand-alone risk. In the next section, we discuss three techniques for assessing a project's stand-alone risk: (1) sensitivity analysis, (2) scenario analysis, and (3) Monte Carlo simulation.

Sensitivity Analysis

Intuitively, we know that many of the variables which determine a project's cash flows are based on some type of probability distribution rather than being known with certainty. We also know that if a key input variable, such as units

Figure 11-1   Sensitivity Analysis (Thousands of Dollars)

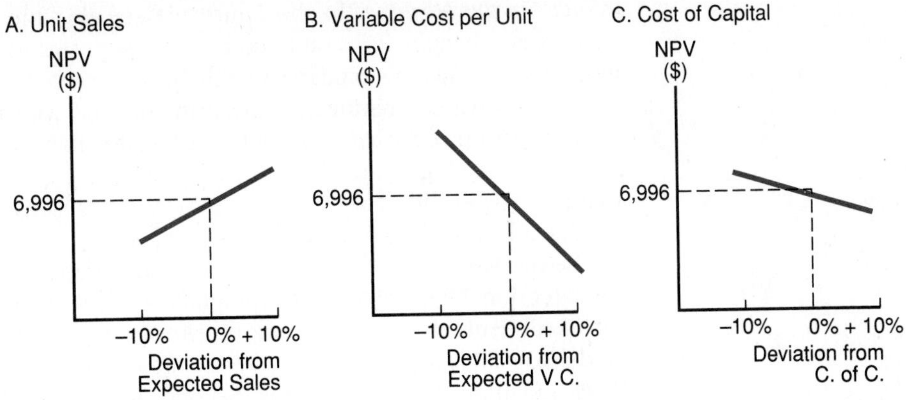

A. Unit Sales

NPV
($)

6,996

−10%   0% + 10%
Deviation from
Expected Sales

B. Variable Cost per Unit

NPV
($)

6,996

−10%   0% + 10%
Deviation from
Expected V.C.

C. Cost of Capital

NPV
($)

6,996

−10%   0% + 10%
Deviation from
C. of C.

Deviation from Base Level (%)	Net Present Value		
	Units Sold	Variable Cost/Unit	Cost of Capital
− 10	$4,080	$11,369	$8,035
− 5	5,538	9,183	7,509
0 (base case)	6,996	6,996	6,996
+ 5	8,454	4,809	6,494
+10	9,911	2,622	6,003

Note: This analysis was performed using *Lotus 1-2-3*, so the values are slightly different than those that would be obtained using interest factor tables because of rounding differences.

---

sensitivity analysis
A risk analysis technique in which key variables are changed and the resulting changes in the NPV and the rate of return are observed.

sold, changes, the project's NPV also will change. **Sensitivity analysis** is a technique which indicates exactly how much the NPV will change in response to a given change in an input variable, other things held constant.

Sensitivity analysis begins with a *base case* situation, which is developed using the *expected* values for each input. To illustrate, consider the data given in Table 10-2 back in Chapter 10, in which projected income statements for Brandt-Quigley's computer project are shown. The values presented in the table for unit sales, sales price, fixed costs, and variable costs are the most likely, or base case, values, and the resulting $6,996,000 NPV shown in Table 10-2 is called the *base case NPV*. Now we ask a series of "what if" questions: "What if unit sales fall 20 percent below the most likely level?" "What if the sales price per unit falls?" "What if variable costs are 65 percent of dollar sales rather than the expected 60 percent?" Sensitivity analysis is designed to provide the decision maker with answers to questions such as these.

In a sensitivity analysis, each variable is changed by several specific percentages above and below the expected value, holding other things constant, then a new NPV is calculated for each of these values, and, finally, the set of NPVs is plotted against the variable that was changed. Figure 11-1 shows the computer project's sensitivity graphs for three of the key input variables. The table below the graphs gives the NPVs that were used to construct the graphs.

The slopes of the lines in the graphs show how sensitive NPV is to changes in each of the inputs: *the steeper the slope, the more sensitive the NPV is to a change in the variable*. In the figure we see that the project's NPV is very sensitive to changes in variable costs, fairly sensitive to changes in unit sales, and not very sensitive to changes in the cost of capital.

If we were comparing two projects, the one with the steeper sensitivity lines would be regarded as riskier, because for that project a relatively small error in estimating a variable such as the variable cost per unit would produce a large error in the project's expected NPV. Thus, sensitivity analysis can provide useful insights into the riskiness of a project.

Before we move on, three additional points about sensitivity analysis warrant attention. First, spreadsheet computer models, such as *Lotus 1-2-3* models, are ideally suited for performing sensitivity analysis. We used a *Lotus 1-2-3* model to conduct the analyses represented in Figure 11-1; it generated the NPVs and then drew the graphs. Second, we could have plotted all of the sensitivity lines on one graph. This would have facilitated direct comparisons of the sensitivities among different input variables. Third, it is easy to vary more than one variable at a time, and thus to do "multivariable sensitivity analysis," although one cannot easily construct graphs to illustrate each variable's effect.

Scenario Analysis

Although sensitivity analysis is probably the most widely used risk analysis technique, it does have limitations. Consider, for example, a proposed coal mine project whose NPV is highly sensitive to any change in output, variable costs, or sales price. If a utility company has contracted to buy a fixed amount of coal at an inflation-adjusted price per ton, however, the mining venture may be quite safe in spite of its steep sensitivity lines. *In general, a project's stand-alone risk depends on both (1) the sensitivity of its NPV to changes in key variables and (2) the range in likely values of these variables as reflected in their probability distributions*. Because sensitivity analysis considers only the first factor, it is incomplete.

scenario analysis
A risk analysis technique in which "bad" and "good" sets of financial circumstances are compared with a most likely, or base case, circumstance.

Scenario analysis is a risk analysis technique that considers both the sensitivity of NPV to changes in key variables and the range of likely variable values. In a scenario analysis, the financial analyst asks operating managers to pick a "bad" set of circumstances (low unit sales, low sales price, high variable cost per unit, high construction cost, and so on) and a "good" set. The NPVs under the bad and good conditions are then calculated and compared to the unexpected, or base case, NPV.

worst case scenario
An analysis in which all of the input variables are set at their worst reasonably forecasted values.

As an example, let us return to the appliance control computer project. Assume that Brandt-Quigley's managers are fairly confident of their estimates of all the project's cash flow variables except price and unit sales. Further, they regard a drop in sales below 15,000 units or a rise above 25,000 units as being extremely unlikely. Similarly, they expect the sales price as set in the marketplace to fall within the range of $1,500 to $2,500. Thus, 15,000 units at a price of $1,500 defines the lower bound, or the **worst case scenario**, whereas 25,000

Table 11-1   Scenario Analysis

Scenario	Probability of Outcome (P_i)	Sales Volume (Units)	Sales Price	NPV (in Thousands)
Worst case	0.25	15,000	$1,500	($ 5,761)
Base case	0.50	20,000	2,000	6,996
Best case	0.25	25,000	2,500	23,397
			Expected NPV =	$ 7,907
			σ_{NPV} =	$10,349

best case scenario
An analysis in which all of the input variables are set at their best reasonably forecasted values.

base case
An analysis in which all of the input variables are set at their most likely values.

units at a price of $2,500 defines the upper bound, or the **best case scenario.** Remember that the **base case** values are 20,000 units and a price of $2,000.

To carry out the scenario analysis, we use the worst case variable values to obtain the worst case NPV and the best case variable values to obtain the best case NPV.[2] We actually performed the analysis using a *Lotus* model, and Table 11-1 summarizes the results of this analysis. We see that the base case forecasts a positive NPV; the worst case produces a negative NPV; and the best case results in a very large positive NPV.

We can use the results of the scenario analysis to determine the expected NPV, the standard deviation of NPV, and the coefficient of variation. To begin, we need an estimate of the probabilities of occurrence of the three scenarios, the P_i values. Suppose management estimates that there is a 25 percent probability of the worst case scenario occurring, a 50 percent probability of the base case, and a 25 percent probability of the best case. Of course, it is *very difficult* to estimate scenario probabilities accurately.

With the probabilities and the scenario NPVs, we have a discrete probability distribution of returns just like those we dealt with in Chapter 4, except that the returns are measured in dollars instead of in percentages (rates of return). The expected NPV (in thousands of dollars) is $7,907.[3]

$$\text{Expected NPV} = \sum_{i=1}^{n} P_i(NPV_i)$$

$$= 0.25(-\$5,761) + 0.50(\$6,996) + 0.25(\$23,397)$$

$$= \$7,907.$$

---

[2]We could have included worst and best case values for fixed and variable costs, income tax rates, salvage values, and so on. For illustrative purposes, we limited the changes to only two variables. Also, note that we are treating sales price and quantity as independent variables; that is, a low sales price could occur when unit sales were low, and a high sales price could be coupled with high unit sales, or vice versa. As we discuss in the next section, it is relatively easy to vary these assumptions if the facts of the situation suggest a different set of conditions.

[3]Note that the expected NPV is *not* the same as the base case NPV, $6,996 (in thousands). This is because the two uncertain variables, sales volume and sales price, are multiplied together to obtain dollar sales, and this process causes the NPV distribution to be skewed to the right. A big number times another big number produces a very big number, which in turn causes the average, or expected value, to be increased.

The standard deviation of the NPV is $10,349 (in thousands of dollars):

$$\sigma_{NPV} = \sqrt{\sum_{i=1}^{n} P_i(NPV_i - \text{Expected NPV})^2}$$

$$= \sqrt{\begin{array}{c} (0.25(-\$5,761 - \$7,907)^2 + 0.50(\$6,996 - \$7,907)^2 \\ + 0.25(\$23,397 - \$7,907)^2) \end{array}}$$

$$= \$10,349.$$

Finally, the project's coefficient of variation is 1.3:

$$CV_{NPV} = \frac{\sigma_{NPV}}{E(NPV)} = \frac{\$10,349}{\$7,907} = 1.3.$$

Now the project's coefficient of variation can be compared with the coefficient of variation of Brandt-Quigley's "average" project to get an idea of the relative riskiness of the appliance control computer project. Brandt-Quigley's existing projects, on average, have a coefficient of variation of about 1.0. Thus, on the basis of this stand-alone risk measure, Brandt-Quigley's managers would conclude that the appliance computer project is 30 percent riskier than the firm's "average" project.

Scenario analysis provides useful information about a project's stand-alone risk. However, it is limited in that it only considers a few discrete outcomes (NPVs) for the project, although there really are an infinite number of possibilities. In the next section, we describe a more rigorous method of assessing a project's stand-alone risk.

Monte Carlo Simulation

Monte Carlo simulation A risk analysis technique in which probable future events are simulated on a computer, generating estimated rates of return and risk indexes.

Monte Carlo simulation, so named because this type of analysis grew out of work on the mathematics of casino gambling, ties together sensitivities and input variable probability distributions.[4] However, simulation requires a relatively powerful computer, coupled with an efficient financial planning software package, whereas scenario analysis can be done using a PC with a spreadsheet program or even using a calculator.

The first step in a computer simulation is to specify the probability distribution of each uncertain cash flow variable. Once this has been done, the simulation proceeds as follows:

1. The computer chooses at random a value for each uncertain variable based on the variable's specified probability distribution. For example, a value for unit sales would be chosen and used in the first model run.

---

[4]The use of simulation analysis in capital budgeting was first reported by David B. Hertz, "Risk Analysis in Capital Investments," *Harvard Business Review,* January–February 1964, 95–106. Usually, continuous distributions are used in simulations.

Figure 11-2   NPV Probability Distribution (Millions of Dollars)

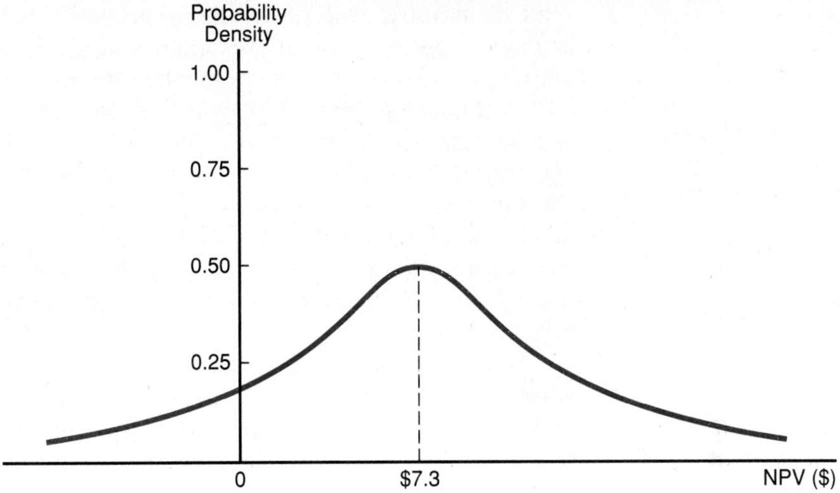

Expected NPV = $7.3
σ_{NPV} = $10.2
CV_{NPV} = $10.2/$7.3 = 1.40

2. The value selected for each uncertain variable, along with values for fixed factors such as the tax rate and depreciation charges, are then used by the model to determine the net cash flows for each year, and these cash flows are then used to determine the project's NPV in the first run.

3. Steps 1 and 2 are repeated many times, say 500, resulting in 500 NPVs, which make up a probability distribution.

Using this procedure, we performed a simulation analysis on Brandt-Quigley's appliance control computer project. As in the scenario analysis, we simplified the illustration by specifying a probability distribution for only one key variable — unit sales. For all of the other variables, we simply used their expected values. The resulting NPV distribution is graphed in Figure 11-2.

The primary advantage of simulation is that it shows us the range of possible outcomes with their attached probabilities, rather than merely a point estimate of the NPV. From Figure 11-2 we can see that the expected NPV is $7.3 million and that the standard deviation of the NPV is $10.2 million. Thus, the coefficient of variation is $10.2 million/$7.3 million = 1.40. These figures differ slightly from those developed in the scenario analysis. Simulation software packages can be used to estimate the probability of NPV > 0, of IRR > 0, and so on. This additional information can be quite helpful in assessing the riskiness of a project.

Limitations of Scenario and Simulation Analysis

In spite of its obvious appeal, Monte Carlo simulation has not been widely used in industry. One of the major problems is specifying the correlations among the uncertain cash flow variables. Mechanically, it is easy to incorporate any type of correlation among variables into a simulation analysis; for example, *IFPS,* a simulation software program, permits one to specify both intervariable and intertemporal correlations. However, it is *not* easy to specify what the correlations should be. Indeed, people who have tried to obtain such relationships from the operating managers who must estimate them have eloquently emphasized the difficulties involved. Clearly, the problem is not insurmountable, as simulation is used in business. Still, it is important not to underestimate the difficulty of obtaining valid estimates of probability distributions and correlations among the variables.[5]

Another problem with both scenario and simulation analyses is that even when the analysis has been completed, no clear-cut decision rule emerges. We end up with an expected NPV and a distribution about this expected value, which we can use to judge the project's stand-alone risk. However, the analysis provides no mechanism to indicate whether a project's profitability as measured by the expected NPV is sufficient to compensate for its risk as measured by σ_{NPV} or CV_{NPV}.

Finally, scenario and simulation analyses ignore the effects of diversification, both among projects within the firm and by investors in their personal investment portfolios. Thus, an individual project might have highly uncertain returns when evaluated on a stand-alone basis, but if those returns are not correlated with the returns on the firm's other assets, the project may not be very risky in terms of either within-firm or market risk. Indeed, if the project's returns are negatively correlated with the returns on the firm's other assets, it actually may decrease the firm's corporate risk, and the larger its σ_{NPV}, the more it will reduce the firm's overall risk. Similarly, if a project's returns are not positively correlated with the stock market, even a project with highly variable returns might not be regarded as risky by well-diversified stockholders, who are normally more concerned with market risk than with total risk.

BETA (OR MARKET) RISK

The types of risk analysis discussed thus far in the chapter provide insights into projects' risks and thus help managers make better accept/reject decisions. However, as we noted previously, these risk measures do not take account of portfolio risk, and they are subjective rather than objective in that they do not

---

[5]For more insight into the difficulties involved in estimating probability distributions and correlations in practice, see K. Larry Hastie, "One Businessman's View of Capital Budgeting," *Financial Management,* Winter 1974, 36–43. Hastie was treasurer of Bendix Corporation.

state specifically which projects should be accepted and which rejected. In this section, we show how the CAPM can be used to help overcome those shortcomings. Of course, the CAPM has shortcomings of its own, but it nevertheless offers useful insights into risk analysis in capital budgeting.

To begin, recall from Chapter 4 that the Security Market Line equation expresses the risk/return relationship as follows:

$$k_s = k_{RF} + (k_M - k_{RF})b_i.$$

As an example, consider the case of Erie Steel Company, an integrated steel producer operating in the Great Lakes region. Erie Steel's beta = 1.1, k_{RF} = 8%, and k_M = 12%. Thus, Erie's cost of equity is 12.4 percent:

$$k_s = 8\% + (12\% - 8\%)1.1$$

$$= 8\% + (4\%)1.1$$

$$= 12.4\%.$$

This suggests that investors would be willing to give Erie money to invest in average-risk projects if the company could earn 12.4 percent or more on this money. Here again, by average risk we mean projects having risk similar to the firm's existing assets. *Therefore, as a first approximation, Erie should invest in capital projects if and only if these projects have an expected return of 12.4 percent or more.*[6] In other words, Erie should use 12.4 percent as its discount rate to determine the NPVs of any average-risk project which it is considering.

Suppose, however, that taking on a particular project would cause a change in Erie's beta coefficient and hence change the company's cost of equity. For example, suppose Erie is considering the construction of a fleet of barges to haul iron ore, and barge operations have betas of 1.5 rather than 1.1. Since the firm itself may be regarded as a "portfolio of assets," and since the beta of any portfolio is a weighted average of the betas of the individual assets, taking on the barge project would cause the overall corporate beta to rise to somewhere between the original beta of 1.1 and the barge project's beta of 1.5. The exact value of the new beta would depend on the relative size of the investment in barge operations versus Erie's other assets. If 80 percent of Erie's total funds were to end up in basic steel operations with a beta of 1.1 and 20 percent in barge operations with a beta of 1.5, the new corporate beta would be 1.18:

$$\text{New beta} = 0.8(1.1) + 0.2(1.5)$$

$$= 1.18.$$

This increase in Erie's beta coefficient would cause the stock price to decline *unless the increased beta were offset by a higher expected rate of return.*

---

[6]To simplify things somewhat, we assume at this point that the firm uses only equity capital. If debt is used, the cost of capital used must be a weighted average of the costs of debt and equity. This point is discussed at length in Chapter 16.

Specifically, taking on the new project would cause the overall corporate cost of capital to rise from the original 12.4 percent to 12.72 percent:

$$k_s = 8\% + (4\%)1.18$$

$$= 12.72\%.$$

Therefore, to keep the barge investment from lowering the value of the firm, Erie's overall expected rate of return would also have to rise from 12.4 to 12.72 percent.

If investments in basic steel must earn 12.4 percent, how much must the barge investment earn for the new overall rate of return to equal 12.72 percent? We know that if Erie undertakes the barge investment, it will have 80 percent of its assets invested in basic steel projects earning 12.4 percent and 20 percent in barge operations earning X percent, and the average required rate of return will be 12.72 percent. Therefore,

$$0.8(12.4\%) + 0.2X = 12.72\%$$

$$0.2X = 2.8\%$$

$$X = 14\%.$$

This shows that the barge project must have an expected return of at least 14 percent if the corporation is to earn its new cost of capital.

In summary, if Erie takes on the barge project, its corporate beta will rise from 1.1 to 1.18; the overall required rate of return will rise from 12.4 to 12.72 percent; and the barge investment will have to earn 14 percent if the company is to earn its new overall cost of capital.

This line of reasoning leads to the conclusion that if the beta coefficient for each project, b_p, could be determined, then an individual project's cost of capital, k_p, could be found as follows:

$$k_p = k_{RF} + (k_M - k_{RF})b_p.$$

Thus, for basic steel projects with b = 1.1, Erie should use 12.4 percent as the discount rate. The barge project, with b = 1.5, should be evaluated at a 14 percent discount rate:

$$k_{Barge} = 8\% + (4\%)1.5$$

$$= 8\% + 6\%$$

$$= 14\%.$$

On the other hand, a low-risk project such as a new steel distribution center with a beta of only 0.5 would have a cost of capital of 10 percent:

$$k_{Center} = 8\% + (4\%)0.5$$

$$= 10\%.$$

***

Figure 11-3   Using the Security Market Line Concept in Capital Budgeting

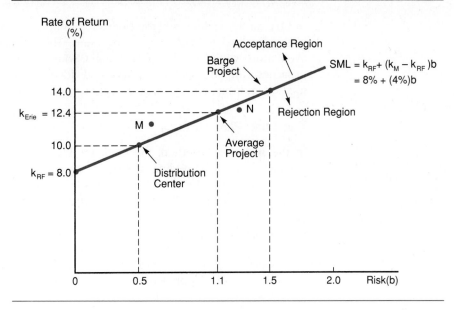

Figure 11-3 gives a graphic summary of these concepts as applied to Erie Steel. Note the following points:

1. The SML is the same Security Market Line that we developed in Chapter 4. It shows how investors are willing to make trade-offs between risk, as measured by beta, and expected returns. The higher the beta risk, the higher the rate of return needed to compensate investors for bearing this risk. The SML specifies the nature of this relationship.

2. Erie Steel initially has a beta of 1.1, so its required rate of return on average-risk investments is 12.4 percent.

3. High-risk investments such as the barge line require higher rates of return, whereas low-risk investments such as the distribution center require lower rates of return. It is not shown on the graph, but if Erie makes relatively large investments in either high- or low-risk projects as opposed to average-risk ones, the corporate beta, and therefore the required rate of return on the common stock (k_s), will change.

4. If the expected rate of return on a given capital project lies *above* the SML, the expected rate of return on the project is more than enough to compensate for its risk, and the project should be accepted. Conversely, if the project's rate of return lies *below* the SML, it should be rejected. Thus, Project M in Figure 11-3 is acceptable, whereas Project N should be rejected. N has a higher expected return than M, but the differential is not enough to offset its much higher risk.

TECHNIQUES FOR MEASURING BETA RISK

In Chapter 4, we discussed the estimation of betas for stocks and indicated that it is difficult to estimate true future betas. The estimation of project betas is even more difficult, and more fraught with uncertainty. However, two approaches can be used to estimate individual assets' betas — the pure play method and the accounting beta method.

The Pure Play Method

pure play method
An approach used for estimating the beta of a project in which a firm identifies several companies whose only business is the product in question, calculates the beta for each firm, and then averages the betas to find an approximation of its own project's beta.

In the **pure play method**, the company tries to find several single-product companies in the same line of business as the project being evaluated, and it then applies these betas to determine the cost of capital for its own project. For example, suppose Erie could find three existing single-product firms that operate barges, and suppose also that Erie's management believes its barge project would be subject to the same risks as these firms. Erie could then determine the betas of those firms, average them, and use this average beta as a proxy for the barge project's beta.[7]

The pure play approach can only be used for major assets such as whole divisions, and even then it is frequently difficult to implement because it is often impossible to find pure play proxy firms. However, when IBM was considering going into personal computers, it was able to obtain data on Apple Computer and several other essentially pure play personal computer companies. This is often the case when a firm considers a major investment outside its primary field.

The Accounting Beta Method

accounting beta method
A method of estimating a project's beta by running a regression of the company's rate of return on assets against the average ROA for a large sample of firms.

As noted above, it is often impossible to find single-product, publicly traded firms suitable for the pure play approach. If that is the case, we may be able to use the **accounting beta method**. Betas normally are found as described in Appendix 4A — by regressing the returns of a particular company's stock against returns on a stock market index. However, we could run a regression of the company's rate of return on assets (EBIT/Total assets) over time against the average return on assets for a large sample of companies, such as those included in the S&P 400. Betas determined in this way (that is, by using accounting data rather than stock market data) are called *accounting betas*.

Accounting betas for projects can be calculated only after the project has been accepted, has been placed in operation, and has begun to generate output and accounting results. However, to the extent that management thinks a given project is similar to other projects the firm has undertaken in the past,

---

[7]If the pure play firms employ different capital structures than that of Erie, this fact must be dealt with by adjusting the beta coefficients. See Eugene F. Brigham and Louis C. Gapenski, *Intermediate Financial Management,* 2nd ed., Chapter 9, for a discussion of this aspect of the pure play method.

other projects' accounting betas can be used as proxies for that of the project in question. In practice, accounting betas are normally calculated for divisions or other large units, not for single assets, and divisional betas then are imputed to the asset. This point is discussed later in the chapter.

PORTFOLIO EFFECTS WITHIN THE FIRM

As we learned in Chapter 4, a security might be quite risky if held in isolation but not very risky if held as part of a well-diversified portfolio. The same thing is true of capital budgeting; the returns on an individual project might be highly uncertain, but if the project is small relative to the total firm, and if its returns are not highly correlated with the firm's other assets, the project may not be very risky in either the corporate or the beta sense.

Many firms do make serious efforts to diversify; often this is a specific objective of the long-run strategic plan. For example, Du Pont diversified into both coal and oil to broaden its operating base, and real estate developers have diversified geographically to lessen the effect of a slowdown in one region. The major objective of many such moves is to stabilize earnings, reduce corporate risk, and thereby raise the value of the firm's stock.

The wisdom of corporate diversification designed to reduce risk has been questioned — why should a firm diversify when stockholders can so easily diversify on their own? In other words, although it may be true that if the returns on Du Pont's and Conoco's stock are not perfectly positively correlated then merging the companies (as happened recently) will reduce their risks somewhat, would it not be just as easy for investors to carry out this risk-reducing diversification directly, without all the trouble and expense of a merger?

As you might suspect, the answer is not so simple. Although stockholders could directly obtain some of the risk-reducing benefits through personal diversification, other benefits can be gained only by diversification at the corporate level. For example, a relatively stable corporation might be able to attract a better work force and also might be able to use more low-cost debt than could two less stable firms. And, of course, there may also be spillover effects from diversification. For example, Du Pont provided Conoco with a more stable market for its oil, while Conoco provided Du Pont with a stable supply of raw materials. Further, the two companies' research departments are reported to have gained economies of scale from combined operations.

CONCLUSIONS ON PROJECT RISK

We have discussed the three types of risk normally considered in capital budgeting analysis — stand-alone risk, within-firm risk, and market risk — and we have discussed ways of assessing each. However, two important questions remain: (1) Is it correct for a firm to be concerned with stand-alone and within-firm risk in its capital budgeting decisions, and (2) what do we do when the stand-alone or within-firm assessments and the market risk assessment lead to different conclusions?

These questions do not have easy answers. From a theoretical standpoint, well-diversified investors should be concerned only with market risk, managers should be concerned only with stock price maximization, and these two factors should lead to the conclusion that market, or beta, risk ought to be given virtually all the weight in capital budgeting decisions. However, if investors are not well diversified, if the CAPM does not really operate as theory says it should, or if measurement problems keep managers from implementing the CAPM approach in capital budgeting, it may be appropriate to give stand-alone and within-firm risk more weight than financial theorists suggest. Note that the CAPM ignores financial distress costs, even though such costs can be substantial, and that the probability of financial distress depends on a firm's total risk, not on its beta risk. Therefore, one can easily conclude that even well-diversified investors want a firm's management to give at least some consideration to a project's within-firm risk instead of concentrating entirely on market risk.

Although it would be desirable to reconcile these problems and to measure project risk on some absolute scale, the best we can do in practice is to determine project risk in a somewhat nebulous, relative sense. For example, we can generally say with a fair degree of confidence that a particular project has more or less stand-alone risk than the firm's average project. Then, assuming that stand-alone and within-firm, or corporate, risk are highly correlated (which is typical), a project's stand-alone risk is a good measure of its corporate risk. Finally, assuming that market risk and corporate risk are highly correlated (as studies suggest), a project with more corporate risk than average will also have more market risk, and vice versa for projects with low corporate risk.[8]

INCORPORATING PROJECT RISK AND CAPITAL STRUCTURE INTO CAPITAL BUDGETING DECISIONS

Thus far, we have seen that capital budgeting can affect a firm's market risk, its corporate risk, or both. We have also seen that it is extremely difficult to quantify either type of risk. In other words, although it may be possible to reach the general conclusion that one project is riskier than another (in either the market or the corporate sense), it is difficult to develop a really good *measure*

---

[8]For example, see M. Chapman Findlay III, Arthur E. Gooding, and Wallace Q. Weaver, Jr., "On the Relevant Risk for Determining Capital Expenditure Hurdle Rates," *Financial Management,* Winter 1976, 9–16.

of project risk. This lack of precision in measuring project risk makes it difficult to incorporate differential risk into capital budgeting decisions.

There are two methods for incorporating project risk into the capital budgeting decision process. In the *certainty equivalent* approach, the expected cash flows in each year are adjusted to reflect project risk; cash flows that are not known with certainty are scaled down, and the riskier the flows, the lower their certainty equivalent values. However, the certainty equivalent approach is difficult to implement in practice, and hence we will focus on the **risk-adjusted discount rate** approach. In this method, differential project risk is dealt with by changing the discount rate. Average risk projects are discounted at the firm's required rate of return, above-average risk projects are discounted at a higher cost of capital, and below-average risk projects are discounted at a rate below the firm's required rate of return. Unfortunately, because risk cannot be measured precisely, there is no good way of specifying exactly *how much* higher or lower these discount rates should be; given the present state of the art, risk adjustments are necessarily judgmental and somewhat arbitrary.

Capital structure also must be taken into account if a firm finances different assets in different ways. For example, one division might have a lot of real estate, which is well suited as collateral for loans, whereas some other division might have most of its capital tied up in special-purpose machinery, which is not good collateral. As a result, the division with the real estate might have a higher *debt capacity* than the division with the machinery and hence an optimal capital structure which contains a higher percentage of debt. In this case, the division with more real estate contributes more to the overall debt capacity of the firm, and management might calculate its required return using a higher debt ratio than for the other division.[9]

Although the process is not exact, many companies use a two-step procedure to develop risk-adjusted discount rates for use in capital budgeting. First, *divisional costs of capital* are established for each of the major operating divisions on the basis of each division's estimated riskiness and capital structure. Second, within each division, all projects are classified into three categories — high risk, average risk, and low risk. Then, each division uses its basic divisional cost of capital as the discount rate for average-risk projects, reduces the divisional cost of capital by one or two percentage points when evaluating low-risk projects, and raises the cost of capital by several percentage points for high-risk projects. For example, if a division's basic cost of capital is estimated to be 10 percent, a 12 percent discount rate might be used for a high-risk project and a 9 percent rate for a low-risk project. Average-risk projects, which constitute about 80 percent of most capital budgets, would be evaluated at the 10 percent divisional cost of capital. This procedure is far from precise, but it does at least recognize that different divisions have different characteristics and hence different costs of capital, and it also acknowledges differential project riskiness within divisions.

---

[9]We will say much more about optimal capital structure and debt capacity in Chapters 16 and 17.

risk-adjusted discount rate
The discount rate that applies to a particular risky (uncertain) stream of income; the risk-free rate of interest plus a risk premium appropriate to the level of risk attached to a particular project's income stream.

International

RISK AND INTERNATIONAL CAPITAL BUDGETING

Although the same basic principles of capital budgeting analysis apply to both foreign and domestic operations, there are three crucial differences: (1) cash flow estimation is generally much more difficult for overseas investments; (2) foreign cash flows are in foreign currencies, so exchange rate fluctuations add to the riskiness of overseas investments; and (3) the possibility of deliberate government acts that truncate or divert cash flows adds another dimension to risk analysis for foreign investments. In this section, we briefly discuss risk analysis of foreign capital projects.

The first issue to be addressed in foreign project analysis is the definition of the relevant cash flows. Is the relevant flow the net cash generated by the foreign subsidiary, or is it the incremental cash flows that will be sent back to the U.S. parent? As long as there are no restrictions on the repatriation of cash flows, these two cash flow streams will be the same. However, if there are local withholding taxes on dividends, restrictions on return of capital, or other blockages of international cash flows, both the timing and magnitude of the cash flows sent back to the parent will be different from the operating cash flows of the project. The parent corporation cannot use cash flows blocked in a foreign country to pay current dividends to its shareholders, nor does it have the flexibility to reinvest the capital in its other subsidiaries. Hence, from the perspective of the parent organization, *the relevant capital budgeting cash flows are the dollar cash flows that are expected to be turned over to the parent.*

The foreign currency cash flows to be turned over to the parent must be converted into U.S. dollar values by translating them at expected future exchange rates. Sensitivity or simulation analyses should be conducted to ascertain the effects of exchange rate variations, and based on these analyses, an exchange rate risk premium should be added to the domestic cost of capital to reflect the *exchange rate risk* inherent in the investment.

Sovereignty risk also differentiates international investment decisions from domestic capital budgeting. Sovereignty refers to the supreme and independent political authority of a nation state to do as it pleases within its own borders. Since foreign subsidiaries are physically located within the jurisdiction of the host country, they are subject to rules and regulations established by local government authorities, no matter how arbitrary and apparently unfair such regulations may be. Sovereignty risk includes both the possibility of expropriation or nationalization without adequate compensation and the possibility of unanticipated restrictions of cash flows to the parent company, such as tighter controls on repatriation of dividends or higher taxes. The risk of expropriation of U.S. assets abroad is small in traditionally friendly and stable countries, such as the United Kingdom or Switzerland. However, in Eastern Bloc countries and in most developing nations in Latin America, Africa, and the Far East, the risk may be substantial. Past expropriations include those of ITT and Anaconda Copper in Chile, Gulf Oil in Bolivia, Occidental Petroleum in Libya, Enron Corporation in Peru, and many companies in both Cuba and Iran.

Generally, sovereignty risk premiums are not added to the cost of capital to adjust for sovereignty risk. If a company's management has a serious concern that a given country might expropriate foreign assets, it simply will not make significant investments in that country. Expropriation is viewed as a catastrophic or ruinous event, and managers have been shown to be extraordinarily risk averse in the presence of ruinous loss possibilities. However, companies can take steps to reduce the potential loss from expropriation in three major ways: (1) by financing the subsidiary with local sources of capital, (2) by structuring operations so that the subsidiary has value only as a part of the integrated corporate system, and (3) by obtaining insurance against economic losses from expropriation from a source such as the Overseas Private Investment Corporation (OPIC). In the latter case, insurance premiums would have to be added to the project's cost.

SUMMARY AND KEY CONCEPTS

Our analysis of risk has focused on three important issues: (1) the variability of a project's cash flows and, consequently, its riskiness on a stand-alone basis; (2) its effect on the variability of the firm's cash flows (within-firm, or corporate, risk); and (3) the effect of a given project on the firm's beta coefficient (market risk). The key concepts covered are listed below.

- **Market risk** is that part of a project's risk which cannot be eliminated by diversification. It is measured by the project's beta coefficient. In theory, market risk should have the greatest effect on the value of the stock.

- **Within-firm total risk (corporate risk)** reflects the effects of a project on the firm's total risk, and it is measured by the project's effect on the firm's earnings variability. Stockholder diversification is not considered.

- **Corporate risk** affects the firm's financial strength, and this, in turn, influences its ability to use debt, to maintain smooth operations over time, and to avoid crises that might consume management's energy and disrupt employees, customers, suppliers, and the community.

- A project's **stand-alone risk** is the risk the project would have if it were the firm's only asset and if the firm's stockholders held only that one stock. Stand-alone risk is measured by the variability of the asset's expected returns.

- Stand-alone risk is often used as a proxy for market risk, because (1) market risk is difficult to measure and (2) the two are usually highly correlated.

- **Sensitivity analysis** is a technique which shows how much NPV will change in response to a given change in an input variable, other things held constant.

- **Scenario analysis** is a risk analysis technique in which the best and worst case NPVs are compared with a most likely NPV.

- **Monte Carlo simulation** is a risk analysis technique which uses a computer to simulate probable future events and to generate estimated rates of return and risk indexes based on these probabilities.

- Projects which are riskier than the firm's average project require higher rates of return, while low-risk projects require lower rates of return. The Security Market Line can be used to determine the exact return required for a project, given its estimated beta coefficient.

- The **pure play method** and the **accounting beta method** can be used to estimate betas for large projects.

- The **risk-adjusted discount rate** is that rate which is used to evaluate a particular stream of cash flows. The discount rate is increased for projects which are riskier than the firm's average project, and it is decreased for less risky projects.

- Investment in **international capital projects** is more risky than purely domestic investments because of **exchange rate risk** and **sovereignty risk.** The relevant cash flows in international capital budgeting are the dollar cash flows which are expected to be turned over to the parent company.

Both the measurement of risk and its incorporation into capital budgeting involve judgment. It is possible to use a quantitative technique such as simulation as an aid to judgment, but in the final analysis the assessment of risk in capital budgeting will always remain a subjective process.

Questions

11-1 Differentiate between (a) simulation analysis, (b) scenario analysis, and (c) sensitivity analysis. If AT&T were considering two investments, one calling for the expenditure of $200 million to develop a satellite communications system and the other involving the expenditure of $12,000 for a new truck, on which one would the company be more likely to use simulation analysis?

11-2 Distinguish between beta (or market) risk, within-firm (or corporate) risk, and stand-alone risk for a project being considered for inclusion in the capital budget. Which type do you believe should be given the greatest weight in capital budgeting decisions?

11-3 Suppose Reading Engine Company, which has a high beta as well as a great deal of corporate risk, merged with Simplicity Patterns, Inc. Simplicity's sales rise during recessions, when people are more likely to make their own clothes, and, consequently, its beta is zero but its corporate risk is relatively high. What would the merger do to the costs of capital in the consolidated company's locomotive engine division and in its patterns division?

11-4 Suppose a firm estimates its cost of capital for the coming year to be 10 percent. What are reasonable costs of capital for evaluating average-risk projects, high-risk projects, and low-risk projects?

Self-Test Problems   *(Solutions Appear on Page 433)*

Key terms

ST-1 Define each of the following terms:
a. Stand-alone total risk; within-firm total risk; market risk
b. Corporate risk
c. Sensitivity analysis
d. Scenario analysis
e. Monte Carlo simulation analysis
f. Coefficient of variation versus standard deviation
g. Project beta versus corporate beta
h. Pure play method of estimating divisional betas; accounting beta method
i. Corporate diversification versus stockholder diversification
j. Risk-adjusted discount rate; project cost of capital

Corporate risk analysis

ST-2 The staff of Scampini Manufacturing has estimated the following net cash flows and probabilities for a new manufacturing process:

	Net Cash Flow		
Year	P = 0.2	P = 0.6	P = 0.2
0	($100,000)	($100,000)	($100,000)
1	20,000	30,000	40,000
2	20,000	30,000	40,000
3	20,000	30,000	40,000
4	20,000	30,000	40,000
5	20,000	30,000	40,000
5*	0	20,000	30,000

Line 0 gives the cost of the process, Lines 1 through 5 give operating cash flows, and Line 5* contains the estimated salvage values. Scampini's cost of capital for an average-risk project is 10 percent.

a. Assume that the project has average risk. Find the project's expected NPV. (Hint: Use expected values for the net cash flow in each year.)
b. Find the best case and worst case NPVs. What is the probability of occurrence of the worst case if the cash flows are perfectly dependent (perfectly positively correlated) over time? If they are independent over time?
c. Assume that all the cash flows are perfectly positively correlated, that is, there are only three possible cash flow streams over time: (1) the worst case, (2) the most likely, or base, case, and (3) the best case, with probabilities of 0.2, 0.6, and 0.2, respectively. These cases are represented by each of the columns in the table. Find the expected NPV, its standard deviation, and its coefficient of variation.
d. The coefficient of variation of Scampini's average project is in the range 0.8 to 1.0. If the coefficient of variation of a project being evaluated is greater than 1.0, 2 percentage points are added to the firm's cost of capital. Similarly, if the coefficient of variation is less than 0.8, 1 percentage point is deducted from the cost of capital. What is the project's cost of capital? Should Scampini accept or reject the project?

Problems

Risk adjustment

11-1   The risk-free rate of return is 8 percent, and the market risk premium is 5 percent. The beta of the project under analysis is 1.6, with expected net cash flows after taxes estimated to be $1,100 per year for 5 years. The required investment outlay on the project is $3,200.
a. What is the required risk-adjusted return on the project?
b. Should the project be accepted?

Risky cash flows

11-2   The Hamsmith Company must decide between two mutually exclusive investment projects. Each project costs $4,500 and has an expected life of 3 years. Annual net cash flows from each project begin 1 year after the initial investment is made and have the following probability distributions:

Project A		Project B	
Probability	Cash Flow	Probability	Cash Flow
0.2	$4,000	0.2	$ 0
0.6	4,500	0.6	4,500
0.2	5,000	0.2	12,000

Hamsmith has decided to evaluate the riskier project at a 12 percent rate and the less risky project at a 10 percent rate.

a. What is the expected value of the annual net cash flows from each project? What is the coefficient of variation (CV)? (Hint: Use Equation 4-3 from Chapter 4 to calculate the standard deviation of Project A. $\sigma_B = \$3,865$ and $CV_B = 0.76$.)

b. What is the risk-adjusted NPV of each project?

c. If it were known that Project B was negatively correlated with other cash flows of the firm whereas Project A was positively correlated, how would this knowledge affect the decision? If Project B's cash flows were negatively correlated with gross national product (GNP), would that influence your assessment of its risk?

Divisional required rates of return   **11-3**   Chabut Computer Corporation, a producer of office equipment, currently has assets of $10 million and a beta of 1.4. The risk-free rate is 7 percent and the market risk premium is 5 percent. Chabut would like to expand into the risky home computer market. If the expansion is undertaken, Chabut would create a new division with $2.5 million in assets. The new division would have a beta of 1.9.

a. What is Chabut's current required rate of return?

b. If the expansion is undertaken, what would be the firm's new beta? What is the new overall required rate of return, and what rate of return must the home computer division produce to leave the new overall required rate of return unchanged?

Divisional required rates of return   **11-4**   National Products, Inc., an all-equity firm, is considering the formation of a new division which will increase the assets of the firm by 50 percent. National Products currently has a required rate of return of 15 percent, the risk-free rate is 6 percent, and the market risk premium is 6 percent.

a. What is National Products' current beta?

b. If National Products would like to lower its overall required rate of return to 13 percent, what is the maximum beta coefficient the new division could have?

CAPM approach to risk adjustments   **11-5**   Goodtread Rubber Company has two divisions: the tire division, which manufactures tires for new autos, and the recap division, which manufactures recapping materials that are sold to independent tire recapping shops throughout the United States. Since auto manufacturing fluctuates with the general economy, the tire division's earnings contribution to Goodtread's stock price is highly correlated with returns on most other stocks. If the tire division were operated as a separate company, its beta coefficient would be about 1.60. The sales and profits of the recap division, on the other hand, tend to be countercyclical, because recap sales boom when people cannot afford to buy new tires. The recap division's beta is estimated to be 0.80. Approximately 75 percent of Goodtread's corporate assets are invested in the tire division and 25 percent are invested in the recap division.

Currently, the rate of interest on Treasury securities is 8 percent, and the expected rate of return on an average share of stock is 13 percent. Goodtread uses only common equity capital, and hence it has no debt outstanding.

a. What is the required rate of return on Goodtread's stock?

b. What discount rate should be used to evaluate capital budgeting projects? Explain your answer fully, and, in the process, illustrate your answer with a project which costs $100,000, has a 10-year life, and provides expected after-tax net cash flows of $20,000 per year.

Sensitivity analysis   **11-6**   Your firm, Agrico, is considering the purchase of a tractor which will have a net cost of $30,000, will increase pretax operating cash flows exclusive of depreciation effects by $10,000 per year, and will be depreciated on a straight line basis to zero over 5 years at the rate of $6,000 per year, beginning the first year. (Annual cash flows will be $10,000, reduced by taxes, plus the tax savings that result from $6,000 of depreciation.) The board of directors is having a heated debate about whether the tractor will actually last 5 years. Specifically, Wayne Castano insists that he knows of some tractors that have lasted only 4 years. Tom Molinero agrees with Castano, but he argues that most tractors do give 5 years of service. Laura Evans says she has known some to last for as long as 8 years.

Given this discussion, the board asks you to prepare a scenario analysis to ascertain the importance of the uncertainty about the tractor's life. Assume a 40 percent marginal federal-plus-state tax rate, a zero salvage value, and a cost of capital of 10 percent. (Hint: Here straight line depreciation is based on the ACRS class life of the tractor and is not affected by the actual life. Also, ignore the half-year convention for this problem.)

Risk analysis
(Integrative)   **11-7**   Steve Johnson was recently assigned to analyze a fresh lemon juice product for Citrus Grove Corporation. The project requires an initial investment of $240,000 in fixed assets (including shipping and installation charges) and $20,000 in net working capital. The machinery is to be used for 4 years, it will be depreciated over its 3-year ACRS class life, and it is expected to have a salvage value of $25,000. If the project is undertaken, the firm expects gross profits (before taxes and depreciation) to increase by $125,000 in each of the next 4 years. Citrus Grove's tax rate is 40 percent, and its cost of capital is 10 percent. Johnson's base case results are given in the following table.

Citrus Grove Corporation's Lemon Juice Project (Thousands of Dollars)

		Year			
	0	1	2	3	4
Gross profit		$125	$125	$125	$125
Depreciation		79	108	36	17
Net income before taxes		$ 46	$ 17	$ 89	$108
Taxes (40%)		18	7	36	43
Net income		$ 28	$ 10	$ 53	$ 65
Plus depreciation		79	108	36	17
Net operating cash flows		$107	$118	$ 89	$ 82
Fixed assets	($240)				
Salvage value					$ 25
Tax on salvage value (40%)					(10)
Net working capital	(20)				20
Project net cash flows	($260)	$107	$118	$ 89	$117

NPV at 10% cost of capital = $82.

Now Johnson's boss would like some information on the riskiness of the project. It appears to be profitable, but what are the chances that it might be a failure, and how should risk be analyzed and worked into the decision process? Johnson has been asked to discuss risk analysis, both in general terms and as applied to the lemon juice project. To structure his analysis, he has decided to answer the following questions and to perform the following tasks.

a. Why should firms be concerned with the riskiness of individual projects? What are the three levels, or types, of project risk that are normally considered? Which type is the most relevant? Which type is the easiest to measure? Are the three types of risk generally highly correlated?

b. What is sensitivity analysis? Perform a sensitivity analysis on the project's data, varying net operating revenue, salvage value, and the cost of capital. Assume that each of these variables can deviate from its base case expected value by ±10%, by ±20%, and by ±30%. Prepare sensitivity diagrams, and interpret the results. What is the primary weakness of sensitivity analysis? What is its primary advantage?

c. Assume that Johnson feels confident about all of the input estimates in the analysis except gross profits. If product acceptance is poor, gross profits will be only $90,000 a year, but a strong consumer response will produce gross profits of $160,000 a year. Assume that there is a 25 percent chance of poor acceptance, a 25 percent chance of excellent acceptance, and a 50 percent chance of average acceptance (the base case). What is the worst case NPV? The best case NPV? Use the worst, base, and best case NPVs, and their probabilities of occurrence, to find the project's expected NPV, standard deviation, and coefficient of variation.

d. Assume that Citrus Grove's average project has a coefficient of variation (CV) in the range of 0.4 to 0.6. Would the lemon juice project be classified as high risk, average risk, or low risk? What type of risk is being measured here? What factors would affect the project's within-firm risk?

e. Citrus Grove typically adds or subtracts 3 percentage points to the cost of capital to adjust for risk. Now assume, contrary to the facts as you have developed them, that the lemon juice project has a CV of 1.2 and is judged to be of high risk. Should it be accepted under these modified conditions? What if it has a CV of only 0.15 and is judged to be a low-risk project?

f. What is scenario analysis? What are its primary advantages and disadvantages? What is Monte Carlo simulation, and what are simulation's advantages and disadvantages as compared with scenario analysis?

g. Assume that the risk-free rate is 8 percent and that the market risk premium is 5 percent. If Johnson's estimate of the lemon juice project's beta is 0.6, what is the project's market risk, and its required rate of return?

h. Citrus Grove is also evaluating two different systems for disposing of wastes associated with another product, fresh grapefruit juice. Plan L requires more workers but less capital, whereas Plan C requires more capital but fewer workers. Both systems have an estimated 3-year life, but the one selected can and will be replicated. Because the waste disposal choice has no effect on revenues, Johnson believes that the decision should be based on the relative present value of future costs of the two systems. These expected costs are as follows:

Year	Expected Net Costs	
	Plan L	Plan C
0	($500)	($1,000)
1	(500)	(300)
2	(500)	(300)
3	(500)	(300)

Assume initially that the two systems are both of average risk. Which one should be chosen? Now assume that the labor-intensive project (L) is judged to be riskier than an average project, because future labor costs are difficult to forecast. Project C, however, is still of average risk. Citrus Grove typically adds 3 percentage points to its cost of capital when evaluating high-risk projects. Now which system should be chosen?

Computer-Related Problem

(Work the problems in this section only if you are using the computer problem diskette.)

Sensitivity analysis

C11-1   Use the computerized model for Problem C11-1 in the file C11 to solve this problem.
   a. Refer back to Problem 11-6. Agrico's board of directors would like to know how sensitive the analysis is to the cost of capital. Assume that the tractor's life is 5 years, and analyze the effects of a change in the cost of capital to 8 percent or to 12 percent. Is the project very sensitive to changes in the cost of capital?
   b. The board also would like to determine the sensitivity of the project to changes in the increase in pretax operating revenues. The directors believe that the increase will be no less than $7,000 per year and no more than $13,000 per year. Analyze the project at these levels of operating revenue, assuming a 5-year project life and a 10 percent cost of capital.

Solutions to Self-Test Problems

ST-1   Refer to the marginal glossary definitions and relevant sections of the text to check your responses.

ST-2   **a.** First, find the expected cash flows:

Year	Expected Cash Flow			
0	0.2(− $100,000) + 0.6(− $100,000) + 0.2(− $100,000)	=	($100,000)
1	0.2($20,000)	+ 0.6($30,000)	+ 0.2($40,000)	=	$30,000
2					$30,000
3					$30,000
4					$30,000
5					$30,000
5*	0.2($0)	+ 0.6($20,000)	+ 0.2($30,000)	=	$18,000

Next, determine the NPV based on the expected cash flows:

$$NPV = -\$100,000 + \frac{\$30,000}{(1.10)^1} + \frac{\$30,000}{(1.10)^2} + \frac{\$30,000}{(1.10)^3}$$

$$+ \frac{\$30,000}{(1.10)^4} + \frac{\$30,000 + \$18,000}{(1.10)^5} = \$24,900.$$

b. For the worst case, the cash flow values from the cash flow column farthest on the left are used to calculate NPV:

$$NPV = -\$100,000 + \frac{\$20,000}{(1.10)^1} + \frac{\$20,000}{(1.10)^2} + \frac{\$20,000}{(1.10)^3}$$

$$+ \frac{\$20,000}{(1.10)^4} + \frac{\$20,000 + \$0}{(1.10)^5} = -\$24,184.$$

Similarly, for the best case, use the values from the column farthest on the right. Here the NPV is $70,259.

If the cash flows are perfectly dependent, then the low cash flow in the first year will mean a low cash flow in every year. Thus, the probability of the worst case occurring is the probability of getting the $20,000 net cash flow in Year 1, or 20 percent. If the cash flows are independent, the cash flow in each year can be low, high, or average, and the probability of getting all low cash flows will be

$$0.2(0.2)(0.2)(0.2)(0.2) = 0.2^5 = 0.00032 = 0.032\%.$$

c. The base case NPV is found using the most likely cash flows and is equal to $26,142. This value differs from the expected NPV of $24,900 because the Year 5 cash flows are not symmetric. Under these conditions, the NPV distribution is as follows:

P	NPV
0.2	($24,184)
0.6	26,142
0.2	70,259

Thus, the expected NPV is $0.2(-\$24,184) + 0.6(\$26,142) + 0.2(\$70,259) = \$24,900$. As is generally the case, the expected NPV is the same as the NPV of the expected cash flows found in Part a. The standard deviation is $29,904:

$$\sigma^2_{NPV} = 0.2(-\$24,184 - \$24,900)^2 + 0.6(\$26,142 - \$24,900)^2$$

$$+ 0.2(\$70,259 - \$24,900)^2$$

$$= \$894,261,126.$$

$$\sigma_{NPV} = \sqrt{\$894,261,126} = \$29,904.$$

The coefficient of variation, CV, is $29,904/$24,900 = 1.20.

d. Since the project's coefficient of variation is 1.20, the project is riskier than average, and hence the project's risk-adjusted cost of capital is $10\% + 2\% = 12\%$. The project now should be evaluated by finding the NPV of the expected cash flows, as in Part a, but using a 12 percent discount rate. The risk-adjusted NPV is $18,357, and therefore the project should be accepted.

IV Strategic Long-Term Financing Decisions

12 Common Stock and the Investment Banking Process

COMPAQ COMPUTERS: HIGH GROWTH CAUSES NEED FOR NEW CAPITAL

Compaq Computer Corporation was organized in 1982 to produce IBM-compatible portable computers. Compaq's founders had the right product at the right time, and in 1983 the Company's sales hit $100 million; this was the fastest any start-up company ever reached that level. Compaq went on to set another record in 1987, sales of more than $1 billion in only 5 years, and it expects to break the $2 billion barrier in 1989.

Compaq started out with a good supply of capital provided by several venture capitalists, but because of its phenomenal growth and the need to build plant and to purchase inventories, it soon ran short of money. Therefore, it "went public" in December 1983, selling 6.5 million shares at $11 each to raise a total of $71.5 million. The two lead underwriters were L. F. Rothschild, Unterberg, Towbin, an investment banking house with expertise in taking small high-tech companies public, and E. F. Hutton, a large brokerage house with a broad retail customer base.

The timing of the offer was absolutely perfect for Compaq; just after the sale, the bottom fell out of the new issue market, and the stock price dropped from $11 to only $3.50 per share. Compaq had its money, though, and it was therefore able to push ahead with its expansion while would-be competitors were left at the starting gate, unable to get the capital needed for their own expansion programs. Even as Compaq's stock price fell, its sales and profits were increasing sharply. Operationally, the Company was doing well.

Compaq was profitable after its first year, but because of its high growth rate, it used up the initial $71.5 million, and by early 1985 the Company had to go back to the market to raise more capital. Because its stock price was down, Compaq decided to sell convertible bonds to raise $75 million. The convertibles carried an interest rate of only 5¼ percent, which was far below the 12 percent rate that nonconvertible bonds would have carried. Investors were willing to buy the convertibles, despite the low interest rate, because they were hopeful that Compaq's stock price would soar, making it possible for them to convert the bonds into stock and earn sizable capital gains. That strategy has worked out well thus far; Compaq's stock rose from $3.50 in 1984 to $78.50 in 1987, before the October 19 crash, and it sells for about $55 as this is written in the fall of 1988.

Compaq's success resulted in part from its good management, but its access to the capital markets was equally important. If the Company had not been able to obtain the two capital infusions, it could not have taken off, and if it had not grown so rapidly, it could not have captured the lion's share of the portable PC market. Compaq's success provides a good example of why the topics covered in this chapter, common stock and the investment banking process, are so important.

IN Part III we examined the analysis firms employ when making capital budgeting decisions. Any decision to acquire new assets necessitates the raising of new capital, and, generally, long-term assets are financed with long-term capital. In this chapter, we consider in some detail decisions regarding common stock financings. As a part of this analysis, we also examine in detail the procedures used by firms to raise new long-term capital, or the investment banking process.

BALANCE SHEET ACCOUNTS AND DEFINITIONS

common equity
The sum of the firm's common stock, paid-in capital, and retained earnings, which equals the common stockholders' total investment in the firm.

An understanding of legal and accounting terminology is vital to both investors and financial managers if they are to avoid misinterpretations and possibly costly mistakes. Therefore, we begin our analysis of common stock with a discussion of accounting and legal issues. Consider first Table 12-1, which shows the **common equity** section of National Paper Company's balance sheet. National Paper's owners, its stockholders, have authorized management to issue a total of 60 million shares, and management has thus far actually issued (or

Table 12-1   National Paper Company:
Stockholders' Equity Accounts as of December 31, 1988

Common stock (60 million shares authorized, 50 million shares outstanding, $1 par)	$ 50,000,000
Additional paid-in capital	100,000,000
Retained earnings	750,000,000
Total common stockholders' equity (or common net worth)	$900,000,000

$$\text{Book value per share} = \frac{\text{Total common stockholders' equity}}{\text{Shares outstanding}} = \frac{\$900,000,000}{50,000,000} = \$18.$$

par value
The nominal or face value of a stock or bond.

retained earnings
The balance sheet account which indicates the total amount of earnings the firm has not paid out as dividends throughout its history; these earnings have been reinvested in the firm.

additional paid-in capital
Funds received in excess of par value when a firm sells new stock.

book value per share
The accounting value of a share of common stock; equal to the common equity (common stock plus paid-in capital plus retained earnings) of the firm divided by the number of shares outstanding.

sold) 50 million shares. Each share has a **par value** of $1; this is the minimum amount for which new shares can be issued.[1]

National Paper is an old company — it was established back in 1873. Its initial equity capital consisted of 5,000 shares sold at the $1 par value, so on its first balance sheet the total stockholders' equity was $5,000. The initial paid-in capital and retained earnings accounts showed zero balances. Over the years National Paper retained some of its earnings, and the firm issued new stock to raise capital from time to time. During 1988 National Paper earned $120 million, paid $100 million in dividends, and retained $20 million. The $20 million was added to the $730 million accumulated **retained earnings** shown on the year-end 1987 balance sheet to produce the $750 million retained earnings at year-end 1988. Thus, since its inception in 1873, National Paper has retained, or plowed back, a total of $750 million. This is money that belongs to the stockholders and that they could have received in the form of dividends. Instead, the stockholders chose to let management reinvest the $750 million in the business.

Now consider the $100 million **additional paid-in capital**. This account shows the difference between the stock's par value and what new stockholders paid when they bought newly issued shares. As has been noted, National Paper was formed in 1873 with 5,000 shares issued at the $1 par value; thus, the first balance sheet showed a zero balance for additional paid-in capital. By 1888 the company had demonstrated its profitability, and it was earning 50 cents per share. Further, it had built up the retained earnings account to a total of $10,000, so the total stockholders' equity was $5,000 of par value plus $10,000 of retained earnings = $15,000, and the **book value per share** was $15,000/ 5,000 shares = $3. National Paper had also borrowed heavily, and in spite of its retained earnings, the company's debt ratio had risen to an unacceptable level, precluding further use of debt without an infusion of equity.

---

[1]A stock's par value is an arbitrary figure that originally indicated the minimum amount of money stockholders had put up. Today, firms are not required to establish a par value for their stock. Thus, National Paper could have elected to use "no par" stock, in which case the common stock and additional paid-in capital accounts would have been consolidated under one account called *common stock,* which would show a 1988 balance of $150 million.

Table 12-2   Effects of Stock Sale on National Paper's Equity Accounts

---

Before Sale of Stock

Common stock (5,000 shares outstanding, $1 par)	$ 5,000
Additional paid-in capital	0
Retained earnings	10,000
Total stockholders' equity	$15,000
Book value per share = $15,000/5,000 =	$ 3.00

After Sale of Stock

Common stock (7,000 shares outstanding, $1 par)	$ 7,000
Additional paid-in capital ($4 − $1) × 2,000 shares	6,000
Retained earnings	10,000
Total stockholders' equity	$23,000
Book value per share = $23,000/7,000 =	$ 3.29

The company had profitable investment opportunities, so to take advantage of them, management decided to issue another 2,000 shares of stock. The market price at the time was $4 per share, which was eight times the 50 cents earnings per share (the price/earnings ratio was 8×). This $4 market value per share was well in excess of the $1 par value and also higher than the $3 book value per share, demonstrating that par value, book value, and market value are not necessarily equal. Had the company lost money since its inception, it would have had negative retained earnings, the book value would have been below par, and the market price may well have been below book. After the 2,000 new shares had been sold to investors back in 1888 at the market price of $4 per share, National Paper's partial balance sheet changed as shown in Table 12-2. Each share brought in $4, of which $1 represented the par value and $3 represented the excess of the sale price above par. Since 2,000 shares were involved, a total of $2,000 was added to common stock, whereas $6,000 was entered in additional paid-in capital. Also, book value per share rose from $3 to $3.29; whenever stock is sold at a price above book, the book value increases, and vice versa if stock is sold below book value.[2]

Similar transactions have taken place through the years to produce the current situation, as shown on National Paper's latest balance sheet in Table 12-1.[3]

---

[2]The effects of stock sales on book value are not important for industrial firms, but they are *very* important for utility companies, whose allowable earnings per share are in effect determined by regulators as a percentage of book value. Thus, if a utility's stock is selling below book value and the company sells stock to raise new equity, this will dilute the book value per share of its existing stockholders and drive down their allowable earnings per share, which in turn will drive down the market price. Most U.S. electric utilities' stocks sold below book value during the late 1970s and early 1980s. The firms needed to raise large amounts of capital, including equity, because they had to keep their capital structures in balance. This meant selling stock at prices below book, which tended to depress the market value of the stock still further.

[3]Stock dividends, stock splits, and stock repurchases (the reverse of stock issues) also affect the capital accounts. However, we shall defer a discussion of these topics until Chapter 18.

LEGAL RIGHTS AND PRIVILEGES OF COMMON STOCKHOLDERS

The common stockholders are the *owners* of a corporation, and as such they have certain rights and privileges. The most important of these rights are discussed in this section.

Control of the Firm

The stockholders have the right to elect the firm's directors, who in turn elect the officers who will manage the business. In a small firm, the major stockholder typically assumes the positions of president and chairperson of the board of directors. In a large, publicly owned firm, the managers typically have some stock, but their personal holdings are insufficient to exercise voting control. Thus, the managements of most publicly owned firms can be removed by the stockholders if they decide a management team is not effective.

Various state and federal laws stipulate how stockholder control is to be exercised. First, corporations must hold an election of directors periodically, usually once a year, with the vote taken at the annual meeting. Frequently, one-third of the directors are elected each year for a three-year term. Each share of stock has one vote; thus, the owner of 1,000 shares has 1,000 votes. Stockholders can appear at the annual meeting and vote in person, but typically they transfer their right to vote to a second party by means of an instrument known as a **proxy**. Management always solicits stockholders' proxies and usually gets them. However, if earnings are poor and stockholders are dissatisfied, an outside group may solicit the proxies in an effort to overthrow management and take control of the business. This is known as a **proxy fight**.

The question of control has become a central issue in finance in recent years. The frequency of proxy fights has increased, as have attempts by one corporation to take over another by purchasing a majority of the outstanding stock. This latter action, which is called a **takeover**, is discussed in detail in Chapter 15. Some well-known examples of recent takeover battles include Du Pont's acquisition of Conoco, Chevron's acquisition of Gulf Oil, and CBS's successful defense against a takeover attempt by Ted Turner. (Subsequently, though, CBS's management lost control to another group headed by Larry Tisch.)

Managers who do not have majority control (more than 50 percent of their firms' stock) are very much concerned about proxy fights and takeovers, and many of them are attempting to get stockholder approval for changes in their corporate charters that would make takeovers more difficult. For example, a number of companies tried in 1988 to get their stockholders to agree (1) to elect only one-third of the directors each year (rather than electing all directors each year), (2) to require 75 percent of the stockholders (rather than 50 percent) to approve a merger, and (3) to vote in a "poison pill" provision which would allow the stockholders of a firm that is taken over by another firm to buy shares in the second firm at a reduced price; this provision makes

proxy
A document giving one person the authority to act for another, typically the power to vote shares of common stock.

proxy fight
An attempt by a person or group of people to gain control of a firm by getting the stockholders to grant that person or group the authority to vote their shares in order to vote a new management into office.

takeover
An action whereby a person or group succeeds in ousting a firm's management and taking control of the company.

the acquisition unattractive and, thus, wards off hostile takeover attempts. Managements seeking such changes generally cite a fear that the firm will be picked up at a bargain price, but it often appears that managers' concern about their own positions might be an even more important consideration.

The Preemptive Right

preemptive right
A provision in the corporate charter or bylaws that gives common stockholders the right to purchase on a pro rata basis new issues of common stock (or convertible securities).

Common stockholders often have the right, called the **preemptive right**, to purchase any additional shares sold by the firm. In some states the preemptive right is automatically included in every corporate charter; in others it is necessary to specifically insert it into the charter.

The purpose of the preemptive right is twofold. First, it protects the power of control of current stockholders. If it were not for this safeguard, the management of a corporation under criticism from stockholders could prevent stockholders from removing it from office by issuing a large number of additional shares and purchasing these shares itself. Management could thereby secure control of the corporation and frustrate the will of the current stockholders.

The second, and by far the most important, reason for the preemptive right is that it protects stockholders against a dilution of value. For example, suppose 1,000 shares of common stock, each with a price of $100, were outstanding, making the total market value of the firm $100,000. If an additional 1,000 shares were sold at $50 a share, or for $50,000, this would raise the total market value of the firm to $150,000. When the total market value is divided by the new total shares outstanding, a value of $75 a share is obtained. The old stockholders thus lose $25 per share, and the new stockholders have an instant profit of $25 per share. Thus, selling common stock at a price below the market value would dilute its price and would transfer wealth from the present stockholders to those who purchase the new shares. The preemptive right prevents such occurrences.[4]

TYPES OF COMMON STOCK

classified stock
Common stock that is given special designations, such as Class A, Class B, and so forth, to meet special needs of the company.

Although most firms have only one type of common stock, in some instances **classified stock** is used to meet the special needs of the company. Generally, when special classifications of stock are used, one type is designated *Class A,* another *Class B,* and so on. Small, new companies seeking to obtain funds from outside sources frequently use different types of common stock. For example, when Genetic Concepts, Inc., went public in 1987, its Class A stock was sold to the public and paid a dividend, but it had no voting rights for five

---

[4]For a discussion of the procedures for issuing stock to existing stockholders, called a "rights offering," see Eugene F. Brigham and Louis C. Gapenski, *Intermediate Financial Management,* 2nd ed., Chapter 12.

years. Its Class B stock was retained by the organizers of the company; it had full voting rights for five years, but the legal terms stated that dividends could not be paid on the Class B stock until the company had established its earning power by building up retained earnings to a designated level. Because of the use of classified stock, the public was able to take a position in a conservatively financed growth company without sacrificing income, while the founders retained absolute control during the crucial early stages of the firm's development. At the same time, outside investors were protected against excessive withdrawals of funds by the original owners. As is often the case in such situations, the Class B stock was also called **founders' shares**.

founders' shares
Stock owned by the firm's founders that has sole voting rights but has restricted dividends for a specified number of years.

Note that "Class A," "Class B," and so on, have no standard meanings. Most firms have no classified shares, but a firm that does could designate its Class B shares as founders' shares and its Class A shares as those sold to the public, whereas another could reverse these designations. Still other firms could use the A and B designations for entirely different purposes.

General Motors recently introduced yet another type of common stock. When GM acquired Hughes Aircraft for $5 billion in 1985, it paid in part with a new Class H common, GMH, which had limited voting rights and whose dividends were tied in part to the performance of Hughes as it operated as a GM subsidiary. The reasons for the new stock were reported to be these: (1) GM wanted to limit voting privileges on the new stock because of management's concern about a possible takeover and (2) Hughes employees and stockholders wanted to participate more directly in Hughes' own performance than would have been possible through regular GM stock.

GM's deal posed a problem for the NYSE, which had a rule against listing any company's common stock if the company had any nonvoting common stock outstanding. GM made it clear that it was willing to delist if the Exchange did not change its rules. The NYSE concluded that arrangements like the one GM had made were logical and were likely to be made by other companies in the future, so it changed its rules to accommodate GM.

EVALUATION OF COMMON STOCK AS A SOURCE OF FUNDS

Thus far this chapter has covered the main characteristics of common stock. Now we will appraise stock financing both from the viewpoint of the corporation and from a social perspective.

From the Corporation's Viewpoint

Advantages. There are several advantages to the corporation associated with common stock financing:

1. Common stock does not obligate the firm to make fixed payments to stockholders. If the company generates earnings and has no pressing internal needs for them, it can pay common stock dividends. Had it used

debt, it would have incurred a legal obligation to pay interest, regardless of its operating conditions and cash flows.

2. Common stock carries no fixed maturity date — it never has to be "repaid" as would a debt issue.

3. Since common stock provides a cushion against losses from the creditors' viewpoint, the sale of common stock increases the creditworthiness of the firm. This, in turn, raises its bond rating, lowers its cost of debt, and increases its future ability to use debt.

4. If a company's prospects look bright, then common stock can often be sold on better terms than debt. Stock appeals to certain groups of investors because (a) it typically carries a higher expected total return (dividends plus capital gains) than does preferred stock or debt and (b) since stock represents the ownership of the firm, it provides the investor with a better hedge against unanticipated inflation than does preferred stock or bonds. Ordinarily, common stock increases in value, and dividends also rise, during inflationary periods.[5]

5. When a company is having operating problems, it often needs new funds to overcome its problems. However, investors are reluctant to supply capital to a troubled company, and if they do, they generally require some type of security. From a practical standpoint, this means that a firm which is experiencing problems can often obtain new capital only by issuing debt, which is safer from the investor's standpoint. Because corporate treasurers are well aware of this, they often opt to finance with common stock during good times in order to maintain a **reserve borrowing capacity**. Indeed, surveys have indicated that maintenance of an adequate reserve of borrowing capacity is the primary consideration in most financing decisions.

reserve borrowing capacity
Unused debt capacity that permits borrowing if a firm needs capital in troubled times.

Disadvantages. Disadvantages associated with issuing common stock include the following:

1. The sale of common stock extends voting rights, and perhaps even control, to new stockholders. For this reason, additional equity financing is often avoided by managers who are concerned about maintaining control. The use of founders' shares and shares such as those GM issued can mitigate this problem, however.

2. Common stock gives new owners the right to share in the income of the firm; if profits soar, the new stockholders get to share in this bonanza, whereas if debt had been used, new investors would have received only a fixed return, no matter how profitable the company had been.[6]

---

[5]For common stock in general, the rate of increase in dividends has exceeded the rate of inflation on average over time.

[6]This point has given rise to this interesting new theory: "If a firm sells a large issue of bonds, this is a *signal* that management expects the company to earn high profits on investments financed by the new capital, and that it does not wish to share these profits with new stockholders. On the other hand, if the firm issues stock, this is a signal that its prospects are not so bright." This issue will be discussed further in Chapters 17 and 18.

3. As we shall see, the costs of underwriting and distributing common stock are usually higher than those for underwriting and distributing preferred stock or debt. Flotation costs associated with the sale of common stock are characteristically higher because: (a) the costs of investigating an equity security investment are higher than those for a comparable debt security; and (b) stocks are riskier than debt, meaning that investors must diversify their equity holdings, which in turn means that a given dollar amount of new stock must be sold to a larger number of purchasers than the same amount of debt.

4. As we will see in Chapter 17, if the firm has more equity than is called for in its optimal capital structure, the average cost of capital will be higher than necessary. Therefore, a firm would not want to sell stock to the point where its equity ratio exceeded the optimal level.

5. Under current tax laws, common stock dividends are not deductible as an expense for calculating the corporation's taxable income, but bond interest is deductible. As we will see in Chapter 16, the impact of this factor is reflected in the relative cost of equity as compared with debt.

From a Social Viewpoint

From a social viewpoint, common stock is a desirable form of financing because it renders business firms less vulnerable to the consequences of declines in sales and earnings. Common stock financing involves no fixed charge payments which might force a faltering firm into reorganization or bankruptcy. From the standpoint of the economy as a whole, if too many firms used too much debt, business fluctuations would be amplified, and minor recessions could turn into major ones. During 1988, when many mergers and management buyouts financed largely with debt were occurring and were raising the aggregate debt ratio (the average debt ratio of all firms), the Federal Reserve and other authorities voiced concern over the situation, and congressional leaders debated the wisdom of social controls over corporations' use of debt. Like most important issues, this one is debatable, and the debate centers around who can better determine "appropriate" capital structures — corporate managers or government officials.[7]

THE MARKET FOR COMMON STOCK

Some companies are so small that their common stocks are not actively traded; they are owned by only a few people, usually the companies' managers. Such firms are said to be *privately owned,* or **closely held, corporations,** and their stock is called *closely held stock.* In contrast, the stocks of most larger compa-

closely held corporation
A corporation that is owned by a few individuals who are typically associated with the firm's management.

---

[7]When business executives hear someone say, "I'm from Washington and I'm here to help you," they generally cringe, and often with good reason. On the other hand, a stable national economy requires sound businesses, and too much debt can lead to corporate instability.

publicly owned corporation
A corporation that is owned by a relatively large number of individuals who are not actively involved in its management.

over-the-counter (OTC) market
An electronically connected network of dealers that provides for trading in unlisted securities.

organized security exchange
A formal organization, having a tangible physical location, that facilitates trading in designated ("listed") securities. The two major U.S. security exchanges are the New York Stock Exchange (NYSE) and the American Stock Exchange (AMEX).

secondary market
The market in which securities are traded after they have been issued by corporations.

primary market
The market in which firms issue new securities to raise corporate capital.

nies are owned by a large number of investors, most of whom are not active in management. Such companies are said to be **publicly owned corporations**, and their stock is called *publicly held stock.*

As we saw in Chapter 3, the stocks of smaller publicly owned firms are not listed on an exchange; they trade in the **over-the-counter (OTC) market**, and the companies and their stocks are said to be *unlisted.* However, larger publicly owned companies generally apply for listing on an **organized security exchange**, and they and their stocks are said to be *listed.* As a general rule, companies are first listed on a regional exchange, such as the Pacific Coast or Midwest Exchange, then they move up to the American Stock Exchange (AMEX), and, finally, if they grow large enough, they are listed on the "Big Board," the New York Stock Exchange (NYSE). About 7,000 stocks are traded in the OTC market, but in terms of market value of both outstanding shares and daily transactions, the NYSE is most important, having about 60 percent of the business.

Institutional investors such as pension trusts, insurance companies, and mutual funds own about 35 percent of all common stocks. These institutions buy and sell relatively actively, however, so they account for about 75 percent of all transactions. Thus, the institutional investors have a heavy influence on the prices of individual stocks. In a real sense, they determine the prices of individual stocks and hence set the tone of the market.

Types of Stock Market Transactions

We can classify stock market transactions into three distinct categories:

1. *Trading in the outstanding shares of established, publicly owned companies: the secondary market.* National Paper Company has 50 million shares of stock outstanding. If the owner of 100 shares sells his or her stock, the trade is said to have occurred in the **secondary market**. Thus, the market for outstanding shares, or *used shares,* is the secondary market. The company receives no new money when sales occur in this market.

2. *Additional shares sold by established, publicly owned companies: the primary market.* If National Paper decides to sell (or issue) an additional 1 million shares to raise new equity capital, this transaction is said to occur in the **primary market.**[8]

3. *New public offerings by privately held firms: the primary market.* In 1975 the Coors Brewing Company, which was owned by the Coors family at the time, decided to sell some stock to raise capital needed for a major

---

[8]Recall that National Paper has 60 million shares authorized but only 50 million outstanding; thus, it has 10 million authorized but unissued shares. If it had no authorized but unissued shares, management could increase the authorized shares by obtaining stockholders' approval, which would generally be granted without any arguments.

going public
The act of selling stock to the public at large by a closely held corporation or its principal stockholders.

new issue market
The market consisting of stocks of companies that have just gone public.

expansion program.[9] This type of transaction is called **"going public"** — whenever stock in a closely held corporation is offered to the public for the first time, the company is said to be going public. The market for stock that has recently gone public is often called the **new issue market**.

Firms can go public without raising any additional capital. For example, the Ford Motor Company was once owned exclusively by the Ford family. When Henry Ford died, he left a substantial part of his stock to the Ford Foundation. When the Foundation later sold some of this stock to the general public, the Ford Motor Company went public, even though the company raised no capital in the transaction.

The Decision to Go Public

As noted in Chapter 2, most businesses begin life as proprietorships or partnerships, and the more successful ones, as they grow, find it desirable at some point to convert into corporations. Initially these new corporations' stocks are owned by the firms' officers, key employees, and a few investors who are not actively involved in management. If growth continues, however, the companies may decide at some point to go public. The advantages and disadvantages of public ownership are discussed next.

Advantages of Going Public

1. *Facilitates stockholder diversification.* As a company grows and becomes more valuable, its founders often have most of their wealth tied up in the company. By selling some of their stock in a public offering, the founders can diversify their holdings and thereby reduce somewhat the riskiness of their personal portfolios.

2. *Increases liquidity.* The stock of a closely held firm is illiquid: no ready market exists for it. If one of the holders wants to sell some shares to raise cash, it is hard to find potential buyers, and even if a buyer is located, there is no established price at which to complete the transaction. These problems do not exist with publicly held firms.

3. *Makes it easier to raise new corporate cash.* If a privately held company wants to raise cash by a sale of new stock, it must either go to its existing owners, who may neither have any money nor want to put any more eggs into this particular basket, or it must shop around for wealthy investors who are willing to make an investment in the company. However, it is usually difficult to get outsiders to put money into a

---

[9]The stock Coors offered to the public was designated Class B, and it was nonvoting. The Coors family retained the founders' shares, called Class A stock, which carried full voting privileges. The company was large enough to obtain a NYSE listing, but at that time the Exchange had a requirement that listed common stock have full voting rights, which precluded Coors from obtaining a NYSE listing. Now that GM has forced the Exchange to change its rules, Coors could presumably list its stock.

closely held company, because if they do not have voting control (over 50 percent) of the stock, then the inside stockholders-managers can run roughshod over them. The insiders can pay or not pay dividends, pay themselves exorbitant salaries, have private deals with the company, and so on. For example, the president might buy a warehouse and lease it to the company at a high rental, get the use of a Rolls Royce, and enjoy all-the-frills travel to conventions. The insiders can even keep the outsiders from knowing the company's actual earnings or its real worth. There are not many positions more vulnerable than that of an outside stockholder in a closely held company, and for this reason it is hard for closely held companies to raise new equity capital. Going public, which brings with it disclosure and regulation by the Securities and Exchange Commission (SEC), greatly reduces these problems and thus makes people more willing to invest in the company.

4. *Establishes a value for the firm.* For a number of reasons, it is often useful to establish a firm's value in the marketplace. For one thing, when the owner of a privately owned business dies, state and federal inheritance tax appraisers must set a value on the company for estate tax purposes. Often, these appraisers set too high a value, which creates all sorts of problems. A company that is publicly owned, however, has its value established, with little room for argument. Similarly, if a company wants to give incentive stock options to key employees, it is useful to know the exact value of these options; employees much prefer to own stock, or options on stock, that is publicly traded, because public trading increases liquidity.

Disadvantages of Going Public

1. *Cost of reporting.* A publicly owned company must file quarterly and annual reports with the SEC, with various state officials, or with both. These reports can be costly, especially for very small firms.

2. *Disclosure.* Management may not like the idea of reporting operating data, because such data will then be available to competitors. Similarly, the owners of the company may not want people to know their net worth. Because publicly owned companies must disclose the number of shares owned by officers, directors, and major stockholders, it is easy enough for anyone to multiply shares held by price per share to estimate the net worth of an insider.

3. *Self-dealings.* The owners-managers of closely held companies have many opportunities for various types of questionable but legal self-dealings, including the payment of high salaries, nepotism, personal transactions with the business (such as leasing arrangements), excellent retirement programs, and not-truly-necessary fringe benefits. Such self-dealings are much harder to arrange if a company is publicly owned — they must be disclosed, and the managers are also subject to stockholder suits.

4. *Inactive market/low price.* If a firm is very small, and if its shares are not traded with much frequency, then its stock will not really be liquid, and the market price may not be representative of the stock's true value. Security analysts and stockbrokers simply will not follow the stock, because there will not be sufficient trading activity to generate enough sales commissions to cover the analysts' or brokers' costs of keeping up with it.

5. *Control.* Because of the dramatic increase in tender offers and proxy fights in the 1980s, the managers of publicly owned firms who do not have at least 50 percent of the stock must be concerned about maintaining control. Further, there is pressure on such managers to produce annual earnings gains, even when it would be in the shareholders' best long-term interests to adopt a strategy that might penalize short-run earnings but lead to higher earnings in future years. These factors have led a number of public companies to "go private" in leveraged buyout (LBO) deals in which the managers borrow the money to buy out the nonmanagement stockholders. Currently, RJR Nabisco is planning a $20 billion LBO, the largest on record.

Conclusions on Going Public

It should be obvious from this discussion that there are no hard and fast rules about whether a company should go public or when it should do so. This is an individual decision that should be made on the basis of the company's and its stockholders' own unique circumstances.

If a company does decide to go public, either by the sale of newly issued stock to raise new capital for the corporation or by the sale of stock by the current owners, setting the price at which shares will be offered to the public is a key issue. The company and its current owners want to set the price as high as possible — the higher the offering price, the smaller the fraction of the company the current owners will have to give up to obtain any specified amount of money. On the other hand, potential buyers will want to buy the stock at as low a price as possible. We will return to the establishment of the offering price later in the chapter, after we have described some other aspects of common stock financing.

The Decision to List the Stock

The decision to go public, as discussed previously, is a truly significant milestone in a company's life; it marks a major transition in the relationship between the firm and its owners. The decision to *list,* on the other hand, is not a major event. The company will have to file a few new reports with an exchange, it will have to abide by the rules of the exchange, and the stock's price will be quoted in the newspaper under a stock exchange rather than in the over-the-counter section. These are not very important differences.

In order to have its stock listed, a company must apply to an exchange, pay a relatively small fee, and meet the exchange's minimum requirements.

These requirements relate to the size of the company's net income as well as to the number of shares outstanding and in the hands of outsiders (as opposed to the number held by insiders, who generally do not trade their stock very actively). The company also must agree to disclose certain information to the exchange; this information is designed to help the exchange track trading patterns and thus try to prevent manipulation of the stock's price.[10] The size qualifications increase as one moves from the regional exchanges to the AMEX and on to the NYSE.

Assuming that a company qualifies, many people believe that listing is beneficial both to it and to its stockholders. Listed companies receive a certain amount of free advertising and publicity, and their status as a listed company enhances their prestige and reputation. This may have a beneficial effect on the sales of the firm's products, and it is probably advantageous in terms of lowering the required rate of return on its common stock. Investors respond favorably to increased information, increased liquidity, and confidence that the quoted price is not being manipulated. By providing investors with these benefits in the form of listing their companies' stock, financial managers may lower their firms' costs of capital and increase the value of their stocks.

Regulation of Securities Markets

Securities and Exchange Commission (SEC)
The U.S. government agency that regulates the issuance and trading of stocks and bonds.

registration statement
A statement of facts filed with the SEC about a company planning to issue securities.

prospectus
A document describing a new security issue and the issuing company.

Sales of new securities, as well as operations in the secondary markets, are regulated by the **Securities and Exchange Commission (SEC)** and, to a lesser extent, by each of the 50 states. The following are the primary elements of SEC regulation.

1. The SEC has jurisdiction over all interstate offerings of new securities to the public in amounts of $1.5 million or more.

2. Newly issued securities must be registered with the SEC at least 20 days before they are publicly offered. The **registration statement** provides financial, legal, and technical information about the company. A **prospectus** summarizes this information for use in selling the securities. SEC lawyers and accountants analyze both the registration statement and the prospectus; if the information is inadequate or misleading, the SEC will delay or stop the public offering.

3. After the registration has become effective, new securities may be offered, but any sales solicitation must be accompanied by the

---

[10]It is illegal for anyone to attempt to manipulate the price of a stock. Prior to the creation of the SEC in the 1930s, syndicates would buy and sell stock back and forth at rigged prices for the purpose of deceiving the public into thinking that a particular stock was worth more or less than its true value. The exchanges, with the encouragement and support of the SEC, utilize sophisticated computer programs to help spot any irregularities that suggest manipulation. They can identify the exact day and time of each trade and the broker who executed it, and they can require the broker to disclose the name of the person for whom the trade was made. Such a system can obviously help identify manipulators. This same system also helps to identify illegal insider trading, as discussed in the next section.

"red herring" prospectus
A preliminary prospectus distributed to potential buyers of a new security issue prior to approval of the registration statement by the SEC.

prospectus. Preliminary, or **"red herring," prospectuses** may be distributed to potential buyers during the 20-day waiting period, but no sales may be finalized during this time. The red herring prospectus contains all the key information that will appear in the final prospectus except the price.

4. If the registration statement or prospectus contains misrepresentations or omissions of material facts, any purchaser who suffers a loss may sue for damages. Severe penalties may be imposed on the issuer or its officers, directors, accountants, engineers, appraisers, underwriters, and all others who participated in the preparation of the registration statement or prospectus.

5. The SEC also regulates all national securities exchanges, and companies whose securities are listed on an exchange must file annual reports similar to the registration statement with both the SEC and the exchange.

insiders
Officers, directors, major stockholders, or others who may have inside information on a company's operations.

6. The SEC has control over stock trades by corporate **insiders**. Officers, directors, and major stockholders must file monthly reports of changes in their holdings of the stock of the corporation. Any short-term profits from such transactions are payable to the corporation.

7. The SEC has the power to prohibit manipulation by such devices as pools (aggregations of funds used to affect prices artificially) or wash sales (sales between members of the same group to record artificial transaction prices).

8. The SEC has control over the form of the proxy and the way the company uses it to solicit votes.

Control over the flow of credit into securities transactions is exercised by the Board of Governors of the Federal Reserve System. The Fed exercises this control through **margin requirements**, which stipulate the maximum percentage of the purchase price of a security that can be borrowed. If a great deal of margin borrowing has been going on, a decline in stock prices can result in inadequate coverages; this forces stock brokers to issue **margin calls**, which in turn require investors either to put up more money or to have their margined stock sold to pay off their loans. Such forced sales further depress the stock market and can set off a downward spiral. The margin requirement has been 50 percent since 1974.

margin requirements
Rules that determine the maximum percentage of debt that can be used to purchase a security.

margin call
Call from a broker asking for more money to support a stock purchase loan.

States also have some control over the issuance of new securities within their boundaries. This control is usually exercised by a "corporation commissioner" or someone with a similar title. State laws relating to securities sales are called **blue sky laws**, because they were put into effect to keep unscrupulous promoters from selling securities that offered the "blue sky" but which actually had little or no asset backing.

blue sky laws
State laws that prevent the sale of securities having little or no asset backing.

The securities industry itself realizes the importance of stable markets, sound brokerage firms, and the absence of stock manipulation. Therefore, the various exchanges work closely with the SEC to police transactions on the exchanges and to maintain the integrity and credibility of the system. Similarly, the **National Association of Securities Dealers (NASD)** cooperates with the SEC to police trading in the OTC market. These industry groups also cooperate with regulatory authorities to set net worth and other standards for securities firms, to develop insurance programs to protect the customers of brokerage houses, and the like.

In general, government regulation of securities trading, as well as industry self-regulation, is designed to insure that investors receive information that is as accurate as possible, that no one artificially manipulates the market price of a given stock, and that corporate insiders do not take advantage of their position to profit in their companies' stocks at the expense of other stockholders. Neither the SEC, the state regulators, nor the industry itself can prevent investors from making foolish decisions or from having bad luck, but the regulators can and do help investors obtain the best data possible for making sound investment decisions.

THE INVESTMENT BANKING PROCESS

The role of investment bankers was discussed in general terms in Chapter 3. There we learned (1) that investment banking is quite different from commercial banking, (2) that the major investment banking houses are often divisions of large financial service corporations engaged in a wide range of activities, and (3) that investment bankers help firms issue new securities in the primary markets and also operate as brokers in the secondary markets. Sears, Roebuck is one of the largest financial services corporations; in addition to its insurance and credit card operations, it owns a large brokerage house and a major investment banking house. Similarly, Merrill Lynch has a brokerage department which operates thousands of offices as well as an investment banking department which helps companies issue securities. Of course, Merrill Lynch's and Sears' brokers also sell securities that have been issued through their investment banking departments. In this section we describe how securities are issued and explain the role of investment bankers in this process.

Stage I Decisions

The firm itself makes some preliminary decisions on its own, including the following:

1. *Dollars to be raised.* How much new capital is needed?
2. *Type of securities used.* Should stock, bonds, or a combination be used? Further, if stock is to be issued, should it be offered to existing stockholders or sold directly to the general public? (See Chapters 13 and 14 for a discussion of different types of securities.)

Table 12-3   Ten Largest Investment Bankers, 1987

1. Salomon Brothers
2. First Boston
3. Merrill Lynch
4. Morgan Stanley
5. Goldman Sachs
6. Drexel Burnham Lambert
7. Shearson Lehman
8. Kidder Peabody
9. Prudential-Bache
10. Bear, Sterns

Note: Rankings are based on the dollar volume of underwritings by U.S. firms worldwide managed in 1987.

Source: IDD Information Services, January 2, 1988.

---

3. *Competitive bid versus negotiated deal.* Should the company simply offer a block of its securities for sale to the highest bidder, or should it sit down with an investment banker and negotiate a deal? These two procedures are called *competitive bids* and *negotiated deals.* Only about 100 of the largest firms on the NYSE, whose securities are already well-known to the investment banking community, are in a position to use the competitive bid process. The investment banks would have to do a large amount of investigative work in order to bid on an issue unless they were already quite familiar with the firm, and the costs involved would be too high to make it worthwhile unless the investment bank was sure of getting the deal. Therefore, except for the very largest firms, offerings of stock or bonds are generally made on a negotiated basis.

4. *Selection of an investment banker.* Assuming the issue is to be negotiated, which investment banker should the firm use? Older firms that have "been to market" before will have already established a relationship with an investment banker, although it is easy enough to change bankers if the firm is dissatisfied. However, a firm that is just going public will have to choose an investment bank, and different investment banking houses are better suited for different companies. The older, larger "establishment houses" like Morgan Stanley deal mainly with large companies like AT&T, IBM, and Exxon. Other bankers, such as Drexel Burnham Lambert, handle more speculative issues. There are some houses that specialize in new issues and others that are not well suited to handle new issues because their brokerage clients are relatively conservative. (Because the investment banking firms sell the issues largely to their own regular investment customers, the nature of these customers has a major effect on the house's ability to do a good job for a corporate security issuer.) Table 12-3 lists in ranked order the ten largest investment bankers for 1987.

Stage II Decisions

Stage II decisions, which are made jointly by the firm and its selected investment banker, include the following:

1. *Reevaluating the initial decisions.* The firm and its banker will reevaluate the initial decisions about the size of the issue and the type of securities to use. For example, the firm may have initially decided to raise $50 million by selling common stock, but the investment banker may convince management that it would be better off, in view of current market conditions, to limit the stock issue to $25 million and to raise the other $25 million as debt.

2. *Best efforts or underwritten issues.* The firm and its investment banker must decide whether the banker will work on a best efforts basis or underwrite the issue. In a **best efforts arrangement**, the banker does not guarantee that the securities will be sold or that the company will get the cash it needs. On an **underwritten arrangement**, the company does get a guarantee, so the banker bears significant risks in such an offering. For example, the very day IBM signed an underwritten agreement to sell $1 billion of bonds in 1979, interest rates rose sharply and bond prices fell. IBM's investment bankers lost somewhere between $10 million and $20 million. Had the offering been on a best efforts basis, IBM would have been the loser. This well-known instance of risk-bearing by investment bankers is described in more detail later in the chapter.

3. *Issuance costs.* The investment banker's fee must be negotiated, and the firm also must estimate the other expenses it will incur in connection with the issue — lawyers' fees, accountants' costs, printing and engraving, and so on. Usually, the banker will buy the issue from the company at a discount below the price at which the securities are to be offered to the public, and this spread covers the banker's costs and provides a profit.

Table 12-4 gives an indication of the **flotation costs** associated with public issues of bonds, preferred stock, and common stock. As the table shows, costs as a percentage of the proceeds are higher for stocks than for bonds, and costs are also higher for small issues than for large issues. The relationship between size of issue and flotation costs is primarily due to the existence of fixed costs: certain costs must be incurred regardless of the size of the issue, so the percentage of flotation costs is quite high for small issues.

When relatively small companies go public to raise new capital, the investment bankers frequently take part of their compensation in the form of options to buy stock in the firm. For example, when Data Technologies, Inc., went public with a $10 million issue in 1988 by selling 1 million shares at a price of $10, its investment bankers bought the stock from the company at a price of $9.75, so the direct underwriting fee was only $1,000,000($10.00 − $9.75) = $250,000, or 2.5 percent. However, the bankers also received a 5-year option to buy

best efforts arrangement
Agreement for the sale of securities in which the investment bank handling the transaction gives no guarantee that the securities will be sold.

underwritten arrangement
Agreement for the sale of securities in which the investment bank guarantees the sale of the securities, thus agreeing to bear any risks involved in the transaction.

flotation costs
The costs of issuing new stocks or bonds.

Table 12-4   Costs of Flotation for Underwritten, Nonrights Offerings (Expressed as a Percentage of Gross Proceeds)

Size of Issue (Millions of Dollars)	Bonds			Preferred Stock			Common Stock		
	Underwriting Commission	Other Expenses	Total Costs	Underwriting Commission	Other Expenses	Total Costs	Underwriting Commission	Other Expenses	Total Costs
Under 1.0	10.0%	4.0%	14.0%	—	—	—	13.0%	9.0%	22.0%
1.0–1.9	8.0	3.0	11.0	—	—	—	11.0	5.9	16.9
2.0–4.9	4.0	2.2	6.2	—	—	—	8.6	3.8	12.4
5.0–9.9	2.4	0.8	3.2	1.9%	0.7%	2.6%	6.3	1.9	8.1
10.0–19.9	1.2	0.7	1.9	1.4	0.4	1.8	5.1	0.9	6.0
20.0–49.9	1.0	0.4	1.4	1.4	0.3	1.7	4.1	0.5	4.6
50.0 and over	0.9	0.2	1.1	1.4	0.2	1.6	3.3	0.2	3.5

Notes:

1. Small issues of preferred are rare, so no data on preferred issues below $5 million are given.

2. Flotation costs tend to rise somewhat when interest rates are cyclically high, because when money is in relatively tight supply, the investment bankers will have a hard time placing issues with permanent investors. Thus, the figures shown in the table represent averages, and actual flotation costs vary somewhat over time.

Sources: Securities and Exchange Commission, *Cost of Flotation of Registered Equity Issues* (Washington, D.C.: U.S. Government Printing Office, December 1974); Richard H. Pettway, "A Note on the Flotation Costs of New Equity Capital Issues of Electric Companies," *Public Utilities Fortnightly,* March 18, 1982; Robert Hansen, "Evaluating the Costs of a New Equity Issue," *Midland Corporate Finance Journal,* Spring 1986; and informal surveys of common stock, preferred stock, and bond issues conducted by the author.

200,000 shares at a price of $10, so if the stock goes up to $15, which the bankers expect it to do, they will make a $1 million profit on top of the $250,000 underwriting fee.

4. *Setting the offering price.* If the company is already publicly owned, the **offering price** will be based on the existing market price of the stock or the yield on the bonds. For common stock, the most typical arrangement calls for the investment banker to buy the securities at a prescribed number of points below the closing price on the last day of registration. For example, on November 1, 1988, the stock of National Paper Company had a current price of $28.50, and it had traded between $25 and $30 a share during the previous three months. National Paper and its underwriter agreed that the investment banker would buy 10 million new shares at $1 below the closing price on the last day of registration, which was expected to be in early 1989. The stock actually closed at $25 on the day the SEC released the issue, so the company received $24 a share. The shares were then sold to the public at a price of $25. As is typical, National Paper's agreement had an escape clause that provided for the contract to be voided if the price of the stock had fallen below a predetermined figure. In the illustrative case, this "upset" price was set at $23 a share. Thus, if the closing price of the shares on the last day of registration had been $22.50, National Paper would have had the option of withdrawing from the agreement.

Investment bankers have an easier job if an issue is priced relatively low, but the issuer of the securities naturally wants as high a price as possible. Therefore, an inherent conflict of interest on price exists

offering price
The price at which common stock is sold to the public.

between the investment banker and the issuer. However, if the issuer is financially sophisticated and makes comparisons with similar security issues, the investment banker will be forced to price close to the market.

As we shall discuss in Chapters 16, 17, and 18, the announcement of a new stock offering by a mature firm is generally taken as a negative signal. If the firm's prospects were very good, management would not want to issue new stock and thus share the rosy future with new stockholders. Because the announcement of a new stock offering is generally taken as bad news, the price will probably fall when the announcement is made; therefore, the offering price will probably have to be set at a price well below the preoffering market price. Consider Figure 12-1, in which d_0 is the estimated market demand curve for National Paper's stock and S_0 is the number of shares currently outstanding. Initially, there are 50 million shares outstanding, and the initial equilibrium price of the stock is $28.57. As we saw in Chapter 6, the equilibrium price of a constant-growth stock is found in accordance with this equation:

$$P_0 = \hat{P}_0 = \frac{D_1}{k_s - g}$$

$$= \frac{\$2.00}{0.12 - 0.05}$$

$$= \$28.57.$$

The values shown for D_1, k_s, and g are *estimates made by a marginal stockholder*. Some stockholders doubtlessly regard National Paper as being less risky than others and hence assign it a lower value for k_s. Similarly, some stockholders have a higher estimate of the company's growth rate than others, and so they will use g > 5 percent when calculating the stock's intrinsic value. Thus, there are some investors who think National Paper's stock is worth more than $28.57 and others who think it is worth less, but **marginal investors** think the stock is worth $28.57. Accordingly, this is its current price.

When National Paper announces that it plans to sell another 10 million shares, this is taken as a negative signal, so k_s rises from 12 to 12.5 percent and the expected g declines from 5 to 4.7 percent. Consequently, the demand curve drops from d_0 to d_1, and the price falls. The new equilibrium price, if 50 million shares were outstanding, would be $25.64:

$$P_1 = \frac{\$2.00}{0.125 - 0.047} = \$25.64.$$

However, if National Paper is to sell another 10 million shares of stock, it will have to either attract some investors who would not be willing to own the stock at the $25.64 price or else induce present

marginal investor
A representative investor whose actions reflect the beliefs of those people who are currently trading a stock. It is the marginal investor who determines a stock's price.

**Figure 12-1   Estimated Demand Curves for
National Paper Company's Common Stock**

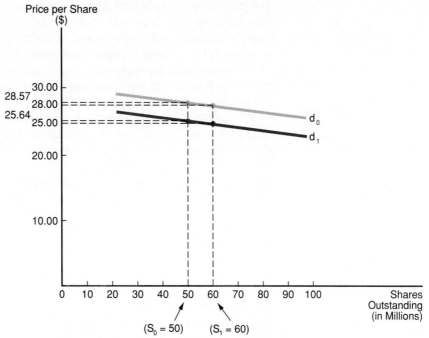

stockholders to buy additional shares. There are two ways this can be
accomplished: (1) by reducing the price of the stock or (2) by
"promoting" the company and thus shifting the demand curve to the
right.[11] If the demand curve does not shift at all from d_1, we see from
Figure 12-1 that the only way the 10 million additional shares can be sold
will be by setting the offering price at $25 per share. However, if the
investment bankers can promote the stock sufficiently to shift the

---

[11]It should be noted that investors can buy newly issued stock without paying normal brokerage
commissions, and brokers are careful to point this out to potential purchasers. Thus, if an
investor were to buy National Paper's stock at $28.57 in the regular market, the commission
would be about 1 percent, or 28 cents per share. If the stock were purchased in an underwriting,
this commission would be avoided.

For years many academicians argued that the demand curve for a firm's stock is either
horizontal or has only a slight downward slope, and that signaling effects are minimal. Most
corporate treasurers, on the other hand, think that both effects exist for mature companies, and
recent empirical studies have confirmed the treasurers' position. One such study is Andrei
Shleifer, "Do Demand Curves for Stocks Slope Down?" *Journal of Finance,* July 1986, 579–590.

demand curve back to d_0, the offering price can be set at $28, which is close to the pre-announcement equilibrium price.[12]

The extent to which the demand curve can be shifted depends primarily on two factors: (1) what investors think the company can do with the money brought in by the stock sale and (2) how effectively the brokers promote the issue. If investors can be convinced that the new money will be invested in highly profitable projects that will substantially raise earnings and the earnings growth rate, then the demand curve may be shifted back to or even to the right of the original curve, d_0, so the stock price might even go above the initial price of $28.57. Even if investors do not radically change their expectations about the company's fundamental factors, the fact that thousands of stockbrokers telephone their clients with suggestions that they consider purchasing National Paper's stock might shift the demand curve. The extent to which this promotional campaign succeeds in shifting the demand curve depends, of course, on the effectiveness of the investment banking firm. Therefore, National Paper's financial manager's perceptions about the effectiveness of different investment bankers will be an important factor in its choice of an underwriter.

One final point should be made: *If pressure from the new shares drives down the price of the stock, all shares outstanding, and not just the new shares, will be affected.* Thus, if National Paper's stock fell from $28.57 to $25 as a result of the financing, and if the price remained at that new level, the company would incur a loss of $3.57 on each of the 50 million shares previously outstanding, or a total market value loss of $178.5 million. In a sense, that loss would be a *flotation cost,* because it would be a cost associated with the new issue. However, if the company's prospects really were poorer than investors thought, then most of the price decline would have occurred sooner or later anyway. On the other hand, if the company's prospects were not really all that bad (if the signal was incorrect), then over time National Paper's demand curve would move back to d_0, or even to the right of d_0, and in that case the company would not suffer a permanent loss anywhere close to $178.5 million.

If the company is going public for the first time, there will be no established price (or demand curve), so the bankers will have to estimate the *equilibrium price* at which the stock will sell after issue. Problem 12-4 at the end of this chapter illustrates in some detail the process involved. If the offering price is set below the true equilibrium price, the stock will rise sharply after issue, and the company and its original stockholders will have given away too much stock to raise the required capital. If the offering price is set above the true equilibrium price, either the issue will fail or, if the bankers succeed in selling the stock, their

---

[12]The supply curve is a vertical line, first at 50 million shares and then, after the new issue, at 60 million.

investment clients will be unhappy when the stock subsequently falls to its equilibrium level. Therefore, it is important that the equilibrium price be approximated as closely as possible.

Selling Procedures

Once the company and its investment bankers have decided how much money to raise, the type of securities to issue, and the basis for pricing the issue, they will prepare and file with the SEC a registration statement and prospectus as described earlier in the chapter. It generally takes about 20 days for the issue to be approved by the SEC. The final price of the stock (or the interest rate on the bond issue) is set at the close of business the day the issue clears the SEC, and the securities are then offered to the public the following day.

Investors are not required to pay for the stock until ten days after they place their buy orders, but the investment bankers must pay the issuing firm within four days of the time the offering officially begins. Typically, the bankers sell the stock within a day or two after the offering begins, but on occasion they miscalculate, set the offering price too high, and are unable to move the issue. Similarly, the market might decline during the offering period, which again would force the bankers to reduce the price of the stock. In either instance, on an underwritten offering the firm receives the price that was agreed upon, and the bankers must absorb any losses that are incurred.

Because they are exposed to large potential losses, investment bankers typically do not handle the purchase and distribution of an issue singlehandedly unless it is a very small one. If the amount of money involved is large and the risk of price fluctuations substantial, investment bankers form an **underwriting syndicate** in an effort to minimize the amount of risk each one carries. The banking house which sets up the deal is called the **lead, or managing, underwriter.**

In addition to the underwriting syndicate, on larger offerings still more investment bankers are included in a **selling group**, which handles the distribution of securities to individual investors. The selling group includes all members of the underwriting syndicate plus additional dealers who take relatively small participations (or shares of the total issue) from the syndicate members. Thus, the underwriters act as *wholesalers,* whereas members of the selling group act as *retailers.* The number of houses in a selling group depends partly on the size of the issue; for example, the one set up when Communications Satellite Corporation (Comsat) went public consisted of 385 members.

Shelf Registrations

The selling procedures described previously, including the 20-day minimum waiting period between registration with the SEC and sale of the issue, apply to most security sales. However, large, well-known public companies which issue securities frequently may file a *master registration statement* with the SEC and then update it with a *short-form statement* just prior to each individual

underwriting syndicate
A syndicate of investment firms formed to spread the risk associated with the purchase and distribution of a new issue of securities.

lead, or managing, underwriter
The member of an underwriting syndicate that actually arranges a new security issue.

selling group
A group that stock brokerage firms formed for the purpose of distributing a new issue of securities.

shelf registration
A procedure under which a large, well-established firm can sell new securities on very short notice.

offering. In such a case, a company that decided at 10 A.M. to sell registered securities could have the sale completed before noon. This procedure is known as **shelf registration**, because in effect the company puts its new securities "on the shelf" and then sells them to investors when it thinks the market is right.

Maintenance of the Secondary Market

In the case of a large, established firm like National Paper, the investment banking firm's job is finished once it has disposed of the stock and turned the net proceeds over to the company. However, in the case of a company going public for the first time, the investment banker is under an obligation to maintain a market for the shares after the issue has been completed. Such stocks are typically traded in the over-the-counter market, and the lead underwriter generally agrees to "make a market" in the stock to keep it reasonably liquid. The company wants a good market to exist for its stock, as do the stockholders. Therefore, if the banking house wants to do business with the company in the future, to keep its own brokerage customers happy, and to have future referral business, it will hold an inventory of the shares and help to maintain an active secondary market in the stock.

IBM'S INITIAL DEBT OFFERING

IBM's first public debt offering provides an interesting case study of investment banking.[13] The offering, at the time the largest in U.S. corporate history, represented a combination of $500 million in 7-year notes and $500 million in 25-year debentures (unsecured long-term debt) for a total of $1 billion. IBM's customary investment banker had been Morgan Stanley & Co. However, for this offering IBM requested separate underwriting proposals from Morgan Stanley and from Salomon Brothers, another major investment banking house; these proposals were presented in September 1979. IBM's financial staff was of the opinion that two managers would provide better execution of the sale and would back it up with a larger amount of capital. John H. Gutfreund, Salomon Brothers' managing partner, is quoted as stating, "A major corporation is best served by two sets of eyes and ears." Robert H. B. Baldwin, president of Morgan Stanley, is said to have responded, "You need only one brain surgeon." Morgan Stanley dropped out, refusing to participate if it could not be sole manager, and Salomon Brothers and Merrill Lynch became co-managers, with an underwriting group totaling 227 members.

---

[13]This summary is based on contemporary accounts in the financial press and in the article by Walter Guzzardi, Jr., "The Bomb IBM Dropped on Wall Street," *Fortune,* November 19, 1979, 52–56.

During the month of September, the prime rate was increased five times, reaching a level of 13.5 percent on September 28. A "pricing meeting" took place on Wednesday, October 3, 1979. At the time, rapidly rising yields were being experienced in the money markets. It was agreed that the prices on IBM's 7-year notes would be based on a yield of 7 basis points above Treasury notes and that prices for the 25-year debentures would be based on a yield of 12 basis points above Treasury bonds.[14] This meant that IBM would have to pay 9.62 percent for the 7-year notes and 9.41 percent for the 25-year debentures. The underwriting spread, or commission, was set at ⅝ of 1 percent, or $6.25, per note and ⅞ of 1 percent, or $8.75, per debenture. Since there were $500,000,000/$1,000 = 500,000 notes and an equal number of debentures, the total underwriting fees were ($6.25)(500,000) + ($8.75)(500,000) = $7,500,000.

Only hours after the meeting in which the securities' yields and prices had been fixed, and the contracts signed, the market yield for Treasury bonds moved up by 5 basis points. The IBM offering began the next day, Thursday, October 4. On that same day, the Treasury auctioned $2.5 billion of 4-year notes yielding 9.79 percent, which was higher than the 9.62 percent on the IBM 7-year notes. Naturally, the IBM securities did not sell at all well.

On Saturday, October 6, the Federal Reserve System announced an increase in its discount rate from 11 percent to 12 percent in an effort to combat the high rate of inflation that was developing. At the same time, a number of other credit-tightening policies, which Wall Street experts called "draconian" in their severity, were implemented. As a result of the Fed's weekend actions, on Tuesday, October 9, the New York banks announced a full percentage point increase in the prime rate, to 14.5 percent. The next morning, the underwriting syndicate was disbanded, and the prices of both the notes and the debentures fell by about $50 each, with yields rising to 10.65 percent on the notes and to 10.09 percent on the debentures.

When the syndicate was disbanded, it was estimated that only $650 million of the $1 billion issue had been sold, earning syndicate members less than $5 million in underwriting fees. The remaining $350 million portion of the issue was sold after prices fell, and the investment bankers had an estimated loss of between $10 and $20 million. To put it mildly, the underwriters "took a bath."

A controversy arose over whether the IBM issue was priced "too tight." During the entire month preceding the offering, the prime rate and the discount rate had both been increasing, and the financial markets were hectic, if not chaotic. Undoubtedly, the severe measures taken by the Federal Reserve System on Saturday, October 6, 1979, were being anticipated. Whether the underwriters should have given themselves more cushion to avoid a subsequent price decline is a matter of judgment. Differences in judgment are natural, and differences are what make markets.

---

[14]One basis point is equal to one one-hundredth of 1 percent. Therefore, IBM's notes were priced to yield 0.07 percent more than Treasury notes of the same maturity.

The IBM offering illustrates a number of basic characteristics of investment banking. First, the risks are real. Second, competition among investment bankers continues to be vigorous and tough. Third, an offering by a well-managed, financially strong firm which is taking on debt for the first time, and in moderate quantity in relation to its total assets, will be rated high and priced close to Treasury issues. Fourth, turbulence in the financial markets during the period immediately preceding the offering makes the task of the underwriters extremely difficult, and great risk-taking and judgment are required when making decisions in an extremely volatile financial environment. In sum, the episode illustrates the high drama, the considerable financial sophistication, and the continued great challenges that exist in the field of financial decision making.[15]

EMERGING TRENDS

Important new developments are taking place in the financial markets. Some of these developments have resulted from legislative changes, others have arisen from fundamental shifts in the nature of economic and financial relationships, and still others are due to technological developments in the computer and telecommunications areas.

Important changes in the banking environment were brought by the Depository Institutions Deregulation and Monetary Control Act of 1980. The law directed the Federal Reserve to lower reserve requirements and to phase out deposit interest rate ceilings. It permitted depository institutions to offer interest-bearing checking accounts, it gave savings and loan associations expanded lending and investing powers, and it allowed commercial banks to offer money market funds and some brokerage services.

Competition has increased dramatically among the different types of financial institutions, as "financial service corporations," which encompass investment banking, brokerage operations, insurance, and commercial banking, are dominating the scene. Investment banking firms often earn more income in the form of interest on customer balances than in commissions, and additional new sources of income for those firms include credit card operations, money market funds, and counseling on corporate merger activity.

When the SEC ordered the end of fixed commission schedules on May 1, 1975, investment bankers were placed under severe financial pressure. To avoid financial disaster, numerous "mergers of necessity" took place, as is ev-

---

[15]To close out the story, at least some of the underwriters had hedged their IBM positions in the futures market, so they were protected against rising interest rates. Salomon Brothers, the lead underwriter, was at the time aggressively (and successfully) seeking to expand its operations, and that required taking some chances. Salomon's overall strategy has certainly worked well, even if this one issue did not, for by 1987 Salomon had surpassed Morgan Stanley as the world's leading underwriter.

ident in the compound names of some of the surviving firms: Merrill Lynch White Weld Capital Markets Group, Blyth Eastman Paine Webber, and Dean Witter Reynolds, Inc. In addition to mergers within the investment banking and brokerage business, mergers between different types of financial institutions have taken place. Bache and Co., once the eighth largest investment banking firm, was taken over by Prudential Insurance; American Express acquired and merged together three very large firms to form Shearson Lehman Hutton, which in 1988 was the fourth largest investment banking firm; and Sears, Roebuck bought out Dean Witter. There is a very clear trend toward *financial service conglomerates.* At the same time, institutional investors, especially pension funds, are continuing to replace individuals on the buying side — about 75 percent of all stock transactions are among institutions, and competition for institutional business has changed the way both brokerage and investment banking houses operate. Finally, the investment banking industry is becoming increasingly global in scope, and Japanese firms, because of Japan's huge trade surplus, have become dominant in world finance. These trends, in turn, have changed and are continuing to change the types of securities that nonfinancial corporations offer to raise capital, as well as where they go for capital. We shall discuss some of these changes in the following chapters.

Small Business

RAISING EQUITY CAPITAL FOR THE SMALL FIRM

Small firms are generally disadvantaged when competing for funds in public equity markets. Nevertheless, as the Compaq Computer example illustrates, the public markets are accessible, and the Securities and Exchange Commission also makes available some special facilities to help small firms raise equity funds at a reduced cost. So, although it is true that smaller firms are at a disadvantage, the public equity markets are by no means the exclusive domain of giant companies.

When Compaq went public and raised $75 million in 1983, it had been losing money. In fact, the company had lost $4.6 million the previous year. How could a firm with no earnings go public and obtain $75 million? How could the public decide on a value for the shares? Finding answers to these questions is difficult, yet Compaq's case illustrates several features of a public offering that can have a major effect on its success for a young, small firm. The features we highlight in this section are market timing, the public's interest in different types of business, and the company's perceived ability to develop a new product. Another point the Compaq case illustrates is the great difficulty of valuing the shares of a start-up company by traditional means.

Market timing is a critical element in the success of a new public offering. The year 1983 was phenomenally successful for the stock market. The Dow Jones Industrial Average reached an all-time historical high, and many investors told stories of huge gains in their equity investments. Pension funds and other large institutional investors shifted huge sums into the equity markets. As interest in the equity markets grew, public participation in new equity offerings increased concurrently, and 1983 was by far the most successful year in history for new public offerings. New offerings are especially interesting to investors during bull market periods. New issue prices tend to be highly volatile, and volatility is attractive to investors who are optimistic.

Of course, investors have to keep in mind that price volatility also means a higher probability of unusually large losses, and indeed, the bull market of 1983 quickly soured, turning into a bear market in 1984. As investor concerns about general economic conditions worsened, prices tumbled. Companies that had delayed their offerings during the bull market, waiting for prices to rise still more, suddenly found that the markets were no longer receptive to new issues. Many firms that had planned to go public found that they had to sell their issues at disappointingly low prices or even postpone their offerings indefinitely.

Compaq made its offering in December 1983, just before the market turned sour. At that time the market was still receptive to new issues, although subsequent events indicate how volatile the initial market reception can be. Compaq was able to sell its shares at a reasonable price, and the firm successfully raised $75 million. Had Compaq waited and come to market three or four months later, however, the shares could not have been sold at all.

The firm's *line of business* is second in importance only to timing in determining the success of a new issue. Personal computers were selling like hot cakes in 1983, and everyone knew that a good portable computer would have a ready market. Thus, Compaq's outlook was excellent, and in the new issue market, such "story stocks" — stocks whose prospects for future success sound good despite financial ratios which look bad on paper — are what investors are willing to buy.

The third factor is the existence of a *promising product:* Does the company actually have a product, or merely dreams? At the time of its public offering, Compaq's first product had been well received. The firm needed funds for continued product develop-ment, and it had already demonstrated its ability to deliver.

We are still left with the question of how Compaq's underwriters came up with a market value for the stock. The answer is unclear. Although the firm was two years old at the time, it had never paid a dividend. In fact, there could be no reasonable expectation of dividends for the foreseeable future, so clearly one could not apply the valuation models discussed in Chapter 6. One could not even apply a price/earnings multiple to current earnings, because there were no current earnings. In essence, the underwriters had to do the best they could to set a price at which the issue would be appealing to the public in spite of the huge uncertainty about the future financial performance of the firm. As it was, the issue price was lowered from $15–$17 to $11 per share even before the offering was made public. If the firm had not had a good product, it is doubtful that the issue would have been offered at all. Compaq's decision to sell stock illustrates the value of being in the right place at the right time.

We see that there can be a market for the stock of promising small and young firms. A number of factors figure in the success of a public offering of a small firm's equity, and not all of these factors are under the firm's control. Still, small firms do have access to public markets if they have a chance to grow into more substantial enterprises. Managing those growth opportunities is something that *is* under the control of the firm and its managers.

SUMMARY AND KEY CONCEPTS

This chapter is more descriptive than analytical, but a knowledge of the issues discussed here is essential to an understanding of finance. The key concepts covered are listed below.

- **Stockholders' equity** consists of the firm's common stock, paid-in capital (funds received in excess of the par value), and retained earnings (earnings not paid out as dividends).

- **Book value per share** is equal to stockholders' equity divided by the number of shares of stock outstanding. A stock's book value is often different from its par value and its market value.

- A **proxy** is a document which gives one person the power to act for another person, typically the power to vote shares of common stock. A proxy fight occurs when an outside group solicits stockholders' proxies in order to vote a new management team into office.

- Stockholders often have the right to purchase any additional shares sold by the firm. This right, called the **preemptive right**, protects the control of the present stockholders and prevents dilution of the value of their stock.

- The major **advantages of common stock financing** are as follows: (1) there is no obligation to make fixed payments, (2) common stock never matures, (3) the use of common stock increases the credit worthiness of the firm, (4) stock often can be sold on better terms than debt, and (5) using stock helps the firm to maintain its reserve borrowing capacity.

- The major **disadvantages of common stock financing** are (1) it extends voting privileges to new stockholders, (2) new stockholders share in the firm's profits, (3) the costs of stock financings are high, (4) using stock can raise the firm's cost of capital, and (5) dividends paid on common stock are not tax deductible.

- **Going public** facilitates stockholder diversification, increases liquidity for the firm's stock, makes it easier for the firm to raise capital, and establishes a value for the firm. However, reporting costs are high, operating data must be disclosed, management self-dealings are harder to arrange, the price may sink to a low level if the stock is not traded actively, and it may be harder for management to maintain control of the firm.

- Security markets are regulated by the **Securities and Exchange Commission (SEC)**.

- An **investment banker** assists in the issuing of securities by helping the firm determine the size of the issue and the type of securities to be used, establishing the selling price, selling the issue, and, in some cases, maintaining an after-market for the stock.

- A **small firm can successfully issue common stock** if its timing is right and if it has a promising product in an industry which is of interest to investors.

Questions

12-1   Examine Table 12-1. Suppose National Metals sold 2 million shares, with the company netting $25 per share. Construct a pro forma statement of the equity accounts to reflect this sale.

12-2   Is it true that the flatter, or more nearly horizontal, the demand curve for a particular firm's stock, and the less important investors regard the signaling effect of the offering, the more important the role of investment bankers when the company sells a new issue of stock?

12-3   The SEC attempts to protect investors who are purchasing newly issued securities by making sure that the information put out by a company and its investment bankers is correct and is not misleading. However, the SEC does not provide an opinion about the real value of the securities; hence, an investor might pay too much for some stock and consequently lose heavily. Do you think the SEC should, as a part of every new stock or bond offering, render an opinion to investors on the proper value of the securities being offered? Explain.

12-4   How do you think each of the following items would affect a company's ability to attract new capital and the flotation costs involved in doing so?
a. A decision to list a company's stock; the stock now trades in the over-the-counter market.
b. A decision of a privately held company to go public.
c. The increasing number of institutions which participate as buyers in the stock and bond markets.
d. The trend toward financial conglomerates as opposed to stand-alone investment banking houses.
e. Elimination of the preemptive right.
f. The introduction of shelf registrations in 1981.

12-5   Before entering a formal agreement, investment bankers carefully investigate the companies whose securities they underwrite; this is especially true of the issues of firms going public for the first time. Since the bankers do not themselves plan to hold the securities but intend to sell them to others as soon as possible, why are they so concerned about making careful investigations?

12-6   It is frequently stated that the primary purpose of the preemptive right is to allow individuals to maintain their proportionate share of the ownership and control of a corporation.
a. How important do you suppose this consideration is for the average stockholder of a firm whose shares are traded on the New York or American Stock Exchanges?
b. Is the preemptive right likely to be of more importance to stockholders of publicly owned or closely held firms? Explain.

12-7   a. Is a firm likely to get a wider distribution of shares if it sells new stock through a preemptive rights offering to existing stockholders or directly to underwriters?
b. Why would management be interested in getting a wider distribution of its shares?

Self-Test Problem   *(Solution Appears on Page 470)*

Key terms

ST-1   Define each of the following terms:
a. Common equity; paid-in capital; retained earnings
b. Par value; book value per share; market value per share
c. Proxy; proxy fight; takeover
d. Preemptive right
e. Classified stock; founders' shares
f. Closely held corporation; publicly owned corporation

g. Over-the-counter (OTC) market; organized security exchange
h. Primary market; secondary market
i. Going public; new issue market
j. Securities and Exchange Commission (SEC); registration statement; shelf registration; blue sky laws; margin requirements; insiders
k. Prospectus; "red herring" prospectus
l. National Association of Securities Dealers (NASD)
m. Best efforts arrangement; underwritten arrangement
n. Spread; flotation costs; offering price
o. Underwriting syndicate; lead, or managing, underwriter; selling group

Problems

Book value per share   **12-1**   The Harmonic Recording Company had the following balance sheet at the end of 1988:

Harmonic Recording Company:
Balance Sheet
December 31, 1988

		Accounts payable	$ 46,000
		Notes payable	51,000
		Long-term debt	108,000
		Common stock (30,000 shares authorized, 20,000 shares outstanding)	260,000
		Retained earnings	240,000
Total assets	$705,000	Total liabilities and equity	$705,000

a. What is the book value per share of Harmonic's common stock?
b. Suppose the firm sold the remaining authorized shares and netted $23.25 per share from the sale. What would be the new book value per share?

Profit (loss) on new   **12-2**   Security Brokers, Inc., specializes in underwriting new issues by small
stock issue   firms. On a recent offering of Meran, Inc., the terms were as follows:

Price to public	$5 per share
Number of shares	3 million
Proceeds to Meran	$14,000,000

The out-of-pocket expenses incurred by Security Brokers in the design and distribution of the issue were $300,000. What profit or loss would Security Brokers incur if the issue were sold to the public at an average price of
a. $5 per share?
b. $6 per share?
c. $4 per share?

Underwriting and   **12-3**   The Malitz Company, whose stock price is now $30, needs to raise $20
flotation expenses   million in common stock. Underwriters have informed Malitz's

management that it must price the new issue to the public at $27 per share because of a downward-sloping demand curve. The underwriters' compensation will be 5 percent of the issue price, so Malitz will net $25.65 per share. Malitz will also incur expenses in the amount of $520,000.

How many shares must Malitz sell to net $20 million after underwriting and flotation expenses?

Setting the price of a new stock issue   **12-4**   The Boro Company, a small garden supply manufacturer, has been successful and has enjoyed a good growth trend. Now Boro is planning to go public with an issue of common stock, and it faces the problem of setting an appropriate price on the stock. The company's management and its investment bankers believe that the proper procedure is to select several similar firms with publicly traded common stock and to make relevant comparisons.

Several garden supply manufacturers are reasonably similar to Boro with respect to product mix, size, asset composition, and debt/equity proportions. Of these companies, Lawn Girl and Roto Tiller are most similar. When analyzing the following data, assume that 1983 and 1988 were reasonably normal years for all three companies; that is, these years were neither especially good nor especially bad in terms of sales, earnings, and dividends. At the time of the analysis, k_{RF} was 10 percent and k_M was 15 percent. Lawn Girl is listed on the AMEX and Roto Tiller on the NYSE, whereas Boro will be traded in the OTC market.

	Lawn Girl	Roto Tiller	Boro (Totals)
Earnings per share			
1988	$ 4.50	$ 7.50	$1,200,000
1983	3.00	5.50	816,000
Price per share			
1988	$36.00	$65.00	—
Dividends per share			
1988	$ 2.25	$ 3.75	$ 600,000
1983	1.50	2.75	420,000
Book value per share, 1988	$30.00	$55.00	$9,000,000
Market/book ratio, 1988	120%	118%	—
Total assets, 1988	$28 million	$ 82 million	$20 million
Total debt, 1988	$12 million	$ 30 million	$11 million
Sales, 1988	$41 million	$140 million	$37 million

a. Assume that Boro has 100 shares of stock outstanding. Use this information to calculate earnings per share (EPS), dividends per share (DPS), and book value per share for Boro. (Hint: Boro's 1988 EPS = $12,000.)

b. Calculate earnings and dividend growth rates for the three companies. (Hint: Boro's EPS g is 8%.)

c. On the basis of your answer to Part a, do you think Boro's stock would sell at a price in the same "ballpark" as that of Lawn Girl and Roto Tiller — that is, in the range of $25 to $100 per share?

d. Assuming that Boro's management can split the stock so that the 100 shares could be changed to 1,000 shares, 100,000 shares, or any other number, would such an action make sense in this case? Why?

e. Now assume that Boro did split its stock and has 400,000 shares. Calculate new values for EPS, DPS, and book value per share. (Hint: Boro's new 1988 EPS is $3.00.)

f. Return on equity (ROE) can be measured as EPS/book value per share or as total earnings/total equity. Calculate ROEs for the three companies for 1988. (Hint: Boro's 1988 ROE = 13.3%.)

g. Calculate dividend payout ratios for the three companies. (Hint: Boro's 1988 payout ratio is 50%.)

h. Calculate debt/total assets ratios for the three companies. (Hint: Boro's 1988 debt ratio is 55%.)

i. Calculate the P/E ratios for Lawn Girl and Roto Tiller. Are these P/E ratios reasonable in view of relative growth, payout, and ROE data? If not, what other factors might explain them? (Hint: Lawn Girl's P/E = 8×.)

j. Now determine a range of values for Boro's stock price, with 400,000 shares outstanding, by applying Lawn Girl's and Roto Tiller's P/E ratios, price/dividends ratios, and price/book value ratios to your data for Boro. For example, one possible price for Boro's stock is (P/E Lawn Girl)(EPS Boro) = 8($3) = $24 per share. Similar calculations would produce a range of prices based on both Lawn Girl's and Roto Tiller's data. (Hint: Our range was $24 to $27.)

k. Using the equation $k = D_1/P_0 + g$, find approximate k values for Lawn Girl and Roto Tiller. Then use these values in the constant growth stock price model to find a price for Boro's stock. (Hint: We averaged the EPS and DPS g's for Boro.)

l. At what price do you think Boro's shares should be offered to the public? You will want to select a price that will be low enough to induce investors to buy the stock but not so low that it will rise sharply immediately after it is issued. Think about relative growth rates, ROEs, dividend yields, and total returns ($k = D_1/P_0 + g$).

Investment banking process (*Integrative*)

12-5   Gonzales Food Stores, a family-owned grocery store chain headquartered in El Paso, has grown to the point where it would like to expand its operations throughout the southwest. The proposed expansion would require Gonzales to raise $10 million in additional capital. Because Gonzales currently has a debt ratio of 50 percent, and because the family members already have all their funds tied up in the business, the owners would like to sell stock to the public. However, they want to insure that they retain control of the company. This would be Gonzales' first stock sale, and the owners are not sure just what would be involved. Therefore, they have asked you to research the process and to help them decide exactly how to raise the needed capital. In doing so, you should answer the following questions.

a. What are the advantages to Gonzales of financing with stock rather than bonds? What are the disadvantages of using stock?

b. Is the stock of Gonzales Food Stores currently publicly held or privately owned? If the firm sells stock to the public, will it then be publicly held or privately owned?

c. What is meant by classified stock? Would there be any advantages to Gonzales from designating the stock currently outstanding as "founders' shares"? What type of common stock should Gonzales sell to the public to allow the family to retain control over the operations of the business?

d. What is meant when a firm is said to be "going public"? What would be the advantages to the Gonzales family of having the firm go public? What would be the disadvantages?

e. What does it mean for a stock to be "listed"? Do you think that Gonzales' stock would be listed as soon as it goes public? If not, where would the stock trade?

f. Suppose the firm has decided to issue $10 million of Class B nonvoting stock. Now Gonzales must select an investment banker. Do you think it should select a banker on the basis of a competitive bid? What is the difference between a competitive bid and a negotiated deal?

g. Without doing any calculations, describe the procedure by which Gonzales and its investment banker will determine the price at which the stock will be offered to the public.

h. What is the difference between a registration statement and a prospectus? What is a "red herring" prospectus? Why does the SEC require all firms to file registration statements and distribute prospectuses to prospective stockholders before selling stock? What steps does the SEC take to ensure that the information in the prospectus presents a fair and accurate portrayal of the issuing firm's financial position?

i. If Gonzales goes public, and sells shares which the public buys at a price of $10 per share, what will be the approximate percentage cost, including both underwriting costs and other costs? Assume the company sells 1.5 million shares. Would the cost be higher or lower if the company were already publicly owned?

j. Would you recommend that Gonzales have the issue underwritten or sold on a best efforts basis? Why? What would be the difference in costs between the two procedures?

k. If some of the Gonzales family members wanted to sell some of their own shares in order to diversify at the same time the company was selling new shares to raise expansion capital, would this be feasible?

l. Would it be a good idea to use a rights offering for the issue? Why or why not?

Solution to Self-Test Problem

ST-1   Refer to the marginal glossary definitions and relevant chapter sections to check your responses.

13 Long-Term Debt

RAISING DEBT CAPITAL

On any given day, corporations go to the markets for vast amounts of new debt capital, and they use many types and forms of securities. To illustrate, on April 29, 1988, *The Wall Street Journal* announced the following debt-related actions:

1. IBM sold $500 million of 9 percent, 10-year bonds priced at $987.50 per $1,000 bond for a yield to maturity of 9.194 percent. These bonds are not callable for 7 years, they are rated triple-A, and they were priced to yield 35 basis points (0.35%) more than 10-year Treasury notes.

2. General Electric sold $500 million of 8.25 percent bonds with a final maturity date of 2018. However, investors have the option in 1991 of turning the bonds in and receiving their par value ($1,000). In 1991 the coupon rate will be reset at up to 120 percent of the rate on comparable maturity Treasury bonds (provided that GE still carries a triple-A rating). Interest rates will be reset every 3 years thereafter until maturity. Thus, these bonds amount to a series of 3-year notes, each with a rate set at the prevailing (future) rate at the time the note is reissued.

3. Compaq Computers sold $200 million of 25-year subordinated convertible debentures. The issue was rated B+, which is a junk bond

rating and indicates that a security is quite risky, yet its coupon rate was only 6.5 percent versus 9.25 percent for 25-year Treasury bonds and about 13 percent for other B+ 25-year bonds. The reason Compaq could sell the bonds with such a low coupon was the convertible feature: holders of the convertibles can turn them in and receive 15.3846 shares of Compaq stock for each $1,000 bond. The stock was selling for $53 on the day of the sale, but if it recovers to its 1987 high of $78.50, the bonds will have a value of $78.50 × 15.3846 = $1,208 versus the $1,000 purchase price. Thus, the purchaser of a Compaq convertible buys a low-yield (6.5%), risky bond but obtains with it the potential for a substantial capital gain.

4. The bond rating of Public Service Electric & Gas, the largest utility in New Jersey, was lowered to single-A from double-A. The Company had been experiencing operating problems that lowered expected future profits, which in turn increased the risk inherent in the bonds. A Wall Street analyst noted that rating agencies "are quick to cut ratings but slow to raise them, so this downgrade will hurt the company for a long time."

5. Valley National Corporation, an Arizona bank holding company, was placed on *CreditWatch,* a rating agency publication which lists and discusses developing situations that are likely to lead to ratings changes. Valley National is being reviewed for a possible downgrading. On the same day, however, *CreditWatch* reaffirmed the rating of Chicago & Western Railroad and removed it from the watch list.

6. Wells Fargo, a banking corporation, called for redemption on June 1, 1988, $100 million of 14.5 percent notes due in 1991. Wells Fargo probably will sell a new $100 million issue at a cost of about 9 percent to obtain the funds to pay off the issue that it called.

Why do companies use so many different types of debt? How are bond ratings determined, and how do they affect the cost of debt? How does a company decide when to call a bond or, at the time of issue, decide whether or not to make the bond callable? These are some of the issues discussed in this chapter.

DIFFERENT groups of investors prefer different types of securities, and investors' tastes change over time. Thus, astute financial managers offer a variety of securities, and they package their new security offerings at each point in time to appeal to the greatest possible number of potential investors in order to hold their costs of capital to a minimum. In this chapter, we consider various types of long-term debt available to financial managers.

funded debt
Long-term debt; "funding" means replacing short-term debt with securities of longer maturity.

Long-term debt is often called **funded debt.** When a firm is planning to "fund" its short-term debt, this means it is planning to replace short-term debt with securities of longer maturity. Funding does not imply that the financial manager places money with a trustee or other repository; it is simply part of the jargon of finance, and it means that the manager replaces short-term debt with permanent capital. Pacific Gas & Electric Company (PG&E) provides a good example of funding. PG&E has a continuous construction program, and it typically uses short-term debt to finance construction expenditures. However, once short-term debt has built up to about $100 million, the company sells a stock or bond issue, uses the proceeds to pay off (or fund) its bank loans, and starts the cycle again. There is a fixed cost involved in selling stocks or bonds which makes it quite expensive to issue small amounts of these securities. Therefore, the process used by PG&E and other companies is quite logical.

TRADITIONAL DEBT INSTRUMENTS

There are many types of long-term debt instruments: term loans, bonds, secured and unsecured notes, marketable and nonmarketable debt, and so on. In this section, we discuss briefly the traditional long-term debt instruments, after which we discuss some important features of debt contracts. Finally, we discuss recent innovations in long-term debt financing.

Term Loans

term loan
A loan, generally obtained from a bank or insurance company, with a maturity period greater than one year.

A **term loan** is a contract under which a borrower agrees to make a series of interest and principal payments on specific dates to the lender.[1] Term loans are usually negotiated directly between the borrowing firm and a financial institution — generally a bank, an insurance company, or a pension fund. Although term loans' maturities vary from 2 to 30 years, most are for periods in the 3-year to 15-year range.

Term loans have three major advantages over public offerings — *speed, flexibility,* and *low issuance costs.* Also, because they are negotiated directly between the lender and the borrower, formal documentation is minimized. The key provisions of a term loan can be worked out much more quickly than those for a public issue, and it is not necessary for the loans to go through the Securities and Exchange Commission registration process. A further advantage

---

[1]Most term loans are *amortized,* which means they are paid off in equal installments over the life of the loan. Amortization protects the lender against the possibility that the borrower will not make adequate provisions for the loan's retirement during the life of the loan. See Chapter 5 for a review of amortization. Also, if the interest and principal payments required under a term loan agreement are not met on schedule, the borrowing firm is said to have *defaulted,* and it can then be forced into bankruptcy. See Appendix 13A for a discussion of bankruptcy.

of term loans has to do with future flexibility. If a bond issue is held by many different bondholders, it is virtually impossible to obtain permission to alter the terms of the agreement, even though new economic conditions may make such changes desirable. With a term loan, the borrower can generally sit down with the lender and work out mutually agreeable modifications to the contract.

The interest rate on a term loan can either be fixed for the life of the loan or be variable. If a fixed rate is used, it will generally be set close to the rate on bonds of equivalent maturity and risk. If the rate is variable, it will usually be set at a certain number of percentage points over the prime rate, the commercial paper rate, the T-bill rate, the T-bond rate, or the London Inter-Bank Offered Rate (LIBOR). Thus, when the index rate goes up or down, so does the rate charged on the outstanding balance of the term loan. Rates may be adjusted annually, semiannually, quarterly, monthly, or on some other basis, depending on what the contract specifies. In 1988, about 60 percent of the dollar amount of all term loans made by banks had floating rates, up from virtually zero in 1970. Banks obtain most of the funds they themselves lend by selling certificates of deposit, and because the CD rate rises when other market rates rise, banks need to increase the rate they charge in order to meet their own interest costs. With the increased volatility of interest rates in recent years, banks and other lenders have become increasingly reluctant to make long-term, fixed-rate loans.

Bonds

bond
A long-term debt instrument.

A bond is a long-term contract under which a borrower agrees to make payments of interest and principal on specific dates to the holder of the bond. Although bonds have traditionally been issued with maturities of between 20 and 30 years, in the 1980s shorter maturities, such as 7 to 10 years, have been used to an increasing extent. Bonds are similar to term loans, but a bond issue is generally advertised, offered to the public, and actually sold to many different investors. Indeed, thousands of individual and institutional investors may purchase bonds when a firm sells a bond issue, whereas there is generally only one lender in the case of a term loan.[2] With bonds the interest rate is generally fixed, although in recent years there has been an increase in the use of various types of floating rate bonds. There are also a number of different types of bonds, the more important of which are discussed next.

mortgage bond
A bond backed by fixed assets. *First mortgage bonds* are senior in priority to claims of *second mortgage bonds.*

Mortgage Bonds. Under a **mortgage bond**, the corporation pledges certain assets as security for the bond. To illustrate, in 1988 Besley Corporation needed $10 million to purchase land and to build a major regional distribution center. Bonds in the amount of $4 million, secured by a mortgage on the property, were issued. (The remaining $6 million was financed with equity

---

[2]However, for very large term loans, 20 or more financial institutions may form a syndicate to grant the credit. Also, it should be noted that a bond issue can be sold to one lender (or to just a few); in this case, the issue is said to be "privately placed." Companies that place bonds privately do so for the same reasons that they use term loans — speed, flexibility, and low issuance costs.

capital.) If Besley defaults on the bonds, the bondholders can foreclose on the property and sell it to satisfy their claims.

If Besley chose to, it could issue *second mortgage bonds* secured by the same $10 million plant. In the event of liquidation, the holders of these second mortgage bonds would have a claim against the property, but only after the first mortgage bondholders had been paid off in full. Thus, second mortgages are sometimes called *junior mortgages,* because they are junior in priority to the claims of *senior mortgages,* or *first mortgage bonds.*

indenture
A formal agreement between the issuer of a bond and the bondholders.

All mortgage bonds are written subject to an **indenture**, which is a legal document that spells out in detail the rights of both the bondholders and the corporation. The indentures of most major corporations were written 20, 30, 40, or more years ago. These indentures are generally "open ended," meaning that new bonds may be issued from time to time under the existing indenture. However, the amount of new bonds that can be issued is virtually always limited to a specified percentage of the firm's total "bondable property," which generally includes all plant and equipment.

An example is provided by Savannah Electric Company. Savannah Electric can issue first mortgage bonds totaling up to 60 percent of its fixed assets. If its fixed assets totaled $1 billion, and if it had $500 million of first mortgage bonds outstanding, it could, by the property test, issue another $100 million of bonds (60% of $1 billion = $600 million).

At times, Savannah Electric has been unable to issue any new first mortgage bonds because of another indenture provision: its times-interest-earned (TIE) ratio was below 2.5, the minimum coverage that it must maintain in order to sell new bonds. Thus, although Savannah Electric passed the property test, it failed the coverage test; hence, it could not issue first mortgage bonds, and it had to finance with junior securities. Since first mortgage bonds carry lower rates of interest than junior long-term debt, this restriction was a costly one.

Savannah Electric's neighbor, Georgia Power Company, has more flexibility under its indenture — its interest coverage requirement is only 2.0. In hearings before the Georgia Public Service Commission, it was suggested that Savannah Electric change its indenture coverage to 2.0 so that it could issue more first mortgage bonds. However, this is simply not possible — the holders of the outstanding bonds would have to approve the change, and it is inconceivable that they would vote for a change that would seriously weaken their position.

debenture
A long-term debt instrument that is not secured by a mortgage on specific property.

Debentures. A **debenture** is an unsecured bond, and as such it provides no lien against specific property as security for the obligation. Debenture holders are, therefore, general creditors whose claims are protected by property not otherwise pledged. In practice, the use of debentures depends both on the nature of the firm's assets and on its general credit strength. An extremely strong company, such as IBM, will tend to use debentures; it simply does not need to put up property as security for its debt. Debentures are also issued by companies in industries in which it would not be practical to provide security through a mortgage on fixed assets. Examples of such industries are the large mail-order houses and commercial banks, which characteristically hold most of their assets in the form of inventory or loans, respectively, neither of which is satisfactory security for a mortgage bond.

Subordinated Debentures. The term *subordinate* means "below," or "inferior to," and in the event of bankruptcy, subordinated debt has claims on assets only after senior debt has been paid off. **Subordinated debentures** may be subordinated either to designated notes payable (usually bank loans) or to all other debt. In the event of liquidation or reorganization, holders of subordinated debentures cannot be paid until all senior debt, as named in the debentures' indenture, has been paid. Precisely how subordination works, and how it strengthens the position of senior debtholders, is explained in Appendix 13A.

Other Types of Bonds. Several other types of bonds are used sufficiently often to warrant mention. First, **convertible bonds** are securities that are convertible into shares of common stock, at a fixed price, at the option of the bondholder. Basically, convertibles provide investors with a chance for capital gains in exchange for a lower coupon rate, while the issuing firm gets the advantage of that lower rate. Bonds issued with warrants are similar to convertibles. **Warrants** are options which permit the holder to buy stock for a stated price, thereby providing a capital gain if the price of the stock rises. Bonds that are issued with warrants, like convertibles, carry lower coupon rates than straight bonds. Warrants and convertibles are discussed in detail in Chapter 14. **Income bonds** pay interest only when the interest is earned. Thus, these securities cannot bankrupt a company, but from an investor's standpoint they are riskier than "regular" bonds. **Putable bonds** may be turned in and exchanged for the bond's par value at the *holder's* option; generally, the put option can be exercised only if the issuer takes some specified action, such as being acquired by a weaker company or increasing its outstanding debt by a large amount.[3]

Another type of bond that has been discussed in the United States but not yet used here to any extent is the **indexed**, or **purchasing power**, **bond**, which is popular in Brazil, Israel, and a few other countries long plagued by high rates of inflation. The interest rate paid on these bonds is based on an inflation index such as the consumer price index, so the interest paid rises when the inflation rate rises, thus protecting the bondholders against inflation. In a similar vein, Mexico has used bonds whose interest rate is pegged to the price of oil to finance the development of its huge petroleum reserves; because oil

---

[3]Putable bonds have not been used to a large extent in the United States, but the recent spate of leveraged buyouts (LBOs) will probably increase their use dramatically in the coming years. A good example of why putable bonds are needed is the situation that arose with RJR Nabisco in 1988. RJR's management announced that it planned to undertake an LBO in which it would issue billions of new debt and use the proceeds to buy all the publicly held stock. The company's debt ratio would thus be changed, instantly, from about 40 percent to about 95 percent. The currently outstanding bonds were rated A+, but as soon as the announcement was made, investors knew that they would soon be junk bonds, and their price fell by about 20 percent in two days. That event virtually paralyzed the bond market, and it will probably lead to widespread use of putable bonds in the future.

---

subordinated debenture
A bond having a claim on assets only after the senior debt has been paid off in the event of liquidation.

convertible bond
A bond that is exchangeable, at the option of the holder, for common stock of the issuing firm.

warrant
A long-term option to buy a stated number of shares of common stock at a specified price.

income bond
A bond that pays interest to the holder only if the interest is earned.

putable bond
A bond that can be redeemed at the bondholder's option.

indexed (purchasing power) bond
A bond that has interest payments based on an inflation index so as to protect the holder from inflation.

prices and inflation are correlated, these bonds also protect investors against inflation. At the same time, Mexico's ability to pay interest depends on the price of oil, so it too is protected by this indexing scheme. The British government has issued an indexed bond whose interest rate is set equal to the British inflation rate plus 3 percent. Thus, these bonds provide a "real rate" of 3 percent.

SPECIFIC DEBT CONTRACT FEATURES

A firm's managers are vitally concerned about the effective cost of debt and any restrictions or provisions which might limit the firm's future alternatives. In this section, we discuss features which could affect either the cost of the firm's debt or its future flexibility.

Bond Indentures

In Chapter 1, we discussed the issue of *agency problems,* which relate to conflicts of interest among stakeholders (stockholders, bondholders, and managers) in an enterprise. Bondholders have a legitimate fear that once they lend money to a company and are "locked in" for up to 20 years, the company will take some action that is designed to benefit stockholders but that harms bondholders. For example, RJR Nabisco, when it was rated triple-A, sold 30-year bonds with a low coupon rate, and investors bought those bonds in spite of the low yield because of their low risk. Then, after the bonds had been sold, the company announced plans to issue a great deal more debt, increasing the expected rate of return to stockholders but also increasing the riskiness of the bonds. RJR's bonds fell 20 percent the week the announcement was made. Safeway Stores did the same thing, and its original bondholders also lost heavily as the market yield of the bonds rose and drove the price of the bonds down.

Investors attempt to mitigate agency problems by use of legal restrictions designed to ensure, insofar as possible, that the company does nothing to cause the quality of its bonds to deteriorate after they have been issued. The legal document which spells out the rights of bondholders and the issuing corporation is the indenture. A **trustee**, usually a bank officer, is assigned to represent the bondholders and to make sure that the terms of the indenture are carried out. The indenture may be several hundred pages in length, and it will include **restrictive covenants** that cover such points as the conditions under which the issuer can pay off the bonds prior to maturity, the level at which the issuer's times-interest-earned ratio must be maintained if the company is to sell additional bonds, and restrictions against the payment of dividends when earnings do not meet certain specifications.

The trustee is responsible both for making sure the covenants are not violated and for taking appropriate action if they are. What constitutes "appropriate action" varies with the circumstances. It might be that to insist on im-

trustee
An official who ensures that the bondholders' interests are protected and that the terms of the indenture are carried out.

restrictive covenant
A provision in a debt contract that constrains the actions of the borrower.

mediate compliance would result in bankruptcy, which in turn might lead to large losses on the bonds. In such a case, the trustee might decide that the bondholders would be better served by giving the company a chance to work out its problems rather than by forcing it into bankruptcy.

The Securities and Exchange Commission approves indentures for publicly-traded bonds and makes sure that all indenture provisions are met before allowing a company to sell new securities to the public. The indentures of many larger corporations were written back in the 1930s or 1940s, and many issues of new bonds, all covered by the same indenture, have been sold down through the years. The interest rates on the bonds, and perhaps also the maturities, will change from issue to issue, but bondholders' protection as spelled out in the indenture will be the same for all bonds of a given type.[4]

Call Provisions

call provision
A provision in a bond contract that gives the issuer the right to redeem the bonds under specified terms prior to the normal maturity date.

Most bonds contain a **call provision**, which gives the issuing corporation the right to call the bonds for redemption. The call provision generally states that the company must pay the bondholder an amount greater than the par value for the bond when it is called. The additional sum, which is termed a *call premium,* is typically set equal to one year's interest if the bond is called during the first year. The premium declines at a constant rate of I/n each year thereafter, where I = annual interest and n = original maturity in years. For example, the call premium on a $1,000 par value, 10-year, 10 percent bond would generally be $100 if it were called during the first year, $90 during the second year (calculated by reducing the $100, or 10 percent, premium by one-tenth), and so on. However, bonds are often not callable until several years (generally 5 to 10) after they were issued.

Suppose a company sold bonds or preferred stock when interest rates were relatively high. Provided the issue is callable, the company could sell a new issue of low-yielding securities if and when interest rates drop. It could then use the proceeds to retire the high-rate issue and thus reduce its interest or preferred dividend expenses. This process is called a *refunding operation,* and it is discussed in detail in Appendix 13B.

The call privilege is valuable to the firm but potentially detrimental to the investor, especially if the bond was issued in a period when interest rates were cyclically high. Accordingly, the interest rate on a new issue of callable bonds will exceed that on a new issue of noncallable bonds. For example, on April 28, 1988, Great Falls Timber Company sold a bond issue yielding 10.375 percent; these bonds were callable immediately. On the same day, Midwest Milling Company sold an issue of similar risk and maturity which yielded 10 percent; its bonds were noncallable for 10 years. (This is known as a *deferred call,* and the bonds are said to have *call protection.*) Investors were apparently willing to accept a 0.375 percent lower interest rate on Midwest's bonds for

---

[4]A firm will have different indentures for each of the major types of bonds it issues, including its first mortgage bonds, its debentures, its convertibles, and so on.

the assurance that the relatively high (by historic standards) rate of interest would be earned for at least 10 years. Great Falls, on the other hand, had to incur a 0.375 percent higher annual interest rate to obtain the option of calling the bonds in the event of a subsequent decline in interest rates.

Sinking Funds

sinking fund
A required annual payment designed to amortize a bond or preferred stock issue.

A **sinking fund** is a provision that facilitates the orderly retirement of a bond issue (or, in some cases, an issue of preferred stock). Typically, the sinking fund provision requires the firm to retire a portion of the bond issue each year. On rare occasions the firm may be required to deposit money with a trustee, who invests the funds and then uses the accumulated sum to retire the bonds when they mature. Usually, though, the sinking fund is used to buy back a certain percentage of the issue each year. A failure to meet the sinking fund requirement causes the bond issue to be thrown into default, which may force the company into bankruptcy. Obviously, then, a sinking fund can constitute a dangerous cash drain on the firm.

In most cases, the firm is given the right to handle the sinking fund in either of two ways:

1. The company may call in for redemption (at par value) a certain percentage of the bonds each year; for example, it might be able to call 2 percent of the total original amount of the issue at a price of $1,000 per bond. The bonds are numbered serially, and those called for redemption are determined by a lottery administered by the trustee.

2. The company may buy the required amount of bonds on the open market.

The firm will choose the least-cost method. If interest rates have risen, causing bond prices to fall, it will buy bonds in the open market at a discount; if interest rates have fallen, it will call the bonds. Note that a call for sinking fund purposes is quite different from a refunding call as discussed previously. A sinking fund call requires no call premium, but only a small percentage of the issue is normally callable in any one year.

Although sinking funds are designed to protect bondholders by insuring that an issue is retired in an orderly fashion, it must be recognized that sinking funds will at times work to the detriment of bondholders. For example, suppose the bond carries a 15 percent interest rate and yields on similar bonds have fallen to 10 percent. A sinking fund call at par would require an investor to give up $150 of interest and reinvest in a bond that pays only $100 per year. This obviously disadvantages those bondholders whose bonds are called. On balance, however, securities that provide for a sinking fund are regarded as being safer than those without such a provision, so at the time they are issued they have lower coupon rates than otherwise similar bonds without sinking funds.

RECENT INNOVATIONS

Zero (or Very Low) Coupon Bonds

Some bonds pay no interest but are offered at a substantial discount below their par values and hence provide capital appreciation rather than interest income. These securities are called **zero coupon bonds** *("zeros")*, or *original issue discount bonds (OIDs)*. Zeros were first used in a major way in 1981. In recent years IBM, Alcoa, J. C. Penney, ITT, Cities Service, GMAC, Martin-Marietta, and many other companies have used them to raise billions of dollars. Municipal governments also sell "zero minus," and investment bankers have in effect created zero coupon Treasury bonds.

zero coupon bond
A bond that pays no annual interest but is sold at a discount below par, thus providing compensation to investors in the form of capital appreciation.

To understand how zeros are used and analyzed, consider the zeros that were issued by Kiefer Corporation, a shopping center developer, on January 1, 1988. Kiefer was developing a new shopping center in Orange County, California, and it needed $50 million. The company did not anticipate major cash flows from the project for about 5 years. However, Carol Kiefer, the president, plans to sell the center once it is fully developed and rented, which should take about 5 years. Therefore, Kiefer wants to use a financing vehicle that will not require cash outflows for 5 years, and she has decided on a 5-year zero coupon bond.

Kiefer Corporation is an A-rated company, and A-rated zeros with 5-year maturities yielded 9 percent in January 1989 (5-year coupon bonds also yielded 9 percent.) The company is in the 40 percent federal-plus-state tax bracket. Carol Kiefer wants to know the firm's after-tax cost of capital if it uses 9 percent, 5-year maturity zeros, and she also wants to know what the bond's cash flows will be. Table 13-1 provides an analysis of the situation, and the following numbered items explain the table itself.

1. The information in the "Basic Data" section, except the issue price was given in the preceding paragraph, and the information in the "Analysis" section was calculated using the known data. The maturity value of the bond is always set at $1,000 or some multiple thereof.

2. The issue price is the PV of $1,000, discounted back 5 years at the rate $k_d = 9\%$. Using the tables, we find PV = $1,000(0.6499) = $649.90. Using a financial calculator, we input FV = 1,000, i = 9, and n = 5, then press the PV key to find PV = $649.93. Note that $649.93 compounded annually for 5 years at 9 percent will grow to $1,000.

3. The accrued values as shown on Line 1 in the analysis section represent the compounded value of the bond at the end of each year. The accrued value for Year 0 is the issue price; the accrued value for Year 1 is found as $649.93(1.09) = $708.42; the accrued value at the end of Year 2 is $649.93(1.09)^2 = $772.18; and, in general, the value at the end of any Year n is

Accrued value at the end of Year n = Issue price $\times (1 + k_d)^n$.

Table 13-1   Analysis of a Zero Coupon Bond

Basic Data:

Maturity value	$1,000
k_d	9.00%
Maturity	5 years
Tax rate	40.00%
Issue price	$649.93

Analysis:

			Years			
	0	1	2	3	4	5
(1) Accrued value	$649.93	$708.42	$772.18	$841.68	$917.43	$1,000.00
(2) Interest deduction		58.49	63.76	69.50	75.75	82.57
(3) Tax savings		23.40	25.50	27.80	30.30	33.03
(4) Cash flow	+649.93	+23.40	+25.50	+27.80	+30.30	−966.97
After-tax cost of debt	5.40%					

Number of $1,000 zeros the company must issue to raise $50 million = Amount needed/Price per bond

$$= \$50,000,000/\$649.93$$

$$= 76,931 \text{ bonds.}$$

4. The interest deduction as shown on Line 2 represents the increase in accrued value during the year. Thus, interest in Year 1 = $708.42 − $649.93 = $58.49. In general,

$$\text{Interest in Year n} = \text{Accrued value}_n - \text{Accrued value}_{n-1}.$$

This method of calculating taxable interest is specified by Congress.

5. The company can deduct interest each year, even though the payment is not made in cash. This deduction lowers the taxes that would otherwise be paid, producing the following:

$$\text{Tax savings} = (\text{Interest deduction})(T)$$

$$= \$58.49(0.4)$$

$$= \$23.40 \text{ in Year 1.}$$

6. Line 4 represents a time line; it shows the cash flow at the end of Years 0 through 5. At Year 0, the company receives the $649.93 issue price. The company also has positive cash inflows equal to the tax savings during Years 1 through 4. Finally, in Year 5, it must pay the $1,000 maturity value, but it gets one more tax savings on interest (increase in accrued value) for the year. Therefore, the net cash flow in Year 5 is − $1,000 + $33.03 = − $966.97.

7. We can find the IRR of the cash flows shown on Line 4 using the IRR function of a financial calculator. The IRR is the after-tax cost of debt to the company, and it is 5.4 percent. Conceptually, here is the situation:

$$\sum_{t=0}^{n} \frac{CF_n}{(1 + k_{d(AT)})^n} = 0.$$

$$\frac{\$649.93}{(1 + k_{d(AT)})^0} + \frac{\$23.40}{(1 + k_{d(AT)})^1} + \frac{\$25.50}{(1 + k_{d(AT)})^2} + \frac{\$27.80}{(1 + k_{d(AT)})^3} + \frac{\$30.30}{(1 + k_{d(AT)})^4} + \frac{-\$966.97}{(1 + k_{d(AT)})^5} = 0.$$

The value $k_{d(AT)} = 0.054 = 5.4\%$, found with a financial calculator, produces the equality.

8. Note that $k_d(1 - T) = 9\%(0.6) = 5.4\%$. As we shall see in Chapter 16, the cost of capital for regular coupon debt is found using the formula $k_d(1 - T)$. Thus, there is symmetrical treatment for tax purposes for zero coupon and regular coupon debt; that is, both types of debt have the same after-tax cost effects. This was Congress's intent, and it is why the Tax Code specifies the treatment set forth in Table 13-1.[5]

Not all original issue discount bonds (OIDs) have zero coupons. For example, Kiefer might have sold an issue of 5-year bonds with a 5 percent coupon at a time when other bonds with similar ratings and maturities were yielding 9 percent. These bonds would have had a value of $844.41:

$$\text{Value} = \sum_{t=1}^{5} \frac{\$50}{(1.09)^t} + \frac{\$1,000}{(1.09)^5} = \$844.41.$$

If an investor had purchased these bonds at a price of $844.41, the yield to maturity would have been 9 percent. The discount of $1,000 - $844.41 = $155.59 would have been amortized over the bond's 5-year life, and it would have been handled by both Kiefer and the bondholders exactly as the discount on the zeros was handled.

Thus, zero coupon bonds are just one type of original issue discount bond. Any nonconvertible bond whose coupon rate is set below the going market rate at the time of its issue will sell at a discount, and it will be classified (for tax and other purposes) as an OID.

Shortly after corporations began to issue zeros, investment bankers figured out a way to create zeros from U.S. Treasury bonds, which are issued only in

---

[5]The purchaser of a zero coupon bond must calculate interest income on the bond in the same manner as the issuer calculates the interest deduction. Thus, in Year 1, a buyer of a bond would report interest income of $58.49 and would pay taxes in the amount of T(Interest income), even though no cash was received. T, of course, would be the bondholder's personal tax rate. Because of the tax situation, most zero coupon bonds are bought by pension funds and other tax-exempt entities. Individuals do, however, buy taxable zeros for their Individual Retirement Accounts (IRAs). Also, state and local governments issue "tax exempt muni zeros," which are purchased by individuals in high tax brackets.

Note too that we have analyzed the bond as if the cash flows accrued annually. Generally, to facilitate comparisons with semiannual payment coupon bonds, the analysis is conducted on a semiannual basis.

coupon form. In 1982 Salomon Brothers bought $1 billion of 12 percent, 30-year Treasuries. Each bond had 60 coupons worth $60 each, which represented the interest payments due every 6 months. Salomon then clipped the coupons and placed them in 60 piles; the last pile also contained the now "stripped" bond itself, which represented a promise of $1,000 in the year 2012. These 60 piles of U.S. Treasury promises were then placed with the trust department of a bank and used as collateral for "zero coupon U.S. Treasury Trust Certificates," which are, in essence, zero coupon Treasury bonds. A pension fund that expected to need money in 1993 could have bought 11-year certificates backed by the interest the Treasury will pay in 1993. Treasury zeros are, of course, safer than corporate zeros, so they are very popular with pension fund managers.

Corporate (and municipal) zeros are generally callable at the option of the issuer, just like coupon bonds, after some stated call protection period. The call price is set at a premium over the accrued value at the time of the call. Stripped U.S. Treasury bonds (Treasury zeros) generally are not callable because the Treasury normally sells noncallable bonds. Thus, Treasury zeros are completely protected against reinvestment risk (the risk of having to invest cash flows from a bond at a lower rate because of a decline in interest rates).

Floating Rate Debt

In the early 1980s, inflation pushed interest rates up to unprecedented levels, causing sharp declines in the prices of long-term bonds. Even some supposedly "risk-free" U.S. Treasury bonds lost fully half their value, and a similar situation occurred with corporate bonds, mortgages, and other fixed rate, long-term securities. As a result, many lenders became reluctant to lend money at fixed rates on a long-term basis, and they would do so only at high rates.

There is normally a *maturity risk premium* embodied in long-term interest rates; this is a risk premium designed to offset the risk of declining bond prices if interest rates rise. Prior to the 1970s, the maturity risk premium on 30-year bonds was about one percentage point, meaning that under normal conditions, a firm might expect to pay about one percentage point more to borrow on a long-term than on a short-term basis. However, in the early 1980s, the maturity risk premium is estimated to have jumped to about three percentage points, which made long-term debt very expensive relative to short-term debt. Lenders were able and willing to lend on a short-term basis, but corporations were correctly reluctant to borrow short-term to finance long-term assets — such action is extremely dangerous. Therefore, there was a situation in which lenders did not want to lend on a long-term basis, but corporations needed long-term money. The problem was solved by the introduction of long-term, floating rate debt.

floating rate bond
A bond whose interest rate fluctuates with shifts in the general level of interest rates.

A typical **floating rate bond** works as follows. The coupon rate is set for, say, the initial six-month period, after which it is adjusted every six months based on some market rate. For example, the GE issue discussed at the beginning of the chapter was tied to the Treasury bond rate. Other companies' issues have been tied to short-term rates. Many additional provisions can be included in floating rate issues; for example, some are convertible to fixed rate debt, whereas others have upper and lower limits ("caps" and "collars") on how high or low the yield can go.

Floating rate debt is advantageous to investors because the interest rate moves up if market rates rise. This causes the market value of the debt to be stabilized, and it also provides lenders such as banks more income to meet their own obligations (for example, a bank which owns floating rate bonds can use the interest it earns to pay interest on its own deposits). Moreover, floating rate debt is advantageous to corporations, because by using it, firms can issue debt with a long maturity without committing themselves to paying a historically high rate of interest for the entire life of the loan. Of course, if interest rates were to move even higher after a floating rate note had been signed, the borrower would have been better off issuing conventional, fixed rate debt.

Junk Bonds

junk bond
A high-risk, high-yield bond used to finance mergers, leveraged buyouts, and troubled companies.

Another new type of bond is the **junk bond**, a high-risk, high-yield bond issued to finance a leveraged buyout, a merger, or a troubled company. For example, when Ted Turner attempted to buy CBS, he planned to finance the acquisition by issuing junk bonds to CBS's stockholders in exchange for their shares. Similarly, Merrill Lynch helped Public Service of New Hampshire finance construction of its troubled Seabrook nuclear plant with junk bonds, and People Express used junk bonds to finance its expansion program. In junk bond deals, the debt ratio is generally extremely high, so the bondholders must bear as much risk as stockholders normally would. The bonds' yields reflect this fact — Merrill Lynch reported that a coupon rate of 25 percent was required to sell the Public Service of New Hampshire bonds.

The emergence of junk bonds as an important type of debt is another example of how the investment banking industry adjusts to and facilitates new developments in capital markets. In the 1980s, mergers and takeovers increased dramatically. People like T. Boone Pickens and Ted Turner thought that certain old-line, established companies were run inefficiently and were financed too conservatively, and they wanted to take these companies over and restructure them. To help finance these takeovers, the investment banking firm of Drexel Burnham Lambert began an active campaign to persuade certain institutions to purchase high-yield bonds. Drexel developed expertise in putting together deals that were attractive to the institutions yet feasible in the sense that projected cash flows were sufficient to meet the required interest payments. The fact that interest on the bonds was tax deductible, combined with the much higher debt ratios of the restructured firms, also increased after-tax cash flows and helped make the deals feasible.

The development of junk bond financing has done as much as any single factor to reshape the U.S. financial scene. The existence of these securities led directly to the loss of independence of Gulf Oil and hundreds of other companies, and it led to major shake-ups in such companies as CBS, Union Car-

---

Table 13-2   Comparison of Bond Ratings

| | High Quality | | Investment Grade | | Substandard | | Junk Bonds | |
							Speculative	
Moody's	Aaa	Aa	A	Baa	Ba	B	Caa	C
S&P	AAA	AA	A	BBB	BB	B	CCC	D

Note: Both Moody's and S&P use "modifiers" for bonds rated below triple A. S&P uses a plus and minus system; thus, A+ designates the strongest A-rated bonds and A− the weakest. Moody's uses a 1, 2, or 3 designation, with 1 denoting the strongest and 3 the weakest; thus, within the double-A category, Aa1 is the best, Aa2 is average, and Aa3 is the weakest.

---

bide, and USX (formerly U.S. Steel). It also caused Drexel Burnham Lambert to leap from essentially nowhere in the 1970s to a position of leadership in the investment banking industry in the 1980s. Note, though, that high quality bonds such as those of RJR Nabisco can be transformed into junk bond status in an LBO, and this is causing investors to insist on put provisions as protection against actions such as that of RJR Nabisco.

BOND RATINGS

Since the early 1900s, bonds have been assigned quality ratings that reflect their probability of going into default. The two major rating agencies are Moody's Investors Service (Moody's) and Standard & Poor's Corporation (S&P). These agencies' rating designations are shown in Table 13-2.[6] The triple- and double-A bonds are extremely safe. Single-A and triple-B bonds are strong enough to be called **investment grade bonds,** and they are the lowest-rated bonds that many banks and other institutional investors are permitted by law to hold. Double-B and lower bonds are speculations, or junk bonds; they have a significant probability of going into default, and many financial institutions are prohibited from buying them.

investment grade bonds
Bonds rated A or triple-B; many banks and other institutional investors are permitted by law to hold only investment grade or better bonds.

Bond Rating Criteria

Bond ratings are based on both qualitative and quantitative factors, some of which are as follows:

1. Debt ratio.
2. Times-interest-earned ratio.
3. Fixed charge coverage ratio.
4. Current ratio.

---

[6]In the discussion to follow, reference to the S&P code is intended to imply the Moody code as well. Thus, for example, triple-B bonds mean both BBB and Baa bonds; double-B bonds mean both BB and Ba bonds; and so on.

5. Mortgage provisions: Is the bond secured by a mortgage? If it is, and if the property has a high value in relation to the amount of bonded debt, the bond's rating is enhanced.

6. Subordination provisions: Is the bond subordinated to other debt? If so, it will be rated at least one notch below the rating it would have if it were not subordinated. Conversely, a bond with other debt subordinated to it will have a somewhat higher rating.

7. Guarantee provisions: Some bonds are guaranteed by other firms. If a weak company's debt is guaranteed by a strong company (usually the weak company's parent), the bond will be given the strong company's rating.

8. Sinking fund: Does the bond have a sinking fund to insure systematic repayment? This feature is a plus factor to the rating agencies.

9. Maturity: Other things the same, a bond with a shorter maturity will be judged less risky than a longer-term bond, and this will be reflected in the ratings.

10. Stability: Are the issuer's sales and earnings stable?

11. Regulation: Is the issuer regulated, and could an adverse regulatory climate cause the company's economic position to decline? Regulation is especially important for utilities, railroads, and telephone companies.

12. Antitrust: Are any antitrust actions pending against the firm that could erode its position?

13. Overseas operations: What percentage of the firm's sales, assets, and profits are from overseas operations, and what is the political climate in the host countries?

14. Environmental factors: Is the firm likely to face heavy expenditures for pollution control equipment?

15. Pension liabilities: Does the firm have unfunded pension liabilities that could pose a future problem?

16. Labor unrest: Are there potential labor problems on the horizon that could weaken the firm's position? As this is written, a number of airlines face this problem, and it has caused their ratings to be lowered.

17. Resource availability: Is the firm likely to face supply shortages that could force it to curtail operations?

18. Accounting policies: If a firm uses relatively conservative accounting policies, its reported earnings will be of "higher quality" than if it uses less conservative procedures. Thus, conservative accounting policies are a plus factor in bond ratings.

Representatives of the rating agencies have consistently stated that no precise formula is used to set a firm's rating; all the factors listed, plus others, are taken into account, but not in a mathematically precise manner. Statistical studies have borne out this contention, for researchers who have tried to predict bond ratings on the basis of quantitative data have had only limited success, indicating that the agencies use subjective judgment when establishing a firm's rating.[7]

Importance of Bond Ratings

Bond ratings are important both to firms and to investors. First, because a bond's rating is an indicator of its default risk, the rating has a direct, measurable influence on the bond's interest rate and the firm's cost of debt capital. Second, most bonds are purchased by institutional investors rather than individuals, and many institutions are restricted to investment-grade securities. Thus, if a firm's bonds fall below BBB, it will have a difficult time selling new bonds, since many potential purchasers will not be allowed to buy them.

As a result of their higher risk and more restricted market, lower-grade bonds have higher required rates of return, k_d, than high-grade bonds. Figure 13-1 illustrates this point. In each of the years shown on the graph, U.S. government bonds have had the lowest yields, AAAs have been next, and BBB bonds have had the highest yields. The figure also shows that the gaps between yields on the three types of bonds vary over time, indicating that the cost differentials, or risk premiums, fluctuate from year to year. This point is highlighted in Figure 13-2, which gives the yields on the three types of bonds and the risk premiums for AAA and BBB bonds in June 1963, June 1975, and April 1988.[8] Note first that the risk-free rate, or vertical axis intercept, rose more than 5 percentage points from 1963 to 1988, primarily reflecting the increase in realized and anticipated inflation. Second, the slope of the line also has increased since 1963, indicating an increase in investors' risk aversion. This increase was quite pronounced from 1963 to 1975, but it fell somewhat between 1975 and 1988. Thus, the penalty for having a low credit rating varies over time. Occasionally, as in 1963, the penalty is quite small, but at other times, as in 1975, it is very large. These slope differences reflect investors' risk aversion. In 1975 the country's economy was emerging from a severe recession caused by a quadrupling of oil prices in 1973–1974, and investors were afraid the economy would slip back into a slump. At such times there is a

---

[7]See Ahmed Belkaoui, *Industrial Bonds and the Rating Process* (London: Quorum Books, 1983).

[8]The term *risk premium* ought to reflect only the difference in expected (and required) returns between two securities that results from differences in their risk. However, the differences between *yields to maturity* on different types of bonds consist of (1) a true risk premium; (2) a liquidity premium, which reflects the fact that U.S. Treasury bonds are more readily marketable than most corporate bonds; (3) a call premium, because most Treasury bonds are not callable whereas corporate bonds are; and (4) an expected loss differential, which reflects the probability of loss on the corporate bonds. As an example of the last point, suppose the yield to maturity on a BBB bond was 10 percent versus 7 percent on government bonds, but there was a 5 percent probability of total default loss on the corporate bond. In this case, the expected return on the BBB bond would be 0.95(10%) + 0.05(0%) = 9.5%, and the risk premium would be 2.5 percent, not the full 3 percentage point difference in "promised" yields to maturity. Because of all these points, the risk premiums given in Figure 13-2 overstate somewhat the true (but unmeasurable) risk premiums.

Figure 13-1   Yields on Selected Long-Term Bonds, 1953–1988

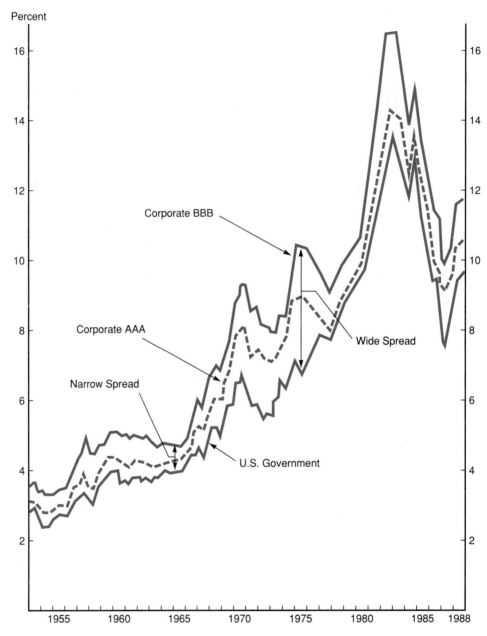

Figure 13-2   Relationship between Bond Ratings and Bond Yields, 1963, 1975, and 1988

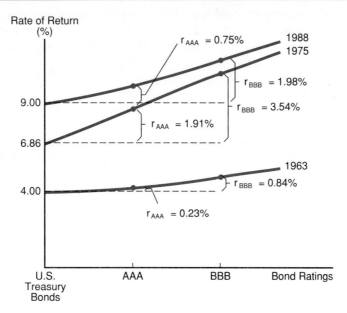

r_{AAA} = risk premium on AAA bonds.
r_{BBB} = risk premium on BBB bonds.

	Long-Term Government Bonds (Default-Free) (1)	AAA Corporate Bonds (2)	BBB Corporate Bonds (3)	Risk Premiums	
				AAA (4) = (2) − (1)	BBB (5) = (3) − (1)
June 1963	4.00%	4.23%	4.84%	0.23%	0.84%
June 1975	6.86	8.77	10.40	1.91	3.54
April 1988	9.00	9.75	10.98	0.75	1.98

Sources: *Federal Reserve Bulletin*, December 1963 and December 1975; *Federal Reserve Statistical Release*, April 1988.

"flight to quality," Treasuries are in great demand, and the premium on low-quality over high-quality bonds increases.

Changes in Ratings

Changes in a firm's bond rating will have notable effects both on its ability to borrow long-term capital and on the cost of that capital. Rating agencies review outstanding bonds on a periodic basis, occasionally upgrading or downgrading a bond as a result of its issuer's changed circumstances. For example, in February 1988, when Texas Utilities (TU) agreed to buy out a minority holder of its troubled Comanche Peak nuclear power plant, S&P placed TU on its *CreditWatch* list. (*CreditWatch* is S&P's weekly publication that discusses developing situations that may lead to upgradings or downgradings.) The statement made by S&P was that the purchase would increase TU's investment in a problem-plagued nuclear power plant, and that it might also cause TU to take on additional debt. However, on the same day the warning about TU was issued, Coastal Corporation's bonds were upgraded, because it announced an offering of new common stock whose proceeds would be used to refund high-cost debt, an action which would reduce the firm's financial risk and provide greater protection to its bondholders.

RATIONALE FOR USING DIFFERENT TYPES OF SECURITIES

Why are there so many different types of long-term securities? At least a partial answer to this question may be seen from Figure 13-3, which depicts the now familiar risk/return trade-off function drawn to show the risk and the expected after-personal-tax returns for the various securities of the McAlhany Company.[9] First, U.S. Treasury bills, representing the risk-free rate, are shown for reference. The lowest-risk long-term securities offered by McAlhany are its floating rate notes; these securities are free of interest rate risk, but they are exposed to some risk of default. The first mortgage bonds are somewhat riskier than the notes (because the bonds are exposed to interest rate risk), and they sell at a somewhat higher required and expected after-tax return. The second mortgage bonds are even riskier, so they have a still higher expected return. Subordinated debentures, income bonds, and preferred stocks are all increasingly risky, and their expected returns increase accordingly. The firm's convertible preferred is riskier than its straight preferred, but less risky than its common stock. McAlhany's warrants, the riskiest security it issues, have the highest required return of any of its offerings. (Preferred stock, warrants, and convertibles are all discussed in Chapter 14.)

Why does McAlhany issue so many different classes of securities? Why does it not offer just one type of bond plus common stock? The answer lies in the fact that different investors have different risk/return trade-off preferences, so to appeal to the broadest possible market, McAlhany must offer securities that attract as many different types of investors as possible. Also, different securities are more popular and hence in demand at different points in time, and firms tend to issue whatever is popular at the time they need money. Used wisely, a

---

[9]The yields in Figure 13-3 are shown on an after-tax basis to the recipient. If yields were on a before-personal-tax basis, those on preferred stocks would lie below those on bonds because of the tax treatment of preferreds. In essence, 70 percent of preferred dividends are tax exempt to corporations owning preferred shares, so a preferred stock with a 10 percent pre-tax yield will have a higher after-tax return to a corporation in the 34 percent tax bracket than will a bond with a 12 percent yield. This point will be discussed in more detail in Chapter 14.

Figure 13-3   McAlhany Company: Risk and Expected Returns on Different Classes of Securities

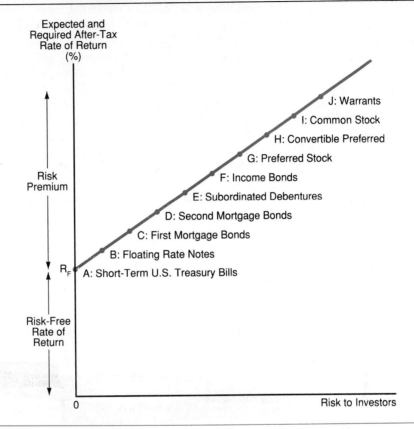

policy of selling differentiated securities to take advantage of market conditions can lower a firm's overall cost of capital below what it would be if the firm used only one class of debt.

FACTORS INFLUENCING LONG-TERM FINANCING DECISIONS

As we show in this section, many factors influence a firm's long-term financing decisions. The factors' relative importance varies among firms at any point in time and for any given firm over time, but any company planning to raise new long-term capital should consider each of these points.

Target Capital Structure

As we shall see in Chapter 17, firms typically establish target capital structures, or target debt/equity mixes. One of the most important considerations in any financing decision is how the firm's actual capital structure compares to its target structure. However, few firms in any one year finance exactly in accordance with their target capital structures, primarily because exact adherence would increase their flotation costs; since smaller issues of new securities have proportionally larger flotation costs, firms tend to use debt one year and stock the next.

For example, Consolidated Tools, Inc., a Cincinnati machine tool manufacturer, requires $20 million of new external capital in each of the next two years. Its target capital structure calls for 40 percent debt, so if Consolidated were to raise debt each year, it would issue $8 million of new bonds each year. The flotation costs, based on data back in Table 12-4, would be 3.2 percent of each $8 million issue. To net $8 million, Consolidated would have to sell $8,000,000/0.968 = $8,264,463 each year and thus pay $264,463 in flotation costs on each issue, for a total of $528,926 in flotation costs over the two years. Alternatively, Consolidated could elect to raise the total $16 million of debt in one year. The flotation cost for a $16 million issue would be about 1.9 percent, so the firm would float an issue for $16,000,000/0.981 = $16,309,888 and pay $309,888 in total flotation costs. By issuing debt only once, Consolidated could cut its debt flotation costs by more than 40 percent. The same relationship would apply to sales of preferred stock and to new common equity issues.

Making fewer but larger security offerings would cause Consolidated's capital structure to fluctuate about its optimal level rather than stay right on target. However, as we shall see in Chapter 17, small fluctuations about the optimal capital structure have little effect either on a firm's required returns on debt and equity or on its overall cost of capital. Also, investors would recognize that its actions were prudent and that the firm would save substantial amounts of flotation costs by financing in this manner. Therefore, even though firms like Consolidated do tend to finance over the long haul in accordance with their target capital structures, flotation costs plus the other factors discussed in the following sections have a definite influence on the specific financing decisions in any given year.

Maturity Matching

Assume that Consolidated decides to float a single $16 million nonconvertible bond issue with a sinking fund. It must next choose a maturity for the issue, taking into consideration the shape of the yield curve, management's own expectations about future interest rates, and the maturity of the assets being financed. In the case at hand, Consolidated's capital projects during the next two years consist primarily of new, automated milling and stamping machinery for its Cincinnati plant. This machinery has an expected economic life of 10 years (even though it falls into the ACRS 5-year class life). Should Consolidated finance the debt portion of the capital raised for this equipment with 5-year, 10-year, 20-year, or 30-year debt, or with debt of some other maturity? *One approach is to match the maturity of the liabilities with the maturity of the assets being financed.*

Note that some of the new capital for the machinery will come from common stock, which is generally considered to be a perpetual security with an infinite maturity. Of course, common stock can always be repurchased on the open market or by a tender offer, so its effective maturity can be reduced significantly.

Debt maturities, however, are specified at the time of issue. If Consolidated financed its capital budgets over the next two years with 10-year sinking fund bonds, it would be matching its asset and liability maturities. The cash flows resulting from the new machinery should be sufficient to make the interest and sinking fund payments on the issue, and the bonds would be retired as the machinery wore out. If Consolidated used 1-year debt, it would have to pay off the loan with cash flows derived from assets other than the machinery in question. If its operations were stable, the company could probably roll over the 1-year debt, but if it did so and interest rates rose, then it would have to pay a higher rate. If Consolidated subsequently experienced difficulties, its lenders might be hesitant to extend the loan, and the company might be unable to obtain new short-term debt at any reasonable rate. On the other hand, if it used 20-year or 30-year debt, Consolidated would still have to service the debt long after the assets that were purchased with it had been scrapped and had ceased providing cash flows, and this would worry potential lenders.

For all these reasons, one commonly used financing strategy is to match debt maturities with asset maturities. In recognition of this fact, firms do consider maturity relationships, and this factor has a major influence on the type of debt securities used.

Interest Rate Levels

Financial managers also consider interest rate levels, both absolute and relative, when making financing decisions. For example, long-term interest rates were high by historic standards in 1981 and 1982, so many managers were reluctant to issue long-term debt and thus lock in those costs for long periods. We already know that one solution to this problem is to use long-term debt with a call provision. Callability permits the company to refund the issue should interest rates drop, but there is a cost, because firms must pay more if they make their debt callable. Alternatively, a firm may finance with short-term debt whenever long-term rates are historically high, and then, assuming that interest rates subsequently fall, sell a long-term issue to replace the short-term debt. Of course, this strategy has its risks. If interest rates move even higher, the firm will be forced to renew the short-term debt at higher and higher rates, or to replace the short-term debt with a long-term bond which will now cost more than it would have when the original decision was made.

Forecasted Interest Rates

In the mid-1980s, the interest rate on AAA corporate bonds was about 12.5 percent, which was high by historical standards. Exxon's investment bankers advised the company to tap the Eurodollar bond market for relatively cheap fixed rate financing.[10] At the time, Exxon could have issued its bonds in London at 0.4 percentage points *below* comparable-maturity Treasury bonds. However, one of Exxon's officers was quoted as saying, "I say so what. The absolute level of rates is too high. We would rather wait." The managers of Exxon, as well as those of many other companies, were betting that the next move in interest rates would be down. This belief was also openly expressed by executives of ITT, Ontario Hydro, and RCA, among others.

This example illustrates that many firms base their financing decisions on expectations about future interest rates. In Exxon's case, the financial staff turned out to be correct. However, the success of such a strategy requires interest rate forecasts to be right more often than they are wrong, and it is very difficult to find someone with a long-term forecasting record better than 50-50.

The Firm's Current and Forecasted Conditions

If a firm's current financial condition is poor, its managers may be reluctant to issue new long-term debt, because (1) a new bond issue would probably trigger a review by the rating agencies, and (2) long-term debt issued when a firm is in poor financial condition costs more and is subject to more severe restrictive covenants than debt issued from strength. Thus, a firm that is in a weakened condition but is forecasting a better situation in the future would be inclined to delay permanent financing of any type until things improved. Conversely, a firm that is strong now but whose forecasts indicate a potentially bad time in the period just ahead would be motivated to finance long-term now rather than to wait. These scenarios imply that the capital markets are inefficient in the sense that investors do not have as much information about the firm's future as does its financial manager. This situation is undoubtedly true at times.

The firm's earnings outlook, and the extent to which forecasted higher earnings per share are reflected in stock prices, also has an effect on the choice of securities. If a successful R&D program has just been concluded and, consequently, management forecasts higher earnings than do most investors, the firm would not want to issue common stock. It would use debt, and then, after earnings had risen and pushed up the stock price, it would sell common stock to restore the capital structure to its target level.[11]

---

[10]A *Eurodollar bond* is a bond sold outside of the United States but denominated in U.S. dollars.

[11]Many of the factors discussed in this section imply an ability on the part of the managers to forecast capital market conditions. Managers can generally forecast their own firms' internal conditions better than outside investors, but no one can consistently forecast interest rates and the general level of stock prices. Note also that financial managers can minimize the adverse effects of changes in capital costs through transactions in the *futures market,* a topic discussed in advanced corporate finance and investments texts.

Restrictions in Existing Debt Contracts

Earlier we discussed the fact that Savannah Electric has at times been restricted from issuing new first mortgage bonds by its indenture coverage requirements. This is just one example of how indenture covenants can influence a firm's financing decision. Restrictions on the current ratio, the debt ratio, and so on, can also restrict a firm's ability to use different types of financing at a given time. Also, as a result of the November 1988 RJR Nabisco LBO announcement, we expect an increased use of putable bonds in the future, along with tighter debt ratio restrictions.

Availability of Collateral

Generally, secured long-term debt will be less costly than unsecured debt. Thus, firms with large amounts of general-purpose (as opposed to specialized) fixed assets that have a ready resale value are likely to use a relatively large amount of debt, especially mortgage bonds. Additionally, each year's financing decision will be influenced by the amount of newly acquired assets that are available as security for new bonds.

International

INTERNATIONAL MARKETS FOR LONG-TERM DEBT

Thus far, we have concentrated on the U.S. capital markets, in which firms raise most of their long-term capital. However, many firms, both multinational and domestic, raise large sums of debt capital in the international markets. For example, General Electric recently raised more than $1 billion in the Eurobond market. These bonds were dollar denominated but issued in Europe to European holders of dollars. What was the big attraction that caused GE to look to Europe for its borrowing needs? As you might suspect, the answer was lower cost. To illustrate, one GE issue cost the firm only 20 basis points more than the U.S. Treasury was paying on its bonds. Had it borrowed in the U.S. bond market, GE, a AAA-rated firm, would have paid about 50 basis points over Treasury rates. In this section we briefly describe the international bond markets.

Any bond sold outside the country of the borrower is called an *international bond,* but it is necessary to distinguish further between two types of international bonds.

Foreign Bonds

Borrowers sometimes raise long-term debt capital in the domestic capital market of a foreign country.

For instance, Bell Canada may need U.S. dollars to finance its operations in the United States. If it decides to raise the needed capital in the domestic U.S. bond market, the bond would be underwritten by a syndicate of U.S. investment bankers, would be denominated in (that is, pay interest and principal in terms of) U.S. dollars, and would be sold to investors in the United States in accordance with SEC and applicable state regulations. Except for the foreign origin of the borrower — Canada — such a bond would be indistinguishable from bonds issued by equivalent U.S. corporations. Because Bell Canada is a foreign corporation, though, its bond would be called a *foreign bond.* In summary, a foreign bond is a bond that is (1) issued by a foreign borrower, (2) underwritten by a syndicate whose members all come from the country where the funds are raised, (3) denominated in the currency of that same country, and (4) sold entirely within that country.

Eurobonds

The second type of international bond is the *Eurobond,* which is sold through an international syndicate and is denominated in a currency *other than* that of the country in which it is sold. For example, when GE sold U.S. dollar–denominated bonds in Europe through investment bankers who operate worldwide to people who paid for the bonds with dollars, that was a Eurobond issue. The institutional arrangements by which Eurobonds are brought to market are different from those for most other bond issues. To a corporation issuing a Eurobond, perhaps the most important feature of the process is a far lower level of required disclosure than would be required for bonds issued in domestic markets, particularly in the United States. Also, governments tend not to apply as strict a set of regulations to securities denominated in foreign currencies but sold in domestic markets to investors holding foreign currencies. This often leads to lower total transaction costs for the issue.

Eurobonds appeal to investors for several reasons. Generally, they are issued in bearer form rather than as registered bonds, so the names and nationalities of investors are not recorded. Individuals who desire anonymity, whether for privacy reasons or for tax avoidance, find Eurobonds to their liking. Similarly, most governments do not withhold taxes on interest payments associated with Euro-

bonds. If the investor requires an effective yield of 10 percent, a Eurobond that is exempt from tax withholding would need a coupon rate of 10 percent. Another type of bond — for instance, a domestic issue subject to a 30 percent withholding tax on interest paid to foreigners — would need a coupon rate of 14.3 percent to yield an after-withholding rate of 10 percent. Investors who desire secrecy would not want to file for a refund of the tax, so they would prefer to hold the Eurobond.

More than half of all Eurobonds are denominated in dollars; bonds in Japanese yen, German marks, and Dutch guilders account for most of the rest. Although centered in Europe, Eurobonds are truly international. Their underwriting syndicates include investment bankers from all parts of the world, and the bonds are sold to investors not only in Europe but also in such faraway places as Bahrain and Singapore. Up to a few years ago, Eurobonds were issued solely by multinational firms, by international financial institutions, or by national governments. Today, however, the Eurobond market is also being tapped by purely domestic U.S. firms such as electric utilities, who find that by borrowing overseas they can lower their debt costs.

SUMMARY AND KEY CONCEPTS

This chapter described the characteristics, advantages, and disadvantages of the major types of long-term debt securities. The key concepts covered are listed below.

- **Term loans** and **bonds** are long-term debt contracts under which a borrower agrees to make a series of interest and principal payments on specific dates to the lender or bondholders. A term loan is generally sold to one (or a few) lenders, while a bond is typically offered to the public and sold to many different investors.

- There are many different types of bonds. They include **mortgage bonds**, **debentures**, **convertibles**, **income bonds**, **putable bonds**, and **purchasing power (indexed) bonds**. The return required on each type of bond is determined by the bond's riskiness.

- A bond's **indenture** is a legal document that spells out the rights of the bondholders and of the issuing corporation. A **trustee** is assigned to make sure that the terms of the indenture are carried out.

- A **call provision** gives the issuing corporation the right to redeem the bonds prior to maturity under specified terms, usually at a price greater than the maturity value. A firm will typically call a bond and refund it if interest rates fall substantially.

- A **sinking fund** provision may be included in a bond indenture which requires the corporation to retire a portion of the bond issue each year. The purpose of the sinking fund is to provide for the orderly retirement of the issue. No call premium is paid to the holders of bonds called for sinking fund purposes.

- Some recent innovations in long-term financing include **zero coupon bonds**, which pay no annual interest but which are issued at a discount; **floating rate debt**, whose interest payments fluctuate with changes in the general level of interest rates; and **junk bonds**, which are high-risk, high-yield instruments used by firms whose debt ratios are very high.

- Bonds are assigned **ratings** that reflect the probability of their going into default. The higher a bond's rating, the lower its required interest rate.

- A firm's long-term financing decisions are influenced by its **target capital structure**, the **maturity of its assets**, current and forecasted **interest rate levels**, the firm's current and forecasted **financial condition, restrictions** in its existing debt contracts, and the amount of its **assets available for use as collateral.**

- U.S. firms often find that they can raise long-term capital at a lower cost outside the United States by selling bonds in the **international capital markets**. International bonds may be either **foreign bonds**, which are exactly like regular domestic bonds except that the issuer is a foreign company, or **Eurobonds**, which are bonds sold in a foreign country but denominated in the currency of the issuing company's home country.

Two related issues are discussed in Appendixes 13A and 13B: bankruptcy and bond refundings. Bankruptcy is an important consideration both to companies that issue debt and to investors, for it has a profound effect on all parties. Refunding, or paying off high interest rate debt with new, lower cost debt, is also an important consideration, especially today (1988), for many firms that issued long-term debt in the early 1980s at rates of 18 percent or more now have an opportunity to refund this debt at a cost of 10 percent or less.

Questions

13-1 What effect would each of the following items have on the interest rate a firm must pay on a new issue of long-term debt? Indicate whether each factor would tend to raise, lower, or have an indeterminate effect on the interest rate, and then explain *why*.
a. The firm uses bonds rather than a term loan.
b. The firm uses nonsubordinated debentures rather than first mortgage bonds.
c. The firm makes its bonds convertible into common stock.

   d. The firm makes its debentures subordinate to its bank debt. What will
      the effect be
      1. On the cost of the debentures?
      2. On the cost of the bank debt?
      3. On the average cost of total debt?
   e. The firm sells income bonds rather than debentures.
   f. The firm must raise $100 million, all of which will be used to
      construct a new plant, and it is debating the sale of first mortgage
      bonds or debentures. If it decides to issue $50 million of each type,
      as opposed to $75 million of first mortgage bonds and $25 million of
      debentures, how will this affect
      1. The cost of debentures?
      2. The cost of mortgage bonds?
      3. The average cost of the $100 million?
   g. The firm puts a call provision on its new issue of bonds.
   h. The firm uses zero coupon bonds rather than coupon bonds.
   i. The firm includes a sinking fund on its new issue of bonds.
   j. The firm's bonds are downgraded from A to BBB.
   k. The firm sells Eurobonds rather than U.S. domestic bonds.

13-2   Rank the following securities from lowest (1) to highest (9) in terms of
       their riskiness for an investor. All securities (except the government
       bond) are for a given firm. If you think two or more securities are
       equally risky, indicate so.

       a. Income bond   _____
       b. Subordinated debentures — noncallable   _____
       c. First mortgage bond — no sinking fund   _____
       d. Common stock   _____
       e. U.S. Treasury bond   _____
       f. First mortgage bond — with sinking fund   _____
       g. Subordinated debentures — callable   _____
       h. Amortized term loan   _____
       i. Nonamortized term loan   _____

13-3   A sinking fund can be set up in one of two ways:
       1. The corporation makes annual payments to the trustee, who invests
          the proceeds in securities (frequently government bonds) and uses
          the accumulated total to retire the bond issue at maturity.
       2. The trustee uses the annual payments to retire a portion of the issue
          each year, either calling a given percentage of the issue by a lottery
          and paying a specified price per bond or buying bonds on the open
          market, whichever is cheaper.

       Discuss the advantages and disadvantages of each procedure from the
       viewpoint of both the firm and the bondholders.

13-4   Draw an SML graph. Put dots on the graph to show (approximately)
       where you think a particular company's (a) common stock and (b)
       bonds would lie. Now put on dots to represent a riskier company's stock
       and bonds.

Self-Test Problems   *(Solutions Appear on Page 502)*

Key terms

ST-1   Define each of the following terms:
a. Funded debt
b. Term loan; bond
c. Mortgage bond
d. Debenture; subordinated debenture
e. Convertible bond; warrant; income bond; putable bond; indexed, or purchasing power, bond
f. Indenture; restrictive covenant
g. Trustee
h. Call provision; sinking fund
i. Zero coupon bond; original issue discount bond (OID)
j. Floating rate bond
k. Junk bond
l. Bond rating; rating agency; investment grade bonds
m. Maturity matching
n. Foreign bond; Eurobond

Sinking fund

ST-2   The Vancouver Development Company has just sold a $100 million, 10-year, 12 percent bond issue. A sinking fund will retire the issue over its life. Sinking fund payments are of equal amounts and will be made *semiannually,* and the proceeds will be used to retire bonds as the payments are made. Bonds can be called at par for sinking fund purposes, or the funds paid into the sinking fund can be used to buy bonds in the open market.
a. How large must each semiannual sinking fund payment be?
b. What will happen, under the conditions of the problem thus far, to the company's debt service requirements per year for this issue over time?
c. Now suppose Vancouver Development set up its sinking fund so that *equal annual amounts,* payable at the end of each year, are paid into a sinking fund trust held by a bank, with the proceeds being used to buy government bonds that pay 9 percent interest. The payments, plus accumulated interest, must total $100 million at the end of 10 years, and the proceeds will be used to retire the bonds at that time. How large must the annual sinking fund payment be now?
d. What are the annual cash requirements for covering bond service costs under the trusteeship arrangement described in Part c? (Note: Interest must be paid on Vancouver's outstanding bonds but not on bonds that have been retired.)
e. What would have to happen to interest rates to cause the company to buy bonds on the open market rather than call them under the original sinking fund plan?

Problems

Loan amortization

13-1   Suppose a firm is setting up an amortized term loan. What are the annual payments for a $10 million loan under the following terms:
a. 9 percent, 5 years?
b. 9 percent, 10 years?

c. 12 percent, 5 years?

d. 12 percent, 10 years?

13-2   Set up an amortization schedule for a $1 million, 3-year, 10 percent loan.

13-3   Six years ago Sirmans Company sold a 20-year bond issue with a 15 percent annual coupon rate and a 10 percent call premium. Today Sirmans called the bonds. The bonds originally were sold at their face value of $1,000. Compute the realized rate of return for investors who purchased the bonds when they were issued and will surrender them today in exchange for the call price.

13-4   In 1936 the Canadian government raised $55 million by issuing bonds at a 3 percent annual rate of interest. Unlike most bonds issued today, which have a specific maturity date, these bonds can remain outstanding forever; they are, in fact, perpetuities.

At the time of issue, the Canadian government stated in the bond indenture that cash redemption was possible at face value ($100) on or after September 1966; in other words, the bonds were callable at par after September 1966. Believing that the bonds would in fact be called, many investors purchased these bonds in 1965 with expectations of receiving $100 in 1966 for each perpetual bond they had. In 1965 the bonds sold for $55, but a rush of buyers drove the price to just below the $100 par value by 1966. Prices fell dramatically, however, when the Canadian government announced that these perpetual bonds were indeed perpetual and would not be paid off. A new, 30-year supply of coupons was sent to each bondholder.

The bonds' market price declined to $42 in December 1966. Because of their severe losses, hundreds of Canadian bondholders formed the Perpetual Bond Association to lobby for face value redemption of the bonds, claiming that the government had reneged on an implied promise to redeem the bonds. Government officials in Ottawa insisted that claims for face value payment were nonsense, for the bonds were and always had been clearly identified as perpetuals. One Ottawa official stated, "Our job is to protect the taxpayer. Why should we pay $55 million for less than $25 million worth of bonds?"

The issue heats up again every few years, and it recently resurfaced once more. Here are some questions relating to the Canadian issue that will test your understanding of bonds in general:

a. Would it make sense for a business firm to issue bonds like the Canadian bonds described here? Would it matter whether the firm was a proprietorship or a corporation?

b. Suppose the U.S. government today sold $100 million each of these four types of bonds: 5-year bonds, 50-year bonds, "regular" perpetuities, and Canadian-type perpetuities. What do you think the relative order of interest rates would be? In other words, rank the bonds from the one with the lowest to the one with the highest rate of interest. Explain your answer.

c. 1. Suppose that because of pressure by the Perpetual Bond Association, you believe that the Canadian government will redeem this particular perpetual bond issue in 5 years. Which course of action would be more advantageous to you if you owned the bonds: (a) sell your bonds today at $42, or (b) wait 5 years and have them redeemed? Assume that similar-risk bonds earn 8 percent today and that interest rates are expected to remain at this level for the next 5 years.

2. If you had the opportunity to invest your money in bonds of similar risk, at what rate of return would you be indifferent to the choice of selling your perpetuals today or having them redeemed in 5 years — that is, what is the expected yield to maturity on the Canadian bonds?

d. Show mathematically the perpetuities' value if they yield 7.15 percent, pay $3 interest annually, and are considered "regular" perpetuities. Show what would happen to the price of the bonds if the going interest rate fell to 2 percent.

e. Are the Canadian bonds more likely to be valued as "regular" perpetuities if the going rate of interest is above or below 3 percent? Why?

f. Do you think the Canadian government would have taken the same action with regard to retiring the bonds if the interest rate had fallen rather than risen after they were issued?

g. Do you think the Canadian government was fair or unfair in its actions? Give the pros and cons, and justify your reason for thinking that one outweighs the other. Would it matter if the bonds had been sold to "sophisticated" as opposed to "naive" purchasers?

Zero coupon bond	**13-5**	Tri-State Farm Equipment needs to raise $3 million for expansion, and its investment bankers have indicated that 5-year zero coupon bonds could be sold at a price of $520 for each $1,000 bond. Tri-State's federal-plus-state tax rate is 40 percent.

a. How many $1,000 par value zero coupon bonds would Tri-State have to sell to raise the needed $3 million?

b. What would be the after-tax yield on the zeros (1) to an investor who is tax exempt and (2) to a taxpayer in the 33 percent marginal tax bracket?

c. What would be the after-tax cost of debt to Tri-State if it decides to issue the zeros?

Long-term debt financing *(Integrative)*	**13-6**	Hospital Development Corporation (HDC) needs $10 million to build a new regional medical center in Birmingham. Once the center is completed and fully operational, which should take about 5 years, HDC will sell it to Southeast Healthcare Providers, a hospital management company operating in Alabama, Florida, and Georgia. HDC plans to raise the $10 million by selling 5-year bonds. Its investment bankers have stated that HDC could sell either regular or zero coupon bonds. Regular coupon bonds would require annual interest payments of 12 percent. Zero coupon bonds would also have to be priced to yield 12 percent. HDC will make the bonds callable after 3 years. If called, the bonds would be redeemed on the anniversary date of the issue at a premium of 6 months' interest for regular bonds or 5 percent over the accrued value on the call date for zero coupon bonds. HDC's federal-plus-state tax rate is 40 percent.

You have been assigned the task of helping HDC decide what type of bonds to issue. In doing the analysis, you should answer the following questions:

a. What is the difference between a bond and a term loan? What are the advantages of a term loan over a bond?

b. Suppose HDC issues bonds and uses the medical center as collateral for the issue. What type of bond would this be? Suppose that instead of using a secured bond, HDC had decided to sell debentures. How would this affect the interest rate that HDC would have to pay on the debt?

c. What is a bond indenture? What are some examples of provisions the bondholders would require HDC to include in its indenture?

d. HDC's bonds will be callable after 3 years. If the bonds were not callable, would the interest rate required be higher or lower than 12 percent? What would be the effect if the bonds were callable immediately? What are the advantages to HDC of making the bonds callable?

e. If HDC's indenture included a sinking fund provision which required HDC to retire one-fifth of the bonds each year, would this provision raise or lower the interest rate required on the bonds? How would the sinking fund operate? Why might HDC's investors require it to use a sinking fund? For this particular issue, would it make sense to include a sinking fund?

f. If HDC were to issue zero coupon bonds, what initial price would cause the zeros to yield 12 percent? How many $1,000 par value zeros would HDC have to sell to raise the needed $10 million? How many regular 12 percent coupon bonds would HDC have to sell?

g. Set up a time line which shows the accrued value of the zeros at the end of Years 1 through 5, along with the annual after-tax cash flows from the zeros (1) to an investor in the 28 percent tax bracket and (2) to HDC.

h. What would be the after-tax yield to maturity on each type of bond to an investor in the 28 percent tax bracket? What would be the after-tax cost of debt to HDC?

i. If interest rates were to fall and HDC called the bonds at the end of Year 3, what would be the after-tax yield to call on each type of bond to an investor in the 28 percent tax bracket?

j. HDC is an A-rated firm. Suppose HDC's bond rating was (1) lowered to triple-B or (2) raised to double-A. What would be the effect of these changes on the interest rate required on HDC's new long-term debt and on the market value of HDC's outstanding debt?

k. What are some of the factors a firm like HDC should consider when deciding whether to issue long-term debt, short-term debt, or equity? Why might long-term debt be HDC's best choice in this situation?

Solution to Self-Test Problems

ST-1   Refer to the marginal glossary definitions or relevant chapter sections to check your responses.

ST-2 a. $100,000,000/10 = $10,000,000$ per year, or $5 million each 6 months. Since the $5 million will be used to retire bonds immediately, no interest will be earned on it.

b. The debt service requirements will decline. As the amount of bonds outstanding declines, so will the interest requirements (amounts given in millions of dollars):

Semiannual Payment Period (1)	Sinking Fund Payment (2)	Outstanding Bonds on Which Interest Is Paid (3)	Interest Payment[a] (4)	Total Bond Service (2) + (4) = (5)
1	$5	$100	$6.0	$11.0
2	5	95	5.7	10.7
3	5	90	5.4	10.4
.	.	.	.	.
.	.	.	.	.
.	.	.	.	.
20	5	5	0.3	5.3

[a]Interest is calculated as $(0.5)(0.12)$(Column 3); for example: interest in Period 2 = $(0.5)(0.12)($95) = 5.7.

The company's total cash bond service requirement will be $21.7 million per year for the first year. The requirement will decline by $0.12($10,000,000) = $1,200,000$ per year for the remaining years.

c. Here we have a 10-year, 9 percent annuity whose compound value is $100 million, and we are seeking the annual payment, PMT, in this equation:

$$\$100,000,000 = \sum_{t=1}^{10} PMT(1 + k)^t$$

$$= PMT(FVIFA_{9\%,10})$$

$$= PMT(15.193)$$

$$PMT = \$6,581,979 = \text{sinking fund payment.}$$

The solution could also be obtained with a financial calculator. Input $FV = 100,000,000$, $n = 10$, and $i = 9$, and press the PMT key to obtain $6,582,009. The difference is due to rounding the FVIFA to 3 decimal places.

d. Annual debt service costs will be $100,000,000(0.12) + $6,582,009 = $18,582,009.

e. If interest rates rose, causing the bond's price to fall, the company would use open market purchases. This would reduce its debt service requirements.

13A   Bankruptcy and Reorganization

In the event of bankruptcy, debtholders have a prior claim over the claims of both common and preferred stockholders to a firm's income and assets. Further, different classes of debtholders are treated differently in the event of bankruptcy. Since bankruptcy is a fairly common occurrence, and since it affects both the bankrupt firm and its customers, suppliers, and creditors, it is important to know who gets what if a firm fails. These topics are discussed in this appendix.[1]

Federal Bankruptcy Laws

Bankruptcy actually begins when a firm is unable to meet scheduled payments on its debt or when the firm's cash flow projections indicate that it will soon be unable to meet payments. As the bankruptcy proceedings go forward, the following central issues arise:

1. Does the firm's inability to meet scheduled payments result from a temporary cash flow problem, or does it represent a permanent problem caused by asset values having fallen below debt obligations?

2. If the problem is a temporary one, then an agreement which stretches out payments may be worked out to give the firm time to recover and to satisfy everyone. However, if basic long-run asset values have truly declined, economic losses will have occurred. In this event, who should bear the losses?

3. Is the company "worth more dead than alive" — that is, would the business be more valuable if it were maintained and continued in operation or if it were liquidated and sold off in pieces?

4. Who should control the firm while it is being liquidated or rehabilitated? Should the existing management be left in control, or should a trustee be placed in charge of operations?

These are the primary issues that are addressed in the federal bankruptcy statutes.

Our bankruptcy laws were first enacted in 1898, modified substantially in 1938, changed again in 1978, and further fine-tuned in 1984. The 1978 act, which provides the basic laws which govern bankruptcy today, was a major revision designed to streamline and expedite proceedings, and it consists of eight odd-numbered chapters, the even-numbered chapters of the earlier act having been deleted. Chapters 1, 3, and 5 of the 1978 act contain general provisions applicable to the other

---

This appendix was coauthored by Arthur L. Herrmann of the University of Hartford.

[1]Much of the current work in this area is based on writings by Edward I. Altman. For a summary of his work, and that of others, see Edward I. Altman, "Bankruptcy and Reorganization," in *Financial Handbook,* Edward I. Altman, ed. (New York: Wiley, 1986), Chapter 19.

chapters; Chapter 7 details the procedures to be followed when liquidating a firm; Chapter 9 deals with financially distressed municipalities; Chapter 11 is the business reorganization chapter; Chapter 13 covers the adjustment of debts for "individuals with regular income"; and Chapter 15 sets up a system of trustees who help administer proceedings under the new act.

Chapters 11 and 7 are the most important ones for financial management purposes. When you read in the paper that Manville Corporation or some other company has "filed for Chapter 11," this means that the company is bankrupt and is trying to reorganize under Chapter 11 of the Act. If a reorganization plan cannot be worked out, then the company will be liquidated as prescribed in Chapter 7 of the Act.

The 1978 act is quite flexible, and it provides a great deal of scope for informal negotiations between a company and its creditors. Under this act, a case is opened by the filing of a petition with a federal district bankruptcy court. The petition may be either voluntary or involuntary — that is, it may be filed either by the firm's management or by its creditors. A committee of unsecured creditors is then appointed by the court to negotiate with management for a reorganization, which may include the restructuring of debt and other claims against the firm. (A "restructuring" could involve extending the maturity of debt, lowering the interest rate on it, reducing the principal amount owed, exchanging common or preferred stock for debt, or some combination of these actions.) A trustee may be appointed by the court if that is deemed to be in the best interests of the creditors and stockholders; otherwise, the existing management will retain control. If no fair and feasible reorganization can be worked out under Chapter 11, the firm will be liquidated under the procedures spelled out in Chapter 7.

Financial Decisions in Bankruptcy

When a business becomes insolvent, a decision must be made whether to dissolve the firm through *liquidation* or to keep it alive through *reorganization*. Fundamentally, this decision depends on a determination of the value of the firm if it is rehabilitated versus the value of its assets if they are sold off individually. The procedure that promises higher returns to the creditors and owners will be adopted. If the decision is made to reorganize the firm, the courts and possibly the SEC will be called upon to determine the fairness and the feasibility of the proposed reorganization plan.

Standard of Fairness. The basic doctrine of *fairness* states that claims must be recognized in the order of their legal and contractual priority. Carrying out this concept of fairness in a reorganization (as opposed to a liquidation) involves the following steps.

1. Future sales must be estimated.

2. Operating conditions must be analyzed so that the future earnings and cash flows can be predicted.

3. A capitalization (or discount) rate to be applied to these future cash flows must be determined.

4. This capitalization rate must then be applied to the estimated cash flows to obtain a present value figure, which is the indicated value for the reorganized company.

5. Provision for distribution of the restructured firm's securities to its claimants must be made.

Standard of Feasibility. The primary test of *feasibility* in a reorganization is whether the fixed charges after reorganization can be covered by cash flows. Adequate coverage generally requires an improvement in operating earnings, a reduction of fixed charges, or both. Among the actions that must generally be taken are the following:

1. Debt maturities are usually lengthened, interest rates may be scaled back, and some debt may be converted into equity.

2. When the quality of management has been substandard, a new team must be given control of the company.

3. If inventories have become obsolete or depleted, they must be replaced.

4. Sometimes the plant and equipment must be modernized before the firm can operate on a competitive basis.

Liquidation Procedures

If a company is too far gone to be reorganized, it must be liquidated. Liquidation should occur if a business is worth more dead than alive, or if the possibility of restoring it to financial health is so remote that the creditors would face a high risk of even greater losses if operations were continued.

Chapter 7 of the Bankruptcy Act is designed to do three things: (1) provide safeguards against the withdrawal of assets by the owners of the bankrupt firm; (2) provide for an equitable distribution of the assets among the creditors; and (3) allow insolvent debtors to discharge all of their obligations and to start over unhampered by a burden of prior debt.

The distribution of assets in a liquidation under Chapter 7 of the Bankruptcy Act is governed by the following priority of claims:

1. *Secured creditors, who are entitled to the proceeds of the sale of specific property pledged for a lien or a mortgage.* If the proceeds do not fully satisfy the secured creditors' claims, the remaining balance is treated as a general creditor claim. (See Item 9.)

2. *Trustee's costs to administer and operate the bankrupt firm.*

3. *Expenses incurred after an involuntary case has begun but before a trustee is appointed.*

4. *Wages due workers if earned within three months prior to the filing of the petition of bankruptcy.* The amount of wages is limited to $2,000 per person.

5. *Claims for unpaid contributions to employee benefit plans that were to have been paid within six months prior to filing.* However, these claims, plus wages in Item 4, are not to exceed the $2,000 per wage earner limit.

Table 13A-1   Pringle, Inc.:
Balance Sheet Just before Liquidation
(Thousands of Dollars)

Current assets	$80,000	Accounts payable	$20,000
Net fixed assets	10,000	Notes payable (to bank)	10,000
		Accrued wages, 1,400 @ $500	700
		U.S. taxes	1,000
		State and local taxes	300
		Current liabilities	$32,000
		First mortgage	$ 6,000
		Second mortgage	1,000
		Subordinated debentures[a]	8,000
		Total long-term debt	$15,000
		Preferred stock	$ 2,000
		Common stock	26,000
		Paid-in capital	4,000
		Retained earnings	11,000
		Total equity	$43,000
Total assets	$90,000	Total liabilities and equity	$90,000

[a]Subordinated to $10 million of notes payable to the bank.

Note: Unfunded pension liabilities are $15 million; this is not reported on the balance sheet.

6. *Unsecured claims for customer deposits, not to exceed a maximum of $900 per individual.*

7. *Taxes due to federal, state, county, and any other government agency.*

8. *Unfunded pension plan liabilities.* Unfunded pension plan liabilities have a claim above that of the general creditors for an amount up to 30 percent of the common and preferred equity; any remaining unfunded pension claims rank with the general creditors.

9. *General, or unsecured, creditors.* Holders of trade credit, unsecured loans, the unsatisfied portion of secured loans, and debenture bonds are classified as *general creditors.* Holders of subordinated debt also fall into this category, but they must turn over required amounts to the holders of senior debt, as discussed later in this section.

10. *Preferred stockholders, who can receive an amount up to the par value of the issue.*

11. *Common stockholders, who receive any remaining funds.*

To illustrate how this priority system works, consider the balance sheet of Pringle, Incorporated, shown in Table 13A-1. The assets have a book value of $90 million. The claims are indicated on the right-hand side of the balance sheet. Note that the debentures are subordinate to the notes payable to banks. Pringle had filed for reorganization under Chapter 11, but since no fair and feasible reorganization could be arranged, the trustee is liquidating the firm under Chapter 7. The firm also has $15 million of unfunded pension liabilities.[2]

The assets as reported in the balance sheet in Table 13A-1 are greatly overstated; they are, in fact, worth about half of the $90 million at which they are carried. The following amounts are realized on liquidation:

Proceeds from sale of current assets	$41,950,000
Proceeds from sale of fixed assets	5,000,000
Total receipts	$46,950,000

The allocation of available funds is shown in Table 13A-2. The holders of the first mortgage bonds receive the $5 million of net proceeds from the sale of fixed assets. Note that a $1 million unsatisfied claim of the first mortgage holders remains; this claim is added to those of the other general creditors. Next come the fees and expenses of administration, which are typically about 20 percent of gross proceeds; in this example, they are assumed to be $6 million. Next in priority are wages due workers, which total $700,000; taxes due, which amount to $1.3 million; and unfunded pension liabilities of up to 30 percent of the common plus preferred equity, or $12.9 million. Thus far, the total of claims paid from the $46.95 million is $25.90 million, leaving $21.05 million for the general creditors.

The claims of the general creditors total $42.1 million. Since $21.05 million is available, claimants will initially be allocated 50 percent of their claims, as shown in Column 2 of Table 13A-2, before the subordination adjustment. This adjustment requires that the holders of subordinated debentures turn over to the holders of notes payable all amounts received until the notes are satisfied. In this situation, the claim of the notes payable is $10 million, but only $5 million is available; the deficiency is therefore $5 million. After transfer of $4 million from the subordinated debentures, there remains a deficiency of $1 million on the notes. This amount will remain unsatisfied.

---

[2]Under the federal statutes which regulate pension funds, corporations are required to estimate the amount of money needed to provide for the pensions which have been promised to their employees. This determination is made by professional actuaries, taking into account when employees will retire, how long they are likely to live, and the rate of return that can be earned on pension fund assets. If the assets currently in the pension fund are deemed sufficient to make all required payments, the plan is said to be *fully funded*. If assets in the plan are less than the present value of expected future payments, an *unfunded liability* exists. Under federal laws, companies are given up to 30 years to fund any unfunded liabilities. (Note that if a company were fully funded in 1988 but then agreed, in 1989, to double pension benefits, this would immediately create a large unfunded liability, and it would need time to make the adjustment. Otherwise, it would be difficult for companies to agree to increase pension benefits.)

Unfunded pension liabilities, including medical benefits to retirees, represent a time bomb ticking in the bowels of many companies. If a company has a relatively old labor force, and if it has promised them substantial retirement benefits but has not set aside assets in a funded pension fund to cover these benefits, it could experience severe trouble in the future. These unfunded pension benefits could even drive the company into bankruptcy, at which point the pension plan would be subject to the bankruptcy laws.

Table 13A-2   Pringle, Inc.:
Order of Priority of Claims

Distribution of Proceeds on Liquidation

1. Proceeds from sale of assets		$46,950,000
2. First mortgage, paid from sale of fixed assets	$5,000,000	
3. Fees and expenses of administration of bankruptcy	6,000,000	
4. Wages due workers earned within three months prior to filing of bankruptcy petition	700,000	
5. Taxes	1,300,000	
6. Unfunded pension liabilities	12,900,000[a]	25,900,000
7. Available to general creditors		$21,050,000

Distribution to General Creditors

Claims of General Creditors	Claim[b] (1)	Application of 50 Percent[c] (2)	After Subordination Adjustment[d] (3)	Percentage of Original Claims Received[e] (4)
Unsatisfied portion of first mortgage	$ 1,000,000	$ 500,000	$ 500,000	92%
Unsatisfied portion of second mortgage	1,000,000	500,000	500,000	50
Notes payable	10,000,000	5,000,000	9,000,000	90
Accounts payable	20,000,000	10,000,000	10,000,000	50
Subordinated debentures	8,000,000	4,000,000	0	0
Pension plan	2,100,000	1,050,000	1,050,000	93
	$42,100,000	$21,050,000	$21,050,000	

[a]Unfunded pension liabilities are $15,000,000, and common and preferred equity total $43,000,000. Unfunded pension liabilities have a prior claim of up to 30 percent of the equity, or $12,900,000, with the remainder, $2,100,000, being treated as a general creditor claim.

[b]Column 1 is the claim of each class of general creditor. Total claims equal $42.1 million.

[c]From Line 7 in the upper section of the table, we see that $21.05 million is available for general creditors. This sum, divided by the $42.1 million of claims, indicates that general creditors will initially receive 50 percent of their claims; this is shown in Column 2.

[d]The debentures are subordinated to the notes payable, so $4 million is reallocated from debentures to notes payable in Column 3.

[e]Column 4 shows the results of dividing the amount in Column 3 by the original claim amount given in Column 1, except for the first mortgage, for which the $5 million received from the sale of fixed assets is included, and the pension plan, for which the $12.9 million is included.

Note that 90 percent of the bank claim and 93 percent of the unfunded pension fund claims are satisfied, whereas a maximum of 50 percent of other unsecured claims will be satisfied. These figures illustrate the usefulness of the subordination provision to the security to which the subordination is made. Because no other funds remain, the claims of the holders of preferred and common stock are completely wiped out. Studies of bankruptcy liquidations indicate that unsecured creditors receive on the average about 15 cents on the dollar, whereas common stockholders generally receive nothing.

Problems

13A-1 The Florida Tile Company has the following balance sheet:

Current assets	$4,200	Accounts payable	$ 900
Fixed assets	2,250	Notes payable (to bank)	450
		Accrued taxes	150
		Accrued wages	150
		Total current liabilities	$1,650
		First mortgage bonds	$ 750
		Second mortgage bonds	750
		Total mortgage bonds	$1,500
		Subordinated debentures	900
		Total debt	$4,050
		Preferred stock	300
		Common stock	2,100
Total assets	$6,450	Total liabilities and equity	$6,450

The debentures are subordinated only to the notes payable. Suppose Florida Tile goes bankrupt and is liquidated, with $1,500 being received from the sale of the fixed assets, which were pledged as security for the first and second mortgage bonds, and $2,400 received from the sale of current assets. The trustee's costs total $400. How much will each class of investors receive?

13A-2 Southern Textiles, Inc., has the following balance sheet:

Current assets	$1,500,000	Notes payable	$ 600,000
Fixed assets	1,500,000	Accounts payable	300,000
		Subordinated debentures	600,000
		Total debt	$1,500,000
		Common equity	1,500,000
Total assets	$3,000,000	Total liabilities and equity	$3,000,000

The trustee's costs total $225,000, and Southern has no accrued taxes or wages. The debentures are subordinated only to the bank debt. If the firm goes bankrupt, how much will each class of investors receive under each of the following conditions?

a. A total of $2 million is received from sale of the assets.

b. A total of $1.5 million is received from sale of the assets.

Computer-Related Problems

(Work the problems in this section only if you are using the computer problem diskette.)

C13A-1 Use the computerized model for Problem C13A-1 in the file C13A to solve this problem.

a. Rework Problem 13A-1, assuming that $800 is received from the sale of fixed assets and $1,700 from the sale of current assets.

b. Rework Problem 13A-1, assuming that $1,400 is received from the sale of fixed assets and $3,100 from the sale of current assets.

Bankruptcy distributions   **C13A-2** Use the computerized model for Problem C13A-2 in the file C13A to solve this problem.

    a. Rework Problem 13A-2, assuming that $1 million is received from the sale of assets.

    b. Rework Problem 13A-2, assuming that $500,000 is received from the sale of assets.

    c. What is the significance of these findings for the banks, the trade creditors, the debenture holders, and the common stockholders?

13B   Refunding Operations

A great deal of long-term debt was sold during the period 1979–1984 at interest rates going up to 18 percent for double-A companies. Because the period of call protection on much of this debt is, or soon will be, ending, many companies are analyzing the pros and cons of bond refundings. Refunding decisions actually involve two separate questions: (1) Is it profitable to call an outstanding issue in the current period and replace it with a new issue; and (2) even if refunding is currently profitable, would the expected value of the firm be increased even more if the refunding were postponed to a later date? We consider both questions in this appendix.

    Note that the decision to refund a security is analyzed in much the same way as a capital budgeting expenditure. The costs of refunding (the investment outlays) are (1) the call premium paid for the privilege of calling the old issue, (2) the tax savings from writing off the unexpensed flotation costs on the old issue, and (3) the net interest that must be paid while both issues are outstanding (the new issue is often sold one month before the refunding to insure that the funds will be available). The annual cash flows, in a capital budgeting sense, are the interest payments that are saved each year plus the net tax savings which the firm receives for amortizing the flotation expenses. For example, if the interest expense on the old issue is $1,000,000 whereas that on the new issue is $700,000, the $300,000 reduction in interest savings constitutes an annual benefit. The annual cash flows will be somewhat higher, however, because of the tax savings associated with the flotation expenses.

    The net present value method is used to analyze the advantages of refunding: the future cash flows are discounted back to the present, and then this discounted value is compared with the cash outlays associated with the refunding. The firm should refund the bond if the present value of the savings exceeds the cost — that is, if the NPV of the refunding operation is positive.

In the discounting process, the after-tax cost of the new debt, $k_{d,}$ should be used as the discount rate. The reason is that there is relatively little risk to the savings — cash flows in a refunding are known with relative certainty, which is quite unlike the situation with cash flows in most capital budgeting decisions.

The easiest way to examine the refunding decision is through an example. Perkins Publishing Company has a $60 million bond issue outstanding that has a 15 percent coupon interest rate and 20 years remaining to maturity. This issue, which was sold 5 years ago, had flotation costs of $3 million that the firm has been amortizing on a straight line basis over the 25-year original life of the issue. The bond has a call provision, which makes it possible for the company to retire the issue at this time by calling the bonds in at a 10 percent call premium. Investment bankers have assured the company that it could sell an additional $60 million to $70 million worth of new 20-year bonds at an interest rate of 12 percent. To insure that the funds required to pay off the old debt will be available, the new bonds will be sold one month before the old issue is called, so for one month, interest will have to be paid on two issues. Current short-term interest rates are 11 percent. Predictions are that long-term interest rates are unlikely to fall below 12 percent.[1] Flotation costs on a new refunding issue will amount to $2,650,000. Perkin's marginal tax rate is 40 percent. Should the company refund the $60 million of 15 percent bonds?

The following steps outline the decision process; they are summarized in worksheet form in Table 13B-1.

Step 1. Determine the investment outlay required to refund the issue.

a.   *Call premium:*

$$\text{Before tax: } 0.10(\$60,000,000) = \$6,000,000.$$

$$\text{After tax: } \$6,000,000(1 - T) = \$6,000,000(0.6)$$

$$= \$3,600,000.$$

Although Perkins must expend $6 million on the call premium, this is a deductible expense in the year the call is made. Because the company is in the 40 percent tax bracket, it saves $2.4 million in taxes; therefore, the after-tax cost of the call is only $3.6 million. This amount is shown on Line 1 of Table 13B-1.

b.   *Flotation costs on new issue:*
Flotation costs on the new issue will be $2,650,000. This is shown on Line 2 of Table 13B-1.

c.   *Flotation costs on old issue:*
The old issue has an unamortized flotation cost of $(20/25)(\$3,000,000) = \$2,400,000$ at this time. If the issue is retired, the unamortized flotation cost may be recognized immediately as an expense, thus creating an after-tax savings of $\$2,400,000(T) = \$960,000$. Because this is a cash inflow, it is shown as a negative outflow on Line 3 of Table 13B-1.

---

[1] The firm's management has estimated that interest rates will probably remain at their present level of 12 percent or else rise; there is only a 25 percent probability that they will fall further.

Table 13B-1   Worksheet for the Bond Refunding Decision

	Amount before Tax	Amount after Tax
Cost of Refunding at t = 0		
1. Call premium on old bond	$ 6,000,000	$3,600,000
2. Flotation costs on new issue	2,650,000	2,650,000
3. Immediate tax savings on old flotation cost expense	(2,400,000)	(960,000)
4. Extra interest on old issue	750,000	450,000
5. Interest on short-term investment	(550,000)	(330,000)
6. Total after-tax investment		$ 5,410,000
Savings over Life of New Issue: t = 1 to 20		
7. Interest on old bond	$ 9,000,000	$ 5,400,000
8. Interest on new bond	(7,200,000)	(4,320,000)
9. Flotation costs, new	132,500	53,000
10. Flotation costs, old	(120,000)	(48,000)
11. Net savings of interest	$ 1,812,500	$ 1,085,000

Refunding NPV

12. NPV = PV of cash flows − Investment

$$= \$1,085,000(10.4313) - \$5,410,000$$

$$= \$11,317,961 - \$5,410,000$$

$$= \$5,907,961.$$

d. *Additional interest:*

One month's "extra" interest on the old issue, after taxes, costs $450,000:

$$(\text{Dollar amount})(1/12 \text{ of } 15\%)(1 - T) = \text{Interest cost}$$

$$(\$60,000,000)(0.0125)(0.6) = \$450,000.$$

However, the proceeds from the new issue can be invested in short-term securities for one month. Thus, $60 million invested at a rate of 11 percent will return $330,000 in after-tax interest:

$$(\$60,000,000)(1/12 \text{ of } 11\%)(1 - T) = \text{Interest earned}$$

$$(\$60,000,000)(0.009167)(0.6) = \$330,000.$$

The net after-tax additional interest cost is thus $120,000:

Interest paid on old issue	$450,000
Interest earned on short-term securities	(330,000)
Net additional interest	$120,000

These figures are reflected on Lines 4 and 5 of Table 13B-1.

e. *Total after-tax investment:*
    The total investment outlay required to refund the bond issue, which will be
    financed by debt, is thus $5,410,000.[2]

Call premium	$3,600,000
Flotation costs, new	2,650,000
Flotation costs, old, tax savings	(960,000)
Net additional interest	120,000
Total investment	$5,410,000

This total is shown on Line 6 of Table 13B-1.

Step 2. Calculate the PV of the annual cash flow savings.

a. *Interest on old bond, after tax:*
    The annual after-tax interest on the old issue is $5.4 million:

    $$(\$60,000,000)(0.15)(0.6) = \$5,400,000.$$

    This is shown on Line 7 of Table 13B-1.

b. *Interest on new bond, after tax:*
    The new issue has an annual after-tax cost of $4,320,000:

    $$(\$60,000,000)(0.12)(0.6) = \$4,320,000.$$

    This is shown on Line 8 as a negative saving.

c. *Tax savings on flotation costs on the new issue:*
    For tax purposes, flotation costs must be amortized over the life of the new
    bond, or for 20 years. Therefore, the annual tax deduction is

    $$\frac{\$2,650,000}{20} = \$132,500.$$

    Because Perkins is in the 40 percent tax bracket, it has a tax savings of
    $132,500(0.4) = $53,000 a year for 20 years. This is an annuity of $53,000 for
    20 years, and it is shown on Line 9.

d. *Tax benefits lost on flotation costs on the old issue:*
    The firm, however, will no longer receive a tax deduction of $120,000 a year
    for 20 years, so it loses an after-tax benefit of $48,000 a year. This is shown
    on Line 10.

e. *Net annual cash flows:*
    Thus, the net annual after-tax cash flow is $1,085,000:

---

[2]The investment outlay (in this case, $5,410,000) is usually obtained by increasing the amount of
the new bond issue. In the example given, the new issue would be $65,410,000. However, the
interest on the additional debt *should not* be deducted at Step 2, because the $5,410,000 itself
will be deducted at Step 3. If additional interest on the $5,410,000 were deducted at Step 2,
interest would, in effect, be deducted twice. The situation here is exactly like that in regular
capital budgeting decisions. Even though some debt may be used to finance a project, interest on
that debt is not subtracted when developing the annual cash flows. Rather, the annual cash flows
are *discounted* by the project's cost of capital.

Interest on old bonds, after tax	$5,400,000
Interest on new bonds, after tax	(4,320,000)
Tax savings, flotation costs, new	53,000
Tax benefits lost, flotation costs, old	(48,000)
Annual net savings	$1,085,000

This is shown on Line 11.

f.   *PV of annual savings:*
  The PV of $1,085,000 a year for 20 years is $11,317,961:[3]

$$PV = \$1,085,000(PVIFA_{7.2\%,20})$$

$$= \$1,085,000(10.4313) = \$11,317,961.$$

This value is used on Line 12 to find the NPV of the refunding operation.

Step 3. Determine the NPV of the refunding.

PV of annual savings	$11,317,961
Net investment	(5,410,000)
NPV from refunding	$ 5,907,961

Because the net present value of the refunding is positive, it will be profitable to refund the old bond issue.

Several other points should be made. First, because the cash flows are based on differences between contractual obligations, their risk is the same as that of the underlying obligations. Therefore, the present values of the cash flows should be found by discounting at the firm's least risky rate — its after-tax cost of marginal debt. Second, since the refunding operation is advantageous to the firm, it must be disadvantageous to bondholders; they must give up their 15 percent bonds and reinvest in new ones yielding 12 percent. This points out the danger of the call provision to bondholders, and it also explains why bonds without a call feature command higher prices than callable bonds. Third, although it is not emphasized in the example, we assumed that the firm raises the investment required to under-take the refunding operation (the $5,410,000 shown on Line 6 of Table 13B-1) as debt. This should be feasible, because the refunding operation will improve the interest coverage ratio, even though a larger amount of debt is outstanding.[4] Fourth, we set up our example in such a way that the new issue had the same maturity as the remaining life of the old one. Often the old bonds have only a

---

[3]The PVIFA for 7.2 percent over 20 years is 10.4313, found with a financial calculator.

[4]See Ahron R. Ofer and Robert A. Taggart, Jr., "Bond Refunding: A Clarifying Analysis," *Journal of Finance,* March 1977, 21–30, for a discussion of how the method of financing the refunding affects the analysis. Ofer and Taggart prove that if the refunding investment outlay is to be raised as common equity, the before-tax cost of debt is the proper discount rate, whereas if these funds are to be raised as debt, the after-tax cost of debt is the proper discount rate. Since a profitable refunding will virtually always raise the firm's debt-carrying capacity (because total interest charges after the refunding will be lower than before it), it is more logical to use debt than either equity or a combination of debt and equity to finance the operation. Therefore, firms generally do use additional debt to finance refunding operations, and we assume debt financing for the costs of refunding and discount at the after-tax cost of debt.

relatively short time to maturity (say, 5 to 10 years), whereas the new bonds have a much longer maturity (say, 25 to 30 years). In such a situation, the analysis should be set up similarly to a replacement chain analysis in capital budgeting.[5] Fifth, refunding decisions are well suited for analysis with a computer spreadsheet such as *Lotus 1-2-3*. The spreadsheet is simple to set up, and once it is, it is easy to vary the assumptions (especially the assumption about the interest rate on the refunding issue) and to see how such changes affect the NPV. See Problem C13B-1 for an example.

One final point should be addressed: Although our analysis shows that the refunding would increase the value of the firm, would refunding *at this time* truly maximize the firm's expected value? If interest rates continue to fall, the company might be better off waiting, for this could increase the NPV of the refunding operation even more. The mechanics of calculating the NPV of a refunding are easy, but the decision of *when* to refund is not a simple one at all, because it requires a forecast of future interest rates. Thus, the final decision on refunding now versus waiting for a possibly more favorable time is a judgmental decision.

Problems

Refunding analysis

13B-1 Copeland Can Corporation (CCC) is considering whether or not to refund a $60 million, 14 percent coupon, 30-year bond issue that was sold 5 years ago. It is amortizing $3 million of flotation costs on the 14 percent bonds over the issue's 30-year life. CCC's investment bankers have indicated that the company could sell a new 25-year issue at an interest rate of 12 percent in today's market. Neither they nor CCC's management anticipates that interest rates will fall below 12 percent any time soon, but there is a chance that rates will increase.

A call premium of 14 percent would be required to retire the old bonds, and flotation costs on the new issue would amount to $3 million. CCC's marginal federal-plus-state tax rate is 40 percent. The new bonds would be issued one month before the old bonds are called, with the proceeds being invested in short-term government securities returning 10 percent annually during the interim period.

a. Perform a complete bond refunding analysis. What is the bond refunding's NPV?

b. What factors would influence CCC's decision to refund now rather than later?

Bond refunding
(Integrative)

13B-2 Chuck Penrose, financial manager of Tidewater Gas and Electric (TG&E), has been asked by his boss to review TG&E's outstanding debt issues for possible bond refunding. Five years ago, TG&E issued $50,000,000 of 12 percent, 30-year debt. The issue, with semiannual coupons, is currently callable at a premium of 10 percent, or $100 for each $1,000 par value bond. Flotation costs on this issue were 3 percent, or $1,500,000.

Penrose believes that TG&E could issue 25-year debt today with a coupon rate of 10 percent. The firm has placed many issues in the

---

[5]For a discussion of bond refunding where the old and new bonds have different lives, see Chapter 13, "Bond Refunding Models," of *Finance with Lotus 1-2-3* (The Dryden Press, 1988), by E. F. Brigham, D. A. Aberwald, and S. E. Ball.

capital markets during the last 10 years, and its debt flotation costs are currently estimated to be 2 percent of the issue's value. TG&E's tax rate is 40 percent.

Help Penrose conduct the refunding analysis by answering the following questions:

a. What is the total dollar call premium required to call the old issue? Is it tax deductible? What is the net after-tax cost of the call?

b. What is the dollar flotation cost on the new issue? Is it immediately tax deductible? What is the after-tax flotation cost?

c. What amount of old-issue flotation costs have not been expensed? Can these deferred costs be expensed immediately if the old issue is refunded? What is the value of the tax savings?

d. What is the net after-tax cash outlay required to refund the old issue?

e. What is the semiannual tax savings which arises from amortizing the flotation costs on the new issue? What is the forgone semiannual tax savings on the old-issue flotation costs?

f. What is the semiannual after-tax interest savings that would result from the refunding?

g. Thus far, Penrose has identified three future cash flows: (1) new-issue flotation cost tax savings; (2) old-issue flotation cost tax savings which are lost if refunding occurs; and (3) after-tax interest savings. What is the sum of these three semiannual cash flows? What is the appropriate discount rate to apply to these future cash flows? What is the present value of these cash flows?

h. What is the NPV of refunding? Should TG&E refund now or wait until later?

Computer-Related Problem

(Work this problem only if you are using the computer problem diskette.)

Refunding analysis

C13B-1 Use the computerized model for Problem C13B-1 in the file C13B to solve this problem.

a. Refer back to Problem 13B-1. Determine the interest rate on new bonds at which CCC would be indifferent to refunding the bond issue. (Hint: You will need to perform this analysis using different rates of interest on new bonds until you find the one which causes the NPV to be zero.)

b. How would the refunding decision be affected if the corporate tax rate were lowered from 40 percent to 30 percent, assuming the rate on new bonds was 12 percent? At what interest rate on new bonds would CCC be indifferent to refunding at a 30 percent corporate tax rate?

14

Hybrid Financing: Preferred Stock, Leasing, and Option Securities

USING HYBRID FINANCING TO MEET DIFFERENT FIRMS' NEEDS: COMPAQ, APPLE, AND DATAPOINT

Apple Computer and Compaq Computer are two stars of the stock market; anyone who has purchased and held the shares of either company has done quite well. The primary reason for both companies' success has been their abilities to identify the potential demand for a new product and then to design, produce, and market that product more effectively than their competitors. Still, financial skills also have been important to both companies, for both have needed large amounts of capital to buy the assets necessary for low-cost, profitable operations. Compaq decided to use convertible debentures, and, to date, it has raised $350 million of long-term bonds with an average coupon rate of less than 6 percent as compared with about 12 percent had it used pure, nonconvertible debt. Thus, Compaq was able to hold its interest expenses down during its critical early years. Apple considered convertibles but decided instead to employ another type of financing; rather than using its money to buy all of its assets, Apple arranged to have others buy assets, which Apple then leased. In 1988, Apple was making lease payments of almost $50 million per year on assets with a value of close to $500 million.

Datapoint Corporation, another computer company, has been experiencing difficulties in recent years. Its stock price had soared from $1.25 in 1974

519

to $67.50 in 1981, but then earnings tumbled and the stock price has dropped to $4.50 in 1988. Datapoint badly needed new capital to shore up its operations. In its heyday, it had issued convertibles, and it had also used leasing, but those sources of funds dried up. The market was unwilling to buy more of its common stock, and because the company had been running large losses, the interest tax shelter of debt did it no good. Investment bankers suggested, and Datapoint used, preferred stock.

In this chapter, we will see how companies like Compaq, Apple, and Datapoint analyze such hybrid securities, and how the use of these securities can benefit both firms and investors.

IN the two preceding chapters, we examined the use of common stock and various types of debt. In this chapter, we examine three other types of long-term capital which financial managers can use to lower their firms' costs of capital: *preferred stock,* which is a hybrid security that represents a cross between debt and equity; *leasing,* which is similar to a loan and which is used by financial managers as an alternative to borrowing to purchase fixed assets; and *option-type securities,* particularly warrants and convertibles, which are attractive to investors because they allow debtholders to acquire common stock at bargain prices and thus to share in the capital gains if a company is especially successful.[1]

PREFERRED STOCK

Preferred stock is a *hybrid* — it is similar to bonds in some respects and to common stock in others. The hybrid nature of preferred stock becomes apparent when we try to classify it in relation to bonds and common stock. Like bonds, preferred stock has a par value. Preferred dividends are also similar to interest payments in that they are fixed in amount and generally must be paid before common stock dividends can be paid. However, if the preferred dividend is not earned, the directors can omit (or "pass") it without throwing the company into bankruptcy. So, although preferred stock has a fixed payment like bonds, a failure to make this payment will not lead to bankruptcy.

Accountants classify preferred stock as equity and report it in the equity portion of the balance sheet under the title "Preferred Stock" or "Preferred

---

[1]Even though all three of the topics covered in this chapter are important, time pressures may preclude a class's detailed coverage of all of them. Accordingly, the chapter is written in a modular form so as to permit instructors to cover one, two, or all three topics. When we are under time pressure in the basic course at Florida, we require students to read the entire chapter but to know for exam purposes only how to answer the end-of-chapter questions, not how to work the problems.

Equity." However, financial analysts sometimes treat preferred stock as debt and sometimes treat it as equity, depending on the type of analysis being made. If the analysis is being made by a common stockholder, the key consideration is the fact that the preferred dividend is a fixed charge which must be paid ahead of common stock dividends, so from the common stockholder's point of view, preferred stock is similar to debt. Suppose, however, that the analysis is being made by a bondholder studying the firm's vulnerability to failure in the event of a decline in sales and income. If the firm's income declines, the debtholders have a prior claim to the available income ahead of preferred stockholders, and if the firm fails, debtholders have a prior claim to assets when the firm is liquidated. Thus, to a bondholder, preferred stock is similar to common equity.

From management's perspective, preferred lies between debt and common equity. Since the dividends on preferred stock are not a fixed charge in the sense that failure to pay them represents a default on an obligation, preferred stock is safer to use than debt. At the same time, if the firm is highly successful, the common stockholders will not have to share that success with the preferred stockholders, because preferred dividends are fixed. Remember, however, that the preferred stockholders do have a higher priority claim than the common stockholders. We see, then, that preferred stock has some of the characteristics of debt and some of the characteristics of common stock, and it is used in situations in which conditions are such that neither debt nor common stock is entirely appropriate.

Major Provisions of Preferred Stock Issues

Preferred stock has a number of features, the most important of which are discussed in the following sections.

Priority to Assets and Earnings. Preferred stockholders have priority over common stockholders with regard to earnings and assets. Thus, dividends must be paid on preferred stock before they can be paid on the common stock, and in the event of bankruptcy, the claims of the preferred shareholders must be satisfied before the common stockholders receive anything. To reinforce these features, most preferred stocks have coverage requirements similar to those on bonds. These restrictions limit the amount of preferred stock a company can use, and they also require the balance sheet to show a minimum level of retained earnings before common dividends can be paid.

Par Value. Unlike common stock, preferred stock always has a par value (or its equivalent under some other name), and this value is important. First, the par value establishes the amount due the preferred stockholders in the event of liquidation. Second, the preferred dividend is frequently stated as a percentage of the par value. For example, Pennsylvania Power & Light's preferred stock has a par value of $100 and a stated dividend of 8.6 percent of par. The same results would, of course, be produced if the PP&L preferred stock simply called for an annual dividend of $8.60.

cumulative dividends
A protective feature on preferred stock that requires past preferred dividends to be paid before any common dividends can be paid.

Cumulative Dividends. Most preferred stock provides for **cumulative dividends**; that is, all preferred dividends in arrears must be paid before common dividends can be paid. The cumulative feature is a protective device, for if the preferred stock dividends were not cumulative, a firm could avoid paying preferred and common stock dividends for, say, 10 years and thus plow back all of its earnings, then pay a huge common stock dividend but pay only the stipulated annual dividend to the preferred stockholders. Obviously, such an action would effectively void the preferred position the preferred stockholders are supposed to have. The cumulative feature helps prevent such abuses.[2]

Convertibility. Approximately 40 percent of the preferred stock that has been issued in recent years is convertible into common stock. For example, each share of Enron's $10.50 Class J preferred stock can be converted into 3.413 shares of its common stock at the option of the preferred shareholders. (Convertibility is discussed in detail later in this chapter.)

Other Provisions. Some other provisions one occasionally encounters in preferred stocks include the following:

1. *Voting rights.* Preferred stockholders are generally given the right to vote for directors if the company has not paid the preferred dividend for a specified period, such as ten quarters. This feature motivates management to make every effort to pay preferred dividends.

2. *Participating.* A rare type of preferred stock is one that participates with the common stock in sharing the firm's earnings. Participating preferred stocks generally work as follows: (a) the stated preferred dividend is paid — for example, $5 a share; (b) the common stock is then entitled to a dividend in an amount equal to the preferred dividend; (c) if the common dividend is raised, say to $5.50, the preferred dividend must likewise be raised to $5.50.

3. *Sinking fund.* In the past (before the mid-1970s), few preferred issues had sinking funds. Today, however, most newly issued preferred stocks have a sinking fund which calls for the purchase and retirement of a given percentage of the preferred stock each year. If the amount is 2 percent, which is used frequently, the preferred issue will have an average life of 25 years and a maximum life of 50 years.

4. *Maturity.* Before the mid-1970s, most preferred stock was perpetual — it had no maturity and never needed to be paid off. However, today most new preferred has a sinking fund and thus an effective maturity date.

5. *Call provision.* A call provision gives the issuing corporation the right to call in the preferred stock for redemption. As in the case of bonds, call

---

[2]Note, however, that compounding is absent in most cumulative plans—in other words, the arrearages themselves earn no return. Also, many preferred issues have a limited cumulative feature; for example, arrearages might accumulate for only three years.

provisions generally state that the company must pay an amount greater than the par value of the preferred stock, the additional sum being termed a **call premium**. For example, Trivoli Corporation's 12 percent, $100 par value preferred stock, issued in 1988, is noncallable for 10 years, but it may be called at a price of $112 after 1998.

call premium
The amount in excess of par value that a company must pay when it calls a security.

Evaluation of Preferred Stock

No tax shelter / But interest expense is.

There are both advantages and disadvantages to financing with preferred stock. They are discussed in the following sections.

Issuer's Viewpoint. By using preferred stock, a firm can fix its financial costs and thus keep more of the potential future profits for its existing set of common stockholders, yet avoid the danger of bankruptcy if earnings are too low to meet these fixed charges. Also, by selling preferred rather than common stock, the firm avoids sharing control with new investors.

However, preferred does have a major disadvantage from the issuer's standpoint: It has a higher after-tax cost of capital than debt. The reason for this higher cost is taxes. Preferred dividends are not deductible as a tax expense, whereas interest expense is deductible.[3] This makes the component cost of preferred stock much greater than that of bonds; the after-tax cost of debt is approximately two-thirds of the stated coupon rate for profitable firms, whereas the cost of preferred stock is the full percentage amount of the preferred dividend. Of course, the deductibility differential is most important for issuers that are in relatively high tax brackets. If a company pays little or no taxes because it is unprofitable or because it has a great deal of accelerated depreciation, the deductibility of interest does not make much difference. Thus, the lower a company's tax bracket, the more likely it is to issue preferred stock. *TEST — if Δ then what??*

Investor's Viewpoint. In designing securities, the financial manager must consider the investor's point of view. It is sometimes asserted that preferred stock

---

[3]One would think that a given firm's preferred stock would carry a higher coupon rate than its bonds because of the preferred's greater risk from the holder's viewpoint. However, the fact that 70 percent of preferred dividends received by corporate owners are exempt from income taxes has made preferred stock very attractive to corporate investors. Therefore, most preferred stock is owned by corporations, and in recent years high-grade preferreds, on average, have sold on a lower-yield basis than high-grade bonds. As an example, Alabama Power recently sold a preferred issue yielding 11 percent to investors. On the day the preferred was issued, Alabama Power's bonds yielded 13 percent, or two percentage points more than the preferred. The tax treatment accounted for this differential; the *after-tax* yield to a corporate investor was greater on the preferred stock than on the bonds. For a corporate investor in the 40 percent tax bracket,

$$\text{After-tax yield on bonds} = \text{Yield} - \text{Yield}(T)$$
$$= \text{Yield}(1 - T) = 13\%(0.6) = 7.8\%.$$
$$\text{After-tax yield on preferred} = \text{Yield} - \text{Yield}(1 - \text{Exclusion})(T)$$
$$= 11\% - 11\%(0.3)(0.4)$$
$$= 11\%(1 - 0.12) = 11\%(0.88) = 9.68\%.$$

has so many disadvantages to both the issuer and the investor that it should never be issued. Nevertheless, preferred stock is issued in substantial amounts. It provides investors with a steadier and more assured income than common stock, and it has a preference over common in the event of liquidation. In addition, 70 percent of the preferred dividends received by corporations are not taxable. For this reason, most preferred stock is owned by corporations.

The principal disadvantage of preferred stock from an investor's standpoint is that although preferred stockholders bear some of the ownership risks, their returns are limited. Other disadvantages are that (1) preferred stockholders have no legally enforceable right to dividends, even if a company earns a profit, and (2) for individual as opposed to corporate investors, after-tax bond yields are generally higher than those of even riskier preferred stock.

Recent Trends

Because preferred dividends are not tax deductible, many companies have retired their preferred stocks and replaced them with debentures or subordinated debentures. However, as the following examples illustrate, preferred is still used to raise long-term capital when conditions are such that neither common stock nor long-term debt can be issued on reasonable terms and a hybrid such as preferred is useful.

1. Chrysler's issue of preferred stock with warrants in the late 1970s proved a successful means of raising capital in the face of adverse circumstances. Because of its losses, Chrysler's common stock was depressed and very much out of favor. Investors were so worried about the company's ability to survive that they were unwilling to make additional commitments without receiving some sort of senior position. Therefore, common stock was ruled out. Chrysler had already borrowed to the hilt, and it could not obtain any more debt without first building its equity base (and preferred is equity from the bondholders' viewpoint). Various incentives were offered to the brokers who handled the preferred issue, and a relatively high yield was set. As a result, the issue was so successful that its size was raised from $150 to $200 million while the underwriting was underway. Chrysler got the money it needed, and that money helped the company regain profitability. Chrysler's common stock is currently priced at $25, up from about $5 when the preferred was issued. The preferred stock helped the company survive and achieve that gain in the common stock price.

2. Utility companies often use preferred stock to bolster the equity component of their capital structures. These companies are capital intensive, and they make heavy use of debt financing, but lenders and rating agencies require minimum equity ratios as a condition for further sales of bonds. Also, the utilities have made very heavy investments in fixed assets and thus have high depreciation charges, which has held

down their effective tax rates and thus has lowered the tax disadvantage of preferred stock in relation to debt.

3. In recent years there has also been a pronounced movement toward convertible preferred, which is used often in connection with mergers. For example, when Belco Petroleum was negotiating its acquisition by Enron, it was pointed out that if the buyout were for cash, Belco's stockholders (one of whom owned about 40 percent of the stock and thus could block the merger) would be required to immediately pay huge capital gains taxes. However, under U.S. tax laws, if preferred stock is exchanged, this constitutes a tax-free exchange of securities. Thus, Belco's stockholders could obtain a fixed-income security yet postpone the payment of taxes on their capital gains.

    Enron actually offered a choice of straight or convertible preferred to Belco's stockholders. Those stockholders who were interested primarily in income could take the straight preferred, whereas those interested in capital gains could take the convertible preferred. After the exchange, both preferred issues traded on the NYSE; the straight preferred had a yield of 11 percent, and the convertible preferred yielded 7.5 percent. However, the convertibles had a chance of gains — indeed, in 1988 the Enron convertible preferred had risen from its initial price of $100 to $150 per share because of an increase in the price of the common into which it could be converted. Meanwhile, the price of the nonconvertible preferred declined from $100 to $97 because of an increase in interest rates.

floating rate preferred stock
Preferred stock whose dividend rate fluctuates with changes in the general level of interest rates.

4. In 1984, Alabama Power introduced a new type of security, **floating rate preferred stock**. Since this stock has a floating rate, its price stays relatively constant, making it suitable for liquidity portfolios (marketable securities held by corporations to provide funds either for planned expenditures or to meet emergencies, as will be discussed in Chapter 19). The combination of a floating rate, and hence a stable price, plus the 70 percent tax exemption for corporations, makes this preferred quite attractive, and it enabled Alabama Power to obtain capital at a low cost.

LEASING

Firms generally own fixed assets and report them on their balance sheets, but it is the *use* of buildings and equipment that is important, not their ownership per se. One way of obtaining the use of facilities and equipment is to buy them, but an alternative is to lease them. Prior to the 1950s, leasing was generally associated with real estate — land and buildings. Today, however, it is possible to lease virtually any kind of fixed asset, and in 1988 about 25 percent of all new capital equipment acquired by businesses was financed through lease arrangements.

Types of Leases

Leasing takes several different forms, the three most important of which are (1) *sale-and-leaseback* arrangements, (2) *operating leases,* and (3) straight *financial,* or *capital, leases.*

sale and leaseback
An operation whereby a firm sells land, buildings, or equipment and simultaneously leases the property back for a specified period under specific terms.

Sale and Leaseback. Under a **sale and leaseback**, a firm that owns land, buildings, or equipment sells the property to another party and simultaneously executes an agreement to lease the property back for a specified period under specific terms. The purchaser of the property could be an insurance company, a commercial bank, a specialized leasing company, or even an individual investor. The sale-and-leaseback plan is an alternative to a mortgage.

lessee
The party that uses, rather than owns, the leased property.

The firm which is selling the property, or the **lessee**, immediately receives the purchase price put up by the buyer, or the **lessor**.[4] At the same time, the seller-lessee retains the use of the property just as if it had borrowed and used the property to secure the loan. Note that under a mortgage loan arrangement, the financial institution would normally receive a series of equal payments just sufficient to amortize the loan while providing a specified rate of return to the lender on the outstanding balance. Under a sale-and-leaseback arrangement, the lease payments are set up in exactly the same way; the payments are set so as to return the full purchase price to the investor-lessor while providing a specified rate of return on the lessor's outstanding investment.

lessor
The owner of the leased property.

operating lease
A lease under which the lessor maintains and finances the property; also called a *service lease.*

Operating Leases. Operating leases, sometimes called *service leases,* provide for both *financing* and *maintenance.* IBM is one of the pioneers of the operating lease contract, and computers and office copying machines, together with automobiles and trucks, are the primary types of equipment involved. Ordinarily, these leases call for the lessor to maintain and service the leased equipment, and the cost of providing maintenance is built into the lease payments.

Another important characteristic of operating leases is the fact that they are frequently *not fully amortized;* in other words, the payments required under the lease contract are not sufficient to recover the full cost of the equipment. However, the lease contract is written for a period considerably shorter than the expected economic life of the leased equipment, and the lessor expects to recover all investment costs through subsequent renewal payments, through subsequent leases to other lessees, or by selling the leased equipment.

A final feature of operating leases is that they frequently contain a *cancellation clause,* which gives the lessee the right to cancel the lease before the expiration of the basic agreement. This is an important consideration to the lessee, for it means that the equipment can be returned if it is rendered obsolete by technological developments or if it is no longer needed because of a decline in the lessee's business.

financial lease
A lease that does not provide for maintenance services, is not cancelable, and is fully amortized over its life; also called a *capital lease.*

Financial, or Capital, Leases. Financial leases, sometimes called *capital leases,* are differentiated from operating leases in three respects: (1) they do *not* pro-

(handwritten margin note: "cost of debt because "lease" is a lower-risk debt")

---

[4]The term *lessee* is pronounced "less-ee," not "lease-ee," and *lessor* is pronounced "less-or."

Table 14-1   Balance Sheet Effects of Leasing

Before Asset Increase				After Asset Increase							
Firms B and L				Firm B, Which Borrows and Purchases				Firm L, Which Leases			
Current assets	$ 50	Debt	$ 50	Current assets	$ 50	Debt	$150	Current assets	$ 50	Debt	$ 50
Fixed assets	50	Equity	50	Fixed assets	150	Equity	50	Fixed assets	50	Equity	50
Total	$100		$100	Total	$200		$200	Total	$100		$100
		Debt ratio: 50%				Debt ratio: 75%				Debt ratio: 50%	

[handwritten: lessor buys lease to a lessee]

vide for maintenance service, (2) they are *not* cancelable, and (3) they *are* fully amortized (that is, the lessor receives rental payments which are equal to the full price of the leased equipment plus a return on the investment). In a typical financial lease arrangement, the firm that will use the equipment (the lessee) selects the specific items it requires and negotiates the price and delivery terms with the manufacturer. The user firm then negotiates terms with a leasing company and, once the lease terms are set, arranges to have the lessor buy the equipment from the manufacturer or the distributor. When the equipment is purchased, the user firm simultaneously executes the lease agreement.

Financial leases are similar to sale-and-leaseback arrangements, the major difference being that the leased equipment is new and the lessor buys it from a manufacturer or a distributor instead of from the user-lessee. A sale and leaseback may thus be thought of as a special type of financial lease, and both sale and leasebacks and financial leases are analyzed in the same manner.[5]

Financial Statement Effects

off balance sheet financing
Financing in which the assets and liabilities under the lease contract do not appear on the firm's balance sheet.

Lease payments are shown as operating expenses on a firm's income statement, but under certain conditions, neither the leased assets nor the liabilities under the lease contract appear on the firm's balance sheet. For this reason, leasing is often called **off balance sheet financing**. This point is illustrated in Table 14-1 by the balance sheets of two hypothetical firms, B (for Buy) and L (for Lease). Initially, the balance sheets of both firms are identical, and both have debt ratios of 50 percent. Each firm then decides to acquire fixed assets which cost $100. Firm B borrows $100 to make the purchase, so both an asset and a liability are recorded on its balance sheet, and its debt ratio is increased to 75 percent. Firm L leases the equipment, so its balance sheet is unchanged. The lease may call for fixed charges as high as or even higher than those on the loan, and the obligations assumed under the lease may be equally or more

---

[5]For a lease transaction to qualify as a lease for tax purposes, and thus for the lessee to be able to deduct the lease payments, the life of the lease must approximate the life of the asset, and the lessee cannot be permitted to buy the asset at a nominal value. It is important to consult lawyers and accountants to insure that a lease is valid under current IRS regulations.

dangerous from the standpoint of financial safety, but the firm's debt ratio remains at 50 percent.

To correct this problem, the Financial Accounting Standards Board issued **FASB #13**, which requires that for an unqualified audit report, firms that enter into financial (or capital) leases must restate their balance sheets to report leased assets as fixed assets and the present value of future lease payments as a debt.[6] This process is called *capitalizing the lease,* and its net effect is to cause Firms B and L to have similar balance sheets, both of which will in essence resemble the one shown for Firm B after the asset increase.

The logic behind FASB #13 is as follows. If a firm signs a lease contract, its obligation to make lease payments is just as binding as if it had signed a loan agreement. The failure to make lease payments can bankrupt a firm just as surely as can the failure to make principal and interest payments on a loan. Therefore, for all intents and purposes, a financial lease is identical to a loan.[7] This being the case, when a firm signs a lease agreement, it has, in effect, raised its "true" debt ratio and thereby has changed its "true" capital structure. Accordingly, if the firm had previously established a target capital structure, and if there is no reason to think that the optimal capital structure has changed, then using lease financing requires additional equity backing in exactly the same manner as does the use of debt financing.

If a disclosure of the lease in the Table 14-1 example were not made, then investors could be deceived into thinking that Firm L's financial position is stronger than it actually is. Even if the lease were disclosed (in a footnote), investors might not fully recognize its impact and might not see that Firms B and L are in essentially the same financial position. If this were the case, Firm L would have increased its true amount of debt through a lease arrangement, but its required return on debt, k_d, its required return on equity, k_s, and consequently its average required rate of return, would have increased less than those required returns for Firm B, which borrowed directly. Thus, investors would be willing to accept a lower return from Firm L because they would view it as being in a stronger financial position than Firm B. These benefits of leasing would accrue to existing investors at the expense of new investors,

FASB #13
The statement of the Financial Accounting Standards Board that details the conditions and procedures for capitalizing leases.

---

[6]FASB #13, "Accounting for Leases," November 1976, spells out in detail the conditions under which leases must be capitalized, and the procedures for doing so.

[7]There are, however, certain legal differences between loans and leases. In a bankruptcy liquidation, the lessor is entitled to take possession of the leased asset, and if the value of the asset is less than the required payments under the lease, the lessor can enter a claim (as a general creditor) for one year's lease payments. In a bankruptcy reorganization, the lessor receives the asset plus three year's lease payments if needed to bring the value of the asset up to the remaining investment in the lease. Under a secured loan arrangement, on the other hand, the lender has a security interest in the asset, meaning that if it is sold, the lender will be given the proceeds, and the full unsatisfied portion of the lender's claim will be treated as a general creditor obligation (see Appendix 13A). It is not possible to state as a general rule whether a supplier of capital is in a stronger position as a secured creditor or as a lessor. Since one position is usually regarded as being about as good as the other at the time the financial arrangements are being made, a lease is about as risky as a secured term loan from both the lessor-lender's and the lessee-borrower's viewpoints.

who were, in effect, being deceived by the fact that the firm's balance sheet did not fully reflect its true liability situation. This is why FASB #13 was issued.

A lease will be classified as a capital lease, and hence be capitalized and shown directly on the balance sheet, if any one of the following conditions exists:

1. Under the terms of the lease, ownership of the property is effectively transferred from the lessor to the lessee.

2. The lessee can purchase the property or renew the lease at less than a fair market price when the lease expires.

3. The lease runs for a period equal to or greater than 75 percent of the asset's life. Thus, if an asset has a 10-year life and if the lease is written for more than 7.5 years, then the lease must be capitalized.

4. The present value of the lease payments is equal to or greater than 90 percent of the initial value of the asset.[8]

These rules, together with strong footnote disclosures for operating leases, are sufficient to insure that no one will be fooled by lease financing. Thus, leases are recognized to be essentially the same as debt, and they have the same effects as debt on the firm's required rate of return. Therefore, leasing will not generally permit a firm to use more financial leverage than could be obtained with conventional debt.

Evaluation by the Lessee

Any prospective lease must be evaluated by both the lessee and the lessor. The lessee must determine whether leasing an asset will be less costly than buying it; the lessor must decide whether or not the lease will provide a reasonable rate of return. Since our focus in this book is primarily on financial management as opposed to investments, we restrict our analysis to that conducted by the lessee.[9]

In the typical case, the events leading to a lease arrangement follow the sequence described in the following list. We should note that a great deal of literature exists about the theoretically correct way to evaluate lease versus purchase decisions, and some very complex decision models have been developed to aid in the analysis. The analysis given here, however, leads to the correct decision in every case we have ever encountered.

---

[8]The discount rate used to calculate the present value of the lease payments must be the lower of (1) the rate used by the lessor to establish the lease payments or (2) the rate of interest which the lessee would have paid for new debt with a maturity equal to that of the lease.

[9]The lessee is typically offered a set of lease terms by the lessor, which is generally a bank, a finance company such as General Electric Credit Corporation (the largest U.S. lessor), or some other institutional lender. It can accept or reject the lease, or shop around for a better deal. In this chapter, we take the lease terms as given for purposes of our analysis. See Chapter 14 of Eugene F. Brigham and Louis C. Gapenski, *Intermediate Financial Management,* 2nd ed., for a discussion of lease analysis from the lessor's standpoint, including a discussion of how a potential lessee can use such an analysis in bargaining for better terms.

1. The firm decides to acquire a particular building or piece of equipment. This decision is based on regular capital budgeting procedures, and it is not an issue in the typical lease analysis. In a lease analysis, we are concerned simply with whether to finance the machine by lease or by a loan. However, if the effective cost of the lease is substantially lower than that of debt — and this could occur for several reasons, including the situation in which the lessor is able to utilize the depreciation tax shelters but the lessee is not — then the capital budgeting decision would have to be reevaluated, and projects formerly deemed unacceptable might become acceptable.

2. Once the firm has decided to acquire the asset, the next question is how to finance it. Well-run businesses do not have excess cash lying around, so new assets must be financed in some manner.

3. Funds to purchase the asset could be obtained by borrowing, by retaining earnings, or by issuing new stock. Alternatively, the asset could be leased. Because of the FASB #13 capitalization/disclosure provision for leases, we assume that a lease would have the same capital structure effect as a loan.

Financing options

As indicated earlier, a lease is comparable to a loan in the sense that the firm is required to make a specified series of payments, and a failure to make these payments will result in bankruptcy. Thus, it is most appropriate to compare the cost of lease financing with that of debt financing.[10] The lease versus borrow-and-purchase analysis is illustrated with data on the Porter Electronics Company. The following conditions are assumed:

(assumed)

1. Porter plans to acquire equipment with a 5-year life which has a cost of $10,000,000, delivered and installed.

2. Porter can borrow the required $10 million using a 10 percent loan to be amortized over 5 years. Therefore, the loan will call for payments of $2,637,965.60 per year, calculated as follows:

$$\text{Payment} = \frac{\$10,000,000}{\text{PVIFA}_{10\%,5}} = \frac{\$10,000,000}{3.7908} = \$2,637,965.60.$$

With a financial calculator, input PV = 10,000,000, i = 10, and n = 5, and then press PMT to find the payment, $2,637,974.81. Note the rounding difference.

3. Alternatively, Porter can lease the equipment for 5 years at a rental charge of $2,800,000 per year, payable at the end of the year, but the

---

[10]The analysis should compare the cost of leasing to the cost of debt financing *regardless* of how the asset is actually financed. The asset may actually be purchased with available cash if it is not leased, but because leasing is a substitute for debt financing, the comparison between the two is still appropriate.

lessor will own it upon the expiration of the lease.[11] (The lease payment schedule is established by the potential lessor, and Porter can accept it, reject it, or negotiate.)

4. The equipment will definitely be used for 5 years, at which time its estimated net salvage value will be $715,000. Porter plans to continue using the equipment, so (1) if it purchases the equipment, the company will keep it, and (2) if it leases the equipment, the company will exercise an option to buy it at its estimated salvage value, $715,000.

5. The lease contract stipulates that the lessor will maintain the equipment. However, if Porter borrows and buys, it will have to bear the cost of maintenance, which will be performed by the equipment manufacturer at a fixed contract rate of $500,000 per year, payable at year-end.

6. The equipment falls in the ACRS 5-year class life, and for this analysis we assume that Porter's effective tax rate is 40 percent. Also, the depreciable basis is the original cost of $10,000,000.

NPV Analysis. Table 14-2 shows the outflows that would be incurred each year under the two financing plans. The table is set up to produce a time line of cash flows:

Year	1	2	3	4	5
Cash flows	CF_1	CF_2	CF_3	CF_4	CF_5

All cash flows occur at the end of the year, and the CF_t values are shown on Lines 12 and 18 of Table 14-2 for buying and leasing respectively.

   The top section of the table (Lines 1–15) is devoted to the costs of borrowing and buying. Lines 1–4 provide the loan amortization schedule, and on Lines 5–7 we calculate the annual depreciation charges. Lines 8–11 show the individual cash outflow items; note that the interest and depreciation tax savings are shown as negative outflows, because they are actually cash inflows resulting from the deductibility of interest and depreciation expenses. Line 12 summarizes the annual net cash outflows that Porter will incur if it finances the equipment with a loan. The present values of these outflows are found by multiplying each cash flow by the appropriate present value interest factor shown on Line 13. The annual present values are given on Line 14, and the sum of these annual figures, which is the *present value of the cost of owning,* is shown on Line 15 in the Year 1 column.

   Section II of the table calculates the present value cost of leasing. The lease payments are $2,800,000 per year; this rate, which in this example but not in all cases includes maintenance, was established by the prospective lessor and

---

[11]Lease payments can occur at the beginning of the year or at the end of the year. In this example, we assume end-of-year payments, but we demonstrate beginning-of-year payments in Self-Test Problem ST-2.

Table 14-2   Porter Electronics Company: NPV Lease Analysis (Thousands of Dollars)

	Year 1	Year 2	Year 3	Year 4	Year 5
I. Borrow and Purchase Analysis					
a. Loan amortization schedule					
(1) Loan payment	$2,638	$2,638	$2,638	$2,638	$2,638
(2) Interest	1,000	836	656	458	240
(3) Principal payment	1,638	1,802	1,982	2,180	2,398
(4) Remaining balance	8,362	6,560	4,578	2,398	0
b. Depreciation schedule					
(5) Depreciable basis	10,000	10,000	10,000	10,000	10,000
(6) Allowance	0.20	0.32	0.19	0.12	0.11
(7) Depreciation	2,000	3,200	1,900	1,200	1,100
c. Cash outflows					
(8) Loan payment	$2,638	$2,638	$2,638	$2,638	$2,638
(9) Interest tax savings	(400)	(334)	(262)	(183)	(96)
(10) Depreciation tax savings	(800)	(1,280)	(760)	(480)	(440)
(11) Maintenance (AT)	300	300	300	300	300
(12) Net cash outflows (buy)	$1,738	$1,324	$1,916	$2,275	$2,402
(13) PVIF	0.9434	0.8900	0.8396	0.7921	0.7473
(14) PV of owning cash flows	$1,640	$1,178	$1,609	$1,802	$1,795
(15) Total PV cost of owning	$8,024 = Sum of Line 14				
II. Lease Analysis					
(16) Lease cost after taxes	$1,680	$1,680	$1,680	$1,680	$1,680
(17) Purchase option price					715
(18) Net cash outflows (lease)	$1,680	$1,680	$1,680	$1,680	$2,395
(19) PVIF	0.9434	0.8900	0.8396	0.7921	0.7473
(20) PV of leasing cash flows	$1,585	$1,495	$1,411	$1,331	$1,790
(21) Total PV cost of leasing	$7,612 = Sum of Line 20				

III. Cost Comparison

Net advantage to leasing = NAL

= Total PV cost of owning − Total PV cost of leasing

= $8,024 − $7,612

= $412.

Note: See next page for a line-by-line explanation of the table.

Explanation of Lines

(1) Payments under the loan were determined as explained in the text.

(2) Interest is calculated as 10 percent of the prior year's remaining balance. Initially, the remaining balance (at Year 0) is $10 million, so the first year's interest is 0.1($10,000,000) = $1,000,000, written as $1,000.

(3) The principal payment is equal to the payment minus the interest component, $2,638 − $1,000 = $1,638 in Year 1.

(4) The remaining balance is calculated as the remaining balance from the prior year minus the principal repayment, $10,000 − $1,638 = $8,362 in Year 1.

(5) The depreciable basis is equal to the purchase price.

(6 and 7) Depreciation is calculated by ACRS, using rates of 0.20, 0.32, 0.19, 0.12, and 0.11. Refer back to Chapter 2 for a discussion of the ACRS depreciation system.

(8) The loan payment is taken from Line 1.

(9) The interest tax savings is calculated as Interest(Tax rate) = Interest(0.40). This amount is shown as a negative because it reduces outflows. Looked at another way, the after-tax cost of interest in Year 1 is $1,000 − $400 = $600. We included the $1,000 on Line 2, so we must subtract the $400 on Line 9.

(10) The depreciation tax savings is equal to Depreciation(Tax rate) = Depreciation(0.40). It is also shown as a negative number because it too reduces outflows. The company does not write a check to pay for depreciation, but the fact that it has depreciation does reduce its taxes, and in this sense depreciation provides a cash flow.

(11) Maintenance costs are $500 per year on a pre-tax basis, or $300 on an after-tax basis: $500(1 − T) = $500(0.6) = $300.

(12) Net cash outflows if Porter borrows and buys are calculated as follows: Line 12 = Line 8 + Line 9 + Line 10 + Line 11.

(13) PVIFs are based on the 6 percent after-tax cost of debt and are taken from Appendix Table A-1. The reason that 6 percent is used is discussed later in the chapter.

(14) The PV of the cost of owning for each year is the product of Line 12 times Line 13.

(15) The total PV cost of owning is the sum of the entries on Line 14.

(16) The lease payment is given in the text as $2,800,000 before taxes and $1,680,000 after taxes. This payment includes all maintenance costs.

(17) Porter may purchase the machinery for $715,000 at the end of 5 years. Because it plans to continue the operation, it must incur this expense in Year 5. No taxes are involved.

(18) Net cash outflows if Porter elects to lease consist of the after-tax amount of the lease payment plus the Year 5 purchase option cost.

(19) PVIFs are the same as those shown on Line 13.

(20) PV costs of leasing are found as Line 18 times Line 19.

(21) The total PV cost of leasing is the sum of the entries on Line 20.

① 215,000

② 181,157

③ 143,253

④ 100,800   (684)

⑤ 53,253

offered to Porter Electronics. If Porter accepts the lease, the full $2,800,000 will be a deductible expense, so the after-tax cost of the lease is calculated as follows:

$$\text{After-tax cost} = \text{Lease payment} - \text{Tax savings}$$

$$= \text{Lease payment} - (\text{Tax rate})(\text{Lease payment})$$

$$= \text{Lease payment}(1 - \text{Tax rate})$$

$$= \$2,800,000(1 - 0.4)$$

$$= \$1,680,000.$$

This amount is shown on Line 16.

Line 17 in the lease section shows the $715,000 which Porter expects to pay in Year 5 to purchase the equipment. We include this amount as a cost of leasing because Porter will almost certainly want to continue the operation and thus will be forced to purchase the equipment from the lessor. If we had assumed that the operation would not be continued, then no entry would have appeared on this line. However, in that case, we would have included the $715,000, minus taxes, as a Year 5 inflow (with parentheses around it) in the purchase analysis, because if the asset were purchased originally, it would be sold after 5 years. It would be subtracted because it would then be an inflow, whereas all other cash flows are outflows. Line 20 calculates the present value of the cost of leasing for each year, and Line 21 sums these costs and shows the total PV cost of leasing.

The rate used to discount the cash flows is a critically important issue. In Chapter 4, we saw that the riskier a cash flow, the higher the discount rate used to find its present value. This same principle was observed in our discussion of capital budgeting, and it also applies in lease analysis. Just how risky are the cash flows under consideration here? Most of them are relatively certain, at least when compared with the types of cash flow estimates that were developed in capital budgeting. For example, the loan payment schedule is set by contract, as is the lease payment schedule. The depreciation expenses are also established by law and are not subject to change, and the $500,000 annual maintenance cost is fixed by contract as well. The tax savings are somewhat uncertain because tax rates may change, although tax rates do not change very often. The residual value is the least certain of the cash flows, but even here Porter's management is fairly confident that it will want to acquire the property and also that the cost of doing so will be close to $715,000.

Since the cash flows under both the lease and the borrow-and-purchase alternatives are all reasonably certain, they should be discounted at a relatively low rate. Most analysts recommend that the company's cost of debt be used, and this rate seems reasonable in our example. Further, since all the cash flows are on an after-tax basis, *the after-tax cost of debt, which is 6 percent, should be used.* Accordingly, in Table 14-2 we multiplied the cash outflows by the 6 percent PVIFs shown below each set of cash flows, and we summed these discounted cash flows to obtain the present values of the costs of owning and leasing. The financing method that produces the smaller present value of costs is the one that should be selected. The example shown in Table 14-2 indicates that leasing has a net advantage over buying: the present value of the cost of leasing is $412,000 less than that of buying. Therefore, it is to Porter's advantage to lease.

Factors That Affect Leasing Decisions

The basic method of analysis set forth in Table 14-2 is sufficient to handle most situations. However, certain factors warrant additional comments.

residual value
The value of leased property at the end of the lease term.

Estimated Residual Value. It is important to note that the lessor will own the property upon the expiration of the lease. The estimated end-of-lease value of the property is called the **residual value**. Superficially, it would appear that if residual values are expected to be large, owning would have an advantage over leasing. However, if expected residual values are large — as they may be under inflation for certain types of equipment as well as if real property is involved — then competition among leasing companies will force leasing rates down to the point where potential residual values will be fully recognized in the lease contract rates. Thus, the existence of large residual values on equipment is not likely to bias the decision against leasing.

Increased Credit Availability. As noted earlier, leasing is sometimes said to have an advantage for firms that are seeking the maximum degree of financial leverage. First, it is sometimes argued that firms can obtain more money, and for a longer period, under a lease arrangement than under a loan secured by a specific piece of equipment. Second, because some leases do not appear on the balance sheet, lease financing has been said to give the firm a stronger appearance in a *superficial* credit analysis, thus permitting it to use more leverage than it could if it did not lease. There may be some truth to these claims for smaller firms. However, now that larger firms are required to capitalize major leases and to report them on their balance sheets, this point is of questionable validity.

OPTIONS

option
A contract that gives the option holder the right to buy or sell an asset at some predetermined price within a specified period of time.

An **option** is a contract that gives its holder the right to buy (or sell) an asset at some predetermined price within a specified period of time. "Pure options" are instruments that are created by outsiders (generally investment banking firms) rather than by the firm itself; they are bought and sold primarily by investors (or speculators). However, financial managers should understand the nature of options, because this will help them structure warrant and convertible financings.

Option Types and Markets

striking (exercise) price
The price that must be paid for a share of common stock when it is bought by exercising an option.

There are many types of options and option markets. To understand how options work, suppose you owned 100 shares of IBM stock which on February 10, 1988, sold for $111.875 per share. You could sell to someone else the right to buy your 100 shares at any time during the next 2 months at a price of, say, $120 per share. The $120 is called the **striking**, or **exercise**, **price**. Such options exist, and they are traded on a number of stock exchanges, with the Chicago Board Options Exchange (CBOE) being the oldest and largest. This type of option is known as a **call option**, as the purchaser has a "call" on 100 shares of stock. The seller of a call option is known as an *option writer*. An investor who writes a call option against stock held in his or her portfolio is said to be selling *covered options;* options sold without the stock to back them up are called *naked options*.

call option
An option to buy, or "call," a share of stock at a certain price within a specified period.

On February 10, 1988, IBM's 2-month, $120 call options sold on the CBOE for $2.875 each. Thus, for ($2.875)(100) = $287.50, you could buy an option contract that would give you the right to purchase 100 shares of IBM at a price of $120 per share at any time during the next 2 months. If the stock price stayed below $120 during that period, you would lose your $287.50, but if it rose to $130, your $287.50 investment would be worth ($130 − $120)(100) = $1,000. That translates into a very healthy rate of return on your $287.50 investment. Incidentally, if the stock price did go up, you would probably not actually exercise your options and buy the stock; rather, you would sell the options, which would then each have a price of at least $10 versus the $2.875 you had paid, to another option buyer.

put option
An option to sell a share of stock at a certain price, within a specified period.

You can also buy an option which gives you the right to *sell* a stock at a specified price at some time in the future — this is called a **put option**. For example, suppose you expect IBM's stock price to decline from its current level sometime during the next 2 months. For $275 you could buy a 2-month put option giving you the right to sell 100 shares (which you would not necessarily own) at a price of $105 per share ($105 is the put option striking price). If you bought a 100-share put contract for $275 and IBM's stock price actually fell to $95, you would make ($105 − $95)(100) = $1,000 minus the $275 you paid for the put option, for a net profit (before taxes and commissions) of $725.

Options trading is one of the hottest financial activities in the United States today. The leverage involved makes it possible for speculators with just a few dollars to make a fortune almost overnight. Also, investors with sizable portfolios can sell options against their stocks and earn the value of the options (minus brokerage commissions) even if the stocks' prices remain constant. Yet, perhaps those who have profited most from the development of options trading are security brokers, who earn very healthy commissions on such trades.

The corporations on whose stocks options are written, such as IBM, have nothing to do with the options market. They neither raise money in that market nor have any direct transactions in it, and option holders do not vote for corporate directors (unless they exercise their options to purchase the stock, which few actually do). There have been studies by the SEC and others as to whether options trading stabilizes or destabilizes the stock market and whether it helps or hinders corporations seeking to raise new capital. The studies have not been conclusive, but options trading is here to stay, and many regard it as the most exciting game in town.[12]

Formula Value Versus Option Price

formula value
The value of an option security on its expiration date, calculated as the stock price minus the striking, or exercise, price.

How is the actual price of an option determined in the market? To begin, we define an option's **formula value** as follows:

$$\text{Formula value} = \text{Current price of the stock} - \text{Striking price.}$$

For example, if a stock sells for $50 and its options have a striking price of $20, then the formula value of the option is $30. As we shall see, options generally sell at a price greater than their formula value.

Now consider Figure 14-1, which presents some data on Space Technology, Inc. (STI), a company which recently went public and whose stock has fluctuated widely during its short history. Column 1 in the lower section shows the trading range of the stock; Column 2 shows the striking price of the option; Column 3 shows the formula values for STI's options when the stock sells at different prices; Column 4 gives the actual market prices of the option; and Column 5 shows the premium, or excess of the actual option price over its formula value. These data are plotted in the graph.

In this example, for any stock price below $20, the formula value is negative; above $20, each $1 increase in the price of the stock brings with it a $1 increase in the option's formula value. Note, however, that the actual market price of the option lies above the formula value at all prices of the common stock, but that the premium declines as the price of the stock increases. For example, when the common stock sold for $20 and the option had a zero formula value, its actual price, and the premium, was $9. Then, as the price of the stock rose, the formula value matched the increase dollar for dollar, but the market price of the option climbed less rapidly, causing the premium to decline. Thus, the premium was $9 when the stock sold for $20 a share, but it had declined to $1 by the time the stock price reached $73 a share, and beyond that point the premium virtually disappeared.

Why does this pattern exist? Why should the option ever sell for more than its formula value, and why does the premium decline as the price of the stock increases? The answer lies in the speculative appeal of options; they provide an investor with a high degree of leverage when buying securities. To illustrate, suppose STI's stock was selling for $21, and its options sold for ex-

---

[12]Closely related to options are *futures*. A future is a contract to buy (or to sell) an asset at a specified price at some future date. Thus, if IBM stock were selling at $111.875 today, and you thought it was going to fall, you could buy a put option contract which would give you the right to sell IBM stock at a price of $105 within a 2-month period. Alternatively, you could sell a 2-month future — meaning that you would promise to sell IBM stock 2 months from now — at a price specified today. Futures are not commonly used for individual stocks, but they are commonly used for stock indices such as the S & P index, for U.S. Treasury bonds, and for commodities such as wheat and corn. We will discuss futures later in Chapter 19.

Figure 14-1   Space Technology, Inc.:
              Option Price and Formula Value

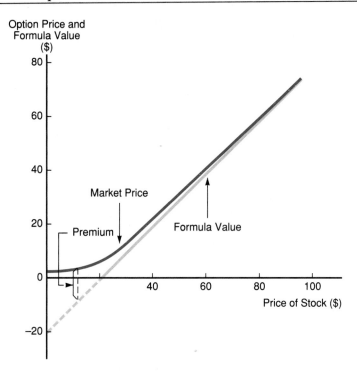

Price of Stock (1)	Striking Price (2)	Formula Value of Option (1) − (2) = (3)	Market Price of Option (4)	Premium (4) − (3) = (5)
$12.00	$20.00	− $ 8.00	$ 5.00	$13.00
20.00	20.00	0.00	9.00	9.00
21.00	20.00	1.00	9.75	8.75
22.00	20.00	2.00	10.50	8.50
35.00	20.00	15.00	21.00	6.00
42.00	20.00	22.00	26.00	4.00
50.00	20.00	30.00	32.00	2.00
73.00	20.00	53.00	54.00	1.00
98.00	20.00	78.00	78.50	0.50

actly their formula value, $1. Now suppose you were thinking of investing in the company. If you bought a share of stock and the price rose to $42, you would make a 100 percent capital gain. However, if you bought the option at its $1 formula value, your capital gain would be $21 on a $1 investment, a 2,100 percent gain! At the same time, your total loss potential with the option would be only $1, whereas the potential loss if you purchased the stock would be $21. The huge capital gains potential, combined with the loss limitation, is clearly worth something; the exact amount it is worth to investors is the amount of the premium.

Why does the premium decline as the price of the stock rises? Part of the answer is that both the leverage effect and the loss protection feature decline at high stock prices. For example, if you were thinking of buying the stock when its price was $73 a share, the formula value of the option would be $53. If the stock price doubled to $146, the formula value of STI's option would go from $53 to $126, an increase of 138 percent versus the 2,100 percent gain when the stock price doubled from $21. Notice also that the potential loss on the option is much greater when the option is selling at high prices. These two factors — the declining leverage effect and the increasing danger of losses — help explain why the premium diminishes as the price of the common stock rises.

In addition to the stock price and the striking price, the value of an option also depends on (1) the option's time to maturity and (2) the variability of the underlying stock's price:

1. The longer an option has to run, the greater its value and the larger its premium. If an option expires at 4 p.m. today, there is not much chance that the stock price will go way up. Therefore, the option will sell at close to its formula value, and its premium will be small. On the other hand, if it has a year to go, the stock price could rise sharply, pulling the option's value up with it.

2. An option on an extremely volatile stock will be worth more than one on a very stable stock. We know that an option on a stock whose price rarely moves will not offer much chance for a large gain. On the other hand, an option on a stock that is highly volatile could provide a large gain, so such an option will be valuable. Note also that because losses on options are limited, large declines in a stock's price do not have a corresponding bad effect on option holders. Therefore, stock price volatility can only enhance the value of an option.[13]

---

[13]To illustrate this point, suppose that for $2 you could buy an option on a stock now selling for $20. The striking price is also $20. Now suppose the stock is highly volatile, and you think it has a 50 percent probability of selling for either $10 or $30 when the option expires in one month. What is the expected value of the option? If the stock sells for $30, the option will be worth $30 − $20 = $10. Since there is a 50-50 chance that the stock will be worth $10 or $30, the expected value of the option is $5:

$$\text{Expected value of option} = 0.5(0) + 0.5(\$10) = \$5.$$

To be exactly correct, we would have to discount the $5 back for one month.

Now suppose the stock was more volatile, with a 50-50 chance of being worth zero or $40. Here the option would be worth

$$\text{Expected value of option} = 0.5(0) + 0.5(\$20) = \$10.$$

This demonstrates that the higher the volatility of the stock, the greater the value of the option. The reason this result occurs is that the large loss on the stock (− $20) had no more of an adverse effect on the option holder than the small loss (− $10). Thus, option holders benefit greatly if a stock goes way up, but they do not lose too badly if it drops all the way to zero. These concepts have been used to develop formulas for pricing options, with the most widely used formula being the Black-Scholes model, which is discussed in most investments texts.

3. If everything else was held constant, then in a graph like Figure 14-1, the longer an option's life, the higher its market price line would be above the formula value line. Also, the more volatile the price of the underlying stock, the higher the market price line would be.

WARRANTS

A **warrant** is an option issued by a company which gives the holder the right to buy a stated number of shares of the company's stock at a specified price. Generally, warrants are distributed along with debt, and they are used to induce investors to buy a firm's long-term debt at a lower interest rate than would otherwise be required. For example, when Pan-Pacific Airlines (PPA) wanted to sell $50 million of 20-year bonds in 1988, the company's investment bankers informed the financial vice-president that straight bonds would be difficult to sell and that an interest rate of 14 percent would be required. However, the bankers suggested as an alternative that investors would be willing to buy bonds with a coupon rate as low as 10⅜ percent if the company would offer 30 warrants with each $1,000 bond, each warrant entitling the holder to buy one share of common stock at a price of $22 per share. The stock was selling for $20 per share at the time, and the warrants would expire in 1995 if they had not been exercised previously.

Why would investors be willing to buy Pan-Pacific's bonds at a yield of only 10⅜ percent in a 14 percent market just because warrants were offered as part of the package? Because warrants are long-term *options,* they have a value for the reasons set forth in the previous section. In the PPA case, this value offset the low interest rate on the bonds and made the entire package of below-market-yield bonds plus warrants attractive to investors.

Initial Market Price of Bond with Warrants

If the PPA bonds had been issued as straight debt, they would have carried a 14 percent interest rate. With warrants attached, however, the bonds were sold to yield 10⅜ percent. Someone buying one of the bonds at its $1,000 initial offering price would thus have been receiving a package consisting of a 10⅜ percent, 20-year bond plus 30 warrants. Since the going interest rate on bonds as risky as those of PPA was 14 percent, we can find the pure-debt value of the bonds, assuming an annual coupon, as follows:

$$\text{Pure-debt value} = \sum_{t=1}^{20} \frac{\$103.75}{(1.14)^t} + \frac{\$1,000}{(1.14)^{20}}$$

$$= \$103.75(\text{PVIFA}_{14\%,20}) + \$1,000(\text{PVIF}_{14\%,20})$$

$$= \$687.15 + \$72.80$$

$$= \$759.95 \approx \$760.$$

Thus, a person buying the bonds in the initial underwriting would pay $1,000 and receive in exchange a pure bond worth about $760 plus warrants presumably worth about $1,000 − $760 = $240:

$$\frac{\text{Price paid for}}{\text{bond with warrants}} = \frac{\text{Straight-debt}}{\text{value of bond}} + \frac{\text{Value of}}{\text{warrants}}$$

$$\$1,000 = \$760 + \$240.$$

Because investors receive 30 warrants with each bond, each warrant has an implied value of $240/30 = $8.

The key issue in setting the terms of a bond-with-warrants offering is finding the value of the warrants. The pure-debt value of the bond can be estimated quite accurately. However, it is much more difficult to estimate the value of the warrants. If their value is overestimated relative to their true market value, it will be difficult to sell the issue at its par value. Conversely, if the warrants' value is underestimated, investors in the issue will receive a windfall profit, because they can sell the warrants in the market for more than they implicitly paid for them; this windfall profit would come out of the pockets of PPA's current stockholders.

Use of Warrants in Financing

Warrants are generally used by small, rapidly growing firms as "sweeteners" to help sell either debt or preferred stock. Such firms are frequently regarded as being highly risky, and their bonds can be sold only if the firms are willing to pay extremely high rates of interest and to accept very restrictive indenture provisions. To avoid this, firms such as Pan-Pacific often have offered warrants along with their bonds. However, some strong firms also have used warrants. In the largest financing of any type ever undertaken by a business firm, AT&T raised $1.57 billion by selling bonds with warrants. This marked the first use ever of warrants by a large, strong corporation.

Getting warrants along with bonds enables investors to share in a company's growth if that firm does in fact grow and prosper; therefore, investors are willing to accept a lower bond interest rate and less restrictive indenture provisions. A bond with warrants has some characteristics of debt and some of equity. It is a hybrid security that provides the financial manager with an opportunity to expand the firm's mix of securities and to appeal to a broader group of investors, thus possibly lowering the firm's cost of capital.

detachable warrant
A warrant that can be detached from a bond and traded independently of it.

Virtually all warrants today are **detachable warrants,** meaning that after a bond with attached warrants has been sold, the warrants can be detached and traded separately from the bond. Further, when these warrants are exercised, the bonds themselves (with their low coupon rate) will remain outstanding. Thus, the warrants will bring in additional equity while leaving low interest rate debt on the books.

The warrants' exercise price is generally set from 10 to 30 percent above the market price of the stock on the date the bond is issued. For example, if the stock sells for $10, the exercise price will be set in the $11 to $13 range.

If the firm does grow and prosper, and if its stock price rises above the exercise price at which shares may be purchased, warrant holders will turn in their warrants, along with cash equal to the stated exercise price, in exchange for stock. Without some incentive, however, many warrants would never be exercised prior to maturity. Their value in the market would be greater than their formula, or exercise, value, and hence holders would sell warrants rather than exercise them.

There are three conditions which encourage holders to exercise their warrants: (1) Warrant holders will *surely* exercise warrants and buy stock if the warrants are about to expire with the market price of the stock above the exercise price. This means that if a firm wants its warrants exercised soon in order to raise capital, it should set a relatively short expiration date. (2) Warrant holders will tend to exercise *voluntarily* and buy stock if the company raises the dividend on the common stock by a sufficient amount. Since no dividend is paid on the warrant, it provides no current income. However, if the common stock pays a high dividend, it provides an attractive dividend yield. Therefore, the higher the stock's dividend, the greater the opportunity cost of holding the warrant rather than exercising it. Thus, if a firm wants its warrants exercised, it can raise the common stock's dividend. (3) Warrants sometimes have **stepped-up exercise prices**, which prod owners into exercising them. For example, the Williamson Scientific Company has warrants outstanding with an exercise price of $25 until December 31, 1990, at which time the exercise price will rise to $30. If the price of the common stock is over $25 just before December 31, 1990, many warrant holders will exercise their options before the stepped-up price takes effect.

Another useful feature of warrants is that they generally bring in funds only if such funds are needed. If the company grows, it will probably need new equity capital. At the same time, this growth will cause the price of the stock to rise and the warrants to be exercised, thereby allowing the firm to obtain additional cash. If the company is not successful and cannot profitably employ additional money, the price of its stock will probably not rise sufficiently to induce exercise of the options.

stepped-up exercise price
An exercise price that is specified to be higher if a warrant is exercised after a designated date.

CONVERTIBLES

convertible security
A security, usually a bond or preferred stock, that is exchangeable at the option of the holder for the common stock of the issuing firm.

Convertible securities are bonds or preferred stocks that can be exchanged for common stock at the option of the holder. Unlike the exercise of warrants, which provides the firm with additional funds, conversion does not bring in additional capital — debt (or preferred stock) is simply replaced by common stock. Of course, this reduction of debt or preferred stock will strengthen the firm's balance sheet and make it easier to obtain additional capital, but this is a separate action.

Conversion Ratio and Conversion Price

conversion ratio, CR
The number of shares of common stock that may be obtained by converting a convertible bond or share of convertible preferred stock.

conversion price, P_c
The effective price paid for common stock obtained by converting a convertible security.

One of the most important provisions of a convertible security is the **conversion ratio, CR**, defined as the number of shares of stock the convertible holder receives upon conversion. Related to the conversion ratio is the **conversion price, P_c**, which is the effective price the company receives for its common stock when conversion occurs. The relationship between the conversion ratio and the conversion price can be illustrated by the Adams Electronics Company's convertible debentures, issued at their $1,000 par value in 1988. At any time prior to maturity on July 1, 2008, a debenture holder can exchange a bond for 20 shares of common stock; therefore, CR = 20. The bond has a par value of $1,000, so the holder would be relinquishing this amount upon conversion. Dividing the $1,000 par value by the 20 shares received gives a conversion price of $P_c = \$50$ a share:

$$\text{Conversion price} = P_c = \frac{\text{Par value of bond}}{\text{CR}}$$

$$= \frac{\$1,000}{20} = \$50.$$

Similarly, if we know the conversion price, we can find CR:

$$\text{CR} = \frac{\$1,000}{P_c} = \frac{\$1,000}{\$50} = 20 \text{ shares.}$$

Once CR is set, the value of P_c is established, and vice versa.

Like a warrant's exercise price, the conversion price is characteristically set at from 10 to 30 percent above the prevailing market price of the common stock at the time the convertible issue is sold. Generally, the conversion price and ratio are fixed for the life of the bond, although sometimes a stepped-up conversion price is used. Litton Industries' convertible debentures, for example, were convertible into 12.5 shares until 1972; into 11.76 shares from 1972 until 1982; and into 11.11 shares from 1982 until maturity in 1987. The conversion price thus started at $80, rose to $85 in 1972, and then went to $90 in 1982. Litton's convertibles, like most, became callable at the option of the company after a 3-year call protection period.

Another factor that may cause a change in the conversion price and ratio is a standard feature of almost all convertibles — the clause protecting the convertible against dilution from stock splits, stock dividends, and the sale of common stock at prices below the conversion price. The typical provision states that if common stock is sold at a price below the conversion price, the conversion price must be lowered (and the conversion ratio raised) to the price at which the new stock was issued. Also, if the stock is split (or if a stock dividend is declared), the conversion price must be lowered by the percentage amount of the stock dividend or split. For example, if Adams Electronics were to have a two-for-one stock split, the conversion ratio would automatically be adjusted from 20 to 40, and the conversion price lowered from $50 to $25. If this protection were not contained in the contract, a company could completely thwart conversion by the use of stock splits. Warrants are similarly protected against such dilution.

The standard protection against dilution from selling new stock at prices below the conversion price can, however, get a company into trouble. For example, Litton Industries' stock was selling for only $64 in 1987 versus the conversion price of $90. Thus, Litton would have had to give its bondholders a tremendous break if it wanted to sell new common stock. Problems like this must be kept in mind by firms considering the use of convertibles or bonds with warrants.[14]

Convertible Bond Model

In 1988 Adams Electronics Company was thinking of issuing 20-year convertible bonds at a price of $1,000 each. Each bond would pay a 10 percent annual coupon interest rate, or $100 per year, and each would be convertible into 20 shares of stock. Thus, the conversion price would be $1,000/20 = $50. If the bonds did not have the conversion feature, investors would require a yield of 12 percent, because k_d = 12%. Knowing k_d, the coupon rate, and the maturity, we can find the pure-debt value of the convertibles at the time of issue, B_0, using the bond valuation model developed back in Chapter 6. The bonds would initially sell at a price of $851:

$$\begin{matrix} \text{Pure-debt value at} \\ \text{time of issue} \end{matrix} = B_0 = \sum_{t=1}^{20} \frac{\$100}{(1.12)^t} + \frac{\$1,000}{(1.12)^{20}} = \$851.$$

Adams's stock is expected to pay a dividend of $2.80 in the coming year; it currently sells at $35 per share, and this price is expected to grow at a constant rate of 8 percent per year. Thus, the stock price expected in each future Year t is $P_t = P_0(1 + g)^t = \$35(1.08)^t$. Further, since Adams's convertibles would allow their holders to convert them into 20 shares of stock, the value a bondholder would expect to receive if he or she converted, defined as C_t, would be $\$35(1.08)^t(20)$.

The convertible bonds would not be callable for 10 years, after which they could be called at a price of $1,000. If after 10 years the conversion value exceeded the call price by at least 20 percent, management has indicated that it would call the bonds.

Figure 14-2 shows the expectations of both an average investor and the company:

1. The horizontal line at M = $1,000 represents the par (and maturity) value. Also, $1,000 is the price at which the bond would initially be offered to the public.

---

[14]For a more complete discussion of how the terms are set on a convertible offering, see M. Wayne Marr and G. Rodney Thompson, "The Pricing of New Convertible Bond Issues," *Financial Management,* Summer 1984, 31–37.

Figure 14-2   Model of a Convertible Bond

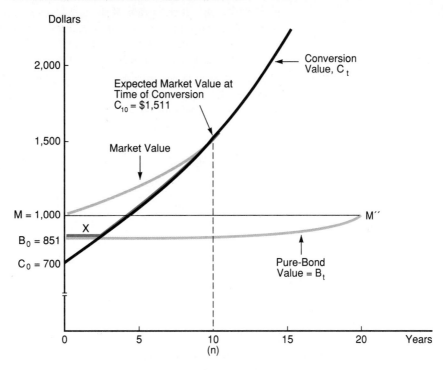

Year	Pure-Bond Value, B_t	Conversion Value, C_t	Maturity Value, M	Market Value
0	$ 851	$ 700	$1,000	$1,000
1	853	756	1,000	1,042
2	855	816	1,000	1,086
3	858	882	1,000	1,132
4	861	952	1,000	1,180
5	864	1,029	1,000	1,229
6	867	1,111	1,000	1,281
7	872	1,200	1,000	1,335
8	876	1,296	1,000	1,391
9	881	1,399	1,000	1,450
10	887	1,511	1,000	1,511
11	893	1,632	1,000	1,632
.	.	.	.	.
.	.	.	.	.
.	.	.	.	.
20	1,000	3,263	1,000	3,263

2. The pure-debt value of the convertible would initially be $851, but it would rise to $1,000 over the 20-year life of the bond. The bond's pure-debt value is shown by the line B_t in Figure 14-2.

3. The bond's initial **conversion value**, C_t, or the value of the stock the investor would receive if the bond were converted at t = 0, is $700:

Conversion value $= P_0(CR) = \$35(20$ shares$) = \$700$. As indicated previously, the stock's price is expected to grow at an 8 percent rate, so $P_t = \$35(1.08)^t$. If the price of the stock rises over time, so will the conversion value of the bond. For example, in Year 3 the conversion value should be $C_3 = P_3(CR) = \$35(1.08)^3(20) = \$882$. The expected conversion value over time is given by the line C_t in Figure 14-2.

4. The actual market price of the bond must always be equal to or greater than the *higher* of its pure-debt value or its conversion value. Therefore, the higher of the bond value or the conversion value curves in Figure 14-2 represents a "floor price" for the bond; this is represented by the heavy line B_0XC_t.

5. The market value of a convertible generally will exceed the floor price for the same reasons that an option's or a warrant's price will exceed its formula value. Investors are willing to pay a premium over the pure-debt value (which establishes the initial floor) because of the possibility of earning large capital gains if the stock price shoots up. After Year 3, when the conversion value exceeds the pure-bond value and thus establishes the floor, the market price will still exceed the floor. This is because the convertible is safer than the stock, for even if profits decline and the stock price drops, the bond's value will never fall below its pure-debt value.[15]

6. The gap between the market price of the convertible and the floor, or the premium investors are willing to pay, declines over time and is zero in Year 10. This decline occurs for two reasons. First, the dividends received on the stock presumably are growing at 8 percent a year, whereas the interest on the bond is fixed at $100 annually. After 8 years, the dividends which would be received from 20 shares of stock, $\$2.80(1.08)^8(20) = \$103.65$, would exceed the $100 of interest paid by the bond; beyond that point the opportunity cost of holding the bond rather than converting it would become increasingly heavy. Second, after 10 years the bond would become callable at a price of $1,000. If Adams called the issue, the bondholder could either convert the bond to common stock worth $C_{10} = \$1,511$ or receive $1,000 in cash. The holder would, of course, choose the $1,511 of stock. Note, however, that if the convertible were selling at a price greater than $C_{10} = \$1,511$ when the call occurred, the holder would suffer an immediate loss equal to the difference between the bond's price and $1,511. Therefore, because of the call provision, the market value of the bond cannot logically exceed the higher of the call price and the conversion price after the bond becomes callable.

7. If someone purchased Adams's stock, they would expect a return of $k_s = D_1/P_0 + g = \$2.80/\$35 + 8\% = 16\%$. If they bought a pure bond, they

---

[15]Note, however, that the bond value line B_0M'' would fall if interest rates rose in the economy or if the company's credit risk deteriorated, both of which would cause k_d to rise.

would earn 12 percent. The convertible has some guaranteed interest plus the expectation of some capital gains, so its risk and therefore its expected rate of return should lie between $k_d = 12\%$ and $k_s = 16\%$. We can find the expected return on the convertible by solving for k_c in the following equation:

$$\text{Initial price} = \sum_{t=1}^{10} \frac{\text{Interest}}{(1 + k_c)^t} + \frac{\text{Conversion value}}{(1 + k_c)^{10}}$$

$$\$1,000 = \sum_{t=1}^{10} \frac{\$100}{(1 + k_c)^t} + \frac{\$1,511}{(1 + k_c)^{10}}.$$

Using a financial calculator, we find $k_c = 12.8\%$. Therefore, under the assumptions of this example, an investor who purchased the convertible at its initial $1,000 offering price could expect to earn a rate of return of 12.8 percent.

Use of Convertibles in Financing

Convertibles offer two important advantages from the issuer's standpoint. First, convertibles, like bonds with warrants, permit a company to sell debt with a lower interest rate and with less restrictive covenants than straight bonds. Second, convertibles provide a way of selling common stock at prices higher than those currently prevailing. Many companies actually want to sell common stock and not debt, but they believe that the price of their stock is temporarily depressed. The financial manager may know, for example, that earnings are depressed because of start-up costs associated with a new project, but he or she may expect earnings to rise sharply during the next year or so, pulling the price of the stock along. In this case, if the company sold stock now it would be giving up too many shares to raise a given amount of money. However, if it sets the conversion price at 20 to 30 percent above the present market price of the stock, then 20 to 30 percent fewer shares will have to be given up when the bonds are converted. Notice, however, that management is counting on the stock price's rising sufficiently above the conversion price to make the bonds attractive in conversion. If earnings do not rise and pull the stock price up, and hence if conversion does not occur, the company could be saddled with debt in the face of low earnings, which could be disastrous.

How can the company be sure that conversion will occur if the price of the stock rises above the conversion price? Typically, convertibles contain a call provision that enables the issuing firm to force bondholders to convert. Suppose the conversion price is $50, the conversion ratio is 20, the market price of the common stock has risen to $60, and the call price on the convertible bond is $1,050. If the company calls the bond, bondholders can either convert into common stock with a market value of $1,200 or allow the company to redeem the bond for $1,050. Naturally, bondholders prefer $1,200 to $1,050, so conversion will occur. The call provision therefore gives the company a means of forcing conversion, but only if the market price of the stock is greater than the conversion price.

Convertibles are useful, but they do have three important disadvantages. (1) The use of a convertible security does in effect give the issuer the opportunity to sell common stock at a price higher than it could sell stock otherwise. However, if the common stock increases greatly in price, the company would probably have been better off if it had used straight debt in spite of its higher interest rate and then later sold common stock to refund the debt. (2) If the company truly wants to raise equity capital, and if the price of the stock does not rise sufficiently after the bond is issued, then the firm will be stuck with debt. (3) Convertibles typically have a low coupon interest rate, an advantage that will be lost when conversion occurs. Warrant financings, on the other hand, permit the company to continue to use the low-coupon debt for a longer period.

REPORTING EARNINGS WHEN WARRANTS OR CONVERTIBLES ARE OUTSTANDING

If warrants or convertibles are outstanding, a firm can theoretically report earnings per share in one of three ways:

1. *Simple EPS.* The earnings available to common stockholders are divided by the average number of shares actually outstanding during the period.

2. *Primary EPS.* The earnings available are divided by the average number of shares that would have been outstanding if warrants and convertibles likely to be converted in the near future had actually been exercised or converted.

3. *Fully diluted EPS.* This is similar to primary EPS except that *all* warrants and convertibles are assumed to be exercised or converted regardless of the likelihood of either occurring.

However, simple EPS is virtually never reported by firms which have warrants or convertibles likely to be exercised or converted; the SEC prohibits use of this figure, and it requires that primary and fully diluted earnings be shown on the income statement.

Small Business

LEASE FINANCING FOR SMALL BUSINESSES

In Chapter 14 we saw that, under certain conditions, leasing an asset can be less costly than borrowing to purchase the asset. For the small firm, leasing often offers these additional advantages: (1) conserves cash, (2) makes better use of managers' time, and (3) provides financing quickly.

Conserving Cash

Small firms often have limited cash resources. Because many leasing companies do not require the lessee to make even a small down payment, and because leases are often for longer terms and thus require lower payments than bank loans, leasing can help the small firm conserve its cash. Leasing companies also may be willing to work with a company to design a flexible leasing package that will help the lessee preserve its cash during critical times. For example, when Surgicare of Central Jersey opened its first surgical center in 1984, the firm did not have cash to pay for the necessary equipment. Surgicare's options were to borrow at a high interest rate, to sell stock to the public (which is difficult for a start-up firm), or to lease the equipment. Surgicare's financial vice-president, John Rutzel, decided to lease the needed equipment from Copelco Financial Services, a leasing company which specializes in health care equipment. Copelco allowed Surgicare to pay a reduced rate for the first six months, a slightly higher rate during the second six months, and a level payment thereafter. Rutzel stated that these unique lease terms "got Surgicare through the start-up phase, when cash flow was the critical consideration."

Freeing Managers for Other Tasks

Most small business owners find that they never have enough time to get everything done — they are simply spread too thin, being in charge of sales, operations, budgeting, and everything else. If an asset is owned, the firm must maintain it in good working condition and also keep records on its use for tax depreciation purposes. However, leasing assets frees the business's owner of these duties. First, paperwork is reduced, because maintenance records, depreciation schedules, and other records do not have to be maintained on leased assets. Second, less time may have to be spent "shopping around" for the right equipment, because leasing companies, which generally specialize in a particular industry, can often provide the manager with the information necessary to select the needed assets. Third, since the assets can be traded in if they become obsolete, the initial choice of equipment is less critical. Fourth, the burden of servicing and repairing the equipment can be passed on to the lessor.

Obtaining Assets More Quickly and at a Lower Cost

Many new, small firms find that banks are unwilling to lend them money at a reasonable cost. Because leasing companies retain the ownership of the equipment, they may be more willing to take chances with start-up firms. When Ed Lavin started Edwards Offset Printing Company in 1984, his bank would not lend him the money to purchase the necessary printing presses — the bank wanted to lend only to firms with proven track records. Lavin arranged to lease the needed presses from Eaton Financial Corporation, which also advised him on the best type of equipment to meet his needs. In 1987, Lavin's firm achieved sales of $250,000: as his company grew, he expanded by leasing additional equipment. Thus, (1) leasing allowed Lavin to go into business when his bank was unwilling to help, (2) his leasing company provided him with help in selecting equipment, and (3) the leasing company also provided additional capital to meet his expansion needs.

SUMMARY AND KEY CONCEPTS

This chapter discussed three hybrid forms of long-term financing: (1) preferred stock, (2) leasing, and (3) option securities. The key concepts covered are listed below.

- **Preferred stock** is a hybrid security having some characteristics of debt and some of equity. Equity holders view preferred stock as debt because it has a claim on the firm's earnings ahead of the claim of the common stockholders. Bondholders, however, view preferred as equity because debtholders have a prior claim on the firm's income and, in the event of bankruptcy, on the firm's assets.

- The primary **advantages of preferred stock** to the issuer are (1) that preferred dividends are limited and (2) that failure to pay them will not bankrupt the firm. The primary disadvantage to the issuer is that the cost of preferred is higher than that of debt because preferred dividend payments are not tax deductible.

- To the investor, preferred stock offers the advantage of **more dependable income** than common stock, and, to a corporate investor, **70 percent of such dividends are not taxable.** The principal disadvantages to the investor are that the **returns are limited** and that the investor has **no legally enforceable right to a dividend.**

- **Leasing** is a means of obtaining the use of an asset without purchasing that asset. The three most important forms of leasing are: (1) **sale-and-leaseback** arrangements, under which a firm sells an asset to another party and leases the asset back for a specified period under specific terms, (2) **operating leases**, under which the lessor both maintains and finances the asset, and (3) **financial leases**, under which the asset is fully amortized over the life of the lease, the lessor does not normally provide maintenance, and the lease is not cancelable.

- The **decision as to whether to lease or buy an asset** is made by comparing the costs of the two alternatives and choosing the financing method with the lower cost. All cash flows should be discounted at the **after-tax cost of debt**, because lease analysis cash flows are relatively certain and are on an after-tax basis.

- An **option** is a contract that gives its holder the right to buy (or sell) an asset at some predetermined price within a specified period of time. Options are used by firms to "sweeten" debt offerings.

- A **warrant** is an option issued along with a bond which gives the holder the right to purchase a stated number of shares of stock at a specified price within a specified period. A warrant will be exercised if it is about to expire and the stock price is above the exercise price.

- A **convertible security** is a bond or preferred stock which can be exchanged for common stock at the option of the holder. When a security is converted, debt or preferred stock is replaced with common stock, and no money changes hands.

- **The conversion of bonds or preferred stock** by their holders **does not provide additional funds** to the company, but it does result in a lower debt ratio. The **exercise of warrants provides additional funds**, which strengthens the firm's equity position, but it still leaves the debt or preferred stock on the balance sheet. Low interest rate debt remains outstanding when warrants are exercised, but the firm loses this advantage when convertibles are converted.

- For the small firm, leasing offers the following advantages: (1) **cash is conserved**, (2) **managers' time is freed** for other tasks, and (3) **financing can be obtained** more **quickly** and at a **lower cost.**

Questions

14-1   For purposes of measuring a firm's leverage, should preferred stock be classified as debt or equity? Does it matter if the classification is being made (a) by the firm's management, (b) by creditors, or (c) by equity investors?

14-2   You are told that one corporation just issued $100 million of preferred stock and another purchased $100 million of preferred stock as an investment. You are also told that one firm has an effective tax rate of 20 percent whereas the other is in the 34 percent bracket. Which firm is more likely to have bought the preferred? Explain.

14-3   One often finds that a company's bonds have a higher yield than its preferred stock, even though the bonds are considered to be less risky than the preferred to an investor. What causes this yield differential?

14-4   Why would a company choose to issue floating rate as opposed to fixed rate preferred stock?

14-5   Distinguish between operating leases and financial leases. Would a firm be more likely to finance a fleet of trucks or a manufacturing plant with an operating lease?

14-6   One alleged advantage of leasing voiced in the past was that it kept liabilities off the balance sheet, thus making it possible for a firm to obtain more leverage than it otherwise could have. This raised the question of whether or not both the lease obligation and the asset involved should be capitalized and shown on the balance sheet. Discuss the pros and cons of capitalizing leases and related assets.

14-7   Suppose there were no IRS restrictions on what constitutes a valid lease. Explain in a manner that a legislator might understand why some restrictions should be imposed.

14-8   Suppose Congress changed the tax laws in a way that (1) permitted equipment to be depreciated over a shorter period, (2) lowered corporate tax rates, and (3) reinstated the investment tax credit. Discuss how each of these changes would affect the relative use of leasing versus conventional debt in the U.S. economy.

14-9   Why do options typically sell at prices higher than their formula values?

14-10   What effect does the expected growth rate of a firm's stock price (subsequent to issue) have on its ability to raise additional funds through (a) convertibles and (b) warrants?

14-11   a. How would a firm's decision to pay out a higher percentage of its earnings as dividends affect each of the following?
   1. The value of its long-term warrants.
   2. The likelihood that its convertible bonds will be converted.
   3. The likelihood that its warrants will be exercised.
   b. If you owned the warrants or convertibles of a company, would you be pleased or displeased if it raised its payout rate from 20 percent to 80 percent? Why?

14-12   Evaluate the following statement: "Issuing convertible securities represents a means by which a firm can sell common stock at a price above the existing market price."

14-13   Suppose a company simultaneously issues $50 million of convertible bonds with a coupon rate of 9 percent and $50 million of pure bonds with a coupon rate of 12 percent. Both bonds have the same maturity. Does the fact that the convertible issue has the lower coupon rate suggest that it is less risky than the pure bond? Would you regard its cost of capital as being lower on the convertible than on the pure bond? Explain. (Hint: Although it might appear at first glance that the convertible's cost of capital is lower, this is not necessarily the case, because the interest rate on the convertible understates its cost. Think about this.)

Self-Test Problems   *(Solutions Appear on Page 560)*

Key terms

ST-1   Define each of the following terms:
  a. Cumulative dividends; floating rate preferred stock
  b. Call premium
  c. Lessee; lessor
  d. Sale and leaseback; operating lease; financial lease
  e. Off balance sheet financing
  f. FASB #13
  g. Residual value
  h. Option; striking, or exercise, price; call option; put option
  i. Formula value; warrant; detachable warrant; stepped-up exercise price
  j. Convertible security; conversion ratio, CR; conversion price, P_c; conversion value, C_t; pure-debt value, B_t
  k. Simple EPS; primary EPS; fully diluted EPS

Lease analysis

ST-2   The Olsen Company has decided to acquire a new truck. One alternative is to lease the truck on a 4-year contract for a lease payment of $10,000 per year, with payments to be made at the *beginning* of each year. The lease would include maintenance. Alternatively, Olsen could purchase the truck outright for $40,000, financing with a bank loan for the net purchase price, amortized over a 4-year period at an interest rate of 10 percent per year, payments to be made at the *end* of each year. Under the borrow-to-purchase arrangement, Olsen would have to maintain the truck at a cost of $1,000 per year, payable at year-end. The truck falls into the ACRS 3-year class. It has a salvage value of $10,000, which is the expected market value after 4 years, at which time Olsen plans to replace the truck irrespective of whether it leases or buys. Olsen has a tax rate of 40 percent.
  a. What is Olsen's PV cost of leasing?
  b. What is Olsen's PV cost of owning? Should the truck be leased or purchased?
  c. The appropriate discount rate for use in Olsen's analysis is the firm's after-tax cost of debt. Why?
  d. The salvage value is the least certain cash flow in the analysis. How might Olsen incorporate the higher riskiness of this cash flow into the analysis?

Problems

Balance sheet effects
of leasing

14-1   Two textile companies, Spencer Manufacturing and Elkton Mills, began operations with identical balance sheets. A year later, both required additional manufacturing capacity at a cost of $100,000. Spencer obtained a 5-year, $100,000 loan at an 8 percent interest rate from its bank. Elkton, on the other hand, decided to lease the required $100,000 capacity from National Leasing for 5 years; an 8 percent return was built into the lease. The balance sheet for each company, before the asset increases, is as follows:

		Debt	$100,000
		Equity	100,000
Total assets	$200,000	Total liabilities and equity	$200,000

a. Show the balance sheet of each firm after the asset increase, and calculate each firm's new debt ratio.
b. Show how Elkton's balance sheet would have looked immediately after the financing if it had capitalized the lease.
c. Would the rate of return (1) on assets and (2) on equity be affected by the choice of financing? How?

Lease versus buy

14-2   Silverton Mining Company must install $1 million of new machinery in its Colorado mine. It can obtain a bank loan for 100 percent of the required amount. Alternatively, a Denver investment banking firm which represents a group of investors believes that it can arrange for a lease financing plan. Assume that the following facts apply:
1. The equipment falls in the ACRS 3-year class.
2. Estimated maintenance expenses are $50,000 per year.
3. Silverton's tax rate is 34 percent.
4. If the money is borrowed, the bank loan will be at a rate of 14 percent, amortized in 3 equal installments to be paid at the end of each year.
5. The tentative lease terms call for payments of $320,000 per year for 3 years.
6. Under the proposed lease terms, the lessee must pay for insurance, property taxes, and maintenance.
7. Silverton must use the equipment if it is to continue in business, so it will almost certainly want to acquire the property at the end of the lease. If it does, then under the lease terms it can purchase the machinery at its fair market value at that time. The best estimate of this market value is the $200,000 salvage value, but it could be much higher or lower under certain circumstances.

To assist management in making the proper lease-versus-buy decision, you are asked to answer the following questions:
a. Assuming that the lease can be arranged, should Silverton lease or should it borrow and buy the equipment? Explain. (Hints: PV cost of owning = $729,952 versus $685,750 for leasing; use these as check figures. Also, we used a discount rate of 9.24%. $PVIF_{9.24\%,1} = 0.9154$, $PVIF_{9.24\%,2} = 0.8380$, and $PVIF_{9.24\%,3} = 0.7671$. Loan payment = $430,731.)

b. Consider the $200,000 estimated salvage value. Is it appropriate to discount it at the same rate as the other cash flows? What about the other cash flows — are they all equally risky? (Hints: Riskier cash flows are normally discounted at higher rates, but when the cash flows are *costs* rather than *inflows,* the normal procedure must be reversed.)

Lease analysis   **14-3**   As part of its overall plant modernization and cost reduction program, the management of Confederate Mills has decided to install a new automated weaving loom. In the capital budgeting analysis of this equipment, the IRR of the project was found to be 29 percent versus a project required return of 14 percent.

The loom has an invoice price of $100,000, including delivery and installation charges. The funds needed could be borrowed from the bank through a 4-year amortized loan at a 15 percent interest rate, with payments to be made at the end of each year. In the event that the loom is purchased, the manufacturer will contract to maintain and service it for a fee of $8,000 per year paid at the end of each year. The loom falls in the ACRS 5-year class, and Confederate's marginal tax rate is 34 percent.

Brooks Automation, Inc., maker of the loom, has offered to lease the loom to Confederate for $31,500 upon delivery and installation (at t = 0) plus 4 additional annual lease payments of $31,500 to be made at the end of Years 1 to 4. (Note that there are 5 lease payments in total.) The lease agreement includes maintenance and servicing. Actually, the loom has an expected life of 8 years, at which time its expected salvage value is zero; however, after 4 years, its market value is expected to equal its book value of $17,000. Confederate plans to build an entirely new plant in 4 years, so it has no interest in either leasing or owning the proposed loom for more than that period.

a. Should the loom be leased or purchased?

b. The salvage value is clearly the most uncertain cash flow in the analysis. Assume that the appropriate salvage value pretax discount rate is 18 percent. What would be the effect of a salvage value risk adjustment on the decision?

c. The original analysis assumed that Confederate would not need the loom after 4 years. Now assume that the firm will continue to use it after the lease expires. Thus, if it leased, Confederate would have to buy the asset after 4 years at the then existing market value, which is assumed to equal the book value. What effect would this requirement have on the basic analysis? (No numerical analysis is required; just verbalize.)

Warrants   **14-4**   Weatherford Industries, Inc., has warrants outstanding that permit its holders to purchase one share of stock per warrant at a price of $30.

a. Calculate the formula value of Weatherford's warrants if the common stock sells at each of the following prices: $25, $30, $35, and $100.

b. At what approximate price do you think the warrants would actually sell under each condition indicated in Part a? What premium is implied in your price? Your answer will be a guess, but your prices and premiums should bear reasonable relationships to each other.

c. How would each of the following factors affect your estimates of the warrants' prices and premiums in Part b?
   1. The life of the warrant is lengthened.
   2. The expected variability (σ_p) in the stock's price decreases.
   3. The expected growth rate in the stock's EPS increases.
   4. The company announces the following change in dividend policy: whereas it formerly paid no dividends, henceforth it will pay out *all* earnings as dividends.

d. Assume Weatherford's stock now sells for $26 per share. The company wants to sell some 20-year, annual interest, $1,000 par value bonds. Each bond will have 50 warrants, each exercisable into one share of stock at an exercise price of $30. Weatherford's pure bonds yield 10 percent. Regardless of your answer to Part b, assume that the warrants will have a market value of $2 when the stock sells at $26. What coupon interest rate and dollar coupon must the company set on the bonds with warrants if they are to clear the market? Round to the nearest dollar or percentage point.

Convertibles

14-5   The Boca Grande Company was planning to finance an expansion in the summer of 1988. The principal executives of the company agreed that an industrial company like theirs should finance growth by means of common stock rather than by debt. However, they believed that the price of the company's common stock did not reflect its true worth, so they decided to sell a convertible security. They considered a convertible debenture but feared the burden of fixed interest charges if the common stock did not rise enough to make conversion attractive. They decided on an issue of convertible preferred stock, which would pay a dividend of $2.10 per share.

The common stock was selling for $42 a share at the time. Management projected earnings for 1988 at $3 a share and expected a future growth rate of 10 percent a year in 1989 and beyond. It was agreed by the investment bankers and management that the common stock would continue to sell at 14 times earnings, the current price/earnings ratio.

a. What conversion price should be set by the issuer? The conversion rate will be 1.0; that is, each share of convertible preferred can be converted into one share of common. Therefore, the convertible's par value (as well as the issue price) will be equal to the conversion price, which in turn will be determined as a percentage over the current market price of the common. Your answer will be a guess, but make it a reasonable one.

b. Should the preferred stock include a call provision? Why or why not?

Financing alternatives

14-6   The Drake Computer Company has grown rapidly during the past 5 years. Recently its commercial bank urged the company to consider increasing its permanent financing. Its bank loan under a line of credit has risen to $300,000, carrying a 10 percent interest rate, and Drake has been 30 to 60 days late in paying trade creditors.

Discussions with an investment banker have resulted in the decision to raise $500,000 at this time. Investment bankers have assured Drake that the following alternatives are feasible (flotation costs will be ignored):

- *Alternative 1:* Sell common stock at $10 per share.
- *Alternative 2:* Sell convertible bonds at a 10 percent coupon, convertible into 80 shares of common stock for each $1,000 bond (that is, the conversion price is $12.50 per share).
- *Alternative 3:* Sell debentures with a 10 percent coupon; each $1,000 bond will have 80 warrants to buy one share of common stock at $12.50.

Melissa Dunlop, the president, owns 80 percent of Drake's common stock and wishes to maintain control of the company; 100,000 shares are outstanding. The following are summaries of Drake's latest financial statements:

Balance Sheet

		Current liabilities	$400,000
		Common stock, $1 par	100,000
		Retained earnings	50,000
Total assets	$550,000	Total liabilities and equity	$550,000

Income Statement

Sales	$1,100,000
All costs except interest	990,000
EBIT	$ 110,000
Interest	20,000
EBT	$ 90,000
Taxes at 40%	36,000
Net income	$ 54,000
Shares outstanding	100,000
Earnings per share	$0.54
Price/earnings ratio	16×
Market price of stock	$8.64

a. Show the new balance sheet under each alternative. For Alternatives 2 and 3, show the balance sheet after conversion of the debentures or exercise of the warrants. Assume that $300,000 of the funds raised will be used to pay off the bank loan and the rest to increase total assets.

b. Show Dunlop's control position under each alternative, assuming that she does not purchase additional shares.

c. What is the effect on earnings per share of each alternative if it is assumed that profits before interest and taxes will be 20 percent of total assets?

d. What will be the debt ratio under each alternative?

e. Which of the three alternatives would you recommend to Dunlop, and why?

Convertibles   **14-7**   Isberg Computers, Inc., needs to raise $35 million to begin producing a new microcomputer. Isberg's straight, nonconvertible debentures currently yield 12 percent. Its stock sells for $38 per share; the last dividend was $2.46; and the expected growth rate is a constant 8 percent.

Investment bankers have tentatively proposed that Isberg raise the $35 million by issuing convertible debentures. These convertibles would have a $1,000 par value, carry a coupon rate of 10 percent, have a 20-year maturity, and be convertible into 20 shares of stock. The bonds would be noncallable for 5 years, after which they would be callable at a price of $1,075; this call price would decline by $5 per year in Year 6 and each year thereafter. Management has called convertibles in the past (and presumably will call them again in the future), once they were eligible for call, as soon as their conversion value was about 20 percent above their par value (not their call price).

a. Draw an accurate graph similar to Figure 14-2 representing the expectations set forth in the problem.

b. Suppose the previously outlined projects work out on schedule for 2 years, but then Isberg begins to experience extremely strong competition from Japanese firms. As a result, Isberg's expected growth rate drops from 8 percent to zero. Assume that the dividend at the time of the drop is $2.87. The company's credit strength is not impaired, and its value of k_s is also unchanged. What would happen (1) to the stock price and (2) to the convertible bond's price? Be as precise as you can.

680-681

Lease analysis
(Integrative)

14-8   Kathy Allen, capital acquisitions manager for C. R. Jones Financial Services, Inc., has been asked to perform a lease-versus-buy analysis on a new quotation display system for Jones's Tampa branch office. The system would receive current pricing information from several on-line data services, record the information for retrieval by the branch's brokers, and display current prices in the lobby.

The equipment costs $1,000,000, and, if it is purchased, Jones could obtain a term loan for the full amount at a 10 percent cost. The loan would be amortized over the 4-year life of the equipment, with payments made at the end of each year. The equipment is classified as special purpose and hence falls into the ACRS 3-year class. If the equipment is purchased, a maintenance contract would be obtained at a cost of $20,000, payable at the beginning of each year.

After 4 years the equipment will be sold, and Allen's best estimate of its residual value at that time is $100,000. Because technology is changing rapidly in real-time display systems, however, the residual value is very uncertain.

As an alternative, Consolidated Leasing is willing to write a 4-year lease on the equipment, including maintenance, for payments of $280,000 at the *beginning* of each year. Jones's marginal federal-plus-state tax rate is 40 percent. Help Allen conduct her analysis by answering the following questions:

a. 1. Why is leasing sometimes referred to as "off balance sheet" financing?
    2. What effect does leasing have on a firm's capital structure?

b. 1. What is Jones's present value cost of owning the equipment?
    2. Explain the rationale for the discount rate you used.

c. 1. What is Jones's present value cost of leasing the equipment?
    2. What is the net advantage to leasing? Should Jones buy or lease the equipment?

d. Now assume that Allen believes the equipment's residual value could be as low as $0 or as high as $200,000, but she stands by $100,000 as her expected value. She concludes that the residual value is riskier than the other cash flows in the analysis, and she wants to incorporate this differential risk into her analysis. Describe how this could be accomplished. What effect would it have on Jones's lease decision?

e. Allen knows that her firm has been considering moving to a new downtown location for some time. Thus, she is concerned that these plans may come to fruition prior to the expiration of the lease. If the move occurs, Jones would buy or lease all new equipment, and hence she would like to include a cancellation clause in the lease contract. What effect would a cancellation clause have on the riskiness of the lease to C. R. Jones?

Warrants and convertibles (Integrative)

14-9   Mark Logan, financial manager of CompuEd, Inc., is facing a dilemma. His firm was founded 5 years ago to provide educational software for the rapidly expanding primary and secondary school markets. Although CompuEd has done well, the firm's founder and chairman believes that an industry shake-out is imminent. To survive, the firm must capture market share now, and this requires a large infusion of new capital.

Because of uncertainties in the near term, Logan does not want to issue new common stock. On the other hand, interest rates are currently very high by historical standards, and with the firm's B rating, the interest payments on a new debt issue would be too much to handle if sales took a downturn. Thus, Logan has narrowed his choice of securities to bonds with warrants or convertible bonds. He has asked you to help in the decision process by answering the following questions:

a. What is a call option? Why does a knowledge of call options help one to understand warrants and convertibles?

b. Computerized Teaching Aids, Inc. (CTAI), has options listed on the Chicago Board Options Exchange. The following table gives the option price for its 6-month, $20 call option at 3 different stock prices:

Stock Price	Option Price
$20	$ 4
30	12
40	20

1. What is the option's theoretical value and premium at each stock price? Why do call options sell for more than their theoretical value?

2. Assume that CTAI's stock price increased from $20 to $30. What rate of return would this provide to a stock investor? An option investor? What is the loss potential on the stock? On the option?

3. Now assume that CTAI's stock price increased from $30 to $40. What would be the rate of return to a stock investor? To an option investor? What is the loss potential on the stock? On the option? Why does the premium over theoretical value decline as the stock price increases?

c. One of Logan's alternatives is to issue a bond with warrants attached. CompuEd's current stock price is $20, and its cost of 20-year, annual coupon debt without warrants is estimated by its investment bankers to be 12 percent. The bankers suggest attaching 50 warrants per bond, with each having an exercise price of $25. It is estimated that each warrant, when detached and traded separately, will have a value of $3.

1. What coupon rate should be set on the bond with warrants if the total package is to sell for $1,000?
2. Suppose the bonds are issued and the warrants immediately trade for $5 each. What does this imply about the terms of the issue?
3. When will the warrants be exercised?
4. Will the warrants bring in additional capital when exercised? If so, what type of capital?
5. Because warrants lower the cost of the accompanying debt issue, shouldn't all debt be issued with warrants? What is the expected cost of the bond with warrants if the warrants are expected to be exercised in 5 years, when CompuEd's stock price is expected to be $35?

d. As an alternative to the bond with warrants, Logan is considering convertible bonds. The firm's investment bankers estimate that CompuEd could sell a 20-year, 10.5 percent, annual coupon, callable convertible bond for its $1,000 par value, whereas a straight debt issue would require a 12 percent coupon. CompuEd's current stock price is $20, its last dividend was $1.48, and the dividend is expected to grow at a constant 8 percent. The convertible could be converted into 40 shares of CompuEd stock at the owner's option.

1. What conversion price, P_c, is implied in the convertible's terms?
2. What is the straight debt value of the convertible? What is the implied value of the convertibility feature?
3. What is the bond's conversion value in any year? At Year 0? At Year 10?
4. What is meant by the "floor value" of a convertible? What is the convertible's expected floor value at Year 0? At Year 10?
5. Assume that CompuEd intends to force conversion by calling the bond when its conversion value is 20 percent above its par value, or at $1.2(\$1,000) = \$1,200$. When is the issue expected to be called? Answer to the closest year.
6. What is the expected cost of the convertible to CompuEd? Does this cost appear consistent with the riskiness of the issue? Assume conversion in Year 5 at a conversion value of $1,200.

e. Logan believes that the costs of both a bond with warrants and a convertible bond are similar. Thus, his decision must be based on other factors. What are some of the factors that he should consider in making his decision?

Computer-Related Problems

(Work the problems in this section only if you are using the computer problem diskette.)

Lease versus buy   **C14-1**   Use the model for Problem C14-1 in the file C14 to work this problem.

a. Refer back to Problem 14-2. Determine the lease payment at which Silverton would be indifferent to buying or leasing; that is, find the lease payment which equates the NPV of leasing to that of buying. (Hint: Use trial-and-error.)

b. Using the $320,000 lease payment, what would be the effect if Silverton's tax rate fell to 20 percent? What would be the effect if the tax rate fell to zero percent? What do these results suggest?

Lease analysis

C14-2 Use the model for Problem C14-2 in the file C14 to work this problem.

a. Refer back to Problem 14-3. Suppose Confederate's managers disagree on the appropriate discount rate to use in the analysis. What effect would a discount rate change have on the lease-versus-buy decision? At what discount rate would Confederate's managers be indifferent to buying or leasing? (The model is set up to use the same discount rate for evaluating both the operating cash flows and the salvage value, so you only need enter the new rate for the operating cash flows.)

b. Under the original lease terms, it was to Confederate's advantage to purchase the loom. However, if you had analyzed the lease from the lessor's viewpoint, you would have found that it was more profitable for Brooks Automation to lease the machine than to sell it. In fact, the manager of Brooks has found that the company can lower the lease payment to $29,900 and still make more by leasing the machine than by selling it. With an annual lease payment of $29,900 should the loom be leased or bought?

c. Perform the lease analysis assuming that Confederate's marginal tax rate is (1) 0 percent and (2) 40 percent. Assume a lease payment of $31,500 and a 15 percent pretax discount rate. What effect, if any, would the lessee's tax rate have on the lease-versus-buy decision?

Solutions to Self-Test Problems

ST-1 Refer to the marginal glossary definitions and appropriate sections of the text to check your responses.

ST-2

a. *Cost of leasing:*

	Beginning of Year			
	0	1	2	3
Lease payment (AT)[a]	$ 6,000	$6,000	$6,000	$6,000
PVIFs (6%)[b]	1.000	0.9434	0.8900	0.8396
PV of leasing	$ 6,000	$5,660	$5,340	$5,038
Total PV cost of leasing =	$22,038			

[a]After-tax payment = $10,000(1 − T) = $10,000(0.60) = $6,000.
[b]This is the after-tax cost of debt: 10%(1 − T) = 10%(0.60) = 6.0%.

b. *Cost of owning:*

$$\text{Purchase price} = \$40,000.$$

$$\text{Loan payment} = \$40,000/(\text{PVIFA}_{10\%,4})$$

$$= \$40,000/(3.1699)$$

$$= \$12,619.$$

$$\text{Depreciable basis} = \$40,000.$$

Here are the cash flows under the borrow-and-buy alternative:

	End of Year			
	1	2	3	4
1. Amortization schedule				
(a) Loan payment	$12,619	$12,619	$12,619	$12,619
(b) Interest	4,000	3,138	2,190	1,147
(c) Principal payment	8,619	9,481	10,429	11,472
(d) Remaining balance	31,381	21,900	11,472	0
2. Depreciation schedule				
(e) Depreciable basis	$40,000	$40,000	$40,000	$40,000
(f) Allowance	0.33	0.45	0.15	0.07
(g) Depreciation	13,200	18,000	6,000	2,800
3. Cash outflows				
(h) Loan payment	$12,619	$12,619	$12,619	$12,619
(i) Interest tax savings	(1,600)[a]	(1,255)	(876)	(459)
(j) Depreciation tax savings	(5,280)[b]	(7,200)	(2,400)	(1,120)
(k) Maintenance (AT)	600	600	600	600
(l) Salvage value (AT)				(6,000)
(m) Total cash outflows	$ 6,339	$ 4,764	$ 9,943	$ 5,640
PVIFs	0.9434	0.8900	0.8396	0.7921
PV of owning	$ 5,980	$ 4,240	$ 8,348	$ 4,467

$$\text{Total PV cost of owning} = \underline{\$23,035}$$

[a]Interest(T) = \$4,000(0.40) = \$1,600.
[b]Depreciation(T) = \$13,200(0.40) = \$5,280.

Because the present value of the cost of leasing is less than that of owning, the truck should be leased: $23,035 − $22,038 = $997, net advantage to leasing.

c. The discount rate is based on the cost of debt because most cash flows are fixed by contract and, consequently, are relatively certain. Thus, the lease cash flows have about the same risk as the firm's debt. Also, leasing is considered to be a substitute for debt. We use an after-tax cost rate because the cash flows are stated net of taxes.

d. Olsen could increase the discount rate on the salvage value cash flow. This would increase the PV cost of owning and make leasing even more advantageous.

15

Mergers, Divestitures, Holding Companies, and LBOs

LOW STOCK PRICE AND UNDERVALUED ASSETS MAKE FEDERATED ATTRACTIVE FOR TAKEOVER

If you have ever shopped in Bloomingdale's, Filene's, Rich's, Bulloch's, Burdines, Lazarus, Foleys, or I. Magnum, you have shopped in Federated Department Stores. Federated is the largest department store chain in the United States, but its performance has been lackluster in recent years, and its stock price fell by more than 50 percent during 1987. Some analysts blamed Federated's problems on its chairman, Howard Goldfeder, claiming that he had failed to take the proper steps to keep up with the competition, while others argued that Goldfeder had taken all the right steps, but that he simply had not moved quickly enough. At any rate, most analysts agreed that Federated was undervalued and that it was a prime acquisition target.

What made Federated attractive to a potential buyer? First, the steps that Goldfeder took to make Federated more efficient and competitive were paying off at last; net earnings for 1987 were 11 percent higher than 1986 net earnings, and 1988 started off even better. Second, Federated has some of the best-known names in retailing, and they are organized as divisions, some of which could easily be sold to allow a buyer to recoup a great deal of cash in a short time period. Third, Federated owns buildings which were acquired years ago at low prices, so its balance sheet does not reflect its true worth.

As a result of all this, in the spring of 1988, Campeau Corporation, a Toronto-based real estate development firm, and R. H. Macy & Company, a long-time rival of Federated, made separate bids for control of Federated. Campeau was primarily interested in acquiring Federated's undervalued real-estate assets. Macy, on the other hand, saw the situation as an opportunity to merge the operations of the two retailing chains, to thereby gain economies of scale in purchasing and operations, and thus to become the preeminent retailer in the United States. Eventually, Campeau and Macy joined forces to acquire Federated and then split up the company. Goldfeder and his top managers lost their positions and were not happy with developments, but Federated's stockholders were quite pleased, as the stock climbed from its 1987 low of $28 to a final purchase price of $73.50.

IN the text thus far, we have discussed some of the operating and financing decisions financial managers must make. Firms also occasionally undertake massive restructuring programs in which major new businesses are acquired, large segments of the firm are sold off, or the capital structure is changed radically. Such events can occur either separately or in combination, and they can be decided by management or be forced on management by outsiders. We discuss such restructurings in this chapter, examining mergers, divestitures, the holding company form of organization, and leveraged buyouts (LBOs).

RATIONALE FOR MERGERS

merger
The combination of two firms to form a single firm.

Many reasons have been given to account for the high level of U.S. **merger** activity. In this section we present some of the motives behind corporate mergers.[1]

Synergy

synergy
The condition wherein the whole is greater than the sum of its parts; in a synergistic merger, the postmerger value exceeds the sum of the separate companies' premerger values.

The primary motivation for most mergers is to increase the value of the combined enterprise. If Companies A and B merge to form Company C, and if C's value exceeds that of A and B taken separately, then **synergy** is said to exist.[2] Such a merger should be beneficial to both A's and B's stockholders. Synergis-

---

[1]As we use the term, *merger* means any combination that forms one firm from two or more existing firms. For legal purposes, there are distinctions among the various ways these combinations can occur, but our emphasis is on the fundamental business and financial aspects of mergers.

[2]If synergy exists, the whole is greater than the sum of the parts. Synergy is also called the "2 plus 2 equals 5 effect." The distribution of the synergistic gain between A's and B's stockholders is determined by negotiation, a point discussed later in the chapter.

tic effects can arise from four sources: (1) *operating economies of scale* in management, production, or distribution; (2) *financial economies,* which could include a higher price/earnings ratio, a lower cost of debt, or a greater debt capacity; (3) *differential management efficiency,* which implies that the management of one firm is relatively inefficient, so the profitability of the acquired assets can be improved by merger; and (4) *increased market power* resulting from reduced competition. Operating and financial economies are socially desirable, as are mergers that increase managerial efficiency, but mergers that reduce competition are both undesirable and illegal.[3]

Tax Considerations

Tax considerations have stimulated a number of mergers. For example, a firm which is highly profitable and in the highest corporate tax bracket could acquire a company with large accumulated tax losses, then use those losses to shelter its own income.[4] Similarly, a company with large losses could acquire a profitable firm. Also, tax considerations could result in mergers being a desirable use for excess cash. For example, if a firm has a shortage of internal investment opportunities compared to its cash flows, it will have excess cash, and its options for disposing of this excess cash are (1) paying an extra dividend, (2) investing in marketable securities, (3) repurchasing its own stock, or (4) purchasing another firm. If the firm pays an extra dividend, its stockholders will have to pay taxes on the distribution. Marketable securities such as Treasury bonds provide a good temporary parking place for money, but the rate of return on such securities is less than that required by stockholders. A stock repurchase might result in a capital gain for the remaining stockholders, but it could be disadvantageous if the company had to pay a high price to acquire the stock, and, if the repurchase was designed solely to avoid paying dividends, it might be challenged by the IRS. However, using surplus cash to acquire another firm has no immediate tax consequences either for the acquiring firm or for its stockholders, and this fact has motivated a number of mergers.

Purchase of Assets below Their Replacement Cost

Sometimes a firm will become an acquisition candidate because the replacement value of its assets is considerably higher than its market value. For example, in the 1980s oil companies could acquire reserves more cheaply by

---

[3]In the 1880s and 1890s, many mergers occurred in the United States, and some of them were clearly directed toward gaining market power rather than increasing operating efficiency. As a result, Congress passed a series of acts designed to insure that mergers are not used as a method of reducing competition. The principal acts include the Sherman Act (1890), the Clayton Act (1914), and the Celler Act (1950). These acts make it illegal for firms to combine in any manner if the combination will tend to lessen competition. They are administered by the antitrust division of the Justice Department and by the Federal Trade Commission.

[4]Mergers undertaken only to use accumulated tax losses would probably be challenged by the IRS. However, because many factors are present in any given merger, it is hard to prove that a merger was motivated only, or even primarily, by tax considerations.

buying out other oil companies than by exploratory drilling. This factor was a motive in Chevron's acquisition of Gulf Oil.

The acquisition of Republic Steel (the sixth largest steel company) by LTV (the fourth largest) provides another example of a firm's being purchased because its purchase price was less than the replacement value of its assets. LTV found that it was less costly to purchase Republic Steel for $700 million than it would have been to construct a new steel mill. At the time, Republic's stock was selling for less than one-third of its book value.

Even though LTV bought Republic's capacity at a lower cost than would have been required to build new plants, the purchase will not benefit LTV's stockholders unless management can operate Republic's assets better than they were being operated. LTV's management has argued that sufficient economies of scale exist to make the merger synergistic. The least efficient plants of both companies are being closed; plants that make similar products (say, sheet steel for autos or oil drilling pipe) are being consolidated; and distribution systems are being integrated. If these moves result in sizable cost savings, the merger will be successful. Otherwise, the fact that LTV bought Republic's assets at below their replacement value will be immaterial, and the consolidated company will have trouble. Currently (1988) LTV is doing well, but its future is far from assured.

Diversification

Managers often claim that diversification helps to stabilize the firm's earnings stream and thus reduces corporate risk. Therefore, diversification is often given as a reason for mergers. Stabilization of earnings is certainly beneficial to a firm's employees, suppliers, and customers, but its value to the firm's stockholders and debtholders is less clear. If an investor is worried about earnings variability, he or she could probably diversify through stock purchases more easily than could the firm through acquisitions. Why should Firms A and B merge to stabilize earnings when a stockholder in Firm A could sell half of his or her stock in A and use the proceeds to purchase stock in Firm B, especially since the stockholder could take this action at a much lower cost than would be involved if the firms merged?

Of course, if you were the owner-manager of a closely held firm, it might be virtually impossible for you to sell part of your stock to diversify, because this would dilute your ownership and also generate a large tax liability. In this case, a merger might well be the best way to achieve personal diversification. However, for publicly held firms, diversification alone is not a valid motive for any merger.

Control

As we discuss in the following section, in recent years many hostile mergers and takeovers have occurred. The managers of the acquired companies generally lose their jobs, or at least their autonomy. Therefore, managers who own less than 51 percent of the stock in their firms look to devices that will lessen the chances of their firms' being taken over. Mergers can serve as such a device. For example, when Enron was under attack, it arranged to buy Houston Natural Gas Company, paying for Houston primarily with debt. That merger made Enron much larger and hence harder for any potential acquirer to "digest." Also, the much higher debt level resulting from the merger made it hard for any acquiring company to use debt to buy Enron. Such **defensive mergers** are difficult to defend on economic grounds. The managers involved invariably argue that synergy, not a desire to protect their own jobs, motivated the acquisition, but there can be no question that many mergers today are designed more for the benefit of managers than for that of stockholders.

defensive merger
A merger designed to make a company less vulnerable to a takeover.

TYPES OF MERGERS

horizontal merger
A combination of two firms that produce the same type of good or service.

vertical merger
A merger between a firm and one of its suppliers or customers.

congeneric merger
A merger of firms in the same general industry, but for which no customer or supplier relationship exists.

conglomerate merger
A merger of companies in totally different industries.

Economists classify mergers into four groups: (1) horizontal, (2) vertical, (3) congeneric, and (4) conglomerate. A **horizontal merger** occurs when one firm combines with another in its same line of business — for example, the 1988 merger of Shearson Lehman and E. F. Hutton was a horizontal merger because both firms are brokerage houses. An example of a **vertical merger** is a steel producer's acquisition of one of its own suppliers, such as an iron or coal mining firm, or an oil producer's acquisition of a company which uses its products, such as a petrochemical firm. *Congeneric* means "allied in nature or action"; hence, a **congeneric merger** involves related enterprises but not producers of the same product (horizontal) or firms in a producer-supplier relationship (vertical). Examples of congeneric mergers include Unilever's takeover of Chesebrough-Ponds, a toiletry maker, and Philip Morris's acquisition of General Foods. A **conglomerate merger** occurs when unrelated enterprises combine, as illustrated by Mobil Oil's acquisition of Montgomery Ward.

Operating economies (and also anticompetitive effects) are at least partially dependent on the type of merger involved. Vertical and horizontal mergers generally provide the greatest synergistic operating benefits, but they are also the ones most likely to be attacked by the U.S. Department of Justice. In any event, it is useful to think of these economic classifications when analyzing the feasibility of a prospective merger.

LEVEL OF MERGER ACTIVITY

Four major "merger waves" have occurred in the United States. The first was in the late 1800s, when consolidations occurred in the oil, steel, tobacco, and other basic industries. The second was in the 1920s, when the stock market

Table 15-1   The Five Biggest Mergers (Billions of Dollars)

Companies	Value	Percent of Book Value	Type of Transaction
Chevron-Gulf	$13.3	136%	Acquisition for cash
Texaco-Getty	10.1	191	Acquisition for cash and notes
British Petroleum-Standard Oil	8.0	253	Acquisition for cash and warrants
Du Pont-Conoco	7.2	156	Acquisition for cash and common stock
General Electric-RCA	6.4	242	Acquisition for cash

boom helped financial promoters consolidate firms in a number of industries, including utilities, communications, and autos. The third was in the 1960s, when conglomerate mergers were the rage. The fourth began in the early 1980s, and it is still going strong.

The "merger mania" of the 1980s has been sparked by six factors: (1) the depressed level of the dollar relative to Japanese and European currencies, which made U.S. companies look cheap to foreign buyers; (2) the unprecedented level of inflation that existed during the 1970s and early 1980s, which increased the replacement value of firms' assets even while a weak stock market reduced their market values; (3) the Reagan administration's stated view that "bigness is not necessarily badness," which resulted in a more tolerant attitude toward large mergers; (4) the general belief among the major natural resource companies that it is cheaper to "buy reserves on Wall Street" through mergers than to explore and find them in the field; (5) attempts to ward off raiders by use of defensive mergers; and (6) the development of the junk bond market, which made it possible to use far more debt in acquisitions than had been possible earlier. Financial historians have not yet compiled the statistics and done the analysis necessary to compare the 1980s merger wave with the earlier ones, but it is virtually certain that the current wave will rank among the largest. Table 15-1 lists the top five mergers of all time, and they all have occurred in the 1980s.

Brief descriptions of some different types of recent mergers will help explain how the deals are worked out:

1. Getty Oil, the fourteenth largest U.S. oil company, was acquired by Texaco, the fourth largest, at a cost of $10.1 billion. Prior to the merger activity, Getty's shares were selling at around $65, and the descendants of J. Paul Getty, the founder, were complaining of inefficient management. Then the controlling trustees of the Sarah C. Getty Trust, together with Pennzoil, announced plans to take the firm private by buying the shares which they did not already control at a price of $112.50 per share. Texaco then jumped in with an offer of $125 per share.

    The merger doubled Texaco's domestic oil and gas reserves, and, with Getty's retail outlets, gave Texaco a larger share of the gasoline market. Some analysts claimed that Texaco, with its sprawling network of refineries and rapidly dwindling reserves, made the correct decision by acquiring Getty, with its large reserves and minimal refining operations. Other analysts contended that Texaco paid too much for Getty. Acquiring Getty's reserves may have been cheaper for Texaco than finding new oil, but the value of these reserves depends on the price of oil, which by 1988 was down by more than 40 percent.

Two side issues arose at the end of the Getty merger. The first concerned the Bass Brothers of Texas, an immensely wealthy family that had acquired over $1 billion of Texaco stock during all the action. Texaco's management was afraid the Basses would try to take over Texaco, so they bought out the Bass interests at a premium of about 20 percent over the market value. Some of Texaco's stockholders argued that the payment amounted to "greenmail," or a payoff made with stockholders' money just to insure that Texaco's managers could keep their jobs. This situation, along with several similar ones, has led to the introduction of bills in Congress to limit the actions that a management group can take in its efforts to avoid being taken over. However, Congress has not actually taken any action to date. The second side issue was a suit by Pennzoil, which charged that Texaco caused Getty to breach its contract with Pennzoil. Pennzoil won a $12 billion judgment, but Texaco appealed, and in 1988 Pennzoil settled for $3 billion, of which Pennzoil's lawyers will get $400 million. Texaco was forced into bankruptcy. At this time it appears that Texaco will survive, but that its top managers will lose their jobs.

2. Conoco, which had assets with a book value of $11 billion and which was, based on sales, the fourteenth largest company in the United States, was the target of three other giants: Mobil (the second largest U.S. corporation), Du Pont (the fifteenth largest U.S. corporation), and Seagram (a large Canadian company). This merger alone almost surpassed in dollar amount the previous record for all mergers in a single year (book value assets of $12 billion in 1968). Conoco's stock sold for about $50 just before the bidding started; the bid price got up to over $100 per share before it was over, because Conoco's oil and coal reserves, plus its plant and equipment, were worth far more than the company's initial stock market value.

If Mobil had won, this would have been a horizontal merger. If Seagram had won, it would have been a conglomerate merger. Yet Du Pont won, and it was classified as a vertical merger because Du Pont uses petroleum in its production processes. The Justice Department would have fought a merger with Mobil, but it indicated that it would not do so in the case of Seagram or Du Pont. For this reason, even though Mobil made the highest bid of $115 per share, Du Pont ended up the winner with a bid of $98. Stockholders chose the Du Pont bid over that of Mobil because they were afraid a Mobil merger would be blocked, causing Conoco's stock to fall below the level of the Du Pont bid.

This was a *hostile merger* — Conoco's management would rather have had the company remain an independent entity. Obviously, though, that was not to be, and Conoco's top managers found themselves working for someone else (or out of a job). This is a good illustration of a point made in Chapter 1, namely, that managers have a strong motivation to operate in a manner that will maximize the value of their firms' stock, for otherwise they can find themselves in the same boat as Conoco's managers.

3. Marathon Oil, a company only slightly smaller than Conoco, was the object of an attempted acquisition by Mobil after that company lost its bid for Conoco. Marathon's management resisted strongly, and again other bidders entered the picture. U.S. Steel picked up Marathon for about $6 billion, making this the fourth largest merger up to that time. U.S. Steel's bid for Marathon was unusual in that the firm offered to purchase only 51 percent of the stock and to exchange bonds for the remainder, with cash going to those stockholders who agreed to the merger at the earliest date. This is called a **two-tier offer**, and it prompted many stockholders to tender their stock to U.S. Steel out of fear of having to accept bonds if they waited to see if the bid might go higher.

two-tier offer
A merger offer which provides different (better) terms to those who tender their stock earliest.

4. Schlitz, once the largest U.S. brewer, had been losing both money and market share. By the 1980s it had become only the fourth largest brewer, with a market share of 8.5 percent, and it seemed to be on a collision course with bankruptcy. Schlitz's troubles arose from its poor marketing strategy, a problem that it was unable to conquer. G. Heileman, the sixth largest brewer, with a market share of 7.5 percent, was better managed, and its sales were growing rapidly. (Heileman's ROE was 27.3 percent; Schlitz's was negative.) Because of its successful marketing programs, Heileman needed more brewing capacity, whereas, because of its poor sales performance, Schlitz had 50 percent excess capacity. Heileman offered to buy Schlitz's common stock for $494 million. If the takeover attempt had been successful, Heileman would have acquired capacity at an effective cost of $19 per barrel versus a construction cost of about $50 per barrel. The merger would also have made Heileman the third largest in the nation. Although the Justice Department under the Reagan administration had previously taken the position that "bigness is not necessarily badness," it opposed this merger because in its judgment the resulting concentration would substantially reduce competition in the brewing industry. Therefore, Heileman abandoned the merger effort. However, Schlitz was still in trouble, and it was later acquired by Stroh Brewery, another good marketer.

5. General Motors recently acquired Electronics Data Systems (EDS), the world's largest data processing company, for $2.2 billion. GM had excess cash, and it wanted to diversify outside the auto industry to stabilize earnings. Also, its management believed that EDS could help GM set up better internal management control systems and help with the company's

planned automation of manufacturing operations. Ross Perot, the founder and a 50 percent owner of EDS, was offered more than $1 billion plus a seat on the GM board for his stock, as well as a chance to continue running EDS. After the merger, Perot clashed with Roger Smith, GM's chairman, and GM bought Perot's stock at a substantial premium over the market price to get him off the board.

6. Shortly after the EDS merger, GM also acquired Hughes Aircraft, a privately held company that was started by the late Howard Hughes in the 1930s, for $4.7 billion. Hughes was one of the largest defense contractors and was highly profitable, but what GM really wanted was its expertise in high-tech electronic controls. GM must utilize such technology in its design and manufacturing of autos if it is to compete effectively with the Japanese. Investment analysts believe that there are tremendous potential synergistic benefits to GM from both the Hughes and the EDS mergers, but at this point one can only wait and see if the $7 billion of investments will really pay off.

As we write this, the merger wave of the 1980s is still alive and well. However, as we discuss later in the chapter, recent tax law changes may have a negative effect on merger activity.

PROCEDURES FOR COMBINING FIRMS

In the vast majority of merger situations, one firm (generally the larger of the two) simply decides to buy another company, negotiates a price, and then acquires the target company. Occasionally, the acquired firm will initiate the action, but it is much more common for a firm to seek acquisitions than to seek to be acquired.[5] Following convention, we shall call a company that seeks to acquire another the **acquiring company** and the one which it seeks to acquire the **target company**.

acquiring company
A company that seeks to acquire another.

target company
A firm that another company seeks to acquire.

Once an acquiring company has identified a possible target, it must establish a suitable price, or range of prices, that it is willing to pay. With this in mind, its managers must decide how to approach the target company's managers. If the acquiring firm has reason to believe that the target's management will approve the merger, then it will simply propose a merger and try to work out some suitable terms. If an agreement can be reached, the two management groups will issue statements to their stockholders recommending that they approve the merger. Assuming that the stockholders do approve, the acquiring

---

[5]However, if a firm is in financial difficulty, if its managers are elderly and do not think that suitable replacements are on hand, or if it needs the support (often the capital) of a larger company, then it may seek to be acquired. Thus, when a number of Texas banks were in trouble in the late 1980s, they lobbied to get the state legislature to pass a law that made it easier for them to be acquired. Out-of-state banks then moved in to help salvage the situation and minimize depositor losses.

firm will simply buy the target company's shares from its stockholders, paying for them either with its own shares (in which case the target company's stockholders become stockholders of the acquiring company), with cash, or with bonds. Such a transaction is defined as a **friendly merger**.

Under other circumstances, the target company's management may resist the merger. Perhaps the managers believe that the price offered for the stock is too low, or perhaps they simply want to keep their jobs. In either case, the target firm's management is said to be *hostile* rather than friendly, and in a **hostile merger**, the acquiring firm must make a direct appeal to the target firm's stockholders. In a hostile merger, the acquiring company generally makes a **tender offer**, in which it asks the stockholders of the firm it is seeking to control to submit, or "tender," their shares in exchange for a specified price. The price is generally stated as so many dollars per share of the stock to be acquired, although it can be stated in terms of shares of stock of the acquiring firm. Because the tender offer is a direct appeal to stockholders, it need not be approved by the target firm's management. Tender offers are not new, but their frequency of use has increased greatly in recent years.[6]

MERGER ANALYSIS

In theory, merger analysis is quite simple. The acquiring firm simply performs a capital budgeting analysis to determine whether the present value of the cash flows expected to result from the merger exceeds the price that must be paid for the target company; if the net present value is positive, the acquiring firm should take steps to acquire the target firm. The target company's stockholders, on the other hand, should accept the proposal if the price offered exceeds the present value of the cash flows they expect to receive in the future if the firm continues to operate independently. Theory aside, however, some difficult issues are involved: (1) The acquiring company must estimate the cash flows that will result from the acquisition; (2) it must also determine what effect, if any, the merger will have on its own required rate of return on equity; (3) it must decide how to pay for the merger — with cash, with its own stock, or with some other type or package of securities; and (4) having estimated the benefits of the merger, the acquiring and target firms' managers and stockholders must bargain (or fight) over how to share these benefits. The Conoco, Marathon, and other cases discussed previously illustrate just how complex this analysis can be.

Operating Mergers versus Financial Mergers

From the standpoint of financial analysis, there are two basic types of mergers: operating mergers and financial mergers.

---

[6]Tender offers can be friendly, with the target firm's management recommending that stockholders go ahead and tender their stock.

operating merger
A merger in which operations of the firms involved are integrated in hope of achieving synergistic benefits.

pure financial merger
A merger in which the firms involved will not be operated as a single unit and from which no operating economies are expected.

1. An **operating merger** is one in which the operations of two companies are integrated with the expectation of obtaining synergistic effects. The GM mergers provide good examples of operating mergers.

2. A **pure financial merger** is one in which the merged companies will not be operated as a single unit and from which no significant operating economies are expected. Coca-Cola's acquisition of Columbia Pictures with $748 million of surplus cash is an example of a financial merger.

Of course, mergers may actually combine these two features. Thus, if Mobil had acquired either Conoco or Marathon, the merger would have been primarily an operating one. However, with Du Pont and U.S. Steel emerging as the victors in those acquisitions, the mergers were more financial than operating in nature.

Estimating Future Operating Income

In a pure financial merger, the postmerger cash flows are simply the sum of the expected cash flows of the two companies if they were to continue to operate independently. However, if the two firms' operations are to be integrated, or if the acquiring firm plans to change the target firm's management to get better results, then accurate estimates of future cash flows, which are absolutely essential to sound merger decisions, will be difficult to construct.

The basic rationale for any operating merger is synergy. Del Monte Corporation provides a good example of a series of well-thought-out, favorable operating mergers. Del Monte successfully merged and integrated numerous small canning companies into a highly efficient, profitable organization. It used standardized production techniques to increase the efficiency of all of its plants, a national brand name and national advertising to develop customer brand loyalty, a consolidated distribution system, and a centralized purchasing office to obtain substantial discounts from volume purchases. Because of these economies, Del Monte became the most efficient and profitable U.S. canning company, and its merger activities helped make possible the size that produced these economies. Consumers also benefited, because Del Monte's efficiency enabled the company to sell high-quality products at relatively low prices.

An example of a poor pro forma analysis that resulted in a disastrous merger was the consolidation of the Pennsylvania and New York Central railroads. The premerger analysis suggested that large cost savings would result, but it was grossly misleading because it failed to recognize that certain key elements in the two rail systems were incompatible and hence could not be meshed together. Thus, rather than gaining synergistic benefits, the combined system actually incurred additional overhead costs that led to bankruptcy. *In planning operating mergers, the development of accurate pro forma cash flows is the single most important aspect of the analysis.*[7]

---

[7]Firms heavily engaged in mergers have "acquisition departments" whose functions include (1) seeking suitable merger candidates and (2) taking over and integrating acquired firms into the parent corporation. The first step involves the development of both pro forma cash flows and a plan for making the projections materialize. The second step involves streamlining the operations of the acquired firm and instituting a system of controls that will permit the parent to effectively manage the new division and to coordinate its operations with those of other units.

Merger Terms

The terms of a merger include two important elements: (1) Who will control the combined enterprise? (2) How much will the acquiring firm pay for the acquired company? These points are discussed next.

Postmerger Control. The employment/control situation is often of vital interest. First, consider the situation in which a small, owner-managed firm sells out to a larger concern. The owner-manager may be anxious to retain a high-status position, and he or she may also have developed a camaraderie with the employees and thus be concerned about keeping operating control of the organization after the merger. Thus, these points are likely to be stressed during the merger negotiations.[8] When a publicly owned firm not controlled by its managers is merged into another company, the acquired firm's management also is worried about its postmerger position. If the acquiring firm agrees to retain the old management, then management may be willing to support the merger and to recommend its acceptance to the stockholders. If the old management is to be removed, it will probably resist the merger.[9]

The Price Paid. The second key element in a merger is the price to be paid for the target company — the cash or securities to be given to the target firm's stockholders. The analysis is similar to a regular capital budgeting analysis: The incremental earnings are estimated; a discount rate is applied to find the present value of those earnings; and, if the present value of the future incremental earnings exceeds the price to be paid for the target firm, the merger is approved. Thus, only if the target firm is worth more to the acquiring firm than its market value as a separate entity will the merger be feasible. Obviously, the acquiring firm tries to buy at as low a price as possible, whereas the target firm tries to sell out at the highest possible price. The final price is determined

---

[8] The acquiring firm may also be concerned about this point, especially if the acquired firm's management is quite good. A condition of the merger may be that the management team agree to stay on for a period, such as five years, after the merger. Also, the price paid may be contingent on the acquired firm's performance subsequent to the merger. For example, when International Holdings acquired Walker Products, the price paid was 100,000 shares of International Holdings stock (which sold for $63 per share) at the time the deal was closed plus an additional 30,000 shares each year for the next three years, provided Walker Products earned at least $1 million during each of these years. Since Walker's managers owned the stock and would receive the bonus, they had a strong incentive to stay on and help the firm meet its targets.

If the managers of the target company are highly competent but do not wish to remain on after the merger, the acquiring firm may build into the merger contract a noncompetitive agreement with the old management. Thus, Walker Products' principal officers had to agree not to affiliate with a new business which is competitive with the one they sold for a period of five years. Such agreements are especially important with service-oriented businesses.

[9] Managements of firms that are thought to be attractive merger candidates occasionally arrange "golden parachutes" for themselves. Golden parachutes are extremely lucrative retirement plans which take effect if a merger is consummated. Thus, when Bendix was acquired by Allied, Bill Agee, Bendix's chairman, "pulled the ripcord of his golden parachute" and walked away with $4 million. Congress is currently considering controls on golden parachutes as a part of its "greenmail" legislative proposals.

by negotiations, with the party that negotiates best capturing most of the incremental value. *The larger the synergistic benefits, the more room there is for bargaining, and the higher the probability that the merger actually will be consummated.*[10]

VALUING THE TARGET FIRM

To determine the value of the target firm, two key items are needed: (1) a set of pro forma financial statements which develop the expected cash flows, and (2) a discount rate, or cost of capital, to apply to the projected cash flows.

Pro Forma Income Statements

Table 15-2 contains the projected income statements for Microchip Corporation, which is being considered for acquisition by Allied Technologies, a large conglomerate. The projected data are postmerger, so all synergistic effects are included. Microchip currently uses 30 percent debt, but if it were acquired, Allied would increase Microchip's debt ratio to 50 percent. Both Allied and Microchip have a 34 percent marginal tax rate.

The net cash flows shown in Table 15-2 are the flows that would be available to Allied's stockholders, and these are the basis of the valuation.[11] Of course, the postmerger cash flows attributable to the target firm are extremely difficult to estimate. In a complete merger valuation, just as in a complete capital budgeting analysis, the component cash flow probability distributions would be specified, and sensitivity, scenario, and simulation analyses would be conducted. Indeed, in a friendly merger, the acquiring firm would send a team consisting of literally dozens of accountants, engineers, and finance people, to the target firm's headquarters to go over its books, to estimate required maintenance expenditures, to set values on assets such as petroleum reserves, and the like.

Estimating the Discount Rate

Because the bottom line net cash flows shown in Table 15-2 are equity flows, they should be discounted at the cost of equity rather than at the overall cost of capital. Further, the cost of equity used must reflect the riskiness of the net

---

[10]It has been estimated that of all merger negotiations seriously begun, fewer than one-third actually result in mergers. Also, in contested merger situations, the company that offers the most will usually make the acquisition, and the company that will gain the greatest synergistic benefits can generally bid the most.

[11]We purposely kept the cash flows simple to help focus in on the key issues of the valuation process. In an actual merger valuation, the cash flows would be much more complex, normally including such items as additional capital furnished by the acquiring firm, tax loss carry-forwards, tax effects of plant and equipment valuation adjustments, and the proceeds of any planned asset sales.

Table 15-2   Microchip Corporation: Projected Postmerger Income
             Statements as of December 31
             (Millions of Dollars)

	1989	1990	1991	1992	1993
Net sales	$105	$126	$151	$174	$191
Cost of goods sold	80	94	111	127	137
Selling and administrative expenses	10	12	13	15	16
EBIT	$ 15	$ 20	$ 27	$ 32	$ 38
Interest[a]	3	4	5	6	6
EBT	$ 12	$ 16	$ 22	$ 26	$ 32
Taxes[b]	4	5	7	9	11
Net income	$ 8	$ 11	$ 15	$ 17	$ 21
Retentions for growth[c]	4	4	7	9	12
Cash available to Allied	$ 4	$ 7	$ 8	$ 8	$ 9
Terminal value[d]					$121
Net cash flow[e]	$ 4	$ 7	$ 8	$ 8	$130

[a]Interest payment estimates are based on Microchip's existing debt plus additional debt to increase the debt ratio to 50 percent, plus additional debt after the merger to finance asset expansion but subject to the 50 percent target capital structure.

[b]Allied will file a consolidated tax return after the merger. Thus, the taxes shown here are the full corporate taxes attributable to Microchip's operations; there will be no additional taxes on the cash flowing from Microchip to Allied.

[c]Some of the net income generated by Microchip after the merger will be retained to finance its own asset growth, and some will be transferred to Allied to pay dividends on its stock or for redeployment within the corporation. It is assumed that Microchip's depreciation-generated funds are used to replace its worn-out and obsolete plant and equipment.

[d]Microchip's available cash flows are expected to grow at a constant 10 percent after 1993. The value of all post-1993 cash flows to Allied, as of December 31, 1993, is estimated by use of the constant growth model to be $121 million:

$$V_{1993} = \$9(1.10)/(0.1815 - 0.10) = \$121 \text{ million.}$$

In the next section, we discuss the estimation of the 18.15 percent cost of equity.

[e]These are the net cash flows which are available to Allied by virtue of the acquisition of Microchip. They may be used for dividend payments to Allied's stockholders or for financing asset expansion in Allied's other divisions and subsidiaries.

cash flows in the table; thus, the appropriate discount rate is Microchip's cost of equity, not that of Allied or the consolidated postmerger firm. Microchip's market-determined premerger beta was 1.30; however, this reflects its premerger 30 percent debt ratio, whereas its postmerger debt ratio will increase to 50 percent. Allied's investment bankers estimate that Microchip's beta will rise to 1.63 if its debt ratio is increased to 50 percent.

We can use the Security Market Line to determine Microchip's approximate cost of equity. If the risk-free rate is 10 percent and the market risk premium is 5 percent, then Microchip's cost of equity, k_s, after the merger would be 18.15 percent:[12]

---

[12]In actual merger situations, the companies often hire investment banking firms to help develop valuation estimates. For example, when General Electric acquired Utah International in the largest merger up to that time, it hired Morgan Stanley to determine Utah's value. The author

$$k_s = k_{RF} + (RP_M)b$$
$$= 10\% + (5\%)1.63$$
$$= 18.15\%.$$

Valuing the Cash Flows

The value of Microchip to Allied is the present value of the cash flows expected to accrue to Allied, discounted at 18.15 percent (in millions of dollars):

$$\text{Value} = \frac{\$4}{(1.1815)^1} + \frac{\$7}{(1.1815)^2} + \frac{\$8}{(1.1815)^3}$$
$$+ \frac{\$8}{(1.1815)^4} + \frac{\$130}{(1.1815)^5} = \$74.$$

Thus, if Allied can acquire Microchip for $74 million or less, the merger appears to be acceptable from Allied's standpoint.

THE ROLE OF INVESTMENT BANKERS

The investment banking community is involved with mergers in a number of ways: (1) helping to arrange mergers, (2) aiding target companies in resisting mergers, and (3) helping to value target companies. These merger-related activities have been quite profitable. For example, the investment bankers who assisted British Petroleum in its recent acquisition of Standard Oil earned fees of $9.6 million, and those who represented Standard Oil were paid $8 million. Du Pont's investment banker in the Conoco contest, First Boston, earned fees of more than $15 million, whereas Morgan Stanley, Conoco's investment banker, had an arrangement under which it would earn fees of about $15 million regardless of who won. No wonder investment banking houses are able to make top offers to finance graduates!

Arranging Mergers

The major investment banking firms have merger and acquisition groups which operate within their corporate finance departments. (Corporate finance departments offer advice, as opposed to underwriting or brokerage services,

---

discussed the valuation process with the Morgan Stanley analyst in charge of the appraisal. Morgan Stanley considered using the CAPM but chose instead to base the discount rate on DCF methodology. However, other analysts, and Morgan Stanley people in other situations, have used CAPM analysis as we describe it here. Merger analysis, like the analysis of any other complex issue, requires judgment, and people's judgments differ as to which method is most appropriate for any given situation.

to business firms.) Members of these groups strive to identify firms with excess cash that might want to buy other firms, companies that might be willing to be bought, and firms that might, for a number of reasons, be attractive to others. If an oil company, for instance, decided to expand into coal mining, it might enlist the aid of an investment banker to help it locate and then negotiate with a target coal company. Similarly, dissident stockholders of firms with poor track records may work with investment bankers to oust management by helping to arrange a merger. Drexel Burnham Lambert, the investment banking house that developed junk bond financing, has offered packages of financing to corporate raiders, with the package including both designing the securities to be used in the tender offer and getting people and firms to buy the target firm's stock now and then tender it once the final offer is made.

Fighting Off Mergers

Target firms that do not want to be acquired generally enlist the help of an investment banking firm, along with a law firm that specializes in helping to block mergers. Defenses include such tactics as (1) changing the by-laws so that only one-third of the directors are elected each year and/or so that a 75 percent approval (a "supermajority") versus a simple majority is required to approve a merger, (2) trying to convince the target firm's stockholders that the price being offered is too low, (3) raising antitrust issues in the hope that the Justice Department will intervene, (4) issuing debt and using the proceeds to repurchase stock in the open market in an effort to push the price above that being offered by the potential acquirer, (5) getting a **white knight** that is more acceptable to the target firm's management to compete with the potential acquirer, and (6) taking a "poison pill," as described below.

white knight
A company that is more acceptable to the management of a firm subject to a hostile takeover attempt.

poison pill
An action which will seriously hurt a company if it is acquired by another.

golden parachutes
Large payments made to the managers of a firm if it is acquired.

Some examples of **poison pills** — which really do amount to virtually committing suicide to avoid a takeover — are such tactics as borrowing on terms that require immediate repayment of all loans if the firm is acquired, selling off at bargain prices the assets that originally made the firm a desirable target, granting such lucrative **golden parachutes** to their executives that the cash drain from these payments would render the merger infeasible, and planning defensive mergers which would leave the firm with new assets of questionable value and a huge amount of debt to service. Companies are even giving their stockholders the right to buy at half-price the stock of an acquiring firm should the firm be acquired. The blatant use of poison pills is constrained by directors' awareness that such use could trigger personal suits by stockholders against directors who voted for them, and, perhaps in the near future, by laws that would limit management's use of these tactics. Still, investment bankers are busy thinking up new poison pill formulas, and others are just as actively trying to come up with antidotes.[13]

---

[13]In large part because of shareholder suits arising out of poison pills, greenmail, or other attempts to block mergers that would be profitable to stockholders, it is becoming both harder and more expensive for companies to buy insurance which protects directors from stockholder

Establishing a Price

If a friendly merger is being worked out between two firms' managements, it is important to be able to document that the agreed-upon price is a fair one; otherwise, the stockholders of either company could sue to block the merger. Therefore, in many large mergers, each side will hire an investment banking firm to evaluate the target company and to help establish the fair price. For example, General Electric employed Morgan Stanley to determine a fair price for Utah International, as did Royal Dutch to help establish the price it paid for Shell Oil. Even if the merger is not friendly, investment bankers may still be asked to help establish a price. If a surprise tender offer is to be made, the acquiring firm will want to know the lowest price at which it might be able to acquire the stock, whereas the target firm may seek help in proving that the price being offered is too low.[14]

The 1986 Tax Reform Act

Prior to the Tax Reform Act of 1986, an acquired company could pay more than book value for a target firm's assets, write up those assets, depreciate the marked-up value for tax purposes, and thus lower the post-merger firm's taxes as compared to the taxes of the two firms operating separately. At the same time, the target firm did not have to pay any taxes on the capital gains at the time of the mergers, although its stockholders were subject to a capital gains liability if and when they sold their stock, assuming they got more for it than they had originally paid.

Under the new law, if the acquiring company writes up the target company's assets for tax purposes, then the target company must pay capital gains taxes in the year the merger occurs. (These immediate capital gains taxes can be avoided if the acquiring company elects not to write up acquired assets and hence depreciates them on their old basis.) So, under the new law, the firms will have to pay more taxes than under the old law, and this fact has made mergers less profitable. Also, the maximum capital gains tax rate rose from 20

---

suits. This, in turn, is forcing directors to be more careful about approving management's proposals, and the whole situation is making it harder for companies to get good people to serve as directors. The final result, however, will probably be less rubber stamping by directors and more concern for stockholder as opposed to management interests. As an example, in August 1988, GM's board refused to go along with Chairman Roger Smith's request that three GM senior VP's be added to the board. The existing board wanted to keep a majority of "outside" as opposed to "inside" (that is, officer) directors.

[14]Such investigations must obviously be done in secret, for if someone knew that Company A was thinking of offering, say, $50 per share for Company T, which was currently selling at $35 per share, huge profits could be made. The biggest scandal to hit Wall Street thus far in the 1980s was the disclosure that Ivan Boesky, a well-known investor, was buying from Dennis Levine, a senior member of the investment banking house Drexel Burnham Lambert, information about prospective takeovers of companies that Drexel Burnham was analyzing for others. Boesky's purchases, of course, raised the prices of the stocks and thus forced Drexel's clients to pay more than they otherwise would have had to pay. Incidentally, Boesky and Levine went to jail for improper use of inside information.

percent to 28 percent in 1987, a 40 percent increase. This, of course, means that target companies' stockholders will now net less from mergers than they would have under the old law.

When one considers the joint effects of the corporate and personal tax changes, it is clear that the tax treatment of mergers is significantly less favorable today than it was before 1987. This means that a great deal less money will end up in the pockets of selling stockholders, so they will be much less anxious to sell out. Taken alone, the tax law changes probably would reduce the level of merger activity, but other forces, such as the declining value of the dollar, have thus far kept the "urge to merge" very much alive.

JOINT VENTURES

joint venture
An undertaking in which two or more independent companies combine their resources to achieve a specific, limited objective.

A merger is not the only way in which the resources of two firms can be combined. In contrast to a merger, in which all resources are combined under a single management, a **joint venture** involves the joining together of parts of two companies to accomplish a specific, limited objective.[15] Joint ventures are controlled by the combined management of the two (or more) parent companies.

In one widely publicized joint venture, General Motors and Toyota, the first and third largest automakers in the world, set up an operation to produce 200,000 cars annually at an idle GM plant in Fremont, California. Toyota contributed an estimated $150 million to the venture, whereas GM put up $20 million in cash plus the California plant. Although both firms appointed an equal number of directors, Toyota got to name the chief executive. GM is reported to have sought the venture to gain better insights into how the Japanese can produce higher-quality cars at a substantially lower cost than U.S. automakers, while Toyota wanted to increase its production in the United States because of import quota limitations. Both companies apparently are realizing their goals.

DIVESTITURES

Although corporations do more buying than selling of operating assets, quite a bit of selling also occurs. In this section we briefly discuss the major types of divestitures, and then we present some recent examples and rationales for divestitures.

---

[15]Cross-licensing, consortia, joint bidding, and franchising are still other ways for firms to combine resources. For more information on joint ventures, see Sanford V. Berg, Jerome Duncan, and Phillip Friedman, *Joint Venture Strategies and Corporate Innovation* (Cambridge, Mass.: Oelgeschlager, Gunn, and Hain, 1982).

Types of Divestitures

divestiture
The sale of some of a company's operating assets.

There are four types of **divestitures**: (1) sale of an operating unit to another firm, (2) sale to the managers of the unit being divested, (3) setting up the business to be divested as a separate corporation and then giving (or "spinning off") its stock on a pro rata basis to the divesting firm's stockholders, and (4) outright liquidation of assets.

Sale to another firm generally involves the sale of an entire division or unit, usually for cash but sometimes for stock of the acquiring firm. In a *managerial buyout,* the managers of the division purchase the division themselves, usually for cash plus notes. Then, as owners/managers, they reorganize it as a closely held firm. In a **spin-off**, the firm's existing stockholders are given new stock representing separate ownership rights in the company that was divested. The new company establishes its own board of directors and officers and operates as a separate company. The stockholders end up owning shares of two firms instead of one, but no cash has been transferred. Finally, in a *liquidation,* the assets of a division are sold off piecemeal rather than as a single entity. We present some recent examples of the different types of divestitures in the next section.

spin-off
A divestiture in which the stock of a subsidiary is given to the parent company's stockholders.

Divestiture Illustrations

1. Esmark, Inc., a holding company which owned such consumer products companies as Swift meats and Playtex, recently sold off several of its nonconsumer-oriented divisions, including petroleum properties for which Mobil and some other oil companies paid $1.1 billion. Investors generally thought of Esmark as a meat packing and consumer products company, and its stock price reflected this image rather than that of a company with huge holdings of valuable oil reserves carried at low balance sheet values. Thus, Esmark's stock was undervalued, according to its managers, and the company was in danger of a Conoco-type takeover bid. Selling the oil properties helped Esmark raise its stock price from $19 to $45. The improved stock price did not prevent Esmark from being taken over by Beatrice Companies shortly thereafter, however.

2. ITT, in a move to streamline and rationalize its holdings, divested itself of 27 separate companies with a value of $1.2 billion. Some of these units were suffering losses and were holding down the parent company's earnings, whereas others simply no longer fitted into ITT's corporate strategy. Also, ITT had a debt ratio that many regarded as excessive, and it used some of the proceeds from the asset sales to reduce its debt.

3. International Paper (IP) recently sold its Canadian subsidiary to Canadian Pacific for $1.1 billion. IP planned to spend $4 billion to modernize its facilities, and the sale of the Canadian unit helped finance these expenditures.

4. IU International, a multimillion-dollar conglomerate listed on the NYSE, recently spun off three major subsidiaries — Gotaas-Larson, an ocean

shipping company, which owned Carnival Cruise Lines; Canadian Utilities, an electric utility; and Echo Bay Mining, a gold mining company. IU also owned (and retained) some major trucking companies (Ryder and PIE), several manufacturing businesses, and some large agribusiness operations. IU's management originally acquired and combined several highly cyclical businesses such as ocean shipping and gold mining with stable ones such as utilities in order to gain overall corporate stability through diversification. The strategy worked reasonably well from an operating standpoint, but it failed in the financial markets. According to its management, IU's very diversity kept it from being assigned to any particular industrial classification, so security analysts tended not to follow the company and therefore did not understand it or recommend it to investors. (Analysts tend to concentrate on an industry, and they do not like to recommend — and investors do not like to invest in — a company they do not understand.) As a result, IU had a low P/E ratio and a low market price. After the spin-offs, IU's stock price plus those of the spun-off companies rose from $10 to over $75.

5. U.S. Steel recently sold certain coal properties to Standard Oil of Ohio for $600 million. Sohio wanted the properties to diversify its energy base, and U.S. Steel needed money to modernize its core businesses.

6. In 1986 the managers of Beatrice Companies and some private investors borrowed $6.9 billion from a group of banks and used this money to buy all of the firm's stock. This type of debt-financed transaction is called a **leveraged buyout**, and Beatrice was said to have "gone private" because the public stockholders were bought out and all of the stock is now in the hands of the management group. The new Beatrice has been busily selling off divisions to raise money to reduce its bank loans; its loan agreements required it to sell off at least $1.45 billion in assets by mid-1987, but Beatrice beat that schedule. The company sold Avis for $250 million just 12 days after it went private, and it later sold off its Coca-Cola bottling operations for about $1 billion. Beatrice also sold its refrigerated warehouse network, its Max Factor cosmetic line, its dairy products line, and its Playtex operations, raising another $2.4 billion in total. It now appears that the management group will net several billion dollars in profits from the deal.

7. In 1984 AT&T was broken up to settle a Justice Department antitrust suit filed in the 1970s. For almost 100 years AT&T had operated as a holding company which owned Western Electric (its manufacturing subsidiary), Bell Labs (its research arm), a huge long-distance network system, and 22 Bell operating companies, such as Pacific Telephone, New York Telephone, Southern Bell, and Southwestern Bell. AT&T was reorganized into eight separate companies: a slimmed-down AT&T, which kept Western Electric, Bell Labs, and all interstate long-distance operations, and seven new regional telephone holding companies that were created from the 22 old operating telephone companies. The stock of the seven

leveraged buyout
A situation in which a firm's managers borrow heavily against the firm's assets and purchase the company themselves.

new telephone companies was then spun off to the old AT&T's stockholders. Thus, a person who held 100 shares of old AT&T stock owned, after the divestiture, 100 shares of the "new" AT&T plus 10 shares of each of the seven new operating companies. These 170 shares were backed by the same assets that had previously backed 100 shares of AT&T common.

The AT&T divestiture occurred as a result of a suit by the Justice Department, which wanted to break up the Bell System into a regulated monopoly segment (the seven regional telephone companies) and a manufacturing/long-distance segment which would be subjected to competition. The breakup was designed to strengthen competition in those parts of the telecommunications industry which are not natural monopolies.[16]

The preceding examples illustrate the varied reasons for divestitures. Sometimes the market does not appear to properly recognize the value of a firm's assets when they are held as part of a conglomerate; the Esmark oil properties case was an example. Similarly, IU International's management thought that the company had become so complex and diverse that analysts and investors did not understand it and consequently ignored it. Other companies need cash either to finance expansion in their primary business lines or to reduce a large debt burden, and divestitures can be used to raise this cash; the International Paper and Beatrice examples illustrated this point. The ITT actions showed that running a business is a dynamic process — conditions change, corporate strategies change in response, and, as a result, firms alter their asset portfolios by acquisitions, divestitures, or both.

HOLDING COMPANIES

holding company
A corporation that owns sufficient common stock of another firm to achieve working control of it.

parent company
A holding company; a firm which controls another firm by owning large blocks of its stock.

operating company
A subsidiary of a holding company; a separate legal entity.

Strictly defined, any company that owns stock in another firm could be called a holding company. However, as the term is generally used, a **holding company** is a firm that holds large blocks of stock in other companies and exercises control over those firms. The holding company is often called the **parent company,** and the controlled companies are known as *subsidiaries* or **operating companies.** The parent can own 100 percent of the subsidiaries' stock, but often control is exercised with only a fraction of the shares.

Many of the advantages and disadvantages of holding companies are identical to those of large-scale operations already discussed in connection with mergers and consolidations. However, as we show next, the holding company

---

[16]Another forced divestiture involved Du Pont and General Motors. In 1921, GM was in serious financial trouble, and Du Pont supplied capital plus managerial talent in exchange for 23 percent of the stock. Many years later, the Justice Department won an antitrust suit which required Du Pont to spin off (to Du Pont stockholders) its GM stock.

form of large-scale operation has some distinct advantages (as well as a few disadvantages) over those of completely integrated, divisionalized operations.

Advantages of Holding Companies

Holding companies have three potential advantages: (1) control with fractional ownership, (2) isolation of risks, and (3) legal and accounting separation when regulations make such separation desirable.

1. **Control with fractional ownership.** Through a holding company operation, a firm may buy 5, 10, or 50 percent, or any other amount, of another corporation's stock. Such fractional ownership may be sufficient to give the acquiring company effective working control over the operations of the firm in which it has acquired stock ownership. Working control is often considered to require more than 25 percent of the common stock, but it can be as low as 10 percent if the stock is widely distributed. One financier recently made this statement: "The attitude of management is more important than the number of shares you own. If they think you can control the company, then you do."

2. **Isolation of risks.** Because the various operating companies in a holding company system are separate legal entities, the obligations of any one unit are separate from those of the others. Therefore, catastrophic losses incurred by one unit might not be transmitted as claims on the assets of the other units. However, although this is a customary generalization, it is not always valid. First, the parent company may feel obligated to make good on the subsidiary's debts, even though it may not be legally bound to do so, to keep its good name and thus retain customers. Examples of this would include American Express's payment of more than $100 million in connection with a swindle that was the responsibility of one of its subsidiaries, and United California Bank's coverage of a multimillion-dollar fraud loss incurred by its Swiss affiliate. Second, a parent company may feel obligated to supply capital to an affiliate to protect its initial investment; General Public Utilities' continued support of its subsidiaries' Three Mile Island nuclear plant is an example. Third, when lending to one of the units of a holding company system, an astute loan officer may require a guarantee by the parent holding company. Finally, an accident such as the one at Union Carbide's Bhopal, India, plant may be deemed the responsibility of the parent company, voiding the limited liability rules that would otherwise apply. Still, holding companies can at times be used to prevent losses in one unit from bringing down other units in the system.

3. **Legal separation.** Certain regulated companies such as utilities and financial institutions find it easier to operate as holding companies than as divisional corporations. For example, an electric utility such as Southern Company, which operates in and is regulated by several states, found it most practical to set up a holding company (Southern) which in

turn owns a set of subsidiaries (Georgia Power, Alabama Power, Mississippi Power, and Gulf Power). All of the Bell telephone companies are part of holding company systems, and even utilities which operate only within a single state are finding it beneficial to operate within a holding company format in order to separate those assets under the control of regulators from those not subject to utility commission regulation. Thus, Florida Power & Light recently reorganized as a holding company called FPL Group, which owns a utility (Florida Power & Light) plus subsidiaries engaged in insurance, real estate development, orange groves, and the like.

Banks, insurance companies, and other financial service corporations have also found it convenient to be organized as holding companies. Thus, Citicorp is a holding company which owns Citibank of New York, a leasing company, a mortgage service company, and so on. Transamerica is a holding company which owns insurance companies, small loan companies, title companies, auto rental companies, and an airline.

Disadvantages of Holding Companies

Holding companies have two disadvantages: (1) partial multiple taxation and (2) ease of enforced dissolution.

1. **Partial multiple taxation.** Provided the holding company owns at least 80 percent of a subsidiary's voting stock, the Tax Code permits the filing of consolidated returns, in which case dividends received by the parent are not taxed. However, if less than 80 percent of the stock is owned, returns cannot be consolidated, and taxes must be paid on 30 percent of the dividends received by the holding company. With a tax rate of 34 percent, this means that the effective tax rate on intercorporate dividends is $0.30 \times 34\% = 10.2\%$. This partial double taxation somewhat offsets the benefits of holding company control with limited ownership, but whether or not the penalty of 10.2 percent of dividends received is sufficient to offset other possible advantages is a matter that must be decided in individual situations.

2. **Ease of enforced dissolution.** It is relatively easy for the Justice Department to require dissolution by disposal of stock ownership of a holding company operation that it finds unacceptable. Thus, in 1955 Du Pont was required to dispose of its 23 percent stock interest in General Motors Corporation, an interest that had been acquired back in the early 1920s. Because there had been no fusion between the two corporations, there were no difficulties, from an operating standpoint, in requiring their separation. If complete amalgamation had taken place, however, it would have been much more difficult to break up the company after so many years, and the likelihood of forced divestiture would have been reduced. Still, the forced breakup of AT&T shows that even fully integrated companies can be broken up.

Holding Companies as a Leveraging Device

The holding company vehicle has been used to obtain huge amounts of financial leverage. In the 1920s, several tiers of holding companies were established in the electric utility and other industries. In those days, an operating company at the bottom of the pyramid might have had $100 million of assets, financed by $50 million of debt and $50 million of equity. A first-tier holding company might have owned the stock of the operating firm as its only asset and then been financed with $25 million of debt and $25 million of equity. A second-tier holding company, which owned the $25 million of stock of the first-tier company as its only asset, might have been financed with $12.5 million of debt and $12.5 million of equity. Such systems were extended to four or more levels, but even with only two holding companies, we see that $100 million of operating assets could be controlled at the top by $12.5 million of second-tier equity, and $100 million of operating assets would have had to provide enough cash flow to support $87.5 million of debt. Such a holding company system is highly leveraged, even though the individual components each report 50 percent debt/assets ratios. Because of this *consolidated leverage,* even a small decline in profits at the operating company level could bring the whole system down like a house of cards.

LEVERAGED BUYOUTS (LBOs)

The 1980s have witnessed a huge increase in the number and size of leveraged buyouts, or LBOs. This development has occurred for the same reasons that mergers and divestitures occurred — the existence of potential bargains, situations in which companies were using insufficient leverage, and the development of the junk bond market, which facilitated the use of leverage in takeovers.

LBOs can be initiated in one of two ways: (1) The firm's own managers set up a new company whose equity comes from the managers themselves and some pension funds and other institutions. This new company then arranges to borrow a large amount of money by selling junk bonds through an investment banking firm such as Drexel Burnham Lambert. With the financing in place, the management group then makes an offer to purchase all the publicly owned shares through a tender offer. (2) A specialized LBO firm, with Kohlberg, Kravis, and Roberts (KKR) being the largest and best known, will identify a potential target company, go to the management, and suggest that an LBO deal be done. KKR and other LBO firms have billions of dollars of equity, most put up by pension funds, available for the equity portion of the deals, and they arrange junk bond financing just as would a management-led group. Generally, the newly formed company will have at least 80 percent debt, and sometimes the debt ratio is as high as 98 percent. Thus, the term "leveraged" is most appropriate.

Often, an LBO is an alternative to a merger. For example, in late 1988, Kraft Foods was approached by Philip Morris about a merger. Kraft's management resisted, and Philip Morris announced that it would undertake a hostile tender offer, and Kraft's management announced that it would undertake an LBO to compete with Philip Morris. Philip Morris then raised its offer, and it now looks as though the merger will go through.

It is not clear if LBOs are, on balance, a good or a bad idea. Some government officials, and others, have stated a belief that the leverage involved might destabilize the economy. On the other hand, they have certainly stimulated some lethargic managements, and that is good. Good or bad, though, LBOs are helping to reshape the face of corporate America.

International

INTERNATIONAL MERGERS

1988 has been a banner year for mergers in the United States, with takeover deals having a total value of $135 billion. One reason for the high level of merger activity was that foreign firms spent $40.6 billion buying American companies. For example, British Petroleum took over Standard Oil, Unilever acquired Chesebrough-Pond's, and Blue Arrow (a London employment agency) bought Manpower (another employment agency).

Foreign companies were interested in U.S. firms for several reasons. First, many companies wanted to gain a foothold in the U.S. market to avoid being shut out if Congress should pass protectionist legislation. Second, the purchase of an American firm can provide the overseas parent with a tax shelter. For example, the average Japanese firms pays 56 percent of its income in federal and local taxes. If that same firm operates in the United States, the income is generally subject to U.S. taxes of only 34 percent. Third, the decline in the value of the dollar relative to most foreign currencies has made U.S. firms more attractive to foreign purchasers. For example, in early 1988 British retailer Marks & Spencer PLC paid $750 million for American retailer Brooks Brothers. At the prevailing exchange rate of $1.86 per pound, the deal cost Marks

& Spencer 403 million pounds. If the purchase had been made in 1985, when a pound was worth only $1.10, it would have cost Marks & Spencer 682 million pounds. Thus, the price of Brooks Brothers to a British company declined by 40.9 percent due to the decline in the value of the dollar. Similar exchange rate drops have occurred in the German mark, the Swiss franc, and the Japanese yen.

Investment analysts predicted at the beginning of 1988 that it would be a record year for foreign acquisition of U.S. firms, and thus far they appear to be correct. Indeed, foreign buyers are literally fighting over U.S. targets. For example, one highly publicized foreign takeover involved a fight between Japan's Bridgestone Corporation and Italy's Pirelli for ownership of Firestone Tire & Rubber Company. Bridgestone began the bidding at $1.25 billion. Then, Pirelli came in, aided by France's Michelin. In the end, Bridgestone won, paying $2.6 billion for Firestone, more than double its original offer. Jeffrey Rosen, head of the international mergers and acquisitions department at First Boston, was quoted in *Business Week* as saying, "1988 will be the year of the foreign acquirer." So far, his prediction is holding true.

SUMMARY AND KEY CONCEPTS

This chapter discussed mergers, divestitures, and holding companies. The key concepts covered are listed below.

- A **merger** occurs when two firms combine to form a single company. The primary motives for mergers are (1) synergy, (2) tax considerations, (3) purchase of assets below their replacement costs, (4) diversification, and (5) control.

- Mergers can provide economic benefits through **economies of scale** or through the **concentration of assets** in the hands of more efficient managers. However, mergers also have the potential for reducing competition, and for this reason they are carefully regulated by governmental agencies.

- In most mergers, one company (**the acquiring firm**) initiates action to take over another (**the target firm**).

- A **horizontal merger** occurs when two firms in the same line of business combine.

- A **vertical merger** is the combination of a firm with one of its customers or suppliers.

- A **congeneric merger** involves firms in related industries, but for which no customer-supplier relationship exists.

- A **conglomerate merger** occurs when firms in totally different industries combine.

- In a **friendly merger**, the managements of both firms approve the merger, while in a **hostile merger** the target firm's management opposes the merger.

- An **operating merger** is one in which the operations of the two firms are combined. A **pure financial merger** is one in which the firms continue to operate separately, and hence no operating economies are expected.

- In a **merger analysis**, the price to be paid for the target firm and the employment/control situation are the two key issues to be resolved.

- To determine the **value of the target firm**, the acquiring firm must (1) forecast the cash flows that will result after the merger and (2) develop a discount rate to apply to the projected cash flows.

- **Poison pills** are actions a firm can take that will make the firm less valuable if it is acquired in a hostile takeover. **Golden parachutes** are a form of poison pill in which large payments are made to a firm's managers if it is acquired.

- A **joint venture** is an undertaking in which two or more companies combine some of their resources to achieve a specific, limited objective.

- A **divestiture** is the sale of some of a company's operating assets. A divestiture may involve (1) selling an operating unit to another firm, (2) selling a unit to that unit's managers, (3) **spinning off** a unit as a separate company, or (4) the outright liquidation of a unit's assets.

- The **reasons for divestitures** include antitrust, the improvement of a company's image, and the raising of capital needed to strengthen the corporation's core business.

- A **holding company** is a corporation which owns sufficient stock of another firm to achieve working control of it. The holding company is also known as the **parent company**, and the companies which it controls are called **subsidiaries**, or operating companies.

- Advantages to holding company operations are (1) that control can often be obtained for a smaller cash outlay, (2) that risks may be separated, and (3) that regulated companies can separate regulated from unregulated assets.

- Disadvantages to holding company operations include (1) tax penalties and (2) the fact that incomplete ownership, if it exists, can lead to control problems.

- A **leveraged buyout (LBO)** is a transaction in which a firm's publicly owned stock is bought up in a mostly debt-financed tender offer, and a privately owned, highly leveraged firm results. Often, the firm's own management initiates the LBO.

- Foreign firms have been acquiring U.S. firms at a record pace in recent years due to **the lower value of the dollar** and **a desire to gain a foothold in the U.S. market.**

Questions

15-1   Four economic classifications of mergers are (1) horizontal, (2) vertical, (3) conglomerate, and (4) congeneric. Explain the significance of these terms in merger analysis with regard to (a) the likelihood of governmental intervention and (b) possibilities for operating synergy.

15-2   Firm A wants to acquire Firm B. Firm B's management agrees that the merger is a good idea. Might a tender offer be used?

15-3   Distinguish between operating mergers and pure financial mergers.

15-4   In the spring of 1984, Disney Productions' stock was selling for about $12.50 per share (all prices have been adjusted for a 4:1 split in March 1986). Then Saul Steinberg, a New York financier, began acquiring it, and after he had 12 percent he announced a tender offer for another 37 percent of the stock — which would bring his holdings up to 49 percent — at a price of $16.88 per share. Disney's management then announced plans to buy Gibson Greeting Cards and Arvida Corporation, paying for them with stock. It also lined up bank credit and (according to Steinberg) was prepared to borrow up to $2 billion and use the funds to repurchase shares at a higher price than Steinberg was offering. All of these efforts were designed to keep Steinberg from taking control. In June, Disney's management agreed to pay Steinberg $19.36 per share, which gave him a gain of about $60 million on a two-month investment of about $26.5 million.

When Disney's buyback of Steinberg's shares was announced, the stock price fell almost instantly from $17 to $11.50. Many Disney stockholders were irate, and they sued to block the buyout. Also, the Disney affair added fuel to the fire in a Congressional committee that was holding hearings on proposed legislation that would (1) prohibit someone from acquiring more than 10 percent of a firm's stock without making a tender offer for all the remaining shares, (2) prohibit poison pill tactics such as those Disney's management had used to fight off Steinberg, (3) prohibit buybacks such as the deal eventually offered to Steinberg (greenmail) unless there was an approving vote by stockholders, and (4) prohibit (or substantially curtail) the use of golden parachutes (the one thing Disney's management did not try).

Set forth the arguments for and against this type of legislation. What provisions, if any, should it contain? Also, look up Disney's current stock price to see how its stockholders have actually fared.

15-5   Two large, publicly owned firms are contemplating a merger. No operating synergy is expected. However, since returns on the two firms are not perfectly positively correlated, the standard deviation of earnings would be reduced for the combined corporation. One group of consultants argues that this risk reduction is sufficient grounds for the merger. Another group thinks this type of risk reduction is irrelevant because stockholders can themselves hold the stock of both companies and thus gain the risk reduction benefits without all the hassles and expenses of the merger. Whose position is correct?

Self-Test Problem   *(Solution Appears on Page 593)*

Key terms

ST-1   Define each of the following terms:
a. Synergy
b. Horizontal merger; vertical merger; congeneric merger; conglomerate merger
c. Friendly merger; hostile merger; defensive merger; tender offer; two-tier offer; target company
d. Operating merger; pure financial merger
e. White knight; poison pill; golden parachute
f. Joint venture
g. Divestiture; spin-off; leveraged buyout
h. Holding company; operating company; parent company

Problems

Capital
budgeting analysis

15-1   Anderson's Gifts & Stationery Shoppe wishes to acquire Cindi's Card Gallery for $500,000. Anderson expects the merger to provide incremental earnings of about $80,000 a year for 10 years. Mary Anderson has calculated the marginal cost of capital for this investment

to be 12 percent. Conduct a capital budgeting analysis for Anderson to
determine whether or not she should purchase Cindi's Card Gallery.

Merger analysis   **15-2**   Dallas Appliance Corporation is considering a merger with the Alamo
Vacuum Company. Alamo is a publicly traded company, and its current
beta is 1.40. Alamo has been barely profitable, so it has paid an average
of only 20 percent in taxes during the last several years. In addition, it
uses little debt, having a market value debt ratio of just 25 percent.

    If the acquisition were made, Dallas would operate Alamo as a
separate, wholly owned subsidiary. Dallas would pay taxes on a
consolidated basis, and the tax rate would therefore increase to 34
percent. Dallas also would increase the debt capitalization in the Alamo
subsidiary on a market value basis to 40 percent of assets, which would
increase its beta to 1.48. Dallas's acquisition department estimates that
Alamo, if acquired, would produce the following net cash flows to
Dallas's shareholders (in millions of dollars):

Year	Net Cash Flow
1	$1.20
2	1.40
3	1.65
4	1.80
5 and beyond	Constant growth at 5%

These cash flows include all acquisition effects. Dallas's cost of equity is
16 percent, its beta is 1.0, and its cost of debt is 12 percent. The risk-free
rate is 10 percent.
a. What discount rate should be used to discount the estimated cash
   flows? (Hint: Use Dallas's k_s to determine the market risk premium.)
b. What is the dollar value of Alamo to Dallas?
c. Alamo has 1.2 million common shares outstanding. What is the
   maximum price per share that Dallas should offer for Alamo? If the
   tender offer is accepted at this price, what will happen to Dallas's
   stock price?

Merger analysis   **15-3**   Worldwide Products, Inc., a large conglomerate, is evaluating the
possible acquisition of Gainesville Siding Company (GSC), a small
aluminum siding manufacturer. Worldwide's analysts project the
following postmerger data for GSC (in thousands of dollars):

	1989	1990	1991	1992
Net sales	$300	$345	$370	$400
Selling and administrative expense	30	35	40	45
Interest	12	14	16	18

Tax rate after merger:	34%
Cost of goods sold as a percent of sales:	65%
Beta after merger:	1.50
Risk-free rate:	7%
Market risk premium:	5%
Terminal growth rate of cash flow available to Worldwide:	10%

If the acquisition is made, it will occur on January 1, 1989. All cash flows shown in the income statements are assumed to occur at the end of the year. GSC currently has a market value capital structure of 40 percent debt, but Worldwide would increase that to 50 percent if the acquisition were made. GSC, if independent, would pay taxes at 20 percent, but its income would be taxed at 34 percent if it were consolidated. GSC's current market-determined beta is 1.40, and its investment bankers think that its beta would rise to 1.50 if the debt ratio were increased to 50 percent. The cost of goods sold is expected to be 65 percent of sales, but it could vary somewhat. Depreciation-generated funds would be used to replace worn-out equipment, so they would not be available to Worldwide's shareholders. The risk-free rate is 7 percent, and the market risk premium is 5 percent.

a. What is the appropriate discount rate for valuing the acquisition?
b. What is the terminal value? What is the value of GSC to Worldwide?

Merger analysis   **15-4**   The Fix-It-Up Company, a regional hardware supplies chain which
(Integrative)   specializes in "do-it-yourself" materials and equipment rentals, is cash
rich because of several consecutive good years. One of the alternative uses for the excess funds is an acquisition. Karen Wright, a recent business school graduate, has been asked to place a value on Hooper Hardware, a small chain which operates in an adjacent state.

The following are Wright's estimates of Hooper's earnings potential (in millions of dollars):

	1989	1990	1991	1992
Net sales	$40.0	$60.0	$75.0	$85.0
Cost of goods sold (60%)	24.0	36.0	45.0	51.0
Selling/administrative expense	3.0	4.0	5.0	6.0
Interest expense	2.0	3.0	3.0	4.0
Necessary earnings retentions	0.0	5.0	4.0	3.0

The interest expense listed here includes the interest (1) on Hooper's existing debt, (2) on new debt that Fix-It-Up would issue to help finance the acquisition, and (3) on new debt expected to be issued over time to help finance expansion within the new "H division," the code name given to the target firm. The retentions represent earnings that will be reinvested within the H division to help finance its growth.

Hooper Hardware currently uses 40 percent debt financing and pays taxes at a 30 percent rate. Security analysts estimate Hooper's beta to be 1.2. If the acquisition were to take place, Fix-It-Up would increase Hooper's debt ratio to 50 percent, increasing its beta to 1.3. Further, because Fix-It-Up is highly profitable, taxes on the consolidated firm would be 40 percent. Wright realizes that Hooper also generates depreciation cash flows, but she believes that these funds would have to be reinvested within the division to replace worn-out equipment.

Wright estimates the risk-free rate to be 10 percent and the market risk premium to be 5 percent. She also estimates that net cash flows after 1992 will grow at a constant rate of 10 percent. Fix-It-Up's management is new to the merger game, so Wright was asked to answer some basic questions about mergers as well as to perform the merger analysis. To structure the task, Wright developed the following questions, which she now wants you to answer:

a. Several reasons have been proposed to justify mergers. Among the more prominent are (1) tax considerations, (2) diversification, (3) control, (4) purchase of assets at below replacement cost, and (5) synergy. Which of the reasons are economically justifiable? Which are not? Explain.

b. Briefly describe the differences between a hostile merger and a friendly merger.

c. Use the data in the table to construct the H division's cash flow statements for 1989 through 1992. Why is interest expense deducted in merger cash flow statements, whereas it is not normally deducted in capital budgeting cash flow analysis? Why are retentions deducted in the cash flow statement?

d. Conceptually, what is the appropriate discount rate to apply to the cash flows developed in Part c? What is your actual estimate of this discount rate?

e. What is the terminal value of the acquisition; that is, what is the value of the H division's cash flows beyond 1992? What is Hooper's value to Fix-It-Up? Suppose another firm were evaluating Hooper as an acquisition candidate. Would it obtain the same value? Explain.

f. Assume that Hooper has 10 million shares outstanding. These shares are traded relatively infrequently, but the last trade, made several weeks ago, was at a price of $6 per share. Should Fix-It-Up make an offer for Hooper? If so, how much should it offer per share?

Computer-Related Problem

(Work the problem in this section only if you are using the computer problem diskette.)

C15-1   Use the model for Problem C15-1 in the file C15 to work this problem.

a. Refer back to Problem 15-3. Rework the problem assuming that sales in each year were $100 higher than the base case amounts and that the cost of goods sold/sales ratio was 60 percent rather than 65 percent. What would be the value of GSC to Worldwide under these assumptions?

b. With sales and the cost of goods sold ratio at the levels specified in Part a, what would be GSC's value if its beta were 1.65, k_{RF} rose to 8 percent, and RP_M rose to 6 percent?

c. Leaving all values at their Part b levels, what would be the value of the acquisition if the terminal growth rate rose to 15 percent or dropped to 3 percent?

Solution to Self-Test Problem

ST-1   Refer to the marginal glossary definitions or relevant chapter sections to check your responses.

V The Cost of Capital, Leverage, and Dividend Policy

16 The Cost of Capital

SUPPLYING POWER TO FLORIDA REQUIRES COST OF CAPITAL ESTIMATE

Forecasters estimate that if Florida's 1988 growth rate is maintained, a severe shortage of electric power will occur in the late 1990s. Although new generating capacity will soon be needed, officials have been having trouble finding suitable sites for power plants in the environmentally sensitive South Florida region. A consortium of equipment manufacturers has proposed constructing a huge generating station on one of the Bahama Islands, about 50 miles off the coast of Miami, and running a transmission cable under the Gulf Stream from the plant to the mainland. Coal could be brought in by ship at a reasonable cost, and there would be no serious environmental problems.

A critical issue, though, relates to financing — how could the facility be financed, what would be the cost of the required capital, and would the rate of return on the investment be high enough to cover the cost of capital? The cost of capital information was needed for the type of capital budgeting analysis that would determine the economic feasibility of the project. The techniques discussed in this chapter were used to develop the cost of capital figure used in the analysis. No final decision has been made, but preliminary reports indicate that this multi-billion dollar project does have a good chance of getting the green light.

THE cost of capital is a critically important topic for three main reasons: (1) to maximize a firm's value, its managers must minimize the costs of all inputs, including capital, and to minimize the cost of capital, the managers must be able to measure it; (2) financial managers require an estimate of the cost of capital to make correct capital budgeting decisions; and (3) many other types of decisions made by financial managers, including those related to leasing, to bond refunding, and to working capital policy, require estimates of the cost of capital.[1]

Our first topic in this chapter is the logic of the weighted average cost of capital. Next, we consider the costs of the major types of capital, after which we see how the costs of the individual components of the capital structure are brought together to form a weighted average cost of capital. Finally, we examine the relationship between capital budgeting and the cost of capital.

It should be noted that the cost of capital models and formulas used in this chapter are the same ones we developed back in Chapter 6. In the earlier chapter we were concerned with the rates of return investors require on different securities. Now we use those same models and formulas to estimate the firm's cost of capital. Indeed, the rate of return on a security to an investor is the same as the cost of capital to a firm, so the same models are used by investors and corporate treasurers.

THE LOGIC OF THE WEIGHTED AVERAGE COST OF CAPITAL

When we discussed capital budgeting, we assumed that the firm under consideration was financed entirely with equity funds. In that case, the cost of capital used to analyze capital budgeting decisions should be the company's required return on equity. However, most firms finance a substantial portion of their capital budgets with long-term debt, and many also use preferred stock. For these firms, the cost of capital must reflect the average cost of the various sources of long-term funds used, not just the firms' costs of equity.

Assume that Universal Machine Company, a world-wide producer of computer-controlled machine tools whose major customers include Chrysler, Ford, Volvo, Saab, and others, has a 10 percent cost of debt and a 15 percent cost of equity. Further assume that Universal has made the decision to finance next year's projects by selling debt. The argument is sometimes made that the cost of capital for these projects is 10 percent, because only debt will be used to

---

[1]The cost of capital is also vitally important in regulated industries, including electric, gas, telephone, and water companies. In essence, a regulatory commission first seeks to measure a utility's cost of capital, and it then sets prices so that the company will just earn this rate of return. If the estimate of the cost of capital is too low, the company will not be able to attract sufficient capital to meet long-run demands for service, and the public will suffer. If the cost of capital estimate is too high, customers will have to pay too much for service.

finance them. However, this position is incorrect. If Universal finances a particular set of projects with debt, the firm will be using up some of its potential for obtaining new debt in the future. As expansion occurs in subsequent years, Universal will at some point find it necessary to use additional equity financing to prevent the debt ratio from becoming too large.

To illustrate, suppose Universal borrows heavily at 10 percent during 1989, using up its debt capacity in the process, to finance projects yielding 12 percent. In 1990 it has new projects available that yield 14 percent, well above the return on 1989 projects, but it cannot accept them because they would have to be financed with 15 percent equity money. To avoid this problem, Universal should be viewed as an ongoing concern, and the cost of capital used in capital budgeting should be calculated as a weighted average, or composite, of the various types of funds it generally uses, regardless of the specific financing used to fund a particular project.

BASIC DEFINITIONS

capital component
One of the types of capital used by firms to raise money.

The items on the right-hand side of a firm's balance sheet — various types of debt, preferred stock, and common equity — are its **capital components**. Any increase in total assets must be financed by an increase in one or more capital components.

Capital is a necessary factor of production, and, like any other factor, it has a cost. The cost of each component is called the *component cost* of that particular type of capital; for example, if Universal Machine can borrow money at 10 percent, its component cost of debt is 10 percent.[2] Throughout this chapter we concentrate on debt, preferred stock, retained earnings, and new issues of common stock, which are the four major capital structure components; their component costs are identified by the following symbols:

k_d = interest rate on the firm's new debt = before-tax component cost of debt. For Universal Machine, k_d = 10%.

$k_d(1 - T)$ = after-tax component cost of debt, where T is the firm's marginal tax rate. $k_d(1 - T)$ is the debt cost used to calculate the weighted average cost of capital. For Universal Machine, T = 40%, so $k_d(1 - T) = 10\%(1 - 0.4) = 10\%(0.6) = 6.0\%$.

k_p = component cost of preferred stock. For Universal, k_p = 12%.

k_s = component cost of retained earnings (or internal equity). It is identical to the k_s developed in Chapter 4 and defined there as the required rate of return on common stock. It is quite difficult to estimate k_s, but, as we shall see shortly, for Universal $k_s \approx 15\%$.

---

[2]We will see shortly that there are both a before-tax and an after-tax cost of debt; for now it is sufficient to know that 10 percent is the before-tax component cost of debt.

k_e = component cost of external capital obtained by issuing new common stock, or external equity as opposed to internal equity. As we shall see, it is necessary to distinguish between equity raised by retained earnings and that raised by selling new stock. This is why we distinguish between k_s and k_e. Further, k_e is always greater than k_s. For Universal, $k_e \approx 15.9\%$.

k_a = WACC = the weighted average, or composite, cost of capital. If Universal Machine raises new capital to finance asset expansion, and if it is to keep its capital structure in balance (that is, if it is to keep the same percentage of debt, preferred stock, and common equity funds), then it must raise part of its new funds as debt, part as preferred stock, and part as common equity (with equity coming either from retained earnings or from the issuance of new common stock).[3] We will calculate k_a = WACC for Universal Machine shortly.

These definitions and concepts are explained in detail in the remainder of the chapter, where we develop a marginal cost of capital (MCC) schedule that can be used in capital budgeting. Then, in Chapter 16, we extend the analysis to determine the mix of types of capital that will minimize the firm's cost of capital and thereby maximize its value.

COST OF DEBT, $k_d(1 - T)$

after-tax cost of debt, $k_d(1 - T)$
The relevant cost of new debt financing, taking into account the tax deductibility of interest; used to calculate the WACC.

The **after-tax cost of debt, $k_d(1 - T)$**, used to calculate the weighted average cost of capital is the interest rate on debt, k_d, multiplied by $(1 - T)$, where T is the firm's marginal tax rate:[4]

$$\text{After-tax component cost of debt} = \text{Interest rate} - \text{Tax savings}$$

$$= k_d - k_d T$$

$$= k_d(1 - T). \qquad (16\text{-}1)$$

In effect, the government pays part of the cost of debt because interest is deductible. Therefore, if Universal can borrow at an interest rate of 10 percent,

---

[3]Firms try to keep their debt, preferred stock, and common equity in optimal proportions; we will learn how they establish these proportions in Chapter 17. However, firms do not try to maintain any proportional relationship between the common stock and retained earnings accounts as shown on the balance sheet — for capital structure purposes, common equity is common equity, whether it is represented by common stock or by retained earnings.

[4]The federal tax rate for most corporations is 34 percent. However, most corporations are also subject to state income taxes, so the marginal tax rate on most corporate income is about 40 percent. For illustrative purposes, we assume that the effective federal-plus-state tax rate on marginal income is 40 percent. Also, note that the cost of debt is considered in isolation. The effect of debt on the cost of equity, as well as on future increments of debt, is ignored when the weighted cost of a combination of debt and equity is derived in this chapter, but it will be treated in Chapter 17, "Capital Structure and Leverage."

and if it has a marginal federal-plus-state tax rate of 40 percent, then its after-tax cost of debt is 6 percent:

$$k_d(1 - T) = 10\%(1.0 - 0.4)$$

$$= 10\%(0.6)$$

$$= 6.0\%.$$

The reason for using the after-tax cost of debt is as follows. The value of the firm's stock, which we want to maximize, depends on *after-tax* cash flows. Because interest is a deductible expense, it produces tax savings which reduce the net cost of debt, so the after-tax cost of debt is less than the before-tax cost. We are concerned with after-tax cash flows, and since cash flows and rates of return should be on a comparable basis, we adjust the interest rate downward to take account of the preferential tax treatment of debt.[5]

Note that the cost of debt is the interest rate on *new* debt, not that on already outstanding debt; in other words, we are interested in the *marginal* cost of debt. Our primary concern with the cost of capital is to use it in a decision-making process — for example, a decision about whether or not to obtain the capital needed to install a new production line. The rate at which the firm has borrowed in the past is irrelevant for this purpose.

COST OF PREFERRED STOCK, k_p

cost of preferred stock,
k_p
The preferred dividend,
D_p, divided by the net
issuing price, P_n.

The component **cost of preferred stock, k_p,** used to calculate the weighted cost of capital is the preferred dividend, D_p, divided by the net issuing price, P_n, or the price the firm receives after deducting flotation costs:

$$\text{Component cost of preferred stock} = k_p = \frac{D_p}{P_n}. \qquad (16\text{-}2)$$

For example, Universal Machine has preferred stock that pays an $11.70 dividend per share which sells for $100 per share in the market. If it issues new

---

[5]The tax rate is *zero* for a firm with losses. Therefore, for a company that does not pay taxes, the cost of debt is not reduced; that is, in Equation 16-1 the tax rate equals zero, so the after-tax cost of debt is equal to the interest rate.

It should also be noted that we have ignored flotation cost on debt because the vast majority of debt (over 99 percent) is privately placed and hence has no flotation cost. However, if bonds are publicly placed and do involve flotation costs, the solution value of k_d in this formula is used as the after-tax cost of debt:

$$M(1-F) = \sum_{t=1}^{n} \frac{I(1-T)}{(1+k_d)^t} + \frac{M}{(1+k_d)^n}.$$

Here F is the percentage amount of the bond flotation cost, n is the number of periods to maturity, I is the dollars of interest per period, T is the corporate tax rate, M is the maturity value of the bond, and k_d is the after-tax cost of debt adjusted to reflect flotation costs. If we assume that the bond in the example calls for annual payments, that it has a 20-year maturity, and that F = 2%, then the flotation-adjusted, after-tax cost of debt is 6.18 percent versus 6 percent before the flotation adjustment.

shares of preferred, it will incur an underwriting (or flotation) cost of 2.5 percent, or $2.50 per share, so it will net $97.50 per share. Therefore, Universal's cost of preferred stock is 12 percent:

$$k_p = \$11.70/\$97.50 = 12\%.$$

No tax adjustments are made when calculating k_p because preferred dividends, unlike interest expense on debt, are *not* deductible.

COST OF RETAINED EARNINGS, k_s

cost of retained earnings, k_s
The rate of return required by stockholders on a firm's common stock.

The costs of debt and preferred stock are based on the returns investors require on these securities. Similarly, the **cost of retained earnings, k_s**, is the rate of return stockholders require on the firm's common stock.[6]

The reason we must assign a cost of capital to retained earnings involves the *opportunity cost principle*. The firm's after-tax earnings literally belong to the stockholders. Bondholders are compensated by interest payments and preferred stockholders by preferred dividends, but the earnings remaining after interest and preferred dividends have been paid belong to the common stockholders and serve to compensate them for the use of their capital. Management may either pay out the earnings in the form of dividends or retain earnings and reinvest them in the business. If management decides to retain earnings, there is an opportunity cost involved — stockholders could have received the earnings as dividends and invested this money in other stocks, in bonds, in real estate, or in anything else. Thus, the firm should earn on its retained earnings at least as much as the stockholders themselves could earn in alternative investments of comparable risk.

What rate of return can stockholders expect to earn on equivalent-risk investments? First, recall from Chapter 6 that stocks are normally in equilibrium, with the expected and required rates of return being equal: $\hat{k}_s = k_s$. Therefore, we can assume that Universal Machine's stockholders expect to earn a return of k_s on their money. *If the firm cannot invest retained earnings and earn at least k_s, it should pay these funds to its stockholders and let them invest directly in other assets that do provide this return.*[7]

---

[6]The term *retained earnings* can be interpreted to mean either the balance sheet item "retained earnings," consisting of all the earnings retained in the business throughout its history, or the income statement item "additions to retained earnings." The income statement item is used in this chapter; for our purpose, *retained earnings* refers to that part of current earnings not paid out in dividends and hence available for reinvestment in the business this year.

[7]Prior to 1987, dividends and capital gains were taxed differently, with long-term gains being taxed at a much lower rate than dividends. That made it beneficial for companies to retain earnings rather than to pay them out as dividends, and that, in turn, resulted in a relatively low cost of capital for retained earnings. Beginning in 1987, however, the differential tax rate was eliminated, so this tax incentive to retain earnings rather than pay them out as dividends no longer exists. It may, however, be reinstated by Congress. This point is discussed in detail in Chapter 18.

Whereas debt and preferred stocks are contractual obligations that have easily determined costs, it is not at all easy to measure k_s. However, we can employ the principles developed in Chapters 4 and 6 to produce reasonably good cost of equity estimates. To begin, we know that if a stock is in equilibrium (which is the typical situation), the required rate of return, k_s, is also equal to the expected rate of return, $\hat{k}_s$. Further, the required return is equal to a risk-free rate, k_{RF}, plus a risk premium, RP, whereas the expected return on a constant growth stock is equal to a dividend yield, D_1/P_0, plus an expected growth rate, g:

Required rate of return = Expected rate of return

$$k_s = k_{RF} + RP = D_1/P_0 + g = \hat{k}_s. \qquad (16\text{-}3)$$

Since the two must be equal, we can estimate k_s either as $k_s = k_{RF} + RP$ or as $k_s = \hat{k}_s = D_1/P_0 + g$. Actually, three methods are commonly used for finding the cost of retained earnings: (1) the CAPM approach, (2) the bond-yield-plus-risk-premium approach, and (3) the discounted cash flow (DCF) approach. These three approaches are discussed in the following sections.

The CAPM Approach

To use the Capital Asset Pricing Model (CAPM) as developed in Chapter 4, we proceed as follows:

Step 1. Estimate the risk-free rate, k_{RF}, generally taken to be either the U.S. Treasury bond rate or the short-term (30-day) Treasury bill rate.

Step 2. Estimate the stock's beta coefficient, b_i, and use this as an index of the stock's risk. The i signifies the *i*th company's beta.

Step 3. Estimate the expected rate of return on the market, or on an "average" stock, k_M.

Step 4. Substitute the preceding values into the CAPM equation to estimate the required rate of return on the stock in question:

$$k_s = k_{RF} + (k_M - k_{RF})b_i. \qquad (16\text{-}4)$$

Equation 16-4 shows that the CAPM estimate of k_s begins with the risk-free rate, k_{RF}, to which is added a risk premium set equal to the risk premium on an average stock, $k_M - k_{RF}$, scaled up or down to reflect the stock's relative risk as measured by its beta coefficient.

To illustrate the CAPM approach, assume that $k_{RF} = 8\%$, $k_M = 14\%$, and $b_i = 0.7$ for a given stock. The stock's k_s is calculated as follows:

$$k_s = 8\% + (14\% - 8\%)(0.7)$$

$$= 8\% + (6\%)(0.7)$$

$$= 8\% + 4.2\%$$

$$= 12.2\%.$$

Had b_i been 1.8, indicating that the stock was riskier than average, k_s would have been

$$k_s = 8\% + (6\%)(1.8)$$

$$= 8\% + 10.8\%$$

$$= 18.8\%.$$

For an average stock,

$$k_s = k_M = 8\% + (6\%)(1.0) = 14\%.$$

It should be noted that although the CAPM approach appears to yield accurate, precise estimates of k_s, there are actually several problems with it. First, as we saw in Chapter 4, if a firm's stockholders are not well diversified, they may be concerned with *total risk* rather than with market risk only; in this case the firm's true investment risk will not be measured by beta, and the CAPM procedure will understate the correct value of k_s. Further, even if the CAPM method is valid, it is hard to obtain correct estimates of the inputs required to make it operational: (1) there is uncertainty about whether to use long-term or short-term Treasury bonds for k_{RF}; (2) it is hard to estimate the beta that investors expect the company to have in the future; and (3) it is difficult to estimate the market risk premium. This latter problem has been especially vexing in the 1980s, because the riskiness of stocks versus bonds has been changing, making the market risk premium unstable.

Bond-Yield-plus-Risk-Premium Approach

Although it is essentially an ad hoc, subjective procedure, analysts often estimate a firm's cost of common equity by adding a risk premium of from two to four percentage points to the interest rate on the firm's own long-term debt. It is logical to think that firms with risky, low-rated, and consequently high-interest-rate debt will also have risky, high-cost equity, and the procedure of basing the cost of equity on a readily observable debt cost utilizes this precept. For example, if an Aaa-rated firm's bonds yield 9 percent, its cost of equity might be estimated as follows:

$$k_s = \text{Bond rate} + \text{Risk premium} = 9\% + 3\% = 12\%.$$

A Baa firm's debt might carry a yield of 12 percent, making its estimated cost of equity 15 percent:

$$k_s = 12\% + 3\% = 15\%.$$

Because the 3 percent risk premium is a judgmental estimate, the estimated value of k_s is also judgmental. Empirical work in recent years suggests that the over-own-debt risk premium has generally ranged from 2.0 to 4.0 percentage points, so this method is not likely to produce a precise cost of equity — about all it can do is get us "into the right ballpark."

Dividend-Yield-plus-Growth-Rate, or Discounted Cash Flow (DCF), Approach

In Chapter 6 we learned that both the price and the expected rate of return on a share of common stock depend, ultimately, on the dividends expected to be paid on the stock:

$$P_0 = \frac{D_1}{(1 + k_s)^1} + \frac{D_2}{(1 + k_s)^2} + \cdots$$

$$= \sum_{t=1}^{\infty} \frac{D_t}{(1 + k_s)^t}. \qquad (16\text{-}5)$$

Here P_0 is the current price of the stock; D_t is the dividend expected to be paid at the end of Year t; and k_s is the required rate of return. If dividends are expected to grow at a constant rate, then, as we saw in Chapter 6, Equation 16-5 reduces to this important formula:

$$P_0 = \frac{D_1}{k_s - g}. \qquad (16\text{-}6)$$

We can solve for k_s to obtain the required rate of return on common equity, which for the marginal investor is also equal to the expected rate of return:

$$k_s = \hat{k}_s = \frac{D_1}{P_0} + \text{Expected g}. \qquad (16\text{-}7)$$

Thus, investors expect to receive a dividend yield, D_1/P_0, plus a capital gain, g, for a total expected return of $\hat{k}_s$, and in equilibrium this expected return is also equal to the required return, k_s. This method of estimating the cost of equity is called the *discounted cash flow, or DCF, method*. Henceforth, we will assume that equilibrium exists, and we will use the terms k_s and $\hat{k}_s$ interchangeably.

It is relatively easy to determine the dividend yield, but it is difficult to establish the proper growth rate. If past growth rates in earnings and dividends have been relatively stable, and if investors appear to be projecting a continuation of past trends, then g may be based on the firm's historic growth rate. *However, if the company's past growth has been abnormally high or low, either because of its own unique situation or because of general economic conditions, then investors will not project the past growth rate into the future.* In this case, g must be estimated in some other manner.

Security analysts regularly make earnings and dividend growth forecasts, looking at such factors as projected sales, profit margins, and competitive factors. For example, *Value Line,* which is available in most libraries, provides growth rate forecasts for 1,700 companies. Someone making a cost of capital estimate can obtain some analysts' forecasts, average them, use the average as a proxy for the growth expectations of investors in general, and then combine g with the current dividend yield to estimate $\hat{k}_s$ as follows:

$$\hat{k}_s = \frac{D_1}{P_0} + \text{Growth rate as projected by security analysts.}$$

Again, note that this estimate of $\hat{k}_s$ is based on the assumption that g is expected to remain constant in the future.[8]

To illustrate the DCF approach, suppose Universal's stock sells for $20; its next expected dividend is $1.60; and its expected growth rate is 7 percent. Universal's expected and required rate of return, and hence its cost of retained earnings, is 15.0 percent:

$$\hat{k}_s = k_s = \frac{\$1.60}{\$20} + 7.0\%$$

$$= 8.0\% + 7.0\%$$

$$= 15\%.$$

This 15 percent is the minimum rate of return that management must expect to earn to justify retaining earnings and plowing them back into the business rather than paying them out to stockholders as dividends.

In practice, it is often easier to obtain reliable inputs for the DCF model than for the other methods. Therefore, financial analysts estimating the cost of equity tend to rely most heavily upon the DCF approach, and if they use the other methods at all, they normally give estimates obtained with them less weight than they give the DCF estimates. Further, people experienced in estimating equity capital costs recognize that both careful analysis and sound judgment are required. It would be nice to pretend that judgment is unnecessary and to specify an easy, precise way of determining the exact cost of equity capital. Unfortunately, this is not possible; finance is in large part a matter of judgment, and we simply must face that fact.

---

[8]Analysts' growth rate forecasts are usually for five years into the future, and the rates provided represent the average growth rate over that 5-year horizon. Studies have shown that analysts' forecasts represent the best source of growth rate data for DCF cost of capital estimates. See Robert Harris, "Using Analysts' Growth Rate Forecasts to Estimate Shareholder Required Rates of Return," *Financial Management,* Spring 1986.

Another method for estimating g involves first forecasting the firm's average future dividend payout ratio and its complement, the *retention rate,* and then multiplying the retention rate by the company's average future projected rate of return on equity (ROE):

$$g = (\text{Retention rate})(\text{ROE}) = (1.0 - \text{Payout rate})(\text{ROE}).$$

Security analysts often use this procedure when they estimate growth rates.

COST OF NEWLY ISSUED COMMON STOCK, OR EXTERNAL EQUITY, k_e

cost of new common equity, k_e
The cost of external equity; based on the cost of retained earnings, but increased for flotation costs.

The **cost of new common equity, k_e,** or external equity capital, is higher than the cost of retained earnings, k_s, because of flotation costs involved in selling new common stock. What rate of return must be earned on funds raised by selling stock in order to make issuing new stock worthwhile? To put it another way, what is the cost of new common stock?

In general, the answer is found by applying the following formula:[9]

$$k_e = \frac{D_1}{P_0(1 - F)} + g. \qquad (16\text{-}8)$$

flotation cost, F
The percentage cost of issuing new common stock.

Here F is the percentage **flotation cost** incurred in selling the new stock issue, so $P_0(1 - F)$ is the net price per share received by the company when it sells a new stock issue.

Assuming that Universal has a flotation cost of 10 percent, its cost of new outside equity is computed as follows:

$$k_e = \frac{\$1.60}{\$20(1 - 0.10)} + 7.0\%$$

$$= \frac{\$1.60}{\$18} + 7.0\%$$

$$= 8.9\% + 7.0\% = 15.9\%.$$

---

[9]Equation 16-8 is derived as follows:

Step 1. The old stockholders expect the firm to pay a stream of dividends, D_t, which will be derived from existing assets with a per-share value of P_0. New investors will likewise expect to receive the same stream of dividends, but the funds available to invest in assets will be less than P_0 because of flotation costs. For new investors to receive their expected dividend stream *without impairing the D_t stream of the old investors,* the new funds obtained from the sale of stock must be invested at a return high enough to provide a dividend stream whose present value will be equal to the price the firm will receive:

$$P_0(1 - F) = P_n = \sum_{t=1}^{\infty} \frac{D_t}{(1 + k_e)^t}. \qquad (16\text{-}9)$$

Here D_t is the dividend stream to new (and old) stockholders and k_e is the cost of new outside equity.

Step 2. When growth is constant, Equation 16-9 reduces to

$$P_n = P_0(1 - F) = \frac{D_1}{k_e - g}. \qquad (16\text{-}9a)$$

Step 3. Equation 16-9a may be solved for k_e to produce Equation 16-8:

$$k_e = \frac{D_1}{P_0(1 - F)} + g. \qquad \textbf{(16-8)}$$

Note that Equation 16-8 is based on the constant growth DCF model. However, very little error is induced if growth is not constant, provided that the growth rate used is the *average* expected future growth rate.

Investors require a return of k_s = 15% on the stock. However, because of flotation costs the company must earn *more* than 15 percent on funds obtained by selling stock to provide this return. Specifically, if the firm earns 15.9 percent on funds obtained from new common stock issues, then earnings per share will not fall below previously expected earnings, the firm's expected dividend can be maintained, and, as a result, the price per share will not decline. If the firm earns less than 15.9 percent, then earnings, dividends, and growth will fall below expectations, causing the price of the stock to decline. If it earns more than 15.9 percent, the price of the stock will rise.[10]

The reason for the flotation adjustment can perhaps be made clear by a simple example. Suppose Weaver Realty Company has $100,000 of assets and no debt, earns a 15 percent return (or $15,000) on its assets, pays all earnings out as dividends, and hence has g = 0. The company has 1,000 shares of stock outstanding, so EPS = DPS = $15, and P_0 = $100. The firm's cost of equity is k_s = $15/$100 + 0 = 15%. Now suppose Weaver can get a return of 15 percent on new assets. Should it sell new stock to acquire new assets? If it sold 1,000 new shares of stock to the public for $100 per share but incurred a 10 percent flotation cost on the issue, it would net $100 − 0.10($100) = $90 per share, or $90,000 in total. It would then invest this $90,000 and earn 15 percent, or $13,500. Its new total earnings would be $15,000 from the old assets plus $13,500 from the new, or $28,500 in total, but it would now have 2,000 shares of stock outstanding. Therefore, its EPS and DPS would decline from $15 to $14.25:

$$\text{New EPS and DPS} = \frac{\$28,500}{2,000} = \$14.25.$$

Because EPS and DPS would have fallen, the price of the stock also would fall, from P_0 = $100 to P_1 = $14.25/0.15 = $95.00. This result occurs because investors have put up $100 per share, but the company has received and invested only $90 per share. Therefore, the $90 must earn more than 15 percent to provide investors with a 15 percent return on the $100 they put up.

Now suppose Weaver earned a return of k_e based on Equation 16-8 on the $90,000 of new assets:

$$k_e = \frac{D_1}{P_0(1 - F)} + g$$

$$= \frac{\$15}{\$100(0.90)} + 0 = 16.667\%.$$

On occasion it is useful to use another equation to calculate the cost of external equity:

$$k_e = \frac{\text{Dividend yield}}{(1 - F)} + g = \frac{D_1/P_0}{(1 - F)} + g. \qquad (16\text{-}8a)$$

Equation 16-8a is derived algebraically from 16-8, and it is useful when information on dividend yields, but not on dollar dividends and stock prices, is available.

Here is the new situation:

$$\text{New total earnings} = \$15,000 + \$90,000(0.1667)$$
$$= \$15,000 + \$15,000$$
$$= \$30,000.$$
$$\text{New EPS and DPS} = \$30,000/2,000 = \$15.$$
$$\text{New price} = \$15/0.15 = \$100.$$

Thus, if the return on the new assets is equal to k_e as calculated by Equation 16-8, then EPS, DPS, and the stock price will all remain constant. If the return on the new assets exceeds k_e, then EPS, DPS, and P_0 will rise. This confirms the fact that the cost of external equity, which involves flotation costs, exceeds the cost of equity raised internally from retained earnings.

WEIGHTED AVERAGE, OR COMPOSITE, COST OF CAPITAL, WACC = k_a

target (optimal) capital structure
The percentages of debt, preferred stock, and common equity that will maximize the price of the firm's stock.

weighted average cost of capital, WACC = k_a
A weighted average of the component costs of debt, preferred stock, and common equity.

As we shall see in Chapter 17, each firm has an optimal capital structure, which is that mix of debt, preferred, and common equity that causes its stock price to be maximized. Therefore, a rational, value-maximizing firm will establish its **target (optimal) capital structure** and then raise new capital in a manner that will keep the actual capital structure on target over time. In this chapter we assume that the firm has identified its optimal capital structure, that it uses this optimum as the target, and that it finances so as to remain constantly on target. How the target is established will be examined in Chapter 17.

The target proportions of debt, preferred stock, and common equity, along with the component costs of capital, are used to calculate the firm's **weighted average cost of capital, WACC = k_a**. To illustrate, suppose Universal Machine Company has a target capital structure calling for 30 percent debt, 10 percent preferred stock, and 60 percent common equity (retained earnings plus common stock). Its before-tax cost of debt, k_d, is 10 percent; its cost of preferred stock, k_p, is 12 percent; its cost of common equity from retained earnings, k_s, is 15 percent; and its marginal tax rate is 40 percent. First, note that Universal's after-tax, or component, cost of debt = $k_d(1 - T) = 10\%(0.6) = 6.0\%$. Now we can calculate Universal's weighted average cost of capital, WACC = k_a, as follows:

$$\text{WACC} = k_a = w_d k_d(1 - T) + w_p k_p + w_s k_s \qquad (16\text{-}10)$$
$$= 0.3(10\%)(0.6) + 0.1(12\%) + 0.6(15\%)$$
$$= 12\%.$$

Here w_d, w_p, and w_s are the weights used for debt, preferred, and common equity, respectively.

Every dollar of new capital that Universal Machine obtains consists of 30 cents of debt with an after-tax cost of 6 percent, 10 cents of preferred stock with a cost of 12 percent, and 60 cents of common equity (all from additions to retained earnings) with a cost of 15 percent. The average cost of each whole dollar, WACC = k_a, is 12 percent.

The weights could be based either on the accounting values shown on the firm's balance sheet (book values) or on the market values of the different securities. Theoretically, the weights should be based on market values, but if a firm's book value weights are reasonably close to its market value weights, book value weights can be used as a proxy for market value weights. This point is discussed further in Chapter 17, but in the remainder of this chapter we shall assume that the firm's market values are approximately equal to its book values and then use book value capital structure weights.

THE MARGINAL COST OF CAPITAL

marginal cost of capital, MCC
The cost of obtaining another dollar of new capital; the weighted average cost of the last dollar of new capital raised.

The *marginal cost* of any item is the cost of another unit of that item; for example, the marginal cost of labor is the cost of adding one additional worker. The marginal cost of labor may be $25 per person if 10 workers are added but $35 per person if the firm tries to hire 100 new workers, because it will be harder to find that many people willing and able to do the work. The same concept applies to capital. As the firm tries to attract more new dollars, the cost of each dollar will at some point rise. *Thus, the marginal cost of capital, MCC, is defined as the cost of the last dollar of new capital that the firm raises, and the marginal cost rises as more and more capital is raised during a given period.*

We can use Universal Machine to illustrate the marginal cost of capital concept. The company's target capital structure and other data follow:[11]

Debt	$ 3,000,000	30%
Preferred stock	1,000,000	10
Common equity	6,000,000	60
Total capital	$10,000,000	100%

$k_d = 10\%$.
$k_p = 12\%$.
$T = 40\%$.
$P_0 = \$20$.
$g = 7\%$, and growth is expected to remain constant.

---

[11]Because we assume that Universal has only a negligible amount of payables and accruals, which have no explicit cost, these items are ignored. For a discussion of how these items are handled, see Eugene F. Brigham and Louis C. Gapenski, *Intermediate Financial Management,* 2nd ed., Chapter 4. In general, though, they are ignored.

$D_0 = \$1.495 =$ dividends per share in the *last* period. D_0 has already been paid, so someone who purchased this stock today would *not* receive D_0 — rather, he or she would receive D_1, the *next* dividend.

$D_1 = D_0(1 + g) = \$1.495(1.07) = \$1.60.$

$k_s = D_1/P_0 + g = (\$1.60/\$20.00) + 0.07 = 0.08 + 0.07 = 0.15 = 15\%.$

Based on these data, the weighted average cost of capital, WACC $= k_a$, is 12 percent:

$$\text{WACC} = k_a = \begin{pmatrix} \text{Fraction} \\ \text{of} \\ \text{debt} \end{pmatrix}\begin{pmatrix} \text{Interest} \\ \text{rate} \end{pmatrix}(1 - T) + \begin{pmatrix} \text{Fraction} \\ \text{of} \\ \text{preferred} \\ \text{stock} \end{pmatrix}\begin{pmatrix} \text{Cost} \\ \text{of} \\ \text{preferred} \\ \text{stock} \end{pmatrix} + \begin{pmatrix} \text{Fraction of} \\ \text{common} \\ \text{equity} \end{pmatrix}\begin{pmatrix} \text{Cost} \\ \text{of} \\ \text{equity} \end{pmatrix}$$

$= 0.3(10\%)(0.6) + 0.1(12\%) + 0.6(15\%)$

$= 1.8\% + 1.2\% + 9.0\%$

$= 12\%.$

As long as Universal keeps its capital structure on target, and as long as its debt has an after-tax cost of 6 percent, its preferred stock a cost of 12 percent, and its common equity a cost of 15 percent, then its weighted average cost of capital will be $k_a =$ WACC $= 12\%$. Each dollar that the firm raises will consist of some debt, some preferred stock, and some common equity, and the cost of the dollar will be 12 percent.

A graph which shows how the WACC changes as more and more new capital is raised during a given year is called the **marginal cost of capital schedule**. The graph shown in Figure 16-1 is Universal's MCC schedule. Here the dots represent dollars raised, and because each dollar of new capital has a cost of 12 percent, the marginal cost of capital (MCC) for Universal is constant at 12 percent under the assumptions we have used thus far.[12]

marginal cost of capital (MCC) schedule
A graph that relates the firm's weighted average cost of each dollar of capital to the total amount of new capital raised.

Breaks in the MCC Schedule

Could Universal raise an unlimited amount of new capital at the 12 percent cost? The answer is no. As a practical matter, as a company raises larger and larger sums during a given time period, the costs of debt, preferred stock, and common equity begin to rise, and as this occurs, the weighted average cost of each new dollar also rises. Thus, just as corporations cannot hire unlimited numbers of workers at a constant wage, they cannot raise unlimited amounts of capital at a constant cost. At some point, the cost of each new dollar will increase.

Where will this point occur for Universal? As a first step to determining the point at which the MCC begins to rise, recognize that although the com-

[12]Universal's MCC schedule in Figure 16-1 would be different (higher) if the company used any capital structure other than 30 percent debt, 10 percent preferred, and 60 percent equity. This point will be developed in Chapter 17. However, as a general rule, a different MCC schedule exists for every possible capital structure, and the optimal structure is the one that produces the lowest MCC schedule.

**Figure 16-1   Marginal Cost of Capital (MCC) Schedule
for Universal Machine Company**

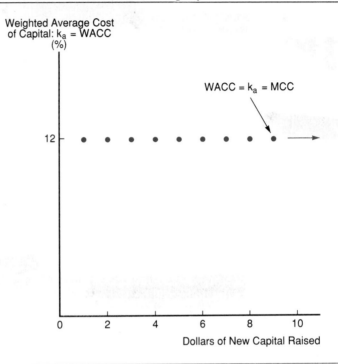

pany's balance sheet shows total long-term capital of $10 million, all of this capital was raised in the past, and it has been invested in assets which are being used in operations. New (or marginal) capital will presumably be raised so as to maintain the 30/10/60 debt/preferred/common relationship. Therefore, if Universal wants to raise $1,000,000 in new capital, it should obtain $300,000 of debt, $100,000 of preferred stock, and $600,000 of common equity. The new common equity could come from two sources: (1) retained earnings, defined as that part of this year's profits which management decides to retain in the business rather than use for dividends (but not earnings retained in the past, for these have already been invested in plant, equipment, inventories, and so on); or (2) proceeds from the sale of new common stock.

The debt will have an interest rate of 10 percent, or an after-tax cost of 6 percent, whereas the preferred stock will have a cost of 12 percent. *The cost of common equity will be k_s = 15% as long as the equity is obtained as retained earnings, but it will jump to k_e = 15.9% once the company uses up all of its retained earnings and is thus forced to sell new common stock.*

Consider first the case in which all the new equity comes from retained earnings. Universal's stock now sells for $20 per share; its last dividend (D_0)

Table 16-1   Universal's WACC Using New Retained Earnings and New Common Stock

---

I. WACC When Equity Is from New Retained Earnings

	Weight	Component Cost	Product
Debt	0.3	6.0%	1.8%
Preferred stock	0.1	12.0	1.2
Common equity (Retained earnings)	0.6	15.0	9.0
	1.0	$\text{WACC}_1 = k_{a1} =$	12.0%

II. WACC When Equity Is from Sale of New Common Stock

	Weight	Component Cost	Product
Debt	0.3	6.0%	1.8%
Preferred stock	0.1	12.0	1.2
Common equity (New common stock)	0.6	15.9	9.5
	1.0	$\text{WACC}_2 = k_{a2} =$	12.5%

---

was $1.495; its expected growth rate is 7 percent; and its next expected dividend is $1.60. Thus, we estimate the expected and required rate of return on its common equity, k_s, to be 15 percent:

$$k_s = \frac{D_1}{P_0} + g = \frac{\$1.60}{\$20} + 7\% = 8\% + 7\% = 15\%.$$

Now suppose the company expands so rapidly that its retained earnings for the year are not sufficient to meet its needs for new equity, forcing it to sell new common stock. Since the flotation cost on new stock is $F = 10$ percent, Universal's cost of equity after it exhausts its retained earnings will jump from 15 to 15.9 percent:

$$k_e = \frac{D_1}{P_0(1 - F)} + g = \frac{\$1.60}{\$20(0.9)} + 7\% = \frac{\$1.60}{\$18} + 7\% = 15.9\%.$$

The company will net $18 per share when it sells new stock, and it must earn 15.9 percent on this $18 in order to provide investors with a 15.0 percent return on the $20 they actually put up.

Universal's weighted average cost of capital, using first new retained earnings (earnings retained this year, not in the past) and then new common stock, is shown in Table 16-1. We see that the weighted average cost of each dollar is 12 percent as long as retained earnings are used, but it jumps to 12.5 percent as soon as the firm exhausts its retained earnings and is forced to sell new common stock.[13]

---

[13]At relatively low growth rates, expansion could be financed by spontaneously generated debt and retained earnings, but at higher growth rates, external capital is needed. If Universal needed no external equity, its cost of capital would be a constant $\text{WACC}_1 = 12\%$. However, if its growth rate were rapid enough to require it to sell new common stock, its cost of capital would rise to $\text{WACC}_2 = 12.5\%$.

How much new capital can Universal raise before it exhausts its retained earnings and is forced to sell new common stock; that is, where will an increase in the MCC schedule occur? We find this point as follows:

1. The company expects to have total earnings of $840,000 for the year, and it has a policy of paying out half of its earnings as dividends. Thus, the addition to retained earnings will be $420,000 during the year.

2. We now want to know how much *total new capital* — debt, preferred stock, and retained earnings — can be raised before the $420,000 of retained earnings is exhausted and Universal is forced to sell new common stock. In effect, we are seeking some amount of capital, X, which is called a **break point (BP)** and which represents the total financing that can be done before Universal is forced to sell new common stock.

break point (BP)
The dollar value of new capital that can be raised before an increase in the firm's weighted average cost of capital occurs.

3. We know that 60 percent, or 0.6, of X, the total capital raised, will be retained earnings, whereas 40 percent will be debt plus preferred. We also know that retained earnings will amount to $420,000. Therefore,

$$\text{Retained earnings} = 0.6X = \$420,000.$$

4. Solving for X, which is the *retained earnings break point,* we obtain $BP_{RE} = \$700,000$:

$$X = BP_{RE} = \frac{\text{Retained earnings}}{\text{Equity fraction}} = \frac{\$420,000}{0.6} = \$700,000.$$

5. Thus, Universal can raise a total of $700,000, consisting of $0.6(\$700,000) = \$420,000$ of retained earnings plus $0.10(\$700,000) = \$70,000$ of preferred stock and $0.30(\$700,000) = \$210,000$ of new debt supported by these new retained earnings, without altering its capital structure:

New debt supported by retained earnings	$210,000	30%
Preferred stock supported by retained earnings	70,000	10
Retained earnings	420,000	60
Total expansion supported by retained earnings, or break point for retained earnings.	$700,000	100%

6. The value of X, or $BP_{RE} = \$700,000$, is the *retained earnings break point,* defined as the amount of total capital at which a break, or jump, occurs in the MCC schedule.

Figure 16-2 graphs Universal's marginal cost of capital schedule with the retained earnings break point. Each dollar has a weighted average cost of 12 percent until the company has raised a total of $700,000. This $700,000 will consist of $210,000 of new debt with an after-tax cost of 6 percent, $70,000 of preferred stock with a cost of 12 percent, and $420,000 of retained earnings with a cost of 15 percent. However, if Universal raises $700,001 or more, each new dollar will contain 60 cents of equity *obtained by selling new common equity at a cost of 15.9 percent;* therefore, WACC = k_a rises from 12 percent to 12.5 percent, as calculated in Table 16-1.

Figure 16-2   Marginal Cost of Capital Schedule for Universal Machine Company Using Both Retained Earnings and New Common Stock

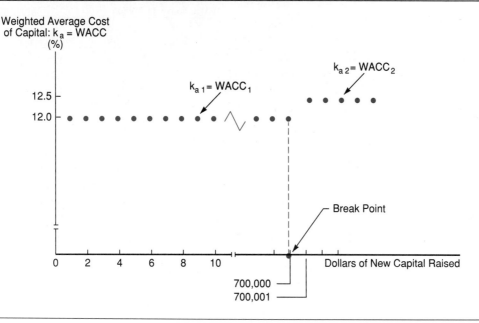

Other Breaks in the MCC Schedule

There is a jump, or break, in Universal's MCC schedule at $700,000 of new capital. Could there be other breaks in the schedule? Yes, there could. For example, suppose Universal could obtain only $300,000 of debt at a 10 percent interest rate, with additional debt costing 12 percent. This would result in a second break point in the MCC schedule at the point where the $300,000 of 10 percent debt is exhausted. At what amount of *total financing* would the 10 percent debt be used up? If we let BP_{Debt} represent the total financing at this second break point, then we know that 30 percent, or 0.3, of BP_{Debt} will be debt, so

$$0.3(BP_{Debt}) = \$300,000,$$

and, solving for BP_{Debt}, we obtain

$$BP_{Debt} = \frac{\text{Amount of 10\% debt}}{\text{Debt fraction}} = \frac{\$300,000}{0.3} = \$1,000,000.$$

Thus, there will be another break in the MCC schedule after Universal has raised a total of $1 million, and this second break results from a jump in the cost of debt.

As we have seen, from $0 to $700,000 of new capital the WACC is 12 percent, whereas just beyond $700,000 the WACC rises to 12.5 percent. Then, as a result of the increase in k_d from 10 percent to 12 percent, the WACC rises again at $1,000,001 to 12.9 percent:

WACC above $1 Million

Component	Weight		Component Cost		Product
Debt	0.3	×	7.2[a]	=	2.2%
Preferred stock	0.1	×	12.0	=	1.2
Common equity	0.6	×	15.9	=	9.5
			WACC$_3$ = k_{a3}	=	12.9%

[a]12%(1 − T) = 12%(0.6) = 7.2%, up from 6%.

In other words, the next dollar beyond $1 million will consist of 30 cents of 12 percent debt (7.2 percent after taxes), 10 cents of 12 percent preferred stock, and 60 cents of new common stock at a cost of 15.9 percent (retained earnings were used up much earlier), and this marginal dollar will have a cost of WACC$_3$ = 12.9%.

The effect of this second WACC increase is shown in Figure 16-3. Now there are two break points, one caused by using up all the retained earnings and the other by using up all the 10 percent debt. With the two breaks, there are three different WACCs: WACC$_1$ = 12% for the first $700,000 of new capital; WACC$_2$ = 12.5% in the interval between $700,001 and $1 million; and WACC$_3$ = 12.9% for all new capital beyond $1 million.[14]

There could, of course, be still more break points; they would occur if the interest rate continued to rise, if the cost of preferred stock rose, or if the cost of common stock rose.[15] *In general, a break point will occur whenever the cost of one of the capital components rises, and the break point can be determined by the following equation:*

---

[14]When we use the term *weighted average cost of capital,* we are referring to k_a, which is the cost of $1 raised partly as debt, partly as preferred, and partly as equity. We could also calculate the average cost of all the capital the firm raised during a given year. For example, if Universal raised $2 million, the first $700,000 would have a cost of 12 percent, the next $300,000 a cost of 12.5 percent, and the last $1 million a cost of 12.9 percent. The entire $2 million would have an average cost of

$$(0.7/2)(12\%) + (0.3/2)(12.5\%) + (1/2)(12.9\%) = 12.53\%.$$

In general, this particular cost of capital should not be used for financial decisions — it usually has no relevance in finance. The only exception to this rule occurs when the firm is considering a very large asset which must be accepted in total or else rejected, and the capital required for it includes capital with different WACCs. For example, if Universal was considering one $2 million project, that project should be evaluated with a 12.53 percent cost.

[15]The first break point is not necessarily the point at which retained earnings are used up; it is possible for low-cost debt to be exhausted *before* retained earnings have been used up. For example, if Universal had available only $150,000 of 10 percent debt, BP$_{Debt}$ would occur at $500,000:

$$BP_{Debt} = \frac{\$150,000}{0.3} = \$500,000.$$

This is well before the break point for retained earnings, which occurs at $700,000.

Figure 16-3   Marginal Cost of Capital Schedule for Universal Machine Company Using Retained Earnings, New Common Stock, and Higher-Cost Debt

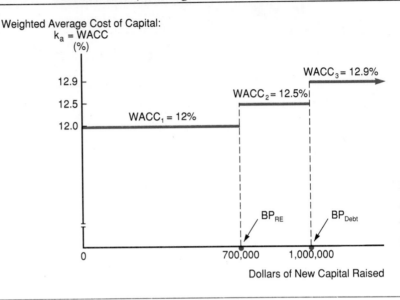

$$\text{Break point} = \frac{\text{Total amount of lower-cost capital of a given type}}{\text{Fraction of this type of capital in the capital structure}}. \quad (16\text{-}11)$$

We see, then, that numerous break points can occur. At the limit, we can even think of an MCC schedule with so many break points that it rises almost continuously beyond some given level of new financing. Such an MCC schedule is shown in Figure 16-4.

The easiest sequence for calculating MCC schedules is as follows:

1. Identify the points at which breaks occur. A break will occur any time the cost of one of the capital components rises. (It is possible, however, that two capital components could both increase at the same point.) Use Equation 16-11 to determine the exact break points, and make a list of them.

2. Determine the cost of capital for each component in the intervals between breaks.

3. Calculate the weighted averages of these component costs to obtain the WACCs in each interval. The WACC is constant within each interval, but it rises at each break point.

Notice that if there are n separate breaks, there will be n + 1 different WACCs. For example, in Figure 16-3 we see two breaks and three different WACCs.

Before closing this section, we should note again that a different MCC schedule would result if a different capital structure were used. As we will

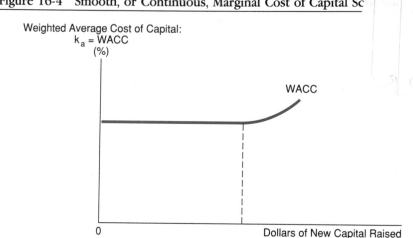

Figure 16-4   Smooth, or Continuous, Marginal Cost of Capital Sc

show in Chapter 17, the optimal capital structure produces the lowest MCC schedule.

COMBINING THE MCC AND INVESTMENT OPPORTUNITY SCHEDULES

Now that we have calculated the MCC schedule, we can use it to develop a discount rate for use in the capital budgeting process; *that is, we can use the MCC schedule to find the cost of capital for determining projects' net present values (NPVs) as discussed in Chapter 9.*

To understand how the MCC schedule is used in capital budgeting, assume that Universal has three financial executives: a financial vice-president (VP), a treasurer, and a director of capital budgeting (DCB). The financial VP asks the treasurer to develop the firm's MCC schedule, and the treasurer produces the schedule shown earlier in Figure 16-3. At the same time, the financial VP asks the DCB to draw up a list of all projects that are potentially acceptable. The list shows each project's cost, projected annual net cash inflows, life, and IRR. These data are presented at the bottom of Figure 16-5. For example, Project A has a cost of $200,000, it is expected to produce inflows of $55,757 per year for 5 years, and, therefore, it has an IRR of 12.2 percent. Similarly, Project B has a cost of $150,000, it is expected to produce inflows of $33,917 per year for 7 years, and thus it has an IRR of 13 percent. (NPVs and IRR*s cannot be shown yet, because we do not yet know the marginal cost of capital.) For simplicity, we assume now that all projects are independent as opposed to

**Figure 16-5   Combining Universal Machine Company's
MCC and IOS Curves to Determine
Its Optimal Capital Budget**

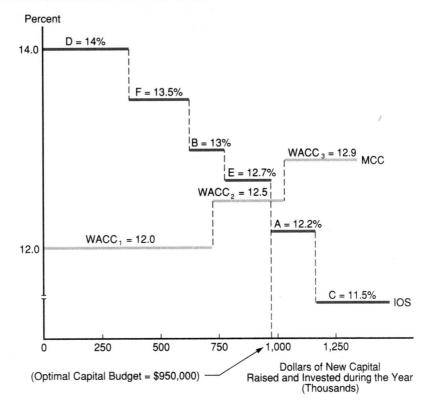

(Optimal Capital Budget = $950,000)

Dollars of New Capital
Raised and Invested during the Year
(Thousands)

Project	Cost	Annual Inflows	Project Life (Years)	IRR, or Discount Rate at which NPV = 0
A	$200,000	$ 55,757	5	12.2%
B	150,000	33,917	7	13.0
C	250,000	43,344	10	11.5
D	350,000	90,005	6	14.0
E	200,000	41,250	8	12.7
F	250,000	106,781	3	13.5

mutually exclusive, that they are equally risky, and that their risks are all equal to those of the firm's average existing assets.

The DCB then plots the IRR data shown at the bottom of Figure 16-5 as the **investment opportunity schedule (IOS)** shown in the graph. The IOS schedule shows how much money Universal could invest at different rates of return. Figure 16-5 also shows Universal's MCC schedule as it was developed by the treasurer and plotted in Figure 16-3. First, consider Project D: its IRR is 14 percent, and it can be financed with capital that costs only 12 percent;

investment opportunity schedule (IOS)
A graph of the firm's investment opportunities ranked in order of the projects' rates of return.

consequently, it should be accepted. Recall from Chapter 9 that if a project's IRR exceeds its cost of capital, its NPV will also be positive; therefore, Project D is also acceptable by the NPV criterion. Projects F, B, and E can be analyzed similarly; they are all acceptable because IRR > MCC and hence NPV > 0. Projects A and C, on the other hand, should be rejected because for them IRR < MCC and NPV < 0.

Notice that if the cost of capital had started at a point above 14 percent, none of the available projects would have had positive NPVs; hence, none of them should be accepted. In that case, Universal simply should not expand. However, in the actual situation, where the MCC starts at 12 percent and then rises, Universal should accept the four projects (D, F, B, and E) which have rates of return in excess of the cost of the capital that would be used to finance them, ending up with a capital budget of $950,000.

People sometimes ask this question: "If we took Project A first, it would be acceptable, because its 12.2 percent return would exceed the 12 percent cost of money used to finance it. Why couldn't we do this?" The answer is that we are seeking, in effect, to maximize the *excess of returns over costs,* or the area that is above the WACC but below the IOS. We accomplish this by graphing (and accepting) the most profitable projects first.

Another question that sometimes arises is this: "What would happen if the MCC cut through one of the projects? For example, suppose the second break point in the MCC schedule had occurred at $900,000 rather than at $1 million, causing the MCC schedule to cut through Project E. Should we then accept Project E?" If Project E could be accepted in part, we would take on only part of it. Otherwise, the answer would be determined by (1) finding the average cost of the funds needed to finance Project E (some of the money would cost 12.5 percent and some 12.9 percent) and (2) comparing the average cost of this money to the 12.7 percent return on the project. We should accept Project E if its return exceeds the average cost of the $200,000 needed to finance it.

The preceding analysis as summarized in Figure 16-5 reveals a very important point: *The cost of capital used in the capital budgeting process as discussed in Chapter 9 is actually determined at the intersection of the IOS and MCC schedules. If the cost of capital at the intersection (WACC$_2$ = 12.5% in Figure 16-5) is used, then the firm will make correct accept/reject decisions, and its level of financing and investment will be optimal. If it uses any other rate, its capital budget will not be optimal.*

If Universal had fewer good investment opportunities, its IOS schedule would be shifted to the left, causing the intersection to occur at a lower level on the MCC curve. Conversely, if the firm had more and better investment opportunities, the IOS would be shifted to the right, and the intersection would occur at a higher WACC. In either event, the WACC at the intersection could change. *Thus, we see that the cost of capital used in capital budgeting is influenced both by the shape of the MCC curve and by the set of available projects.*

We have, of course, abstracted from differential project riskiness in this chapter; for simplicity, we have assumed that all projects are equally risky. As we learned in Chapter 11, the cost of capital used to evaluate riskier projects should be adjusted upward, whereas a lower rate should be used for projects with below-average risk. The intersection WACC as determined in Figure 16-5 should be used to find the NPVs of new projects that are about as risky as the firm's existing assets, but this corporate cost of capital should be adjusted up or down to find NPVs for projects with higher or lower risk than the average project. This point was discussed in Chapter 11, in connection with the Brandt-Quigley Corporation appliance control computer example.[11]

Some Problem Areas in Cost of Capital

A number of difficult issues relating to the cost of capital either have not been mentioned or were glossed over lightly in this chapter. These topics are covered in advanced finance courses, but they deserve some mention now to alert you to potential dangers as well as to provide you with a preview of some of the matters dealt with in advanced courses.

Depreciation-Generated Funds. The largest single source of capital for many firms is depreciation, yet we have not discussed the cost of funds from this source. In brief, depreciation cash flows can either be reinvested or returned to investors (stockholders *and* creditors). The cost of depreciation generated funds is approximately equal to the weighted average cost of capital in the interval in which capital comes from retained earnings and low-cost debt. See Eugene F. Brigham and Louis C. Gapenski, *Intermediate Financial Management,* 2nd ed., Chapter 4, for a discussion.

Privately Owned Firms. Our whole discussion of the cost of equity was related to publicly owned corporations, and we have concentrated on the rate of return required by stockholders at large. However, there is a serious question about how one should measure the cost of equity for a firm whose stock is not traded. Tax issues also become especially important in these cases. As a general rule, the same principles of cost of capital estimation apply to both privately held and publicly owned firms, but the problems of obtaining input data are somewhat different for each.

Small Businesses. Small businesses are generally privately owned, making it difficult to estimate their cost of equity, and some of them also obtain debt from government sources, such as the Small Business Administration. The section on the next page, on small business, discusses this issue.

Measurement Problems. One cannot overemphasize the practical difficulties encountered when one actually attempts to estimate the cost of equity. It is very difficult to obtain good input data for the CAPM, for g in the formula $k_s = D_1/P_0 + g$, and for the risk premium in the formula k_s = Bond yield + Risk premium.

Costs of Capital for Projects of Differing Riskiness. As noted in Chapter 11, care must be taken to assign different risk-adjusted discount rates to capital budgeting projects of differing degrees of riskiness.

Capital Structure Weights. In this chapter we have simply taken as given the target capital structure and used this target to obtain the weights used to calculate k. As we shall see in Chapter 17, establishing the target capital structure is a major task in itself.

Dynamic Considerations. Capital budgeting and cost of capital estimates are a part of the *planning process* — they deal with ex ante, or estimated, data rather than ex post, or historical data. Hence, we can be wrong about the location of the IOS and the MCC. For example, we can underestimate the MCC and hence accept projects that, with 20-20 hindsight, we should have rejected. In a dynamic, changing world this is a real problem. Interest rates and money costs could be low at the time plans are being laid and contracts to build plants are being let, but six or eight months later these capital costs could have risen substantially. Thus, a project that formerly looked good could turn out to be a bad one because we improperly forecasted the MCC schedule.

Although this listing of problem areas may appear formidable, the state of the art in cost of capital estimation is really not in bad shape. The procedures outlined in this chapter can be used to obtain cost of capital estimates that are sufficiently accurate for practical purposes, and the problems listed here merely indicate the desirability of certain refinements. The refinements are not unimportant, but the problems we have identified do not invalidate the usefulness of the procedures outlined in the chapter.

**Small
Business**

COST OF EQUITY CAPITAL FOR SMALL FIRMS

The three equity cost estimating techniques that were discussed in this chapter have serious limitations when applied to small firms, thus increasing the need for the small-business manager to use judgment. Consider first the constant growth model, $k_s = D_1/P_0 + g$. Imagine a small, rapidly growing firm, such as Bio-Technology General (BTG), which does not now and will not in the foreseeable future pay dividends. For firms like this, the constant growth model is simply not applicable. In fact, it is difficult to imagine any dividend model that would

be of practical benefit for such a firm because of the difficulty of estimating growth rates.

The method which calls for adding a risk premium of about 3 percent to the firm's cost of debt can be used for some small firms, but problems arise if the firm does not have a fixed rate issue outstanding. BTG, for example, has no such debt issue outstanding, so we could not use the bond-yield-plus-risk-premium approach for BTG.

The third approach, the CAPM, is also often unusable because if the firm's stock is not publicly traded, then we cannot calculate the firm's beta. For the privately owned firm, we might use the so-called "pure play" CAPM technique. This involves finding a firm in the same line of business that does have public equity, estimating its beta, and then using this beta as a proxy for that of the small business in question.

To illustrate the pure play approach, again consider BTG. The firm is not publicly traded, so we cannot estimate its beta. However, data are available on more established firms, such as Genentech and Genetic Industries, so we could use their betas as representative of the biological and genetic engineering industry. Of course, these firms' betas would have to be subjectively modified to reflect their larger sizes and more established positions, as well as to take account of the differences in the nature of their products and their capital structures as compared to those of BTG. Still, as long as there are public companies in similar lines of business available for comparison, the estimates of their betas can be used to help estimate the cost of capital of a firm whose equity is not publicly traded. Note that a "liquidity premium" as discussed in Chapter 3 would also have to be added to reflect the illiquidity of the small, nonpublic firm's stock.

Flotation Costs for Small Issues

When external equity capital is raised, flotation costs increase the cost of equity capital beyond what it would be for internal funds. These external flotation costs are especially significant for smaller firms, and they can substantially affect capital budgeting decisions involving external equity funds. To illustrate this point, consider a firm that is expected to pay constant dividends forever, and hence whose growth rate is zero. In this case, if F is the percentage flotation cost, then the cost of equity capital is $k_e = D_1/[P_0(1 - F)]$. The higher the flotation cost, the higher the cost of external equity.

How big is F? According to the latest Securities and Exchange Commission data, the average flotation cost of large common stock offerings (more than $50 million) is only about 4 percent. For a firm that is expected to provide a 15 percent dividend yield (that is, $D_1/P_0 = 15\%$), the cost of equity is $15\%/(1 - 0.04)$, or 15.6 percent. However, the

SEC's data on small stock offerings (less than $1 million) show that flotation costs for such issues average about 21 percent. Thus, the cost of equity capital in the preceding example would be $15\%/(1 - 0.21)$, or about 19 percent. When we compare this to the 15.6 percent for large offerings, it is clear that a small firm would have to earn considerably more on the same project than a large firm. Small firms are therefore at a substantial disadvantage because of the effects of flotation costs.

The Small-Firm Effect

A number of researchers have observed that portfolios of small-firm stocks have earned consistently higher average returns than those of large-firm stocks; this is called the "small-firm effect." On the surface, it would seem to be advantageous to the small firm to provide average returns in the stock market that are higher than those of large firms. In reality, it is bad news for the small firm; what the small-firm effect means is that the capital market demands higher returns on stocks of small firms than on otherwise similar stocks of large firms. Therefore, the cost of equity capital is higher for small firms. This compounds the high flotation cost problem noted above.

It may be argued that stocks of small firms are riskier than those of large ones and that this accounts for the differences in returns. It is true that academic research usually finds that betas are higher on average for small firms than for large ones. However, the larger returns for small firms remain larger even after adjusting for the effects of their higher risks as reflected in their beta coefficients.

The small-firm effect is an anomaly in the sense that it is not consistent with the CAPM theory. Still, higher returns reflect a higher cost of capital, so we must conclude that smaller firms do have higher capital costs than otherwise similar larger firms. The manager of a small firm should take this factor into account when estimating his or her firm's cost of equity capital. In general, the cost of equity capital appears to be about four percentage points higher for small firms (those with market values of less than $20 million) than for large, New York Stock Exchange firms with similar risk characteristics.

SUMMARY AND KEY CONCEPTS

This chapter showed how the MCC schedule is developed and used in the capital budgeting process. The key concepts covered are listed below.

- The cost of capital to be used in capital budgeting decisions is the **weighted average** of the various types of capital the firm uses, typically debt, preferred stock, and common equity.

- The **component cost of debt** is the **after-tax** cost of new debt. It is found by multiplying the cost of new debt by $(1 - T)$, where T is the firm's marginal tax rate: $k_d(1 - T)$.

- The **component cost of preferred stock** is calculated as the preferred dividend divided by the net issuing price, where the net issuing price is the price the firm receives after deducting flotation costs: $k_p = D_p/P_n$.

- The **cost of common equity** is the cost of retained earnings as long as the firm has retained earnings, but it is the cost of new common stock once the firm has exhausted its retained earnings.

- The **cost of retained earnings**, or the rate of return required by stockholders on the firm's common stock, can be estimated using one of three methods: (1) the **CAPM approach**, (2) the **bond-yield-plus-risk-premium approach**, and (3) the **dividend-yield-plus-growth-rate**, or DCF, approach.

- To use the **CAPM approach**, one (1) estimates the firm's beta, (2) multiplies this beta by the market risk premium to determine the firm's risk premium, and (3) adds the firm's risk premium to the risk-free rate to obtain the firm's cost of retained earnings: $k_s = k_{RF} + (k_M - k_{RF})b_i$.

- The **bond-yield-plus-risk-premium approach** requires one to add a risk premium of from 2 to 4 percentage points to the firm's interest rate on long-term debt: $k_s = $ Bond rate $+$ RP.

- To use the **dividend-yield-plus-growth-rate approach**, also called the **DCF approach**, one adds the firm's expected growth rate to its expected dividend yield: $k_s = D_1/P_0 + g$.

- The **cost of new common equity** is higher than the cost of retained earnings because the firm must incur **flotation expenses** to sell stock. To find the cost of new common equity, the selling price is reduced by the flotation expense, the dividend yield is then calculated based on the price the firm actually will receive, and the expected growth rate is added to this **adjusted dividend yield**: $k_e = D_1/[P_0(1 - F)] + g$.

- Each firm has an **optimal capital structure**, defined as that mix of debt, preferred stock, and common equity which minimizes the firm's **weighted average cost of capital (WACC)**:

$$k_a = \text{WACC} = w_d k_d (1 - T) + w_p k_p + w_e (k_s \text{ or } k_e).$$

- The **marginal cost of capital, MCC,** is defined as the cost of the last dollar of new capital that the firm raises. The MCC increases as the firm raises more and more capital during a given period. A graph of the MCC plotted against dollars raised is the **MCC schedule.**

- A **break point** will occur in the MCC schedule each time the cost of one of the capital components increases.

- A firm's **investment opportunity schedule (IOS),** is a graph of the firm's investment opportunities, with the projects having the highest returns plotted first.

- The MCC schedule is combined with the IOS schedule, and the intersection defines the **cost of capital** used to evaluate average risk capital budgeting projects.

The concepts developed in this chapter are extended in Chapter 17, where we consider the effect of the capital structure on the cost of capital.

Questions

16-1 In what sense does the marginal cost of capital schedule represent a series of average costs?

16-2 How would each of the following affect a firm's cost of debt, $k_d(1 - T)$; its cost of equity, k_s; and its weighted average cost of capital, k_a? Indicate by a plus ($+$), a minus ($-$), or a zero (0) if the factor would raise, lower, or have an indeterminate effect on the item in question. Assume other things are held constant. Be prepared to justify your answer, but recognize that several of the parts probably have no single correct answer; these questions are designed to stimulate thought and discussion.

	Effect on		
	$k_d(1 - T)$	k_s	k_a = WACC
a. The corporate tax rate is lowered.	_____	_____	_____
b. The Federal Reserve tightens credit.	_____	_____	_____
c. The firm uses more debt; that is, it increases its debt/assets ratio.	_____	_____	_____
d. The dividend payout ratio is increased.	_____	_____	_____
e. The firm doubles the amount of capital it raises during the year.	_____	_____	_____
f. The firm expands into a risky new area.	_____	_____	_____
g. The firm merges with another firm whose earnings are countercyclical both to those of the first firm and to the stock market.	_____	_____	_____
h. The stock market falls drastically, and the firm's stock falls along with the rest.	_____	_____	_____
i. Investors become more risk averse.	_____	_____	_____
j. The firm is an electric utility with a large investment in nuclear plants. Several states propose a ban on nuclear power generation.	_____	_____	_____

16-3 Suppose that a firm estimates its MCC and IOS schedules for the coming year and finds that they intersect at the point 10%, $10 million. What cost of capital should be used to evaluate average projects, high-risk projects, and low-risk projects?

Self-Test Problems *(Solutions Appear on Page 633)*

Key terms   **ST-1**   Define each of the following terms:
a. After-tax cost of debt, $k_d(1 - T)$; component cost
b. Cost of preferred stock, k_p
c. Cost of retained earnings, k_s
d. Cost of new common equity, k_e
e. Flotation cost, F
f. Target capital structure; capital structure components
g. Weighted average cost of capital, WACC $= k_a$
h. Marginal cost of capital, MCC
i. Marginal cost of capital schedule; break point
j. Investment opportunity schedule (IOS)

Optimal capital budget   **ST-2**   Lancaster Engineering, Inc., (LEI) has the following capital structure, which it considers to be optimal:

Debt	25%
Preferred stock	15
Common equity	60
	100%

LEI's expected net income this year is $34,285.72; its established dividend payout ratio is 30 percent; its federal-plus-state tax rate is 40 percent; and investors expect earnings and dividends to grow at a constant rate of 9 percent in the future. LEI paid a dividend of $3.60 per share last year, and its stock currently sells at a price of $60 per share.

LEI can obtain new capital in the following ways:

- *Common:* New common stock has a flotation cost of 10 percent for up to $12,000 of new stock and 20 percent for all common over $12,000.

- *Preferred:* New preferred stock with a dividend of $11 can be sold to the public at a price of $100 per share. However, flotation costs of $5 per share will be incurred for up to $7,500 of preferred, rising to $10 per share, or 10 percent, on all preferred over $7,500.

- *Debt:* Up to $5,000 of debt can be sold at an interest rate of 12 percent; debt in the range of $5,001 to $10,000 must carry an interest rate of 14 percent; and all debt over $10,000 will have an interest rate of 16 percent.

LEI has the following investment opportunities:

Project	Cost at t = 0	Annual Net Cash Flow	Project Life	IRR
A	$10,000	$2,191.20	7 years	12.0%
B	10,000	3,154.42	5	17.4
C	10,000	2,170.18	8	14.2
D	20,000	3,789.48	10	13.7
E	20,000	5,427.84	6	

a. Find the break points in the MCC schedule.
b. Determine the cost of each capital structure component.
c. Calculate the weighted average cost of capital in the interval between each break in the MCC schedule.
d. Calculate the IRR for Project E.
e. Construct a graph showing the MCC and IOS schedules.
f. Which projects should LEI accept?

Problems

After-tax cost of debt   **16-1**   Calculate the after-tax cost of debt under each of the following conditions:
a. Interest rate, 12 percent; tax rate, 0 percent.
b. Interest rate, 12 percent; tax rate, 20 percent.
c. Interest rate, 12 percent; tax rate, 34 percent.

After-tax cost of debt   **16-2**   The Besley Company's financing plans for next year include the sale of long-term bonds with a 12 percent coupon. The company believes it can sell the bonds at a price that will provide a yield to maturity of 14 percent. If the federal-plus-state tax rate is 34 percent, what is Besley's after-tax cost of debt?

Cost of preferred stock   **16-3**   Scott Industries plans to issue some $100 par preferred stock with a 10 percent dividend. The stock is selling on the market for $94.50, and Scott must pay flotation costs of 5 percent of the market price. What is the cost of the preferred stock for Scott?

Cost of retained earnings   **16-4**   The earnings, dividends, and stock price of the Abbott Company are expected to grow at 8 percent per year after this year. Abbott's common stock sells for $26 per share, its last dividend was $2.00, and the company will pay a dividend of $2.16 at the end of the current year.
a. Using the discounted cash flow approach, what is its cost of retained earnings?
b. If the firm's beta is 2.0, the risk-free rate is 9 percent, and the average return on the market is 12 percent, what will be the firm's cost of equity using the CAPM approach?
c. If the firm's bonds earn a return of 13 percent, what will k_s be using the bond-yield-plus-risk-premium approach?
d. Based on the results of Parts a through c, what would you estimate Abbott's cost of retained earnings to be?

Cost of retained earnings   **16-5**   The Iverson Company's EPS was $5 in 1988 and $3.40 in 1983. The company pays out 40 percent of its earnings as dividends, and the stock sells for $30.
a. Calculate the past growth rate in earnings. (Hint: This is a 5-year growth period.)
b. Calculate the *next* expected dividend per share, D_1. ($D_0 = 0.4(\$5) = \$2.00$) Assume that the past growth rate will continue.
c. What is the cost of retained earnings, k_s, for the Iverson Company?

Break point calculations   **16-6**   The O'Brien Company expects earnings of $25 million next year. Its dividend payout ratio is 40 percent, and its debt/assets ratio is 50 percent. O'Brien uses no preferred stock.

a. What amount of retained earnings does O'Brien expect next year?
b. At what amount of financing will there be a break point in the MCC schedule?
c. If O'Brien can borrow $10 million at an interest rate of 10 percent, another $10 million at a rate of 11 percent, and any additional debt at a rate of 12 percent, at what points will rising debt costs cause breaks in the MCC schedule?

Cost of new common stock   **16-7**   The Sorenson Company's next expected dividend, D_1, is $2.70; its growth rate is 8 percent; and the stock now sells for $40. New stock can be sold to net the firm $35 per share.
a. What is Sorenson's percentage flotation cost, F?
b. What is Sorenson's cost of new common stock, k_e?

Weighted average cost of capital   **16-8**   The Teweles Company's cost of equity is 15 percent. Its before-tax cost of debt is 12 percent, and its average tax rate is 40 percent. The stock sells at book value. Using the following balance sheet, calculate Teweles's after-tax weighted average cost of capital:

$\frac{1}{3}$ DEBT

$.33(.12)(1-.40) + .67(.15)$

$.0238 + .1005$

$.1243$

$-33 \quad (.12)(1-.40) + (.67)(.15)$

$.0238 + .1005$

$.1243$

Assets		Liabilities and Equity	
Cash	$ 100		
Accounts receivable	200		
Inventories	300	Long-term debt	33% $ 800
Plant and equipment, net	1,800	Equity	67% 1,600
Total assets	$2,400	Total liabilities and equity	$2,400

Return on common stock $.1243$ **16-9**   Isberg Products' stock is currently selling for $40 a share. The firm is expected to earn $4 per share and to pay a year-end dividend of $2.00.

12.4%

a. If investors require a 10 percent return, what rate of growth must be expected for Isberg?
b. If Isberg reinvests retained earnings in projects whose average return is equal to the stock's expected rate of return, what will be next year's EPS? (Hint: g = b(ROE), where b = fraction of earnings retained.)

Optimal capital budget   **16-10**   On January 1, 1989, the total assets of the Shipley Company were $180 million. During the year, the company plans to raise and invest $90 million. The firm's present capital structure, which follows, is considered to be optimal. Assume that there is no short-term debt.

Long-term debt	$ 90,000,000
Common equity	90,000,000
Total liabilities and equity	$180,000,000

New bonds will have a 10 percent coupon rate and will be sold at par. Common stock, currently selling at $40 a share, can be sold to net the company $36 a share. Stockholders' required rate of return is estimated to be 12 percent, consisting of a dividend yield of 4 percent and an expected growth rate of 8 percent. (The next expected dividend is $1.60, so $1.60/$40 = 4%.) Retained earnings are estimated to be $9 million. The marginal corporate tax rate is 40 percent. Assuming that all asset expansion (gross expenditures for fixed assets plus related working capital) is included in the capital budget, the dollar amount of the capital budget, ignoring depreciation, is $90 million.
a. To maintain the present capital structure, how much of the capital budget must Shipley finance by equity?

b. How much of the new equity funds needed must be generated internally? Externally?

c. Calculate the cost of each of the equity components.

d. At what level of capital expenditure will there be a break in Shipley's MCC schedule?

e. Calculate the WACC (1) below and (2) above the break in the MCC schedule.

f. Plot the MCC schedule. Also, draw in an IOS schedule that is consistent with the MCC schedule and the projected capital budget. (Any IOS schedule that is consistent will do.)

Marginal cost of capital   **16-11**   The following tabulation gives earnings per share figures for the Prock Company during the preceding 10 years. The firm's common stock, 6 million shares outstanding, is now (1/1/89) selling for $50 per share, and the expected dividend at the end of the current year (1989) is 50 percent of the 1988 EPS. Because investors expect past trends to continue, g may be based on the earnings growth rate. (Note that nine years of growth are reflected in the data.)

Year	EPS	Year	EPS
1979	$3.00	1984	$4.41
1980	3.24	1985	4.76
1981	3.50	1986	5.14
1982	3.78	1987	5.55
1983	4.08	1988	6.00

The current interest rate on new debt is 10 percent. The firm's marginal tax rate is 40 percent. Its capital structure, considered to be optimal, is as follows:

Debt	$ 80,000,000
Common equity	120,000,000
Total liabilities and equity	$200,000,000

a. Calculate Prock's after-tax cost of new debt and of common equity, assuming that new equity comes only from retained earnings. Calculate the cost of equity as $k_s = D_1/P_0 + g$.

b. Find Prock's weighted average cost of capital, again assuming that no new common stock is sold and that all debt costs 10 percent.

c. How much can be spent on capital investments before external equity must be sold? (Assume that retained earnings available for 1989 are 50 percent of 1988 earnings. Obtain 1988 earnings by multiplying 1988 EPS by the shares outstanding.)

d. What is Prock's weighted average cost of capital (cost of funds raised in excess of the amount calculated in Part c) if new common stock can be sold to the public at $50 a share to net the firm $45 a share? The cost of debt is constant.

Optimal capital budget   **16-12**   Austen Enterprises has the following capital structure, which it considers to be optimal under present and forecasted conditions:

Debt (long-term only)	40%
Common equity	60
Total liabilities and equity	100%

For the coming year, management expects after-tax earnings of $2 million. Austen's past dividend policy of paying out 60 percent of earnings will continue. Present commitments from its banker will allow Austen to borrow according to the following schedule:

Loan Amount	Interest Rate
$0 to $500,000	10% on this increment of debt
$500,001 to $900,000	12% on this increment of debt
$900,001 and above	14% on this increment of debt

The company's average tax rate is 40 percent, the current market price of its stock is $24 per share, its *last* dividend was $2.05 per share, and the expected growth rate is 6 percent. External equity (new common) can be sold at a flotation cost of 15 percent.

Austen has the following investment opportunities for the next year:

Project	Cost	Annual Cash Flows	Project Life	IRR
1	$ 900,000	$186,210	10 years	
2	1,200,000	316,904	6	15.0%
3	500,000	303,644	2	
4	750,000	246,926	4	12.0
5	1,000,000	194,322	8	11.0

Management asks you to help determine which projects (if any) should be undertaken. You proceed with this analysis by answering the following questions (or performing the tasks) as posed in a logical sequence:

a. How many breaks are there in the MCC schedule?
b. At what dollar amounts do the breaks occur, and what causes them?
c. What is the weighted average cost of capital, k_a, in each of the intervals between the breaks?
d. What are the IRR values for Projects 1 and 3?
e. Graph the IOS and MCC schedules.
f. Which projects should Austen's management accept?
g. What assumptions about project risk are implicit in this problem? If you learned that Projects 1, 2, and 3 were of above-average risk, yet Austen chose the projects which you indicated in Part f, how would this affect the situation?
h. The problem stated that Austen pays out 60 percent of its earnings as dividends. In words, how would the analysis change if the payout ratio were changed to zero, to 100 percent, or somewhere in between?

Cost of capital
(*Integrative*)

16-13 Assume that you were recently hired as an analyst by Goulbourne Technologies, and you were asked by the firm's financial vice-president, Jerry Lahman, to estimate Goulbourne's cost of capital. You were provided with the following data, which Lahman believes may be relevant to your task:

1. The firm's tax rate is 40 percent.
2. The current price of Goulbourne's 12 percent semiannual coupon bonds with 15 years remaining to maturity is $1,153.72. Goulbourne does not use short-term interest-bearing debt on a permanent basis.

3. The current price of the firm's 10 percent, $100 par value, quarterly dividend, perpetual preferred stock is $113.10. Goulbourne would incur flotation costs of $2.00 per share on a new issue.
4. Goulbourne's common stock is currently selling at $50 per share. Its last dividend (D_0) was $4.19, and dividends are expected to grow at a constant rate of 5 percent in the foreseeable future. Goulbourne's beta is 1.2; the current yield on T-bonds is 7 percent; and the market risk premium is 6 percent. When using the bond-yield-plus-risk-premium approach, the firm's estimate of the risk premium is 4 percentage points.
5. Up to $300,000 of new common stock can be sold at a flotation cost of 15 percent. Above $300,000, the flotation cost would be 25 percent.
6. Goulbourne's target capital structure is 30 percent long-term debt, 10 percent preferred stock, and 60 percent common stock.
7. The firm is forecasting retained earnings of $300,000 for the coming year.

To structure the task somewhat, Lahman has asked you to answer the following questions:

a. 1. What sources of capital should be included in the estimate of Goulbourne's overall cost of capital?
   2. Should the component cost estimates be before-tax or after-tax costs?
   3. Should the costs be historical (embedded) costs or new (marginal) costs?
b. What is Goulbourne's component cost of debt?
c. 1. What is the firm's cost of preferred stock?
   2. Goulbourne's preferred stock is riskier to investors than its debt, yet the yield to investors is lower than the yield to maturity on the debt. Does this suggest that you have made a mistake?
d. 1. Why is there a cost associated with retained earnings?
   2. What is Goulbourne's estimated cost of retained earnings using the CAPM approach?
   3. Why is the T-bond rate a better estimate of the risk-free rate for our purposes than the T-bill rate?
e. What is the estimated cost of retained earnings using the discounted cash flow (DCF) approach?
f. What is the bond-yield-plus-risk-premium estimate for Goulbourne's cost of retained earnings?
g. What is your final estimate for k_s?
h. What is Goulbourne's cost for up to $300,000 of newly issued common stock, k_{e1}? What happens to the cost of equity if Goulbourne sells more than $300,000 of new common stock?
i. 1. What is the firm's overall, or weighted average, cost of capital (WACC) when retained earnings are used as the equity component?
   2. What is the firm's WACC when up to $300,000 of new common stock with a 15 percent flotation cost is used?
   3. What is the WACC if more than $300,000 of new common equity is sold?

4. Would Goulbourne prefer to use retained earnings or new common stock as the common equity component, and does it have a choice?

j. 1. At what amount of new investment would Goulbourne be forced to issue new common stock?

2. At what amount of new investment would Goulbourne be forced to issue new common stock with a 25 percent flotation cost?

3. What is a marginal cost of capital (MCC) schedule? Construct Goulbourne's MCC schedule.

4. Would Goulbourne's MCC schedule remain constant at 12.8 percent beyond $2 million regardless of the amount of capital required?

k. Goulbourne's Director of Capital Budgeting has identified the four following potential projects:

Project	Cost	Life	Cash Flow	IRR
A	$700,000	5 years	$218,795	17.0%
B	500,000	5	152,705	16.0
B'	500,000	20	79,881	15.0
C	800,000	5	219,185	11.5

Projects B and B' are mutually exclusive, whereas the remainder are independent. All of the projects are equally risky.

1. Plot the IOS schedule on the same graph that contains your MCC schedule. What is the firm's marginal cost of capital?

2. What is Goulbourne's optimal capital budget? Explain your answer fully.

3. If $WACC_3$ had been 18.5 percent rather than 12.8 percent, but its break point had still occurred at $1,000,000, how would that have affected the analysis?

4. If the four projects had differential riskiness, how would that have affected the analysis?

Computer-Related Problem

(Work this problem only if you are using the computer problem diskette.)

C16-1 Use the model for Problem C16-1 in the file C16 to work this problem.

a. Refer back to Problem 16-12. Now assume that the debt ratio is increased to 65 percent, causing all interest rates to rise by 1 percentage point, to 11 percent, 13 percent, and 15 percent, and causing g to increase from 6 to 7 percent. What happens to the MCC schedule and the capital budget?

b. Suppose that Austen's tax rate falls (1) to 20 percent and (2) to 0 percent. How would this affect the MCC schedule and the capital budget?

c. Austen's management now would like to know what the optimal capital budget should be if earnings are as high as $3 million or as low as $1 million. Assume a 40 percent tax rate.

  d. Would it be reasonable to use the model to analyze the effects of a change in the payout ratio without changing other variables?

Solutions to Self-Test Problems

ST-1   Refer to the marginal glossary definitions or relevant chapter sections to check your responses.

ST-2   a. A break point will occur each time a low-cost type of capital is used up. We establish the break points as follows, after first noting that LEI has $24,000 of retained earnings:

$$\text{Retained earnings} = (\text{Total earnings})(1.0 - \text{Payout})$$

$$= \$34,285.72(0.7)$$

$$= \$24,000.$$

$$\text{Break point} = \frac{\text{Total amount of low-cost capital of a given type}}{\text{Fraction of this type of capital in the capital structure}}.$$

Capital Used Up	Break Point Calculation		Break Number
Retained earnings	$BP_{RE} = \dfrac{\$24,000}{0.60}$	$= \$40,000$	2
10% flotation common	$BP_{10\%E} = \dfrac{\$24,000 + \$12,000}{0.60}$	$= \$60,000$	4
5% flotation preferred	$BP_{5\%P} = \dfrac{\$7,500}{0.15}$	$= \$50,000$	3
12% debt	$BP_{12\%D} = \dfrac{\$5,000}{0.25}$	$= \$20,000$	1
14% debt	$BP_{14\%D} = \dfrac{\$5,000 + \$5,000}{0.25}$	$= \$40,000$	2

Summary of Break Points

1. There are three common equity costs and hence two changes, and, therefore, two equity-induced breaks in the MCC. There are two preferred costs and hence one preferred break. There are three debt costs and hence two debt breaks.
2. The numbers in the third column of the table designate the sequential order of the breaks, determined after all the break points were calculated. Note that the second debt break and the break for retained earnings both occur at $40,000.
3. The first break point occurs at $20,000, when the 12 percent debt is used up. The second break point, $40,000, results from using up both retained earnings and the 14 percent debt. The MCC curve also rises at $50,000 and $60,000, as preferred stock with a 5 percent flotation cost and common stock with a 10 percent flotation cost, respectively, are used up.

  b. Component costs within indicated total capital intervals are as follows: Retained earnings (used in interval $0 to $40,000):

$$k_s = \frac{D_1}{P_0} + g = \frac{D_0(1 + g)}{P_0} + g$$

$$= \frac{\$3.60(1.09)}{\$60} + 0.09$$

$$= 0.0654 + 0.09 \qquad\qquad = 15.54\%.$$

Common with F = 10% ($40,001 to $60,000):

$$k_e = \frac{D_1}{P_0(1.0 - F)} + g = \frac{\$3.924}{\$60(0.9)} + 9\% \qquad = 16.27\%.$$

Common with F = 20% (over $60,000):

$$k_e = \frac{\$3.924}{\$60(0.8)} + 9\% \qquad\qquad = 17.18\%.$$

Preferred with F = 5% ($0 to $50,000):

$$k_p = \frac{\text{Preferred dividend}}{P_n} = \frac{\$11}{\$100(0.95)} \qquad = 11.58\%.$$

Preferred with F = 10% (over $50,000):

$$k_p = \frac{\$11}{\$100(0.9)} \qquad\qquad = 12.22\%.$$

Debt at k_d = 12% ($0 to $20,000):

$$k_d(1 - T) = 12\%(0.6) \qquad\qquad = 7.20\%.$$

Debt at k_d = 14% ($20,001 to $40,000):

$$k_d(1 - T) = 14\%(0.6) \qquad\qquad = 8.40\%.$$

Debt at k_d = 16% (over $40,000):

$$k_d(1 - T) = 16\%(0.6) \qquad\qquad = 9.60\%.$$

c. WACC calculations within indicated total capital intervals:
  1. $0 to $20,000 (debt = 7.2%, preferred = 11.58%, and retained earnings (RE) = 15.54%):

$$\text{WACC}_1 = w_d k_d(1 - T) + w_p k_p + w_s k_s$$

$$= 0.25(7.2\%) + 0.15(11.58\%) + 0.60(15.54\%) = 12.86\%.$$

  2. $20,001 to $40,000 (debt = 8.4%, preferred = 11.58%, and RE = 15.54%):

$$\text{WACC}_2 = 0.25(8.4\%) + 0.15(11.58\%) + 0.60(15.54\%) = 13.16\%.$$

  3. $40,001 to $50,000 (debt = 9.6%, preferred = 11.58%, and equity = 16.27%):

$$\text{WACC}_3 = 0.25(9.6\%) + 0.15(11.58\%) + 0.60(16.27\%) = 13.90\%.$$

  4. $50,001 to $60,000 (debt = 9.6%, preferred = 12.22%, and equity = 16.27%):

MCC and IOS Schedules for Lancaster Engineering, Inc.

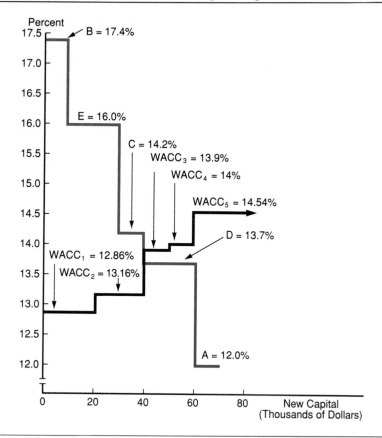

$$\text{WACC}_4 = 0.25(9.6\%) + 0.15(12.22\%) + 0.60(16.27\%) = 14.00\%.$$

5. Over $60,000 (debt = 9.6%, preferred = 12.22%, and equity = 17.18%):

$$\text{WACC}_5 = 0.25(9.6\%) + 0.15(12.22\%) + 0.60(17.18\%) = 14.54\%.$$

d. IRR calculation for Project E:

$$\text{PVIFA}_{k,6} = \frac{\$20,000}{\$5,427.84} = 3.6847.$$

This is the factor for 16 percent, so $\text{IRR}_E = 16\%$.

e. See the graph of the MCC and IOS schedules for LEI at the top of this page.

f. LEI should accept Project B, E, and C. It should reject Projects A and D, because their IRRs do not exceed the marginal costs of funds needed to finance them. The firm's capital budget would total $40,000.

17

Capital Structure and Leverage

HAS THE DEBT BINGE GONE TOO FAR?

In April 1988, a *Fortune* article entitled "Has the Debt Binge Gone Too Far?" reported that the debt ratio of the average U.S. company had risen from 49 percent in 1972 to 56 percent in 1988. When questioned about this trend, a number of respected business and academic leaders concluded that corporations are using too much debt. For example, Henry Kaufman, a well-known Wall Street worrier whose nickname is "Dr. Gloom," argued that debt levels are so high that an otherwise minor economic setback could turn into a major recession. However, John Paulus, Morgan Stanley's chief economist, countered that debt is the cheapest source of capital and that if U.S. firms are to compete effectively, they should use even more debt. Still others questioned *Fortune*'s basic data. Robert Taggart, a finance professor at Boston University, argued that accounting data like those *Fortune* used tell us nothing, and that "market value debt ratios are the only comparisons that make sense."

Fortune also noted that, while the median rating of companies followed by Standard & Poors (a leading bond-rating agency) was A in 1981, it had dropped to the "junk" level, BB, by 1988. However, Michael Milken, the Drexel Burnham Lambert executive who literally created the junk bond market (and whose annual income is reported to be $40 million), correctly pointed out that in 1981 most smaller, riskier companies were simply unable to obtain capital in the public bond markets, and hence they did not have rated debt in 1981. Milken went on to argue that the junk bond market has benefited the nation by making capital available to creative and venturesome companies.

After reading this chapter, you should be able to appraise the positions of Kaufman, Paulus, Taggart, and Milken. More important, you should understand the issues in establishing a company's target capital structure.

In Chapter 16, when we calculated the weighted average cost of capital for use in capital budgeting, we took the capital structure weights as given. However, if the weights are changed, the calculated cost of capital and thus the set of acceptable projects also will change. Further, changing the capital structure will affect the riskiness inherent in the firm's common stock and thus will affect k_s and P_0. Therefore, the choice of a capital structure, or the mix of securities the firm uses to finance its assets, is an important decision.

target capital structure
The optimal capital structure; the capital structure that will maximize the price of the firm's stock.

As we shall see, the firm first analyzes a number of factors and then establishes a **target capital structure**. This target may change over time as conditions vary, but at any given moment the firm's management has a specific capital structure in mind, and individual financing decisions should be consistent with this target. If the actual debt ratio is below the target level, expansion capital will probably be raised by issuing debt, whereas if the debt ratio is currently above the target, stock will probably be sold.

Capital structure policy involves a trade-off between risk and return. Using more debt raises the riskiness of the firm's earnings stream, but it can also lead to a higher expected rate of return. Higher risk tends to lower the stock's price, but a higher expected rate of return raises it. *The optimal capital structure is the one that strikes a balance between risk and return and thereby maximizes the price of the stock and simultaneously minimizes the cost of capital.*

Several factors influence capital structure decisions. The first is the firm's *business risk,* or the riskiness inherent in its type of business. The greater the firm's business risk, the lower its optimal debt ratio. A second key factor is the firm's *tax position.* A major reason for using debt is that interest is deductible, which lowers the effective cost of debt. However, if much of a firm's income is already sheltered from taxes by accelerated depreciation or tax loss carryforwards, its tax rate will be low, and in this case debt will not be as advantageous as it would be to a firm with a higher effective tax rate. A third important consideration is *financial flexibility,* or the ability to raise capital on reasonable terms under adverse conditions. Corporate treasurers know that a steady supply of capital is necessary for stable operations, which in turn is vital for long-run success. They also know that when money is tight in the economy, or when a firm is experiencing operating difficulties, suppliers of capital prefer to advance funds to companies with strong balance sheets. Therefore, potential future availability of funds, and the consequences of a funds shortage, have a major influence on the target capital structure. In this chapter we show how business risk, taxes, and financial flexibility, along with other factors, combine to determine the firm's optimal capital structure.

BUSINESS AND FINANCIAL RISK

In Chapter 4, when we examined risk from the viewpoint of the individual investor, we distinguished between *market risk,* which is measured by the firm's beta coefficient, and *total risk,* which includes both beta risk and an element of risk which can be eliminated by diversification. Then, in Chapter 11, we examined risk from the viewpoint of the corporation, and we considered how capital budgeting decisions affect the riskiness of the firm. There again we distinguished between beta risk (the effect of a project on the firm's beta) and corporate risk (the effect of the project on the firm's total risk).

Now we introduce two new dimensions of risk: (1) *business risk,* which is the riskiness of the firm's operations if it uses no debt, and (2) *financial risk,* which is the additional risk placed on the common stockholders as a result of the firm's decision to use debt. Conceptually, the firm has a certain amount of risk inherent in its operations; this is its business risk. When it uses debt, it partitions this risk and concentrates most of it on one class of investors — the common stockholders. However, the common stockholders must be compensated for this extra risk by a higher expected return.[1]

Business Risk

business risk
The risk associated with projections of a firm's future operating income.

Business risk, which is defined as the uncertainty inherent in projections of future *operating income,* or *earnings before interest and taxes (EBIT),* is the single most important determinant of a firm's capital structure. Figure 17-1 gives some clues about Porter Electronics Company's business risk. The top graph shows the trend in EBIT over the past 11 years; this gives both security analysts and Porter's management an idea of the degree to which EBIT has varied in the past and might vary in the future. The bottom graph shows a subjectively estimated probability distribution of Porter's EBIT for 1988. The estimate was made at the beginning of 1988, and the expected value of $275 million was read from the trend line in the top section of the figure. As the graphs indicate, actual EBIT in 1988 fell below the expected value.

Porter's past fluctuations in EBIT were caused by many factors — booms and recessions in the national economy, successful new products introduced both by Porter and by its competitors, labor strikes, a fire in Porter's major plant, and so on. Similar events will doubtless occur in the future, and when they do, EBIT will rise or fall. Further, there is always the possibility that a

---

[1]Using preferred stock also adds to financial risk. To simplify matters somewhat, in this chapter we shall consider only debt and common equity. Also, if a firm uses an especially large amount of debt in an LBO, as RJR Nabisco will apparently do, then its debt will be classified as "junk bonds," and the bondholders will also be exposed to financial risk. Some junk bonds practically amount to equity.

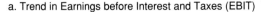

Figure 17-1   Porter Electronics Company: Trend in EBIT, 1978–1988, and Subjective Probability Distribution of EBIT, 1988

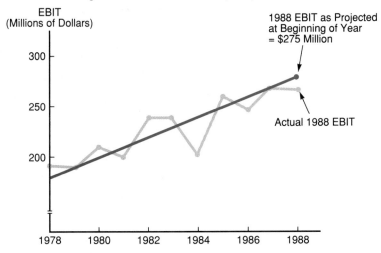

a. Trend in Earnings before Interest and Taxes (EBIT)

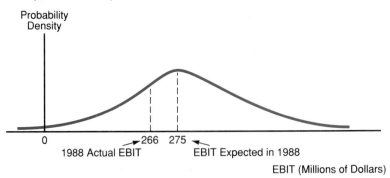

b. Subjective Probability Distribution of EBIT

long-term disaster might strike, permanently depressing the company's earning power. For example, a competitor could introduce a new product that would permanently lower Porter's earnings.[2] This element of uncertainty about Porter's future operating income is the company's *basic business risk*.

Business risk varies both from one industry to another and among firms in a given industry. Further, business risk can change over time. For example,

---

[2]Two examples of "safe" industries that turned out to be risky are the railroads just before automobiles, airplanes, and trucks took away most of their business and the telegraph business just before telephones came on the scene. Numerous individual companies have been hurt, if not destroyed, by antitrust actions, fraud, or just plain bad management.

the electric utilities were regarded for years as having little business risk, but a combination of events in the 1970s and 1980s altered their situation, producing huge losses for some companies, and greatly increasing the industry's business risk. Today food processors and grocery retailers are frequently given as examples of industries with low business risks, whereas cyclical manufacturing industries, such as steel, are regarded as having especially high business risks. Smaller companies and single-product firms also have a relatively high degree of business risk.[3]

Business risk depends on a number of factors, the more important of which include the following:

1. *Demand variability.* The more stable the demand for a firm's products, other things held constant, the lower the firm's business risk.
2. *Sales price variability.* Firms whose products are sold in highly volatile markets are exposed to more business risk than similar firms whose output prices are relatively stable.
3. *Input price variability.* Firms whose input prices are highly uncertain are exposed to a high degree of business risk.
4. *Ability to adjust output prices for changes in input prices.* Some firms have little difficulty in raising their own output prices when input costs rise, and the greater the ability to adjust output prices, the lower the degree of business risk. This factor is especially important during periods of high inflation.
5. *The extent to which costs are fixed: operating leverage.* If a high percentage of a firm's costs are fixed and hence do not decline when demand falls off, this increases the company's business risk. This factor is called *operating leverage,* and it is discussed at length in the next section.

Each of these factors is determined partly by the firm's industry characteristics, but each is also controllable to some extent by management. For example, most firms can, through their marketing policies, take actions to stabilize both unit sales and sales prices; however, this stabilization may require either large expenditures on advertising or price concessions to induce customers to commit to purchasing fixed quantities at fixed prices in the future. Similarly, firms like Porter Electronics can reduce the volatility of future input costs by negotiating long-term labor and materials supply contracts, but they may have to agree to pay prices above the current spot price level to obtain these contracts.[4]

---

[3]We have avoided any discussion of market versus company-specific risk in this section. We note now (1) that any action which increases business risk will generally increase a firm's beta coefficient but (2) that a part of business risk as we define it will generally be company specific and hence subject to elimination through diversification by the firm's stockholders.

[4]For example, in 1988 utilities could buy coal in the spot market for about $30 per ton, but under a 5-year contract, coal cost about $50 per ton. Clearly, the price for reducing uncertainty was high!

Operating Leverage

As noted previously, business risk depends in part on the extent to which a firm's costs are fixed. If fixed costs are high, even a small decline in sales can lead to a large decline in EBIT. Therefore, other things held constant, the higher a firm's fixed costs, the greater its business risk. Higher fixed costs are generally associated with more highly automated, capital-intensive firms and industries; electric utilities, telephone companies, and airlines are three examples.

operating leverage
The extent to which fixed costs are used in a firm's operations.

If a high percentage of a firm's total costs are fixed, the firm is said to have a high degree of operating leverage. In physics, leverage implies the use of a lever to raise a heavy object with a small amount of force. In politics, people who have leverage can accomplish a great deal with their smallest word or action. *In business terminology, a high degree of operating leverage, other things held constant, means that a relatively small change in sales will result in a large change in operating income.*

Figure 17-2 illustrates the concept of operating leverage by comparing the results that a new firm can expect if it uses different degrees of operating leverage. Plan A calls for a relatively small amount of fixed charges. Here the firm would not have much automated equipment, so its depreciation, maintenance, property taxes, and so on, would be low. Note, however, that under Plan A the total cost line has a relatively steep slope, indicating that variable costs per unit are higher than they would be if the firm used more leverage. Plan B calls for a higher level of fixed costs. Here the firm uses automated equipment (with which one operator can turn out a few or many units at the same labor cost) to a much larger extent. The **breakeven point** is higher under Plan B: Breakeven occurs at 40,000 units under Plan A versus 60,000 units under Plan B.

breakeven point
The volume of sales at which total costs equal total revenues, so profits equal zero.

We can develop a formula to find the breakeven quantity by recognizing that breakeven occurs when operating income (EBIT) is equal to zero, which implies that sales revenues are equal to costs:

$$Sales = Costs$$

$$PQ = VQ + F$$

$$PQ - VQ - F = 0. \qquad (17\text{-}1)$$

Here P is sales price per unit of output, Q is units of output, V is variable cost per unit, and F is fixed operating costs. We can solve Equation 17-1 for the breakeven quantity, Q_{BE}:

$$Q_{BE} = \frac{F}{P - V}. \qquad (17\text{-}1a)$$

Thus for Plan A,

$$Q_{BE} = \frac{\$20,000}{\$2.00 - \$1.50} = 40,000 \text{ units,}$$

Figure 17-2   Illustration of Operating Leverage

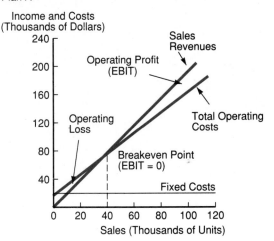

Plan A

Income and Costs
(Thousands of Dollars)

Selling price = $2.00

Fixed costs = $20,000

Variable costs = $1.50/Q

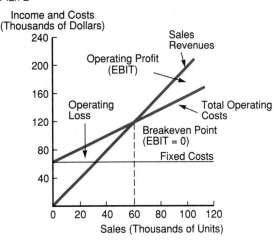

Plan B

Income and Costs
(Thousands of Dollars)

Selling price = $2.00

Fixed costs = $60,000

Variable costs = $1.00/Q

Units Sold, Q	Sales	Operating Costs	Operating Profit (EBIT)	Units Sold, Q	Sales	Operating Costs	Operating Profit (EBIT)
0	$ 0	$ 20,000	$(20,000)	0	$ 0	$ 60,000	$(60,000)
40,000	80,000	80,000	0	40,000	80,000	100,000	(20,000)
60,000	120,000	110,000	10,000	60,000	120,000	120,000	0
110,000	220,000	185,000	35,000	110,000	220,000	170,000	50,000
160,000	320,000	260,000	60,000	160,000	320,000	220,000	100,000
180,000	360,000	290,000	70,000	180,000	360,000	240,000	120,000
220,000	440,000	350,000	90,000	220,000	440,000	280,000	160,000

and for Plan B,

$$Q_{BE} = \frac{\$60,000}{\$2.00 - \$1.00} = 60,000 \text{ units.}$$

How does operating leverage affect business risk? *Other things held constant, the higher a firm's operating leverage, the higher its business risk.* This point is demonstrated in Figure 17-3, where we show how probability distributions for EBIT under Plans A and B are developed.

The top section of Figure 17-3 shows the probability distribution of sales. This distribution depends on how demand for the product varies and not on whether the product is manufactured by Plan A or by Plan B. Therefore, the same sales probability distribution applies to both production plans: expected

Figure 17-3   Analysis of Business Risk

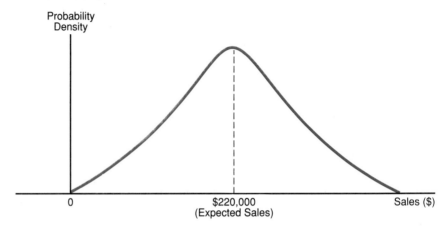

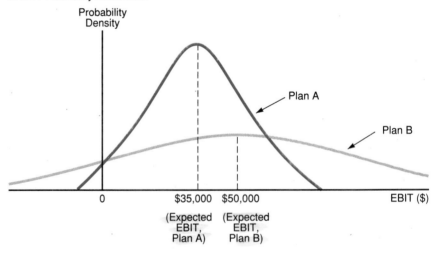

sales are $220,000 but with a range of from zero to about $500,000 under either plan.

If we had actually specified the sales probability distribution, then we could have used this information, together with the operating profit (EBIT) at each sales level as shown in the lower part of Figure 17-2, to develop probability distributions for EBIT under Plans A and B. Typical EBIT distributions are shown in the lower section of Figure 17-3. Plan B has a higher expected level of EBIT, but it also entails a much higher probability of large losses. Therefore, Plan B, the one with more fixed costs and a higher degree of operating leverage, is riskier. *In general, holding other things constant, the higher the degree of operating leverage, the greater the degree of business risk as measured by variability of EBIT.*

To what extent can firms control their operating leverage? To a large degree, operating leverage is determined by technology. Electric utilities, telephone companies, airlines, steel mills, and chemical companies simply *must* make heavy investments in fixed assets, and as a result they have high fixed costs and operating leverage. Grocery stores, on the other hand, have substantially lower fixed costs and hence lower operating leverage. Still, all firms have some control over their operating leverage. For example, an electric utility can expand its generating capacity by building either a nuclear reactor or a coal-fired plant. The nuclear generator would require a larger investment and hence higher fixed costs, but its variable operating costs would be relatively low. The coal-fired plant, on the other hand, would require a smaller investment and have lower fixed costs, but its variable costs (for coal) would be high. Thus, by its capital budgeting decisions, the utility (or any other company) can influence its operating leverage and hence its basic business risk.

The concept of operating leverage was in fact originally developed for use in capital budgeting. Alternative methods for producing a given product often have different degrees of operating leverage and hence different breakeven points and different degrees of risk. Porter Electronics and other companies regularly undertake a type of breakeven analysis (the sensitivity analysis discussed in Chapter 11) as a part of their capital budgeting process. Still, once a corporation's operating leverage has been established, this factor influences its capital structure decisions.

Financial Risk

financial leverage
The extent to which fixed-income securities (debt and preferred stock) are used in a firm's capital structure.

financial risk
The portion of stockholders' risk, over and above basic business risk, resulting from financial leverage.

Financial leverage refers to the use of fixed-income securities — debt and preferred stock — and **financial risk** is the additional risk placed on the common stockholders as a result of using financial leverage. Conceptually, the firm has a certain amount of risk inherent in its operations; this is its business risk, which is defined as the uncertainty inherent in projections of future EBIT. By using debt and preferred stock (financial leverage), the firm concentrates its business risk on the common stockholders. To illustrate, suppose 10 people decide to form a corporation to manufacture running shoes. There is a certain amount of business risk in the operation. If the firm is capitalized only with common equity, and if each person buys 10 percent of the stock, then each investor will bear an equal share of the business risk. However, suppose the firm is capitalized with 50 percent debt and 50 percent equity, with 5 of the investors putting up their capital as debt and the other 5 putting up their money as equity. In this case, the investors who put up the equity will have to bear essentially all of the business risk, so their common stock will be twice as risky as it would have been had the firm been financed only with equity. Thus, the use of debt concentrates the firm's business risk on its stockholders.

In the next section, we will learn how financial leverage affects a firm's expected earnings per share, the riskiness of those earnings, and, conse-

Table 17-1   Data on Firm B

I. Balance Sheet on 12/31/88

Current assets	$100,000	Debt	$ 0
Net fixed assets	100,000	Common equity (10,000 shares)	200,000
Total assets	$200,000	Total liabilities and equity	$200,000

II. Income Statement for 1988

Sales		$200,000
Fixed operating costs	$ 40,000	
Variable operating costs	120,000	160,000
Earnings before interest and taxes (EBIT)		$ 40,000
Interest		0
Taxable income		$ 40,000
Taxes (40%)		16,000
Net income after taxes		$ 24,000

III. Other Data

1. Earnings per share = EPS = $24,000/10,000 shares = $2.40.
2. Dividends per share = DPS = $24,000/10,000 shares = $2.40. (Thus, Firm B pays out all of its earnings as dividends.)
3. Book value per share = $200,000/10,000 shares = $20.
4. Market price per share = P_0 = $20. (Thus, the stock sells at its book value, so M/B = 1.0.)
5. Price/earnings ratio = P/E = $20/$2.40 = 8.33 times.

quently, the price of the firm's stock. As we shall see, the value of a firm that has no debt first rises as it substitutes debt for equity, then hits a peak, and finally declines as the use of debt becomes excessive. The objective of our analysis is to determine the capital structure at which value is maximized; this point is then used as the *target capital structure*.[5]

DETERMINING THE OPTIMAL CAPITAL STRUCTURE

We can illustrate the effects of financial leverage using the data for an illustrative company which we shall call Firm B. As shown in the top section of Table 17-1, the company has no debt. Should it continue the policy of using no debt,

---

[5]In this chapter we examine capital structures on a *book value* (or *balance sheet) basis*. An alternative approach is to calculate the market values of debt, preferred stock, and common equity and then to reconstruct the balance sheet on a *market value basis*. Although the market value approach is more consistent with financial theory, bond rating agencies and most financial executives focus their attention on book values. Moreover, the conversion from book to market values is a complicated process, and market value capital structures are thought by many to be too unstable to serve as operationally useful targets. Finally, exactly the same insights are gained from the book value and market value analyses. For all these reasons, the market value analysis of capital structure is better suited for advanced than for introductory finance courses.

Table 17-2   Interest Rates for Firm B with Different Debt/Assets Ratios

Amount Borrowed	Debt/Assets Ratio[a]	Interest Rate, k_d, on All Debt
$ 20,000	10%	8.0%
40,000	20	8.3
60,000	30	9.0
80,000	40	10.0
100,000	50	12.0
120,000	60	15.0

[a]We assume that the firm must borrow in increments of $20,000. We also assume that Firm B is unable to borrow more than $120,000, or 60 percent of assets, because of restrictions in its corporate charter.

or should it start using financial leverage? If it does decide to substitute debt for equity, how far should it go? As in all such decisions, *the correct answer is that it should choose the capital structure that will maximize the price of its stock.*

EBIT/EPS Analysis of the Effects of Financial Leverage

Changes in the use of debt will cause changes in earnings per share (EPS) and consequently in the stock price. To understand the relationship between financial leverage and EPS, first consider Table 17-2, which shows how Firm B's cost of debt would vary if it used different percentages of debt in its capital structure. Naturally, the higher the percentage of debt, the riskier the debt, and hence the higher the interest rate lenders will charge.

Now consider Table 17-3, which shows how expected EPS varies with changes in financial leverage. Section I of the table begins with a probability distribution of sales; we assume for simplicity that sales can take on only three values, $100,000, $200,000, or $300,000. Next, the table calculates EBIT at each of the three sales levels. Note that the Section I data are assumed to be independent of financial leverage. Therefore, the three EBIT figures ($0, $40.0, and $80.0) will always be the same, no matter how much debt Figure B uses.[6]

---

[6]In the real world, capital structure *does* at times affect EBIT. First, if debt levels are excessive, the firm will probably not be able to finance at all if its earnings are low at a time when interest rates are high. This could lead to stop-start construction and R&D programs, as well as to the necessity of passing up good investment opportunities. Second, a weak financial condition (i.e., too much debt) could cause a firm to lose sales. For example, when Eastern Airlines was thought to be on the verge of bankruptcy — and a forced shutdown — because it was unable to meet scheduled interest and principal payments on its huge debt, many travelers switched to other airlines. Third, financially strong companies are able to bargain hard with unions as well as with their suppliers, whereas weaker ones may have to give in simply because they do not have the financial resources to carry on the fight. Finally, a company with so much debt that bankruptcy is a serious threat will have difficulty attracting and retaining managers and employees, or it will have to pay premium salaries. People value job security, and financially weak companies simply cannot provide such protection. For these reasons, it is not totally correct to say that a firm's financial policy has no effect on its operating income.

Note also that EBIT is dependent on operating leverage. If we were analyzing a firm with either more or less operating leverage, the top section of Table 17-3 would be quite different: fixed and variable costs would be different, and the range of EBIT over the various sales levels would be narrower if the company used a lower degree of operating leverage but wider if it used more operating leverage.

Table 17-3   Firm B: EPS with Different Amounts of Financial Leverage (Thousands of Dollars, except Per-Share Figures)

I. Calculation of EBIT

Probability of indicated sales	0.2	0.6	0.2
Sales	$100.0	$200.0	$300.0
Fixed costs	40.0	40.0	40.0
Variable costs (60% of sales)	60.0	120.0	180.0
Total costs (except interest)	$100.0	$160.0	$220.0
Earnings before interest and taxes (EBIT)	$ 0.0	$ 40.0	$ 80.0

II. Debt/Assets (D/A) = 0%

EBIT (from Section I)	$ 0.0	$ 40.0	$ 80.0
Less interest	0.0	0.0	0.0
Earnings before taxes	$ 0.0	$ 40.0	$ 80.0
Taxes (40%)	0.0	(16.0)	(32.0)
Net income after taxes	$ 0.0	$ 24.0	$ 48.0
Earnings per share on 10,000 shares (EPS)[a]	$ 0.0	$ 2.40	$ 4.80
Expected EPS		$ 2.40	
Standard deviation of EPS		$ 1.52	
Coefficient of variation		0.63	

III. Debt/Assets (D/A) = 50%

EBIT (from Section I)	0.0	$ 40.0	$ 80.0
Less interest (0.12 × $100,000)	12.0	12.0	12.0
Earnings before taxes	$(12.0)	$ 28.0	$ 68.0
Taxes (40%; tax credit on losses)	4.8	(11.2)	(27.2)
Net income after taxes	$(7.2)	$ 16.8	$ 40.8
Earnings per share on 5,000 shares (EPS)[a]	$(1.44)	$ 3.36	$ 8.16
Expected EPS		$ 3.36	
Standard deviation of EPS		$ 3.04	
Coefficient of variation		0.90	

[a]For those who like algebra, the EPS figures can also be obtained using the following formula, in which the numerator amounts to an income statement at a given sales level laid out horizontally:

$$EPS = \frac{(Sales - Fixed\ costs - Variable\ costs - Interest)(1 - Tax\ rate)}{Shares\ outstanding}$$

$$= \frac{(EBIT - I)(1 - T)}{Shares\ outstanding}.$$

For example, with zero debt and Sales = $200,000, EPS is $2.40:

$$EPS_{D/A=0} = \frac{(\$200,000 - \$40,000 - \$120,000 - 0)(0.6)}{10,000} = \$2.40.$$

With 50 percent debt and Sales = $200,000, EPS is $3.36:

$$EPS_{D/A=0.5} = \frac{(\$200,000 - \$40,000 - \$120,000 - \$12,000)(0.6)}{5,000} = \$3.36.$$

Since the equation is linear, the sales level at which EPS will be equal under the two financing policies, or the indifference level of sales, S_I, can be found by setting $EPS_{D/A=0}$ equal to $EPS_{D/A=0.5}$ and solving for S_I:

$$EPS_{D/A=0} = \frac{(S_I - \$40,000 - 0.6S_I - 0)(0.6)}{10,000} = \frac{(S_I - \$40,000 - 0.6S_I - \$12,000)(0.6)}{5,000} = EPS_{D/A=0.5}.$$

$$S_I = \$160,000.$$

By substituting this value of sales into either equation, we can find EPS_I, the earnings per share at this indifference point, as $EPS_I = \$1.44$.

Section II of Table 17-3, the zero-debt case, calculates Firm B's earnings per share at each sales level under the assumption that the company continues to use no debt. Net income after taxes is divided by the 10,000 shares outstanding to obtain EPS. If sales are as low as $100,000, EPS will be zero, but it will rise to $4.80 at a sales level of $300,000. The EPS at each sales level is then multiplied by the probability of that sales level to calculate the expected EPS, which is $2.40 if Firm B uses no debt. We also show the standard deviation of EPS and the coefficient of variation to provide an idea of the firm's risk at a zero debt ratio: $\sigma_{EPS} = \$1.52$, and $CV_{EPS} = 0.63$.[7]

Section III of the table shows the financial results that would occur if Firm B were financed with a debt/assets ratio of 50 percent. In this situation, $100,000 of the $200,000 total capital is debt. The interest rate on the debt, 12 percent, is taken from Table 17-2. With $100,000 of 12 percent debt outstanding, the company's interest expense in Table 17-3 will be $12,000 per year. This is a fixed cost — it is the same regardless of the level of sales — and it is deducted from the EBIT values as calculated in the top section. Next, taxes are taken out to derive net income. EPS is then calculated as net income after taxes divided by shares outstanding. With debt = 0, there were 10,000 shares outstanding. However, if half of the equity were replaced by debt (debt = $100,000), there would be only 5,000 shares outstanding, and we use this fact to determine the EPS figures that would result at each of the three possible sales levels.[8] With a debt/assets ratio of 50 percent, EPS would be −$1.44 if sales were as low as $100,000; it would rise to $3.36 if sales were $200,000; and it would soar to $8.16 if sales were as high as $300,000.

The EPS distributions under the two financial structures are graphed in Figure 17-4, where we use continuous distributions rather than the discrete distributions contained in Table 17-3. Although expected EPS would be much higher if financial leverage were employed, the graph makes it clear that the risk of low or even negative EPS would also be higher if debt were used.

Another view of the relationships among expected EPS, risk, and financial leverage is presented in Figure 17-5. The tabular data in the lower section were calculated in the manner set forth in Table 17-3, and the graphs plot these data. Here we see that expected EPS rises until the firm is financed with 50 percent debt. Interest charges rise, but this effect is more than offset by the declining number of shares outstanding as debt is substituted for equity. How-

---

[7]See Chapter 4 for a review of procedures for calculating standard deviations and coefficients of variation. Recall that the advantage of the coefficient of variation is that it permits better comparisons when the expected values of EPS vary, as they do here for the two capital structures.

[8]We assume in this example that the firm could repurchase common stock at its book value of $100,000/5,000 shares = $20 per share. However, the firm may actually have to pay a higher price to repurchase its stock on the open market. If Firm B had to pay $22 per share, then it could repurchase only $100,000/$22 = 4,545 shares, and in this case, expected EPS would be only $16,800/(10,000 − 4,545) = $16,800/5,455 = $3.08. A model in which the stock repurchase price is a variable is discussed in Eugene F. Brigham and Louis C. Gapenski, *Intermediate Financial Management*, 2nd ed., Chapter 6.

Figure 17-4   Firm B: Probability Distribution of EPS with Different Amounts of Financial Leverage

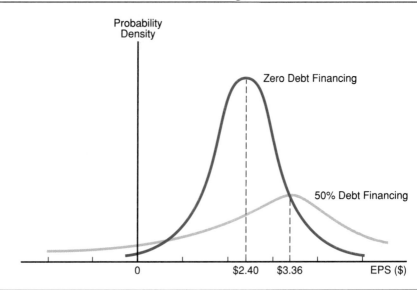

ever, EPS peaks at a debt ratio of 50 percent. Beyond this amount, interest rates rise so rapidly that EPS is depressed in spite of the falling number of shares outstanding.

The right panel of Figure 17-5 shows that risk, as measured by the coefficient of variation of EPS, rises continuously, and at an increasing rate, as debt is substituted for equity.

We see, then, that using leverage has both good and bad effects: higher leverage increases expected earnings per share (until the D/A ratio equals 50 percent), but it also increases the firm's risk. Clearly, the debt ratio should not exceed 50 percent, but where, in the range of 0 to 50 percent, should it be set? This issue is discussed in the next section.

EPS Indifference Analysis

EPS indifference point
The level of sales at which EPS will be the same whether the firm uses debt or common stock financing.

Another way of considering the data on Firm B's two financing methods is shown in Figure 17-6, which depicts the **EPS indifference point** — that is, the point at which EPS is the same regardless of whether the firm uses debt or common stock. At a low level of sales, EPS is much higher if stock rather than debt is used. However, the debt line has a steeper slope, showing that earnings per share will go up faster with increases in sales if debt is used. The two lines cross at sales of $160,000. Below that level, EPS would be higher if the firm used more common stock; above it, debt financing would produce higher earnings per share.

Figure 17-5   Firm B: Relationships among Expected EPS, Risk, and Financial Leverage

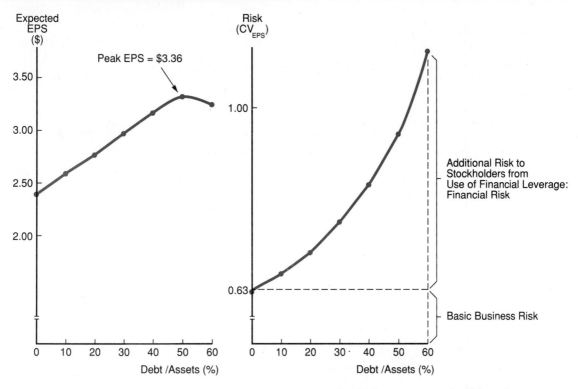

Debt/Assets Ratio	Expected EPS	Standard Deviation of EPS	Coefficient of Variation
0%[a]	$2.40[a]	$1.52[a]	0.63[a]
10	2.56	1.69	0.66
20	2.75	1.90	0.69
30	2.97	2.17	0.73
40	3.20	2.53	0.79
50[a]	3.36[a]	3.04[a]	0.90[a]
60	3.30	3.79	1.15

[a]Values for D/A = 0 and D/A = 50 percent are taken from Table 17-3. Values at other D/A ratios were calculated similarly.

If it were certain that sales would never again fall below $160,000, bonds would be the preferred method of financing the asset increase. But we cannot know this for certain. In fact, investors know that in a number of previous years, sales have fallen below this critical level, and if any of several detrimental events should occur in the future, sales would again fall below $160,000. On the other hand, if sales continued to expand, higher earnings per share would result from the use of bonds, an advantage that no investor would want to forgo.

Figure 17-6   Earnings per Share for Stock and Debt Financing

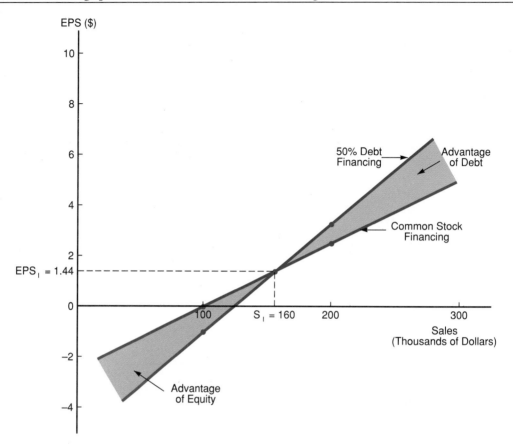

1. These values of the indifference level of sales, S_I and EPS_I, are the same as those obtained algebraically in Table 17-3. These relationships would be somewhat different if we did not assume that stock can be repurchased at book value.
2. For those who like math, we can develop an equation to find the sales level at which EPS is the same under different degrees of financial leverage:

$$EPS_1 = \frac{S_{BE} - F - V - I_1}{Shares_1} = \frac{S_{BE} - F - V - I_2}{Shares_2} = EPS_2.$$

Here, EPS_1 and EPS_2 are the EPSs at two debt levels; S_{BE} is the sales breakeven (or indifference) level at which $EPS_1 = EPS_2$; I_1 and I_2 are interest charges at the two debt levels; $Shares_1$ and $Shares_2$ are shares outstanding at the two debt levels; F is the fixed costs; and V = variable costs = Sales × v, where v is the variable cost percentage. Solving for S_{BE}, we obtain this expression:

$$S_{BE} = \left(\frac{(Shares_2)(I_1) - (Shares_1)(I_2)}{Shares_2 - Shares_1} + F \right) \left(\frac{1}{1 - v} \right)$$

In our example,

$$S_{BE} = \left(\frac{(5,000)(0) - (10,000)(\$12,000)}{-5,000} + \$40,000 \right) \left(\frac{1}{0.4} \right)$$

$$= \$160,000.$$

It should be noted that in our example we assume that the price at which shares are issued is $20, regardless of the amount of leverage employed.

**Table 17-4   Stock Price and Cost of Capital Estimates for Firm B
with Different Debt/Assets Ratios**

Debt/ Assets (1)	k_d (2)	Expected EPS (and DPS)[a] (3)	Estimated Beta (4)	$k_s = [k_{RF} + (k_M - k_{RF})b]$[b] (5)	Estimated Price[c] (6)	Resulting P/E Ratio (7)	Weighted Average Cost of Capital,[d] WACC (8)
0%	—	$2.40	1.50	12.0%	$20.00	8.33	12.00%
10	8.0%	2.56	1.55	12.2	20.98	8.20	11.46
20	8.3	2.75	1.65	12.6	21.83	7.94	11.08
30	9.0	2.97	1.80	13.2	22.50	7.58	10.86
40	10.0	3.20	2.00	14.0	22.86	7.14	10.86
50	12.0	3.36	2.30	15.2	22.11	6.58	11.20
60	15.0	3.30	2.70	16.8	19.64	5.95	12.12

[a]Firm B pays all of its earnings out as dividends, so EPS = DPS.

[b]We assume that k_{RF} = 6% and k_M = 10%. Therefore, at debt/assets equal to zero, k_s = 6% + (10% − 6%)1.5 = 6% + 6% = 12%. Other values of k_s are calculated similarly.

[c]Since all earnings are paid out as dividends, no retained earnings will be plowed back into the business, and growth in EPS and DPS will be zero. Hence, the zero growth stock price model developed in Chapter 6 can be used to estimate the price of Firm B's stock. For example, at debt/assets = 0,

$$P_0 = \frac{DPS}{k_s} = \frac{\$2.40}{0.12} = \$20.$$

Other prices were calculated similarly.

[d]Column 8 is found by use of the weighted average cost of capital (WACC) equation developed in Chapter 16:

$$WACC = w_d k_d (1 - T) + w_s k_s$$

For example, at D/A = 40%,

$$= (D/A)(k_d)(1 - T) + (1 - D/A)k_s.$$
$$WACC = 0.4(10\%)(0.6) + 0.6(14.0\%) = 10.80\%.$$

The Effect of Capital Structure on Stock Prices and the Cost of Capital

As we saw in Figure 17-5, Firm B's expected EPS is maximized at a debt/assets ratio of 50 percent. Does this mean that Firm B's optimal capital structure calls for 50 percent debt? The answer is a resounding no—*the optimal capital structure is the one that maximizes the price of the firm's stock, and this always calls for a debt ratio which is lower than the one that maximizes expected EPS.*

This statement is demonstrated in Table 17-4, which develops Firm B's estimated stock price and weighted average cost of capital at different debt/assets ratios. The debt cost and EPS data in Columns 1, 2, and 3 were taken from Table 17-2 and Figure 17-5. The beta coefficients shown in Column 4 were estimated. Recall from Chapter 4 that a stock's beta measures its relative volatility as compared with that of an average stock. It has been demonstrated both theoretically and empirically that a firm's beta increases with its degree of financial leverage. The exact nature of this relationship for a given firm is difficult to estimate, but the values given in Column 4 do show the approximate nature of the relationship for Firm B.

Assuming that the risk-free rate of return, k_{RF}, is 6 percent and that the required return on an average stock, k_M, is 10 percent, we use the CAPM equation to develop estimates of the required rates of return, k_s, for Firm B as shown in Column 5. Here we see that k_s is 12 percent if no financial leverage is used, but k_s rises to 16.8 percent if the company finances with 60 percent debt, the maximum permitted by its charter.

The zero growth stock valuation model developed in Chapter 6 is used, along with the Column 3 values of DPS and the Column 5 values of k_s, to develop the estimated stock prices shown in Column 6. Here we see that the expected stock price first rises with financial leverage, hits a peak of $22.86 at a debt/assets ratio of 40 percent, and then begins to decline. *Thus, Firm B's optimal capital structure calls for 40 percent debt.*

The price/earnings ratios shown in Column 7 were calculated by dividing the price in Column 6 by the expected earnings given in Column 3. We use the pattern of P/E ratios as a check on the "reasonableness" of the other data. Other things held constant, P/E ratios should decline as the riskiness of a firm increases, and that pattern does exist in our own illustrative case. Also, at the time Firm B's data were being analyzed, the P/Es shown here were generally consistent with those of zero growth companies with varying amounts of financial leverage. Thus, the data in Column 7 reinforce our confidence that the estimated prices shown in Column 6 are reasonable.

Finally, Column 8 shows Firm B's weighted average cost of capital, WACC, calculated as described in Chapter 16, at the different capital structures. If the company uses zero debt, its capital is all equity; hence, WACC = k_s = 12%. As the firm begins to use lower-cost debt, its weighted average cost of capital declines. However, as the debt ratio increases, the costs of both debt and equity rise, and the increasing costs of the two components begin to offset the fact that larger amounts of the lower-cost component are being used. At 40 percent debt, WACC hits a minimum, and it rises after that as the debt ratio is increased.

The EPS, cost of capital, and stock price data shown in Table 17-4 are plotted in Figure 17-7. As the graph shows, the debt/assets ratio that maximizes Firm B's expected EPS is 50 percent. However, the expected stock price is maximized, and the cost of capital is minimized, at a 40 percent debt ratio. *Thus, the optimal capital structure calls for 40 percent debt and 60 percent equity.* Management should set its target capital structure at these ratios, and if the present ratios are off target, it should move toward the target when new security offerings are made.

DEGREE OF LEVERAGE

In our discussion of operating leverage earlier in this chapter, we made no mention of financial leverage, and when we discussed financial leverage, operating leverage was assumed to be given. Actually, the two types of leverage are interrelated. For example, if Firm B *reduced* its operating leverage, this

**Figure 17-7   Relationship between Firm B's Capital Structure and
Its EPS, Cost of Capital, and Stock Price**

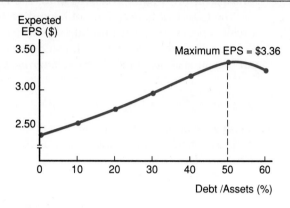

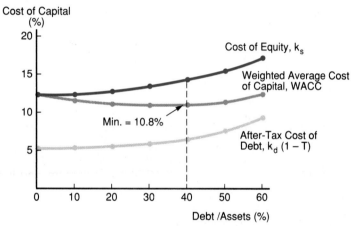

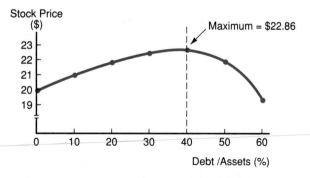

would probably lead to an *increase* in its optimal amount of financial leverage. On the other hand, if it decided to *increase* its operating leverage, its optimal capital structure would probably call for *less* debt.

The theory of finance has not been developed to the point where we can actually specify simultaneously the optimal levels of operating and financial leverage. However, we can see how operating and financial leverage interact through an analysis of the *degree of leverage concept.*

Degree of Operating Leverage (DOL)

degree of operating leverage (DOL)
The percentage change in EBIT resulting from a one percent change in sales.

The **degree of operating leverage (DOL)** is defined as the percentage change in operating income (or EBIT) associated with a given percentage change in sales volume:

$$DOL = \frac{\text{Percentage change in EBIT}}{\text{Percentage change in sales}} = \frac{\dfrac{\Delta EBIT}{EBIT}}{\dfrac{\Delta Q}{Q}}. \qquad (17\text{-}2)$$

In effect, the DOL is an index number which measures the effect of a change in sales on operating income, or EBIT.

DOL can be calculated by using Equation 17-3, which is derived from Equation 17-2:[9]

$$DOL_Q = \text{Degree of operating leverage at Point Q}$$

$$= \frac{Q(P - V)}{Q(P - V) - F}, \qquad (17\text{-}3)$$

or, based on dollar sales rather than units,

$$DOL_S = \frac{S - VC}{S - VC - F}. \qquad (17\text{-}3a)$$

Here Q is units of output, P is the average sales price per unit of output, V is the variable cost per unit, F is fixed operating costs, S is sales in dollars, and

---

[9]For those interested in proofs, Equation 17-3 is developed from 17-2 as follows. The change in units of output is defined as ΔQ. In equation form, $EBIT = Q(P - V) - F$, where Q is units sold, P is the price per unit, V is the variable cost per unit, and F is the total fixed cost. Since both price and fixed costs are constant, the change in EBIT is $\Delta EBIT = \Delta Q(P - V)$. The initial EBIT is $Q(P - V) - F$, so the percentage change in EBIT is

$$\%\Delta EBIT = \frac{\Delta Q(P - V)}{Q(P - V) - F}.$$

The percentage change in output is $\Delta Q/Q$, so the ratio of the percentage change in EBIT to the percentage change in output is

$$DOL = \frac{\dfrac{\Delta Q(P - V)}{Q(P - V) - F}}{\dfrac{\Delta Q}{Q}} = \left(\frac{\Delta Q(P - V)}{Q(P - V) - F}\right)\left(\frac{Q}{\Delta Q}\right) = \frac{Q(P - V)}{Q(P - V) - F}. \qquad (17\text{-}3)$$

VC is total variable costs. Equation 17-3 is normally used to analyze a single product, such as IBM's PC, whereas Equation 17-3a is used to evaluate an entire firm with many types of products and hence for which "quantity in units" and "sales price" are not meaningful.

Applying Equation 17-3 to data for Firm B at a sales level of $200,000 as shown back in Table 17-3, we find its degree of operating leverage to be 2.0:

$$DOL_{\$200,000} = \frac{\$200,000 - \$120,000}{\$200,000 - \$120,000 - \$40,000}$$

$$= \frac{\$80,000}{\$40,000} = 2.0.$$

Thus, an X percent increase in sales will produce a 2X percent increase in EBIT. For example, a 50 percent increase in sales, starting from sales of $200,000, will result in a 50%(2.0) = 100% increase in EBIT. This situation is confirmed by examining Section I of Table 17-3, where we see that a 50 percent increase in sales, from $200,000 to $300,000, causes EBIT to double. Notice also that the DOL is specific to the beginning sales level; thus, if we evaluate it from a sales base of $300,000, there will be a different DOL:

$$DOL_{\$300,000} = \frac{\$300,000 - \$180,000}{\$300,000 - \$180,000 - \$40,000}$$

$$= \frac{\$120,000}{\$80,000} = 1.5.$$

In general, if a firm is operating at close to its breakeven level, the degree of operating leverage will be high, but DOL declines the higher the base level of sales is above breakeven sales. Looking back at the top section of Table 17-3, we see that the company's breakeven point (before consideration of financial leverage) is at sales of $100,000. At that level, DOL is infinite:

$$DOL_{\$100,000} = \frac{\$100,000 - \$60,000}{\$100,000 - \$60,000 - \$40,000}$$

$$= \frac{\$40,000}{0} = \text{undefined but} \approx \text{infinity.}$$

When evaluated at higher and higher sales levels, DOL progressively declines.

Degree of Financial Leverage (DFL)

Operating leverage affects earnings before interest and taxes (EBIT), whereas financial leverage affects earnings after interest and taxes, or the earnings available to common stockholders. In terms of Table 17-3, operating leverage affects the top section, whereas financial leverage affects the lower sections. Thus, if Firm B decided to use more operating leverage, its fixed costs would be higher than $40,000, its variable cost ratio would be lower than 60 percent of sales, and its EBIT would vary with sales to a greater extent. Financial leverage takes over where operating leverage leaves off, further magnifying the effects on earnings per share of changes in the level of sales. For this reason, operating leverage is sometimes referred to as *first-stage leverage* and financial leverage as *second-stage leverage.*

degree of financial leverage (DFL)
The percentage change in earnings available to common stockholders associated with a given percentage change in earnings before interest and taxes.

The **degree of financial leverage (DFL)** is defined as the percentage change in earnings per share that is associated with a given percentage change in earnings before interest and taxes (EBIT), and it may be calculated as follows:[10]

$$\text{DFL} = \frac{\%\Delta \text{EPS}}{\%\Delta \text{EBIT}}$$

$$= \frac{\text{EBIT}}{\text{EBIT} - \text{I}}. \qquad (17\text{-}4)$$

For Firm B at sales of $200,000 and an EBIT of $40,000, the degree of financial leverage with a 50 percent debt ratio is

$$\text{DFL}_{\text{S} = \$200,000, \, \text{D} = 50\%} = \frac{\$40,000}{\$40,000 - \$12,000}$$

$$= 1.43.$$

Therefore, a 100 percent increase in EBIT would result in a $100(1.43) = 143$ percent increase in earnings per share. This may be confirmed by referring to the lower section of Table 17-3, where we see that a 100 percent increase in EBIT, from $40,000 to $80,000, produces a 143 percent increase in EPS:

---

[10]For those who like proofs, Equation 17-4 is developed as follows:

1. Recall that EBIT = Q(P − V) − F.

2. Earnings per share are found as EPS = [(EBIT − I)(1 − T)]/N, where I is interest paid, T is the corporate tax rate, and N is the number of shares outstanding.

3. I is a constant, so ΔI = 0; hence, ΔEPS, the change in EPS, is

$$\Delta \text{EPS} = \frac{(\Delta \text{EBIT} - \Delta \text{I})(1 - \text{T})}{\text{N}} = \frac{\Delta \text{EBIT}(1 - \text{T})}{\text{N}}.$$

4. The percentage change in EPS is the change in EPS divided by the original EPS:

$$\frac{\dfrac{\Delta \text{EBIT}(1 - \text{T})}{\text{N}}}{\dfrac{(\text{EBIT} - \text{I})(1 - \text{T})}{\text{N}}} = \left[\frac{\Delta \text{EBIT}(1 - \text{T})}{\text{N}}\right]\left[\frac{\text{N}}{(\text{EBIT} - \text{I})(1 - \text{T})}\right] = \frac{\Delta \text{EBIT}}{\text{EBIT} - \text{I}}.$$

5. The degree of financial leverage is the percentage change in EPS over the percentage change in EBIT:

$$\text{DFL} = \frac{\dfrac{\Delta \text{EBIT}}{\text{EBIT} - \text{I}}}{\dfrac{\Delta \text{EBIT}}{\text{EBIT}}} = \left(\frac{\Delta \text{EBIT}}{\text{EBIT} - \text{I}}\right)\left(\frac{\text{EBIT}}{\Delta \text{EBIT}}\right) = \frac{\text{EBIT}}{\text{EBIT} - \text{I}}. \qquad (17\text{-}4)$$

6. This equation must be modified if the firm has preferred stock outstanding.

$$\%\Delta EPS = \frac{\Delta EPS}{EPS_0} = \frac{\$8.16 - \$3.36}{\$3.36} = \frac{\$4.80}{\$3.36} = 1.43 = 143\%.$$

If no debt were used, the degree of financial leverage would by definition be 1.0, so a 100 percent increase in EBIT would produce exactly a 100 percent increase in EPS. This can be confirmed from the data in Section II of Table 17-3.

Combining Operating and Financial Leverage (DTL)

We have seen that operating leverage causes a change in sales volume to have a magnified effect on EBIT, and that if financial leverage is superimposed on operating leverage, changes in EBIT will have a magnified effect on earnings per share. Therefore, if a firm uses a considerable amount of both operating and financial leverage, then even small changes in sales will produce wide fluctuations in EPS.

Equation 17-3 for the degree of operating leverage can be combined with Equation 17-4 for the degree of financial leverage to produce the equation for the **degree of total leverage (DTL)**, which shows how a given change in sales will affect earnings per share. Here are three equivalent equations for DTL:[11]

degree of total leverage (DTL)
The percentage change in EPS brought about by a given percentage change in sales; the product of the degree of operating leverage times the degree of financial leverage.

$$DTL = (DOL)(DFL). \tag{17-5}$$

$$DTL = \frac{Q(P - V)}{Q(P - V) - F - I}. \tag{17-5a}$$

$$DTL = \frac{S - VC}{S - VC - F - I}. \tag{17-5b}$$

For Firm B at sales of $200,000, we can substitute data from Table 17-3 into Equation 17-5b to find the degree of total leverage if the debt ratio is 50 percent:

----

[11]For those interested in proofs, Equation 17-5 is true by definition. Equations 17-5a and 17-5b are developed as follows:

1. Recognize that $EBIT = Q(P - V) - F$; then rewrite Equation 17-4 as follows:

$$DFL = \frac{EBIT}{EBIT - I} = \frac{Q(P - V) - F}{Q(P - V) - F - I} = \frac{S - VC - F}{S - VC - F - I}. \tag{17-4a}$$

2. The degree of total leverage is equal to the degree of operating leverage times the degree of financial leverage, or Equation 17-3 times Equation 17-4a:

$$DTL = (DOL)(DFL) \tag{17-5}$$

$$= (\text{Equation 17-3})(\text{Equation 17-4a})$$

$$= \left[\frac{Q(P - V)}{Q(P - V) - F}\right]\left[\frac{Q(P - V) - F}{Q(P - V) - F - I}\right]$$

$$= \frac{Q(P - V)}{Q(P - V) - F - I} \tag{17-5a}$$

$$= \frac{S - VC}{S - VC - F - I}. \tag{17-5b}$$

$$DTL_{\$200,000,\ 50\%} = \frac{\$200,000\ -\ \$120,000}{\$200,000\ -\ \$120,000\ -\ \$40,000\ -\ \$12,000}$$

$$= \frac{\$80,000}{\$28,000} = 2.86.$$

Equivalently, using Equation 17-5, we find

$$DTL_{\$200,000,\ 50\%} = (2.00)(1.43) = 2.86.$$

We can now use the degree of total leverage (DTL) to find the new earnings per share (EPS_1) for any given percentage increase in sales (%Δ Sales), proceeding as follows:

$$EPS_1 = EPS_0 + EPS_0[(DTL)(\%\Delta Sales)]$$

$$= EPS_0[1.0 + (DTL)(\%\Delta Sales)].$$

For example, a 50 percent (or 0.5) increase in sales, from \$200,000 to \$300,000, would cause EPS_0 (\$3.36 as shown in Section III of Table 17-3) to increase to \$8.16:

$$EPS_1 = \$3.36[1.0 + (2.86)(0.5)]$$

$$= \$3.36(2.43)$$

$$= \$8.16.$$

This figure agrees with the one for EPS shown in Table 17-3.

The degree of leverage concept is useful primarily for the insights it provides into the joint effects of operating and financial leverage on earnings per share. The concept could be used to show the management of a business, for example, that a decision to automate a plant and to finance the new equipment with debt would result in a situation wherein a 10 percent decline in sales would produce a 50 percent decline in earnings, whereas a different operating and financial leverage package would be such that a 10 percent sales decline would cause earnings to decline by only 20 percent. Having the alternatives stated in this manner might give the decision maker a better idea of the ramifications of alternative actions.[12]

---

[12]The degree of leverage concept is also useful for investors. If firms in an industry are classified as to their degrees of total leverage, an investor who is optimistic about prospects for the industry might favor those firms with high leverage, and vice versa if industry sales are expected to decline. However, it is very difficult to separate fixed from variable costs. Accounting statements simply do not make this breakdown, so the analyst must make the separation in a necessarily judgmental manner. Note that costs are really fixed, variable, and "semivariable," for if times get tough enough, firms will sell off depreciable assets and thus reduce depreciation charges (a fixed cost), lay off "permanent" employees, reduce salaries of the remaining personnel, and so on. For this reason, the degree of leverage concept is generally more useful in explaining the general nature of the relationship than in developing precise numbers, and any numbers developed should be thought of as approximations rather than as exact specifications.

LIQUIDITY AND CASH FLOW ANALYSIS

There are some practical difficulties with the types of analyses described thus far in the chapter, including the following:

1. It is virtually impossible to determine exactly how either P/E ratios or equity capitalization rates (k_s values) are affected by different degrees of financial leverage. The best we can do is make educated guesses about these relationships. Therefore, management rarely, if ever, has sufficient confidence in the type of analysis set forth in Table 17-3 and Figure 17-7 to use it as the sole determinant of the target capital structure.

2. The managers may be more or less conservative than the average stockholder, and hence management may set a somewhat different target capital structure than the one that would maximize the stock price. The managers of a publicly owned firm would never admit this, for unless they owned voting control, they would quickly be removed from office. However, in view of the uncertainties about what constitutes the value-maximizing capital structure, management could always say that the target capital structure employed is, in its judgment, the value-maximizing structure, and it would be difficult to prove otherwise. Still, if management is far off target, especially on the low side, then chances are very high that some other firm or management group will take over the company, increase its leverage, and thereby raise its value. This point is discussed in more detail later in the chapter.

3. Managers of large firms, especially those providing vital services such as electricity or telephones, have a responsibility to provide *continuous* service; therefore, they must refrain from using leverage to the point where the firms' long-run viability is endangered. Long-run viability may conflict with short-run stock price maximization and capital cost minimization.[13]

For all of these reasons, managers are concerned about the effects of financial leverage on the risk of bankruptcy, and an analysis of this factor is therefore an important input in all capital structure decisions. Accordingly, managements

---

[13]Recognizing this fact, most public service commissions require utilities to obtain the commission's approval before issuing long-term securities, and Congress has empowered the SEC to supervise the capital structures of public utility holding companies. However, in addition to concern over the firms' safety, which suggests low debt ratios, both managers and regulators recognize a need to keep all costs as low as possible, including the cost of capital. Since a firm's capital structure affects its cost of capital, regulatory commissions and utility managers try to select capital structures that will minimize the cost of capital, subject to the constraint that the firm's financial flexibility not be endangered.

Figure 17-8   Firm B: Probability Distributions of Times-Interest-Earned Ratios with Different Capital Structures

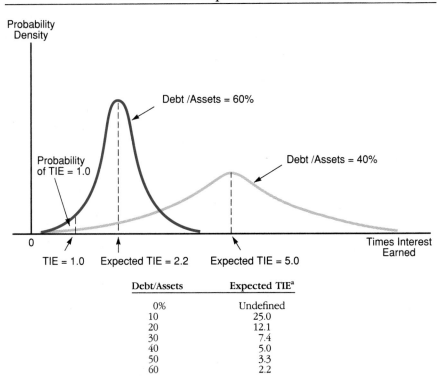

Debt/Assets	Expected TIE[a]
0%	Undefined
10	25.0
20	12.1
30	7.4
40	5.0
50	3.3
60	2.2

[a]TIE = EBIT/Interest. For example, when debt/assets = 50%, TIE = $40,000/$12,000 = 3.3. Data are from Tables 17-2 and 17-3.

times-interest-earned (TIE) ratio
A ratio that measures the firm's ability to meet its annual interest obligations, calculated by dividing earnings before interest and taxes by interest charges.

give considerable weight to financial strength indicators such as the **times-interest-earned (TIE) ratio**. The lower this ratio, the higher the probability that a firm will default on its debt and be forced into bankruptcy.

The tabular material in the lower section of Figure 17-8 shows Firm B's expected TIE ratio at several different debt/assets ratios. If the debt/assets ratio were only 10 percent, the expected TIE would be a high 25 times, but the interest coverage ratio would decline rapidly if the debt ratio were increased. Note, however, that these coverages are expected values at different debt ratios; the actual TIE for any debt ratio will be higher if sales exceed the expected $200,000 level but lower if sales fall below $200,000.

The variability of the TIE ratio is highlighted in the graph in Figure 17-8, which shows the probability distributions of the TIEs at debt/assets ratios of 40 percent and 60 percent. The expected TIE is much higher if only 40 percent debt is used. Even more important, with less debt there is a much lower probability of a TIE of less than 1.0, the level at which the firm is not earning enough to meet its required interest payment and thus is seriously exposed to the threat of bankruptcy.[14]

CAPITAL STRUCTURE THEORY

Modern capital structure theory began in 1958, when Professors Franco Modigliani and Merton Miller (hereafter MM) published what has been called the most influential finance article ever written.[15] MM proved, under a very restrictive set of assumptions, that because of the tax deductibility of interest on debt, a firm's value rises continuously as it uses more debt, and hence its value will be maximized by financing almost entirely with debt. MM's assumptions included the following:

1. There are no brokerage costs;

2. There are no personal taxes;

3. Investors can borrow at the same rate as corporations;

4. Investors have the same information as management about the firm's future investment opportunities;

5. All the firm's debt is riskless, regardless of how much debt it uses; and

6. EBIT is not affected by the use of debt.

Since several of these assumptions were obviously unrealistic, MM's position was only a beginning.

Subsequent researchers, and MM themselves, extended the basic theory by relaxing the assumptions. Other researchers attempted to test the various theoretical models with empirical data to see exactly how stock prices and capital costs are affected by capital structure. Both the theoretical and the empirical results have added to our understanding of capital structure, but none of these studies has produced results that can be used to precisely identify a firm's optimal capital structure. A summary of the theoretical and empirical research to date is expressed graphically in Figure 17-9. Here are the key points in the figure:

1. The fact that interest is a deductible expense makes debt less expensive than common or preferred stock. In effect, the government pays part of

---

[14]Note that cash flows, which include depreciation, can be sufficient to cover required interest payments even though the TIE is less than 1.0. Thus, at least for a while, a firm may be able to avoid bankruptcy even though its operating income is less than its interest charges. However, most debt contracts stipulate that firms must maintain the TIE ratio above some minimum level, say, 2.0 or 2.5, or else they cannot borrow any additional funds, which can severely constrain operations. Such potential constraints, as much as the threat of actual bankruptcy, limit the use of debt.

[15]Franco Modigliani and Merton H. Miller, "The Cost of Capital, Corporation Finance, and the Theory of Investment," *American Economic Review,* June 1958.

Figure 17-9   Effect of Leverage on the Value of Firm B's Stock

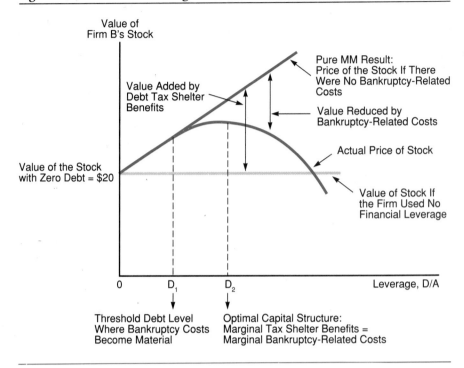

the cost of debt capital, or, to put it another way, debt provides tax shelter benefits. As a result, more of the firm's operating income (EBIT) flows through to investors, so the more debt a company uses, the higher its value, and the higher the price of its stock. Under the assumptions of the original Modigliani-Miller paper, their analysis led to the conclusion that the firm's stock price will be maximized if it uses virtually 100 percent debt, and the line labeled "Pure MM Result" in Figure 17-9 expresses the relationship between stock prices and debt.

2. The MM assumptions do not hold in the real world. First, interest rates rise as the debt ratio rises. Second, EBIT declines at extreme levels of leverage. Third, expected tax rates fall, thus reducing the value of the debt tax shelter. And, fourth, the probability of bankruptcy, which brings with it lawyers' fees and other costs, increases as the debt ratio rises.

3. There is some threshold level of debt, labeled D_1 in Figure 17-9, below which the effects noted in Point 2 are immaterial. Beyond D_1, however, the bankruptcy-related costs become increasingly important, and they reduce the tax benefits of debt at an increasing rate. In the range from D_1 to D_2, bankruptcy-related costs reduce but do not completely offset the tax benefits of debt, so the firm's stock price rises (but at a decreasing rate) as the debt ratio increases. However, beyond D_2,

bankruptcy-related costs exceed the tax benefits, so from this point on increasing the debt ratio lowers the value of the stock. Therefore, D_2 denotes the optimal capital structure.

4. Both theory and empirical evidence support the preceding discussion. However, statistical problems prevent researchers from identifying Points D_1 and D_2, both for firms in general and for any given firm.

5. While theoretical and empirical work supports the general shape of the curves in Figures 17-7 and 17-9, these graphs must be taken as approximations, not as precisely defined functions. The numbers in Figure 17-7 are shown out to two decimal places, but that is merely for illustrative purposes — the numbers are not nearly that accurate in view of the fact that the data on which the graph is based are judgmental estimates.

6. Perhaps the most disturbing aspect of capital structure theory as expressed in Figure 17-9 is the fact that many large, successful firms, such as IBM and Eastman Kodak, use far less debt than the theory suggests. However, leveraged mergers and LBOs are changing this.

ASYMMETRIC INFORMATIONAL EFFECTS

symmetric information
The situation in which investors and managers have the same information about the firm's prospects.

asymmetric information
The situation in which managers have different (better) information about their firm's prospects than do investors.

MM assumed that investors have the same information about a firm's prospects as its managers — this is called **symmetric information**. However, we know that in fact managers often have better information about their firms than outside investors. This is called **asymmetric information**, and it has an important effect on the optimal capital structure. To see why, consider two situations, one in which the company's prospects are extremely favorable (Firm F) and one in which they are very unfavorable (Firm U). Suppose, for example, that Firm F's R&D labs have just discovered a nonpatentable cure for the common cold. Firm F's managers want to keep the new product a secret for as long as possible to delay competitors' entry into the market. New plants and distribution facilities must be built to exploit the new product, so capital must be raised. How should Firm F's needed capital be raised? If the firm sells stock, then, when profits from the new product start flowing in (or, really, when the new product is announced), the price of the stock will rise sharply, and the purchasers of the new stock will have made a bonanza. The current stockholders (including the managers) will also do well, but not as well as they would have done if the company had not sold stock before the price increased, because then they would not have had to share the benefits of the new product with the new stockholders. *Therefore, one would expect a firm with very favorable prospects to try to avoid selling stock and, rather, to attempt to raise any required new capital by other means, including using debt beyond the normal target capital structure.* (Note: It would be illegal for Firm F's managers to purchase more shares on the basis of their inside knowledge of the new product. They could be sent to jail if they did.)

Now let's consider Firm U. Suppose its managers have information that new orders are off sharply because a competitor has installed new technology which has improved its products' quality. Firm U must upgrade its own facilities, at a high cost, just to maintain its recent sales level. As a result, its return on investment will fall (but not by as much as if it took no action, which would lead to a 100 percent loss through bankruptcy). How should Firm U raise the needed capital? Here the situation is just the reverse of that facing Firm F, which did not want to sell stock so as to avoid having to share the benefits of future developments. *A firm with unfavorable prospects should sell stock, which would mean bringing in new investors to share the losses!*[16]

The conclusions from all this are that firms with extremely bright prospects prefer not to finance through new stock offerings, whereas firms with poor prospects do like to finance with outside equity. How would you, as an investor, react to this conclusion? You ought to say, "If I see that a company plans to issue new stock, this should worry me, because I know that management would not want to issue stock if future prospects looked good, but it would want to issue stock if things looked bad. Therefore, I would lower my estimate of the firm's value, other things held constant, if I read an announcement of a new stock offering. Of course, my negative reaction would be stronger if the stock sale was by a large, established company such as GM or IBM, which surely has many financing options, than if it was by a small company such as Lotus Development. For Lotus, a stock sale might mean truly extraordinary investment opportunities that were so large that they just could not be financed without a stock sale." If you gave that answer, your views are completely consistent with those of sophisticated portfolio managers of institutions such as Morgan Guaranty Trust, Prudential Insurance, and so forth. *So, in a nutshell, the announcement of a stock offering by a mature firm that seems to have financing alternatives is taken as a* **signal** *that the firm's prospects as seen by its management are not bright.* This, in turn, suggests that when a mature firm announces a new stock offering, the price of its stock should decline. Empirical studies have shown that this situation does indeed exist.[17]

What are the implications of all this for capital structure decisions? The answer is that firms should, in normal times, maintain a **reserve borrowing capacity** which can be used in the event that some especially good investment opportunities come along. This means that firms should, in normal times, carry less debt than would be suggested by the tax benefit/bankruptcy cost trade-off expressed in Figure 17-9.

There are also implications of signaling/asymmetric information concepts for the marginal cost of capital (MCC) curve as discussed in Chapter 16. There

signal
An action taken by a firm's management which provides clues to investors about how management views the firm's prospects.

reserve borrowing capacity
The ability to borrow money at a reasonable cost when good investment opportunities arise; firms often carry less debt than specified by their optimal capital structures to insure that they can obtain debt capital later.

---

[16]Of course, Firm U would have to make certain disclosures when it offered new shares to the public, but it could probably meet the legal requirements without fully disclosing management's worst fears. Disclosure requirements were discussed in Chapter 12.

[17]Paul Asquith and David W. Mullins, Jr., "The Impact of Initiating Dividend Payments on Shareholders' Wealth," *Journal of Business,* January 1983, 77–96.

we saw that the weighted average cost of capital (WACC) jumped when retained earnings were exhausted and the firm was forced to sell new common stock to raise equity. The jump in the WACC, or break in the MCC schedule, was attributed only to flotation costs. However, if the announcement of a stock sale causes a decline in the price of the stock, then k as measured by $k = D_1/P_0 + g$ will rise because of the decline in P_0. This factor reinforces the effects of flotation costs, and perhaps it is an even more important explanation for the break in the MCC schedule at the point at which new stock must be issued. For example, suppose that $P_0 = \$10$, $D_1 = \$1$, $g = 5\%$, and $F = 10\%$. Therefore, $k_s = 10\% + 5\% = 15\%$, and k_e, the cost of external equity, is 16.1 percent:

$$k_e = \frac{D_1}{P_0(1 - F)} + g = \frac{\$1}{\$10(1.0 - 0.10)} + 5\% = 16.1\%.$$

Suppose, however, that the announcement of a stock sale causes the market price of the stock to fall from $P_0 = \$10$ to $P_0 = \$8$. This will produce an increase in the costs of both retained earnings (k_s) and external equity:

$$k_s = \frac{D_1}{P_0} + g = \frac{\$1}{\$8} + 5\% = 17.5\%.$$

$$k_e = \frac{D_1}{P_0(1 - F)} + g = \frac{\$1}{\$8(0.9)} + 5\% = 18.9\%.$$

This would, of course, have further implications for capital budgeting. Specifically, it would make it even more difficult for a marginal project to show a positive NPV (or IRR > WACC) if the project required the firm to sell stock to raise capital.

Although a new equity offering should alert investors to the possibility that the issuing firm's management predicts a downturn, investors also should consider other reasons for a stock sale. For example, the declining value of the dollar in early 1988 made U.S. firms more competitive in world markets, and, as a result, U.S. steel companies' profits and stock prices soared in the spring of 1988. Bethlehem Steel's stock price rose from $6.375 in early 1987 to more than $20 in April 1988. Because Bethlehem's rising sales were straining its capacity, the company decided to expand. Debt and preferred stock represented a high 70 percent of Bethlehem's capital, and that fact, together with the strong stock price, led management to decide to issue stock. Therefore, in May 1988, Bethlehem sold 10 million shares at a price of $19 per share, to raise $190 million. This move improved the common equity ratio from 30 to 37 percent, increased the expected times-interest-earned ratio, and generally strengthened the company's financial position. As a result, its stock price rose sharply just after the stock offering was announced.

If you find our discussion of capital structure theory somewhat confusing, or at least imprecise, you are not alone. In truth, no one knows how to identify precisely the optimal capital structure for a firm, or how to measure precisely the effect of the firm's capital structure on either its value or its cost of capital. In real life, capital structure decisions must be made more on the basis of judgment than numerical analysis. Still, an understanding of the theoretical issues as presented in this chapter is essential to making sound judgments on capital structure issues.[18]

CAPITAL STRUCTURE AND MERGERS

One of the most exciting developments in the financial world during the 1980s has been the high levels of merger activity, especially hostile takeovers, and leveraged buyouts. The target firm's stock is considered to be undervalued, so the acquiring firm will pay a premium of 50 to 100 percent to gain control. For example, General Electric recently offered $66.50 per share for RCA (which owns the NBC television network, among other things) versus RCA's preannouncement price of $45 per share, and RJR Nabisco's stock is up 70 percent since its LBO was announced. Mergers were discussed at length in Chapter 15, but it is useful to reiterate several points now: (1) very often the acquiring firm issues debt and uses it to buy the target firm's stock; (2) the new debt effectively changes the enterprise's capital structure; and (3) the value enhancement resulting from the use of debt is sufficient to cover the premium offered for the stock and still leave a profit for the acquiring company.

A recognition of the validity of the analysis described in this chapter has led to the creation of companies whose major function is to acquire other companies through debt-financed takeovers. The managers of these acquiring companies have made huge personal fortunes, and shrewd individual investors, including a few finance professors, have selected stock portfolios heavily weighted with prime acquisition targets and have done well in the market. Of course, the managements of firms with low leverage ratios who do not want to be taken over can be expected to react by attempting to find their optimal debt levels and then issuing debt and repurchasing stock, thus bringing their firms' actual debt ratios up to the levels that maximize the prices of their stocks, which will make these companies less attractive acquisition targets. This is called *restructuring*, and a great deal of it has been going on lately. CBS, for example, did this when it was fighting off an acquisition attempt by Ted Turner, and Phillips Petroleum did likewise to fend off T. Boone Pickens.

---

[18]We can report first-hand the usefulness of financial theory in the actual establishment of corporate capital structures. During 1987 and 1988, the author served as a consultant to several of the regional telephone companies established as a result of the breakup of AT&T, as well as to several large electric utilities, including Consolidated Edison, the utility serving New York City. On the basis of finance theory and computer models which simulated results under a range of conditions, the companies were able to specify "optimal capital structure ranges" with at least a reasonable degree of confidence. Without finance theory, setting a target capital structure would have amounted to little more than throwing darts.

CHECKLIST FOR CAPITAL STRUCTURE DECISIONS

In addition to the types of analysis discussed previously, a firm must consider the following factors, which have an important, though difficult-to-measure, bearing on the choice of a target capital structure:

1. *Sales stability.* A firm whose sales are relatively stable can safely take on more debt and incur higher fixed charges than a company with unstable sales. Utility companies, because of their stable demand, have historically been able to use more financial leverage than industrial firms.

2. *Asset structure.* Firms whose assets are suitable as security for loans tend to use debt rather heavily. General purpose assets which can be used by many businesses make good collateral, whereas special purpose assets do not. Thus, real estate companies are usually highly leveraged, whereas companies involved in technological research employ less debt.

3. *Operating leverage.* Other things the same, a firm with less operating leverage is better able to employ financial leverage because, as we saw, the interaction of operating and financial leverage determines the overall effect of a decline in sales on operating income and net cash flows.

4. *Growth rate.* Other things the same, faster-growing firms must rely more heavily on external capital (see Chapter 8). Further, the flotation costs involved in selling common stock exceed those incurred when selling debt. Thus, rapidly growing firms tend to use somewhat more debt than slower-growing companies.

5. *Profitability.* One often observes that firms with very high rates of return on investment use relatively little debt. Although there is no theoretical justification for this fact, one practical explanation is that very profitable firms such as IBM, 3M, and Kodak simply do not need to do much debt financing. Their high rates of return enable them to do most of their financing with retained earnings.

6. *Taxes.* Interest is a deductible expense, and deductions are most valued by firms with high tax rates. Hence, the higher a firm's corporate tax rate, the greater the advantage of using debt.

7. *Control.* The effect that issuing debt versus stock might have on a management's control position may influence its capital structure. If management currently has voting control (over 50 percent of the stock) but is not in a position to buy any more stock, it may choose debt for new financings. On the other hand, a management group that is not concerned about voting control may decide to use equity rather than debt if the firm's financial situation is so weak that the use of debt might subject the firm to serious risk of default. If the firm goes into default, the managers will almost surely lose their jobs. However, if too little debt is used, management runs the risk of a takeover. Control considerations

do not necessarily suggest the use of debt or equity, because the type of capital that best protects management will vary from situation to situation. However, if management is at all insecure, it will take into account the effects of capital structure on control.

8. *Management attitudes.* In the absence of proof that one capital structure will lead to higher stock prices than another, management can exercise its own judgment about a proper choice. Some managements tend to be more conservative than others and thus use less debt than the average firm in their industry, whereas for other managements the reverse is true.

9. *Lender and rating agency attitudes.* Regardless of managers' own analyses of the proper leverage factors for their firms, there is no question that lenders' and rating agencies' attitudes frequently influence financial structure decisions. In the majority of cases, the corporation discusses its financial structure with lenders and rating agencies and gives much weight to their advice. For example, one large utility was told by Moody and Standard & Poor that its bonds would be downgraded if it issued more bonds, so it financed its 1988 expansion with common equity.

10. *Market conditions.* Conditions in the stock and bond markets undergo both long- and short-run changes that can have an important bearing on a firm's optimal capital structure. For example, during the credit crunch in the fall of 1987, there was simply no market at any "reasonable" interest rate for new long-term bonds rated below A. Therefore, low-rated companies in need of capital were forced to go to the stock market or to the short-term debt market, regardless of their target capital structures. When conditions eased, however, these companies were able to bring their capital structures back to their target levels.

11. *The firm's internal condition.* As we discussed earlier in the section on asymmetric information, a firm's own internal condition can also have a bearing on its target capital structure. For example, suppose a firm has just successfully completed an R&D program, and it projects higher earnings in the immediate future. However, the new earnings are not yet anticipated by investors and hence are not reflected in the price of the stock. This company would not want to issue stock. It would prefer to finance with debt until the higher earnings materialize and are reflected in the stock price, at which time it would want to sell an issue of common stock, retire the debt, and return to its target capital structure.

12. *Financial flexibility.* An astute corporate treasurer made this statement to the author:

> "Our company can earn a lot more money from good capital budgeting and operating decisions than from good financing decisions. Indeed, we are not sure exactly how financing decisions affect our stock price, but we do know that having to turn down a promising venture because funds are not available will reduce our long-run profitability. For this reason, my primary goal as treasurer is to always be in a position to raise the capital needed to support operations.

Table 17-5   Capital Structure Percentages, 1986: Selected Industries Ranked by Common Equity Ratios

Industry	Common Equity (1)	Preferred Stock (2)	Total Debt (3)	Long-Term Debt (4)	Short-Term Debt (5)	Times-Interest-Earned Ratio (6)
Drugs	73.5%	1.9%	24.6%	14.0%	10.6%	10.3 ×
Electrical/electronics	71.9	0.5	27.6	18.9	8.7	5.0
Automotive	70.9	0.7	28.4	23.2	5.2	6.7
Retailing	55.1	1.0	43.9	30.4	13.5	3.6
Utilities (electric, gas, and telephone)	45.1	5.6	49.3	46.5	2.8	3.0
Steel	50.8	2.7	46.5	42.1	4.4	1.6
Composite (average of all industries, not just those listed above)	42.5%	2.1%	55.4%	32.5%	22.9%	2.2 ×

Note: These ratios are based on accounting (or book) values. Stated on a market-value basis, the results would be somewhat different. Most important, the equity ratio would rise, and the debt ratios would fall, because most stocks sell at prices that are much higher than their book values.

Source: *Industrial Compustat Data Tape,* 1987.

We also know that when times are good, we can raise capital with either stocks or bonds, but when times are bad, suppliers of capital are much more willing to make funds available if they are given a secured position, and this means bonds. Further, when we sell a new issue of stock, this sends a negative signal to investors, so stock sales by a mature company such as ours are not generally desirable."

Putting these thoughts together gives rise to the goal of *maintaining financial flexibility,* which, from an operational viewpoint, means *maintaining adequate reserve borrowing capacity.* Determining an "adequate" reserve borrowing capacity is judgmental, but it clearly depends on the factors mentioned previously in the chapter, including the firm's forecasted need for funds, predicted capital market conditions, management's confidence in its forecasts, and the consequences of a capital shortage.

VARIATIONS IN CAPITAL STRUCTURES AMONG FIRMS

As might be expected, wide variations in the use of financial leverage occur both among industries and among the individual firms in each industry. Table 17-5 illustrates differences for selected industries; the ranks are in descending order of equity ratios, as shown in Column 1.[19]

---

[19]Information on capital structures and financial strength is available from a multitude of sources. We used the *Compustat* data tapes to develop Table 17-5, but other published sources include *The Value Line Investment Survey, Robert Morris Association Annual Studies,* and *Dun & Bradstreet Key Business Ratios.*

The drug and electronics companies do not use much debt; these companies have generally been quite profitable and hence have been able to finance through retained earnings. Also, the uncertainties inherent in industries that are both oriented toward research and subject to huge product liability suits render the heavy use of debt unwise. Retailers, steel, and utility companies, on the other hand, use debt relatively heavily, but each for a different reason. Retailers use short-term debt to finance inventories and long-term debt secured by mortgages on their stores. The steel companies have been losing money in recent years, and these losses have reduced their equity positions and also have made it difficult for them to sell new common stock, hence requiring them to use debt financing. The utilities use large amounts of debt because their relatively stable sales and profits enable them to carry more debt than would be possible for firms in less stable industries.

Particular attention should be given to the times-interest-earned ratio. This ratio is a joint function of financial leverage and profitability. Generally, the least-leveraged industries, such as the drug industry, have the highest coverage ratios, whereas industries such as steel, which finance heavily with debt, have low ratios.

Wide variations in capital structures among firms within given industries also exist. For example, although the average common equity ratio in 1986 for the drug industry was 73.5 percent, Warner-Lambert's equity ratio was 61 percent versus Bristol-Myers' 88 percent ratio. Thus, factors unique to individual firms, including management attitudes, play an important role in setting target capital structures.

International

INTERNATIONAL FINANCIAL MANAGEMENT

Significant differences have been observed in the capital structures of U.S. corporations in comparison to their German and Japanese counterparts. For example, the Organization for Economic Cooperation and Development (OECD) recently reported that, on average, Japanese firms use 85 percent debt to total assets (in book value terms), German firms use 64 percent, and U.S. firms use 55 percent. Of course, different countries use somewhat different accounting conventions with regard to (1) reporting assets on a historical versus a replacement cost basis, (2) the treatment of leased assets, (3) pension plan funding, and (4) capitalizing versus expensing R&D costs, and these differences make comparisons difficult. Still, even after adjusting for accounting differences, researchers find that Japanese and German firms use considerably more financial leverage than U.S. companies.

Why do international differences in financial leverage exist? Since taxes are thought to be a major reason for using debt, the effects of differential tax structures in the three countries have been examined. The interest on corporate debt is deductible in each country, and individuals must pay taxes on dividends and interest received. However, capital gains are not taxed in either Germany or Japan. The conclusions from this analysis are as follows: (1) From a tax standpoint, corporations should be equally inclined to use debt in all three countries. (2) Since capital gains are not taxed in Germany or Japan, but are taxed in the United States, and since capital gains are associated more with stocks than with bonds, investors in Germany and Japan should show a preference for stocks as compared with U.S. investors. (3) Investor preferences should lead to relatively low equity capital costs in Germany and Japan, and this, in turn, should cause German and Japanese firms to use more equity capital than their U.S. counterparts. Of course, this is exactly the opposite of the actual capital structures, so differential tax laws cannot explain the observed capital structure differences.

If tax rates cannot explain differential capital structures, what else might explain the observed differences? Another possibility is differences in bankruptcy costs. Earlier in this chapter we saw that actual bankruptcy, and even the threat of potential bankruptcy, imposes a costly burden on firms with large amounts of debt. Note, though, that the threat of bankruptcy is dependent on the *probability* of bankruptcy. Now recall our discussion of *agency costs* in Chapter 1. There we saw that agency costs arise from two agency relationships: (1) the relationship between shareholders and managers, and (2) the relationship between bondholders and shareholders. In the United States, equity agency costs are comparatively low — corporations produce quarterly reports, pay quarterly dividends, and must comply with relatively stringent audit requirements. These conditions are less prevalent in the other countries. Conversely, debt agency costs are probably lower in Germany and Japan than in the United States. In these countries, the bulk of corporate debt consists of bank loans as opposed to publicly-issued bonds, but, more important, the banks are closely linked to the corporations which borrow from them. German and Japanese banks often (1) hold major equity positions in their debtor corporations, (2) vote the shares of individual shareholders for whom banks hold shares in trust, and (3) have bank officers sit on the boards of debtor corporations. Given these close relationships, the banks are much more directly involved with the debtor firms' affairs, and as a result they are also more accommodating in the event of financial distress than U.S. bondholders would be. This, in turn, suggests that a given amount of debt brings with it a lower threat of bankruptcy for a German or a Japanese firm than for a U.S. firm with the same amount of business risk. Thus, an analysis of both bankruptcy and equity agency costs leads to the conclusion that U.S. firms ought to have more equity and less debt than firms in Japan and Germany.

We cannot state that one financial system is better or worse than another in the sense of making the firms in one country more efficient than those in another. However, as U.S. firms become increasingly involved in worldwide operations, they must become increasingly aware of worldwide conditions, and they must be prepared to adapt to conditions in the various countries in which they do business.

SUMMARY AND KEY CONCEPTS

In this chapter we examined the effects of financial leverage on stock prices, earnings per share, and the cost of capital. The key concepts covered are summarized below:

- A firm's **optimal capital structure** is that mix of debt and equity which (1) results in the lowest weighted average cost of capital and (2) maximizes the price of the firm's stock. At any point in time, the firm's management has a specific optimal, or **target**, capital structure in mind, although this target may change over time.

- Several factors influence a firm's capital structure decisions. These factors include (1) the firm's **business risk**, (2) its **tax position**, and (3) its need for **financial flexibility**.

- **Business risk** is the uncertainty associated with a firm's projections of its future operating income. A firm will tend to have low business risk if the demand for its products is stable, if the prices of its inputs and products remain relatively constant, if it can adjust its prices freely as its costs increase, and if a high percentage of its costs are variable and hence decrease as its output and sales decrease. Other things the same, the lower a firm's business risk, the higher its optimal debt ratio.

- **Operating leverage** is a measure of the extent to which fixed costs are used in a firm's operations. A firm with a high percentage of fixed costs is said to have a high *degree of operating leverage.* In general, the higher a firm's operating leverage, the greater its business risk.

- The **breakeven point** is the sales volume at which total costs equal total revenues, and profits equal zero.

- **Financial leverage** is the extent to which fixed-income securities (debt and preferred stock) are used in a firm's capital structure. **Financial risk** is the added risk to stockholders which results from financial leverage.

- The **EPS indifference point** is the level of sales at which EPS will be the same whether the firm uses debt or common stock financing. Equity financing will increase EPS if the firm's sales end up below the EPS indifference point, whereas debt financing will increase EPS at higher sales levels.

- The **degree of operating leverage (DOL)** shows how a change in sales will affect operating income, whereas the **degree of financial leverage (DFL)** shows how a change in operating income will affect earnings per share. The **degree of total leverage (DTL)** is the percentage change in EPS caused by a given percentage change in sales: DTL = DOL × DFL.

- Modigliani and Miller, among others, showed that the value of a firm will rise as it moves from using no debt to using some moderate amount of debt. This increase in value arises because interest is a tax deductible expense. As a firm uses more debt, however, the risk of bankruptcy increases, causing the cost of equity to increase. At some point, rising bankruptcy costs outweigh the benefits of the debt tax shelter, and the weighted average cost of capital begins to increase, causing the value of the firm to decrease. **The optimal capital structure is the one at which the debt tax shelter benefits are just equal to the bankruptcy-related costs.**

Although it is theoretically possible to determine the optimal capital structure, as a practical matter we cannot estimate this structure with precision. Accordingly, financial executives generally treat the optimal capital structure as a range — for example, 40 to 50 percent debt — rather than as a precise point, such as 45 percent. The concepts discussed in this chapter should help you understand the factors that influence managers when they set the optimal capital structure ranges for their firms.

Questions

17-1   "One type of leverage affects both EBIT and EPS. The other type affects only EPS." Explain what this statement means.

17-2   Explain why the following statement is true: "Other things being the same, firms with relatively stable sales are able to carry relatively high debt ratios."

17-3   Why do public utility companies usually pursue a different financial policy than retail firms?

17-4   Why is EBIT generally considered to be independent of financial leverage? Why might EBIT actually be influenced by financial leverage at high debt levels?

17-5   If a firm went from zero debt to successively higher levels of debt, why would you expect its stock price to first rise, then hit a peak, and then begin to decline?

17-6   Why is the debt level that maximizes a firm's expected EPS generally higher than the one that maximizes its stock price?

17-7   The Bell System was recently broken up, with the old AT&T being split into a new AT&T plus seven regional telephone companies. The specific reason for forcing the breakup was to increase the degree of competition in the telephone industry. AT&T had had a monopoly in local service, long distance, and the manufacture of all the equipment used by telephone companies, and the breakup was expected to open most of these markets to competition. In the court order that laid out the terms of the breakup, the capital structures of the surviving companies were specified, and much attention was given to the increased competition telephone companies could expect in the future. Do you think the optimal capital structure after the breakup was the same as the pre-breakup optimal capital structure? Do you think competition could force companies to use more debt in order to reduce taxes? Explain your position.

17-8   Assume that you are advising the management of a firm that is about to double its assets to serve its rapidly growing market. It must choose between a highly automated production process and a less automated one, and it must also choose a capital structure for financing the expansion. Should the asset investment and financing decisions be jointly determined, or should each decision be made separately? How would these decisions affect one another? How could the degree of leverage concept be used to help management analyze the situation?

17-9   Your firm's R&D department has been working on a new process which, if it works, can convert coal to oil at a cost of about $5 per barrel versus a current market price of $15 per barrel. The company needs $10 million of external funds at this time to complete the research. The results of the research will be known in about a year, and there is about a 50-50 chance of success. If the research is successful, your company will need to raise a substantial amount of new money to put the idea into production. Your economists forecast that although the economy will be depressed next year, interest rates will be high because of international monetary problems. You must recommend how the currently needed $10 million should be raised — as debt or as equity. How would the situation influence your decision?

Self-Test Problems   *(Solutions Appear on Page 683)*

Key terms

ST-1   Define each of the following terms:
a. Target capital structure; optimal capital structure; target range
b. Business risk; financial risk; total risk
c. Operating leverage; financial leverage; total leverage
d. EPS indifference point
e. Degree of operating leverage (DOL)
f. Degree of financial leverage (DFL)
g. Degree of total leverage (DTL)
h. Times-interest-earned (TIE) ratio
i. Modigliani-Miller (MM) theory
j. Reserve borrowing capacity
k. Asymmetric information; signal

Operating leverage

ST-2   Simmons Electronics, Inc., produces stereo components which sell for P = $100 per unit. Simmons' fixed costs are $200,000; 5,000 units are produced and sold each year; profits total $50,000; and Simmons' assets (all equity financed) are $500,000. Simmons estimates that it can change its production process, adding $400,000 to investment and $50,000 to fixed operating costs. This change will reduce variable costs per unit by $10 and increase output by 2,000 units, but the sales price on all units will have to be lowered to $95 to permit sales of the additional output. Simmons has tax loss carry-forwards that cause its tax rate to be zero. It uses no debt, and its average cost of capital is 10 percent.
a. Should Simmons make the change?
b. Would Simmons' operating leverage as measured by DOL increase or decrease if it made the change? What about its breakeven point?
c. Suppose the investment totaled $800,000, and Simmons had to borrow $400,000 at an interest rate of 10 percent. Find the ROE on the $400,000 incremental equity investment. Should Simmons make the change if debt financing must be used?

Financial leverage

ST-3   Gentry Motors, Inc., a producer of turbine generators, is in this situation: EBIT = $4 million; tax rate = T = 35%; debt outstanding = D = $2 million; k_d = 10%; k_s = 15%; shares of stock outstanding = N_0 = 600,000; and book value per share = $10. Since Gentry's product market is stable and the company expects no growth, all earnings are paid out as dividends. The debt consists of perpetual bonds.
a. What are Gentry's earnings per share (EPS) and its price per share (P_0)?
b. What is Gentry's weighted average cost of capital (k_a)?
c. Gentry can increase its debt by $8 million, to a total of $10 million, using the new debt to buy back and retire some of its shares at the current price. Its interest rate on debt will be 12 percent (it will have to call and refund the old debt), and its cost of equity will rise from

15 percent to 17 percent. EBIT will remain constant. Should Gentry change its capital structure?

d. If Gentry did not have to refund the $2 million of old debt, how would this affect things? Assume that the new and the still outstanding debt are equally risky, with $k_d = 12\%$, but that the coupon rate on the old debt is 10 percent.

e. What is Gentry's TIE coverage ratio under the original situation and under the conditions in Part c above?

Problems

Risk analysis

17-1   a. Given the following information, calculate the expected value for Firm C's EPS: $EPS_A = \$3.40$, and $\sigma_A = \$2.41$; $EPS_B = \$2.80$, and $\sigma_B = \$1.97$; and $\sigma_C = \$2.74$.

	Probability				
	0.1	0.2	0.4	0.2	0.1
Firm A: EPS_A	($1.00)	$1.20	$3.40	$5.60	$7.80
Firm B: EPS_B	(0.80)	1.00	2.80	4.60	6.40
Firm C: EPS_C	(1.60)	0.90	3.40	5.90	8.40

b. Discuss the relative riskiness of the three firms' earnings.

Degree of leverage

17-2   a. Refer back to Figure 17-2. Calculate the degree of operating leverage for Plans A and B at sales of $120,000 and $160,000. At sales of $80,000, DOL_A = undefined (or ∞) and $DOL_B = -2.0$, whereas at sales of $240,000, $DOL_A = 1.50$ and $DOL_B = 2.0$.

b. Is it true that the DOL is approximately equal to infinity just above the breakeven point, implying that a very small change in sales will produce a huge percentage increase in EBIT, but that DOL will decline when calculated at higher levels of sales?

c. Is it true that, for all sales levels at which DOL > 0 for both plans, $DOL_B < DOL_A$? Explain.

d. Assume that Plans A and B can be financed in either of the following ways: (1) no debt or (2) $90,000 of debt at 10 percent. Calculate the DFL for Plan A at sales of $120,000 and $160,000. The DFLs for Plan B at these sales levels with debt are 0 and 1.82, respectively.

e. Calculate the degree of total leverage (DTL) under Plan A with debt at sales of $120,000 and $160,000. The DTLs under Plan B at these sales levels are -6.67 and 7.27, respectively.

f. Several of the degree of leverage figures were negative; for example, DTL_B at S = $120,000 in Part e was -6.67. Does a negative degree of leverage imply that an increase in sales will *lower* profits?

Operating leverage effects

17-3   Perkins Corporation will begin operations next year to produce a single product at a price of $16 per unit. Perkins has a choice of two methods of production: Method A, with variable costs of $9 per unit and fixed operating costs of $900,000; and Method B, with variable costs of $11 per unit and fixed operating costs of $535,000. To support operations under either production method, the firm requires $3,000,000 in assets, and it has established a debt ratio of 40 percent. The cost of debt is $k_d = 10$

percent. The tax rate is irrelevant for the problem, and fixed *operating* costs do not include interest.

a. Calculate the breakeven point for each method, and then find the level of sales in units at which the firm should be indifferent between the two methods with respect to expected operating income (that is, EBIT).

b. The sales forecast for the coming year is 200,000 units. Under which method would EBIT be most adversely affected if sales did not reach the expected levels? (Hint: Compare DOLs under the two production methods.)

c. Given the firm's present debt, which method would produce the greatest percentage increase in earnings per share for a given increase in EBIT? (Hint: Compare DFLs under the two methods.)

d. Calculate DTL under each method, and then evaluate the firm's total risk under each method.

e. Is there some debt ratio under Method A which would produce the same DTL_A as the DTL_B that you calculated in Part d? (Hint: Let $DTL_A = DTL_B$ as calculated in Part d, solve for I, and then determine the amount of debt that is consistent with this level of I. Conceivably, debt could be *negative,* which implies holding liquid assets rather than borrowing. Also, you should have found $DTL_B = 2.90$ in Part d.)

Degree of leverage   17-4   Astrocom Corporation supplies headphones to airlines for use with movie and stereo programs. The headphones sell for $240 per set, and this year's sales are expected to be 45,000 units. Variable production costs for the expected sales under present production methods are estimated at $8,500,000, and fixed production (operating) costs at present are $1,300,000. Astrocom has $4,000,000 of debt outstanding at an interest rate of 8 percent. There are 200,000 shares of common stock outstanding, and there is no preferred stock. The dividend payout ratio is 70 percent, and Astrocom is in the 40 percent federal-plus-state tax bracket.

The company is considering investing $6,000,000 in new equipment. Sales would not increase, but variable costs per unit would decline by 20 percent. Also, fixed operating costs would increase from $1,300,000 to $1,500,000. Astrocom could raise the required capital by borrowing $6,000,000 at 10 percent or by selling 200,000 additional shares at $30 per share.

a. What would be Astrocom's EPS (1) under the old production process, and (2) under the new process if it uses debt or (3) under the new process if it uses common stock?

b. Calculate DOL, DFL, and DTL under the existing setup and under the new setup with each type of financing. Assume that the expected sales level is 45,000 units, or $10,800,000.

c. Calculate the operating breakeven point (which does not consider interest expenses) under each setup. Explain how the breakeven volume could decline even though fixed costs increase. (Hint: Units sold = Sales revenues/Sales price.)

d. At what unit sales level would Astrocom have the same EPS, assuming it undertakes the investment and finances it with debt or with stock? (Hint: V = variable cost per unit = $6,800,000/45,000, and EPS = $[(PQ - VQ - F - I)(1 - T)]/N$. Set EPS$_{Stock}$ = EPS$_{Debt}$ and solve for Q.)

e. At what unit sales level would EPS = 0 under the three production/financing setups — that is, under the old plan, the new plan with debt financing, and the new plan with stock financing? (Hint: Note that V$_{Old}$ = $8,500,000/45,000, and use the hints for Part d, setting the EPS equation equal to zero.)

f. On the basis of the analysis in Parts a through e, which plan is the riskiest, which has the highest expected EPS, and which would you recommend? Assume here that there is a fairly high probability of sales falling as low as 25,000 units, and determine EPS$_{Debt}$ and EPS$_{Stock}$ at that sales level to help assess the riskiness of the two financing plans.

Financial leverage effects   **17-5**   The Firms HL and LL are identical except for their leverage ratios and interest rates on debt. Each has $25 million in assets, earned $5 million before interest and taxes in 1988, and has a 40 percent average federal-plus-state tax rate. Firm HL, however, has a leverage ratio (D/TA) of 50 percent and pays 12 percent interest on its debt, whereas LL has a 30 percent leverage ratio and pays only 10 percent interest on debt.

a. Calculate the rate of return on equity (net income/equity) for each firm.

b. Observing that HL has a higher return on equity, LL's treasurer decides to raise the leverage ratio from 30 to 60 percent, which will increase LL's interest rate on all debt to 15 percent. Calculate the new rate of return on equity for LL.

Effects of financial leverage on ROE   **17-6**   The Tanner Company wishes to calculate next year's return on equity under different leverage ratios. Tanner's total assets are $10 million, and its average tax rate is 40 percent. The company is able to estimate next year's earnings before interest and taxes for three possible states of the world: $3 million with a 0.2 probability, $2 million with a 0.5 probability, and $500,000 with a 0.3 probability. Calculate Tanner's expected return on equity, standard deviation, and coefficient of variation for each of the following leverage ratios, and evaluate the results:

Leverage (Debt/Total Assets)	Interest Rate
0%	—
10	10%
50	12
60	15

Financing alternatives   **17-7**   The Nordlund Company plans to raise a net amount of $180 million to finance new equipment and working capital in early 1989. Two alternatives are being considered: Common stock may be sold to net $40 per share, or debentures yielding 12 percent may be issued. The balance sheet and income statement of the Nordlund Company prior to financing are as follows:

The Nordlund Company
Balance Sheet as of December 31, 1988
(Millions of Dollars)

Current assets	$600	Accounts payable	$115
Net fixed assets	300	Notes payable to bank	170
		Other current liabilities	150
		Total current liabilities	$435
		Long-term debt (10%)	200
		Common stock, $2 par	40
		Retained earnings	225
Total assets	$900	Total liabilities and equity	$900

The Nordlund Company:
Income Statement for Year Ended December 31, 1988
(Millions of Dollars)

Sales	$1,650
Operating costs	1,485
Earnings before interest and taxes (10%)	$ 165
Interest on short-term debt	10
Interest on long-term debt	20
Earnings before taxes	$ 135
Federal-plus-state tax (40%)	54
Net income after tax	$ 81

The probability distribution for annual sales is as follows:

Probability	Annual Sales (Millions of Dollars)
0.30	$1,500
0.40	1,800
0.30	2,100

Assuming that EBIT is equal to 10 percent of sales, calculate earnings per share under both the debt financing and the stock financing alternatives at each possible level of sales. Then calculate expected earnings per share and σ_{EPS} under both debt and stock financing. Also, calculate the debt ratio and the times-interest-earned (TIE) ratio at the expected sales level under each alternative. The old debt will remain outstanding. Which financing method do you recommend?

Optimal capital structure   **17-8**
(Integrative)

Janice Underwood, an MBA student at Southeastern University, has just been hired as night manager of Campus Deli and Sub Shop (CDSS), which is located adjacent to the campus. Sales were $875,000 last year; variable costs were 60 percent of sales; and fixed costs were $50,000. Therefore, EBIT totalled $300,000. Since the university's enrollment is capped, the store's EBIT is expected to be constant over time. Since no expansion capital is required, CDSS pays out all earnings as dividends.

CDSS is currently all-equity financed, and its 100,000 shares outstanding sell at a price of $10 per share. The firm's tax rate is 34 percent. Underwood, who is taking her first corporate finance course, believes that the firm's shareholders would be better off if some debt financing were used. When she suggested this to the principal stockholder, who is also her uncle, she was encouraged to pursue the idea, but to provide justification for her suggestion.

Janice, along with her finance professor, developed the following estimates of the costs of debt and equity at different debt levels (in thousands of dollars):

Amount Borrowed	k_d	k_s
$ 0	—	15.0%
200	10.0%	15.5
400	11.0	16.5
500	13.0	18.0
600	16.0	20.0

If the firm were recapitalized, the borrowed funds would be used to repurchase stock. Stockholders, in turn, would use funds provided by the repurchase to buy equities in other fast food companies similar to CDSS.

Underwood planned to conduct her analysis by asking and then answering the following questions. Your job is to help her out.

a. 1. What is business risk? What factors affect the amount of business risk inherent in a firm?
   2. What is operating leverage? How does the use of operating leverage affect the level of business risk?

b. What is meant by the term financial leverage? What is financial risk? How does financial risk differ from business risk?

c. Consider two hypothetical firms, Firm U with zero debt financing and Firm L with $10,000 of 12 percent debt. Both firms have $20,000 in total assets and a 40 percent tax rate, and they face the following EBIT distribution for next year:

Probability	EBIT
0.25	$2,000
0.50	3,000
0.25	4,000

1. Construct partial income statements for the two firms at each level of EBIT.
2. Now calculate the ratio of EBIT to total assets, and the ROE, for each firm at each EBIT level.
3. What does this example illustrate concerning the impact of financial leverage on expected return and risk?

d. With the above points in mind, Underwood began to consider the optimal capital structure for CDSS.
   1. To begin, define optimal capital structure.
   2. Describe briefly, without using numbers, the sequence of events which will occur if CDSS recapitalizes.
   3. Calculate CDSS's expected EPS at debt levels of $0, $200,000, $400,000, $500,000, and $600,000. How many shares would remain after recapitalization under each scenario? Assume that shares could be repurchased at the current market price of $10 per share.

 4. What would be the new stock price if CDSS recapitalizes at $200,000 of debt? $400,000? $500,000? $600,000?
 5. Considering only the levels of debt discussed, what is CDSS's optimal capital structure?
 6. Is EPS maximized at the debt level which maximizes share price?

e. 1. What is meant by the degree of operating leverage? If CDSS's fixed costs total $50,000, what is its degree of operating leverage?
 2. What is the degree of financial leverage? What will be CDSS's degree of financial leverage if it increases its debt to the optimal level of $500,000?
 3. What is the degree of total leverage? What is CDSS's degree of total leverage with EBIT of $300,000 and $500,000 of debt?

f. Modigliani and Miller proved, under a very restrictive set of assumptions, that the value of a firm will be maximized by financing almost entirely with debt.
 1. Why is it beneficial for a firm to finance with debt?
 2. What were the assumptions MM needed to prove their theory? Are these assumptions realistic?
 3. When MM and other researchers relaxed these assumptions, they found that most firms should use considerably less than 100 percent debt. What factor(s) cause the optimal amount of debt in the capital structure to be less than 100 percent?
 4. In theory, how is the optimal capital structure determined?

g. Asymmetric information is the situation in which the managers of a firm have different (better) information about the firm's prospects than do outside investors.
 1. How does the existence of asymmetric information influence a manager's decision about whether to finance with debt or equity?
 2. What would you expect to happen to the price of the stock of a mature firm if that firm announces a stock offering? Would you expect the stock price to react differently if the issuing firm were a young firm experiencing rapid growth?

h. What are some factors managers should consider when determining the optimal capital structures for their firms?

Computer-Related Problem

(Work this problem only if you are using the computer problem diskette.)

Effects of financial leverage

C17-1   Use the model for Problem C17-1 in the file C17 to work this problem.
 a. Rework Problem 17-7, assuming that the old long-term debt will not remain outstanding but, rather, that it must be refinanced at the new long-term interest rate of 12 percent. What effect does this have on the decision to refinance?
 b. What would be the effect on the refinancing decision if the rate on long-term debt fell to 5 percent or rose to 20 percent, assuming that all long-term debt must be refinanced?
 c. Which financing method would be recommended if the stock price

(1) rose to \$70 or (2) fell to \$20? (Assume that all debt will have an interest rate of 12 percent.)

d. With $P_0 = \$40$ and $k_d = 12\%$, change the sales probability distribution to the following:

| Alternative 1 | | Alternative 2 | |
Sales	Probability	Sales	Probability
\$1,500	0	\$ 0	0.3
1,800	1.0	1,800	0.4
2,100	0	5,000	0.3

What are the implications of these changes?

Solutions to Self-Test Problems

ST-1   Refer to the marginal glossary definitions and relevant chapter sections to check your responses.

ST-2   a. 1. Determine the variable cost per unit at present, using the following definitions and equations:

P = average sales price per unit of output = \$100.

F = fixed operating costs = \$200,000.

Q = units of output (sales) = 5,000.

V = variable costs per unit, found as follows:

$$\text{Profit} = P(Q) - F - V(Q)$$

$$\$50,000 = \$100(5,000) - \$200,000 - V(5,000)$$

$$5,000V = \$250,000$$

$$V = \$50.$$

2. Determine the new profit level if the change is made:

$$\text{New profit} = P_2(Q_2) - F_2 - V_2(Q_2)$$

$$= \$95(7,000) - \$250,000 - \$40(7,000)$$

$$= \$135,000.$$

3. Determine the incremental profit:

$$\Delta\text{Profit} = \$135,000 - \$50,000 = \$85,000.$$

4. Estimate the approximate rate of return on the new investment:

$$\text{ROI} = \frac{\Delta\text{Profit}}{\text{Investment}} = \frac{\$85,000}{\$400,000} = 21.25\%.$$

Because the ROI exceeds Simmons' average cost of capital, this analysis suggests that Simmons should go ahead and make the investment.

b.
$$DOL = \frac{Q(P - V)}{Q(P - V) - F}.$$

$$DOL_{Old} = \frac{5,000(\$100 - \$50)}{5,000(\$100 - \$50) - \$200,000} = 5.00.$$

$$DOL_{New} = \frac{7,000(\$95 - \$40)}{7,000(\$95 - \$40) - \$250,000} = 2.85.$$

This indicates that operating income will be less sensitive to changes in sales if the production process is changed, suggesting that the change would reduce risks. However, the change would increase the breakeven point. Still, with a lower sales price, it might be easier to achieve the higher new breakeven volume:

$$Old: Q_{BE} = \frac{F}{P - V} = \frac{\$200,000}{\$100 - \$50} = 4,000 \text{ units.}$$

$$New: Q_{BE} = \frac{F_2}{P_2 - V_2} = \frac{\$250,000}{\$95 - \$40} = 4,545 \text{ units.}$$

c. The incremental ROE is:

$$ROE = \frac{\Delta Profit}{\Delta Equity}.$$

Using debt financing, the incremental profit associated with the equity investment is equal to that found in Part a minus the interest expense incurred as a result of the investment:

$$\Delta Profit = New\ profit - Old\ profit - Interest$$
$$= \$135,000 - \$50,000 - 0.10(\$400,000)$$
$$= \$45,000.$$

$$ROE = \frac{\$45,000}{\$400,000} = 11.25\%.$$

The return on the new equity investment still exceeds the average cost of capital, so Simmons should make the investment.

ST-3

a.

EBIT	$4,000,000
Interest ($2,000,000 × 0.10)	200,000
Net income before taxes	$3,800,000
Taxes (35%)	1,330,000
Net income after taxes	$2,470,000

$$EPS = \$2,470,000/600,000 = \$4.12.$$

$$P_0 = \$4.12/0.15 = \$27.47.$$

b.
$$Equity = 600,000 \times (\$10) = \$6,000,000.$$

$$Debt = \$2,000,000.$$

$$Total\ capital = \$8,000,000.$$

$$k_a = w_d k_d (1 - T) + w_s k_s$$

$$= (2/8)(10\%)(1 - 0.35) + (6/8)(15\%)$$

$$= 1.63\% + 11.25\%$$

$$= 12.88\%.$$

c.

EBIT	$4,000,000
Interest ($10,000,000 × 0.12)	1,200,000
Net income before taxes	$2,800,000
Taxes (35%)	980,000
Net income after taxes	$1,820,000

Shares bought and retired:

$$\Delta N = \Delta Debt/P_0 = \$8,000,000/\$27.47 = 291,227.$$

New outstanding shares:

$$N_1 = N_0 - \Delta N = 600,000 - 291,227 = 308,773.$$

New EPS:

$$EPS = \$1,820,000/308,773 = \$5.89.$$

New price per share:

$$P_0 = \$5.89/0.17 = \$34.65 \text{ versus } \$27.47.$$

Therefore, Gentry should change its capital structure.

d. In this case, the company's net income after taxes would be higher by $(0.12 - 0.10)(\$2,000,000)(1 - 0.35) = \$26,000$, because its interest charges would be lower. The new price would be

$$P_0 = \frac{(\$1,820,000 + \$26,000)/308,773}{0.17} = \$35.18.$$

In the first case, in which debt had to be refunded, the bondholders were compensated for the increased risk of the higher debt position. In the second case, the old bondholders were not compensated; their 10 percent coupon perpetual bonds would now be worth

$$\$100/0.12 = \$833.33,$$

or $1,666,667 in total, down from the old $2 million, or a loss of $333,333. The stockholders would have a gain of

$$(\$35.18 - \$34.65)(308,773) = \$163,650.$$

This gain would, of course, be at the expense of the old bondholders. (There is no reason to think that bondholders' losses would exactly offset stockholders' gains.)

e.

$$TIE = \frac{EBIT}{I}.$$

$$\text{Original TIE} = \frac{\$4,000,000}{\$200,000} = 20 \text{ times.}$$

$$\text{New TIE} = \frac{\$4,000,000}{\$1,200,000} = 3.33 \text{ times.}$$

18 Dividend Policy

UNITED BRANDS: HOW ONE COMPANY SETS ITS DIVIDEND POLICY

In May 1988, United Brands (UB), a NYSE-listed company with 1988 sales of $3.5 billion, reported a year-to-year earnings gain of 26 percent because of improved performance in its Chiquita banana division. The company's earnings had been on a strong upward trend since the early 1980s, and its stock was selling for $48, up from $6.50 in 1982. UB's financial position had also improved substantially: its debt ratio had been lowered from almost 60 percent to only 27 percent, and its times-interest-earned ratio had gone up from less than 1.0 times to more than 4.1 times. The company paid a dividend of $0.50 in 1981, but the dividend was eliminated in the mid-1980s because of financial difficulties. An annual dividend of $0.60 was restored in 1987, but at that level the payout was only 13 percent of earnings, versus a payout of 40 percent for other major food companies.

When UB's directors met and were briefed on the higher earnings, one of the topics discussed was the possibility of a dividend increase. The company's debt ratio was in good shape (27 percent), and it had ample funds available to meet projected capital budgeting requirements. Thus, it seemed reasonable to increase the dividend. However, the company also considered giving its surplus cash flows to stockholders by repurchasing shares: because stockholders could elect either to sell back their shares or to keep them, a repurchase would transmit cash only to those stockholders who wanted it and were willing to pay taxes on it. A dividend increase, on the other hand, would go to all stockholders, whether they needed cash or not, and all taxable owners would be required to pay taxes on the dividends received.

The directors also considered the issue of a stock dividend or a stock split, an action which gives stockholders additional shares at no cost. Normally, stock dividends or splits are declared after a sharp increase in the price of a firm's stock, especially if management thinks the conditions which caused the stock's price to increase are likely to continue.

Do you think United Brands should increase its cash dividend, repurchase some of its stock, or declare a stock dividend or split? Keep this question in mind, and see if you can answer it when you have finished reading the chapter.

DIVIDEND policy involves the decision to pay out earnings or to retain them for reinvestment in the firm. The basic stock price model, $P_0 = D_1/(k_s - g)$, shows that if the firm adopts a policy of paying out more cash dividends, D_1 will rise, which will tend to increase the price of the stock. However, if cash dividends are increased, then less money will be available for reinvestment, the expected future growth rate will be lowered, and this will depress the price of the stock. Thus, changing the dividend has two opposing effects. *The optimal dividend policy for a firm strikes that balance between current dividends and future growth which maximizes the price of the stock.*

optimal dividend policy
The dividend policy that strikes the balance between current dividends and future growth which maximizes the firm's stock price.

In this chapter, we first examine factors which affect the optimal dividend policy, after which we discuss stock repurchases as an alternative to cash dividends.

DIVIDEND POLICY THEORIES

A number of factors influence dividend policy, including the investment opportunities available to the firm, alternative sources of capital, and stockholders' preferences for current versus future income. Our major goal in this chapter is to show how these factors interact to determine a firm's optimal dividend policy. We begin by examining two theories of dividend policy: (1) the dividend irrelevance theory and (2) the "bird-in-the-hand" theory.

Dividend Irrelevance Theory

dividend irrelevance theory
The theory that a firm's dividend policy has no effect on either its value or its cost of capital.

It has been argued that dividend policy has no effect on either the price of a firm's stock or its cost of capital — that is, that dividend policy is *irrelevant*. The principal proponents of the **dividend irrelevance theory** are Merton Miller and Franco Modigliani (MM).[1] They argued that the value of the firm is determined only by its basic earning power and its business risk; in other words, MM argued that the value of the firm depends only on the income produced by its assets, not on how this income is split between dividends and retained earnings (and hence growth).

MM based their proposition on theoretical grounds. However, as in all theoretical work, they had to make some assumptions in order to develop a manageable theory. Specifically, they assumed (1) that there are no personal or corporate income taxes, (2) that there are no stock flotation or transactions costs, (3) that financial leverage has no effect on the cost of capital, (4) that investors and managers have the same information about the firm's future prospects, (5) that the distribution of income between dividends and retained earnings has no effect on the firm's cost of equity (k_s), and (6) that a firm's capital budgeting policy is independent of its dividend policy. Obviously these assumptions do not hold precisely. Firms and investors do pay income taxes; firms do incur flotation costs; managers often know more about the firm's future prospects than outside investors know; investors do incur transactions costs; and both taxes and transactions costs may cause k_s to be affected by dividend policy. MM argued (correctly) that all economic theories are based on simplifying assumptions and that the validity of a theory must be judged on empirical tests, not on the realism of its assumptions. We will discuss empirical tests of the MM dividend theory shortly.

"Bird-in-the-Hand" Theory

The fifth assumption in MM's dividend irrelevance theory is that dividend policy does not affect investors' required rate of return on equity, k_s. This particular assumption has been hotly debated in academic circles. For example, Myron Gordon and John Lintner argued that k_s increases as the dividend payout is reduced, because investors are less certain of receiving the capital gains which should result from retained earnings than they are of receiving dividend payments.[2] Gordon and Lintner said, in effect, that investors value a dollar of expected dividends more highly than a dollar of expected capital gains, because the dividend yield component, D_1/P_0, is less risky than the g component in the total expected return equation, $\hat{k}_s = D_1/P_0 + g$.

MM disagreed. They argued that k_s is independent of dividend policy, which implies that investors are indifferent between D_1/P_0 and g, and, hence, between dividends and capital gains. They called the Gordon-Lintner argument the **"bird-in-the-hand"** fallacy because, in MM's view, most investors plan to reinvest their dividends in stock of the same or similar firms anyway, and, in

"bird-in-the-hand" theory
MM's name for the theory that a firm's value will be maximized by a high dividend payout ratio because investors regard dividends as being less risky than capital gains.

---

[1]Merton H. Miller and Franco Modigliani, "Dividend Policy, Growth, and the Valuation of Shares," *Journal of Business,* October 1961, 411–433.

[2]Myron J. Gordon, "Optimal Investment and Financing Policy," *Journal of Finance,* May 1963, 264–272, and John Lintner, "Dividends, Earnings, Leverage, Stock Prices, and the Supply of Capital to Corporations," *Review of Economics and Statistics,* August 1962, 243–269.

**Figure 18-1   The Miller-Modigliani and Gordon-Lintner
Dividend Hypotheses**

---

a. Dividends Are Irrelevant (MM)

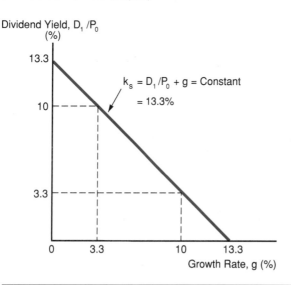

b. Dividends Are Relevant: Investors
Like Dividends (GL)

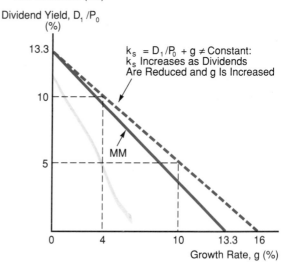

any event, the riskiness of the firm's cash flows to investors in the long run is determined only by the riskiness of its operating cash flows and not by its dividend payout policy.

Figure 18-1 presents two graphs which highlight the MM versus Gordon-Lintner arguments. The left panel shows the Miller-Modigliani position. Here the company has $k_s = D_1/P_0 + g = $ a constant 13.3 percent for any dividend policy. Thus, the equilibrium total return, k_s, is assumed to be a constant 13.3 percent regardless of whether it comes entirely as a dividend yield (the vertical axis intercept, 13.3 percent), entirely as expected capital gains (the horizontal axis intercept, also 13.3 percent), or in any combination of the two. For example, MM believed that a representative investor would be indifferent between a 13.3 percent dividend yield with zero expected capital gains, a 10 percent dividend yield plus a 3.3 percent expected capital gains, a 3.3 percent dividend yield and 10 percent expected capital gains, and a zero dividend yield with a 13.3 percent expected capital gains return.

The graph in the right panel repeats the MM relationship, but it also shows, as the dashed line, the Gordon-Lintner view. Gordon-Lintner argued that a dividend in the hand is less risky than a possible capital gain in the bush, so investors require a larger total return, k_s, if that return has a larger capital gains component, g, than dividend yield, D_1/P_0. In other words, Gordon-Lintner argued that *more than 1 percent* of additional growth is required to offset a 1 percent reduction of dividend yield. Thus, the required rate of return, or cost of equity, would be 13.3 percent if the firm paid all of its earnings out in dividends, but as it lowered the payout and hence the dividend portion of the total return, the cost of equity would increase. In our example, k_s would be 16 percent at a zero payout, the point at which the dividend yield was zero.

At this time, we are not prepared to say which of these two positions is more correct. Before reaching such a conclusion, we must examine the empirical evidence.

TESTS OF DIVIDEND THEORIES

In the preceding section, we presented two dividend theories:

1. MM argued that dividend policy is irrelevant; that is, it does not affect a firm's value or its cost of capital. Thus, according to MM, there is no optimal dividend policy — one dividend policy is as good as any other.

2. Gordon and Lintner disagreed with MM, arguing that dividends are less risky than capital gains, so a firm should set a high dividend payout ratio and offer a high dividend yield in order to minimize its cost of capital. MM called this the "bird-in-the-hand" fallacy.

Because these two theories offer contradictory advice to corporate managers, which one should we believe? The most logical way to proceed is to test the theories empirically. Actually, many empirical tests have been used in attempts to determine the true relationship between dividend yield and required return. The earliest type of test was designed along the lines set forth in Figure 18-1.[3] In theory, we could take a sample of companies which have different dividend policies, and hence different dividend yield and growth rate components, and plot them in graphs such as those shown in Figure 18-1. If all the points fell on the line labeled MM in Panel b, so the slope of the resulting regression line was −1.0, this would support the MM irrelevance hypothesis. If all the points fell on the dashed line, so the slope was less negative (less steep) than −1.0 (say, −0.8), this would support the Gordon-Lintner hypothesis. If the slope was more negative (steeper) than −1.0 (say, −1.2), this would suggest that investors preferred retained earnings and capital gains to dividends; when capital gains were taxed at a lower rate than dividends (before 1987), that position was not unreasonable.

Such tests have been conducted, but the results have been unclear. With one set of data the slope would be low, say −0.5; a second data set would

---

[3]The earliest such test was that described in Eugene F. Brigham and Myron J. Gordon, "Leverage, Dividend Policy, and the Cost of Capital," *Journal of Finance,* March 1968, 85–104. In work done in conjunction with writing this chapter, we reexamined the issue and reached the conclusions reported in this section.

show a high slope, say −1.5; and a third data set would show a slope close to −1.0; and so forth. In all cases, the standard deviations were too large to permit much confidence in the slope coefficients. For example, one test we conducted showed a slope coefficient of −1.2 but a standard deviation of 0.5, which meant that we could say only that the true slope was probably within the range of −0.7 and −1.7. These results in turn meant that either of the theories could be correct, or that they could both be incorrect. There are two reasons for this situation: (1) For a valid statistical test, things other than dividend policy must be held constant; that is, the sample companies must differ only in their dividend policies. (2) We must be able to measure with a high degree of accuracy the expected growth rates for the sample firms. Neither of these two conditions actually holds: we can neither find a set of publicly owned firms that differ only in their dividend policies nor can we obtain precise estimates of investors' expected growth rates. Therefore, we cannot determine with much precision what effect dividend policy has on the cost of equity. Hence, this particular type of test has been unable to solve the dividend policy puzzle.

Academic researchers have also studied the dividend yield effect from a CAPM perspective. These studies hypothesize that required returns are a function of both market risk, as measured by beta, and dividend yield. As with the earlier studies, the results of this line of research have been mixed. Using NYSE data from 1936 through 1977, Litzenberger and Ramaswamy showed that stocks with high dividend yields had higher total returns than stocks with low dividend yields, after adjusting for market risk.[4] Their study indicated that required total returns increased by about 0.24 percentage points for every percentage point increase in dividend yield. Thus, a company might have had a 10 percent cost of equity if it retained all of its earnings but a cost of over 12.4 percent if it paid out all of its earnings as dividends. Other studies, however, have reached the opposite conclusion.[5]

The major problem with the CAPM studies is that they generally used historic earned rates of return as proxies for required returns, and with such a poor proxy, the tests were almost bound to have mixed results. Thus, the CAPM-based empirical tests, like the purely DCF-based ones, have not led to definitive conclusions about which dividend theory is more correct. As a result, the issue is still unresolved; academicians at this time simply cannot tell corporate decision makers how dividend policy affects stock prices and capital costs.

---

[4]Robert H. Litzenberger and Krishna Ramaswamy, "The Effect of Personal Taxes and Dividends on Capital Asset Prices," *Journal of Financial Economics,* June 1979, 163–196. These authors argued that the lower tax on capital gains led to a preference for capital gains, hence higher prices and lower k values for stocks that paid less dividends and consequently offered higher capital gains. Under current tax laws, this situation is much less likely.

[5]For example, see Fischer Black and Myron Scholes, "The Effects of Dividend Yield and Dividend Policy on Common Stock Prices and Returns," *Journal of Financial Economics,* May 1974, 1–22.

OTHER DIVIDEND POLICY ISSUES

Before discussing dividend policy in practice, we must examine two other theoretical issues that could affect our views toward the dividend policy theories presented earlier: (1) the *information content,* or *signaling, hypothesis* and (2) the *clientele effect.*

Information Content, or Signaling, Hypothesis

If investors expect a company's dividend to increase by 5 percent per year, and if the dividend is in fact increased by 5 percent, then the stock price generally will not change significantly on the day the dividend increase is announced. In Wall Street parlance, the dividend increase is "discounted," or anticipated, by the market. However, if investors expect a 5 percent increase, but the company actually increases the dividend by 25 percent — say from $2 to $2.50 — this generally is accompanied by an increase in the price of the stock. Conversely, a less-than-expected dividend increase, or a reduction, generally leads to a price decline.

The fact that large dividend increases generally cause stock price increases suggests to some that investors in the aggregate prefer dividends to capital gains. However, MM argued differently. They noted the well-established fact that corporations are always reluctant to cut dividends, and, consequently, that managers do not raise dividends unless they anticipate higher, or at least stable, earnings in the future. Therefore, according to MM (and many others), this meant that a larger-than-expected dividend increase is taken by investors as a "signal" that the firm's management forecasts improved future earnings, whereas a dividend reduction signals a poor earnings forecast. Thus, MM claimed that investor reactions to changes in dividend payments do not show that investors prefer dividends to retained earnings; rather, the stock price changes simply indicate that there is important information inherent in dividend announcements. This theory is referred to as the **information content, or signaling, hypothesis.**

Like most other aspects of dividend policy, empirical studies on this topic have been inconclusive. Although there clearly is some information content in dividend announcements, this is not necessarily the complete explanation for the stock price changes that follow increases or decreases in dividends, especially if these dividend changes include a change in the percentage payout ratio as well as in the dollars of dividends paid.

information content (signaling) hypothesis
The theory that investors regard dividend changes as signals of management's earnings forecasts.

Clientele Effect

clientele effect
The tendency of a firm to attract the type of investor who likes its dividend policy.

MM also suggested that a **clientele effect** might exist, and, if so, this might help explain why stock prices change after announced changes in dividend policy. Their argument went like this: A firm sets a particular dividend payout policy, which then attracts a "clientele" consisting of those investors who like this particular dividend policy. For example, some stockholders, such as university endowment funds and retired individuals, prefer current income to future capital gains, so they want the firm to pay out a higher percentage of its earnings. Other stockholders have no need for current investment income — they simply reinvest any dividend income received, after first paying income taxes on it, so they favor a low payout ratio.

If the firm retained and reinvested income rather than paying dividends, those stockholders who need current income would be disadvantaged. They would presumably receive capital gains, but they would also have to go to the trouble and expense of selling some of their shares to obtain cash. Since brokerage costs are quite high on small transactions, selling a few shares to obtain periodic income would be expensive and inefficient. Also, some institutional investors (or trustees for individuals) are precluded from selling stock and then "spending capital." However, if the firm paid out most of its income, those stockholders who did not need current cash income would be forced to receive such income, pay taxes on it, and then go to the trouble and expense of reinvesting what's left of their dividends after taxes. MM concluded from all this that those investors who desired current investment income would own shares in high-dividend-payout firms, whereas those who did not need current cash income would invest in low-payout firms.

To the extent that stockholders can shift their investments among firms, a firm can establish the specific policy that its management deems most appropriate and then have stockholders who do not like this policy sell their shares to other investors who do. However, switching is inefficient because of (1) brokerage costs, (2) the likelihood that selling stockholders will have to pay taxes on their capital gains, and (3) a possible shortage of investors in the aggregate who like the firm's newly stated dividend policy. This means that if a firm makes a significant change in dividend policy, some buying and selling can be expected, and there will be some net losses because of brokerage costs and taxes. If there are enough investors in the economy who favor the new policy, however, then their demand for the stock could more than offset the costs associated with the change and lead to an increase in the price of the stock.

Several studies have investigated the importance of the clientele effect.[6] Like most other issues in the dividend arena, the implications of the clientele effect are still up in the air.

DIVIDEND POLICY IN PRACTICE

We noted earlier that there are two conflicting theories as to what dividend policy firms *should* follow: (1) Miller and Modigliani's theory that dividend policy is irrelevant, and (2) the bird-in-the-hand theory that dividends are less

---

[6]For example, see R. Richardson Pettit, "Taxes, Transactions Costs, and the Clientele Effect of Dividends," *Journal of Financial Economics,* December 1977, 419–436.

risky than capital gains and hence that k_s rises as dividend payments are reduced. We also saw that dividend payments send signals to investors — an unexpectedly large dividend increase conveys management optimism, whereas a cut conveys pessimism — and that companies' dividend policies attract clienteles of stockholders who prefer a dividend policy similar to the one the company is following. All of this provides insights that aid corporate decision makers. However, no one has been able to develop a formula that can be used to tell management how a given dividend policy will affect a firm's stock price.

Even though no dividend policy formula exists, managements must still establish dividend policies. This section discusses several alternative policies as applied in practice.

Residual Dividend Policy

(leftover)

residual dividend policy
A policy in which dividends paid equals actual earnings minus the amount of retained earnings necessary to finance the firm's optimal capital budget.

In practice, dividend policy is very much influenced by investment opportunities and by the availability of funds with which to finance them. This fact has led to the development of a **residual dividend policy**, which states that a firm should follow these four steps when deciding on its payout ratio: (1) determine the optimal capital budget; (2) determine the amount of capital needed to finance that budget; (3) use retained earnings to supply the equity component to the extent possible; and (4) pay dividends only if more earnings are available than are needed to support the optimal capital budget. The word *residual* means "left over," and the residual policy implies that dividends should be paid only out of "leftover" earnings.

The basis of the residual policy is the belief that *investors prefer to have the firm retain and reinvest earnings rather than pay them out in dividends if the rate of return the firm can earn on reinvested earnings exceeds the rate investors on average can themselves obtain on other investments of comparable risk.* For example, if the corporation can reinvest retained earnings at a 14 percent rate of return, whereas the best rate the average stockholder can obtain if the earnings are passed on in the form of dividends is 12 percent, then stockholders will prefer to have the firm retain the profits.

To continue, we saw in Chapter 16 that the cost of retained earnings is an *opportunity cost* which reflects rates of return available to equity investors. If a firm's stockholders can buy other stocks of equal risk and obtain a 12 percent dividend-plus-capital-gains yield, then 12 percent is the firm's cost of retained earnings. The cost of new outside equity raised by selling common stock will be higher than 12 percent because of the costs of floating the issue.

Most firms have a target capital structure that calls for at least some debt, so new financing is done partly with debt and partly with equity. As long as the firm finances with the optimal mix of debt and equity, and as long as it uses only internally generated equity (retained earnings), its marginal cost of each new dollar of capital will be minimized. Internally generated equity is available for financing a certain amount of new investment, but beyond that amount the firm must turn to more expensive new common stock. At the point

**Figure 18-2   Texas and Western Transport Company:
Marginal Cost of Capital**

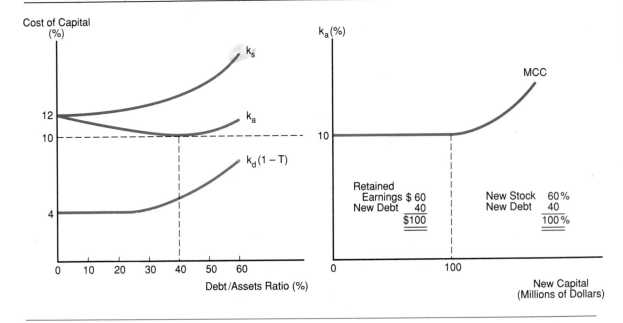

where new stock must be sold, the cost of equity, and consequently the marginal cost of capital, rises.

These concepts, which were developed in Chapter 16, are illustrated in Figure 18-2 with data from the Texas and Western (T&W) Transport Company. T&W has a marginal cost of capital of 10 percent. However, this cost rate assumes that all new equity comes from retained earnings. Therefore, MCC = 12% as long as retained earnings are available, but MCC begins to rise at the point where new stock must be sold.

T&W has $60 million of net income and a 40 percent optimal debt ratio. Provided that it does not pay cash dividends, T&W can make net investments (investments in addition to asset replacements financed from depreciation) of $100 million, consisting of $60 million from retained earnings plus $40 million of new debt supported by the retained earnings, at a 10 percent marginal cost of capital. Therefore, its MCC is constant at 10 percent up to $100 million of capital, beyond which it rises as the firm begins to use more expensive new common stock.

Of course, if T&W does not retain all of its earnings, then its MCC will begin to rise before $100 million. For example, if T&W retains only $30 million, its MCC will begin to rise at $50 million: $30 million of retained earnings + $20 million of debt = $50 million.

Figure 18-3   Texas and Western Transport Company:
Investment Opportunity (or IRR) Schedules

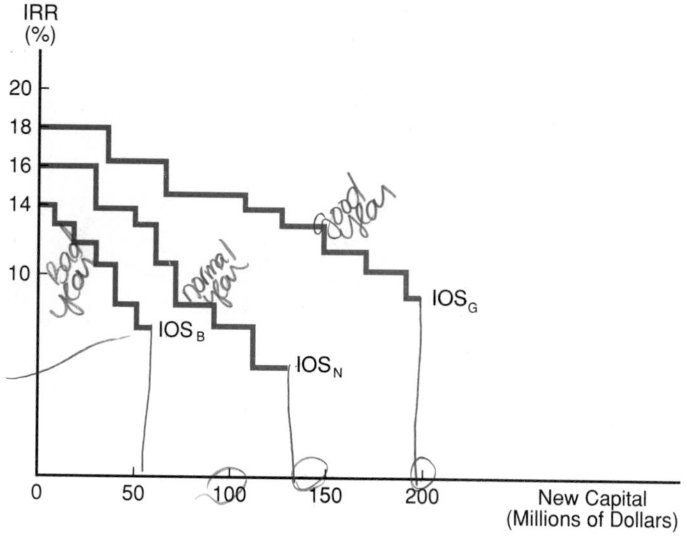

Now suppose T&W's director of capital budgeting constructs an investment opportunity schedule each year and plots it on a graph. The investment opportunity schedules for three different years — a good year (IOS_G), a normal year (IOS_N), and a bad year (IOS_B) — are shown in Figure 18-3. T&W can invest the most money, and earn the highest rates of return, when the investment opportunities are given as IOS_G.

In Figure 18-4, we combine these investment opportunity schedules with the cost of capital schedule that would exist if the company retained all of its earnings. The point where the relevant IOS curve cuts the MCC curve defines the proper level of new investment. When investment opportunities are relatively bad (IOS_B), the optimal level of investment is $40 million; when opportunities are normal (IOS_N), $70 million should be invested; and when opportunities are relatively good (IOS_G), T&W should make new investments in the amount of $150 million.[7]

Consider the situation in which IOS_G is the appropriate schedule. T&W should raise and invest $150 million. It has $60 million in earnings and a 40 percent target debt ratio. Thus, if it retained all of its earnings, it could finance $100 million, consisting of $60 million of retained earnings plus $40 million

_____

[7]Figure 18-4 shows one MCC schedule and three IOS schedules for three possible sets of investment opportunities. Actually, both the MCC and the IOS schedules would normally change from year to year as interest rates and stock prices change. Figure 18-4 is designed to illustrate a point, not to duplicate reality. In reality there would be one MCC and one IOS schedule for each year, but those schedules would change from year to year.

Figure 18-4   Texas and Western Transport Company: Interrelationships between Cost of Capital, Investment Opportunities, and New Investment

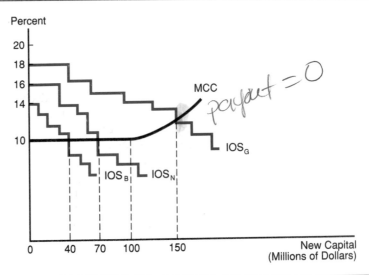

of new debt at an average cost of 10 percent. The remaining $50 million would include external equity and thus would have a higher cost. If T&W paid out part of its earnings in dividends, it would have to begin to use more costly new common stock earlier than need be, so its MCC curve would rise earlier than it otherwise would. This suggests that under the conditions of IOS$_G$, T&W should retain all of its earnings. According to the residual policy, T&W's payout ratio should be zero if IOS$_G$ applies.

Under the conditions of IOS$_N$, however, T&W should invest only $70 million. How should this investment be financed? First, notice that if T&W retained all of its earnings, $60 million, it would need to sell only $10 million of new debt. However, if T&W retained $60 million and sold only $10 million of new debt, it would move away from its target capital structure. To stay on target, T&W must finance 60 percent of the required $70 million with equity—retained earnings—and 40 percent with debt. This means that it would retain only $42 million and sell $28 million of new debt. Since T&W would retain only $42 million of its $60 million total earnings, it would have to distribute the residual, $18 million, to its stockholders. Thus, its optimal payout ratio would be $18/$60 = 30% if IOS$_N$ prevailed.

Under the conditions of IOS$_B$, T&W should invest only $40 million. Because it has $60 million in earnings, it could finance the entire $40 million out of retained earnings and still have $20 million available for dividends. Should this be done? Under our assumptions this would not be a good decision, because it would force T&W away from its optimal capital structure. To stay at the 40 percent target debt/assets ratio, T&W must retain $24 million of earnings and sell $16 million of debt. When the $24 million of retained earnings is subtracted from the $60 million total earnings, T&W would be left with a residual of $36 million, the amount that should be paid out in dividends. Thus, under IOS$_B$, the payout ratio as prescribed by the residual policy would be $36/$60 = 60 percent.

Since both the IOS schedule and the earnings level vary from year to year, strict adherence to the residual dividend policy would result in dividend variability — one year the firm might declare zero dividends because investment opportunities were good, but the next year it might pay a large dividend because investment opportunities were poor. Similarly, fluctuating earnings would also lead to variable dividends even if investment opportunities were stable over time. Thus, following the residual dividend policy would be optimal only if investors were not bothered by fluctuating dividends; if they preferred stable, dependable dividends, k_s would be higher, and the stock price lower, if the firm followed the residual theory in a strict sense rather than attempted to stabilize its dividends over time.

Constant, or Steadily Increasing, Dividends

In the past, many firms set a specific annual dollar dividend per share and then maintained it, increasing the annual dividend only if it seemed clear that future earnings would be sufficient to allow the new dividend to be maintained. A corollary of that policy was this rule: *Never reduce the annual dividend.*

More recently, inflation has tended to push earnings up, so many firms that would otherwise have followed the stable dividend payment policy have switched over to what is called the "stable growth rate" policy. Here the firm sets a target growth rate for dividends (for example, 6 percent per year, which is close to the long-run average inflation rate) and strives to increase dividends by this amount each year. Obviously, earnings must be growing at about the same rate for this policy to be feasible, but such a policy provides investors with a stable real income.

A fairly typical dividend policy, that of Eastman Kodak, is illustrated in Figure 18-5. Kodak's payout ratio ranged from 41.1 to 52.5 percent from 1972 to 1982, and it averaged 47.6 percent during those 11 years. Although the payout ratio fluctuated somewhat, dividends clearly tracked earnings. Dividends were increased sharply in 1973 and 1974, following large earnings gains in 1972 and 1973; the dividend was stabilized during the mid-1970s when earnings were flat; and dividends were again increased rapidly from 1978 to 1981, when a high inflation rate pushed up earnings.

Kodak's earnings fell sharply from 1981 to 1983, and again in 1985, because of increased competition. The 1985 drop included a $494 million writeoff that resulted when Kodak lost a suit to Polaroid and had to close down its instant photography business. Management stopped increasing the dividend when earnings fell, but did not cut the dividend, even when earnings failed to

Figure 18-5   Eastman Kodak:
Earnings and Dividends, 1972–1992

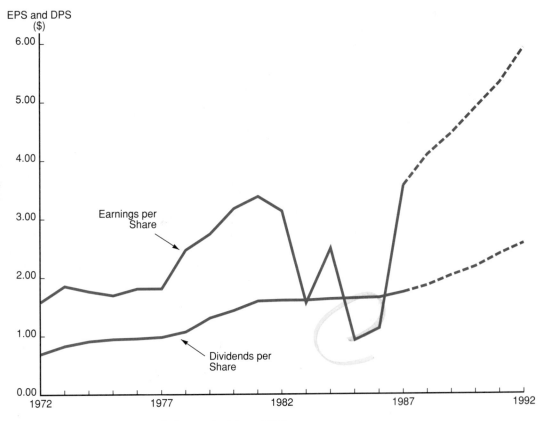

Source: *Value Line*, March 25, 1988. Projected values are shown beyond 1987.

cover the dividend. Thus, from 1983 to 1985, the payout ratio averaged more than 100 percent. Maintaining the dividend was Kodak's way of signaling to stockholders that management was confident that the earnings decline was only temporary and that earnings would soon resume their upward trend. This was, indeed, the case. Kodak's earnings increased by 14 percent in 1986 and then by more than 200 percent in 1987. The 1987 dividend payout ratio was down to 48 percent, which is about where Kodak likes to keep it.

The dashed lines beyond 1987 in Figure 18-5 represent the forecasts of a major investment advisory service, *Value Line*, whose analysts believe that Kodak's earnings will continue to grow at a rate of about 10 percent per year and that, over the long run, Kodak will increase dividends as earnings grow. During the forecast period, 1988–1992, *Value Line* projects that Kodak will pay out just under 50 percent of earnings.

There are several logical reasons for following a stable, predictable dividend policy. First, given the existence of the information content, or signaling, idea, a fluctuating payment policy would lead to greater uncertainty, and hence to a higher k_s and a lower stock price, than would exist under a stable policy. Second, some stockholders use dividends for current consumption, and they would be put to trouble and expense if they had to sell part of their shares to obtain cash if the company cut the dividend; this is in addition to the signaling anxiety a dividend cut would cause them. Third, even though the optimal dividend as prescribed by the residual policy might vary somewhat from year to year, actions such as delaying some investment projects, departing from the target capital structure during a particular year, or even issuing new common stock make it possible for a company to avoid the problems associated with signaling and unstable cash flow effects.

Constant Payout Ratio

A few firms follow a policy of paying out a constant percentage of earnings. Since earnings will surely fluctuate, following this policy necessarily means that the dollar amount of dividends will vary. For example, if it had paid out a constant percentage of earnings, Eastman Kodak would have had to cut its dividend in several different years, and this would undoubtedly have caused its stock price to fall sharply. (Kodak's stock price was stable in the 1982–1985 period, in spite of the sharp earnings decline. Had it cut the dividend to keep the payout ratio constant, the stock price would have fallen out of bed, because investors would have taken the dividend reduction as a signal that management thought the earnings drop was permanent.)

Note, though, that Kodak's long-run payout ratio appears to be relatively constant; except for the depressed period in the mid-1980s, it has fluctuated narrowly about 50 percent. Kodak, like most companies, conducts an analysis similar to the residual analysis set forth earlier in the chapter and then establishes a target payout ratio based on the most likely set of conditions. The target is not hit in every year, but over time the average payout has been close to the target level. Of course, the target would change if fundamental changes in the company's position were to occur.

Low Regular Dividend plus Extras

A policy of paying a low regular dividend plus a year-end extra in good years is a compromise between a stable dividend (or stable growth rate) and a constant payout rate. Such a policy gives the firm flexibility, yet investors can count on receiving at least a minimum dividend. Therefore, if a firm's earnings and cash flows are quite volatile, this policy may well be its best choice. The directors can set a relatively low regular dividend — low enough so that it can be maintained even in low-profit years or in years when a considerable amount of retained earnings is needed — and then supplement it with an **extra dividend** in years when excess funds are available. Ford, General Motors, and

extra dividend
A supplementary dividend paid in years when excess funds are available.

other auto companies, whose earnings fluctuate widely from year to year, used to follow such a policy, but in recent years they have joined the crowd and now follow a stable dividend policy.

Payment Procedures

Dividends are normally paid quarterly, and if conditions permit, the dividend is increased once each year. For example, Kodak paid $1.68 per share in 1987, or $0.42 per quarter. In common financial parlance, we say that in 1987 Kodak's *regular quarterly dividend* was $0.42, and its *annual dividend* was $1.68. In late 1987, Kodak's board of directors met, reviewed projections for 1988, and raised the dividend for 1988 to $1.80, or $0.45 per quarter. The directors announced that rate, so stockholders could count on receiving it unless the company experienced major operating problems.

The actual payment procedure is as follows:

declaration date
The date on which a firm's directors issue a statement declaring a dividend.

1. **Declaration date.** On the declaration date — say, on November 14 — the directors meet and declare the regular dividend, issuing a statement similar to the following: "On November 14, 1988, the directors of the XYZ Company met and declared the regular quarterly dividend of 50 cents per share, payable to holders of record on December 9, payment to be made on January 2, 1989." For accounting purposes, the declared dividend becomes an actual liability on the declaration date, and if a balance sheet were constructed, the amount ($0.50) (number of shares outstanding) would appear as a current liability, and retained earnings would be reduced by a like amount.

holder-of-record date
If the company lists the stockholder as an owner on this date, then the stockholder receives the dividend.

2. **Holder-of-record date.** At the close of business on the holder-of-record date, December 9, the company closes its stock transfer books and makes up a list of shareholders as of that date. If XYZ Company is notified of the sale and transfer of some stock before 5 P.M. on December 9, then the new owner receives the dividend. However, if notification is received on or after December 10, the previous owner of the stock gets the dividend check.

ex-dividend date
The date on which the right to the current dividend no longer accompanies a stock; it is usually four working days prior to the holder-of-record date.

3. **Ex-dividend date.** Suppose Jean Buyer buys 100 shares of stock from John Seller on December 7. Will the company be notified of the transfer in time to list Buyer as the new owner and thus pay the dividend to her? To avoid conflict, the securities industry has set up a convention of declaring that the right to the dividend remains with the stock until four business days prior to the holder-of-record date; on the fourth day before that date, the right to the dividend no longer goes with the shares. The date when the right to the dividend leaves the stock is called the *ex-dividend date.* In this case, the ex-dividend date is four days prior to December 9, or December 5:

		December 4 Buyer receives dividend

- -

	Ex-dividend date:	December 5 Seller receives dividend

- -

		December 6
		December 7
		December 8
	Holder-of-record date:	December 9

Therefore, if Buyer is to receive the dividend, she must buy the stock on or before December 4 (actually December 2, since stocks are not traded over the weekend). If she buys it on December 5 or later, Seller will receive the dividend because he will be the holder of record.

The XYZ dividend amounts to $0.50, so the ex-dividend date is important. Barring fluctuations in the stock market, one would normally expect the price of a stock to drop by approximately the amount of the dividend on the ex-dividend date. Thus, if XYZ closed at $30½ on Friday, December 2, it would probably open at about $30 on Monday, December 5.[8]

payment date
The date on which a firm actually mails dividend checks.

4. **Payment date**. The company actually mails the checks to the holders of record on January 2, the payment date.

Dividend Reinvestment Plans

dividend reinvestment plan (DRP)
A plan that enables a stockholder to automatically reinvest dividends received back into the stock of the paying firm.

During the 1970s most of the larger companies instituted **dividend reinvestment plans (DRPs)**, whereby stockholders can automatically reinvest dividends received in the stock of the paying corporation.[9] There are two types of DRPs:

---

[8]Tax effects cause the price decline on average to be less than the full amount of the dividend. Suppose you were an investor in the 40 percent federal-plus-state tax bracket. If you bought XYZ's stock on December 2, you would receive the dividend, but you would almost immediately pay 40 percent of it out in taxes. Thus, you would want to wait until December 5 to buy the stock if you thought you could get it for $0.50 less per share. Your reaction, and that of others, would influence stock prices around dividend payment dates: Here is what would happen:

1. Other things held constant, a stock's price should rise during the quarter, with the daily price increase (for XYZ) equal to $0.50/90 = $0.005556. Therefore, if the price started at $30 just after its last ex-dividend date, it would rise to $30.50 on December 2.

2. In the absence of taxes, the stock's price would fall to $30 on December 5 and then start up as the next dividend accrual period began. Thus, over time, if everything else were held constant, the stock's price would follow a sawtooth pattern if it were plotted on a graph.

3. Because of taxes, the stock's price would neither rise by the full amount of the dividend nor fall by the full dividend amount when it goes ex-dividend.

4. The amount of the rise and subsequent fall would depend on the average investor's marginal tax rate.

See Edwin J. Elton and Martin J. Gruber, "Marginal Stockholder Tax Rates and the Clientele Effect," *Review of Economics and Statistics,* February 1970, 68–74, for an interesting discussion of all this.

[9]See Richard H. Pettway and R. Phil Malone, "Automatic Dividend Reinvestment Plans," *Financial Management,* Winter 1973, 11–18, for an excellent discussion of this topic.

(1) plans which involve only "old" stock that is already outstanding, and (2) plans which involve newly issued stock. In either case, the stockholder must pay income taxes on the amount of the dividends even though stock rather than cash is received.

Under the "old-stock" type of plan, the stockholder chooses between receiving dividend checks or having the company use the dividends to buy more stock in the corporation. If the stockholder elects reinvestment, a bank, acting as trustee, takes the total funds available for reinvestment (minus a fee), purchases the corporation's stock on the open market, and allocates the shares purchased to the participating stockholders' accounts on a pro rata basis. The transactions costs of buying shares (brokerage costs) are low because of volume purchases, so these plans benefit small stockholders who do not need cash dividends for current consumption.

The "new-stock" type of DRP provides for dividends to be invested in newly issued stock; hence, these plans raise new capital for the firm. AT&T, Florida Power & Light, Union Carbide, and many other companies have had such plans in effect in recent years, using them to raise substantial amounts of new equity capital. No fees are charged to stockholders, and many companies offer stock at a discount of 5 percent below the actual market price. The companies absorb these costs as a trade-off against the flotation costs that would have been incurred had they sold stock through investment bankers rather than through the dividend reinvestment plans.[10]

SUMMARY OF FACTORS INFLUENCING DIVIDEND POLICY

Thus far in the chapter we have described the major theories that deal with the effects of dividend policy on the value of a firm, and we have discussed alternative payment policies. Firms choose a particular policy based on managements' beliefs concerning the dividend theories, plus a host of other factors. All of the factors which are taken into account may be grouped into four broad categories: (1) constraints on dividend payments, (2) investment opportunities, (3) availability and cost of alternative sources of capital, and (4) effects of dividend policy on k_s. Each of these categories has several subparts, which we discuss in the following paragraphs.

---

[10]One interesting aspect of DRPs is that they are forcing corporations to reexamine their basic dividend policies. A high participation rate in a DRP suggests that stockholders might be better off if the firm simply reduced cash dividends, as this would save stockholders some personal income taxes. Quite a few firms are surveying their stockholders to learn more about their preferences and to find out how they would react to a change in dividend policy. A more rational approach to basic dividend policy decisions may emerge from this research.

Also, it should be noted that companies either use or stop using new-stock DRPs depending on their need for equity capital. Florida Power & Light recently stopped offering a new-stock DRP with a 5 percent discount because its need for equity capital declined once it had completed a nuclear-powered generating plant.

Constraints

1. *Bond indentures.* Debt contracts generally limit dividend payments to earnings generated after the loan was granted. Also, contracts often stipulate that no dividends can be paid unless the current ratio, times-interest-earned ratio, and other safety ratios exceed stated minimums.

2. *Impairment of capital rule.* Dividend payments cannot exceed the balance sheet item "retained earnings." This legal restriction, known as the *impairment of capital rule,* is designed to protect creditors. Without the rule, a company that was in trouble might distribute most of its assets to stockholders and leave its debtholders out in the cold. (*Liquidating dividends* can be paid out of capital, but they must be indicated as such, and they must not reduce capital below the limits stated in debt contracts.)

3. *Availability of cash.* Cash dividends can be paid only with cash. Thus, a shortage of cash in the bank can restrict dividend payments. However, the ability to borrow can offset this factor.

4. *Penalty tax on improperly accumulated earnings.* To prevent wealthy individuals from using corporations to avoid personal taxes, the Tax Code provides for a special surtax on improperly accumulated income. Thus, if the IRS can demonstrate that a firm's dividend payout ratio is being deliberately held down to help its stockholders avoid personal taxes, the firm is subject to heavy penalties. To date, this factor has been applied only to privately owned firms.

Investment Opportunities

1. *Location of the IOS schedule.* If the relevant IOS schedule, as shown in Figure 18-4 above, is far to the right, this will tend to produce a low payout ratio, and vice versa if the IOS is far to the left.

2. *Possibility of accelerating or delaying projects.* The ability to accelerate or postpone projects will permit more flexibility in a firm's dividend policy.

Alternative Sources of Capital

1. *Cost of selling new stock.* If a firm needs to finance a given level of investment, it can obtain equity by retaining earnings or by selling new common stock. If flotation costs (including any negative signaling effects of a stock offering) are high, k_e will be well above k_s, making it better to set a low payout ratio and to finance through retention rather than through sale of new common stock. On the other hand, a high dividend payout ratio is more feasible for a firm whose flotation costs are low. Flotation costs differ among firms — for example, the flotation percentage is generally higher for small firms.

2. *Ability to substitute debt for equity.* A firm can finance a given level of investment with either debt or equity. As we have seen, low stock flotation costs permit a more flexible dividend policy because equity can be raised either by retaining earnings or by selling new stock. A similar situation holds for debt policy: if the firm can adjust its debt ratio without raising costs sharply, it can maintain a constant dollar dividend by using a variable debt ratio. The shape of the average cost of capital curve (in the left-hand panel of Figure 18-2 above) determines the practical extent to which the debt ratio can be varied. If the average cost of capital curve is relatively flat over a wide range, then a higher payout ratio is more feasible than it would be if the curve had a distinct minimum.

3. *Control.* If management is concerned about maintaining control, it may be reluctant to sell new stock, and hence the company may retain more earnings than it otherwise would. However, if stockholders want higher dividends and a proxy fight looms, then the dividend will be increased.

Effects of Dividend Policy on k_s

The effects of dividend policy on k_s may be considered in terms of these three factors: (1) stockholders' desire for current versus future income, (2) perceived riskiness of dividends versus capital gains, and (3) the information content of dividends (signaling). Since we discussed each of these factors in detail earlier, we need only note here that the importance of each factor in terms of its effect on k_s varies from firm to firm depending on the makeup of its current and possible future stockholders.

It should be apparent from our discussion thus far that dividend policy decisions are truly exercises in informed judgment, not decisions that can be quantified precisely. Even so, to make rational dividend decisions, financial managers need to take account of all the points discussed in the preceding sections.

STOCK DIVIDENDS AND STOCK SPLITS

Stock dividends and stock splits are related to the firm's cash dividend policy. The rationale for stock dividends and splits can best be explained through an example. We will use Porter Electronic Controls, Inc., a $700 million electronic components manufacturer, for this purpose. Since its inception, Porter's markets have been expanding, and the company has enjoyed growth in sales and earnings. Some of the earnings were paid out in dividends, but some were also retained each year, causing earnings per share and market price per share to grow. The company began its life with only a few thousand shares outstanding. After some years of growth, each of Porter's shares had a very high EPS and DPS. When a "normal" P/E ratio was applied, the derived market price was

[handwritten margin notes at top: growth ≥ = PO there people not to high cannot afford a block]

so high that few people could afford to buy a "round lot" of 100 shares. This limited the demand for the stock and thus kept the total market value of the firm below what it would have been if more shares, at a lower price, had been outstanding. To correct this situation, Porter "split its stock," as described in the next section.

Stock Splits

stock split
An action taken by a firm to increase the number of shares outstanding, such as doubling the number of shares outstanding by giving each stockholder two new shares for each one formerly held.

Although there is little empirical evidence to support the contention, there is nevertheless a widespread belief in financial circles that an *optimal price range* exists for stocks. "Optimal" means that if the price is within this range, the price/earnings ratio, and hence the value of the firm, will be maximized. Many observers, including Porter's management, believe that the best range for most stocks is from $20 to $80 per share. Accordingly, if the price of Porter's stock rose to $80, management would probably declare a two-for-one **stock split**, thus doubling the number of shares outstanding, halving the earnings and dividends per share, and thereby lowering the price of the stock. Each stockholder would have more shares, but each share would be worth less. If the post-split price were $40, Porter's stockholders would be exactly as well off as they were before the split. However, if the price of the stock were to stabilize above $40, stockholders would be better off. Stock splits can be of any size — for example, the stock could be split two-for-one, three-for-one, one-and-a-half-for-one, or in any other way.[11]

Stock Dividends

stock dividend
A dividend paid in the form of additional shares of stock rather than of cash.

Stock dividends are similar to stock splits in that they "divide the pie into smaller slices" without affecting the fundamental position of the current stockholders. On a 5 percent stock dividend, the holder of 100 shares would receive an additional 5 shares (without cost); on a 20 percent stock dividend, the same holder would receive 20 new shares; and so on. Again, the total number of shares is increased, so earnings, dividends, and price per share all decline.

[handwritten margin notes: Splits ≥ large reduction stock dividend ; keep PO constrained "not to high" maintain optimal trading range]

If a firm wants to reduce the price of its stock, should it use a stock split or a stock dividend? Stock splits are generally used after a sharp price run-up to produce a large price reduction. Stock dividends are frequently used on a regular annual basis to keep the stock price more or less constrained. For example, if a firm's earnings and dividends were growing at about 10 percent per year, the price would tend to go up at about that same rate, and it would soon be outside the desired trading range. A 10 percent annual stock dividend would maintain the stock price within the optimal trading range.

---

[11]*Reverse splits,* which reduce the shares outstanding, can even be used. For example, a company whose stock sells for $5 might employ a one-for-five reverse split, exchanging 1 new share for 5 old ones and raising the value of the shares to about $25, which is within the optimal range. LTV Corporation did this after several years of losses had driven its stock price down below the optimal range.

**Table 18-1   Porter Electronic Controls, Inc.:
Stockholders' Equity Accounts,
Pro Forma, December 31, 1989**

Before a Stock Split or Stock Dividend

Common stock (6 million shares authorized, 5 million outstanding, $1 par)	$ 5,000,000
Additional paid-in capital	10,000,000
Retained earnings	155,000,000
Total common stockholders' equity	$170,000,000

After a Two-for-One Stock Split

Common stock (12 million shares authorized, 10 million outstanding, $0.50 par)	$ 5,000,000
Additional paid-in capital	10,000,000
Retained earnings	155,000,000
Total common stockholders' equity	$170,000,000

After a 20 Percent Stock Dividend

Common stock (6 million shares authorized, 6 million outstanding, $1 par)[a]	$ 6,000,000
Additional paid-in capital[b]	89,000,000
Retained earnings[b]	75,000,000
Total common stockholders' equity	$170,000,000

[a]Shares outstanding are increased by 20 percent, from 5 million to 6 million.

[b]A transfer equal to the market value of the new shares is made from the retained earnings account to the additional paid-in capital and common stock accounts:

$$\text{Transfer} = (5{,}000{,}000 \text{ shares})(0.2)(\$80) = \$80{,}000{,}000.$$

Of this $80 million, ($1 par)(1,000,000 shares) = $1,000,000 goes to common stock and $79 million to paid-in capital.

Balance Sheet Effects

Although the economic effects of stock splits and stock dividends are virtually identical, accountants treat them somewhat differently. On a two-for-one split, the shares outstanding are doubled and the stock's par value is halved. This treatment is shown in the middle section of Table 18-1 for Porter Electronic Controls, using a pro forma 1989 balance sheet.

The bottom section of Table 18-1 shows the effect of a 20 percent stock dividend. With a stock dividend, the par value is not reduced, but an accounting entry is made transferring capital from the retained earnings account to the common stock and paid-in capital accounts. The transfer from retained earnings is calculated as follows:

$$\begin{pmatrix}\text{Dollars} \\ \text{transferred from} \\ \text{retained earnings}\end{pmatrix} = \begin{pmatrix}\text{Number} \\ \text{of shares} \\ \text{outstanding}\end{pmatrix}\begin{pmatrix}\text{Percentage} \\ \text{of the} \\ \text{stock dividend}\end{pmatrix}\begin{pmatrix}\text{Market} \\ \text{price of} \\ \text{the stock}\end{pmatrix}.$$

Porter has 5 million shares outstanding, and they sell for $80 each, so a 20 percent stock dividend would require the transfer of $80 million:

$$\text{Dollars transferred} = (5{,}000{,}000)(0.2)(\$80) = \$80{,}000{,}000.$$

Table 18-2   Price Effects of Stock Dividends

	Price at Selected Dates (Percent)		
	6 Months before Ex-Dividend Date	At Ex-Dividend Date	6 Months after Ex-Dividend Date
Cash dividend increase after stock dividend	$100	$109	$108
No cash dividend increase after stock dividend	100	99	88

As shown in the table, $1 million of this $80 million is added to the common stock account and $79 million to the additional paid-in capital account. The retained earnings account is reduced from $155 million to $75 million.[12]

Price Effects

Several empirical studies have examined the effects of stock splits and stock dividends on stock prices.[13] The findings of one, the Barker study, are presented in Table 18-2. When stock dividends were associated with a cash dividend increase, the value of the company's stock rose by 8 percent six months after the ex-dividend date. On the other hand, when stock dividends were not accompanied by cash dividend increases, stock values fell by 12 percent within six months, which approximated the percentage of the average stock dividend.

These data suggest that investors see stock dividends for what they are — simply additional pieces of paper. When stock dividends are accompanied by higher earnings and cash dividends, investors bid up the price of the stock. However, when stock dividends are not accompanied by increases in earnings and cash dividends, the dilution of earnings and dividends per share causes the price of the stock to drop by the same percentage as the stock dividend. The fundamental determinants of price are the underlying earnings and cash dividends per share.

---

[12]Note that Porter could not pay a stock dividend that exceeded 38.75 percent; a stock dividend of that percentage would exhaust the retained earnings. Thus, a firm's ability to declare stock dividends is constrained by the amount of its retained earnings. Of course, if Porter had wanted to pay a 50 percent stock dividend, it could have just switched to a 1.5-for-one stock split and accomplished the same thing.

[13]See C. A. Barker, "Evaluation of Stock Dividends," *Harvard Business Review,* July–August 1958, 99–114. Barker's study has been replicated several times in recent years, and his results are still valid — they have withstood the test of time. Another excellent study, using an entirely different methodology, reached similar conclusions; see Eugene F. Fama, Lawrence Fisher, Michael C. Jensen, and Richard Roll, "The Adjustment of Stock Prices to New Information," *International Economic Review,* February 1969, 1–21.

STOCK REPURCHASES

A recent *Fortune* article entitled "Beating the Market by Buying Back Stock" discussed the fact that during a one-year period, more than 600 major companies had repurchased significant amounts of their own stock. It also gave illustrations of some specific companies' repurchase programs and their effects on stock prices. The article's conclusion was that "buybacks have made a mint for shareholders who stay with the companies carrying them out." This section explains what a **stock repurchase** is, how a repurchase is carried out, and how the financial manager should analyze a possible repurchase program.

There are two principal types of repurchases: (1) situations in which the firm has cash available for distribution to its stockholders, and it distributes this cash by repurchasing shares rather than by paying cash dividends; and (2) situations in which the firm concludes that its capital structure is too heavily weighted with equity, and therefore it sells debt and uses the proceeds to buy back its stock.

Stock that has been repurchased by a firm is called *treasury stock*. If some of the outstanding stock is repurchased, fewer shares will remain outstanding. Assuming that the repurchase does not adversely affect the firm's future earnings, the earnings per share on the remaining shares will increase, resulting in a higher market price per share. As a result, capital gains will have been substituted for dividends.

stock repurchase
A means by which a firm distributes cash to stockholders by buying back shares of its own stock, thereby decreasing shares outstanding, increasing EPS, and, often, increasing the price of the stock.

The Effects of Stock Repurchases

Many companies have been repurchasing their stock in recent years. Until the 1980s, most repurchases amounted to a few million dollars, but in 1985 Phillips Petroleum announced plans for the largest repurchase on record — 81 million of its shares with a market value of $4.1 billion. Other large repurchases have been made by Texaco, IBM, CBS, Coca Cola, Teledyne, Atlantic Richfield, and Goodyear.

The effects of a repurchase can be illustrated with data on American Development Corporation (ADC). The company expected to earn $4.4 million in 1988, and 50 percent of this amount, or $2.2 million, was allocated for distribution to common shareholders. There were 1.1 million shares outstanding, and the market price was $20 a share. ADC believed that it could either use the $2.2 million to repurchase 100,000 of its shares through a tender offer for $22 a share or else pay a cash dividend of $2 a share.[14]

---

[14]Stock repurchases are generally made in one of three ways: (1) A publicly owned firm can simply buy its own stock through a broker on the open market. (2) It can make a *tender offer,* under which it permits stockholders to send in (that is, "tender") their shares to the firm in exchange for a specified price per share. When a firm makes a tender offer, it generally indicates that it will buy up a specified number of shares within a particular time period (usually about two weeks); if more shares are tendered than the company wishes to purchase, purchases are made on a pro rata basis. (3) The firm can purchase a block of shares from one large holder on

The effect of the repurchase on the EPS and market price per share of the remaining stock can be analyzed in the following way:

1. $\text{Current EPS} = \dfrac{\text{Total earnings}}{\text{Number of shares}} = \dfrac{\$4.4 \text{ million}}{1.1 \text{ million}} = \$4 \text{ per share.}$

2. $\text{P/E ratio} = \dfrac{\$20}{\$4} = 5\times.$

3. $\text{EPS after repurchase of 100,000 shares} = \dfrac{\$4.4 \text{ million}}{1 \text{ million}}$
    $= \$4.40 \text{ per share.}$

4. $\text{Expected market price after repurchase} = (\text{P/E})(\text{EPS}) = (5)(\$4.40)$
    $= \$22 \text{ per share.}$

It should be noted from this example that investors would receive benefits of $2 per share in any case, either in the form of a $2 cash dividend or a $2 increase in the stock price. This result would occur because we assumed, first, that shares could be repurchased at exactly $22 a share and, second, that the P/E ratio would remain constant. If shares could be bought for less than $22, the operation would be even better for *remaining* stockholders, but the reverse would hold if ADC paid more than $22 a share. Furthermore, the P/E ratio might change as a result of the repurchase operation, rising if investors viewed it favorably and falling if they viewed it unfavorably. Some factors that might affect P/E ratios are considered next.

Advantages of Repurchases from the Stockholder's Viewpoint

From the stockholder's viewpoint, advantages of repurchases are as follows:

1. Repurchase announcements are often viewed as positive signals by investors because the repurchase is often motivated by management's belief that the firm's shares are undervalued. For example, Teledyne, a $3 billion conglomerate which earned almost $400 million in 1987, paid its first cash dividend ever in that year. Prior to 1987, all profits had either been reinvested in the firm or used to repurchase stock and thus stimulate growth in earnings. Teledyne's stock price increased from $4 per share in 1972 to $390 in 1987, so its stockholders apparently have been happy with this policy. Although the company began paying dividends in 1987, the dividend was only $4 per share versus an EPS of

---

a negotiated basis. If a negotiated purchase is employed, care must be taken to insure that this one stockholder does not receive preferential treatment over other stockholders, or that any preference given can be justified by "sound business reasons." Texaco's management recently was sued by stockholders who were unhappy over the company's repurchase of about $600 million of stock from the Bass Brothers' interests at a substantial premium over the market price. The suit charged that Texaco's management, afraid the Bass Brothers would attempt a takeover, used the buyback to get them off its back. Such payments have been dubbed "greenmail."

$31.68; thus, the payout ratio was only 12.6 percent. *Value Line* predicts that Teledyne will follow a policy in the future of paying out a small percentage of earnings in dividends while continuing to repurchase its own stock.

2. The stockholders have a choice when the firm *repurchases* stock — to sell or not to sell. However, stockholders must accept a *dividend payment* and pay the tax. Thus, in the previous example, those Teledyne stockholders who need cash can sell back some of their shares, whereas those who do not want additional cash can simply retain their stock. From a tax standpoint, in a repurchase both types of stockholders come out ahead. Under Teledyne's low-cash-dividend-plus-repurchases policy, the clientele effect will steer investors who want regular and substantial cash dividends away from the company, but those who do not need current cash dividends (and taxes) will be attracted to it.

3. A qualitative advantage reported by market practitioners is that a repurchase can often remove a large block of stock which is overhanging the market and keeping the price per share down.

Advantages of Repurchases from Management's Viewpoint

From management's viewpoint, the major advantages of repurchases are these:

1. Dividends are "sticky" in the short run because managements are reluctant to raise the dividend if it cannot be maintained in the future — managements dislike cutting cash dividends. Hence, if the excess cash flow is thought to be only temporary, management may prefer to make the distribution in the form of a share repurchase rather than to declare a cash dividend that cannot be maintained.

2. Repurchased stock can be used for acquisitions or to provide shares when stock options are exercised, when convertibles are converted, or when warrants are exercised. Discussions with financial managers indicate that they often like to use repurchased stock rather than newly issued stock for these purposes in order to avoid dilution in earnings per share.

3. If directors have large holdings themselves, they may have especially strong preferences for repurchases rather than dividend payments because of the tax factor.

4. Repurchases can be used to produce large-scale changes in capital structures. For example, Consolidated Edison recently decided to repurchase up to $400 million of its common stock in order to increase its debt ratio. The repurchase was necessary because even if the company financed its capital budget only with debt, it would still have taken years to get the debt ratio up to the target level. Con Ed used a repurchase program to produce an instantaneous change in its capital structure. Goodyear and GenCorp followed similar strategies in 1987.

Disadvantages of Repurchases from the Stockholder's Viewpoint

From the stockholder's viewpoint, disadvantages of repurchases include the following:

1. Stockholders may not be indifferent between the choices of dividends and capital gains, and the price of the stock might benefit more from cash dividends than from repurchases. Cash dividends are generally thought to be relatively dependable, but repurchases are not. Further, if a firm was to announce a regular, dependable repurchase program, the improper accumulation tax would probably become more of a threat. Although Teledyne has apparently had no problems in this regard, its repurchases are irregular, which may make a difference.

2. The *selling* stockholders may not be fully aware of all the implications of a repurchase, or they may not have all pertinent information about the corporation's present and future activities. However, firms generally announce a repurchase program before embarking on it to avoid potential stockholder suits.

3. The corporation may pay too high a price for the repurchased stock, to the disadvantage of remaining stockholders. If the shares are inactively traded, and if the firm seeks to acquire a relatively large amount of its own stock, the price may be bid above its equilibrium price and then fall after the firm ceases its repurchase operations. Con Ed attempted to minimize this problem by authorizing its investment banker, Goldman Sachs, to buy shares if and only if they could be acquired at or below a stipulated price, and then by taking close to a year to complete the repurchase program.

Disadvantages of Repurchases from Management's Viewpoint

From management's viewpoint, disadvantages of repurchases are as follows:

1. Repurchases might involve some risk from a legal standpoint. If the Internal Revenue Service established that the primary purpose of the repurchases was to avoid paying taxes on dividends, penalties could then be imposed on the firm under the improper accumulation of earnings provision of the Tax Code. Congress would also probably act if tax avoidance implications were blatant. IRS suits have been brought against privately held companies, but no actions have been instituted against publicly owned firms, even though some have retired more than half of their outstanding stock.

2. The SEC could raise questions if it appears that the firm may be manipulating the price of its shares. This factor keeps firms from doing much repurchasing if they plan offerings of other types of securities in the near future, or if they contemplate merger negotiations in which their stock would be exchanged for that of the acquired company.

Conclusions on Stock Repurchases

When all the pros and cons on stock repurchases have been totaled, where do we stand? Our conclusions may be summarized as follows:

1. Because of uncertainties about their tax treatment, repurchases on a regular, systematic, dependable basis may not be feasible.

2. However, repurchases do offer investors the opportunity to delay taxes on their profits, and for this reason alone they should be given careful consideration.

3. Repurchases can be especially valuable to a firm that wants to make a significant shift in its capital structure within a short period of time.

On balance, companies probably ought to be doing more repurchasing and distributing less cash as dividends than they are. Increases in the size and frequency of repurchases in recent years suggest that companies are increasingly reaching this same conclusion.

Small Business

DIVIDEND POLICY FOR SMALL BUSINESSES

The dividend policy decision involves determining the amount of earnings to distribute to stockholders. While most large, mature firms do pay out some portion of earnings each year, many small, rapidly growing firms pay no dividends whatsoever. As the small firm grows, so does its need for financing. However, small businesses have limited access to the capital markets, so they must rely on internal financing (retained earnings) to a greater extent than larger firms. Over time, though, as the firm and its products mature, its growth will slow, its financing requirements will lessen, and at some point it will begin to pay dividends.

Apple Computer can be used to illustrate this process. Apple was founded in 1977, and its first year sales were $660,000. In 1978, sales increased by 550 percent, to $3.6 million, and the company earned a profit of $660,000. Growth continued at a rapid pace in the following years. Initially, all of the stock was owned by the founders and a few venture capitalists. These investors wanted to insure the company's success, and they also were more interested in capital gains than in taxable dividends, so the firm did not pay any dividends. Indeed, from 1978 to 1987, all earnings were plowed back and used to support growth, which averaged about 50 percent annually. We should also point out that Apple has never issued debt; it has chosen instead to support its growth by retaining earnings and by occasionally issuing additional shares of common stock. Apple had 126 million shares of stock outstanding in 1988, up from 33 million in 1978.

By 1987, new competitors had entered the market, and Apple's growth was slowing down. *Value Line's* analysts estimated that Apple's revenues would grow at an annual rate of 19 percent during the period 1987 to 1992. While a growth rate of 19 percent per year is well above average, it is far below Apple's earlier growth rate of 50 percent. On the basis of these growth forecasts, Apple's board of directors met early in 1987 and declared a quarterly dividend of $0.06 per share. The stock price reacted favorably, so the dividend was raised in the fourth quarter to $0.08 per quarter, or $0.32 per year.

This story illustrates three points. First, small, rapidly growing firms generally need to retain all their earnings, and to obtain additional capital from outside sources, to support growth. Growth requires cash, and even highly profitable companies like Apple have difficulty generating enough cash from earnings to support rapid growth. Second, as the firm matures, and as its growth slows down, its need for funds diminishes. Thus, when Apple's growth began to slow down, it no longer needed to retain all of its earnings, so it began to pay a small dividend. Third, as we saw earlier in the chapter, the sale of stock by a mature firm is often interpreted by investors to mean that management expects bad times ahead. However, this is not the case when the issuer is a young, rapidly growing firm: the market recognizes that new, profitable firms often grow so fast that they simply must issue common stock, and that such issues indicate that the firm's managers see good investment opportunities.

SUMMARY AND KEY CONCEPTS

Dividend policy involves the decision to pay out earnings versus retaining them for reinvestment in the firm. Dividend policy decisions can have either favorable or unfavorable effects on the price of the firm's stock. The key factors influencing a firm's dividend policy are as follows:

- The **optimal dividend policy** is that policy which strikes a balance between current dividends and future growth and thereby maximizes the price of the firm's stock.

- Miller and Modigliani developed the **dividend irrelevance theory**, which holds that a firm's dividend policy has no effect either on the value of the firm or on its cost of capital.

- The **"bird-in-the-hand" theory** advocated by Gordon and Lintner holds that the value of the firm will be maximized by a high dividend payout ratio, because investors regard actual dividends as being less risky than potential capital gains.

- Because **empirical tests** of the two theories **have been inconclusive**, academicians simply cannot tell corporate managers with any degree of precision how a change in dividend policy will affect stock prices and capital costs.

- Dividend policy may also be influenced by the **information content of dividends (signaling)** and by the **clientele effect**. The information content, or signaling, hypothesis states that investors regard dividend changes as a signal of management's forecast of future earnings. The clientele effect suggests that a firm will tend to attract the type of investor who likes the firm's dividend policy.

- In practice, most firms try to follow a policy of paying a **constant, or steadily increasing, dividend**. This policy provides investors with a stable real income and, if the signaling theory is correct, also tells investors that management expects earnings to grow at this same rate.

- Other dividend policies used include: (1) the **residual dividend policy**, in which dividends are paid out of earnings left over after the capital budget has been financed; (2) the **constant payout ratio policy**, in which a constant percentage of earnings are paid out each year; and (3) the **low-regular-dividend-plus-extras policy**, in which the firm pays a constant, low dividend which can be maintained even in bad years, and then pays an extra dividend in good years.

- **Dividend reinvestment plans (DRPs)** allow stockholders to have the company automatically use dividends to purchase additional shares of the firm's stock for them. DRPs are popular with investors who do not need current income because the plans allow stockholders to acquire additional shares without incurring normal brokerage fees.

- Other factors, such as **legal constraints, investment opportunities, availability and cost of funds from other sources**, and **taxes**, are considered by managers when dividend policies are established.

- A **stock split** is an action taken by a firm to increase the number of shares outstanding. Normally, splits reduce the price per share in proportion to the share increase because they merely "divide the pie into smaller slices." A **stock dividend** is a dividend paid in additional shares of stock rather than in cash. Stock dividends and splits are used by managers to keep stock prices within an "optimal" range.

- Under a **stock repurchase plan**, a firm buys back some of its outstanding stock, thereby decreasing the number of shares, which in turn increases both EPS and the stock price. Repurchases are useful for making major changes in a firm's capital structure, as well as for allowing stockholders to delay paying taxes on their share of the firm's profits.

Questions

18-1   As an investor, would you rather invest in a firm that has a policy of maintaining (a) a constant payout ratio, (b) a constant dollar dividend per share, (c) a target dividend growth rate, or (d) a constant regular quarterly dividend plus a year-end extra when earnings are sufficiently high or corporate investment needs sufficiently low? Explain your answer, stating how these policies would affect your k_s. Discuss also how your answer might change if you were a student, a 50-year-old professional with peak earnings, or a retiree.

18-2   How would each of the following changes tend to affect aggregate (that is, the average for all corporations) payout ratios, other things held constant? Explain your answers.
a. An increase in the personal income tax rate.
b. A liberalization of depreciation for federal income tax purposes — that is, faster tax write-offs.
c. A rise in interest rates.
d. An increase in corporate profits.
e. A decline in investment opportunities.
f. Permission for corporations to deduct dividends for tax purposes as they now do interest charges.

g. A change in the Tax Code so that both realized and unrealized capital gains in any year were taxed at the same rate as dividends.

18-3   Discuss the pros and cons of having the directors formally announce what a firm's dividend policy will be in the future.

18-4   Most firms would like to have their stock selling at a high P/E ratio, and they would also like to have extensive public ownership (many different shareholders). Explain how stock dividends or stock splits may help achieve these goals.

18-5   What is the difference between a stock dividend and a stock split? As a stockholder, would you prefer to see your company declare a 100 percent stock dividend or a two-for-one split? Assume that either action is feasible.

18-6   "The cost of retained earnings is less than the cost of new outside equity capital. Consequently, it is totally irrational for a firm to sell a new issue of stock and to pay dividends during the same year." Discuss this statement.

18-7   Would it ever be rational for a firm to borrow money in order to pay dividends? Explain.

18-8   "Executive salaries have been shown to be more closely correlated to the size of the firm than to its profitability. If a firm's board of directors is controlled by management instead of by outside directors, this might result in the firm's retaining more earnings than can be justified from the stockholders' point of view." Discuss the statement, being sure (a) to use Figure 18-4 in your answer and (b) to explain the implied relationship between dividend policy and stock prices.

18-9   Modigliani and Miller (MM) on the one hand and Gordon and Lintner (GL) on the other have expressed strong views regarding the effect of dividend policy on a firm's cost of capital and value.
   a. In essence, what are the MM and GL views regarding the effect of dividend policy on the cost of capital and stock prices?
   b. According to the text, which of these theories, if any, has received statistical confirmation from empirical tests?
   c. How could MM use the *information content,* or *signaling, hypothesis* to counter their opponents' arguments? If you were debating MM, how would you counter them?
   d. How could MM use the *clientele effect* concept to counter their opponents' arguments? If you were debating MM, how would you counter them?

18-10   More NYSE companies had stock dividends and stock splits during the first 9 months of 1985 than during the whole 12 months of the previous record high year, 1983. Would you guess that the stock market was strong or weak in 1985? Explain the rationale that a financial vice-president might give his or her board of directors to support a stock split/dividend recommendation.

18-11   Refer to the chapter-opening vignette, where we discussed United Brands' dividend policy. Do you think UB should increase its dividend, repurchase shares, or declare either a stock dividend or split?

Self-Test Problems   *(Solutions Appear on Page 723)*

Key terms

ST-1   Define each of the following terms:
   a. Optimal dividend policy
   b. Dividend irrelevance theory; "bird-in-the-hand" theory
   c. Information content, or signaling, hypothesis; clientele effect
   d. Residual dividend policy
   e. Extra dividend
   f. Declaration date; holder-of-record date; ex-dividend date; payment date
   g. Dividend reinvestment plan (DRP)
   h. Stock split; stock dividend
   i. Stock repurchase

Alternative dividend policies

ST-2   Components Manufacturing Corporation (CMC) has an all-common-equity capital structure. It has 200,000 shares of $2 par value common stock outstanding.

   When CMC's founder, who was also its research director and most successful inventor, retired unexpectedly to the South Pacific in late 1988, CMC was left suddenly and permanently with materially lower growth expectations and relatively few attractive new investment opportunities. Unfortunately, there was no way to replace the founder's contributions to the firm. Previously, CMC found it necessary to plow back most of its earnings to finance growth, which averaged 12 percent per year. Future growth at a 5 percent rate is considered realistic, but that level would call for an increase in the dividend payout. Further, it now appears that new investment projects with at least the 14 percent rate of return required by CMC's stockholders ($k_s = 14\%$) would amount to only $800,000 for 1989 in comparison to a projected $2,000,000 of net income after taxes. If the existing 20 percent dividend payout were continued, retained earnings would be $1.6 million in 1989, but, as noted, investments which yield the 14 percent cost of capital would amount to only $800,000.

   The one encouraging thing is that the high earnings from existing assets are expected to continue, and net income of $2 million is still expected for 1989. Given the dramatically changed circumstances, CMC's management is reviewing the firm's dividend policy.

   a. Assuming that the acceptable 1989 investment projects would be financed entirely by earnings retained during the year, calculate DPS in 1989, assuming that CMC uses the residual payment policy.
   b. What payout ratio does your answer to Part a imply for 1989?
   c. If a 60 percent payout ratio is maintained for the foreseeable future, what is your estimate of the present market price of the common stock? How does this compare with the market price that should have prevailed under the assumptions existing just before the news about the founder's retirement? If the two values of P_0 are different, comment on why.
   d. What would happen to the price of the stock if the old 20 percent payout were continued? Assume that if this payout is maintained, the average rate of return on the retained earnings will fall to 7.5 percent and the new growth rate will be

$$g = (1.0 - \text{Payout ratio})(\text{ROE})$$
$$= (1.0 - 0.2)(7.5\%)$$
$$= (0.8)(7.5\%) = 6.0\%.$$

Problems

Residual policy   **18-1**   One position expressed in the financial literature is that firms set their dividends as a residual after using income to support new investment.

    a. Explain what a residual dividend policy implies, illustrating your answer with a graph showing how different conditions could lead to different dividend payout ratios.

    b. Could the residual dividend policy be consistent with (1) a constant growth-rate policy, (2) a constant payout policy, and/or (3) a low-regular-dividend-plus-extras policy? Answer in terms of both short-run, year-to-year consistency and longer-run consistency.

    c. Think back to Chapter 17, in which we considered the relationship between capital structure and the cost of capital. If the k_a versus debt ratio plot was shaped like a sharp V, would this have a different implication for the importance of setting dividends according to the residual policy than if the plot was shaped like a shallow bowl (or a flattened U)?

    d. Assume that Companies A and B both have IOS schedules that intersect their MCC schedules at a point which, under the residual policy, calls for a 20 percent payout. In both cases, a 20 percent payout would require a cut in the annual dividend from $2 to $1. One company cuts its dividend, whereas the other does not. One company has a relatively steep IOS curve, whereas the other has a relatively flat one. Explain which company probably has the steeper curve.

External equity financing   **18-2**   Arizona Heating and Cooling, Inc., has a six-month backlog of orders for its patented solar heating system. To meet this demand, management plans to expand production capacity by 40 percent with an $8 million investment in plant machinery. The firm wants to maintain a 40 percent debt-to-total-assets ratio in its capital structure; it also wants to maintain its past dividend policy of distributing 40 percent of last year's after-tax earnings. In 1988, after-tax earnings were $4 million. How much external equity must Arizona seek at the beginning of 1989 to expand capacity as desired?

Dividend payout   **18-3**   Warner Systems, Inc., expects next year's after-tax income to be $10 million. The firm's debt ratio is currently 40 percent. Warner has $8 million of profitable investment opportunities, and it wishes to maintain its existing debt ratio. According to the residual dividend policy, how large should Warner's dividend payout ratio be next year?

Stock split   **18-4**   After a four-for-one stock split, the Kish Company paid a dividend of $1 per new share, which represents an 8 percent increase over last year's pre-split dividend. What was last year's dividend per share?

Stock dividend   **18-5**   Guira Corporation declared a 4 percent stock dividend plus a cash dividend of $0.60 per share. The cash dividend was paid on both the old shares and the new shares received from the stock dividend. Construct a pro forma balance sheet showing the effect of these actions; use one new balance sheet that incorporates both actions. The stock was selling for $25 per share, and a condensed version of Guira's balance sheet as of December 31, 1988, before the dividends, follows (millions of dollars):

Cash	$ 75	Debt	$1,000
Other assets	1,925	Common stock (60 million shares authorized, 50 million shares outstanding, $1 par)	50
		Paid-in capital	200
		Retained earnings	750
Total assets	$2,000	Total liabilities and equity	$2,000

Alternative dividend policies

18-6   In 1988 the Kahn Company paid dividends totaling $3,000,000 on after-tax income of $9 million. 1988 was a normal year, and for the past 10 years, earnings have grown at a constant rate of 10 percent. However, in 1989, earnings are expected to jump to $12 million, and the firm expects to have profitable investment opportunities of $7 million. It is predicted that Kahn will not be able to maintain the 1989 level of earnings growth — the high 1989 earnings level is attributable to an exceptionally profitable new product line introduced that year — and the company will return to its previous 10 percent growth rate. Kahn's target debt ratio is 40 percent.

a. Calculate Kahn's total dividends for 1989 if it follows each of the following policies:
  1. Its 1989 dividend payment is set to force dividends to grow at the long-run growth rate in earnings.
  2. It continues the 1988 dividend payout ratio.
  3. It uses a pure residual dividend policy (40 percent of the $7 million investment is financed with debt).
  4. It employs a regular-dividend-plus-extras policy, with the regular dividend being based on the long-run growth rate and the extra dividend being set according to the residual policy.

b. Which of the preceding policies would you recommend? Restrict your choices to the ones listed, but justify your answer.

c. Assume that investors expect Kahn to pay total dividends of $7,500,000 in 1989 and to have the dividend grow at 10 percent after 1989. The total market value of the stock is $150 million. What is the company's cost of equity?

d. What is Kahn's long-run average return on equity? (Hint: $g = b(\text{ROE})$.)

e. Does a 1989 dividend of $7,500,000 seem reasonable in view of your answers to Parts c and d? If not, should the dividend be higher or lower?

Dividend policy and capital structure

18-7   Tampa Tobacco Company has for many years enjoyed a moderate but stable growth in sales and earnings. However, cigar consumption and consequently Tampa's sales have been falling recently, primarily because of an increasing awareness of the dangers of smoking to health.

Anticipating further declines in tobacco sales for the future, Tampa's management hopes eventually to move almost entirely out of the tobacco business and into a newly developed, diversified product line in growth-oriented industries. The company is especially interested in the prospects for pollution-control devices, because its research department has already done much work on the problems of filtering smoke. Right now the company estimates that an investment of $12 million is necessary to purchase new facilities and to begin operations on these products, but the investment could be earning a return of about 18 percent within a short time. The only other available investment opportunity totals $4.8 million, is expected to return about 10.2 percent, and is indivisible — that is, it must be accepted in its entirety or else be rejected.

The company is expected to pay a $2.40 dividend on its 3 million outstanding shares, the same as its dividend last year. The directors might, however, change the dividend if there are good reasons for doing so. Total earnings for the year are expected to be $11.4 million; the common stock is currently selling for $45; the firm's target debt ratio (debt/assets ratio) is 45 percent; and its tax rate is 40 percent. The costs of various forms of financing are as follows:

New bonds, $k_d = 11\%$. This is a before-tax rate.

New common stock sold at $45 per share will net $41.

Required rate of return on retained earnings, $k_s = 14\%$.

a. Calculate Tampa's expected payout ratio, the break point at which MCC rises, and its marginal cost of capital above and below the point of exhaustion of retained earnings at the current payout. (Hint: k_s is given, and D_1/P_0 can be found. Then, knowing k_s and D_1/P_0, g can be determined.)

b. How large should Tampa's capital budget be for the year?

c. What is an appropriate dividend policy for Tampa? How should the capital budget be financed?

d. How might risk factors influence Tampa's cost of capital, capital structure, and dividend policy?

e. What assumptions, if any, do your answers to the preceding parts make about investors' preferences for dividends versus capital gains (in other words, their preferences regarding the D_1/P_0 and g components of k_s)?

Dividend policy
(Integrative)

18-8   Information Systems, Inc., (ISI), was founded 5 years ago by Michael Taylor and Karen Black, who are still its only stockholders. ISI has now reached the stage where outside equity capital is necessary to maintain its optimal capital structure of 60 percent equity and 40 percent debt. Therefore, Taylor and Black have decided to take the company public. Up to this point, Taylor and Black have routinely reinvested all earnings in the firm and hence dividend policy has not been an issue, but now they must decide on a dividend policy.

Assume that you were recently hired by Arthur Adamson & Company, a consulting firm which has been asked to help ISI prepare for its public offering. Tom Nickols, the senior consultant in your group, has asked you to review some basic dividend policy issues and to answer the following questions:

a. 1. What is meant by a firm's dividend policy?
    2. What are the two major theories regarding dividend policy's effect on a firm's value? Briefly describe each theory.
    3. What do the two theories indicate regarding an optimal dividend policy?
    4. Construct a graph with dividend yield on the Y axis and capital gains yield on the X axis. Now assume that if the company paid out all earnings as dividends, it would have a required rate of return of 15 percent. Plot dividend yield versus capital gains yield for alternative payout ratios under each dividend policy theory. Explain your plots.
    5. Has empirical testing been able to prove which theory, if any, is correct?

b. 1. Discuss the information content, or signaling, hypothesis.
    2. Discuss the clientele effect.

c. 1. Explain in general terms what the residual dividend policy is.
    2. Assume that ISI has an $800,000 capital budget planned for the coming year. You have determined that its present capital structure (60 percent equity and 40 percent debt) is optimal, and its net income is forecasted at $600,000. What would be the total dollar dividend and the payout ratio if the firm used the residual policy. What if net income were forecasted at $400,000? $800,000?
    3. How would a change in investment opportunities affect the residual payment policy?
    4. What are the advantages and disadvantages of the residual policy? (Hint: Think about signaling and the clientele effect.)

d. What are the three other dividend payment policies? What are their advantages and disadvantages? Which are more widely used in practice?

e. Briefly describe dividend reinvestment plans.

f. Briefly describe how most firms set their dividend policy in practice.

g. What are stock repurchases? Discuss the advantages and disadvantages of stock repurchases.

h. What are stock dividends and stock splits? When should a firm consider using a stock dividend? When should a firm consider splitting its stock?

Computer-Related Problem

(Work the problem in this section only if you are using the computer problem diskette.)

Dividend policy and capital structure

C18-1   Use the model for Problem C18-1 in the file C18 to work this problem. Refer back to Problem 18-7. Assume that Tampa's management is considering a change in the firm's capital structure to include more debt; thus, management would like to analyze the effects of an increase in the debt ratio to 65 percent. The treasurer believes that such a move would cause lenders to increase the required rate of return on new bonds to 12 percent and that k_s would rise to 14.5 percent.

a. How would this change affect the optimal capital budget?

b. If k_s rose to 16 percent, would the low-return project be acceptable?

c. Would the project selection be affected if the dividend was reduced to $1.50 from $2.40, still assuming $k_s = 16$ percent?

Solutions to Self-Test Problems

ST-1 Refer to the marginal glossary definitions and the relevant sections of your text to check your responses.

ST-2 a.

Projected net income	$2,000,000
Less projected capital investments	800,000
Available residual	$1,200,000
Shares outstanding	200,000

$$\text{DPS} = \$1,200,000/200,000 \text{ shares} = \$6 = D_1.$$

b. $\text{EPS} = \$2,000,000/200,000 \text{ shares} = \$10.$

$\text{Payout ratio} = \text{DPS/EPS} = \$6/\$10 = 60\%, \text{ or}$

$\text{Total dividends/NI} = \$1,200,000/\$2,000,000 = 60\%.$

c. Currently, $P_0 = \dfrac{D_1}{k_s - g} = \dfrac{\$6}{0.14 - 0.05} = \dfrac{\$6}{0.09} = \$66.67.$

Under the former circumstances, D_1 would be based on a 20 percent payout on $10 EPS, or $2. With $k_s = 14\%$ and $g = 12\%$, we solve for P_0:

$$P_0 = \frac{D_1}{k_s - g} = \frac{\$2}{0.14 - 0.12} = \frac{\$2}{0.02} = \$100.$$

Although CMC has suffered a severe setback, its existing assets will continue to provide a good income stream. More of these earnings should now be passed on to the shareholders, as the slowed internal growth has reduced the need for funds. However, the net result is a 33 percent decrease in the value of the shares.

d. If the payout ratio were continued at 20 percent, even after internal investment opportunities had declined, the price of the stock would drop to $2/(0.14 − 0.06) = $25 rather than to $66.67. Thus, an increase in the dividend payout is consistent with maximizing shareholder wealth.

Because of the downward-sloping IOS curve (see Figure 18-4), the greater the firm's level of investment, the lower the average ROE. Thus, the more money CMC retains and invests, the lower its average ROE will be. We can determine the average ROE under different conditions as follows:

Old situation (with founder active and a 20 percent payout):

$$g = (1.0 - \text{Payout ratio})(\text{Average ROE})$$

$$12\% = (1.0 - 0.2)(\text{Average ROE})$$

$$\text{Average ROE} = 12\%/0.8 = 15\% > k_s = 14\%.$$

Note that the *average* ROE is 15 percent whereas the *marginal* ROE is presumably equal to 14 percent. In terms of a graph like Figure 18-4, the intersection of the MCC and IOS curves would be 14 percent, and the average of the IOS curve above the intersection would be 15 percent.

New situation (with founder retired and a 60 percent payout):

$$g = 6\% = (1.0 - 0.6)(\text{ROE})$$

$$\text{ROE} = 6\%/0.4 = 15\% > k_s = 14\%.$$

This suggests that the new payout is appropriate and that the firm is taking on investments down to the point at which marginal returns are equal to the cost of capital. In terms of a graph like Figure 18-4, the IOS curve shifted to the left after the founder retired. Note that if the 20 percent payout was maintained, the *average* ROE would be only 7.5 percent, which would imply a marginal ROE far below the 14 percent cost of capital.

VI Working Capital Management

19 Working Capital Policy and Short-Term Credit

AFTER RIDING THE WAVE OF SHORT-TERM INTEREST RATES, TRANSAMERICA'S DEBT EXPENSES TAKE A REFRESHING PLUNGE

Several years ago Transamerica Corporation, a major financial services company, was financing a substantial portion of its total assets with short-term, variable-rate debt. Short-term rates had generally been lower than long-term rates, and thus Transamerica had reduced its interest expense by following this financing policy. Then, however, short-term interest rates soared to unprecedented levels, and Transamerica's interest costs rose equally sharply, contributing to a severe drop in profits. Transamerica's chairman later described the situation as follows:

> In the past two years we have reduced our variable-rate [short-term] debt by about $450 million. We aren't going to go through the enormous increase in debt expense again. Our earnings fell sharply when money rates rose to record levels because we were almost entirely in variable-rate debt. Now, out of total debt of slightly more than $1 billion, about 65 percent is fixed rate and 35 percent variable. We've come a long way, and we'll keep plugging away at it.

Transamerica's earnings and stock price had been hurt by the rise in interest rates, but other companies were even less fortunate — they simply could not pay the rising interest charges, and this forced them into bankruptcy.

WORKING capital policy involves decisions relating to these questions: (1) How much should we invest in current assets, and (2) how should we finance that investment? About 40 percent of the typical firm's capital is invested in current assets, so providing correct answers to these questions is vitally important to the firm's profitability.

WORKING CAPITAL TERMINOLOGY

We begin our discussion of working capital by defining some basic terms and concepts:

working capital
A firm's investment in short-term assets — cash, marketable securities, inventory, and accounts receivable.

net working capital
Current assets minus current liabilities.

working capital policy
Basic policy decisions regarding target levels for each category of current assets, and regarding how current assets will be financed.

1. **Working capital**, sometimes called *gross working capital*, simply means current assets.
2. **Net working capital** is defined as current assets minus current liabilities.
3. One key working capital ratio is the *current ratio*, which was defined in Chapter 7 as current assets divided by current liabilities. This ratio measures a firm's liquidity, or its ability to meet current obligations.
4. The *quick ratio*, or *acid test*, is current assets minus inventories divided by current liabilities. This ratio, which also measures liquidity, removes inventories from current assets because they are the least liquid of those assets, and it thus provides an "acid test" of a company's ability to meet its current obligations.
5. **Working capital policy** refers to the firm's basic policies regarding (1) target levels for each category of current assets and (2) how current assets will be financed.
6. *Working capital management* involves the administration, within policy guidelines, of current assets and current liabilities.

The term *working capital* originated with the old Yankee peddler, who would load up his wagon with goods and then go off on his route to peddle his wares. The merchandise was his working capital because it was what he actually sold, or "turned over," to produce his profits. The wagon and horse were his fixed assets. He generally owned the horse and wagon, so they were financed with "equity" capital, but he borrowed the funds to buy the merchandise. These borrowings were called *working capital loans,* and they had to be repaid after each trip to demonstrate to the bank that the credit was sound. If the peddler was able to repay the loan, then the bank would make another one, and banks that followed this rule were said to be employing sound banking practices.

We must distinguish between those current liabilities which are specifically used to finance current assets and those current liabilities which represent (1) current maturities of long-term debt, (2) financing associated with a construction program which will, after the project is completed, be funded with the proceeds of a long-term security issue, or (3) the financing of fixed assets.

Table 19-1   Drexel Card Company:
Balance Sheet as of January 1 and June 30, 1989
(Thousands of Dollars)

	January 1 (Actual)	June 30 (Projected)		January 1 (Actual)	June 30 (Projected)
Cash and marketable securities	$ 20	$ 20	Accounts payable	$ 30[a]	$ 50[a]
Accounts receivable	80	20	Accrued wages	15	10
Inventories	100	200	Accrued taxes	15	10
			Notes payable	50	80
			Current maturities of long-term debt	40	40
Total current assets	$200	$240	Total current liabilities	$150	$190
Fixed assets	500	500	Long-term debt	150	140
			Stockholders' equity	400	410
Total assets	$700	$740	Total liabilities and equity	$700	$740

[a]DCC takes discounts, so this is "free" trade credit. This point is discussed in detail later in the chapter, but it should be noted here that accounts payable represent an interest-free loan to a firm that takes discounts. This is because the firm gets credit but pays no interest on this credit, whereas it would pay interest on bank credit.

Table 19-1 contains the actual and projected balance sheets of Drexel Card Company (DCC), a manufacturer of greeting cards, as of January 1 and June 30 of 1989. According to the preceding definitions, DCC's January 1 working capital is $200,000, whereas its net working capital is $200,000 − $150,000 = $50,000. Also, DCC's initial current ratio is 1.33, and its initial quick ratio is 0.67. However, the total current liabilities of $150,000 include the current portion of long-term debt, which is $40,000. This account is unaffected by changes in working capital policy, since it is a function of the firm's long-term financing decisions. Thus, even though the long-term debt coming due in the next accounting period is defined as a current liability, it is not a working capital decision variable. Similarly, if DCC were building a new factory and financing it with short-term loans that were to be converted to a mortgage bond when the building was completed, the construction loans would be separated from the current liabilities associated with working capital management.

REQUIREMENT FOR EXTERNAL WORKING CAPITAL FINANCING

The manufacture of greeting cards is a seasonal business. In June of each year, DCC begins producing Christmas and New Year cards for sale in the July–November period, and by the end of the year it has sold most of them; thus, its inventories are relatively low at year-end. However, most of its buyers purchase on credit, so the year-end receivables are at a seasonal high. Now look again at Table 19-1, this time at DCC's projected balance sheet for June 30, 1989. Here we see that inventories will be relatively high ($200,000 versus $100,000), as will accounts payable ($50,000 versus $30,000), but receivables are projected to be relatively low ($20,000 versus $80,000).

Now consider what happens to DCC's current assets and current liabilities during the period from January 1 to June 1989. Total current assets are projected to increase from $200,000 to $240,000, so the firm must finance this $40,000. However, during the same period, payables and accruals will spontaneously increase by $10,000 — from $30,000 + $15,000 + $15,000 = $60,000 to $50,000 + $10,000 + $10,000 = $70,000 — so the company is left with only a $30,000 projected net working capital financing requirement. This requirement could be obtained from various sources, but because such seasonal needs are typically met by bank financing, we assume that the $30,000 will be obtained from the bank. Therefore, on June 30, 1989, we project notes payable of $80,000, up from $50,000 on January 1.

The fluctuations in DCC's working capital position as shown in Table 19-1 resulted from seasonal variations. Similar fluctuations in working capital requirements, and hence in financing needs, also occur during business cycles; working capital needs typically decline during recessions and increase during booms. In the following sections we look in more detail at working capital variations, at alternative plans for establishing the target level of current assets, and at strategies for financing current assets.

THE WORKING CAPITAL CASH FLOW CYCLE

As we noted above, the concept of working capital management originated with the old Yankee peddler, who would borrow to buy inventory, sell the inventory and obtain cash, pay off the bank loan, and then repeat the cycle. That general concept has been applied to more complex businesses, and it is useful when analyzing the effectiveness of a firm's working capital management process.

We can illustrate the process with data from Real Time Computer Corporation (RTC), which in early 1988 introduced a new super-minicomputer that can perform 15 million instructions per second and that will sell for $250,000. The effects of this new product on RTC's working capital position were analyzed in terms of its *working capital cash flow cycle*. RTC anticipated a demand for 100 of the new machines. The following are the steps in the cash flow cycle and the effects of the production decision on RTC's working capital position:

1. RTC will order and then receive the raw materials that it needs to produce the 100 computers. Because RTC and most other firms purchase raw materials on credit, this transaction will create an account payable, but the decision will have no immediate cash flow effect.

2. Labor will be used to convert the raw materials into finished computers. However, wages will not be fully paid at the time the work is done, so accrued wages will build up.

3. The finished computers will be sold, usually on credit, so sales will create receivables, not immediate cash inflows.

4. At some point during the cycle, RTC must pay off its accounts payable and accrued wages. Because these payments will normally be required before RTC has collected cash from its receivables, a net cash outflow will occur, and this outflow must be financed.

5. The working capital cash flow cycle will be completed when RTC's receivables have been collected; at this point, the company will be in a position to pay off the loans that were used to finance production, and it can then repeat the cycle.

This approach centers on the conversion of operating events to cash flows, and it is thus called the **cash conversion cycle** model.[1] The following are some terms used in the model:

cash conversion cycle
The length of time between the payment for the purchase of raw materials and the collection of accounts receivable generated by the sale of the final product.

1. *Inventory conversion period,* which is the average length of time required to convert raw materials into finished goods and then to sell these goods. Note that the inventory conversion period can be calculated as 360 divided by the inventory turnover ratio (Sales/Inventory). For example, if sales are $10 million and average inventories are $1.39 million, then the inventory turnover ratio is $10 million/$1.39 million = 7.2, and the inventory conversion period is 360/7.2 = 50 days:

$$\text{Inventory conversion period} = \frac{360}{\text{Sales/Inventory}}$$

$$= \frac{360}{\$10 \text{ million}/\$1.39 \text{ million}}$$

$$= 360/7.2 = 50 \text{ days.}$$

Thus, it takes an average of 50 days from the purchase of raw materials to the sale of finished goods.

2. *Receivables conversion period,* which is the average length of time required to convert the firm's receivables into cash, that is, to collect cash following a sale. The receivables conversion period is also called the average collection period (ACP), and it was calculated in Chapter 7 as receivables/sales per day = receivables/(sales/360). If receivables are $1.11 million and sales are $10 million, the ACP is

---

[1]See Verlyn D. Richards and Eugene J. Laughlin, "A Cash Conversion Cycle Approach to Liquidity Analysis," *Financial Management,* Spring 1980, 32–38.

Figure 19-1   The Cash Conversion Cycle

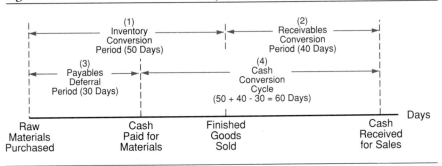

$$ACP = \text{Receivables conversion period} = \frac{\$1.11 \text{ million}}{\$10 \text{ million}/360} = 40 \text{ days.}$$

Thus, it takes 40 days after a sale to convert the receivables into cash.

3. *Payables deferral period,* which is the average length of time between the purchase of raw materials and labor and the payment of cash for them. For example, the firm might on average have 30 days to pay for labor and materials.

4. *Cash conversion cycle,* which nets out the three periods just defined and which therefore equals the length of time between the firm's actual cash expenditures on productive resources (raw materials and labor) and its own cash receipts from the sale of products (that is, from the day labor and/or suppliers are paid to the day receivables are collected). The cash conversion cycle thus equals the length of time the firm has funds tied up in working capital.

We can now use these definitions to analyze the cash conversion cycle. First, the concept is diagrammed in Figure 19-1. Each component is given a number, and the cash conversion cycle can be expressed by this equation:

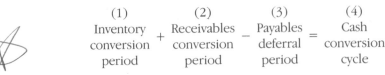

To illustrate, suppose it takes Real Time Computers an average of 50 days to convert raw materials to computers and to make a sale, and it takes another 40 days to collect on receivables (ACP = 40), while 30 days normally lapse between receipt of raw materials and payment of the associated account payable. In this case, the cash conversion cycle is 60 days:

$$50 \text{ days} + 40 \text{ days} - 30 \text{ days} = 60 \text{ days.}$$

To look at it another way,

Receipts delay   − Payment delay = Net delay
(50 days + 40 days) −   (30 days)   = 60 days.

Given these data, RTC knows when it decides to produce a computer that it will have to finance the costs of processing the computer for a 60-day period. The firm's goal should be to shorten its cash conversion cycle as much as possible without hurting operations. This would improve profits, because the longer the cash conversion cycle, the greater the need for external financing — and such financing has a cost.

The cash conversion cycle can be shortened (1) by reducing the inventory conversion period, that is, by processing and selling goods more quickly; (2) by reducing the receivables conversion period (or ACP) by speeding up collections; or (3) by lengthening the payables deferral period by slowing down its own payments. To the extent that these actions can be taken *without increasing costs or depressing sales,* they should be carried out.

We can illustrate the benefits of shortening the cash conversion cycle by looking again at Real Time Computers. Suppose RTC must spend $200,000 on materials and labor to produce one computer, and it will produce three computers per day. Thus, it must invest $600,000 into each day's production. This investment must be financed for 60 days — the length of the cash conversion cycle — so the company's working capital financing needs will be 60 × $600,000 = $36 million. If RTC could reduce the cash conversion cycle to 50 days, say by deferring payment of its accounts payable an additional 10 days, or by speeding up either the production process or the collection of its receivables, it could reduce its working capital financing requirements by $6 million. We see, then, that actions which affect the inventory conversion period, the receivables conversion period, and the payables deferral period all affect the cash conversion cycle, and hence they influence the firm's need for working capital. You should keep the cash conversion cycle in mind as you go through the remainder of this chapter and the other chapters on working capital.

WORKING CAPITAL INVESTMENT AND FINANCING POLICIES

Working capital policy involves two basic questions: (1) What is the appropriate level of current assets, both in total and by specific accounts? and (2) How should the required level of current assets be financed? In this section we examine alternative policies regarding the level of investment in current assets and the types of liabilities that can be used to finance those assets.

Alternative Current Asset Investment Policies

Figure 19-2 shows three alternative policies regarding the level of current assets. Under each policy, a different amount of working capital is carried to support each level of sales. The line with the steepest slope in Figure 19-2

Figure 19-2   Alternative Current Asset Investment Policies
(Millions of Dollars)

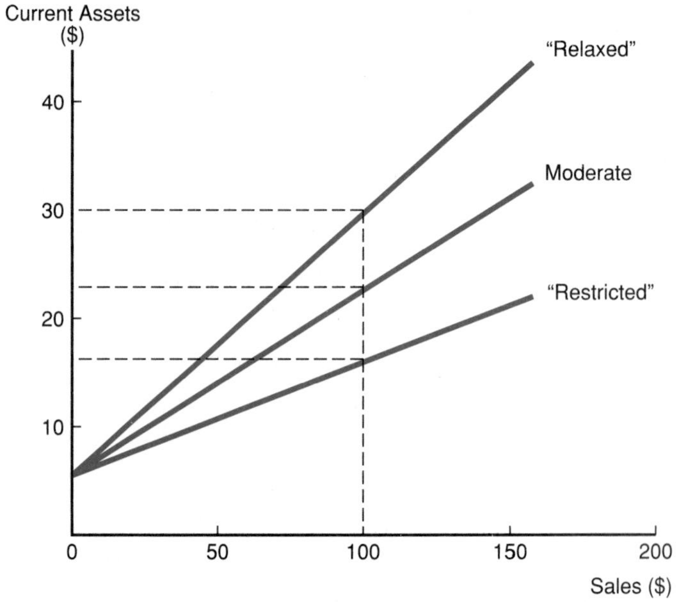

Policy	Current Assets to Support Sales of $100
Relaxed	$30
Moderate	23
Restricted	16

Note: The sales/current assets relationship is shown here as being linear. However, this is often not the case.

---

represents a relatively "relaxed" working capital policy. The word *relaxed* as used here has no negative connotation; we merely mean that relatively large amounts of cash, marketable securities, and inventories are carried, and that sales are stimulated by the use of a credit policy which provides liberal financing to customers and thus results in a corresponding high level of receivables. Conversely, under the "restricted" policy, the holdings of cash, securities, inventories, and receivables are minimized. The moderate policy is between these two extremes.

Under conditions of certainty — that is, if sales, costs, order lead times, collection periods, and so on, were known for sure — all firms would hold the same level of current assets. Any larger amounts would increase the need for external funding without a corresponding increase in profits, whereas any smaller holdings would involve late payments to suppliers, lost sales, and production inefficiencies because of inventory shortages.

However, the picture changes when uncertainty is introduced. Here the firm requires some minimum amount of cash and inventories based on expected payments, sales, order lead times, and so on, plus additional amounts, or *safety stocks,* to account for deviations from expected values. Similarly, accounts receivable are based on credit terms, and the tougher those terms, the lower the receivables for any given level of sales. With a restricted working capital policy, the firm would hold minimal levels of safety stocks for cash and inventories, and it would have a tight credit policy, even though this would mean running the risk of a decline in sales. Generally, a restricted, or tight, policy provides the highest expected return on investment, but it also entails the greatest risk. The reverse is true under a relaxed policy. The moderate policy falls in between the two extremes in terms of risk and expected return.

The policy with regard to the level of current assets is never set in a vacuum; it is always established in conjunction with the firm's working capital financing policy. This is the topic we consider next.

Alternative Working Capital Financing Policies

Most businesses experience seasonal or cyclical fluctuations, or both. For example, construction firms have peaks in the spring and summer, retail sales often peak around Christmas, and manufacturers who supply either construction companies or retailers follow patterns similar to those of their customers. Similarly, virtually all businesses must build up working capital when the economy is strong, but their inventories and receivables fall when the economy slacks off. However, even when business is seasonally or cyclically low, current assets do not drop to zero; this realization has led to the development of the idea of **permanent current assets**.

permanent current assets
Current assets that are still on hand at the trough of a firm's cycles.

Applying this idea to Drexel Card Company, we see from Table 19-1, presented earlier, that DCC's total assets fluctuate between $700,000 and $740,000. Thus, DCC has $700,000 in permanent assets, composed of $500,000 of fixed assets plus a minimum of $200,000 in current assets — the *permanent level of current assets* — plus additional seasonal, or **temporary**, **current assets**, which fluctuate from zero to a maximum of $40,000. The manner in which the permanent and temporary current assets are financed constitutes the firm's *working capital financing policy*.

temporary current assets
Current assets that fluctuate with seasonal or cyclical variations in a firm's business.

Maturity Matching, or "Self-Liquidating," Approach. One commonly used financing policy is that of matching asset and liability maturities, as shown in Panel a of Figure 19-3. Permanent assets are financed with long-term capital. This reduces risk. To illustrate, suppose a firm borrows $1 million at 10 percent on a 1-year basis and uses the funds obtained to build and equip a plant. The firm expects to earn 15 percent after taxes on its investment, and it will depreciate the building by the straight line method over 20 years. Thus, expected cash flows are $150,000 net income + $50,000 depreciation = $200,000. However, the firm must pay off or refinance the $1 million loan plus pay interest of $100,000, so it will have cash flows of $200,000 versus a cash

Figure 19-3   Alternative Working Capital Financing Policies

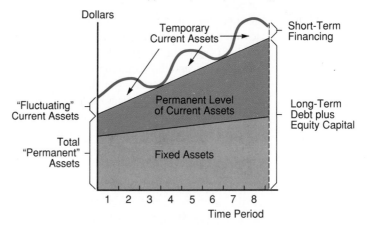

a. Moderate Approach (Maturity Matching)

Dollars

Temporary Current Assets

Short-Term Financing

"Fluctuating" Current Assets

Permanent Level of Current Assets

Long-Term Debt plus Equity Capital

Total "Permanent" Assets

Fixed Assets

Time Period: 1 2 3 4 5 6 7 8

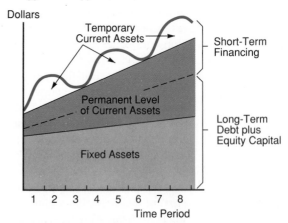

b. Aggressive Approach

Dollars

Temporary Current Assets

Short-Term Financing

Permanent Level of Current Assets

Long-Term Debt plus Equity Capital

Fixed Assets

Time Period: 1 2 3 4 5 6 7 8

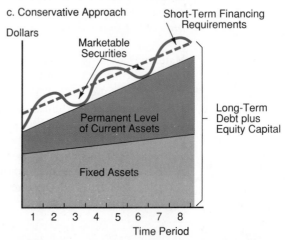

c. Conservative Approach

Short-Term Financing Requirements

Dollars

Marketable Securities

Permanent Level of Current Assets

Long-Term Debt plus Equity Capital

Fixed Assets

Time Period: 1 2 3 4 5 6 7 8

requirement of $1.1 million. In this case, as in most similar situations in which long-term assets are financed with short-term loans, cash flows from the plant are not sufficient to pay off the loan at the end of only one year, so the loan must be renewed. If for some reason the lender refuses to renew the loan, the firm will have problems. Had the plant been financed with long-term debt, however, the required loan payments (interest plus part of the principal) would have been better matched with cash flows from profits and depreciation, and the problem of renewal would not have arisen.

At the limit, a firm could attempt to exactly match the maturity structure of its assets and liabilities. Inventory expected to be sold in 30 days would be financed with a 30-day bank loan; a machine expected to last for 5 years would be financed with a 5-year loan; a 20-year building would be financed with a 20-year mortgage bond; and so forth. In effect, each loan would be paid off with the cash flows generated by the assets financed by the loan, so loans would be "self-liquidating." Actually, of course, uncertainty about the lives of assets prevents this exact maturity matching in an ex post sense. For example, a firm may finance inventories with a 30-day loan, expecting to sell the inventories and to use the cash generated to retire the loan. If sales are slow, however, the cash will not be forthcoming, and the use of short-term credit may end up causing a problem. Still, if the firm attempts to match asset and liability maturities, we call this a *moderate (maturity matching, or self-liquidating) working capital financing policy.*

Aggressive Approach. Panel b of Figure 19-3 illustrates the situation for an aggressive firm which finances all of its fixed assets with long-term capital but part of its permanent current assets with short-term credit. A look back at Table 19-1 will show that DCC follows this strategy. Even at the low point in operations, DCC has $200,000 of current assets plus $500,000 of fixed assets, or $700,000 of permanent assets. At the same time, its equity plus long-term debt (including the current portion of long-term debt) is only about $590,000, so about $110,000 of short-term credit is being used to finance permanent assets.

Returning to Figure 19-3, the dashed line in Panel b could have been drawn *below* the line designating fixed assets, indicating that all of the current assets plus part of the fixed assets were financed with short-term credit. This would be a risky, nonconservative position, and the firm would be very much exposed to the danger of rising interest rates as well as to loan renewal problems. However, short-term debt is often cheaper than long-term debt, and some firms are willing to sacrifice safety for the chance of higher profits.

Conservative Approach. As shown in Panel c of Figure 19-3, the dashed line could also have been drawn *above* the line designating permanent current assets, indicating that long-term capital is being used to finance all permanent asset requirements and also to meet some or all of the seasonal demands. In the situation depicted in this graph, the firm uses a small amount of short-term credit to meet its peak requirements, but it also meets a part of its seasonal needs by "storing liquidity" in the form of marketable securities during the off-season. The humps above the dashed line represent short-term financing; the troughs below it represent short-term security holdings. Panel c represents a very safe, conservative working capital financing policy.

ADVANTAGES AND DISADVANTAGES OF SHORT-TERM CREDIT

The three possible financing policies described previously differ primarily in the relative amount of short-term debt financing used under each. The aggressive policy called for the greatest amount of short-term debt, the conservative policy required the least, and maturity matching (self-liquidating) fell in between. Although using short-term credit is generally riskier than using long-term credit, short-term credit does have some notable advantages. The advantages and disadvantages of short-term credit are considered in this section.

Speed

A short-term loan can be obtained much more quickly than a long-term loan. Lenders will insist on a more thorough financial examination before granting long-term credit, and the loan agreement will have to be spelled out in considerably more detail, because a great deal can happen during the life of a 10- to 20-year loan. Therefore, if funds are needed in a hurry, the firm should look to the short-term markets.

Flexibility

If its needs for funds are seasonal or cyclical, a firm may not want to commit itself to long-term debt for the following reasons. (1) Flotation costs are generally higher for long-term debt. (2) Although long-term debt can be repaid early, provided the loan agreement includes a prepayment provision, prepayment penalties can be expensive. Accordingly, if a firm thinks its need for funds will diminish in the near future, it should choose short-term debt for the repayment flexibility it provides. (3) Long-term loan agreements always contain provisions, or covenants, which constrain the firm's future actions, but short-term credit agreements are generally less restrictive.

Cost of Long-Term versus Short-Term Debt

In Chapter 3, we saw that the yield curve is normally upward sloping, indicating that interest rates are generally lower on short-term than on long-term debt. Thus, interest charges at the time the funds are obtained are normally lower if the firm borrows on a short-term rather than a long-term basis.

Risk to the Borrowing Firm

Even though short-term debt is often less expensive than long-term debt, financing with short-term debt subjects the borrowing firm to greater risk than does financing with long-term debt. This added risk occurs for two reasons. First, if a firm borrows on a long-term basis, its interest costs will be fixed and therefore stable over time, but if it uses short-term credit, its interest expense will fluctuate widely, at times going quite high. Second, if a firm borrows heavily on a short-term basis, it may find itself unable to repay this debt, and it may be in such a weak financial position that the lender will not renew the loan; this could force the firm into bankruptcy. Braniff Airlines, which failed several years ago during a credit crunch, is an example.

Statements about the flexibility, cost, and riskiness of short-term versus long-term credit depend to a large extent on the type of short-term credit that is actually used. The major types of short-term credit are discussed in the following sections.

ACCRUALS

accruals
Continually recurring short-term liabilities, especially accrued wages and accrued taxes.

Because firms generally pay employees on a weekly, biweekly, or monthly basis, the balance sheet will typically show some accrued wages. Similarly, the firm's own estimated income taxes, plus social security and income taxes withheld from employee payrolls, are generally paid on a weekly, monthly, or quarterly basis, so the balance sheet will typically show some accrued taxes along with its accrued wages. These **accruals** increase automatically as a firm's operations expand. Further, this type of debt is "free" in the sense that no explicit interest is paid on funds raised through accruals. However, a firm cannot ordinarily control its accruals: the timing of wage payments is set by economic forces and industry custom, whereas tax payment dates are established by law. Thus, firms use all the accruals they can, but they have little control over the level of these accounts.

ACCOUNTS PAYABLE, OR TRADE CREDIT

trade credit
Interfirm debt arising through credit sales and recorded as an account receivable by the seller and as an account payable by the buyer.

Firms generally make purchases from other firms on credit, recording the debt as an *account payable*. Accounts payable, or **trade credit**, as it is commonly called, is the largest single category of short-term debt, representing about 40 percent of the current liabilities of the average nonfinancial corporation. This percentage is somewhat larger for smaller firms; because small companies often do not qualify for financing from other sources, they rely especially heavily on trade credit.[2]

Trade credit is a spontaneous source of financing in the sense that it arises from ordinary business transactions. For example, suppose a firm makes average purchases of $2,000 a day on terms of "net 30," meaning that it must pay for goods 30 days after the invoice date. On average it will owe 30 times $2,000, or $60,000, to its suppliers. If its sales, and consequently its purchases, were to double, its accounts payable would also double, to $120,000. Simply by growing, the firm would have *spontaneously* generated an additional $60,000 of financing. Similarly, if the terms under which it bought goods were extended from 30 to 40 days, its accounts payable would expand from $60,000 to $80,000. Therefore, lengthening the credit period also generates additional financing.

The Cost of Trade Credit

Firms that sell on credit have a *credit policy* that includes certain *terms of credit*. For example, Porter Electronics sells on terms of "2/10, net 30," meaning that a 2 percent discount is given if payment is made within 10 days of the invoice date but the full invoice amount is due and payable within 30 days if the discount is not taken.

Suppose Pineapple Computers, Inc., buys an average of $12 million of electronic components from Porter each year, minus a 2 percent discount, for net purchases of $11,760,000/360 = $32,666.67 per day. For simplicity, suppose Porter is Pineapple's only supplier. If Pineapple takes the discount, paying at the end of the tenth day, its payables will average (10)($32,666.67) = $326,667, so it will on average be receiving $326,667 of credit from its only supplier, Porter Electronics Company.

Now suppose Pineapple decides *not* to take the discount — what will happen? First, Pineapple will begin paying invoices after 30 days, so its accounts payable will increase to (30)($32,666.67) = $980,000.[3] Porter Electronics will now be supplying Pineapple with an *additional* $980,000 − $326,667 = $653,333 of credit. Pineapple could use this additional credit to pay off bank loans, to expand inventories, to increase fixed assets, to build up its cash account, or even to increase its own accounts receivable.

---

[2]In a credit sale, the seller records the transaction as a receivable and the buyer records it as a payable. We will examine accounts receivable as an asset investment in Chapter 21. Our focus in this chapter is on accounts payable, a liability item. We might also note that if a firm's accounts payable exceed its receivables, it is said to be *receiving net trade credit,* whereas if its receivables exceed its payables, it is *extending net trade credit.* Smaller firms frequently receive net credit; larger firms extend it.

[3]A question arises here: Should accounts payable reflect gross purchases or purchases net of discounts if a company does not plan to take discounts? Although generally accepted accounting practices permit either treatment, most accountants prefer recording both inventories and payables net of discounts and then reporting the higher payments that result from not taking discounts as an additional expense, called "discounts lost." *Thus, we show accounts payable net of discounts even when the company does not expect to take the discount.*

Pineapple's new credit from Porter Electronics has a cost. Because Pineapple is forgoing a 2 percent discount on its $12 million of purchases, its costs will rise by $240,000 per year. Dividing this $240,000 by the additional credit, we find the implicit cost of the added trade credit as follows:

$$\text{Approximate percentage cost} = \frac{\$240,000}{\$653,333} = 36.7\%.$$

Assuming that Pineapple can borrow from its bank (or from other sources) at an interest rate of less than 36.7 percent, it should not borrow the additional $653,333 by forgoing discounts.

The following equation may be used to calculate the approximate percentage cost, on an annual basis, of not taking discounts:

$$\begin{matrix}\text{Approximate} \\ \text{percentage} \\ \text{cost}\end{matrix} = \frac{\text{Discount percent}}{100 - \text{Discount percent}} \times \frac{360}{\begin{matrix}\text{Days credit is} \\ \text{outstanding} - \text{Discount} \\ \text{period}\end{matrix}}. \qquad (19\text{-}1)$$

The numerator of the first term, discount percent, is the cost per dollar of credit, while the denominator (100 − discount percent) represents the funds made available by not taking the discount. The second term shows how many times each year this cost is incurred. To illustrate the equation, the approximate cost of not taking a discount when the terms are 2/10, net 30, is computed as follows:[4]

$$\text{Approximate percentage cost} = \frac{2}{98} \times \frac{360}{20} = 0.0204(18)$$

$$= 0.367 = 36.7\%.$$

Notice, however, that the calculated cost of trade credit is reduced by paying late. Thus, if Pineapple can get away with paying in 60 days rather than in the specified 30, the effective credit period becomes 60 − 10 = 50 days, and the approximate cost drops from 36.7 percent to (2/98)(360/50) = 14.7%. If their suppliers have excess capacity, firms may be able to get away with late payments, but this is an unethical practice, and it will lead to a variety of problems associated with **"stretching" accounts payable** and being branded a "slow payer" account. These problems are discussed later in the chapter.

stretching accounts payable The practice of deliberately paying accounts payable late.

---

[4]In terms of effective annual interest, the rate is even higher. In the case of trade discounts, the discount amounts to interest, and with terms of 2/10, net 30, the firm gains use of the funds for 30 − 10 = 20 days, so there are 360/20 = 18 "interest periods" per year. The first term in the equation is (Discount percent)/(100 − Discount percent) = 0.02/0.98 = 0.0204. This "interest rate" is the periodic rate which is "paid" 18 times each year. Therefore, the effective annual rate cost of trade credit is

$$\text{Effective rate} = (1.0204)^{18} - 1.0 = 1.438 - 1.0 = 43.8\%.$$

Thus, the 36.7 percent cost calculated by the approximation formula, Equation 19-1, understates the true cost of trade credit. Equation 19-1 would be correct if the full cost of the discounts was incurred at the end of the year, but in actuality these costs are incurred all during the year.

The cost of the additional trade credit obtained by not taking discounts can be worked out for other purchase terms. Some illustrative costs are as follows:

Credit Terms	Approximate Cost
1/10, net 30	18%
1/10, net 20	36
2/10, net 30	37
2/10, net 20	73

As these figures show, the cost of not taking discounts can be substantial. Incidentally, throughout the chapter we assume that payments are made either on the *last day* for taking discounts or on the *last day* of the credit period unless otherwise noted. It would be foolish to pay, say, on the fifth day or on the twentieth day if the credit terms were 2/10, net 30.

Effects of Trade Credit on the Financial Statements

A firm's policy with regard to taking or not taking discounts can have a significant effect on its financial statements. To illustrate, let us assume that Pineapple Computers is just beginning its operations. On the first day, it makes net purchases of $32,666.67; this amount is recorded on its balance sheet under accounts payable.[5] The second day it buys another $32,666.67 of goods. The first day's purchases are not yet paid for, so at the end of the second day, accounts payable total $65,333.34. Accounts payable increase by another $32,666.67 on the third day, for a total of $98,000, and after 10 days they are up to $326,666.70.

If Pineapple takes discounts, then on the eleventh day it will have to pay for the $32,666.67 of purchases made on the first day, which will reduce accounts payable. However, it will buy another $32,666.67 of goods, which will increase payables. Thus, after the tenth day of operations, Pineapple's balance sheet will level off, showing a balance of $326,666.70 in accounts payable, assuming it pays on the tenth day in order to take discounts.

Now suppose Pineapple decides not to take discounts. In this case, on the eleventh day it will add another $32,666.67 to payables, but it will not pay for the purchases made on the first day. Thus, the balance sheet figure for accounts payable will rise to $(11)($32,666.67) = $359,333.37$. This buildup will continue through the thirtieth day, at which point payables will total $(30)($32,666.67) = $980,000$. On the thirty-first day, Pineapple will buy another $32,666.67 of goods, thus increasing accounts payable, but it will also pay for the purchases made the first day, which will reduce payables. Thus, the balance sheet item "accounts payable" will stabilize at $980,000 after 30 days, assuming Pineapple does not take discounts.

---

[5]Inventories also increase by $32,666.67, but we are not now concerned with this account.

Table 19-2   Pineapple Computers' Financial Statements with Different Trade Credit Policies

	Does Not Take Discounts; Uses Maximum Trade Credit	Takes Discounts; Borrows from Bank	Difference
I. Balance Sheets			
Cash	$ 500,000	$ 500,000	$ 0
Receivables	1,000,000	1,000,000	0
Inventories	2,000,000	2,000,000	0
Fixed assets	2,980,000	2,980,000	0
Total assets	$ 6,480,000	$ 6,480,000	$ 0
Accounts payable	$ 980,000	$ 326,667	$ + 653,333
Notes payable (10%)	0	653,333	− 653,333
Accruals	500,000	500,000	0
Common equity	5,000,000	5,000,000	0
Total claims	$ 6,480,000	$ 6,480,000	$ 0
II. Income Statements			
Sales	$15,000,000	$15,000,000	$ 0
Less: Purchases	11,760,000	11,760,000	0
Labor	2,000,000	2,000,000	0
Interest	0	65,333	− 65,333
Discounts lost	240,000	0	+ 240,000
Net income before tax	$ 1,000,000	$ 1,174,667	$ + 174,667
Federal-plus-state tax (40%)	400,000	469,867	+ 69,867
Net income	$ 600,000	$ 704,800	$ + 104,800

Part I of Table 19-2 shows Pineapple's balance sheet after it reaches a steady state under the two trade credit policies. Total assets are unchanged by this policy decision, and we also assume that accruals and the common equity account are unchanged. The differences show up in accounts payable and notes payable; when Pineapple elects to take discounts and thus gives up some of the trade credit it otherwise could have obtained, it will have to raise $653,333 from some other source. It could have sold more common stock or used long-term bonds, but we assume that it chose to use bank credit, which has a 10 percent cost and is reflected in the notes payable account.

Part II of Table 19-2 shows Pineapple's income statement under the two policies. If the company does not take discounts, its interest expense will be zero, but it will have a $240,000 expense for discounts lost. On the other hand, if it does take discounts, it will incur an interest expense of $65,333, but it will avoid the cost of the discounts lost. Because the discounts lost would exceed the interest expense, the take-discounts policy would result in a higher net income and thus in a higher stock price.

Components of Trade Credit: Free versus Costly

free trade credit
Credit received during the discount period.

costly trade credit
Credit taken in excess of free trade credit, thereby necessitating a forfeit of the discount offered.

On the basis of the preceding discussion, trade credit can be divided into two components: (1) **free trade credit**, which involves credit received during the discount period and which for Pineapple amounts to 10 days' net purchases, or $326,667; and (2) **costly trade credit**, which involves credit in excess of the free credit and whose cost is the discounts lost. Pineapple could obtain $653,333, or 20 days' net purchases, of nonfree trade credit at a cost of approximately 37 percent. *Financial managers should always use the free component, but they should use the costly component only after analyzing its cost to make sure that it is less than the cost of funds that could be obtained from other sources.* Under the terms of trade found in most industries, the costly component involves a relatively high percentage cost; therefore, firms with access to bank credit should use only the free component of trade credit.

We noted earlier that firms sometimes can and do deviate from the stated credit terms, thus altering the percentage cost figures cited previously. For example, a California manufacturing company that buys on terms of 2/10, net 30, makes a practice of paying in 15 days (rather than 10), but it still takes discounts — its treasurer simply waits until 15 days after receipt of the goods and still writes a check for the invoiced amount less the 2 percent discount. Because the company's suppliers want its business, they tolerate this practice. Similarly, a Wisconsin firm that also buys on terms of 2/10, net 30, does not take discounts, but it pays in 60 rather than 30 days, thus stretching its trade credit. As we saw earlier, both practices reduce the calculated cost of trade credit. However, neither of these firms is "loved" by its suppliers, and neither could continue these practices in times when suppliers were operating at full capacity and had order backlogs. Indeed, both firms have bad reputations in their industries, and both will have a hard time getting deliveries when their suppliers are operating at full capacity.

SHORT-TERM BANK LOANS

Commercial banks, whose loans generally appear on firms' balance sheets under the notes payable account, are second in importance to trade credit as a source of short-term financing. Their influence is actually greater than appears from the dollar amounts they lend because banks provide *nonspontaneous* funds. As a firm's financing needs increase, it requests its bank to provide the additional funds. If the request is denied, the firm may be forced to abandon attractive growth opportunities.[6]

---

[6]Although commercial banks remain the primary source of short-term loans, other sources are available. For example, in 1988 General Electric Credit Corporation (GECC) had several billion dollars of commercial loans outstanding. Firms such as GECC, which was initially established to finance consumers' purchases of GE's durable goods, often find business loans to be more profitable than consumer loans.

Bank Loan Features

Some features of bank loans are discussed in the following paragraphs.

Maturity. Although banks do make longer-term loans, the bulk of their lending is on a short-term basis; about two-thirds of all bank loans mature in a year or less. Bank loans to businesses are frequently written as 90-day notes, so the loans must be repaid or renewed at the end of 90 days. Note, though, that if a borrower's financial position has deteriorated, the bank may refuse to renew the loan. This can mean serious trouble for the borrower.

promissory note
A document specifying the terms and conditions of a loan, including the amount, interest rate, and repayment schedule.

Promissory Note. When a bank loan is approved, the agreement is executed by signing a **promissory note**. The note specifies: (1) the amount borrowed; (2) the percentage interest rate; (3) the repayment schedule, which can involve either a lump sum or a series of installments; (4) any collateral that might be put up as security for the loan; and (5) any other terms and conditions to which the bank and the borrower have agreed. When the note is signed, the bank credits the borrower's checking account with the amount of the loan, so on the borrower's balance sheet, both the cash and the notes payable accounts increase.

compensating balance
A minimum checking account balance that a firm must maintain with a commercial bank, generally equal to 10 to 20 percent of the amount of loans outstanding.

Compensating Balances. Banks typically require that a regular borrower maintain an average demand deposit balance equal to a specified percentage of the face amount of the loan; generally, the required balance is set at from 10 to 20 percent. This is called a **compensating balance** (CB), and it raises the effective interest rate on the loan. For example, if a firm needs $80,000 to pay off outstanding obligations, but it must maintain a 20 percent compensating balance, then it must borrow $100,000 to obtain a usable $80,000. If the stated interest rate is 8 percent, the effective cost is actually 10 percent: $8,000 interest divided by $80,000 of usable funds equals 10 percent.[7] The effective cost of a loan with a compensating balance will be discussed in more detail in the next section.

line of credit
An arrangement in which a financial institution commits itself to lend up to a specified maximum amount of funds during a designated period.

Line of Credit. A **line of credit** is a formal or informal understanding between the bank and the borrower indicating the maximum amount of credit the bank will extend to the borrower. It works just like a credit card limit. For example, on December 31 a bank loan officer may indicate to a corporate treasurer that the bank regards the firm as being "good" for up to $80,000 for the forthcoming year. On January 10 the treasurer signs a promissory note for $15,000 for 90 days; this is called "taking down" $15,000 of the total line of credit. This amount is credited to the firm's checking account at the bank. The firm then has $65,000 of unused credit, because it can borrow additional amounts up to

---

[7]Note, however, that the compensating balance may be set as a minimum monthly *average;* if the firm maintains this average anyway, the compensating balance requirement will not raise the effective interest rate.

a total of $80,000 outstanding at any one time. Also, if the firm has surplus cash, it can pay down the loan, which will both reduce its interest expense and increase its available credit.

revolving credit agreement
A formal line of credit extended to a firm by a bank or other lending institution.

Revolving Credit Agreement. A revolving credit agreement is a formal line of credit used by large firms. To illustrate, Porter Electronics negotiated a revolving credit agreement for $100 million with a group of banks. The banks were formally committed for 4 years to lend Porter up to $100 million if the funds were needed. Porter in turn paid a commitment fee of one-quarter of 1 percent on the unused balance of the committed funds to compensate the banks for making the commitment. Thus, if Porter did not take down any of the $100 million commitment during a given year, it would still be required to pay a $250,000 fee. If it borrowed $50 million, the unused portion of the line of credit would fall to $50 million, and the fee would fall to $125,000. Of course, interest also had to be paid on the amount of money Porter actually borrowed. As a general rule, the rate of interest on "revolvers" is pegged to the T-bill rate or some other open-market rate, so the cost of the loan "floats" over time as interest rates vary. Porter's rate was set at the T-bill rate plus 1.5 percentage points, to be adjusted on the first of every month.

A revolving credit agreement is very similar to a line of credit. However, there is an important distinguishing feature: The bank has a legal obligation to honor a revolving credit agreement, and it charges a fee for this commitment. No legal obligation exists under the less formal line of credit.

The Cost of Bank Loans

The cost of bank loans varies for different types of borrowers at a given point in time, and for all borrowers over time. Interest rates are higher for riskier borrowers, and they are also higher on smaller loans because of the fixed costs involved in making and servicing loans. If a firm can qualify as a "prime risk" because of its size and financial strength, it can borrow at the **prime rate**, which has traditionally been the lowest rate banks charge. Rates on other loans tend to be scaled up from the prime rate.[8]

prime rate
A published rate of interest charged by commercial banks to very large, strong corporations.

---

[8]Each bank sets its own prime rate, but because of competitive forces, most banks' prime rates are identical. Further, most banks follow the rate set by the large New York City banks, which in turn often follow the rate set by Citibank, New York's largest. Citibank at one time had a policy of setting the prime rate each week at $1\frac{1}{4}$ to $1\frac{1}{2}$ percentage points above the average rate paid on large certificates of deposit (CDs) during the preceding three weeks. CD rates represent the "price" of money in the open market; since they rise and fall with the supply and demand of money, CD rates are "market-clearing" rates. By tying the prime rate to CD rates, the banking system insured that the prime rate would also be a market-clearing rate.

However, in recent years the prime rate has been held relatively constant even though open market rates have fluctuated sharply. Also, in recent years many banks have been lending to the very strongest companies at rates well below the prime rate. As we note later in this chapter, large firms have ready access to the commercial paper market, and if banks want to do a significant volume of business with these firms, they must match or at least come close to the commercial paper rate.

Bank lending rates vary widely over time, depending on economic conditions and Federal Reserve policy. When the economy is weak, loan demand is usually slack, and the Fed also makes an ample supply of money available to the system. As a result, interest rates on all types of loans decline. Conversely, when the economy is booming, loan demand is typically strong, and the Fed restricts the money supply; the result is an increase in interest rates. As an indication of the kinds of fluctuations that can occur, in just five months (August to December of 1980) the prime rate rose from 11 percent to 21 percent.

Interest rates on bank loans are quoted in three ways: (1) *simple interest,* (2) *discount interest,* and (3) *add-on interest.* These three methods are explained next.

Regular, or Simple, Interest. Simple interest is charged on many bank loans, and it also provides a basis of comparison for all other loan rates. In a **simple interest** loan, the borrower receives the face value of the loan and then repays the principal and interest at maturity. For example, on a simple interest loan of $10,000 at 12 percent for 1 year, the borrower receives the $10,000 upon approval of the loan and pays back the $10,000 principal plus $10,000(0.12) = $1,200 of interest at maturity (1 year later). The 12 percent is the stated, or nominal, rate. The effective annual rate is also 12 percent:

> **simple interest**
> Interest that is charged on the basis of the amount borrowed; it is paid when the loan ends rather than when it begins.

$$\text{Effective rate}_{\text{Simple}} = \frac{\text{Interest}}{\text{Amount received}} = \frac{\$1,200}{\$10,000} = 12\%.$$

On a simple interest loan of 1 year or more, the nominal rate equals the effective rate. However, if the loan has a term of less than 1 year — say, 90 days — the effective rate will be higher. To see why, suppose someone borrowed $10,000 at a 12 percent simple interest rate for 90 days. The interest charge would be $(0.12/360)(90)(\$10,000) = \$300$. If this loan was then "rolled over" three more times, the total interest for the year would be $(4)(\$300) = \$1,200$, the same as the interest paid on the 1-year, 12 percent loan. However, with the 90-day loan, some of the interest would have to be paid every 90 days rather than all at the end of the year. Because of compounding effects, the 90-day, 12 percent loan would have a higher effective rate, calculated as follows:

$$\text{Effective rate}_{\text{Simple}} = \left(1 + \frac{k_{\text{Nom}}}{m}\right)^m - 1.0$$

$$= (1 + 0.12/4)^4 - 1.0$$

$$= 12.55\%.$$

Here k_{Nom} is the nominal, or stated, rate, and m is the number of loan periods per year, or $360/90 = 4$. The bank gets the interest sooner under a 90-day loan than under a 1-year loan, which makes the effective rate higher.

> **discount interest**
> Interest that is calculated on the face amount of a loan but is deducted in advance.

Discount Interest. In a **discount interest** loan, the bank deducts the interest in advance; this is called *discounting.* Thus, the borrower receives less than the face value of the loan. On a 1-year, $10,000 loan with a 12 percent (nominal) rate, discount basis, the interest is $10,000(0.12) = $1,200$, so the borrower obtains the use of only $10,000 - $1,200 = $8,800$. The effective rate is 13.64 percent versus 12 percent on a 1-year, simple interest loan:[9]

$$\text{Effective rate}_{\text{Discount}} = \frac{\text{Interest}}{\text{Amount received}} = \frac{\text{Interest}}{\text{Face value} - \text{Interest}}$$

$$= \frac{\$1,200}{\$10,000 - \$1,200} = 13.64\%.$$

An alternative procedure for finding the effective annual rate on a discount interest loan is

$$\text{Effective rate}_{\text{Discount}} = \frac{\text{Nominal rate (\%)}}{1.0 - \text{Nominal rate (fraction)}}$$

$$= \frac{12\%}{1.0 - 0.12} = \frac{12\%}{0.88} = 13.64\%.$$

If the discount loan was for a period of less than 1 year, its effective annual rate would be found as follows:

$$\text{Effective rate}_{\text{Discount}} = \left(1.0 + \frac{\text{Interest}}{\text{Face value} - \text{Interest}}\right)^{m} - 1.0.$$

For example, if a firm borrowed $10,000 face value at a nominal rate of 12 percent, discount interest, for 3 months, then $m = 12/3 = 4$, the interest payment would be $(0.12/4)(\$10,000) = \$300$, and the effective rate would be 12.96 percent:

$$\text{Effective rate}_{\text{Discount}} = \left(1.0 + \frac{\$300}{\$10,000 - \$300}\right)^{4} - 1.0$$

$$= 0.1296 = 12.96\%.$$

Thus, discount interest imposes less of a penalty on shorter-term than on longer-term loans. This result occurs because the interest is paid closer to the average date of use of the funds (half the life of the loan).

add-on interest
Interest calculated and added to funds received to determine the face amount of an installment loan.

Installment Loans: Add-on Interest. Lenders typically charge **add-on interest** on automobile, appliance, and other types of small installment loans. The term

---

[9]If the borrowing firm actually requires $10,000, it must borrow $11,363.64:

$$\text{Face value} = \frac{\text{Funds required}}{1.0 - \text{Nominal rate (fraction)}}$$

$$= \frac{\$10,000}{1.0 - 0.12} = \frac{\$10,000}{0.88} = \$11,363.64.$$

The borrower will sign a note for $11,363.64 but receive only $11,363.64 - 0.12(\$11,363.64) = \$10,000$. Increasing the face value of the loan does not change the effective rate of 13.64 percent on the $10,000 of usable funds.

add-on means that the interest is calculated based on the nominal rate and then added to the amount received to obtain the loan's face value. To illustrate, suppose that to buy a car you borrow $10,000 on an add-on basis at a nominal rate of 12 percent, with the loan to be repaid in 12 monthly installments. At a 12 percent nominal rate, you pay a total interest charge of $1,200; thus, the face amount of the note is $10,000 + $1,200 = $11,200. However, since the loan is paid off in monthly installments, you have the use of the full $10,000 for only the first month. The amount of usable funds declines by $10,000/12 = $833.33 per month, and the average amount of usable funds during the year is $10,000 − ($833.33 × 6) = $10,000 − $5,000 = $5,000. Thus, you pay $1,200 for the use of only about half the amount of funds initially borrowed. Therefore, we can approximate the effective rate as follows:

$$\text{Approximate effective rate}_{\text{Add-on}} = \frac{\text{Interest}}{(\text{Amount received})/2}$$

$$= \frac{\$1,200}{\$10,000/2} = 24\%.$$

The main point to note here is that interest is paid on the *original* amount of funds received, not on the average amount actually outstanding, which causes the effective rate to be almost double the stated rate.[10]

---

[10]This is only an approximation of the true rate of interest. To determine the precise effective rate under add-on interest, we proceed as follows:

1. The total loan to be repaid is $10,000 of principal plus $1,200 of interest, or $11,200.

2. The monthly payment is $11,200/12 = $933.33.

3. The bank is in effect buying a 12-period annuity of $933.33 for $10,000, so $10,000 is the PV of the annuity. Expressed in equation form,

$$PV = \$10,000 = \sum_{t=1}^{12} \$933.33\left(\frac{1}{1 + k_d}\right)^t.$$

4. This equation can be solved for k_d, which is the rate per month, using a financial calculator. Here $k_d = 1.788\% = 0.01788$.

5. The effective annual rate is then found as follows:

$$\text{Effective rate}_{\text{Add-on}} = (1 + k_d)^{12} - 1.0$$

$$= (1.01788)^{12} - 1.0$$

$$= 1.2370 - 1.0 = 23.7\%.$$

6. Under the truth-in-lending laws, banks, department stores, and other installment lenders are required to report the *annual percentage rate (APR)* in boldface type on the first page of all installment loan contracts to prevent lenders from calling a loan with an effective rate of 23.7 percent a 12 percent loan. However, existing laws do not in all cases define the effective rate the same way we do. For example, many institutions would report our sample add-on loan as having an APR of 12 × 1.788 = 21.46% versus the 23.7 percent we calculated.

7. Note that if an installment loan is paid off ahead of schedule, additional complications will arise. The issue is, how much of the prepaid interest does the borrower get back? For a discussion of this point, see Dick Bonker, "The Rule of 78," *Journal of Finance,* June 1976, 877–888.

Simple Interest with Compensating Balances. Compensating balances tend to raise the effective rate on a loan. To illustrate this, suppose a firm needs $10,000 to pay for some equipment that it recently has purchased. A bank offers to lend the company money for one year at a 12 percent simple rate, but the firm must maintain a compensating balance (CB) equal to 20 percent of the loan amount. If the firm did not take the loan, it would keep no deposits with the bank. What is the effective annual rate on the loan?

First, note that if the firm requires $10,000, it must borrow $12,500, assuming that it does not have spare cash to use as the compensating balance:

$$\text{Face value} = \frac{\text{Funds required}}{1.0 - \text{CB (fraction)}}$$

$$= \frac{\$10,000}{1.0 - 0.20} = \$12,500.$$

The interest paid at the end of the year will be $12,500(0.12) = $1,500, but the firm will get the use of only $10,000. Therefore, the effective annual rate is 15 percent:

$$\text{Effective rate}_{\text{Simple/CB}} = \frac{\text{Interest}}{\text{Amount received}}$$

$$= \frac{\$1,500}{\$10,000} = 15\%.$$

An alternative formulation is

$$\text{Effective rate}_{\text{Simple/CB}} = \frac{\text{Nominal rate (\%)}}{1.0 - \text{CB (fraction)}}$$

$$= \frac{12\%}{1.0 - 0.2} = 15\%.$$

Discount Interest with Compensating Balances. The preceding analysis can be extended to the case in which compensating balances are required and the loan is also on a discount basis. In this situation, if a firm requires $10,000 for 1 year, and a 20 percent compensating balance (CB) is required on a 12 percent discount loan, the firm will have to borrow $14,705.88:

$$\text{Amount borrowed} = \frac{\text{Funds required}}{1.0 - \text{Nominal rate (fraction)} - \text{CB (fraction)}}$$

$$= \frac{\$10,000}{1.0 - 0.12 - 0.2}$$

$$= \$10,000/0.68 = \$14,705.88.$$

The firm would record this $14,705.88 under current liabilities as a note payable, which would be offset by these asset accounts:

To cash account; subsequently write check	$10,000.00
Prepaid interest (12% of $14,705.88)	1,764.70
Frozen cash balance (20% of $14,705.88)	2,941.18
	$14,705.88

The effective annual rate on this loan would be 17.65 percent:

$$\text{Effective rate}_{\text{Discount/CB}} = \frac{\text{Nominal rate}}{1.0 - \text{Nominal rate (fraction)} - \text{CB (fraction)}}$$

$$= \frac{12\%}{1.0 - 0.12 - 0.2}$$

$$= 12\%/0.68 = 17.65\%.$$

In this example, compensating balances and discount interest combined to push the effective rate of interest up from 12 to 17.65 percent. Note, however, that in our analysis we assumed that the compensating balance requirements forced the firm to increase its bank deposits. Had the company had transactions balances which could have been used to supply all or part of the compensating balance, the effective annual rate would have been less than 17.65 percent. Also, if the firm earned interest on its bank deposits, including the compensating balance, the effective annual rate would be decreased.

Choosing a Bank

Individuals whose only contact with their bank is through the use of its checking services generally choose a bank for the convenience of its location and the competitive cost of its services. However, businesses that borrow from banks must look at other criteria, for important differences exist among banks. Some of these differences are considered in this section.

Willingness to Assume Risks. Banks have different basic policies toward risk. Some follow relatively conservative lending practices, whereas others engage in what are often termed "creative banking practices." These policies reflect both the personalities of the bank's officers and the characteristics of the bank's deposit liabilities. Thus, a bank with fluctuating deposit liabilities in a static community should tend to be a conservative lender, whereas a bank whose deposits are growing with little interruption can more safely follow liberal credit policies. A large bank with broad diversification over geographic regions and across industries served can obtain the benefit of combining and averaging risks. Thus, marginal credit risks that might be unacceptable to a small, specialized bank can be pooled by a branch banking system to reduce the overall risk of a group of marginal accounts.

Advice and Counsel. Some bank loan officers are active in providing counsel and in making developmental loans to firms in their early and formative years. Certain banks have specialized departments which make loans to firms that are expected to grow and thus become more important customers. The personnel of these departments can provide valuable counseling to customers; their experience with other firms in growth situations may enable them to spot, and then warn their customers about, developing problems.

Merchant Banking. The term "merchant bank" was originally applied to a bank which not only loaned depositors' money but also provided its customers with equity capital and financial advice. Prior to 1933, U.S. commercial banks performed all types of merchant banking functions. However, about one-third of the U.S. banks failed during the Great Depression, in part because of these activities, so in 1933 the Glass-Steagall Act was passed in an effort to reduce banks' exposure to risk. In recent years, commercial banks have been attempting to get back into merchant banking, in part because their foreign competitors offer such services, and U.S. banks need to be able to compete with their foreign counterparts for multinational corporations' business. Currently, the larger banks, often through holding companies, are being permitted to get back into merchant banking, at least to a limited extent. This trend will probably continue, and, if it does, corporations will need to consider a bank's ability to provide a full range of commercial and merchant banking services when choosing a bank.

Loyalty to Customers. Banks differ in the extent to which they will support the activities of their borrowers in bad times. This characteristic is referred to as the bank's degree of *loyalty*. Some banks may put great pressure on a business to liquidate its loans when the firm's outlook becomes clouded, whereas others will stand by the firm and work diligently to help it get back on its feet. An especially dramatic illustration of this point was Bank of America's bailout of Memorex Corporation. The bank could have forced Memorex into bankruptcy, but instead it loaned the company additional capital and helped it survive a bad period. Since Memorex's stock price subsequently rose on the New York Stock Exchange from $1.50 to $68, Bank of America's help was indeed substantial.

Note, though, that a bank's loyalty to weak customers can lead to loan losses, and Bank of America, after being the largest and most profitable U.S. bank for many years, almost went bankrupt during the 1980s. So, "loyalty" and "willingness to assume risks" go hand in hand, and banks should and do charge a price in the form of higher interest rates for loyalty in times of stress. Still, the point remains that some banks are more willing to assume the risk of standing by their customers in times of stress than are other banks, so companies can choose between higher-cost but more "loyal" and lower-cost but less "loyal" banks.

Specialization. Banks differ greatly in their degree of loan specialization. Larger banks have separate departments that specialize in different kinds of loans (for example, real estate, farm, and commercial loans). Within these broad categories there may be a further specialization by line of business, such as steel, machinery, cattle, or textiles. The banks' strengths are also likely to reflect the nature of the business and the economic environment in which the banks operate. For example, Seattle banks have become specialists in lending to timber companies, while many midwestern banks are agricultural specialists. A sound firm can obtain more creative cooperation and more active support by going to the bank that has the greatest experience and familiarity with its particular type of business, and financial managers should take this factor into account. A bank that is excellent for one firm may be unsatisfactory for another.

Maximum Loan Size. The size of a bank can be an important factor. Since the maximum loan a bank can make to any one customer is limited to 15 percent of the bank's capital accounts (capital stock plus retained earnings), it is generally not appropriate for large firms to develop borrowing relationships with small banks.

Other Services. Banks also provide lockbox systems (see Chapter 20), assist with electronic funds transfers, help firms obtain foreign currencies, and the like, and such services should be taken into account when selecting a bank. Also, if the firm is a small business whose manager owns most of its stock, the bank's willingness and ability to provide trust and estate services should also be considered.

COMMERCIAL PAPER

commercial paper
Unsecured, short-term promissory notes of large firms, usually issued in denominations of $100,000 or more and having an interest rate somewhat below the prime rate.

Commercial paper is the name given to the unsecured promissory notes of large, strong firms; it is sold primarily to other business firms, to insurance companies, to pension funds, to money market mutual funds, and to banks. Commercial paper is traded in the secondary markets, and a firm which holds the commercial paper of another firm can sell it to raise cash in a matter of hours — it is highly liquid. Although the amount of commercial paper outstanding is smaller than bank loans outstanding, this form of financing has grown rapidly in recent years. At the end of 1987, there was approximately $350 billion of commercial paper outstanding versus about $570 billion of bank loans to businesses.

Maturity and Cost

Maturities of commercial paper generally vary from two to six months, with an average of about five months.[11] The rates on commercial paper fluctuate with

---

[11]The maximum maturity that can be used without going through the SEC registration process is 270 days. Also, commercial paper can be sold only to "sophisticated" investors; otherwise, SEC registration would be required even for maturities of 270 days or less.

supply and demand conditions; they are determined in the marketplace, varying daily as conditions change. Recently, commercial paper rates have generally ranged from one to two percentage points below the stated prime rate, and about one-quarter of a percentage point above the T-bill rate. For example, in March 1988, the average rate on 3-month commercial paper was 6.6 percent, while the stated prime rate was 8.50 percent and the T-bill rate was 5.76 percent. Also, since compensating balances are not required for commercial paper, the *effective* cost differential is still wider.[12]

Use of Commercial Paper

The use of commercial paper is restricted to a comparatively small number of concerns that are exceptionally good credit risks. Purchasers of commercial paper hold it in their temporary marketable securities portfolios or as liquidity reserves, as discussed in Chapter 20, and for these purposes safety is a paramount concern. Dealers prefer to handle the paper of firms whose net worth is $50 million or more and whose annual borrowing exceeds $10 million.

One potential problem with commercial paper is that a debtor who is in temporary financial difficulty may receive little help, because commercial paper dealings are generally less personal than bank relationships. Thus, banks are usually more able and willing to help a good customer weather a temporary storm than are the commercial paper dealers. On the other hand, using commercial paper permits a corporation to tap a wide range of credit sources, including both financial institutions outside its own area and industrial corporations across the country, and this can reduce interest costs.

USE OF SECURITY IN SHORT-TERM FINANCING

Thus far we have not addressed the question of whether or not loans should be secured. Commercial paper is never secured by specific collateral, but all the other types of loans can be secured if this is deemed necessary or desirable. Given a choice, it is ordinarily better to borrow on an unsecured basis, since the bookkeeping costs of **secured loans** are often high. However, weak firms may find that they can borrow only if they put up some type of security to protect the lender or that by using security they can borrow at a much lower rate.

secured loan
A loan backed by collateral, often inventories or receivables.

Several different kinds of collateral can be employed, including marketable stocks or bonds, land or buildings, equipment, inventory, and accounts

---

[12]However, this factor is offset to some extent by the fact that firms issuing commercial paper are required by commercial paper dealers to have unused revolving credit agreements to back up their outstanding commercial paper, and fees must be paid to obtain these credit lines. In other words, to sell $1 million of commercial paper, a firm must have revolving credit available to pay off the paper when it matures, and commitment fees on this unused credit line (about 0.5 percent) increase the paper's effective cost.

receivable. Marketable securities make excellent collateral, but few firms hold portfolios of stocks and bonds. Similarly, real property (land and buildings) and equipment are good forms of collateral, but they are generally used as security for long-term loans rather than for working capital loans. Therefore, most secured short-term business borrowing involves the use of accounts receivable and inventories as collateral.

To understand the use of security, consider the case of a Chicago hardware dealer who wanted to modernize and expand his store. He requested a $200,000 bank loan. After examining his business's financial statements, the bank indicated that it would lend him a maximum of $100,000 and that the interest rate would be 12 percent, discount interest, for an effective rate of 13.6 percent. The owner had a substantial personal portfolio of stocks, and he offered to put up $300,000 of high-quality stocks to support the $200,000 loan. The bank then granted the full $200,000 loan, and at a rate of only 10 percent, simple interest. The store owner might also have used his inventories or receivables as security for the loan, but processing costs would have been high. Procedures for using accounts receivable and inventories as security for short-term credit are described in Appendix 19A.[13]

---

[13]The term "asset-based financing" is often used as a synonym for "secured financing". Also, in recent years accounts receivable have been used as collateral for long-term bonds; this is called "collateralizing" debt, and it permits corporations to borrow from lenders such as pension funds rather than being restricted to banks and other short-term lenders. In collateralized loans, some arrangement must be made either to replace paid-off receivables or else to transfer such proceeds to the lender.

**Small
Business**

GROWTH AND WORKING CAPITAL NEEDS

The working capital requirements of a new firm are often underestimated by the entrepreneur seeking funds to start the business. The entrepreneur makes provisions for research and development and for plant and equipment required to produce the firm's products. But working capital is frequently a surprise. The entrepreneur expects to come up with a product that the market will immediately accept and for which it will pay a substantial premium. This premium price is expected to lead to a high profit margin, which will in turn "finance" all of the firm's other needs. This point of view is naive, but it is nevertheless common among less experienced founders of new businesses.

Mike Wilson was one of the founders of a new microcomputer software company that began seek-ing venture capital to support its products in the latter part of 1988. In discussions with a venture capitalist who was concerned about the low level of funding being sought, Mike explained that the company's products would have such a high profit margin that the firm would be essentially self-financing after marketing was under way — in fact, there would even be funds available from internal sources to support continued new product development. The venture capitalist, John Solomon, was a little disconcerted. He asked which firm was currently most successful in the microcomputer software business. Mike instantly responded, "Personal Software." John asked, "Why, then, do you suppose that Personal Software has just raised an additional $2,500,000 in new venture capital? Isn't it as profitable as you expect to be?" Mike fumbled around for a while with no answer; to his credit, he got the point.

Rapid growth consumes cash rather than generating it. Rapid growth does generate profits, but profits do not pay the bills — cash does. Consider what a firm must do to sustain a very high growth rate. If it is a manufacturing firm, its assets include raw materials inventory, work-in-process inventory, finished goods inventory, and accounts receivable, as well as fixed assets. With the exception of fixed assets, these items are all components of gross working capital. When the firm produces a product, it must make an investment in each of these working capital items *before* any cash is received from collection of receivables, assuming that all sales are credit sales.

Now imagine a small firm that has limited access to external financing or that chooses to finance itself internally from its retained earnings. It initially secures enough funding to acquire its fixed assets and to get started producing its product. When receivables are collected, the company will have a little more money than it needed to create the products that generated the collections. Excluding any noncash expenses, suppose that for each dollar of sales the company spends about 95 cents. That leaves a nickel in profit. Of course, the firm's silent partner (Uncle Sam) takes a cut, and perhaps the firm pays out a little to its stockholders. The bottom line is that the firm has 3 cents left in cash from each dollar of sales. Since the firm puts in 97 cents for each dollar that it has left at the end of a single manufacture and sales cycle, it now has about 3 percent more to put into manufacturing and selling the next round of production. In other words, after one sales cycle, the firm can afford another sales cycle with about a 3 percent increase in sales without external financing.

Now recall our cash conversion cycle analysis. Suppose the firm has an average of 120 days of sales in inventory and an average of 60 days of sales tied up in accounts receivable. If the firm pays cash for all of its materials and labor, it essentially "turns" cash about twice a year (360/180). In other words, from the time new investment is made in inventory and receivables, it takes 180 days on average before the invested cash is returned. The firm then has two complete cash cycles per year, and at the end of each of them it ends up with 3 percent more available funds. Therefore, the firm can grow at about a 6 percent annual rate from internal sources. If the firm is actually growing at, say, 20 percent, it will be experiencing a constant need for new funds. These funds must come from the sale of new equity or debt; retained earnings will not be adequate.

The preceding analysis is only a crude approximation of the firm's internally fundable growth rate, but it does show how working capital requirements constrain growth. The small firm planning for supernormal growth must therefore make provisions to obtain capital to support its growth. The manager has some alternatives, and each of them should be considered. For example, the firm can vary its working capital policy. Tightening the credit policy, for instance, may cost it some sales, but this will also reduce the average collection period, thereby increasing the number of cash cycles per year. Reducing inventory investment will probably cost the firm some lost sales in the event of stockouts, but it will again reduce the cash cycle and increase the number of cycles per year. Both of these measures will tend to reduce sales growth but also to increase the rate at which sales growth can be financed internally. For the firm with constraints on available financing, these discretionary policies may help bring its rate of growth into balance with its ability to finance that growth.

SUMMARY AND KEY CONCEPTS

This chapter examined (1) working capital management and (2) methods of financing current assets. The key concepts covered are listed below.

- **Working capital** refers to current assets, and **net working capital** is defined as current assets minus current liabilities. **Working capital policy** refers to decisions relating to the level and financing of current assets.

- The **cash conversion cycle** is the length of time between the payment for raw materials purchased and the receipt of cash from the sale of finished goods.

- Under a "**relaxed**" **working capital policy**, a firm holds relatively large amounts of each type of current asset. A "**restricted**" **working capital policy** entails holding minimal amounts of these items.

- **Permanent current assets** are those current assets that the firm holds even during slack times, whereas **temporary current assets** are the additional current assets that are needed during seasonal or cyclical peaks. The methods used to finance permanent and temporary current assets define the firm's working capital financing policy.

- A **moderate**, or **self-liquidating**, approach to working capital financing involves matching the maturities of assets and liabilities, so that temporary current assets are financed with short-term debt and permanent current assets and fixed assets are financed with long-term debt. Under an **aggressive** approach, some permanent current assets and perhaps even fixed assets are financed with short-term debt. A **conservative** approach would be to use long-term debt to finance some of the temporary current assets.

- The advantages of short-term credit are (1) the **speed** with which short-term loans can be arranged, (2) their **flexibility**, and (3) the fact that short-term **interest rates** are generally **lower** than long-term rates. The principal disadvantage of short-term credit is the **extra risk** that the borrower must bear because (1) the lender can demand payment on short notice and (2) the cost of the loan will increase if interest rates rise.

- **Accruals**, which are continually recurring short-term liabilities, represent free, spontaneous credit.

- Accounts payable, or **trade credit**, is the largest category of short-term debt. This credit arises spontaneously as a result of purchases on credit. Firms should use all the free trade credit they can obtain, but they should use costly trade credit only if it is less expensive than other forms of short-term debt.

- **Bank loans** are an important source of short-term credit. Interest on bank loans may be quoted as **simple interest**, **discount interest**, or **add-on interest**. The effective rate on a discount or add-on interest loan always exceeds the stated nominal rate. Banks are required by law to report the effective **annual percentage rate (APR)** on all loans.

- Banks often require borrowers to maintain **compensating balances**, which are deposit accounts set equal to between 10 and 20 percent of the loan amount. Compensating balances raise the effective rate of interest on bank loans.

- **Commercial paper** is unsecured, short-term debt issued by large, financially strong corporations. Although the cost of commercial paper is lower than the cost of bank loans, commercial paper's maturity is limited to 270 days, and it can be used only by large firms with exceptionally strong credit ratings.

● Sometimes a borrower will find that it is necessary to borrow on a **secured basis**, in which case the borrower pledges assets such as real estate, securities, equipment, inventories, or accounts receivable as collateral for the loan.

The next two chapters focus on the management of specific types of current assets — cash, marketable securities, accounts receivable, and inventories.

Questions

19-1 "Firms can control their accruals within fairly wide limits; depending on the cost of accruals, financing from this source will be increased or decreased." Discuss.

19-2 It is true that both trade credit and accruals represent a spontaneous source of capital for financing growth? Explain.

19-3 Is it true that most firms are able to obtain some free trade credit and that additional trade credit is often available, but at a cost? Explain.

19-4 What kinds of firms use commercial paper? Could Mama and Papa Gus's Corner Grocery borrow using this form of credit?

19-5 From the standpoint of the borrower, is long-term or short-term credit riskier? Explain. Would it ever make sense to borrow on a short-term basis if short-term rates were above long-term rates?

19-6 If long-term credit exposes a borrower to less risk, why would people or firms ever borrow on a short-term basis?

19-7 Suppose a firm can obtain funds by borrowing at the prime rate or selling commercial paper.
a. If the prime rate is 12 percent, what is a reasonable estimate for the cost of commercial paper?
b. If a substantial cost differential exists, why might a firm like this one actually borrow some of its funds from both markets?

19-8 What are the advantages of matching the maturities of assets and liabilities? What are the disadvantages?

Self-Test Problems *(Solutions Appear on Page 767)*

Key terms

ST-1 Define each of the following terms:
a. Working capital; net working capital; working capital policy
b. Cash conversion cycle
c. Permanent current assets; temporary current assets
d. Accruals
e. Trade credit; free trade credit; stretching accounts payable
f. Promissory note; line of credit; revolving credit agreement
g. Compensating balance
h. Prime rate

i. Simple interest; discount interest; add-on interest
j. Commercial paper
k. Secured loan

Working capital
financing

ST-2   Nelson Press, Inc., and the Craig Publishing Company had the following balance sheets as of December 31, 1988 (thousands of dollars):

	Nelson Press	Craig Publishing
Current assets	$100,000	$100,000
Fixed assets (net)	100,000	100,000
Total assets	$200,000	$200,000
Current liabilities	$ 20,000	$ 80,000
Long-term debt	80,000	20,000
Common stock	50,000	50,000
Retained earnings	50,000	50,000
Total claims	$200,000	$200,000

Earnings before interest and taxes for both firms are $30 million, and the effective federal-plus-state tax rate is 40 percent.
a. What is the return on equity for each firm if the interest rate on current liabilities is 10 percent and the rate on long-term debt is 13 percent?
b. Assume that the short-term rate rises to 20 percent. While the rate on new long-term debt rises to 16 percent, the rate on existing long-term debt remains unchanged. What would be the return on equity for Nelson Press and for Craig Publishing under these conditions?
c. Which company is in a riskier position? Why?

Working capital policy

ST-3   The Calgary Company is attempting to establish a current assets policy. Fixed assets are $600,000, and the firm plans to maintain a 50 percent debt-to-assets ratio. The interest rate is 10 percent on all debt. Three alternative current asset policies are under consideration: 40, 50, and 60 percent of projected sales. The company expects to earn 15 percent before interest and taxes on sales of $3 million. Calgary's effective federal-plus-state tax rate is 40 percent. What is the expected return on equity under each alternative?

Problems

Cash conversion cycle

19-1   For the Belvedere Company, the average age of accounts receivable is 48 days, the average age of accounts payable is 38 days, and the average age of inventory is 60 days.
a. What is the length of the firm's cash conversion cycle?
b. If Belvedere's annual sales are $1,440,000, what is the firm's investment in accounts receivable?
c. How many times per year does Belvedere turn over its inventory?

Working capital
cash flow cycle

19-2   The Kantrowitz Corporation is trying to determine the effect of its inventory turnover ratio and average collection period (ACP) on its cash flow cycle. Kantrowitz's 1988 sales (all on credit) were $2.4 million, and it earned a net profit after tax of 5 percent, or $120,000. It turned over its inventory 5 times during the year, and its ACP was 40 days. The firm had fixed assets totaling $1 million. Kantrowitz's payables deferral period is 30 days.

a. Calculate Kantrowitz's cash conversion cycle.

b. Assuming Kantrowitz holds negligible amounts of cash and marketable securities, calculate its total asset turnover ratio and ROA.

c. Suppose Kantrowitz's managers believe that the inventory turnover can be raised to 6 times. What would Kantrowitz's cash conversion cycle, total asset turnover ratio, and ROA have been if the inventory turnover had been 6 for 1988?

Working capital investment   **19-3**   Dellvoe Corporation is a leading U.S. producer of automobile batteries. Dellvoe turns out 2,000 batteries a day at a cost of $7 per battery for materials and labor. It takes the firm 20 days to convert raw materials into a battery. Dellvoe allows its customers 30 days in which to pay for the batteries, and the firm generally pays its suppliers in 20 days.

a. What is the length of Dellvoe's cash conversion cycle?

b. At a steady state in which Dellvoe produces 2,000 batteries a day, what amount of working capital must it finance?

c. By what amount could Dellvoe reduce its working capital financing needs if it was able to stretch its payables deferral period to 25 days?

d. Dellvoe's management is trying to analyze the effect of a proposed new production process on the working capital investment. The new production process would allow Dellvoe to decrease its inventory conversion period to 18 days and to increase its daily production to 2,200 batteries. However, the new process would cause the cost of materials and labor to increase to $8. Assuming the change does not affect the receivables conversion period (30 days) or the payables deferral period (20 days), what will be the length of the cash conversion cycle and the working capital financing requirement if the new production process is implemented?

Working capital policy   **19-4**   The Jefferson Roofing Corporation is attempting to determine the optimal level of current assets for the coming year. Management expects sales to increase to approximately $1.2 million as a result of an asset expansion presently being undertaken. Fixed assets total $500,000, and the firm wishes to maintain a 60 percent debt ratio. Jefferson's interest cost is currently 10 percent on both short-term and longer-term debt (which the firm uses in its permanent structure). Three alternatives regarding the projected current asset level are available to the firm: (1) an aggressive policy requiring current assets of only 45 percent of projected sales; (2) a moderate policy of 50 percent of sales in current assets; and (3) a conservative policy requiring current assets of 60 percent of sales. The firm expects to generate earnings before interest and taxes at a rate of 12 percent on total sales.

a. What is the expected return on equity under each current asset level? (Assume a 40 percent effective federal-plus-state tax rate.)

b. In this problem we have assumed that the level of expected sales is independent of current asset policy. Is this a valid assumption?

c. How would the overall riskiness of the firm vary under each policy?

Cost of trade credit   **19-5**   Calculate the implicit cost of nonfree trade credit under each of the following terms. Assume payment is made either on the due date or on the discount date.

a. 1/15, net 20
b. 2/10, net 60
c. 3/10, net 30
d. 2/10, net 45
e. 1/10, net 40

Cost of credit   **19-6**   a. If a firm buys under terms of 2/10, net 30, but actually pays on the 15th day and *still takes the discount,* what is the cost of its nonfree trade credit?
b. Does it receive more or less credit than it would if it paid within 10 days?

Cash discounts   **19-7**   Suppose Sunshine Aluminum, Inc., makes purchases of $3 million per year under terms of 2/10, net 30, and takes discounts.
a. What is the average amount of accounts payable net of discounts? (Assume that the $3 million of purchases is net of discounts — that is, gross purchases are $3,061,225, discounts are $61,225, and net purchases are $3 million. Also, use 360 days in a year.)
b. Is there a cost of the trade credit the firm uses?
c. If Sunshine did not take discounts, what would be its average payables and the cost of this nonfree trade credit?
d. What would its cost of not taking discounts be if it could stretch its payments to 40 days?

Cost of bank loans   **19-8**   Green Thumb Garden Shop is negotiating with First City Bank for a $50,000, 1-year loan. First City has offered Green Thumb the following alternatives. Which alternative has the lowest effective interest rate?
1. A 13 percent annual rate on a simple interest loan, with no compensating balance required and interest due at the end of the year.
2. An 11 percent annual rate on a simple interest loan, with a 15 percent compensating balance required and interest again due at the end of the year.
3. A 10 percent annual rate on a discounted loan with a 10 percent compensating balance.
4. Interest is figured as 11 percent of the $50,000 amount, payable at the end of the year, but the $50,000 is repayable in monthly installments during the year.

Trade credit versus bank credit   **19-9**   Selfridge Corporation projects an increase in sales from $2 million to $3 million, but it needs an additional $600,000 of current assets to support this expansion. The money can be obtained from the bank at an interest rate of 12 percent, discount interest; no compensating balance is required. Alternatively, Selfridge can finance the expansion by no longer taking discounts, thus increasing accounts payable. Selfridge purchases under terms of 3/10, net 30, but it can delay payment for an additional 30 days — paying in 60 days and thus becoming 30 days past due — without a penalty because of its suppliers' current excess capacity problems.
a. Based strictly on an interest rate comparison, how should Selfridge finance its expansion?
b. What additional qualitative factors should Selfridge consider before reaching a decision?

Bank financing

19-10   The Kriebel Corporation had sales of $7 million last year, and it earned a 5 percent return, after taxes, on sales. Recently the company has fallen behind in its accounts payable. Although its terms of purchase are net 30 days, its accounts payable represent 60 days' purchases. The company's treasurer is seeking to increase bank borrowings in order to become current in meeting its trade obligations (that is, to have 30 days' payables outstanding). The company's balance sheet is as follows (thousands of dollars):

Cash	$ 200	Accounts payable	$1,200
Accounts receivable	600	Bank loans	1,400
Inventory	2,800	Accruals	400
Current assets	$3,600	Current liabilities	$3,000
Land and buildings	1,200	Mortgage on real estate	1,400
Equipment	1,200	Common stock, $0.10 par	600
		Retained earnings	1,000
Total assets	$6,000	Total claims	$6,000

a. How much bank financing is needed to eliminate the past-due accounts payable?
b. Would you as a bank loan officer make the loan? Why?

Cost of trade credit

19-11   C. Charles Smith & Sons sells on terms of 2/10, net 40. Gross sales last year were $6 million, and accounts receivable averaged $583,333. Half of Smith's customers paid on the tenth day and took discounts. What is the cost of trade credit to Smith's nondiscount customers? (Hint: Calculate sales/day based on a 360-day year; then get average receivables of discount customers; then find the ACP for the nondiscount customers.)

Short-term financial analysis

19-12   Granulated Grain, Inc., buys on terms of 1/10, net 30, but it has not been taking discounts and has actually been paying in 60 rather than 30 days. Granulated's balance sheet follows (thousands of dollars):

Cash	$ 50	Accounts payable[a]	$ 500
Accounts receivable	450	Notes payable	50
Inventories	750	Accruals	50
Current assets	$1,250	Current liabilities	$ 600
		Long-term debt	150
Fixed assets	750	Common equity	1,250
Total assets	$2,000	Total claims	$2,000

[a]Stated net of discounts.

Now Granulated's suppliers are threatening to stop shipments unless the company begins making prompt payments (that is, paying in 30 days or less). The firm can borrow on a 1-year note (call this a current liability) from its bank at a rate of 13 percent, discount interest, with a 20 percent compensating balance required. (Granulated's $50,000 of cash is needed for transactions; it cannot be used as part of the compensating balance.)

a. Determine what action Granulated should take by calculating (1) the costs of nonfree trade credit and (2) the cost of the bank loan.
b. Assume that Granulated forgoes discounts and then borrows the amount needed to become current on its payables from the bank. How large will the bank loan be?

c. Based on your conclusion in Part b, construct a pro forma balance sheet. (Hint: You will need to include an account entitled "prepaid interest" under current assets.)

Alternative financing arrangements

19-13   Sunlight Sailboats estimates that because of the seasonal nature of its business, it will require an additional $350,000 of cash for the month of July. Sunlight has the four following options available for raising the needed funds:

1. Establish a one-year line of credit for $350,000 with a commercial bank. The commitment fee will be 0.5 percent per year on the unused portion, and the interest charge on the used funds will be 12 percent per annum. Assume that the funds are needed only in July, and that there are 30 days in July and 360 days in the year.
2. Forgo the trade discount of 3/10, net 40, on $350,000 of purchases during July.
3. Issue $350,000 of 30-day commercial paper at an 11.4 percent per annum interest rate. The total transactions fee, including the cost of a backup credit line, on using commercial paper is 0.5 percent of the amount of the issue.
4. Issue $350,000 of 60-day commercial paper at an 11.0 percent per annum interest rate, plus a transactions fee of 0.5 percent. Since the funds are required for only 30 days, the excess funds ($350,000) can be invested in 10.8 percent per annum marketable securities for the month of August. The total transactions cost of purchasing and selling the marketable securities is 0.4 percent of the amount of the issue.

a. What is the cost of each financing arrangement?
b. Is the source with the lowest expected cost necessarily the one to select? Why or why not?

Working capital policy and financing (Integrative)

19-14   Timothy Wong was recently hired as the financial manager of Browning Office Furnishings, Inc., a small manufacturer of metal office furniture. His first assignment is to develop a rational working capital policy.

Wong has identified three potential policies: (1) an aggressive policy which calls for a minimum amount of working capital and for substantial use of short-term debt, (2) a conservative policy which calls for a high working capital level and primary reliance on long-term as opposed to short-term debt, and (3) a moderate policy which falls between the two extremes. Wong estimates that the balance sheet will look like this under the three policies (in thousands of dollars):

	Balance Sheet		
	Aggressive	Moderate	Conservative
Current assets	$300	$400	$500
Net fixed assets	400	400	400
Total assets	$700	$800	$900
Short-term debt (8.0%)	$400	$200	$ 0
Long-term debt (10.0%)	0	200	400
Common equity	300	400	500
Total claims	$700	$800	$900

Short-term debt would have a cost of 8.0 percent, while long-term debt would cost 10.0 percent. Variable costs are expected to be 60 percent of sales regardless of which working capital policy is adopted, but fixed costs would increase when more current assets are held, because of increased storage and insurance costs. Annual fixed costs would be $200,000 under an aggressive policy, $210,000 with a moderate policy, and $220,000 under a conservative policy.

Because its working capital policy would influence the firm's ability to respond to customers' needs, sales are expected to vary under different economic scenarios as follows (in thousands of dollars):

	Sales with Each Working Capital Policy		
Economy	Aggressive	Moderate	Conservative
Strong	$1,000	$1,050	$1,100
Average	800	900	1,000
Weak	600	750	900

As Wong's assistant, you have been asked to draft a report which answers the following questions:

a. What are the two basic decisions in formulating a working capital policy? Describe how a firm that is willing to take relatively high risks in the hope of earning high returns would make these two decisions, and then describe the policy decisions of a highly risk-averse (conservative) firm and a moderate firm.

b. Construct income statements for Browning for each working capital policy assuming an average economy. Also, calculate ROE. Use the following format:

	Income Statements with Each Policy		
	Aggressive	Moderate	Conservative
Sales			
Cost of goods sold	———	———	———
EBIT			
Interest expense	———	———	———
Taxable income			
Taxes (40%)	———	———	———
Net income	———	———	———
ROE	———	———	———

c. Rework the income statements for weak and strong economies.

d. Assume that there is a 50 percent chance for an average economy and a 25 percent probability for both a strong and a weak economy. What is the expected ROE under each policy? Are the policies equally risky?

e. Now suppose that, after Browning has established its working capital policy, the Federal Reserve reacts to increasing inflationary expectations and begins to tighten monetary policy. As a result, interest rates increase. If Browning were following the conservative policy, it would have locked-in its 10.0 percent long-term debt cost. However, if it were following the aggressive policy, and if short-term rates increased by 4 percentage points, then this would push Browning's short-term debt cost up to 12.0 percent. What impact would this have on the firm's profitability under each of the working capital policies, in an average economy, as measured by ROE?

f. Like most small companies, Browning has two primary sources of short-term debt: trade credit and bank loans. One supplier, which supplies Browning with $25,000 of materials a year, offers Browning terms of 3/10, net 60.

1. What are Browning's net daily purchases from this supplier?
2. What is the average level of Browning's accounts payable to this supplier if the discount is taken? If the discount is not taken? What are the amounts of free credit and costly credit under both discount policies?
3. What is the approximate cost of the costly trade credit? What is the effective annual cost?

g. In discussing a possible loan with the firm's banker, Wong has found that the bank is willing to lend Browning up to $400,000 for 1 year at an 8 percent nominal, or stated, rate. However, he forgot to ask what the specific terms would be.

1. Assume the firm will borrow $400,000. What would be the effective interest rate if the loan were based on simple interest? If the loan had been an 8 percent simple interest loan for 6 months rather than for a year, would that have affected the effective annual rate?
2. What would be the effective rate if the loan were a discount interest loan? What would be the face amount of a loan large enough to net the firm $400,000 of usable funds?
3. Assume now that the terms call for an installment (or add-on) loan with equal monthly payments. What would be Browning's monthly payment? What would be the approximate cost of the loan? What would be the effective annual rate?
4. Now assume that the bank charges simple interest, but it requires the firm to maintain a 20 percent compensating balance. How much must Browning borrow to obtain its needed $400,000 plus meet the compensating balance requirement? What is the effective annual rate on the loan?
5. Now assume that the bank charges discount interest and also requires a compensating balance. How much must Browning borrow, and what is the effective annual rate under these terms?
6. Now assume all the conditions in Part (4), that is, a 20 percent compensating balance and an 8 percent simple interest loan, but assume also that Browning has $50,000 of cash balances which it normally holds for transactions purposes and which can be used as part of the required compensating balance. How does this affect (a) the size of the required loan and (b) the effective cost of the loan?

Computer-Related Problems

(Work the problems in this section only if you are using the computer problem diskette.)

Working capital policy
C19-1 Use the model for Problem C19-1 in the file C19 to work this problem.
  a. Refer back to Problem 19-4. What would be the return on equity under each current asset level if actual sales were (1) $1.6 million or (2) $800,000?

b. What would be the return on equity under each current asset level if sales were $1.2 million under the moderate policy, $1.6 million under the conservative policy, and $800,000 under the aggressive policy?

c. Which current asset level is the least risky over the range of probable sales from $800,000 to $1.6 million? Which current asset level do you recommend that Jefferson Roofing maintain? Why?

C19-2 Three companies — Aggressive, Moderate, and Conservative — have different working capital management policies as implied by their names. For example, Aggressive employs only minimal current assets, and it finances almost entirely with current liabilities plus equity. This "restricted" approach has a dual effect. It keeps total assets low, which tends to increase return on assets; but because of stock-outs and credit rejections, total sales are reduced, and because inventory is ordered more frequently and in smaller quantities, variable costs are increased. Condensed balance sheets for the three companies follow.

	Aggressive	Moderate	Conservative
Current assets	$150,000	$200,000	$300,000
Fixed assets	200,000	200,000	200,000
Total assets	$350,000	$400,000	$500,000
Current liabilities (cost = 12%)	$200,000	$100,000	$ 50,000
Long-term debt (cost = 10%)	0	100,000	200,000
Total debt	$200,000	$200,000	$250,000
Equity	150,000	200,000	250,000
Total claims on assets	$350,000	$400,000	$500,000
Current ratio	0.75:1	2:1	6:1

The cost of goods sold functions for the three firms are as follows:

$$\text{Cost of goods sold} = \text{Fixed Costs} + \text{Variable costs.}$$

Aggressive: Cost of goods sold = $200,000 + 0.70(Sales).

Moderate: Cost of goods sold = $270,000 + 0.65(Sales).

Conservative: Cost of goods sold = $385,000 + 0.60(Sales).

Because of the working capital differences, sales for the three firms under different economic conditions are expected to vary as follows:

	Aggressive	Moderate	Conservative
Strong economy	$1,200,000	$1,250,000	$1,300,000
Average economy	900,000	1,000,000	1,150,000
Weak economy	700,000	800,000	1,050,000

a. Construct income statements for each company for strong, average, and weak economies using the following format:

Sales
Less cost of goods sold
Earnings before interest and taxes (EBIT)
Less interest expense
Taxable income
Less taxes (at 40%)
Net income

b. Compare the basic earning power (EBIT/assets) and return on equity for the companies. Which company is best in a strong economy? In an average economy? In a weak economy?

c. Suppose that, with sales at the normal-economy level, short-term interest rates rose to 25 percent. How would this affect the three firms?

d. Suppose that because of production slowdowns caused by inventory shortages, the aggressive company's variable cost ratio rose to 80 percent. What would happen to its ROE? Assume a short-term interest rate of 12 percent.

e. What considerations for management of working capital are indicated by this problem?

Solutions to Self-Test Problems

ST-1   Refer to the marginal glossary definitions to check your responses.

ST-2   a. and b.

	Income Statements For Year Ended December 31, 1988 (Thousands of Dollars)			
	Nelson Press		Craig Publishing	
	a	b	a	b
EBIT	$ 30,000	$ 30,000	$ 30,000	$ 30,000
Interest	12,400	14,400	10,600	18,600
Taxable income	$ 17,600	$ 15,600	$ 19,400	$ 11,400
Federal-plus-state taxes (40%)	7,040	6,240	7,760	4,560
Net income	$ 10,560	$ 9,360	$ 11,640	$ 6,840
Equity	$100,000	$100,000	$100,000	$100,000
Return on equity	10.56%	9.36%	11.64%	6.84%

The Nelson Press has a higher ROE when short-term interest rates are high, whereas Craig Publishing does better when rates are lower.

c. Craig's position is riskier. First, its profits and return on equity are much more volatile than Nelson's. Second, Craig must renew its large short-term loan every year, and if the renewal comes up at a time when money is very tight, when its business is depressed, or both, then Craig could be denied credit, which could put it out of business.

ST-3

	The Calgary Company: Alternative Balance Sheets		
	Restricted (40%)	Moderate (50%)	Relaxed (60%)
Current assets	$1,200,000	$1,500,000	$1,800,000
Fixed assets	600,000	600,000	600,000
Total assets	$1,800,000	$2,100,000	$2,400,000
Debt (10%)	$ 900,000	$1,050,000	$1,200,000
Equity	900,000	1,050,000	1,200,000
Total claims	$1,800,000	$2,100,000	$2,400,000

continued

	The Calgary Company: Alternative Income Statements		
	Restricted	Moderate	Relaxed
Sales	$3,000,000	$3,000,000	$3,000,000
EBIT (15% of sales)	450,000	450,000	450,000
Interest (10%)	90,000	105,000	120,000
Earnings before taxes	$ 360,000	$ 345,000	$ 330,000
Federal-plus-state taxes (40%)	144,000	138,000	132,000
Net income	$ 216,000	$ 207,000	$ 198,000
ROE	24.0%	19.7%	16.5%

19A Secured Short-Term Financing

This appendix discusses procedures for using accounts receivable and inventories as security for short-term loans. As noted in Chapter 19, secured loans involve quite a bit of paperwork and other administrative costs, which makes them relatively expensive. However, this is often the only type of financing available to weaker firms.

Accounts Receivable Financing

pledging receivables
Putting accounts receivables up as security for a loan.

recourse
The lender can seek payment from the selling firm if an account receivable is uncollectable.

factoring
Outright sale of accounts receivable.

Accounts receivable financing involves either the pledging of receivables or the selling of receivables (factoring). The **pledging of accounts receivable** is characterized by the fact that the lender not only has a claim against the receivables but also has **recourse** to the borrower: If the person or firm that bought the goods does not pay, the selling firm must take the loss. Therefore, the risk of default on the pledged accounts receivable remains with the borrower. The buyer of the goods is not ordinarily notified about the pledging of the receivables, and the financial institution that lends on the security of accounts receivable is generally either a commercial bank or one of the large industrial finance companies.

Factoring, or *selling accounts receivable,* involves the purchase of accounts receivable by the lender, generally without recourse to the borrower, which means that if the purchaser of the goods does not pay for them, the lender rather than the seller of the goods takes the loss. Under factoring, the buyer of the goods is typically notified of the transfer and is asked to make payment directly to the financial institution. Since the factoring firm assumes the risk of default on bad accounts, it must make the credit check. Accordingly, factors provide not only money but also a credit department for the borrower. Incidentally, the same financial institutions that make loans against pledged receivables also serve as factors. Thus, depending on the circumstances and the wishes of the borrower, a financial institution will provide either form of receivables financing.

Procedure for Pledging Accounts Receivable. The financing of accounts receivable is initiated by a legally binding agreement between the seller of the goods and the financing institution. The agreement sets forth in detail the procedures to be followed and the legal obligations of both parties. Once the working relationship has been established, the seller periodically takes a batch of invoices to the financing institution. The lender reviews the invoices and makes credit appraisals of the buyers. Invoices of companies that do not meet the lender's credit standards are not accepted for pledging.

The financial institution seeks to protect itself at every phase of the operation. First, selection of sound invoices is one way the lender safeguards itself. Second, if the buyer of the goods does not pay the invoice, the lender still has recourse against the seller. Third, additional protection is afforded the lender because the loan will generally be less than 100 percent of the pledged receivables; for example, the lender may advance the selling firm only 75 percent of the amount of the pledged invoices.

Procedure for Factoring Accounts Receivable. The procedures used in factoring are somewhat different from those for pledging. Again, an agreement between the seller and the factor specifies legal obligations and procedural arrangements. When the seller receives an order from a buyer, a credit approval slip is written and immediately sent to the factoring company for a credit check. If the factor approves the credit, shipment is made and the invoice is stamped to notify the buyer to make payment directly to the factoring company. If the factor does not approve the sale, the seller generally refuses to fill the order; if the sale is made anyway, the factor will not buy the account.

The factor normally performs three functions: (1) credit checking, (2) lending, and (3) risk bearing. However, the seller can select various combinations of these functions by changing provisions in the factoring agreement. For example, a small- or medium-sized firm may have the factor perform the risk-bearing function and thus avoid having to establish a credit department. The factor's service might well be less costly than a credit department that would have excess capacity for the firm's credit volume. At the same time, if the selling firm uses someone who is not really qualified for the job to perform credit checking, then that person's lack of education, training, and experience could result in excessive losses.

The seller may have the factor perform the credit-checking and risk-taking functions without performing the lending function. The following procedure illustrates the handling of a $10,000 order under this arrangement. The factor checks and approves the invoices. The goods are shipped on terms of net 30. Payment is made to the factor, who remits to the seller. If the buyer defaults, however, the $10,000 must still be remitted to the seller, and if the $10,000 is never paid, the factor sustains a $10,000 loss. Note that in this situation, the factor does not remit funds to the seller until either they are received from the buyer of the goods or the credit period has expired. Thus, the factor does not supply any credit.

Now consider the more typical situation in which the factor performs the lending, risk-bearing, and credit-checking functions. The goods are shipped, and even though payment is not due for 30 days, the factor immediately makes funds available to the seller. Suppose $10,000 worth of goods are shipped. Further assume that the factoring commission for credit checking and risk bearing is 2.5 percent of the invoice price, or $250, and that the interest expense is computed at a 9 percent annual rate on the invoice balance, or $75.[1] The selling firm's accounting entry is as follows:

Cash	$9,175	
Interest expense	75	
Factoring commission	250	
Reserve due from factor on collection of account	500	
Accounts receivable		$10,000

The $500 due from the factor upon collection of the account is a reserve established by the factor to cover disputes between the seller and buyers over damaged goods, goods returned by the buyers to the seller, and the failure to make an outright sale of goods. The reserve is paid to the selling firm when the factor collects on the account.

Factoring is normally a continuous process instead of the single cycle just described. The firm that sells the goods receives an order; it transmits this order to the factor for approval; upon approval, the firm ships the goods; the factor advances the invoice amount minus withholdings to the seller; the buyer pays the factor when payment is due; and the factor periodically remits any excess in the reserve to the seller of the goods. Once a routine has been established, a continuous circular flow of goods and funds takes place between the seller, the buyers of the goods, and the factor. Thus, once the factoring agreement is in force, funds from this source are *spontaneous* in the sense that an increase in sales will automatically generate additional credit.

Cost of Receivables Financing. Both accounts receivable pledging and factoring are convenient and advantageous, but they can be costly. The credit-checking and risk-bearing fee is 1 to 3 percent of the amount of invoices accepted by the factor, and it may be even more if the buyers are poor credit risks. The cost of money is reflected in the interest rate (usually 2 to 3 percentage points over the prime rate) charged on the unpaid balance of the funds advanced by the factor.

Evaluation of Receivables Financing. It cannot be said categorically that accounts receivable financing is always either a good or a poor method of raising funds for an individual business. Among the advantages is, first, the flexibility of this source of financing: As the firm's sales expand, causing more financing to be needed, a larger volume of invoices, and hence a larger amount of receivables financing, is generated automatically. Second, receivables can be used as security for a loan that

---

[1]Since the interest is only for 1 month, we multiply 1/12 of the stated rate (9 percent) by the $10,000 invoice price:

$$(1/12)(0.09)(\$10,000) = \$75.$$

The effective rate of interest is really above 9 percent because (1) the term is for less than 1 year and (2) a discounting procedure is used and the borrower does not get the full $10,000. In many instances, however, the factoring contract calls for interest to be computed on the invoice price minus the factoring commission and the reserve account.

a firm might otherwise not be able to obtain. Third, factoring can provide the services of a credit department that might otherwise be available to the firm only under much more expensive conditions.

Accounts receivable financing also has disadvantages. First, when invoices are numerous and relatively small in dollar amount, the administrative costs involved may be excessive. Second, since the firm is using its most liquid noncash assets as security, some trade creditors may refuse to sell on credit to firms that are factoring or pledging their receivables on the grounds that this practice weakens the position of other creditors.

Future Use of Receivables Financing. We may make a prediction at this point: In the future, accounts receivable financing will increase in relative importance. Computer technology is rapidly advancing toward the point where credit records of individuals and firms can be kept on disks and magnetic tapes. For example, one device used by retailers consists of a box which, when an individual's magnetic credit card is inserted, gives a signal that the credit is "good" and that a bank is willing to "buy" the receivable created as soon as the store completes the sale. The cost of handling invoices will be greatly reduced over present-day costs because the new systems will be so highly automated. This will make it possible to use accounts receivable financing for very small sales, and it will reduce the cost of all receivables financing. The net result will be a marked expansion of accounts receivable financing. In fact, when consumers use credit cards such as MasterCard or Visa, the seller is in effect factoring receivables. The seller receives the amount of the purchase, minus a percentage fee, the next working day. The buyer receives 30 days' (or so) credit, at which time he or she remits payment directly to the credit card company or sponsoring bank.

Inventory Financing

A substantial amount of credit is secured by business inventories. If a firm is a relatively good credit risk, the mere existence of the inventory may be a sufficient basis for receiving an unsecured loan. However, if the firm is a relatively poor risk, the lending institution may insist upon security in the form of a *lien* against the inventory. Methods for using inventories as security are discussed in this section.

Blanket Liens. The *inventory blanket lien* gives the lending institution a lien against all of the borrower's inventories. However, the borrower is free to sell inventories, and thus the value of the collateral can be reduced below the level that existed when the loan was granted.

Trust Receipts. Because of the inherent weakness of the blanket lien, another procedure for inventory financing has been developed — the *trust receipt,* which is an instrument acknowledging that the goods are held in trust for the lender. Under this method the borrowing firm, as a condition for receiving funds from the lender, signs and delivers a trust receipt for the goods. The goods can be stored in a public warehouse or held on the premises of the borrower. The trust receipt states that the goods are held in trust for the lender or are segregated on the borrower's premises on the lender's behalf and that any proceeds from the sale of the goods must be transmitted to the lender at the end of each day. Automobile dealer financing is one of the best examples of trust receipt financing.

One defect of trust receipt financing is the requirement that a trust receipt be issued for specific goods. For example, if the security is autos in a dealer's inventory, the trust receipts must indicate the cars by registration number. In order to validate its trust receipts, the lending institution must send someone to the borrower's premises periodically to see that the auto numbers are correctly listed, because auto dealers who are in financial difficulty have been known to sell cars backing trust receipts and then use the funds obtained for other operations rather than to repay the bank. Problems are compounded if borrowers have geographically diversified operations or if they are separated geographically from the lender. To offset these inconveniences, *warehousing* has come into wide use as a method of securing loans with inventory.

Warehouse Receipts. Like trust receipts, warehouse receipt financing uses inventory as security. A *public warehouse* is an independent third-party operation engaged in the business of storing goods. Items which must age, such as tobacco and liquor, are often financed and stored in public warehouses. Sometimes a public warehouse is not practical because of the bulkiness of goods and the expense of transporting them to and from the borrower's premises. In such cases, a *field warehouse* may be established on the borrower's grounds. To provide inventory supervision, the lending institution employs a third party in the arrangement, the field warehousing company, which acts as its agent.

Field warehousing can be illustrated by a simple example. Suppose a firm which has iron stacked in an open yard on its premises needs a loan. A field warehouse can be established by the field warehousing concern's merely placing a temporary fence around the iron, erecting a sign stating "This is a field warehouse supervised and conducted by the Smith Field Warehousing Corporation," and assigning an employee to supervise and control the inventory.

This example illustrates the three essential elements for the establishment of a field warehouse: (1) public notification, (2) physical control of the inventory, and (3) supervision by a custodian of the field warehousing concern. When the field warehousing operation is relatively small, the third condition is sometimes violated by hiring an employee of the borrower to supervise the inventory. This practice is viewed as undesirable by most lenders, because there is no control over the collateral by a person independent of the borrowing firm.[2]

The field warehouse financing operation is best described by an actual case. A California tomato cannery was interested in financing its operations by bank borrowing. It had sufficient funds to finance 15 to 20 percent of its operations during the canning season. These funds were adequate to purchase and process an initial batch of tomatoes. As the cans were put into boxes and rolled into the storerooms, the cannery needed additional funds for both raw materials and labor. Because of the cannery's poor credit rating, the bank decided that a field warehousing operation was necessary to secure its loans.

---

[2]This absence of independent control was the main cause of the breakdown that resulted in more than $200 million of losses on loans to the Allied Crude Vegetable Oil Company by Bank of America and other banks. American Express Field Warehousing Company was handling the operation, but it hired men from Allied's own staff as custodians. Their dishonesty was not discovered because of another breakdown — the fact that the American Express touring inspector did not actually take a physical inventory of the warehouses. As a consequence, the swindle was not discovered until losses running into the hundreds of millions of dollars had been suffered.

The field warehouse was established, and the custodian notified the bank of the description, by number, of the boxes of canned tomatoes in storage and under warehouse control. With this inventory as collateral, the lending institution established for the cannery a deposit on which it could draw. From this point on, the bank financed the operations. The cannery needed only enough cash to initiate the cycle. The farmers brought in more tomatoes; the cannery processed them; the cans were boxed; the boxes were put into the field warehouse; field warehouse receipts were drawn up and sent to the bank; the bank established further deposits for the cannery on the basis of the additional collateral, and the cannery could draw on the deposits to continue the cycle.

Of course, the cannery's ultimate objective was to sell the canned tomatoes. As it received purchase orders, it transmitted them to the bank, and the bank directed the custodian to release the inventories. It was agreed that as remittances were received by the cannery, they would be turned over to the bank. These remittances thus paid off the loans.

Note that a seasonal pattern existed. At the beginning of the tomato harvesting and canning season, the cannery's cash needs and loan requirements began to rise, and they reached a peak just as the season ended. It was hoped that well before the new canning season began, the cannery would have sold a sufficient volume to pay off the loan. If the cannery had had a bad year, the bank might have carried the loan over for another year to enable the company to work off its inventory.

Acceptable Products. In addition to canned foods, which account for about 17 percent of all field warehouse loans, many other types of products provide a basis for field warehouse financing. Some of these are miscellaneous groceries, which represent about 13 percent; lumber products, about 10 percent; and coal and coke, about 6 percent. These products are relatively nonperishable and are sold in well-developed, organized markets. Nonperishability protects the lender if it should have to take over the security. For this reason, a bank would not make a field warehousing loan on perishables such as fresh fish; however, frozen fish, which can be stored for a long time, can be field warehoused.

Cost of Financing. The fixed costs of a field warehousing arrangement are relatively high; such financing is therefore not suitable for a very small firm. If a field warehousing company sets up a field warehouse, it will typically set a minimum charge of about $5,000 per year, plus about 1 to 2 percent of the amount of credit extended to the borrower. Furthermore, the financing institution will charge an interest rate of two to three percentage points over the prime rate. An efficient field warehousing operation requires a minimum inventory of at least $1 million.

Evaluation of Inventory Financing. The use of inventory financing, especially field warehouse financing, as a source of funds for business firms has many advantages. First, the amount of funds available is flexible because the financing is tied to the growth of inventories, which in turn is related directly to financing needs. Second, the field warehousing arrangement increases the acceptability of inventories as loan collateral; some inventories simply would not be accepted by a bank as security without such an arrangement. Third, the necessity for inventory control and safekeeping as well as the use of specialists in warehousing often results in improved warehouse practices, which in turn save handling costs, insurance charges, theft losses, and so on. Thus, field warehousing companies have often saved money for firms in spite of the costs of financing that we have discussed. The major disadvantages of a field warehousing operation are the paperwork, physical separation requirements, and, for small firms, the fixed-cost element.

Problems

Receivables financing   **19A-1**   The Funtime Company manufactures plastic toys. It buys raw materials, manufactures the toys in the spring and summer, and ships them to department stores and toy stores by late summer or early fall. Funtime factors its receivables; if it did not, its October 1988 balance sheet would appear as follows (thousands of dollars):

Cash	$ 40	Accounts payable	$1,200
Receivables	1,200	Notes payable	800
Inventory	800	Accruals	80
Current assets	$2,040	Current liabilities	$2,080
		Mortgages	200
		Common stock	400
Fixed assets	800	Retained earnings	160
Total assets	$2,840	Total claims	$2,840

Funtime provides extended credit to its customers, so its receivables are not due for payment until January 31, 1989. Also, Funtime would have been overdue on some $800,000 of its accounts payable if the preceding situation had actually existed.

Funtime has an agreement with a finance company to factor the receivables for the period October 31 through January 31 of each selling season. The factoring company charges a flat commission of 2 percent, plus 6 percent per year interest on the outstanding balance; it deducts a reserve of 8 percent for returned and damaged materials. Interest and commissions are paid in advance. No interest is charged on the reserved funds or on the commission.

a. Show Funtime's balance sheet on October 31, 1988, including the purchase of all the receivables by the factoring company and the use of the funds to pay accounts payable.

b. If the $1.2 million is the average level of outstanding receivables, and if they turn over four times a year (hence the commission is paid four times a year), what are the total dollar costs of receivables financing (factoring) and the effective annual interest rate?

Factoring arrangement   **19A-2**   Weaver Industries needs an additional $500,000, which it plans to obtain through a factoring arrangement. The factor would purchase Weaver's accounts receivable and advance the invoice amount, minus a 2 percent commission, on the invoices purchased each month. Weaver sells on terms of net 30 days. In addition, the factor charges a 12 percent annual interest rate on the total invoice amount, to be deducted in advance.

a. What amount of accounts receivable must be factored to net $500,000?

b. If Weaver can reduce credit expenses by $3,500 per month and avoid bad debt losses of 2.5 percent on the factored amount, what is the total dollar cost of the factoring arrangement?

c. What would be the total cost of the factoring arrangement if Weaver's funds needed rose to $750,000? Would the factoring arrangement be profitable under these circumstances?

Field warehousing arrangement

19A-3   Because of crop failures last year, the San Joaquin Packing Company has no funds available to finance its canning operations during the next six months. It estimates that it will require $1,200,000 from inventory financing during the period. One alternative is to establish a six-month, $1,500,000 line of credit with terms of 9 percent annual interest on the used portion, a 1 percent commitment fee on the unused portion, and a $300,000 compensating balance at all times. The other alternative is to use field warehouse financing. The costs of the field warehouse arrangement in this case would be a flat fee of $2,000, plus 8 percent annual interest on all outstanding credit, plus 1 percent of the maximum amount of credit extended.

Expected inventory levels to be financed are as follows:

Month	Amount
July 1989	$ 250,000
August	1,000,000
September	1,200,000
October	950,000
November	600,000
December	0

a. Calculate the cost of funds from using the line of credit. Be sure to include interest charges and commitment fees. Note that each month's borrowings will be $300,000 greater than the inventory level to be financed because of the compensating balance requirement.

b. Calculate the total cost of the field warehousing operation.

c. Compare the cost of the field warehousing arrangement to the cost of the line of credit. Which alternative should San Joaquin choose?

20 Cash and Marketable Securities

HOW SOME SUCCESSFUL FIRMS DETERMINE HOW MUCH CASH TO HOLD

Cash is absolutely essential to businesses, for without cash, operations would quickly grind to a halt. Because companies recognize this, they try to make sure that they always have enough cash on hand to meet daily needs. However, cash earns either no return or a very low return, so firms try to hold their cash balances to the bare minimum. Still, *Business Week* reported that many companies, including the following ones, had huge cash positions at the end of 1987:

	Cash	Total Assets	Percentage of Assets
	(millions of dollars)		
Ford	$9,145	$33,511	27.3%
IBM	6,772	63,688	10.6
Texaco	3,715	32,012	11.6
Boeing	3,269	17,665	18.5
INC Pharmaceuticals	299	650	46.0
Golden Nugget	353	840	42.0

Why would these companies have so much cash, both in absolute dollars and as a percentage of total assets? The reasons vary. However, you should recognize that *Business Week* defines *cash* to include such "near-cash" marketable securities as Treasury bills and commercial paper, and that if a firm's cash holdings are more than 2 percent of its assets, most of the "cash" is

777

really near-cash securities, not currency and checking account balances. Thus, one reason these cash balances appear large is that they include short-term marketable securities.

Two reasons for holding large cash balances are to meet anticipated needs and to take advantage of investment opportunities that might arise. Texaco built up its cash balance because it anticipated having to pay about $4 billion to settle a lawsuit with Pennzoil. Ford was said to be looking for companies to acquire, as were INC and Golden Nugget. Boeing needed cash to support a large increase in the number of jet airplanes it was producing, whereas IBM was rumored to have plans to buy back some of its own stock on the open market. Finally, all of these companies planned to use some of their cash to pay off their maturing debts. According to *Business Week,* the stock of overleveraged companies was selling at a discount because the threat of an economic downturn, along with rising interest rates, was worrying investors. Therefore, these firms planned to use some of their cash to lower their debt ratios, with the expectation that investors would respond favorably and bid up the prices of their stocks.

Whether or not these cash-rich companies were correct remains to be seen. Certainly they were playing it safe, but they were also sacrificing potential earnings by investing capital in low-yielding securities. When you finish this chapter, you will have a better idea about how firms should determine the optimal cash and marketable securities balance.

APPROXIMATELY 1.5 percent of the average industrial firm's assets are held in the form of cash, which is defined as the total of bank demand deposits plus currency. In addition, sizable holdings of near-cash marketable securities such as U.S. Treasury bills (T-bills) or bank certificates of deposit (CDs) are often reported on corporations' financial statements. However, cash balances vary widely both among industries and among the firms within a given industry, depending on the individual firms' specific conditions and on their owners' and managers' aversion to risk. In this chapter, we analyze the factors that determine firms' cash and marketable securities balances. These same factors, incidentally, apply to the cash holdings of individuals and nonprofit organizations, including government agencies.

CASH MANAGEMENT

Cash is generally called a "nonearning" asset; although it is needed to pay for labor and raw materials, to buy fixed assets, to pay taxes, to service debt, to pay dividends, and so on, cash itself (and most commercial checking accounts) earns no interest. Thus, the goal of cash management is to reduce the amount of cash held to the minimum necessary to conduct business. We begin our analysis with a discussion of reasons for holding cash.

Rationale for Holding Cash

Firms hold cash for two primary reasons:

transactions balance
A cash balance associated with payments and collections; the balance necessary for day-to-day operations.

1. *Transactions.* Cash balances are necessary in business operations. Payments must be made in cash, and receipts are deposited in the cash account. Those cash balances associated with routine payments and collections are known as **transactions balances**.

2. *Compensation to banks for providing loans and services.* A bank makes money by lending out funds that have been deposited with it; thus, depositing money in a bank helps improve the bank's profit position. As we saw in the last chapter, banks often require borrowing firms to hold **compensating balances**. Similarly, if a bank is providing services to a customer, it generally requires the customer to leave a minimum compensating balance on deposit to help offset the costs of providing the services.

compensating balance
A checking account balance that a firm must maintain with a commercial bank.

Two other reasons for holding cash have been noted in the finance and economics literature: for precaution and for speculation. Cash inflows and outflows are somewhat unpredictable, with the degree of predictability varying among firms and industries. Therefore, firms need to hold some cash in reserve for random, unforeseen fluctuations in inflows and outflows. These "safety stocks" are called **precautionary balances**, and the less predictable the firm's cash flows, the larger such balances should be. However, if the firm has easy access to borrowed funds — that is, if it can borrow on short notice — its need to hold cash for precautionary purposes is reduced. Also, as we note later in this chapter, firms that would otherwise need large precautionary balances tend to hold highly liquid marketable securities rather than cash per se; such holdings accomplish the same purposes as cash balances, but they provide greater interest income than bank deposits.

precautionary balance
A cash balance held in reserve for random, unforeseen fluctuations in cash inflows and outflows.

Some cash balances may be held to enable the firm to take advantage of any bargain purchases that might arise; these funds are called **speculative balances**. However, as with precautionary balances, firms today are more likely to rely on reserve borrowing power and on marketable securities portfolios than on cash per se for speculative purposes.

speculative balance
A cash balance that is held to enable the firm to take advantage of any bargain purchases that might arise.

Although the cash accounts of most firms can be thought of as consisting of transactions, compensating, precautionary, and speculative balances, we cannot calculate the amount needed for each purpose, sum them, and produce a total desired cash balance, because the same money often serves more than one purpose. For instance, precautionary and speculative balances can also be used to satisfy compensating balance requirements. Firms do, however, consider these four factors when establishing their target cash positions.

THE CASH BUDGET

The firm estimates its needs for cash as a part of its general budgeting, or forecasting, process. First, it forecasts sales. Next, it forecasts the fixed assets and inventories that will be required to meet the forecasted sales levels. Asset purchases and the actual payments for them are then put on a time scale, along with the actual timing of the sales and the timing of collections for sales. For example, the typical firm makes a 5-year sales forecast, which is then used to help plan fixed asset acquisitions (capital budgeting). Next, the firm develops an annual forecast, in which sales and inventory purchases are projected on a monthly basis, along with the times when payments for both fixed assets and inventory purchases must be made. These forecasts are combined with projections about the timing of the collection of accounts receivable, the schedule for payment of taxes, the dates when dividend and interest payments will be made, and so on. Finally, all of this information is summarized in the **cash budget**, which shows the firm's projected cash inflows and outflows over some specified period of time.

Cash budgets can be constructed on a monthly, weekly, or even daily basis. Generally, firms use a monthly cash budget forecasted over the next 6 to 12 months, plus a more detailed daily cash budget for the coming month. The longer-term budget is used for planning purposes, and the shorter-term one for actual cash control.

cash budget
A schedule showing cash flows (receipts, disbursements, and net cash) for a firm over a specified period.

Constructing the Cash Budget

We shall illustrate the process with a monthly cash budget covering the last six months of 1989 for the Drexel Card Company, a leading producer of greeting cards. Drexel's birthday and get-well cards are sold year round, but the bulk of sales occurs during September, when retailers are stocking up for Christmas. All sales are made on terms that allow a cash discount for payments made within 10 days, but if the discount is not taken, the full amount must be paid in 40 days. However, Drexel, like most other companies, finds that some of its customers delay payment up to 70 days. Indeed, its experience shows that on 20 percent of the sales, payment is made during the month in which the sale is made; on 70 percent of the sales, payment is made during the first month after the month of the sale; and on 10 percent of the sales, payment is made during the second month after the month of the sale. Drexel offers a 2 percent discount for payments received within 10 days of sales. Typically, payments received in the month of sale are on discount sales.

Rather than produce at a uniform rate throughout the year, Drexel prints cards immediately before they are required for delivery. Paper, ink, and other materials amount to 70 percent of sales and are bought the month before the company expects to sell the finished product. Its own purchase terms permit Drexel to delay payment on its purchases for 1 month. Accordingly, if July sales are forecasted at $10 million, purchases during June will amount to $7 million, and this amount will actually be paid in July.

Such other cash expenditures as wages and rent are also built into the cash budget. Further, Drexel must make tax payments of $2 million on September 15 and December 15, as well as a payment for a new plant in October. Assuming that it needs to keep a **target cash balance** of $2.5 million at all times and that it will have $3 million on July 1, what are Drexel's financial requirements for the period July through December?[1]

target cash balance
The desired cash balance that a firm plans to maintain in order to conduct business.

The monthly cash flow forecasts are worked out in Table 20-1. Section I of the table provides a worksheet for calculating collections on sales and payments for purchases. Line 1 gives the sales forecast for the period May through December; May and June sales are necessary to determine collections for July and August. Next, on Lines 2 through 5, cash collections are given. Line 2 shows that 20 percent of the sales during any given month are collected during that month. Customers who pay in the first month, however, typically take the discount, so the cash collected in the month of sale is reduced by 2 percent; for example, collections during July for the $10 million of sales in that month will be 20% of total sales less the 2% discount = $(0.2)(0.98)($10,000,000) =$ $1,960,000. Line 3 shows the collections on the previous month's sales, or 70 percent of sales in the preceding month; for example, in July, 70 percent of the $5,000,000 June sales, or $3,500,000, will be collected. Line 4 gives collections from sales two months earlier, or 10 percent of sales in that month; for example, the July collections for May sales are $(0.10)($5,000,000) = $500,000$. The collections during each month are summed and shown on Line 5; thus, the July collections represent 20 percent of July sales (minus the discount) plus 70 percent of June sales plus 10 percent of May sales, or $5,960,000 in total.

Next, payments for purchases of raw materials are shown. July sales are forecasted at $10 million, so Drexel will purchase $7 million of materials in June (Line 6) and pay for these purchases in July (Line 7). Similarly, Drexel will purchase $10.5 million of materials in July to produce cards to meet August's forecasted sales of $15 million.

With Section I completed, Section II can be constructed. Cash from collections is shown on Line 8. Lines 9 through 14 list payments made during each month, and these payments are summed on Line 15. The difference between cash receipts and cash payments (Line 8 minus Line 15) is the net cash gain or loss during the month; for July there is a net cash loss of $2,140,000, as shown on Line 16.

In Section III, we first determine Drexel's cumulative cash balance at the end of each month, assuming no borrowing is done. Then we determine the company's forecasted cash surplus or the loan balance, if any, that is needed to force Drexel's cash balance to equal the target cash balance. The cash on hand at the beginning of the month is shown on Line 17. We assume that Drexel will have $3 million on hand on July 1, but thereafter the beginning cash

---

[1]Setting the target cash balance is an important part of cash management. We will discuss this topic later in the chapter.

Table 20-1   Drexel Card Company: Cash Budget
(Thousands of Dollars)

	May	June	July	Aug.	Sept.	Oct.	Nov.	Dec.
I. Collections and Payments								
(1) Sales (gross)[a]	$5,000	$5,000	$10,000	$15,000	$20,000	$10,000	$10,000	$5,000
Collections:								
(2) During month of sale: 20% minus 2% discount = (0.2)(0.98)(month's sales)	980	980	1,960	2,940	3,920	1,960	1,960	980
(3) During first month after sale month: 70% = 0.7 (previous month's sales)		3,500	3,500	7,000	10,500	14,000	7,000	7,000
(4) During second month after sale month: 10% = 0.1 (sales 2 months ago)	——	——	500	500	1,000	1,500	2,000	1,000
(5) Total collections	$ 980	$4,480	$ 5,960	$10,440	$15,420	$17,460	$10,960	$8,980
(6) Purchases (70% of next month's sales)	$3,500	$7,000	$10,500	$14,000	$ 7,000	$ 7,000	$ 3,500	
(7) Payments (1-month lag)		$3,500	$ 7,000	$10,500	$14,000	$ 7,000	$ 7,000	$3,500
II. Cash Gain or Loss for Month								
(8) Collections (from Section I)			$ 5,960	$10,440	$15,420	$17,460	$10,960	$8,980
Payments:								
(9) Purchases (from Section I)			$ 7,000	$10,500	$14,000	$ 7,000	$ 7,000	$3,500
(10) Wages and salaries			750	1,000	1,250	750	750	500
(11) Rent			250	250	250	250	250	250
(12) Other expenses			100	150	200	100	100	50
(13) Taxes					2,000			2,000
(14) Payment for plant construction						5,000		
(15) Total payments			$ 8,100	$11,900	$17,700	$13,100	$ 8,100	$6,300
(16) Net cash gain (loss) during month (Line 8 − Line 15)			($ 2,140)	($ 1,460)	($ 2,280)	$ 4,360	$ 2,860	$2,680
III. Cash Surplus or Loan Requirements								
(17) Cash at start of month if no borrowing is done[b]			3,000	860	(600)	(2,880)	1,480	4,340
(18) Cumulative cash (cash at start + gain or − loss = Line 16 + Line 17)			$ 860	($ 600)	($ 2,880)	$ 1,480	$ 4,340	$7,020
(19) Target cash balance			2,500	2,500	2,500	2,500	2,500	2,500
(20) Surplus cash or total loans outstanding required to maintain $2,500 target cash balance (Line 18 − Line 19)[c]			($ 1,640)	($ 3,100)	($ 5,380)	($ 1,020)	$ 1,840	$4,520

Notes:

[a]Although the budget period is July through December, sales and purchases data for May and June are needed to determine collections and payments during July and August.

[b]The amount shown on Line 17 for the first budget period month, the $3,000 balance on July 1, is assumed to be on hand initially. The values shown for each of the following months on Line 17 are equal to the cumulative cash as shown on Line 18 for the preceding month; for example, the $860 shown on Line 17 for August is taken from Line 18 in the July column.

[c]When the target cash balance of $2,500 (Line 19) is deducted from the cumulative cash balance (Line 18), a resulting negative figure on Line 20 represents a required loan, whereas a positive figure represents surplus cash. Loans are required from July through October, and surpluses are expected during November and December. Note also that firms can borrow or pay off loans on a daily basis, so the $1,640 borrowed during July would be done on a daily basis, as needed, and during October the $5,380 loan that existed at the beginning of the month would be reduced daily to the $1,020 ending balance, which in turn would be completely paid off during November.

balance is taken as the cumulative cash balance (Line 18) from the previous month. The beginning cash balance (Line 17) is added to the net cash gain or loss during the month (Line 16) to obtain the cumulative cash that would be on hand if no financing were done (Line 18); at the end of July, Drexel forecasts a cumulative cash balance of $860,000 in the absence of borrowing.

The target cash balance, $2.5 million, is then subtracted from the cumulative cash balance to determine the firm's borrowing requirements or surplus cash. Because Drexel expects to have cumulative cash, as shown on Line 18, of $860,000 in July, it will have to borrow $1,640,000 to bring the cash account up to the target balance of $2,500,000. Assuming that this amount is indeed borrowed, loans outstanding will total $1,640,000 at the end of July. (We assume that Drexel did not have any loans outstanding on July 1, because its beginning cash balance exceeded the target balance.) The cash surplus or required loan balance is given on Line 20; a positive value indicates a cash surplus, whereas a negative value indicates a loan requirement. Note that the surplus cash or loan requirement shown on Line 20 is a *cumulative amount.* Thus, Drexel must borrow $1,640,000 in July; it has a cash shortfall during August of $1,460,000 as reported on Line 16; and, therefore, its total loan requirement at the end of August is $1,640,000 + $1,460,000 = $3,100,000, as reported on Line 20. Drexel's arrangement with the bank permits it to increase its outstanding loans on a daily basis, up to a prearranged maximum, just as you could increase the amount you owe on a credit card. Drexel will use any surplus funds it generates to pay off its loans, and because the loan can be paid down at any time, Drexel will never have both a cash surplus and an outstanding loan balance.

This same procedure is used in the following months. Sales will peak in September, accompanied by increased payments for purchases, wages, and other items. Receipts from sales will also go up, but the firm will still be left with a $2,280,000 net cash outflow during the month. The total loan requirement at the end of September will be $5,380,000, the cumulative cash plus the target cash balance. This amount is also equal to the $3,100,000 needed at the end of August plus the $2,280,000 cash deficit for September. Thus, loans outstanding will hit a high of $5,380,000 at the end of September.

Sales, purchases, and payments for past purchases will fall sharply in October, but collections will be the highest of any month because they will reflect the high September sales. As a result, Drexel will enjoy a healthy $4,360,000 net cash gain during October. This net gain will be used to pay off borrowings, so loans outstanding will decline by $4,360,000, to $1,020,000.

Drexel will have another cash surplus in November, which will permit it to pay off all of its loans. In fact, the company is expected to have $1,840,000 in surplus cash by the month's end, and another cash surplus in December will swell the extra cash to $4,520,000. With such a large amount of unneeded funds, Drexel's treasurer will certainly want to invest in interest-bearing securities, or to put the funds to use in some other way.

Before concluding our discussion of the cash budget, we should make some additional points:

1. Our cash budget example does not reflect interest on loans or income from the investment of surplus cash. This refinement could easily be added.

2. If cash inflows and outflows are not uniform during the month, we could be seriously understating the firm's peak financing requirements. The data in Table 20-1 show the situation expected on the last day of each month, but on any given day during the month it could be quite different. For example, if all payments had to be made on the fifth of each month, but collections came in uniformly throughout the month, the firm would need to borrow much larger amounts than those shown in Table 20-1. In this case, we would have to prepare a cash budget identifying requirements on a daily basis.

3. Since depreciation is a noncash charge, it does not appear on the cash budget other than through its effect on taxes paid.

4. Since the cash budget represents a forecast, all the values in the table are *expected* values. If actual sales, purchases, and so on, are different from the forecasted levels, then the projected cash deficits and surpluses will also be incorrect. Thus, Drexel might end up needing to borrow larger amounts than are indicated on Line 20, so it should arrange a line of credit in excess of that amount.

5. Computerized spreadsheet programs such as *Lotus 1-2-3* are particularly well suited for constructing and analyzing the cash budget, especially with respect to the sensitivity of cash flows to changes in sales levels, collection periods, and the like. We could change any assumption, say the projected monthly sales or the time when customers pay, and the cash budget would automatically and instantly be recalculated. This would show us exactly how the firm's borrowing requirements would change if various other things changed. We have written such a model; see Computer-Related Problem C20-1. Also, with a computer model, it is easy to add features like interest on loans, bad debts, and so on.

6. Finally, we should note that the target cash balance probably will be adjusted over time, rising and falling with seasonal patterns and with long-term changes in the scale of the firm's operations. Thus, Drexel will probably plan to maintain larger cash balances during August and September than at other times, and as the company grows, so will its required cash balance. Factors that influence the target cash balance are discussed in the following sections.

Other Factors Influencing the Target Cash Balance

Any firm's target cash balance is normally set as the larger of (1) its transactions balances plus its precautionary (safety stock) balances or (2) its required compensating balances as determined by its agreements with its banks. Both the transactions balances and the precautionary balances depend on the firm's volume of business, the degree of uncertainty inherent in its forecasts of cash inflows and outflows, and its ability to borrow on short notice to meet cash shortfalls. Consider again the cash budget for the Drexel Card Company. The target cash balance (or desired cash balance) is shown on Line 19 of Table 20-1. Other things held constant, the target cash balance would increase if Drexel expanded, but it would decrease if it contracted. Similarly, Drexel could afford to operate with a smaller target balance if it could forecast better and thus be more certain that inflows will come in as scheduled and that no unanticipated outflows, such as might result from uninsured fire losses, lawsuits, and the like, will occur. The higher the cash balance, the smaller the probability that reduced inflows or unexpected outflows will cause the firm to actually run out of cash.

Statistics are not available on whether transactions balances or compensating balances actually control most firms' target cash balances, but compensating balance requirements do often dominate, especially during periods of high interest rates and tight money.[2] Also, even though our discussion of the target cash balance in this section has been more intuitive than rigorous, formal models designed to optimize cash holdings have been developed. One of these models is discussed later in the chapter.

INCREASING THE EFFICIENCY OF CASH MANAGEMENT

Although a carefully prepared cash budget is a necessary starting point, there are other elements of a good cash management program, some of which we describe in this section.

Cash Flow Synchronization

If you as an individual were to receive income once a year, you would probably put it in the bank, draw down your account periodically, and have an average balance during the year equal to half your annual income. If you received income monthly, or even daily, instead of once a year, you would operate with a lower average checking account balance. Indeed, if you could

---

[2]This point is underscored by an incident that occurred at a professional finance meeting. A professor presented a scholarly paper that used operations research techniques to determine "optimal cash balances" for a sample of firms. He then reported that the firms' actual cash balances greatly exceeded their optimal balances, suggesting inefficiency and the need for more refined techniques. The discussant of the paper made her comments short and sweet. She reported that she had written each of the sample firms and asked them why they had so much cash; they had uniformly replied that their cash holdings were set by compensating balance requirements. Thus, the model might have been useful to determine the optimal cash balance in the absence of compensating balance requirements, but it was precisely those requirements that determined actual balances.

arrange to receive income daily and to pay rent, tuition, and other charges on a daily basis, and if you were quite confident of your forecasted inflows and outflows, this would enable you to hold a very small average cash balance. Exactly the same situation holds for business firms. By improving their forecasts and by arranging things so that cash receipts coincide with cash outflows, firms can hold their transactions balances to a minimum. Recognizing this point, utility companies, oil companies, and others arrange to bill customers and to pay their own bills on regular "billing cycles" throughout the month. In our cash budgeting example, if the Drexel Card Company could arrange more **synchronized cash flows** and increase the certainty of its forecasts, it could reduce its target cash balance and therefore its required bank loans.

synchronized cash flows
A situation in which inflows coincide with outflows, thereby permitting a firm to hold transactions balances to a minimum.

Using Float

Suppose you have $1,000 in your bank account, and you then write a check for $600 and mail it to a company to pay for some clothes. You will reduce your balance by $600, to $400. However, during the time before the payee receives the check and deposits it, and until the check is cleared through the banking system, your bank will think that you still have $1,000 in your account. If your bank pays interest on checking accounts, you will continue to earn interest on the $600 until the check has cleared. The $600 is called *disbursement float,* and it is defined as the amount of funds tied up in checks that you (or any firm or individual) have written but that are still in process and have not yet been deducted from your checking account balance by the bank. Similarly, when you receive a check, it takes time for you to deposit it, and for the bank to process it and credit your account with "good" funds; the delay on the collections side is known as *collection float.*

At any given time, a business has a number of checks that it has written but that have not been deducted by the bank from its account (disbursement float), as well as a number of checks that it has received but that have not yet been credited to its account (collection float). The difference between disbursement float and collection float is called **net float:**

net float
The difference between a firm's checkbook balance and the balance shown on the bank's books.

$$\text{Net float} = \text{Disbursement float} - \text{Collection float.}$$

Net float can also be defined as the difference between a firm's (or an individual's) checkbook balance and the balance shown on the bank's books.

In general, it is good to operate with *positive net float;* this means that the firm is able to collect checks written to it, and thus to get the use of money paid to it, relatively rapidly. Those to whom it writes checks are relatively less efficient in clearing checks, allowing the firm to use the funds for a while after it has written checks. One large manufacturer of construction equipment has stated that although its account, according to its bank's records, shows an average cash balance of about $20 million, its *book* cash balance is *minus* $20 million. Therefore, it has $40 million of net float. Obviously the firm must be able to forecast its positive and negative clearings accurately in order to make such a heavy use of float.[3]

Basically, a firm's net float is a function of its ability to speed up collections on checks received and to slow down collections on checks written. Efficient firms go to great lengths to speed up the processing of incoming checks, thus putting the funds to work faster, and they try to stretch their own payments out as long as possible.

Note also that when a customer writes and mails a check, this does *not* mean that the funds are immediately available to the receiving firm. Most of us have been told by someone that "the check is in the mail," and we have also deposited a check in our account and then been told that we cannot write our own checks against this deposit until the **check-clearing** process has been completed. Our bank must first make sure that the check we deposited is good and then receive funds itself from the customer's bank before releasing funds for us to spend.

As shown on the left side of Figure 20-1, quite a bit of time may be required for a firm to process incoming checks and obtain the use of the money. A check must first be delivered through the mail and then be cleared through the banking system before the money can be put to use. Checks received from customers in distant cities are especially subject to delays because of mail time and also because more parties are involved. For example, assume that we receive a check and deposit it in our bank. Our bank must send the check to the bank on which it was drawn. Only when this latter bank transfers funds to our bank are the funds available for us to use. Checks are generally cleared through the Federal Reserve System or through a clearinghouse set up by the banks in a particular city. Of course, if the check is deposited in the same bank on which it was drawn, that bank merely transfers funds by bookkeeping entries from one of its depositors to another. The length of time required for checks to clear is thus a function of the distance between the payer's and the payee's banks. In the case of private clearinghouses, it can range from one to three days. The maximum time required for checks to clear through the Federal Reserve System is two days, but mail delays can slow down things on each end of the Fed's involvement in the process.

The right side of Figure 20-1 shows how the process can be speeded up. First, to reduce mail and clearing delays, a **lockbox plan** can be used. Suppose a New York firm makes sales to customers all across the country. It can arrange to have its customers send payments to post office boxes (lockboxes) in their

check clearing
The process of converting a check that has been written and mailed into cash in the payee's account.

lockbox plan
A procedure used to speed up collections and reduce float through the use of post office boxes in payers' local areas.

---

[3]The distinction between using float and kiting checks should be made clear. *Kiting* is a situation in which a firm has accounts in two or more banks, and it deposits a bad check written on one bank with another bank to inflate its balance in the second bank. It then writes checks on the second bank account to pay debts. Kiting requires a continuous process, and it can only work if banks allow a firm to write checks against deposits based on checks which have not yet been cleared through the system. Kiting is illegal, and those who engage in the practice can be sent to jail. Using float is perfectly legitimate — you can legally write a check on Saturday for more than the balance in your account, provided that you are sure you can deposit the funds to cover the check on Monday before the check you wrote clears.

Figure 20-1   Diagram of the Check-Clearing Process

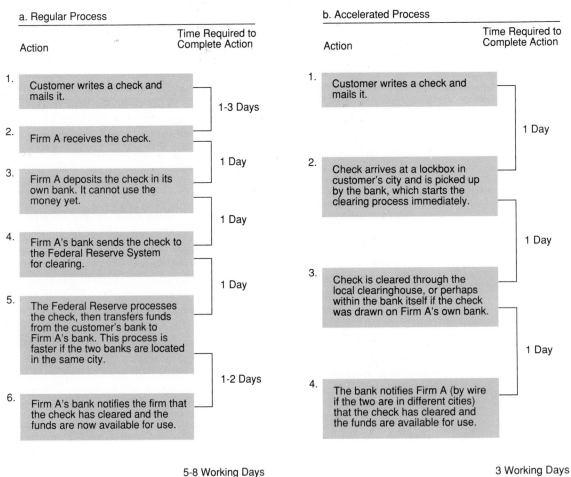

a. Regular Process

Action	Time Required to Complete Action
1. Customer writes a check and mails it.	1-3 Days
2. Firm A receives the check.	1 Day
3. Firm A deposits the check in its own bank. It cannot use the money yet.	1 Day
4. Firm A's bank sends the check to the Federal Reserve System for clearing.	1 Day
5. The Federal Reserve processes the check, then transfers funds from the customer's bank to Firm A's bank. This process is faster if the two banks are located in the same city.	1-2 Days
6. Firm A's bank notifies the firm that the check has cleared and the funds are now available for use.	

5-8 Working Days

b. Accelerated Process

Action	Time Required to Complete Action
1. Customer writes a check and mails it.	1 Day
2. Check arrives at a lockbox in customer's city and is picked up by the bank, which starts the clearing process immediately.	1 Day
3. Check is cleared through the local clearinghouse, or perhaps within the bank itself if the check was drawn on Firm A's own bank.	1 Day
4. The bank notifies Firm A (by wire if the two are in different cities) that the check has cleared and the funds are available for use.	

3 Working Days

own local areas. A local bank will pick up the checks, have them cleared in the local area, and then transfer the funds by wire to the company's New York bank. In this way, collection time can be reduced by several days. Examples of freeing funds in the amount of $5 million or more by this method are not uncommon.

Just as expediting the collection process conserves cash, slowing down disbursements accomplishes the same thing by keeping cash on hand for longer periods. One obviously could simply delay payments, but this would involve equally obvious difficulties. Firms have in the past devised rather ingenious methods for "legitimately" lengthening the collection period on their own checks, primarily by writing checks on banks in distant locations. For example, until a lawsuit forced it to stop the practice, Merrill Lynch paid customers located west of the Mississippi with checks drawn on an East Coast bank, and paid Eastern customers with a West Coast bank's checks. Since such practices are usually recognized for what they are, there are severe limits to their use.

Another widely used procedure for delaying payouts is the use of *drafts*. Although a check is payable on demand, a draft must be transmitted to the issuer, who approves it and deposits funds to cover it, after which it can be collected. Insurance companies often use drafts in handling claims. For instance, Aetna can pay a claim by draft on Friday. The recipient deposits the draft at a local bank, which must then send it to Aetna's Hartford bank. It may be Wednesday or Thursday before the draft arrives. The bank then sends it to the company's accounting department, which has until 3 P.M. that day to inspect and approve it. Not until then does Aetna have to deposit funds in its bank to pay the draft.

Cash Management in the Multidivisional Firm

The concepts, techniques, and procedures described thus far in the chapter must be extended when applied to large, national firms. Such corporations have plants and sales offices all across the nation (or around the world), and they deal with banks in all of their operating territories. These companies must maintain compensating balances in each of their banks, and they must be sure that no bank account becomes overdrawn. Cash inflows and outflows are subject to random fluctuations, so in the absence of close control and coordination, there would be a tendency for some accounts to have shortages while others had excess balances. Thus, a sound cash management program for such a multibank corporation necessarily includes provisions for keeping strict control over the level of funds in each account and for shifting funds among accounts so as to minimize the total corporate cash balance. Mathematical models and electronic connections between a central computer and each branch location have been developed to help with such situations, but a discussion of these topics goes beyond the scope of this book.

BANK RELATIONSHIPS

Banks provide a great many services to firms — they clear checks, operate lockbox plans, supply credit information, and the like. Because these services cost the bank money, the bank must be compensated for rendering them.

Compensating Balances

Banks earn most of their income by lending money at interest, and most of the funds they lend are obtained in the form of deposits. If a firm maintains a deposit account with an average balance of $100,000, and if the bank can lend these funds at a net return of $8,000, then the account is, in a sense, worth $8,000 to the bank. Thus, it is to the bank's advantage to provide services worth up to $8,000 to attract and hold the account.

Banks first determine the costs of the services rendered to their larger customers and then estimate the average account balances necessary to provide enough income to compensate for these costs. Firms can make direct payments for these services, but they often find it cheaper to maintain compensating balances in order to avoid paying cash service charges to the bank.[4]

As we saw in Chapter 19, compensating balances are also required by some banks under loan agreements. During periods when the supply of credit is restricted and interest rates are high, banks frequently insist that borrowers maintain accounts averaging a specified percentage of the loan amount as a condition for granting a loan; 10 percent is a typical figure. If the balance is larger than the firm would otherwise maintain, the effective cost of the loan is increased; the excess balance presumably "compensates" the bank for making a loan at a rate below what it could earn on the funds if they were invested elsewhere.[5]

Compensating balances can be established (1) as an *absolute minimum* — say, $100,000 — below which the actual balance must never fall or (2) as a *minimum average* balance — perhaps $100,000 — over some period, generally a month. The absolute minimum is a much more restrictive requirement, because the total amount of cash held during the month must be above $100,000 by the amount of the firm's transactions balances. The $100,000 in this case is "dead money" from the firm's standpoint. With a minimum average balance, however, the account could fall to zero on one day provided it was $200,000 on some other day, with the average working out to $100,000. Thus, the $100,000 in this case is available for transactions.

Statistics on compensating balance requirements are not available, but average balances are typical and absolute minimums rare for business accounts. Discussions with bankers, however, indicate that absolute balance requirements are less rare during times of extremely tight money.

Overdraft Systems

overdraft system
A system whereby depositors may write checks in excess of their balances, with the banks automatically extending loans to cover the shortages.

Most countries outside the United States use **overdraft systems**. In such systems depositors write checks in excess of their actual balances, and their banks automatically extend loans to cover the shortages. The maximum amount of such loans must, of course, be established beforehand. Although statistics are not available on the usage of overdrafts in the United States, a number of firms have worked out informal, and in some cases formal, overdraft arrangements.

---

[4]Compensating balance arrangements apply to individuals as well as to business firms. Thus, you might get "free" checking services if you maintain a minimum balance of $500 but be charged 25 cents per check if your balance falls below that amount during the month.

[5]The interest rate effect of compensating balances was discussed in Chapter 19.

Also, both banks and credit card companies regularly establish cash reserve systems for individuals. In general, the use of overdrafts has been increasing in recent years, and, if this trend continues, it will lead to a reduction of cash balances.

Zero Balance Account

Larger corporations often set up accounts for special purposes, such as paying dividends. Suppose IBM planned to pay dividends of $1.25 per share on 600 million shares, or $750 million in total, on September 10, 1989. It could deposit $750 million in an account and then write checks to its 790,000 stockholders, but because some stockholders would surely delay cashing their dividend checks, a great deal of money would be sitting idle in the account. One alternative would be for IBM to write the checks, forecast how rapidly they would be cashed and presented for payment, and then make a series of daily deposits based on those forecasts. Another alternative would be to set up a *zero balance account,* in which (1) it would write the dividend checks, (2) each day the bank would notify IBM by 11 A.M. of the total dollar amount of checks that had been received for payment that day, and (3) IBM would have until 4 P.M. to deposit the funds to cover those checks. IBM could obtain the funds by transferring them to the account from an active account, by selling marketable securities, or by borrowing in the commercial paper market. IBM could even arrange to borrow the necessary funds from the bank itself. In any event, the account would be zeroed out at the end of each day. This type of account is being used with increasing frequency.

MATCHING THE COSTS AND BENEFITS OF CASH MANAGEMENT

Although a number of procedures may be used to hold down cash balance requirements, implementing these methods is not a costless operation. How far should a firm go in making its cash operations more efficient? As a general rule, the firm should incur these expenses as long as marginal returns exceed marginal expenses.

For example, suppose that by establishing a lockbox system and increasing the accuracy of cash inflow and outflow forecasts, a firm can reduce its investment in cash by $1 million without increasing the risk of running short of cash. Further, suppose the firm borrows at a cost of 12 percent. The steps taken have released $1 million, which can be used to reduce bank loans and thus save $120,000 per year. If the costs of the procedures necessary to release the $1 million are less than $120,000, the move is a good one; if they exceed $120,000, the greater efficiency is not worth the cost. It is clear that larger firms, which have larger cash balances, can better afford to hire the personnel necessary to maintain tight control over their cash positions. Cash management is thus one element of business operations in which economies of scale are present.

Clearly, the value of careful cash management depends on the costs of funds invested in cash, which in turn depend on the current rate of interest. In the 1980s, when interest rates have often been near their historic highs, firms have been devoting a great deal of care to cash management.

MARKETABLE SECURITIES

marketable securities
Securities that can be sold on short notice for close to their quoted market prices.

As noted at the beginning of the chapter, sizable holdings of such short-term **marketable securities** as U.S. Treasury bills (T-bills) or bank certificates of deposit (CDs) are often reported on corporations' financial statements. The reasons for such holdings, as well as the factors that influence the choice of securities held, are discussed in this section.

Reasons for Holding Marketable Securities

Marketable securities typically provide much lower yields than operating assets. For example, International Business Machines (IBM) holds a multibillion-dollar portfolio of marketable securities that yields about 8 percent, whereas its operating assets have recently been providing a return of about 18 percent. Why would a company like IBM have such large holdings of low-yielding assets? There are two basic reasons for these holdings: (1) they serve as a substitute for cash balances, and (2) they are used as a temporary investment. These points are considered next.

Marketable Securities as a Substitute for Cash. Some firms hold portfolios of marketable securities in lieu of larger cash balances, then sell some securities from the portfolios to increase the cash account when cash outflows exceed inflows.

Marketable Securities as a Temporary Investment. Temporary investments in marketable securities generally occur in one of the three following situations:

1. *When the firm must finance seasonal or cyclical operations.* Firms engaged in seasonal operations frequently have surplus cash flows during one part of the year and deficit cash flows during the other. Such firms may purchase marketable securities during their surplus periods and then liquidate them when cash deficits occur. Other firms, however, choose to use bank financings to cover such shortages.

2. *When the firm must meet some known financial requirements.* If a major plant construction program is planned for the near future, or if a bond issue is about to mature, a firm may build up its marketable securities portfolio to provide the required funds. Furthermore, marketable

securities holdings are frequently built up immediately preceding quarterly corporate tax payment dates.

3. *When the firm has just sold long-term securities.* Expanding firms generally have to sell long-term securities (stocks or bonds) periodically. The proceeds from such sales are often invested in marketable securities, which are then sold off to provide cash as it is needed to pay for operating assets.

Holding Marketable Securities versus Borrowing

Actually, each of the needs listed above can be met either by taking out short-term loans or by holding marketable securities. Consider a firm such as the Drexel Card Company, whose cash budget was discussed earlier. Drexel's sales are growing over time, but they fluctuate on a seasonal basis; as we saw from Drexel's cash budget (Table 20-1), the firm plans to borrow to meet seasonal needs. As an alternative financial policy, Drexel could hold a portfolio of marketable securities and then liquidate these securities to meet its peak cash needs.

A firm's marketable securities policy is an integral part of its overall working capital policy. If the firm has a conservative working capital financing policy, its long-term capital will exceed its permanent assets, and it will hold marketable securities when inventories and receivables are low. With an aggressive policy, it will never carry any securities and will borrow heavily to meet peak needs. With a moderate policy, under which maturities are matched, the firm will match permanent assets with long-term financing, and it will meet most seasonal increases in inventories and receivables with short-term loans, but it will also carry marketable securities at certain times.

Figure 20-2, which is similar to Figure 19-2 in Chapter 19, illustrates three alternative policies for a firm like Drexel. Under Plan A, which represents an aggressive financing policy, Drexel would hold no marketable securities, relying completely on bank loans to meet seasonal peaks. Under the conservative Plan B, Drexel would stockpile marketable securities during slack periods and then sell them to raise funds for peak needs. Plan C is a compromise: Under this alternative, the company would hold some securities but not enough to meet all of its peak needs. Drexel actually follows Plan C.

There are advantages and disadvantages to each of these strategies. Plan A is clearly the most risky; the firm's current ratio is always lower than under the other plans, indicating that it might encounter difficulties either in borrowing the funds needed or in repaying the loan. On the other hand, Plan A requires no holdings of low-yielding marketable securities, and this will probably lead to a relatively high expected rate of return on both total assets and equity.

Exactly the same types of choices are involved with regard to meeting known financial needs such as plant construction, as well as to deciding whether to issue long-term securities before or after the actual need for the

Figure 20-2 Alternative Strategies for Meeting Seasonal Cash Needs

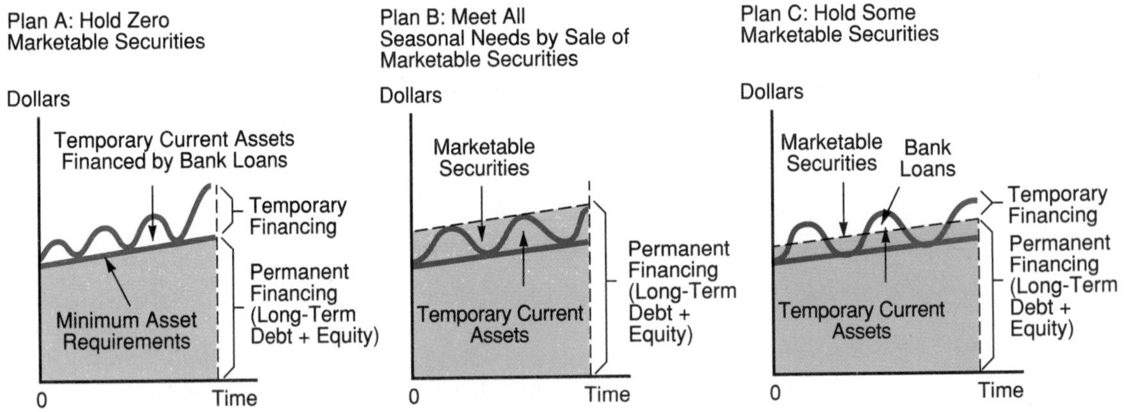

Plan A: Hold Zero Marketable Securities

Plan B: Meet All Seasonal Needs by Sale of Marketable Securities

Plan C: Hold Some Marketable Securities

funds arises. We can use Commonwealth Edison, the electric utility serving Chicago, to illustrate the issues involved in timing the sale of long-term securities. Commonwealth has a continuous, ongoing construction program, generating a continuous need for new outside capital. As we saw in Chapters 12 and 13, there are substantial fixed costs involved in stock or bond flotations, so these securities are issued infrequently and in large amounts. During the 1970s, Commonwealth followed the practice of selling bonds and stocks *before* the capital was needed, investing the proceeds in marketable securities, and then liquidating these assets to finance plant construction. Plan B in Figure 20-3 illustrates this procedure. However, during the 1980s Commonwealth encountered financial stress. It was forced to use up its liquid assets and to switch to its present policy of financing plant construction with short-term bank loans, then selling long-term securities to retire these loans when they have built up to some target level. This policy is illustrated by Plan A of Figure 20-3.

Plan B is the more conservative, less risky one. First, the company is minimizing its liquidity problems because it has no short-term debt hanging over its head. Second, it is sure of having the funds available to meet construction payments as they come due. On the other hand, when firms borrow, they generally have to pay interest rates that are higher than the return they receive on marketable securities; following the less risky strategy therefore does have a cost. Again, firms are faced with a risk/return trade-off.

It is difficult to prove that one strategy is better than another. In principle, the practice of holding marketable securities reduces the firm's expected rate of return, but it also reduces k_s, the required rate of return on its stock. Although we can quantify the cost of following a more conservative policy — it is the average percentage differential between the return received on marketable securities and the interest rate paid on the long-term debt — it is almost impossible to quantify the benefits in terms of how much such a policy re-

Figure 20-3   Alternative Methods of Financing a Continuous Construction Program

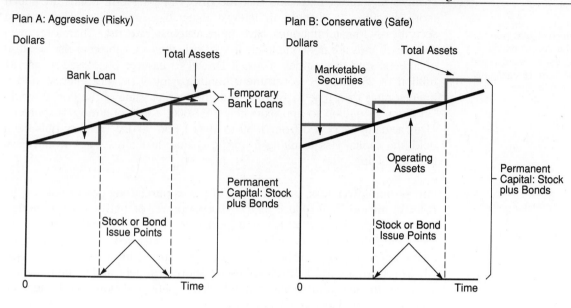

duces risk and how this risk reduction affects k_s. Further, it is impossible to measure the higher sales and profits, if any, that a liquid asset portfolio might make possible should a credit crunch occur. Accordingly, the basic policies with regard to securities holdings are generally set either on the basis of judgment or, as in the case of Commonwealth Edison, by circumstances beyond the company's control.

Criteria for Selecting Marketable Securities

A wide variety of securities, differing in terms of default risk, interest rate risk, liquidity risk, and expected rate of return, are available to firms that choose to hold marketable securities. In this section, we first consider the characteristics of different securities, and then we show how the financial manager selects the specific instruments to be held in the portfolio.

default risk
The risk that a borrower will not pay the interest or principal on a loan.

Default Risk. The risk that a borrower will be unable to make interest payments, or to repay the principal amount upon maturity, is known as **default risk.** If the issuer is the U.S. Treasury, default risk is negligible, so Treasury securities are regarded as being free of such risk. Corporate securities and bonds issued by state and local governments are subject to some degree of default risk, and they are rated with regard to their chances of going into default.[6]

---

[6]Bond ratings were discussed in detail in Chapter 13.

interest rate risk
The risk to which investors are exposed because of changing interest rates.

Interest Rate Risk. We learned in Chapter 6 that bond prices vary with changes in interest rates, and that the prices of long-term bonds are much more sensitive to changes in interest rates than are prices of short-term securities — long-term bonds have more **interest rate risk**. Therefore, even Treasury bonds are not completely free of risk; they are subject to risk because of interest rate fluctuations. Thus, if Drexel's treasurer purchased at par $1 million of 25-year U.S. government bonds paying 9 percent interest, and if interest rates then rose to 14.5 percent, the market value of the bonds would fall from $1 million to approximately $638,000, a loss of almost 40 percent. (This actually happened from 1980 to 1982.) Had 90-day Treasury bills been held, the capital loss resulting from the change in interest rates would have been negligible.

purchasing power risk
The risk that inflation will reduce the purchasing power of a given sum of money.

Purchasing Power Risk. Another type of risk is **purchasing power risk,** or the risk that inflation will reduce the purchasing power of a given sum of money. Purchasing power risk, which is important both to firms and to individual investors during times of inflation, is generally regarded as being lower on assets whose returns can be expected to rise during inflation than on assets whose returns are fixed. Thus, real estate, short-term debt, and common stocks are often thought of as being better hedges against inflation than bonds and other long-term fixed-income securities.

Liquidity, or Marketability, Risk. An asset that can be sold on short notice for close to its quoted market price is considered to be highly liquid. If Drexel purchased $1 million of infrequently traded bonds of a relatively obscure company such as Gainesville Pork Products, it would probably have to accept a price reduction in order to sell the bonds on short notice. On the other hand, if Drexel invested in U.S. Treasury bonds or bonds issued by AT&T, General Motors, or Exxon, it would be able to dispose of them almost instantaneously at close to the quoted market price. These latter bonds are therefore said to have very little **liquidity, or marketability, risk**.[7]

liquidity (marketability) risk
The risk that securities cannot be sold at a reasonable price on short notice.

Returns on Securities. As we know from earlier chapters, the higher a security's risk, the higher its expected and required return. Thus, corporate treasurers, like other investors, must make a trade-off between risk and return when choosing investments for their marketable securities portfolios. Since the liquidity portfolio is generally held for a specific known need or for use in emergencies, the firm might be financially embarrassed should the portfolio decline in value. Further, most nonfinancial corporations do not have investment departments specializing in appraising securities and determining the probability

---

[7]Some people define *liquidity* as encompassing an absence of default risk, interest rate risk, and marketability risk, as well as market risk such as any stock would have. By this definition, short-term Treasury bills, CDs, and the like are the only liquid assets. IBM stock is not liquid because its stock price could fall sharply in a down market. These definitions are not really important, but the characteristics of different securities are important.

Table 20-2   Securities Available for Investment of Surplus Cash

Security	Typical Maturity at Time of Issue	Approximate Yields as of:		
		6/10/77	2/10/82	4/8/88
Suitable to Hold as Near-Cash Reserve				
U.S. Treasury bills	91 days to 1 year	4.8%	15.1%	6.2%
Commercial paper	Up to 270 days	5.5	15.3	6.7
Negotiable certificates of deposit (CDs) of U.S. banks	Up to 1 year	6.0	15.5	6.9
Money market mutual funds	Instant liquidity	5.1	14.0	5.8
Floating rate preferred stock mutual funds[a]	Instant liquidity	n.a.	n.a.	7.0
Eurodollar market time deposits	Up to 1 year	6.1	16.2	7.3
Not Suitable to Hold as Near-Cash Reserve				
U.S. Treasury notes	3 to 5 years	6.8	14.8	7.9
U.S. Treasury bonds	Up to 30 years	7.6	14.6	8.9
Corporate bonds (AAA)[b]	Up to 40 years	8.2	16.0	9.8
State and local government bonds (AAA)[b,c]	Up to 30 years	5.7	12.8	7.9
Preferred stocks (AAA)[b,c]	30 years to perpetual	7.5	14.0	8.8
Common stocks of other corporations	Unlimited	Variable	Variable	Variable
Common stock of the firm in question	Unlimited	Variable	Variable	Variable

[a]Floating rate preferred stock is a recent innovation in near-cash securities, first marketed in 1983. It is held by corporations (often through money funds designed for this purpose) because of the 70 percent dividend tax exclusion.

[b]Rates shown for corporate and state/local government bonds and preferred stock are for longer maturities rated AAA. Lower-rated securities have higher yields. The slope of the yield curve determines whether shorter- or longer-term securities of a given rating have higher yields.

[c]Rates are lower on state and municipal government bonds because the interest they pay is exempt from federal taxes and on preferred stocks because 70 percent of the dividends paid on them is exempt from federal taxes for corporate owners, who own most preferred stocks.

of their going into default. Accordingly, the marketable securities portfolio is generally confined to safe, highly liquid, short-term securities issued by either the U.S. government or the very strongest corporations. Given the purpose of the securities portfolio, treasurers are generally unwilling to sacrifice safety for higher rates of return.

Types of Marketable Securities

Table 20-2 provides a listing of the major types of securities available for investment, with yields as of June 10, 1977, February 10, 1982, and April 8, 1988. Giving careful consideration to how long they will probably be held, the financial manager decides on a suitable maturity pattern for the firm's holdings. Because the securities' characteristics change with shifts in financial market conditions, it would be misleading to attempt to give detailed descriptions of them here.

It should be noted that large corporations that have substantial amounts of surplus cash tend to make direct purchases of Treasury bills, commercial paper, and CDs, as well as Euromarket securities. Smaller firms are more likely to use money market mutual funds as **near-cash reserves** because their volume

near-cash reserves
Reserves that can be quickly and easily converted to cash.

of investment simply does not warrant their hiring investment specialists to manage the portfolios and to make sure that the securities held mature (or can be sold) at the same time cash is required. Such firms can use money funds and then literally write checks on them to meet cash needs as they arise. Interest rates on money funds are somewhat lower than those on direct investments of equivalent risk, but net returns, from which the expenses of managing the portfolio are already deducted, are often higher on money funds for smaller companies.

THE BAUMOL MODEL FOR BALANCING CASH AND MARKETABLE SECURITIES

Earlier in the chapter, when we discussed the Drexel Card Company's cash budget, we took as a given the $2.5 million target cash balance. Subsequently, we discussed how the use of lockboxes, the synchronization of cash inflows and outflows, and the use of float can reduce the size of the required cash balance. Now we shall consider a formal model which can be used as the starting point for establishing a target cash balance.

William Baumol first noted that cash balances are in many respects similar to inventories, and that the EOQ inventory model, which will be developed in Chapter 21, can be used to establish a target cash balance.[8] Baumol's model assumes that the firm uses cash at a steady, predictable rate — say, $1 million per week — and that the firm's cash inflows from operations also occur at a steady, predictable rate — say, $900,000 per week. Therefore, the firm's net cash outflows, or net need for cash, also occur at a steady rate — in this case, $100,000 per week.[9] Under these steady-state assumptions, the firm's cash position will resemble the situation shown in Figure 20-4.

If our illustrative firm started at Time 0 with a cash balance of C = $300,000, and if its outflows exceeded its inflows by $100,000 per week, then its cash balance would drop to zero at the end of Week 3, and its average cash balance would be C/2 = $300,000/2 = $150,000. Therefore, at the end of Week 3 the firm would have to replenish its cash balance, either by selling marketable securities, if it had any, or by borrowing.

If C were set at a higher level, say, $600,000, then the cash supply would last longer (6 weeks) and the firm would have to sell securities (or borrow)

---

[8]William J. Baumol, "The Transactions Demand for Cash: An Inventory Theoretic Approach," *Quarterly Journal of Economics,* November 1952, 545–556.

[9]Our hypothetical firm is experiencing a $100,000 weekly cash shortfall, but this does not necessarily imply that it is headed for bankruptcy. The firm could, for example, be highly profitable and be enjoying high earnings, but be expanding so rapidly that it is experiencing chronic cash shortages that must be made up by borrowing or by selling common stock. (See Chapter 8 for examples.) Or the firm could be in the construction business and therefore receive major cash inflows at wide intervals, but have net cash outflows of $100,000 per week between major inflows.

Figure 20-4   Cash Balances under the Baumol Model's Assumptions

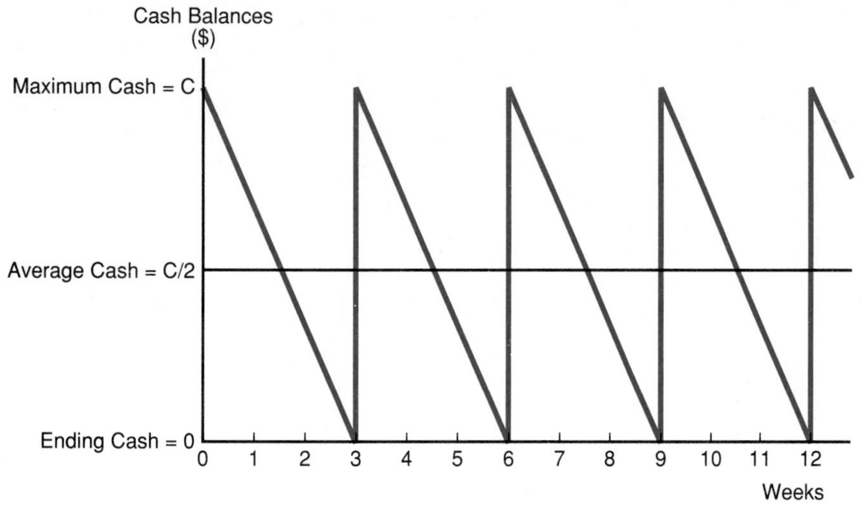

less frequently, but its average cash balance would rise from $150,000 to $300,000. Brokerage or some other type of transactions cost must be incurred to sell securities (or to borrow), so holding larger cash balances will lower the transactions costs associated with obtaining cash. On the other hand, cash provides no income, so the larger the average cash balance, the higher the opportunity cost, which is the return that could have been earned on securities or other assets held in lieu of cash. Thus, we have the situation that is graphed in Figure 20-5. The optimal cash balance is found by using the following variables and equations:

C = amount of cash raised by selling marketable securities or by borrowing. $C/2$ = average cash balance.

C^* = optimal amount of cash to be raised by selling marketable securities or by borrowing. $C^*/2$ = optimal average cash balance.

F = fixed costs of making a securities trade or of obtaining a loan.

T = total amount of net new cash needed for transactions during the entire period (usually a year).

k = opportunity cost of holding cash, set equal to the rate of return forgone on marketable securities or the cost of borrowing to hold cash.

The total costs of cash balances consist of a holding (or opportunity) cost plus a transactions cost:[10]

---

[10]Total costs can be expressed on both a before-tax and an after-tax basis. Both methods lead to the same conclusions regarding target cash balances and comparative costs. For simplicity, we present the model here on a before-tax basis.

Figure 20-5   Determination of the Target Cash Balance

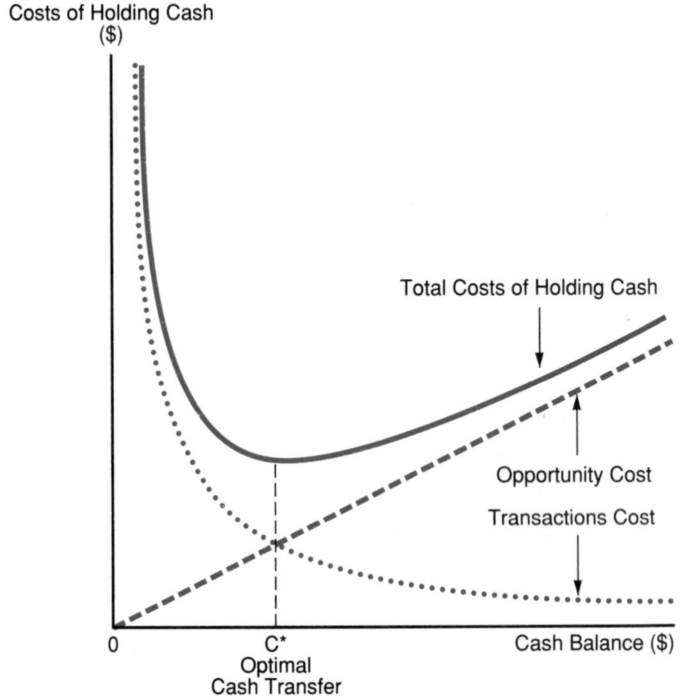

Total costs =   Holding cost   +   Transactions cost

$$= \begin{pmatrix} \text{Average cash} \\ \text{balance} \end{pmatrix} \begin{pmatrix} \text{Opportunity} \\ \text{cost} \end{pmatrix} + \begin{pmatrix} \text{Number of} \\ \text{transactions} \end{pmatrix} \begin{pmatrix} \text{Cost per} \\ \text{transaction} \end{pmatrix}$$

$$= \frac{C}{2}(k) + \frac{T}{C}(F). \tag{20-1}$$

The minimum total costs are achieved when C is set equal to C*, the optimal cash transfer. C* is found as follows:[11]

$$C^* = \sqrt{\frac{2(F)(T)}{k}}. \tag{20-2}$$

---

[11]Equation 20-1 is differentiated with respect to C. The derivative is set equal to zero, and we then solve for C = C* to derive Equation 20-2. This model, applied to inventories and called the EOQ model, is discussed further in Chapter 21.

Baumol model
An economic model that determines the optimal cash balance by using economic ordering quantity (EOQ) concepts.

Equation 20-2 is the **Baumol model** for determining optimal cash balances. To illustrate its use, suppose F = $150; T = 52 weeks × $100,000/week = $5,200,000; and k = 15% = 0.15. Then

$$C^* = \sqrt{\frac{2(\$150)(\$5,200,000)}{0.15}} = \$101,980.$$

Therefore, the firm should sell securities in the amount of $101,980 when its cash balance approaches zero, thus building its cash balance back up to $101,980. If we divide T by C*, we have the number of transactions per year: $5,200,000/$101,980 = 50.99 ≈ 51, or about once a week. The firm's average cash balance is $101,980/2 = $50,990 ≈ $51,000.

Notice that the optimal cash balance increases less than proportionately with increases in the amount of cash needed for transactions. For example, if the firm's size and consequently its net new cash needs doubled from $5,200,000 to $10,400,000 per year, average cash balances would increase by only 41 percent, from $51,000 to $72,000. This suggests that there are economies of scale in holding cash balances, and this in turn gives larger firms an edge over smaller ones.[12]

Of course, the firm would probably want to hold a safety stock of cash designed to reduce the probability of a cash shortage to some specified level. However, if the firm is able to sell securities or to borrow on short notice — and most larger firms can do so in a matter of just a couple of hours simply by making a telephone call — the safety stock of cash can be quite low.

The Baumol model is obviously simplistic in many respects. Most important, it assumes relatively stable, predictable cash inflows and outflows, and it does not take into account any seasonal or cyclical trends. Other models have been developed to deal both with uncertainty in the cash flows and with trends. Any of these models, including the Baumol model, can provide a useful starting point for establishing a target cash balance, but all of them have limitations and must be applied with a great deal of judgment.

---

[12]This edge may, of course, be more than offset by other factors — after all, cash management is only one aspect of running a business.

International

INTERNATIONAL CASH MANAGEMENT

The objectives of cash management in a multinational corporation are similar to those in a purely domestic corporation — namely (1) to speed up collections and to slow down disbursements as much as is feasible, and hence to maximize net float; (2) to shift cash from those parts of the business where it is not needed to parts where it is needed as rapidly as possible; and (3) to obtain the highest possible risk-adjusted rate of return on temporary cash balances. Multinational companies use the same general procedures for achieving these goals as domestic firms, but because of longer distances and more serious mail delays, lockbox systems and electronic funds transfers are especially important.

Although multinational and domestic corporations have the same objectives and use similar procedures, the multinational corporation faces a more complex task. First, domestic governments often place restrictions on transfers of funds out of the country, so although IBM can transfer money from its Salt Lake City office to its New York concentration bank just by pressing a few buttons, a similar transfer from its Buenos Aires office is far more complex. Buenos Aires funds are denominated in australs (Argentina's equivalent of the dollar), so the australs must be converted to dollars before the transfer. If there is a shortage of dollars in Argentina, or if the Argentinean government wants to conserve the dollars in the country to use for the purchase of strategic materials, then conversion, and hence the transfer, may be blocked. Even if no dollar shortage exists in Argentina, the government may still restrict funds outflows if those funds represent profits or depreciation rather than payments for purchased materials or equipment. The reason is that many countries, especially the less developed countries, want profits reinvested in the country in which they were made in order to stimulate economic growth.

Once it has been determined what funds can be transferred out of the various nations in which a multinational corporation operates, it is important to get those funds to locations where they will earn the highest returns. Whereas domestic corporations tend to think in terms of the alternatives listed in Table 20-2, multinationals are more likely to be aware of investment opportunities all around the world. Most multinational corporations use one or more global concentration banks, located in money centers such as London, New York, Tokyo, Zurich, or Singapore, and their staffs in those cities, working with international bankers, know of and are able to take advantage of the best rates available anywhere in the world.

SUMMARY AND KEY CONCEPTS

This chapter discussed cash management. In it we examined the motives for holding cash, cash budgets, several ways in which firms can minimize their cash holdings, the different types of marketable securities that can be used as substitutes for cash, and the Baumol model for determining optimal cash balances. The key concepts covered in the chapter are listed below.

- The primary **goal of cash management** is to reduce the amount of cash held to the minimum necessary to conduct business. This minimum is usually set as the larger of transactions plus precautionary balances or required compensating balances.

- The **transactions balance** is the cash necessary to conduct day-to-day business, whereas the **precautionary balance** is a cash reserve held to meet random, unforeseen needs. A **compensating balance** is a minimum checking account balance that a bank requires a customer to maintain as compensation either for services provided or as part of a loan agreement. Firms also hold **speculative balances**, which allow them to take advantage of bargain purchases, but borrowing capacity and marketable securities reduce the need for speculative balances.

- A **cash budget** is a schedule showing cash inflows and outflows over a specified period. The cash budget is used to determine when the firm will have cash surpluses and shortfalls, and thus to help management plan to invest surpluses or to cover shortages.

- A firm can minimize its cash balances if it can **synchronize** its cash outflows and inflows. The use of **lockboxes** can speed collections and thus reduce a firm's required cash holdings.

- **Disbursement float** is the amount of funds associated with checks written by the firm that are still in process and hence have not yet been deducted by the bank from the firm's account.

- **Collection float** is the amount of funds associated with checks written to the firm that have not been cleared and are not yet available for use.

- **Net float** is the difference between disbursement float and collection float, and it also is equal to the difference between the balance in a firm's checkbook and the balance on the bank's records. The larger the net float, the smaller the cash balances the firm must maintain.

- Firms can reduce their cash balances by holding **marketable securities**, which can be sold on short notice at close to their quoted market values. Marketable securities serve both as a substitute for cash and as a temporary investment for funds that will be needed in the near future. Safety is the primary consideration when treasurers select marketable securities.

- The **Baumol model** is an economic model used to determine the optimal cash balance. This model balances the opportunity cost of holding cash against the transactions costs associated with replenishing the cash account either by selling off marketable securities or by borrowing.

Questions

20-1   What are the two principal reasons for holding cash? Can a firm estimate its target cash balance by summing the cash held to satisfy each of the two?

20-2   Explain how each of the following factors would probably affect a firm's target cash balance if all other factors were held constant.
   a. The firm institutes a new billing procedure which better synchronizes its cash inflows and outflows.
   b. The firm develops a new sales forecasting technique which improves its forecasts.
   c. The firm reduces its portfolio of U.S. Treasury bills.
   d. The firm arranges to use an overdraft system for its checking account.
   e. The firm borrows a large amount of money from its bank and also begins to write far more checks than it did in the past.
   f. Interest rates on Treasury bills rise from 5 percent to 10 percent.

20-3   In the cash budget shown in Table 20-1, is the projected maximum funds requirement of $5,380,000 in September known with certainty, or should it be regarded as the expected value of a probability distribution? Consider how this peak would probably be affected by each of the following:

    a. A lengthening of the average collection period.

    b. An unanticipated decline in sales that occurred in a month when sales were supposed to peak.

    c. A sharp drop in sales prices required to meet competition.

    d. A sharp increase in interest rates for a firm with a large amount of short-term debt outstanding.

20-4   Would a lockbox plan make more sense for a firm that makes sales all over the United States or for a firm with the same volume of business but concentrated in its home city?

20-5   Would a corporate treasurer be more tempted to invest the firm's liquidity portfolio in long-term as opposed to short-term securities when the yield curve was upward sloping or downward sloping?

20-6   What does the term *liquidity* mean? Which would be more important to a firm that held a portfolio of marketable securities as precautionary balances against the possibility of losing a major lawsuit — liquidity or rate of return? Explain.

20-7   Firm A's management is very conservative, whereas Firm B's is more aggressive. Is it true that, other things the same, Firm B would probably have larger holdings of short-term marketable securities? Explain.

20-8   Is it true that interest rate risk refers to the risk that a firm will be unable to pay the interest on its bonds? Explain.

20-9   When selecting securities for portfolio investments, corporate treasurers must make a trade-off between risk and returns. Is it true that most treasurers are willing to assume a fairly high exposure to risk to gain higher expected returns?

Self-Test Problems   *(Solutions Appear on Page 811)*

Key terms

ST-1   Define each of the following terms:

    a. Transactions balance; compensating balance; precautionary balance; speculative balance

    b. Cash budget; target cash balance

    c. Synchronized cash flows

    d. Check clearing; net float

    e. Lockbox plan

    f. Overdraft system

    g. Marketable securities; near-cash reserves

    h. Default risk; interest rate risk; purchasing power risk; liquidity (marketability) risk

    i. Baumol model

Comparison of transfer methods

ST-2   Olinde, Inc., has grown from a small Boston firm with customers concentrated in New England to a large, national firm serving customers throughout the United States. It has, however, kept its central billing system in Boston. On average, 5 days elapse from the time customers mail payments until Olinde is able to receive, process, and deposit them. To shorten the collection period, Olinde is considering the installation of a lockbox system consisting of 30 local depository banks, or lockbox operators, and 8 regional concentration banks. The fixed costs of operating the system are estimated to be $14,000 per month. Under this system, customers' checks should be received by the lockbox operator 1 day after they are mailed, and daily collections should average $30,000 at each location. The collections would be transferred daily to the regional concentration banks. One transfer mechanism would involve having the local depository banks use "mail depository transfer checks," or DTCs, to move the funds to the concentration banks; the alternative would be to use electronic (wire) transfers. A DTC would cost only 75 cents, but it would take 2 days before funds were in the concentration bank and thus available to Olinde. Therefore, float time under the DTC system would be 1 day for mail plus 2 days for transfer, or 3 days total, down from 5 days. A wire transfer would cost $11, but funds would be available immediately, so float time would be only 1 day. If Olinde's opportunity cost is 11 percent, should it initiate the lockbox system? If so, which transfer method should be used? (Assume that there are $52 \times 5 = 260$ working days in a year.)

Problems

Net float

20-1   The McShane-Blarney Company is setting up a new checking account with the First National Bank. McShane-Blarney plans to issue checks in the amount of $1 million each day and to deduct them from its own records at the close of business on the day they are written. On average, the bank will receive and clear (that is, deduct from the firm's bank balance) the checks at 5 P.M. the fourth day after they are written; for example, a check written on Monday will be cleared on Friday afternoon. The firm's agreement with the bank requires it to maintain a $750,000 average compensating balance; this is $250,000 greater than the cash balance the firm would otherwise have on deposit. It makes a $750,000 deposit at the time it opens the account.

a. Assuming that the firm makes deposits at 4 P.M. each day (and the bank includes them in that day's transactions), how much must it deposit daily in order to maintain a sufficient balance once it reaches a steady state? Indicate the required deposit on Day 1, Day 2, Day 3, Day 4, if any, and each day thereafter, assuming that the company will write checks for $1 million on Day 1 and each day thereafter.

b. How many days of float does McShane-Blarney carry?

c. What ending daily balance should the firm try to maintain (1) on the bank's records and (2) on its own records?

d. Explain how net float can help increase the value of the firm's common stock.

Cash budgeting

20-2   Mark Reardon recently leased space in the Westgate Mall and opened a new business, Reardon's Hobby Shop. Business has been good, but Reardon has frequently run out of cash. This has necessitated late payment on certain orders, which in turn is beginning to cause a problem with suppliers. Reardon plans to borrow from the bank to have cash ready as needed, but first he needs a forecast of just how much he must borrow. Accordingly, he has asked you to prepare a cash budget for the critical period around Christmas, when needs will be especially high.

Sales are made on a cash basis only. Reardon's purchases must be paid for the following month. Reardon pays himself a salary of $3,000 per month, and the rent is $2,000 per month. In addition, he must make a tax payment of $8,000 in December. The current cash on hand (on December 1) is $400, but Reardon has agreed to maintain an average bank balance of $4,500; this is his target cash balance. (Disregard till cash, which is insignificant because Reardon keeps only a small amount on hand to lessen the chances of robbery.)

The estimated sales and purchases for December, January, and February are as follows. Purchases during November amounted to $80,000.

	Sales	Purchases
December	$110,000	$25,000
January	25,000	35,000
February	40,000	30,000

a. Prepare a cash budget for December, January, and February.
b. Now suppose that Reardon was to start selling on a credit basis on December 1, giving customers 30 days to pay. All customers accept these terms, and all other facts in the problem are unchanged. What will the company's loan requirements be at the end of December in this case? (Hint: The calculations required to answer this question are minimal.)

Cash budgeting   **20-3**   The Kramer Company is planning to request a line of credit from its bank. The following sales forecasts have been made for 1988 and 1989:

May 1988	$150,000
June	150,000
July	300,000
August	450,000
September	600,000
October	300,000
November	300,000
December	75,000
January 1989	150,000

Collection estimates were obtained from the credit and collection department as follows: collected within the month of sale, 5 percent; collected the month following the month of sale, 80 percent; and collected the second month following the month of sale, 15 percent. Payments for labor and raw materials are typically made during the month following the month in which these costs are incurred. Total labor and raw materials costs are estimated for each month as follows (payments are made the following month):

May 1988	$ 75,000
June	75,000
July	105,000
August	735,000
September	255,000
October	195,000
November	135,000
December	75,000

General and administrative salaries amount to approximately $22,500 a month; lease payments under long-term lease contracts are $7,500 a month; depreciation charges are $30,000 a month; miscellaneous expenses are $2,250 a month; income tax payments of $52,500 are due in both September and December; and a progress payment of $150,000 on a new research laboratory must be paid in October. Cash on hand on July 1 amounts to $110,000, and a minimum cash balance of $75,000 should be maintained throughout the cash budget period.

a. Prepare a monthly cash budget for the last six months of 1988. How much money will Kramer need to borrow (or how much will it have available to invest) each month?

b. Suppose receipts from sales come in uniformly during the month — that is, cash payments come in 1/30 each day — but all outflows are paid on the fifth of the month. Would this have an effect on the cash budget; in other words, would the cash budget you have prepared be valid under these assumptions? If not, what could be done to make a valid estimation of financing requirements? No calculations are required, although calculations can be used to illustrate the effects.

c. Kramer produces on a seasonal basis, just ahead of sales. Without making any calculations, discuss how the company's current ratio and debt ratio would vary during the year, assuming that all financial requirements were met by short-term bank loans. Could changes in these ratios affect the firm's ability to obtain bank credit?

d. If you prepared the cash budget in Part a correctly, you should show a surplus of $85,250 at the end of July. Suggest some alternative investments for this money. Be sure to consider the pros and cons of long-term versus short-term debt instruments and the appropriateness of investing in common stock.

e. Would your choice of securities in Part d be affected if the cash budget showed continuous cash surpluses versus alternating surpluses and deficits?

Lockbox system

20-4 Lardner, Inc., currently has a centralized billing system located in Los Angeles. However, over the years its customers gradually have become less concentrated on the West Coast and now cover the entire United States. On average, it requires 5 days from the time customers mail payments until Lardner is able to receive, process, and deposit them. To shorten this period, Lardner is considering the installation of a lockbox collection system. It estimates that the system will reduce the time lag from customer mailing to deposit by 3 days, to 2 days. Lardner has a daily average collection of $125,000.

a. How many days of float now exist (Lardner's customers' float, really), and what would it be under the lockbox system? What reduction in cash balances could Lardner achieve by initiating the lockbox system?

b. If Lardner has an opportunity cost of 12 percent, how much is the lockbox system worth on an annual basis?

c. What is the maximum monthly charge Lardner should pay for the lockbox system?

Optimal cash transfer   **20-5**   Northern Industries projects that cash outlays of $3,375,000 will occur uniformly throughout the coming year. Northern plans to meet its cash requirements by periodically selling marketable securities from its portfolio. The firm's marketable securities are invested to earn 10 percent, and the cost per transaction of converting securities to cash is $30.

a. Use the Baumol model to determine the optimal transaction size for transfers from marketable securities to cash.

b. What will be Northern's average cash balance?

c. How many transfers per year will be required?

d. What will be Northern's total annual cost of maintaining cash balances? What would the total cost be if the company maintained an average cash balance of $50,000 or of $0 (it deposits funds daily to meet cash requirements)?

Comparison of transfer methods   **20-6**   The San Diego field office of Rothwell Silver and Gems, Inc., has sold a quantity of silver ingots for $45,000. Rothwell wants to transfer this amount to its concentration bank in New York as economically as possible. Two means of transfer are being considered:

1. A mail depository transfer check (DTC), which costs $0.75 and takes 2 days.

2. A wire transfer, which costs $10 and for which funds are immediately available in New York.

a. Rothwell earns 12 percent annual interest on funds in its concentration bank. Which transfer method should Rothwell use to minimize the total cost of the transfer?

b. At what dollar transfer amount would Rothwell be indifferent to the two transfer procedures?

Lockbox system   **20-7**   Hammermeister Brothers, Inc., operates a mail-order firm doing business on the East Coast. Hammermeister receives an average of $250,000 in payments per day. On average it takes 4 days from the time customers mail checks until Hammermeister receives and processes them. Hammermeister is considering the use of a lockbox system to reduce collection and processing float. The system will cost $5,000 per month and will consist of 10 local depository banks and a concentration bank located in Atlanta. Under this system, customers' checks should be received at the lockbox locations 1 day after they are mailed, and they will be transferred to Atlanta using wire transfers costing $8 each. Assume that Hammermeister has an opportunity cost of 10 percent and that there are $52 \times 5 = 260$ working days, hence 260 transfers from each lockbox location, in a year.

a. What is the total cost of operating the lockbox system?

b. What is the benefit of the lockbox system to Hammermeister?

c. Should Hammermeister initiate the system?

Cash management   **20-8**   Peter Anderson, financial manager of Swimwear, Inc., is currently
(Integrative)   forecasting the company's cash needs for the first half of next year. Swimwear's sales are highly seasonal, with most of its sales occurring in the spring, just prior to the summer swimming season. The firm's marketing department forecasts sales as follows:

November	$100,000
December	150,000
January	300,000
February	400,000
March	550,000
April	900,000
May	700,000
June	450,000
July	250,000

The firm's credit terms are 2/10, net 30, and the credit department provided Peter with the following collections estimates: 20 percent of dollar sales will be collected in the month of sale (these are the discount sales); 70 percent will be collected the month following the sale; 9 percent will be collected two months following the sale; and 1 percent will end up as bad debt losses.

Wages and material costs are related to production, and hence to sales. The production department has estimated these costs as follows:

December	$175,000
January	175,000
February	250,000
March	325,000
April	425,000
May	125,000
June	75,000

Note, however, that payments for wages and materials are typically paid in the month following the one in which the costs are incurred.

Administrative salaries are projected at $25,000 a month; lease payments amount to $20,000 a month; depreciation expenses are $30,000 per month; and miscellaneous expenses total $10,000 a month. Quarterly tax payments of $125,000 must be made in March and June, and $250,000 will be needed in April to purchase a new fabric cutting machine.

Peter expects the firm to have $50,000 on hand at the beginning of January, and he wants to start each month with that amount on hand. As Peter's assistant, you have been asked to assist him by completing the following tasks and answering the following questions:

a. Construct the collections worksheet for the months of January through June.

b. Construct the remainder of the cash budget for the months of January through June. What is Swimwear's maximum loan requirement? What is the firm's maximum surplus balance?

c. 1. Should depreciation expense be explicitly included in the cash budget?

2. Suppose the outflows all occur on the 5th day of each month, but the inflows all occur on the 25th day. How would this affect January's cash budget? What could Peter do to incorporate such nonuniform flows?

3. Swimwear's only receipts are collections. What are some other types of inflows that could occur?

4. Most firms would "sweep" excess cash balances into marketable securities. Further, Swimwear would have to pay interest on its short-term borrowings. How would interest income and/or interest expense be incorporated into the cash budget?

d. The cash budget is a forecast, so many of the flows are *expected* values rather than amounts known with certainty. If actual sales, and hence collections and production, are different from the forecasted levels, then the projected surpluses and deficits will also be incorrect. What would you expect the impact on the cash budget to be if sales were 20 percent above those originally forecast? What about sales 20 percent below those originally forecast? How could scenario analyses such as these be used to help set the target cash balance?

e. If Peter's cash budget is correct, Swimwear will generate large surpluses in May and June, and these surpluses will be invested temporarily in marketable securities. What are the characteristics typically associated with marketable security investments? What types of securities are typically used?

f. Explain how each of the following could be used to reduce the target cash balance:
   1. Efforts to reduce collection float, including lockboxes and wire transfers, and to increase disbursement float, including remote disbursements and drafts.
   2. Better synchronization of cash inflows and outflows.
   3. Better forecasts of cash inflows and outflows.
   4. Larger holdings of marketable securites, and better access to the credit markets.

g. Swimwear's target cash balance was given as $50,000. Discuss the potential use of the Baumol model to determine the company's optimal cash balance. To apply the model, what additional information would you need, and what is the likelihood of getting good data?

Computer-Related Problems

(Work the problems in this section only if you are using the computer problem diskette.)

Cash budgeting

C20-1   Use the model for Problem C20-1 in the file C20 to work this problem.
   a. Refer back to Problem 20-3. Suppose that by offering a 2 percent cash discount for paying within the month of sale, the credit manager believes that Kramer can speed up its collections. The credit manager's revised collection percentages are 50 percent in the month of sale, 35 percent in the following month, and 15 percent in the third month. How are the loan requirements affected by this change in policy?
   b. What would be the effect on loan requirements if instead of the preceding percentages, 20 percent of customers paid in the month of the sale and took the discount, 70 percent paid in the following month, and 10 percent paid in the third month?
   c. Suppose that collection percentages were the same as those given in Part a but that sales in each month fell to 90 percent of the forecasted

level. Production is maintained, so cash outflows are unchanged. How
does this affect Kramer's financial requirements?

Lockbox system   **C20-2**   Use the model for Problem C20-2 in the file C20 to work this problem.

    a. Refer back to Problem 20-7. Would the lockbox system be beneficial
if Hammermeister could operate it with only 8 lockbox locations
while achieving the same reduction in float?

    b. Suppose that interest rates rise so that Hammermeister can now earn
11 percent on its invested funds. What will be the benefit (or loss) of
operating the lockbox system with 8 lockbox locations?

Solutions to Self-Test Problems

ST-1   Refer to the marginal glossary definitions and the appropriate sections of
the text to check your responses.

ST-2   First, determine the annual benefit to Olinde from the reduction in cash
balances under each plan:

$$\text{Average daily collections} = (30)(\$30,000)$$

$$= \$900,000.$$

DTC:

Current collection float:	$900,000 per day × 5 days =	$4,500,000
New collection float:	$900,000 per day × 3 days =	2,700,000
Float reduction:		$1,800,000

Olinde can reduce its average cash balances by $1,800,000 by using
DTCs, and it can earn 11 percent, which will provide $198,000 of
additional income:

$$\text{Additional income} = (\$1,800,000)(0.11)$$

$$= \$198,000.$$

Wire Transfer:

Current collection float:	$900,000 per day × 5 days =	$4,500,000
New collection float:	$900,000 per day × 1 day =	900,000
Float reduction:		$3,600,000

Olinde can reduce its cash balances by $3,600,000 by using wire
transfers, which will increase income by $396,000:

$$\text{Additional income} = (\$3,600,000)(0.11)$$

$$= \$396,000.$$

Next, compute the annual cost of each transfer method:

$$\text{Number of transfers} = 30 \times 260 = 7,800 \text{ per year.}$$

$$\text{Fixed lockbox cost} = \$14,000 \times 12 = \$168,000 \text{ per year.}$$

DTC:

$$(7,800)(\$0.75) + \$168,000 = \$173,850.$$

Wire Transfer:

$$(7,800)(\$11) + \$168,000 = \$253,800.$$

Finally, calculate the net additional income resulting from each transfer method:

DTC:

$$\$198,000 - \$173,850 = \$24,150.$$

Wire Transfer:

$$\$396,000 - \$253,800 = \$142,200.$$

Therefore, Olinde should adopt the lockbox system and transfer funds from the lockbox operators to the regional concentration banks using wire transfers.

21 Receivables and Inventory Management

HOW A BETTER INVENTORY CONTROL SYSTEM CAN IMPROVE A FIRM'S PROFITABILITY

Fireplace Manufacturers, Inc., a Santa Ana, California, producer of prefabricated metal fireplaces, was recently experiencing serious profit and cash flow problems. Arthur Young & Company, the accounting and consulting firm, was called in. The Arthur Young analysts concluded that Fireplace's inventory control system was inadequate, and, as a result, the company was required to carry $1.1 million of inventories to support only $8 million of sales. The $1.1 million invested in inventories had been borrowed, and interest charges, along with warehousing, insurance, and other costs associated with inventories, were eating up cash and profits.

Arthur Young recommended that Fireplace adopt a just-in-time (JIT) inventory control system, under which the company would arrange for its suppliers to deliver parts and materials in a smooth flow just about the time they were needed, rather than in large periodic lots. The JIT system — which had been pioneered by the Japanese and had helped make Japan the world's most efficient manufacturing nation — allowed Fireplace to cut inventories by 35 percent in 1988, even as sales were doubling to $16 million. According to Don Bowker, Fireplace Manufacturers' vice-president, "Without JIT, I don't think we'd be here today."

The JIT system is used primarily to control raw materials and work-in-process inventories, but firms are also using a system called *electronic data interchange (EDI)* to help control finished goods inventories. EDI systems allow specially formatted documents such as purchase orders to be sent from one company's computer to another's. Wal-Mart is one firm which uses an EDI system. Most items sold by Wal-Mart have magnetic bar codes which are scanned by a reader when a customer checks out. While the register is processing the customer's payment, information about the items that have been sold (such as color and size) is being transmitted to Wal-Mart's inventory control computers. The inventory control computers record the inventory reduction, and when the inventory level of an item falls to a specified amount, the computer automatically places an order with the manufacturer's computer through the EDI system.

Wal-Mart recently set up an EDI system with Seminole Manufacturing Company, a clothing maker. The system cut the average delivery time for various garments by 50 percent, from 44 days to 22 days. Previously, Wal-mart had to choose between holding large stocks and thus incurring high carrying costs or holding smaller stocks and then periodically running out of stock and losing profitable sales. The EDI system allowed Wal-Mart to reduce inventory levels without increasing the danger of stock-outs. Seminole was glad to cooperate — it gained a major competitive advantage over other Wal-Mart suppliers, and it tied the EDI system in with its own JIT system. Seminole can now determine how its various products are selling and obtain up-to-date information on its inventory positions. It uses this information to schedule arrivals of its raw materials and to set up its manufacturing plans. Because of its reduced costs, Seminole was able to lower its prices to Wal-Mart, and Wal-Mart, in turn, was able to both lower prices to its customers and raise its profit margins. Thus, everyone benefited — except Wal-Mart's and Seminole's less efficient competitors.

SINCE the typical firm has about 20 percent of its assets in receivables and another 20 percent in inventories, its effectiveness in managing these two accounts is obviously important to its profitability and risk — and thus to its stock price. Techniques for managing receivables and inventories are covered in this chapter.

RECEIVABLES MANAGEMENT

In general, firms would rather sell for cash than on credit, but competitive pressures force most companies to offer credit. When goods are shipped, in-

account receivable
A balance due from a customer.

ventories are reduced, and an **account receivable** is created.[1] Eventually the customer will pay the account, at which time receivables will decline and cash will increase. Managing receivables has both direct and indirect costs, but granting credit normally increases sales. The optimal credit policy is the one that maximizes the value of the firm.

The Accumulation of Receivables

The total amount of accounts receivable outstanding at any given time is determined by two factors: (1) the volume of credit sales and (2) the average length of time between sales and collections. For example, suppose you open a store on January 1 and, starting the first day, make sales of $100 each day. Customers are given 10 days in which to pay. At the end of the first day, accounts receivable will be $100; they will rise to $200 by the end of the second day; and by January 10 they will have risen to $10 \times \$100 = \$1,000$. On January 11 another $100 will be added to receivables, but payments for sales made on January 1 will reduce receivables by $100; total accounts receivable will therefore remain constant at $1,000. In general, once your firm's operations are stable, this situation will exist:

$$\text{Accounts receivable} = \frac{\text{Credit sales}}{\text{per day}} \times \frac{\text{Length of}}{\text{collection period}}$$

$$= \$100 \times 10 \text{ days} = \$1,000.$$

Note, however, that any changes in either sales or the collection period will cause accounts receivable to change.

Notice that the $1,000 investment in receivables must be financed. To illustrate, suppose that when you started on January 1, you put up $100 as common stock and used the money to buy the goods sold the first day. Thus, your initial balance sheet would be as follows:

Inventories	$100	Common equity	$100
Total assets	$100	Total liabilities and equity	$100

At the end of the day, the balance sheet would look like this:[2]

Accounts receivable	$100		
Inventories	0	Common equity	$100
Total assets	$100	Total liabilities and equity	$100

---

[1]Whenever goods are sold on credit, two accounts actually are created — an asset item entitled *accounts receivable* appears on the books of the selling firm, and a liability item called *accounts payable* appears on the books of the purchaser. At this point we are analyzing the transaction from the viewpoint of the seller, so we are concentrating on the variables under its control, in this case, the receivables. We examined the transaction from the viewpoint of the purchaser in Chapter 19, where we discussed accounts payable as a source of funds and considered their cost relative to the cost of funds obtained from other sources.

[2]Of course, a profit might have been earned on the sales, but for a retail business it would amount to only about 2 percent, or $2. Also, the firm would need other assets, such as cash, fixed assets, and a permanent stock of inventory. We abstract from these details so that we may focus on receivables.

In order to remain in business, you must replenish inventories. To do so requires that $100 of goods be purchased, and this requires $100. Assuming that you borrow the $100 from the bank, your balance sheet at the start of the second day will be as follows:

Accounts receivable	$100	Notes payable to bank	$100
Inventories	100	Common equity	100
Total assets	$200	Total liabilities and equity	$200

At the end of the day, the inventories will have been converted to receivables, and you will have to borrow another $100 to restock for the third day.

This process will continue, provided the bank is willing to lend the necessary funds, until the eleventh day, when the balance sheet will read as follows:

Accounts receivable	$1,000	Notes payable to bank	$1,000
Inventories	100	Common equity	100
Total assets	$1,100	Total liabilities and equity	$1,100

This balance sheet is in a steady-state condition; from now on, $100 of receivables will be collected every day, and the money will be used to finance the sales made that day. Thus, the balance sheet will remain stable until the situation changes.

Now suppose your sales double to $200 per day. After a brief transition period (10 days), your balance sheet would be as follows:

Accounts receivable	$2,000	Notes payable to bank	$2,100
Inventories	200	Common equity	100
Total assets	$2,200	Total liabilities and equity	$2,200

These examples should make it clear that accounts receivable depend jointly on the level of sales and the collection period, and that any increase in receivables must be financed in some manner. We assumed bank financing, but other possibilities include having the firm itself buy on credit (in which case the financing would be done by accounts payable rather than notes payable), by selling bonds, or by selling more common stock.[3]

CREDIT POLICY

The success or failure of a business depends primarily on demand for its products — as a rule, the higher its sales, the greater its profits and the healthier the firm. Sales, in turn, depend on a number of factors, some exogenous but others controllable by the firm. The major controllable variables that affect

---

[3]In time, profits will presumably be earned and reinvested in the business, but with normal profit margins, external funds will always be needed to support rapid growth. This point was discussed in Chapter 8 in connection with the Telecomp Corporation.

sales are sales prices, product quality, advertising, and the firm's credit policy. **Credit policy,** in turn, consists of these four elements:

credit policy
A set of decisions that include a firm's credit period, credit standards, collection procedures, and discounts offered.

1. The *credit period,* which is the length of time buyers have before they must pay for their purchases.
2. *Discounts* given to encourage early payment.
3. *Credit standards,* which refers to the minimum financial strength of acceptable credit customers.
4. The *collection policy,* which reflects the firm's toughness or laxity in following up on slow-paying accounts.

credit terms
A statement of the credit period and any discounts offered — for example, 2/10, net 30.

The credit period and the discount allowed (if any), when combined, are called the **credit terms.** Thus, if a company allows its customers 30 days in which to pay, but then gives a 2 percent discount if payment is made within 10 days, it is said to offer credit terms of 2/10, net 30. The credit manager has the responsibility for enforcing the credit terms and administering the firm's credit policy. However, because of the pervasive importance of credit, the credit policy itself — both setting the credit terms and specifying the credit standards and collection policy — is established by the executive committee, which usually consists of the president and the vice-presidents in charge of finance, marketing, and production.

Credit Period

credit period
The length of time for which credit is granted.

The **credit period** is the length of time a company gives its customers to pay; for example, credit might be extended for 30, 60, or 90 days. Generally there is a relationship between the normal inventory holding period of the customer and the credit period. Thus, fresh fruits and vegetables are normally sold on very short credit terms, whereas jewelry may involve a 90-day credit period.

Cash Discounts

cash discount
A reduction in the price of goods given to encourage early payment.

Another element in the credit policy decision is the use of **cash discounts** designed to encourage early payment. Decisions on the size of the discount are analyzed by balancing the costs and benefits of different discount terms. For example, Stylish Fashions might decide to change its credit terms from "net 30," which means that customers must pay within 30 days, to "2/10, net 30," which means that it will allow a 2 percent discount if payment is received within 10 days, whereas the full invoice price must otherwise be paid within 30 days. This change should produce two benefits: (1) it should attract new customers who consider discounts a type of price reduction; and (2) it should cause a reduction in the average collection period, since some old customers will pay more promptly to take advantage of the discount. Offsetting these benefits is the dollar cost of the discounts taken. The optimal discount is the one at which the costs and benefits are exactly offsetting. The methodology for analyzing changes in the discount is developed later in the chapter.

Offering cash discounts for prompt payment may lead to increased profits for the selling firm if its customers follow the terms of credit, but discounts can be quite costly if buyers pay late and still take the discount. One such case, involving Carter Hawley Hale Stores, Inc., was reported in the press recently. Arizona Wholesale Supply Company, a distributor of household products such as television sets, sold merchandise to Carter Hawley Hale on terms which allowed a 2 percent discount on invoices paid within 20 days. Arizona Wholesale filed a lawsuit charging that Carter Hawley Hale had illegally deducted $53,000 in discounts on invoices which were not paid within the stated 20-day credit period. It was also charged in the case that federal antitrust laws were being violated, because firms which allow some customers to take discounts on late payments are discriminating against other customers who are not allowed to take such discounts. Thus, Arizona Wholesale would be guilty of antitrust violations if it permitted Carter Hawley Hale to take discounts after the 20-day credit period but did not allow other customers to also take such discounts. Therefore, firms have two incentives to enforce their credit policies: profitability and avoidance of antitrust violations.

seasonal dating
A procedure for inducing customers to buy early by not requiring payment until the purchaser's selling season, regardless of when the merchandise is shipped.

If sales are seasonal, a firm may use **seasonal dating** on discounts. For example, Slimwear, Inc., a swimsuit manufacturer, sells on terms of 2/10, net 30, May 1 dating. This means that the effective invoice date is May 1 even if the sale was made back in January. If the discount is not taken by May 10, the full amount must be paid on May 30. Slimwear produces throughout the year, but retail sales of bathing suits are concentrated in the spring and early summer. By offering seasonal datings, the company induces some customers to stock up early, saving itself storage costs and also "nailing down" sales.

Credit Standards

credit standards
Standards that stipulate the minimum financial strength that an applicant must demonstrate in order to be granted credit.

Credit standards refer to the strength and creditworthiness a customer must exhibit in order to qualify for credit. If a customer does not qualify for the regular credit terms, it can still purchase from the firm, but under more restrictive terms. For example, a firm's "regular" credit terms might call for payment after 30 days, and these terms might be extended to all qualified customers. The firm's credit standards would be applied to determine which customers qualified for the regular credit terms and how much credit each customer should receive. The major factors considered when setting credit standards relate to the likelihood that a given customer will pay slowly or perhaps even end up as a bad debt loss.

Setting credit standards implicitly requires a measurement of *credit quality,* which is defined in terms of the probability of a customer's default. The probability estimate for a given customer is for the most part a subjective judgment. Nevertheless, credit evaluation is a well-established practice, and a good credit manager can make reasonably accurate judgments of the probability of default by different classes of customers. In this section we discuss some of the methods used by firms to measure credit quality.

Credit Scoring. Companies that sell to large numbers of small customers often use statistical procedures to determine the probability that a given customer will default if granted credit. For example, a credit card company or a department store might obtain information such as the following on each credit applicant: type of job, length of time the job has been held, whether the applicant owns his or her home or rents, income, amount of debt outstanding, and past credit experience (for example, does the applicant pay bills on time, has he or she ever gone through bankruptcy, and the like). This information is then fed into a computer, and a statistical "credit score" is generated. A score of 1 might, for example, indicate a very low probability of default, a 2 might indicate that, although there is some probability of default, the customer is still an acceptable credit risk, and a 3 might indicate too high a probability of default to justify extending credit.

Credit scoring systems are used extensively by credit card companies, by retailers such as Sears, which grant credit to large numbers of customers, and by manufacturers and wholesalers which sell to large numbers of customers such as builders or small retailers. Large numbers are necessary to obtain statistical validity, and mechanically derived scores are useful because of the cost that would be involved in determining the credit quality of thousands of individual customers "by hand".

The Five Cs System. The traditional method of measuring credit quality, where no computerized system is to be used, is to investigate potential credit customers with respect to five factors called the **five Cs of credit**:

five Cs of credit
The factors used to evaluate credit risk: character, capacity, capital, collateral, and conditions.

1. *Character* refers to the probability that customers will *try* to honor their obligations. This factor is of considerable importance, because every credit transaction implies a *promise* to pay. Will debtors make an honest effort to pay their debts, or are they likely to try to get away with something? Experienced credit managers frequently insist that the moral factor is the most important issue in a credit evaluation. Thus, credit reports provide background information on people's and firms' past performances. Often credit analysts will seek this type of information from a firm's bankers, its other suppliers, its customers, and even its competitors.

2. *Capacity* is a subjective judgment of customers' ability to pay. It is gauged in part by the customers' past records and business methods, and it may be supplemented by physical observation of their plants or stores. Again, credit analysts will obtain judgmental information on this factor from a variety of sources.

3. *Capital* is measured by the general financial condition of a firm as indicated by an analysis of its financial statements. Special emphasis is given to the risk ratios — the debt/assets ratio, the current ratio, and the times-interest-earned ratio.

4. *Collateral* is represented by assets that customers may offer as security in order to obtain credit.

5. *Conditions* refers both to general economic trends and to special developments in certain geographic regions or sectors of the economy that might affect a customer's ability to meet its obligations.

Information on these five factors comes from the firm's previous experience with its customers, and it is supplemented by a well-developed system of external information gatherers. Of course, once the information on the five Cs is developed, the credit manager must still make a final decision on the potential customer's overall credit quality. This decision is normally judgmental in nature, and credit managers must rely on their background knowledge and instincts.

Sources of Credit Information. Two major sources of external information are available. The first is the work of the *credit associations,* which are local groups of credit managers that meet frequently and correspond with one another to exchange information on credit customers. These local groups have also banded together to create Credit Interchange, a system developed by the National Association of Credit Management for assembling and distributing information about customers' past payment performances. The interchange reports show the paying records of different debtors, the industries from which they are buying, and the geographic areas in which they are making purchases. The second source of external information is the work of the *credit-reporting agencies,* which collect credit information and sell it for a fee. The best known of these agencies are Dun & Bradstreet (D&B) and TRW, Inc. D&B, TRW, and other agencies supply factual data that can be used in credit analysis, and they also provide ratings similar to those available on corporate bonds.[4]

Managing a credit department requires fast, accurate, up-to-date information. To help make it available, the National Association of Credit Management (a group with 43,000 member firms) persuaded TRW, Inc., to develop a computer-based telecommunications network for the collection, storage, retrieval, and distribution of credit information. The TRW system transmits credit reports electronically, so they are available within seconds to its thousands of subscribers. Dun & Bradstreet has a similar system, plus a service which provides more detailed reports through the U.S. mail.

A typical credit report would include the following pieces of information:

1. A summary balance sheet and income statement.

2. A number of key ratios, with trend information.

3. Information obtained from the firm's banks and suppliers about whether it tends to pay promptly or slowly, and whether it has recently failed to make a payment.

4. A verbal description of the physical condition of the firm's operations.

---

[4]For additional information, see Christie and Bracuti, *Credit Management,* a publication of the National Association of Credit Management.

5. A verbal description of the backgrounds of the firm's owners, including any previous bankruptcies, lawsuits, fraud, and the like.

6. A summary rating, ranging from A+ for the best credit risks down to F for those who are most likely to default.

Although a great deal of credit information is available, it must still be processed in a judgmental manner. Computerized information systems can assist managers in making better credit decisions, especially where the amounts are small, but in the final analysis large credit determinations are exercises in informed judgment.

Management by Exception. Modern credit managers often practice *management by exception.* Under such a system, statistical procedures are used to classify customers into five or six categories according to degree of risk, and the credit manager then concentrates time and attention on the customers that are most likely to cause problems. For example, the following classes might be established:

Risk Class	Percentage of Uncollectable Credit Sales	Percentage of Customers in This Class
1	0–½%	60%
2	½–2	20
3	2–5	10
4	5–10	5
5	Over 10	5

Firms in Class 1 might be extended credit automatically, and their credit status might be reviewed only once a year. Those in Class 2 might also receive credit (up to specified limits) automatically, but a ratio analysis of their financial condition would be conducted more frequently (perhaps every quarter), and they would be moved down to Class 3 if their position deteriorated. Specific approvals might be required for credit sales to Classes 3 and 4, whereas sales to Class 5 might be on a COD (cash-on-delivery) basis only.

Collection Policy

collection policy
The procedures that a firm follows to collect accounts receivable.

Collection policy refers to the procedures used to collect receivables. For example, a letter might be sent to any account holder that is 10 days past due; a more severe letter, followed by a telephone call, might be used if payment is not received within 30 days; and the account might be turned over to a collection agency after 90 days. The collection process can be expensive in terms of both out-of-pocket expenditures and lost goodwill, but some firmness is needed to prevent an undue lengthening of the collection period and to minimize outright losses. A balance must be struck between the costs and benefits of different collection policies.

Changes in collection policy influence the level of sales, the collection period, the bad debt loss percentage, and the percentage of customers who take discounts. The effects of a change in collection policy, along with changes in the other credit policy variables, will be analyzed later in the chapter.

Other Factors Influencing Credit Policy

In addition to the factors discussed previously, several other factors also influence a firm's overall credit policy.

Profit Potential. Thus far we have emphasized the costs of granting credit. *However, if it is possible to sell on credit and also to assess a carrying charge on the receivables that are outstanding, then credit sales can actually be more profitable than cash sales.* This is especially true for consumer durables (autos, appliances, clothing, and so on), but it is also true for certain types of industrial equipment. Thus, General Motors Acceptance Corporation (GMAC), which finances automobiles, is highly profitable, as is Sears, Roebuck's credit subsidiary.[5] Some encyclopedia companies even lose money on cash sales but more than make up these losses from the carrying charges on their credit sales; obviously, such firms would rather sell on credit than for cash.

The carrying charges on outstanding credit are generally about 18 percent on an annual interest rate basis (1.5 percent per month, so $1.5\% \times 12 = 18\%$). Unless the bad debt percentage is quite high, having receivables outstanding that earn more than 18 percent is highly profitable.

Legal Considerations in Granting Credit. Under the Robinson-Patman Act, it is illegal for a firm to offer more favorable credit terms to one customer or one class of customers than to another unless the differences are cost justified. Therefore, managers must be careful not to discriminate against any of their customers in granting credit or in offering special credit terms. This point was illustrated by the Carter Hawley Hale case described previously.

open account
A credit instrument consisting simply of an invoice that is signed by the buyer upon receipt of goods, after which both the buyer and the seller record the purchase on their books.

Credit Instruments. Most credit is offered on **open account**, which means that the only formal evidence of the credit is an invoice which accompanies the shipment and which the buyer signs to indicate that goods have been received. The buyer and the seller then each record the purchase on their books. Under

---

[5]Companies that do a large volume of sales financing, typically set up subsidiary companies called *captive finance companies* to do the actual financing. General Motors, Chrysler, and Ford all have captive finance companies, as do Sears and Montgomery Ward. The reason for this is that consumer finance companies, because their assets are highly liquid, tend to use far more debt — especially short-term debt — than manufacturers or retailers. Thus, if GM did not use a captive finance company, its balance sheet would show an exceptionally high debt ratio and a low current ratio. By having General Motors Acceptance Corporation (GMAC) as a separate but wholly owned corporation, GM avoids distorting its own balance sheet, which presumably helps it raise capital on more favorable terms. However, the Financial Accounting Standards Board may soon require firms to show consolidated financial statements, which would eliminate this advantage of captive finance companies.

promissory note
A document specifying the amount, percentage interest rate, repayment schedule, and other terms and conditions of a loan.

certain circumstances, the selling firm may require the buyer to sign a **promissory note** evidencing the credit obligation. Promissory notes are useful (1) if the order is very large; (2) if the seller anticipates the possibility of having trouble collecting, because a note is a stronger legal claim than a simple invoice; and (3) if the buyer wants a longer than usual time period in which to pay for the order, for in that case, interest charges can be built into a promissory note.

Another instrument used in trade credit, especially in international trade, is the **commercial draft**. Here the seller draws up a draft, which looks like a check written by the buyer and made payable to the seller, but dated some time in the future. This draft is then sent to the buyer's bank, along with the shipping invoices necessary for taking possession of the goods. The bank forwards the draft to the buyer, who signs it and returns it to the bank. The bank then delivers the shipping documents to the customer, who at this point can claim the goods. If the draft is a **sight draft**, then upon delivery of the shipping documents and acceptance of the draft by the buyer, the bank actually withdraws money from the buyer's account and forwards it to the selling firm. If the draft is a **time draft**, or **trade acceptance**, payable on a specified future date, the bank returns the draft to the selling firm, which can hold it for future payment, use it as collateral for a loan, or sell it on the open market to raise immediate cash. In each of these situations, the bank has served as an intermediary, making sure that the buyer does not receive title to the goods until the note (or draft) has been executed for the benefit of the seller.

A seller who lacks confidence in the ability or willingness of the buyer to pay off a time draft may refuse to ship goods without a guarantee of payment by the buyer's bank. Presumably the bank knows its customer and, for a fee, will guarantee payment of the draft. In this instance, the draft is called a **banker's acceptance**. Such instruments are widely used, especially in foreign trade. They have a low degree of risk if guaranteed by a strong bank, and there is a ready market for them, making it easy for the seller of the goods to sell the acceptance to raise immediate cash. (Because banker's acceptances as well as trade acceptances are sold at a discount below face value and then paid off at face value when they mature, the discount amounts to interest on the acceptance. The effective interest rate on a strong banker's acceptance is a little above the Treasury bill rate of interest.)

A final type of credit instrument that should be mentioned is the **conditional sales contract**. Here the seller retains legal ownership of the goods until the buyer has completed payment. Conditional sales contracts are used primarily for sales of such items as machinery, dental equipment, and the like, which are often paid for on an installment basis over a period of two or three years. The primary advantage of a conditional sales contract is that it is easier for the seller to repossess the equipment in the event of default because title remains with the seller until payment has been completed. This feature makes possible some credit sales that otherwise would not be feasible. Conditional sales contracts generally carry an interest rate that is equivalent to what the buyer would have to pay on a bank loan.

commercial draft
A draft drawn up by and made out to the seller that must be signed by the buyer before taking possession of goods.

sight draft
A draft that is payable upon acceptance by the buyer.

time draft (trade acceptance)
A draft that is payable on a specified future date.

banker's acceptance
A time draft that has been guaranteed by a bank. It is a promissory note by a business debtor arising out of a business transaction; a bank, by endorsing it, assumes the obligation of payment at the due date.

conditional sales contract
A method of financing in which the seller retains title to the goods until the buyer has completed payment.

MONITORING THE RECEIVABLES POSITION

The optimal credit policy, and hence the optimal level of accounts receivable, depends on the firm's own unique operating conditions. Thus, a firm with excess capacity and low variable production costs should extend credit more liberally, and thus carry a higher level of accounts receivable, than a firm operating at full capacity or having a slim profit margin. However, although optimal credit policies vary among firms, or even for a single firm over time, it is still useful to analyze the effectiveness of the firm's credit policy in an aggregate sense.

As we saw in connection with the Du Pont analysis in Chapter 7, an excessive investment in any asset account will lead to a low rate of return on equity. For comparative purposes, we can focus on the average collection period (ACP) as discussed in Chapter 7. There we saw that National Metals Company's average collection period was 42 days compared to an industry average of 36 days. If National Metals lowered its ACP by 6 days, to 36 days, this would mean a reduction of (6)($8,333,333) = $50,000,000 in the amount of capital tied up in receivables. If the cost of the funds tied up in receivables was 10 percent, this would mean a savings of $5 million per year, other things held constant.

The ACP can also be compared with National Metals' credit terms. National Metals typically sells on terms of 1/10, net 30. Since the 42-day average collection period is greater than the 30-day maximum credit period, its customers, on average, are not paying their bills on time. Note also that if some of the customers are paying within 10 days to take advantage of the discount, then others must be taking much longer than 42 days to pay; some accounts may, in fact, be so old as to suggest that they really represent bad debts. One way to get a better view of the situation is to construct an **aging schedule**, which breaks down accounts receivable according to how long they have been outstanding. National Metals' aging schedule is shown in Table 21-1. Most of the accounts pay on schedule or after only a slight delay, but a significant number are more than 1 month past due. This indicates that even though the average collection period is close to the 30-day credit period, National Metals has quite a bit of capital tied up in slow-paying accounts, some of which may turn out to be bad debts.

aging schedule
A report showing how long accounts receivable have been outstanding; gives the percentage of receivables currently past due, and the percentages past due by specified periods.

Management should constantly monitor the firm's average collection period and aging schedule to detect trends, to see how the firm's collection experience compares with its credit terms, and to see how effectively the credit department is operating in comparison with other firms in the industry. If the ACP starts to lengthen, or if the aging schedule begins to show an increasing percentage of past-due accounts, then the firm's credit policy may have to be tightened.

Although a change in the ACP or the aging schedule should be a signal to the firm to investigate its credit policy, a deterioration in either of these measures does not necessarily indicate that the firm's credit policy has weakened. In fact, if a firm experiences sharp seasonal variations, or if it is growing rap-

Table 21-1   National Metal's Aging Schedule
             as of December 31, 1988

Age of Account (Days)	Percentage of Total Value of Accounts Receivable
0–10	52%
11–30	20
31–45	13
46–60	4
Over 60	11
	Total 100%

idly, then both the aging schedule and the ACP may be distorted. This point can be illustrated using Drexel Card Company. Recall from Chapter 19 that Drexel's peak selling season was in the fall, so receivables were high, at $80,000, in January just after the peak season ended and were low, at $20,000, at the end of June just before the peak season began. If Drexel's average daily sales were $2,000, then its ACP would have been $80,000/$2,000 = 40 days on January 1 but only 10 days on June 30. This dramatic decline in ACP would not indicate that Drexel had tightened its credit policy, only that its sales had fallen due to seasonal factors. Similar problems arise with the aging schedule when sales fluctuate widely. Therefore, a deterioration in either the ACP or the aging schedule should be taken as a signal to investigate further, but not necessarily as a sign that the firm's credit policy has weakened. Still, the average collection period and the aging schedule are useful tools for reviewing the credit department's performance.[6]

Investors — both stockholders and bank loan officers — should pay close attention to accounts receivable management; otherwise, they could be misled by the firm's financial statements and later suffer serious losses on their investments. When a sale is made, the following events occur: (1) Inventories are reduced by the cost of the goods sold, (2) accounts receivable are increased by the sales price, and (3) the difference is recorded as a profit. If the sale is for cash, the profit is definitely earned, but if the sale is on credit, the profit is not actually earned unless and until the account is collected. Firms have been known to use credit policy to encourage "sales" to very weak customers in order to inflate reported profits. This can boost the stock price, at least until credit losses begin to show up and to lower earnings, at which time the stock price will fall. An analysis along the lines suggested previously will detect any such questionable practices, as well as any unconscious deteriora-

---

[6]See Eugene F. Brigham and Louis C. Gapenski, *Intermediate Financial Management,* 2nd ed., Chapter 19, for a more complete discussion of the problems with the ACP and aging schedule and how to correct for them. Also, note that the ACP is often called the DSO, for Days Sales Outstanding. ACP and DSO mean exactly the same thing.

tion in the quality of accounts receivable. Such early detection can help both investors and bankers avoid losses.[7]

ANALYZING CHANGES IN THE CREDIT POLICY VARIABLES

If the firm's credit policy is *eased* by such actions as lengthening the credit period, relaxing credit standards, following a less tough collection policy, or offering cash discounts, sales should increase: *Easing the credit policy normally stimulates sales.* However, if credit policy is eased and sales do indeed rise, then costs will also rise (1) because more labor, more materials, and so on will be required to produce more goods; (2) because receivables outstanding will increase, which will raise carrying costs; and (3) because bad debt or discount expenses will also rise. Thus, the key question when deciding on a credit policy change is this: Will sales revenues rise more than costs, causing net income to increase, or will the increase in sales revenues be more than offset by higher costs?

Table 21-2 illustrates the general idea behind credit policy analysis. Column 1 shows the projected 1989 income statement for Monroe Office Equipment Company under the assumption that the firm's current credit policy is maintained throughout the year. Column 2 shows the expected effects of easing the credit policy by extending the credit period, offering larger discounts, relaxing credit standards, and easing collection efforts. Specifically, Monroe is analyzing the effects of changing its credit terms from 1/10, net 30 to 2/10, net 40, of relaxing its credit standards, and of putting less pressure on slow-paying customers. Column 3 shows the projected 1989 income statement incorporating the expected effects of this easier credit policy. The change is expected to increase sales and lower collection costs, but discounts and several other types of costs would rise. The overall, bottom-line effect is an $8.7 million increase in projected profits. In the following paragraphs, we explain how the numbers in the table were calculated.

Monroe's annual sales are currently projected at $400 million. Under its current credit policy, 50 percent of those customers who pay do so on Day 10 and take the discount, 40 percent pay on Day 30, and 10 percent pay late, on Day 40. Thus, Monroe's average collection period is $(0.50)(10) + (0.40)(30) + (0.10)(40) = 21$ days.

Even though Monroe spends $5 million annually to analyze accounts and to collect bad debts, 2.5 percent of sales will never be collected. Bad debt losses therefore amount to $(0.025)(\$400,000,000) = \$10.0$ million. In

---

[7]Accountants are increasingly interested in these matters. Investors have sued several of the Big Eight accounting firms for substantial damages in cases in which (1) profits were overstated and (2) it could be shown that the auditors should have conducted an analysis along the lines described here and then reported the results to stockholders on the audited financial statements.

Table 21-2   Monroe Office Equipment Company:
Analysis of Credit Policy
(Millions of Dollars)

	Projected 1989 Income Statement under Current Credit Policy (1)	Effect of Credit Policy Change (2)	Projected 1989 Income Statement under New Credit Policy (3)
Gross sales	$400.0	+ $130.0	$530.0
Less discounts	2.0	+ 4.0	6.0
Net sales	$398.0	+ $126.0	$524.0
Production costs, including overhead	280.0	+ 91.0	371.0
Profit before credit costs and taxes	$118.0	+ $ 35.0	$153.0
Credit-related costs:			
Cost of carrying receivables	3.3	+ 1.6	4.9
Credit analysis and collection expenses	5.0	− 3.0	2.0
Bad debt losses	10.0	+ 22.0	32.0
Profit before taxes	$ 99.7	+ $ 14.4	$114.1
Taxes (40%)	39.9	+ 5.7	45.6
Net income	$ 59.8	+ $ 8.7	$ 68.5

addition, Monroe's cash collections will be reduced by the amount of discounts taken. Fifty percent of the customers who pay (and 97.5 percent of all customers pay) take the 1 percent discount, so discounts equal ($400,000,000)(0.975)(0.01)(0.50) = $1,950,000 ≈ $2.0 million. Notice that total sales are multiplied by (1 − Bad debt ratio) to obtain collected sales, and collected sales are then multiplied by the discount percentage times the percentage of paying customers who take the discount.

The annual cost of carrying receivables is equal to the average amount of receivables times the variable cost percentage, which gives the dollars of capital invested in receivables, times the cost of money used to carry receivables:

$$\left(\begin{array}{ccccc} \text{Average} & & \text{Variable} & \text{Cost} & \text{Cost of} \\ \text{amount of} & \times & \text{cost} & \times & \text{of} & = & \text{carrying} \\ \text{receivables} & & \text{ratio} & \text{funds} & \text{receivables} \end{array} \right)$$

The average amount of receivables, in turn, is equal to the average collection period times sales per day. Monroe's ACP is 21 days, its variable cost ratio is 70 percent, and its cost of funds invested in receivables is 20 percent. Therefore, its annual cost of carrying receivables is approximately $3.3 million:

$$(\text{ACP}) \left(\begin{array}{c} \text{Sales} \\ \text{per} \\ \text{day} \end{array} \right) \left(\begin{array}{c} \text{Variable} \\ \text{cost} \\ \text{ratio} \end{array} \right) \left(\begin{array}{c} \text{Cost} \\ \text{of} \\ \text{funds} \end{array} \right) = \begin{array}{c} \text{Cost of} \\ \text{carrying} \\ \text{receivables} \end{array}$$

$$(21) \left(\frac{\$400,000,000}{360} \right) (0.70)(0.20) = \$3,266,667 \approx \$3.3 \text{ million.}$$

Only variable costs enter into this calculation because this is the only cost element that must be financed as a result of a change in the credit policy. In other words, if a new customer buys goods worth $100, Monroe will have to invest only $70 (in labor and materials); therefore, it will have to finance only $70, even though accounts receivable rise by $100. Variable costs thus represent the company's investment in the goods sold.

Monroe's new credit policy calls for a larger discount, a longer payment period, a relaxed collection effort, and lower credit standards. The company believes that these changes will lead to an increase in sales to $530 million per year. Under the new credit terms, management believes that 60 percent of the customers who pay will take the 2 percent discount, and that bad debt losses will total 6 percent of sales, so discounts will increase to ($530,000,000)(0.94)(0.02)(0.60) = $5,978,400 ≈ $6 million. Half of the remaining paying customers (20 percent of paying customers) will pay on the fortieth day, and the remainder on the fiftieth day. The new ACP is thus estimated to be 24 days:

$$(0.6)(10) + (0.2)(40) + (0.2)(50) = 24 \text{ days.}$$

Also, the cost of carrying receivables will increase to $4.9 million:

$$(24)\left(\frac{\$530,000,000}{360}\right)(0.70)(0.20) = \$4,946,667 \approx \$4.9 \text{ million.}$$

Since the credit policy change will result in a longer ACP, Monroe will have to wait longer to receive its profit on the goods it sells. Therefore, the firm will incur an opportunity cost as a result of not having the cash from these profits available for investment. The dollar amount of this opportunity cost is equal to the old sales per day times the change in ACP times the contribution margin times the cost of the funds invested in receivables:[8]

$$\text{Opportunity cost} = (\text{Old sales}/360)(\Delta \text{ACP})(1 - v)(k)$$

$$= (\$400 \text{ million}/360)(3)(0.3)(0.20) = \$0.2 \text{ million.}$$

Here v = variable cost ratio and k = cost of funds. For simplicity, we ignored opportunity costs in Table 21-2.

Because it will relax credit standards (hence credit checking expenses) and also ease up on collections, the company expects to reduce its annual credit analysis and collection expenditures from $5 million to $2 million. However, the reduced credit standards and the relaxed collection effort are expected to raise bad debt losses from 2.5 percent to 6 percent of sales, or to (0.06)($530,000,000) = $32.0 million.

The combined effect of all the changes in credit policy is a projected $8.7 million increase in net income. There would, of course, be corresponding changes on the projected balance sheet. The higher sales would necessitate

---

[8]The contribution margin is equal to 1 minus the variable cost ratio, and it represents the pre-tax gross profit margin.

somewhat larger cash balances and inventories and perhaps (depending on capacity conditions) more fixed assets. Accounts receivable would also increase. Since these asset increases would have to be financed, certain liability accounts or equity would also have to be increased. *therefore – less liquid*

The $8.7 million expected increase in net income is, of course, an estimate, and the actual effects of the change could be quite different. In the first place, there is uncertainty about the projected $130 million increase in sales. Conceivably, if Monroe's competitors matched its changes, sales would not rise at all. Similar uncertainties must be attached to the number of customers who would take discounts, to production costs at higher or lower sales levels, to the costs of carrying additional receivables, and to the bad debt loss ratio. In view of all the uncertainties, management might deem the projected $8.7 million increase in net income insufficient to justify the change. In the final analysis, the decision to make the change will be based on judgment, but the type of quantitative analysis set forth here is essential to good judgmental decisions.

Competitors

INVENTORY MANAGEMENT

Inventories may be grouped into three classifications: (1) *raw materials,* (2) *work-in-process,* and (3) *finished goods.* As is true of accounts receivable, inventory levels depend heavily upon sales. However, whereas receivables build up *after* sales have been made, inventories must be acquired *ahead of* sales. This is a critical difference, and the necessity of forecasting sales before establishing target inventory levels makes inventory management a difficult task. Also, because errors in establishing inventory levels can lead either to lost sales and profits or to excessive costs and hence profit problems, inventory management is as important as it is difficult.

Inventory management focuses on three basic questions. (1) How many units of each inventory item should the firm hold in stock? (2) How many units should be ordered (or produced) at a given time? (3) At what point should inventory be ordered (or produced)? The remainder of this chapter is devoted to answering these questions.

Typical Inventory Decisions

Two examples, one of a retail store and one of a manufacturer, will make clear both the types of issues involved in inventory management and the problems poor inventory control can cause.

Retail Clothing Store. Glamour Galore Boutique must order bathing suits in January for sales the following summer, and it must take delivery by April to be sure of having enough suits to meet the heavy May-June demand. Bathing suits come in many styles, colors, and sizes. If the buyer stocks incorrectly, either in total or in terms of the style-color-size distribution, then the store will have trouble; it will lose potential sales if it stocks too few suits, and it will be forced to mark them down and take losses if it stocks either too many or the wrong types.

The effects of inventory changes on the balance sheet are important. For simplicity, assume that Glamour Galore has a $100 base stock of inventories, financed by common stock. Its initial balance sheet is as follows:

Inventories (base stock)	$100	Common stock	$100
Total assets	$100	Total liabilities and equity	$100

Now the store anticipates a seasonal increase in sales of $300, and it takes on additional inventories in that amount, financing them with a bank loan:

Inventories	$400	Notes payable to bank	$300
		Common stock	100
Total assets	$400	Total liabilities and equity	$400

If everything works out as planned, sales will be made, inventories will be converted to cash, the bank loan will be retired, and the company will earn a profit. The balance sheet after a successful season might look like this:

Cash and marketable securities	$ 50	Notes payable to bank	$ 0
Inventories (base stock)	100	Common stock	100
		Retained earnings	50
Total assets	$150	Total liabilities and equity	$150

The company is now in a highly liquid position and is ready to begin a new season.

But what if the season has not gone well? Suppose sales have been slow, and as fall approaches, the balance sheet looks like this:

Inventories	$300	Notes payable to bank	$200
		Common stock	100
Total assets	$300	Total liabilities and equity	$300

Now suppose the bank insists on repayment of its loan, and it wants cash, not bathing suits. If the bathing suits did not sell well in the summer, how will out-of-style suits sell in the fall? Assume that Glamour Galore is forced to mark the suits down to half price in order to sell them to raise cash to repay the bank loan. The result will be as follows:

Cash	$150	Notes payable to bank	$200
		Common equity	(50)
Total assets	$150	Total liabilities and equity	$150

At this point, Glamour Galore goes bankrupt. The banks gets the $150 of cash and takes a $50 loss on its loan. The stockholders are wiped out, and the company goes out of business.

Appliance Manufacturer. Now consider a different type of situation, that of Whirlwind Corporation, a well-established appliance manufacturer, whose inventory position follows (millions of dollars):

Raw materials	$ 200
Work-in-process	200
Finished goods	600
	$1,000

Suppose Whirlwind anticipates that the economy is about to get much stronger and that the demand for appliances is likely to rise sharply. If it is to share in the expected boom, Whirlwind will have to increase production. This means it will have to increase inventories and, since that increase will precede sales, additional financing will be required. The details are not shown here, but some liability account, probably notes payable, will have to be increased to support the inventory buildup.

Proper inventory management requires close coordination among the sales, purchasing, production, and finance departments. The sales/marketing department is generally the first to spot changes in demand. These changes must be worked into the company's purchasing and manufacturing schedules, and the financial manager must arrange any financing that will be needed to support the inventory buildup. Either improper coordination among departments or poor sales forecasts can lead to disaster. For example, Varner Corporation, a manufacturer of home computers, was recently forced into bankruptcy because of a poor system of internal controls. The company set its production schedules for 1989 on the basis of 1988 sales. However, the introduction of new, improved computers by competitors caused sales to drop sharply during the first half of 1989. Production schedules were not adjusted downward, so both inventories and bank debt built up. By the time the situation had been properly assessed, inventories of now obsolete components had risen to $10 million. The situation was like this (millions of dollars):

Cash	$ 1	Accounts payable	$ 3
Receivables	8	Notes payable to bank	15
Inventories: Good	6		
Bad	10		
Total current assets	$25	Total current liabilities	$18
		Long-term debt	10
Fixed assets	10	Common equity	7
Total assets	$35	Total liabilities and equity	$35

The bank insisted upon payment of the note. Varner simply could not generate the necessary cash, and it was thus forced into bankruptcy.[9] The company had some good products on the drawing board, but it did not survive to bring them to fruition.

Inventory Costs

The goal of inventory management is to provide the inventories required to sustain operations at the minimum cost. The first step is to identify all the costs

---

[9]As we saw in Chapter 19, bank loans are generally written as 90-day notes. Thus, the loan must be repaid or renewed every 90 days. If the bank thinks the firm's situation has deteriorated, as Varner's had, it will refuse to renew. Then, if the firm cannot raise cash to repay the loan, it will be bankrupt.

Table 21-3   Costs Associated with Inventories

	Approximate Annual Percentage Cost
Carrying Costs	
Cost of capital tied up	12.0%
Storage and handling costs	0.5
Insurance	0.5
Property taxes	1.0
Depreciation and obsolescence	12.0
Total	26.0%
Ordering, Shipping, and Receiving Costs	
Cost of placing orders, including production and set-up costs	varies
Shipping and handling costs	2.5%
Costs of Running Short	
Loss of sales	varies
Loss of customer goodwill	varies
Disruption of production schedules	varies

Note: These costs vary from firm to firm, from item to item, and over time. The figures shown are U.S. Department of Commerce estimates for an average manufacturing firm. Where costs vary so widely that no meaningful numbers can be assigned, we simply report "varies."

---

involved in purchasing and maintaining inventories. Table 21-3 gives a listing of the typical costs associated with inventories, broken down into three categories: costs associated with carrying inventories, costs associated with ordering and receiving inventories, and costs associated with running short of inventory, called stock-out costs.

Although they may well be the most important element, we shall at this point disregard stock-out costs; these are dealt with by adding safety stocks, as we will discuss later. The costs that remain for consideration at this stage, then, are carrying costs and ordering, shipping, and receiving costs.

carrying costs
The costs associated with carrying inventories, including storage, capital, and depreciation costs; these costs generally increase in proportion to the average amount of inventory held.

Carrying Costs. **Carrying costs** generally rise in direct proportion to the average amount of inventory carried, which in turn depends on the frequency with which orders are placed. To illustrate, if a firm sells S units per year and places equal-sized orders of Q units N times per year, then, assuming no safety stocks are carried, the average inventory, A, is:

$$A = \frac{\text{Quantity ordered}}{2} = \frac{Q}{2}. \qquad (21\text{-}1)$$

Note also that the quantity ordered, Q, is equal to S divided by N, the number of orders placed per year, and substituting for Q in Equation 21-1, we get:

$$A = \frac{\text{Annual sales/Number of orders}}{2} = \frac{S/N}{2}. \qquad (21\text{-}1a)$$

For example, if the firm sells S = 120,000 units in a year and orders inventory N = 4 times a year, its average inventory will be A = 15,000 units:

$$A = \frac{Q}{2} = \frac{S/N}{2} = \frac{120,000/4}{2} = \frac{30,000}{2} = 15,000 \text{ units.}$$

Inventory will range from a high of 30,000 units just after an order arrives to a low of 0 just before the next order arrives, and it will average 15,000 units. If the firm purchases its inventory at a price P = $2 per unit, the average inventory value will be (P)(A) = ($2)(15,000) = $30,000.

If the firm has a cost of capital of 10 percent, it incurs $3,000 in capital costs to carry the inventory. Assume that each year the firm incurs $2,000 of storage costs (space, utilities, security, taxes, and so forth), $500 of inventory insurance costs, and $1,000 of depreciation and obsolescence costs. The firm's total cost of carrying the $30,000 average inventory is thus $3,000 + $2,000 + $500 + $1,000 = $6,500, and its percentage cost of carrying inventory is $6,500/$30,000 = 0.2167 = 21.67%. Calling the percentage cost C, we can in general find the annual total carrying costs, TCC, as the percentage carrying cost, C, times the purchase price per unit, P, times the average number of units, A:

$$\text{Total carrying costs} = \text{TCC} = (C)(P)(A). \tag{21-2}$$

In our example,

$$\text{TCC} = (0.2167)(\$2)(15,000)$$

$$\approx \$6,500.$$

Ordering Costs. Although carrying costs are entirely variable and rise in direct proportion to the average size of inventories, **ordering costs** per order are fixed.[10] For example, the costs of placing and receiving an order — interoffice memos, long-distance telephone calls, setting up a production run, taking delivery, and executive time — are essentially a fixed amount for each order, so this part of total inventory cost is simply the fixed cost of placing and receiving orders times the number of orders placed. We call the fixed costs associated with ordering inventories F, and if we place N orders per year, the annual total ordering costs, TOC, are

ordering costs
The costs of placing and receiving an order; this cost is fixed regardless of the average size of inventories.

$$\text{Total ordering costs} = \text{TOC} = (F)(N). \tag{21-3}$$

Equation 21-1a may be solved for N to produce N = S/2A, which may then be substituted for N in Equation 21-3:

---

[10]For certain purposes it is useful to add another term to the inventory cost model — *shipping and receiving costs*. This term should be added if there are economies of scale in shipping so that the cost of shipping a unit is smaller if shipments are larger. In most situations, however, shipping costs are not sensitive to order size, so total shipping costs are simply the shipping cost per unit times the units ordered (and sold) during the year. Under this condition, shipping costs are not influenced by inventory policy and hence may be disregarded for purposes of determining the optimal inventory level and order size.

$$TOC = \text{Total ordering costs} = F\left(\frac{S}{2A}\right) = (F)(N). \qquad (21\text{-}4)$$

To evaluate Equation 21-4, suppose $F = \$100$, $S = 120,000$ units, and $A = 15,000$ units. Then TOC, the total annual ordering costs, will be $\$400$:

$$TOC = (F)(S/2A) = (F)(N) = \$100\left(\frac{120,000}{30,000}\right) = \$100(4) = \$400.$$

Total Inventory Costs. Total carrying costs, TCC, as defined in Equation 21-2, and total ordering costs, TOC, as defined in Equation 21-4, may be combined to find total inventory costs, TIC, as follows:

$$\text{Total inventory costs} = TIC = TCC + TOC$$

$$= (C)(P)(A) + F\left(\frac{S}{2A}\right). \qquad (21\text{-}5)$$

Therefore, if the firm orders 30,000 units four times a year, its total inventory costs will be $\$6,900$:

$$TIC = \$6,500 + \$400$$

$$= \$6,900.$$

Recalling from Equation 21-1 that the average inventory carried is $A = Q/2$, or one-half the size of each order quantity, Equation 21-5 may be rewritten as follows:

$$TIC = (C)(P)\left(\frac{Q}{2}\right) + (F)\left(\frac{S}{Q}\right). \qquad (21\text{-}6)$$

Using Equation 21-6, we calculate the firm's total inventory costs to be $\$6,900$, which matches the value found using Equation 21-5:

$$TIC = (0.2167)(\$2)\left(\frac{30,000}{2}\right) + \$100\left(\frac{120,000}{30,000}\right) = \$6,900.$$

This equation is used in the next section to find the policy which results in the minimum total inventory cost.

THE OPTIMAL ORDERING QUANTITY

Inventories are obviously necessary, but it is equally obvious that a firm will suffer if it has too much or too little inventory. How can we determine the *optimal* inventory level? One commonly used approach utilizes the *economic ordering quantity (EOQ) model,* which is described in this section.

Figure 21-1 illustrates the basic premise on which inventory theory is built, namely, that some costs rise with larger inventories whereas other costs de-

Figure 21-1   Determination of the Optimal Order Quantity

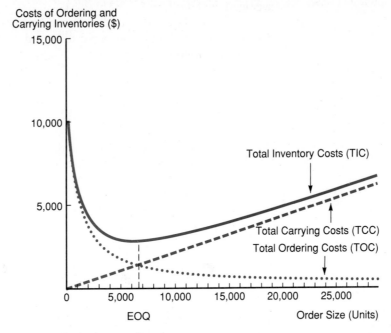

Q	Average Inventory	Total Carrying Costs (TCC)	Total Ordering Costs (TOC)	Total Inventory Costs (TIC)
5,000	2,500	$1,085.00	$2,400.00	$3,485.00
10,000	5,000	2,170.00	1,200.00	3,370.00
15,000	7,500	3,255.00	800.00	4,055.00
20,000	10,000	4,340.00	600.00	4,940.00
25,000	12,500	5,425.00	480.00	5,905.00
30,000	15,000	6,510.00	400.00	6,910.00

cline, and that there is an optimal order size which minimizes the total costs associated with inventories, TIC. First, as noted earlier, the average investment in inventories depends on how frequently orders are placed. If a firm places a small order every day, average inventories will be much smaller than if it places one large order once a year. Further, as Figure 21-1 shows, some of the firm's costs rise with larger orders. Larger orders mean larger average inventories, so warehousing costs, interest on funds tied up in inventory, insurance costs, and obsolescence costs all will increase. At the same time, ordering costs decline with larger orders and inventories, because the costs of placing orders, setting up production runs, and handling shipments all will decline if the firm orders infrequently and consequently holds larger quantities.

When the carrying and ordering cost curves in Figure 21-1 are added together, the sum represents the total cost of ordering and carrying inventories,

economic ordering quantity (EOQ)
The optimal, or least-cost, quantity of inventory that should be ordered.

TIC. The point at which the total cost curve is minimized represents the **economic ordering quantity (EOQ)**, and this, in turn, determines the optimal average inventory level.

It can be shown that under reasonable assumptions, the order quantity that minimizes the total cost curve in Figure 21-1, or the EOQ, can be found by using the following formula:[11]

$$EOQ = \sqrt{\frac{2(F)(S)}{(C)(P)}}. \qquad (21\text{-}7)$$

Here

EOQ = the economic ordering quantity, or the optimum quantity to be ordered each time an order is placed.

F = fixed costs of placing and receiving an order.

S = annual sales in units.

C = carrying cost expressed as a percentage of inventory value.

P = purchase price that the firm must pay per unit of inventory.

EOQ model
A formula for determining the order quantity that will minimize total inventory cost: $EOQ = \sqrt{2FS/(CP)}$.

The assumptions of the **EOQ model**, which will be relaxed shortly, include the following: (1) sales can be forecasted perfectly; (2) sales are evenly distributed throughout the year; and (3) orders are received with no delays whatever.

To illustrate the EOQ model, let us consider the following data supplied by Romantic Books, Inc., publisher of the classic novel *Madame Boudoir*:

S = sales = 26,000 copies per year.

C = carrying cost = 20 percent of inventory value.

P = purchase price per book to Romantic Books from a printing company = $6.1538 per copy. (The sales price Romantic Books charges is $9, but this is irrelevant for our purposes.)

F = fixed cost per order = $1,000. The bulk of this cost is the labor cost of setting the page plates on the presses as well as of setting up the binding equipment for the production run. The printer bills this cost separately from the $6.1538 cost per copy.

Substituting these data into Equation 21-7, we obtain an EOQ of 6,500 copies:

$$EOQ = \sqrt{\frac{2(F)(S)}{(C)(P)}}$$

$$= \sqrt{\frac{(2)(\$1,000)(26,000)}{(0.2)(\$6.1538)}}$$

$$= \sqrt{42,250,317}$$

$$= 6,500 \text{ copies.}$$

---

[11]The total cost function as set forth in Equation 21-6 is differentiated with respect to Q, and the first derivative is set equal to zero to locate the minimum point on the total cost curve in Figure 21-1. Equation 21-7 results from this operation.

Figure 21-2   Inventory Position without Safety Stock

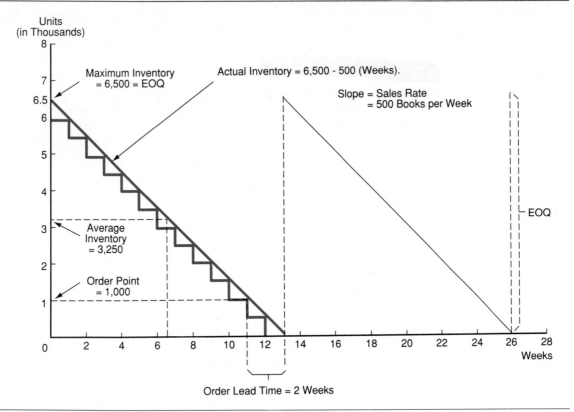

The average inventory depends directly on the EOQ; this relationship is illustrated graphically in Figure 21-2. Immediately after an order is received, 6,500 copies are in stock. The usage rate, or sales rate, is 500 copies per week (26,000/52 weeks), so inventories are drawn down by this amount each week, and this determines the slope of the line. Thus, if the sales rate increases, the line will become steeper.

The actual number of units held in inventory will vary from 6,500 books just after an order is received to zero just before the next order arrives. On average, the number of units held will be 6,500/2 = 3,250 books. At a cost of $6.1538 per book, the average investment in inventories will be (3,250)($6.1538) = $19,999.85 ≈ $20,000. If inventories are financed by a bank loan, the loan will vary from a high of $40,000 to a low of $0, but the average amount outstanding over the course of a year will be $20,000.

The EOQ, and hence average inventory holdings, rises not with sales but with the square root of sales. Therefore, a given increase in sales will result in a less than proportionate increase in inventories, and the inventory/sales ratio will thus decline as sales grow. For example, Romantic Books' EOQ is 6,500 copies at an annual sales level of 26,000, and the average inventory is 3,250 copies, worth $20,000. However, if sales increase by 100 percent, to 52,000 copies per year, the EOQ will rise to only 9,192 copies, or by 41 percent, and the average inventory will rise by this same percentage. This suggests that there are economies of scale in the holding of inventories.[12]

Setting the Reorder Point

reorder point
The point at which stock on hand must be replenished.

If a 2-week lead time is required for production and shipping, what is Romantic Books' **reorder point**, or the inventory level at which an order should be placed? Romantic Books sells 26,000/52 = 500 books per week. Thus, if a 2-week lag occurs between the order and the delivery, Romantic Books must place the order when there are 1,000 books on hand:

$$\text{Order point} = \text{Lead time in weeks} \times \text{Weekly usage}$$

$$= 2 \times 500 = 1,000.$$

At the end of the 2-week production and shipping period, the inventory balance will be down to zero — but just at that time, the order of new books will arrive.

Goods in Transit

goods in transit
Goods which have been ordered but have not been received.

If a new order must be placed before the previous order is received, a **goods-in-transit** inventory will build up. Goods in transit are goods which have been ordered but have not been received. A goods-in-transit inventory will exist if the normal delivery lead time is longer than the time between orders. This complicates matters somewhat, but the simplest solution to the problem is to deduct goods in transit when calculating the order point. In other words, the order point is calculated as follows:

$$\text{Order point} = (\text{Lead time in weeks} \times \text{Weekly usage}) - \text{Goods in transit}.$$

Goods in transit is not an issue for Romantic Books because the firm orders 26,000/6,500 = 4 times a year, or once every 13 weeks, and the delivery lead time is 2 weeks. However, suppose that Romantic Books ordered 1,000 copies of *Madame Boudoir* every 2 weeks and the delivery lead time was 3 weeks. Then, whenever an order was placed, another order of 1,000 books would be in transit. Therefore, Romantic Books' order point would be

$$\text{Order point} = (3 \times 500) - 1,000$$

$$= 1,500 - 1,000$$

$$= 500.$$

---

[12]Note, however, that these scale economies relate to the particular item, not to the entire firm. Thus, a large publishing company with $500 million of sales may have a higher inventory/sales ratio than a much smaller company if the small company has only a few high-volume books whereas the large one publishes a great many low-volume books.

Figure 21-3   Inventory Position with Safety Stock Included

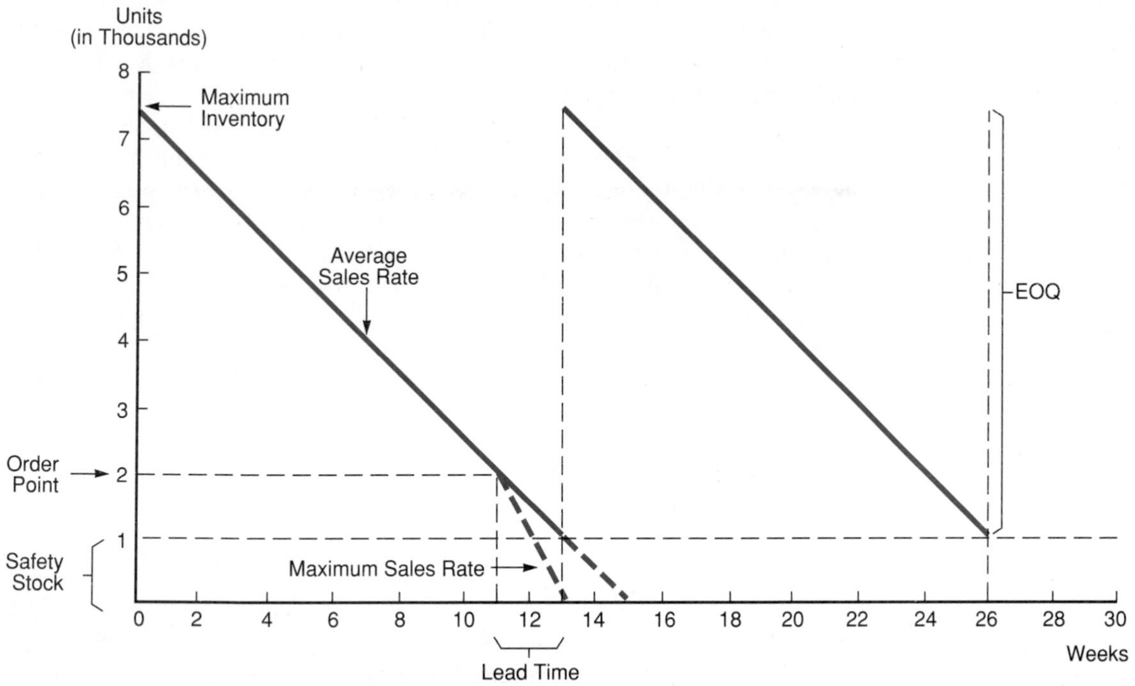

Safety Stocks

If Romantic Books knew for certain that both the sales rate and the order lead time would never vary, it could operate exactly as shown in Figure 21-2. However, because sales do change, and because production and shipping delays are encountered, the firm must carry additional inventories, or **safety stocks**.

The concept of a safety stock is illustrated in Figure 21-3. First, note that the slope of the sales line measures the expected rate of sales. The company *expects* sales of 500 copies per week, but let us assume that the maximum possible sales rate is twice that amount, or 1,000 copies each week. Further, assume that Romantic Books sets the safety stock at 1,000 books. Thus, it initially orders 7,500, which is the EOQ of 6,500 copies plus the safety stock. Subsequently, it reorders the EOQ whenever the inventory level falls to 2,000 copies, which is the safety stock of 1,000 copies plus the 1,000 copies expected to be used while awaiting delivery of the order. The company could, over the 2-week delivery period, sell 1,000 copies a week, or double its normal expected sales; this maximum rate of sales is shown by the steep, dashed line in Figure 21-3. The condition that makes it possible to achieve this higher sales rate is the safety stock of 1,000 copies; without it, the firm would run out of stock if the sales rate rose from 500 to 1,000 copies per week.

safety stocks
Additional inventories carried to guard against changes in sales rates or production/shipping delays.

The safety stock is also useful for guarding against delays in receiving orders. The expected delivery time is 2 weeks, but with a 1,000-copy safety stock the company could maintain sales at the expected rate of 500 copies per week for an additional 2 weeks if shipping delays held up an order.

Safety stocks are obviously useful, but they do have a cost. For Romantic Books, the average inventory is now EOQ/2 plus a safety stock of 1,000, or 6,500/2 + 1,000 = 3,250 + 1,000 = 4,250 books, and the average inventory value is (4,250)($6.1538) = $26,154. The increase in average inventory resulting from the safety stock causes an increase in inventory carrying costs.

The optimum safety stock varies from one situation to another, but in general it *increases* (1) with the uncertainty of the sales forecast, (2) with the costs (in terms of lost sales and lost goodwill) that would result from an inventory shortage, and (3) with the probability of delays in receiving shipments. The optimum safety stock *decreases* as the cost of carrying it increases.[13]

Inventory Control Systems

The EOQ model, along with an analysis of safety stocks, can be used to establish the proper inventory level, but inventory management also involves the *inventory ordering and control system.* One simple control procedure is the **red-line method.** Here inventory items are stocked in a bin, a red line is drawn around the inside of the bin at the level of the order point, and the inventory clerk places an order when the red line shows. For the **two-bin method,** inventory items are stocked in two bins; when the working bin is empty, an order is placed and inventory is drawn from the second bin. These procedures work well for items like bolts in a manufacturing process and for many items in retail businesses.

Companies are increasingly employing **computerized inventory control systems.** A computer starts with an inventory count in memory. Withdrawals are recorded by the computer as they are made, and the inventory balance is constantly revised. When the order point is reached, the computer automatically places an order; when this new order is received, the recorded balance is increased. Retail stores have carried this system quite far; each item has a magnetic code, and as an item is checked out, it passes over an electronic reader, which then adjusts the computer's inventory balance at the same time the price is fed to the cash register tape. When the balance drops to the order point, an order is placed. Also, as we noted at the beginning of the chapter,

red-line method
An inventory control procedure in which a red line is drawn around the inside of an inventory-stocked bin to indicate the order point level.

two-bin method
An inventory control procedure in which the order point is reached when one of two inventory-stocked bins is empty.

computerized inventory control system
A system of inventory control in which computers are used to determine order points and to adjust inventory balances.

---

[13] If we knew the probability distribution of usage rates and the probability distribution of order lead times, we could determine joint probabilities of inventory shortages with various safety stock levels. With a safety stock of 1,000 copies, for example, the probability of a shortage for *Madame Boudoir* might be 5 percent. If the safety stock was reduced to 500 copies, the probability of a shortage might rise to 15 percent, whereas it might be reduced to 1 percent with a safety stock of 2,000 copies. If we had additional information on the precise cost of running out of inventory, we could compare it with the cost of carrying larger safety stocks. The optimum safety stock is determined at the point where the marginal cost of a shortage is equal to the marginal inventory carrying cost.

companies such as Wal-Mart even have their computers hooked up with their suppliers' computers, so the order can be placed electronically.

A good inventory control system is dynamic. Companies such as IBM and General Motors stock hundreds of thousands of different items, and the sales (or use) of these items can rise or fall quite separately from fluctuating overall corporate sales. As the usage rate for an individual item begins to fall, the inventory manager must adjust this item's balance to avoid ending up with obsolete items — either finished goods or parts and materials for use in producing them.

The EOQ model is useful for establishing order sizes and average inventory levels *given a correctly forecasted sales or usage rate.* However, usage rates change over time, and a good inventory management system must respond promptly to any change in sales. One system that is used to monitor inventory usage rates and in turn to modify EOQs and inventory item levels is the **ABC system**. Under this system, the firm analyzes each inventory item on the basis of its cost, frequency of usage, seriousness of a stock-out, order lead time, and other criteria. Items that are expensive, are frequently used, and have long order lead times are put in the A category; less important items are put in the B category; and the least important items are designated C. Management reviews the A items' recent usage rates, stock positions, and delivery time situations quite frequently — say, monthly — and adjusts the EOQ as necessary. Category B items are reviewed and adjusted less frequently — say, every quarter — and C items are reviewed perhaps annually. Thus, the inventory control group's resources are concentrated where they will do the most good.

Efficient inventory management will result in a relatively high inventory turnover ratio, in low write-offs of obsolete or deteriorated inventories, and in few instances of work stoppages or lost sales because of stock-outs. All this, in turn, will contribute to a high profit margin, a high total assets turnover, a high rate of return on investment, and a strong stock price.

ABC system
A system used to categorize inventory items to insure that the most important ones are reviewed most often.

Effects of Inflation on Inventory Management

Moderate inflation — say, 3 percent per year — can largely be ignored for purposes of inventory management, but at higher rates of inflation it becomes important to consider this factor. If the rate of inflation in the types of goods the firm stocks tends to be relatively constant, it can be dealt with easily; one simply deducts the expected annual rate of inflation from the carrying cost percentage, C, in Equation 21-7 and uses this modified version of the EOQ model to establish the working stock. The reason for making this deduction is that inflation causes the value of the inventory to rise, thus offsetting somewhat the effects of depreciation and other carrying cost factors. Since C will now be smaller, the calculated EOQ and hence the average inventory will increase. However, the higher the rate of inflation, the higher interest rates will be, and this will cause C to increase and thus lower the EOQ and average inventories.

On balance, there is no evidence that inflation either raises or lowers the optimal level of inventories of firms in the aggregate. It should still be thoroughly considered, however, for it will raise the individual firm's optimal holdings if the rate of inflation for its own inventories is above average (and is greater than the effects of inflation on interest rates), and vice versa.

Other Inventory Issues

just-in-time system
A system of inventory control in which a manufacturer coordinates production with suppliers so that raw materials or components arrive just as they are needed in the production process.

Two other inventory-related issues should be mentioned. The first is the **just-in-time system**, in which a manufacturer coordinates production with suppliers so that raw materials or components arrive from suppliers just as they are needed in the production process. This point was illustrated with the Fireplace example at the beginning of the chapter. Another example is Anheuser-Busch, which makes Budweiser and Michelob beer. It has a just-in-time arrangement with Ball Corporation, a container company. Ball has set up can manufacturing plants near breweries, and the individual can plants and breweries coordinate their production schedules. The Japanese have carried the just-in-time system to great lengths, and U.S. companies are increasingly adopting this system in their manufacturing plants. To some extent, the just-in-time system reduces the need for the purchaser to carry inventories by passing the problem back to its suppliers. Nevertheless, coordination between suppliers and users lessens total inventory requirements.

out-sourcing
The practice of purchasing components rather than making them in-house.

Another important development related to inventories is **out-sourcing**, which is the practice of purchasing components rather than making them in-house. Thus, if General Motors arranges to buy radiators, axles, and other parts from suppliers rather than making them itself, it has increased its use of out-sourcing. Out-sourcing is often combined with just-in-time systems to reduce inventory levels. However, perhaps the major reason for out-sourcing has nothing to do with inventory policy — a heavily unionized company like GM can often buy parts from a non-unionized supplier at a lower cost than it could make them because of wage-rate differentials.

A final point relating to inventory levels is *the relationship between production scheduling and inventory levels.* A firm like Drexel Card Company, whose cash budget was discussed in Chapter 20, has sales which are highly seasonal. Drexel could produce on a steady, year-round basis, or it could let production rise and fall with sales. If it established a level production schedule, its inventories would rise sharply during periods when sales were low and then would decline during peak sales periods, but the average inventory held would be substantially higher than if production were geared to rise and fall with sales.

Our discussion of just-in-time systems, out-sourcing, and production scheduling all point out the necessity of coordinating inventory policy with manufacturing/procurement policies. Companies try to minimize *total production and distribution costs,* and inventory costs are just one part of total costs. Still, they are an important cost, and financial managers should be aware of the determinants of inventory costs and how they can be minimized.

International

INTERNATIONAL CREDIT MANAGEMENT AND INVENTORY MANAGEMENT

International Credit Management

Like most other aspects of finance, credit management in the multinational corporation is similar to but more complex than that in a purely domestic business. First, granting credit is riskier in an international context because, in addition to the normal risks of default, the multinational firm must also worry about exchange rate changes between the time a sale is made and the time a receivable is collected. For example, if IBM sold a computer to a Japanese customer for 160 million yen when the exchange rate was 160 yen per $1, IBM would obtain 160,000,000/160 = $1,000,000 for the computer. However, if it sold the computer on terms of net/6 months, and if the yen fell against the dollar so that one dollar would now buy 200 yen, IBM would end up realizing only 160,000,000/200 = $800,000 when it collected the receivable.

In addition to being riskier, credit policy is generally more important for a multinational than for a purely domestic firm for two reasons. First, much of the United States' trade is with poorer, less-developed nations, and in such situations granting credit is generally a necessary condition for doing business. Second, and in large part as a result of the first point, nations whose economic health depends upon exports often help their manufacturing firms compete internationally by granting credit to foreign countries. In Japan, for example, the major manufacturing firms have direct ownership ties with large "trading companies" engaged in international trade, as well as with giant commercial banks. In addition, a government agency, the Ministry of International Trade and Industry (MITI), helps Japanese firms identify potential export markets and helps potential customers arrange credit for purchases from Japanese firms. In effect, the huge Japanese trade surpluses are used to finance Japanese exports, thus helping to perpetuate their favorable trade balance. The United States has attempted to counter with the Export-Import Bank, which is funded by Congress, but the fact that the United

States expects a balance of payments deficit in 1988 in excess of $100 billion is clear evidence that it has been less successful than others in world markets in recent years.

The huge debt which countries such as Brazil, Mexico, and Argentina owe the international banks, including many U.S. banks, is well known, and this situation illustrates how credit policy (by banks in this case) can go astray. The banks face a particularly sticky problem with these loans, because if a sovereign nation defaults, the banks cannot lay claim to the assets of the country as they could if a corporate customer defaulted. Note too that although the banks' loans to foreign governments are getting most of the headlines, many multinational corporations are also in trouble as the result of granting credit to business customers in the same countries in which the bank loans are on shaky ground.

By pointing out the risks inherent in granting credit internationally, we are by no means suggesting that such credit is necessarily bad. Quite the contrary, for on balance, the potential gains from international operations far outweigh the risks, at least for companies (and banks) that truly have the expertise to engage in these activities.

International Inventory Management

Inventory management in a multinational setting is also more complex than that in a purely domestic firm for several reasons. First, there is the matter of the physical location of inventories. For example, where should Exxon keep its stockpiles of crude oil and refined products? It has refineries and marketing centers located worldwide, and one alternative is to keep items concentrated in a few strategic spots from which they can then be shipped to the locations where they will be used as needs arise. Such a strategy may minimize the total amount of inventories needed to operate the global business and thus may minimize the firm's total investment in inventories. Note, though, that consideration will have to be given to potential delays in getting goods from central storage locations to user locations all around the world. Both working stocks and safety stocks will have to be maintained at each user location, as well as at the strategic storage centers. Problems like the Iran–Iraq war, which brings with it the potential for a shutdown of production of about 25 percent of the world's oil supply, complicate matters even more.

Exchange rates also influence inventory policy. If a local currency, say the Danish krone, was expected to rise in value against the dollar, a U.S. company operating in Denmark would want to increase stocks of local products before the rise in the krone, and vice versa if the krone was expected to fall.

Another factor that must be considered is the possibility of import or export quotas or tariffs. For example, if Apple Computer Company was obtaining 256k memory chips from Japanese suppliers at bargain prices, but U.S. chipmakers had just charged the Japanese with dumping chips in the U.S. market at prices below cost and were seeking to force the Japanese to raise prices, Apple might decide to increase its chip inventory.[14]

Yet another issue in certain countries is the threat of expropriation. If that threat is large, inventory holdings will be minimized, and goods will be brought in only as needed. Similarly, if the operation involves extraction of raw material such as oil or bauxite, production may be stepped up and stockpiles moved offshore rather than left close to the production site.

Taxes have two effects on multinational inventory management. First, countries often impose property taxes on assets, including inventories, and when this is done, the tax is based on holdings as of a specific date, say January 1 or March 1. Such rules make it advantageous for a multinational firm (1) to schedule production so that inventories are low on the assessment date, and (2) where assessment dates vary among countries in a region, to hold safety stocks in different countries at different times during the year.

Finally, firms may consider the possibility of at-sea storage. Oil, chemical, grain, and other companies that deal in a bulk commodity that must be stored in some type of tank can often buy tankers at a cost not much greater — or perhaps even cheaper, considering land cost — than land-based facilities. Loaded tankers can then be kept at sea or at anchor in some strategic location. This eliminates the danger of expropriation, minimizes the property tax problem, and maximizes flexibility with regard to shipping to areas where needs are greatest or prices highest.

This discussion has only scratched the surface of inventory management in the multinational corporation. As we noted at the outset, the task is much more complex than for a purely domestic firm, but the greater the degree of complexity, the greater the rewards from superior performance. If you want challenge along with potentially high rewards, look to the international arena.

---

[14]The term *dumping* warrants explanation, because the practice is so potentially important in international markets. Suppose Japanese chipmakers have excess capacity. A particular chip has a variable cost of $25, and its "fully allocated cost," which is the $25 plus total fixed cost per unit of output, is $40. Now suppose the Japanese firm can sell chips in the United States at $35 per unit, but if it charges $40 it will not make any sales because U.S. chipmakers sell for $35.50. If the Japanese firm sells at $35, it will cover variable cost plus make a contribution to fixed overhead, so selling at $35 makes sense. Continuing, if the Japanese firm can sell in Japan at $40, but U.S. firms are excluded from Japanese markets by import duties or other barriers, the Japanese will have a huge advantage over U.S. manufacturers. The practice of selling goods at lower prices in foreign markets than at home is called "dumping." U.S. firms are required by anti-trust laws to offer the same price to all customers and, therefore, cannot engage in dumping.

SUMMARY AND KEY CONCEPTS

This chapter has examined methods of managing the firm's accounts receivable and inventories. Because the typical manufacturing firm has about 40 percent of its assets invested in these two current asset accounts, the management of these assets is obviously important. The key concepts covered in this chapter are listed below.

- When a firm sells goods to a customer on credit, an **account receivable** is created.

- Firms can use an **aging schedule** and the **average collection period (ACP)** to help keep track of their receivables position and to avoid the buildup of possible bad debts.

- A firm's **credit policy** consists of four elements: (1) credit period, (2) discounts given for early payment, (3) credit standards, and (4) collection policy.

- If a firm **eases its credit policy**, its sales should increase. Actions which ease the credit policy include lengthening the credit period, relaxing credit standards and collection policy, and offering cash discounts. Each of these actions, however, increases costs. This is because a longer credit period increases both the cost of carrying receivables and bad debt losses; relaxed credit standards and an easier collection policy also lead to higher bad debt costs; and higher cash discounts reduce the amount that the firm receives on each sale. A firm should ease its credit policy only if the costs of doing so will be more than offset by higher sales revenues.

- **Inventory management** involves determining how much inventory to hold, when to place orders, and how many units to order at a time. Because the cost of holding inventory is high, inventory management is important.

- **Inventory costs** can be divided into three categories: carrying costs, ordering costs, and stock-out costs. In general, carrying costs increase as the level of inventory rises, but ordering costs and stock-out costs decline with larger inventory holdings.

- **Total carrying costs (TCC)** are equal to the percentage cost of carrying inventory (C) times the purchase price per unit of inventory (P) times the average number of units held (A): TCC = (C)(P)(A).

- **Total ordering costs (TOC)** are equal to the fixed cost of placing an order (F) times the number of orders placed per year (N): TOC = (F)(N).

- **Total inventory costs (TIC)** are equal to carrying costs plus ordering costs.

- The **economic ordering quantity (EOQ) model** is a formula for determining the order quantity that will minimize total inventory costs:

$$EOQ = \sqrt{\frac{2(F)(S)}{(C)(P)}}.$$

Here F is the fixed cost per order, S is annual sales in units, C is the percentage cost of carrying inventory, and P is the purchase price per unit.

- The **costs of running short of inventory** include lost sales and lost customer goodwill. These costs can be avoided by carrying safety stocks. The cost of carrying safety stocks is equal to the percentage cost of carrying inventories times the purchase price per unit times the number of units held as the safety stock. These costs are separate from those used in the EOQ model.

- Firms use inventory control systems, such as the **red-line method**, the **two-bin method**, and **computerized inventory control systems**, to help them keep track of actual inventory levels and to insure that inventory levels are adjusted as sales change. **Just-in-time (JIT)** systems are also used to hold down inventory costs.

Questions

21-1 Is it true that when one firm sells to another on credit, the seller records the transaction as an account receivable while the buyer records it as an account payable and that, disregarding discounts, the receivable typically exceeds the payable by the amount of profit on the sale?

21-2 What are the four elements in a firm's credit policy? To what extent can firms set their own credit policies as opposed to having to accept policies that are dictated by "the competition"?

21-3 Suppose that a firm makes a purchase and receives the shipment on February 1. The terms of trade as stated on the invoice read "2/10, net 40, May 1 dating." What is the latest date on which payment can be made and the discount can still be taken? What is the date on which payment must be made if the discount is not taken?

21-4 a. What is the average collection period (ACP) for a firm whose sales are $2,880,000 per year and whose accounts receivable are $312,000? (Use 360 days per year.)

  b. Is it true that if this firm sells on terms of 3/10, net 40, its customers probably all pay on time?

21-5 Is it true that if a firm calculates its average collection period, it has no need for an aging schedule?

21-6 Firm A had no credit losses last year, but 1 percent of Firm B's accounts receivable proved to be uncollectible and resulted in losses. Should Firm B fire its credit manager and hire A's?

21-7 Indicate by (+), (−), or (0) whether each of the following events would probably cause accounts receivable (A/R), sales, and profits to increase, decrease, or be affected in an indeterminant manner:

	A/R	Sales	Profits
a. The firm tightens its credit standards.	_____	_____	_____
b. The terms of trade are changed from 2/10, net 30, to 3/10, net 30.	_____	_____	_____
c. The terms are changed from 2/10, net 30, to 3/10, net 40.	_____	_____	_____
d. The credit manager gets tough with past-due accounts.	_____	_____	_____

21-8   If a firm calculates its optimal inventory of widgets to be 1,000 units
when the general rate of inflation is 2 percent, is it true that the optimal
inventory (in units) will almost certainly rise if the general rate of
inflation climbs to 10 percent?

21-9   Indicate by a (+), (−), or (0) whether each of the following events
would probably cause average annual inventories (the sum of the
inventories held at the end of each month of the year divided by 12) to
rise, fall, or be affected in an indeterminant manner:
a. Our suppliers switch from delivering by train to air freight.   _____
b. We change from producing just in time to meet seasonal
   sales to steady, year-round production. (Sales peak at
   Christmas.)   _____
c. Competition in the markets in which we sell increases.   _____
d. The rate of general inflation increases.   _____
e. Interest rates rise; other things are constant.   _____

Self-Test Problems   *(Solutions Appear on Page 853)*

Key terms

ST-1   Define each of the following terms:
a. Account receivable
b. Aging schedule
c. Credit policy; credit period; credit standards; five Cs of credit;
   collection policy
d. Cash discounts
e. Seasonal dating
f. Open account; promissory note; commercial draft; sight draft; time
   draft, or trade acceptance; banker's acceptance; conditional sales
   contract
g. Carrying costs; ordering costs; total inventory costs
h. Economic ordering quantity (EOQ); EOQ model
i. Reorder point; safety stock
j. Red-line method; two-bin method; computerized inventory control
   system; ABC system
k. Average collection period (ACP)
l. Just-in-time system; out-sourcing

Change in credit policy

ST-2   The Mallory Company expects to have sales of $10 million this year
under its current operating policies. Its variable costs as a percentage of
sales are 80 percent, and its cost of capital is 16 percent. Currently,
Mallory's credit policy is net 25 (no discount for early payment).
However, its ACP is 30 days, and its bad debt loss percentage is 2
percent. Mallory spends $50,000 per year to collect bad debts, and its
effective federal-plus-state tax rate is 40 percent.

The credit manager is considering two alternative proposals for
changing Mallory's credit policy. Find the expected change in net
income, taking into consideration anticipated changes in carrying costs
for accounts receivable, the probable bad debt losses, and the discounts
likely to be taken, for each proposal. Should a change in credit policy be
made?

Proposal 1: Lengthen the credit period by going from net 25 to net 30. Collection expenditures will remain constant. Under this proposal, sales are expected to increase by $1 million annually, and the bad debt loss percentage on *new* sales is expected to rise to 4 percent (the loss percentage on old sales should not change). In addition, the ACP is expected to increase from 30 to 45 days on all sales.

Proposal 2: Shorten the credit period by going from net 25 to net 20. Again, collection expenses will remain constant. The anticipated effects of this change are a decrease in sales of $1 million per year, a decline in the ACP from 30 to 22 days, and a decline in the bad debt loss percentage to 1 percent on all sales.

EOQ and total
inventory costs

ST-3   The Best Breads Company buys and then sells (as bread) 2.6 million bushels of wheat annually. The wheat must be purchased in multiples of 2,000 bushels. Ordering costs, which include grain elevator removal charges of $3,500, are $5,000 per order. Annual carrying costs are 2 percent of the purchase price of $5 per bushel. The company maintains a safety stock of 200,000 bushels. The delivery time is 6 weeks.

a. What is the EOQ?

b. At what inventory level should a reorder be placed to prevent having to draw on the safety stock?

c. What are the total inventory costs, including the costs of carrying the safety stock?

d. The wheat processor agrees to pay the elevator removal charges if Best Breads will purchase wheat in quantities of 650,000 bushels. Would it be to Best Breads' advantage to order under this alternative?

Problems

Receivables investment

21-1   Wood Carvers, Inc., sells on terms of 2/10, net 30. Total sales for the year are $600,000. Forty percent of the customers pay on the tenth day and take discounts; the other 60 percent pay, on average, 40 days after their purchases.

a. What is the average collection period?

b. What is the average amount of receivables?

c. What would happen to the average investment in receivables if Wood Carvers toughened up on its collection policy with the result that all nondiscount customers paid on the thirtieth day?

Easing credit terms

21-2   Mayberry Auto Parts is considering changing its credit terms from 2/15, net 30, to 3/10, net 30, in order to speed collections. At present, 50 percent of Mayberry's customers take the 2 percent discount. Under the new terms, discount customers are expected to rise to 60 percent. Regardless of the credit terms, half of the customers who do not take the discount are expected to pay on time, whereas the remainder will pay 10 days late. The change does not involve a relaxation of credit standards; therefore, bad debt losses are not expected to rise above their present 2 percent level. However, the more generous cash discount terms are expected to increase sales from $2 million to $2.3 million per year. Mayberry's variable cost ratio is 80 percent, the interest rate on funds invested in accounts receivable is 12 percent, and the firm's federal-plus-state tax rate is 40 percent.

a. What is the average collection period before and after the change?

b. Calculate the discount costs before and after the change.
c. Calculate the dollar cost of carrying receivables before and after the change.
d. Calculate the bad debt losses before and after the change.
e. What is the incremental profit from the change in credit terms? Should Mayberry change its credit terms?

Credit analysis **21-3** Bay Area Distributors makes all sales on a credit basis, selling on terms of 2/10, net 30. Once a year it evaluates the creditworthiness of all its customers. The evaluation procedure ranks customers from 1 to 5, with 1 indicating the best customers. Results of the ranking are as follows:

Customer Category	Percentage of Bad Debts	Average Collection Period (Days)	Credit Decision	Annual Sales Lost Because of Credit Restrictions
1	None	10	Unlimited credit	None
2	1.0	12	Unlimited credit	None
3	3.0	20	Limited credit	$365,000
4	9.0	60	Limited credit	$182,500
5	16.0	90	Limited credit	$230,000

The variable cost ratio is 75 percent. The cost of capital invested in receivables is 15 percent. Bay Area Distributors' tax rate is 40 percent. What would be the effect on the profitability of extending unlimited credit to each of Categories 3, 4, and 5? (Hint: Determine the effect of changing each policy separately on the income statement. In other words, find the change in sales, change in production costs, change in receivables and cost of carrying receivables, change in bad debt costs, and so forth, down to the change in net profits. Assume that none of the customers in these three categories will take the discount.)

Tightening credit terms **21-4** Mark Beasley, the new credit manager of the Haskell Corporation, was alarmed to find that Haskell sells on credit terms of net 60 days while industrywide credit terms have recently been lowered to net 30 days. On annual credit sales of $3 million, Haskell currently averages 70 days' sales in accounts receivable. Beasley estimates that tightening the credit terms to 30 days would reduce annual sales to $2.7 million, but accounts receivable would drop to 35 days of sales and the savings on investment in them should more than overcome any loss in profit.

Haskell's variable cost ratio is 75 percent, and federal-plus-state taxes are 40 percent. If the interest rate on funds invested in receivables is 14 percent, should the change in credit terms be made?

Relaxing collection efforts **21-5** The Kavoc Corporation has annual credit sales of $3.4 million. Current expenses for the collection department are $60,000, bad debt losses are 2 percent, and the average collection period is 30 days. Kavoc is considering easing its collection efforts so that collection expenses will be reduced to $40,000 per year. The change is expected to increase bad debt losses to 2.5 percent and to increase the average collection period to 45 days. In addition, sales are expected to increase to $3.6 million per year.

Should Kavoc relax collection efforts if the opportunity cost of funds is 13 percent, the variable cost ratio is 75 percent, and federal-plus-state taxes are 40 percent?

<table>
<tr><td>Economic ordering
quantity</td><td>**21-6**</td><td>The Green Thumb Nursery sells 45,000 bags of lawn fertilizer annually. The optimal safety stock (which is on hand initially) is 2,000 bags. Each bag costs Green Thumb $1, inventory carrying costs are 20 percent, and the cost of placing an order with the nursery's supplier is $20.</td></tr>
</table>

Economic ordering quantity

21-6   The Green Thumb Nursery sells 45,000 bags of lawn fertilizer annually. The optimal safety stock (which is on hand initially) is 2,000 bags. Each bag costs Green Thumb $1, inventory carrying costs are 20 percent, and the cost of placing an order with the nursery's supplier is $20.
a. What is the economic ordering quantity?
b. What is the maximum inventory of fertilizer?
c. What will Green Thumb's average inventory be?
d. How often must the company order?

EOQ and total ordering costs

21-7   The following inventory data have been established for the Balik Corporation:
1. Orders must be placed in multiples of 100 units.
2. Annual sales are 338,000 units.
3. The purchase price per unit is $3.
4. Carrying cost is 20 percent of the purchase price of goods.
5. Cost per order placed is $24.
6. Desired safety stock is 14,000 units; this amount is on hand initially.
7. Two weeks are required for delivery.
a. What is the EOQ?
b. How many orders should Balik place each year?
c. At what inventory level should a reorder be made? [Hint: Reorder point = Safety stock + (Weeks to deliver × Weekly usage) − Goods in transit.]
d. Calculate the total cost of ordering and carrying inventories if the order quantity is (1) 4,000 units, (2) 4,800 units, or (3) 6,000 units. What are the total costs if the order quantity is the EOQ?

Credit policy
(Integrative)

21-8   Beverly Garcia took over as financial manager for the Learning Aids Company, which supplies computer software to public and private schools, about a year ago. She has questioned the firm's credit policy, which includes credit terms of 2/10, net 30, for some time. Thus, customers buying from Learning Aids receive a 2 percent discount if they pay within 10 days of purchase, and they must pay the full amount in 30 days if they do not take the discount. If the current credit policy is maintained, next year's sales are expected to be $1,000,000. Currently, 50 percent of Learning Aids' paying customers normally take the discount and pay on Day 10, 40 percent pay the full amount on Day 30, and the remaining 10 percent of those who pay do so (on average) on Day 40. Two percent of Learning Aids sales end up as bad debt losses.

Garcia is thinking about tightening the firm's credit policy, and her proposed new policy would entail changing the credit terms to 4/10, net 20, and enforcing stricter credit standards. Thus, customers who paid within 10 days would receive a 4 percent discount, but all others would have to pay the full amount after only 20 days. Garcia believes that the increased discount would bring in more customers and would also encourage some existing customers to take the discount. The net result, she believes, would be to increase next year's sales to $1,100,000, with 60 percent of the paying customers taking the discount, 30 percent paying the full amount on Day 20, and 10 percent paying late on Day 30. Also, she believes that bad debt losses would be reduced from 2 percent to 1 percent of gross sales. Learning Aids' operating cost ratio is 75 percent, and the cost of funds used to carry receivables is 12 percent; neither of these ratios would change under the new credit policy. Learning Aids' tax rate is 40 percent.

If Garcia's assumptions are correct, should Learning Aids' credit policy be changed? To help her decide on this issue, complete the following tasks, and answer each of the following questions:

a. Briefly describe the four variables which make up a firm's credit policy.

b. What is Learning Aids' current average collection period? What is the expected ACP if the credit policy change is made?

c. What are the current bad debt losses? What losses are expected under the new policy?

d. What are the current costs of granting discounts? What costs are expected under the new policy?

e. What is Learning Aids' current dollar cost of carrying receivables? Under the proposed terms?

f. What is the incremental profit associated with the change in credit terms? Should Learning Aids make the change?

g. Suppose Learning Aids makes the change, but the firm's competitors react by making similar changes in their credit terms, with the net result being that Learning Aids' gross sales remain at the current $1,000,000 level. What would be the impact on Learning Aids' post-tax profitability?

EOQ model
(Integrative)

21-9   Andrew McDonald, financial manager of Stevenson Electronics, has been asked by the CEO to evaluate the firm's inventory management. He has decided to begin by looking at Stevenson's "big ticket" items. One such item is a customized computer microchip which the firm uses in its laptop computer. Each chip costs Stevenson $300, but it must pay its supplier an $800 set-up fee on each order. Further, the supplier requires a minimum order of 250 units on custom chips. Stevenson's annual usage forecast is 6,000 units, and the annual carrying cost on this item is estimated to be 20 percent of inventory value.

McDonald's first step is to apply the EOQ model. As his assistant, he has asked you to answer the following questions:

a. What are the assumptions behind the EOQ model?

b. What is the formula for total inventory costs?

c. What is the EOQ for the custom microchips? What will the total inventory costs be if the EOQ is ordered?

d. What is Stevenson's added cost if it orders 300 units at a time rather than the EOQ quantity? What if it orders 500 per order?

e. Suppose it takes 2 weeks for Stevenson's supplier to set up production, make and test the chips, and deliver them to Stevenson's plant. Assuming certainty in delivery times and usage, at what inventory level should Stevenson reorder? (Assume a 52-week year, and assume that Stevenson orders the EOQ amount.)

f. Of course, there is uncertainty in Stevenson's usage rate, as well as in delivery times, so the company must carry a safety stock to avoid running out of chips and having to halt production. If a 200-unit safety stock is carried, what effect would this have on total inventory costs? What is the new reorder point? What protection does the safety stock provide if usage increases or if delivery is delayed?

g. Now suppose Stevenson's supplier offers a discount of 1 percent on orders of 1,000 or more. Should the company take the discount? Why or why not?

h. For many firms, inventory usage is not uniform throughout the year, but rather follows some seasonal pattern. Can the EOQ model be used in this situation? If so, how?

i. How would these factors affect EOQ analysis?

1. "Just-in-time" procedures.
2. The use of air freight for deliveries.
3. Computerized inventory control systems.
4. Flexible plant designs which reduce setup costs and make small production runs more feasible.

Computer-Related Problems

(Work the problems in this section only if you are using the computer problem diskette.)

Easing credit terms   **C21-1**   Use the model for Problem C21-1 in the file C21 to work this problem.

a. Refer back to Problem 21-2. Suppose that Mayberry's customers did not change their payment pattern when Mayberry adopted its new credit policy; that is, 50 percent still took the discount, 25 percent paid on time, and 25 percent paid late. How would this affect the decision, assuming that sales did increase to $2.3 million as forecasted?

b. At what level of sales would the new credit policy become profitable if the customers' payment pattern remained constant, as specified in Part a?

Tightening credit terms   **C21-2**   Use the model for Problem C21-2 in the file C21 to work this problem.

a. Refer back to Problem 21-4. When Beasley analyzed his proposed credit policy changes, he found that they would reduce Haskell's profits and, therefore, should not be enacted. Beasley has reevaluated his sales estimates since all other firms in the industry have recently tightened their credit policies. He now estimates that sales would decline to only $2,875,000 if he tightened the credit policy to net 30 days. Would the credit policy change be profitable under these circumstances?

b. On the other hand, Beasley believes that he could tighten the credit policy to net 45 days and pick up some sales from his competitors. He estimates that sales would increase to $3.2 million and that the average collection period would fall to 50 days under this policy. What would be Haskell's profits if Beasley enacted this change?

c. Beasley also believes that if he leaves the credit policy as it is, sales will increase to $3.3 million and the average collection period will remain at 70 days. Should Beasley leave the credit policy alone or tighten it as described in either Part a or Part b? Which credit policy produces the largest profits for Haskell Corporation?

EOQ and total inventory costs   **C21-3**   Use the model for Problem C21-3 in the file C21 to work this problem. Doll Makers Unlimited, Inc., uses large quantities of flesh-colored cloth in its doll production process. Throughout the year, the firm uses

1,000,000 square yards of this cloth. The fixed costs of placing and receiving an order are $2,000, including a $1,500 setup charge at the mill. The price of this cloth is $2.00 per square yard, and the annual cost of carrying this inventory item is 20 percent of the price. Doll Makers maintains a 10,000 square yard safety stock. The cloth supplier requires a two-week lead time from order to delivery.

a. What is the EOQ for this cloth? What is the total cost of ordering and carrying the inventory, including the safety stock? (Assume that the safety stock is on hand at the beginning of the year.)

b. Suppose the mill offers to lower the fixed cost to $500 if Doll Makers will increase its order size to 200,000 square yards. Would it be to Doll Makers' advantage to order under this alternative?

c. Now suppose the mill offers to lower the fixed cost to $1,200 if Doll Makers will order 125,000 yards at a time. Should Doll Makers accept this alternative?

Solutions to Self-Test Problems

ST-1   Refer to the marginal glossary definitions or relevant chapter sections to check your responses.

ST-2   Under the current credit policy, the Mallory Company has no discounts, has collection expenses of $50,000, has bad debt losses of $(0.02)($10,000,000) = $200,000$, and has average accounts receivable of (ACP)(Average sales per day) = $(30)($10,000,000/360) = $833,333$. The firm's cost of carrying these receivables is (Variable cost ratio)(A/R)(Cost of capital) = $(0.80)($833,333)(0.16) = $106,667$. It is necessary to multiply by the variable cost ratio because the actual *investment* in receivables is less than the dollar amount of the receivables.

Proposal 1: Lengthen the credit period to net 30 so that
1. Sales increase by $1 million.
2. Discounts = $0.
3. Bad debt losses = $(0.02)($10,000,000) + (0.04)($1,000,000)$

$$= $200,000 + $40,000$$

$$= $240,000.$$

4. ACP = 45 days on all sales.
5. New average receivables = $(45)($11,000,000/360)$

$$= $1,375,000.$$

6. Cost of carrying receivables = (v)(k)(Average accounts receivable)

$$= (0.80)(0.16)($1,375,000)$$

$$= $176,000.$$

7. Collection expenses = $50,000.
Analysis of proposed change:

	Income Statement under Current Policy	Effect of Change	Income Statement under New Policy
Gross sales	$10,000,000	+ $1,000,000	$11,000,000
Less discounts	0	+ 0	0
Net sales	$10,000,000	+ $1,000,000	$11,000,000
Production costs (80%)	8,000,000	+ 800,000	8,800,000
Profits before credit costs and taxes	$ 2,000,000	+ $ 200,000	$ 2,200,000
Credit-related costs:			
Cost of carrying receivables	106,667	+ 69,333	176,000
Collection expenses	50,000	+ 0	50,000
Bad debt losses	200,000	+ 40,000	240,000
Profits before taxes	$ 1,643,333	+ $ 90,667	$ 1,734,000
Federal-plus-state taxes (40%)	657,333	+ 36,267	693,600
Net income	$ 986,000	+ $ 54,400	$ 1,040,400

The proposed change appears to be a good one, assuming the assumptions are correct.

Proposal 2: Shorten the credit period to net 20 so that
1. Sales decrease by $1 million.
2. Discount = $0.

3. Bad debt losses = $(0.01)($9,000,000)$

$$= \$90,000.$$

4. ACP = 22 days.

5. New average receivables = $(22)($9,000,000/360)$

$$= \$550,000.$$

6. Cost of carrying receivables = (v)(k)(Average accounts receivable)
   = $(0.80)(0.16)($550,000)$
   = $70,400.

7. Collection expenses = $50,000.

Analysis of proposed change:

	Income Statement under Current Policy	Effect of Change	Income Statement under New Policy
Gross sales	$10,000,000	− $1,000,000	$9,000,000
Less discounts	0	− 0	0
Net sales	$10,000,000	− $1,000,000	$9,000,000
Production costs (80%)	8,000,000	− 800,000	7,200,000
Profits before credit costs and taxes	$ 2,000,000	− $ 200,000	$1,800,000
Credit-related costs:			
Cost of carrying receivables	106,667	− 36,267	70,400
Collection expenses	50,000	− 0	50,000
Bad debt losses	200,000	− 110,000	90,000
Profits before taxes	$ 1,643,333	− $ 53,733	$1,589,600
Federal-plus-state taxes (40%)	657,333	− 21,493	635,840
Net income	$ 986,000	− $ 32,240	$ 953,760

This change reduces net income, so it should be rejected. Mallory will increase profits by accepting Proposal 1 and lengthening the credit period from 25 days to 30 days, assuming all assumptions are correct. This may or may not be the *optimal,* or profit-maximizing, credit policy, but it does appear to be a movement in the right direction.

ST-3

a.
$$EOQ = \sqrt{\frac{2(F)(S)}{(C)(P)}}$$

$$= \sqrt{\frac{(2)(\$5,000)(2,600,000)}{(0.02)(\$5.00)}}$$

$$= 509,902 \text{ bushels.}$$

Because the firm must order in multiples of 2,000 bushels, it should order in quantities of 510,000 bushels.

b.
$$\text{Average weekly sales} = 2,600,000/52$$

$$= 50,000 \text{ bushels.}$$

$$\text{Reorder point} = 6 \text{ weeks' sales} + \text{Safety stock}$$

$$= 6(50,000) + 200,000$$

$$= 300,000 + 200,000$$

$$= 500,000 \text{ bushels.}$$

c. Total inventory costs:

$$TIC = CP\left(\frac{Q}{2}\right) + F\left(\frac{S}{Q}\right) + CP(\text{Safety stock})$$

$$= (0.02)(\$5)\left(\frac{510,000}{2}\right) + (\$5,000)\left(\frac{2,600,000}{510,000}\right)$$

$$+ (0.02)(\$5)(200,000)$$

$$= \$25,500 + \$25,490.20 + \$20,000$$

$$= \$70,990.20.$$

d. Ordering costs would be reduced by $3,500, to $1,500. By ordering 650,000 bushels at a time, the firm can bring its total inventory costs to

$$TIC = (0.02)(\$5)\left(\frac{650,000}{2}\right) + (\$1,500)\left(\frac{2,600,000}{650,000}\right)$$

$$+ (0.02)(\$5)(200,000)$$

$$= \$32,500 + \$6,000 + \$20,000$$

$$= \$58,500.$$

Because the firm can reduce its total inventory costs by ordering 650,000 bushels at a time, it should accept the offer and place larger orders. (Incidentally, this same type of analysis is used to consider any quantity discount offer.)

A   Mathematical Tables

Table A-1   Present Value of $1 Due at the End of n Periods:

$$PVIF_{k,n} = \frac{1}{(1 + k)^n}$$

Period	1%	2%	3%	4%	5%	6%	7%	8%	9%	10%
1	.9901	.9804	.9709	.9615	.9524	.9434	.9346	.9259	.9174	.9091
2	.9803	.9612	.9426	.9246	.9070	.8900	.8734	.8573	.8417	.8264
3	.9706	.9423	.9151	.8890	.8638	.8396	.8163	.7938	.7722	.7513
4	.9610	.9238	.8885	.8548	.8227	.7921	.7629	.7350	.7084	.6830
5	.9515	.9057	.8626	.8219	.7835	.7473	.7130	.6806	.6499	.6209
6	.9420	.8880	.8375	.7903	.7462	.7050	.6663	.6302	.5963	.5645
7	.9327	.8706	.8131	.7599	.7107	.6651	.6227	.5835	.5470	.5132
8	.9235	.8535	.7894	.7307	.6768	.6274	.5820	.5403	.5019	.4665
9	.9143	.8368	.7664	.7026	.6446	.5919	.5439	.5002	.4604	.4241
10	.9053	.8203	.7441	.6756	.6139	.5584	.5083	.4632	.4224	.3855
11	.8963	.8043	.7224	.6496	.5847	.5268	.4751	.4289	.3875	.3505
12	.8874	.7885	.7014	.6246	.5568	.4970	.4440	.3971	.3555	.3186
13	.8787	.7730	.6810	.6006	.5303	.4688	.4150	.3677	.3262	.2897
14	.8700	.7579	.6611	.5775	.5051	.4423	.3878	.3405	.2992	.2633
15	.8613	.7430	.6419	.5553	.4810	.4173	.3624	.3152	.2745	.2394
16	.8528	.7284	.6232	.5339	.4581	.3936	.3387	.2919	.2519	.2176
17	.8444	.7142	.6050	.5134	.4363	.3714	.3166	.2703	.2311	.1978
18	.8360	.7002	.5874	.4936	.4155	.3503	.2959	.2502	.2120	.1799
19	.8277	.6864	.5703	.4746	.3957	.3305	.2765	.2317	.1945	.1635
20	.8195	.6730	.5537	.4564	.3769	.3118	.2584	.2145	.1784	.1486
21	.8114	.6598	.5375	.4388	.3589	.2942	.2415	.1987	.1637	.1351
22	.8034	.6468	.5219	.4220	.3418	.2775	.2257	.1839	.1502	.1228
23	.7954	.6342	.5067	.4057	.3256	.2618	.2109	.1703	.1378	.1117
24	.7876	.6217	.4919	.3901	.3101	.2470	.1971	.1577	.1264	.1015
25	.7798	.6095	.4776	.3751	.2953	.2330	.1842	.1460	.1160	.0923
26	.7720	.5976	.4637	.3604	.2812	.2198	.1722	.1352	.1064	.0839
27	.7644	.5859	.4502	.3468	.2678	.2074	.1609	.1252	.0976	.0763
28	.7568	.5744	.4371	.3335	.2551	.1956	.1504	.1159	.0895	.0693
29	.7493	.5631	.4243	.3207	.2429	.1846	.1406	.1073	.0822	.0630
30	.7419	.5521	.4120	.3083	.2314	.1741	.1314	.0994	.0754	.0573
35	.7059	.5000	.3554	.2534	.1813	.1301	.0937	.0676	.0490	.0356
40	.6717	.4529	.3066	.2083	.1420	.0972	.0668	.0460	.0318	.0221
45	.6391	.4102	.2644	.1712	.1113	.0727	.0476	.0313	.0207	.0137
50	.6080	.3715	.2281	.1407	.0872	.0543	.0339	.0213	.0134	.0085
55	.5785	.3365	.1968	.1157	.0683	.0406	.0242	.0145	.0087	.0053

Table A-1 (continued)

Period	12%	14%	15%	16%	18%	20%	24%	28%	32%	36%
1	.8929	.8772	.8696	.8621	.8475	.8333	.8065	.7813	.7576	.7353
2	.7972	.7695	.7561	.7432	.7182	.6944	.6504	.6104	.5739	.5407
3	.7118	.6750	.6575	.6407	.6086	.5787	.5245	.4768	.4348	.3975
4	.6355	.5921	.5718	.5523	.5158	.4823	.4230	.3725	.3294	.2923
5	.5674	.5194	.4972	.4761	.4371	.4019	.3411	.2910	.2495	.2149
6	.5066	.4556	.4323	.4104	.3704	.3349	.2751	.2274	.1890	.1580
7	.4523	.3996	.3759	.3538	.3139	.2791	.2218	.1776	.1432	.1162
8	.4039	.3506	.3269	.3050	.2660	.2326	.1789	.1388	.1085	.0854
9	.3606	.3075	.2843	.2630	.2255	.1938	.1443	.1084	.0822	.0628
10	.3220	.2697	.2472	.2267	.1911	.1615	.1164	.0847	.0623	.0462
11	.2875	.2366	.2149	.1954	.1619	.1346	.0938	.0662	.0472	.0340
12	.2567	.2076	.1869	.1685	.1372	.1122	.0757	.0517	.0357	.0250
13	.2292	.1821	.1625	.1452	.1163	.0935	.0610	.0404	.0271	.0184
14	.2046	.1597	.1413	.1252	.0985	.0779	.0492	.0316	.0205	.0135
15	.1827	.1401	.1229	.1079	.0835	.0649	.0397	.0247	.0155	.0099
16	.1631	.1229	.1069	.0980	.0708	.0541	.0320	.0193	.0118	.0073
17	.1456	.1078	.0929	.0802	.0600	.0451	.0258	.0150	.0089	.0054
18	.1300	.0946	.0808	.0691	.0508	.0376	.0208	.0118	.0068	.0039
19	.1161	.0829	.0703	.0596	.0431	.0313	.0168	.0092	.0051	.0029
20	.1037	.0728	.0611	.0514	.0365	.0261	.0135	.0072	.0039	.0021
21	.0926	.0638	.0531	.0443	.0309	.0217	.0109	.0056	.0029	.0016
22	.0826	.0560	.0462	.0382	.0262	.0181	.0088	.0044	.0022	.0012
23	.0738	.0491	.0402	.0329	.0222	.0151	.0071	.0034	.0017	.0008
24	.0659	.0431	.0349	.0284	.0188	.0126	.0057	.0027	.0013	.0006
25	.0588	.0378	.0304	.0245	.0160	.0105	.0046	.0021	.0010	.0005
26	.0525	.0331	.0264	.0211	.0135	.0087	.0037	.0016	.0007	.0003
27	.0469	.0291	.0230	.0182	.0115	.0073	.0030	.0013	.0006	.0002
28	.0419	.0255	.0200	.0157	.0097	.0061	.0024	.0010	.0004	.0002
29	.0374	.0224	.0174	.0135	.0082	.0051	.0020	.0008	.0003	.0001
30	.0334	.0196	.0151	.0116	.0070	.0042	.0016	.0006	.0002	.0001
35	.0189	.0102	.0075	.0055	.0030	.0017	.0005	.0002	.0001	*
40	.0107	.0053	.0037	.0026	.0013	.0007	.0002	.0001	*	*
45	.0061	.0027	.0019	.0013	.0006	.0003	.0001	*	*	*
50	.0035	.0014	.0009	.0006	.0003	.0001	*	*	*	*
55	.0020	.0007	.0005	.0003	.0001	*	*	*	*	*

*The factor is zero to four decimal places.

Table A-2   Present Value of an Annuity of $1 per Period for n Periods:

$$PVIFA_{k,n} = \sum_{t=1}^{n} \frac{1}{(1 + k)^t} = \frac{1 - \dfrac{1}{(1 + k)^n}}{k} = \frac{1}{k} - \frac{1}{k(1 + k)^n}$$

Number of Periods	1%	2%	3%	4%	5%	6%	7%	8%	9%
1	0.9901	0.9804	0.9709	0.9615	0.9524	0.9434	0.9346	0.9259	0.9174
2	1.9704	1.9416	1.9135	1.8861	1.8594	1.8334	1.8080	1.7833	1.7591
3	2.9410	2.8839	2.8286	2.7751	2.7232	2.6730	2.6243	2.5771	2.5313
4	3.9020	3.8077	3.7171	3.6299	3.5460	3.4651	3.3872	3.3121	3.2397
5	4.8534	4.7135	4.5797	4.4518	4.3295	4.2124	4.1002	3.9927	3.8897
6	5.7955	5.6014	5.4172	5.2421	5.0757	4.9173	4.7665	4.6229	4.4859
7	6.7282	6.4720	6.2303	6.0021	5.7864	5.5824	5.3893	5.2064	5.0330
8	7.6517	7.3255	7.0197	6.7327	6.4632	6.2098	5.9713	5.7466	5.5348
9	8.5660	8.1622	7.7861	7.4353	7.1078	6.8017	6.5152	6.2469	5.9952
10	9.4713	8.9826	8.5302	8.1109	7.7217	7.3601	7.0236	6.7101	6.4177
11	10.3676	9.7868	9.2526	8.7605	8.3064	7.8869	7.4987	7.1390	6.8052
12	11.2551	10.5753	9.9540	9.3851	8.8633	8.3838	7.9427	7.5361	7.1607
13	12.1337	11.3484	10.6350	9.9856	9.3936	8.8527	8.3577	7.9038	7.4869
14	13.0037	12.1062	11.2961	10.5631	9.8986	9.2950	8.7455	8.2442	7.7862
15	13.8651	12.8493	11.9379	11.1184	10.3797	9.7122	9.1079	8.5595	8.0607
16	14.7179	13.5777	12.5611	11.6523	10.8378	10.1059	9.4466	8.8514	8.3126
17	15.5623	14.2919	13.1661	12.1657	11.2741	10.4773	9.7632	9.1216	8.5436
18	16.3983	14.9920	13.7535	12.6593	11.6896	10.8276	10.0591	9.3719	8.7556
19	17.2260	15.6785	14.3238	13.1339	12.0853	11.1581	10.3356	9.6036	8.9501
20	18.0456	16.3514	14.8775	13.5903	12.4622	11.4699	10.5940	9.8181	9.1285
21	18.8570	17.0112	15.4150	14.0292	12.8212	11.7641	10.8355	10.0168	9.2922
22	19.6604	17.6580	15.9369	14.4511	13.1630	12.0416	11.0612	10.2007	9.4424
23	20.4558	18.2922	16.4436	14.8568	13.4886	12.3034	11.2722	10.3711	9.5802
24	21.2434	18.9139	16.9355	15.2470	13.7986	12.5504	11.4693	10.5288	9.7066
25	22.0232	19.5235	17.4131	15.6221	14.0939	12.7834	11.6536	10.6748	9.8226
26	22.7952	20.1210	17.8768	15.9828	14.3752	13.0032	11.8258	10.8100	9.9290
27	23.5596	20.7069	18.3270	16.3296	14.6430	13.2105	11.9867	10.9352	10.0266
28	24.3164	21.2813	18.7641	16.6631	14.8981	13.4062	12.1371	11.0511	10.1161
29	25.0658	21.8444	19.1885	16.9837	15.1411	13.5907	12.2777	11.1584	10.1983
30	25.8077	22.3965	19.6004	17.2920	15.3725	13.7648	12.4090	11.2578	10.2737
35	29.4086	24.9986	21.4872	18.6646	16.3742	14.4982	12.9477	11.6546	10.5668
40	32.8347	27.3555	23.1148	19.7928	17.1591	15.0463	13.3317	11.9246	10.7574
45	36.0945	29.4902	24.5187	20.7200	17.7741	15.4558	13.6055	12.1084	10.8812
50	39.1961	31.4236	25.7298	21.4822	18.2559	15.7619	13.8007	12.2335	10.9617
55	42.1472	33.1748	26.7744	22.1086	18.6335	15.9905	13.9399	12.3186	11.0140

Number of Periods	10%	12%	14%	15%	16%	18%	20%	24%	28%	32%
1	0.9091	0.8929	0.8772	0.8696	0.8621	0.8475	0.8333	0.8065	0.7813	0.7576
2	1.7355	1.6901	1.6467	1.6257	1.6052	1.5656	1.5278	1.4568	1.3916	1.3315
3	2.4869	2.4018	2.3216	2.2832	2.2459	2.1743	2.1065	1.9813	1.8684	1.7663
4	3.1699	3.0373	2.9137	2.8550	2.7982	2.6901	2.5887	2.4043	2.2410	2.0957
5	3.7908	3.6048	3.4331	3.3522	3.2743	3.1272	2.9906	2.7454	2.5320	2.3452
6	4.3553	4.1114	3.8887	3.7845	3.6847	3.4976	3.3255	3.0205	2.7594	2.5342
7	4.8684	4.5638	4.2883	4.1604	4.0386	3.8115	3.6046	3.2423	2.9370	2.6775
8	5.3349	4.9676	4.6389	4.4873	4.3436	4.0776	3.8372	3.4212	3.0758	2.7860
9	5.7590	5.3282	4.9464	4.7716	4.6065	4.3030	4.0310	3.5655	3.1842	2.8681
10	6.1446	5.6502	5.2161	5.0188	4.8332	4.4941	4.1925	3.6819	3.2689	2.9304
11	6.4951	5.9377	5.4527	5.2337	5.0286	4.6560	4.3271	3.7757	3.3351	2.9776
12	6.8137	6.1944	5.6603	5.4206	5.1971	4.7932	4.4392	3.8514	3.3868	3.0133
13	7.1034	6.4235	5.8424	5.5831	5.3423	4.9095	4.5327	3.9124	3.4272	3.0404
14	7.3667	6.6282	6.0021	5.7245	5.4675	5.0081	4.6106	3.9616	3.4587	3.0609
15	7.6061	6.8109	6.1422	5.8474	5.5755	5.0916	4.6755	4.0013	3.4834	3.0764
16	7.8237	6.9740	6.2651	5.9542	5.6685	5.1624	4.7296	4.0333	3.5026	3.0882
17	8.0216	7.1196	6.3729	6.0472	5.7487	5.2223	4.7746	4.0591	3.5177	3.0971
18	8.2014	7.2497	6.4674	6.1280	5.8178	5.2732	4.8122	4.0799	3.5294	3.1039
19	8.3649	7.3658	6.5504	6.1982	5.8775	5.3162	4.8435	4.0967	3.5386	3.1090
20	8.5136	7.4694	6.6231	6.2593	5.9288	5.3527	4.8696	4.1103	3.5458	3.1129
21	8.6487	7.5620	6.6870	6.3125	5.9731	5.3837	4.8913	4.1212	3.5514	3.1158
22	8.7715	7.6446	6.7429	6.3587	6.0113	5.4099	4.9094	4.1300	3.5558	3.1180
23	8.8832	7.7184	6.7921	6.3988	6.0442	5.4321	4.9245	4.1371	3.5592	3.1197
24	8.9847	7.7843	6.8351	6.4338	6.0726	5.4509	4.9371	4.1428	3.5619	3.1210
25	9.0770	7.8431	6.8729	6.4641	6.0971	5.4669	4.9476	4.1474	3.5640	3.1220
26	9.1609	7.8957	6.9061	6.4906	6.1182	5.4804	4.9563	4.1511	3.5656	3.1227
27	9.2372	7.9426	6.9352	6.5135	6.1364	5.4919	4.9636	4.1542	3.5669	3.1233
28	9.3066	7.9844	6.9607	6.5335	6.1520	5.5016	4.9697	4.1566	3.5679	3.1237
29	9.3696	8.0218	6.9830	6.5509	6.1656	5.5098	4.9747	4.1585	3.5687	3.1240
30	9.4269	8.0552	7.0027	6.5660	6.1772	5.5168	4.9789	4.1601	3.5693	3.1242
35	9.6442	8.1755	7.0700	6.6166	6.2153	5.5386	4.9915	4.1644	3.5708	3.1248
40	9.7791	8.2438	7.1050	6.6418	6.2335	5.5482	4.9966	4.1659	3.5712	3.1250
45	9.8628	8.2825	7.1232	6.6543	6.2421	5.5523	4.9986	4.1664	3.5714	3.1250
50	9.9148	8.3045	7.1327	6.6605	6.2463	5.5541	4.9995	4.1666	3.5714	3.1250
55	9.9471	8.3170	7.1376	6.6636	6.2482	5.5549	4.9998	4.1666	3.5714	3.1250

Table A-3 Future Value of $1 at the End of n Periods:

$$FVIF_{k,n} = (1 + k)^n$$

Period	1%	2%	3%	4%	5%	6%	7%	8%	9%	10%
1	1.0100	1.0200	1.0300	1.0400	1.0500	1.0600	1.0700	1.0800	1.0900	1.1000
2	1.0201	1.0404	1.0609	1.0816	1.1025	1.1236	1.1449	1.1664	1.1881	1.2100
3	1.0303	1.0612	1.0927	1.1249	1.1576	1.1910	1.2250	1.2597	1.2950	1.3310
4	1.0406	1.0824	1.1255	1.1699	1.2155	1.2625	1.3108	1.3605	1.4116	1.4641
5	1.0510	1.1041	1.1593	1.2167	1.2763	1.3382	1.4026	1.4693	1.5386	1.6105
6	1.0615	1.1262	1.1941	1.2653	1.3401	1.4185	1.5007	1.5869	1.6771	1.7716
7	1.0721	1.1487	1.2299	1.3159	1.4071	1.5036	1.6058	1.7138	1.8280	1.9487
8	1.0829	1.1717	1.2668	1.3686	1.4775	1.5938	1.7182	1.8509	1.9926	2.1436
9	1.0937	1.1951	1.3048	1.4233	1.5513	1.6895	1.8385	1.9990	2.1719	2.3579
10	1.1046	1.2190	1.3439	1.4802	1.6289	1.7908	1.9672	2.1589	2.3674	2.5937
11	1.1157	1.2434	1.3842	1.5395	1.7103	1.8983	2.1049	2.3316	2.5804	2.8531
12	1.1268	1.2682	1.4258	1.6010	1.7959	2.0122	2.2522	2.5182	2.8127	3.1384
13	1.1381	1.2936	1.4685	1.6651	1.8856	2.1329	2.4098	2.7196	3.0658	3.4523
14	1.1495	1.3195	1.5126	1.7317	1.9799	2.2609	2.5785	2.9372	3.3417	3.7975
15	1.1610	1.3459	1.5580	1.8009	2.0789	2.3966	2.7590	3.1722	3.6425	4.1772
16	1.1726	1.3728	1.6047	1.8730	2.1829	2.5404	2.9522	3.4259	3.9703	4.5950
17	1.1843	1.4002	1.6528	1.9479	2.2920	2.6928	3.1588	3.7000	4.3276	5.0545
18	1.1961	1.4282	1.7024	2.0258	2.4066	2.8543	3.3799	3.9960	4.7171	5.5599
19	1.2081	1.4568	1.7535	2.1068	2.5270	3.0256	3.6165	4.3157	5.1417	6.1159
20	1.2202	1.4859	1.8061	2.1911	2.6533	3.2071	3.8697	4.6610	5.6044	6.7275
21	1.2324	1.5157	1.8603	2.2788	2.7860	3.3996	4.1406	5.0338	6.1088	7.4002
22	1.2447	1.5460	1.9161	2.3699	2.9253	3.6035	4.4304	5.4365	6.6586	8.1403
23	1.2572	1.5769	1.9736	2.4647	3.0715	3.8197	4.7405	5.8715	7.2579	8.9543
24	1.2697	1.6084	2.0328	2.5633	3.2251	4.0489	5.0724	6.3412	7.9111	9.8497
25	1.2824	1.6406	2.0938	2.6658	3.3864	4.2919	5.4274	6.8485	8.6231	10.835
26	1.2953	1.6734	2.1566	2.7725	3.5557	4.5494	5.8074	7.3964	9.3992	11.918
27	1.3082	1.7069	2.2213	2.8834	3.7335	4.8223	6.2139	7.9881	10.245	13.110
28	1.3213	1.7410	2.2879	2.9987	3.9201	5.1117	6.6488	8.6271	11.167	14.421
29	1.3345	1.7758	2.3566	3.1187	4.1161	5.4184	7.1143	9.3173	12.172	15.863
30	1.3478	1.8114	2.4273	3.2434	4.3219	5.7435	7.6123	10.063	13.268	17.449
40	1.4889	2.2080	3.2620	4.8010	7.0400	10.286	14.974	21.725	31.409	45.259
50	1.6446	2.6916	4.3839	7.1067	11.467	18.420	29.457	46.902	74.358	117.39
60	1.8167	3.2810	5.8916	10.520	18.679	32.988	57.946	101.26	176.03	304.48

Table A-3 (continued)

Period	12%	14%	15%	16%	18%	20%	24%	28%	32%	36%
1	1.1200	1.1400	1.1500	1.1600	1.1800	1.2000	1.2400	1.2800	1.3200	1.3600
2	1.2544	1.2996	1.3225	1.3456	1.3924	1.4400	1.5376	1.6384	1.7424	1.8496
3	1.4049	1.4815	1.5209	1.5609	1.6430	1.7280	1.9066	2.0972	2.3000	2.5155
4	1.5735	1.6890	1.7490	1.8106	1.9388	2.0736	2.3642	2.6844	3.0360	3.4210
5	1.7623	1.9254	2.0114	2.1003	2.2878	2.4883	2.9316	3.4360	4.0075	4.6526
6	1.9738	2.1950	2.3131	2.4364	2.6996	2.9860	3.6352	4.3980	5.2899	6.3275
7	2.2107	2.5023	2.6600	2.8262	3.1855	3.5832	4.5077	5.6295	6.9826	8.6054
8	2.4760	2.8526	3.0590	3.2784	3.7589	4.2998	5.5895	7.2058	9.2170	11.703
9	2.7731	3.2519	3.5179	3.8030	4.4355	5.1598	6.9310	9.2234	12.166	15.917
10	3.1058	3.7072	4.0456	4.4114	5.2338	6.1917	8.5944	11.806	16.060	21.647
11	3.4785	4.2262	4.6524	5.1173	6.1759	7.4301	10.657	15.112	21.199	29.439
12	3.8960	4.8179	5.3503	5.9360	7.2876	8.9161	13.215	19.343	27.983	40.037
13	4.3635	5.4924	6.1528	6.8858	8.5994	10.699	16.386	24.759	36.937	54.451
14	4.8871	6.2613	7.0757	7.9875	10.147	12.839	20.319	31.691	48.757	74.053
15	5.4736	7.1379	8.1371	9.2655	11.974	15.407	25.196	40.565	64.359	100.71
16	6.1304	8.1372	9.3576	10.748	14.129	18.488	31.243	51.923	84.954	136.97
17	6.8660	9.2765	10.761	12.468	16.672	22.186	38.741	66.461	112.14	186.28
18	7.6900	10.575	12.375	14.463	19.673	26.623	48.039	85.071	148.02	253.34
19	8.6128	12.056	14.232	16.777	23.214	31.948	59.568	108.89	195.39	344.54
20	9.6463	13.743	16.367	19.461	27.393	38.338	73.864	139.38	257.92	468.57
21	10.804	15.668	18.822	22.574	32.324	46.005	91.592	178.41	340.45	637.26
22	12.100	17.861	21.645	26.186	38.142	55.206	113.57	228.36	449.39	866.67
23	13.552	20.362	24.891	30.376	45.008	66.247	140.83	292.30	593.20	1178.7
24	15.179	23.212	28.625	35.236	53.109	79.497	174.63	374.14	783.02	1603.0
25	17.000	26.462	32.919	40.874	62.669	95.396	216.54	478.90	1033.6	2180.1
26	19.040	30.167	37.857	47.414	73.949	114.48	268.51	613.00	1364.3	2964.9
27	21.325	34.390	43.535	55.000	87.260	137.37	332.95	784.64	1800.9	4032.3
28	23.884	39.204	50.066	63.800	102.97	164.84	412.86	1004.3	2377.2	5483.9
29	26.750	44.693	57.575	74.009	121.50	197.81	511.95	1285.6	3137.9	7458.1
30	29.960	50.950	66.212	85.850	143.37	237.38	634.82	1645.5	4142.1	10143.
40	93.051	188.88	267.86	378.72	750.38	1469.8	5455.9	19427.	66521.	*
50	289.00	700.23	1083.7	1670.7	3927.4	9100.4	46890.	*	*	*
60	897.60	2595.9	4384.0	7370.2	20555.	56348.	*	*	*	*

*FVIF > 99,999.

Table A-4 Sum of an Annuity of $1 per Period for n Periods:

$$\text{FVIFA}_{k,n} = \sum_{t=1}^{n}(1 + k)^{n-t} = \frac{(1 + k)^n - 1}{k}$$

Number of Periods	1%	2%	3%	4%	5%	6%	7%	8%	9%	10%
1	1.0000	1.0000	1.0000	1.0000	1.0000	1.0000	1.0000	1.0000	1.0000	1.0000
2	2.0100	2.0200	2.0300	2.0400	2.0500	2.0600	2.0700	2.0800	2.0900	2.1000
3	3.0301	3.0604	3.0909	3.1216	3.1525	3.1836	3.2149	3.2464	3.2781	3.3100
4	4.0604	4.1216	4.1836	4.2465	4.3101	4.3746	4.4399	4.5061	4.5731	4.6410
5	5.1010	5.2040	5.3091	5.4163	5.5256	5.6371	5.7507	5.8666	5.9847	6.1051
6	6.1520	6.3081	6.4684	6.6330	6.8019	6.9753	7.1533	7.3359	7.5233	7.7156
7	7.2135	7.4343	7.6625	7.8983	8.1420	8.3938	8.6540	8.9228	9.2004	9.4872
8	8.2857	8.5830	8.8923	9.2142	9.5491	9.8975	10.260	10.637	11.028	11.436
9	9.3685	9.7546	10.159	10.583	11.027	11.491	11.978	12.488	13.021	13.579
10	10.462	10.950	11.464	12.006	12.578	13.181	13.816	14.487	15.193	15.937
11	11.567	12.169	12.808	13.486	14.207	14.972	15.784	16.645	17.560	18.531
12	12.683	13.412	14.192	15.026	15.917	16.870	17.888	18.977	20.141	21.384
13	13.809	14.680	15.618	16.627	17.713	18.882	20.141	21.495	22.953	24.523
14	14.947	15.974	17.086	18.292	19.599	21.015	22.550	24.215	26.019	27.975
15	16.097	17.293	18.599	20.024	21.579	23.276	25.129	27.152	29.361	31.772
16	17.258	18.639	20.157	21.825	23.657	25.673	27.888	30.324	33.003	35.950
17	18.430	20.012	21.762	23.698	25.840	28.213	30.840	33.750	36.974	40.545
18	19.615	21.412	23.414	25.645	28.132	30.906	33.999	37.450	41.301	45.599
19	20.811	22.841	25.117	27.671	30.539	33.760	37.379	41.446	46.018	51.159
20	22.019	24.297	26.870	29.778	33.006	36.786	40.995	45.762	51.160	57.275
21	23.239	25.783	28.676	31.969	35.719	39.993	44.865	50.423	56.765	64.002
22	24.472	27.299	30.537	34.248	38.505	43.392	49.006	55.457	62.873	71.403
23	25.716	28.845	32.453	36.618	41.430	46.996	53.436	60.893	69.532	79.543
24	26.973	30.422	34.426	39.083	44.502	50.816	58.177	66.765	76.790	88.497
25	28.243	32.030	36.459	41.646	47.727	54.865	63.249	73.106	84.701	98.347
26	29.526	33.671	38.553	44.312	51.113	59.156	68.676	79.954	93.324	109.18
27	30.821	35.344	40.710	47.084	54.669	63.706	74.484	87.351	102.72	121.10
28	32.129	37.051	42.931	49.968	58.403	68.528	80.698	95.339	112.97	134.21
29	33.450	38.792	45.219	52.966	62.323	73.640	87.347	103.97	124.14	148.63
30	34.785	40.568	47.575	56.085	66.439	79.058	94.461	113.28	136.31	164.49
40	48.886	60.402	75.401	95.026	120.80	154.76	199.64	259.06	337.88	442.59
50	64.463	84.579	112.80	152.67	209.35	290.34	406.53	573.77	815.08	1163.9
60	81.670	114.05	163.05	237.99	353.58	533.13	813.52	1253.2	1944.8	3034.8

Number of Periods	12%	14%	15%	16%	18%	20%	24%	28%	32%	36%
1	1.0000	1.0000	1.0000	1.0000	1.0000	1.0000	1.0000	1.0000	1.0000	1.0000
2	2.1200	2.1400	2.1500	2.1600	2.1800	2.2000	2.2400	2.2800	2.3200	2.3600
3	3.3744	3.4396	3.4725	3.5056	3.5724	3.6400	3.7776	3.9184	4.0624	4.2096
4	4.7793	4.9211	4.9934	5.0665	5.2154	5.3680	5.6842	6.0156	6.3624	6.7251
5	6.3528	6.6101	6.7424	6.8771	7.1542	7.4416	8.0484	8.6999	9.3983	10.146
6	8.1152	8.5355	8.7537	8.9775	9.4420	9.9299	10.980	12.136	13.406	14.799
7	10.089	10.730	11.067	11.414	12.142	12.916	14.615	16.534	18.696	21.126
8	12.300	13.233	13.727	14.240	15.327	16.499	19.123	22.163	25.678	29.732
9	14.776	16.085	16.786	17.519	19.086	20.799	24.712	29.369	34.895	41.435
10	17.549	19.337	20.304	21.321	23.521	25.959	31.643	38.593	47.062	57.352
11	20.655	23.045	24.349	25.733	28.755	32.150	40.238	50.398	63.122	78.998
12	24.133	27.271	29.002	30.850	34.931	39.581	50.895	65.510	84.320	108.44
13	28.029	32.089	34.352	36.786	42.219	48.497	64.110	84.853	112.30	148.47
14	32.393	37.581	40.505	43.672	50.818	59.196	80.496	109.61	149.24	202.93
15	37.280	43.842	47.580	51.660	60.965	72.035	100.82	141.30	198.00	276.98
16	42.753	50.980	55.717	60.925	72.939	87.442	126.01	181.87	262.36	377.69
17	48.884	59.118	65.075	71.673	87.068	105.93	157.25	233.79	347.31	514.66
18	55.750	68.394	75.836	84.141	103.74	128.12	195.99	300.25	459.45	700.94
19	63.440	78.969	88.212	98.603	123.41	154.74	244.03	385.32	607.47	954.28
20	72.052	91.025	102.44	115.38	146.63	186.69	303.60	494.21	802.86	1298.8
21	81.699	104.77	118.81	134.84	174.02	225.03	377.46	633.59	1060.8	1767.4
22	92.503	120.44	137.63	157.41	206.34	271.03	469.06	812.00	1401.2	2404.7
23	104.60	138.30	159.28	183.60	244.49	326.24	582.63	1040.4	1850.6	3271.3
24	118.16	158.66	184.17	213.98	289.49	392.48	723.46	1332.7	2443.8	4450.0
25	133.33	181.87	212.79	249.21	342.60	471.98	898.09	1706.8	3226.8	6053.0
26	150.33	208.33	245.71	290.09	405.27	567.38	1114.6	2185.7	4260.4	823.13
27	169.37	238.50	283.57	337.50	479.22	681.85	1383.1	2798.7	5624.8	11198.0
28	190.70	272.89	327.10	392.50	566.48	819.22	1716.1	3583.3	7425.7	15230.3
29	214.58	312.09	377.17	456.30	669.45	984.07	2129.0	4587.7	9802.9	20714.2
30	241.33	356.79	434.75	530.31	790.95	1181.9	2640.9	5873.2	12941.	28172.3
40	767.09	1342.0	1779.1	2360.8	4163.2	7343.9	22729.	69377.	*	*
50	2400.0	4994.5	7217.7	10436.	21813.	45497.	*	*	*	*
60	7471.6	18535.	29220.	46058.	*	*	*	*	*	*

*FVIFA > 99,999.

B

Answers to Selected End-of-Chapter Problems

We present here some intermediate steps and final answers to selected end-of-chapter problems. Please note that your answer may differ slightly from ours due to rounding errors. Also, although we hope not, some of the problems may have more than one correct solution, depending upon what assumptions are made in working the problem. Finally, many of the problems involve some verbal discussion as well as numerical calculations; this verbal material is not presented here.

2-1	Tax = $104,150; $205,850.
2-2	a. Tax = $204,000.
	b. $17,000.
	c. $5,100.
2-5	a. Cash flow = $2,200,000.
2-6	a. 1989 advantage as a corporation = $799; 1990 advantage = $3,399; 1991 advantage = $6,199.
2-7	a. $17,303.
	c. IBM yield = 7.37%, or $7,370.
	d. 18.2%.
2-9	a. $20,000; $32,000; $19,000; $12,000; $11,000; $6,000.
2-10	b. $5,550; $6,375; $25,175.
	c. $64,450; $81,125; $97,325.
3-1	a. k_1 = 10.20%; k_5 = 8.20%.
3-3	a. k_1 in Year 2 = 12%.

3-4   Year 2 inflation $= 12\%$; k_1, in Year 2 $= 15\%$.

3-5   a. 8.40%.
     b. 10.40%.
     c. $k_5 = 10.9\%$.

4-1   a. $k_B = 17\%$.
     b. $\sigma_a = 17.75\%$.

4-2   a. $k_C = 14.2\%$.
     b-1. $k_M = 14\%$; $k_C = 15.2\%$.
     c-1. $k_M = 15\%$; $k_C = 17.0\%$.

4-4   a. $k_i = 7\% + (5\%)b_i$.
     b. 15.75%.
     c. Indifference rate $= 19.5\%$.

4-5   a. $\bar{k}_A = 11.4\%$.
     c. $\sigma_A = 21.9\%$; $\sigma_P = 21.3\%$.

4A-1   a. $b = 0.62$.

4A-2   a. $b_A = 1.0$; $b_B = 0.5$.
     c. $k_A = 15\%$; $k_B = 12.5\%$.

5-1   a. $324.
     d. $257.20.

5-2   a. $647.67.
     b. $1,323.42.
     c. $138.96.
     d. $300.02; $613.01.

5-3   a. 10 years.
     c. 6 years

5-4   a. $3,187.48.
     d(a). $3,506.23.

5-5   a. $1,228.92.
     c. $1,000.
     d(a). $1,351.81.

5-6   a. Stream A: $1,181.46.

5-7 $3,638.78.

5-9   a. 15% (or 14.87%).

5-10   b. 8%.
     c. 8%.
     d. 12%.

5-12   7.18%.

5-13   9%.

5-15   a. $26,496.80.
     b. $20,616.54 and $0.

5-16   10 years.

5-17   5.2 years.

5-18   a. $352.46.
b. $358.16.
c. $361.22.
d. $225.36.

5-19   a. $111.68.
b. $110.74.
c. $177.48.

5-21   a. 1st City = 9%; 2nd City = 8.24%.

5-22 $PV_{5\%} = \$2,000$; $PV_{10\%} = \$1,000$.

5-23   a. PMT = $8,042.30.

5-25   d. PMT = $5,673.

5-26   a. PV Costs = $25.02 billion.
b. PV Benefits = $20.78 billion.

6-1   a. V_L at 6 percent = $1,388.52; V_L at 9 percent = $1,080.57; V_L at 12 percent = $863.79.

6-2   a. YTM at $825 = 14%.

6-3   a. $1,233.04.
b. $905.50.

6-4   a. $1,200.
b. $800.
d. At 10%, V = $1,170.23.

6-6   b. PV = $5.29.
d. $30.01.

6-8   a-1. $7.60.
a-2. $10.00.
b-1. Undefined.

6-10   a. YTM = 3.4%.
b. YTM = 7%.
c. $852.

6-11 $21.60.

6-12   a. Div. 1991 = $2.60.
b. $P_0 = \$71.20$.
c. Div. yield 1989 = 2.53%; 1993 = 4%.

6-13   a. $P_0 = \$36.46$.

6-14   a. YTM = 9%; YTC = 7.75%.

6-15   a. $19.23.
b. $P_0 = \$20.83$.
d. $P_0 = \$30.73$.

6-16   a. New price = $31.34.
b. beta = 0.49865.

6-17   a. $k_C = 10.6\%$; $k_D = 7\%$.

7-1   a. Current ratio = $1.98\times$; ACP = 75 days; Total assets turnover = $1.7\times$; Debt ratio = 61.9%.

7-2 $350,000; 1.19.

7-3   Sales = $2,160,000; ACP = 36 days.

7-6   Decrease in cash + marketable securities = $38.

7-7   a. 16%.
   b. Profit margin = 7.33%; Equity multiplier = 1.39;
      Industry D/A = 44%.

7-8   a. Quick ratio = 0.8×; ACP = 37 days; ROE = 13.1%;
      Debt ratio = 54.8%.

8-1   a. Total assets = $3.6 million.
   b. $1,790,000.

8-2   a. $1,920,000.
   b. $150,000.

8-3   a. $13.3 million.
   b. Notes payable = $30.8 million.
   c. Current ratio = 2.00×; ROE = 14.2%.
   d. (1) − $14.40 million; (2) Total assets = $147 million; Notes pay-
      able = $3.1 million; (3) Current ratio = 4.25×; ROE = 10.8%.

8-4   a. Total assets = $42,240,000.
   b. $1,440,000.
   c. Notes payable = $5,840,000.

8-5   a. Total assets = $78,480,000.
   b. 25%.
   c. Additional external capital = $3,888,000.
   d. ROE = 10.7%.

8-7   a. AFN = $578,200.
   b. Increase in notes payable = $49,000.

9-1   a. 4 years.
   b. NPV = $4,583.50.
   c. IRR = 16%.

9-2 NPV_T = $417; IRR_T = 16%; Accept; NPV_P = $2,928; IRR_P = 20%; Accept.

9-3 NPV_E = $6,745; IRR_E = 20%; NPV_G = $5,483; IRR_G = 20%; The electric-
   powered forklift has a higher NPV.

9-4   a. NPV_S = $814.33; NPV_L = $1,675.34. At k = 12%, IRR^*_S = 13.77% and
      IRR^*_L = 13.46%.

9-5   b. IRR_A = 18.1%; IRR_B = 24.0%.
   c. At k = 10%, choose A; at k = 17%, choose B.
   d. IRR^*_A = 14.07% and IRR^*_B = 15.89% at k = 10%.
   e. 14.53%.

9-7   a. NPV_A = $18,108,510; IRR_B = 22.26%.
   b. NPV_Δ = $4,162,393; IRR_Δ = 11.71%.
   c. Crossover rate = 11.7%.

9-8   a. IRR_1 = 9.2%; IRR_2 = 420%.

9-9 IRR_1 = 13%; IRR_2 = 76%.

9-10   a. IRR is undefined.
  b. PV(cost) of conveyor = −$939,198.

10-1 $\Delta Dep_1 = 0$; $\Delta Dep_2 = \$4,000,000$; $\Delta Dep_{11} = \$1,500,000$;
  PV at 10% = $674,311.

10-2   a. $89,000.
  b. $26,220, $30,300, $20,100.
  c. $24,380.
  d. No, NPV = −$6,705.

10-3   a. $212,500.
  b. $CF_1 = \$72,501$; $CF_2 = \$80,865$; $CF_3 = \$59,955$.
  c. $65,179.
  d. NPV = $14,256.

10-4   NPV = $9,901.

10-5   NPV = $32,227.

10-6   a. $88,400.
  c. −$10,000.
  d. NPV = $46,051.

10-8   a. EAA (190-3) = $5,161; EAA (360-6) = $5,723.

11-1   a. 16%.
  b. Yes; NPV = $402.

11-2   a. P.C.F.$_A$ = $4,500; P.C.F.$_B$ = $5,100.
  b. NPV$_B$ = $7,749.

11-3   a. k = 14%.
  b. $b_{Firm} = 1.50$; $k_{New\ division} = 16.5\%$.

11-4   a. 1.50.
  b. $b_{New} = 0.50$.

11-5   a. $k_S = 15\%$.
  b. NPV$_{RD}$ = $13,004; NPV$_{TD}$ = −$3,335.

12-1   a. $25.00.
  b. $24.42.

12-2   a. $700,000.
  b. $3,700,000.
  c. −$2,300,000.

12-3   800,000 shares.

12-4   a. EPS$_{1988}$ = $12,000; DPS$_{1988}$ = $6,000; BV$_{1988}$ = $90,000/share.
  b. g_{EPS}: Lawn Girl = 8.4%; RotoTiller = 6.4%; Boro = 8.0%;
    g_{DPS}: Lawn Girl = 8.4%; RotoTiller = 6.4%; Boro = 7.4%.
  f. ROE$_{LG}$ = 15%; ROE$_{RT}$ = 13.64%; ROE$_B$ = 13.33%.
  i. P/E$_{LG}$ = 8×; P/E$_{RT}$ = 8.67×.
  k. $k_{Lawn\ Girl}$ = 15.2%; $k_{RotoTiller}$ = 12.5%; Boro's price: P_0 (Lawn Girl) =
    $21.54; P_0 (RotoTiller) = $33.66.

13-1   a. $2,570,892.
  c. $2,774,079.

13-2   Payment = $402,107.04.

13-3   16.1%.

13-4   d. At k_d = 2% , V = $150.

13-5   a. Number of zeros = 5,769.
      b. YTM on zeros: Tax-exempt holder = 14%,
         33% holder = 9.38%.

13B-1 a. 1,173,121.

14-1   a. D/A_s = 67%; D/A_E = 50%.
      b. D/A_E = 67%.

14-3   a. PV of owning = − $82,262.
        PV of leasing = − $86,834.

14-4   a. − $5; $0; $5; $70.
      d. 9%; $90.

14-6   b. Percent ownership: Original = 80%; Plan 1 = 53%;
        Plans 2 and 3 = 57%.
      c. EPS_0 = $0.54; EPS_1 = $0.60; EPS_2 = $0.64; EPS_3 = $0.86.
      d. D/A_1 = 13%; D/A_2 = 13%; D/A_3 = 48%.

15-1   NPV = − $47,984.

15-2   a. 18.9%.
      c. P_{Max} = $8.91.

15-3   a. 14.5%.
      b. Terminal value = $1,242; Value to Worldwide = $857.

16-1   a. 12%.
      b. 9.6%.
      c. 7.9%.

16-2   9.24%.

16-3   11.14%.

16-4   a. 16.3%.
      b. 15%.
      c. 16%.
      d. ≈16%.

16-5   a. g = 8%.
      b. $2.16.
      c. 15.20%.

16-6   a. $15 million.
      b. $30 million.
      c. $20 million; $40 million.

16-7   a. 12.5%.
      b. 15.7%.

16-8   12.4%.

16-9   a. 5%.
      b. $4.20.

16-10   a. $45 million.
        c. k_s = 12%.
        d. $18 million.

16-11   a. k_d = 6%; k_s = 14%.
        d. k_e = 14.67%; k_a = 11.2%.

16-12   a. 3.
        c. 11.4%; 11.9%; 12.9%; 13.4%.
        d. 16%; 14%.

17-1   a. $3.40.

17-2   a. DOL_A at $120,000 = 3.0.
        e. DTL_A at $120,000 = 30.

17-3   a. BE_A = 128,571 units; BE_B = 107,000 units; indifference Q = 182,500 units.
        b. DOL_A = 2.80; DOL_B = 2.15; Method A.
        c. DFL_A = 1.32; DFL_B = 1.35; Method B.
        d. DTL_A = 3.68; DTL_B = 2.90.
        e. Debt = $172,410; D/A = 5.75%.

17-4   a. EPS_{Old} = $2.04; New: EPS_D = $4.74; EPS_s = $3.27.
        b. DOL_{Old} = 2.30; DOL_{New} = 1.60; DFL_{Old} = 1.47; $DFL_{New, Stock}$ = 1.15; $DTL_{New, Debt}$ = 2.53.
        c. $Q_{BE(Old)}$ = 25,435 units; $Q_{BE(New)}$ = 16,875 units.
        d. 33,975 units.
        e. Q_{Stock} = 20,475 units.

17-5   a. ROE_{LL} = 14.6%; ROE_{HL} = 16.8%.
        b. ROE_{LL} = 16.5%.

17-6   No leverage: ROE = 10.5%; σ^2 = 0.00293; CV = 0.5; 50% leverage: ROE = 13.8%; σ^2 = .01170; CV = 0.78.

18-2 $2,400,000.

18-3   52%.

18-4 $3.70.

18-6   a. (1) $3,300,000; (2) $4,000,000; (3) $7,800,000.
        c. k_s = 15%.
        d. ROE = 15%.

18-7   a. Payout = 63.16%; Break point = $7.64 million; 10.67%, 10.96%.
        b. $12 million.

19-1   a. 70.
        b. $192,000.
        c. 6.

19-2   a. 82.
        b. ROA = 6.9%.
        c. ROA = 7.2%.

19-3   a. 30 days.
        b. $420,000.
        d. $492,800.

19-4 a. ROE(Aggressive) = 11.8%; ROE(Moderate) = 10.6%; ROE(Conservative) = 8.7%.

19-5 a. 72.73%.
c. 55.67%.
e. 12.12%.

19-6 a. 48.98%.

19-7 a. $83,333.
b. no.
d. 24.49%.

19-8 Alternative 3 has the lowest effective interest rate = 12.50%.

19-9 a. Obtain bank financing.

19-10 a. $600,000.

19-11 14.69%.

19-12 b. $373,134.

19-13 a. 1. $5,104; 2. $10,824; 3. $5,075; 4. $6,417.

19A-1 b. Total dollar cost = $160,800.

19A-2 a. $515,464.

19A-3 a. $46,167.
b. $40,667.
c. Field warehousing.

20-1 a. Deposit $1,000,000 each day.
b. 4 days.
c. Bank's balance = $750,000; Firm's balance = −$3,250,000.

20-2 a. December surplus = $12,900.

20-3 a. July surplus = $85,250; October loans = $26,500.

20-4 a. $375,000 reduction in cash.
b. $45,000.
c. $3,750.

20-5 a. $C^* = \$45,000$.
c. 75.
d. Total cost = $4,500.

20-6 a. Wire transfer.
b. $13,875.

20-7 a. $80,800.
c. Net loss = −$5,800.

21-1 a. 28 days.
b. $46,666.67.
c. $36,666.67.

21-2 a. $ACP_O = 25$ days; $ACP_N = 20$ days.
b. New discounts = $40,572.
d. Bad debt loss$_O$ = $40,000.
e. $NI_O = \$196,240$; $NI_N = \$216,697$.

21-3 a. NI_3 = $46,811; NI_4 = $15,467; NI_5 = $8,539.

21-4 a. NI_O = $413,250; NI_N = $388,462.

21-5 a. NI_O = $416,625; NI_N = $435,675.

21-6 a. EOQ = 3,000 bags.
      b. 5,000 bags.
      c. 3,500 bags.
      d. Every 24 days.

21-7 a. EOQ = 5,200 units.
      c. 16,600 units.

C Selected Equations

Chapter 2

	ACRS Class	
Year	3-Year	5-Year
1	33%	20%
2	45	32
3	15	19
4	7	12
5		11
6		6

Chapter 3

$$k = k^* + IP + DRP + LP + MRP.$$

Chapter 4

$$\text{Expected rate of return} = \hat{k} = \sum_{i=1}^{n} P_i k_i.$$

$$\text{Variance} = \sigma^2 = \sum_{i=1}^{n} (k_i - \hat{k})^2 P_i.$$

$$\text{Standard deviation} = \sigma = \sqrt{\sum_{i=1}^{n} (k_i - \hat{k})^2 P_i}.$$

$$CV = \frac{\sigma}{\hat{k}}.$$

$$\hat{k}_p = \sum_{i=1}^{n} w_i \hat{k}_i.$$

$$\sigma_p = \sqrt{\sum_{j=1}^{n} (k_{pj} - \hat{k}_p)^2 P_j}.$$

$$b_p = \sum_{i=1}^{n} w_i b_i.$$

$$k_i = k_{RF} + (k_M - k_{RF})b_i.$$

Security Market Line (SML): $k_i = k_{RF} + (k_M - k_{RF})b_i.$

Chapter 5

$$FV_n = PV(1 + k)^n = PV(FVIF_{k,n}).$$

$$PV = FV_n \left(\frac{1}{1 + k}\right)^n = FV_n(1 + k)^{-n} = FV_n(PVIF_{k,n}).$$

$$PVIF_{k,n} = \frac{1}{FVIF_{k,n}}.$$

$$FVIFA_{k,n} = [(1 + k)^n - 1]/k.$$

$$PVIFA_{k,n} = [1 - (1/(1 + k)^n)]/k.$$

$$\frac{\text{Present value}}{\text{of a perpetuity}} = \frac{\text{Payment}}{\text{Discount rate}} = \frac{PMT}{k}.$$

$$FVA_n = PMT(FVIFA_{k,n}).$$

$$FVA_n \text{ (Annuity due)} = PMT(FVIFA_{k,n})(1 + k).$$

$$PVA_n = PMT(PVIFA_{k,n}).$$

$$PVA_n \text{ (Annuity due)} = PMT(PVIFA_{k,n})(1 + k).$$

$$FV_n = PV\left(1 + \frac{k_{Nom}}{m}\right)^{mn}.$$

$$\text{Effective annual rate} = \left(1 + \frac{k_{Nom}}{m}\right)^m - 1.0.$$

$$FV_n = PVe^{kn}.$$

$$PV = FV_n e^{-kn}.$$

Chapter 6

$$V = \sum_{t=1}^{n} I\left(\frac{1}{1 + k_d}\right)^t + M\left(\frac{1}{1 + k_d}\right)^n$$

$$= I(\text{PVIFA}_{k_d,n}) + M(\text{PVIF}_{k_d,n}).$$

$$V = \sum_{t=1}^{2n} \frac{I}{2}\left(\frac{1}{1 + \dfrac{k_d}{2}}\right)^t + M\left(\frac{1}{1 + \dfrac{k_d}{2}}\right)^{2n}$$

$$= \frac{I}{2}(\text{PVIFA}_{k_d/2,2n}) + M(\text{PVIF}_{k_d/2,2n}).$$

$$V_p = \frac{D_p}{k_p}.$$

$$\hat{P}_0 = \sum_{t=1}^{\infty} \frac{D_t}{(1 + k_s)^t}.$$

$$\hat{P}_0 = \frac{D}{k_s}.$$

$$\hat{k}_s = \frac{D}{P_0}.$$

$$\hat{P}_0 = \frac{D_0(1 + g)}{k_s - g} = \frac{D_1}{k_s - g}.$$

$$\hat{k}_s = \frac{D_1}{P_0} + g.$$

Chapter 7

$$\text{ROE} = \left(\begin{array}{c}\text{Profit}\\\text{margin}\end{array}\right)\left(\begin{array}{c}\text{Total asset}\\\text{turnover}\end{array}\right)\left(\begin{array}{c}\text{Equity}\\\text{multiplier}\end{array}\right)$$

$$= \left(\frac{\begin{array}{c}\text{Net income}\\\text{available to}\\\text{common stockholders}\end{array}}{\text{Sales}}\right)\left(\frac{\text{Sales}}{\text{Total assets}}\right)\left(\frac{\text{Total assets}}{\text{Common equity}}\right)$$

$$= \frac{\begin{array}{c}\text{Net income}\\\text{available to}\\\text{common stockholders}\end{array}}{\text{Common equity}}.$$

$$\text{Current ratio} = \frac{\text{Current assets}}{\text{Current liabilities}}.$$

$$\begin{array}{c}\text{Quick, or acid}\\\text{test, ratio}\end{array} = \frac{\text{Current assets} - \text{Inventories}}{\text{Current liabilities}}.$$

$$\begin{array}{c}\text{Inventory turnover,}\\\text{or utilization, ratio}\end{array} = \frac{\text{Sales}}{\text{Inventory}}.$$

$$\text{ACP} = \text{Average collection period} = \frac{\text{Receivables}}{\text{Average sales per day}} = \frac{\text{Receivables}}{\text{Annual sales}/360}.$$

$$\frac{\text{Fixed assets turnover ratio}} = \frac{\text{Sales}}{\text{Net fixed assets}}.$$

$$\frac{\text{Total assets turnover ratio}} = \frac{\text{Sales}}{\text{Total assets}}.$$

$$\text{Debt ratio} = \frac{\text{Total debt}}{\text{Total assets}}.$$

$$\text{D/E} = \frac{\text{D/A}}{1 - \text{D/A}}, \text{ and D/A} = \frac{\text{D/E}}{1 + \text{D/E}}.$$

$$\frac{\text{Times-interest-earned (TIE) ratio}} = \frac{\text{EBIT}}{\text{Interest charges}}.$$

$$\frac{\text{Fixed charge coverage ratio}} = \frac{\text{EBIT} + \text{Lease payments}}{\text{Interest charges} + \text{Lease payments.}}$$

$$\frac{\text{Cash flow coverage ratio}} = \frac{\text{Cash inflows}}{\text{Fixed charges} + \dfrac{\text{Preferred dividends}}{1 - \text{T}} + \dfrac{\text{Debt repayment}}{1 - \text{T}}}.$$

$$\text{Profit margin} = \frac{\text{Net income available to common stockholders}}{\text{Sales}}.$$

$$\text{Basic earning power ratio} = \frac{\text{EBIT}}{\text{Total assets}}.$$

$$\text{Return on total assets (ROA)} = \frac{\text{Net income available to common stockholders}}{\text{Total assets}}.$$

$$\frac{\text{Return on equity (ROE)}} = \frac{\text{Net income available to common stockholders}}{\text{Common equity}}.$$

$$\frac{\text{Price/earnings (P/E) ratio}} = \frac{\text{Price per share}}{\text{Earnings per share}}.$$

$$\text{Book value per share} = \frac{\text{Common equity}}{\text{Shares outstanding}}.$$

$$\text{Market/book ratio} = \frac{\text{Market price per share}}{\text{Book value per share}}.$$

Chapter 8

$$AFN = (A/S)\Delta S - (L/S)\Delta S - MS_1(1 - d).$$

$$\frac{\text{Full capacity}}{\text{sales}} = \frac{\text{Current sales}}{\text{Percentage of capacity at}}.$$
$$\text{which fixed assets were operated}$$

$$\text{Target fixed assets/Sales ratio} = \frac{\text{Fixed assets}}{\text{Full capacity sales}}.$$

Chapter 9

$$NPV = \sum_{t=0}^{n} \frac{CF_t}{(1 + k)^t}.$$

$$IRR: \sum_{t=0}^{n} \frac{CF_t}{(1 + r)^t} = 0.$$

$$IRR^*: PV_{Costs} = \frac{TV}{(1 + IRR^*)^n} = \sum_{t=0}^{n} \frac{COF_t}{(1 + k)^t} = \frac{\sum_{t=0}^{n} CIF_t (1 + k)^{n-t}}{(1 + IRR^*)^n}.$$

Chapter 11

$$CV = \frac{\sigma_{NPV}}{\text{Expected NPV}}.$$

$$k_p = k_{RF} + (k_M - k_{RF})b_p.$$

Chapter 15

$$\text{Formula value} = \frac{\text{Current price}}{\text{of the stock}} - \frac{\text{Striking}}{\text{price}}.$$

$$\frac{\text{Price paid for}}{\text{bond with warrants}} = \frac{\text{Straight-debt}}{\text{value of bond}} + \frac{\text{Value of}}{\text{warrants}}.$$

$$\text{Conversion price} = P_c = \frac{\text{Par value of bond}}{\text{Shares received}}.$$

$$\frac{\text{Price paid for}}{\text{convertible bond}} = \sum_{t=1}^{n} \frac{I}{(1 + k_c)^t} + \frac{\text{Expected market value at}}{\text{time of conversion}}.$$
$$\frac{}{(1 + k_c)^n}$$

Chapter 16

$$\text{Component cost of debt} = k_d(1 - T).$$

$$\frac{\text{Component cost}}{\text{of preferred stock}} = k_p = \frac{D_p}{P_n}.$$

$$k_s = \hat{k}_s = \frac{D_1}{P_0} + g.$$

$$k_s = k_{RF} + (k_M - k_{RF})b_i.$$

$$k_s = \text{Bond yield} + \text{Risk premium.}$$

$$\hat{k}_e = \frac{D_1}{P_0(1 - F)} + g.$$

$$\text{WACC} = k_a = w_d k_d(1 - T) + w_p k_p + w_s(k_s \text{ or } k_e).$$

Chapter 17

$$Q_{BE} = \frac{F}{P - V}.$$

$$\text{EPS} = \frac{(\text{EBIT} - I)(1 - T)}{\text{Shares outstanding}}.$$

$$\text{WACC} = k_a = w_d k_d(1 - T) + w_s k_s$$

$$= (D/A)k_d(1 - T) + (1 - D/A)k_s.$$

$$\text{DOL} = \frac{Q(P - V)}{Q(P - V) - F}$$

$$= \frac{S - VC}{S - VC - F}.$$

$$\text{DFL} = \frac{\text{EBIT}}{\text{EBIT} - I}.$$

$$\text{DTL} = \frac{Q(P - V)}{Q(P - V) - F - I} = (\text{DOL})(\text{DFL}).$$

Chapter 19

$$\frac{\text{Percentage}}{\text{cost}} = \frac{\text{Discount percent}}{100 - \text{Discount percent}} \times \frac{360}{\text{Days credit is} - \text{Discount outstanding period}}.$$

$$\text{Effective rate}_{\text{Simple}} = \frac{\text{Interest}}{\text{Amount borrowed}}.$$

$$\text{Effective rate}_{\text{Discount}} = \frac{\text{Nominal rate (\%)}}{1.0 - \text{Nominal rate (fraction)}}.$$

$$\text{Effective rate}_{\text{Simple/CB}} = \frac{\text{Nominal rate (\%)}}{1.0 - \text{CB(fraction)}}.$$

$$\text{Effective rate} = \frac{\text{Nominal rate (\%)}}{1 - \text{CB (fraction)} - \text{Nominal rate (fraction)}}.$$

$$\text{Approximate effective rate}_{\text{Installment}} = \frac{\text{Interest}}{\text{Amount received}/2}.$$

Chapter 20

Total costs = Holding cost + Transaction cost

$$= \frac{C}{2}(k) + \frac{T}{C}(F).$$

$$C^* = \sqrt{\frac{2(F)(T)}{k}}.$$

Chapter 21

Cost of carrying receivables = (ACP)(Sales/360)(v)(k).

Opportunity cost = (Old sales/360)(ΔACP)(1 − v)(k).

TCC = (C)(P)(A).

TOC = (F)(N) = F(S/2A).

TIC = TCC + TOC.

$$= (C)(P)\left(\frac{Q}{2}\right) + \frac{F(S)}{Q}.$$

$$\text{EOQ} = \sqrt{\frac{2(F)(S)}{(C)(P)}}.$$

Index

Running glossary items are set in bold face type. They are indexed either under their main
subject heading or as individual items, or in both those ways.